The Life of CHRIST

FREDERIC WILLIAM FARRAR

The Life of CHRIST

FREDERIC W. FARRAR

BOOKCRAFT

Salt Lake City, Utah

Originally published in 1874
by Cassell & Company, Limited, London, England

First issued in the United States in 1875
by E. P. Dutton & Company, New York, New York

Fourth Bookcraft printing, 1998

ISBN 0-88494-939-7

Printed in the United States of America

PREFACE.

In fulfilling a task so difficult and so important as that of writing the Life of Christ, I feel it to be a duty to state the causes which led me to undertake it, and the principles which have guided me in carrying it to a conclusion.

1. It has long been the desire and aim of the publishers of this work to spread as widely as possible the blessings of knowledge; and, in special furtherance of this design, they wished to place in the hands of their readers such a sketch of the Life of Christ on earth as should enable them to realize it more clearly, and to enter more thoroughly into the details and sequence of the Gospel narratives. They therefore applied originally to an eminent theologian, who accepted the proposal, but whose elevation to the Episcopate prevented him from carrying it out.

Under these circumstances application was made to me, and I could not at first but shrink from a labor for which I felt that the amplest leisure of a lifetime would be insufficient, and powers incomparably greater than my own would still be utterly inadequate. But the considerations that were urged upon me came no doubt with additional force from the deep interest with which, from the first, I contemplated the design. I consented to make the effort, knowing that I could at least promise to do my best, and believing that he who does the best he can, and also seeks the blessing of God upon his labors, cannot finally and wholly fail.

And I have reason to be thankful that I originally entered upon the task, and, in spite of all obstacles, have still persevered in it. If the following pages in *any* measure fulfil the objects with which such a

Life ought to be written, they should fill the minds of those who read them with solemn and not ignoble thoughts; they should "add sunlight to daylight by making the happy happier;" they should encourage the toiler; they should console the sorrowful; they should point the weak to the one true source of moral strength. But whether this book be thus blessed to high ends, or whether it be received with harshness and indifference, nothing at least can rob me of the deep and constant happiness which I have felt during almost every hour that has been spent upon it. Though, owing to serious and absorbing duties, months have often passed without my finding an opportunity to write a single line, yet, even in the midst of incessant labor at other things, nothing forbade that the subject on which I was engaged should be often in my thoughts, or that I should find in it a source of peace and happiness different, alike in kind and in degree, from any which other interests could either give or take away.

2. After I had in some small measure prepared myself for the task, I seized, in the year 1870, the earliest possible opportunity to visit Palestine, and especially those parts of it which will be forever identified with the work of Christ on earth. Amid those scenes wherein He moved — in the

> *   *   *   " holy fields
> Over whose acres walked those blessed feet
> Which, eighteen hundred years ago, were nailed
> For our advantage, on the bitter cross " —

in the midst of those immemorial customs which recalled at every turn the manner of life He lived — at Jerusalem, on the Mount of Olives, at Bethlehem, by Jacob's Well, in the Valley of Nazareth, along the bright strand of the Sea of Galilee, and in the coasts of Tyre and Sidon — many things came home to me, for the first time, with a reality and vividness unknown before. I returned more than ever confirmed in the wish to tell the full story of the Gospels in such a manner and with such illustrations as — with the aid of all that was within my reach of that knowledge which has been accumulating for centuries — might serve to enable at least the simple and the unlearned to understand and enter into the human surroundings of the life of the Son of God.

3. But, while I say this to save the book from being judged by a false standard, and with reference to ends which it was never intended to accomplish, it would be mere affectation to deny that I have hoped to furnish much which even learned readers may value. Though the following pages do not pretend to be exhaustive or specially erudite, they yet contain much that men of the highest learning have thought or ascertained. The books which I have consulted include the researches of divines who have had the privilege of devoting to this subject, and often to some small fragment of it, the best years of laborious and uninterrupted lives. No one, I hope, could have reaped, however feebly, among such harvests, without garnering at least something, which must have its value for the professed theologian as well as for the unlearned. And because I believed — and indeed most earnestly hoped — that this book might be acceptable to many of my brother-clergymen, I have admitted into the notes some quotations and references which will be comparatively valueless to the ordinary reader. But, with this double aim in view, I have tried to avoid "moving as in a strange diagonal," and have never wholly lost sight of the fact that I had to work with no higher object than that thousands, who have even fewer opportunities than myself, might be the better enabled to read that one Book, beside which even the best and profoundest treatises are nothing better than poor and stammering fragments of imperfect commentary.

4. It is perhaps yet more important to add that this Life of Christ is avowedly and unconditionally the work of a believer. Those who expect to find in it new theories about the divine personality of Jesus, or brilliant combinations of mythic cloud tinged by the sunset imagination of some decadent belief, will look in vain. It has not been written with any *direct* and *special* reference to the attacks of sceptical criticism. It is not even intended to deal otherwise than indirectly with the serious doubts of those who, almost against their will, think themselves forced to lapse into a state of honest disbelief. I may indeed venture to hope that such readers, if they follow me with no unkindly spirit through these pages, may here and there find considerations of real weight and importance, which will solve imaginary difficulties and supply an answer to real objections. Although this book is not mainly controversial, and would,

had it been intended as a contribution to polemical literature, have been written in a very different manner, I do not believe that it will prove wholly valueless to any honest doubter who reads it in a candid and uncontemptuous spirit. Hundreds of critics, for instance, have impugned the authority of the Gospels on the score of the real or supposed contradictions to be found in them. I am of course familiar with such objections, which may be found in all sorts of books, from Strauss's *Leben Jesu* and Renan's *Vie de Jésus*, down to Sir R. Hanson's *Jesus of History*, and the English *Life of Jesus*, by Mr. Thomas Scott. But, while I have never consciously evaded a distinct and formidable difficulty, I have constantly endeavored to show by the mere silent course of the narrative itself that many of these objections are by no means insuperable, and that many more are unfairly captious or altogether fantastic.

5. If there are questions wider and deeper than the minutiæ of criticism, into which I have not fully and directly entered, it is not either from having neglected to weigh the arguments respecting them, or from any unwillingness to state the reasons why, in common with tens of thousands who are abler and wiser than myself, I can still say respecting every fundamental doctrine of the Christian faith, Manet immota fides.[1] Writing as a believer to believers, as a Christian to Christians, surely, after nearly nineteen centuries of Christianity, any one may be allowed to rest a fact of the Life of Jesus on the testimony of St. John without stopping to write a volume on the authenticity of the Fourth Gospel; or may narrate one of the Gospel miracles without deeming it necessary to answer all the arguments which have been urged against the possibility of the supernatural. After the long labors, the powerful reasoning, and the perfect historical candor with which this subject has been treated by a host of apologists, it is surely as needless as it is impossible to lay again, on every possible occasion, the very lowest foundations of our faith. As regards St. John, therefore, I have contented myself with the merest and briefest summary of some of the evidence which to me still seems adequate to prove that he was the author of the Gospel which passes by his name,* and minuter indications tending to strengthen

---

* See pp. 128, 129, *passim.*

that conviction will be found scattered throughout the book. It would indeed be hypocrisy in me to say with Ewald that " *every argument, from every quarter to which we can look, every trace and record*, combine together to render any serious doubt upon the question absolutely impossible ; " but I do say that, after the fairest and fullest consideration which I have been able to give to a question beset with difficulties, the arguments in favor of the Johannine authorship seem to me to be immensely preponderant.

Nor have I left the subject of the credibility of miracles and the general authenticity of the Gospel narratives entirely untouched, although there was the less need for my entering fully upon those questions in the following pages from my having already stated elsewhere, to the best of my ability, the grounds of my belief. The same remark applies to the yet more solemn truth of the Divinity of Christ. That — not indeed as surrounded with all the recondite inquiries about the περιχώρησις[2] or *communicatio idiomatum*,[3] the hypostatic union, the abstract impeccability, and such scholastic formulæ, but in its broad scriptural simplicity — was the subject of the Hulsean Lectures before the University of Cambridge in the year 1870. In those lectures I endeavored to sketch what has ever seemed to my mind the most convincing external evidence of our faith, namely, " *The Witness of History to Christ.*" Those who have rejected the creed of the Church in this particular, approach the subject from a totally opposite point to our own. They read the earlier chapters of St. Luke and St. Matthew, and openly marvel that any mind can believe what to them appears to be palpable mythology ; or they hear the story of one of Christ's miracles of power — the walking on the Sea of Galilee, or turning the water into wine — and scarcely conceal their insinuated misgiving as to honesty of those who can accept such narratives as true. Doubtless we should share their convictions in these respects, if we approached the subject in the same spirit and by the same avenues. To show that we *do not* and *why* we do not so approach it, is — incidentally at least — one of the objects of this book.

The sceptic — and let me here say at once that I hope to use no single word of anger or denunciation against a scepticism which I know to be in many cases perfectly honest and self-sacrificingly noble — approaches the examination of the question from a point of view the very opposite to that of the believer. He looks at the majestic order and apparently unbroken uniformity of Law, until the Universe becomes to him but the result mechanically evolved from tendencies at once irreversible and self-originated. To us such a conception is wholly inconceivable. Law to us involves the necessity of postulating a Law-giver, and "Nature," which we only use as an unscientific and imaginative synonym for the sum total of observed phenomena, involves in our conceptions the Divine Power of whose energy it is but the visible translucence. We believe that the God and Creator of "Nature" has made Himself known to us, if not by a primitive intuition, at any rate by immediate revelation to our hearts and consciences. And therefore such narratives as those to which I have alluded are not nakedly and singly presented to us in all their unsupported and startling difficulty. To us they are but incidental items in a faith which lies at the very bases of our being — they are but fragments of that great whole which comprises all that is divine and mysterious and supernatural in the two great words, Christianity and Christendom. And hence, though we no longer prominently urge the miracles of Christ as the proofs of our religion, yet, on the other hand, we cannot regard them as stumbling-blocks in the path of an historical belief. We study the sacred books of all the great religions of the world; we see the effect exercised by those religions on the minds of their votaries; and in spite of all the truths which even the worst of them enshrined, we watch the failure of them all to produce the inestimable blessings which we have ourselves enjoyed from infancy, which we treasure as dearly as our life, and which we regard as solely due to the spread and establishment of the faith we hold. We read the systems and treatises of ancient philosophy, and in spite of all the great and noble elements in which they abound, we see their total incapacity to console, or support, or deliver, or regenerate the world. Then we see the light of Christianity dawning like a tender dayspring amid the universal and intolerable darkness. From the first, that new religion allies itself with the world's utter feeblenesses, and those feeblenesses it shares;

yet without wealth, without learning, without genius, without arms, without anything to dazzle and attract — the religion of outcasts and exiles, of fugitives and prisoners — numbering among its earliest converts not many wise, not many noble, not many mighty, but such as the gaoler of Philippi, and the runaway slave of Colossæ — with no blessing apparently upon it save such as cometh from above — with no light whatever about it save the light that comes from heaven — it puts to flight kings and their armies; it breathes a new life, and a new hope, and a new and unknown holiness into a guilty and decrepit world. This we see; and we see the work grow, and increase, and become more and more irresistible, and spread "with the gentleness of a sea that caresses the shore it covers." And seeing this, we recall the faithful principle of the wise and tolerant Rabbi, uttered more than 1,800 years ago — "If this counsel or this work be of men, it will come to nought; but if it be of God, ye cannot overthrow it, lest haply ye be found to fight against God."[1]

And when we have thus been led to see and to believe that the only religion in the world which has established the ideal of a perfect holiness, and rendered common the attainment of that ideal, has received in conspicuous measure the blessing of God, we examine its truths with a deeper reverence. The record of these truths — the record of that teaching which made them familiar to the world — we find in the Gospel narrative. And that narrative reveals to us much more. It not only furnishes us with an adequate reason for the existence and for the triumphs of the faith we hold, but it also brings home to us truths which affect our hearts and intellects no less powerfully than "the starry heavens above and the moral law within." Taught to regard ourselves as children of God, and common brothers in his great family of man, we find in the Gospels a revelation of God in His Son which enables us to know Him more, and to trust Him more absolutely, and to serve Him more faithfully, than all which we can find in all the other books of God, whether in Scripture, or history, or the experience of life, or those unseen messages which God has written on every individual heart. And finding that

[1] Acts v. 38, 39.

this revelation has been recorded by honest men in narratives which, however fragmentary, appear to stand the test of history, and to bear on the face of them every mark of transparent simplicity and perfect truthfulness — prepared for the reception of these glad tidings of God's love in man's redemption by the facts of the world without, and the experiences of the heart within — we thus cease to find any overwhelming difficulty in the record that He whom we believe to have been the Son of God — He who alone has displayed on earth the transcendent miracle of a sinless life — should have walked on the Sea of Galilee or turned the water into wine.

And when.we thus accept the truth of the miracles they become to us moral lessons of the profoundest value. In considering the miracles of Jesus we stand in a wholly different position to the earlier disciples. To them the evidence of the miracles lent an overwhelming force to the teachings of the Lord ; they were as the seal of God to the proclamation of the new kingdom. But to us who, for nineteen centuries, have been children of that kingdom, such evidence is needless. To the Apostles they were the credentials of Christ's mission; to us they are but fresh revelations of His will. To us they are works rather than signs, revelations rather than portents. Their historical importance lies for us in the fact that without them it would be impossible to account for the origin and spread of Christianity. We appeal to them not to prove the truth of Christianity, but to illustrate its dissemination. But though to us Christianity rests on the basis of a Divine approval far more convincing than the display of supernatural power — though to us the providence which for these two millenniums has ruled the destinies of Christendom is a miracle far more stupendous in its evidential force than the raising of the dead or the enlightenment of the blind — yet a belief in these miracles enables us to solve problems which would otherwise be insolvable, as well as to embrace moral conceptions which would otherwise have found no illustration. To one who rejects them — to one who believes that the loftiest morals and the divinest piety which mankind has ever seen were evoked by a religion which rested on errors or on lies — the world's history must remain, it seems to me, a hopeless enigma or a revolting fraud.[1]

6. Referring to another part of the subject, I ought to say I do not regard as possible any final harmony of the Gospels. Against *any* harmony which can be devised some plausible objection could be urged. On this subject no two writers have ever been exactly agreed, and this alone is sufficient to prove that the Gospel notices of chronology are too incomplete to render certainty attainable. I have, of course, touched directly, as well as indirectly, on such questions as the length of the ministry ; and wherever the narrative required some clear and strong reason for adopting one view rather than another on some highly disputed point — such, for instance, as the Feast alluded to in John v. 1 — I have treated the question as fully as was consistent with brevity, and endeavored to put the reader in possession of the main facts and arguments on which the decision rests. But it would have been equally unprofitable and idle to encumber my pages with endless controversy on collateral topics which, besides being dreary and needless, are such as admit of no final settlement. In deciding upon a particular sequence of events, we can only say that such a sequence appears to us a *probable* one, not by any means that we regard it as *certain.* In every instance I have carefully examined the evidence for myself, often compressing into a few lines, or even

---

[1] " Que la philosophie est ingénieuse et profonde dans ses conjectures ! " writes De Lamennais in his scornful style. " Comme les événemens qui paraissaient les plus extraordinaires, deviennent simple dès qu'elle daigne les expliquer ! Vous ne concevez pas que le Christianisme se soit propagé naturellement : elle va vous le faire comprendre. Les Apôtres ont dit, ' Nous vous annonçons l'Évangile au nom de l'Éternel, et vous devez nous croire, car nous sommes doués du pouvoir miraculeux. Nous rendons la santé aux malades, aux perclus l'usage de leurs membres, la vue aux aveugles, l'ouïe aux sourds, la vie aux morts.' A ce discours le peuple est accouru de toutes parts, pour être témoin des miracles promis avec tant de confiance. Les malades n'ont point été guéris, les perclus n'ont point marché, les aveugles n'ont point vu, les sourds n'ont point entendu, les morts n'ont point ressuscité. Alors, transporté d'admiration, le peuple est tombé aux pieds des Apôtres, et s'est écrié, ' Ceux-ci sont manifestement les envoyés de Dieu, les ministres de sa puissance ! ' et sur le champ brisant ses idoles, il a quitté le culte des plaisirs pour le culte de la croix ; il a renoncé à ses habitudes, à ses préjugés, à ses passions ; il a réformé ses mœurs et embrassé la pénitence ; les riches ont vendu leurs biens, pour en distribuer le prix aux indigens, et tous ont préféré les plus horribles tortures et une mort infâme aux remords d'abandonner une religion qui leur était si solidement prouvée." (*Ess. sur l'Indifférence*, iv. 458.) [4]

into an incidental allusion, the results of a long inquiry. To some extent I agree with Stier and Lange in the order of events which they have adopted, and in this respect, as well as for my first insight into the character of several scenes (acknowledged in their place), I am perhaps more indebted to the elaborate work of Lange than to any others who have written on the same subject. When an author is writing from the results of independent thought on the sum total of impressions formed during a course of study, it is not always possible to acknowledge specific obligations; but whenever I was consciously indebted to others, I have, throughout the book, referred especially to Ewald, Neander, Schenkel, Strauss, Hase, Sepp, Stier, Ebrard, Wieseler, Hofmann, Keim, Caspari, Ullmann, Delitzsch, De Pressensé, Wallon, Dupanloup, Capecelatro, Ellicott, Young, Andrews, Wordsworth, Alford, and many others; as well as to older writers like Bonaventura and Jeremy Taylor. I have also to acknowledge the assistance which I have gained from the writings of Dean Stanley, Canons Lightfoot and Westcott, Professor Plumptre, Dr. Ginsburg, Mr. Grove, and the authors of articles in the Encyclopædias of Ersch and Grube, Herzog, Zeller, Winer, and Dr. W. Smith. Incidental lights have of course been caught from various archæological treatises, as well as works of geography and travel, from the old Itineraries and Reland down to Dr. Thomson's *Land and Book*, and Mr. Hepworth Dixon's *Holy Land*.

7. It is needless to add that this book is almost wholly founded on an independent study of the four Gospels side by side. In quoting from them I have constantly and intentionally diverged from the English version, because my main object has been to bring out and explain the scenes as they are described by the original witnesses. The minuter details of those scenes, and therewith the accuracy of our reproduction of them, depend in no small degree upon the discovery of the true reading, and the delicate observance of the true usage of words, particles, and tenses. It must not be supposed for a moment that I offer these translations — which are not unfrequently paraphrases — as preferable to those of the English version, but only that, consistently with the objects which I had in view, I have aimed at representing with more rigid accuracy the force and meaning of

the true text in the original Greek. It will be seen, too, that I have endeavored to glean in illustration all that is valuable or trustworthy in Josephus, in the Apocryphal Gospels, and in traditional particulars derived from the writings of the Fathers.

8. Some readers will perhaps be surprised by the frequency of the allusions to Jewish literature. Without embarking on "the sea of the Talmud" (as the Rabbis themselves call it) — a task which would require a lifetime — a modern reader may find not only the amplest materials, but probably *all* the materials it can offer for the illustration of the Gospel history, in the writings not of Christians only, but also of learned and candid Rabbis. Not only in the well-known treatises of Lightfoot, Schöttgen, Surenhuys, Wagenseil, Buxtorf, Otho, Reland, Budæus, Gfrörer, Herzfeld, McCaul, Etheridge, but also in those of Jews by birth or religion, or both, like Geiger, Jost, Grätz, Derenbourg, Munk, Frankl, Deutsch, Raphall, Schwab, Cohen, any one may find large quotations from the original authorities collected as well by adversaries as by reverent and admiring students. Further, he may read the entire Mishna (if he have the time and patience to do so) in the Latin version of Surenhusius, and may now form his judgment respecting large and important treatises even of the Gemara, from such translations as the French one of the Berachôth by M. Moïse Schwab. I have myself consulted all the authorities here named, and have gained from them much information which seems to me eminently useful. Their researches have thrown a flood of light on some parts of the Gospels, and have led me to some conclusions which, so far as I am aware, are new. I have, indeed, in the second Excursus of the Appendix, shown that nothing of the slightest importance can be gleaned from the Talmudists about our Lord Himself. The real value of the Rabbinic writings in illustrating the Gospels is indirect, not direct — archæological, not controversial. The light which they throw on the fidelity of the Evangelists is all the more valuable because it is derived from a source so unsuspected and so hostile.[1]

9. If in any part of this book I have appeared to sin against the

---

[1] I take this opportunity of saying that the reader will not find in the following pages any one rigid or uniform system of *transliteration* of Hebrew words into English. This is due to the fact that, in most instances, my references to the

divine law of charity, I must here ask pardon for it. But at least I may say that whatever trace of asperity may be found in any page of it, has never been directed against men, but against principles, or only against those men or classes of men in long-past ages whom we solely regard as the representatives of principles. It is possible that this book may fall into the hands of some Jewish readers, and to these particularly I would wish this remark to be addressed. I have reason to believe that the Jewish race have long since learnt to look with love and reverence on Him whom their fathers rejected; nay, more, that many of them, convinced by the irrefragable logic of history, have openly acknowledged that He was indeed their promised Messiah, although they still reject the belief in His divinity. I see, in the writings of many Jews, a clear conviction that Jesus, to whom they have quite ceased to apply the terms of hatred found in the Talmud, was at any rate the greatest religious Teacher, the highest and noblest Prophet whom their race produced. They, therefore, would be the last to defend that greatest crime in history — the Crucifixion of the Son of God. And while no Christian ever dreams of visiting upon them the horror due to the sin of their ancestors, so no Jew will charge the Christians of to-day with looking with any feeling but that of simple abhorrence on the long, cruel, and infamous persecutions to which the ignorance and brutality of past ages have subjected their great and noble race. We may humbly believe that the day is fast approaching when He whom the Jews crucified, and whose divine revelations the Christians have so often and so grievously disgraced, will break down the middle wall of partition between them, and make both races one in religion, in heart, and life — Semite and Aryan, Jew and Gentile, united to bless and to evangelize the world.

Talmud have been derived from the numerous sources mentioned in the above paragraphs, and in referring such passages to the author who is responsible for their accuracy, I have generally adopted his mode of spelling. Scripture names I have mostly left in the form in which they occur in our English version; and in many terms that have acquired a common currency, like Mishna, Gemara, Talmud, &c., I have left the words in the shape most usually adopted. Besides these sources of difference there may doubtless be others " quas aut incuria fudit aut humana parum cavit natura." [5] For these errors, where they occur, as well as for all others, I must ask the indulgence of the candid reader, who will appreciate the difficulties of a task accomplished under conditions far from favorable.

10. One task alone remains — the pleasant task of thanking those friends to whose ready aid and sympathy I owe so much, and who have surrounded with happy memories and obligations the completion of my work. First and foremost, my heartiest and sincerest thanks are due to my friends, Mr. C. J. Monro, late Fellow of Trinity College, Cambridge, and Mr. R. Garnett, of the British Museum. They have given me an amount of time and attention which leaves me most largely indebted to their unselfish generosity; and I have made claims on their indulgence more extensive than I can adequately repay. To my old pupil, Mr. H. J. Boyd, late scholar of Brasenose College, Oxford, I am indebted for the table of Contents. I have also to thank the Rev. Professor Plumptre and Mr. George Grove not only for the warm interest which they have taken in my work, but also for some valuable suggestions. There are many others, not here named, who will believe, without any assurance from me, that I am not ungrateful for the help which they have rendered; and I must especially offer my best acknowledgments to the Rev. T. Teignmouth Shore — but for whose kind encouragement the book would not have been undertaken — and to those who with so much care and patience have conducted it through the press.

And now I send these pages forth not knowing what shall befall them, but with the earnest prayer that they may be blessed to aid the cause of truth and righteousness, and that He in whose name they are written may, of His mercy,

" Forgive them where they fail in truth,
And in His wisdom make me wise."

F. W. F.

THE LODGE, MARLBOROUGH COLLEGE,
Monday before Easter, 1874.

LIST OF AUTHORITIES.

The following (without any attempt at completeness in the list) are some of the books and editions frequently referred to in this work:—

Akerman, *Numism. Illustr. of the New Testament.* London, 1846.

Alford, *Greek Testament.* Second Edition. London, 1854.

Andrews, *Bible Student's Life of our Lord.* London, 1867.

Bengel, *Gnomon.* Second Edition. Tübingen, 1759.

Bible Educator, The. London, 1874.

Bloomfield, *Greek Testament.* Eighth Edition, 1850.

Bonaventura, *Vita Christi.*

Browne, H., *Ordo Saeclorum.* London, 1844.

Browning, R., *A Death in the Desert.*

Bruce, *Training of the Twelve.*

Budacus, *Philosoph. Hebraeorum.* 1720.

Buxtorf, *Lexicon Talmudicum.*

—— *Synag. Judaica.* Basle, 1661.

Capecelatro, *La Vita di Gesù Cristo.* Napoli, 1868.

Caspari, *Chronologische-Geographische Einleitung in das Leben Jesu.* Hamburg, 1869.

Cohen, *Les Déicides.* E. Tr. London, 1872.

Cowper, B. H., *The Apocryphal Gospels.*

Davidson, *Introd. to New Testament.* 2 vols. London, 1868.

Delitzsch, F., *Jesus und Hillel.* Erlangen, 1867.

De Pressensé, *Jésus Christ.*

Dérenbourg, *L' Hist. et la Géogr. de la Palestine d'après les Thalmuds.* Paris, 1867.

De Saulcy, *Hist. d'Herode.* Paris, 1872.

Deutsch, *Literary Remains* [The Talmud, &c.]. London, 1874.

Dixon, W. Hepworth, *The Holy Land.* 2 vols. London, 1865.

Döllinger, *The Jew and the Gentile.* E. Tr. 2 vols.

—— *The First Age of the Church.* Second Edition. London, 1867.

Dupanloup, *Hist. de Notre Sauveur Jésus Christ.* Paris, 1870.

Ebrard, *Gospel History.* Edinb., 1869.

Ecce Homo. 1867.

Ellicott, Bishop, *Historical Lectures on the Life of our Lord Jesus Christ.* Fifth Edition. London, 1869.

Etheridge, *Introduction to Hebrew Literature.* London, 1858.

Ewald, *Geschichte Christus und seiner Zeit (Gesch. des Volkes Israel. V.). Dritte Ausgabe.* Göttingen, 1867.

Frankl, *The Jews in the East.* E. Tr. London, 1859.

Gaussen, *Theopneustia.* E. Tr. London, 1866.

Gfrörer, *Das Jahrhundert des Heils.* Stuttgard, 1838.

Glass, *Philologia Sacra.* Amsterdam, 1694.

Graetz, *Geschichte des Juden.*

Guder, *König Herodes der Grosse.*

Guizot, *Méditations sur l' Esprit de Christianisme.*

Hanna, Dr., *Life of Jesus.* 1869.

Hanson, Sir R., *The Jesus of History,* London, 1869.

Hase, *Leben Jesu. Fünfte Auflage.* Leipzig, 1865.

Hervey, Rev. Lord A., (Bishop of Bath and Wells), *The Genealogies of. Our Lord.* Cambridge, 1853.

Herzfeld, *Geschichte des Volkes Israel.*

Herzog, *Encyclopœdia.* E. Tr. Ed. Bomberger, 1860.

Hilgenfeld, *Messia Judaeorum.* Leipzig, 1869.

Hofmann, *Das Leben Jesu nach den Apokryphen.* Leipzig, 1851.

Jahn, *Hebrew Commonwealth.* London, 1828.

—— *Archaeologia Biblica.* Third Edition. E. Tr. Oxford, 1836.

Josephus, *Antiquitates Judaicae, Bellum Judaicum, Vita Contra Apionem.* Edit. Richter, 1826, and Whiston's Translation.

Jost, *Geschichte des Judenthums.*

Judged by His Words.

Keim, *Geschichte Jesu von Nazara.* Zürich, 1867.

Kitto, *Biblical Cyclopœdia.* Third Edition. Edinburgh, 1862.

Lange, *Leben Jesu.* E. Tr. 6 vols. Edinburgh, 1864.

Lightfoot, *Horae Hebraicae.* Cantab., 1658.

Lightfoot, *The Revision of the New Testament.*

Lynch, *Exploration of the Jordan and Dead Sea.* Philadelphia, 1849.

Madden, *History of Jewish Coinage.* London, 1864.

Maurice, *Unity of the New Testament.* London, 1854.

McCaul, *The Old Paths.*

McGregor, *The Rob Roy on the Jordan.*

Messiah, The. London, 1864.

Mill, *Mythical Interpretation of the Gospels.* Cambridge, 1861.

Milman, *History of Christianity.*

Monod, Adolphe, *Enfance de Jésus.*

Munk, *Palestine.* Didot frères. Paris.

Neander, *The Life of Jesus Christ.* E. Tr. 1869.

Otho, *Lexicon Rabbinicum.*

Pearson, *On the Creed.* Twenty-first Edition. London, 1839.

Perrone, Joan, *De D. N. Jesu Christi Divinitate.* Turin, 1870.

Plumptre, *Christ and Christendom.* Boyle Lectures. London, 1866.

Porter, J. L., *Handbook for Syria and Palestine.* London, 1868.

Raphall, *History of the Jews.*

Reland, *Antiq. Hebraicae.* Ed. 3. 1717.

—— *Analecta Rabbinica.* 1711.

Renan, *Vie de Jésus.* 13me éd. Paris, 1867.

—— *L'Antechrist.* Paris, 1873.

Robinson, *Biblical Researches.* Boston, 1856.

Salvador, J., *Jésus Christ et sa Doctrine.* Two vols. Paris, 1861.

Sanday, *The Authorship and Historical Character of the Fourth Gospel.* London, 1872.

Schenkel, *Character of Jesus.* E. Tr. London, 1869.

Schleusner, *Lex. Nov. Testamenti.* Third Edition. Leipzig, 1808.

Schöttgen, Horae Hebraicae. Dresden, 1733.

Scott, *English Life of Jesus.*

Scrivener, *Introduction to the Criticism of the New Testament.* Cambridge, 1861.

Sepp, *Das Leben Jesu.* Regensburg, 1852-62.

Smith, *Dictionary of the Bible.* London, 1860.

Stanley, *Sinai and Palestine.* London, 1866.

Stier, R., *Reden Jesu.* 8 vols. E. Tr. Edinburgh, 1855.

Strauss, *Leben Jesu;* and *A New Life of Jesus.* E. Tr. London, 1865.

Surenhusius, *Mischna.* 6 vols., fol. Amsterdam, 1700.

Thomson, *The Land and the Book.* New York, 1859.

Tischendorf, *Synopsis Evangelica.* Ed. Tert. Leipzig, 1871.

Trench, *On the Miracles.* Ninth Edition, 1870.

—— *On the Parables.* Tenth Edition, 1866.

—— *Sermon on the Mount.*

—— *Studies in the Gospels.*

Turpie, *The Old Testament in the New.* London, 1868-1872.

Ullmann, *Die Sündlosigkeit Jesu.* Gotha, 1863. 7te Aufl.

—— *Historisch oder Mythisch?* 2te Aufl. Gotha, 1866.

Waehner's *Antiq. Hebraicae.* 2 vols. Göttingen, 1742.

Wagenseil, *Tela Ignea Satanae.* 2 vols. Altdorf, 1861.

Wallon, H., *Vie de Notre Seigneur Jésus Christ.* Paris, 1865.

Westcott, *Introduction to the Study of the Gospels.* Third Edition, 1867.

—— *Characteristics of the Gospel Miracles.* Cambridge, 1859.

—— *Gospel of the Resurrection.* London, 1866.

Wieseler, *Synopsis of the Four Gospels.* E. Tr. Cambridge, 1864.

Williams, *The Nativity.* London, 1844.

Winer, *Realwörterbuch.* Leipzig, 1847.

—— *Grammar of the New Testament.* E. Tr. Sixth Edition, 1866.

Wordsworth, Bishop, *The Four Gospels.* Seventh Edition. London, 1870.

Young, *The Christ of History.*

CONTENTS.

CHAPTER XII.

The Scene of the Ministry.

CHAPTER XIII.

Jesus at the Passover.

CHAPTER XIV.

Nicodemus.

CHAPTER XV.

The Woman of Samaria.

CHAPTER XVI.

Rejected by the Nazarenes.

CHAPTER XVII.

The Beginning of the Galilæan Ministry.

CHAPTER XLII.

FAREWELL TO GALILEE.   PAGE.

CHAPTER XLIII.

INCIDENTS OF THE JOURNEY.

CHAPTER XLIV.

TEACHINGS OF THE JOURNEY.

CHAPTER XLV.

THE FEAST OF DEDICATION.

CHAPTER XLVI.

THE LAST STAY IN PERÆA.

CHAPTER XLVII.

THE RAISING OF LAZARUS.

CHAPTER XLVIII.

JERICHO AND BETHANY.

CHAPTER XLIX.

PALM SUNDAY.

CHAPTER L.

MONDAY IN PASSION WEEK.—A DAY OF PARABLES.

CHAPTER LX.

JESUS BEFORE PILATE.

CHAPTER LXI.

THE CRUCIFIXION.

CHAPTER LXII.

THE RESURRECTION.

APPENDIX.

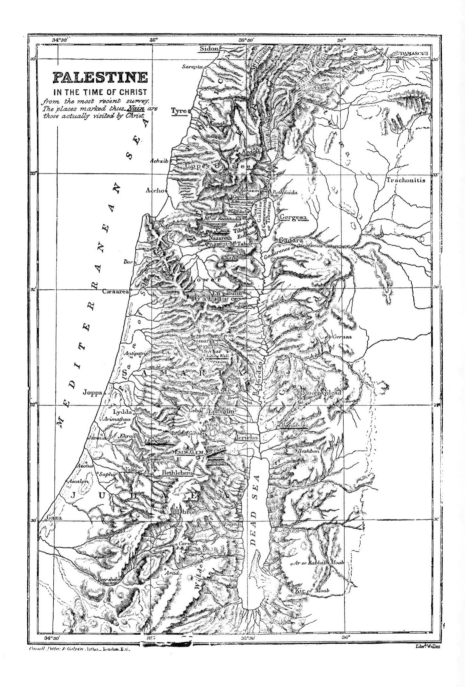

PALESTINE

IN THE TIME OF CHRIST

from the most recent survey.
The places marked thus. <u>Nain</u> are
those actually visited by Christ.

Sidon

DAMASCUS

Sarepta

Tyre

Kanah

M E D I T E R R A N E A N   S E A

Achzib

Kedesh

Trachonitis

Upper Galilee

Accho

Chorazin
Capernaum
Bethsaida

Bethsaida

Magdala

Gergesa

M^t of Beatitudes

Galilee
(Gennesaret)
or Tiberias

Cana
Tiberias

Nazareth
Endor

Gadara

Japha

M^tTabor

Gadarenes or Gergesenes

<u>Nain</u>

Dor

Lower
Galilee

Caesarea

En gannim

Gerasa

Salim

Enon

Samaria
Mt Ebal
Sychar
Jacobs Well
Gerizim

S A M A R I A

Antipatris

Shiloh

J O R D A N

Ramoth Gilead

Joppa

Lydda

Gebal
Ephraim

Arimathea

Bethel
Gibeah

Rabbath

Jamnia

Elron

Jericho

Emmaus

Heshbon

JERUSALEM
Bethany

Azotus

Saphir

Valley of

Bethlehem

Ascalon

J U D Æ A

Gaza

Hebron

D E A D   S E A

Engedi

R. Arnon

Carmel

Ar or Rabbath Moab

Beersheba

Arad

Kir of Moab

34°30' 35° 35°30' 36°

Cassell Petter & Galpin Litho London E.C.

Edwd Weller

THE

LIFE OF CHRIST.

CHAPTER I.

THE NATIVITY.

Αὐτὸς ἐνηνθρωπήσεν ἵνα ἡμεῖς θεοποιηθῶμεν.[6] — ATHAN., *De Incarn.*, p.
54 (*Opp.* i. 108).

ONE mile from Bethlehem is a little plain, in which, under a grove
of olives, stands the bare and neglected chapel known by the name
of "the Angel to the Shepherds."[1] It is built over the traditional
site of the fields where, in the beautiful language of St. Luke — more
exquisite than any idyl to Christian ears — "there were shepherds
keeping watch over their flock by night, when, lo, the angel of the
Lord came upon them, and the glory of the Lord[2] shone round about
them," and to their happy ears were uttered the good tidings of great
joy, that unto them was born that day in the city of David a Saviour,
which was Christ the Lord.

The associations of our Lord's nativity were all of the humblest
character, and the very scenery of His birthplace was connected with
memories of poverty and toil. On that night, indeed, it seemed as
though the heavens must burst to disclose their radiant minstrelsies ;
and the stars, and the feeding sheep, and the "light and sound in the

---

[1] "*Angelus ad Pastores.*" Near this spot once stood a tower called Migdal
Eder, or "Tower of the Flock " (Gen. xxxv. 21). The present rude chapel is,
perhaps, a mere fragment of a church built over the spot by Helena. (See Caspari, *Chronologisch-Geographische Einleitung*, p. 57.) The prophet Micah (iv. 8 ;
v. 2) had looked to Migdal Eder with Messianic hopes ; and St. Jerome (*De Loc.
Hebr.*), writing with views of prophecy which were more current in the ancient
than in the modern Church, ventures to say " that by its very name it fore-signi-
fied by a sort of prophecy the shepherds at the birth of the Lord."

[2] By *δόξα Κυρίου* (Luke ii. 9) is probably meant the Shechînah or cloud of
brightness which symbolized the Divine presence.

darkness and stillness," and the rapture of faithful hearts, combine to furnish us with a picture painted in the colors of heaven. But in the brief and thrilling verses of the Evangelist we are not told that those angel songs were heard by any except the wakeful shepherds of an obscure village; — and those shepherds, amid the chill dews of a winter night, were guarding their flocks from the wolf and the robber, in fields where Ruth, their Saviour's ancestress, had gleaned, sick at heart, amid the alien corn, and David, the despised and youngest son of a numerous family, had followed the ewes great with young.[1]

"And suddenly," adds the sole Evangelist who has narrated the circumstances of that memorable night in which Jesus was born, amid the indifference of a world unconscious of its Deliverer, "there was with the angel a multitude of the heavenly host, praising God, and saying, Glory to God in the highest, and on earth peace among men of good will."[2]

It might have been expected that Christian piety would have marked the spot by splendid memorials, and enshrined the rude grotto of the shepherds in the marbles and mosaics of some stately church. But, instead of this, the Chapel of the Herald Angel is a mere rude crypt; and as the traveller descends down the broken steps, which lead from the olive-grove into its dim recess, he can hardly persuade himself that he is in a consecrated place. Yet a half

---

[1] Ps. lxxviii. 71.

[2] Luke ii. 14, ἐν ἀνθρώποις εὐδοκίας: such is the reading of the best MSS.. א, A, B, D, and some of the best versions, the Vetus Itala, Vulgate, Gothic, &c. Moreover, however dear the other reading may be to us from long and delightful association, this best maintains the obvious poetic parallelism :

Glory　to God　　　　　　　　in the highest,
Peace　to men of good will　on earth.

By ἀνθρώποις εὐδοκίας we may perhaps understand with Valcknaer, "men with whom God is pleased." As I shall not unfrequently refer to the text of the Greek Testament, I may take this opportunity of telling the ordinary reader that by א is meant the *Codex Sinaiticus*, now at St. Petersburgh, discovered by Tischendorf in 1844, and perhaps as old as the fourth century ; by A, the *Codex Alexandrinus* in the British Museum, written in the middle of the fifth century ; by B, the *Codex Vaticanus* in the Vatican, which belongs to the middle of the fourth century ; by C, the *Codex Ephraemi*, a palimpsest in the Imperial Library at Paris, not later than the fifth century ; by D, the *Codex Bezae* in the University Library at Cambridge, not later than the seventh century ; by E, the *Codex Basiliensis*, about the eighth century ; by F, the *Codex Boreeli* at Utrecht ; by L, the *Codex Regius Parisiensis*, an accurate and important MS. of the eighth century. I shall seldom refer to the readings of any later MSS. A full and convenient account of them may be found in the Rev. F. Scrivener's *Plain Introduction to the Criticism of the New Testament* (1861), and in the Prolegomena to Alford's *Greek Testament*, i. pp. 83—90.

unconscious sense of fitness has, perhaps, contributed to this apparent neglect. The poverty of the chapel harmonizes well with the humble toil of those whose radiant vision it is intended to commemorate.

"Come now! let us go into Bethlehem,[1] and see this thing which has come to pass, which the Lord made known to us," said the shepherds, when those angel songs had ceased to break the starry silence. Their way would lead them up the terraced hill, and through the moonlit gardens of Bethlehem, until they reached the summit of the grey ridge on which the little town is built. On that summit stood the village inn. The khan (or caravansary) of a Syrian village, at that day, was probably identical, in its appearance and accommodation, with those which still exist in modern Palestine. A khan is a low structure, built of rough stones, and generally only a single story in height. It consists for the most part of a square enclosure, in which the cattle can be tied up in safety for the night, and an arched recess for the accommodation of travellers. The *leewan*, or paved floor of the recess, is raised a foot or two above the level of the courtyard. A large khan — such, for instance, as that of which the ruins may still be seen at Khan Minyeh, on the shore of the Sea of Galilee — might contain a series of such recesses, which are, in fact, low small rooms with no front wall to them. They are, of course, perfectly public; everything that takes place in them is visible to every person in the khan. They are also totally devoid of even the most ordinary furniture. The traveller may bring his own carpet if he likes, may sit cross-legged upon it for his meals, and may lie upon it at night.[2] As a rule, too, he must bring his own food, attend to his own cattle, and draw his own water from the neighboring spring. He would neither expect nor require attendance, and would pay only the merest trifle for the advantage of shelter, safety, and a floor on which to lie. But if he chanced to arrive late, and the *leewans* were

---

[1] Luke ii. 15, διέλθωμεν δή = *agedum*. I must remark at the outset that in most of my quotations from the Gospels I do not slavishly follow the English version, but translate from the original Greek.

[2] "It is common to find two sides of the one room where the native farmer resides with his cattle, and the remainder elevated about two feet higher for the accommodation of the family" (Thomson, *Land and Book*, II., ch. xxxiii.). See, too, Lane's *Modern Egyptians*, i. 18.—*Leewan* is a corruption *el-eewán*, which signifies any raised place to sit upon. My description is, however, drawn directly from my own experiences, especially one night at a poor and lonely place called Khan Hulda, between Sidon and Beyrout, at which we found ourselves belated. A distinction has been drawn between κατάλυμα (Luke ii. 7), and πανδοχεῖον (Luke x. 34), but probably the only distinction is that the former was a *free* place of shelter, and had no host.

all occupied by earlier guests, he would have no choice but to be content with such accommodation as he could find in the court-yard
below, and secure for himself and his family such small amount of
cleanliness and decency as are compatible with an unoccupied corner
on the filthy area, which must be shared with horses, mules, and
camels. The litter, the closeness, the unpleasant smell of the crowded
animals, the unwelcome intrusion of the pariah dogs, the necessary
society of the very lowest hangers-on of the caravansery, are
adjuncts to such a position which can only be realized by any traveller
in the East who happens to have been placed in similar circumstances.

In Palestine it not unfrequently happens that the entire khan, or
at any rate the portion of it in which the animals are housed, is one
of those innumerable caves which abound in the limestone rocks of
its central hills. Such seems to have been the case at the little town
of Bethlehem-Ephratah, in the land of Judah. Justin Martyr the
Apologist, who, from his birth at Shechem, was familiar with Palestine, and who lived less than a century after the time of our Lord,[1]
places the scene of the nativity in a cave. This is, indeed, the
ancient and constant tradition both of the Eastern and the Western
Churches, and it is one of the few to which, though unrecorded in
the Gospel history, we may attach a reasonable probability.[2] Over
this cave has risen the Church and Convent of the Nativity, and it
was in a cave close beside it that one of the most learned, eloquent,
and holy of the Fathers of the Church — that great St. Jerome to
whom we owe the received Latin translation of the Bible — spent
thirty of his declining years in study, and fast, and prayer.[3]

From their northern home at Nazereth, in the mountains of Zabu-
lon, Joseph, the village carpenter, had made his way along the wintry
roads with Mary his espoused wife, being great with child.[4] Fallen

---

[1] Justin Martyr was born at Flavia Neapolis, A. D. 103, and died A. D. 166. The
date of his First Apology was about A. D. 138. (Gieseler, *Ch. Hist.* i. 153, E. Tr.)

[2] It is impossible to stand in the little Chapel of the Nativity, and to look without emotion on the silver star let into the white marble, encircled by its sixteen
ever-burning lamps, and surrounded by the inscription, "*Hic de Virgine Maria
Jesus Christus natus est.*" [7]

[3] He settled in Bethlehem A. D. 386 and died A. D. 420. His allusions to the
sacredness of the spot are very touching, and the most splendid offers of prefer-
ment were insufficient to tempt him away from that holy ground (*Ep.* 24 *ad
Marcell.*).

[4] It appears to be uncertain whether the journey of Mary with her husband was
obligatory or voluntary. From Dion. Hal. iv. 15 (*ed. Sylb.*, p. 221) and Lact. *De
mort. persec.* 23, the former seems not unlikely. Women were liable to a capitation tax, if this enrolment (ἀπογραφή) also involved taxation (ἀποτίμησις).

as were their fortunes, they were both of the house and lineage of
David, and they were traversing a journey of eighty miles to the village which had been the home of their great ancestor while he was
still a ruddy shepherd lad, tending his flocks upon the lonely hills.
The object of that toilsome journey, which could not but be disagreeable to the settled habits of Oriental life, was to enrol their names as
members of the house of David in a census which had been ordered
by the Emperor Augustus. In the political condition of the Roman
Empire, of which Judæa then formed a part, a single whisper of the
Emperor was sufficiently powerful to secure the execution of his
mandates in the remotest corners of the civilized world. Great as
are the historic difficulties in which this census is involved, there seem
to be good independent grounds for believing that it may have been
originally ordered by Sentius Saturninus,[1] that it was *begun* by Pub-
lius Sulpicius Quirinus,[2] when he was for the first time legate of

But, apart from any legal necessity, it may easily be imagined that at such a
moment Mary would desire not to be left alone. The cruel suspicion of which she
had been the subject, and which had almost led to the breaking off of her betrothal
(Matt. i. 19), would make her cling all the more to the protection of her husband.

[1] Tert. *Adv. Marc.* v. 19. It has been held impossible that there should have
been a census in the kingdom of an independent prince; yet the case of the
Clitae (" Clitarum natio, Cappadoci Archelao subjecta, quia *nostrum in modum
deferre census, pati tributa* adigebatur," [3] &c., Tac. *Ann.* vi. 41) seems to be closely
parallel. That the enrollment should be conducted in the Jewish fashion at the
place of family origin, and not in the Roman fashion at the place of residence,
may have been a very natural concession to the necessities of Herod's position.
It may be perfectly true that this plan would give more trouble; but, in spite of
this, it was far less likely to cause offence. Yet although the whole proceeding
was probably due to a mere desire on the part of Augustus to make a *breviarium
imperii*, or Domesday Book, which should include the *regna* as well as the provinces (Tac. *Ann.* i. 11), it is very doubtful whether it actually did not cause disturbances at this very time (Jos. *Antt.* xvii. 2, § 2), as we know that it did ten years
later. How deeply the disgrace of a heathen census was felt is shown by
the Targum of Jonathan, Hab. iii. 17, where for " The flock shall be cut off
from the folds, and there shall be no herd in the stalls," he has, " The Romans
shall be rooted out ; they shall collect no more tribute from Jerusalem " (*Kesooma*
= census, v. Buxtorf, s. v.; Gfrörer, *Jahrhund. des Heils*, i. 42).

[2] Cyrenius (P. Sulp. Quirinus) was a man of low extraction, at once ambitious
and avaricious, but faithful to Augustus (Tac. *Ann.* ii. 30 ; iii. 22—48). Other
passages bearing more or less directly on this famous census are Tac. *Ann.* i. 11 ;
Suet. *Aug.* 28, 101; Dio Cass. liv. 35, &c. ; Suidas, s. v. ἀπογραφη. No less
than three censuses of Roman citizens are mentioned in the Monumentum Ancyranum ; and Strabo (under Tiberius) speaks of them as common. Zumpt has,
with incredible industry and research, all but established in this matter the
accuracy of St. Luke, by proving the extreme *probability* that Quirinus was *twice*
governor of Syria — viz., 750—753 A. U. C., and again 760—765. It was during
the *former* period that he completed the first census which had been commenced

Syria, and that it was completed during his second term of office. In deference to Jewish prejudices, any infringement of which was the certain signal for violent tumults and insurrection, it was not carried out in the ordinary Roman manner, at each person's place of residence, but according to Jewish custom, at the town to which their family originally belonged. The Jews still clung to their genealogies and to the memory of long-extinct tribal relations; and though the journey was a weary and distasteful one, the mind of Joseph may well have been consoled by the remembrance of that heroic descent which would now be authoritatively recognized, and by the glow of those Messianic hopes to which the marvellous cir-

---

by Varus (Zumpt, *Das Geburtsjahr Christi; Hist. Chronol. Untersuchungen*, Leipz., 1870). The argument mainly turns on the fact that in A. U. C. 742, Quirinus was consul and afterwards (not before A. U. C. 747) proconsul of Africa: yet some time between this year and A. U. C. 753 (in which year he was appointed *rector* to C. Cæsar, the grandson of Augustus) he conquered the Homonadenses in Cilicia (Tac. *Ann.* iii. 48). He must therefore have been at this time *propraetor* of the *imperial* province of Syria, to which Cilicia belonged. The other provinces near Cilicia (Asia, Bithynia, Pontus, Galatia) were senatorial, *i. e., proconsular,* and as a man could not be *proconsul* twice, Quirinus could not have been governor in any of these. It is not possible here to give the ingenious and elaborate arguments by which Zumpt shows that the Homonadenses must at this time have been under the jurisdiction of the Governor of Syria. Further than this, we know that P. Q. Varus was propraetor of Syria, between B. C. 6 and B. C. 4 (A. U. C. 748 — 750), and it is extremely likely that Varus may have been displaced in favor of Quirinus in the latter year, because the close friendship of the former with Archelaus, who resembled him in character, might have done mischief. It may therefore be regarded as all but certain, on independent grounds, that Quirinus was propraetor of Syria between B. C. 4 and B. C. 1. And if such was the case, instead of having been guilty of a flagrant historical error by antedating, by ten years, the propraetorship of Quirinus in Syria,.St. Luke has preserved for us the *historical fact* of his having been *twice* propraetor, or, to give the full title, Legatus Augusti pro praetore a fact which we should have been unable to learn from Josephus or Dio Cassius, whose histories are here imperfect. For the full arguments on this point the reader must, however, consult the exhaustive treatise of A. W. Zumpt. The appeals of Tertullian to census-records of Saturninus, and of Justin Martyr to the tables of Quirinus, as proving the genealogy of our Lord, are (so far as we can attach any importance to them) an additional confirmation of these conclusions, which are not overthrown by Mommsen (*Res. Gest. Div. Aug.*, p. 123) and Strauss (*Leben Jesu*, i. 28); see Merivale, Hist. iv. 45. Quirinus, not Quirinius, is probably the true form of the name (Orelli ad Tac. *Ann.* ii. 30) For further discussion of the question see Wieseler, *Synops. of the Four Gospels*, E. Tr., pp. 65—106. I may, however, observe in passing that, although no error has been proved, and, on the contrary, there is much reason to believe that the reference is perfectly accurate, yet I hold no theory of inspiration which would prevent me from frankly admitting, in such matters as these, any mistake or inaccuracy which could be shown really to exist.

cumstances of which he was almost the sole depositary would give a tenfold intensity.[1]

Travelling in the East is a very slow and leisurely affair, and was likely to be still more so if, as is probable, the country was at that time agitated by political animosities. Beeroth, which is fifteen miles distant from Bethlehem,[2] or possibly even Jerusalem, which is only six miles off, may have been the resting-place of Mary and Joseph before this last stage of their journey. But the heavy languor, or

---

[1] That Joseph alone knew these facts appears from Matt. i. 19, where the best reading seems to be not παραδειγματίσαι, but δειγματίσαι — i. e., not "make her an example," but, as Eusebius points out, "reveal her condition to the world." The ἐνθυμηθέντος of verse 20 means that this intention continued until the explanation had been revealed to him. There is nothing surprising in the fact that the descendant of a royal house should be in a lowly position. Hillel, the great Rabbi, though he, too, was a descendant of David, spent a great part of his life in the deepest poverty as a common workman. The green turban, which marks a descendant of Mahomet, may often be seen in Egypt and Arabia on the head of paupers and beggars. Similar facts exist quite commonly among ourselves ; and, ages before this time, we find that the actual *grandson* of the great Lawgiver himself (Judg. xviii. 30, where the true reading is "Moses," not "Manasseh") was an obscure, wandering, semi-idolatrous Levite, content to serve an irregular ephod for a double suit of apparel and ten shekels (*i. e.* about thirty shillings) a year (Judg. xvii. 10). On the genealogies given in St. Matthew and St. Luke, see the learned and admirable article by the Bishop of Bath and Wells in Smith's *Dict. of the Bible*, and his more elaborate work on the same subject. Here I need only add that remarkable confirmations of the descent of Jesus from David are found (1) in the story of Domitian and the Desposyni, alluded to in *infr.* Chap. IV. ; and (2) in a statement by Ulla, a Rabbi, of the third century, that "Jesus was treated exceptionally *because of His royal extraction*" (שאני ישו דקרוב למלכות הוה, *Sanhedrin*, 43 *a*, in non-expurgated editions) (Derenbourg, *L'Hist. de la Palestine,* p. 349). It is now almost certain that the genealogies in both Gospels are genealogies of Joseph, which, if we may rely on early traditions of their consanguinity, *involve* genealogies of Mary also. The Davidic descent of Mary is implied in Acts ii. 30 ; xiii. 23; Rom. i. 3; Luke i. 32, &c. St. Matthew gives the legal descent of Joseph, through the elder and regal line, as heir to the throne of David; St. Luke gives the natural descent. Thus the real father of Salathiel was heir of the house of Nathan, but the childless Jeconiah (Jer. xxii. 30) was the last lineal representative of the elder kingly line. The omission of some obscure names and the symmetrical arrangement into tesseradecads were common Jewish customs. It is not too much to say that after the labors of Mill (*On the Mythical Interpretation of the Gospels*, pp. 147—217) and Lord A. C. Hervey (*On the Genealogies of Our Lord*, 1853), scarcely a single serious difficulty remains in reconciling the apparent divergencies. And thus, in this, as in so many other instances, the very discrepancies which appear to be most irreconcilable, and most fatal to the historic accuracy of the four Evangelists, turn out, on closer and more patient investigation, to be fresh proofs that they are not only entirely independent, but also entirely trustworthy.

[2] St. Matthew calls it Bethlehem of Judæa (ii. 1) to distinguish it from Bethlehem in Zebulun (Josh. xix. 15). It is the Ephrath of Gen. xlviii. 7. Cf. Micah v. 2.

even the commencing pangs of travail, must necessarily have retarded the progress of the maiden-mother. Others who were travelling on the same errand, would easily have passed them on the road, and when, after toiling up the steep hill-side, by David's well, they arrived at the khan — probably the very one which had been known for centuries as the House of Chimham,[1] and if so, covering perhaps the very ground on which, one thousand years before, had stood the hereditary house of Boaz, of Jesse, and of David — every *leewan* was occupied. The enrolment had drawn so many strangers to the little town, that "there was no room for them in the inn." In the rude limestone grotto attached to it as a stable, among the hay and straw spread for the food and rest of the cattle, weary with their day's journey, far from home, in the midst of strangers, in the chilly winter night — in circumstances so devoid of all earthly comfort or splendor that it is impossible to imagine a humbler nativity — Christ was born.[2]

Distant but a few miles, on the plateau of the abrupt and singular hill now called *Jebel Fureidîs*, or "Little Paradise Mountain," towered the palace-fortress of the Great Herod. The magnificent houses of his friends and courtiers crowded around its base. The humble wayfarers, as they passed near it, might have heard the hired and voluptuous minstrelsy with which its feasts were celebrated, or the shouting of the rough mercenaries whose arms enforced obedi-

---

[1] Or rather "hostel" (גֵּרוּת) (Jer. xli. 17 ; 2 Sam. xix. 37, 38). One tradition says that the khan was on the ruins of a fortress built by David which had gradually fallen to ruin. The suggestion that the House of Chimham was the khan of Bethlehem is made by Mr. W. Hepworth Dixon (*Holy Land*, I., ch. xiii.). He gives a good description of Syrian khans.

[2] That "it was the winter wild," at the end of B. C. 5 or the beginning of B. C. 4 of our Dionysian era, is all but certain ; but neither the day nor the month can be fixed (εἰσὶν δὲ οἱ περιεργότερον . . . καὶ τὴν ἡμέραν προστιθέντες;[9] Clem. Alex. *Strom.* i. 21, § 145). That the actual place of Christ's birth was a cave is, as we have seen, a very ancient tradition, and this cave used to be shown as the scene of the event even so early (A. D. 150) as the time of Justin Martyr (*Dial. c. Tryph.*, c. 78, 304, ἐν σπηλαίῳ τινι συνεγγὺς τῆς κώμης.[10] Cf. Orig. *c. Cels.*, i. 51). There is therefore nothing improbable in the tradition which points out the actual cave as having been the one now covered by the Church of the Nativity at Bethlehem. Hadrian is said to have profaned it by establishing there the worship of Adonis. (Sepp, *Leben Jesu*, i. 7.) It is fair, however, to add that the tradition of the cave *may* have arisen from the LXX. rendering of Isa. xxxiii. 16, just as the subsequent words in the LXX., ἄρτος δοθήσεται αὐτῷ, were fancifully referred to Bethlehem, "the house of bread." There seems to be no proof of the assertion (mentioned by Stanley, *Sin. and Pal.*, p. 441), that the Arabs, when they plundered the church, found that the Grotto of the Nativity was an ancient sepulchre. If such had been the case, is it likely that the Empress Helena (A. D. 330) would have built her church there ?

ence to its despotic lord. But the true King of the Jews — the rightful Lord of the Universe — was not to be found in palace or fortress. They who wear soft clothing are in kings' houses. The cattle-stables of the lowly caravansery were a more fitting birthplace for Him who came to reveal that the soul of the greatest monarch was no dearer or greater in God's sight than the soul of his meanest slave; for Him who had not where to lay His head; for Him who, from His cross of shame, was to rule the world.[1]

Guided by the lamp which usually swings from the center of a rope hung across the entrance of the khan, the shepherds made their way to the inn of Bethlehem, and found Mary, and Joseph, and the Babe lying in the manger. The fancy of poet and painter has revelled in the imaginary glories of the scene. They have sung of the "bright harnessed angels" who hovered there, and of the stars lingering beyond their time to shed their sweet influences upon that smiling infancy. They have painted the radiation of light from His manger-cradle, illuminating all the place till the bystanders are forced to shade their eyes from that heavenly splendor.[2] But all this is wide of the reality. Such glories as the simple shepherds saw were seen only by the eye of faith; and all which met their gaze was a peasant of Galilee, already beyond the prime of life, and a young mother, of whom *they* could not know that she was wedded maid and virgin wife, with an Infant Child, whom, since there were none to help her, her own hands had wrapped in swaddling-clothes. The light that shined in the darkness was no physical, but a spiritual beam ;

---

[1] Ps. xcvi. 10, LXX. *ἐβασίλευσεν* [*ἀπὸ τοῦ ξύλου*] (J. Mart., *Dial c. Tryph.* § 73, p. 298). Tert. *Adv. Marc.* iii. 19, "Age nunc si legisti penes David ' *Dominus regnavit a ligno,*' exspecto quid intelligas nisi forte lignarium aliquem regem Judaeorum et non Christum, qui exinde a passione ligni superata morte regnavit." [11] Some suggest that the LXX. read עץ for אז, but it is more probable that the words were added by Christians, than that they were erased by Jews. The admission of the rendering quoted by Tertullian from the Vetus Itala, made some of the Western fathers attach great importance to a phrase which, though interesting, is certainly spurious.

[2] As in the splendid picture, " La Notte," of Correggio. See Arab. Gospel of the Infancy, ch. iii. : " And, lo! it (the cave) was filled with lights more beautiful than the glittering of lamps and candles, and brighter than the light of the sun." Protev. ch. xix. : " There appeared a great light in the cave, so that their eyes could not bear it." Gospel Pseud. Matth. xiii. : "A cave below a cavern, in which there was never any light, but always darkness. And when the blessed Mary had entered it, it began to become all light with brightness," &c. " Praesepe jam fulget tuum " [12] (Ambros. *De Adv. Dom.* 86). " Quando Christus natus est corpus ejus resplenduit ut sol quando oritur " [13] (Vincent Lerin. *Serm. de Nativitate,* referring to Isa. ix. 2).

the Dayspring from on high, which had now visited mankind, dawned only in a few faithful and humble hearts.[1]

And the Gospels, always truthful and bearing on every page that simplicity which is the stamp of honest narrative, indicate this fact without comment. There is in them nothing of the exuberance of marvel, and mystery, and miracle, which appears alike in the Jewish imaginations about their coming Messiah, and in the apocryphal narratives about the Infant Christ. There is no more decisive criterion of their absolute credibility as simple histories, than the marked and violent contrast which they offer to all the spurious gospels of the early centuries, and all the imaginative legends which have clustered about them. Had our Gospels been unauthentic, they too must inevitably have partaken of the characteristics which mark, without exception, every early fiction about the Saviour's life. To the unilluminated fancy it would have seemed incredible that the most stupendous event in the world's history should have taken place without convulsions and catastrophes. In the Gospel of St. James[2] there is a really striking chapter, describing how, at the awful moment of the nativity, the pole of the heaven stood motionless, and the birds were still, and there were workmen lying on the earth with their hands in a vessel, "and those who handled did not handle it, and those who took did not lift, and those who presented it to their mouth did not present it, but the faces of all were looking up; and I saw the sheep scattered and the sheep stood, and the shepherd lifted up his hand to strike, and his hand remained up; and I looked at the stream of the river, and the mouths of the kids were down, and were not drinking; and everything which was being propelled forward was intercepted in its course." But of this sudden hush and pause of awe-struck Nature,[3] of the parhelions and mysterious splendors which blazed in many places of the world, of the painless childbirth,[4] of the perpetual virginity,[5] of the

---

[1] The apocryphal Gospels, with their fondness for circumstantiality, and their readiness on all occasions to invent imaginary names, say that there were four shepherds, and that their names were Misael, Acheel, Cyriacus, and Stephanus (see Hofmann, *Leben Jesu nach den Apokryphen,* p. 117). The little village of Beit-Sahur is pointed out as their native place.

[2] Commonly known as the Protevangelium, ch. xviii.

[3] "Credibile est in aliis partibus mundi aliqua indicia nativitatis Christi apparuisse"[14] (S. Thom. Aquin., *Summa* iii. qu. 36, art. 3. Hofmann, p. 115, seqq.).

[4] "Nulla ibi obstetrix, nulla muliercularum sedulitas intercessit"[15] (Jer. *Adv. Helvid.*), probably with reference to Ps. xxii. 9 — "Thou art He who tookest me out of my mother's womb." This is, however, involved in Luke ii. 7, ἐσπαργάνωσεν.

[5] "Virgo ante partum, in partu, post partum"[16] (Aug. *Serm.* 123). "Claustrum

ox and the ass kneeling to worship Him in the manger,[1] of the voice
with which immediately after His birth He told His mother that He
was the Son of God,[2] and of many another wonder which rooted itself
in the earliest traditions, there is no trace whatever in the New Testament. The inventions of man differ wholly from the dealings of
God. In His designs there is no haste, no rest, no weariness, no dis-
continuity; all things are done by Him in the majesty of silence, and
they are seen under a light that shineth quietly in the darkness,
"showing all things in the slow history of their ripening." "The
unfathomable depths of the Divine counsels," it has been said, "were
moved; the fountains of the great deep were broken up; the healing of the nations was issuing forth: but nothing was seen on the
surface of human society but this slight rippling of the water: the
course of human things went on as usual, while each was taken up
with little projects of his own."

How long the Virgin Mother and her holy Child stayed in this
cave, or cattle-inclosure, we cannot tell, but probably it was not for
long. The word rendered "manger" in Luke ii. 7,[3] is of very
uncertain meaning, nor can we discover more about it than that it
means a place where animals were fed.[4] It is probable that the crowd
in the khan would not be permanent, and common humanity would
have dictated an early removal of the mother and her child to some

---

pudoris permanet" [17] (Ambros. *De Adv. Dom.* 10). This was a mere fantastic
inference from Ezek. xliv. 2. (See Jer. Taylor, *Life of Christ*, ed. Eden, p. 65, *n.*)
  [1] Gosp. Pseud. Matth. xiv. An incident imagined with reference to Isa. i. 3,
"The ox knoweth his owner," &c., and Hab. iii. 2, mistranslated in the LXX.,
"Between two animals Thou shalt be made known" (ἐν μέσῳ δύο ζώων
γνωσθήσῃ), and the Vet. Itala ("In medio duorum animalium innotesceris." [18])
"Cognovit bos et asinus Quod puer erat Dominus" [19] (Pister, *De Nativ. Dom.* 5).
  [2] Arab. Gosp. of Inf. i.
  [3] φάτνη (from πατέομαι, "I eat:" Curtius, *Grundzüge Griech. Etym.*, ii. 84).
It is used for אֵבוּס A. V., "crib," in Prov. xiv. 4 (Targ. אורותא, "barn;" cf. Isa.
i. 3; Job xxxix. 9), and for אֻרְוָה, "stable," in 2 Chron. xxxii. 28; cf. Hab. iii. 17.
In Luke xiii. 15 it is rendered "stall." But actual mangers, built as they are in
the shape of a kneading-trough, may be, and are, used as cradles in the East
(Thomson, *Land and Book*, ii. 533). Even where these are wanting, there is often
a projecting ledge on which the cattle can rest their nosebags. Mangers are certainly ancient (Hom. *Il.* x. 568; Hdt. ix. 70). On the whole I conclude that
φάτνη means primarily "an enclosure where cattle are fed;" and secondly, "the
place from which they eat," and hence is used both for a stable and a manger.
  [4] Vulg. "praesepe." Hence Mr. Grove (*Bibl. Dict.* s. v. "Bethlehem") goes a
little too far in saying that "the stable and its accompaniments are the creation
of the imagination of poets and painters, with *no support* from the Gospel narrative."

more appropriate resting-place. The magi, as we see from St. Mat
thew, visited Mary in "the house." [1]   But on all these minor incidents the Gospels do not dwell.   The fullest of them is St. Luke,
and the singular sweetness of his narrative, its almost idyllic grace,
its sweet calm tone of noble reticence, seemed clearly to indicate that
he derived it, though but in fragmentary notices, from the lips of
Mary herself.   It is, indeed, difficult to imagine from whom else it
could have come, for mothers are the natural historians of infant
years; but it is interesting to find, in the actual style, that "coloring
of a woman's memory and a woman's view," which we should naturally have expected in confirmation of a conjecture so obvious and so
interesting.[2]   To one who was giving the reins to his imagination,
the minutest incidents would have claimed a description; to Mary
they would have seemed trivial and irrelevant.   Others might wonder, but in her all wonder was lost in the one overwhelming revelation — the one absorbing consciousness.   Of such things she could
not lightly speak ; " she kept all these things, and pondered them in
her heart." [3]   The very depth and sacredness of that reticence is the
natural and probable explanation of the fact, that some of the details
of the Saviour's infancy are fully recorded by St. Luke alone.

---

[1] Matt. ii. 11.   [2] See Lange i. 325.   [3] Luke ii. 19.

CHAPTER II.

THE PRESENTATION IN THE TEMPLE.

"He who with all heaven's heraldry whilere
Entered the world, now bleeds to give us ease.
Alas! how soon our sin
Sore doth begin
His infancy to seize!" — MILTON, *The Circumcision.*

FOUR events only of our Lord's infancy are narrated by the Gospels —namely, the Circumcision, the Presentation in the Temple, the Visit of the Magi, and the Flight into Egypt. Of these the first two occur only in St. Luke, the last two only in St. Matthew. Yet no single particular can be pointed out in which the two narratives are necessarily contradictory. If, on other grounds, we have ample reason to accept the evidence of the Evangelists, as evidence given by witnesses of unimpeachable honesty, we have every right to believe that, to whatever cause the confessed fragmentariness of their narratives may be due, those narratives may fairly be regarded as supplementing each other. It is as dishonest to assume the existence of irreconcilable discrepancies, as it is to suggest the adoption of impossible harmonies. The accurate and detailed sequence of biographical narrative from the earliest years of life was a thing wholly unknown to the Jews, and alien alike from their style and temperament. Anecdotes of infancy, incidents of childhood, indications of future greatness in boyish years, are a very rare phenomenon in ancient literature. It is only since the dawn of Christianity that childhood has been surrounded by a halo of romance.

The exact order of the events which occurred before the return to Nazareth can only be a matter of uncertain conjecture. The Circumcision was on the eighth day after the birth (Luke i. 59; ii. 21); the Purification was thirty-three days after the circumcision [1] (Lev. xii. 4); the Visit of the Magi was "when Jesus was born in Bethlehem" (Matt. ii. 1); and the Flight into Egypt immediately after their departure. The supposition that the return from Egypt was previ-

---

[1] Not after the *birth*, as Caspari says.

ous to the Presentation in the Temple, though not absolutely impossible, seems most improbable. To say nothing of the fact that such a postponement would have been a violation (however necessary) of the Levitical law,[1] it would either involve the supposition that the Purification was long postponed, which seems to be contradicted by the twice-repeated expression of St. Luke (ii. 22, 39); or it supposes that forty days allowed sufficient time for the journey of the wise men from "the East," and for the flight to, and return from, Egypt. It involves, moreover, the extreme improbability of a return of the Holy Family to Jerusalem — a town but six miles distant from Bethlehem — within a few days after an event so frightful as the Massacre of the Innocents. Although no supposition is entirely free from the objections which necessarily arise out of our ignorance of the circumstances, it seems almost certain that the Flight into Egypt, and the circumstances which led to it, did not occur till after the Presentation. For forty days, therefore, the Holy Family were left in peace and obscurity, in a spot surrounded by so many scenes of interest, and hallowed by so many traditions of their family and race.

Of the Circumcision no mention is made by the apocryphal gospels, except an amazingly repulsive one in the Arabic Gospel of the Infancy.[2] It was not an incident which would be likely to interest those whose object it was to intrude their own dogmatic fancies into the sacred story. But to the Christian it has its own solemn meaning. It shows that Christ came not to destroy the Law, but to fulfil. Thus it became Him to fulfil all righteousness.[3] Thus early did He suffer pain for our sakes, to teach us the spiritual circumcision — the circumcision of the heart — the circumcision of all our bodily senses.[4] As the East catches at sunset the colors of the

---

[1] For by the law a woman was obliged to stay in the house during the forty days before the purification (Lev. xii. 1—8).

[2] Arab. Ev. Inf. ch. v.— It was doubtless performed by Joseph, and the presence of witnesses was necessary. Special prayers were offered on the occasion, a chair was placed for the prophet Elijah, as the precursor of the Messiah, and a feast terminated the ceremony. Lange (i. 399) well observes the contrast between the slight notice of the circumcision of Jesus, and the great festivities with which that of St. John was solemnized. " In John the rite of circumcision solemnized its last glory."

[3] Matt. iii. 15.

[4] See the somewhat fanciful, yet beautiful remarks of St. Bonaventura in his *Vita Christi*, ch. v.: " We Christians have baptism, a rite of fuller grace, and free from pain. Nevertheless, we ought to practice the circumcision of the heart."

West, so Bethlehem is a prelude to Calvary, and even the Infant's cradle is tinged with a crimson reflection from the Redeemer's cross.[1] It was on this day, too, that Christ first publicly received that name[2] of Jesus, which the command of the angel Gabriel had already announced. " Hoshea " meant salvation; Joshua, " whose salvation is Jehovah ; "[3] Jesus is but the English modification of the Greek form of the name. At this time it was a name extraordinarily common among the Jews. It was dear to them as having been borne by the great Leader who had conducted them into victorious possession of the Promised Land, and by the great High Priest who had headed the band of exiles who returned from Babylon;[4] but henceforth — not for Jews only, but for all the world — it was destined to acquire a significance infinitely more sacred as the mortal designation of the Son of God. The Hebrew " Messiah " and the Greek " Christ " were names which represented His office as the Anointed Prophet, Priest, and King ; but " Jesus " was the personal name which He bore as one who " emptied Himself of His glory " to become a sinless man among sinful men.[5]

On the fortieth day after the nativity — until which time she could not leave the house — the Virgin presented herself with her Babe for

---

[1] See Williams, *Nativity*, p. 87.

[2] Among the Greeks, and Romans also, the $\gamma\varepsilon\nu\acute{\varepsilon}\theta\lambda\iota\alpha$, or nominalia, were on the eighth or ninth day after birth. Among the Jews this was due to the fact mentioned in Gen. xvii. 5, 15 (Abraham and Sarah).

[3] יְהוֹשׁוּעַ, יֵשׁוּעַ, and יֵשׁוּ (Jehoshua, Jeshua, Jeshu) are the forms in which it occurs. It was sometimes Grecized into Jason, sometimes into Jesus. Its meaning is given in Philo ($\sigma\omega\tau\eta\rho\acute{\iota}\alpha$ $K\nu\rho\acute{\iota}o\nu$, *De Mutat. Nomin.*, § 21), and in Ecclus. xlvi. 1, $\mu\acute{\varepsilon}\gamma\alpha\varsigma$ $\grave{\varepsilon}\pi\grave{\iota}$ $\sigma\omega\tau\eta\rho\acute{\iota}\alpha$), just as in Matt. i. 21. In the New Testament " Jesus " twice stands for Joshua (Acts vii. 45 ; Heb. iv. 8). The name thus resembles the German *Gotthilf*. The Valentinians, by the cabalistic system, *notarikon*, made it equivalent to Jehovah shammaim va-aretz (see *Iren.* II., xxxiv 4); and Osiander makes it the ineffable name, the " Shemhammephorash," rendered utterable by an inserted שׁ.

[4] See Ezra ii. 2; iii. 2; Zech. iii. 1, &c. For other bearers of the name, see 1 Chron. xxiv. 11 ; 1 Sam. vi. 14; 2 Kings xxiii. 8 ; Luke iii. 29. A son of Saul is said to have been so called (Jos. *Antt.* vi. 6, § 6). In the New Testament we have " Jesus which is called Justus " (Col. iv. 11) ; Bar-Jesus (Acts xiii. 6); and probably *Jesus* Barabbas, if the reading be right in Matt. xxvii. 16. Possibly the name might have been omitted by transcribers from feelings of reverence ; on the other hand, it might have been inserted by heretics to spoil the fancy (alluded to by Origen *ad loc.*) that " in tantâ multitudine Scripturarum *neminem invenimus Jesum peccatorem.*"[20] (See Keim, *Geschichte Jesu*, i. 384—387.) No less than twelve people of the name (besides those mentioned in Scripture) are alluded to in Josephus alone..

[5] "Jesus mel in ore, in aure melos, in corde jubilum."[21] (St. Bern.)

their Purification in the Temple at Jerusalem.[1] "Thus, then," says
St. Bonaventura, "do they bring the Lord of the Temple to the
Temple of the Lord." The proper offering on such occasions was a
yearling lamb for a burnt-offering, and a young pigeon or a turtle-
dove for a sin-offering;[2] but with that beautiful tenderness, which
is so marked a characteristic of the Mosaic legislation, those who
were too poor for so comparatively costly an offering, were allowed
to bring instead two turtle-doves or two young pigeons.[3] With this
humble offering Mary presented herself to the priest. At the same
time Jesus, as being a first-born son, was presented to God, and in
accordance with the law, was redeemed from the necessity of Temple
service by the ordinary payment of five shekels of the sanctuary
(Numb. xviii. 15, 16), amounting in value to about fifteen shillings.
Of the purification and presentation no further details are given to
us, but this visit to the Temple was rendered memorable by a double
incident — the recognition of the Infant Saviour by Simeon and Anna.

Of Simeon we are simply told that he was a just and devout
Israelite endowed with the gift of prophecy, and that having received
divine intimation that his death would not take place till he had
seen the Messiah,[4] he entered under some inspired impulse into the
Temple, and there, recognizing the Holy Child, took Him in his arms,
and burst into that glorious song — the "Nunc Dimittis" — which
for eighteen centuries has been so dear to Christian hearts. The
prophecy that the Babe should be "a light to lighten the *Gentiles*,"
no less than the strangeness of the circumstances, may well have
caused astonishment to His parents, from whom the aged prophet did
not conceal their own future sorrows — warning the Virgin Mother
especially, both of the deadly opposition which that Divine Child was
destined to encounter, and of the national perils which should agitate
the days to come.[4]

---

[1] τοῦ καθαρισμοῦ αὐτῶν. The reading, αὐτῆς, adopted by the E. V., is of
ve y inferior authority, and probably due to dogmatic prejudice. Αὐτοῦ, the
reading of the Codex Bezae, is singular, but improbable.

[2] Luke ii. 22 ; Lev. xii. 1—8 ; Numb. xviii. 16.

[3] Lev. xii. 6—8.

[4] Hence he has received in early Christian writers the surname of Θεοδόκος.
The expression, "waiting for the consolation of Israel," resembles what St. Mark
says of Joseph of Arimathea, "who also waited for the kingdom of God" (Mark
xv. 43). A prayer for the coming of the Messiah formed a part of the daily *gĕul-
lah ;* and "may I see the consolation of Israel," was a common formula of hope
Sepp quotes *Chagigah*, fol. 16, and other rabbinical authorities.

[5] The word κεῖται (Luke ii. 34) has been taken to mean, "this child who lies in
my arms;" but the E. V. is probably nearer to the true meaning, and the meta-

Legend has been busy with the name of Simeon. In the Arabic Gospel of the Infancy, he recognizes Jesus because he sees Him shining like a pillar of light in His mother's arms.¹ Nicephorus tells us that, in reading the Scriptures, he had stumbled at the verse, ' Behold, a virgin shall conceive, and bear a son" (Isa. vii. 14), and had then received the intimation that he should not die till he had seen it fulfilled. All attempts to identify him with other Simeons have failed.² Had he been a High Priest, or President of the Sanhedrin, St. Luke would not have introduced him so casually as "a man (ἄνθρωπος) in Jerusalem whose name was Simeon." The statement in the Gospel of the Nativity of Mary that he was 113 years old is wholly arbitrary; as is the conjecture that the silence of the Talmud about him is due to his Christian proclivities. He could not have been Rabban Simeon, the son of Hillel, and father of Gamaliel, who would not at this time have been so old. Still less could he have been the far earlier Simeon the Just, who was believed to have prophesied the destruction of Jerusalem, and who was the last survivor of the great Sanhedrin.³ It is curious that we should be told nothing respecting him, while of Anna the prophetess several interesting particulars are given, and among others that she was of the tribe of Asher — a valuable proof that tribal relations still lived affectionately in the memory of the people.⁴

phor involved is that of a stone — whether for stumbling or for edification (v. Wordsworth *ad loc.*). In the sad prophecy, " Yea, a sword shall pierce through thy own soul also," the same word, *ῥομφαία*, is used as in Zech. xiii. 7, LXX.

¹ Ev. Inf. Arab. ch. vi.

² Gospel of James xxvi., and of Nicodemus xvi. They call him ὁ μέγας διδάσκαλος.²² It is a curious coincidence that the Jews say that " Christ was born in the days of R. Simeon, the son of Hillel."

³ I spell this word, Sanhedrin throughout, because it is evidently a mere transliteration of the Greek συνέδριον.

⁴ I can see no ground for the conjecture of Schleiermacher, approved by Neander, that the narrative was derived from Anna herself.

CHAPTER III.

THE VISIT OF THE MAGI.

" O Jerusalem, look about thee toward the east, and behold the joy that cometh
unto thee from God."— BARUCH iv. 36.

THE brief narrative of the Visit of the Magi, recorded in the
second chapter of St. Matthew, is of the deepest interest in the history
of Christianity. It is, in the first place, the Epiphany, or Manifestation of Christ to the Gentiles. It brings the facts of the Gospel
history into close connection with Jewish belief, with ancient prophecy, with secular history, and with modern science; and in doing so
it furnishes us with new confirmations of our faith, derived incidentally, and therefore in the most unsuspicious manner, from indisputable and unexpected quarters.

Herod the Great, who, after a life of splendid misery and criminal
success, had now sunk into the jealous decrepitude of his savage old
age, was residing in his new palace on Zion, when, half maddened as
he was already by the crimes of his past career, he was thrown into
a fresh paroxysm of alarm and anxiety by the visit of some Eastern
Magi, bearing the strange intelligence that they had seen in the East [1]
the star of a new-born king of the Jews, and had come to worship
him. Herod, a mere Idumæan usurper, a more than suspected apostate, the detested tyrant over an unwilling people, the sacrilegious
plunderer of the tomb of David [2] — Herod, a descendant of the

---

[1] The expression might, perhaps, be rendered, " at its rising" (the plural
ἀνατολαὶ, not ἀνατολή, is used for " the east," in Matt. ii. 1); but this would
seem to require αὐτοῦ, and does not well suit verse 9.

[2] Jos. *Antt.* xvi. 7, § 1. On seizing the throne, with the support of the Romans,
and specially of Antony, more than thirty years before (A. U. C. 717), Herod
(whose mother, Cypros, was an Arabian, and his father, Antipater, an Idumæan)
had been distinctly informed by the Sanhedrin that, in obedience to Deut. xvii.
15, they could not accept a stranger for their king. This faithfulness cost a great
many of them their lives. (See Jos. *Antt.* xiv. 9, § 4; xv. 1, &c., and rabbinic
authorities quoted by Sepp.) The political and personal relations of Herod were
evidently well adapted for the furtherance of a new religion. The rulers of the
Jews, since the Captivity, had been Persian between B.C. 536—332; Egypto-
Greek and Syro-Greek between B.C. 332—142; Asmonæan and independent

despised Ishmael and the hated Esau, heard the tidings with a terror and indignation which it was hard to dissimulate. The grandson of one who, as was believed, had been a mere servitor in a temple at Ascalon, and who in his youth had been carried off by Edomite brigands, he well knew how worthless were his pretensions to an historic throne which he held solely by successful adventure. But his craft equalled his cruelty, and finding that all Jerusalem shared his suspense, he summoned to his palace the leading priests and theologians of the Jews — perhaps the relics of that Sanhedrin which he had long reduced to a despicable shadow — to inquire of them where the Messiah [1] was to be born. He received the ready and confident answer that Bethlehem was the town indicated for that honor by the prophecy of Micah. [2] Concealing, therefore, his desperate intention, he dispatched the wise men to Bethlehem, bidding them to let him know as soon as they had found the child, that he too might come and do him reverence.

Before continuing the narrative, let us pause to inquire who these Eastern wanderers were, and what can be discovered respecting their mysterious mission.

---

between B. C. 142—63; and under Roman influences since the conquest of Jerusalem by Pompey, B.C. 63. Under Herod (from B.C. 37 to the birth of Christ) the government might fairly be called cosmopolitan. In him the East and the West were united. By birth an Edomite on the father's side, and an Ishmaelite on the mother's, he represented a *third* great division of the Semitic race by his nominal adoption of the Jewish religion. Yet his life was entirely moulded by conceptions borrowed from the two great *Aryan* races of the ancient world; his conceptions of policy and government were entirely Roman; his ideal of life and enjoyment entirely Greek. And, in addition to this, he was surrounded by a body-guard of barbarian mercenaries. At no previous or subsequent period could a world-religion have been more easily preached than it was among the heterogeneous elements which were brought together by his singular tyranny. (Guder, *König Herodes der Grosse*, i.) His astuteness, however, had early taught him that his one best security was to truckle to the all-powerful Romans (οἱ πάντων κρατοῦντες Ῥωμαῖοι, Jos. *Antt.* xv. 11, § 1).

[1] Not as in the English version, "where *Christ* should be born;" for it is ὁ Χριστός, "the Anointed." "Christ" in the Gospels, even when without the article in Greek, which is only in four passages, is *almost* without exception (John xvii. 3), an appellative and not a proper name ("non proprium nomen est, sed nuncupatio potestatis et regni," [23] Lact. *Instt. Div.* iv. 7). (See Lightfoot *on Revision*, 100.)

[2] Micah v. 2; cf. John vii. 42. The latter passage shows how familiarly this prophecy was known to the people. The Jewish authorities quote the text loosely, but give the sense. (See Turpie, *The Old · Test. in the New*, p. 189.) The version of Gen. xlix. 27 in the Targum of Onkelos is, "The Shechinah shall dwell in the land of Benjamin." (Gfrörer, *Jahrh. d. Heils*, i. 55.)

The name " Magi," by which they are called in the Greek of St.
Matthew, is perfectly vague.   It meant originally a sect of Median
and Persian scholars ; it was subsequently applied (as in Acts xiii.
6) to pretended astrologers, or Oriental soothsayers.   Such characters
were well known to antiquity, under the name of Chaldæans, and
their visits were by no means unfamiliar even to the Western
nations.   Diogenes Laertius reports to us a story of Aristotle, that a
Syrian *mage* had predicted to Socrates that he would die a violent
death ;[1] and Seneca informs us that magi, " *qui forte Athenis
erant*," [2a] had visited the tomb of Plato, and had there offered incense
to him as a divine being.[2]   There is nothing but a mass of confused
and contradictory traditions to throw any light either on their rank,
their country, their number, or their names.   The tradition which
makes them kings was probably founded on the prophecy of Isaiah
(lx. 3) : "And the Gentiles shall come to thy light, and kings to the
brightness of thy rising."   The fancy that they were Arabians may
have arisen from the fact that myrrh and frankincense are Arabian
products, joined to the passage in Ps. lxxii. 10, " The kings of Thar-
shish and of the isles shall give presents ; the kings of Arabia and
Saba shall bring gifts." [3]

There was a double tradition as to their number.   Augustine and
Chrysostom say that there were twelve, but the common belief, arising perhaps from the triple gifts, is that they were three in number.[4]
The Venerable Bede even gives us their names, their country, and
their personal appearance.   Melchior was an old man with white hair
and long beard ; Caspar, a ruddy and beardless youth ; Balthasar,
swarthy and in the prime of life.[5]   We are further informed by tradition that Melchior was a descendant of Shem, Caspar of Ham, and
Balthasar of Japheth.   Thus they are made representatives of the
three periods of life, and the three divisions of the globe ; and valueless as such fictions may be for direct historical purposes, they have
been rendered interesting by their influence on the most splendid
productions of religious art.[6]   The skulls of these three kings, each

---

[1] Diog. Laert. ii. 45.

[2] Sen. *Ep.* 58.

[3] In the original נשָׁבֶא, *i. e.* Arabia Felix.   One MS. of the Protevangelium makes
them come from Persia (ἐκ Περσίδος) ; Theodoret calls them Chaldæans ; Hilary,
Æthiopians ; some more recent writers make them Indians. (See Hofmann, p. 127.)

[4] See all the authorities for these legends or fancies quoted with immense learning and accuracy by Hofmann.

[5] Bede, *Opp.* iii. 649.

[6] The art student will at once recall the glorious pictures of Paul Veronese,
Giovanni Bellini, &c.

circled with its crown of jewelled gold, are still exhibited among the relics in the cathedral at Cologne.[1]

It is, however, more immediately to our purpose to ascertain the causes of their memorable journey.

We are informed by Tacitus, by Suetonius, and by Josephus,[2] that there prevailed throughout the entire East at this time an intense conviction, derived from ancient prophecies, that ere long a powerful monarch would arise in Judæa, and gain dominion over the world. It has, indeed, been conjectured that the Roman historians may simply be echoing an assertion, for which Josephus was in reality their sole authority; but even if we accept this uncertain supposition, there is still ample proof, both in Jewish and in Pagan writings, that a guilty and weary world was dimly expecting the advent of its Deliverer. "The dew of blessing falls not on us, and our fruits have no taste," exclaimed Rabban Simeon, the son of Gamaliel; and the expression might sum up much of the literature of an age which was, as Niebuhr says, "effete with the drunkenness of crime." The splendid vaticination in the fourth Eclogue of Virgil proves the intensity of the feeling, and has long been reckoned among the "unconscious prophecies of heathendom."

There is, therefore, nothing extraordinary in the fact that these Eastern magi should have bent their steps to Jerusalem, especially if there were any circumstances to awaken in the East a more immediate conviction that this wide-spread expectation was on the point of fulfilment. If they were disciples of Zoroaster, they would see in the Infant King the future conqueror of Ahriman, the destined Lord of all the World. The story of their journey has indeed been set down with contemptuous confidence as a mere poetic myth; but though its actual historic verity must rest on the testimony of the Evangelist alone, there are many facts which enable us to see that in its main outlines it involves nothing either impossible or even improbable.

---

[1] They were said to have been found by Bishop Reinald in the twelfth century.

[2] "Pluribus persuasio inerat, antiquis sacerdotum libris contineri, fore ut valesceret oriens, et e Judaea profecti rerum potirentur"[25] (Tac. *Hist.* v. 13). "Percrebuerat oriente toto vetus et constans opinio esse in fatis, ut eo tempore Judaea profecti rerum potirentur,[26] (Suet. *Vesp.* 4). χρησμὸς . . . ὡς κατὰ τὸν καιρὸν ἐκεῖνον ἀπὸ τῆς χώρας τις αὐτῶν ἄρξει τῆς οἰκουμένης[27] (Jos. *B. J.* vi. 5, § 4). Josephus steadily and characteristically interprets the prophecy of Vespasian. It is true that these historians refer to the days of the Flavian dynasty (A. D. 79); but the "vetus" of Suetonius, and the 4th Eclogue of Virgil, taken in connection with the possible date of the Third Book of the Sibylline Oracles, are signs that the expectation had existed half a century earlier.

Now St. Matthew tells us that the cause of their expectant attitude was that they had seen the star of the Messiah in the East, and that to discover Him was the motive of their journey.

That any strange siderial phenomenon should be interpreted as the signal of a coming king, was in strict accordance with the belief of their age. Such a notion may well have arisen from the prophecy of Balaam,[1] the Gentile sorcerer — a prophecy which from the power of its rhythm, and the splendor of its imagery, could hardly fail to be disseminated in eastern countries. Nearly a century afterwards, the false Messiah, in the reign of Hadrian, received from the celebrated Rabbi Akiba, the surname of Bar-Cocheba, or "Son of a Star," and caused a star to be stamped upon the coinage which he issued. Six centuries afterwards, Mahomet is said to have pointed to a comet as a portent illustrative of his pretensions. Even the Greeks and Romans[2] had always considered that the births and deaths of great men were symbolized by the appearance and disappearance of heavenly bodies, and the same belief has continued down to comparatively modern times. The evanescent star which appeared in the time of Tycho Brahe, and was noticed by him on Nov. 11, 1572, was believed to indicate the brief but dazzling career of some warrior from the north, and was subsequently regarded as having been prophetic of the fortunes of Gustavus Adolphus. Now it so happens that, although the exact year in which Christ was born is not ascertainable with any certainty from Scripture, yet, within a few years of what must, on any calculation, have been the period of His birth, there *undoubtedly* did appear a phenomenon in the heavens so remarkable that it could not possibly have escaped the observation of an astrological people. The immediate applicability of this phenomenon to the Gospel narrative is now generally abandoned; but, whatever other theory may be held about it, it is unquestionably

---

[1] That the Jews and their Rabbis had borrowed many astrological notions from the Chaldæans, and that they connected these notions with the advent of the Messiah, is certain. See the quotations from the tract *Sanhedrin*, R. Abraham, Abarbanel, the *Zohar*, in Münter, Sepp, &c. Comp. Jos. *Antt.* ii. 9, § 2, and i. 7, § 2, where Josephus quotes Berosus as having said that Abram was "skilful in the celestial science."

[2] Luc. i. 529; Suet. *Caes.* 88; Sen. *Nat. Quaest.* i. 1; Serv. ad Virg. *Ecl.* 9, 47, " Ecce Dionaei processit Caesaris astrum,"[25] &c. — Every one will remember the allusions in Shakespeare —

"The Heavens themselves blaze at the death of princes."—*Henry IV.*

and

"Comets portending change of time and state,
Brandish your crystal tresses in the sky,
And with them scourge the bad revolting stars
That have consented to our Henry's death."—1 *Henry VI.*, i. 1.

important and interesting as having furnished one of the data which first led to the discovery, that the birth of Christ took place three or four years before our received era.[1] This appearance, and the circumstances which have been brought into connection with it, we will proceed to notice. They form a curious episode in the history of exegesis, and are otherwise remarkable ; but we must fully warn the reader that the evidence by which this astronomical fact has been brought into immediate connection with St. Matthew's narrative is purely conjectural, and must be received, if received at all, with considerable caution.

On Dec. 17, 1603, there occurred a conjunction of the two largest superior planets, Saturn and Jupiter, in the zodiacal sign of the Fishes, in the watery trigon.[2] In the following spring they were joined in the fiery trigon by Mars, and in Sept., 1604, there appeared in the foot of Ophiuchus, and between Mars and Saturn, a new star of the first magnitude, which, after shining for a whole year, gradually waned in March, 1606, and finally disappeared.[3] Brunowski, the pupil of Kepler, who first noticed it, describes it as sparkling with an interchange of colors like a diamond, and as not being in any way nebulous, or offering any analogy to a comet.[4] These remarkable phenomena attracted the attention of the great Kepler, who, from his acquaintance with astrology, knew the immense importance which such a conjunction would have had in the eyes of the Magi, and wished to discover whether any such conjunction had taken place about the period of our Lord's birth. Now there is a conjunction of

---

[1] This is the date adopted by Ideler, Sanclemente, Wieseler. Herod the Great died in the first week of Nisan, A. U. C. 750, as we can prove, partly from the fact that shortly before his death there was an eclipse of the moon (Jos. *Antt.* xvii. 6, § 4). Ideler and Wurm have shown that the only eclipse visible at Jerusalem in the year 750 A. U. C., B. C. 4, must have taken place in the night between the 12th and 13th of March (Wieseler, p. 56). Our era was invented by Dionysius Exiguus, an abbot at Rome, who died in 556. See Appendix, Excursus I., " Date of Christ's Birth."

[2] Astrologers divided the Zodiac into four trigons — that of fire (Aries, Leo, Sagittarius) ; that of earth (Taurus, Virgo, Capricornus) ; that of air (Gemini, Libra, Aquarius) ; and that of water (Cancer, Scorpio, Pisces). (Wieseler, *Synopsis of the Four Gospels*, E. Tr., p. 57.) — On the astrology of the Jews in general, see Gfrörer, *Jahrh. des Heils*, ii. 116.

[3] The star observed by Tycho lasted from November, 1572, till about April, 1574. Such temporary stars are perhaps due to immense combustions of hydrogen. See Guillemin, *The Heavens*, pp. 310—313 ; Humboldt's *Cosmos*, ii. 323—333 (ed. Sabine).

[4] There may, therefore, be no exaggeration in the language of Ignatius (*Ep. ad Ephes.* § 19), when he says, " The star sparkled brilliantly above all stars "

Jupiter and Saturn in the same trigon about every twenty years, but in every 200 years they pass into another trigon, and are not conjoined in the same trigon again (after passing through the entire Zodiac), till after a lapse of 794 years, four months, and twelve days. By calculating backwards, Kepler discovered that the same conjunction of Jupiter and Saturn, in Pisces, had happened no less than three times in the year A. U. C. 747, and that the planet Mars had joined them in the spring of 748; and the general fact that there was such a combination at this period has been verified by a number of independent investigators,[1] and does not seem to admit of denial. And however we may apply the fact, it is certainly an interesting one. For such a conjunction would at once have been interpreted by the Chaldæan observers as indicating the approach of some memorable event; and since it occurred in the constellation Pisces, which was supposed by astrologers to be immediately connected with the fortunes of Judæa,[2] it would naturally turn their thoughts in that direction. The form of their interpretation would be moulded, both by the astrological opinions of the Jews — which distinctly point to this very conjunction as an indication of the Messiah — and by the expectation of a Deliverer which was so widely spread at the period in which they lived.

The appearance and disappearance of new stars is a phenomenon by no means so rare as to admit of any possible doubt.[3] The fact that St. Matthew speaks of such a star within two or three years, at the utmost, of a time when we know that there was this remarkable

---

[1] He supposed that the other conjunctions would coincide with seven great climacteric years or epochs : Adam, Enoch, the Deluge, Moses, Isaiah (about the commencement of the Greek, Roman, and Babylonian eras), Christ, Charlemagne, and the Reformation.

[2] Kepler's first tract on this subject was *De nova Stella in pede Serpentarii*, Prague, 1606. He was followed by Ideler, *Handbuch der Chronologie*, ii. 406 ; Pfaff, *Das Licht und die Weltgegenden*, Bamb., 1821 ; Münter, *Stern d. Weisen*, Copenhag., 1827 ; Schumacher, Schubert, Encke, Goldschmidt, &c. Professor Pritchard carefully went through Kepler's calculations, and confirms the fact of the conjunction, though he slightly modifies the dates, and, like most recent inquirers, denies that the phenomenon has any bearing on the Gospel narrative. That such astronomical facts are insufficient to explain the language of St. Matthew, if taken with minute and literal accuracy, is obvious ; but that they have *no bearing on* the circumstances as they were reported to the Evangelist perhaps half a century later, is more than can be safely affirmed.

[3] Sepp, who always delights in the most fanciful and unfounded combinations, connects this fact with the *Fish* (ΙΧΘΥΣ = ’Ιησοῦς Χριστὸς Θεοῦ Υἱὸς Σωτήρ) as the well-known symbol of the Church and of Christians. (*Leben Jesu*, p. 7.)

planetary conjunction, and the fact that there was such a star nearly 1,600 years afterwards, at the time of a similar conjunction, can only be regarded as a curious coincidence. We should, indeed, have a strong and strange confirmation of one main fact in St. Matthew's narrative, if any reliance could be placed on the assertion that, in the astronomical tables of the Chinese, a record has been preserved that a new star did appear in the heavens at this very epoch.[1] But it would be obviously idle to build on a datum which is so incapable of verification and so enveloped with uncertainty.

We are, in fact, driven to the conclusion that the astronomical researches which have proved the reality of this remarkable planetary conjunction are only valuable as showing the *possibility* that it may have prepared the Magi for the early occurrence of some great event. And this confident expectation may have led to their journey to Palestine, on the subsequent appearance of an evanescent star, an appearance by no means unparalleled in the records of astronomy, but which in this instance[2] seems to rest on the authority of the Evangelist, alone.

No one, at any rate, need stumble over the supposition that an apparent sanction is thus extended to the combinations of astrology. Apart from astrology altogether, it is conceded by many wise and candid observers, even by the great Niebuhr, the last man in the world to be carried away by credulity or superstition, that great catastrophes and unusual phenomena in nature have, as a matter of fact — however we may choose to interpret such a fact — synchronized in a remarkable manner with great events in human

---

[1] This is mentioned by Wieseler, p. 61. We cannot, however, press the Evangelist's use of ἀστήρ, "a star," rather than ἄστρον, "a constellation;" the two words are loosely used, and often almost indiscriminately interchanged. Further than this it must be steadily borne in mind (v. *supra*, note 2, page 54), that the curious fact of the planetary conjunction, even if it were accompanied by an evanescent star, would not exactly coincide with, though it might to some extent account for, the language used by St. Matthew.

[2] It is remarkable that the celebrated Abarbanel (d. 1508), in his מעיני הישועה, or " wells of salvation "—a commentary on Daniel—distinctly says that the conjunction of Jupiter and Saturn always indicates great events. He then gives five mystic reasons why Pisces should be the constellation of the Israelites, and says that there had been a conjunction of Jupiter and Saturn in Pisces *three years before* the birth of Moses. From a similar conjunction in his own days (1463), he expected the speedy birth of the Messiah. What makes this statement (which is quoted by Münter, *Stern d. Weisen*, § 55 ; and Ideler, *Handb. d. Chronol.*, ii. 405) more remarkable is, that Abarbanel must have been wholly ignorant of the conjunction in A. U. C. 747. (See Ebrard, *Gosp. Hist.*, E. Tr., p. 178.)

history.[1] It would not, therefore, imply any prodigious folly on the part of the Magi to regard the planetary conjunction as something providentially significant. And if astrology be ever so absurd, yet there is nothing absurd in the supposition that the Magi should be led to truth, even through the gateways of delusion, if the spirit of sincerity and truth was in them. The history of science will furnish repeated instances, not only of the enormous discoveries accorded to apparent accident, but even of the immense results achieved in the investigation of innocent and honest error. Saul who, in seeking asses, found a kingdom, is but a type of many another seeker in many another age.[2]

The Magi came to Bethlehem, and offered to the young child in his rude and humble resting-place[3] a reverence which we do not hear that they had paid to the usurping Edomite in his glittering palace. "And when they had opened their treasures they presented unto him gifts, gold, and frankincense, and myrrh." The imagination of early Christians has seen in each gift a special significance: myrrh for the human nature, gold to the king, frankincense to the divinity; or, the gold for the race of Shem, the myrrh for the race of Ham, the incense for the race of Japhet; — innocent fancies, only worthy of mention because of their historic interest, and their bearing on the conceptions of Christian poetry and Christian art.[4]

---

[1] See Niebuhr's *Lect. on Hist. of Rome*, ii. 103, ed. Schmitz.

[2] "Superstition," says Neander, "often paves the way for faith." "How often," says Hamann, "has God condescended not merely to the feelings and thoughts of men, but even to their failings and their prejudices."

[3] Matt. ii. 11 (εἰς τὴν οἰκίαν [29]) seems to show, what would of course be probable, that the stall or manger formed but a brief resting-place. It is needless to call attention to the obvious fact that St. Matthew does not mention the birth in the inn, or the previous journey from Nazareth. It is not *necessary* to assume that he was wholly unaware of these circumstances, though I see no difficulty in the admission that such may have been the case.

[4] "Dant tibi Chaldaei praenuntia munera reges,
   Myrrham homo, rex aurum, suscipe thura Deus." [30]   (Ps. Claudian.)

   "Thus, aurum, myrrham, regique, hominique, Deoque,
   Dona ferunt." [31]   (Juvenc. *Hist. Ev.*, 249.)

   "Aurea nascenti fuderunt munera regi,
   Thura dedere Deo, myrrham tribuere sepulcro." [32]   (Sedulius, ii. 95.)

See, too, Orig *c. Cels.*, p. 47, Iren. iii. 10, and many other ancient fancies in Hofmann, *Das Leben Jesu nach d. Apokr.*, p. 128; and others may be found in the Latin Hymns of Mauburn, &c.

CHAPTER IV.

THE FLIGHT INTO EGYPT, AND THE MASSACRE OF THE INNOCENTS.

" Salvete flores martyrum
Quos, lucis ipso in limine,
Christi insecutor sustulit,
Ceu turbo nascentes rosas." [33]

PRUDENT, *De SS. Innocentt.*

WHEN they had offered their gifts, the Wise Men would naturally have returned to Herod, but being warned of God in a dream, they returned to their own land another way. Neither in Scripture, nor in authentic history, nor even in early apocryphal tradition, do we find any further traces of their existence; but their visit led to very memorable events.

The dream which warned them of danger may very probably have fallen in with their own doubts about the cruel and crafty tyrant who had expressed a hypocritical desire to pay his homage to the Infant King; and if, as we may suppose, they imparted to Joseph any hint as to their misgivings, he too would be prepared for the warning dream which bade him fly to Egypt to save the young child from Herod's jealousy.

Egypt has, in all ages, been the natural place of refuge for all who were driven from Palestine by distress, persecution, or discontent. Rhinokolura, the river of Egypt, or as Milton, with his usual exquisite and learned accuracy, calls it, —

" The brook that parts
Egypt from Syrian ground," [1]

might have been reached by the fugitives in three days; and once upon the further bank, they were beyond the reach of Herod's jurisdiction.

Of the flight, and its duration, Scripture gives us no further par-

---

[1] Milton has, however, been misled by the word *wady,* and its translation by " brook " in our version. Mr. Grove informs me that Rhinocolura, now Wady el-Areesh) the *Nachal Mitzraîm,* or " river of Egypt," (Numb. xxxiv. 5, &c.), is a broad shallow wady with scarcely a trace of a bank. Still, as is usual in desert valleys, a torrent *does* flow through the bottom of it after winter rains.

ticulars; telling us only that the Holy Family fled by night from Bethlehem, and returned when Joseph had again been assured by a dream that it would be safe to take back the Saviour to the land of His nativity. It is left to apocryphal legends, immortalized by the genius of Italian art, to tell us how, on the way, the dragons came and bowed to Him, the lions and leopards adored Him, the roses of Jericho blossomed wherever His footsteps trod, the palm-trees at His command bent down to give them dates, the robbers were overawed by His majesty, and the journey was miraculously shortened.[1] They tell us further how, at His entrance into the country, all the idols of the land of Egypt fell from their pedestals with a sudden crash, and lay shattered and broken upon their faces, and how many wonderful cures of leprosy and demoniac possession were wrought by His word. All this wealth and prodigality of superfluous, aimless, and unmeaning miracle — arising in part from a mere craving for the supernatural, and in part from a fanciful application of Old Testament prophecies — furnishes a strong contrast to the truthful simplicity of the Gospel narrative. St. Matthew neither tells us where the Holy Family abode in Egypt, nor how long their exile continued; but ancient legends say that they remained two[2] years absent from Palestine, and lived at Mataréëh,[3] a few miles north-east of Cairo, where a fountain was long shown of which Jesus had made the water fresh, and an ancient sycamore under which they had rested. The Evangelist alludes only to the causes of their flight and of their return, and finds in the latter a new and deeper significance for the words of the prophet Hosea, " Out of Egypt have I called my Son." [4]

---

[1] See the Gospel of Pseudo-Matthew xviii.— xxiv.; Arab. Gospel of the Infancy, xii.— xxv. ; B. H. Cowper, *The Apocr. Gospels*, pp. 56—64,178—191 ; Hofmann, pp. 140—183. Many of these legends are mere fanciful representations of Ps. cxlviii. 7 ; Isa. xi. 6—9; lxv. 25; xix. 1, &c. From the dissemination of the Gospel of the Infancy in Arabia, many of these fables have exercised a strong influence on the Mohammedan legends of Jesus. Some of the Rabbis took occasion from the visit to Egypt to charge Christ with a knowledge of magic. Matathia, in the *Nizzachon,* says that as Jesus did not know the Tetragrammaton, or ineffable name of God, His miracles (the reality of which is not denied) were due to sorcery learnt in Egypt (Sepp, *Leben Jesu,* § xiii.). It is hardly worth while to refer to the pre posterous story in the *Toldôth Jeshû* (Wagenseil, *Tela Ignea,* ii. p. 7).

[2] St. Bonaventura (*De Vita Christi*) says *seven* years.

[3] This town is sometimes identified with On, or Heliopolis, where lived Asenath, the wife of Joseph, and where, under the name of Osarsiph, Moses had been a priest. Onias, at the head of a large colony of Jewish refugees, flying from the rage of Antiochus, had founded a temple there, and was thus believed to have fulfilled the prophecy of Isa. xix. 19. (Sepp.)

[4] " Finds a new and deeper significance, or, in other words, totally misunder stands," is the marginal comment of a friend who saw these pages. And so, no

The flight into Egypt led to a very memorable event. Seeing that the Wise Men had not returned to him, the alarm and jealousy of Herod assumed a still darker and more malignant aspect. He had no means of identifying the royal infant of the seed of David, and least of all would he have been likely to seek for Him in the cavern stable of the village khan. But he knew that the child whom the visit of the Magi had taught him to regard as a future rival of himself or of his house was yet an infant at the breast; and as Eastern mothers usually suckle their children for two years,[1] he issued his fell mandate to slay all the children of Bethlehem and its neighborhood "from two years old and under." Of the method by which the decree was carried out we know nothing. The children may have been slain secretly, gradually, and by various forms of murder; or, as has been generally supposed, there may have been one single hour of dreadful butchery.[2] The decrees of tyrants like Herod are usually involved in a deadly obscurity; they reduce the world to a torpor in which it is hardly safe to speak above a whisper. But the wild wail of anguish which rose from the mothers thus cruelly robbed of their infant children could not be hushed, and they who heard it might well imagine that Rachel, the great ancestress of their race, whose tomb stands by the roadside about a mile from Bethlehem, once more, as

doubt, it might at first appear to our Western and Northern conceptions and methods of criticism; but not so to an Oriental and an Analogist. Trained to regard every word, nay, every letter of Scripture as mystical and divine, accustomed to the application of passages in various senses, *all* of which were supposed to be latent, in some mysterious fashion, under the original utterance, St. Matthew would have regarded his least apparently relevant quotations from, and allusions to, the Old Testament, not in the light of occasional illustrations, but in the light of most solemn prophetic references to the events about which he writes. And in so doing he would be arguing in strict accordance with the views in which those for whom he wrote had been trained from their earliest infancy. Nor is there, even to our modern conceptions, anything erroneous or unnatural in the fact that the Evangelist transfers to the Messiah the language which Hosea had applied to the ideal Israel. The ideal Israel — *i. e.*, the ideal "Jashar" or " Upright Man "— was the obvious and accepted type of the coming Christ.— The quotation is from Hosea xi. 1, and St. Matthew has here referred to the original, and corrected the faulty rendering of the LXX., which is ἐξ Αἰγύπτου μετεκάλεσα τὰ τέκνα αὐτοῦ.[34] See Excursus XI., " Old Testament Quotations in the Evangelists."

[1] *Ketubhóth,* 59 *b;* 2 Macc. vii. 27, " gave thee suck three years." Others refer the calculation to the previous appearance of the planetary conjunction; and if this took place A. U. C. 747, and Jesus was born (as is all but certain) A. U. C. 750, it is a curious coincidence that Abarbanel, as we have already mentioned, places the astrological " aspect " which foreshadowed the birth of Moses *three years before* that event took place.

[2] The Protevang. says (xxi. 1) that he dispatched the assassins to Bethlehem (ἔπεμψε τοὺς φονευτάς[35].)

in the pathetic image of the prophet, mingled her voice with the mourning and lamentation of those who wept so inconsolably for their murdered little ones.[1]

To us there seems something inconceivable in a crime so atrocious; but our thoughts have been softened by eighteen centuries of Christianity, and such deeds are by no means unparalleled in the history of heathen despots and of the ancient world. Infanticide of a deeper dye than this of Herod's was a crime dreadfully rife in the days of the Empire, and the Massacre of the Innocents, as well as the motives which led to it, can be illustrated by several circumstances in the history of this very epoch. Suetonius, in his Life of Augustus, quotes from the life of the Emperor by his freedman Julius Marathus, a story to the effect that shortly before his birth there was a prophecy in Rome that a king over the Roman people would soon be born. To obviate this danger to the Republic, the Senate ordered that all the male children born in that year should be abandoned or exposed; but the Senators, whose wives were pregnant, took means to prevent the ratification of the statute, because each of them hoped that the prophecy might refer to his own child.[2] Again, Eusebius [3] quotes from Hegesippus, a Jew by birth, a story that Domitian, alarmed by the growing power of the name of Christ, issued an order to destroy all the descendants of the house of David. Two grandchildren of St. Jude — "the Lord's brother" — were still living, and were known as the *Desposyni.*[4] They were betrayed to

---

[1] Jer. xxxi. 15, applied originally to the Captivity. In this quotation also St. Matthew has translated freely from the Hebrew original. The remark of Calvin, that "Matthew *does not mean that the prophet had predicted what Herod should do,* but that, at the advent of Christ, that mourning was renewed which many years before the women of Bethlehem had made," is characterized by his usual strong and honest common sense, and must be borne in mind in considering several of the Gospel references to ancient prophecy. It applies to St. Matthew more strongly than to the other Evangelists. On this, as on other points of exegesis, there can be no question whatever, in the mind of any competent scholar, that the theology of the Reformation, and even of the Fathers, was freer, manlier, less shackled by false theories about inspiration, and less timid of ignorant criticism, than that which claims to be the sole orthodox theology of the present day.

[2] Suet. *Vit. Aug.,* p. 94. — As history, no doubt the anecdote is perfectly worthless, but it is not worthless as illustrating what we otherwise know to have been possible in an age in which, as is still the case in China, infanticide was hardly regarded as a disgrace.

[3] *Hist. Ecc.* iii. 15.

[4] This fact is mentioned by Julius Africanus, who was born at Emmaus, about the beginning of the third century, and who says that he knew some of the Desposyni personally. (Euseb. *Hist. Ecc.* i. 7.)

the Emperor by a certain Jocatus, and other Nazaræan heretics, and were brought into the imperial presence; but when Domitian observed that they only held the rank of peasants, and that their hands were hard with manual toil, he dismissed them in safety with a mixture of pity and contempt.

Although doubts have been thrown on the Massacre of the Innocents, it is profoundly in accordance with all that we know of Herod's character. The master-passions of that able but wicked prince were a most unbounded ambition, and a most excruciating jealousy.[1] His whole career was red with the blood of murder. He had massacred priests and nobles; he had decimated the Sanhedrin; he had caused the High Priest, his brother-in-law, the young and noble Aristobulus, to be drowned in pretended sport before his eyes; he had ordered the strangulation of his favorite wife, the beautiful Asmonæan princess Mariamne, though she seems to have been the only human being whom he passionately loved.[2] His sons Alexander, Aristobulus, and Antipater — his uncle Joseph — Antigonus and Alexander, the uncle and father of his wife — his mother-in-law Alexandra — his kinsman Cortobanus — his friends Dositheus and Gadias, were but a few of the multitudes who fell victims to his sanguinary, suspicious, and guilty terrors. His brother Pheroras and his son Archelaus barely and narrowly escaped execution by his orders. Neither the blooming youth of the prince Aristobulus, nor the white hairs of the king Hyrcanus had protected them from his fawning and treacherous fury. Deaths by strangulation, deaths by burning, deaths by being cleft asunder, deaths by secret assassination, confessions forced by unutterable torture, acts of insolent and inhuman lust, mark the annals of a reign which was so cruel that, in the energetic language of the Jewish ambassadors to the Emperor Augustus, "the survivors during his lifetime were even more miserable than the sufferers."[3] And as in the case of Henry VIII., every dark and brutal instinct of his character seemed to acquire fresh

---

[1] Jos. *Antt.* xvi. 5, § 4.

[2] The feelings of Herod towards Mariamne, who, as a Maccabæan princess, had far more right to the sovereignty than himself, were not unlike those of Henry VII. towards Elizabeth of York, and in a less degree those of William III. towards Mary. Herod was well aware that he owed his sovereignty solely to "the almighty Romans." Aristobulus was murdered at the age of eighteen, Hyrcanus at the age of eighty; and he hated them alike for their popularity, and for their Maccabæan origin. More ghosts must have gathered round the dying bed of this "gorgeous criminal" than those which the fancy of Shakespeare has collected round the bed of Richard III.

[3] Jos. *Antt.* xvii. 11, § 2.

intensity as his life drew towards its close. Haunted by the spectres of his murdered wife and murdered sons, agitated by the conflicting furies of remorse and blood, the pitiless monster, as Josephus calls him, was seized in his last days by a black and bitter ferocity, which broke out against all with whom he came in contact.[1] There is no conceivable difficulty in supposing that such a man — a savage barbarian with a thin veneer of corrupt and superficial civilization — would have acted in the exact manner which St. Matthew describes ; and the belief in the fact receives independent confirmation from various sources. " On Augustus being informed," says Macrobius, " that *among the boys under two years of age whom Herod ordered to be slain in Syria*, his own son also had been slain," " It is better," said he " to be Herod's pig ($\tilde{v}\nu$) than his son ($v\acute{\iota}\grave{o}\nu$)." [2] Although Macrobius is a late writer, and made the mistake of supposing that Herod's son Antipater, who was put to death about the same time as the Massacre of the Innocents, had actually perished *in* that massacre, it is clear that the form in which he narrates the *bon mot* of Augustus points to some dim reminiscence of this cruel slaughter.

Why then, it has been asked, does Josephus make no mention of so infamous an atrocity? Perhaps because it was performed so secretly that he did not even know of it. Perhaps because, in those terrible days, the murder of a score of children, in consequence of a transient suspicion, would have been regarded as an item utterly insignificant in the list of Herod's murders.[3] Perhaps because it was

---

[1] Jos. *Antt.* xvii. 6, § 5, $\mu\acute{\epsilon}\lambda\alpha\iota\nu\alpha$ $\chi o\lambda\grave{\eta}$ $\alpha\grave{v}\tau\grave{o}\nu$ $\mathring{\eta}\rho\epsilon\iota$ $\grave{\epsilon}\pi\grave{\iota}$ $\pi\acute{\alpha}\acute{o}\iota\nu$ $\grave{\epsilon}\xi\alpha\gamma\rho\iota\alpha\acute{\iota}$-$\nu o\nu\acute{o}\alpha$;[36] *B. J.* i. 30, § 4, $\grave{\epsilon}\pi\tau\acute{o}\eta\tau o$ $\tau\tilde{\omega}$ $\varphi\acute{o}\beta\omega$ $\kappa\alpha\grave{\iota}$ $\pi\rho\grave{o}s$ $\pi\tilde{\alpha}\acute{o}\alpha\nu$ $\grave{v}\pi\acute{o}\nu o\iota\alpha\nu$ $\grave{\epsilon}\xi\epsilon\rho\rho\acute{\iota}\pi\tau\acute{\iota}\zeta\epsilon\tau o$.[37]— " Most miserable family, even to the third generation, to be imbued so deep beyond any other in blood ; one steeped in the blood of infant martyrs, the other in that of John the Baptist, and the third who slew James the Apostle with the sword — all three conspicuous in the persecution of Christ." (Williams, *The Natic.* 132.)

[2] *Saturnal.* ii. 4, " Augustus cum audisset, inter pueros, *quos in Syria Herodes infra bimatum* (cf. Matt. ii. 16, $\grave{\alpha}\pi\grave{o}$ $\delta\iota\epsilon\tau o\tilde{v}s$ $\kappa\alpha\grave{\iota}$ $\kappa\alpha\tau\omega\tau\acute{\epsilon}\rho\omega$; Vulg., " a *bimatu et infra* ") *interfici jussit, filium quoque ejus occisum*, ait, Melius est Herodis porcum ($\tilde{v}\nu$) esse quam puerum ($v\acute{\iota}\grave{o}\nu$)." [38] The pun cannot be preserved in English. Augustus meant that Herod's pig, since, as a Jew, he could not eat it, would be safer than his son. Herod had to ask the Emperor's leave before putting his sons to death ; and Antipater, whom he ordered to be executed only five days before his death, was the *third* who had undergone this fate.— Macrobius lived about A. D. 400, but he used early materials, and the pun is almost certainly historical.

[3] The probable number of the Innocents has been extraordinarily exaggerated. An Æthiopian legend makes them 14,000 ! Considering that Bethlehem was but a village of perhaps 2,000 inhabitants, we may safely hope that, even in all its boundaries, not more than twenty were sacrificed, and perhaps not half that num-

passed over in silence by Nikolaus of Damascus, who, writing in the true spirit of those Hellenizing courtiers, who wanted to make a political Messiah out of a corrupt and blood-stained usurper, magnified all his patron's achievements, and concealed or palliated all his crimes.¹ But the more probable reason is that Josephus, whom, in spite of all the immense literary debt which we owe to him, we can only regard as a renegade and a sycophant, did not choose to make any allusion to facts which were even remotely connected with the life of Christ. The single passage in which he alludes to Him is interpolated, if not wholly spurious, and no one can doubt that his silence on the subject of Christianity was as deliberate as it was dishonest.²

But although Josephus does not distinctly mention the event, yet every single circumstance which he does tell us about this very period of Herod's life supports its probability. At this very time two elo-

---

ber; especially as the ἀπὸ διετοῦς may mean (as Greswell supposes) "*just beyond the age of one year.*"

¹ Nikolaus was to Herod what Velleius Paterculus was to Tiberius. Josephus's own opinion of the kind of men who were Herod's creatures and parasites may be found in his *Antt.* xvi. 5, § 4. As to Josephus, his own narrative is his worst condemnation, and De Quincey's estimate of him (*Works*, vi. 272—275) is not too severe. His works betray some of the worst characteristics of the Oriental and the Pharisee. He may have omitted all mention of Christ out of sheer perplexity, although he certainly rejected His Messiahship (Orig. c. *Cels.* i. 35). Nothing is more common in historians and biographers than the deliberate suppression of awkward and disagreeable facts. Justus of Tiberius, another contemporary historian, was also purposely reticent. Does any one doubt the murder of Crispus because Eusebius takes no notice of it in his life of Constantine? But perhaps, after all, there *is* an allusion — though guarded and distant — to this crime, or at any rate to the circumstances which led to it, in the *Antiquities* of Josephus (xvi. 11, § 7 ; xvii. 2, § 4), where it is narrated that Herod slew a number of Pharisees and others because they foretold "how God had decreed that Herod's government should cease, and his posterity should be deprived of it." Possibly another allusion (though out of place) may be found in xiv. 9, § 4, where we hear of a clamor against Herod, raised by "*The mothers* of those who had been slain by him "

² This celebrated passage is as follows: — *Antt.* xviii. 3, § 3 : Γίγνεται δὲ κατὰ τοῦτον τὸν χρόνον Ἰησοῦς, σοφὸς ἀνὴρ [εἴ γε αὐτὸν ἄνδρα λέγειν χρὴ. ἦν γὰρ] παραδόξων ἔργων ποιητὴς [διδάσκαλος ἀνθρώπων τῶν σὺν ἡδονῇ τἀληθῆ δεχομένων] καὶ πολλοὺς μὲν τῶν Ἰουδαίων πολλοὺς δὲ καὶ ἀπὸ τοῦ Ἑλληνικοῦ ἐπηγάγετο [Ὁ Χριστός, οὗτος ἦν.] Καὶ αὐτὸν ἐνδείξει τῶν πρώτων ἀνδρῶν παρ' ἡμῖν σταυρῷ ἐπιτετιμηκότος Πιλάτου, οὐκ ἐπαύσαντο οἵ γε πρῶτον αὐτὸν ἀγαπήσαντες. [Ἐφάνη γὰρ αὐτοῖς τρίτην ἔχων ἡμέραν πάλιν ζῶν, τῶν θείων προφητῶν ταῦτά τε καὶ ἄλλα μυρία περὶ αὐτοῦ θαυμάσια εἰρηκότων.] Εἰς ἔτι νῦν τῶν Χριστιανῶν ἀπὸ τοῦδε ὠνομασμένων οὐκ ἐπέλιπε τὸ φῦλον.³⁹ The only other allusion to Jesus in Josephus is also of dubious authenticity (*Antt.* xx. 9, § 1), where he calls James τὸν ἀδελφὸν Ἰησοῦ τοῦ λεγομένου Χριστοῦ.⁴⁰

quent Jewish teachers, Judas and Matthias, had incited their scholars to pull down the large golden eagle which Herod had placed above the great gate of the Temple. Josephus connects this bold attempt with premature rumors of Herod's death ; but Lardner's conjecture that it may have been further encouraged by the Messianic hopes freshly kindled by the visit of the Wise Men, is by no means impossible. The attempt, however, was defeated, and Judas and Matthias, with forty of their scholars, were burned alive. With such crimes as this before him on every page, Josephus might well have ignored the secret assassination of a few unweaned infants in a little village. Their blood was but a drop in that crimson river in which Herod was steeped to the very lips.

It must have been very shortly after the murder of the Innocents that Herod died. Only five days before his death he had made a frantic attempt at suicide, and had ordered the execution of his eldest son Antipater. His deathbed, which once more reminds us of Henry VIII., was accompanied by circumstances of peculiar horror, and it has been noticed that the loathsome disease [1] of which he died is hardly mentioned in history, except in the case of men who have been rendered infamous by an atrocity of persecuting zeal.[2] On his bed of intolerable anguish, in that splendid and luxurious palace which he had built for himself under the palms of Jericho, swollen with disease and scorched by thirst — ulcerated externally and glowing inwardly with " a soft, slow fire " — surrounded by plotting sons and plundering slaves, detesting all and detested by all — longing for death as a release from his tortures, yet dreading it as the beginning of worse terrors — stung by remorse, yet still unslaked with murder — a horror to all around him, yet in his guilty conscience a worse terror to himself — devoured by the premature corruption of an

---

[1] The *morbus pedicularis*, or phthiriasis. See Lactantius, *De Mortibus persecutorum*, cap. xxxiii., where, describing the disease of Maximian in terms which would serve equally well to record what is told us of the death of Herod, he says, " Percussit eum Deus insanabili plagâ. Nascitur ei ulcus malum in inferiori parte genitalium, serpitque latius . . . . proxima quæque cancer invadit . . . . jam non longe pernicies aberat, et inferiora omnia corripuerat. Computrescunt forinsecus viscera, et in tabem sedes tota dilabitur . . . . Vermes intus creantur. Odor it autem non modo per palatium, sed totam pervadit civitatem." [4] There is more and worse, which I spare the reader, especially since it is very doubtful whether there is such a disease as the *morbus pedicularis.*— There is a somewhat similar account of the deathbed of Henry VIII. in Forster's *Essay on Popular Progress.* " Now Herod died the worst kind of death, suffering punishment for the shed blood of the children," &c. (*Hist. of Jos. the Carpenter*, ix.)

[2] *E. g.*, Antiochus Epiphanes, Sylla, Maximian, Diocletian, Herod the Great, Herod Agrippa, the Duke of Alva, Henry VIII., &c.

anticipated grave — eaten of worms as though visibly smitten by the finger of God's wrath after seventy years of successful villainy — the wretched old man, whom men had called the Great, lay in savage frenzy awaiting his last hour.[1] As he knew that none would shed one tear for *him*, he determined that they should shed many for *themselves*, and issued an order that, under pain of death, the principal families in the kingdom and the chiefs of the tribes should come to Jericho. They came, and then, shutting them in the hippodrome, he secretly commanded his sister Salome that at the moment of his death they should all be massacred. And so, choking as it were with blood, devising massacres in its very delirium, the soul of Herod passed forth into the night.

In purple robes, with crown and sceptre and precious stones, the corpse was placed upon its splendid bier, and accompanied with military pomp and burning incense to its grave in the Herodium, not far from the place where Christ was born. But the spell of the Herodian dominion was broken, and the people saw how illusory had been its glittering fascination. The day of Herod's death was, as he had foreseen, observed as a festival. His will was disputed; his kingdom disintegrated; his last order was disobeyed; his sons died for the most part in infamy and exile; the curse of God was on his house, and though, by ten wives and many concubines, he seems to have had nine sons and five daughters, yet within a hundred years the family of the *hierodoulos* of Ascalon had perished by disease or violence, and there was no living descendant to perpetuate his name.[2]

If the intimation of Herod's death[3] was speedily given to Joseph, the stay in Egypt must have been too short to influence in any way the human development of our Lord. This may perhaps be the reason why St. Luke passes it over in silence.

---

[1] The title first occurs in Jos *Antt.* xviii. 5, § 4. He was beginning the thirty-eighth year of his reign. It has been suggested that " the Great " is a mistaken rendering of רבא, " the elder." " Nur aus Missverständniss eines Hebräischen Ausdruckes ;" cf. Ἑλκίας ὁ μέγας (*Antt.* xviii. 8, § 4). Ewald (*Gesch.* iv. 473) thinks that the name may possibly have originated from coins, as Agrippa I. is called βασιλεὺς μέγας on a coin. In this case it may merely imply that he was not a mere tetrarch, or ethnarch, but a king of Palestine — just as Indian princes call themselves *Maharajah.* In any case, " L'épithète de grand que l'histoire lui a donnée est une amère dérision : sa grandeur consistait à être un magnifique esclave, portant des chaines d'or " [42] (Munk, *Palest.*, 560).

[2] Antipater, father of Herod, is said to have been a *hierodoulos* or servitor in a temple of Apollo at Ascalon. Compare the rapid extinction of the sons of Philip the Fair.

[3] The plural τεθνήκασι may be merely general, or it is perhaps a reference to Exod. iv. 19.

It seems to have been the first intention of Joseph to fix his home in Bethlehem. It was the city of his ancestors, and was hallowed by many beautiful and heroic associations. It would have been easy to find a living there by a trade which must almost anywhere have supplied the simple wants of a peasant family. It is true that an Oriental rarely leaves his home, but when he has been compelled by circumstances to do so, he finds it comparatively easy to settle elsewhere. Having once been summoned to Bethlehem, Joseph might find a powerful attraction in the vicinity of the little town to Jerusalem ; and the more so since it had recently been the scene of such memorable circumstances. But, on his way, he was met by the news that Archelaus ruled in the room of his father Herod.[1] The people would only too gladly have got rid of the whole Idumæan race ; at the worst they would have preferred Antipas to Archelaus. But Augustus had unexpectedly decided in favor of Archelaus, who, though younger than Antipas, was the heir nominated by the last will of his father ; and as though anxious to show that he was the true son of that father, Archelaus, even before his inheritance had been confirmed by Roman authority, " had," as Josephus[2] scornfully remarks, " given to his subjects a specimen of his future virtue, by ordering a slaughter of 3,000 of his own countrymen at the Temple." It was clear that under such a government there could be neither hope nor safety ; and Joseph, obedient once more to an intimation of God's will, seeking once more the original home of himself and Mary, " turned aside into the parts of Galilee,"[3] where, in remote obscurity, sheltered by poverty and insignificance, the Holy Family might live secure under the sway of another son of Herod — the equally unscrupulous, but more indolent and indifferent Antipas.

---

[1] Matt. ii. 22. He was saluted "king " by the army, though he declined the title. Similarly Josephus gives the name of "kingdom " to the tetrarchy of Lysanias (*B. J.* ii. 11, § 5). The word βασιλεύει seems, however — if taken quite strictly — to show that the return from Egypt was very shortly after the flight thither ; for it was only during a short time after his father's death that Archelaus strictly had the title of king (cf Jos. *B. J.* ii. 1, § 1). When he went to Rome for the confirmation of his title, Augustus only allowed him to be called ethnarch ; but before this time his assumptions of royalty, by sitting on a golden throne, &c., were actually part of Antipater's charges against him, and at this period Josephus distinctly calls him the "king " (*Antt.* xvii. 9, § 2). It is remarkable *how near* the Evangelists often seem to be to an inaccuracy, while yet closer inspection shows them to be, in these very points, minutely accurate.

[2] *Antt.* xvii. 11, § 2. Augustus afterwards banished him for his tyranny and insolence, and he died at Vienne in Gaul, A. D. 7 (id. 13, § 2).

[3] Matt. ii 22, ἀνεχώρησεν, not " returned," but " retired." The same word is used of the flight into Egypt (Matt. ii. 14). St. Luke (ii. 39) was either unaware of the flight into Egypt, or passed it over as having no bearing on his subject.

CHAPTER V.

THE BOYHOOD OF JESUS.

" Try to become little with the Little One, that you may increase in stature with Him."— St. Bonaventura, *Vita Christi*, ix.

" Le haut degré de la perfection consiste à participer à l'enfance sacrée de notre très doux, très humble, et très obéissant Serviteur." [43] — St. François de Sales.

The physical geography of Palestine is, perhaps, more distinctly marked than that of any other country in the world. Along the shore of the Mediterranean runs the Shephelah and the maritime plain, broken only by the bold spur of Mount Carmel; parallel to this is a long range of hills, for the most part rounded and featureless in their character; these, on their eastern side, plunge into the deep declivity of El Ghôr, the Jordan valley; and beyond the Jordan valley runs the straight, unbroken, purple line of the mountains of Moab and Gilead. Thus the character of the country from north to south may be represented by four parallel bands — the Sea-board, the Hill country, the Jordan valley, and the Trans-Jordanic range.

The Hill country, which thus occupies the space between the low maritime plain and the deep Jordan valley, falls into two great masses, the continuity of the low mountain-range being broken by the plain of Jezreel. The southern mass of those limestone hills formed the land of Judea; the northern, the land of Galilee.

Gâlil, in Hebrew, means " a circle," and the name was originally applied to the twenty cities in the circuit of Kedesh-Naphtali, which Solomon gave to Hiram in return for his services in transporting timber, and to which Hiram, in extreme disgust, applied the name of *Cabûl*, or "disgusting." [1] Thus it seems to have been always the destiny of Galilee to be despised; and that contempt was likely to be fostered in the minds of the Jews from the fact that this district became, from very early days, the residence of a mixed population, and was distinguished as "Galilee of the Gentiles." [2] Not only

---

[1] See 1 Kings ix. 13. In Hebrew the word *Cabûl* has no meaning, but it seems to be put as an equivalent for a Phœnician word to which this meaning is assigned. Josephus calls it χαβαλών, and explains it οὐκ ἀρέσκον (*Antt.* viii. 5, § 3).

[2] Compare Judg. iv. 2, " Harosheth of the Gentiles;" and Isa. ix. 1 ; Matt. iv. 15 ; 1 Macc. v. 15—27.

were there many Phœnicians and Arabs in the cities of Galilee, but, in the time of our Lord, there were also many Greeks, and the Greek language was currently spoken and understood.

The hills which form the northern limit of the plain of Jezreel run almost due east and west from the Jordan valley to the Mediterranean, and their southern slopes were in the district assigned to the tribe of Zebulun.

Almost in the centre of this chain of hills there is a singular cleft in the limestone, forming the entrance to a little valley. As the traveller leaves the plain he will ride up a steep and narrow pathway, broidered with grass and flowers, through scenery which is neither colossal nor overwhelming, but infinitely beautiful and picturesque. Beneath him, on the right-hand side, the vale will gradually widen, until it becomes about a quarter of a mile in breadth. The basin of the valley is divided by hedges of cactus into little fields and gardens, which, about the fall of the spring rains, wear an aspect of indescribable calm, and glow with a tint of the richest green.[1] Beside the narrow pathway, at no great distance apart from each other, are two wells, and the women who draw water there are more beautiful, and the ruddy, bright-eyed shepherd boys who sit or play by the well-sides, in their gay-colored Oriental costume, are a happier, bolder, brighter-looking race than the traveller will have seen elsewhere. Gradually the valley opens into a little natural amphitheatre of hills, supposed by some to be the crater of an extinct volcano; and there, clinging to the hollows of a hill, which rises to the height of some five hundred feet above it, lie, "like a handful of pearls in a goblet of emerald," the flat roofs and narrow streets of a little Eastern town. There is a small church; the massive buildings of a convent; the tall minaret of a mosque; a clear, abundant fountain; houses built of white stone, and gardens scattered among them, umbrageous with figs and olives, and rich with the white and scarlet blossoms of orange and pomegranate. In spring, at least, everything about the place looks indescribably bright and soft; doves murmur in the trees; the hoopoe flits about in ceaseless activity; the bright blue roller-bird, the commonest and loveliest bird of Palestine, flashes like a living sapphire over fields which

---

[1] An early pilgrim, Antoninus Martyr, speaks of Nazareth with a sincerity of enthusiasm which many a modern traveller would echo. "In civitate tanta est gratia mulierum Hebraearum ut inter Hebraeas pulcriores non inveniantur, et hoc a S. Mariâ sibi concessum dicunt . . . . . *Provincia paradiso similis* in tritico, in frugibus similis Ægypto, sed praecellit in vino et oleo, pomis ac melle." [44] (Quoted by Caspari, p. 53.)

are enamelled with innumerable flowers. And that little town is *En Názirah*, Nazareth,[1] where the Son of God, the Saviour of mankind, spent nearly thirty years of His mortal life. It was, in fact, His home, His native village for all but three or four years of His life on earth ; the village which lent its then ignominious name to the scornful title written upon His cross ; the village from which He did not disdain to draw His appellation when He spake in vision to the persecuting Saul.[2] And along the narrow mountain-path which I have described, His feet must have often trod, for it is the only approach by which, in returning northwards from Jerusalem, He could have reached the home of His infancy, youth, and manhood.

What was His manner of life during those thirty years? It is a question which the Christian cannot help asking in deep reverence, and with yearning love ; but the words in which the Gospels answer it are very calm and very few.

Of the four Evangelists, St. John, the beloved disciple, and St. Mark, the friend and "son" of St. Peter,[3] pass over these thirty years in absolute, unbroken silence. St. Matthew devotes one chapter to the visit of the Magi, and the Flight into Egypt, and then proceeds to the preaching of the Baptist. St. Luke alone, after describing the incidents which marked the presentation in the Temple, preserves for us one inestimable anecdote of the Saviour's boyhood, and one inestimable verse descriptive of His growth till He was twelve years old. And that verse contains nothing for the gratification of our curiosity ; it furnishes us with no details of life, no incidents of adventure ; it tells us only how, in a sweet and holy childhood, "the child grew and waxed strong in spirit, filled with wisdom, and the grace of God was upon Him." To this period of His life, too, we may apply the subsequent verse, "And Jesus increased in wisdom and stature, and in favor with God and man." His development was a strictly human development. He did not come into the world

---

[1] Nazareth is not mentioned in the Old Testament ; unless it be identical with Sarid, which is mentioned as the border of the inheritance of Zebulun in Josh. xix. 10, 12. The position accurately corresponds, but it is philologically difficult to suppose that Nazareth is a corruption — as some have suggested — of *En Sarid* (the fountain or spring of Sarid). It has been more usually connected with *Nēt-ser* (a branch), and perhaps in allusion to this St. Jerome compares it to an opening rose, and calls it "the flower of Galilee." It is not once mentioned by Josephus.

[2] John xix. 19 ; Luke ii. 51 ; Acts xxii. 8.

[3] "Marcus, my son" (1 Pet. v. 13). Papias, quoted by Eusebius, says of Mark, ἑρμηνευτὴς Πέτρου γενόμενος ἀκριβῶς ἔγραψεν οὐ μέντοι τάξει, τὰ ὑπὸ τοῦ Χριστοῦ ἢ λεχθέντα ἢ πραχθέντα[45] (*Hist. Ecc.* iii. 40).

endowed with infinite knowledge, but, as St. Luke tells us, " He gradually advanced in wisdom." [1] He was not clothed with infinite power, but experienced the weaknesses and imperfections of human infancy. He grew as other children grow, only in a childhood of stainless and sinless beauty — " as the flower of roses in the spring of the year, and as lilies by the waters." [2]

There is, then, for the most part a deep silence in the Evangelists respecting this period; but what eloquence in their silence! May we not find in their very reticence a wisdom and an instruction more profound than if they had filled many volumes with minor details?

In the first place, we may see in this their silence a signal and striking confirmation of their faithfulness. We may learn from it that they desired to tell the simple truth, and not to construct an astonishing or plausible narrative. That Christ should have passed thirty years of His brief life in the deep obscurity of a provincial village; that He should have been brought up not only in a conquered land, but in its most despised province; not only in a despised province, but in its most disregarded valley; [3] that during all those thirty years the ineffable brightness of His divine nature should have tabernacled among us, " in a tent like ours, and of the same material," unnoticed and unknown; that during those long years there should have been no flash of splendid circumstance, no outburst of amazing miracle, no " sevenfold chorus of hallelujahs and harping symphonies " to announce, and reveal, and glorify the coming King — this is not what we should have expected — not what *any one* would have been likely to imagine or to invent.

We should not have expected it, but it *was* so; and therefore the Evangelists leave it so; and the very fact of its contradicting all that we should have imagined, is an additional proof that so it must have been. An additional proof, because the Evangelists must inevitably have been — as, indeed, we know that they *were* — actuated by the same *à priori* anticipations as ourselves; and had there been any glorious circumstances attending the boyhood of our Lord, they, as honest witnesses, would certainly have told us of them; and had they *not* been honest witnesses, they would — if none such occurred in

---

[1] Luke ii. 52, προέκοπτε σοφίᾳ. Cf. Heb. v. 8, ἔμαθεν ἀφ᾽ ὧν ἔπαθε. [46].

[2] Comp. Ecclus. xxxix. 13, 14. "Hearken unto me, ye holy children, and bud forth as a rose growing by the brook of the field : and give ye a sweet savor as frankincense, and flourish as a lily, and send forth a smell, and sing a song of praise."

[3] The terms of Isa. ix. 1, 2, show in what estimation Galilee was held. Keim also refers to Jos. *Antt.* xiii. 12, § 1 ; xiv. 9, § 2.

reality — have most certainly invented them. But man's ways are not as God's ways; and because the truth which, by their very silence, the Evangelists record, is a revelation to us of the ways of God, and not of man, therefore it contradicts what we should have invented; it disappoints what, without further enlightenment, we should have desired. But, on the other hand, it fulfils the ideal of ancient prophecy, "He shall grow up before him as a tender plant, and as a root out of a dry ground;" and it is in accordance with subsequent allusion, "He made himself of no reputation, and took upon Him the form of a servant." [1]

We have only to turn to the Apocryphal Gospels, and we shall find how widely different is the false human ideal from the divine fact. There we shall see how, following their natural and unspiritual bent, the fabulists of Christendom, whether heretical or orthodox, surround Christ's boyhood with a blaze of miracle, make it portentous, terror-striking, unnatural, repulsive. It is surely an astonishing proof that the Evangelists were guided by the Spirit of God in telling how *He* lived in whom God was revealed to man, when we gradually discover that no profane, no irreverent, even no imaginative hand can touch the sacred outlines of that divine and perfect picture without degrading and distorting it. Whether the Apocryphal writers meant their legends to be accepted as history or as fiction, it is at least certain that in most cases they meant to weave around the brows of Christ a garland of honor. Yet how do their stories dwarf, and dishonor, and misinterpret Him! How infinitely superior is the noble simplicity of that evangelic silence to all the theatrical displays of childish and meaningless omnipotence with which the Protevangelium, and the Pseudo-Matthew, and the Arabic Gospel of the Infancy are full! [2] They meant to honor Christ; but no invention *can* honor Him; he who invents about Him degrades Him; he mixes the weak, imperfect, erring fancies of man with the unapproachable and awful purposes of God. The boy Christ of the Gospels is simple and sweet, obedient and humble; He is subject to His parents; He is occupied solely with the quiet duties of His home and of His

[1] Isa. liii. 2; Phil. ii. 7.— The Apocryphal Gospels are for the most part mere worthless Hegadôth, in glorification (1) of the birth and virginity of Mary, (2) of the childhood, and (3) of the passion of our Lord. They were widely spread in the East, and traces of them may be found in the Koran (D'Herbelot, *Bibl. Orient.* 499).

[2] "Caveat omnia apocrypha. Sciat multa his admixta vitiosa, *et grandis esse prudentiae aurum in luto quaerere.*" [41] (Jer. *Ep. ad Laetam. Praef. ad Lib. Regg.*). But, as a friend remarks, *aurum in luto quaerere* [48] is, in some sad senses, a business of life.

age; He loves all men, and all men love the pure, and gracious, and noble child. Already He knows God as His Father, and the favor of God falls on Him softly as the morning sun-light, or the dew of heaven, and plays like an invisible aureole round His infantine and saintly brow. Unseen, save in the beauty of heaven, but yet covered with silver wings, and with its feathers like gold, the Spirit of God descended like a dove, and rested from infancy upon the Holy Child.

But how different is the boy Christ of the New Testament Apocrypha! He is mischievous, petulant, forward, revengeful. Some of the marvels told of Him are simply aimless and puerile — as when He carries the spilt water in His robe; or pulls the short board to the requisite length; or moulds sparrows of clay, and then claps His hand to make them fly; or throws all the cloths into the dyer's vat, and then draws them out each stained of the requisite color. But some are, on the contrary, simply distasteful and inconsiderate, as when He vexes and shames and silences those who wish to teach Him; or rebukes Joseph; or turns His playmates into kids: and others are simply cruel and blasphemous, as when He strikes dead with a curse the boys who offend or run against Him, until at last there is a storm of popular indignation, and Mary is afraid to let Him leave the house. In a careful search through all these heavy, tasteless, and frequently pernicious fictions, I can find but one anecdote in which there is a touch of feeling, or possibility of truth; and this alone I will quote because it is at any rate harmless, and it is quite conceivable that it may rest upon some slight basis of traditional fact. It is from the Arabic Gospel of the Infancy, and runs as follows: [1]

"Now in the month of Adar, Jesus assembled the boys as if He were their king; they strewed their garments on the ground, and He sat upon them. Then they put on His head a crown wreathed of flowers, and, like attendants waiting upon a king, they stood in order before Him on His right hand and on His left. And whoever passed that way the boys took him by force, crying, 'Come hither and adore the King, and then proceed upon thy way.'"

Yet I am not sure that the sacredness of the evangelic silence is not rudely impaired even by so simple a fancy as this: for it was in utter stillness, in prayerfulness, in the quiet round of daily duties — like Moses in the wilderness, like David among the sheep-folds, like Elijah among the tents of the Bedawîn, like Jeremiah in his

---

[1] Cap. 41. I quote the translation of Mr. B. Harris Cowper, whose admirable volume has placed the Apocryphal Gospels within easy reach of all readers. unlearned as well as learned.

quiet home at Anathoth, like Amos in the sycamore groves of Tekoa — that the boy Jesus prepared Himself, amid a hallowed obscurity, for His mighty work on earth. His outward life was the life of all those of His age, and station, and place of birth. He l'ved as lived the other children of peasant parents in that quiet town, and in great measure as they live now. He who has seen the children of Nazareth in their red caftans, and bright tunics of silk or cloth, girded with a many-colored sash, and sometimes covered with a loose outer jacket of white or blue — he who has watched their noisy and merry games, and heard their ringing laughter as they wander about the hills of their little native vale, or play in bands on the hill-side beside their sweet and abundant fountain, may perhaps form some conception of how Jesus looked and played when He too was a child. And the traveller who has followed any of those children — as I have done — to their simple homes, and seen the scanty furniture, the plain but sweet and wholesome food, the uneventful, happy patriarchal life, may form a vivid conception of the manner in which Jesus lived. Nothing can be plainer than those houses, with the doves sunning themselves on the white roofs, and the vines wreathing about them. The mats, or carpets, are laid loose along the walls; shoes and sandals are taken off at the threshold; from the centre hangs a lamp which forms the only ornament of the room; in some recess in the wall is placed the wooden chest, painted with bright colors, which contains the books or other possessions of the family; on a ledge that runs round the wall, within easy reach, are neatly rolled up the gay-colored quilts, which serve as beds, and on the same ledge are ranged the earthen vessels for daily use; near the door stand the large common water-jars of red clay with a few twigs and green leaves — often of aromatic shrubs — thrust into their orifices to keep the water cool. At meal-time a painted wooden stool is placed in the centre of the apartment, a large tray is put upon it, and in the middle of the tray stands the dish of rice and meat, or *libbán*, or stewed fruits, from which all help themselves in common. Both before and after the meal the servant, or the youngest member of the family, pours water over the hands from a brazen ewer into a brazen bowl. So quiet, so simple, so humble, so uneventful was the outward life of the family of Nazareth.[1]

---

[1] Some of these facts have been exquisitely represented by Mr. Holman Hunt in his truly noble picture, "The Shadow of Death." The above paragraphs were, however, written before I had seen the picture. Readers of this book may be interested to know that it was in Palestine, and at the author's request, that Mr.

The reverent devotion and brilliant fancy of the early mediæval painters have elaborated a very different picture. The gorgeous pencils of a Giotto and a Fra Angelico have painted the Virgin and her Child seated on stately thrones, upon floors of splendid mosaic, under canopies of blue and gold ; they have robed them in colors rich as the hues of summer or delicate as the flowers of spring, and fitted the edges of their robes with golden embroidery, and clasped them with priceless gems.¹ Far different was the reality. When Joseph returned to Nazareth he knew well that they were going into seclusion as well as into safety ; and that the life of the Virgin and the Holy Child would be spent, not in the full light of notoriety or wealth, but in secrecy,² in poverty, and in manual toil.

Yet this poverty was not pauperism ; there was nothing in it either miserable or abject ; it was sweet, simple, contented, happy, even joyous. Mary, like others of her rank, would spin, and cook food, and go to buy fruit, and evening by evening visit the fountain, still called after her "the Virgin's fountain," with her pitcher of earthenware carried on her shoulder or her head. Jesus would play, and learn, and help His parents in their daily tasks, and visit the synagogues on the Sabbath days. "It is written," says Luther, " that there was once a pious godly bishop, who had often earnestly prayed that God would manifest to him what Jesus had done in His youth. Once the bishop had a dream to this effect. He seemed in his sleep to see a carpenter working at his trade, and beside him a little boy who was gathering up chips. Then came in a maiden clothed in green, who called them both to come to the meal, and set porridge before them. All this the bishop seemed to see in his dream, himself standing behind the door that he might not be perceived. Then the little boy began and said, ' Why does that man stand there? shall he not also eat with us?' And this so frightened the bishop that he awoke." "Let this be what it may," adds Luther, " a true history or a fable, I none the less believe that Christ in His childhood and youth looked and acted like other children, yet without sin, in fashion like a man." ³

Holman Hunt sketched the two engravings which adorn it. It is not often that a chance traveller gets the opportunity, as I was fortunate enough to do on several occasions, of seeing the every-day home life and meals of the inhabitants.

¹ As early as 1679 a monograph was written by Rohr, *Pictor errans in Hist. Sacrâ ;* and in 1689, by Hilscher, *De erroribus pictorum circa Nativ. Christi.*

² John vii. 3—5. Work in Galilee is there called work ἐν κρυπτῷ.⁴⁹

³ Cf. St. Bonaventura, *Vit. Christi,* xii. " Fancy you see Him busied with His parents in the most servile work of their little dwelling. Did He not help them

St. Matthew tells us, that in the settlement of the Holy Family at Nazareth, was fulfilled that which was spoken by the prophets, " He shall be called a Nazarene." It is well known that no such passage occurs in any extant prophecy. If the name implied a contemptuous dislike — as may be inferred from the proverbial question of Nathanael, " Can any good thing come out of Nazareth ? " [1] — then St. Matthew may be summing up in that expression the various prophecies so little understood by his nation, which pointed to the Messiah as a man of sorrows. And certainly to this day " Nazarene " has continued to be a term of contempt. The Talmudists always speak of Jesus as " Ha-nozeri ; " Julian is said to have expressly decreed that Christians should be called by the less honorable appellation of Galilæans; and to this day the Christians of Palestine are known by no other title than Nusâra.[2] But the explanation which refers St. Matthew's allusion to those passages of prophecy in which Christ is called " the Branch" (*nétser*, נֵצֶר) seems far more probable. The village may have derived this name from no other circumstance than its abundant foliage; but the Old Testament is full of proofs that the Hebrews — who in philology accepted the views of the Analogists — attached immense and mystical importance to mere resemblances in the sound of words. To mention but one single instance, the first chapter of the prophet Micah turns almost entirely on such merely external similarities in what, for lack of a better term, I can only call the physiological quantity of sounds. St. Matthew, a Hebrew of the Hebrews, would without any hesitation have seen a prophetic fitness in Christ's residence at this town of Galilee, because its name recalled the title by which He was addressed in the prophecy of Isaiah.[3]

---

in setting out the frugal board, arranging the simple sleeping-rooms, nay, and in other yet humbler offices ? "

[1] Perhaps in this question, and in the citation of St. Matthew, there may be a play upon the possible derivation of the name from *Nazóra,* " despicable."

[2] In the singular, Nusrâny. On the supposed edict of Julian, see Gibbon, ii. 312 (ed. Milman). If we ever passed a particularly ill-conditioned village in Palestine, my Mohammedan dragoman always rejoiced if he could assure me that the inhabitants were not Mbslim, but Nusâra — which he rarely lost an opportunity of doing. Cf. Acts xxviii. 22.

[3] Isa. xi. 1. *Tsemach,* the word used in Jer. xxiii. 5 ; Zech. iii. 8, &c., also means " Branch." Hitzig, with less probability, supposed St. Matthew to allude to Isa. xlix. 6 (Heb.). The explanation of the passage as = Ναζιραῖος, a Nazarite, is philologically erroneous and historically false ; but something may be said for the derivation from *nôtser,* " protecting," so that " he who calls Jesus Nazarene shall, against his will, call Him 'my Saviour,' ' my Protector ' " (Bp. Alexander,

"Shall the Christ come out of Galilee?" asked the wondering people. "Search and look!" said the Rabbis to Nicodemus, "for out of Galilee ariseth no prophet" (John vii. 41, 52). It would not have needed very deep searching or looking to find that these words were ignorant or false ; for not to speak of Barak the deliverer, and Elon the judge, and Anna the prophetess, three, if not four, of the prophets — and those prophets of the highest eminence, Jonah, Elijah, Hosea, and Nahum — had been born, or had exercised much of their ministry, in the precincts of Galilee.[1] And in spite of the supercilious contempt with which it was regarded, the little town of Nazareth, situated as it was in a healthy and secluded valley, yet close upon the confines of great nations, and in the centre of a mixed population, was eminently fitted to be the home of our Saviour's childhood, the scene of that quiet growth " in wisdom, and stature, and favor with God and man."[2]

Ideas of the Gospels, p. 6). — The vague $\delta\iota\grave{\alpha}\ \tau\tilde{\omega}\nu\ \pi\rho o\varphi\eta\tau\tilde{\omega}\nu$ [50] of Matt. ii. 23 perhaps admits of more than one reference and explanation. For a fuller disquisition on the principles of the explanation offered in the text I must refer to my *Chapters on Language* (second edition), pp. 229—247, in which I have attempted to illustrate this difficult and interesting subject.

[1] Jonah was of Gath-hepher (2 Kings xiv. 25), a town of Zebulun (Josh. xix. 10, 13) ; Hosea is said to have been of Issachar, and was a Northern prophet ; Elkosh, the birthplace of Nahum, was probably in Galilee (Jer. *ad Nah.* i. 1) ; Thisbe, the supposed birthplace of Elijah, was believed to be in Naphthali (Tobit i. 2, but it is exceedingly uncertain whether התשבי מתשב may not mean " the stranger, from the strangers ") — at any rate Elijah's main ministry was in Galilee ; Elisha was of Abel-meholah, in the Jordan valley. To get over such flagrant carelessness in the taunting question of the Jews, some have proposed to give a narrower significance to the name Galilee, and make it mean only Upper Galilee, for the limits of which see Jos. *B. J.* iii. 3, § 1. Among other great names connected with Galilee, Keim mentions the philosopher Aristobulus (of Paneas), the Scribe Nithai of Arbela, Alexander Jannæus, Judas the Gaulonite, and John of Giscala (*Gesch. Jes.* i. 317). A legend mentioned by Jerome also connects the family of St. Paul with Giscala (Jer. *De Vir. illustr.* 5).

[2] Luke ii. 52. Cf. Prov. iii. 4 ; Ps. cxi. 10 ; 1 Sam. ii. 26.

CHAPTER VI.

JESUS IN THE TEMPLE.

" Omnes venit salvare, infantes, et parvulos, et pueros, et juvenes, et seniores ; ideo per omnem venit aetatem." [51] — IREN. *Adv. Haeres.* iii. 18.

EVEN as there is one hemisphere of the lunar surface on which, in its entirety, no human eye has ever gazed, while at the same time the moon's librations enable us to conjecture of its general character and appearance, so there is one large portion of our Lord's life respecting which there is no full record; yet such glimpses are, as it were, accorded to us of its outer edge, that from these we are able to understand the nature of the whole.

Again, when the moon is in crescent, a few bright points are visible through the telescope upon its unilluminated part; those bright points are mountain peaks, so lofty that they catch the sunlight. One such point of splendor and majesty is revealed to us in the otherwise unknown region of Christ's youthful years, and it is sufficient to furnish us with a real insight into that entire portion of His life. In modern language we should call it an anecdote of the Saviour's confirmation.

The age of twelve years was a critical age for a Jewish boy. It was the age at which, according to Jewish legend, Moses had left the house of Pharaoh's daughter; and Samuel had heard the Voice which summoned him to the prophetic office; and Solomon had given the judgment which first revealed his possession of wisdom; and Josiah had first dreamed of his great reform. At this age a boy of whatever rank was obliged, by the injunction of the Rabbis and the custom of his nation, to learn a trade for his own support. At this age he was so far emancipated from parental authority that his parents could no longer sell him as a slave. At this age he became a *ben hat-tôrah*, or " son of the Law." Up to this age he was called *katón*, or " little;" henceforth he was *gadôl*, or " grown up," and was treated more as a man ; henceforth, too, he began to wear the *tephillîn*, or " phylacteries," and was presented by his father in the synagogue on a Sabbath, which was called from this circumstance the *shabbath tephillin*. Nay, more, according to one Rabbinical treatise, the *Sepher Gilgulim*, up to this age a boy only possessed the *nephesh,* or animal life; but henceforth he began to acquire the *ruach,* or spirit, which, if his life were virtuous, would develop, at the age of twenty, into the *nishema,* or reasonable soul.[1]

This period, too — the completion of the twelfth year [2]—formed a decisive epoch in a Jewish boy's education. According to Juda Ben Tema,[3] at *five* he was to study the Scriptures (Mikra), at ten the Mishna, at thirteen the Talmud; at eighteen he was to marry, at twenty to acquire riches, at thirty strength, at forty prudence, and so on to the end. Nor must we forget, in considering this narrative, that the Hebrew race, and, indeed, Orientals generally, develop with a precocity unknown among ourselves, and that boys of this age (as we learn from Josephus) could and did fight in battle, and that, to the great detriment of the race, it is, to this day, regarded as a marriageable age among the Jews of Palestine and Asia Minor.

Now it was the custom of the parents of our Lord to visit Jerusalem every year at the feast of the Passover. Women were, indeed, not mentioned in the law which required the annual presence of all males at the three great yearly feasts of Passover, Pentecost, and Tabernacles; but Mary, in pious observance of the rule recommended by Hillel,[4] accompanied her husband every year, and on this occasion they took with them the boy Jesus, who was beginning to be of an age to assume the responsibilities of the Law. We can easily imagine how powerful must have been the influence upon His human development of this break in the still secluded life; of this glimpse into the great outer world; of this journey through a land of which every hill and every village teemed with sacred memories; of this first visit to that Temple of His Father which was associated with so many mighty events in the story of the kings His ancestors and the prophets His forerunners.

---

[1] Fol. 40, 1. Sepp is my authority for these particulars. These roughly correspond to Philo's division of life into the λογικὴ ἕξις, ἄκρως τελείωσις,[52] and ἀκμή,[53] or πέρας αὐξήσεως.[54] — This incident preserved for us by St. Luke is of inestimable value as discountenancing that too-prevalent Apollinarian heresy which denies to Christ the possession of a human soul (νοῦς), and gives Him only the Λόγος in lieu of it. It is as much the object of the Gospels to reveal to us that He was τελέως (man), as that He was ἀληθῶς (God). (See Hooker, *Eccl. Pol.* i. 614, ed. Keble.)— It should be observed that the word used in Luke ii. 40 is πληρούμενον, *implying a course of growth in wisdom,* not πεπληρωμένον, *implying a finished and permanent result.*

[2] Πεπληρωκὼς ἔτος ἤδη δυωδέκατον [55] (Jos. *Antt.* ii. 9, § 6; v. 10, § 4), the instances of Moses and Samuel. (Keim, i. 416.)

[3] *Pirke Abhôth,* v. 21.

Caspari, p 64.—"Pascha feminarum est arbitrarium" [56] (*Kiddushin,* f. 61, 3). (Sepp.)

Nazareth lies from Jerusalem at a distance of about eighty miles, and, in spite of the intense and jealous hostility of the Samaritans, it is probable that the vast caravan of Galilæan pilgrims on their way to the feast would go by the most direct and the least dangerous route, which lay through the old tribal territories of Manasseh and Ephraim.[1] Leaving the garland of hills which encircle the little town in a manner compared by St. Jerome to the petals of an opening rose, they would descend the narrow flower-bordered limestone path into the great plain of Jezreel. As the Passover falls at the end of April and the beginning of May, the country would be wearing its brightest, greenest, loveliest aspect, and the edges of the vast cornfields on either side of the road through the vast plain would be woven, like the High Priest's robe, with the blue and purple and scarlet of innumerable flowers.[2] Over the streams of that ancient river, the river Kishon — past Shunem, recalling memories of Elisha as it lay nestling on the southern slopes of Little Hermon — past royal Jezreel, with the sculptured sarcophagi that alone bore witness to its departed splendor — past the picturesque outline of bare and dewless Gilboa — past sandy Taanach, with its memories of Sisera and Barak — past Megiddo, where He might first have seen the helmets and broadswords and eagles of the Roman legionary — the road would lie to En-Gannîm, where, beside the fountains, and amid the shady and lovely gardens which still mark the spot, they would probably have halted for their first night's rest. Next day they would begin to ascend the mountains of Manasseh, and crossing the "Drowning Meadow," as it is now called, and winding through the rich figyards and olive-groves that fill the valleys round El Jib, they would leave upon the right the hills which, in their glorious beauty, formed the "crown of pride" of which Samaria boasted, but which, as the prophet foretold, should be as a "fading flower." Their second encampment would probably be near Jacob's well, in the beautiful and fertile valley between Ebal and Gerizim, and not far from the ancient Shechem. A third day's journey would take them past Shiloh and Gibeah of Saul and Bethel to Beeroth; and from the pleasant springs by which they would there encamp a short and easy stage would

---

[1] Two other routes were open to them : one by the sea-coast, past Carmel and Cæsarea to Joppa, and so across the plain to Jerusalem; the other to Tiberias, and then on the eastern bank of the Jordan to the fords of Bethabara. Both of these routes were longer, less frequented, and more liable to the attacks of roving bands.

[2] It was at this time of year that the author visited in 1870 the scenes he is here describing. In the year A. D. 8 the Passover began on April 8.

bring them in sight of the towers of Jerusalem. The profane plumage of the eagle-wings of Rome was already overshadowing the Holy City; but, towering above its walls, still glittered the great Temple, with its gilded roofs and marble colonnades, and it was still the Jerusalem of which royal David sang, and for which the exiles by the waters of Babylon had yearned with such deep emotion, when they took their harps from the willows to wail the remorseful dirge that they would remember her until their right hands forgot their cunning. Who shall fathom the unspeakable emotion with which the boy Jesus gazed on that memorable and never-to-be-forgotten scene?

The numbers who flocked to the Passover from every region of the East might be counted by tens of thousands.[1] There were far more than the city could by any possibility accommodate; and then, as now at Eastertime, vast numbers of the pilgrims reared for themselves the little *succôth* — booths of mat, and wicker-work, and interwoven leaves, which provided them with a sufficient shelter for all their wants. The feast lasted for a week — a week, probably, of deep happiness and strong religious emotion; and then, with their mules, and horses, and asses, and camels, the vast caravan would clear away their temporary dwelling-places, and start on the homeward journey. The road was enlivened by mirth and music. They often beguiled the tedium of travel with the sound of drums and timbrels, and paused to refresh themselves with dates, or melons, or cucumbers, and water drawn in skins and waterpots from every springing well and running stream. The veiled women and the stately old men are generally mounted, while their sons or brothers, with long sticks in their hands, lead along by a string their beasts of burden. The boys and children sometimes walk and play by the side of their parents, and sometimes, when tired, get a lift on horse or mule. I can find no trace of the assertion or conjecture[2] that the women, and

---

[1] Josephus (*Bell. Jud.* ii. 1, § 3) calls them "an innumerable multitude;" and in vi. 9, § 3, he mentions the very remarkable fact that Cestius, in order to give Nero some notion of the power of the city, had asked the chief priests to count the number of paschal lambs offered at the Passover, and found that there were no less than 256,500! which (allowing a general average of rather more than ten to each lamb, whereas there were sometimes as many as twenty) would make the number of worshippers no less than 2,700,200, exclusive of all foreigners, and all who were ceremonially unclean, &c. The assertion that Agrippa reckoned 12,000,000 worshippers by counting the kidneys of the lambs offered, is one of the usual Rabbinic exaggerations.

[2] Which first occurs, I believe, in Bede.

boys, and men formed three separate portions of the caravan, and such is certainly not the custom in modern times. But, in any case, among such a sea of human beings, how easy would it be to lose one young boy![1]

The apocryphal legend says that on the journey from Jerusalem the boy Jesus left the caravan and returned to the Holy City.[2] With far greater truth and simplicity St. Luke informs us that — absorbed in all probability in the rush of new and elevating emotions — He "tarried behind in Jerusalem." A day elapsed before the parents[3] discovered their loss; this they would not do until they arrived at the place of evening rendezvous, and all day long they would be free from all anxiety, supposing that the boy was with some other group of friends or relatives in that long caravan. But when evening came, and their diligent inquiries[4] led to no trace of Him, they would learn the bitter fact that He was altogether missing from the band of returning pilgrims. The next day, in alarm and anguish — perhaps, too, with some sense of self-reproach that they had not been more faithful to their sacred charge — they retraced their steps to Jerusalem. The country was in a wild and unsettled state. The ethnarch Archelaus, after ten years of a cruel and disgraceful reign, had recently been deposed by the Emperor, and banished to Vienne, in Gaul. The Romans had annexed the province over which he had ruled, and the introduction of their system of taxation by Coponius, the first procurator, had kindled the revolt which, under Judas of Gamala and the Pharisee Sadoc, wrapped the whole country in a storm of sword and flame.[5] This disturbed state of the political horizon would not only render their journey more difficult when once

---

[1] The incident constantly occurs to this day in the annual expeditions of the pilgrims to bathe in the fords of Jordan. At Easter I met hundreds of Mohammedan pilgrims streaming southwards to the "Tomb of Moses."

[2] Lange here particularizes too much, both in assuming that there was a separate company of boys; and that "the Child — He knew not how — fell out of the train of boys, and went on, led by the Spirit, meditating, longing, attracted, and carried along by His own infinite thoughts until He stood in the Temple, in the midst of the Rabbis."

[3] The proper reading of Luke ii. 43 is almost certainly οἱ γονεῖς,[57] which has for dogmatic reasons been dishonestly altered into Ἰωσὴφ καὶ ἡ μήτηρ αὐτοῦ[58] (see Lightfoot, *Rev. of the New Test.*, p. 29). The place where they first halted might very well be, as tradition says, El Bîreh, the ancient Beeroth, about six miles north of Jerusalem.

[4] Luke ii. 44, ἀνεζήτουν.

[5] The insurrection of Judas was A. D. 6 — *i. e.*, only two years before this event. It will be seen (Exc. I. *infr.*, "The date of Christ's Birth") that A. U. C. 750 (B. C. 4) seems to me the almost certain date of the Nativity.

they had left the shelter of the caravan, but would also intensify their dread lest, among all the wild elements of warring nationalities which at such a moment were assembled about the walls of Jerusalem, their Son should have met with harm. Truly on that day of misery and dread must the sword have pierced through the virgin mother's heart !

Neither on that day, nor during the night, nor throughout a considerable part of the third day, did they discover Him, till at last they found Him in the place which, strangely enough, seems to have been the last where they searched for Him — in the Temple, "sitting in the midst of the doctors, both hearing them and asking them questions; and all that heard Him were astonished at His understanding and answers."

The last expression, no less than the entire context, and all that we know of the character of Jesus and the nature of the circumstances, shows that the Boy was there to inquire and learn — not, as the Arabic Gospel of the Infancy[1] represents it, to cross-examine the doctors "each in turn"— not to expound the number of the spheres and celestial bodies, and their natures and operations — still less to " explain physics and metaphysics, hyperphysics and hypophysics " (!) All these are but the Apollinarian fictions of those who preferred their heretical and pseudo-reverential fancies of what was fitting, to the simple truthfulness with which the Evangelist lets us see that Jesus, like other children, grew up in gradual knowledge, consistently with the natural course of human development. He was there, as St. Luke shows us, in all humility and reverence to His elders, as an eager-hearted and gifted learner, whose enthusiasm kindled their admiration, and whose bearing won their esteem and love.[2] All tinge of

---

[1] Ch. xlviii.—lii. Not of this kind was the wisdom in which He grew. "La sagesse dont il est question, ce n'est pas la sagesse selon le monde mais la sagesse selon Dieu. Ce n'est ni cette philosophie superbe dont se vantait la Grèce, et qu'elle inculquait si soigneusement à la génération naissante ; ni cette prudence de la vie, par laquelle les enfants de ce siècle surpassent les enfants de la lumière ; ni cette instruction des livres que les hommes d'étude ramassent avec tant de travail ; ni même la connaissance speculative de Dieu et des saints mystères de sa Parole. Il s'agit ici de cette sagesse si souvent louée dans les livres du roi Salomon, dont la première leçon est, 'Crains Dieu, et garde ses commandements.'"[59] (Adolphe Monod, *Enfance de Jésus*, p. 9.)

[2] " The Rabbis themselves said," observes Stier, " that the word of God out of the mouths of children is to be received as from the mouth of the Sanhedrin, of Moses, of the Blessed God Himself " (*Bammidbar Rabba*, 14). (Stier, *Words of the Lord Jesus*, i. 20, E. Tr.) — Anything like forwardness in boys was peculiarly distasteful to the Jews (*Abhôth*, v. 12, 15).

arrogance and forwardness was utterly alien to His character, which, from His sweet childhood upward, was meek and lowly of heart. Among those present may have been — white with the snows of well-nigh a hundred years — the great Hillel, one of the founders of the Masôrah, whom the Jews almost reverence as a second Moses ; and his son the Rabban Simeon, who thought so highly of silence ; and his grandson, the refined and liberal Gamaliel ; and Shammai, his great rival, a teacher who numbered a still vaster host of disciples ; and Hanan, or Annas, son of Seth, His future judge ; and Boethus, the father-in-law of Herod ; and Babha Ben Butah, whose eyes Herod had put out ; and Nechaniah Ben Hiskanah, so celebrated for his victorious prayers ; and Johanan Ben Zacchai, who predicted the destruction of the Temple ; and the wealthy Joseph of Arimathea ; and the timid but earnest Nicodemus ; and the youthful Jonathan Ben Uzziel, who subsequently wrote the celebrated Chaldee paraphrase, and was held by his contemporaries in boundless honor.[1] But though none of these might conjecture Who was before them — and though hardly one of them lived to believe on Him, and some to oppose Him in years to come — which of them all would not have been charmed and astonished at a glorious and noble-hearted boy, in all the early beauty of his life, who, though He had never learned in the schools of the Rabbis, yet showed so marvellous a wisdom, and so deep a knowledge in all things Divine ?[2]

Here then — perhaps in the famous *Lishcath hagqazzith,* or " Hall of Squares " — perhaps in the *Chanujôth,* or " Halls of Purchase," or in one of the spacious chambers assigned to purposes of

---

[1] Sepp, *Leben Jesu,* i. § 17 ; but I do not pledge myself to the exactitude of his conjecture in this enumeration. For some further allusions to these Rabbis with Talmudic references to the traditions about them, see Etheridge's *Hebrew Literature,* p. 38. In a blasphemous Jewish book, the *Toldôth Jeshû* (which is not older than the thirteenth century, though Voltaire supposed it to belong to the first), Hillel and Shammai are represented as having reproved Jesus for having come into the Temple with His head uncovered. Nothing whatever new or true respecting Jesus is to be learnt from the Talmud (see Excursus II., *infr.,* " Christ and Christians in the Talmud "), and least of all from this sickening and worthless piece of blasphemy, which he who wills may read in Wagenseil's *Tela Ignea Satanae,* 1681.

[2] Incidents somewhat similar in their external circumstances were by no means unknown. They are narrated of R. Eliezer Ben Azaria, a descendant in the tenth generation of Ezra ; and of R. Ashe, the first compiler of the Babylonian Talmud. (Sepp, *Leben Jesu, ubi supr.*) Josephus (*Vita,* 2), with the imperturbable egotism and naïve self-complacency which characterized him, narrates how, when he was about fourteen years of age, the chief priests and Rabbis at Jerusalem frequently visited him to hear the understanding with which he answered the most difficult questions on the hidden meaning of the Law.

teaching [1] which adjoined the Court of the Gentiles — seated, but doubtless at the feet of his teachers, on the many-colored mosaic which formed the floor, Joseph and Mary found the Divine Boy. Filled with that almost adoring spirit of reverence for the great priests and religious teachers of their day which characterized at this period the simple and pious Galilæans, they were awe-struck to find Him, calm and happy, in so august a presence.[2] They might, indeed, have known that He was wiser than His teachers, and transcendently more great; but hitherto they had only known Him as the silent, sweet, obedient child, and perhaps the incessant contact of daily life had blunted the sense of His awful origin. Yet it is Mary, not Joseph, who alone ventures to address Him in the language of tender reproach. " My child, why dost Thou treat us thus? see, thy father and I were seeking Thee with aching hearts." [3] And then follows His answer, so touching in its innocent simplicity, so unfathomable in its depth of consciousness, so infinitely memorable as furnishing us with the *first recorded words* of the Lord Jesus:

" *Why is it that ye were seeking me? Did ye not know that I must be about my Father's business ?* " [4]

This answer, so divinely natural, so sublimely noble, bears upon itself the certain stamp of authenticity. The conflict of thoughts which it implies; the half-vexed astonishment which it expresses that they should so little understand Him; the perfect dignity, and yet the perfect humility which it combines, lie wholly beyond the possibility of invention. It is in accordance, too, with all His ministry — in accordance with that utterance to the tempter, " Man shall not live by bread alone, but by every word that proceedeth out of the mouth of God," and with that quiet answer to the disciples by the well of Samaria, " My meat is to do the will of Him that sent me, and to finish His work." Mary had said unto Him, " Thy father," but in His reply He recognizes, and henceforth He knows, *no* father except His Father in heaven. In the " Did ye not *know*," He delicately recalls to them the fading memory of all that they *did*

---

[1] The *Lishcath haggazzith* was a basilica of hewn square stones (built B. C. 110 by Simon Ben Shetach), in which both priests and Sanhedrin met, till they were transferred to the *chanujôth.* It opened both on the Court of the Priests and on that of the Gentiles. (*Joma,* 25 *a* ; *Shabbah,* 15 *a,* in Ginsburg, s. v. " Sanhedrin," Kitto's *Cyclop.*)

[2] The word is a strong one, $\dot{\epsilon}\xi\epsilon\pi\lambda\dot{\alpha}\gamma\eta\sigma\alpha\nu$ (Luke ii. 48).

[3] Luke ii. 48, $\dot{o}\delta\upsilon\nu\dot{\omega}\mu\epsilon\nu o\iota$ $\dot{\epsilon}\zeta\eta\tau o\tilde{\upsilon}\mu\epsilon\nu$.[59] †

[4] $\dot{\epsilon}\nu$ $\tau o\tilde{\iota}\varsigma$ $\tau o\tilde{\upsilon}$ $\pi\alpha\tau\rho\dot{o}\varsigma$ $\mu o\upsilon,$ sc. $\pi\rho\dot{\alpha}\gamma\mu\alpha\sigma\iota\nu$ (Luke ii. 49). It *might* mean " in my father's house;" but the other rendering is wider and better. Cf. 1 Tim. iv. 15; Gen. xli. 51, LXX.

know; and in that " *I* must," He lays down the sacred law of self-sacrifice by which He was to walk, even unto the death upon the cross.

" And they understood not the saying which He spake unto them." They — even they — even the old man who had protected His infancy, and the mother who knew the awful secret of His birth — understood not, that is, not in their *deeper* sense, the significance of those quiet words. Strange and mournful commentary on the first recorded utterance of the youthful Saviour, spoken to those who were nearest and dearest to Him on earth! Strange, but mournfully prophetic of all His life: — " He was in the world, and the world was made by Him, and the world knew Him not. He came unto His own, and His own received Him not." [1]

And yet, though the consciousness of His Divine parentage was thus clearly present in His mind — though one ray from the glory of His hidden majesty had thus unmistakably flashed forth — in all dutiful simplicity and holy obedience " He went down with them, and came to Nazareth, and was subject unto them."

---

[1] John i. 10, 11. It should be rather " unto His own possessions (εἰς τὰ ἴδια), and His own people (οἱ ἴδιοι) received Him not."

CHAPTER VII.

THE HOME AT NAZARETH.

Αὐξάνων κατὰ τὸ κοινὸν ἁπάντων ἀνθρώπων.[60] — JUST. MART. *Dial. c. Tryph.* 88.

SUCH, then, is the "solitary floweret out of the wonderful enclosed garden of the thirty years, plucked precisely there where the swollen bud, at a *distinctive crisis*, bursts into flower." [1]

But if of the first twelve years of His human life we have only this single anecdote, of the next eighteen years of His life we possess no record whatever save such as is implied in a single word.

That word occurs in Mark vi. 3: "Is not this *the carpenter?*" [2]

We may be indeed thankful that the word remains, for it is full of meaning, and has exercised a very noble and blessed influence over the fortunes of mankind. It has tended to console and sanctify the estate of poverty; to ennoble the duty of labor; to elevate the entire conception of manhood, as of a condition which in itself alone, and apart from every adventitious circumstance, has its own grandeur and dignity in the sight of God.

1. It shows, for instance, that not only during the three years of His ministry, but throughout the whole of His life, our Lord was

---

[1] Stier, i. 18.

[2] It is, no doubt, on dogmatical grounds that this was altered into "the son of the carpenter" in the later MSS., though not in a single uncial. Some were offended that the Lord of All should have worked in the shop of a poor artisan; but how alien to the true spirit of Christianity is this feeling of offence! Origen, indeed, says (*c. Cels.* vi. 36) that nowhere in the Gospels is Jesus himself called a carpenter; but this is probably a mere slip of memory, or may only prove how early the Christians grew ashamed of their Divine Master's condescension, and how greatly they needed the lessons which it involves. That even "the carpenter's son" became a term of reproach among the Gentiles, is clear from the story of Libanius's question to a Christian during Julian's expedition into Persia, "What is the Carpenter's Son doing now?" The Christian answered, "He is making a coffin;" and soon came the news of Julian's death. The omission of Joseph's name in Mark vi. 3 has been universally accepted as an indication that he was dead; otherwise we might suppose that something contemptuous was intended by only mentioning the mother's name (see Ewald, *Gram. Arabica*, ii. 4, *note*). For this reference I am indebted to.Mr. C. J. Monro.

poor. In the *cities* the carpenters would be Greeks, and skilled workmen; the carpenter of a provincial village — and, if tradition be true, Joseph was "not very skilful" — can only have held a very humble position and secured a very moderate competence.[1] In all ages there has been an exaggerated desire for wealth; an exaggerated admiration for those who possess it; an exaggerated belief of its influence in producing or increasing the happiness of life; and from these errors a flood of cares and jealousies and meannesses have devastated the life of man. And therefore Jesus chose voluntarily "the low estate of the poor" — not, indeed, an absorbing, degrading, grinding poverty, which is always rare, and almost always remediable, but that commonest lot of honest poverty, which, though it necessitates self-denial, can provide with ease for all the necessaries of a simple life. The Idumæan dynasty that had usurped the throne of David might indulge in the gilded vices of a corrupt Hellenism, and display the gorgeous gluttonies of a decaying civilization; but He who came to be the Friend and the Saviour, no less than the King of All, sanctioned the purer, better, simpler traditions and customs of His nation,[2] and chose the condition in which the vast majority of mankind have ever, and must ever live.

2. Again, there has ever been, in the unenlightened mind, a love of idleness; a tendency to regard it as a stamp of aristocracy; a desire to delegate labor to the lower and weaker, and to brand it with the stigma of inferiority and contempt.[3] But our Lord wished to show that labor is a pure and a noble thing; it is the salt of life;

---

[1] Arab. Gosp. Inf. xxxviii. Unfortunately, Pagan writers do not add one single fact to our knowledge of the life of Jesus (Tac. *Ann.* xv. 44; Plin. *Epp.* x. 97; Suet. *Claud.* 25; Lucian, *De Mort. Peregr.* 11; Lamprid. *Alex. Sev.* 29, 43). A few passages in the Vera Hist. of the Pseudo-Lucian are probably meant to ridicule Gospel narratives, and a few passages in the Life of Apollonius of Tyana by Philostratus, and the Life of Pythagoras by Jamblichus — the "cloudy romances of Pagan sophists" — are perhaps intended by way of parallel. Jewish writers are just as barren. Josephus and Justus of Tiberias passed over the subject with obvious and unworthy reticence. The Talmudists simply preserved or invented a few turbid and worthless calumnies.

[2] Philo. *in Flac.* 977 f.

[3] To the Greeks and Romans all mechanical trade was βάναυσος, *i. e.*, mean, vulgar, contemptible, and was therefore left to slaves. The Jews, with a truer and nobler wisdom, enacted that every boy should learn a trade, and said with R. Juda b. Ilai, "the wise," that "labor honors the laborer." Saul was a tentmaker. Up to the age of forty, R. Johanan, son of Zakkai, afterwards president of the Sanhedrin, was, like Mahomet, a merchant; the Rabbis Juda and Menahem were bakers; R. Eliezer, supreme president of the schools of Alexandria, was a smith; R. Ismael, a needle-maker; R. Joza Ben Chalaphta, a tanner. (Sepp, § 19; Ginsburg, in Kitto's *Cyclop.*, s. v. "Education"). The rabbis even assumed and

it is the girdle of manliness; it saves the body from effeminate languor, and the soul from polluting thoughts. And therefore Christ labored, working with His own hands, and fashioned ploughs and yokes for those who needed them. The very scoff of Celsus against the possibility that *He* should have been a carpenter who came to save the world,[1] shows how vastly the world has gained from this very circumstance — how gracious and how fitting was the example of such humility in One whose work it was to regenerate society, and to make all things new.

3. Once more, from this long silence, from this deep obscurity, from this monotonous routine of an unrecorded and uneventful life, we were meant to learn that our *real* existence in the sight of God consists in the inner and not in the outer life. The world hardly attaches any significance to any life except those of its heroes and benefactors, its mighty intellects, or its splendid conquerors. But these are, and must ever be, the few. One raindrop of myriads falling on moor or desert, or mountain — one snowflake out of myriads melting into the immeasurable sea — is, and must be, for most men the symbol of their ordinary lives. They die, and barely have they died, when they are forgotten; a few years pass, and the creeping lichens eat away the letters of their names upon the churchyard stone; but even if those crumbling letters were still decipherable, they would recall no memory to those who stand upon their graves. Even common and ordinary men are very apt to think themselves of much importance; but, on the contrary, not even the greatest man is in any degree necessary, and after a very short space of time —

> " His place, in all the pomp that fills
> The circuit of the summer hills,
> Is that his grave is green."

4. A relative insignificance, then, is, and must be, the destined lot of the immense majority, and many a man might hence be led to

---

rejoiced in the titles of R. Johanan, the shoemaker; R. Simon, the weaver, &c. Labor and learning were, in the eyes of the Rabbis, good antidotes against sinful thoughts (*Pirke Abhôth*, fol. 2, 2). — Even the Rabbis, however, were not far enough advanced to honor labor *without* learning, and, as we shall see hereafter, they spoke contemptuously of uneducated artisans and common tillers of the soil (*vid. infra*, p. 92).

[1] Justin Mart. *Dial c. Tryph.* 88, τεκτονικὰ ἔργα εἰργάζετο ἐν ἀνθρώποις ὤν, ἄροτρα καὶ ζύγα, διὰ τούτων τὰ τῆς δικαιοσύνης σύμβολα διδάσκων καὶ ἐνεργῆ βίον.[61] (There is no necessity, with Neander, to translate ζύγα, " scales.") The supposed allusions to the trade of a carpenter in Matt. vi. 27; Luke xxiii. 31, &c., are obviously too vague to have any bearing on this question.

think, that since he fills so small a space — since, for the vast masses of mankind, he is of as little importance as the ephemerid which buzzes out its little hour in the summer noon — there is nothing better than to eat, and drink, and die. But Christ came to convince us that a *relative* insignificance may be an *absolute* importance.[1] He came to teach that continual excitement, prominent action, distinguished services, brilliant success, are no essential elements of true and noble life, and that myriads of the beloved of God are to be found among the insignificant and the obscure. "*Si vis divinus esse, late ut Deus,*"[2] is the encouraging, consoling, ennobling lesson of those voiceless years. The calmest and most unknown lot is often the happiest, and we may safely infer that these years in the home and trade of the carpenter of Nazareth were happy years in our Saviour's life. Often, even in His later days, it is clear that His words are the words of one who rejoiced in spirit; they are words which seem to flow from the full river of an abounding happiness. But what must that happiness have been in those earlier days, before the storms of righteous anger had agitated His unruffled soul, or His heart burned hot with terrible indignation against the sins and hypocrisies of men? "*Heaven,*" as even a Confucius could tell us, "*means principle;*" and if at all times innocence be the only happiness, how great must have been the happiness of a sinless childhood! "Youth," says the poet-preacher, "danceth like a bubble, nimble and gay, and shineth like a dove's neck, or the image of a rainbow which hath no substance, and whose very image and colors are fantastical." And if this description be true of even a careless youth, with what transcendently deeper force must it apply to the innocent, the sinless, the perfect youth of Christ? In the case of many myriads, and assuredly not least in the case of the saints of God, a sorrowful and stormy manhood has often been preceded by a calm and rosy dawn.

5. And while they were occupied manually, we have positive evidence that these years were not neglected intellectually. No importance can be attached to the clumsy stories of the Apocryphal Gospels, but it is possible that some religious and simple instruction may have been given to the little Nazarenes by the *sopherîm*, or other attendants of the synagogue;[2] and here our Lord, who was made

---

[1] "Tu homo, TANTUM NOMEN, si intelligas te "[63] (Tert. *Apol. adv. Gent.* xlviii.)

"We are greater than we know."— *Wordsworth.*

[2] The Talmud certainly proves their *later* existence, and that the *sopherîm* and *chazanîm* of the synagogues acted as *mikredardike* — i. e., *mikrodidaktici*, or private teachers of the young. But the *chazzan* of our Lord's day was in a much

like unto us in all things, may have learnt, as other children learnt, the elements of human learning. But it is, perhaps, more probable that Jesus received His early teaching at home, and in accordance with the injunctions of the Law (Deut. xi. 19), from His father. He would, at any rate, have often heard in the daily prayers of the synagogue all which the elders of the place could teach respecting the Law and the Prophets. That He had not been to Jerusalem, for purposes of instruction, and had not frequented any of the schools of the Rabbis, is certain from the indignant questions of jealous enemies, " From whence hath this man these things?" " How knoweth this man letters, having never learned?"[1] There breathes throughout these questions the Rabbinic spirit of insolent contempt for the *am ha-aretz* (עַם הָאָרֶץ) or illiterate countryman. The stereotyped intelligence of the nation, accustomed, if I may use the expression, to that mummified form of a dead religion, which had been embalmed by the Oral Law, was incapable of appreciating the divine originality of a wisdom learnt from God alone. They could not get beyond the sententious error of the son of Sirach, that " the wisdom of the learned man cometh by opportunity of leisure."[2] Had Jesus received the slightest tincture of their technical training he would have been *less*, not *more*, effectually armed for putting to shame the supercilious exclusiveness of their narrow erudition.

6. And this testimony of His enemies furnishes us with a convincing and fortunate proof that His teaching was not, as some would insinuate, a mere eclectic system borrowed from the various sects and teachers of His times. It is certain that He was never enrolled among the scholars of those Scribes[3] who made it their main business to teach the traditions of the fathers. Although schools in great

---

humbler position than was the case later. The regular foundation of schools for *infants* is said to have been due to Jesus the son of Gamaliel I. See the whole question examined by Winer, *Realwörterb.*, s. v. *Unterricht; Jost, Gesch. d. Volkes Israel*, iii. 163 ; and Keim, *Jesu*, i. 428. On the familiarity of Jewish children with the Law, see Jos. *Antt.* iv. 8, § 12 ; Gfrörer, *Jahrh d. Heils*, i. 118.

[1] Mark vi. 2 ; John vi. 42 ; vii. 15. The *am ha-aretz*, according to R. Eliezer, is one who does not say the *Shema* (Hear, O Israel) morning and evening. According to R. Joshua, one who wore no *tephillin* (phylacteries) ; according to Ben Assai, one who did not wear *tsitsith* (tassels) ; according to R. Nathan, one who had no *mezuzah* above his door ; according to R. Nathan Ben Joseph, one who did not train his sons in the Law ; but according to R. Hona the true *Halachah* (" rule ") was with those *who, even if they had read the Scriptures and the Mishna, had not attended the school of any Rabbi.* (*Bab. Berachôth*, fol. 47, 6 ; *v. infr.*, p. 324 ; Gfrörer, *Jahrhund. d. Heils*, i. 188.)

[2] Ecclus. xxxviii. 24. For the continuation of the passage, *v. infra*, p. 92.

[3] Jos. *Antt.* xv. 10, § 5. Sometimes an educated slave acted as home-tutor.

towns had been founded eighty years before, by Simon Ben Shatach, yet there could have been no Beth Midrash or Beth Rabban, no "vineyard" or "array" at despised and simple Nazareth.[1] And from whom could Jesus have borrowed? — From Oriental Gymnosophists or Greek Philosophers? No one, in these days, ventures to advance so wild a proposition.[2]— From the *Pharisees?* The very foundations of their system, the very idea of their religion, was irreconcilably alien from all that He revealed.— From the *Sadducees?* Their epicurean insouciance, their "expediency" politics, their shallow rationalism, their polished sloth, were even more repugnant to true Christianity, than they were to sincere Judaism.— From the *Essenes?* They were an exclusive, ascetic, and isolated community, with whose discouragement of marriage, and withdrawal from action, the Gospels have no sympathy, and to whom our Lord never alluded, unless it be in those passages where He reprobates those who abstain from anointing themselves when they fast,[3] and who hide their candle under a bushel.— From *Philo*, and the Alexandrian Jews? Philo was indeed a good man, and a great thinker, and a contemporary of Christ;[4] but (even if his name had ever been heard — which is exceedingly doubtful — in so remote a region as Galilee) it would be impossible, among the world's philosophies, to choose any system less like the doctrines which Jesus taught, than the mystic theosophy and allegorizing extravagance of that "sea of abstractions" which lies congealed in his writings. From *Hillel* and *Shammai?* We know but little of them; but although, in one or two passages of the Gospels, there may be a conceivable allusion to the disputes which agitated their schools, or to one or two of the best and truest maxims which originated in them, such allusions, on the one hand, involve no more than belongs to the common stock of

---

[1] ברם, "vineyard;" סדרא, "array," and other similar names, were given by the Jews to their schools (Dr. Ginsburg, in Kitto's *Cyclop.* i. 728).

[2] For numerous monographs on all these theories, see Hase, *Leben Jesu*, p. 73.

[3] Jos. *B. J.* ii. 8, § 3.

[4] Philo was probably born B. C. 20, and lived till about A. D. 50. As we know that he once visited Jerusalem, it is just possible (no more) that he *may* have seen Jesus. The tendency of his spiritualism was "to exalt knowledge in place of action; its home was in the cells of the recluse, and not in the field or the market; its truest disciples were visionary Therapeutæ, and not Apostles charged with a Gospel to the world." Alexandrianism "was the ideal of heathen religion and the negation of Christianity. . . . It suppressed the instincts of civil and domestic society which Christianity ennobled; it perpetuated the barriers which Christianity removed; it abandoned the conflict which Christianity carries out to victory." (Westcott, *Introd.*, p. 77.)

truth taught by the Spirit of God to men in every age; and, on the other hand, the system which Shammai and Hillel taught was that oral tradition, that dull dead Levitical ritualism, at once arrogant and impotent, at once frivolous and unoriginal, which Jesus both denounced and overthrew.[1] The schools in which Jesus learnt were not the schools of the Scribes, but the school of holy obedience, of sweet contentment, of unalloyed simplicity, of stainless purity, of cheerful toil. The lore in which He studied was not the lore of Rabbinism, in which to find one just or noble thought we must wade through masses of puerile fancy and cabbalistic folly, but the Books of God without Him, in Scripture, in Nature, and in Life; and the Book of God within Him, written on the fleshly tables of the heart.

The education of a Jewish boy of the humbler classes was almost solely scriptural and moral,[2] and his parents were, as a rule, his sole teachers. We can hardly doubt that the child Jesus was taught by Joseph and Mary to read the Shema (Deut. vi. 4), and the Hallel (Ps. cxiv.—cxviii.), and the simpler parts of those holy books, on whose pages His divine wisdom was hereafter to pour such floods of light.

But He had evidently received a further culture than this.

(i.) The art of writing is by no means commonly known, even in these days, in the East; but more than one allusion to the form of the Hebrew letters,[3] no less than the stooping to write with His

---

[1] We shall see hereafter that in all questions such as that respecting divorce, the decisions of Jesus were wholly different from those either of Hillel or of Shammai. Can it be regarded as certain that Hillel occupied among his contemporaries anything like the space which he occupies in tradition? Unless he be the same as Pollio (*Antt.* xv. 1, § 1; 10, § 4) — which, to say the least, is very doubtful, for Pollio seems to be Abtalion who preceded Hillel — Josephus *does not even mention him,* though there could be no possible reason, whether of timidity or of uncertainty, to pass over his name, as he passes over that of Jesus. I shall speak of the supposed relation of Jesus to Hillel in Excursus III., "Jesus and Hillel," and may refer to Ewald, *Gesch. Christ.* 28—39.

[2] Exod. xii. 26; Deut. *passim ;* Acts xxii. 3; 2 Tim. iii. 15. In Ecclus. xxxviii. 24 seqq., there is a striking contrast between the limited studies and opportunities of the poor and the range and leisure of the rich. " The wisdom of a learned man cometh by opportunity of leisure. . . . How can he get wisdom that holdeth the plough, . . . that driveth oxen, . . . and *whose talk is of bullocks ?* . . . *So every carpenter and workmaster* that laboreth night and day. . . . All these trust to their hands. . . . They shall not be sought for in public counsel, nor set high in the congregation, . . . and they shall not be found where parables are spoken ; . . . but . . . their desire is in the work of their craft."

[3] Matt. v. 18. Eusebius (*H. E.* i. 13) gives the spurious letter which Christ was asserted to have written (Cedrenus, *Hist.*, p. 145, adds ἰδίαις χερσὶ [64]) to Abgarus, King of Edessa. Cf. Arab. Gosp. Inf. xlviii.; Ps. Matth. xxxi.

finger on the ground,[1] show that our Lord could write. (ii.) That His knowledge of the sacred writings was deep and extensive — that, in fact, He must almost have known them by heart — is clear, not only from His direct quotations, but also from the numerous allusions which He made to the Law and to the Hagiographa, as well as to Isaiah, Jeremiah, Daniel, Joel, Hosea, Micah, Zechariah, Malachi, and, above all, to the Book of Psalms.[2] It is probable, though not certain, that He was acquainted with the uncanonical Jewish books.[3] This profound and ready knowledge of the Scriptures gave more point to the half-indignant question, so often repeated, " *Have ye not read ?* " (iii.) The language which our Lord commonly spoke was Aramaic ; and at that period Hebrew was completely a dead language, known only to the more educated, and only to be acquired by labor ; yet it is clear that Jesus was acquainted with it, for some of His scriptural quotations[4] directly refer to the Hebrew original. Greek too He must have known, for it was currently spoken in towns so near His home as Sepphoris, Cæsarea, and Tiberias.[5] Meleager, the poet of the Greek anthology, in his epitaph on himself, assumes that his Greek will be intelligible to Syrians and Phœnicians : he also speaks of his native Gadara, which was at no great distance from Nazareth, as though it were a sort of Syrian Athens. Ever since the days of Alexander the Great, alike in the contact of the Jews with Ptolemies, and with Seleucids, Hellenic influences had been at work in Palestine. Greek was, indeed, the common medium of intercourse,

---

[1] John viii. 6 (in MS. U), τῷ δακτύλῳ ἔγραψεν ἑκάστου αὐτῶν τὰς ἁμαρτίας.[65] (See Hofmann, p. 309 ; Fabr. *Cod. ap.* N. T. i. 315 ; Wagenseil, *ad Sot.* p. 33.) The common use of the *mezuzôth* (Deut. vi. 9) and *tephillin* hardly show that the art of writing was common.

[2] These all occur in St. Matthew's Gospel.

[3] Cf. Matt. xi. 28 seq. with Ecclus. li. 26, &c., and Luke xiv. 28 with 2 Macc. ii. 29, 30 (Keim, i. 455). Every respectable family possessed at least a portion of the sacred books. Prof. Plumptre (*Christ and Christendom*, p. 96) has observed that James "the Lord's brother" certainly makes allusions to the Apocrypha (cf. James i. 6, 8, 25 with Ecclus. vii. 10 ; i. 28 ; xiv. 23.)

[4] Mark xii. 29, 30 ; Luke xxii. 37 ; Matt. xxvii. 46.

[5] The coinage of the Herods has Greek inscriptions (De Saulcy, *Hist. d'Herode*, p. 385). The study of Greek was encouraged by some Rabbis ; they said that the *tallîth* of Shem and the *pallium* of Japhet ought to be united (*Midrash Rabba*, Gen. xxxiv.). As a rule, however, they did not value the acquisition of languages (Jos. *Antt.* xx. 11, § 2) ; and the learning of Greek was absolutely forbidden during the Roman war (*Sota*, ix. 14). Gamaliel alone, of the Rabbis, permitted his scholars to study Greek literature (*chochmath Javanith*) ; and Rabbi Ismael said that Greek wisdom should only be taught at the hour which was *neither day nor night*, since the Law was to be studied *day and night* (*Menachôth*, 19 *b*). But see Excursus IV., " Greek Learning."

and without it Jesus could have had no conversation with strangers — with the centurion, for instance, whose servant He healed, or with Pilate, or with the Greeks who desired an interview with Him in the last week of His life.[1] Some too of His scriptural quotations, if we can venture to assume a reproduction of the *ipsissima verba*,[2] are taken directly from the Greek version of the Septuagint, even where it differs from the Hebrew original.[3] Whether He was acquainted with Latin is much more doubtful, though not impossible. The Romans in Judæa must by this time have been very numerous, and Latin was inscribed upon the coins in ordinary use.[4] But to whatever extent He may have known these languages, it is clear that they exercised little or no influence on His human development, nor is there in all His teaching a single indisputable allusion to the literature, philosophy, or history of Greece or Rome.[5] And that Jesus habitually *thought* in that Syriac which was His native tongue may be conjectured, without improbability, from some curious plays on words which are lost in the Greek of the Gospels, but which would have given greater point and beauty to some of His utterances, as spoken in their original tongue.[6]

7. But whatever the boy Jesus may have learned as child or boy in the house of His mother, or in the school of the synagogue, we

---

[1] Matt. viii. 6—9; xxvii. 11; John xii. 21.

[2] Of course we cannot assume this in all cases. χαλεπὸν τὴν ἀκρίβειαν αὐτὴν τῶν λεχθέντων διαμνημονεῦσαι [66] (Thuc. i. 22), and although the Holy Evangelists have been guided from above to reveal all that is essential to our salvation in the life of Christ, yet their variations show that they were not endowed with a verbal exactitude, which would have been at once supernatural and needless.

[3] Matt. iv. 7; xiii. 14, 15.

[4] Matt. xxii. 19. Wernsdorf wrote a treatise *De Christo Latine loquente.* The Latin words, μόδιον, κοδράντην, λεγεών, &c., occur in our Lord's teaching.

[5] It is surely very far-fetched to find, as some have done, a possible allusion to the death of Socrates in Mark xvi. 18. On the other hand, there is a (perhaps accidental) resemblance between the ἄγραφον δόγμα of our Lord preserved by St. Paul in Acts xx. 35, and the Epicurean maxim ἥδιον τὸ εὖ ποιεῖν τοῦ εὖ πάσχειν.[67] (Cf. Athen. *Deipnos.* viii. 5; Arist. *Eth. Nic.* iv. 1.) J. F. Mayer wrote a pamphlet, *Utrum Christus legerit Platonem vel Terentium?*[68] Hamb. 1701.

[6] See Winer, *Realwörterb.* ii. 501. s. v. *Sprache;* Glass, *Philologia Sacra,* p. 918, seq., "We have piped unto you, and ye have not danced (רְקַדְתּוּן, *rakedtoon*); we have mourned unto you, and ye have not wept (אַרְקֵדְתּוּן, *arkêdtoon*);" other supposed instances are adduced in Heinsius's *Aristarchus.* The words, γολγοθᾶ, ταλιθᾶ, κῦμι, ἀββᾶ, κῆφας, &c., are all Aramaic (or, as it is called, Syro-Chaldee); as is the cry upon the cross, "*Eloi, Eloi, lama sabachthani.*" The particular dialect of Galilee was marked by a change of gutturals, and a general πλατειασμός. (Lightfoot and Schöttgen, *Hor. Hebr. in* Matt. xxvi. 73.)

know that His best teaching was derived from immediate insight into His Father's will. In the depths of His inmost consciousness, did that voice of God, which spake to the father of our race as he walked in the cool evening under the palms of Paradise, commune — more plainly, by far — with Him. He heard it in every sound of nature, in every occupation of life, in every interspace of solitary thought. His human life was "an ephod on which was inscribed the one word God." Written on His inmost spirit, written on His most trivial experiences, written in sunbeams, written in the light of stars, He read everywhere His Father's name. The calm, untroubled seclusion of the happy valley, with its green fields and glorious scenery, was eminently conducive to a life of spiritual communion; and we know how from its every incident — the games of its innocent children,[1] the buying and selling in its little market-place, the springing of its perennial fountain, the glory of its mountain lilies in their transitory loveliness, the hoarse cry in their wind-rocked nest of the raven's callow brood — he drew food for moral illustration and spiritual thought.

Nor must we lose sight of the fact that it was in these silent, unrecorded years that a great part of His work was done. He was not only "girding His sword upon His thigh," but also wielding it in that warfare which has no discharge.[2] That noiseless battle, in which no clash of weapons sounds, but in which the combatants against us are none the less terrible because they are not seen, went on through all the years of His redeeming obedience. In these years He "began to do" long before He "began to teach."[3] They were the years of sinless childhood, a sinless boyhood, a sinless youth, a sinless manhood, spent in that humility, toil, obscurity, submission, contentment, prayer, to make them an eternal example to all our race. We cannot imitate Him in the occupations of His ministry, nor can we even remotely reproduce in our own experience the external circumstances of His life during those three crowning years. But the vast majority of us are placed, by God's own appointment, amid those quiet duties of a commonplace and uneventful routine which are most closely analogous to the thirty years of His retirement; it was during these years that His life is for us the main example of how we ought to live. "Take notice here," says the saintly Bonaventura, "that His doing nothing wonderful was in itself a kind of wonder. For

---

[1] Matt. xi. 16.
[2] Ps. xlv. 3; Eccles. viii. 8.
[3] Acts i. 1. See further on this subject the note at the end of Chap. IX, p. 126.

His whole life is a mystery; and as there was power in His actions, so was there power in His silence, in His inactivity, and in His retirement. This sovereign Master, who was to teach all virtues, and to point out the way of life, began from His youth up, by sanctifying in his own person the practice of the virtuous life He came to teach, but in a wondrous, unfathomable, and, till then, unheard-of manner."

His mere presence in that home of His childhood must have made it a happy one. The hour of strife, the hour of the sword, the hour when many in Israel should rise or fall because of Him, the hour when the thoughts of many hearts should be revealed, the hour when the kingdom of heaven should suffer violence, and the violent take it by force, was not yet come. In *any* family circle the gentle influence of one loving soul is sufficient to breathe around it an unspeakable calm; it has a soothing power like the shining of the sunlight, or the voice of doves heard at evening; —

> " It droppeth, like the gentle dew from heaven,
> Upon the place beneath."

Nothing vulgar, nothing tyrannous, nothing restless can permanently resist its beneficent sorcery; no jangling discord can long break in upon its harmonizing spell. But the home of Jesus was no ordinary home. With Joseph to guide and support, with Mary to hallow and sweeten it, with the youthful Jesus to illuminate it with the very light of heaven, we may well believe that it was a home of trustful piety, of angelic purity, of almost perfect peace; a home for the sake of which all the earth would be dearer and more awful to the watchers and holy ones, and where, if the fancy be permitted us, they would love to stay their waving wings. The legends of early Christianity tell us that night and day, where Jesus moved and Jesus slept, the cloud of light shone round about Him. And so it was; but that light was no visible Shechînah; it was the beauty of holiness; it was the peace of God.

8. In the eleventh chapter of the Apocryphal History of Joseph the Carpenter, it is stated that Joseph had four elder sons and several daughters by a previous marriage, and that the elder sons, Justus and Simon, and the daughters, Esther and Thamar, in due time married and went to their houses. " But Judas and James the Less, and the Virgin my mother," continues the speaker, who is supposed to be Jesus Himself, " remained in the house of Joseph. I also continued along with them, not otherwise than if I had been one of his sons.

I passed all my time without fault. I called Mary my mother, and Joseph father, and in all they said I was obedient to them, nor did I ever resist them, but submitted to them . . . nor did I provoke their anger any day, nor return any harsh word or answer to them ; on the contrary, I cherished them with immense love, as the apple of my eye."

This passage, which I quote for the sake of the picture which it offers of the unity which prevailed in the home at Nazareth, reminds us of the perplexed question, Had our Lord any actual uterine brothers and sisters ? and if not, who were those who in the Gospels are so often called " the brethren of the Lord ? " Whole volumes have been written on this controversy, and I shall not largely enter on it here, both because I do not wish these pages to be controversial, and because I have treated it elsewhere.[1] The evidence is so evenly balanced, the difficulties of each opinion are so clear, that to insist very dogmatically on any positive solution of the problem would be uncandid and contentious. Some, in accordance certainly with the *primâ facie* evidence of the Gospels, have accepted the natural supposition that, after the miraculous conception of our Lord, Joseph and Mary lived together in the married state, and that James, and Joses, and Judas, and Simon, with daughters, whose names are not recorded, were subsequently born to them. According to this view, Jesus would be the eldest, and on the death of Joseph, which, if we may follow tradition, took place when He was nineteen, would assume the natural headship and support of the orphaned family.[2] But

---

[1] In Smith's *Dict. of the Bible*, s. v. "Brother." Certainly the Hieronymian and Epiphanian theories (see next note) are an *afterthought*, caused by a growing tendency to magnify the ἀ ειπαρθενία. This notion was partly due to the development of ascetic opinions, partly to a fantastic allegorical interpretation of Ezek. xliv. 2.

[2] So much, and so much that is most easily accessible, has been written on this point — a point which is, after all, incapable of positive solution — that it will be needless to enter elaborately upon it here, especially as Dr. Lightfoot, in an appendix to his edition of the Epistle to the Galatians, has treated it with his usual exhaustive learning and accuracy. Dismissing all minor and arbitrary combinations, there are three main views : (1) The *Helvidian* — that the brethren of the Lord were the actual children of Joseph and Mary ; (2) the *Hieronymian* — that they were his first cousins, being sons of Mary and Alphæus ; (3) the *Epiphanian* — that they were the sons of Joseph by a former marriage. Of these three theories, the second — that of St. Jerome — is decidedly the most popular, and the one which has *least* to be said for it. It has not a particle of tradition before the time of St. Jerome in its favor, since the Papias, who is quoted as having held it, is, as Dr. Lightfoot shows, a writer of the eleventh century. Even St. Jerome, after his residence in Palestine, seems to have abandoned it ; and it is perhaps

according to another view, of which St. Jerome may be called the inventor, these brethren of our Lord were in reality His cousins. Mary, it is believed, had a sister or half-sister of the same name,[1] who was married to Alphæus or Clopas, and these were their children. I have in the note reviewed some of the evidence. Each person can form upon that evidence a decided conviction of his own, but it is too scanty to admit of any positive conclusion in which we may expect a general acquiescence. In any case, it is clear that our Lord, from His earliest infancy, must have been thrown into close connection with sev-

---

sufficient to observe that, as it assumes three at least of these " brethren " to have been actual apostles, it is in flagrant contradiction to John vii. 5, to say nothing of the fact that it depends on a number of very dubious hypotheses. The Epiphanian theory seems to have been the tradition of Palestine, and is the one current in the Apocryphal Gospels (see Hofmann, *Leben Jesu*, 4); but I still believe that the Helvidian has an overwhelming preponderance of argument in its favor. The only two serious arguments against it are : (α) The fact that our Lord entrusted His mother to the care of St. John, not of her own children; but this is accounted for by their acknowledged want of sympathy with Him up to that time. It is true that the appearance of the risen Christ to James (1 Cor. xv. 7, see Lightfoot *ubi supr.*, p. 260) seems to have wholly converted them ; but there may have been many reasons why Mary should still live with the Apostle to whom the Lord had entrusted her. (β) The fact that the names of the sons of Alphæus were identical with those of the Lord's brethren; but this argument loses all force from the extreme commonness of these names, which were as common among the Jews as John and William among us. The genealogies of Joseph show, moreover, that they were in part family and ancestral names. The imagined necessity of the ἀειπαρθενία is no argument whatever, since it is abundantly clear that, had the Evangelists believed in the importance of such a view, or held the superior sacredness of celibacy over marriage, they would either have stated their belief, or would at any rate have abstained from language which, in its obvious and only natural significance, conveys the reverse notion. For undoubtedly the Helvidian view — that they were actual sons of Joseph and Mary — is most in accordance with the simple interpretation of the Gospel narratives. Not to dwell on the πρωτότοκος of Luke ii. 7, and the ἕως οἷ of Matt. i. 25, and the πρὶν ἢ συνελθεῖν αὐτοὺς of Matt. i. 18, we have (α) the fact that they are *always* called ἀδελφοὶ, never ἀνέψιοι or συγγενεῖς (a fact which appears to me to be alone decisive against the Hieronymian view, for reasons which I have given *s. v.* " Brother " in Smith's *Dict. of the Bible*); and (β) the fact that they are always found accompanying the Virgin (John ii. 12; Matt. xii. 46), and not their own (supposed) mother, without the slightest hint that they were not in reality her own children. To these I would add, as against the Epiphanian theory, that, had the " brethren " been elder sons of Joseph, Jesus would not have been regarded by any of His followers as legal heir to the throne of David (see not only Matt i. 16; Luke i. 27; but also Rom. i. 3; 2 Tim. ii. 8; Rev. xxii. 16).

[1] That two sisters should both have received the same name seems very improbable. The custom of the Herodian family would be little likely to prevail among the peasants of Nazareth. I have, however, discovered one modern instance of such a fact, and there are doubtless others.

eral kinsmen, or brothers, a little older or a little younger than Himself, who were men of marked individuality, of burning zeal, of a simplicity almost bordering on Essenic asceticism, of overpowering hostility to every form of corruption, disorder, or impurity, of strong devotion to the Messianic hopes, and even to the ritual observances of their country.[1] We know that, though afterwards they became pillars of the infant Church, at first they did not believe in our Lord's Divinity, or at any rate held views which ran strongly counter to the divine plan of His self-manifestation.[2] Not among these, in any case, did Jesus during His lifetime find His most faithful followers, or His most beloved companions. There seemed to be in them a certain strong opinionativeness, a Judaic obstinacy, a lack of sympathy, a deficiency in the elements of tenderness and reverence. Peter, affectionate even in his worst weakness, generous even in his least controlled impulse; James the son of Zebedee, calm and watchful, reticent and true; above all, John, whose impetuosity lay involved in a soul of the most heavenly tenderness, as the lightning slumbers in the dewdrop — these were more to Him and dearer than His brethren or kinsmen according to the flesh. A hard aggressive morality is less beautiful than an absorbing and adoring love.[3]

9. Whether these little clouds of partial miscomprehension tended in any way to overshadow the clear heaven of Christ's youth in the little Galilæan town, we cannot tell. It may be that these brethren toiled with Him at the same humble trade, lived with Him under the

---

[1] Especially Jude and James, if, as seems at least possible, *they* were " the Lord's brethren," and authors of the epistles which pass by their names, but were not actual apostles (see James i. 1 ; Jude 17).

[2] John vii. 3, 4 ; Mark iii. 21. Can there be any stronger evidence of the perfect simplicity and truthfulness of the Gospel evidence than the fact that they faithfully record what sceptics are pleased to consider so damaging an admission ? It is exactly the reverse of what is said in the Apocr. Gospels, *e. g.* Apocr. Gosp. Matt. xliii.

[3] If, as Wieseler (*Die Sohne Zebedäi, Vettern des Herrn., Stud. und Krit.* 1840) with great probability supposes, there be any truth in the tradition (Nicephorus, *Hist. Ecc.* ii. 3) that Salome was the sister of Mary, delicately alluded to but unnamed in John xix. 25 (as compared with Matt. xxvii. 56; Mark xv. 40), then James and John the sons of Zebedee were actually first cousins of our Lord. In that case there would still be nothing surprising in their having first been disciples of the Baptist, for Mary and Elizabeth were related (Luke i. 36), and the ministry of John preceded that of Jesus. [Ewald even supposes that the Virgin was of the tribe of Levi, and connects with this not only the fact that Jesus wore a seamless coat (John xix. 23), but also the story (Polycrates in Euseb. *Hist. Ecc.* iii. 31, v. 24) that St. John in his old age wore the priestly πέταλον (Deut. xxxiii. 8) (see *Gesch. Christ.*, p. 246). He accepts the conjecture and tradition that St. John was related to Jesus, *id.* p. 239.]

same humble roof. But, however this may be, we are sure that He would often be alone. Solitude would be to him, more emphatically than to any child of man, "the audience-chamber of God;" He would beyond all doubt seek for it on the grey hill-sides, under the figs and olive-trees, amid the quiet fields; during the heat of noonday, and under the stars of night. No soul can preserve the bloom and delicacy of its existence without lonely musing and silent prayer; and the greatness of this necessity is in proportion to the greatness of the soul. There were many times during our Lord's ministry when, even from the loneliness of desert places, He dismissed His most faithful and most beloved, that He might be yet more alone.

10. It has been implied that there are but two spots in Palestine where we may feel an absolute moral certainty that the feet of Christ have trod, namely — the well-side at Shechem, and the turning of that road from Bethany over the Mount of Olives from which Jerusalem first bursts upon the view.[1] But to these I would add at least another — the summit of the hill on which Nazareth is built. That summit is now unhappily marked, not by any Christian monument, but by the wretched, ruinous, crumbling *wely* of some obscure Mohammedan saint.[2] Certainly there is no child of ten years old in Nazareth now, however dull and unimpressionable he may be, who has not often wandered up to it; and certainly there could have been no boy at Nazareth in olden days who had not followed the common instinct of humanity by climbing up those thymy hill-slopes to the lovely and easily accessible spot which gives a view of the world beyond. The hill rises six hundred feet above the level of the sea. Four or five hundred feet below lies the happy valley. The view from this spot would in any country be regarded as extraordinarily rich and lovely; but it receives a yet more indescribable charm from our belief that here, with His feet among the mountain flowers, and the soft breeze lifting the hair from His temples, Jesus must often have watched the eagles poised in the cloudless blue, and have gazed upwards as He heard overhead the rushing plumes of the long line of pelicans, as they winged their way from the streams of Kishon to the Lake of Galilee. And what a vision would be outspread before Him, as He sat at spring-time on the green and thyme-besprinkled turf! To Him every field and fig-tree, every palm and garden, every house and synagogue, would have been a familiar object; and most fondly of all amongst the square flat-roofed houses would His eye single out

---

[1] Stanley, *Sin. and Pal.*, p. 194.   [2] Neby Ismaîl.

the little dwelling-place of the village carpenter. To the north, just beneath them, lay the narrow and fertile plain of Asochis,[1] from which rise the wood-crowned hills of Naphtali, and conspicuous on one of them was Safed, " the city set upon a hill ; "[2] beyond these, on the far horizon, Hermon upheaved into the blue the huge splendid mass of his colossal shoulder, white with eternal snows.[3] Eastward, at a few miles' distance, rose the green and rounded summit of Tabor, clothed with terebinth and oak. To the west He would gaze through that diaphanous air on the purple ridge of Carmel, among whose forests Elijah had found a home ; and on Caifa and Accho, and the dazzling line of white sand which fringes the waves of the Mediterranean, dotted here and there with the white sails of the " ships of Chittim."[4] Southwards, broken only by the graceful outlines of Little Hermon and Gilboa, lay the entire plain of Esdraelon, so memorable in the history of Palestine and of the world ; across which lay the southward path to that city which had ever been the murderess of the prophets, and where it may be that even now, in the dim foreshadowing of prophetic vision, He foresaw the agony in the garden, the mockings and scourgings, the cross and the crown of thorns.

The scene which lay there outspread before the eyes of the youthful Jesus was indeed a central spot in the world which He came to save. It was in the heart of the Land of Israel, and yet — separated from it only by a narrow boundary of hills and streams — Phœnicia, Syria, Arabia, Babylonia, and Egypt lay close at hand. The Isles of the Gentiles, and all the glorious regions of Europe, were almost visible over the shining waters of that Western sea. The standards of Rome were planted on the plain before Him ; the language of Greece was spoken in the towns below. And however peaceful it then might look, green as a pavement of emeralds, rich with its gleams of vivid sunlight, and the purpling shadows which floated over it from the clouds of the latter rain, it had been for centuries a battle-field of nations. Pharaohs and Ptolemies, Emîrs and Arsacids, Judges and Consuls, had all contended for the mastery of that smiling tract. It had glittered with the lances of the Amalekites ; it had trembled

---

[1] Now called El Buttauf.

[2] The present town of Safed is of much later date ; but *a* city or fortress most probably existed there in our Lord's time.

[3] The epithet is so far accurate, that even in September snow would be found in the ravines and crevices of Hermon. (*Report of Pal. Explor. Fund,* 1870 p. 230.)

[4] I describe the scene as I saw it on Easter Sunday, April 17, 1870.

under the chariot-wheels of Sesostris; it had echoed the twanging bowstrings of Sennacherib; it had been trodden by the phalanxes of Macedonia; it had clashed with the broadswords of Rome; it was destined hereafter to ring with the battle-cry of the Crusaders, and thunder with the artillery of England and of France. In that Plain of Jezreel, Europe and Asia, Judaism and Heathenism, Barbarism and Civilization, the Old and the New Covenant, the history of the past and the hopes of the present, seemed all to meet. No scene of deeper significance for the destinies of humanity could possibly have arrested the youthful Saviour's gaze.

CHAPTER VIII.

THE BAPTISM OF JOHN.

" John than which man a sadder or a greater
Not till this day has been of woman born ;
John like some iron peak by the Creator
Fired with the red glow of the rushing morn."— MYERS.

THUS then His boyhood, and youth, and early manhood had passed
away in humble submission and holy silence, and Jesus was now
thirty years old.[1] That deep lesson for all classes of men in every
age, which was involved in the long toil and obscurity of those thirty
years, had been taught more powerfully than mere words could
teach it, and the hour for His ministry and for the great work of His
redemption had now arrived. He was to be the Saviour not only by
example, but also by revelation, and by death.

And already there had begun to ring that Voice in the Wilderness which was stirring the inmost heart of the nation with its cry,
" Repent ye, for the Kingdom of Heaven is at hand."

It was an age of transition, of uncertainty, of doubt. In the
growth of general corruption, in the wreck of sacred institutions, in
those dense clouds which were gathering more and more darkly on
the political horizon, it must have seemed to many a pious Jew as if
the fountains of the great deep were again being broken up.
Already the sceptre had departed from his race; already its high-
priesthood was contemptuously tampered with by Idumæan tetrarchs
or Roman procurators; already the chief influence over his degraded
Sanhedrin was in the hands of supple Herodians or wily Sadducees.
It seemed as if nothing were left for his consolation but an increased
fidelity to Mosaic institutions, and a deepening intensity of Messianic hopes. At an epoch so troubled, and so restless — when old
things were rapidly passing away, and the new continued unre-
vealed — it might almost seem excusable for a Pharisee to watch for
every opportunity of revolution; and still more excusable for an

---

[1] On the elaborate chronological data for the commencement of the Baptist's
ministry given by St. Luke (iii. 1, 2), see Excursus I., " Date of Christ's Birth."

Essene to embrace a life of celibacy, and retire from the society of man. There was a general expectation of that "wrath to come," which was to be the birth-throe of the coming kingdom — the darkness deepest before the dawn.[1] The world had grown old, and the dotage of its paganism was marked by hideous excesses. Atheism in belief was followed, as among nations it has always been, by degradation of morals. Iniquity seemed to have run its course to the very farthest goal. Philosophy had abrogated its boasted functions except for the favored few. Crime was universal, and there was no known remedy for the horror and ruin which it was causing in a thousand hearts. Remorse itself seemed to be exhausted, so that men were "past feeling."[2] There was a callosity of heart, a petrifying of the moral sense, which even those who suffered from it felt to be abnormal and portentous.[3] Even the heathen world felt that "the fulness of the time" had come.

At such periods the impulse to an ascetic seclusion becomes very strong. Solitary communion with God amid the wildest scenes of

---

[1] Mal. iii. 1; iv. 2. The ἐκκόπτεται and βάλλεται of Mat. iii. 10 are the so-called *praesens futurascens* — i. e., they imply that the fiat had gone forth ; that the law had already begun to work ; that the doom was now in course of accomplishment. Probably the words " kingdom of heaven " (*malkûth shamajim*) and " coming time " (*olam ha-ba*) were frequent at this time on pious lips ; but the Zealots were expecting a warrior as Messiah ; and the school of Shammai a legalist ; and the Essenes an ascetic ; and the philosophic schools some divine vision (Philo, *De Execratt.* ii. 435 ; Grätz, *Gesch. d. Juden,* iii. 218). It has been impossible for me here to enter into the vast literature about the Messianic conception prevalent at the time of our Lord ; but it seems clear that Ewald, Hilgenfeld, Keim (as against Volkmar, &c.) are right in believing that there *was* at this time a fully-developed Messianic tradition. The decision depends mainly on the date of various Apocryphal writings — the Book of Enoch, the Fourth Book of Esdras, the Ascension of Moses, the Psalms of Solomon, the third book of the Sibylline prophecies, &c. See especially Hilgenfeld's *Messias Judaeorum.* He certainly proves that the 2nd Psalm of Solomon was written about B. C. 48.

[2] πᾶν εἶδος κακίας διεξελθοῦσα ἡ φύσις ἡ ἀνθρωπίνη ἐδεῖτο θεραπείας [69] (Theophyl.); Eph. iv. 19, ἀπηλγηκότες.[70] I have slightly sketched the characteristics of this age in *Seekers after God,* pp. 36—53 ; a powerful picture of its frightful enormities may be seen in Renan, *L'Antechrist,* or Döllinger, *The Jew and the Gentile.* It were better to know nothing of it, than to seek a notion of its condition in the pages of Juvenal, Martial, Suetonius, Apuleius, and Petronius. Even in the case of Dr. Döllinger's book, one cannot but feel that he might have attended to the noble rule of Tacitus, " Scelera ostendi oportet dum puniuntur, abscondi flagitia " [71] (Tac. *Germ.* 12). Too much of what has been written on the abysmal degradations of a decadent Paganism resembles the Pharos lights which sometimes caused the shipwreck of those whom they were meant to save. There are some things which, as a Church Father says of the ancient pantomimes, " *ne accusari quidem possunt honeste.*" [72]

[3] πώρωσις τῆς καρδίας [73] (Eph. iv. 17—19). ἀπολίθωσις [74] (Epict. *Diss.* i. 53)

nature seems preferable to the harassing speculations of a dispirited society. Self-dependence, and subsistence upon the very scantiest resources which can supply the merest necessities of life, are more attractive than the fretting anxieties and corroding misery of a crushed and struggling poverty. The wildness and silence of indifferent Nature appear at such times to offer a delightful refuge from the noise, the meanness, and the malignity of men. Banus, the Pharisee, who retired into the wilderness, and lived much as the hermits of the Thebaid lived in after years, was only one of many who were actuated by these convictions. Josephus, who for three years [1] had lived with him in his mountain-caves, describes his stern self-mortifications and hardy life, his clothing of woven leaves, his food of the chance roots which he could gather from the soil, and his daily and nightly plunge in the cold water that his body might be clean and his heart pure.

But asceticism may spring from very different motives. It may result from the arrogance of the cynic who wishes to stand apart from all men; or from the disgusted satiety of the epicurean who would fain find a refuge even from himself; or from the selfish terror of the fanatic, intent only on his own salvation. Far different and far nobler was the hard simplicity and noble self-denial of the Baptist. It is by no idle fancy that the mediæval painters represent him as emaciated by a proleptic asceticism.[2] The tendency to the life of a recluse had shown itself in the youthful Nazarite from his earliest years; but in him it resulted from the consciousness of a glorious mission — it was from the desire to fulfil a destiny inspired by burning hopes. St. John was a dweller in the wilderness, only that he might thereby become the prophet of the Highest. The light which was within him should be kindled, if need be, into a self-consuming flame, not for his own glory, but that it might illuminate the pathway of the coming King.

The nature of St. John the Baptist was full of impetuosity and fire. The long struggle which had given him so powerful a mastery over himself — which had made him content with self-obliteration before the presence of his Lord — which had inspired him with fearlessness in the face of danger, and humility in the midst of applause — had left its traces in the stern character, and aspect, and teaching of the man. If he had won peace in the long prayer and

---

[1] Joseph. *Vit.* 2, if the reading παρ' αὐτῷ and not παρ' αυτοῖς be right.

[2] As, for instance, in a fine picture by Sandro Botticelli in the Borghese Palace at Rome. Compare the early life of St. Benedict of Nursia.

penitence of his life in the wilderness, it was not the spontaneous peace of a placid and holy soul. The victory he had won was still encumbered with traces of the battle; the calm he had attained still echoed with the distant mutter of the storm. His very teaching reflected the imagery of the wilderness — the rock, the serpent, the barren tree. "In his manifestation and agency," it has been said, "he was like a burning torch; his public life was quite an earthquake — the whole man was a sermon; he might well call himself a voice — the voice of one crying in the wilderness, Prepare ye the way of the Lord." [1]

While he was musing the fire burned, and at the last he spake with his tongue. Almost from boyhood he had been a voluntary eremite. In solitude he had learnt things unspeakable; there the unseen world had become to him a reality; there his spirit had caught "a touch of phantasy and flame." Communing with his own great lonely heart — communing with the high thoughts of that long line of prophets, his predecessors to a rebellious people — communing with the utterances that came to him from the voices of the mountain and the sea — he had learnt a deeper lore than he could have ever learnt at Hillel's or Shammai's feet. In the tropic noonday of that deep Jordan valley, where the air seems to be full of a subtle and quivering flame — in listening to the howl of the wild beasts in the long night, under the lustre of stars "that seemed to hang like balls of fire in a purple sky" — in wandering by the sluggish cobalt-colored waters of that dead and accursed lake, until before his eyes, dazzled by the saline efflorescence of the shore strewn with its wrecks of death, the ghosts of the guilty seemed to start out of the sulphurous ashes under which they were submerged — he had learnt a language, he had received a revelation, not vouchsafed to ordinary men — attained, not in the schools of the Rabbis, but in the school of solitude, in the school of God. [2]

Such teachers are suited for such times. There was enough and to spare of those respectable, conventional teachers, who spake smooth things and prophesied deceits. The ordinary Scribe or Pharisee, sleek with good living and supercilious with general respect, might get up

---

[1] Lange, ii., p. 11, E. Tr.

[2] The Jews of that day had but little sense of the truth expressed by the very greatest of Greek thinkers, Herakleitos, $\pi o \lambda \upsilon \mu \alpha \theta \acute{\iota} \eta \ \nu \acute{o} o \nu \ o \grave{\upsilon} \ \delta \iota \delta \acute{a} \acute{o} \varkappa \epsilon \iota.$ [15] "Dass aber Jesu auch innerlich der Hohen Schule jener Zeit nicht bedurfte," says Ewald, "zeigt uns nur umso deutlicher welcher Geist von anfang an in Ihm waltete" [16] (*Gesch. Christ.*, p. 250. The remarks which follow are also worthy of profound study).

in the synagogue, with his broad phylacteries and luxurious robes, and might, perhaps, minister to some sleepy edification with his *midrash* of hair-splitting puerilities and threadbare precedents; but the very aspect of John the Baptist would have shown that there was another style of teacher here. Even before the first vibrating tone of a voice that rang with scorn and indignation, the bronzed countenance, the unshorn locks, the close-pressed lips, the leathern girdle, the mantle of camel's hair,[1] would at once betoken that here at last was a man who was a man indeed in all his natural grandeur and dauntless force, and who, like the rough Bedawy prophet who was his antitype, would stand unquailing before purple Ahabs and adulterous Jezebels. And then his life was known. It was known that his drink was water of the river, and that he lived on locusts[2] and wild honey.[3] Men felt in him that power of mastery which is always granted to perfect self-denial. He who is superior to the common ambitions of man is superior also to their common timidities. If he have little to hope from the favor of his fellows he has little to fear from their dislike; with nothing to gain from the administration of servile flattery, he has nothing to lose by the expression of just rebuke. He sits as it were above his brethren, on a sunlit eminence of peace and purity, unblinded by the petty mists that dim their vision, untroubled by the petty influences that disturb their life.

No wonder that such a man at once made himself felt as a power in the midst of his people. It became widely rumored that, in the wilderness of Judæa, lived one whose burning words it was worth while to hear; one who recalled Isaiah by his expressions,[4] Elijah by his life. A Tiberius was polluting by his infamies the throne of the Empire; a Pontius Pilate with his insolences, cruelties, extortions, massacres, was maddening a fanatic people;[5] Herod Antipas was exhibiting to facile learners the example of calculated apostasy and

---

[1] Cf. 2 Kings i. 8; Zech. xiii. 4; Heb. xi. 37.

[2] Lev. xi. 22; Plin. ii. 29. The fancy that it means the pods of the so-called locust-tree (carob) is a mistake. Locusts are sold as articles of food in regular shops for the purpose at Medina , they are plunged into salt boiling water, dried in the sun, and eaten with butter, but only by the poorest beggars. Most Bedawin speak of eating them with disgust and loathing (Thomson, *Land and Book*, II. xxviii.).

[3] 1 Sam. xiv. 25; Ps. lxxxi. 16.

[4] Compare Isa. lix. 5 with Matt. iii. 7; Isa. iv. 4 and xliv. 3 with Matt. iii. 11; Isa. xl. 3 with Luke iii. 4; Isa. lii. 10 with Luke iii. 6, &c.

[5] Τὰς δωροδοκίας, τὰς ὕβρεις, τὰς ἁρπαγὰς, τὰς αἰκίας, τὰς ἐπηρείας, τοὺς ἀκρίτους καὶ ἐπαλλήλους φόνους, τὴν ἀνήνυτον καὶ ἀργαλεωτάτην ὠμότητα, κ. τ. λ.[76] † (Philo, *Leg.* 1033.)

reckless lust; Caiaphas and Annas were dividing the functions of a priesthood which they disgraced. Yet the talk of the new Prophet was not of political circumstances such as these; the lessons he had to teach were deeper and more universal in their moral and social significance. Whatever might be the class who flocked to his stern solitude, his teaching was intensely practical, painfully heart-searching, fearlessly downright. And so Pharisee and Sadducee, scribe and soldier, priest and publican, all thronged to listen to his words.[1] The place where he preached was that wild range of uncultivated and untenanted wilderness, which stretches southward from Jericho and the fords of Jordan to the shores of the Dead Sea. The cliffs that overhung the narrow defile which led from Jerusalem to Jericho were the haunt of dangerous robbers; the wild beasts and the crocodiles were not yet extinct in the reed-beds that marked the swellings of Jordan; yet from every quarter of the country — from priestly Hebron, from holy Jerusalem, from smiling Galilee — they came streaming forth,[2] to catch the accents of this strange voice. And the words of that voice were like a hammer to dash in pieces the flintiest heart, like a flame to pierce into the most hidden thoughts. Without a shadow of euphemism, without an accent of subservience, without a tremor of hesitation, he rebuked the tax-gatherers for their extortionateness; the soldiers for their violence, unfairness, and discontent;[3] the wealthy Sadducees, and stately Pharisees, for a formalism and falsity which made them vipers of a viperous brood.[4] The whole people he warned that their cherished privileges were worse than valueless if, without repentance, they regarded them as a protection against the wrath to come. They prided themselves upon their high descent; but God, as He had created Adam out of the earth, so even out of those flints upon the strand of Jordan was able to raise up children unto Abraham.[5] They listened with accusing consciences

---

[1] But the Pharisees " were not baptized of him " (Luke vii. 30). St. John expresses the frankest and most contemptuous amazement at their presence (Matt. iii. 7). And their brief willingness to listen was soon followed by the violent and summary judgment, "He hath a devil " (Matt. xi. 18). This was not the only age in which such a remark has served as an angry and self-deceiving synonym for " we cannot and will not accept his words."

[2] Matt. iii. 5, ἐξεπορεύετο.

[3] στρατευόμενοι (Luke iii. 14) means " soldiers on the march ; " what the occasion was we do not know.

[4] " Offspring of vipers," " Serpentes e serpentibus " (Lightfoot, *Hor. Hebr.*, in Matt. iii. 7). Cf. Ps. lviii. 4; Isa. xiv. 29.

[5] Cf. John viii. 33 ; Rom. ii. 28 ; iv. 16 ; ix. 6. Comp. Jer. vii. 4. μὴ ἄρξησθε λέγειν ἐν ἑαυτοῖς (Luke iii. 8), " do not even for a moment begin to imagine." " Omnem excusationis etiam *conatum* præcidit " [16]‡ (Bengel).

and stricken hearts; and since he had chosen baptism as his symbol of their penitence and purification, "they were baptized of him in Jordan, confessing their sins." Even those who did not submit to his baptism were yet " willing for a season to rejoice in his light."

But he had another and stranger message — a message sterner, yet more hopeful — to deliver; for himself he would claim no authority save as the forerunner of another; for his own baptism no value, save as an initiation into the kingdom that was at hand.[1] When the deputation from the Sanhedrin asked him who he was — when all the people were musing in their hearts whether he were the Christ or no — he never for a moment hesitated to say that he was not the Christ, nor Elias, neither that prophet.[2] He was "a voice in the wilderness," and nothing more; but after him — and this was the announcement that stirred most powerfully the hearts of men — after him was coming One who was preferred before him, for He was before him[3] — One whose shoe's latchet he was unworthy to unloose[4] — One who should baptize, not with water, but with the Holy Ghost, and with fire[5] — One whose fan was in His hand, and who should thoroughly purge His floor — who should gather His wheat into the garner, but burn up the chaff with unquenchable fire. The hour for the sudden coming of their long-promised, long-expected Messiah was at hand. His awful presence was near them, was among them, but they knew Him not.

Thus repentance and the kingdom of heaven were the two cardinal points of his preaching, and though he did not claim the credentials of a single miracle,[6] yet while he threatened detection to the

---

[1] It was, as Olshausen says, "a baptism of *repentance*," not "a laver of *regeneration*" (Titus iii. 5).

[2] *i. e.*, one of the great prophets like Jeremiah (cf. 2 Macc. ii. 7), whose return was expected as a precursor of the Messiah, and who was especially alluded to in Deut. xviii. 15, 18: Acts iii. 22; vii. 37.

[3] The πρῶτός μου of John i. 30 means something more than merely ἔμπροσθέν μου, viz., "*long* before me." (See Ewald, *Gesch. Christus*, p. 232.)

[4] Or, "to carry his shoes" (Matt. iii. 11). Both were servile functions.

The most immediate and obvious interpretation of these words is to be found in Acts ii. 3; but there may also be a reference to fiery trials (Luke xii. 49; 1 Pet. i. 7) and fiery judgments (1 Cor. iii. 13).

[6] This should be noted as a most powerful argument of the Gospel truthfulness. If, as the schools of modern rationalists argue, the miracles be mere myths woven into a circle of imaginative legends devised to glorify the Founder of Christianity, why was no miracle attributed to St. John? Not certainly from any deficient sense of his greatness, nor from any disinclination to accept miraculous evidence. Surely if it were so easy and so natural as has been assumed to weave a garland of myth and miracle round the brow of a great teacher, John was con-

hypocrite and destruction to the hardened, he promised also pardon to the penitent and admission into the kingdom of heaven to the pure and clean. " The two great utterances," it has been said, " which he brings from the desert, contain the two capital revelations to which all the preparation of the Gospel has been tending. Law and prophecy; denunciation of sin and promise of pardon ; the flame which consumes and the light which consoles — is not this the whole of the covenant ? "

To this preaching, to this baptism, in the thirtieth year of His age,[1] came Jesus from Galilee. John was his kinsman by birth,[2] but the circumstances of their life had entirely separated them. John, as a child in the house of the blameless priest his father, had lived at Juttah, in the far south of the tribe of Judah, and not far from Hebron ;[3] Jesus had lived in the deep seclusion of the carpenter's shop in the valley of Galilee. When he first came to the banks of the Jordan, the great forerunner, according to his own emphatic and twice repeated testimony, "knew Him not." And yet, though Jesus was not yet revealed as the Messiah to His great herald-prophet, there was something in His look, something in the sinless beauty of His ways, something in the solemn majesty of His aspect, which at once overawed and captivated the soul of John. To others he was the uncompromising prophet; kings he could confront with rebuke; Pharisees he could unmask with indignation; but before this Presence all his lofty bearing falls. As when some unknown dread checks the flight of the eagle, and makes him settle with hushed scream and drooping plumage on the ground, so before " the royalty of inward happiness," before the purity of sinless life, the wild prophet of the desert becomes like a submissive and timid child.[4]

---

spicuously worthy of such an honor. Why then ? because " John did no miracle," and because the Evangelists speak the words of soberness and truth.

[1] The arguments in favor of our Lord's having been fifty years of age, although adopted by Irenæus (*Adv. Haer.* ii. 22), partly apparently from tradition, partly on fanciful grounds, and partly by mistaken inference from John viii. 57, are wholly insufficient to outweigh the distinct statement by St. Luke, and the manifold probabilities of the case.

[2] The relationship between Mary and Elisabeth does not prove that Mary was of the tribe of Levi, since intermarriage between the tribes was freely permitted (2 Chron. xxii. 11).

[3] On Juttah, see Luke i. 39, where the reading 'Ιούτα (first suggested by Reland, *Pal.* p. 870), though unconfirmed by any existing MS., is not impossible (Josh. xv. 55) ; it was a *priestly* city (id. xxi. 16).

[4] Stier beautifully says, " He has baptized many ; has seen, and in some sense seen through men of all kinds ; but no one like this had as yet come before him.

The battle-brunt which legionaries could not daunt — the lofty manhood before which hierarchs trembled and princes grew pale — resigns itself, submits, adores before a moral force which is weak in every external attribute and armed only in an invisible mail. John bowed to the simple stainless manhood before he had been inspired to recognize the Divine commission. He earnestly tried to forbid the purpose of Jesus.[1] He who had received the confessions of all others, now reverently and humbly makes his own. " I have need to be baptized of Thee, and comest Thou to me ? " [2]

The answer contains the second recorded utterance of Jesus, and the first word of His public ministry — " Suffer it to be so now : for thus it becometh us to fulfil all righteousness."

" I will sprinkle clean water upon you, and ye shall be clean " [3] — such seems to have been the burden of John's message to the sinners who had become sincerely penitent.

But, if so, why did our Lord receive baptism at His servant's hands ? His own words tell us ; it was to fulfil every requirement to which God's will might seem to point (Ps. xl. 7, 8). He did not accept it as subsequent to a confession, for He was sinless ; and in this respect, even before he recognized Him as the Christ, the Baptist clearly implied that the rite would be in His case exceptional.[4] But He received it as ratifying the mission of His great forerunner — the last and greatest child of the Old Dispensation, the earliest herald of the New ; and He also received it as the beautiful symbol of moral purification, and the humble inauguration of a ministry which came not to destroy the Law, but to fulfil. His own words obviate all possibility of misconception. He does not say, " I must," but, " Thus it becometh us." He does not say, " I *have* need to be baptized ;" nor does He say, " *Thou* hast *no* need to be baptized of me," but He says, " Suffer it to be so now." This is, indeed, but the

---

They have all bowed down before him ; but before this Man bows down, in the irrepressible emotion of his own most profound contrition, the sinful man in the greatest prophet." (*Reden Jesu* i. 28.)

[1] Matt. iii. 14, διεκώλυεν.

[2] " *Tu* ad *me* ? aurum ad lutum ? ad scintillam fax ? ad lucernam sol ? ad servum Filius ? ad peccatorem Agnus sine maculâ ? " [77] (Lucas Brugensis.)

[3] Ezek. xxxvi. 25.

[4] ἵνα τὸ ὕδωρ καθαρί'σῃ[78] (Ignat. *Eph.* 18). " Baptisatur Christus non ut purificetur aquis, sed ut aquas ipse sanctificet " [79] (Maxim. *Serm.* 7 *de Epiphan.*). " In baptismo *non tam lavit aqua quam lota est*, purgantur potius fluenta quam purgant " [80] (Aug. *Serm.* 135, 4 ; Hofmann, p. 166).

baptism of repentance ; yet it may serve to prefigure the "laver of regeneration." [1]

So Jesus descended into the waters of Jordan, and there the awful sign was given that this was indeed "He that should come." From the cloven [2] heaven streamed the Spirit of God in a dovelike radiance that seemed to hover over His head in lambent flame,[3] and the *Bath Kôl*,[4] which to the dull unpurged ear was but an inarticulate thunder, spake in the voice of God to the ears of John — " This is my beloved Son, in whom I am well pleased."

---

[1] πᾶσαν δικαιοσύνην (Matt. iii. 15) has been sometimes taken to mean " every observance " (cf. vi. 1). Others, as Schenkel, have supposed that He submitted to baptism as it were vicariously — *i. e.*, as the representative of a guilty people. Others, again (as Lange), say that the act was solidary in its character — that " social righteousness drew Him down into the stream ; " *i. e.*, that according to the Old Testament legislation, His baptism was required because He was, as it were, ceremonially unclean, as representing an unclean people. Compare the remark of Cato, " Scito dominum pro totâ familiâ rem divinam facere " [81] (*De Re Rusticâ*, 143). Justin Martyr held this view, οὐχ ὡς ἐνδεᾶ . . . ἀλλ' ὑπὲρ τοῦ γένους τοῦ τῶν ἀνθρώπων [82] (*Dial. c. Tryph.* 88). And so, too, the antiphon of the *Benedictus* in the Romish office for the Epiphany : " This day the Church is united to her heavenly Spouse, for in Jordan Christ has washed away her sins." St. Bernard and St. Bonaventura (and perhaps in myriads of instances the profound intuition of a saint may give a view far more true and lofty than the minute criticism of a theologian) mainly see in the act its deep humility. " Thus placing the confirmation of perfect righteousness in the perfection of humility." (St. Bern. *Serm.* 47 *in Cant. ;* St. Bonavent. *Vita Christi*, cap. xiii.)

[2] εἶδε σχιζομένους τοὺς οὐρανούς (Mark i. 10). The whole context seems to show that Theodoret and Jerome were right in supposing that this was a πνευματικὴ θεωρία — a sight seen, " non reseratione elementorum, sed spiritualibus oculis." [83]

[3] " Spiritus Jesu, spiritus columbinus " [84] (Bacon, *Meditt. Sacr.*). Some ancient Christian mystics explained the appearance by Gematria, because περιστερά = 801 = AΩ. We need not necessarily suppose an actual dove, as is clear from John i. 32 ; the expression in the three Gospels is ὡσεὶ περιστεράν, though St. Luke adds σωματικῷ εἴδει. Compare Targum, Cant. ii. 12, " Vox turturis vox spiritus sancti ; " [85] and 2 Esdras v. 26 ; 1 Macc. i. 2 ; and Milton's " with mighty wings outspread, *Dovelike*, sat'st brooding on the vast abyss " (*Par. Lost*, i. 20). In the tract *Chagigah*, we find, " The Spirit of God moved on the face of the waters like a dove " (Gen. i. 2).

[4] On the *Bath Kôl*, see Gfrörer, *Jahrh. d. Heils*, i. 253, seqq.; Otho, *Lex. Rabb.* s. v. The term was sometimes applied to voices from heaven, sometimes to sounds repeated by natural echo, sometimes to chance words overruled to providential significance (Etheridge, *Hebr., Literat.*, p. 39). The Apocryphal Gospels add that a fire was kindled in Jordan (J. Mart. *c. Tryph.* 88 ; Hofmann, p. 299).

CHAPTER IX.

THE TEMPTATION.

"Ideo tentatus est Christus, ne vincatur a Tentatore Christianus." [86] — AUG in Ps. lx.

HIS human spirit filled with overpowering emotions, Jesus sought for retirement, to be alone with God, and once more to think over His mighty work. From the waters of the Jordan He was led — according to the more intense and picturesque expression of St. Mark, He was "driven" — by the Spirit into the wilderness.[1]

A tradition, said to be no older than the time of the Crusades, fixes the scene of the temptation at a mountain to the south of Jericho, which from this circumstance has received the name of Quarantania. Naked and arid like a mountain of malediction, rising precipitously from a scorched and desert plain, and looking over the sluggish, bituminous waters of the Sodomitic sea — thus offering a sharp contrast to the smiling softness of the Mountain of Beatitudes and the limpid crystal of the Lake of Gennesareth — imagination has seen in it a fit place to be the haunt of evil influences [2] — a place where, in the language of the prophets, the owls dwell and the satyrs dance.

---

[1] Cf. Rom. viii. 14; Ezek. iii. 14; Mark i. 12, τὸ *Πνεῦμα ἐκβάλλει αὐτὸν εἰς τὴν ἔρημον*. St. John, perhaps, among other reasons which are unknown to us, from his general desire to narrate nothing of which he had not been an eye-witness, omits the narrative of the temptation, which clearly followed immediately after the baptism. Unless a charge of dishonesty be deliberately maintained, and an adequate reason for such dishonesty assigned, it is clearly unfair to say that a fact is wilfully *suppressed* simply because it is not narrated. It seems probable that on the last day of the temptation came the deputation to John from the priests and Levites, and on the following day Christ returned from the desert, and was saluted by the Baptist as the Lamb of God.

[2] *Bab. Erubhin*, f. 19, 1 *a;* Isa. xiii. 21, 22; xxxiv. 14. The Rabbis said that there were three mouths of Gehenna — *in the Desert* (Numb. xvi. 33), in the sea (Jonah ii. 3), and at Jerusalem (Isa. xxxi. 9). Cf. 4 Macc. xviii., οὐ *διέφθειρέ με λυμεὼν ἐρημίας, φθορεὺς ἐν πεδίῳ*.[81] Azazel (Lev. xvi. 10, Heb.) was a demon of "dry places" (cf. Matt. xii. 43). (Lightfoot, *Hor. Hebr.;* Keim, i. 638.) — Milton's description (*Par. Reg.* iii. 242), probably derived from some authentic source, "would almost seem to have been penned on the spot." (Porter, *Palestine*, i. 185.)

And here Jesus, according to that graphic and pathetic touch of the second Evangelist, " was with the wild beasts." They did not harm Him. " Thou shalt tread upon the lion and the adder: the young lion and the dragon shalt thou trample under feet." So had the voice of olden promise spoken; [1] and in Christ, as in so many of His children, the promise was fulfilled. Those whose timid faith shrinks from all semblance of the miraculous, need find nothing to alarm them here. It is not a natural thing that the wild creatures should attack with ferocity, or fly in terror from, their master man. A poet has sung of a tropical isle that —

> " Nor save for pity was it hard to take
> The helpless life, so wild that it was tame." [2]

The terror or the fury of animals, though continued by hereditary instinct, was begun by cruel and wanton aggression; and historical instances are not wanting in which both have been overcome by the sweetness, the majesty, the gentleness of man. There seems to be no adequate reason for rejecting the unanimous belief of the early centuries that the wild beasts of the Thebaid moved freely and harmlessly among the saintly eremites, and that even the wildest living creatures were tame and gentle to St. Francis of Assisi. Who has not known people whose presence does not scare the birds, and who can approach, without danger, the most savage dog? We may well believe that the mere human spell of a living and sinless personality would go far to keep the Saviour from danger. In the catacombs and on other ancient monuments of early Christians, He is sometimes represented as Orpheus charming the animals with his song. All that was true and beautiful in the old legends found its fulfilment in Him, and was but a symbol of His life and work.

And He was in the wilderness forty days. The number occurs again and again in Scripture, and always in connection with the facts of temptation or retribution. It is clearly a sacred and representative number, and independently of other associations, it was for forty days that Moses had stayed on Sinai, and Elijah in the wilderness. In moments of intense excitement and overwhelming thought the ordinary needs of the body seem to be modified, or even for a time superseded; and unless we are to understand St. Luke's words, " He did eat nothing," as being absolutely literal, we might suppose that Jesus found all that was necessary for His bare sustenance in such

---

[1] Ps. xci. 13. " The beasts of the field shall be at peace with thee " (Job v. 23)
[2] Tennyson's *Enoch Arden.*

scant fruits as the desert might afford ;[1] but however that may be — and it is a question of little importance — at the end of the time He hungered. And this was the tempter's moment. The whole period had been one of moral and spiritual tension.[2] During such high hours of excitement men will sustain, without succumbing, an almost incredible amount of labor, and soldiers will fight through a long day's battle unconscious or oblivious of their wounds. But when the enthusiasm is spent, when the exaltation dies away, when the fire burns low, when Nature, weary and overstrained, reasserts her rights — in a word, when a mighty reaction has begun, which leaves the man suffering, spiritless, exhausted — then is the hour of extreme danger, and that has been, in many a fatal instance, the moment in which a man has fallen a victim to insidious allurement or bold assault. It was at such a moment that the great battle of our Lord against the powers of evil was fought and won.

The struggle was, as is evident, no mere allegory. Into the exact external nature of the temptation it seems at once superfluous and irreverent to enter — superfluous, because it is a question in which any absolute decision is for us impossible ; irreverent, because the Evangelists could only have heard it from the lips of Jesus, or of those to whom He communicated it, and our Lord could only have narrated it in the form which conveys at once the truest impression and the most instructive lessons. Almost every different expositor has had a different view as to the agency employed, and the objective or subjective reality of the entire event.[3] From Origen down to Schleiermacher some have regarded it as a vision or allegory — the symbolic description of a purely inward struggle ; and even so literal and orthodox a commentator as Calvin has embraced this view. On this point, which is a matter of mere exegesis, each must hold the view which seems to him most in accordance with the truth ; but the one essential point is that the struggle was powerful, personal, in-

---

[1] The Jewish hermit Banus lived for years on the spontaneous growth of this very desert (Jos. *Vit.* 2). The νηστεύσας of St. Matthew does not necessarily imply an absolute fast.

[2] Luke iv. 2, " Being *forty days tempted* of the devil."

[3] Very few writers in the present day will regard the story of the temptation as a narrative of objective facts. Even Lange gives the story a natural turn, and supposes that the tempter may have acted through the intervention of human agency. Not only Hase and Weisse, but even Olshausen, Neander, Ullmann, and many orthodox commentators, make the narrative entirely symbolical, and treat it as a profound and eternally significant parable. For a fuller discussion of the subject, see the Excursus " On Different Views of the Temptation " in Ullmann's beautiful treatise on *The Sinlessness of Jesus* (pp. 264—291, third edition, E. Tr.).

tensely real — that Christ, for our sakes, met and conquered the tempter's utmost strength.

The question as to whether Christ was or was not *capable* of sin — to express it in the language of that scholastic and theological region in which it originated, the question as to the peccability or impeccability of His human nature — is one which would never occur to a simple and reverent mind. We believe and know that our blessed Lord was sinless — the Lamb of God, without blemish, and without spot. What can be the possible edification or advantage in the discussion as to whether this sinlessness sprang from a *posse non peccare* or a *non posse peccare?* Some, in a zeal at once intemperate and ignorant, have claimed for Him not only an actual sinlessness, but a nature to which sin was divinely and miraculously impossible. What then? If His great conflict were a mere deceptive phantasmagoria, how can the narrative of it profit us? If *we* have to fight the battle clad in that armor of human free-will which has been hacked and riven about the bosom of our fathers by so many a cruel blow, what comfort is it to us if our great Captain fought not only victoriously, but without real danger; not only uninjured, but without even a possibility of wound? Where is the warrior's courage, if he knows that for him there is but the *semblance* of a battle against the *simulacrum* of a foe? Are we not thus, under an appearance of devotion, robbed of One who, "though He were a son, yet *learned obedience* by the things which He suffered?"[1] Are we not thus, under the guise of orthodoxy, mocked in our belief that we have a High Priest who can be touched with a feeling of our infirmities, " being *tempted in all points like as we are*, yet without sin?"[2] They who would *thus* honor Him rob us of our living Christ, who was very man no less than very God, and substitute for Him a perilous Apollinarian phantom enshrined "in the cold empyrean of theology," and alike incapable of kindling devotion, or of inspiring love.

Whether, then, it comes under the form of a pseudo-orthodoxy, false and pharisaical, and eager only to detect or condemn the supposed heresy of others; or whether it comes from the excess of a dishonoring reverence which has degenerated into the spirit of fear and bondage — let us beware of contradicting the express teaching of the Scriptures, and, as regards this narrative, the express teaching of Christ Himself, by a supposition that He was not liable to real temptation. Nay, He was liable to temptation all the sorer, because it came like agony to a nature infinitely strong yet infinitely pure. In

---

[1] Heb. v. 8.   [2] Heb. iv. 15.

proportion as any one has striven all his life to be, like his great Ensample, holy, harmless, undefiled, separate from sinners, in that proportion will he realize the intensity of the struggle, the anguish of the antipathy which pervade a nobler nature when, either by suggestions from within or from without, it has been dragged into even apparent proximity to the possibilities of evil. There are few passages in the *Pilgrim's Progress* more powerful, or more suggestive of profound acquaintance with the mysteries of the human heart, than that in which Christian in the Valley of the Shadow of Death finds his mind filled with revolting images and blaspheming words, which have indeed been but whispered into his ear, beyond his own powers of rejection, by an evil spirit, but which, in his dire bewilderment, he cannot distinguish or disentangle from thoughts which are his own, and to which his will consents.[1] In Christ, indeed, we suppose that such special complications would be wholly impossible, not because of any transcendental endowments connected with "immanent divinity" or the "communication of idioms," but because He had lived without yielding to wickedness, whereas in men these illusions arise in general from their own past sins. They are, in fact, nothing else but the flitting spectres of iniquities forgotten or unforgotten — the mists that reek upward from the stagnant places in the deepest caverns of hearts not yet wholly cleansed. No, in Christ there could not be this terrible inability to discern that which comes from within us and that which is forced upon us from without — between that which the weak will has entertained, or to which, in that ever-shifting border-land which separates thought from action, it has half assented,

---

[1] There is something of the same conception in Milton's description of the attempts made by the Evil Spirit to assoil the thoughts of Eve while yet she was innocent : —

> " Him there they found
> Squat like a toad, close at the ear of Eve,
> Assaying by his devilish art to reach
> The organs of her fancy, and with them forge
> Illusions as he list, phantasms and dreams,
> At least distempered, discontented thoughts,
> Vain hopes, vain aims, inordinate desires." — *Par. Lost*, iv. 800.

The passage in the *Pilgrim's Progress* is, " Christian made believe that he spake blasphemies, when it was Satan that suggested them into his mind." It is as follows : — " One thing I would not let slip. I took notice that now poor Christian was so confounded that he did not know his own voice, and thus I perceived it. Just when he was come over against the mouth of the burning pit, one of the wicked ones got behind him, and stepped up softly to him, and whisperingly suggested many grievous blasphemies to him, *which he verily thought had proceeded from his own mind* . . . but he had not the discretion either *to stop his ears, or to know from whence those blasphemies came.*"

and that with which it does indeed find itself in immediate contact, but which, nevertheless, it repudiates with every muscle and fibre of its moral being. It must be a weak or a perverted intellect which imagines that "man becomes acquainted with temptation only in proportion as he is defiled by it," or that is unable to discriminate between the severity of a powerful temptation and the stain of a guilty thought. It may sound like a truism, but it is a truism much needed alike for our warning and our comfort, when the poet who, better than any other, has traversed every winding in the labyrinth of the human heart, has told us with such solemnity,

> " 'Tis one thing to be tempted, Escalus,
> Another thing to fall." [1]

And Jesus was tempted. The "Captain of our salvation" was "made perfect through sufferings." [2] "In that He Himself *hath suffered being tempted*, He is able to succor them that are tempted." [3] The wilderness of Jericho and the Garden of Gethsemane — these witnessed His two most grievous struggles, and in these He triumphed wholly over the worst and most awful assaults of the enemy of souls; but during *no* part of the days of His flesh was He free from temptation, since otherwise His life had been no true human life at all, nor would He in the same measure have left us an ensample that we should follow His steps. "Many other were the occasions," says St. Bonaventura, [4] "on which he endured temptations." "They," says St. Bernard, "who reckon only three temptations of our Lord, show their ignorance of Scripture." [5] He refers to John vii. 1, and Heb. iv. 15; he might have referred still more appositely to the express statement of St. Luke, that when the temptation in the wilderness was over, the foiled tempter left Him

---

[1] Shakespeare, *Measure for Measure*, ii. 1. Similarly St. Augustine says, " It is the devil's part to suggest, it is ours not to consent ;" and St. Gregory, " Sin is first by suggestion, then by delight, and lastly by consent." Luther, says Ullmann, " well distinguishes between *sentire tentationem* and *consentire tentationi*. Unless the tempting impression *be felt*, there is no real temptation ; but unless it be *acquiesced in* or *yielded to*, there is no sin " (*ubi supra*, p. 129). " Where then is the point in temptation at which sin begins, or at which it becomes itself sin ? it is there where the evil which is presented *to us begins to make a determining impression upon the heart*" (id.).

[2] Heb. ii. 10.

[3] Heb. ii. 18.

[4] Bonav. *De Vit. Christi*, xiv.

[5] Bern. (Serm. xiv. in Ps. " *Qui habitat*"). Vulg. " Militia est vita hominis super terram." [88] See too Theophylact in *Aur. Cat. in Luc.*

indeed, but left Him only *"for a season,"* [1] or, as the words may perhaps be rendered, "till a new opportunity occurred." Yet we may well believe that when He rose victorious out of the dark wiles in the wilderness, all subsequent temptations, until the last, floated as lightly over His sinless soul as the cloud-wreath of a summer day floats over the blue heaven which it cannot stain.

1. The exhaustion of a long fast would have acted more powerfully on the frame of Jesus from the circumstance that with Him it was not usual. It was with a gracious purpose that He lived, not as a secluded ascetic in hard and self-inflicted pangs, but as a man with men. Nor does he ever enjoin fasting as a positive obligation, although in two passages He more than sanctions it as a valuable aid (Matt. vi. 16—18; ix. 15).[2] But, in general, we know from His own words that He came " eating and drinking ; " practicing, not *abstinence*, but *temperance* in all things, joining in the harmless feasts and innocent assemblages of friends, so that His enemies dared to say of Him, " Behold a gluttonous man and a winebibber," as of John they said, " He hath a devil." After His fast, therefore, of forty days, however supported by solemn contemplation and supernatural aid, His hunger would be the more severe. And then it was that the tempter came ; in what form — whether as a spirit of darkness or as an angel of light, whether under the disguise of a human aspect or an immaterial suggestion, we do not know and cannot pretend to say — content to follow simply the Gospel narrative, and to adopt its expressions, not with dry dogmatic assertion as to the impossibility of such expressions being in a greater or less degree allegorical, but with a view only to learn those deep moral lessons which alone concern us, and which alone are capable of an indisputable interpretation.

---

[1] Luke iv. 13, ἄχρι καιροῦ. Much that I have here said is confirmed by a passage in Greg. M. *Hom.* i. 16 (Wordsw. on Matt. iv. 1), " Tentari Christus potuit, sed ejus mentem peccati delectatio non momordit. Ideo omnis *diabolica illa tentatio foris non intus fuit*." [s9] And yet in spite of these and many more saintly and erudite justifications of such a view from the writings of theologians in all ages, the violent and prejudiced ignorance of modern ἀοραδία still continues to visit all such methods of interpretation with angry anathema and indiscriminate abuse.

[2] Matt. xvii. 21, from which it might seem that Jesus Himself fasted, is omitted by Tischendorf on the authority of א, B, the Cureton Syriac, the Sahidic version, &c. This interpolation arises, however, from Mark ix. 29, where the words of Jesus should also perhaps end at προσευχῇ, and where καὶ νηστείᾳ, though widely sanctioned by the MSS. and versions, are omitted by א, B, K, and rejected by Tischendorf. (When I refer to Tischendorf I mean the readings adopted by him in his *Synopsis Evangelica*, 3d edition, 1871.)

"If Thou be the Son of God, command that these stones be made loaves." So spake the Tempter first. Jesus was hungry, and " these stones " were perhaps those siliceous accretions, sometimes known under the name of *lapides judaici*, which assume the exact shape of little loaves of bread,[1] and which were represented in legend as the petrified fruits of the Cities of the Plain. The pangs of hunger work all the more powerfully when they are stimulated by the added tortures of a quick imagination; and if the conjecture be correct, then the very shape and aspect and traditional origin of these stones would give to the temptation an added force.

There can be no stronger proof of the authenticity and divine origin of this narrative than the profound subtlety and typical universality of each temptation. Not only are they wholly unlike the far cruder and simpler stories of the temptation, in all ages, of those who have been eminent saints, but there is in them a delicacy of insight, an originality of conception, that far transcend the range of the most powerful invention.

It was a temptation to the senses — an appeal to the appetites — an impulse given to that lower nature which man shares with all the animal creation. But so far from coming in any coarse or undisguisedly sensuous form, it came shrouded in a thousand subtle veils. Israel, too, had been humbled, and suffered to hunger in the wilderness, and there, in his extreme need, God had fed him with manna, which was as angels' food and bread from heaven. Why did not the Son of God thus provide Himself with a table in the wilderness? He *could* do so if He liked, and why should He hesitate? If an angel had revealed to the fainting Hagar the fountain of Beer-lahai-roi — if an angel had touched the famishing Elijah, and shown him food — why should *He* await even the ministry of angels to whom such ministry was needless, but whom, if He willed it, angels would have been so glad to serve?

How deep is the wisdom of the reply! Referring to the very lesson which the giving of the manna had been designed to teach, and quoting one of the noblest utterances of Old Testament inspiration, our Lord answered, "It standeth written,[2] Man shall not live by bread alone, but by every word that proceedeth out of the mouth of God." [3] And what a lesson lies herein for us — a lesson enforced by

---

[1] So Matt. iv. 3, ἄρτοι ; Luke iv. 3, " that *this* stone become a loaf." Cf. Stanley's *Sinai and Palestine*, p. 154 (*Elijah's melons*).

[2] Matt. iv. 4, γέγραπται — the perfect indicates an abiding, eternal lesson.

[3] Deut. viii. 3. Alford justly draws attention to the fact that Jesus meets and defeats the temptation in His *humanity ;* " Man shall not," &c

how great an example — that we are not to be guided by the wants of our lower nature; that we may not misuse that lower nature for the purposes of our own sustenance and enjoyment; that we are not our own, and may not do what we will with that which we imagine to be our own; that even those things which may seem lawful, are yet not all expedient; that man has higher principles of life than material sustenance, as he is a higher existence than his material frame.[1] He who thinks that we live by bread alone, will make the securing of bread the chief object of his life — will determine to have it at whatever cost — will be at once miserable and rebellious if even for a time he be stinted or deprived of it, and, because he seeks no diviner food, will inevitably starve with hunger in the midst of it. But he who knows that man doth *not* live by bread alone, will not thus, for the sake of living, lose all that makes life dear — will, when he has done his duty, trust God to preserve with all things needful the body He has made — will seek with more earnest endeavor the bread from heaven, and that living water whereof he who drinketh shall thirst no more.

And thus His first temptation was analogous in form to the last taunt addressed to Him on the cross — " If Thou be the Son of God, come down from the cross." "*If*" — since faith and trust are the mainstay of all human holiness, the tempter is ever strongest in the suggestion of such doubts; strong, too, in his appeal to the free-will and the self-will of man. " You *may*, you *can* — why not do it ? " On the cross our Saviour answers not; here He answers only to express a great eternal principle. He does not say, " I *am* the Son of God; " in the profundity of His humiliation, in the extreme of His self-sacrifice, He made not His equality with God a thing to be grasped at,[2] " but made Himself of no reputation." He foils the tempter, not as very God, but as very man.

2. The order of the temptations is given differently by St. Matthew and St. Luke, St. Matthew placing second the scene on the pinnacle of the Temple, and St. Luke the vision of the kingdoms of the world. Both orders cannot be right, and possibly St. Luke may have been influenced in his arrangement by the thought that a temptation to spiritual pride and the arbitrary exercise of miraculous power was a subtler and less transparent, and therefore more powerful one, than the temptation to fall down and recognize the power of evil.[3] But

---

[1] " We live by admiration, hope, and love." (Wordsworth.)

[2] Phil. ii. 6, οὐχ ἁρπαγμὸν ἡγήσατο τὸ εἶναι ἴσα Θεῷ.

[3] Milton in the *Paradise Regained* may have been influenced to prefer the order

the words, " Get thee behind me, Satan," recorded by both Evangelists (Luke iv. 8; Matt. iv. 10) — the fact that St. Matthew alone
gives a definite sequence (" then," " again ") — perhaps, too, the consideration that St. Matthew, as one of the apostles, is more likely to
have heard the narrative immediately from the lips of Christ — give
greater weight to the order which he adopts.

Jesus had conquered and rejected the first temptation by the
expression of an absolute trust in God. Adapting itself, therefore,
with infinite subtlety to the discovered mood of the Saviour's soul,
the next temptation challenging as it were directly, and appealing
immediately to, this absolute trust, claims the illustration and expression of it, not to relieve an immediate necessity, but to avert an
overwhelming peril. " Then he brought Him to the Holy City,' and
setteth Him on the pinnacle of the Temple." ² Some well-known pinnacle of that well-known mass must be intended; perhaps the roof of
the *Stoa Basilikè*, or Royal Porch, on the southern side of the Temple, which looked down sheer into the valley of the Kidron below it,
from a height so dizzy that, according to the description of Josephus,
if any one ventured to look down, his head would swim at the immeasurable depth; perhaps Solomon's Porch, the *Stoa Anatolikè*, which

---

as given in St. Luke, partly from this reason, and partly from the supposition that
angels rescued our Lord in safety from that dizzy height.

¹ Still called by the Arabs *El-Kúds esh-Shereef*, " the Holy, the Noble."

² Matt. iv. 5, ἐπὶ τὸ πτερύγιον τοῦ ἱεροῦ. The article is used in both Evangelists, and both times omitted by the English version.

> " So saying, he caught Him up, and without wing
> Of hippogrif, bore through the air sublime,
> Over the wilderness, and o'er the plain,
> Till underneath them fair Jerusalem,
> The Holy City, lifted high her towers,
> And higher yet *the glorious Temple reared*
> *Her pile, far off appearing like a mount*
> *Of alabaster, topt with golden spires.*
> *There, on the highest pinnacle,* he set
> The Son of God." (Milton, *Par. Reg.* iv. 462.)

These journeys through the air (though the sacred narrative says nothing
of them, clearly thereby tending to turn our attention wholly from the mere
secondary accidents and external form of the story to its inmost meaning) were
thoroughly in accordance with ordinary Jewish beliefs (1 Kings xviii. 12; 2 Kings
ii. 16; Acts viii. 39; Ezek. iii. 14). See, too, the apocryphal addition to Habakkuk,
and the text interpolated in the Ebionite Gospel of St. Matthew, "My mother the
Holy Ghost took me by a hair of the head and carried me to Mount Tabor." This
is quoted by Origen, *in Joann.* t. ii., § 6; and Jer. *in Mic.* vii. 6. The expression
" My mother " apparently arises from the fact that the Hebrew *ruach* is fem.
Jerome (in Isa. xl. 11) tells us that in Ps. lxviii. 12, the Jews explain " maiden " of
the soul, and "mistress " of the Holy Spirit.

Josephus also has described,[1] and from which, according to tradition, St. James, the Lord's brother, was afterwards precipitated into the court below.[2]

"If"—again that doubt, as though to awake a spirit of pride, in the exercise of that miraculous display to which He is tempted — "if thou be the Son of God, cast Thyself down." "Thou art in danger not self-sought; save Thyself from it, as Thou canst and mayest, and thereby prove Thy Divine power and nature. Is it not written that the angels shall bear Thee up?[3] Will not this be a splendid proof of Thy trust in God?" Thus deep and subtle was this temptation; and thus, since Jesus had appealed to Scripture, did the devil also "quote Scripture for his purpose." For there was nothing vulgar, nothing selfish, nothing sensuous in this temptation. It was an appeal, not to natural appetites, but to perverted spiritual instincts. Does not the history of sects, and parties, and churches, and men of high religious claims, show us that thousands who could not sink into the slough of sensuality, have yet thrust themselves arrogantly into needless perils, and been dashed into headlong ruin from the pinnacle of spiritual pride? And how calm, yet full of warning, was that simple answer, "It is written again, 'Thou shalt not tempt the Lord thy God.'" The word in the original ($\dot{\varepsilon}\varkappa\pi\varepsilon\iota\rho\acute{a}\sigma\varepsilon\iota\varsigma$—Matt. iv. 7; Deut. vi. 16) is stronger and more expressive. It is, "Thou shalt not *tempt to the extreme* the Lord thy God;" thou shalt not, as it were, presume on all that He can do for thee; thou shalt not claim His miraculous intervention to save thee from thine own presumption and folly; thou shalt not challenge His power to the proof. When thou art in the path of duty trust in Him to the utmost with a perfect confidence; but listen not to that haughty seductive whisper, "Ye shall be as gods," and let there be no self-willed and capricious irreverence in thy demand for aid. Then — to add the words so cunningly omitted by the tempter — "shalt thou be safe in all thy ways."[4] And Jesus does not even allude to His apparent danger. Danger not self-sought is safety. The tempter's own words had been a confession of his own impotence — "Cast *Thyself* down." Even from that giddy

---

[1] Jos. *Antt.* xv 11, § 5, $\acute{o}\varkappa o\tau o\delta\iota\nu\iota\tilde{a}\nu$; xx. 9, §7. See Caspari, p. 256.

[2] Hegesippus *ap.* Euseb. *H. E.* ii. 23; Epiphan. *Adv. Hæres.* xxix. 4.

[3] Ps. xci. 11, 12.

[4] Ps. xci. 11, 12. As the psalm is addressed to "Him that dwelleth in the secret place of the Most High," the expression "all thy ways" can only mean ways of innocence and holiness — the ways of God's providence. The only true meaning of the text therefore excludes the insolent gloss put on it by the tempter; and he omits verse 13, which is a prophecy of his own defeat.

height he had no power to hurl Him whom God kept safe. The Scripture which he had quoted was true, though he had perverted it. No amount of temptation can ever *necessitate* a sin. With every temptation God provides also "*the* way to escape" :

> "Also, it is written,
> ' Tempt not the Lord thy God,' He said, and stood :
> But Satan, smitten by amazement, fell." [1]

3. Foiled in his appeal to natural hunger, or to the possibility of spiritual pride, the tempter appealed to "the last infirmity of noble minds," and staked all on one splendid cast. He makes up for the want of subtlety in the form by the apparent magnificence of the issue. From a high mountain he showed Jesus all the kingdoms of the world and the glory of them, and as the κοσμοκράτωρ, the "prince of this world," he offered them all to Him who had lived as the village carpenter, in return for one expression of homage, one act of acknowledgment.[2]

"The kingdoms of the world, and the glory of them!" "There are some that will say," says Bishop Andrewes, "that we are never tempted with kingdoms. It may well be, for it needs not be, when less will serve. It was Christ only that was thus tempted; in Him lay an heroical mind that could not be tempted with small matters. But with us it is nothing so, for we esteem more basely of ourselves. We set our wares at a very easy price; he may buy us even dagger-cheap. He need never carry us so high as the mount. The pinnacle is high enough ; yea, the lowest steeple in all the town would serve the turn. Or let him but carry us to the leads and gutters of our own houses; nay, let us but stand in our windows or our doors, if he will give us so much as we can there see, he will tempt us thoroughly ; we will accept it, and thank him too. . . . . A matter of half-a-crown, or ten groats, a pair of shoes, or some such trifle, will bring us on our knees to the devil."

But Christ taught, "What shall it profit a man, if he gain the whole world, and lose his own soul ? "

---

[1] *Par. Reg.* iv. 481.

[2] See John xii. 31; xvi. 2—30 ; Eph. ii. 2 (τὸν ἄρχοντα τῆς ἐξουσίας τοῦ ἀέρος[90]); 2 Cor. iv. 4; Sar ha-Olam, *Sanhedr.* f. 94. It was done ἐν στιγμῇ χρόνου [91] (Luke iv. 5), for, as St. Ambrose says, "in momento praetereunt." [91] We must bear in mind that the Power of Evil has been disarmed to a very great extent in the kingdom of Christ. Samael in the Talmud is called "the prince of the air." The tract *Zohar* goes so far as to call him אֵל אָחֵר *el âcheer*, "a second god." (See Gfrörer, *Jahrh. d. Heils*, i. 402—420.)

There was one living who, scarcely in a figure, might be said to have the whole world. The Roman Emperor Tiberius was at that moment infinitely the most powerful of living men, the absolute, undisputed, deified ruler of all that was fairest and richest in the kingdoms of the earth. There was no control to his power, no limit to his wealth, no restraint upon his pleasures. And to yield himself still more unreservedly to the boundless self-gratification of a voluptuous luxury, not long after this time he chose for himself a home on one of the loveliest spots on the earth's surface, under the shadow of the slumbering volcano, upon an enchanting islet in one of the most softly delicious climates of the world. What came of it all? He was, as Pliny calls him, "tristissimus ut constat hominum," [1] "confessedly the most gloomy of mankind." And there, from this home of his hidden infamies, from this island where on a scale so splendid he had tried the experiment of what happiness can be achieved by pressing the world's most absolute authority, and the world's guiltiest indulgences, into the service of an exclusively selfish life, he wrote to his servile and corrupted Senate, "What to write to you, Conscript Fathers, or how to write, or what *not* to write, *may all the gods and goddesses destroy me worse than I feel that they are daily destroying me,* if I know." [2] Rarely has there been vouchsafed to the world a more overwhelming proof that its richest gifts are but "fairy gold that turns to dust and dross," and its most colossal edifices of personal splendor and greatness no more durable barrier against the encroachment of bitter misery than are the babe's sandheaps to stay the mighty march of the Atlantic tide.

In such perplexity, in such anguish, does the sinful possession of all riches and all rule end. Such is the invariable Nemesis of unbridled lusts. It does not need the snaky tresses or the shaken torch of the fabled Erinnyes. The guilty conscience is its own adequate avenger; and "if the world were one entire and perfect chrysolite," and that gem ours, it would not console us for one hour of that inward torment, or compensate in any way for those lacerating pangs.

But he who is an inheritor of the kingdom of heaven is lord over vaster and more real worlds, infinitely happy because infinitely

---

[1] *H. N.* xxviii. 5.   For Capreae, see Tac. *Ann.* iv. 61, 62,67.

[2] "Quid scribam vobis, Patres Conscripti, aut quomodo scribam, aut quid omnino non scribam hoc tempore, di me deaeque pejus perdant quam perire me cotidie sentio si scio. Adeo facinora atque flagitia sua ipsi quoque in supplicium verterant. Quippe Tiberium non fortuna, non solitudines protegebant quin tormenta pectoris suasque ipse poenas fateretur." [93]   (Tac. *Ann.* vi. 6.)

pure. And over that kingdom Satan has no power. It is the king-dom of God; and since from Satan not even the smallest semblance of any of his ruinous gifts can be gained except by suffering the soul to do allegiance to him, the answer to all his temptations is the answer of Christ, "Get thee behind me, Satan: for it is written, 'Thou shalt worship the Lord thy God, and Him only shalt thou serve.'"[1]

Thus was Christ victorious, through that self-renunciation through which only can victory be won. And the moments of such honest struggle crowned with victory are the very sweetest and happiest that the life of man can give. They are full of an elevation and a delight which can only be described in language borrowed from the imagery of heaven.

"Then the devil leaveth Him" — St. Luke adds, "till a fitting opportunity" — "and, behold, angels came and ministered unto Him."[2]

---

[1] Deut. vi. 13. This being one of St. Matthew's "cyclic" quotations agrees mainly with the LXX. [except προσκυνήσεις for φοβηθήσῃ and μόνῳ, for the LXX. variations are here, no doubt, *altered* in the Alex. MS. from the N. T.], and is not close to the Hebrew; but his "*peculiar*" quotations are usually from the Hebrew, and differ from the LXX. (See Westcott, *Introd.*, p. 211.) It is remark-able that our Lord's three answers are all from Deut. vi. and viii.

[2] The reader will be glad to see, in connection with this subject, some of the remarks of Ullmann, who has studied it more profoundly, and written on it more beautifully, than any other theologian. "The positive temptations of Jesus," he says, "were not confined to that particular point of time when they assailed Him with concentrated force. . . But still more frequently in after life was He called to endure temptation of the other kind — the temptation of suffering, and this culminated on two occasions, viz., in the conflict of Gethsemane, and in that moment of agony on the cross when He cried, '*My God, my God, why hast thou forsaken me?*'" (*Sinlessness of Jesus*, E. Tr., p. 140.) He had already remarked (p. 128) that "man is exposed in two ways to the possibility and seductive power of evil. On the one hand he may be drawn to actual sin by enticements; and, on the other hand, he may be turned aside from good by threatened as well as by inflicted suffering. The former may be termed positive, the latter negative temptation." "Jesus was tempted in all points — that is, He was tempted in the only two possible ways specified above. On the one hand, allurements were pre-sented which, if successful, would have led Him to actual sin; and, on the other hand, He was beset by sufferings which might have turned Him aside from the divine path of duty. These temptations, moreover, occurred both on great occa-sions and in minute particulars, under the most varied circumstances, from the beginning to the end of His earthly course. But in the midst of them all His spiritual energy and his love to God remained pure and unimpaired" (*id.* p. 30). Ewald, in his *Die drei Ersten Evangelien*, regarding the Temptation from the point of view of public work, makes the three temptations correspond severally to the tendencies to (i.) unscrupulousness, (ii.) rash confidence, (iii.) unhallowed personal ambitions.

CHAPTER X.

THE FIRST APOSTLES.

" Nisi habuisset et in vultu quiddam oculisque sidereum nunquam eum statim secuti fuissent Apostoli, nec qui ad comprehendendum eum venerant corruissent.[94] — JER. *Ep.* lxv.

VICTORIOUS over that concentrated temptation, safe from the fiery ordeal, the Saviour left the wilderness and returned to the fords of Jordan.[1]

The Synoptical Gospels, which dwell mainly on the ministry in Galilee, and date its active commencement from the imprisonment of John, omit all record of the intermediate events, and only mention our Lord's retirement to Nazareth.[2] It is to the fourth Evangelist that we owe the beautiful narrative of the days which immediately ensued upon the temptation. The Judæan ministry is brought by him

---

[1] It is well known that " Bethania " (א, A, B, C, &c.), not " Bethabara," is the true reading of John i. 28; it was altered by Origen (who admits that it was the reading of nearly all the MSS.) on very insufficient grounds, viz., that no Bethany on the Jordan was known, and that there was *said to be* (δείκνυσθαι δὲ λέγουσι) a Bethabara, where John was said to have baptized. Origen is, however, supported by Cureton's Syriac. The two names (בֵּית עֲבָרָה, " house of passage," and בֵּית אֲנָיָה, " house of ship," or ferry-boats) have much the same meaning (see 2 Sam. xv. 23, Heb.). Mr. Grove thinks that Bethabara may be identical with Beth-barah, the fords secured by the Ephraimites (Judg. vii. 24), or with Beth-nimrah (Numb. xxxii. 36). This latter answers to the description, being close to the region round about Jordan, the *Ciccar* of the O. T., the oasis of Jericho. In some edd. of the LXX. this is actually written Βηθαβρά (*Bibl. Dict.* i. 204). Mr. Monro ingeniously suggests that Origen (like his copyists) may have confused Bethabara with Betharaba (Josh. xviii. 22) which was in the Jordan valley. After careful attention, I see no grounds whatever for agreeing with Caspari (*Chron. Geogr. Einl.* 277), and others who place this Bethania at Tellanihje, on the upper Jordan, to the north-east of the Sea of Gennesareth. The reasons for the traditional scene of the baptism, near Jericho, and therefore within easy reach of Jerusalem, seem far more convincing. [The Bethany on the Mount of Olives has another derivation ; it was usually derived from בֵּית הִינִי, " house of unripe dates;" but after the valuable letter of Dr. Deutsch, published by Mr. W. H. Dixon in his *Holy Land* (ii. 217), this conjecture of Lightfoot's must remain at least doubtful.]

[2] Matt. iv. 12 (ἀνεχώρησεν, " withdrew "); Mark i. 14; Luke iv. 14.

into the first prominence.[1] He seems to have made a point of relating nothing of which he had not been a personal witness, and there are some few indications that he was bound to Jerusalem by peculiar

---

[1] Throughout this book it will be seen that I accept unhesitatingly the genuineness of St. John's Gospel. It would be of course impossible, and is no part of my purpose, to enter fully into the controversy about it ; and it is the more needless, because in many books of easy access (I may mention, among others, Professor Westcott's *Introd. to the Study of the Gospels*, and *Hist. of the Canon of the New Testament*, and Mr. Sanday's *Authorship of the Fourth Gospel*) the main arguments which seem decisive in favor of its genuineness may be studied by any one. The other side is powerfully argued by Mr. Tayler in his *Fourth Gospel*. All that I need here say (referring especially to what Professor Westcott has written on the subject), is, that there is *external* evidence for its authenticity in the allusions to or *traces of the influence* of this Gospel in Ignatius and Polycarp ; and later in the second century, of Justin Martyr, Tatian, Theophilus, &c. Papias does not indeed mention it, which is a circumstance difficult to account for; but according to Eusebius (*Hist. Ecc.* iii. 39), he "made use of testimonies" out of the First Epistles, and few will separate the question of the genuineness of the Epistles from that of the genuineness of the Gospel. The very slightness of the Second and Third Epistles is almost a convincing proof of their authenticity, since no one could have dreamed of forging them. The early admission of the Fourth Gospel into the canon both of the East and West, and the acknowledgment of it even by heretics, are additional arguments in its favor. Dr. Lightfoot also notices the further fact that "soon after the middle of the second century divergent readings of a striking kind occur in St. John's Gospel, as for instance, $\mu o \nu o \gamma \varepsilon \nu \grave{\eta} s \ \theta \varepsilon \grave{o} s$ [95] and $\acute{o} \ \mu o \nu o \gamma \varepsilon \nu \grave{\eta} s \ \upsilon \acute{\iota} \acute{o} s$" [96] (i. 18), and this leads us to the conclusion "that the text has already a history, and that the Gospel therefore cannot have been very recent" (*On Revision*, p. 20). But if the external evidence, though less *decisive* than we could have desired, is not inadequate, the internal evidence, derived not only from its entire scope, but also from numberless minute and incidental particulars, is simply overwhelming; and the improbabilities involved in the hypothesis of forgery are so immense, that it is hardly too much to say that we should have recognized in the Gospel the authorship of St. John, even if it had come down to us anonymously, or under some other name. The Hebraic coloring of the style ; the traces of distinctly Judaic training and conceptions (i. 45 ; iv. 22); the naïve faithfulness in admitting facts which might seem to tell most powerfully against the writer's belief (vii. 5); the minute topographical and personal allusions and reminiscences (vi. 10, 19, 23 ; x. 22, 23 ; xi. 1, 44, 54 ; xxi. 2); the faint traces that the writer had been a disciple of John the Baptist, whose title he alone omits (i. 15 ; iii. 23, 25); the vivid freshness of the style throughout, as, for instance, in the account of the blind man, and of the Last Supper — so wholly unlike a philosopheme, and so clearly written *ad narrandum*, not *ad probandum* (ch. ix., xiii.); the preservation of the remarkable fact that Jesus was first tried before Annas (xviii. 13, 19—24), and the correction of the current tradition as to the time of the Last Supper (xiii. 1 ; xviii. 28) ;— these are but a few of numberless internal evidences which bring additional confirmation to the conviction inspired by the character and contents of this great Gospel. They have left no doubt on the minds of many profound and competent scholars, and no one can easily make light of evidence which has satisfied such a philologian as Ewald, and, for twelve editions of his book, satisfied even such a critic

relations.¹ By station St. John was a fisherman, and it is not impossible that, as the fish of the Lake of Galilee were sent in large quantities to Jerusalem, he may have lived there at certain seasons in connection with the employment of his father and his brother, who, as the owners of their own boat and the masters of hired servants, evidently occupied a position of some importance. Be that as it may, it is St. John alone who narrates to us the first call of the earliest Apostles, and he relates it with all the minute particulars and graphic touches of one on whose heart and memory each incident had been indelibly impressed.

The deputation of the Sanhedrin² (to which we have already alluded) seems to have taken place the day previous to our Lord's return from the wilderness; and when, on the following morning,³ the Baptist saw Jesus approaching, he delivered a public and emphatic testimony that this was indeed the Messiah who had been marked out to him by the appointed sign, and that He was "the Lamb of God that taketh away the sin of the world." Whether the prominent conception in the Baptist's mind was the Paschal Lamb, or the Lamb of the morning and evening sacrifice; whether "the world" (κόσμος) was the actual expression which he used, or is merely a Greek rendering of the word "people" (עם); whether he understood the profound and awful import of his own utterance, or was carried by prophetic inspiration beyond himself — we cannot tell. But this much is clear, that since his whole imagery, and indeed the very description of his own function and position, is, as we have already seen, borrowed from the Evangelical prophet, he must have used the expression with distinct reference to the picture of Divine patience and mediatorial suffering in Isa. liii. 7 (cf. Jer. xi. 19). His words could hardly have involved less meaning than this — that the gentle and sinless man to whom he pointed should be a man of sorrows, and

---

as Renan. It is my sincere belief that the difficulties of accepting the Gospel are mainly superficial, and that they are infinitely less formidable than those involved in its rejection. Mr. Sanday has treated the question with great impartiality ; and in his volume many of the points touched upon in this note are developed with much force and skill.

¹ John xix. 27; xviii. 16. Perhaps this explains the fact that James was not with his brother John as a disciple of the Baptist. Andrew, on finding Christ, immediately sought out his brother Simon. John could not do so, for his brother was in Galilee, and was not called till some time subsequently.

² John i. 19—34. See p. 109.

³ John i. 35—43. The οὐκ ᾔδειν αὐτόν ⁹⁷ means that the Baptist did not recognize Jesus as the Messiah, till he had seen (τεθέαμαι, ver. 32 ; ἑώρακα, ver. 34) the heavenly sign.

that these sorrows should be for the salvation of His race.[1] Whatever else the words may have connoted to the minds of his hearers, yet they could hardly have thought them over without connecting Jesus with the conceptions of sinlessness, of suffering, and of a redeeming work.

Memorable as this testimony was, it seems on the first day to have produced no immediate result. But on the second day, when the Baptist was standing accompanied by two of his disciples, Jesus again walked by, and John, fixing upon Him his intense and earnest gaze,[2] exclaimed again, as though with involuntary awe and admiration, "Behold the Lamb of God!"

The words were too remarkable to be again neglected, and the two Galilæan youths who heard them followed the retreating figure of Jesus. He caught the sound of their timid footsteps, and turning round to look at them as they came near, He gently asked, "What seek ye?"

It was but the very beginning of His ministry: as yet they could not know Him for all that He was;[3] as yet they had not heard the gracious words that proceeded out of His lips; in coming to seek Him thus they might be actuated by inadequate motives, or even by mere passing curiosity; it was fit that they should come to Him by spontaneous impulse, and declare their object of their own free will.

But how deep and full of meaning is that question, and how sternly it behooves all who come to their Lord to answer it! One of the holiest of the Church's saints, St. Bernard, was in the habit of constantly warning himself by the solemn query, "*Bernarde, ad quid venisti?*"—"Bernard, for what purpose art thou here?" Self-examination could assume no more searching form; but all the mean-

---

[1] "He felt in the delicacy of Christ's personality all its capability of suffering, and its suffering destiny." (Lange, ii. 283. Comp. Exod. xii. 5; 1 Cor. v. 7; 1 Pet. i. 19.) In the Apocalypse (v. 6; vii. 9, &c.) ἀρνίον,[98] not ἀμνός,[99] is always used. The attempt of Danz to account for the expression as a mistaken rendering of עַמְנוּאֵל in the sense of "strong hero" (see Hase, *Leben Jesu*, p. 101) is only worth noticing as an instance of that fondness for ingenious novelties which is the bane of German theologians. On the word αἴρων, "bearing, and carrying away," "expiating," cf. Exod. xxviii. 30; xxxiv. 7; Lev. v. 1, &c.

[2] ἐμβλέψας. For other instances of the word, see Matt. xix. 26; Luke xx. 17; Mark x. 21.

[3] Even if, as some suppose, St. John the Evangelist was His first cousin. The argument for supposing that Salome, the wife of Zebedee, was a sister of the Virgin Mary, rises from the comparison of Mark xv. 40 with John xix. 25, where *four* women are mentioned; but John, with his usual delicate reserve, does not mention his own mother by name. See *sup.*, p. 99, *n.* 3.

ing which it involved was concentrated in that quiet and simple question, " What seek ye ? "

It was more than the two young Galilæans could answer Him at once; it meant more perhaps than they knew or understood, yet the answer showed that they were in earnest. " Rabbi," they said (and the title of profound honor and reverence [1] showed how deeply His presence had impressed them), " where art thou staying ? "

Where it was we do not know. Perhaps in one of the temporary *succôth*, or booths, covered at the top with the striped *abba*, which is in the East an article of ordinary wear, and with their wattled sides interwoven with green branches of terebinth or palm, which must have given the only shelter possible to the hundreds who had flocked to John's baptism. " He saith to them, Come and see." Again, the words were very simple, though they occur in passages of much significance.[2] Never, however, did they produce a result more remarkable than now. They came and saw where Jesus dwelt, and as it was then four in the afternoon,[3] stayed there that day, and probably slept there that night; and before they lay down to sleep they knew and felt in their inmost hearts that the kingdom of heaven had come, that the hopes of long centuries were now fulfilled, that they had been in the presence of Him who was the desire of all nations, the Priest greater than Aaron, the Prophet greater than Moses, the King greater than David, the true Star of Jacob and Sceptre of Israel.

One of those two youths who thus came earliest to Christ was Andrew.[4] The other suppressed his own name because he was the narrator, the beloved disciple, the Evangelist St. John.[5] No wonder that the smallest details, down even to the very hour of the day, were

---

[1] Among the Jews this title was a sort of degree. One of the myriads of idle conjectures which have defaced the simple narrative of the Gospels is that Jesus had taken this degree among the Essenes. It is clear, on the one hand, that He never sought it ; and on the other, that it was bestowed upon Him even by the most eminent Pharisees (John iii. 2) out of spontaneous and genuine awe.

[2] John xi. 34 ; Cant. iii. 11 ; Rev. vi. 1, 3, 5, 7 ; Ps. lxvi. 5, &c. (see Stier, i. 51).

[3] The tenth hour counting from six in the morning ; there is no ground for supposing, with Wieseler, that John counts from midnight, instead of adopting the ordinary Jewish computation (John iv. 6, 52 ; xi. 9 ; xix. 14). Wieseler seems even to be mistaken in the belief that the Romans ever counted the *hours* of their civil day from midnight. — Mr. Monro refers me to a passage of the *Digests* in which *hora vi. diei* and *hora vi. noctis* are referred to in the very sentence in which a lawyer is expounding civil computation in opposition to natural. (Dig. xli., tit. 3, fr. 6, 7.)

[4] Hence the Fathers call him ὁ πρωτόκλητος.[100]

[5] This exquisite and consistent reticence is one of the many strong arguments in favor of the genuineness of the Gospel. If our view be right, he *did* care

treasured in his memory, never to be forgotten, even in extreme old age.

It was the first care of Andrew to find his brother Simon, and tell him of this great Eureka.[1] He brought him to Jesus, and Jesus looking earnestly on him with that royal gaze which read intuitively the inmost thoughts — seeing at a glance in that simple fisherman all the weakness but also all the splendid greatness of the man — said, giving him a new name, which was long afterwards yet more solemnly confirmed, " Thou art Simon, the Son of Jona ; thou shalt be called Kephas ; " that is, " Thou art Simon, the son of the *dove ;* hereafter thou shalt be as the rock in which the dove hides." [2] It was, indeed, a play upon the word, but one which was memorably symbolic and profound. None but the shallow and the ignorant will see, in such a play upon the name, anything derogatory to the Saviour's dignity. The essential meaning and augury of names had been in all ages a belief among the Jews, whose very language was regarded by themselves as being no less sacred than the oracular gems on Aaron's breast. Their belief in the mystic potency of sounds, of the tongue guided by unalterable destiny in the realms of seeming chance, may seem idle and superstitious to an artificial cultivation, but has been shared by many of the deepest thinkers in every age.[3]

How was it that these youths of Galilee, how was it that a John so fervid yet contemplative, a Peter so impetuous in his affections, yet so timid in his resolves, were thus brought at once — brought, as it were, by a single look, by a single word — to the Saviour's feet ? How came they thus, by one flash of insight or of inspiration, to

---

about the facts of which he is writing, but did not care that his mere name should be remembered among men. M. Renan seems at one time to have held that it was partly written out of jealousy at the primacy popularly ascribed to St. Peter !

[1] *Εὑρήκαμεν τὸν Μεσσίαν* [101] (John i. 41). (Pressensé, *Jésus Christ,* p. 294.) This was indeed a true act of brotherly affection. (See Keble's Hymn on St. Andrew's Day.) It is strange that no one should have alluded (so far as I have seen) to the reason why St. John could not then perform for his brother the same great service. The reason probably is that James was at the time quietly pursuing his calling by the Sea of Galilee.

[2] Lange, ii. 284. Or possibly, " Thou art a Son of Weakness, but shalt become a Rock." Unfortunately, however, there is no sufficient authority for giving this meaning to the word נֵי· (Lücke, i. 450.)

[3] Cf. Æsch. *Agam.* 665, *προνοίαισι τοῦ πεπρωμένου γλῶσσαν ἐν τύχᾳ νέμων.*[102] (See *Origin of Lang.,* ch. iii. ; *Chapters on Lang.,* p. 269—277.) I am not now referring to such recondite fancies as those involved in the Cabbalistic modes of interpretation by *Gematria, notarikon. atbash,* &c., but to something far more antique and spontaneous, of which, for instance, we find specimens not only in the tragedians, but even in the stories of Herodotus ix. 91, &c.).

recognize, in the carpenter of Nazareth, the Messiah of prophecy, the Son of God, the Saviour of the world?

Doubtless in part by what He said, and by what John the Baptist had testified concerning Him, but doubtless also in part by His very look. On this subject, indeed, tradition has varied in a most remarkable manner; but on a point of so much interest we may briefly pause.

Any one who has studied the representations of Christ in mediæval art will have observed that some of them, particularly in missals, are degradingly and repulsively hideous, while others are conceived in the softest and loveliest ideal of human beauty.[1] Whence came this singular divergence?

It came from the prophetic passages which were supposed to indicate the appearance of the Messiah, as well as His life.

The early Church, accustomed to the exquisite perfection of form in which the genius of heathen sculpture had clothed its conceptions of the younger gods of Olympus — aware, too, of the fatal corruptions of a sensual imagination — seemed to find a pleasure in breaking loose from this adoration of personal endowments, and in taking as their ideal of the bodily aspect of our Lord, Isaiah's picture of a patient and afflicted sufferer, or David's pathetic description of a smitten and wasted outcast.[2] His beauty, says Clemens of Alexandria, was in His soul and in His actions, but in appearance He was base. Justin Martyr describes Him as being without beauty, without glory, without honor. His body, says Origen, was small, and ill-shapen, and ignoble. "His body," says Tertullian, "had no human handsomeness, much less any celestial splendor." The heathen Celsus, as we learn from Origen, even argued from His traditional meanness and ugliness of aspect as a ground for rejecting His divine origin.[3] Nay, this kind of distorted inference went to even greater extremities. The Vulgate rendering of Isa. liii. 4 is, "Nos putavimus eum *quasi leprosum*, percussum a Deo et humiliatum;"[107] and

---

[1] See Lecky, *Hist. of Rationalism*, i. 257.

[2] Isa. lii. 14; liii. 4, "We did esteem him *stricken* (נָגוּעַ; cf. נֶגַע, Lev. xiii. 13), smitten of God, and afflicted." Ps. xxii. 6, 7, "I am a worm, and no man. . . . . All they that see me laugh me to scorn;" 15—17, "My strength is dried up like a potsherd. . . . I may tell all my bones they stand staring and looking upon me."

[3] See Keim, i. 460, who quotes Just. Mart. *c. Tryph.* xiv. 36, &c., ἀειδής, ἄδοξος, ἄτιμος;[103] Clem. *Strom.* ii. 440, *Paed.* iii. 1, 3, τὴν ὄψιν αἰσχρός;[104] Tert. *De Car. Christ.* 9, "Nec humanae honestatis corpus fuit, nedum caelestis claritatis;"[105] Orig. *c. Cels.* vi. 75, τὸ σῶμα μικρὸν καὶ δυσειδὲς καὶ ἀγενὲς ἦν.[106]

this gave rise to a wide-spread fancy, of which there are many traces, that He who healed so many leprosies was Himself a leper![1]

Shocked, on the other hand, by these revolting fancies, there were many who held that Jesus, in His earthly features, reflected the charm and beauty of David, His great ancestor; and St. Jerome and St. Augustine preferred to apply to Him the words of Psalm xlv. 2, 3, "Thou art fairer than the children of men."[2] It was natural that, in the absence of positive indications, this view should command a deeper sympathy, and it gave rise both to the current descriptions of Christ, and also to those ideals, so full of mingled majesty and tenderness in —

> "That face
> How beautiful, if sorrow had not made
> Sorrow more beautiful than beauty's self,"

which we see in the great pictures of Fra Angelico, of Michael Angelo, of Leonardo da Vinci, of Raphael, and of Titian.[3]

Independently of all tradition, we may believe with reverent conviction that there could have been nothing mean or repugnant — that there must, as St. Jerome says, have been "something starry" — in the form which enshrined an Eternal Divinity and an Infinite Holiness. All true beauty is but "the sacrament of goodness," and a conscience so stainless, a spirit so full of harmony, a life so purely noble, could not but express itself in the bearing, could not but be reflected in the face, of the Son of Man. We do not indeed find any allusion to this charm of aspect, as we do in the description of the young High-priest Aristobulus whom Herod murdered; but neither, on the other hand, do we find in the language of His enemies a single word or allusion which might have been founded on an unworthy appearance. He of whom John bore witness as the Christ — He whom the multitude would gladly have seized that He might be their king — He whom the city saluted with triumphal

---

[1] In the Talmud *Cod. Sanhedrin,* to the question, "What is the name of the Messias?" it is answered "*The Leper.*" (Pearson *On the Creed,* Art. iv.) See the story of St. Francis in Sir J. Stephen's *Essays on Eccles. Biog.* i. 99 ; Montalembert, *St. Eliz. de Hongrie,* ii. 93—99 (in both of which stories Christ appears as a leper). Hence the extraordinary devotion bestowed on this afflicted class by St. Edmund of Canterbury, St. Louis, St. James de Chantal, &c. In fact, leprosy came to be regarded as a gift of God. In 1541 Henry, organist of Coblenz, begged the council of the city to give a place in the hospital to his son. "Somit dem Us-satz von Gott dem almechtigen begabt."[108] In 1189 Clement III. addressed a bull " dilectis filiis leprosis."[109]

[2] Aug. *in Ep. Joh.,* tract. ix. 9.

[3] See Excursus IV., "Traditional Descriptions of the Appearance of Our Lord."

shouts as the Son of David — He to whom women ministered with
such deep devotion, and whose aspect, even in the troubled images
of a dream, had inspired a Roman lady with interest and awe — He
whose mere word caused Philip and Matthew and many others to
leave all and follow Him — He whose one glance broke into an agony
of repentance the heart of Peter — He before whose presence those
possessed with devils were alternately agitated into frenzy and calmed
into repose, and at whose question, in the very crisis of His weakness
and betrayal, His most savage enemies shrank and fell prostrate in
the moment of their most infuriated wrath [1] — such an One as this
could not have been without the personal majesty of a Prophet and
a Priest. All the facts of His life speak convincingly of that
strength, and endurance, and dignity, and electric influence, which
none could have exercised without a large share of human, no less
than of spiritual, gifts. " Certainly," says St. Jerome, " a flame of
fire and starry brightness flashed from His eye, and the majesty of
the Godhead shone in His face."

The third day after the return from the wilderness seems to have
been spent by Jesus in intercourse with His new disciples. On the
fourth day He wished to start [2] for His return to Galilee, and on the
journey fell in with another young fisherman, Philip of Bethsaida.
Alone of the apostles Philip had a Greek name, derived, perhaps,
from the tetrarch Philip, since the custom of naming children after
reigning princes has always been a common one.[3] If so, he must at
this time have been under thirty. Possibly his Greek name indicates
his familiarity with some of the Greek-speaking population who lived
mingled with the Galilæans on the shores of Gennesareth ; and this
may account for the fact, that he, rather than any of the other Apostles, was appealed to by the Greeks who, in the last week of His life,
wished to see our Lord. One word — the one pregnant invitation,
"*Follow me !* "— was sufficient to attach to Jesus for ever the gentle
and simple-minded Apostle, whom in all probability He had previously known.

The next day a fifth neophyte was added to that sacred and happy

---

[1] John xviii. 6. Cf. Luke iv. 30.

[2] In using the phrase ἠθέλησεν ἐξελθεῖν,[110] it is evident that St. John had in
his mind some slight circumstance unknown to us.

[3] The name Andrew is of Greek origin, but Lightfoot (*Harmony*, Luke v. 10)
shows that it was in use among the Jews. Thomas was also called by the Greek
name Didymus, or " Twin ; " but we know no name of Philip except this Greek
one. The ἀπὸ Βηθσαδίας probably means " a native of ; " for Greswell's attempt
to distinguish ἀπὸ from ἐκ in this sense is untenable.

136 *THE LIFE OF CHRIST.*

band. Eager to communicate the rich discovery which he had made, Philip sought out his friend Nathanael, exercising thereby the divinest prerogative of friendship, which consists in the communication to others of all that we have ourselves experienced to be most divine. Nathanael, in the list of apostles, is generally, and almost indubitably, identified with Bartholomew; for Bartholomew is less a name than a designation — "*Bar-Tolmai*, the son of Tolmai; " and while Nathanael is only in one other place mentioned under this name (John xxi. 2), Bartholomew (of whom, on any other supposition, we should know nothing whatever) is, in the list of apostles, almost invariably associated with Philip.[1] As his home was at Cana of Galilee, the son of Tolmai might easily have become acquainted with the young fishermen of Gennesareth. And yet so deep was the retirement in which up to this time Jesus had lived His life, that though Nathanael knew Philip, he knew nothing of Christ. The simple mind of Philip seemed to find a pleasure in contrasting the grandeur of His office with the meanness of His birth: "We have found Him of whom Moses in the Law, and the Prophets, did write;" whom think you? — a young Herodian prince? — a young Asmonæan priest? — some burning light from the schools of Shammai or Hillel? — some passionate young Emír from the followers of Judas of Gamala? — no, but "*Jesus of Nazareth, the son of Joseph.*"

Nathanael seems to have felt the contrast. He caught at the local designation. It may be, as legend says, that he was a man of higher position than the rest of the Apostles.[2] It has been usually considered that his answer was proverbial; but perhaps it was a passing allusion to the word *nazora*, "despicable;" or it may merely have implied "*Nazareth*, that obscure and ill-reputed town in its little untrodden valley — can anything good come from *thence?*" The answer is in the same words which our Lord had addressed to John and Andrew. Philip was an apt scholar, and he too said, "*Come and see.*"

To-day, too, that question — "*Can any good thing come out of Nazareth?*" — is often repeated, and the one sufficient answer —

---

[1] Some make Tolmai a mere abbreviation of Ptolomæus. On the identity of Nathanael with Bartholomew, see Ewald, *Gesch. Christus*, 327. Donaldson (*Jashar*, p. 9) thinks that Nathanael was Philip's brother.

[2] " Non Petro vili piscatori *Bartholomaeus nobilis* anteponitur "[111] (Jerome, *Ep. ad Eustoch.*). Hence he is usually represented in mediæval art clothed in a purple mantle, adorned with precious stones; but John xxi. 2 is alone sufficient to invalidate the tradition.

almost the only possible answer — is now, as it then was, " *Come and see*." Then it meant, come and see One who speaks as never man spake ; come and see One who, though He be but the Carpenter of Nazareth, yet overawes the souls of all who approach Him — seeming by His mere presence to reveal the secrets of all hearts, yet drawing to Him even the most sinful with a sense of yearning love ; come and see One from whom there seems to breathe forth the irresistible charm of a sinless purity, the unapproachable beauty of a Divine life. " Come and see," said Philip, convinced in his simple faithful heart that to see Jesus was to know Him, and to know was to love, and to love was to adore. In this sense, indeed, we can say " come and see " no longer ; for since the blue heavens closed on the visions which were vouchsafed to St. Stephen and St. Paul, His earthly form has been visible no more. But there is another sense, no less powerful for conviction, in which it still suffices to say, in answer to all doubts, " Come and see." Come and see a dying world revivified, a decrepit world regenerated, an aged world rejuvenescent ; come and see the darkness illuminated, the despair dispelled ; come and see tenderness brought into the cell of the imprisoned felon, and liberty to the fettered slave ; come and see the poor, and the ignorant, and the many, emancipated for ever from the intolerable thraldom of the rich, the learned, and the few ; come and see hospitals and orphanages rising in their permanent mercy beside the crumbling ruins of colossal amphitheatres which once reeked with human blood ; come and see the obscene symbols of an universal degradation obliterated indignantly from the purified abodes ; come and see the dens of lust and tyranny transformed into sweet and happy homes, defiant atheists into believing Christians, rebels into children, and pagans into saints. Ay, come and see the majestic acts of one great drama continued through nineteen Christian centuries ; and as you see them all tending to one great development, long predetermined in the Council of the Divine Will — as you learn in reverent humility that even apparent Chance is in reality *the daughter of Forethought*, as well as, for those who thus recognize her nature, *the sister of Order and Persuasion* [1] — as you hear the voice of your Saviour searching, with the loving accents of a compassion

---

[1] [Τύχα] Εὐνομίας τε καὶ Πειθοῦς ἀδελφὰ καὶ Προμαθείας θυγάτηρ [112] (Alcman, f. 55, ed. Bergk.). " The threefold offspring of Forethought which is described in this noble fragment, appears to represent three of the cardinal relations in which we may regard the working of Providence. It first appears as Chance in regard to its occurrence ; it next works Persuasion as men bow to its decrees ; and at last it issues in Order " (Westcott, *Charact. of the Gosp. Miracles*, p. 35).

which will neither strive nor cry, your very reins and heart — it may
be that you too will unlearn the misery of doubt, and exclaim in
calm and happy confidence, with the pure and candid Nathanael,
" *Rabbi, thou art the Son of God, thou art the King of Israel !* "

The fastidious reluctance of Nathanael was very soon dispelled.
Jesus, as He saw him coming, recognized that the seal of God was
upon his forehead, and said of him, " Behold a true Israelite, in whom
guile is not." " Whence dost thou recognize me ? " asked Nathanael ;
and then came that heart-searching answer, " Before that Philip
called thee, whilst thou wert under the fig-tree, I saw thee."

It was the custom of pious Jews — a custom approved by the Talmud — to study their *crishma*, or office of daily prayer, under a fig-
tree ;[1] and some have imagined that there is something significant
in the fact of the Apostle having been summoned from the shade of
a tree which symbolized Jewish ordinances and Jewish traditions, but
which was beginning already to cumber the ground.[2] But though
something interesting and instructive may often be derived from the
poetic insight of a chastened imagination which can thus observe
allegories which lie involved in the simplest facts, yet no such flash
of sudden perception could alone have accounted for the agitated
intensity of Nathanael's reply. Every one must have been struck, at
first sight, with the apparent disproportionateness between the cause
and the effect. How apparently inadequate was that quiet allusion
to the lonely session of silent thought under the fig-tree, to produce
the instantaneous adhesion, the henceforth inalienable loyalty, of this
" fusile Apostle " to the Son of God, the King of Israel ! But for
the true explanation of this instantaneity of conviction, we must look
deeper ; and then, if I mistake not, we shall see in this incident
another of those indescribable touches of reality which have been to
so many powerful minds the most irresistible internal evidence to
establish the historic truthfulness of the Fourth Gospel.

There are moments when the grace of God stirs sensibly in the
human heart ; when the soul seems to rise upon the eagle-wings of
hope and prayer into the heaven of heavens ; when caught up, as it
were, into God's very presence, we see and hear things unspeakable.

---

[1] *Beresh. Rabba,* f. 62, quoted by Sepp. The accusative, ὑπὸ τὴν συκῆν, [113]
where we should have expected the dative, seems to imply that he had *purposely
gone there* for prayer and meditation. Perhaps some inference as to the time of
year may be drawn from this circumstance.

[2] See 1 Kings iv. 25 ; Mic. iv. 4 ; Zech. iii. 10 ; Matt. xxi. 20 ; Luke xiii. 7.

At such moments we live a lifetime ; for emotions such as these annihilate all time ; they —

> " Crowd Eternity into an hour,
> Or stretch an hour into Eternity."

At such moments we are nearer to God ; we seem to know Him and be known of Him ; and if it were possible for any man at such a moment to see into our souls, he would know all that is greatest and most immortal in our beings. But to see us then is impossible to man ; it is possible only to Him whose hand should lead, whose right hand should guide us, even if we could take the wings of the morning and fly into the uttermost parts of the sea. And such a crisis of emotion must the guileless Israelite have known as he sat and prayed and mused in silence under his fig-tree. To the consciousness of such a crisis — a crisis which could only be known to One to whom it was given to read the very secrets of the heart — our Lord appealed. Let him who has had a similar experience say how he would regard a living man who could reveal to him that he had at such a moment looked into and fathomed the emotions of his heart. That such solitary musings — such penetrating, even in this life, " behind the vail "— such raptures into the third heaven during which the soul strives to transcend the limitations of space and time while it communes, face to face, with the Eternal and the Unseen — such sudden kindlings of celestial lightning which seem to have fused all that is meanest and basest within us in an instant and for ever — that these supreme crises *are* among the recorded experiences of the Christian life, rests upon indisputable evidence of testimony and of fact. And if any one of my readers has ever known this spasm of divine change which annihilates the old and in the same moment creates or re-creates a new-born soul, such a one, at least, will understand the thrill of electric sympathy, the arrow-point of intense conviction, that shot that very instant through the heart of Nathanael, and brought him, as it were, at once upon his knees with the exclamation, "*Rabbi, thou art the Son of God, thou art the King of Israel !* "

We scarcely hear of Nathanael again. His seems to have been one of those calm, retiring, contemplative souls, whose whole sphere of existence lies not here, but —

> " Where, beyond these voices, there is peace."

It was a life of which the world sees nothing, because it was " *hid* with Christ in God ;" but of this we may be sure, that never till the day of his martyrdom, or even during his martyr agonies, did he forget those quiet words which showed that his "Lord had searched him out and known him, and comprehended his thoughts long before." Not once, doubtless, but on many and many a future day,[1] was the promise fulfilled for him and for his companions, that, with the eye of faith, they should "see the heavens opened, and the angels of God ascending and descending upon the Son of Man." [2]

---

[1] ὄψεσθε (א, B, L, &c.). The promise is obviously spiritual, as the ablest Fathers saw. A striking passage of Luther's to this effect is quoted in Alford. The word " *hereafter* shall ye see," &c. (John i. 51), meant "*from this time forth,*" and therefore was a correct translation of ἀπ' ἄρτι at the time when our Version was made. Compare Matt. xxvi. 64, and the petition " that we may *hereafter* live a godly, righteous, and sober life "—*i. e.*, not at some future time, but " from this day forward." The reading, however, is very dubious, and B, L, as well as several versions, and Origen, &c., omit it. The 'Αμὴν is found twenty-five times in St. John, and always doubled. Cf. Isa. lxv. 16 (where God is called the " God of אָמֵן ") ; 2 Cor. i. 20 ; Rev. iii. 14. For the Messianic title Son of Man — a title describing the Messiah as the essential representative of every child in the great human family of God — see Dan. vii. 13, 14 ; Rev. i. 13, &c.

[2] " Son of Man," *Ben-adam*, may, in its general sense, be applied to any man (Job xxv. 6 ; Ps. cxliv. 3, &c.), but it is applied in a *special* sense to Ezekiel in the Old Testament, and to Christ in the New. One very observable fact is, that though used of Ezekiel nearly ninety times, he does not once apply the title to himself ; and though used about eighty times of Christ, it is never used by any but Himself, except in passages which describe His heavenly exaltation (Acts vii. 56 ; Rev. i. 13—20 ; xiv. 14). It seems further clear that though Ezekiel is called Ben-Adam (perhaps, in the midst of his revelations, to remind him of his own nothingness, μέμνησο ἄνθρωπος ὤν), the title in the New Testament, being clearly drawn from Daniel (vii. 13), is the Chaldee *Bar-enôsh*, which represents humanity in its greatest frailty and humility, and is a significant declaration that the exaltation of Christ in His kingly and judicial office is due to His previous self-humiliation in His human nature (Phil. ii. 5—11). (Bishop Wordsworth s. v. in Smith's *Dict. of Bible*, iii. 1359, who quotes Cypr. *De Idol. Vanit.*, p. 538, " hominem induit, quem perducat ad Patrem," [114] and Aug., *Serm.* 121, " Filius Dei factus est filius hominis, ut vos, qui eratis filii hominis, efficeremini filii Dei.[115] The term *beni ish*, found in Ps. iv. 3, &c., means " filii *viri*," [116] not " filii *hominis.*" [117] Bengel, on this verse (John i. 51), referring to 1 Cor. xv. 47, says, " Unus hic nempe homo est, quem Adamus, post lapsum, expectavit." [118]

CHAPTER XI.

THE FIRST MIRACLE.

" Unde rubor vestris et non sua purpura lymphis ?,
Quae rosa mirantes tam nova mutat aquas ?
Numen, convivae, praesens agnoscite numen :
Lympha pudica Deum vidit et erubuit." [119] — CRASHAW.

" On the third day," says St. John, " there was a marriage in Cana of Galilee." Writing with a full knowledge and vivid recollection of every fact that took place during those divinely-memorable days, he gives his indications of time as though all were equally familiar with them. The third day has been understood in different manners : it is simplest to understand it as the third after the departure of Jesus for Galilee. If He were travelling expeditiously He might stop on the first night (supposing him to follow the ordinary route) at Shiloh or at Shechem ; on the second at En-Gannim ; on the third, crossing the plain of Jezreel, He could easily reach Nazareth,[1] and finding that His mother and brethren were not there, might, in an hour and a half longer, reach Cana in time for the ceremonies of an Oriental wedding.[2]

It is well known that those ceremonies began at twilight. It was the custom in Palestine, no less than in Greece,

" To bear away
The bride from home at blushing shut of day,"

---

[1] The author has done this himself, and therefore knows that it is easily possible, although it requires quick travelling. There would, however, be nothing on this occasion to make Jesus linger, and possibly he was journeying with the express intention of being present at the marriage feast. The fact that a wedding will soon take place is usually known throughout an Eastern village, and Jesus might easily have heard about it from one of His disciples, or from some other Galilæan pilgrim.

[2] It will be seen from this paragraph that I consider Kefr Kenna, and not the so-called Kâna el-Jalîl, to be the real Cana. On this point I entirely agree with De Saulcy as against Dr. Robinson. If I am right in the explanation of " the third day," it will be an additional argument in favor of this view. I say " the so-called Kâna el-Jalîl," because certainly the more ordinary name of this ruined

or even later, far on into the night,[1] covered from head to foot in her loose and flowing veil, garlanded with flowers, and dressed in her fairest robes. She was heralded by torchlight, with songs and dances, and the music of the drum and flute, to the bridegroom's home. She was attended by the maidens of her village, and the bridegroom came to meet her with his youthful friends. Legend says that Nathanael was on this occasion the paranymph, whose duty it was to escort the bride; but the presence of Mary, who must have left Nazareth on purpose to be present at the wedding, seems to show that one of the bridal pair was some member of the Holy Family. Jesus too was invited, and His disciples, and the use of the singular ($\dot{\varepsilon}\varkappa\lambda\dot{\eta}\theta\eta$ [120]) implies that they were invited for His sake, not He for theirs. It is not likely, therefore, that Nathanael, who had only heard the name of Jesus two days before, had anything to do with the marriage. All positive conjecture is idle; but the fact that the Virgin evidently took a leading position in the house, and commands the servants in a tone of authority, renders it not improbable that this may have been the wedding of one of her nephews, the sons of Alphæus, or even of one of her daughters, "the sisters of Jesus," [2] to whom tradition gives the names Esther and Thamar. That Joseph himself was dead is evident from the complete silence of the Evangelists, who after Christ's first visit to Jerusalem as a boy, make no further mention of his name.[3]

Whether the marriage festival lasted for seven days, as was usual

---

and deserted village is Khurbet Kâna, and Thomson (*The Land and the Book*) could find no trace worth mentioning of the other name, which rests solely on Robinson's authority; moreover, the name Kenna el-Jalîl is certainly sometimes given to Kefr Kenna, as Osborne testifies. The philological difficulty is by no means insuperable; tradition too, fairly tested, is in favor of Kefr Kenna; and its position (far nearer to Nazareth and Capernaum than Khurbet Kâna, and lying on the direct road) is in every respect more in accordance with the indications of the Gospel narrative than its more remote and desolate rival. Moreover, at Kefr Kenna there are distinct traces of antiquity, and at the other place there are none. If in fact it be a mere hallucination to suppose that Khurbet Kâna is at all known under the designation of Kâna el-Jalîl, more than half of the reasons for identifying it with Cana of Galilee at once fall to the ground. Now on this point Mr. Thomson is far more likely to be right than Dr. Robinson, from his long residence in Palestine, and great knowledge of Arabic.

[1] When in Palestine I arrived at El Jîb about sunset, and found that the festivities of a wedding were just commencing. They lasted till late at night.

[2] Matt. xiii. 56. See, however, Luke iv. 22; John vi. 42.

[3] The notion that the bridegroom was Simon the Canaanite, arises from a complete, but not unnatural, error about his name. An improbable tradition followed by St. Jerome and St. Bonaventura, and adopted by the Mahometans (D'Herbelot s. v. "Johannes"), represents that the bridegroom was the Evangelist St. John.

among those who could afford it,[1] or only for one or two, as was the case among the poorer classes, we cannot tell; but at some period of the entertainment the wine suddenly ran short.[2] None but those who know how sacred in the East is the duty of lavish hospitality, and how passionately the obligation to exercise it to the utmost is felt, can realize the gloom which this incident would have thrown over the occasion, or the misery and mortification which it would have caused to the wedded pair. They would have felt it to be, as in the East it would still be felt to be, a bitter and indelible disgrace.

Now the presence of Jesus and his five disciples may well have been the cause of this unexpected deficiency. The invitation, as we have seen, was originally intended for Jesus alone, nor could the youthful bridegroom in Cana of Galilee have been in the least aware that during the last four days Jesus had won the allegiance of five disciples. It is probable that no provision had been made for this increase of numbers, and that it was their unexpected presence which caused the deficiency in this simple household.[3] Moreover, it is hardly probable that, coming from a hasty journey of ninety miles, the little band could, even had their means permitted it, have conformed to the common Jewish custom of bringing with them wine and other provisions to contribute to the mirthfulness of the wedding feast.

Under these circumstances, therefore, there was a special reason why the mother of Jesus should say to Him, " They have no wine." The remark was evidently a pointed one, and its import could not be misunderstood. None knew, as Mary knew, who her son was ; yet for thirty long years of patient waiting for this manifestation, she had but seen him grow as other children grow, and live, in sweetness indeed and humility and grace of sinless wisdom, like a tender plant before God, but in all other respects as other youths have lived, pre-eminent only in utter stainlessness. But now he was thirty years old ; the voice of the great Prophet, with whose fame the nation rang, had proclaimed Him to be the promised Christ; He was being publicly attended by disciples who acknowledged Him as Rabbi and Lord. Here was a difficulty to be met ; an act of true kindness to be performed ; a disgrace to be averted from friends whom he loved — and that too a disgrace to which His own presence and that of His disciples had unwittingly contributed. Was not His hour yet come ?

---

[1] Judg. xiv. 12 ; Tob. xi. 19.

[2] John ii. 3, ὑστερήσαντος οἴνου.[121]

[3] In some MSS. of the Vetus Itala are added the words " Et factum est per multam turbam vocatorum vinum consummari." [122]

Who could tell what He might do, if He were only made aware of the trouble which threatened to interrupt the feast? Might not some band of hymning angels, like the radiant visions, who had heralded His birth, receive His bidding to change that humble marriage-feast into a scene of heaven? Might it not be that even now He would lead them into His banquet-house, and His banner over them be love?

Her faith was strong, her motives pure, except perhaps what has been called "the slightest possible touch of the purest womanly, motherly anxiety (we know no other word) prompting in her the desire to see *her Son* honored in her presence." [1] And her Son's hour *had* nearly come: but it was necessary now, at once, for ever, for that Son to show to her that henceforth he was not Jesus the Son of Mary, but the Christ the Son of God; that as regarded His great work and mission, as regarded His Eternal Being, the significance of the beautiful relationship had passed away; that His thoughts were not as her thoughts, neither His ways her ways. [2] It could not have been done in a manner more decisive, yet at the same time more entirely tender.

" *Woman, what have I to do with thee ?* " The words at first sound harsh, and almost repellant in their roughness and brevity ; but that is the fault partly of our version, partly of our associations. He does not call her " mother," because, in circumstances such as these, she was His mother no longer ; but the address " Woman " (Γύναι) was so respectful that it might be, and was, addressed to the queenliest ; [3] and so gentle that it might be, and was, addressed at

---

[1] Stier, i. 61, E. Tr.   The germ of the remark is to be found in Chrysostom.

[2] Similarly in Luke ii. 49, the authority of Joseph is wholly subordinated to a truer and loftier one (see p. 83).   The same truth is distinctly shadowed forth in Matt. xii. 48—50 ; Luke xi. 27, 28. St. Bernard, in illustration of this desire of our Lord to indicate that the spiritual life must not be disturbed by earthly relationships, tells a striking story of a hermit who, on being consulted by his brother, referred him to the advice of another brother who had died some time before. " But he is dead," said the other with surprise. " So am I also," replied the hermit. (S. Bernard, *Serm.* 2 *in Dom.* 1 *post Epiphan.*) It may have been their inability to appreciate this very fact that produced a sort of alienation between Christ and His earthly brethren as regards the entire plan of His Messianic manifestation, and made Him imply that even " *in His own house*" a prophet is without honor (Matt. xiii. 57).

[3] As by the Emperor Augustus to Cleopatra, Θάρσει, ὦ γύναι, καὶ θυμὸν ἔχε ἀγαθόν [123] (Dio Cass. *Hist.* li. 12); by the chorus to Queen Clytemnestra (Æsch. *Ag.* 1603); and not unfrequently to princesses in Greek tragedy.

the tenderest moments to the most fondly loved.[1]   And " what have
I to do with thee ? " is a literal version of a common Aramaic phrase
(*mah li velák*), which, while it sets aside a suggestion and waives all
further discussion of it, is yet perfectly consistent with the most delicate courtesy, and the most feeling consideration.[2]

Nor can we doubt that even the slight check involved in these
quiet words was still more softened by the look and accent with which
they were spoken, and which are often sufficient to prevent far harsher
utterances from inflicting any pain.   For with undiminished faith,
and with no trace of pained feeling, Mary said to the servants — over
whom it is clear she was exercising some authority — " Whatever He
says to you, do it at once." [3]

The first necessity after a journey in the East is to wash the feet,
and before a meal to wash the hands ; and to supply these wants
there were standing (as still is usual), near the entrance of the house,
six large stone water-jars, with their orifices filled with bunches of
fresh green leaves to keep the water cool.   Each of these jars contained two or three *baths* [4] of water, and Jesus bade the servants at
once fill them to the brim.[5]   They did so, and He then ordered them
to draw out the contents in smaller vessels,[6] and carry it to the guest
who, according to the festive custom of the time, had been elected

---

[1] As, for instance, by Jesus to Mary Magdalene, in the garden, " *Woman*, why
weepest thou? whom seekest thou?" (John xx. 15); by the angels (Id. 13); and
by Jesus to his mother on the cross, " Woman, behold thy son " (John xix. 26).
Our Lord probably spoke, however, in Aramaic and here the word would be אנתה,
not אישה, *i. e.*, more like *domina* than *femina*.

[2] See for other instances of the phrase, 2 Sam. xvi. 10; xix. 22 ; 1 Kings xvii.
18; Judg. xi. 12; 2 Kings iii. 13; Josh. xxii. 24.

[3] ποιήσατε (John ii. 5).   For the expression, " Mine hour is not yet come," see
the instance in which, with a very similar desire to check the unwarranted suggestions of His earthly relatives, He uses it to His brethren who wished to hurry
His visit to Jerusalem (John vii. 6, where, however, the word is καιρός, not ὥρα)·
Mr. Sanday compares the passage with Matt. xv. 21—28.   " There too a petition
is first refused, and then granted, and there too the petitioner seems to divine that
it will be " (*Authorship of the Fourth Gosp.*, p. 50).

[4] μετρηταὶ.   This is used in the LXX. version of 2 Chron. iv. 5 as a rendering of the Hebrew בת, and was equal to about 7½ gallons.   It is, however, hard to
suppose that each of these stone jars held from fifteen to twenty-two gallons, so
that perhaps μετρητὴς (as Lange suggests) may be the Roman *amphora* = five
gallons.   A " firkin " (E. V.) is eight gallons.

[5] John ii. 7, γεμίσατε.

[6] ἀντλήσατε.   Cf. John iv. 7.   Prof. Westcott thinks that the exact words
exclude the all but universal notion, that *all the water in the six jars* was turned
into wine (*Characteristics of the Gospel Miracles*, p. 15).

"governor of the feast." [1] Knowing nothing of what had taken place, he mirthfully observed that in offering the good wine last, the bridegroom had violated the common practice of banquets. This was Christ's first miracle, and *thus*, with a definite and symbolic purpose,[2] did He manifest His glory, and His disciples believed on Him.

It was His first miracle, yet how unlike all that we should have expected; how simply unobtrusive, how divinely calm! The method, indeed, of the miracle — which is far more wonderful in character than the ordinary miracles of healing — transcends our powers of conception; yet it was not done with any pomp of circumstance, or blaze of adventitious glorification. Men in these days have presumptuously talked as though it were God's duty — the duty of Him to whom the sea and the mountains are a very little thing, and before whose eyes the starry heaven is but as one white gleam in the "intense inane"— to perform His miracles before a circle of competent *savans!* Conceivably it might be so had it been intended that miracles should be the sole, or even the main, credentials of Christ's authority; but to the belief of Christendom the Son of God would still be the Son of God even if, like John, He had done no miracle. The miracles of Christ were miracles addressed, not to a cold and sceptic curiosity, but to a loving and humble faith. They needed not the acuteness of the impostor, or the self-assertion of the thaumaturge. They were indeed the signs — almost, we had said, the accidental signs — of His divine mission; but their primary object was the alleviation of human suffering, or the illustration of sacred truths, or, as in this instance, the increase of innocent joy. An obscure village, an ordinary wedding, a humble home, a few faithful peasant guests — such a scene, and no splendid amphitheatre or stately audience, beheld one of Christ's greatest miracles of power. And in these respects the circumstances of the First Miracle are exactly analogous to the supernatural events recorded of Christ's birth. In the total unlikeness of this to all that we should have imagined —in its absolute contrast with anything which legend would have invented — in all, in short, which most offends the unbeliever, we see

---

[1] The custom may have been originally borrowed from the Greeks (συμποσιάρ-χης, *arbiter bibendi, magister convivii*,[124] &c.), but it had long been familiar to the Jews, and the ἀρχιτρίκλινος [125] here acts exactly as he is advised to do by the son of Sirach: " When thou hast done all thy office, take thy place, that thou mayest be merry with them, and receive a crown for thy well-ordering of the feast " (Ecclus. xxxii. 1, 2).

[2] John ii. 11, ταύτην ἐποίησε ἀρχήν (this *as* a beginning, A, B, L, &c.), not τὴν ἀρχήν.

but fresh confirmation that we are reading the words of soberness and truth.

A miracle is a miracle, and we see no possible advantage in trying to understand the *means* by which it was wrought. In accepting the evidence for it — and it is for each man to be fully persuaded in his own mind, and to accept or to reject at his pleasure, perhaps even it may prove to be at his peril — we are avowedly accepting the evidence for something which transcends, though it by no means necessarily supersedes, the ordinary laws by which Nature works. What is gained — in what single respect does the miracle become, so to speak, easier or more comprehensible — by supposing, with Olshausen, that we have here only an accelerated process of nature ; or with Neander (apparently), that the water was magnetized ; or with Lange (apparently), that the guests were in a state of supernatural exaltation ?[1] Let those who find it intellectually possible, or spiritually advantageous, freely avail themselves of such hypotheses if they see their way to do so : to us they seem, not "irreverent," not "rationalistic," not "dangerous," but simply embarrassing and needless. To denounce them as unfaithful concessions to the spirit of scepticism may suit the exigencies of a violent and Pharisaic theology, but is unworthy of that calm charity which should be the fairest fruit of Christian faith. In matters of faith it ought to be to every one of us "a very small thing to be judged of you or of man's judgment ; " we ought to believe, or disbelieve, or modify belief, with sole reference to that which, in our hearts and consciences, we feel to be the Will of God ; and it is by His judgment, and by His alone, that we should care to stand or to fall. We as little claim a right to scathe the rejector of miracles by abuse and anathema, as we admit *his* right to sneer at us for imbecility or hypocrisy. Jesus has taught to all men, whether they accept or reject Him, the lessons of charity and sweetness ; and what the believer and unbeliever alike can do, is

---

[1] Olshausen, *Comment. on the Gospels,* iii. 368, following Augustine, "Ipse fecit vinum in nuptiis qui omni anno hoc facit in vitibus." [126] Neander, *Life of Jesus Christ,* E. Tr., p. 176. It is to be regretted that this "acceleration" hypothesis has been received with favor by some eminent English divines ; *Nature alone,* as a friend remarks, will never, whatever time you give her, make thirty imperial gallons of wine without at least ten pounds avoirdupois of carbon. Ewald beautifully, but with a perhaps intentional vagueness, says, "Wir würden uns diesen wein der seit jener zeit auch uns noch immer fliessen kann, selbst übel verwässern, wenn wir hier in groben sinne fragen wollten wiedenn aus blossem wasser im augenblicke wein werden könne : soll denn das wasser im besten sinne des wortes nicht überall auch jezt noch zu weine werden wo Sein geist in voller kraft thätig ist ?" [127] (*Gesch. Christ.* p. 329).

calmly, temperately, justly, and with perfect and solemn sincerity —
knowing how deep are the feelings involved, and how vast the issues
at stake between us — to state the reason for the belief that is in
him. And this being so, I would say that if we once understand
that the word Nature has little or no meaning unless it be made to
include the idea of its Author ; if we once realize the fact, which all
science teaches us, that the very simplest and most elementary oper-
ation of the laws of Nature is infinitely beyond the comprehension
of our most exalted intelligence ; if we once believe that the Divine
Providence of God is no far-off abstraction, but a living and loving
care over the lives of man ; lastly, if we once believe that Christ was
the only-begotten Son of God, the Word of God who came to reveal
and declare His Father to mankind, then there is nothing in any
Gospel miracle to shock our faith : we shall regard the miracles of
Christ as resulting from the fact of His Being and His mission, no
less naturally and inevitably than the rays of light stream outwards
from the sun. They were, to use the favorite expression of St. John,
not merely " portents " ($\tau\acute{\epsilon}\rho\alpha\tau\alpha$), or powers ($\delta\upsilon\nu\acute{\alpha}\mu\epsilon\iota\varsigma$), or signs
($\sigma\eta\mu\epsilon\tilde{\iota}\alpha$), but they were works ($\acute{\epsilon}\rho\gamma\alpha$), the ordinary and inevitable
works (whenever He chose to exercise them) of One whose very
Existence was the highest miracle of all.[1] For our faith is that He
was sinless ; and to borrow the words of a German poet, " one might
have thought that the miracle of miracles was to have created the
world such as it is ; yet it is a far greater miracle to have lived a perfectly pure life therein." The greatest of modern philosophers said
that there were two things which overwhelmed his soul with awe and
astonishment, " the starry heaven above, and the moral law within ; "
but to these has been added a third reality no less majestic — the fulfilment of the moral law *without* us in the Person of Jesus Christ.[2]
That fulfilment makes us believe that He was indeed Divine ; and
if He were Divine, we have no further astonishment left when we
are taught that He did on earth that which can be done by the
Power of God alone.

But there are two characteristics of this first miracle which we
ought to notice.

One is its divine unselfishness. His ministry is to be a ministry
of joy and peace ; His sanction is to be given not to a crushing
asceticism, but to a genial innocence ; His approval, not to a compulsory celibacy, but to a sacred union. He who, to appease His

---

[1] See Abp. Trench on *Miracles*, p. 8.

[2] See Ullmann, *Sinlessness of Jesus*, E. Tr. pp. 181—193.

own sore hunger would not turn the stones of the wilderness into bread, gladly exercises, for the sake of others, His transforming power; and but six or seven days afterwards, relieves the perplexity and sorrow of a humble wedding feast by turning water into wine. The first miracle of Moses was, in stern retribution, to turn the river of a guilty nation into blood; the first of Jesus to fill the water-jars of an innocent family with wine.

And the other is its symbolical character. Like nearly all the miracles of Christ, it combines the characteristics of a work of mercy, an emblem, and a prophecy. The world gives its best first, and afterwards all the dregs and bitterness; but Christ came to turn the lower into the richer and sweeter, the Mosaic law into the perfect law of liberty, the baptism of John into the baptism with the Holy Ghost and with fire, the self-denials of a painful isolation into the self-denials of a happy home, sorrow and sighing into hope and blessing, and water into wine. And thus the "holy estate" which Christ adorned and beautified with His presence and first miracle in Cana of Galilee, foreshadows the mystical union between Christ and His Church; and the common element which He thus miraculously changed becomes a type of our life on earth transfigured and ennobled by the anticipated joys of heaven — a type of that wine which He shall drink new with us in the kingdom of God, at the marriage supper of the Lamb.[1]

---

[1] A large school of English Apologists have appealed to the miracles of Christ as proving His mission, and to the Gospels as proving the miracles. This is not the view of the writer, who, in common he believes with many of the more recent authorities who have dealt with the subject, regards "Christianity and Christendom" as the strongest external proofs of the historical reality of that which the Gospels relate. The Gospels supply us with a *vera caussa* for that which otherwise would be to us an inexplicable enigma. This was the argument which I endeavored to state as forcibly as I could in the Hulsean Lectures of 1870 — "The Witness of History to Christ." But I say "the strongest *external* proof," because those who are so ready to assume that any one who believes, for instance, in the Incarnation must necessarily be either morally a hypocrite, or intellectually an imbecile, ought not to forget how strong is that *preparation for belief* which every Christian derives from the experiences of his own life, and from that which he believes to be the Voice of God speaking to his heart, and confirming all which he has learnt of God through Christ, and Christ alone. The force of *this* evidence is indeed valueless as an argument against others; on the other hand, they should bear in mind that their denial of its force in their own case does not invalidate its force in the minds of those for whom it exists.

CHAPTER XII.

THE SCENE OF THE MINISTRY.

" Give true hearts but earth and sky,
And some flowers to bloom and die ;
Homely scenes and simple views
Lowly thoughts may best infuse."
                KEBLE, " *First Sunday after Epiphany.*"

CHRIST's first miracle of Cana was a sign that He came, not to call His disciples *out* of the world and its ordinary duties, but to make men happier, nobler, better *in* the world. He willed that they should be husbands, and fathers, and citizens, not eremites or monks. He would show that He approved the brightness of pure society, and the mirth of innocent gatherings, no less than the ecstasies of the ascetic in the wilderness, or the visions of the mystic in his solitary cell.

And, as pointing the same moral, there was something significant in the place which he chose as the scene of His earliest ministry. St. John had preached in the lonely wastes by the Dead Sea waters ; his voice has been echoed back by the flinty precipices that frown over the sultry Ghôr. The city nearest to the scene of his teaching had been built in defiance of a curse, and the road to it led through " the bloody way." All around him breathed the dreadful associations of a guilty and desolated past ; the very waves were bituminous ; the very fruits crumbled into foul ashes under the touch ; the very dust beneath his feet lay, hot and white, over the relics of an abominable race. There, beside those leaden waters, under that copper heaven, amid those burning wildernesses and scarred ravines, had he preached the baptism of repentance. But Christ, amid the joyous band of His mother, and His brethren, and His disciples, chose as the earliest centre of His ministry a bright and busy city, whose marble buildings were mirrored in a limpid sea.

That little city was Capernaum. It rose under the gentle declivities of hills that encircled an earthly Paradise.[1] There were no such

---

[1] John ii. 12, *κατέβη* [128] — a touch of accuracy, since the road is one long descent.

trees, and no such gardens, anywhere in Palestine as in the land of Gennesareth. The very name means "garden of abundance," [1] and the numberless flowers blossom over a little plain which is "in sight like unto an emerald." It was doubtless a part of Christ's divine plan that His ministry should begin amid scenes so beautiful, and that the good tidings, which revealed to mankind their loftiest hopes and purest pleasures, should be first proclaimed in a region of unusual loveliness. The features of the scene are neither gorgeous nor colossal ; there is nothing here of the mountain gloom or the mountain glory ; nothing of that "dread magnificence" which over-awes us as we gaze on the icy precipices of tropical volcanoes, or the icy precipices of northern hills. Had our life on earth been full of wild and terrible catastrophes, then it might have been fitly symbol-ized by scenes which told only of deluge and conflagration ; but these green pastures and still waters, these bright birds and flowering oleanders, the dimpling surface of that inland sea, so doubly delicious and refreshful in a sultry land, all correspond with the characteristics of a life composed of innocent and simple elements, and brightened with the ordinary pleasures which, like the rain and the sunshine, are granted to all alike.

What the traveller will see, as he emerges from the Valley of Doves, and catches his first eager glimpse of Gennesareth, will be a small inland sea, like a harp in shape,[2] thirteen miles long and six broad. On the farther or eastern side runs a green strip about a quar-ter of a mile in breadth,[3] beyond which rises, to the height of some 900 feet above the level of the lake, an escarpment of desolate hills, scored with grey ravines, without tree, or village, or vestige of culti-vation — the frequent scene of our Lord's retirement when, after His weary labors, He sought the deep refreshment of solitude with God. The lake — with its glittering crystal, and fringe of flowering olean-ders, through whose green leaves shine the bright blue wings of the roller-bird, and the king-fishers may be seen in multitudes dashing down at the fish that glance beneath them — lies at the bottom of a great dent or basin in the earth's surface, more than 500 feet below

---

[1] "Quare vocatur Gennezar? *ob hortos principum (ganne sarim)*" [129] (Lightfoot, *Cent. Chorogr.* lxxix.).

[2] This is said to be the origin of the ancient name "Chinnereth," a beautiful onomatopœia for a harp. The Wady Hammâm, or "Valley of Doves," is a beau-tiful gorge in the hills by which the traveller may descend from Hattin to Mejdel.

[3] Except at one spot, the probable scene of the cure of the Gadarene demoniacs where the hills run close up to the water.

the level of the Mediterranean.[1] Hence the burning and enervating heat of the valley ; but hence, too, the variety of its foliage, the fertility of its soil, the luxuriance of its flora, the abundant harvests that ripen a month earlier than they do elsewhere, and the number of rivulets that tumble down the hill-sides into the lake. The shores are now deserted. With the exception of the small and decaying town of Tiberias — crumbling into the last stage of decrepitude — and the "frightful village" of Mejdel (the ancient Magdala), where the degradation of the inhabitants is best shown by the fact that the children play stark naked in the street — there is not a single inhabited spot on its once crowded shores.[2] One miserable, crazy boat — and that not always procurable — has replaced its gay and numerous fleet. As the fish are still abundant, no fact could show more clearly the dejected inanity and apathetic enervation of the present dwellers upon its shores. But the natural features still remain. The lake still lies unchanged in the bosom of the hills, reflecting every varying gleam of the atmosphere like an opal set in emeralds ; the waters are still as beautiful in their clearness as when the boat of Peter lay rocking on their ripples, and Jesus gazed into their crystal depths ; the cup-like basin still seems to overflow with its flood of sunlight ; the air is still balmy with natural perfumes ; the turtle-dove still murmurs in the valleys, and the pelican fishes in the waves ; and there are palms, and green fields, and streams, and grey heaps of ruin. And what it has lost in population and activity, it has gained in solemnity and interest. If every vestige of human habitation should disappear from beside it, and the jackal and the hyena should howl about the shattered fragments of the synagogues where once Christ taught, yet the fact that He chose it as the scene of His opening ministry [3] will give a sense of sacredness and pathos to its lonely waters till time shall be no more.

Yet widely different must have been its general aspect in the time of Christ, and far more strikingly beautiful, because far more richly

---

[1] Hence the plain of Gennesareth is called by the Arabs El-Ghuweir, or "the little hollow," to distinguish it from El-Ghôr, "the great hollow," i. e. the Jordan valley.

[2] A few Bedawîn may sometimes be found at Ain et-Tâbijah (Bethsaida). Renan truly observes that a furnace such as El Ghuweir now is, could hardly have been the scene of such prodigious activity, had not the climate been modified by the numberless trees, which under the withering influence of Islam have all been destroyed.

[3] Acts x. 37: St. Peter says, "That word which was preached throughout all Judæa, and began from Galilee." Luke xxiii. 5 : "Beginning from Galilee."

cultivated. Josephus, in a passage of glowing admiration, after describing the sweetness of its waters, and the delicate temperature of its air, its palms, and vines, and oranges, and figs, and almonds, and pomegranates, and warm springs, says that the seasons seemed to compete for the honor of its possession, and Nature to have created it as a kind of emulative challenge, wherein she had gathered all the elements of her strength.[1] The Talmudists see in the fact that this plain — "the ambition of Nature"— belonged to the tribe of Naphtali, a fulfilment of the Mosaic blessing, that that tribe should be "satisfied with favor, and full with the blessing of the Lord ; "[2] and they had the proverb, true in a deeper sense than they suppose, that "God had created seven seas in the land of Canaan, but one only — the Sea of Galilee — had he chosen for Himself."

Not, however, for its beauty only, but because of its centrality, and its populous activity, it was admirably adapted for that ministry which fulfilled the old prophecy of Isaiah, that "the land of Zebulun and the land of Naphtali, beyond Jordan, Galilee of the Gentiles," should "see a great light ; " and that to them " who sat in the region and shadow of death" should "light spring up." For Christ was to be, even in His own lifetime, "a light to lighten the Gentiles," as well as "the glory of His people Israel." And people of many nationalities dwelt in and encompassed this neighborhood, because it was "the way of the sea." "The cities," says Josephus, "lie here very thick ; and the very numerous villages are so full of people, because of the fertility of the land . . . . that the very smallest of them contain above 15,000 inhabitants."[3] He adds that the people were active, industrious, and inured to war from infancy, cultivating every acre of their rich and beautiful soil. No less than four roads communicated with the shores of the lake. One led down the Jordan valley on the western side ; another, crossing a bridge at the south of the lake, passed through Peræa to the fords of Jordan near Jericho ; a third led, through Sepphoris, the gay and rising capital of Galilee, to the famous port of Accho on the Mediterranean Sea ; a fourth ran over the mountains of Zebulon to Nazareth, and so through the plain of Esdraelon to Samaria and Jerusalem. Through this district passed the great caravans on their way from Egypt to Damascus ; and the heathens who congregated at Bethsaida Julias and Cæsarea

---

[1] The Rabbis refer to its extraordinary fruitfulness. (*Bab. Pesachim*, f. 8, 2 ; *Berachoth*, f. 44, 1 ; Lightfoot, *ubi supr. ;* Caspari, p. 69, &c.) φιλοτιμίαν ἄν τις εἴποι τῆς φύσεως [130] (Jos. *B. Jud.* iii. 10, §§ 7, 8).

[2] Deut. xxxiii. 23.

[3] Jos. *B. J.* iii. 3, § 2. See note 1, p. 156.

Philippi must have been constantly seen in the streets of Capernaum. In the time of Christ it was for population and activity "the manufacturing district" of Palestine, and the waters of its lake were ploughed by 4,000 vessels of every description, from the war vessel of the Romans to the rough fisher-boats of Bethsaida, and the gilded pinnaces from Herod's palace. Ituræa, Samaria, Syria, Phœnicia were immediately accessible by crossing the lake, the river, or the hills. The town of Tiberias, which Herod Antipas had built to be the capital of Galilee, and named in honor of the reigning emperor, had risen with marvellous rapidity ; by the time that St. John wrote his Gospel it had already given its name to the Sea of Galilee ; and even if Christ never entered its heathenish amphitheatre or grave-polluted streets,[1] He must have often seen in the distance its turreted walls, its strong castle, and the Golden House of Antipas, flinging far into the lake the reflection of its marble lions and sculptured architraves.[2] Europe, Asia, and Africa had contributed to its population, and men of all nations met in its market-place. All along the western shores of Gennesareth Jews and Gentiles were strangely mingled, and the wild Arabs of the desert might there be seen side by side with enterprising Phœnicians, effeminate Syrians, contemptuous Romans, and supple, wily, corrupted Greeks.

The days of delightful seclusion in the happy valley of Nazareth were past ; a life of incessant toil, of deep anxiety, of trouble, and wandering, and opposition, of preaching, healing, and doing good, was now to begin. At this earliest dawn of His public entrance upon His ministry, our Lord's first stay in Capernaum was not for many days ; yet these days would be a type of all the remaining life. He would preach in a Jewish synagogue built by a Roman centurion, and His works of love would become known to men of many nationalities.[3] It would be clear to all that the new Prophet who had arisen was wholly unlike His great forerunner. The hairy mantle,

---

[1] Being built on the site of an old cemetery, no true Jew could enter it without ceremonial pollution (see Lightfoot, *Cent. Chorogr.*, lxxxi.). Josephus (*Antt.* xviii. 2, § 3) expressly says that, from the number of tombs which had to be removed in laying the foundations, every Jew who inhabited it became unclean (Numb. xix. 11); and hence Herod Antipas, who built it (*B. J.* ii. 9, § 1), had to *compel* people to reside in it, or to bribe them by very substantial privileges (*Antt.* xviii. 2, § 3). It is probable that Christ never set foot within its precincts; yet some of the inhabitants were, of course, among His hearers (John vi. 23).

[2] Jos. *Vit.* 9, 12, 13 ; *B. Jud.* ii. 21, § 6.

[3] That some great works were performed during this brief visit seems clear from Luke iv. 23 ; but that they could scarcely be regarded as miracles seems equally clear from John iv. 54.

the ascetic seclusion, the unshorn locks, would have been impossible and out of place among the inhabitants of those crowded and busy shores. Christ came not to revolutionize, but to ennoble and to sanctify. He came to reveal that the Eternal was not the *Future*, but only the *Unseen;* that Eternity was no ocean whither men were being swept by the river of Time, but was around them now, and that their lives were only real in so far as they felt its reality and its presence. He came to teach that God was no dim abstraction, infinitely separated from them in the far-off blue, but that He was the Father in whom they lived, and moved, and had their being ; and that the service which he loved was not ritual and sacrifice, not pompous scrupulosity and censorious orthodoxy, but mercy and justice, humility and love. He came, not to hush the natural music of men's lives, nor to fill it with storm and agitation, but to re-tune every silver chord in that " harp of a thousand strings," and to make it echo with the harmonies of heaven.

And such being the significance of Christ's life in this lovely region, it is strange that the exact size of Capernaum — of Capernaum, " His own city " (Matt. ix. 1), which witnessed so many of His mightiest miracles, which heard so many of His greatest revelations — should remain to this day a matter of uncertainty. That it was indeed *either* at Khan Minyeh *or* at Tell Hûm is reasonably certain; but at which ? Both towns are in the immediate vicinity of Bethsaida and of Chorazin ; both are beside the waves of Galilee; both lie on the " way of the sea ; " the claims of both are supported by powerful arguments; the decision in favor of either involves difficulties as yet unsolved. After visiting the scenes, and carefully studying on the spot the arguments of travellers in many volumes, the preponderance of evidence seems to me in favor of Tell Hûm. There, on bold rising ground, encumbered with fragments of white marble, rise the ruined walls of what was perhaps a synagogue, built in the florid and composite style which marks the Herodian age; and amid the rank grass and gigantic thistles lie scattered the remnants of pillars and architraves which prove that on this spot once stood a beautiful and prosperous town.[1] At Khan Minyeh there is nothing but a common ruined caravansery

---

[1] Major Wilson. R. E., of the *Palestine Exploration Fund,* found that the plan of the large white building at Tell Hûm consisted of " four rows of seven columns each . . surrounded by a blank wall, ornamented outside with pilasters, and apparently a heavy cornice of late date ; . . but what puzzles me is that the entrance was on the south side, which does not seem to be usual in synagogues. The synagogue was surrounded by another building of later date, also well built and ornamented " (see Porter's *Handbook,* ii. 403).

and grey mounded heaps, which may or may not be the ruins of ruins.   But whichever of the two was the site on which stood the home of Peter — which was also the home of Christ (Matt. viii. 14) — either is desolate; even the wandering Bedawy seems to shun those ancient ruins, where the fox and the jackal prowl at night.   The sad and solemn woe that was uttered upon the then bright and flourishing city has been fulfilled: " And thou, Capernaum, which art exalted to heaven, shalt be thrust down to hell: for if the mighty works, which have been done in thee, had been done in Sodom, it had remained unto this day." [1]

---

[1] Luke x. 15; Matt. xi. 23. — The arguments about the site of Capernaum would fill several volumes.   The reader may find most of them in Dr. Robinson's *Bibl. Researches*, iii. 288—294 ; Wilson, *Lands of the Bible*, ii. 139—149 ; Ritter, *Jordan*, 335—343 ; Thomson, *The Land and the Book*, 352 seqq., &c.   Some new arguments are adduced in Mr. McGregor's *Rob Roy on the Jordan*.   The recent researches of the Palestine Exploration Fund, under Major Wilson, seem to me to strengthen the case in favor of Tell Hûm very considerably ; and Tell Hûm, "the ruined mound of Hum," is a very natural corruption of Kefr *Nahûm*, "the village of *Nahûm*." — As this chapter is on the scene of the ministry, it may be well to observe that the true version of the famous prophecy in Isa. ix. 1 is, " As of old He lightly estemed the land of Zebulun and the land of Naphtali ; so, in the latter time, *He hath made her glorious* by the way of the sea," &c. (See Perowne, *On the Psalms*, I. xix.)

CHAPTER XIII.

JESUS AT THE PASSOVER.

" The Lord, whom ye seek, shall suddenly come to His Temple." — MAL iii. 1.

THE stay of Jesus at Capernaum on this occasion was very short,[1] and it is not improbable that He simply awaited there the starting of the great caravan of pilgrims who, at this time, were about to wend their way to the great feast at Jerusalem.

The Synoptists are silent respecting any visit of Christ to the Passover between His twelfth year till His death;[2] and it is St. John alone who, true to the purpose and characteristics of his Gospel, mentions this earliest Passover of Christ's ministry, or gives us any particulars that took place during its progress.[3]

The main event which distinguished it was the purification of the Temple — an act so ineffectual to conquer the besetting vice of the Jews, that he was obliged to repeat it, with expressions still more stern, at the close of His ministry, and only four days before His death.[4]

---

[1] John ii. 12 : " Not many days."

[2] But just as St. John distinctly implies the Galilæan ministry (vii. 3, 4), so the Synoptists distinctly imply that there must have been a Judæan ministry ; *e. g.*, Judas is a Jew, and Joseph of Arimathea ; and our Lord was well known to people at and near Jerusalem (see Matt. iv. 25 ; xxiii. 37 ; Mark iii. 7, 8, 22 ; xi. 2, 3 ; xiv. 14 ; xv. 43—46 ; and compare Matt. xiii. 57). In Luke iv. 44 there is good MS. authority (א, B, C, L, &c.) for the reading, "He preached in the synagogues of Judæa." " The vague and shifting outlines of the Synoptists," says Mr. Sanday, "allow ample room for all the insertions that are made in them with so much precision by St. John" (*Fourth Gospel*, p. 166.) See too the important testimony of St. Peter (Acts x. 37, 39).

[3] Other Passovers mentioned are John vi. 4 ; xi. 55. The feast of v. 1 would make four Passovers, if it were certain that a Passover were intended ; and in any case we shall in the course of the narrative find much to confirm the opinion of Eusebius and Theodoret, that the ministry lasted three years and a few months. The τὸ πάσχα τῶν Ἰουδαίων [131] of St. John may perhaps be regarded as an indication that he wrote when the Passover had ceased to be possible.

[4] Matt. xxi. 12, 13 ; Mark xi. 15—17 ; Luke xix. 45. It seems impossible to believe that the two narratives refer to the same event. The consequences of that act, and the answer which He then gives to the priests who asked for some proof of His commission to exercise this authority, are quite different. To give all the arguments which in each case have led me to a particular conclusion on

We have already seen what vast crowds flocked to the Holy City at the great annual feast. Then, as now, that immense multitude, composed of pilgrims from every land, and proselytes of every nation, brought with them many needs. The traveller who now visits Jerusalem at Easter time will make his way to the gates of the Church of the Sepulchre through a crowd of vendors of relics, souvenirs, and all kinds of objects, who, squatting on the ground, fill all the vacant space before the church and overflow into the adjoining street. Far more numerous and far more noisome must have been the buyers and sellers who choked the avenues leading to the Temple, in the Passover to which Jesus now went among the other pilgrims;[1] for what they had to sell were not only trinkets and knick-knacks, such as now are sold to Eastern pilgrims, but oxen, and sheep, and doves. On both sides of the eastern gate — the gate Shusan — as far as Solomon's porch, there had long been established the shops of merchants and the banks of money-changers. The latter were almost a necessity; for, twenty days before the Passover, the priests began to collect the old sacred tribute of half a shekel paid yearly by every Israelite, whether rich or poor, as atonement money for his soul, and applied to the expenses of the Tabernacle service.[2] Now it would not be lawful to pay this in the coinage brought from all kinds of governments, sometimes represented by wretched counters of brass and copper, and always defiled with heathen symbols and heathen inscriptions. It was lawful to send this money to the priests from a distance, but every Jew who presented himself in the Temple preferred to pay it in person. He was therefore obliged to procure the little silver coin in return for his own currency, and the money-changers charged him five per cent. as the usual *kolbon* or agio.[3]

Had this trafficking been confined to the streets immediately adjacent to the holy building, it would have been excusable, though not altogether seemly. Such scenes are described by heathen writers as occurring round the Temple of Venus at Mount Eryx, and of the Syrian goddess at Hierapolis — nay even, to come nearer home, such scenes once occurred in our own St. Paul's.[4] But the mischief had

disputed points, would require five times the space at my disposal, and would wholly alter the character of the book. I can only ask the reader to believe that I have always tried to weigh with impartiality the evidence on both sides.

[1] The date of this Passover was perhaps April, A. D. 28.

[2] Exod. xxx. 11—16.

[3] κόλλυβος. For full information on this subject, with the Rabbinic authorities, see Lightfoot, *Hor. Hebr.*, in Matt. xxi. 12.

[4] Ælian, *Hist. Animal.* x. 50; Lucian, *De Deâ Syr.*, 41 (Sepp); Dixon's *Holy Land*, ii. 61.

not stopped here. The vicinity of the Court of the Gentiles, with its broad spaces and long arcades, had been too tempting to Jewish greed. We learn from the Talmud that a certain Babha Ben Buta had been the first to introduce " 3,000 sheep of the flocks of Kedar into the Mountain of the House"—*i. e.*, into the Court of the Gentiles, and therefore within the consecrated precincts.[1] The profane example was eagerly followed. The *chanujôth* of the shop-keepers, the exchange booths of the usurers, gradually crept into the sacred enclosure. There, in the actual Court of the Gentiles, steaming with heat in the burning April day, and filling the Temple with stench and filth, were penned whole flocks of sheep and oxen,[2] while the drovers and pilgrims stood bartering and bargaining around them. There were the men with their great wicker cages filled with doves, and under the shadow of the arcades, formed by quadruple rows of Corinthian columns,[3] sat the money-changers with their tables covered with piles of various small coins, while, as they reckoned and wrangled in the most dishonest of trades, their greedy eyes twinkled with the lust of gain. And this was the entrance-court to the Temple of the Most High! The court which was a witness that that house should be a House of Prayer for all nations had been degraded into a place which, for foulness, was more like shambles, and for bustling commerce more like a densely-crowded bazaar; while the lowing of oxen, the bleating of sheep, the Babel of many languages, the huckstering and wrangling, and the clinking of money and of balances (perhaps not always just), might be heard in the adjoining courts, disturbing the chant of the Levites and the prayers of priests!

Filled with a righteous scorn at all this mean irreverence, burning with irresistible and noble indignation, Jesus, on entering the Temple, made a scourge of the rushes that lay on the floor; and in order to cleanse the sacred court of its worst pollutions, first drove out, indiscriminately, the sheep and oxen and the low crowd who tended them.[4]

---

[1] *Jer. Jôm Tobh.*, f. 61, 3, quoted by Lightfoot, *Hor. Hebr.*, ubi supr.

[2] Their number may be conjectured from the fact that Herod alone sacrificed 300 oxen at the consecration of the new Temple (Jos. *Antt.* xv. 11, § 6). Josephus adds that Herod's example was followed by each according to his ability, so that it was impossible to set down correctly the vast number of the sacrifices.

[3] Jos. *Antt.* xv. 11, § 5.

[4] John ii. 15, φραγέλλιον (the Roman *flagellum*), *id.* ἐξέβαλεν. That the scourge was for the men as well as the cattle, is clear from the πάντας[132] (ver. 15). On this occasion, however, our Lord used the expression "a house of merchandise," not, as afterwards, the sterner censure, "a den of robbers." (Cf. Jer. vii. 10, 11.) Luther's comment on this action is somewhat too free. "Ist das nicht aufrührisch?"[133] he asks. " Diese That Christi ist nicht zum Exempel zu

Then going to the tables of the money-changers He overthrew them where they stood, upsetting the carefully-arranged heaps of heterogeneous coinage, and leaving the owners to grope and hunt for their scattered money on the polluted floor. Even to those who sold doves He issued the mandate to depart, less sternly indeed, because the dove was the offering of the poor, and there was less desecration and foulness in the presence there of those lovely emblems of innocence and purity; nor could He overturn the tables of the dove-sellers lest the birds should be hurt in their cages; but still, even to those who sold doves, He authoritatively exclaimed, "Take these things hence," justifying His action to the whole terrified, injured, muttering, ignoble crowd in no other words than the high rebuke, " *Make not my Father's house a house of merchandise.*" [1] And His disciples, seeing this transport of inspiring and glorious anger, recalled to mind what David had once written "to the chief musician upon Shoshannim," for the service of that very Temple, "The zeal of thine house shall even devour me." [2]

Why did not this multitude of ignorant pilgrims resist? Why did these greedy chafferers content themselves with dark scowls and muttered maledictions, while they suffered their oxen and sheep to be chased into the streets and themselves ejected, and their money flung rolling on the floor, by one who was then young and unknown, and in the garb of despised Galilee? Why, in the same way we might ask, did Saul suffer Samuel to beard him in the very presence of his army? Why did David abjectly obey the orders of Joab? Why

---

ziehen; er hat sie nicht als Diener des Neuen, sondern des Alten Testament und Mosis Schüler gethan " [134] (Hase, p. 76). I quote this unbecoming and mistaken remark only to show how even the best and greatest fail to rise to the height of that universal morality of which the life of Jesus is the sole human example.

[1] Cf. Luke ii. 49. We find in the Talmud that doves were usually sold in the *chanujôth*, or "shops," belonging to the family of Annas on the Mount of Olives, who had so multiplied the occasions for offering them, that a single dove cost a gold piece, until this nefarious artificial value was reduced by the teachings of R. Simeon, the son of Gamaliel. Perhaps the profitableness of the trade had caused its extension to the Temple courts (Derenbourg, *Hist. de Palest. d'après les Thalmuds*, 467). He quotes *Keritoth*, i. 7. The expression *chanujôth benî Hanan* is found in *Jer.Pea.* i. 6 (*id. ib.*).

[2] Ps. lxix. 9. There is no doubt that $\kappa\alpha\tau\alpha\varphi\acute{\alpha}\gamma\varepsilon\tau\alpha\iota$ [135] ($\aleph$, A, B, E, F, G, &c.) is the right reading; but it may by a Hebraism really imply the $\kappa\alpha\tau\acute{\varepsilon}\varphi\alpha\gamma\varepsilon$ [136] of the LXX. " The præterite, as a representative of the *present*, is employed also to denote the *future* (Gesen., *Hebr. Gram.*, § 124, 4; Turpie, *The Old Testament in the New*, p. 29). Bishop Wordsworth points out that St. John's phrase in quotation is $\gamma\varepsilon\gamma\rho\alpha\mu\mu\acute{\varepsilon}\nu o\nu$ $\acute{\varepsilon}\sigma\tau\acute{\iota}$ [137] (vi. 31, 45; x. 34, &c.), that of the other Evangelists $\gamma\acute{\varepsilon}\gamma\rho\alpha\pi\tau\alpha\iota$.[138] We may notice that St. John's style is more analytical and more modern than that of the others.

did Ahab not dare to arrest Elijah at the door of Naboth's vineyard?
Because sin is weakness; because there is in the world nothing so
abject as a guilty conscience, nothing so invincible as the sweeping
tide of a Godlike indignation against all that is base, and wrong.
How could these paltry sacrilegious buyers and sellers, conscious of
wrong-doing, oppose that scathing rebuke, or face the lightnings of
those eyes that were enkindled by an outraged holiness? When
Phinehas the priest was zealous for the Lord of Hosts, and drove
through the bodies of the prince of Simeon and the Midianitish
woman with one glorious thrust of his indignant spear, why did not
guilty Israel avenge that splendid murder? Why did not every man
of the tribe of Simeon become a *Goel* to the dauntless assassin?
Because Vice cannot stand for one moment before Virtue's uplifted
arm. Base and grovelling as they were, these money-mongering
Jews felt, in all that remnant of their souls which was not yet eaten
away by infidelity and avarice, that the Son of Man was right.

Nay, even the Priests and Pharisees, and Scribes and Levites,
devoured as they were by pride and formalism, could not condemn
an act which might have been performed by a Nehemiah or a Judas
Maccabæus, and which agreed with all that was purest and best in
their traditions.[1] But when they had heard of this deed, or witnessed
it, and had time to recover from the breathless mixture of admiration,
disgust, and astonishment which it inspired, they came to Jesus, and
though they did not dare to condemn what He had done, yet half
indignantly asked Him for some sign that He had a right to act
thus.[2]

Our Lord's answer in its full meaning was far beyond their comprehension, and in what *appeared* to be its meaning filled them with
a perfect stupor of angry amazement. " Destroy," He said, " this
temple,[3] and in three days I will raise it up."

---

[1] *E. g.*, in the Rabbis we find R. Eliezer Ben Zadok severely blamed for prac-
ticing merchandise in a synagogue which he himself had built at Alexandria
(Sepp). Gfrörer has pointed out the remarkable fact that in the Targum of
Jonathan, at the last verse of Zechariah (xiv. 21), the word " trader " is substi-
tuted for " Canaanite." " There shall be no more the trader in the house of the
Lord." (Ebrard, *Gosp. Hist.*, E. Tr., p. 219.)

[2] " The Jews " in John ii. 18 means, as usual in this Gospel, " the opponents of
Jesus." The term hardly occurs in the other Gospels, except in the title of the
cross, " King of the Jews; " but to St. John " standing within the boundary of the
Christian age, . . the name appears to be the true antithesis to Christianity."
(Westcott, s. v. " Jew " in Smith's *Dict. Bible.*)

[3] John ii. 19. More literally, " shrine " ($\nu\alpha\grave{o}\nu$), not $i\varepsilon\rho\grave{o}\nu$ as before in verse 14.
Consequently the assertion of the Jews was not strictly accurate, for $\acute{o}$ $\nu\alpha\grave{o}s$
$o\H{\nu}\tau os$ (as distinguished from $\tau\grave{o}$ $i\varepsilon\rho\grave{o}\nu$), with all its porticoes, had been finished

Destroy this Temple! — the Temple on which a king pre-eminent for his wealth and magnificence had lavished his most splendid resources, and thereby almost reconciled the Jews to an intolerable tyranny ; the Temple for the construction of which one thousand wagons had been required, and ten thousand workmen enrolled, and a thousand priests in sacerdotal vestments employed to lay the stones which the workmen had already hewn ; the Temple which was a marvel to the world for its colossal substructions of marble, its costly mosaics, its fragrant woods, its glittering roofs, the golden vine with its hanging clusters sculptured over the entrance door, the embroidered vails, enwoven with flowers of purple, the profuse magnificence of its silver, gold, and precious stones.[1] It had been already forty-six years in building, and was yet far from finished; and this unknown Galilæan youth bade them destroy it, and *He* would raise it in three days! Such was the literal and evidently false construction which they chose to put upon His words, though the recorded practice of their own great prophets might have shown them that a mystery lay hidden in this sign which He gave.[2]

How ineffaceable was the impression produced by the words is best proved by the fact that more than three years afterwards it was this, more than all His other discourses, which His accusers and false witnesses tried to pervert into a constructive evidence of guilt; nay, it was even this, more than anything else, with which the miserable

---

in eight or nine years. The Talmud (*Taanith*, f. 23 *a*) says that to aid the building, the rain which fell had been dried with miraculous quickness. The sign which Jesus gives is His prediction. Cf. Micaiah (1 Kings xxii. 24; Jer. xx. 1—6, &c.).

[1] See the elaborate and gloating description of Josephus (*Antt.* xv. 11, §§ 3—5). It appears, however, that the actual Holy Place — the ναός alone — had been "built by the priests in a year and six months" (*id.* 6). The expression of the Jews applied to the whole area with its splendid colonnades, royal citadel, &c. Josephus says (xv. 11, § 1) that Herod had begun the Temple in the eighteenth year of his reign — *i. e.* between Nisan 1, A. U. C. 734 and 735. This would give us A. U. C. 781—782, A. D. 28 or 29, for our Lord's first Passover; and as the Temple was begun in Kisleu, the exact date is probably A. D. 28. This agrees with the date given in Luke iii. 1, if we suppose that he dates from the first year of Tiberius's joint reign, as we seem entitled to infer from the evidence of coins, &c. (Wieseler, *Beiträge*, 177 ff.; see Sanday, *Fourth Gospel*, p. 65). Similarly in Jos. *B. J.*, i. 21, § 1, Herod is said to have begun the Temple in the fifteenth year of his reign, which is no contradiction to *Antt.* xv. 11, § 1, the reign in the former instance being dated from the death of Augustus, in the latter from the confirmation of Herod by the Romans. The ᾠκοδομήθη seems to imply that the works were then *suspended* (cf. Ezra v. 16), but the whole was not *finished* till the time of Herod Agrippa II. (*Antt.* xx. 9, § 7).

[2] See Isa. vii. 11, 14, &c.

robber taunted Him upon the very cross. They were obliged, indeed, entirely to distort His words into "*I am able to destroy* the Temple of God,"¹ or "*I will destroy* this Temple made with hands, and in three days will build another."² He had never used these expressions, and here also their false witness was so self-contradictory as to break down. But they were well aware that this attempt of theirs to infuse a political and seditious meaning into what He said, was best calculated to madden the tribunal before which He was arraigned : indeed, so well adapted was it to this purpose that the mere distant echo, as it were, of the same words was again the main cause of martyrdom to His protomartyr Stephen.³

"But he spake," says St. John, "of the temple of His body," and he adds that it was not until His resurrection that His disciples fully understood His words.⁴ Nor is this astonishing, for they were words of very deep significance. Hitherto there had been but one Temple of the true God, the Temple in which He then stood — the Temple which symbolized, and had once at least, as the Jews believed, enshrined that Shechînah, or cloud of glory, which was the living witness to God's presence in the world. But now the Spirit of God abode in a Temple not made with hands, even in the sacred Body of the Son of God made flesh. He tabernacled among us ; "He had a tent like ours, and of the same material." Even this was to be done away. At that great Pentecost three years later, and thenceforward for ever, the Holy Spirit of God was to prefer

"Before all temples the upright heart and pure."

Every Christian man was to be, in his mortal body, a temple of the Holy Ghost. This was to be the central truth, the sublimest privilege of the New Dispensation ; this was to be the object of Christ's departure, and to make it " better for us that He should go away."

Nothing could have been more amazing to the carnal mind, that walked by sight and not by faith — nothing more offensive to the Pharisaic mind that clung to the material — than this high truth, that his sacred Temple at Jerusalem was henceforth to be no longer, with any special privilege, the place where men were to worship the Father ; that, in fact, it *was* the truest Temple no longer. Yet they might, if they had willed it, have had some faint conception of what Christ meant. They must have known that by the voice of John He had been proclaimed the Messiah ; they might have realized what he afterwards said to them, that " in this place was one greater than

---

¹ Matt. xxvi. 61.   ³ Acts vi. 14.
² Mark xiv. 58.   ⁴ Ps. xvi. 10 ; Hos. vi. 2 ; 1 Cor. xv. 4, &c.

the Temple;" they might have entered into the remarkable utterance of a Rabbi of their own class — an utterance involved in the prophetic language of Daniel ix. 24, and which they ought therefore to have known — that the true Holy of Holies was the Messiah Himself.

And in point of fact there is an incidental but profoundly significant indication that they *had* a deeper insight into Christ's real meaning than they chose to reveal. For, still brooding on these same words — the first official words which Christ had addressed to them — when Jesus lay dead and buried in the rocky tomb, they came to Pilate with the remarkable story, " Sir, we remember that that deceiver said, while He was yet alive, After three days I will rise again." Now there is no trace that Jesus had *ever* used any such words distinctly to them; and unless they had heard the saying from Judas, or unless it had been repeated by common rumor derived from the Apostles — *i. e.*, unless the "we remember" was a distinct falsehood — they could have been referring to no other occasion than this. And that they should have heard it from any of the disciples was most unlikely; for over the slow hearts of the Apostles these words of our Lord seem to have passed like the idle wind. In spite of all that He had told them, there seems to have been nothing which they expected *less* than His death, unless it were His subsequent resurrection. How then came these Pharisees and Priests to understand better than His own disciples what our Lord had meant? Because they were not like the Apostles, loving, guileless, simplehearted men; because, in spite of all their knowledge and insight, their hearts were even already full of the hatred and rejection which ended in Christ's murder, and which drew the guilt of His blood on the heads of them and of their children.

But there was yet another meaning which the words involved, not, indeed, less distasteful to their prejudices, but none the less full of warning, and more clearly within the range of their understandings. The Temple was the very heart of the whole Mosaic system, the head-quarters, so to speak, of the entire Levitical ceremonial. In profaning that Temple, and suffering it to be profaned — in suffering One whom they chose to regard as only a poor Galilæan teacher to achieve that purification of it which, whether from supineness or from self-interest, or from timidity, neither Caiaphas, nor Annas, nor Hillel, nor Shammai, nor Gamaliel, nor Herod had ventured to attempt — were they not, as it were, destroying that Temple, abrogating that system, bearing witness by their very actions that for them its real significance had passed away ? " Finish, then," [1] he might have implied, at once by way of prophecy and of permission, "finish without delay this your work of dissolution : in three days will I, as a risen Redeemer, restore something better and greater ; not a material Temple, but a living Church." Such is the meaning which St. Stephen seems to have seen in these words. Such is the meaning which is expanded in so many passages by the matchless reasoning and passion of St. Paul. But to this and every meaning they were deaf, and dull, and blind. They seem to have gone away silent indeed, but sullen and dissatisfied ; suspicious of, yet indifferent to, the true solution ; ignorant, yet too haughty and too angry to inquire.

What great works Jesus did on this occasion we cannot tell. Whatever they were, they caused some to believe on Him ; but it was not as yet a belief in which He could trust. Their mere intellectual witness to His claims He needed not ; and their hearts, untouched as yet, were, as He knew by divine insight, cold and barren,· treacherous and false. [2]

---

[1] John ii. 19, *Λύσατε*. It is obviously hypothetic. Cf. Matt. xii. 33.

[2] John ii. 23—25.

CHAPTER XIV.

NICODEMUS.

Ο διδάσκαλος τοῦ Ἰσραήλ. [139] — JOHN iii. 10.

A CASTE or a sect may consist for the most part of haughty fanatics and obstinate bigots, but it will be strange indeed if there are to be found among them no exceptions to the general characteristics; strange if honesty, candor, sensibility, are utterly dead among them all. Even among rulers, scribes, Pharisees, and wealthy members of the Sanhedrin, Christ found believers and followers. The earliest and most remarkable of these was Nicodemus, a rich man, a ruler, a Pharisee, and a member of the Sanhedrin.[1]

A constitutional timidity is, however, observable in all which the Gospels tell us about Nicodemus; a timidity which could not be wholly overcome even by his honest desire to befriend and acknowledge One whom he knew to be a Prophet, even if he did not at once recognize in Him the promised Messiah. Thus the few words which he interposed to check the rash injustice of his colleagues are cautiously rested on a general principle, and betray no indication of his personal faith in the Galilæan whom his sect despised. And even when the power of Christ's love, manifested on the cross, had made the most timid disciples bold, Nicodemus does not come forward with his splendid gifts of affection until the example had been set by one of his own wealth, and rank, and station in society.[2]

---

[1] Matt. ix. 18; Mark xii. 28. Strauss considers this conversation with Nicodemus to have been invented to show that the followers of Jesus were not all obscure and poor! But the Fathers and early Christians considered it to be their glory, not their reproach, that to the poor the Gospel was preached (see 1 Cor. i. 26—29). It is with no touch of regret that Jerome writes, " Ecclesia Christi non de Academiâ, et Lycaeo, sed *de vili plebeculâ* congregata est " [140] (Comm. in Gal. iii. 3.)

[2] John vii. 50; xix. 39. I have borrowed a few words from my article on "Nicodemus" in Smith's *Dict. of the Bible.* The name, which seems to have been not uncommon among the Jews (Jos. *Antt.* xiv. 3, § 2), is doubtless, like so many Jewish names at this period, derived from the Greek. In the Talmud it appears under the form Nakdîmôn, and some would derive it from *naki,* " innocent," and *dam,* " blood." (See Wetstein, *N. T.* i. 150.) Tradition says that after

Such was the Rabbi who, with that mingled candor and fear of man which characterize all that we know of him, came indeed to Jesus, but came cautiously by night. He was anxious to know more of this young Galilæan prophet whom he was too honest not to recognize as a teacher come from God ; but he thought himself too eminent a person among his sect to compromise his dignity, and possibly even his safety, by visiting Him in public.

Although he is alluded to in only a few touches, because of that high teaching which Jesus vouchsafed to him, yet the impression left upon us by his individuality is inimitably distinct, and wholly beyond the range of invention. His very first remark shows the indirect character of his mind — his way of suggesting rather than stating what he wished — the half-patronizing desire to ask, yet the half-shrinking reluctance to frame his question — the admission that Jesus had come "from God," yet the hesitating implication that it was only as " a teacher," and the suppressed inquiry, " What must I do ? "

Our Lord saw deep into his heart, and avoiding all formalities or discussion of preliminaries, startles him at once with the solemn uncompromising address, " Verily, verily, I say unto thee, Except a man be born again (or ' from above '),¹ he cannot see the kingdom of God." My disciple must be mine in heart and soul, or he is no disciple at all; the question is not of doing or not doing, but of *being*.

That answer startled Nicodemus into deep earnestness; but like the Jews in the last chapter (ii. 20), he either could not, or would not, grasp its full significance. He prefers to play, with a kind of quer-

---

the Resurrection (which would supply the last outward impulse necessary to confirm his faith and increase his courage) he became a professed disciple of Christ, and received baptism from Peter and John ; that the Jews then stripped him of his office, beat him, and drove him from Jerusalem ; that his kinsman Gamaliel received and sheltered him in his country house till death, and finally gave him honorable burial near the body of St. Stephen. If he be identical with the *Nakdimón Ben Gorión* of the Talmud, he outlived the fall of Jerusalem, and his family were reduced from wealth to such horrible poverty that, whereas the bridal bed of his daughter had been covered with a dower of 12,000 denarii, she was subsequently seen endeavoring to support life by picking the grains from the ordure of cattle in the streets. (*Gittin*, f. 56, 1 ; *Kethubh.*, f. 66, 2, quoted by Otho, *Lex. Rabb.* s. v.)

² The two meanings do not exclude each other. St. John elsewhere always uses ἄνωθεν in the sense of "from above" (i. 13; 1 John ii. 29 ; iii. 9 ; iv. 7; comp. James i. 17); on the other hand, it is clear that Nicodemus here understood Christ to mean also "a second birth" (ver. 4; and cf. Gal. vi. 15 ; 1 Pet. i. 3, 23); and as our Lord probably spoke in Aramaic, and there is, according to Grotius, *no* Aramaic word which has both meanings, Alford is doubtless right in making it = ἀναγεννᾶσθαι.

ulous surprise, about the mere literal meaning of the words which he chooses to interpret in the most physical and unintelligible sense. Mere logomachy like this Jesus did not pause to notice ; He only sheds a fresh ray of light on the reiteration of his former warning. He spoke, not of the fleshly birth, but of that spiritual regeneration of which no man could predict the course or method, any more than they could tell the course of the night breeze that rose and fell and whispered fitfully outside the little tabernacle where they sat,¹ but which must be a birth by water and by the Spirit — a purification, that is, and a renewal — an outward symbol and an inward grace — a death unto sin and a new birth unto righteousness.

Nicodemus could only answer by an expression of incredulous amazement. A Gentile might need, as it were, a new birth when admitted into the Jewish communion ; but he — a son of Abraham, a Rabbi, a zealous keeper of the Law — could *he* need that new birth ? How could such things be ?

" Art thou *the* teacher (ὁ διδάσκαλος) of Israel," asked our Lord, " and knowest not these things ? "² Art thou the third member of the Sanhedrin, the *chákám* or wise man, and yet knowest not the earliest, simplest lesson of the initiation into the kingdom of heaven ? If thy knowledge be thus carnal, thus limited — if thus thou stumblest on the threshold, how canst thou understand those deeper truths which He only who came down from heaven can make known ? The question was half sorrowful, half reproachful ; but He proceeded to reveal to this Master in Israel things greater and stranger than these ; even the salvation of man rendered possible by the sufferings and exaltation of the Son of Man ;³ the love of God manifested in send-

---

¹ That this was the character of the allusion seems to be implied in the use of τὸ πνεῦμα, " the breeze," rather than ὁ ἄνεμος, " the wind." *Ruach* in Hebrew no less than πνεῦμα in Greek, means both spirit and wind. This is, indeed, the only place in the N. T. where πνεῦμα is used in this sense ; but it is found in the LXX. (Gen. viii. 1 ; Wisd. v. 23), and the quotation in Heb. i. 7. But to make it mean as many do, " The Spirit breathes where it wills," &c., gives an inferior sense. The meaning is, " The wind breatheth where it listeth ; so *it is with* every one born of the Spirit." Alford refers to other instances of the same idiom.

² This may, perhaps, be the meaning. The president of the Sanhedrin was called the *Nasi* (נָשִׂיא) ; the vice-president was called Father of the House of Judgment (אֲבִי בֵּית דִּין) ; the third member, who sat on the president's left, bore the title of *chákám*, or " wise man " (חָכָם). On the other hand, ὁ διδάσκαλος *may* be merely generic — " one of οἱ διδάσκαλοι." Cf. Gal. iv. 2.

³ The ὑψωθῆναι ¹⁴¹ (ver. 14) is both literal and metaphorical — uplifted on the cross, exalted to the kingdom. Cf. Gen. xl. 13 ; John xii. 32 ; and ἀπαρθῇ ¹⁴² (Luke v. 35).

ing His only-begotten Son, not to judge but to save;[1] the deliverance for all through faith in Him; the condemnation which must fall on those who wilfully reject the truths He came to teach.

These were indeed the mysteries of the kingdom of heaven — truths once undreamed of, but now fully revealed. And although they violated every prejudice, and overthrew every immediate hope of this aged inquirer — though to learn them he must unlearn the entire intellectual habits of his life and training — yet we know from the sequel that they must have sunk into his inmost soul. Doubtless in the further discussion of them the night deepened around them; and in the memorable words about the light and the darkness with which the interview was closed, Jesus gently rebuked the fear of man which led this great Rabbi to seek the shelter of midnight for a deed which was not a deed of darkness needing to be concealed, but which was indeed a coming to the true and only Light.

Whatever lessons were uttered, or signs were done during the remainder of this First Passover, no further details are given us about them. Finding a stolid and insensate opposition, our Lord left Jerusalem, and went with His disciples " into Judæa," apparently to the banks of the Jordan, for there St. John tells us that His disciples began to baptize.[2] This baptism, a distant foreshadowing of the future sacrament, Christ seems rather to have permitted than to have directly organized. As yet it was the time of Preparation; as yet the inauguration of His ministry had been, if we may be allowed the expression, of an isolated and tentative description. Theologians have sought for all kinds of subtle and profound explanations of this baptism by the disciples. Nothing, however, that has been suggested throws any further light upon the subject, and we can only believe that Jesus permitted for a time this simple and beautiful rite as a sign of discipleship, and as the national symbol of a desire for that lustration of the heart which was essential to all who would enter into the kingdom of heaven.

John the Baptist was still continuing his baptism of repentance. Here, too, theologians have discovered a deep and mysterious dif-

---

[1] The change from ἵνα κρίνῃ [143] (act.) to ἵνα σωθῇ [144] (pass.) indicates that in this great salvation man s free will must take a part. Alford, whose notes on this chapter are specially good, points out in verse 20 the remarkable variation from ὁ φαῦλα πράσσων [145] to ὁ ποιῶν τὴν ἀλήθειαν [146] (cf. v. 29, οἱ τὰ ἀγαθὰ ποιήσαντες — οἱ δὲ τὰ φαῦλα πράξαντες [147]), as indicating the *transient and worthless result* of evil, and the *permanent effect* of good.

[2] He would not *Himself* baptize; the reasons for this would be analogous to those which prevented St. Paul from frequently baptizing, but far deeper, and more peremptory.

ficulty, and have entered into elaborate disquisitions on the relations
between the baptism of Jesus and of John. Nothing, however, has
been elicited from the discussion.[1] Inasmuch as the full activity of
Christ's ministry had not yet begun, the baptism of St. John no less
than that of the disciples must be still regarded as a symbol of
repentance and purity. Nor will any one who is convinced that
Repentance is " the younger brother of Innocence," and that for all
who have sinned repentance is the very work of life, be surprised
that the earliest preaching of Jesus as of John was — " Repent, for
the kingdom of heaven is at hand." [2] The time of preparation, of
preliminary testing, was not over yet; it was indeed drawing to a
conclusion, and this baptism by the disciples was but a transitory
phase of the opening ministry. And the fact that John no longer
preached in the wilderness, or baptized at Bethany, but had found it
desirable to leave the scene of his brief triumph and glory, marked
that there was a waning in the brightness of that star of the Gospel
dawn. The humble spirit of John — in all of whose words a deep
undertone of sadness is traceable — accepted, in entire submissiveness
to the will of God, the destiny of a brief and interrupted mission.

He had removed to Ænon, near Salim, a locality so wholly uncertain that it is impossible to arrive at any decision respecting it.[3]
Some still came to his baptism, though probably in diminished numbers, for a larger multitude now began to flock to the baptism of
Christ's disciples. But the ignoble jealousy which could not darken
the illuminated soul of the Forerunner, found a ready place in the
hearts of his followers. How long it may have smouldered we do
not know, but it was called into active display during the controversy
excited by the fact that two great Teachers, of whom one had testified to the other as the promised Messiah, were baptizing large mul-

---

[1] Tert., *De Baptismo,* xi.; Calvin, *Institt.,* cc. 15, 18; Schneckenburger, *Ueber das Alter der Jüdischen Proselyten-taufe;* Wall, *Hist. of Inf. Bapt.;* R. Hall, *Works,* ii. 175 seqq., &c.— Ewald thinks that the baptism of the disciples only differed from that of John in the two respects that, (i.) it was now directed to Jesus definitely as the Messiah to whom John had borne witness; and (ii.) that it was an initiation not into painful penitences, but into a life of divine joy and love (*Gesch. Christ.,* p. 345.)

[2] Matt. xviii. 3; Mark i. 15.

[3] Jerome, and the great majority of inquirers, place it near Beth-shean, or Scy-thopolis, in the Valley of the Jordan, where there were ruins called Salumias, and a spring. The objection to this is that it would be in the limits of Samaria. Robinson (iii. 298) found a Salim east of Nablous. Others have fancied they found places which might answer the description near Hebron (cf. Josh. xv. 32); and even at Wady Seleim, five miles N. E. of Jerusalem. The identification of the site is of no great importance for the narrative.

titudes of people, although the Sanhedrin and all the appointed authorities of the nation had declared against their claims. Some Jew [1] had annoyed the disciples of John with a dispute about purification, and they vented their perplexed and mortified feelings in a complaint to their great master: "Rabbi, He who was with thee beyond Jordan, to whom thou hast borne witness,[2] lo *He* is baptizing, and all men are coming to Him." The significant suppression of the name, the tone of irritation at what appeared to them an encroachment, the scarcely subdued resentment that any one should be a successful rival to him whose words had for a season so deeply stirred the hearts of men, are all apparent in this querulous address. And in the noble answer to it, all John's inherent greatness shone forth. He could not enter into rivalries, which would be a treachery against his deepest convictions, a falsification of his most solemn words. God was the sole source of human gifts, and in His sight there can be no such thing as human greatness. He reminded them of his asseveration that He was *not* the Christ, but only His messenger; He was not the bridegroom, but the bridegroom's friend, and his heart was even now being gladdened by the bridegroom's voice. Henceforth he was content to decrease; content that his little light should be swallowed up in the boundless Dawn. He was but an earthly messenger; but he had put the seal of his most intense conviction to the belief that God was true, and had given all things to His Son, and that through Him alone could eternal life be won.

---

[1] μετὰ 'Ιουδαίου, " with *a* Jew," seems to be undoubtedly the right reading in John iii. 25. (א, A, B, L, &c.)

[2] μεμαρτύρηκας, a perfect tense (John iii. 26).

CHAPTER XV.

THE WOMAN OF SAMARIA.

"In templo vis orare ? in te ora, sed prius esto templum Dei." [148] — Aug.

The Jew whose discussions had thus deeply moved the followers of John may well have been one of the prominent Pharisees; and our Lord soon became aware that they were watching his proceedings with an unfriendly eye. Their hostility to John was a still deeper hostility against Him, for the very reason that His teaching was already more successful. Perhaps in consequence of this determined rejection of the earliest steps of His teaching — perhaps also out of regard for the wounded feelings of John's followers — but most of all because at this very time the news reached Him that John had been seized by Herod Antipas and thrown into prison — Jesus left Judæa and again departed into Galilee.[1] Being already in the north of Judæa, He chose the route which led through Samaria. The fanaticism of Jewish hatred, the fastidiousness of Jewish Pharisaism, which led His countrymen when travelling alone to avoid that route, could have no existence for Him, and were things rather to be discouraged than approved.

Starting early in the morning, to enjoy as many as possible of the cool hours for travelling, he stopped at length for rest and refreshment in the neighborhood of Sychar,[2] a city not far from the well in the fertile district which the partiality of the patriarch Jacob had bequeathed to his favorite son. The well, like all frequented wells in the East, was doubtless sheltered by a little alcove, in which were seats of stone.

---

[1] The first reasons are emphasized by John (iv. 2, 3), the latter by Matt. iv. 12 ; Mark i. 14. For the imprisonment of John, *vid. infra*, Chap. XX. (see pp. 289, seqq.). The Synoptists markedly make the imprisonment of John the beginning of the Galilæan ministry, but the Fourth Gospel supplies the hiatus which they leave.

[2] The town of Shechem (cf. iv. 5 with Gen. xxxiii. 19 ; xlviii. 22, " one portion," LXX. $\Sigma i \kappa \iota \mu \alpha$ $\dot{\epsilon} \xi \alpha i \rho \epsilon \tau o \nu$) — the modern Nablûs (Neapolis) — corresponds to the description here given of Sychar; and if we imagine that the city extended a little farther eastward than at present, it is not so far from the well as to render it unlikely that the women of the city would sometimes resort to it for the cool and

It was the hour of noon,[1] and weary as He was with the long journey, possibly also with the extreme heat, our Lord sat "thus" on the well. The expression in the original is most pathetically picturesque. It implies that the Wayfarer was quite tired out, and in His exhaustion flung His limbs wearily on the seat, anxious if possible for complete repose. His disciples — probably the two pairs of brothers whom he had called among the earliest, and with them the friends Philip and Bartholomew — had left him, to buy in the neighboring city what was necessary for their wants; and hungry and thirsty, He who bore all our infirmities sat wearily awaiting them, when His solitude was broken by the approach of a woman. In a May noon in Palestine the heat may be indeed intense,[2] but it is not too intense

---

sacred water. From what the name of Sychar is derived is uncertain. The word λεγόμενος in St. John seems to imply a sobriquet (xi. 16; xx. 24; xix. 13). It may be שֶׁקֶר (*sheker*), "a lie," alluding to the false worship of the Temple on Gerizim; or שִׁכּוֹר (*shikkôr*), "drunken," alluding to Isa. xxviii. 1; or סִכַּר (*sûkar*), "a sepulchre," alluding to Joseph's tomb, which is close by (Josh. xxiv. 32). If the designation were common, St. John might use it without any shadow of scorn; or, again, Sychar may possibly have been a village [πόλις is very loosely used; thus Capernaum in the Gospels is called πόλις, though Josephus only calls it a village, κώμη] nearer the well than Sichem, on the site of the village now called El Askar, a name which Mr. Thomson says (*The Land and the Book*, ii. 220) may very easily have been corrupted from Sychar. (See, too, Keim, iii. 15, 16.)

[1] I must here repeat that I see no sufficient reason for supposing that St. John adopts a different computation of hours from that of the other Evangelists. If it had been evening, there would have been many women at the well instead of one; and, as Alford observes, St. John, if he had *meant* six in the evening, would have naturally specified whether he meant 6 a. m. or p. m. It is a pity that such a notion has ever been started. Rettig, followed by Olshausen, Meyer, Tholuck, &c., *assumed* that the Romans had a civil day, the same as the modern. Hug attempted, but quite failed, to prove it. Wieseler, acknowledging that there is no evidence of any such civil reckoning, appeals to the fact that for *scientific* purposes the *hora aequinoctialis* (*i. e.* the twenty-fourth part of a νυχθήμερον) was recognized (*e. g.* by Pliny, *Hist. Nat.* ii. 79), and concludes, from internal evidence — but, as it seems to me, quite unnecessarily — that St. John *must* have done so (*Synops.*, pp. 377 ff., E. Tr.). Ewald also adopts this view in a more summary way (*Gesch. Christ.*, pp. 323, 573; *Alterthümer*, p. 452), though he admits that Josephus (*Vit.* 54) and Philo (*Opp.* i., p. 692) have no such reckoning. Townson conjectured, without sufficient proof, that St. John had found this mode of reckoning in use at Ephesus. St. John reckoned his hours from sunrise, as did the rest of mankind till the fifth century, so far as we know. (See p. 131.)

[2] It is not possible to determine at what time of the year this incident took place. Those who take John iv. 35 literally, suppose that it was in December; those who take verse 36 literally, place it in May. Now one of the two must be metaphorical, and how shall we decide which? Each supposition is surrounded with difficulties; but as the baptizing period seems to have been extremely short, and as the Passover in this year was in April, there is possibly a shade more like-

to admit of moving about; and this woman, either from accident, or, possibly, because she was in no good repute, and therefore would avoid the hour when the well would be thronged by all the women of the city,[1] was coming to draw water. Her national enthusiasm and reverence for the great ancestor of her race, or perhaps the superior coolness and freshness of the water, may have been sufficient motive to induce her to seek this well, rather than any nearer fountain.[2] Water in the East is not only a necessity, but a delicious luxury, and the natives of Palestine are connoisseurs as to its quality.

Jesus would have hailed her approach. The scene, indeed, in that rich green valley, with the great corn-fields spreading far and wide, and the grateful shadow of trees, and the rounded masses of Ebal and Gerizim rising on either hand, might well have invited to lonely musing; and all the associations of that sacred spot—the story of Jacob, the neighboring tomb of the princely Joseph, the memories of Joshua, and of Gideon, and the long line of Israelitish kings—would supply many a theme for such meditations. But the Lord was thirsty and fatigued, and having no means of reaching the cool water which glimmered deep below the well's mouth, He said to the woman, " Give me to drink."

Every one who has travelled in the East knows how glad and ready is the response to this request. The miserable Fellah, even the rough Bedawy, seems to feel a positive pleasure in having it in his power to obey the command of his great prophet, and share with a thirsty traveller the priceless element. But so deadly was the hatred and rivalry between Jews and Samaritans, so entire the absence of all familiar intercourse between them, that the request only elicited from the woman of Samaria an expression of surprise that it should have been made.[3]

---

lihood that it took place in May. If so, " Say ye not, There are yet four months, and then cometh harvest," must be understood as being merely a proverbial expression of the average interval between seed-time and harvest in some parts of Palestine; for which proverb there are parallels both in Hebrew and classic literature.

[1] Gen. xxiv. 11.

[2] $\pi\eta\gamma\tilde{\eta}$ (John iv. 6). $\varphi\rho\acute{e}\alpha\rho$ (ver. 12).

[3] οὐ γὰρ συγχρῶνται (*i.e.* hold no *familiarity* with) Ἰουδαῖοι Σαμαρείταις (John iv. 9); see Ezra iv. 1. Even our Lord speaks of a Samaritan as ἀλλογενής (Luke xvii. 18). The Jews called them Cuthites; coupled the name of " Samaritan " with "devil;" accused them of worshipping the earrings and idolatrous amulets buried by Jacob under the Allonmeonenim or " Enchanter's Oak " (Gen. xxxv. 4); cursed them in their synagogues; did not suffer them to become proselytes; said that to eat their bread was like eating swine's flesh; and denied them all share in the resurrection. The Samaritans, on their part, were accused of

Gently, and without a word of rebuke, our Lord tells her that had she known Him, and asked of Him, He would have given her living water.¹ She pointed to the well, a hundred feet deep. He had nothing to draw with : whence could He obtain this living water? And then, perhaps with a smile of incredulity and national pride, she asked if He were greater than their father Jacob, who had digged and drunk of that very well.² And yet there must have been something which struck and overawed her in His words, for now she addresses Him by the title of respect which had been wanting in her first address.

---

waylaying Jews ; of misleading them by false fire-signals; and of having scattered bones in the Temple (Jos. *Antt.* xx. 6, § 1; xviii. 2, § 2). " Are you a Jew ? " asked Salameh Cohen, the Samaritan high priest of Dr. Frankl ; "and do you come to us, the Samaritans who are despised by the Jews ? " (*Jews in the East*, ii. 329.) He added that they would willingly live in friendship with the Jews, but that the Jews avoided all intercourse with them. Soon after visiting the Sepharedish Jews of Nablous, Dr. Frankl asked one of that sect, " if he had any intercourse with the Samaritans. The women retreated with a cry of horror, and one of them said, ' Have you been among the worshippers of the pigeon ? ' I said that I had. The women again fell back with the same expression of repugnance, and one of them said, ' *Take a purifying bath!* ' " (id., p. 334). I had the pleasure of spending a day among the Samaritans encamped on Mount Gerizim for their annual Passover, and neither in their habits nor apparent character could I see any cause for all this horror and hatred.

¹ Not far from Jacob's well — which is one of the very few precise spots in Palestine actually and closely identified by probability, as well as by unanimous tradition, with our Saviour's presence — there gushes a sweet and abundant stream. The fact that even the close vicinity of the fountain should not have been enough to render needless the toil of Jacob in digging the well — which is of immense depth — forcibly illustrates the jealousy and suspicion that marked his relations to the neighboring Canaanites. I sat by Jacob's well at noon one April day in 1870, hot and thirsty and tired. The well is now dry, and in fact all that can be seen of it is a pit some twenty feet deep ; the true well, or at any rate the mouth of it, having been filled up with masses of rubble and masonry from the basilica once built over it. Captain Anderson descended it to a depth of seventy-five feet, and it may have been twice that depth originally (*Work in Palestine*, p. 201). Riding on to the stream, I asked for some water, and, to my extreme surprise, for it never happened on any other occasion, was refused. I can only suppose that the cup which the Arab had in his hand was in some way sacred, and he did not wish it to be touched by a *Nusrâny*.

² Josephus (*Antt.* ix. 14, § 3 ; xi. 8, § 6 ; xii. 5, § 5) says that the Samaritans were fond of appealing to their descent from Jacob when the Jews were in prosperity, but denied all relationship when the Jews were in adversity. The son of Sirach calls them " the foolish people (ὁ λαὸς ὁ μωρὸς) that dwelleth in Shechem." Wetstein thinks that this was a play on the ancient name *Moreh*. " There be two manner of nations which my heart abhorreth, and the third is no nation : they that sit upon the mountain of Samaria, and they that dwell among the Philistines, and that foolish people that dwell in Sichem " (Ecclus. l. 25, 26).

Our Lord is not deterred by the hard literalism of her reply ; He treats it as He had treated similar unimaginative dulness in the learned Nicodemus, by still drawing her thoughts upward, if possible, to a higher region. She was thinking of common water, of which he who drinketh would thirst again ; but the water He spake of was a fountain within the heart, which quenched all thirst for ever, and sprang up unto eternal life.[1]

She becomes the suppliant now. He had asked her a little favor, which she had delayed, or half declined ; He now offers her an eternal gift. She sees that she is in some great Presence, and begs for this living water, but again with the same unspiritual narrowness — she only begs for it that she might thirst no more, nor come there to draw.

But enough was done for the present to awake and to instruct this poor stranger, and abruptly breaking off this portion of the conversation, Jesus bids her call her husband and return. All that was in His mind when He uttered this command we cannot tell ; it may have been because the immemorial decorum of the East regarded it as unbecoming, if not as positively wrong, for any man, and above all for a Rabbi, to hold conversation with a strange woman ; it may have been also to break a stony heart, to awake a sleeping conscience. For she was forced to answer that she had no husband, and our Lord, in grave confirmation of her sad confession, unbared to her the secret of a loose and wanton life. She had had five husbands, and he whom she now had was not her husband.[2]

She saw that a Prophet was before her, but from the facts of her own history — on which she is naturally anxious to linger as little as possible — her eager mind flies to the one great question which was daily agitated with such fierce passion between her race and that of Him to whom she spake, and which lay at the root of the savage animosity with which they treated each other. Chance had thrown her into the society of a great Teacher : was it not a good opportunity to settle for ever the immense discussion between Jews and Samaritans as to whether Jerusalem or Gerizim was the holy place of Palestine — Jerusalem, where Solomon had built his temple ; or Gerizim,

[1] Cf. Isa. xii. 3. The water is always there ; what is wanting is the sacred thirst. " Ubi sitis recurrit, hominis, non aquae defectus est." [149] (Bengel.)

[2] Keim, and many others, think it indisputable that this is an allegorical reference to the five religions brought by the Asiatic settlers into Samaria, and the hybrid Jehovism into which they were merged ! Strange that an allusion so superfluously dim should have been made at all ! If the Gospels were only intelligible to those who could guess the solution of such enigmas, the study of them might well be discredited altogether.

the immemorial sanctuary, where Joshua had uttered the blessings, and where Abraham had been ready to offer up his son ? [1] Pointing to the summit of the mountain towering eight hundred feet above them, and crowned by the ruins of the ancient temple of Manasseh, which Hyrcanus had destroyed, she put her dubious question, " Our fathers worshipped in this mountain, and ye say that Jerusalem is the place where men ought to worship ? " [2]

Briefly, and merely by way of parenthesis, He resolved her immediate problem. As against the Samaritans, the Jews were unquestionably right. Jerusalem was the place which God had chosen; compared to the hybrid and defective worship of Samaria, Judaism was pure and true; [3] but before and after touching on the earthly and temporal controversy, He uttered to her the mighty and memorable prophecy, that the hour was coming, yea now was, when " neither in this mountain nor yet in Jerusalem " should true worshippers worship the Father, but in every place should worship Him in spirit and in truth.

She was deeply moved and touched; but how could she, at the mere chance word of an unknown stranger, give up the strong faith in which she and her fathers had been born and bred? With a sigh she referred the final settlement of this and of every question to the advent of the Messiah; [4] and then He spake the simple, awful words — " I that speak unto thee am He."

---

[1] Deut. xxvii. 4 (where they read Gerizim). Cf. Gen. xii. 7 ; xxxiii. 18 ; Deut. xii. 5 ; xi. 29. See Stanley, *Sinai and Palestine*, pp. 236, 250, &c., ed. 1866 ; and the remarkable story in Jos. *Antt.* xviii. 4, § 1.

[2] Gen. xii. 6 ; xxxiii. 18, 20 ; Jos. *Antt.* xi. 8, § 4. Some have seen in the woman's question a mere desire to " turn the conversation," and to avoid the personal and searching topics to which it seemed likely to lead. Although there is no sign that her conscience was sufficiently moved to make this likely, we may doubtless see in what she says the common phenomenon of an intense interest in speculative and party questions combined with an utter apathy respecting moral obedience.

[3] John iv. 22, " *We* worship what we know ; for salvation is of the Jews " (Isa. ii. 3 ; compare the phrase of Tacitus, preserved in Sulp. Severus, " Christianos ex Judaeis exstitisse " [150]). It has been pointed out that such a sentence could not conceivably have been written by the Asiatic Gnostic to whom the school of Baur attribute the Fourth Gospel. " The ἡμεῖς is remarkable as being *the only instance* of our Lord thus speaking. . . The nearest approach to it is Matt. xv. 24, 26 " (Alford). Josephus preserves the striking fact that, down to the time of Alexander, the Temple on Gerizim *had no name* (ἀνώνυμον ἱερόν, *Antt.* xii. 5, § 5). The Samaritans actually proposed to Antiochus Epiphanes that it should be dedicated to Jupiter Hellenius.

[4] The Messianic hopes of the Samaritans were founded, not on the Prophets (whom they rejected), but on such passages as Gen. xlix. 10 ; Numb. xxiv. 17 :

His birth had been first revealed by night to a few unknown and ignorant shepherds; the first full, clear announcement by Himself of His own Messiahship was made by a well-side in the weary noon to a single obscure Samaritan woman. And to this poor, sinful, ignorant stranger had been uttered words of immortal significance, to which all future ages would listen, as it were, with hushed breath and on their knees.

Who would have *invented*, who would have merely *imagined*, things so unlike the thoughts of man as these? [1]

And here the conversation was interrupted; for the disciples — and among them he who writes the record — returned to their Master. Jacob's well is dug on elevated ground, on a spur of Gerizim, and in a part of the plain unobstructed and unshaded by trees or buildings. From a distance in that clear air they had seen and had heard their Master in long and earnest conversation with a solitary figure. He a Jew, He a Rabbi, talking to "a woman," and that woman a Samaritan, and that Samaritan a sinner! [2] Yet they dared not suggest anything to Him; they dared not question Him. The sense of His majesty, the love and the faith His very presence breathed, overshadowed all minor doubts or wondering curiosities.

Meanwhile the woman, forgetting even her water-pot in her impetuous amazement, had hurried to the city with her wondrous story.

Deut. xviii. 15. That they had hopes of a character more or less Messianic is independently proved by Jos. *Antt.* xviii. 4, § 1; and both Simon Magus and Dositheus may fairly be regarded as false Messiahs. Yet Sir R. Hanson (*Jesus of History*, pp. 82—85) relies on the supposed absence of Messianic expectations in Samaria as one argument against the genuineness of the Fourth Gospel (see Sanday, p. 88). It is true that the Tirithaba impostor is not said by Josephus (*l. c.*) to have called himself a Christ; but this silence would prove little. Ewald (*Gesch. Christ.* 174, 349) seems to feel a needless difficulty here. If Hausrath (*Neutest. Zeitgesch.*) were right in dating the disturbance about this time, the woman's remark would be still more natural; but probably this event was six or seven years after this date.

[1] A somewhat similar story occurs in the life of Ananda, the favorite disciple of Buddha; but I feel a strong conviction that some of these Buddhist stories are simply distorted echoes of the Gospel interpolated into the Lalita Vistara (see Beal's *Travels of Fah Hian and Sung Yun*, pp. lxxii., lxxiii.), and that others are merely accidental resemblances.

[2] John iv. 27, ὅτι μετὰ γυναικὸς ἐλάλει, "that he was talking with *a* (not *the*) woman." To talk with a woman in public was one of the six things which a Rabbi might not do (*Berachôth*, fol. 43 *b;* Schwab, p. 404); even, adds R. Hisda, with his own wife. Here we have a curious accidental analogy between Pharisaism and Buddhism. In the *Vinaya* a *Bhikshu* is not only forbidden to look at or speak to a woman, but he may not hold out his hand to his own mother if she be drowning! (Wilson, *Essays on the Rel. of the Hindus*, i. 360.)

Here was One who had revealed to her the very secrets of her life. Was not this the Messiah?

The Samaritans — in all the Gospel notices of whom we detect something simpler and more open to conviction than in the Jews — instantly flocked out of the city at her words, and while they were seen approaching,[1] the disciples urged our Lord to eat, for the hour of noon was now past, and He had had a weary walk. But all hunger had been satisfied in the exaltation of His ministry. "*I* have food to eat," He said, " which ye know not." Might they not have understood that, from childhood upwards, He had not lived by bread alone? But again we find the same dull, hard, stolid literalism. Their Scriptures, the very idiom in which they spoke, were full of vivid metaphors, yet they could hit on no deeper explanation of His meaning than that perhaps some one had brought Him something to eat.[2] How hard must it have been for Him thus, at every turn, to find even in His chosen ones such a strange incapacity to see that material images were but the vehicles for deep spiritual thoughts. But there was no impatience in Him who was meek and lowly of heart. " My meat," He said, " is to do the will of Him that sent me, and to finish His work." And then pointing to the inhabitants of Sichem, as they streamed to Him over the plain, he continued, " You talk of there being yet four months to harvest. Look at these fields, white already for the spiritual harvest. Ye shall be the joyful reapers of the harvest which I thus have sown in toil and pain ; but I, the sower, rejoice in the thought of that joy to come." [3]

The personal intercourse with Christ convinced many of these Samaritans far more deeply than the narrative of the woman to whom He had first revealed Himself ; and graciously acceding to their request that He would stay with them, He and His disciples abode there two days. Doubtless it was the teaching of those two days that had a vast share in the rich conversions of a few subsequent years.[4]

---

[1] John iv. 30, ἐξῆλθον —ἤρχοντο.

[2] For similar literal misconstructions see John ii. 20 ; iii. 4 ; iv. 11 ; vi. 42—52 ; Matt. xvi. 6 ; Mark viii. 15. We shall meet with the metaphor again, and even the Rabbis said, " The just *eat* of the glory of the Shechinah," and that Moses in Horeb was *fed* by the music of the spheres (Philo, *De Somn.*, i. 6).

[3] Josh. xxiv. 13. We have already seen that no certain note of time can be drawn from this allusion ; He " in whom is no before or after " might also have seen by imagination the whitening harvest in the springing corn.

[4] Acts viii. 5.

CHAPTER XVI.

REJECTED BY THE NAZARENES.

οἱ ἴδιοι αὐτὸν οὐ παρέλαβον.[151] — JOHN i. 11.

UP to this point of the sacred narrative we have followed the chronological guidance of St. John, and here, for the first time, we are seriously met by the difficult question as to the true order of events in our Lord's ministry.

Is it or is it not possible to construct a harmony of the Gospels which shall remove all the difficulties created by the differing order in which the Evangelists narrate the same events, and by the confessedly fragmentary character of their records, and by the general vagueness of the notes of time which they give, even when such notes are not wholly absent?

It is, perhaps, a sufficient answer to this question that scarcely any two authorities agree in the schemes which have been elaborated for the purpose. A host of writers, in all Christian nations, have devoted years — some of them have devoted well-nigh their whole lives — to the consideration of this and of similar questions, and have yet failed to come to any agreement or to command any general consent.

To enter into all the arguments, on both sides, about the numerous disputed points which must be settled before the problem can be solved, would be to undertake a task which would fill many volumes, would produce no final settlement of the difficulty, and would be wholly beyond the purpose before us. What I have done is carefully to consider the chief *data*, and without entering into controversy or pretending to remove all possible objections, to narrate the events in that order which, after repeated study, seems to be the most intrinsically probable, with due reference to all *definite* indications of time which the Gospels contain. An indisputable or convincing harmony of the Gospels appears to me to be impossible, and as a necessary consequence it can be of no absolute importance. Had it been essential to our comprehension of the Saviour's life that we should know more exactly the times and places where the years of His public ministry were spent, the Christian at least will believe that such knowledge would not have been withheld from us.

The inspiration which guided the Evangelists in narrating the life of Christ was one which enabled them to tell all that was necessary for the peace and well-being of our souls, but very far from all which we might have yearned to know for the gratification of our curiosity, or even the satisfaction of our historic interest. Nor is it difficult to see herein a fresh indication that our thoughts must be fixed on the spiritual more than on the material — on Christ who liveth for ever-more, and is with us always, even to the end of the world, far more than on the external incidents of that human life which, in the council of God's will, was the appointed means of man's redemption. We shall never know all that we could wish to know about

> " The sinless years
> That breathed beneath the Syrian blue."

but we shall still be the children of God and the disciples of His Christ if we keep His sayings and do the things which He commanded.

St. John tells us that after two days' abode among the open-minded Samaritans of Sychar, Jesus went into Galilee, "*for* He himself testified that a prophet hath no honor in his own country," and yet he continues, that, "When he was come into Galilee, the Galilæans received him, having seen all the things that He did at Jerusalem at the feast;" and he adds, immediately afterwards, that Jesus came again into Cana of Galilee, and there healed the nobleman's son. The perplexing "for" seems to point to one of those suppressed trains of thought which are so frequent in St. John. I understand it to mean that at Nazareth, in his own home, rejection awaited Him in spite of the first gleam of transient acceptance; and that for this rejection He was not unprepared, *for* it was one of His distinct statements that "in His own country a Prophet is dishonored." [1]

---

[1] John iv. 43—45. The "*for*" seems at first sight to involve a contradiction, nor is it possible to make it mean "although." Some suppose the meaning to be that " He did *not* go to his own country, Nazareth, but to Cana and Capernaum "— which were in Upper Galilee, to which alone the name Galilee was properly applied (cf. Luke iv. 31 ; Matt. iv. 13, 15 ; Jos. *De Bell. Jud.* iii. 3, § 1) — "*for*," &c. And accordingly the *Galilæans,* properly so called, received Him. [But this would make the καταλιπών of Matt. iv. 13 = παραλιπών.] Possibly, however the particle may refer (as I have stated in the text) to a thought unexpressed in the writer's mind — viz., either that the reason *why he had declared himself first in Judæa,* was that a prophet has no honor in his own country ; or that " He was not unaware of the opposition which would await Him, for He knew that a prophet is least honored among his own." The γάρ may therefore point mentally to the very events which St. John omits, but which are narrated or alluded to in Luke iv. 14—30. " The causal connections in the Fourth Gospel," says Mr. Sanday (p. 98), "are often perplexing." Origen's solution that by Ἰδία πατρίς is

It was not the object of St. John to dwell on the ministry in Galilee, which had been already narrated by the Synoptists; accordingly it is from St. Luke that we receive the fullest account of our Lord's first public act in His native town.[1]

It appears that Jesus did not go direct from Sychar to Nazareth. On His way (unless we take Luke iv. 15 for a general and unchronological reference) He taught continuously, and with general admiration and acceptance, in the synagogues of Galilee.[2] In this way He arrived at Nazareth, and according to His usual custom, for He had doubtless been a silent worshipper in that humble place Sabbath after Sabbath from boyhood upwards, He entered into the synagogue on the Sabbath day.

There was but one synagogue in the little town,[3] and probably it resembled in all respects, except in its humbler aspect and materials, the synagogues of which we see the ruins at Tell Hûm and Irbid. It was simply a rectangular hall, with a pillared portico of Grecian architecture, of which the further extremity (where the "sanctuary" was placed) usually pointed towards Jerusalem, which, since the time of Solomon, had always been the *kibleh* — i. e., the consecrated *direction* — of a Jew's worship, as Mecca is of a Mohammedan's. In wealthier places it was built of white marble, and sculptured on the outside in alto-relievo, with rude ornaments of vine-leaves and grapes, or the budding rod and pot of manna.[4] On

---

meant Judæa, is wholly unsatisfactory. That Christ did not *twice* preach at Nazareth under circumstances so closely analogous, I regard as certain, and that is my reason for considering that Matt. xiii. 53—58; Mark vi. 1—6, refer to this same event, narrated out of its proper order.

[1] Luke iv. 14—30. There *may possibly* (but not certainly) be some unchronological reminiscences of this visit to Nazareth in Matt. xiii. 54—58; Mark vi. 2—6.

[2] Luke iv. 15, ἐδίδασκεν . . . δοξαζόμενος. The old name for a synagogue was *Beth Tephillah*, or "House of Prayer;" but they are now called *Beth Hak-Keneseth*, "House of Assembly." The hours of meeting were the 3d (*shacarith*), the 6th (*mincha*), and the 9th (*arabith*) — i. e., 9, 12, and 3. (Buxt. *De Synag. Jud.*, ch. x., p. 219, ed. 1661.) Without consulting the Latin treatises of Buxtorf, Vitringa, &c., the reader may find many of the most interesting facts about synagogues in the admirable articles on them by Prof. Plumptre (Smith's *Dict. of the Bible*) and Dr. Ginsburg (Kitto's *Bible Cyclop.*).

[3] Luke iv. 16, εἰς τὴν συναγωγὴν.

[4] These emblems were found on the broken slab of the architrave which once stood over the door of the synagogue at Capernaum (Tell Hûm). They have no pretence to architectural beauty ; "le goût en est assez mesquin" [152] (Renan, *Vie de Jésus*, p. 82, ed. pop.). For the reason of the *kibleh*, see 1 Kings viii. 29 ; Dan. vi. 10. The orientation does not now seem to be very carefully attended to, for Mr. Monro tells me that in Algiers the reader's pulpit in the synagogues may look north, east, or south — only not west.

entering there were seats on one side for the men ; on the other, behind a lattice, were seated the women, shrouded in their long veils. At one end was the *tebhah* or ark of painted wood, which contained the sacred scriptures; and at one side was the *bîma*, or elevated seat for the reader or preacher.¹ Clergy, properly speaking, there were none, but in the chief seats were the ten or more *batlanîm*, "men of leisure," or leading elders;² and pre-eminent among these the chief of the synagogue,³ or *rôsh hak-kenéseth.* Inferior in rank to these were the *chazzán*,⁴ or clerk, whose duty it was to keep the sacred books; the *sheliach*, corresponding to our sacristan or verger; and the *parnasîm*, or shepherds, who in some respects acted as deacons.

The service of the synagogue was not unlike our own. After the prayers ⁵ two lessons were always read, one from the Law called *parashah*, and one from the Prophets called *haphtarah;* and as there were no ordained ministers to conduct the services — for the office of priests and Levites at Jerusalem was wholly different — these lessons might not only be read by any competent person who received permission from the *rôsh hak-kenéseth*, but he was even at liberty to add his own *midrash*, or comment.⁶

The reading of the *parashah*, or lesson from the Pentateuch, was apparently over ⁷ when Jesus ascended the steps of the *bîma*. Recognizing his claim to perform the honorable function of a *maphtîr* or reader, the *chazzán* drew aside the silk curtain of the painted ark which contained the sacred manuscripts, and handed Him the *megillah* or roll of the Prophet Isaiah, which contained the *haphtarah* of the day.⁸ Our Lord unrolled the volume, and found the well-known

---

¹ The Jews borrowed the word בימה from the Greek (but compare Neh. viii. 4; ix. 4).

² πρεσβύτεροι (Luke vii. 3); called also *zekénîm* (זקנים). Their " chief seats " (Mark xii. 39, &c.) were placed in front of the ark, and facing the congregation. In the synagogue at Alexandria were seventy-one golden arm-chairs, or seats of honor, for doctors and honorable men (Ginsburg, *l. c.*).

³ ἀρχισυνάγωγος (Mark v. 22; &c.).

⁴ ὑπηρέτης (Luke iv. 20).

⁵ For the prayers, which consisted of the Hymnal group, the *Shema*, the 18 *Berachôth*, or Benedictions, &c., see a full account in Ginsburg, *l. c.*

⁶ See, for these particulars, Surenhusius, *Mishna*, pp. 339, seqq.; Capecelatro, *Vita di Gesù Cristo*, i. 153 ; Keim, *Gesch. Jesu*, ii. 20. — Often the interpreter or expounder was a different person from the *maphtîr*, or reader. The *Tôrah* rolls are now usually adorned with the *ets chajîm*, or "tree of life" (Frankl, *Jews in the East*, ii. 17).

⁷ This may, perhaps, be implied in the word ἐπεδόθη, was handed to him in addition. (Wordsworth.)

⁸ It appears that the Prophecy of Isaiah was generally written on a separate *megillah*. It would be necessary to find the place, because the scroll of the

passage in Isaiah lxi. The whole congregation stood up to listen to Him. The length of the *haphtarah* might be from three to twenty one verses, but Jesus only read the first and part of the second; ¹ stopping short, in a spirit of tenderness, before the stern expression, " The day of vengeance of our God," so that the gracious words, " The acceptable year ² of the Lord," might rest last upon their ears and form the text of His discourse. He then rolled up the *megillah*, handed it back to the *chazzán*, and, as was customary among the Jews, sat down to deliver His sermon.³

The passage which He had read, whether part of the ordinary lesson for the day or chosen by himself,⁴ was a very remarkable one, and it must have derived additional grandeur and solemnity from the lips of Him in whom it was fulfilled. Every eye in the synagogue

---

Prophets had only one roller, the Law had two ; and " every hebdomadal lesson is unrolled from the right roller, and rolled on the left Hence, when the scroll of the Law is opened on the next Sabbath, the portion appointed for the day is at once found." (Ginsburg, s. v. " Haphtarah," Kitto's *Cyclop.* ii. 224.)

¹ Probably it would be read in Hebrew, but translated by the *methurgeman* (" interpreter ") either into Aramaic, which was then the vernacular of Palestine ; or into Greek, which at that time seems to have been generally understood and spoken throughout the country. The passage, as given in St. Luke, agrees mainly with the LXX. or Greek version ; but (as is almost invariably the case in the New Testament quotations from the Old Testament) with some remarkable differences. The deviations from the Hebrew original are at first sight considerable, though the main conception is the same. I do not know of any book where the reader will find a clearer and briefer comparison of the New Testament quotations with the original, with some explanation of the divergences between them, than in Mr. Turpie's *Old Testament in the New* (Williams and Norgate, 1868). Without binding myself by all Mr. Turpie's conclusions, I have found his book very useful.

² This expression led to the mistaken tradition of some Fathers [Clem. Alex. *Strom.* i., p. 147; Orig., *De Princ.* iv. 5 ; Tert. *C. Jud.* 8 ; Lactant. *Instt. Div.* iv. 10 ; Aug. *De Civ. Dei*, xviii. 54 ; together with the Valentinians and the Alogi (see Hase, *Leben Jesu*, p. 21 ; Gieseler, *Ch. Hist.* i. 2, 10, &c.)] that our Lord's ministry lasted but for a single year. Some refer them to that great and beautiful section of His life known as " the Galilæan year." In all probability the expression " year " is merely general. Mr. Browne, in his *Ordo Saeclorum*, argues powerfully for the limitation of our Lord's ministry to a year; but the *three* passovers distinctly mentioned by St. John (without a single important variation in any MS., or version, or quotation by the Fathers in vi. 4) seem conclusive on the other side (John ii. 13 ; vi. 4 ; xi. 55) ; and this was the view of Melito, St. Hippolytus, St. Jerome, &c. (See Hase, *ubi supra;* Westcott, *Introd. to Gosp.*, p. 266.)

³ This was our Lord's usual attitude when teaching (Matt. v. 1 ; Mark xiii. 3, &c.). Probably the audience, as well as the reader, stood at any rate during the reading of the Law (Neh. viii. 5). (Frankl, *ubi supr.*) The sermon was called *derash* (λόγος παρακλήσεως, Acts xiii. 15).

⁴ It appears that this was admissible in the case of the lesson from the Prophets, though no one might select a passage alternative for the *parashah.*

was fixed upon Him with a gaze of intense earnestness,[1] and we may imagine the thrill of awful expectation and excitement which passed through the hearts of the listeners, as, in a discourse of which the subject only is preserved for us by the Evangelist, He developed the theme that He was Himself the Messiah, of whom the great Prophet had sung 700 years before.[2] His words were full of a grace, an authority, a power which was at first irresistible, and which commanded the involuntary astonishment of all. But as He proceeded He became conscious of a change. The spell of His wisdom and sweetness[3] was broken, as these rude and violent Nazarenes began to realize the full meaning of His divine claims. It was customary with the Jews in the worship of their synagogue to give full vent to their feelings, and it was not long before Jesus became sensible of indignant and rebellious murmurs. He saw that those eager glittering eyes, which had been fixed upon Him in the first excitement of attention, were beginning to glow with the malignant light of jealousy and hatred. "Is not this *the carpenter?* is he not the brother of workmen like himself — James and Joses and Simon and Judas — and of sisters who live among us? do not even his own family disbelieve in him?"[4] Such were the whispers which began to be buzzed about among the audience. This was no young and learned Rabbi[5] from the schools of Gamaliel or Shammai, and yet he spoke with an authority which not even the great scribes assumed! Even a Hillel, when his doctrines failed to persuade, could only secure conviction by appealing to the previous authority of a Shemaia or an Abtalion. But *this* teacher appealed to no one — this teacher who had but been their village carpenter! What business had *he* to teach? Whence could he know letters, having never learned?[6]

Jesus did not leave unobserved the change which was passing over

---

(Lightfoot, *Hor. Hebr.*, *ad* Luke iv. 16). In the list of Sabbatic and festival *parshiôth* and *haphtarôth*, Isa. lxi. 1 does not occur; but Isa. lxi. 10—lxiii. 9 was read on the 51st Sunday of the year (Ginsburg, s. v. "Haphtara;" Kitto, *Bib. Cycl.*; Deutsch, *Bible Dict.* iii. 1639 *a*).

[1] Luke iv. 20, ἦσαν ἀτενίζοντες αὐτῷ.

[2] Luke iv. 18, οὗ ἕνεκεν ἔχρισέ με. "M'a messianisée" (Salvador, *Jésus Christ et sa Doctrine*).

[3] Cf. Ps. xlv. 2.

[4] Matt. xiii. 57, "and in his own house." Cf. John vii. 5; Mark iii. 21; Matt. xiii. 56.

[5] The title, together with that of "teacher," was, however, freely allowed to Christ even by his enemies (Matt. viii. 19; xii. 38; xxii. 16; xxiii. 7, &c.).

[6] *Jer. Pesach.*, f. 33, 1; Derenbourg, *Hist. Pal.* 177, seqq.; Keim, *Gesch. Jes.* ii. 12. Cf. John vii. 15, &c.

the feelings of His audience.[1] He at once told them that He-*was* the Jesus whom they described, and yet with no abatement of His Messianic grandeur. Their hardness and unbelief had already depressed His spirit before He had even entered the synagogue. The implied slur on the humility of His previous life He passes by; it was too essentially provincial and innately vulgar to need correction, since any Nazarene of sufficient honesty might have reminded himself of the yet humbler origin of the great herdsman Amos. Nor would He notice the base hatred which weak and bad men always contract for those who shame them by the silent superiority of noble lives. But He was aware of another feeling in their minds; a demand upon Him for some stupendous vindication of His claims; a jealousy that He should have performed miracles at Cana, and given an impression of His power at Capernaum,[2] to say nothing of what He had done and taught at Jerusalem — and yet that He should have vouchsafed no special mark of His favor among them. He knew that the taunting and sceptical proverb, "Physician, heal thyself," was in their hearts, and all but on their lips.[3] But to show them most clearly that He was something more than they — that He was no mere Nazarene like any other who might have lived among them for thirty years, and that He belonged not to them but to the world[4] — He reminds them that miracles are not to be limited by geographical relationships — that Elijah had only saved the Phœnician widow of Sarepta, and Elisha only healed the hostile leper of Syria.

What then? were they in *His* estimation (and He but "the carpenter!") no better than Gentiles and lepers? This was the climax of all that was intolerable to them, as coming from a fellow-townsman

---

[1] "The village beggarly pride of the Nazarenes cannot at all comprehend the humility of the Great One" (Stier, *Reden Jesu,* E. Tr., iii. 446). Their remark savors of the notions of Shammai, who (in opposition to Hillel) held that no one ought even to be admitted into a school unless he was of good family and rich (*Abhôth de Rabbi Nathan,* ii.).

[2] These are unrecorded if our order is right; but remarkable instances of teaching and of powers quite sufficient to establish a strong expectation — especially when taken in connection with the miracle at Cana — may have occurred in the short interval mentioned in John ii. 12. Even at Nazareth it seems that some slight acts of healing, hardly regarded as miracles, had been performed (Mark vi. 5; Matt. xiii. 58). More than this He neither could nor would perform amid a faithless and hostile population.

[3] The proverb finds its analogy in all nations. It was afterwards addressed to Christ upon the cross.

[4] It has been conjectured that His recent favorable reception at Sychar would tend to prejudice the Nazarenes against Him.

whom they wished to rank among themselves; and at these words their long-suppressed fury burst into a flame. The speaker was no longer interrupted by a murmur of disapprobation, but by a roar of wrath. With one of those bursts of sanguinary excitement which characterized that strange, violent, impassioned people — a people whose minds are swept by storms as sudden as those which in one moment lash into fury the mirror surface of their lake — they rose in a body,[1] tore Him out of the city, and then dragged Him to the brow of the hill above. The little town of Nazareth nestles in the southern hollows of that hill; many a mass of precipitous rock lies imbedded on its slopes, and it is probable that the hill-side may have been far more steep and precipitous two thousand years ago.[2] To one of these rocky escarpments they dragged Him, in order to fling Him headlong down.

But His hour was not yet come, and they were saved from the consummation of a crime which would have branded them with everlasting infamy. "He passed through the midst of them, and went on his way." There is no need to suppose an actual miracle; still less to imagine a secret and sudden escape into the narrow and tortuous lanes of the town. Perhaps His silence, perhaps the calm nobleness of His bearing, perhaps the dauntless innocence of His gaze overawed them. Apart from anything supernatural, there seems to have been in the presence of Jesus a spell of mystery and of majesty which even His most ruthless and hardened enemies acknowledged, and before which they involuntarily bowed. It was to this that He owed His escape when the maddened Jews in the Temple took up stones to stone Him; it was this that made the bold and bigoted officers of the Sanhedrin unable to arrest Him as He taught in public during the Feast of Tabernacles at Jerusalem; it was this that made the armed band of His enemies, at His mere look, fall before Him to the ground in the Garden of Gethsemane. Suddenly, quietly He asserted His freedom, waved aside His captors,

---

[1] Luke iv. 28, ἐπλήσθησαν πάντες θυμοῦ, κ. τ. λ. Cf. Acts xxii. 22; xxviii. 25.

[2] Κατακρημνίσαι. The word occurs nowhere else in the New Testament or the LXX., except in 2 Chron. xxv. 12. Κατακρημνισμός was one form of stoning, which was the recognized legal punishment for blasphemy. The scene of this event was certainly not the "Mount of Precipitation," which was *much* beyond a Sabbath-day's journey, being at least two miles off. It may have been the cliff above the Maronite Church, which is about forty feet high. When I was at Nazareth, my horse was hurt, and might easily have been killed, by sliding down a huge mass of rock on the hill-side. What criminal would be hurt by a fall from the Tarpeian rock in its *present* condition?

and overawing them by His simple glance, passed through their midst unharmed. Similar events have occurred in history, and continue still to occur. There is something in defenceless and yet dauntless dignity that calms even the fury of a mob. "They stood — stopped — inquired — were ashamed — fled — separated." [1]

And so He left them, never apparently to return again ; never, if we are right in the view here taken, to preach again in their little synagogue. Did any feelings of merely human regret weigh down His soul while He was wending His weary steps [2] down the steep hill-slope towards Cana of Galilee ? Did any tear start in His eyes unbidden as He stood, perhaps for the last time, to gaze from thence on the rich plain of Esdraelon, and the purple heights of Carmel, and the white sands that fringe the blue waters of the Mediterranean ? Were there any from whom He grieved to be severed, in the green secluded valley where His manhood had labored, and His childhood played ? Did He cast one longing, lingering glance at the humble home in which for so many years He had toiled as the village carpenter ? Did no companion of His innocent boyhood, no friend of His sinless youth, accompany Him with awe, and pity, and regret ? Such questions are not, surely, unnatural ; not, surely, irreverent ; — but they are not answered. Of all merely human emotions of His heart, except so far as they directly affect His mission upon earth, the Gospels are silent. [3] We know only that henceforth other friends awaited him away from boorish Nazareth, among the gentle and noble-hearted fishermen of Bethsaida ; and that thenceforth His home, so far as He had a home, was in the little city of Capernaum, beside the sunlit waters of the Galilæan Lake.

---

[1] Pfenninger, quoted by Stier, iii. 451. Cf. John vii. 30, 46 ; viii. 59 ; x. 39 ; xviii. 6. — Some of my readers may be aware of an instance in which a clergyman, still living, walked untouched through the very midst of a brutal and furious London mob, who had assembled for the express purpose of insulting and assaulting him. It was observed by more than one spectator, that if he had wavered for a single instant, or shown the slightest sign of fear and irresolution, he would in all probability have been struck down, and possibly have not escaped with his life.

[2] Luke iv. 30, ἐπορεύετο.

[3] Whole volumes must lie concealed in that memorable allusion of Heb. ii. 18 {πέπονθεν αὐτὸς πειρασθείς [153]) and iv. 15 (πεπειραμένον κατὰ πάντα καθ᾽ ὁμοιότητα, κ. τ. λ.[154]).

CHAPTER XVII.

THE BEGINNING OF THE GALILÆAN MINISTRY.

πτωχοὶ εὐαγγελίζονται.[155] — MATT. xi. 5.

REJECTED at Nazareth, our Lord naturally turned to the neighboring Cana, where His first miracle had been wrought to gladden friends. He had not long arrived when an officer from the neighboring court of Herod Antipas, hearing of His arrival, came and urgently entreated that He would descend to Capernaum and heal his dying son. Although our Lord never set foot in Tiberias, yet the voice of 'John had more than once been listened to with alarm and reverence in the court of the voluptuous king.[1] We know that Manaen, the foster-brother of Herod, was in after days a Christian, and we know that among the women who ministered to Christ of their substance was Joanna, the wife of Chuza, Herod's steward.[2] As this courtier (βασιλικὸς) believed in Christ with his whole house, in consequence of the miracle now wrought, it has been conjectured with some probability that it was none other than Chuza himself.

The imperious urgency of his request, a request which appears at first to have had but little root in spiritual conviction, needed a momentary check. It was necessary for Jesus to show that He was no mere *hakeem*, no mere benevolent physician, ready at any time to work local cures, and to place His supernatural powers at the beck and call of any sufferer who might come to Him as a desperate resource. He at once rebuked the spirit which demanded mere signs and prodigies as the sole possible ground of faith.[3] But yielding to the father's passionate earnestness, He dismissed him with the assur-

---

[1] In the general obscurity of the chronology, it seems clear (as we have said before) that by *this* time John had been cast into prison (Matt. iv. 12, 13 ; Mark i. 14 ; Luke iii. 20). Comparing these passages of the Synoptists with John iii. 24; iv. 45, and following the order of events given in the text, we may perhaps assume (though this is not absolutely necessary, *v. supr.*, p. 181, *n.*) that Galilee here means *Northern* Galilee, or Galilee proper.

[2] Acts xiii. 1 ; cf. Luke viii. 3.

[3] τέρατα. This is a half-disparaging term for miracles, rarely used in the Gospels, and derived only from the sense of astonishment which they caused

ance that his son lived. The interview had taken place at the seventh hour — *i. e.*, at one o'clock in the day.[1] Even in the short November day it would have been still possible for the father to get to Capernaum ; for if Cana be, as we believe, Kefr Kenna, it is not more than five hours' distance from Capernaum. But the father's soul had been calmed by faith in Christ's promise, and he slept that night at some intermediate spot upon the road.[2] The next day his slaves met him, and told him that, at the very hour when Jesus had spoken, the fever had left his son. This was the second time that Christ had signalized His arrival in Galilee by the performance of a conspicuous miracle. The position of the courtier caused it to be widely known, and it contributed, no doubt, to that joyous and enthusiastic welcome which our Lord received during that bright early period of His ministry, which has been beautifully called the " Galilæan spring." [3]

At this point we are again met by difficulties in the chronology, which are not only serious, but to the certain solution of which there appears to be no clue. If we follow exclusively the order given by one Evangelist, we appear to run counter to the scattered indications which may be found in another. That it should be so will cause no difficulty to the candid mind. The Evangelists do not profess to be scrupulously guided by chronological sequence. The pictures which they give of the main events in the life of Christ are simple and harmonious, and that they should be presented in an informal, and what, with reference to mere literary considerations, would be called inartistic manner, is not only in accordance with the position of the writers, but is an additional confirmation of our conviction that we are reading the records of a life which, in its majesty and beauty, infinitely transcended the capacities of invention or imagination in the simple and faithful annalists by whom it was recorded.

It was not, as we have already observed, the object of St. John to narrate the Galilæan ministry, the existence of which he distinctly implies (vii. 3, 4), but which had already been fully recorded. Circumstances had given to the Evangelist a minute and profound knowl-

---

[1] I here again (*v. supr.*, pp. 131, *n.*, 173, *n.*) assume that the hours, as mentioned by St. John, are calculated from sunrise, according to the *universal* custom of that day.

[2] Perhaps at Lubîyeh, or Hattîn.

[3] Ewald says that " no one can doubt " as to the identity of this incident with that narrated of the centurion's servant. It is, however, seriously doubted — nay, entirely disputed — by many of the ablest commentators, from Chrysostom down to Ebrard and Tischendorf.

edge of the ministry in Judæa, which is by the others presupposed, though not narrated.[1] At this point accordingly (iv. 54) he breaks off, and only continues the thread of his narrative at the return of Jesus to "a" or "the" feast of the Jews (v. 1). If the feast here alluded to were the feast of Purim, as we shall see is probably the case, then St. John here passes over the history of several months. We fall back, therefore, on the Synoptic Gospels for the events of the intervening ministry on the shores of Gennesareth. And since we have often to choose between the order of events as narrated by the three Evangelists, we must here follow that given by St. Luke, both because it appears to us intrinsically probable, and because St. Luke, unlike the two previous Evangelists, seems to have been guided, so far as his information allowed, by chronological considerations.[2]

It seems then, that after leaving Cana, our Lord went at once to Capernaum, accompanied apparently by His mother and His brethren, and made that town His home.[3] His sisters were probably married, and did not leave their native Nazareth; but the dreadful insult which Jesus had received would have been alone sufficient to influence His family to leave the place, even if they did not directly share in the odium and persecution which His words had caused. Perhaps the growing alienation between Himself and them may have been due, in part, to this circumstance. They must have felt, and we know that they did feel, a deeply-seated annoyance, if, refusing to

---

[1] Distinctly, for instance, in Matt. iv. 25; xxiii. 37, "*how often;*" xix. 1; Luke x. 38; &c.; not to mention the extremely interesting and valuable reading of $\tau\tilde{\eta}s$ *Ἰουδαίας*[156] for $\tau\tilde{\eta}s$ *Γαλιλαίας*[157] in Luke iv. 44. This reading is found in ℵ, B, C, L, &c., and in the Coptic version. On the probable character of the reading, see Caspari, *Chronol. Geogr. Einleit.*, p. 111. If the abrupt transition to another scene in Luke v. 1 is against it, yet this very circumstance strengthens the *diplomatic* evidence in its favor. Spannheim well remarks, " Nihil frequentius quam quaedam praetermitti ab his, suppleri ab aliis. . . ne vel scriptores sacri ex compacto scripsisse viderentur, vel lectores uni ab illis, spretis reliquis, haererent" [158] (Wordsworth on Matt. v. 1).

[2] Luke i. 1—3.

[3] " His own city " (Matt. ix. 1 ; cf. Matt. xvii. 24). St. Matthew (iv. 15, 16) sees in this locality of the ministry an idealized fulfilment of Isa. ix. 1. The LXX. is here loose, and the quotation also differs from the Hebrew ; less so, however, than might at first sight appear, because the " did more greviously afflict her " of the English Version (which would utterly contradict the purport of St. Matthew's allusion) should be rather, "made heavy," i. e., "*honored*" (*v. supr.*, pp. 153, 156 ; see Turpie, p. 226). " Way of the sea," because the great caravan road ran along its western shore. St. Luke alone calls the Sea of Galilee $\lambda i\mu\nu\eta$, because he wrote for Gentiles. The Hebrews apply ‏ם‎, to any water (1 Kings xviii. 43 ; Numb. xxxiv. 11). " Beyond Jordan " perhaps refers to Peræa.

admit the full awfulness of His mission, and entirely disapproving the form of its manifestation, they yet felt themselves involved in hatred and ruin as a direct consequence of His actions. Certain it is that, although apparently they were living at Capernaum, *their* home was not *His* home. Home, in the strict sense, He had none; but the house of which He made ordinary use appears to have been that which belonged to His chief apostle. It is true that Simon and Andrew are said to have belonged to Bethsaida, but they may easily have engaged the use of a house at Capernaum, belonging to Peter's mother-in-law; or, since Bethsaida is little more than a suburb or part of Capernaum, they may have actually moved for the convenience of their Master from the one place to the other.

The first three Evangelists have given us a detailed account of the Lord's first sabbath at Capernaum, and it has for us an intrinsic interest, because it gives us one remarkable specimen of the manner in which He spent the days of His active ministry. It is the best commentary on that epitome of His life which presents it to us in its most splendid originality — that "He went about doing good." It is the point which the rarest and noblest of His followers have found it most difficult to imitate; it is the point in which His life transcended most absolutely the ideal of the attainments of His very greatest forerunners. The seclusion of the hermit, the self-maceration of the ascetic, the rapture of the mystic — all these are easier and more common than the unwearied toil of a self-renouncing love.

The day began in the synagogue, perhaps in the very building which the Jews owed to the munificence of the centurion proselyte. If Capernaum were indeed Tell Hûm, then the white marble ruins which still stand on a little eminence above the sparkling lake, and still encumber the now waste and desolate site of the town with their fragments of elaborate sculpture, may possibly be the ruins of this very building. The synagogue, which is not very large, must have been densely crowded; and to teach an earnest and expectant crowd — to teach as He taught, not in dull, dead, conventional formulæ, but with thoughts that breathed and words that burned — to teach as they do who are swayed by the emotion of the hour, while heart speaks to heart — must have required no slight energy of life, must have involved no little exhaustion of the physical powers. But this was not all. While He was speaking, while the audience of simple-hearted yet faithful, intelligent, warlike people were listening to Him in mute astonishment, hanging on His lips with deep and reverential admiration — suddenly the deep silence was broken by the wild cries and obscene ravings of one of those unhappy wretches who were universally believed to be under the influence of impure spirits, and who — in the absence of any retreat for such sufferers — had, perhaps, slipped in unobserved among the throng.[1] Even the poor demoniac, in the depths of his perturbed and degraded nature, had felt the haunting spell of that pure presence, of that holy voice, of that divine and illuminating message. But, distorted as his whole moral being was, he raved against it, as though by the voices of the evil demons who possessed him, and while he· saluted " Jesus the Nazarene " as the Holy One of God, yet, with agonies of terror and hatred, demanded to be let alone, and not to be destroyed.

Then followed a scene of thrilling excitement. Turning to the furious and raving sufferer, recognizing the duality of his consciousness, addressing the devil which seemed to be forcing from him these terrified ejaculations, Jesus said, " Hold thy peace,[2] and come out of

---

[1] Luke iv. 33, "A spirit of an unclean devil," "cried with a loud voice ;" cf. Mark i. 23. The ἔα is, perhaps, not " desist ! let us alone ! " but a wild cry of horror, the Hebr. אֲחָהּ; so Stier, iii. 378. The Jews, like most ancient nations, attributed every evil result immediately to the action of demons, *e. g.*, even Noah's drunkenness. In Ps. xci. 6, the LXX. renders "the destruction that wasteth at noonday," by μεσημβρινὰ δαιμόνια. These mid-day demons are called שִׁיהֲרִין, Targ. Cant. iv. 6. If a woman does not cover her head, demons sit upon her hair. If you do not wash your hands before meals, you become the victim of a demon, *Shibta.* " If a bull rushes at you in the field," says the Talmud, " Satan leaps up from between his horns." All mental aberration, all sudden sickness, all melancholy tendencies, all unexpected obstacles, were, and in the East still are, regarded as due to the direct influence of demons (*devs*). These demons they believed to be the spirits of the wicked (Jos. *B. J.* vii. 6, § 3). Such instances of the Jewish belief might be indefinitely multiplied, and that they shared it with the majority of mankind may be seen in Mr. E. B. Tylor's *Primitive Culture, passim.* That they regarded as demoniacal possession what we regard as epilepsy and mania is certain. This is indeed clear from the passage of Josephus to which I have just referred, but the real controversy turns on the question whether much more than this is not possible, and whether in the days of Christ much more than this was not a common phenomenon. It is not one of those questions which seem to me to be of vital importance, and dogmatism on either side must be left to those who think it necessary. The reader may find the entire question as to the *actuality*, or the mere *semblance* of, and *belief in*, demoniacal possession, fully argued on both sides, with much acuteness and impartiality in Jahn, *Archæologia Biblica*, E. Tr., 3rd edn., pp. 200—216.

[2] φιμώθητι (Luke iv. 35). A strong word, meaning literally " be thou muzzled " (cf. Acts xvi. 18). Those who reject the reality of demoniacal possession, and therefore regard the action as a figurative concession to the sufferers' delusions, appeal to such expressions as Matt. viii. 26 ; Luke iv. 39. On this doctrine of "accommodation," see Suidas s. v. Συγκατάβασις ; Haag, *Hist. des Dogmes*, i. 98. Although it is a principle which has received the sanction of some very eminent Fathers, it must be applied with the most extreme caution.

him." He never accepted or tolerated this ghastly testimony to His origin and office. The calm, the sweetness, the power of the divine utterance were irresistible. The demon fell to the ground in a fearful paroxysm, screaming and convulsed. But it was soon over. The man arose cured; his whole look and bearing showed that he was dispossessed of the over-mastering influence, and was now in his right mind. A miracle so gracious and so commanding had never before been so strikingly manifested, and the worshippers separated with emotions of indescribable wonder.[1]

Rising from the seat of the *maphtîr* in the synagogue, Christ retired into the house of Simon. Here again he was met by the strong appeal of sickness and suffering. Simon, whom he had already bound to Himself on the banks of the Jordan, by the first vague call to his future Apostolate, was a married man,[2] and his wife's mother lay stricken down by a violent access of fever.[3] One request from the afflicted family was sufficient: there was no need, as in the case of the more worldly nobleman, for importunate entreaty.[4] He stood over her; He took her by the hand; He raised her up; He rebuked the fever; His voice stirring her whole being, dominated over the

---

[1] It is worth while to set side by side with this an instance of exorcism, such as was commonly practised by Jews at this very period (cf. Matt. xii. 27; Mark ix. 38; Acts xix. 13), the invention of which Josephus attributes to Solomon, and which he tells us he had himself witnessed. He says that he had seen a Jew named Eleazar casting out demons in the presence of Vespasian, Titus, their officers and army. His method was to draw the demoniac out through the nostrils by a ring and a particular root. Hereupon the man fell down, and Eleazar, with various incantations and in the name of Solomon, adjured the demon not to return. And then, in proof that the cure was effectual, he put a basin of water a little way off, and bade the demon, as he departed, to overturn it! (Jos. *Antt.* viii. 2, § 5). For the root employed see *id. B. J.* vii. 6, § 3. Josephus was a man of astute mind and liberal experience, familiar with heathen culture, and a constant denizen of courts and camps. The Evangelists, on the other hand, were simple, untrained, and ignorant men; yet to what scorn would they have been subjected — how would their credulity and superstition have been derided — if they had told the story of such an exorcism as *this?* And if this was the current mode, we may the better understand the profound sensation caused in the minds of the spectators by the effect of Christ's simple word.

[2] Cf. 1 Cor. ix. 5.

[3] Luke iv. 38, $\sigma υνεχομένη πυρετ ῷ μεγάλῳ$.

[4] *Id.* 38, $ἠρώτησαν$ (implying a single and instantaneous act), not $ἠρώτα$, as in John iv. 47. A careful comparison of this or any similar narrative in the three Synoptists (Matt. viii. 14, 15; Mark i 29—31; Luke iv. 38, 39) will show the inquirer more clearly the resemblances and the differences in the descriptions of the same event, than any number of disquisitions. Often it is only by combining the three independent testimonies that we get a clear and graphic picture.

sources of disease, and, restored instantaneously to health, she rose and busied herself about the household duties.[1]

Possibly the strictness of observance which marked the Jewish Sabbath secured for our Lord a brief interval for refreshment; but no sooner did the sun begin to set, than the eager multitude, barely waiting for the full close of the Sabbath hours, began to seek His aid. The whole city came densely thronging round the doors of the humble home, bringing with them their demoniacs and their diseased. What a strange scene! There lay the limpid lake, reflecting in pale rose-color the last flush of sunset that gilded the western hills; and here, amid the peace of Nature, was exposed, in hideous variety, the sickness and misery of man, while the stillness of the Sabbath twilight was broken by the shrieks of demoniacs who testified to the Presence of the Son of God.[2]

> " A lazar-house it seemed, wherein were laid
> Numbers of all diseased; all maladies
> Of ghastly spasm, and racking tortures, qualms
> Of heart-sick agony, all feverous kinds,
> Demoniac phrenzy, moping melancholy
> And moonstruck madness; "

and amidst them all, not

> " Despair
> Tended the sick, busiest from couch to couch,
> And over them triumphant Death his dart
> Shook," . . . .

but far into the deepening dusk, the only person there who was unexcited and unalarmed — hushing by His voice the delirium of madness and the screams of epilepsy,[3] touching disease into health again by laying on each unhappy and tortured[4] sufferer His pure and gentle hands — moved, in His love and tenderness, the young Prophet of Nazareth, the Christ, the Saviour of the world. Unalarmed indeed, and unexcited, but not free from sorrow and suffering. For sympathy is nothing else than a fellow-feeling with others; a sensible participation in their joy or woe. And Jesus was touched with a feeling of their infirmities. Those cries pierced to His inmost heart; the groans and sighs of all that collective misery filled His

---

[1] This is involved in the aorists and imperfects: $\dot{\alpha}\nu\alpha\sigma\tau\tilde{\alpha}\sigma\alpha$ $\delta\iota\eta\kappa\acute{o}\nu\epsilon\iota$ (Luke iv. 39), $\dot{\eta}\gamma\acute{e}\rho\theta\eta$ $\kappa\alpha\grave{\iota}$ $\delta\iota\eta\kappa\acute{o}\nu\epsilon\iota$ (Matt. viii. 15).

[2] Luke iv. 40, $\dot{\alpha}\sigma\theta\epsilon\nu o\tilde{\upsilon}\nu\tau\alpha\varsigma$ $\nu\acute{o}\sigma o\iota\varsigma$ $\pi o\iota\kappa\acute{\iota}\lambda\alpha\iota\varsigma$.

[3] Matt. iv. 24, $\sigma\epsilon\lambda\eta\nu\iota\alpha\zeta o\mu\acute{e}\nu o\upsilon\varsigma$.

[4] Matt. iv. 24, $\beta\alpha\sigma\acute{\alpha}\nu o\iota\varsigma$ $\sigma\upsilon\nu\epsilon\chi o\mu\acute{e}\nu o\upsilon\varsigma$.

whole soul with pity : He bled for them ; He suffered with them ; their agonies were His ; so that the Evangelist St. Matthew recalls and echoes in this place, with a slight difference of language, the words of Isaiah, " Surely He bore our griefs and carried our sorrows." [1]

The fame of that marvellous day rang through all Galilee and Peræa, and even to the farthest parts of Syria,[2] and we might well have imagined that the wearied Saviour would have needed a long repose. But to Him the dearest and best repose was solitude and silence, where he might be alone and undisturbed with His heavenly Father. The little plain of Gennesareth was still covered with the deep darkness which precedes the dawn,[3] when, unobserved by all, Jesus rose and went away to a desert place, and there refreshed His spirit with quiet prayer. Although the work which He was sent to do obliged Him often to spend His days amid thronging and excited multitudes, He did not love the tumult, and avoided even the admiration and gratitude of those who felt in His presence a spring of life. But He was not suffered thus to remain, even for a brief period, in rest and seclusion. The multitude sought Him persistently ; Simon and his friends almost hunted for Him in their eager desire to see and to hear. They even wished to detain Him among them by gentle force.[4] But he quietly resisted their importunity. It was not His object to become the centre of an admiring populace, or to spend His whole time in working miracles, which, though they were deeds of mercy, were mainly intended to open their hearts to His diviner teaching. His blessings were not to be confined to Capernaum. Dalmanutha, Magdala, Bethsaida, Chorazin were all near at hand. " Let us go," He said, " to the adjoining country towns [5] to preach the kingdom of God there also ; for therefore am I sent."

It is doubtful, however, whether Jesus put His intention into instant effect. It seems as if He so far yielded to the anxiety of the multitude as to give them one more address before He set forth to

---

[1] Matt. viii. 17, *ἔλαβε, ἐβάσταδε* ; Isa. liii. 4 (cf. *ἀνήνεγκεν*, 1 Pet. ii. 24). The LXX. reads *ἁμαρτίας* for *ἀσθενείας*, and makes the sympathy more purely mental (*ὀδυνᾶται περὶ ἡμῶν*). Though no word of the LXX. is found in St. Matthew's quotation, yet he gives one of the possible senses of the original.

[2] Matt. iv. 24.

[3] Mark i. 35, *πρωῒ ἔννυχον λίαν.* One of the many little graphic touches, derived doubtless from the Apostle St. Peter, in which the Gospel of St. Mark abounds.

[4] Luke iv. 42, *ἐπεζήτουν, κατεῖχον* ; Mark i. 36, *κατεδίωξαν.*

[5] Mark i. 38, *κωμοπόλεις.* Cf. Luke iv. 43.

preach in that populous neighborhood.[1] He bent His steps towards the shore, and probably to the spot where the little boats of His earliest disciples were anchored, near the beach of hard white sand which lines the water-side at Bethsaida. At a little distance behind Him followed an ever-gathering concourse of people from all the neighborhood; and while He stopped to speak to them, the two pairs of fisher-brethren, Simon and Andrew, and James and John, pursued the toils by which they earned their daily bread. While Jesus had retired to rest for a few short hours of the night, Simon and his companions, impelled by the necessities of a lot which they seem to have borne with noble-minded cheerfulness, had been engaged in fishing; and, having been wholly unsuccessful, two of them, seated on the shore — probably, in that clear still atmosphere, within hearing of His voice — were occupying their time in washing, and two, seated in their boat with their hired servants, and Zebedee, their father, were mending their nets.[2] As Jesus spoke, the multitude — some in their desire to catch every syllable that fell from the lips of Him who spake as never man spake, and some in their longing to touch Him, and so be healed of whatever plagues they had — thronged upon Him closer and closer, impeding His movements with dangerous and unseemly pressure.[3] He therefore beckoned to Simon to get into his boat and push it ashore, so that He might step on board of it, and teach the people from thence. Seated in this pleasant pulpit, safe from the inconvenient contact with the multitude, he taught them from the little boat as it rocked on the blue ripples, sparkling in the morning sun. And when His sermon was over, He thought not of Himself and of His own fatigue, but of His poor and disap-

---

[1] I must again remark that while adopting the order which appears to me most probable, and which in this part of the narrative is that given by St. Luke, and is followed (among other eminent authorities) by Lange, repeated examination has convinced me of the utter impossibility of any certainty about the *exact* sequence of events. The data of time are far too vague to admit of definiteness in the chronological arrangement.

[2] I have here attempted to combine, as far as it is *possible*, in one continuous narrative, the perfectly comprehensible, but slightly differing accounts of the Synoptists (Matt. iv. 18—22; Mark i. 16—20; Luke v. 1—11). Let me remark — (1) that any one whose faith is shaken by the so-called "discrepancies" of these and similar stories must (*a*) either hold some very rigid, untenable, and superstitious view of inspiration, or (*b*) be wholly unacquainted with the different aspects assumed by perfectly truthful but confessedly fragmentary testimonies; and (2) that the very variety in the narratives, being in no respect inconsistent with essential and truthful unity, is a valuable proof of the independence of the Gospel witnesses.

[3] See Mark iii. 9—12.

pointed disciples. He knew that they had toiled in vain; He had observed that even while he spoke they had been preparing for some future and more prosperous expedition; and with a sympathy which never omitted an act of kindness, He ordered Peter to push out his boat into the deep, and all of them to cast out their nets once more.[1] Peter was in a despondent mood; but the mere word of One whom he so deeply reverenced, and whose power he had already witnessed, was sufficient. And his faith was rewarded. Instantly a vast haul of fishes crowded into the nets.

A busy scene followed. The instinct of work first prevailed. Simon and Andrew beckoned to Zebedee and his sons and servants to come in their boat and help to save the miraculous draught and straining nets; both boats were filled to the gunwale with the load; and at the first moment that the work was finished, and Peter recognized the whole force of the miracle, he falls, with his usual eager impetuosity, at his Master's feet — to thank Him? to offer Him henceforth an absolute devotion? — No; but (and here we have a touch of indescribable truthfulness, utterly beyond the power of the most consummate intellect to have invented) to exclaim, "DEPART FROM ME, for I am a sinful man, O Lord!"[2] A flash of supernatural illumination had revealed to him both his own sinful unworthiness and who HE was who was with him in the boat. It was the cry of self-loathing which had already realized something nobler. It was the first impulse of fear and amazement, before they had had time to grow into adoration and love. St. Peter did not *mean* the "Depart from me;" he only meant — and this was known to the Searcher of hearts — "I am utterly unworthy to be near Thee, yet let me stay." How unlike was this cry of his passionate and trembling humility to the bestial ravings of the unclean spirits, who bade the Lord to let them alone, or to the hardened degradation of the filthy Gadarenes, who preferred to the presence of their Saviour the tending of their swine!

And how gently the answer came: "Fear not; from henceforth thou shalt catch men." Our Lord, as in all His teaching, seized and applied with exquisite significance the circumstances of the moment. Round them in the little boat lay in heaps the glittering spoil of the

---

[1] Luke v. 4, ἐπανάγαγε . . . χαλάσατε.

[2] It is ἀνὴρ ἁμαρτωλός (Luke v. 8), a confession of individual guilt; not ἄνθρωπος. Comp. Exod. xx. 18, 19; Judg. xiii. 22; 1 Kings xvii. 18; Dan. x. 17; Isa. vi. 5.

lake — glittering, but with a glitter that began to fade in death.' Henceforth that sinful man, washed and cleansed, and redeemed and sanctified, was to chase, with nobler labor, a spoil which, by being entangled in the Gospel net, would not die, but be saved alive.² And his brother, and his partners, they, too, were to become "fishers of men." This final call was enough. They had already been called by Jesus on the banks of Jordan; they had already heard the Baptist's testimony; but they had not yet been bidden to forsake all and follow Him; they had not yet grown familiar with the miracles of power which confirmed their faith; they had not yet learned fully to recognize that they who followed Him were not only safe in His holy keeping, but should receive a thousandfold more in all that constitutes true and noble happiness even in this life — in the world to come, life everlasting.

We have already seen that, at the very beginning of His ministry, our Lord had prepared six of His Apostles for a call to His future service; four of whom were on this occasion bidden not only to regard Him as their Master, but henceforth to leave all and follow Him. There was but one other of the Apostles who received a separate call — the Evangelist, St. Matthew. His call, though narrated in different sequences by each of the Synoptists, probably took place about this time.³ At or near Capernaum there was a receipt of custom. Lying as the town did at the nucleus of roads which diverged to Tyre, to Damascus, to Jerusalem, and to Sepphoris, it was a busy centre of merchandise, and therefore a natural place for the collection

---

¹ Hence the extreme frequency of the fish as a symbol of Christians in early Christian art and literature. "Nos pisciculi secundum ἰχθῦν nostrum (*Ἰησοῦν Χριστὸν Θεοῦ υἱὸν Σωτῆρα*) in aquâ (sc. baptismi) nascimur." ¹⁵⁹ (Tert. *De Bapt.* 1).

² Luke v. 10, *ἀνθρώπους ἔσῃ ζωγρῶν.* The word *ζωγρεῖν,* from *ζῶος* and *ἀγρεύω,* means "to take alive;" see Jos. *Antt.* xiii. 6, § 2. Those who had been *ἐζωγρημένοι,* "taken alive" in the deadly snare (*παγὶς*) of the devil (2 Tim. ii. 26), should henceforth be gathered in the net of life. "The Fathers," says Bishop Wordsworth, "call Peter the *σύμβολον πρακτικῆς* and John the *σύμβολον θεωρίας,* and infer that the practical must precede the contemplative life."

³ By St. Matthew himself, after the Sermon on the Mount, the miracle of the Gadarene demoniacs, and the cure of the man sick of the palsy (ix. 9); by St. Mark, after the cure of the paralytic, but some time before the visit to Gergesa (ii. 14); by St. Luke after the cure of the paralytic, but before the choice of the Twelve, and before the Sermon on the Mount (v. 27). It seems, however, to have been the wish of all three to narrate it in immediate connection with the feast which he gave in Christ's honor; but it does not follow that the feast was given *immediately* after his call.

of tribute and taxes. These imposts were to the Jews pre-eminently distasteful. The mere fact of having to pay them wounded their tenderest sensibilities. They were not only a badge of servitude; they were not only a daily and terrible witness that God seemed to have forsaken His land, and that all the splendid Messianic hopes and promises of their earlier history were merged in the disastrous twilight of subjugation to a foreign rule which was cruelly and contemptuously enforced; but, more than this, the mere payment of such imposts wore almost the appearance of apostasy to the sensitive and scrupulous mind of a genuine Jew.[1] It seemed to be a violation of the first principles of the Theocracy, such as could only be excused as the result of absolute compulsion. We cannot, therefore, wonder that the officers who gathered these taxes were regarded with profound dislike. It must be remembered that those with whom the provincials came in contact were not the Roman knights—the real *publicani*, who farmed the taxes—but were the merest subordinates, often chosen from the dregs of the people, and so notorious as a class for their mal-practices, that they were regarded almost with horror, and were always included in the same category with harlots and sinners. When an occupation is thus despised and detested, it is clear that its members are apt to sink to the level at which they are placed by the popular odium. And if a Jew could scarcely persuade himself that it was right to *pay* taxes, how much more heinous a crime must it have been in his eyes to become the questionably-honest instrument for *collecting* them? If a publican was hated, how still more intense must have been the disgust entertained against a publican who was also a Jew?[2]

---

[1] Deut. xvii. 15; Jos. *Antt.* xviii. 2, § 1. "If we can imagine an Irish Roman Catholic in Ireland undertaking the functions of a Protestant tithe proctor, we can realize the detestation in which the publicans were held." (See Prof. Plumptre, Art. "Publican," Smith's *Bibl. Dict.*) These, however, are the *Socii*, or "subordinates," not the "*Mancipes*," who were people of some distinction (Cic. *Pro Plancio*, ix.). Honesty among them was considered so rare that, according to Suetonius, several cities erected statues to Sabinus, "the honest publican" (*Vesp.* i.). Lucian places them only in the worst company round the tribunal of Minos (*Menip.* ii.). But although Matthew held a disreputable office, we may wholly deny the remarks of Ep. Barn. 5 (ὑπὲρ πᾶσαν ἁμαρτίαν ἀνομωτέρους[160]); and Cels. *Ap. Orig.* ii. 46 (τοὺς ἐξωλεστάτους μόνους εἷλε[161]).

[2] The title "publican," as a term of opprobrium, was so thoroughly proverbial that, if we may trust the exact report of His words, it was even used in that sense by our Lord himself: "Let him be unto thee as a heathen man and a publican" (Matt. xviii. 17). The Jews had a proverb, "Take not a wife out of the family where there is a publican, for they are all publicans." The Gentiles did not think much better of them, πάντες τελῶναι, πάντες εἰσὶν ἅρπαγες[162]) Xeno. *Ap. Dicaearch. de Vit. Graec.*, p. 29). Theocritus, in answer to the question,

But He who came to seek and save the lost — He who could evoke Christian holiness out of the midst of heathen corruption — could make, even out of a Jewish publican, the Apostle and the first Evangelist of a new and living Faith. His choice of apostles was dictated by a spirit far different from that of calculating policy or conventional prudence. He rejected the dignified scribe (Matt. viii. 19); He chose the despised and hated tax-gatherer. It was the glorious unworldliness of a Divine insight and a perfect charity, and St. Matthew more than justified it by turning his knowledge of writing to a sacred use, and becoming the earliest biographer of his Saviour and his Lord.

No doubt Matthew had heard some of the discourses, had seen some of the miracles of Christ. His heart had been touched, and to the eyes of Him who despised none and despaired of none, the publican, even as he sat at "the receipt of custom," · was ready for the call. One word was enough. The "Follow me" which showed to Matthew that his Lord loved him, and was ready to use him as a chosen instrument in spreading the good tidings of the kingdom of God, was sufficient to break the temptations of avarice and the routine of a daily calling, and "he left all, rose up, and followed Him," touched into noblest transformation by the Ithuriel-spear of a forgiving and redeeming love.[2]

---

which were the worst kind of wild beasts, said, " On the mountains, bears and lions; in cities, publicans and pettifoggers " (Muson. *Ap. Stob.*). Suidas, s. v. τελώνης, defines the life as ἀνεπιτίμητος ἁρπαγή, ἀναισχυντὸς πλεονεξία, πραγμάτεια λόγον μὴ ἔχουσα, ἀναιδὴς ἐμπορία.[163] (Cave, *Lives of the Apostles.*)

[1] This "receipt of custom" is said to have been at the seaside; hence, in the Hebrew Gospel of St. Matthew, "publican" is rendered בעל עברה, "lord of the passage." The publicans are said to have delivered to those who paid toll, a ticket to free them on the other side. (Buxtorf, *Lex.* s. v. מובס; Cave, *Lives of the Apostles.*)

[2] It is here assumed that Matthew is identical with Levi, although Ewald, on insufficient grounds, denies it (*Gesch. Christus*, 364, 367). The λεγόμενον of Matt. ix. 9 implies a change of name. His name may have been changed by Christ, perhaps, in part to obliterate the painful reminiscences of his late discreditable calling. The name Matthew (if with Gesenius we regard it as equivalent to Mattithjah) means, like Nathanael and Theodore, "gift of God." (Ewald connects it with Amittai, *Gramm.* § 273 *e;* but in *Gesch. Christ.*, p. 397, he says that *Matthias* = Mattijah, and *Matthew* = Mattai, which occurs, by a misreading, as *Nittai* among Christ's disciples in *Chagigah* 2, 2, and is an abbreviation of Mattaniah.) If the Evangelist himself naturally prefers this name, whereas St. Mark and St. Luke call him by the name which he bore when he received Christ's summons, on the other hand we should note the touching humility with which he alone of the Evangelists gives to himself in the list of the Apostles (x. 3) the dishonorable title of "publican."

CHAPTER XVIII.

THE TWELVE, AND THE SERMON ON THE MOUNT.

" Ante Christi adventum Lex jubebat non juvabat ; post et jubet, et juvat." [164]
— AUGUSTINE.

AFTER one of His days of loving and ceaseless toil, Jesus, as was
His wont, found rest and peace in prayer. "He went out into a
mountain "— or, as it should rather be rendered, into *the* mountain [1]
—"to pray, and continued all night in prayer to God." There is
something affecting beyond measure in the thought of these lonely
hours ; the absolute silence and stillness, broken by no sounds of
human life, but only by the hooting of the night-jar or the howl of
the jackal; the stars of an Eastern heaven raining their large lustre
out of the unfathomable depth; the figure of the Man of Sorrows
kneeling upon the dewy grass, and gaining strength for His labors
from the purer air, the more open heaven, of that intense and silent
communing with His Father and His God. [2]

The scene of this lonely vigil, and of the Sermon on the Mount,
was in all probability the singular elevation known at this day as the
Kurn Hattîn, or "Horns of Hattîn." [3] It is a hill with a summit
which closely resembles an oriental saddle with its two high peaks.
On the west it rises very little above the level of a broad and undu-
lating plain ; on the east it sinks precipitately towards a plateau, on
which lies, immediately beneath the cliffs, the village of Hattîn; and
from this plateau the traveller descends through a wild and tropic

---

[1] In Luke vi. 12, τὸ ὄρος is clearly specific, though elsewhere it only means the
hill districts.

[2] "In solitudine aer purior, caelum apertius, familiarior Deus" [165] (Orig.). (Jer.
Taylor, *Life of Christ*, I. § viii. 5.) — It is a mistake of Mede, Hammond, &c., to
suppose that ἐν τῇ προσευχῇ τοῦ Θεοῦ [166] can mean "in a proseucha," or oratory
(cf. Acts xvi. 13 ; Juv. iii. 296, "In quâ te quæro proseuchâ;" [167] Jos. *Vit.* 54)
These were always near water (cf. Jos. *Antt.* xiv. 10, § 23, "and may make their
proseuchae at the sea-side, according to the custom of their forefathers "), and we
know of no instance of their being on hill-tops.

[3] Robinson writes it Kurûn, which as a plural is good dictionary Arabic. I
generally follow Mr. Porter's spelling of modern names in Palestine, as it certainly well represents the actual pronunciation.

gorge to the shining levels of the Lake of Galilee. It is the only conspicuous hill on the western side of the lake, and it is singularly adapted by its conformation, both to form a place for short retirement, and a rendezvous for gathering multitudes. Hitherward, in all probability, our Lord wandered in the evening between the rugged and brigand-haunted crags which form the sides of the Vale of Doves, stopping, perhaps, at times to drink the clear water of the little stream, to gather the pleasant apples of the *nubk*, and to watch the eagles swooping down on some near point of rock. And hither, in the morning, less heedful than their Divine Master of the manifold beauties of the scene, the crowd followed Him — loth even for a time to lose His inspiring presence, eager to listen to the gracious words that proceeded out of His mouth.

It was at dawn of day, and before the crowd had assembled, that our Lord summoned into His presence the disciples who had gradually gathered around Him. Hitherto the relation which bound them to His person seems to have been loose and partial; and it is doubtful whether they at all realized its full significance. But now the hour was come, and out of the wider band of general followers He made the final and special choice of His twelve Apostles. Their number was insignificant compared to the pompous retinue of hundreds who called themselves followers of a Hillel or a Gamaliel, and their position in life was humble and obscure. Simon and Andrew the sons of Jonas, James and John the sons of Zabdîa, and Philip, were of the little village of Bethsaida. If Matthew be the same as Levi, he was a son of Alphæus, and therefore a brother of James the Less and of Jude, the brother of James, who is generally regarded as identical with Lebbæus and Thaddæus. They belonged in all probability to Cana or Capernaum, and if there were any ground for believing the tradition [1] which says that Mary, the wife of Alphæus or Klopas, [2] was a younger sister of the Virgin, then we should have to consider these two brothers as first-cousins of our Lord. Nathanael or Bartholomew was of Cana in Galilee. [3] Thomas and

---

[1] The punctuation of John **xix.** 25 is too uncertain to regard this as undeniable ; nor, since James, Judas, Simon are among the very commonest of Jewish names, does this in any way affect the question of the " Brethren of Jesus."

[2] That Alphæus and Klopas may represent חַלְפַּי seems clear ; and Kleopas (Luke xxiv. 18) may be only another variation. On the other hand, Kleopas may be a shortened form of Kleopater, as Antipas is of Antipater.

[3] This goes against Dr. Donaldson's conjecture that both Philip and Nathanael were sons of Tolmai, and brothers. Dr. Donaldson also argues that Thomas was a twin brother of Matthew, and was originally called Jude ; and that Jude was

Simon Zelotes were also Galilæans. Judas Iscariot was the son of a Simon Iscariot, but whether this Simon is identical with the Zealot cannot be determined.

Of these, "the glorious company of the Apostles," three, James the Less,[1] Jude [the brother [2]] of James, and Simon Zelotes, are almost totally unknown. The very personality of James and Jude is involved in numerous and difficult problems, caused by the extreme frequency of those names among the Jews. Whether they are the authors of the two Catholic Epistles, is a question which, perhaps, will never be determined. Nor is anything of individual interest recorded about them in the Gospels, if we except the single question

---

the *son* of James the Less, and therefore *grandson* of Alphæus (see his arguments in *Jashar*, p. 100). Euseb. *H. E.* i. 13.) — Some legends make Thomas a twin-brother of James.

[1] James should rather be called "the Little" than "the Less." The Greek is ὁ μικρός, which in classical Greek means "the short of stature" (Xen. *Mem.* i. 4, 2; Lightfoot, *Galatians*, p. 250); moreover, James the son of Zebedee is never called the Great.

[2] "Judas of James" *may* mean "*son* of James;" but it is supposed that *both* Judas and the better-known James were sons of Alphæus, as well as Matthew. Judas is almost universally believed (except by Ewald, *Gesch. Christ.*, p. 399) to be the same as Lebbæus and Thaddæus — "the three-named disciple." לֵב (*lebh*) means "heart;" and Jerome renders the name Corculum. (There is absolutely *no* ground for the notion that he received other names because the name Jehuda has three letters of the Tetragrammaton, and so the Jews avoided it; on the contrary, it was one of the very commonest of Jewish names.) The identification rests partly on the fact that in Matt. x. 3, the reading Λεββαῖος is in א, B, Θαδδαῖος; and in some MSS. Λεββ. ὁ ἐπικληθεὶς Θαδδαῖος. In Mark iii. 18, the reading also varies, but the true reading is probably Θαδδαῖος, who, then, in both lists occupies the tenth place. In St. Luke's list, the corresponding name, though it occupies the eleventh place, is "Judas of James." The attempt to make Thaddæus *mean* the same as Lebbæus is a mistake, for the Aram. תַּד (Hebr. שַׁד) means *mamma*, not *pectus* or *cor* (Lam. iv. 3, &c.). Ewald identifies Lebbæus with Levi (Mark ii. 14), where Origen (*c. Cels.* ii. 62) seems to have read Λεβής, and conjectures that Thaddæus died early, and "Judas of James" was appointed in his place (*Gesch. Christ.* 399). Clemens of Alexandria certainly distinguishes between Ματθαῖος and Λευΐς (*Strom.* iv. 9, § 73). But the whole subject is involved in almost incredible obscurity. The lists of the Apostles as given by the three Evangelists and in the Acts are as follow : —

MATT. x. 2—4.	MARK iii. 16—19.	LUKE vi. 14—16.	ACTS i. 13.
1. Simon.	Simon.	Simon.	Peter.
2. Andrew.	James.	Andrew.	James.
3. James.	John.	James.	John.
4. John.	Andrew.	John.	Andrew.
5. Philip.	Philip.	Philip.	Philip.
6. Bartholomew	Bartholomew.	Bartholomew.	Thomas.
7. Thomas.	Matthew	Matthew.	Bartholomew.
8. Matthew.	Thomas.	Thomas.	Matthew.
9. James of Alphæus.	James of Alphæus.	James of Alphæus.	James of Alphæus.
10. Lebbæus.	Thaddæus.	Simon Zelotes	Simon Zelotes.
11. Simon ὁ Καναναῖος.	Simon ὁ Καναναῖος.	Jude of James.	Jude of James.
12. Judas Iscariot.	Judas Iscariot.	Judas Iscariot.	

of " Judas, not Iscariot," which is mentioned by St. John.¹ Simon is
only known by his surnames of Zelotes, " the Zealot," or " the Canaanite "—names which are identical in meaning, and which mark him
out as having once belonged to the wild and furious followers of
Judas of Giscala.² The Greek names of Philip and Andrew, together
with the fact that it was to Philip that the Greeks applied who
wished for an interview with our Lord, and his reference of the
request to Andrew, may possibly point³ to some connection on their
part with the Hellenists ; but, besides their first call, almost nothing
is recorded about them ; and the same remark applies to Nathanael
and to Matthew. Of Thomas, called also Didymus, or "the Twin,"
which is only a Greek version of his Hebrew name, we catch several
interesting glimpses, which show a well-marked character, naïve and
simple, but at the same time ardent and generous ; ready to die, yet
slow to believe. Of Judas, the man of Kerioth,⁴ perhaps the only
Jew in the Apostolic band, we shall have sad occasion to speak here-

---

¹ John xiv. 22.

² קַנְאָה means " zeal." The true reading of Matt. x. 4 ; Mark iii. 18 is *Κανα-
ναῖος,* and the form of the word indicates the member of a sect (Lightfoot,
Revision, p. 138). *Ζηλωταὶ παρὰ ᾽Ιουδαίοις οἱ τοῦ νόμου φύλακες* ¹⁶⁵ (Suid.
s. v.). Nicephorus (*Hist. Eccl.* ii. 40) says that he derived the name *διὰ τὸν πρὸς
τὸν διδάσκαλον διάπυρον ζῆλον.*¹⁶⁹ For a description of this faction, and
their doings, see Jos. *Bell. Jud.* iv. *passim.* " Zealots," he says (iv. 3, § 9), " for
that was the name they went by, as if they were zealous in good deeds, and not
rather zealous in the worst." They took Phinehas as their type (Numb. xxv. 11
—13). Canaanite can hardly mean " of Cana," for that would be *Καναθαῖος*
(Ewald, *Gesch. Christ.,* p. 399). Bruce happily remarks that the choice of an ex-
Zealot as an apostle, giving grounds for political suspicion, is another sign of
Christ's disregard of mere prudential wisdom. Christ wished the apostles to be
the type and germ of the Church ; and therefore we find in it a union of opposites —
the tax-gatherer Matthew, and the tax-hater Simon — the unpatriotic Jew who
served the alien, and the patriot who strove for emancipation (*Training of the
Twelve,* p. 36).

³ But see *supra,* Chap. X., p. 135.

⁴ In John vi. 71, some MSS. read, *ἀπὸ Καρυώτου* (א, al.). In D this is the
reading also of xii. 4 ; xiii. 2, &c., and Tischendorf thinks that St. John may have
always used this form. Kerioth is the name of a town on the southern border of
Judah (Josh. xv. 25). *᾽Ισκαριώτης* then means " man (אִישׁ, *ish*) of Kerioth," just
as *᾽Ιστωβος,* " a man of Tob" (Jos. *Antt.* viii. 6, § 1). Ewald, however (*Gesch.
Christ.,* p. 398), identifies it with *Kartah* in Zebulun (Josh. xxi. 34). Other derivations of the name (*e. g., scortea,* " a leather apron ;" *askara,* " suffocation," &c.;
see Lightfoot, *Hor. Hebr.,* in Matt. x. 4) are hardly worth noticing ; but it must be
admitted that the reading in Josh. xv. 25 is dubious, being probably Kerioth-
Hezron, *i. e.,* " cities of Hezron, which is Hazor." Robinson identifies the place
with *Kuryetein,* " the two cities "—a ruined site, ten miles south of Hebron.

after; and throughout the Gospels he is often branded by the fatal epitaph, so terrible in its very simplicity, " Judas Iscariot, who also betrayed Him." [1]

James, John, and Peter belonged to the innermost circle — the ἐκλεκτῶν ἐκλεκτότεροι [170] — of our Lord's associates and friends.[2] They alone were admitted into His presence when He raised the daughter of Jairus, and at His transfiguration, and during His agony in the garden. Of James we know nothing further except that to him was granted the high honor of being the first martyr in the Apostolic band. He and his brother John seem, although they were fishermen, to have been in easier circumstances than their associates. Zebedee, their father, not only had his own boat, but also his own hired servants; and John mentions incidentally in his Gospel that he " was known to the high priest." [3] We have already noticed the not improbable conjecture that he resided much at Jerusalem, and there managed the importing of the fish which were sent thither from the Sea of Galilee. We should thus be able to account for his more intimate knowledge of those many incidents of our Lord's ministry in Judæa which have been entirely omitted by the other Evangelists.

---

[1] Matt. x. 4. The ὅς ἐγένετο προδότης, " who became a traitor," of Luke vi. 16, is a little less severe. If Simon the Zealot bore also the name Iscariot, as would appear from ℵ, B, C, G, L, &c., in John vi. 71 ; xiii. 26, then he was a father of the traitor. If he were, as some traditions say, a son of " Clopas, or Alphæus," it might appear that nearly all the Apostles were related to each other and to our Lord. If we accept the suggestions of different writers on the subject, James and John, James the Less, Jude, Matthew, and Simon were all His first-cousins, and Judas Iscariot His second-cousin. The notion that Thomas was a twin-brother, according to some of Matthew, according to others of Thaddæus, according to others of Jesus Himself, merely arises from his name. But all these suppositions depend on dubious conjecture or wavering tradition, and it is hardly needful to recount all the various guesses and attempted combinations of modern writers. It is, however, an interesting fact that so many of the Apostles were brothers — two sons of Zabdia, two of Jonas, three (at least), if not four, of Alphæus; besides (possibly) two sons of Tolmai, and a father and son.

[2] I have already mentioned the conjecture derived from John xix. 25, that Salome was a sister of the Virgin (v. supr., p. 130, n. 3). But if the sons of Zebedee were the first-cousins of Jesus, it would be strange that no hint or tradition of the fact should have been preserved. Zebedee probably died shortly after their final call to the Apostolate, as we hear no more of him.

[3] The story of his wearing a πέταλον (Exod. xxviii. 36 ; xxix. 6) at Ephesus, as though he had himself been of priestly race (ὅς ἐγενήθη ἱερεὺς τὸ πέταλον πεφορεκώς, [171] Euseb. H. E. iii. 31), sounds very apocryphal. Yet it is strange that such a story should have been invented, especially as we find the same thing asserted of James the Just, " the Lord's brother " (Epiphan. Haer. xxix. 4 ; Ewald. Gesch. Christus, p. 246, 3rd ed.). Perhaps in this instance, as in others, a symbolic allusion has been too literally interpreted as a fact.

St. John and St. Peter — the one the symbol of the contemplative, the other of the practical life — are undoubtedly the grandest and most attractive figures in that Apostolic band. The character of St. John has been often mistaken. Filled as he was with a most divine tenderness — realizing as he did to a greater extent than any of the Apostles the full depth and significance of our Lord's new commandment — rich as his Epistles and his Gospel are with a meditative and absorbing reverence — dear as he has ever been in consequence to the heart of the mystic and the saint — yet he was something indefinitely far removed from that effeminate pietist which has furnished the usual type under which he has been represented. The name Boanerges, or "Sons of Thunder," which he shared with his brother James,[1] their joint petition for precedence in the kingdom of God, their passionate request to call down fire from heaven on the offending village of the Samaritans,[2] the burning energy of the *patois* in which the Apocalypse is written, the impetuous horror with which, according to tradition, St. John recoiled from the presence of the heretic Cerinthus,[3] all show that in him was the spirit of the eagle, which, rather than the dove, has been his immemorial symbol.[4] And since zeal and enthusiasm, dead as they are, and scorned in these days by an effete and comfortable religionism, yet have ever been indispensable instruments in spreading the Kingdom of Heaven, doubtless it was the existence of these elements in his character, side by side with tenderness and devotion, which endeared him so greatly to his Master, and made him the "disciple whom Jesus loved." The wonderful depth and power of his imagination, the rare combination of contemplativeness and passion, of strength and sweetness, in the same soul — the perfect faith which inspired his devotion, and the perfect love which precluded fear — these were the gifts and graces which rendered him worthy of leaning his young head on the bosom of his Lord.

Nor is his friend St. Peter a less interesting study. We shall have many opportunities of observing the generous, impetuous, wavering, noble, timid, impulses of his thoroughly human but most lovable disposition. Let the brief but vivid summary of another now suffice. "It would be hard to tell," says Dr. Hamilton, "whether most of his fervor flowed through the outlet of adoration or activity. His full

---

[1] *Bene R'aasch* (Grätz, *Gesch. d. Jud.* iii. 231).

[2] Luke ix. 54.

[3] Euseb. *H. E.* iv. 14. The heretic is also said to have been Ebion (Epiph. *Haer.* xxx. 24).

[4] The same spirit appears in Luke ix. 49 ; Rev. xxii. 18 ; 2 John 9, 10.

heart put force and promptitude into every movement. Is his Master encompassed by fierce ruffians? — Peter's ardor flashes in his ready sword, and converts the Galilæan boatman into the soldier instantaneous. Is there a rumor of a resurrection from Joseph's tomb? — John's nimbler foot distances his older friend; but Peter's eagerness outruns the serene love of John, and past the gazing disciple he rushes breathless into the vacant sepulchre. Is the risen Saviour on the strand? — his comrades secure the net, and turn the vessel's head for shore; but Peter plunges over the vessel's side, and struggling through the waves, in his dripping coat falls down at his Master's feet. Does Jesus say, ' Bring of the fish ye have caught?' — ere any one could anticipate the word, Peter's brawny arm is lugging the weltering net with its glittering spoil ashore, and every eager movement unwittingly is answering beforehand the question of his Lord, ' Simon, lovest thou me?' And that fervor is the best, which, like Peter's, and as occasion requires, can ascend in ecstatic ascriptions of adoration and praise, or follow Christ to prison and to death; which can concentrate itself on feats of heroic devotion, or distribute itself in the affectionate assiduities of a miscellaneous industry." [1]

Such were the chief of the Apostles whom their Lord united into one band as He sat on the green summit of Kurn Hattin. We may suppose that on one of those two peaks He had passed the night in prayer, and had there been joined by His disciples at the early dawn. By what external symbol, if by any, our Lord ratified this first great ordination to the Apostolate we do not know; but undoubtedly the present choice was regarded as formal and as final. Henceforth there was to be no return to the fisher's boat or the publican's booth as a source of sustenance; but the disciples were to share the wandering missions, the evangelic labors, the scant meal and uncertain home, which marked even the happiest period of the ministry of their Lord. They were to be weary with Him under the burning noonday, and to sleep, as He did, under the starry sky.

And while the choice was being made, a vast promiscuous multitude had begun to gather. Not only from the densely-populated shores of the Sea of Galilee, but even from Judæa and Jerusalem — nay, even from the distant sea-coasts of Tyre and Sidon — they had crowded to touch His person and hear his words.[2] From the peak

---

[1] Dr. Hamilton, *Life in Earnest*, p. 80.

[2] Luke vi. 17—19. Assuming, with little or no hesitation, that St. Luke intends to record the same great discourse as that given by St. Matthew, I have here, as in so many other places, combined the separate touches in the twofold narrative

He descended to the flat summit of the hill,[1] and first of all occupied Himself with the physical wants of those anxious hearers, healing their diseases, and dispossessing the unclean spirits of the souls which they had seized. And then, when the multitude were seated in calm and serious attention on the grassy sides of that lovely natural amphitheatre, He raised His eyes,[2] which had, perhaps, been bent downwards for a few moments of inward prayer, and opening His mouth,[3] delivered primarily to His disciples, but intending through them to address the multitude, that memorable discourse which will be known for ever as " the Sermon on the Mount."

The most careless reader has probably been struck with the contrast between the delivery of this sermon and the delivery of the Law on Sinai. We think of that as a " fiery law," whose promulgation is surrounded by the imagery of thunders, and lightnings, and the voice of the trumpet sounding long and waxing louder and louder. We think of this as flowing forth in divinest music amid all the calm and loveliness of the clear and quiet dawn. That came dreadfully to the startled conscience from an Unseen Presence, shrouded by wreathing clouds, and destroying fire, and eddying smoke; this was uttered by a sweet human voice that moved the heart most gently in words of peace. That was delivered on the desolate and storm-rent hill which seems with its red granite crags to threaten the scorching wilderness; this on the flowery grass of the green hill-side which slopes down to the silver lake. That shook the heart with terror and agitation; this soothed it with peace and love. And yet the New Commandments of the Mount of Beatitudes were not meant to abrogate, but rather to complete, the Law which was spoken from Sinai to them of old.[4] That Law was founded on the eternal distinctions of right and wrong — distinctions strong and irremovable as the granite bases of the world. Easier would it be to sweep away the heaven

---

The apparent differences are easily accounted for by any reasonable theory of the position of the Evangelists. At the same time I see no objection whatever to the supposition that our Lord may have repeated parts of His teaching at different times and places and to different audiences; or that St. Matthew has combined and summarized not one but many sermons delivered on the Galilæan hills.

[1] The τόπος πεδινός of Luke vi. 17, which is too briefly rendered " the plain " in the English Version. Cf. Isa. xiii. 2. ἐπ᾽ ὄρους πεδινοῦ ἄρατε σημεῖον, LXX.

[2] Luke vi. 20.

[3] Matt. v. 2. The expression marks the solemnity and importance of the discourse.

[4] Τοῖς ἀρχαίοις (Matt. v. 21). Not " by," as in our A. V., but " to " them of old ; " to eld men " (Wiclif). The Rabbis, too, spoke of the abiding permanence of the Law, but they applied the remark materially, not, as Jesus does, spiritually.

and the earth, than to destroy the least letter, one *yod* — or the least point of a letter, one projecting horn — of that code which contains the very principles of all moral life. Jesus warned them that He came, not to abolish that Law, but to obey and to fulfil; while at the same time He taught that this obedience had nothing to do with the Levitical scrupulosity of a superstitious adherence to the letter, but was rather a surrender of the heart and will to the innermost meaning and spirit which the commands involved. He fulfilled that olden Law by perfectly keeping it, and by imparting a power to keep it to all who believe in Him, even though He made its cogency so far more universal and profound.[1]

The sermon began with the word "blessed," and with an octave of beatitudes. But it was a *new* revelation of beatitude. The people were expecting a Messiah who should break the yoke off their necks — a king clothed in earthly splendor, and manifested in the pomp of victory and vengeance. Their minds were haunted with legendary prophecies, as to how He should stand on the shore of Joppa, and bid the sea pour out its pearls and treasure at His feet; how He should clothe them with jewels and scarlet, and feed them with even a sweeter manna than the wilderness had known. But Christ reveals to them another King, another happiness — the riches of poverty, the royalty of meekness, the high beatitude of sorrow and persecution. And this new Law, which should not only command but also aid, was to be set forth in beneficent manifestation — at once as salt to preserve the world from corruption, and as a light to guide it in the darkness. And then follows a comparison of the new Law of mercy with the old Law of threatening; the old was transitory, this permanent; the old was a type and shadow, the new a fulfilment and completion; the old demanded obedience in outward action, the new was to permeate the thoughts; the old contained the rule of conduct, the new the secret of obedience. The command, " Thou shalt not murder," was henceforth extended to angry words and feelings of hatred.[2] The germ of adultery was shown to be involved in a lasciv-

---

[1] See the beautiful remarks of St. Augustine, quoted in Archbishop Trench's *Sermon on the Mount,* p. 186.

[2] The word εἰκῇ (D, many uncials, the Vetus Itala, the Cureton Syriac, &c.) in Matt. v. 22, whether genuine or not, expresses the true sense, for there is such a thing as a righteous anger, and a justifiable indignation (Eph. iv. 26). Augustine finely and truly says, "Non fratri irascitur, qui peccato fratris irascitur" [172] (*Retract.* i. 19). The word μωρὲ in the same verse may be not merely " fool," but " rebel," " apostate ; " the Hebrew *morah* (Numb. xx. 10). (Of course, I do not mean that μωρὸς is *derived from,* but merely that it was *suggested by* the Hebrew word, as is the case very often in LXX. renderings.) But the thing which Jesus forbids is

ious look. The prohibition of perjury was extended to every vain and unnecessary oath. The law of equivalent revenge was superseded by a law of absolute self-abnegation. The love due to our neighbor was extended also to our enemy.[1] Henceforth the children of the kingdom were to aim at nothing less than this — namely, to be *perfect*, as their Father in heaven is perfect.

And the new life which was to issue from this new Law was to be contrasted in all respects with that routine of exaggerated scruples and Pharisaic formalism which had hitherto been regarded as the highest type of a religious conversation. Alms were to be given, not with noisy ostentation, but in modest secrecy.[2] Prayers were to be uttered, not with hypocritic publicity, but in holy solitude. Fasting was to be exercised, not as a belauded virtue, but as a private self-denial. And all these acts of devotion were to be offered with sole reference to the love of God, in a simplicity which sought no earthly reward, but which stored up for itself a heavenly and incor-

---

not the mere use of particular expressions — for if that were all, He might have instanced taunts and libels ten thousand times more deadly — but the spirit of rage and passion out of which such expressions spring. Thus *Raca* (ὦ ἄνθρωπε κενέ) is used, with due cause, by St. James (ii. 20), and μωρός is applied to the blind and wicked, not only by David (Ps. xiv. 1), but by our Lord Himself (Matt. xxiii. 17).

[2] Matt. v. 43, "and hate thine enemy," has been severely criticised by later Jews as a misrepresentation of the Mosaic Law. See, however, Deut. xxiii. 6; vii. 2. And although these precepts were of special significance, certainly many of the Rabbis, including Shammai himself, had made use of the Mosaic Law to justify the most violent national and religious hatred (*v.* Schöttgen, *Hor. Hebr.*, *ad loc.*). He quotes, among other passages from the Talmud, *Midr. Tehillin*, f. 26, 4: "Do not show kindness or pity to Gentiles." Lightfoot, *ib.*, quotes one from Maimonides, and says, "Exemplum hoc unum satis sit pro plurimis, quae praesto sunt ubique." [173] "The Mishna," says Gfrörer (*Jahrh. d. Heils*, i. 114), " is full of such passages." and if the Jews had not acted in the spirit of them, we should not have had the charges against them in Tacitus ("adversus omnes alios hostile odium," [174] *H.* v. 5) and Juvenal (" Non monstrare vias eadem nisi sacra colenti," [175] *Sat.* xiv. 103).

[3] There is no trace in the Talmud or elsewhere that it was a practice of the Pharisees to send a trumpeter before them when they distributed their alms (Lightfoot, *Hor. Hebr. in Matt.* vi. 2). The expression " do not sound a trumpet before thee" is merely a graphic touch for " do not do it publicly and ostentatiously" (cf. Numb. x. 3; Ps. lxxxi. 3; Joel ii. 15, &c.). Mr. Shore, in the *Bible Educator*, approves of Schöttgen's conjecture, which connects it with the trumpet-shaped openings of the alms-boxes in the Temple treasury (Neh. xii. 41); but surely " do not trumpet" could never mean "do not make your shekels rattle in those trumpet-shaped orifices." It is true that they were called *shopheróth* (Reland, *De Spol Templ. Hierosol.* xii.). Grotius connects the expression with Amos iv. 5; and Rashi with a supposed custom (Targ. Hos. xiv. 8) of blowing the trumpet during libations in the Temple.

ruptible treasure. And the service to be sincere must be entire and undistracted. The cares and the anxieties of life were not to divert its earnestness or to trouble its repose. The God to whom it was directed was a Father also, and He who ever feeds the fowls of the air, which neither sow nor reap, and clothes in their more than regal loveliness the flowers of the field,[1] would not fail to clothe and feed, and that without any need for their own toilsome anxiety, the children who seek His righteousness as their first desire.

And what should be the basis of such service? The self-examination which issues in a gentleness which will not condemn, in a charity that cannot believe, in an ignorance that will not know, the sins of others; the reserve which will not waste or degrade things holy; the faith which seeks for strength from above, and knows that, seeking rightly, it shall obtain; the self-denial which, in the desire to increase God's glory and man's happiness, sees the sole guide of its actions towards all the world.

The gate was strait, the path narrow, but it led to life; by the lives and actions of those who professed to live by it, and point it out, they were to judge whether their doctrine was true or false; without this neither words of orthodoxy would avail, nor works of power.

Lastly, He warned them that he who heard these sayings and did them was like a wise man who built a house with foundations dug deeply into the living rock, whose house, because it was founded upon a rock, stood unshaken amid the vehement beating of storm and surge: but he who heard and did them not was likened " unto a foolish man that built his house upon the sand; and the rain descended, and the floods came, and the winds blew and beat upon that house: and it fell, and great was the fall of it." [2]

---

[1] Compare the name *Kaiserkrone* for the imperial martagon. The lilies to which Christ alluded (Matt. vi. 28) are either flowers generally, or, perhaps, the scarlet anemone, or the Huleh lily — a beautiful flower which is found wild in this neighborhood. In verse 27, ἡλικία should be rendered " age," not " stature," as in John ix. 21 ; Eph. iv. 13 ; Heb. xi. 11.   Cf. δάκτυλος ἁμέρα, Alc., and Ps. xxxix. 5.

[2] With this simile compare Ezek. xiii. 11 ; Job xxvii. 18. Schöttgen quotes an analogous comparison from the *Pirke Abhôth* iii. 17, and *Abhôth de Rabbi Nathan,* c. 23 (a late Jewish writer). For an admirable sketch of the topics handled in the Sermon on the Mount, see Westcott's *Introd.*, p. 358. In outline he arranges it thus : — 1. " The Citizens of the Kingdom (v. 1—16) — their character absolutely (3—6); relatively (7—12); and their influence (13—16). 2. The New Law (17—48) as the fulfilment of the Old generally (17—20) and specially (murder, adultery, perjury, revenge, exclusiveness, 21—48). 3. The New Life (vi.—vii. 27); acts of devotion (vi. 1—18), aims (19—34), conduct (vii. 1—12), dangers (vii. 13—23). 4. The Great Contrast." Many Rabbinical parables — always inferior

Such in barest and most colorless outline are the topics of that mighty sermon ; nor is it marvellous that they who heard it " were astonished at the doctrine." Their main astonishment was that He taught " as one having authority, and not as the Scribes.[1] The teach-

---

in beauty, in point, in breadth, and in spirituality — have been compared with separate clauses of the Sermon on the Mount. Since even the Mishna was not committed to writing till the second century, and since it is therefore impossible to estimate the diffusion of Christian thought even among hostile Rabbinic writers, nothing conclusive can be assured from these parallels. It is a great mistake, as a friend observes, to suppose that the world is made in water-tight compartments, even when the divisions seem most absolute. In fact, hostility may be less a barrier than a channel, at least when accompanied by competition. Protestantism has reacted upon Romanism, but nothing like to the extent that Christianity reacted upon Judaism. But even if we suppose the Rabbinic parallels, such as they are, to be independent and precedent, yet, considering the fact that high moral truths have been uttered even by pagans, from the earliest times — and considering that all discovery of moral truths is due to that revealing Spirit which is called in Scripture " the candle of the Lord " (Prov. xx. 27) — the question of " originality," to which some writers attach so much importance, seems to be futile, and devoid of all significance. I have not thought it worth while to adduce these parallels, except in rare and interesting cases. The attack on the score of its not being " original " is the one of all others from which Christianity has least to fear. The question of mere literary precedence in the utterance or illustration of a moral truth is one which has no importance for mankind. A truth so enunciated that it merely lies " in the lumber-room of the memory, side by side with the most exploded errors," is practically no truth at all ; it only becomes real when it is so taught as to become potent among human motives.

> " Though truths in manhood darkly join,
>   Deep-seated in our mystic frame,
>   We yield all honor to the name
>   Of Him who made them current coin."

[1] The Scribes (*Sopherîm*) date as a distinct body from the period of Ezra. The name is derived from *sepher*, " or book," and means " Scripturalists " — those who explained and copied the Law ; not from *saphar*, " to count," because they *counted* all the letters of it (Derenbourg, *Hist. Pal.* 25). Their functions were to copy, read, amend, explain, and protect the Law. It was in the latter capacity that they invented the " fences," which, under the title of *Dibherî Sopherîm*, " words of the Scribes," formed the nucleus of the " tradition of the elders " (Matt. xv. 2 ; Gal. i. 14), or Oral Law (the *Torah shebeal pî*, or " Law upon the lip," as distinguished from the *Torah shebeketeb*, or " Law which is in writing "), any transgression of which is declared by the Mishna to be more heinous than a transgression of the words of the Bible (*Sanhedrin*, x. 3). The *Sopherîm* proper only lasted from Ezra to the death of Simon the Just, B. C. 300, and they were succeeded by the *Tanaîm*, or teachers of the Law — the νομικοὶ and νομοδιδάσκαλοι of the Gospels, who lasted to A. D. 220, and fixed the " Words of the Scribes " into " Halachôth," or " rules of action," chiefly intended to form a *seyag latôrah*, or " hedge about the Law." The *Tanaîm* inherited a splendor of reputation which was reflected on them from their predecessors, who held a most exalted position

ing of their Scribes was narrow, dogmatic, material; it was cold in manner, frivolous in matter, second-hand, and iterative in its very essence; with no freshness in it, no force, no fire; servile to all authority, opposed to all independence; at once erudite and foolish, at once contemptuous and mean; never passing a hair's breadth beyond the carefully-watched boundary line of commentary and precedent; full of balanced inference and orthodox hesitancy, and impossible literalism; intricate with legal pettiness and labyrinthine system; elevating mere memory above genius, and repetition above originality; concerned only about Priests and Pharisees, in Temple and synagogue, or school, or Sanhedrin, and mostly occupied with things infinitely little. It was not indeed wholly devoid of moral significance, nor is it impossible to find here and there, among the *débris* of it, a noble thought; but it was occupied a thousandfold more with Levitical minutiæ about mint, and anise, and cummin, and the length of fringes, and the breadth of phylacteries, and the washing of cups and platters, and the particular quarter of a second when new moons and Sabbath-days began.[1] But this teaching of Jesus was wholly

(Ecclus. xxxix. 1—11). But the name γραμματεύς still continued to exist although in a less lofty meaning than it had previously acquired. Secondhandness, the slavish dependence on precedent and authority, is the most remarkable characteristic of Rabbinical teaching. It very rarely rises above the level of a commentary at once timid and fantastic. R. Eliezer actually made it his boast that he had originated nothing; and Hillel's grand position, as *Nasî*, or President of the Sanhedrin, was simply due to his having remembered a decision of Shemaia and Abtalion. "Get for thyself a teacher," was a characteristic gnome of Joshua Ben Perachia, whom the Talmud calls "the Teacher of Christ."

[1] Any one who chooses to take the trouble, may verify these assertions for himself. Much has been written lately in exaltation of the Talmud. Now the literature to which the general name of Talmud is given, occupies twelve immense folio volumes; and it would be strange indeed if out of this vast encyclopædia of a nation's literature, it were not possible to quote a few eloquent passages, some beautiful illustrations, and a considerable number of just moral sentiments which sometimes rise to the dignity of noble thoughts. But what seems to me absolutely indisputable, and what any one may judge of for himself, is that all that is really valuable in the Talmud is infinitesimally small compared with the almost immeasurable rubbish-heaps in which it is imbedded. Let any one, for instance, take in hand the recent French translation of one of the most important Talmudic treatises. The Talmud — *i. e.*, the Mishna and Gemara — is divided into six *Sedarîm*, or "orders," the first of which is called *Seder Zeraîm*, or "Order of Seeds," and the first treatise of this is called *Berachôth*, or "Blessings," and is composed of nine chapters on "the confession, worship, and service of the one God, and of prayers and benedictions offered to Him as the Giver of the blessings of Life." This has been translated into French by a learned Hebraist, M. Moïse Schwab, of the Bibliothèque Nationale. The subject of this treatise is infinitely more elevating and important than that of any other of the sixty-three *massiktoth*, or "treatises" of which the Mishna is composed. Now I will ask any

different in its character, and as much grander as the temple of the morning sky under which it was uttered was grander than stifling synagogue or crowded school. It was preached, as each occasion rose, on the hill-side, or by the lake, or on the roads, or in the house of the Pharisee, or at the banquet of the Publican; nor was it any sweeter or loftier when it was addressed in the Royal Portico to the Masters of Israel, than when its only hearers were the ignorant people whom the haughty Pharisees held to be accursed. And there was no reserve in its administration. It flowed forth as sweetly and as lavishly to single listeners as to enraptured crowds; and some of its very richest revelations were vouchsafed, neither to rulers nor to multitudes, but to the persecuted outcast of the Jewish synagogue, to the timid inquirer in the lonely midnight, and the frail woman by the noon-day well. And it dealt, not with scrupulous tithes and ceremonial cleansings, but with the human soul, and human destiny, and human life — with Hope and Charity, and Faith. There were no definitions in it, or explanations, or " scholastic systems," or philosophic theoriz-ing, or implicated mazes of difficult and dubious discussion, but a swift intuitive insight into the very depths of the human heart — even a supreme and daring paradox that, without being fenced round with exceptions or limitations, appealed to the conscience with its irresistible simplicity, and with an absolute mastery stirred and dom-inated over the heart. Springing from the depths of holy emotions, it thrilled the being of every listener as with an electric flame. In a word, its authority was the authority of the Divine Incarnate; it was a Voice of God, speaking in the utterance of man; its austere purity was yet pervaded with tenderest sympathy, and its awful severity with an unutterable love. It is, to borrow the image of the wisest of

---

reader or critic who considers that I have spoken too slightingly of the Scribes in the above passage, or have unduly depreciated the Talmud in other parts of this book, merely to take at haphazard any three *perakîm*, or chapters of the *Berachôth*, and make an abstract of them. I shall be indeed surprised if after accepting this little test he still retains the exalted conception of these Jewish writings which some recent writers — notably the late lamented Mr. Deutsch — have endeavored to create. Few English divines have known the Talmud so thoroughly as Dr. Lightfoot, the learned author of the *Horae Hebraicae* (d. 1675). He was a man of eminent candor and simplicity, and his estimate of the Talmud, after an almost lifelong study of it, was as follows : " Volumina ista legentem supra modum cruciant, torquent, et fatigant, styli difficultas tantum non insuperabilis, linguae asperitas tremenda, et rerum tractatarum STUPENDA INANITAS ET VAFRITIES. Nugis ubique scatent ita ac si nollent legi ; obscuris ac difficilibus ac si nollent intelligi ; ita ut ubique patientiâ Lectori sit opus, et nugas ferendo et asperi-tates." [176] (*Dedic. in Hor. Hebr. in Matth.*, 1658.) — See Excursus V., " The Talmud and the Oral Law."

the Latin Fathers, a great sea whose smiling surface breaks into refreshing ripples at the feet of our little ones, but into whose unfathomable depths the wisest may gaze with the shudder of amazement and the thrill of love.[1]

And we, who can compare Christ's teaching — the teaching of One whom some would represent to have been no more than the Carpenter of Nazareth — with all that the world has of best and greatest in Philosophy and Eloquence and Song, must not we too add, with yet deeper emphasis, that teaching as one having authority, He spake as never man spake? Other teachers have by God's grace uttered words of wisdom, but to which of them has it been granted to regenerate mankind? What would the world be now if it had nothing better than the dry aphorisms and cautious hesitations of Confucius, or the dubious principles and dangerous concessions of Plato? Would humanity have made the vast moral advance which it *has* made, if no great Prophet from on High had furnished it with anything better than Sakya Mouni's dreary hope of a *nirvâna*, to be won by unnatural asceticism, or than Mahomet's cynical sanction of polygamy and despotism? Christianity may have degenerated in many respects from its old and great ideal; it may have lost something of its virgin purity — the struggling and divided Church of to-day may have waned, during these long centuries, from the splendor of the New Jerusalem descending out of heaven from God : but is Christendom no better than what Greece became, and what Turkey and Arabia and China are? Does Christianity wither the nations which have accepted it with the atrophy of Buddhism, or the blight of Islam?[2] Even as a moral system — though it is infinitely more than a moral system — we do not concede that Christianity is unor-

---

[1] "Mira profunditas eloquiorum tuorum, quorum ecce ante nos superficies blandiens parvulis : sed mira profunditas, Deus meus, mira profunditas ! Horror est intendere in eam ; horror honoris et tremor amoris "[17] (Augustine, *Conf.* xii. 14). On the general characteristics of Christian teaching there are some very beautiful and interesting remarks in Guizot, *Méditations sur l'Essence de la Religion Chrétienne*, p. 279 ; Dupanloup, *Vie de Notre Seigneur*, pp. lxxiv. seqq. To avoid repetition, I may refer on this subject to the third of my Hulsean Lectures on the *Witness of History to Christ*, pp. 134—149.

[2] A blight certainly in Turkey, Syria, Arabia, and Egypt, and surely everywhere non-progressive ; but Islam being, as it is, a professed modification of Judaism and Christianity, can hardly be counted an independent religion, and is indeed a degeneracy even from Judaism. On Mahomet's teaching in general see some wise remarks in Prof. Mozley's Bampton Lectures *On Miracles*, p. 179. The reader may form some conception of K'ung Foo-tze from Dr. Legge's *Life and Teaching of Confucius*, which contains a translation of the Analects; and of Sakya Mouni from M. B. St. Hilaire's *Le Bouddha et sa Religion* (Paris, 1860).

iginal; and we besides maintain that no faith has ever been able like it to sway the affections and hearts of men. Other religions are demonstrably defective and erroneous; ours has never been proved to be otherwise than perfect and entire; other systems were esoteric and exclusive, ours simple and universal; others temporary and for the few, ours eternal and for the race. K'ung Foo-tze, Sakya Mouni, Mahomet, could not even conceive the ideal of a society without falling into miserable error; Christ established the reality of an eternal and glorious kingdom — whose theory for all, whose history in the world, prove it to be indeed what it was from the first proclaimed to be — the Kingdom of Heaven, the Kingdom of God.[1]

And yet how exquisitely and freshly simple is the actual language of Christ compared with all other teaching that has ever gained the ear of the world! There is no science in it, no art, no pomp of demonstration, no carefulness of toil, no trick of rhetoricians, no wisdom of the schools. Straight as an arrow to the mark His precepts pierce to the very depths of the soul and spirit. All is short, clear, precise, full of holiness, full of the common images of daily life. There is scarcely a scene or object familiar to the Galilee of that day, which Jesus did not use as a moral illustration of some glorious promise or moral law. He spoke of green fields, and springing flowers, and the budding of the vernal trees; of the red or lowering sky; of sunrise and sunset; of wind and rain; of night and storm; of clouds and lightning; of stream and river; of stars and lamps; of honey and salt; of quivering bulrushes and burning weeds; of rent garments and bursting wine-skins; of eggs and serpents; of pearls and pieces of money; of nets and fish. Wine and wheat, corn and oil, stewards and gardeners, laborers and employers, kings and shepherds, travellers and fathers of families, courtiers in soft clothing and brides in nuptial robes — all these are found in His discourses. He knew all life, and had gazed on it with a kindly as well as a kingly glance. He could sympathize with its joys no less than He could heal its sorrows, and the eyes that were so often suffused with tears as they saw the sufferings of earth's mourners beside the bed of death, had shone also with a kindlier glow as they watched the games of earth's happy little ones in the green fields and busy streets.[2]

---

[1] See further *The Witness of History to Christ*, pp. 142. seqq.

[2] Few have spoken more beautifully of our Lord's teaching in these respects than Bishop Dupanloup, *Vie de Notre Seigneur, l. c.*, in whom the main thought of the last paragraph will be found at much greater length. Much that I have

said in this chapter is beautifully illustrated in a little poem by Arthur Hugh Clough, part of which (if it be not known to him) the reader will thank me for quoting · —

> ' 'Across the sea, along the shore,
> In numbers ever more and more,
> From lonely hut and busy town,
> The valley through, the mountain down,
> What was it ye went out to see,
> Ye silly folk of Galilee?
> The reed that in the wind doth shake?
> The weed that washes in the lake?

>   *   *   *   *

> " 'A teacher? Rather seek the feet
> Of those who sit in Moses' seat.
> Go, humbly seek, and bow to them
> Far off in great Jerusalem . . . .
> What is it came ye here to note?
> A young man preaching in a boat.

> " 'A Prophet ! Boys and women weak
>   Declare — and cease to rave —
> Whence is it he hath learnt to speak
>   Say, who his doctrine gave?
> A Prophet? Prophet wherefore he
>   Of all in Israel's tribes?'
> *He teacheth with authority*
>   *And not as do the Scribes.*

CHAPTER XIX.

" He sent forth His word, and healed them." — Ps. cvii. 20.

THE Inauguration of the Great Doctrine was immediately followed and ratified by mighty signs. Jesus went, says one of the Fathers, from teaching to miracle.[1] Having taught as one who had authority, He proceeded to confirm that authority by accordant deeds.

It might have been thought that after a night of ceaseless prayer under the open sky, followed at early dawn by the choice of Twelve Apostles, and by a long address to them and to a vast promiscuous multitude, our Lord would have retired to the repose which such incessant activity required. Such, however, was very far from being the case, and the next few days, if we rightly grasp the sequence of events, were days of continuous and unwearying toil.

When the Sermon was over, the immense throng dispersed in various directions, and those whose homes lay in the plain of Gennesareth would doubtless follow Jesus through the village of Hattin, and across the narrow plateau, and then, after descending the ravine, would leave Magdala on the right, and pass through Bethsaida[2] to Capernaum.

As He descended the mountain,[3] and was just entering one of the little towns,[4] probably a short distance in advance of the multitude, who from natural respect would be likely to leave Him undisturbed after His labors, a pitiable spectacle met His eyes. Suddenly,[5] with agonies of entreaty, falling first on his knees, then, in the anguish of

---

[1] Euthymius. Matt. viii. 1—4 ; Mark i. 40—45 ; Luke v. 12—16. — St. Matthew narrates twenty miracles ; St. Mark, eighteen ; St. Luke, nineteen ; and St. John, seven. The total number of miracles related by the Evangelists is thirty-three.

[2] *i. e.*, the *Western* Bethsaida — probably the pleasant spot on the lake with its gently sloping banks, abundant streams, and strip of bright sand, now called Ain et-Tâbijah.

[3] This definite mark of time and place is furnished by St. Matthew (viii. 1). I have combined with his narrative the incidents alluded to by the two other Synoptists.

[4] Luke v. 12. Hattin, or Magdala, would best suit the conditions mentioned.

[5] This is implied in the καὶ ἰδού of Luke v. 12 ; Matt. viii. 2. The phrase is peculiar to these two Evangelists, of whom St. Matthew uses it twenty-three, and St. Luke sixteen times (Westcott, *Introd*, p. 237, *n.*).

his heart and the intensity of his supplication, prostrating himself upon his face,[1] there appeared before Him, with bare head, and rent garments, and covered lip, a leper — "full of leprosy"—smitten with the worst and foulest form of that loathsome and terrible disease. It must, indeed, have required on the part of the poor wretch a stupendous faith to believe that the young Prophet of Nazareth was One who could heal a disease of which the worst misery was the belief that, when once thoroughly seated in the blood, it was ineradicable and progressive. And yet the concentrated hope of a life broke out in the man's impassioned prayer, "Lord, if Thou wilt, Thou canst make me clean." Prompt as an echo came the answer to his faith, "I will: be thou clean."[2] All Christ's miracles are revelations also. Sometimes, when the circumstances of the case required it, He delayed His answer to a sufferer's prayer. But we are never told that there was a moment's pause when a *leper* cried to him. Leprosy was an acknowledged type of sin, and Christ would teach us that the heartfelt prayer of the sinner to be purged and cleansed is always met by instantaneous acceptance. When David, the type of all true penitents, cried with intense contrition, "I have sinned against the Lord," Nathan could instantly convey to him God's gracious message, "The Lord also hath put away thy sin; thou shalt not die."[3]

Instantly stretching forth His hand, our Lord touched the leper, and he was cleansed.

It was a glorious violation of the *letter* of the Law, which attached ceremonial pollution to a leper's touch;[4] but it was at the same time a glorious illustration of the *spirit* of the Law, which was that mercy is better than sacrifice. The hand of Jesus was not polluted by touching the leper's body, but the leper's whole body was cleansed by the touch of that holy hand. It was even thus that He touched our sinful human nature, and yet remained without spot of sin.[5]

---

[1] προσεκύνει (Matt. viii. 2), γονυπετῶν (Mark i. 40), πεσὼν ἐπὶ πρόσωπον (Luke v. 12). A leper was regarded as one dead (Jos. *Antt.* iii. 11, § 3, μηδενὶ συνδιαιτωμένους καὶ νεκροῦ μηδὲν διαφέροντας[178]).

[2] "Echo prompta ad fidem leprosi maturam"[179] (Bengel). St. Ambrose says, very fancifully, "Dicit volo propter Photinum; imperat propter Arium; tangit propter Manichæum."[180] The prompt, almost impetuous gladness and spontaneity of these miracles contrasts with the sorrow and delay of those later ones, which Jesus wrought when His heart had been utterly saddened, and men's faith in Him had already begun to wane (cf. Matt. xiii. 58; Mark vi. 5). "Prima miracula fecit confestim, ne videretur cum labore facere"[181] (Bengel).

[3] 2 Sam. xii. 13.

[4] Lev. xiii. 26, 46; Numb. v. 2. — "Quia Dominus Legis est non obsequitur Legi, sed Legem facit"[182] (Ambr., *in Luc.*).

[5] H. de Sto. Victore (in Trench *on Miracles,* p. 237).

It was in the depth and spontaneity of His human emotion that our Lord had touched the leper into health. But it was His present desire to fulfil the Mosaic Law by perfect obedience ; and both in proof of the miracle, and out of consideration to the sufferer, and in conformity with the Levitical ordinance, He bade the leper go and show himself to the priest, make the customary offerings, and obtain the legal certificate that he was clean.[1] He accompanied the direction with a strict and even stern injunction to say not one word of it to any one.[2] It appears from this that the suddenness with which the miracle had been accomplished had kept it secret from all, except perhaps a few of our Lord's immediate followers, although it had been wrought in open day, and in the immediate neighborhood of a city, and at no great distance from the following multitudes. But why did our Lord on this, and many other occasions, enjoin on the recipients of the miracles a secrecy which they so rarely observed? The full reason perhaps we shall never know, but that it had reference to circumstances of time and place, and the mental condition of those in whose favor the deeds were wrought, is clear from the fact that on one occasion at least, where the conditions were different, He

---

[1] We shall speak more of leprosy hereafter, when we consider others of our Lord's miracles. Perhaps no conception of it can be derived from any source more fearfully than from Lev. xiii., xiv. The reader will find the subject fully and learnedly treated in Jahn's *Archaeologia Biblica*, §§ 188, 189. The rites which accompanied the sacerdotal cleansing of a leper are described at length in Lev. xiv. It was a long process, in two stages. First the priest had to come to him outside the camp or town, to kill a sparrow over fresh water, to dip a living sparrow with cedar-wood, scarlet wool, and hyssop into the blood-stained water, to sprinkle the leper seven times with this strange aspergillum, and then let the living bird loose, and pronounce the man clean. The man was then to shave off his hair, bathe, remain seven days out of his house ; again shave, and bathe, and return to the priest, bringing one lamb for a trespass-offering, and a second with a ewe-lamb for a burnt and sin-offering (or, if too poor to do this, two young pigeons), and flour and oil for a meat-offering. Some of the blood of the trespass-offering, and some of the oil, was then put, with certain ceremonies, on the tip of his right ear, the thumb of his right hand, and the great toe of his right foot, the rest of the oil being poured upon his head. He was then pronounced clean. There could not well be any dispute about the reality of the cleansing, after ceremonials so elaborate as this, which are the main topic of the Mishnaic tract *Negaîm*, in fourteen chapters. Since writing the above note I have read Delitzsch's *Durch Krankheit zur Genesung*, in which the whole rites are elaborately described.

[2] Ὅρα μηδενὶ μηδὲν εἴπῃς (Mark i. 44). This probably is the correct reading of B. The expression is much stronger than usual (see xiii. 2 ; xiv. 2). For other instances of enjoined secrecy see Mark i. 25, 44 (Luke iv. 35 ; v. 14) ; Mark iii. 12 (Matt. xii. 16) ; v. 43 (Luke viii. 56). It will be seen from this that such commands were mainly given in the early part of the ministry.

even enjoined a publication of the mercy vouchsafed.[1] Was it, as St. Chrysostom conjectures, to repress a spirit of boastfulness, and teach men not to talk away the deep inward sense of God's great gifts? or was it to avoid an over-excitement and tumult in the already astonished multitudes of Galilee?[2] or was it that He might be regarded by them in His true light — not as a mighty Wonder-worker, not as a universal Hakîm, but as a Saviour by Revelation and by Hope?

Whatever may have been the general reasons, it appears that in this case there must have been some reason of special importance. St. Mark, reflecting for us the intense and vivid impressions of St. Peter, shows us, in his terse but most graphic narrative, that the man's dismissal was accompanied on our Saviour's part with some overpowering emotion. Not only is the word, "He straitly charged him" (Mark i. 43), a word implying an extreme earnestness and even vehemence of look and gesture, but the word for "forthwith sent him away" is literally He "pushed" or "drove him forth."[3] What was the cause for this severely inculcated order, for this instantaneous dismissal? Perhaps it was the fact that by touching the leper — though the touch was healing — He would, in the eyes of an unreasoning and unspiritual orthodoxy, be regarded as ceremonially unclean. And that this actually did occur may be assumed from the expressly mentioned fact that, in consequence of the manner in which this incident was blazoned abroad by the cleansed sufferer, "He could not openly enter into a city, but was without in desert places."[4] St. Luke mentions a similar circumstance, though without giving any special

---

[1] The Gadarene demoniac (Mark v. 19; Luke viii. 39).

[2] As is clearly indicated in the beautiful reference to Isa. xlii. in Matt. xii. 15—20. No true Prophet regards such powers as being the real root of the matter. At the best they are *evidential*, and that mainly to the immediate witnesses.

[3] ἐμβριμησάμενος αὐτῷ, εὐθέως ἐξέβαλεν αὐτόν (Mark i. 43). Euthymius explains this word by αὐστηρῶς ἐμβλέψας καὶ ἐπισείσας τὴν κεφαλήν.[183] It is true that both these words occur elsewhere in the picturesque and energetic Greek of the Gospels, but generally in very strong senses — *e. g.* Matt. ix. 30, 38; Mark i. 12; xiv. 5; John xi. 33. In Aquila and Symmachus also the word is used of vehement indignation (Ps. vii. 11; Isa. xvii. 13). (Cf. גָּעַר, implying *sorrow*, Gen. xl. 6, &c.) Some have supposed that ἐκβαλεῖν, merely in the sense of "send forth," is due to the vagueness of the Hebrew words שָׁלַח and גָּרַשׁ; still a certain vehemence and urgency in our Lord's words to the leper is observable in the change from the third to the first person in Luke v. 14. The ἐξέβαλεν does not imply that the miracle was done in a house; it may mean "from the town" (Alf.).

[4] Mark i. 45. "It was," says Lange (*Life of Christ*, E. Tr., ii. 443), "a sort of Levitical quarantine." He is wrong, however, in taking πόλιν to mean "*that* city," for St. Mark has not mentioned any city, and the word has no article.

reason for it, and adds that Jesus spent the time in prayer.[1] If, however, the dissemination of the leper's story involved the necessity for a short period of seclusion, it is clear that the multitude paid but little regard to this Levitical uncleanness, for even in the lonely spot to which Jesus had retired they thronged to Him from every quarter.

Whether the healing of the centurion's servant[2] took place before or after this retirement is uncertain ; but from the fact that both St. Matthew and St. Luke place it in close connection with the Sermon on the Mount, we may suppose that the thronging of the multitudes to seek Him even in desert places, may have shown that it would not be possible for Him to satisfy the scruples of the Legalists by this temporary retirement from human intercourse.

Our Lord had barely reached the town of Capernaum, where He had fixed His temporary home, when He was met by a deputation of Jewish elders[3] — probably the *batlanîm* of the chief synagogue —

---

[1] It is interesting to observe that St. Luke, more than the other Evangelists, *constantly* refers to the private prayers of Jesus (iii. 21 ; vi. 12 ; ix. 18, 28 ; xi. 1 ; xxiii. 34, 46).

[2] Luke vii. 1—10 ; Matt. viii. 5—13. The points of difference between the healing of the nobleman's son and this miracle are too numerous to admit of our accepting the opinion of those who identify them.

[3] St. Matthew's briefer and less accurate narrative represents the request as coming from the centurion himself, on the every-day principle that " qui facit per alium facit per se." [184] For a similar case, comp. Matt. xx. 20 with Mark. x. 35 (Trench, on *Miracles*, p. 236). Of course if Inspiration were a *supernatural, miraculous* interposition, instead of, as we believe, a guiding and illuminating influence, such apparent discrepancies would not exist. But, as the Jews wisely said even of their adored Law תורה דברה בלשון בני אדם, " the Law speaks with the tongue of the sons of men" (*Gittin*, 41, 3 ; *Babha Metsia*, 31, 2 ; *Nedarim*, 2, 1 ; Reland, *Antt. Hebr.* p. 140), so we say with St. Augustine, that the Evangelists are perfectly sober and truthful witnesses, though they were not in trivial matters miraculously exempted from insignificant imperfections of memory, and speak to us as we speak to each other. I would not go so far as St. Augustine in saying that they wrote " ut quisque meminerat vel ut cuique cordi erat ;" [185] but I would ask with him, " An Scriptura Dei aliter nobiscum fuerat quam nostro more locutura ? [186] (*De Cons. Evv.* ii. 20.) In the face of such obvious variations — trivial indeed, yet real — such as exist between them, in recording exact words (*e. g.*, those uttered in Gethsemane, or by the Apostles in the sinking ship), and facts (*e. g.*, the order of the Temptations and the Title on the Cross), I do not see how their *supernatural and infallible accuracy*, as apart from their absolutely truthful evidence, can be maintained. As, once more, is observed by St. Augustine, " Per hujusmodi locutiones *varias sed non contrarias* discimus nihil in cujusque verbis nos inspicere debere nisi voluntatem," [187] &c. (ib. ii. 28). " *Diversa* multa," he says elsewhere, " *adversa* nulla esse possunt." [188] The Manichæans, to whom this narrative was very distasteful, tried to reject it on the ground of this very discrepancy. The free and candid manner in which St. Augustine meets and answers them is

to intercede with Him on behalf of a centurion, whose faithful and beloved slave [1] lay in the agony and peril of a paralytic seizure. It might have seemed strange that Jewish elders should take this amount of interest in one who, whether a Roman or not, was certainly a heathen, and may not even have been a "proselyte of the gate." [2] They explained, however, that not only did he love their nation — a thing most rare in a Gentile, for, generally speaking, the Jews were regarded with singular detestation — but had even, at his own expense, built them a synagogue, which, although there must have been several in Capernaum, was sufficiently beautiful and conspicuous to be called "*the* synagogue." [3] The mere fact of their appealing to Jesus shows that this event belongs to an early period of His ministry when myriads looked to Him with astonishment and hope, and before the deadly exasperation of after days had begun. Christ immediately granted their request. "I will go," He said, "and heal him." But on the way they met other messengers from the humble and devout centurion, entreating Him not to enter the unworthy roof of a Gentile, but to heal the suffering slave (as He had healed the son of the courtier) by a mere word of power. As the centurion, though in a subordinate office, yet had ministers ever ready to do his bidding, so could not Christ bid viewless messengers to perform His will, without undergoing this personal labor? The Lord was struck by so remarkable a faith, greater than any which He had met with even in Israel. He had found in the oleaster what He had not found in the olive; [4] and He drew from this circumstance the lesson, which fell with such a chilling and unwelcome sound on Jewish ears, that when

well worth study. The reader will find some of his most important remarks on this subject quoted or referred to by Archbishop Trench, *Sermon on the Mount,* pp. 48—50.

[1] It has been suggested, and is not impossible, that the ὁ παῖς of St. Matthew's Gospel may have risen out of a confusion from the Hebrew word. St. Luke, however, calls the slave ὁ παῖς μου (vii. 7) as well as St. Matthew.

[2] Alford points out that he is not designated by the terms usually applied to proselytes (*e. g.,* in Acts x. 1, 2). He may have been one of the Samaritan soldiers of Herod Antipas, or he may have been at the head of a small Roman garrison at Capernaum.

[3] Luke vii. 5, τὴν ὀυναγωγὴν αὐτὸς (of his own accord) ᾠκοδόμηϭεν ἡμῖν. There were said to be 400 synagogues in Jerusalem, and if Capernaum be Tell Hûm, there are among its ruins the apparent remains of at least *two* synagogues. Perhaps when the traveller is sitting among the sculptured *débris* of white marble which crown the low bluff on which Tell Hûm stands, he may be in the ruins of the actual building, which by its splendor attested the centurion's liberal and kindly feelings towards the Jews, and which once rang with the echoes of the voice of Christ.

[4] Aug. in Joh. *tr.* xvi.

many of the natural children of the kingdom should be cast into outer darkness, many should come from the East and the West, and sit down with Abraham and Isaac and Jacob in the kingdom of heaven. But the centurion's messengers found on their return that the healing word had been effectual, and that the cherished slave had been restored to health.

It is not strange that, after days so marvellous as these, it was impossible for Jesus to find due repose. From early dawn on the mountain-top to late evening in whatever house He had selected for His nightly rest, the multitudes came crowding about Him, not respecting His privacy, not allowing for His weariness, eager to see Him, eager to share His miracles, eager to listen to His words. There was no time even to eat bread. Such a life is not only to the last degree trying and fatiguing, but to a refined and high-strung nature, rejoicing in noble solitude, finding its purest and most perfect happiness in lonely prayer, this incessant publicity, this apparently illimitable toil becomes simply maddening, unless the spirit be sustained by boundless sympathy and love. But the heart of the Saviour *was* so sustained. It is probably to this period that the remarkable anecdote belongs which is preserved for us by St. Mark alone. The kinsmen and immediate family of Christ, hearing of all that He was doing, came from their home — perhaps at Cana, perhaps at Capernaum — to get possession of His person, to put Him under constraint.[1] Their informants had mistaken the exaltation visible in all His words and actions — the intense glow of compassion — the burning flame of love; they looked upon it as over-excitement, exaggerated sensibility, the very delirium of beneficence and zeal. To the world there has ever been a tendency to confuse the fervor of enthusiasm with the eccentricity of a disordered genius. " Paul, thou art mad," was the only comment which the Apostle's passion of exalted eloquence produced on the cynical and *blasé* intellect of the Roman Procurator.[2] "He hath a devil," was the inference suggested to many dull and worldly hearers after some of the tenderest and divinest sayings of our Lord.[3] " Brother Martin has a

---

[1] Mark iii. 21, οἱ παρ᾽ αὐτοῦ — a somewhat vague expression — seems something like our colloquial expression " his people." From the curious accident that the word κρατῆσαι occurs in the LXX. (2 Kings iv. 8), in immediate connection with " eating bread," Bishop Wordsworth makes the surely too-ingenious conjecture " that the mother of Christ supposed that she was imitating the good Shunamite in her conduct to the prophet Elisha, in endeavoring to *constrain them* [qu. Him ? unless, indeed, he refers αὐτὸν to τὸν ὄχλον, which is impossible] *to eat bread.*"

[2] Acts xxvi. 24. Cf. 2 Cor. v. 13.

[3] John x. 20.

fine genius," was the sneering allusion of Pope Leo X. to Luther. " What crackbrained fanatics," observed the fine gentlemen of the eighteenth century when they spoke of Wesley and Whitefield. Similar, though not so coarse, was the thought which filled the mind of Christ's wondering relatives, when they heard of this sudden and amazing activity after the calm seclusion of thirty unknown and unnoticed years.   As yet they were out of sympathy with Him ; they knew Him not, did not fully believe in Him ; they said, " He is beside Himself."   It was needful that they should be henceforth taught by several decisive proofs that He was not of them ; that this was no longer the Carpenter, the brother of James and Joses and Judas and Simon, but the Son of God, the Saviour of the world.

CHAPTER XX.

JESUS AT NAIN.

" Shall the dead arise, and praise thee ? " — Ps. lxxxviii. 10.

IF the common reading in the text of St. Luke (vii. 11) be right, it was on the very day after these events that our Lord took His way from Capernaum to Nain.[1] Possibly — for, in the dim uncertainties of the chronological sequence, much scope must be left to pure conjecture — the incident of His having touched the leper may have tended to hasten His temporary departure from Capernaum by the comments which the act involved.

Nain — now a squalid and miserable village — is about twenty-five miles from Capernaum, and lies on the north-west slope of Jebel el-Duhy, or Little Hermon. The name (which it still retains) means " fair," and its situation near Endor — nestling picturesquely on the hill-slopes of the graceful mountain, and full in view of Tabor and the heights of Zebulon — justifies the flattering title. Starting, as Orientals always do, early in the cool morning hours, Jesus, in all probability, sailed to the southern end of the lake, and then passed down the Jordan valley, to the spot where the wadies of the Esdraelon slope down to it ; from which point, leaving Mount Tabor on the right hand, and Endor on the left, He might easily have arrived at the little village soon after noon.

At this bright and welcome period of His ministry, He was usually accompanied, not only by His disciples, but also by rejoicing and adoring crowds. And as this glad procession, so full of their high hopes and too-often-erring beliefs about the coming King, was climbing the narrow and rocky ascent which leads to the gate of Nain, they were met by another and a sad procession issuing through it to

---

[1] The narratives of this chapter are mostly peculiar to St. Luke (vii. 11—50). The message of St. John Baptist's disciples is, however, also related by St. Matthew (xi. 2—19). ἐν τῇ ἑξῆς (sc. ἡμέρᾳ) must mean, " on the next day." It is true that the latter word is added in Luke ix. 37 ; but, on the other hand, it is omitted in Acts xxi. 1; xxv. 17, &c. And when a wider range of time is intended, St. Luke uses ἐν τῷ καθεξῆς; on the other hand, according to Meyer, when ἡμέρᾳ is understood, St. Luke never uses ἐν. See Alford, *ad loc.* ʼΕν τῷ is here the reading of A, B, L, &c. ; Tischendorf reads τῇ with ℵ (*primâ manu*), C, D, K, &c.

bury a dead youth outside the walls.[1] There was a pathos deeper than ordinary in the spectacle, and therefore probably, in that emotional race, a wail wilder and sincerer than the ordinary lamentation. For this boy was — in language which is all the more deeply moving from its absolute simplicity, and which to Jewish ears would have involved a sense of anguish yet deeper than to ours [2] — " the only son of his mother, and she a widow." The sight of this terrible sorrow appealed irresistibly to the Saviour's loving and gentle heart. Pausing only to say to the mother, "Weep not," He approached, and — heedless once more of purely ceremonial observances — touched the bier, or rather the open coffin in which the dead youth lay. It must have been a moment of intense and breathless expectation. Unbidden, but filled with indefinable awe, the bearers of the bier stood still. And then through the hearts of the stricken mourners, and through the hearts of the silent multitude, there thrilled the calm utterance, " Young man, arise !" Would that dread monosyllable [3] thrill also through the unknown mysterious solitudes of death ? would it thrill through the impenetrable darkness of the more-than-midnight which has ever concealed from human vision the world beyond the grave ? It did. The dead got up, and began to speak ; and He delivered him to his mother.

No wonder that a great fear fell upon all. They might have thought of Elijah and the widow of Sarepta ; of Elisha and the lady of the not far distant Shunem. They too, the greatest of the Prophets, had restored to lonely women their dead only sons. But *they* had done it with agonies and energies of supplication, wrestling in prayer, and lying outstretched upon the dead ;[4] whereas Jesus had wrought that miracle calmly, incidentally, instantaneously, in His own name, by His own authority, with a single word. Could they judge otherwise than that " God had visited His people ?"

It was about this time, possibly even on this same day,[5] that our

---

[1] The ordinary Jewish custom. The rough path near the entrance of *Nein* must be added to the *certain* sites of events in the life of Christ. The rock-hewn sepulchres on the hill-side may well be as old as the time of Christ, and it is probably to one of them that the youth's body was being carried.

[2] Partly because to die childless was to them a terrible calamity ; partly because the loss of offspring was often regarded as a direct punishment for sin (Jer. vi. 26 ; Zech. xii. 10 ; Amos viii. 10).

[3] קוּם, *kûm !* It is at least natural to suppose that our Lord used the same Aramaic word as to the daughter of Jairus, " Talitha cûmi" (Mark v. 41).

[4] 1 Kings xvii. 21 ; 2 Kings iv. 35.

[5] Matt. xi. 2—19 ; Luke vii. 18—35.— I am well aware of what Stier and others say to the contrary ; but it is impossible and wholly unnecessary to give separate reasons and proofs at each step of the narrative.

Lord received a short but agitated message from His own great Forerunner, John the Baptist. Its very brevity added to the sense of doubt and sadness which it breathed. " Art Thou," he asked, "the coming Messiah, or are we to expect another ? " [1]

Was this a message from him who had first recognized and pointed out the Lamb of God ? from him who, in the rapture of vision, had seen heaven opened and the Spirit descending on the head of Jesus like a dove ?

It may be so. Some have indeed imagined that the message was merely intended to satisfy the doubts of the Baptist's jealous and disheartened followers ; some, that his question only meant, " Art Thou indeed the Jesus to whom I bore my testimony ? " [2] some, that the message implied *no* latent hesitation, but was intended as a timid suggestion that the time was now come for Jesus to manifest Himself as the Messiah of His nation's theocratic hopes — perhaps even as a gentle rebuke to Him for allowing His friend and Forerunner to languish in a dungeon, and not exerting on his behalf the miraculous power of which these rumors told. But these suggestions — all intended, as it were, to save the credit of the Baptist — are at the best wholly unauthorized, and are partly refuted by the actual expressions of the narrative. St. John Baptist in his heroic greatness needs not the poor aid of our charitable suppositions : we conclude from the express words of Him, who at this very crisis pronounced upon him the most splendid eulogy ever breathed over mortal man, that the great and noble prophet had indeed, for the moment, found a stumbling-block to his faith in what he heard about the Christ. [3]

And is this natural ? is it an indecision which any one who knows anything of the human heart will venture for a moment to condemn ? The course of the greatest of the Prophets had been brief and tragical — a sad calendar of disaster and eclipse. Though all men flocked

---

[1] The ἕτερον of Matt. xi. 3 would strictly mean either " a second " or " one quite different ;" but as the messenger doubtless spoke in Aramaic, the variation from the ἄλλον of Luke vii. 19 must not be pressed.

[2] The main argument for this is that in Matt. xi. 2 it says that John had heard in prison the works of the Messiah (τοῦ Χριστοῦ), not as elsewhere in St. Matthew, τοῦ Ἰησοῦ. It must be borne in mind that in the Gospels " Christ " is always a *title*, scarcely ever a *proper name*. It did not become a name till after the Resurrection. Moreover, it appears that some of the rumors about Jesus were that He was Elijah, or Jeremiah, and these may have tended to confuse the prison-clouded mind of John (Just. Mart., *Quaest. ad Orthod.* 34, quoted by Alford). Dr. Lightfoot (*On Revision,* p. 100) says that Χριστός is never found in the Gospels with Ἰησοῦς, except in John xvii. 3 (but add Matt. i. 1, 18 ; Mark i. 1).

[3] Matt. xi. 11

in multitudes to listen to the fiery preacher of the wilderness, the real effect on the mind of the nation had been neither permanent nor deep.' We may say with the Scotch poet —

> " Who listened to his voice ?. obeyed his cry ?
> Only the echoes which he made relent
> Rang from their flinty caves, ' Repent l repent ! ' "

Even before Jesus had come forth in the fulness of His ministry, the power and influence of John had paled like a star before the sunrise. He must have felt very soon — and that is a very bitter thing for any human heart to feel — that his mission for this life was over; that nothing appreciable remained for him to do. Similar moments of intense and heart-breaking despondency had already occurred in the lives of his very greatest predecessors — in the lives of even a Moses and an Elijah. But the case was far worse with John the Baptist than with them. For though his Friend and his Saviour was living, was at no great distance from him, was in the full tide of His influence, and was daily working the miracles of love which attested His mission, yet John saw that Friend and Saviour on earth no more. There were no visits to console, no intercourse to sustain him; he was surrounded only by the coldness of listeners whose curiosity had waned, and the jealousy of disciples whom his main testimony had disheartened. And then came the miserable climax. Herod Antipas — the pettiest, meanest, weakest, most contemptible of titular princelings — partly influenced by political fears, partly enraged by John's just and blunt rebuke of his adulterous life, though at first he had listened to the Baptist with the superstition which is the usual concomitant of cunning, had ended by an uxorious concession to the hatred of Herodias, and had flung him into prison.

Josephus tells us that this prison was the fortress of Machærus, or Makor, a strong and gloomy castle, built by Alexander Jannæus and strengthened by Herod the Great — on the borders of the desert, to the north of the Dead Sea, and on the frontiers of Arabia.' We know enough of solitary castles and Eastern dungeons to realize what horrors must have been involved for any man in such an imprisonment; what possibilities of agonizing torture, what daily risk of a violent and unknown death. How often in the world's history have even the most generous and dauntless spirits been crushed and effeminated by such hopeless captivity. When the first noble rage, or

---

¹ Matt. xi. 18 ; xxi. 23—27 ; John v. 35.

² Hitzig says that קָוֹר means " diadem." The ruins of it have rarely been visited, but were discovered, or at any rate heard of, by Seetzen in 1807.

heroic resignation, is over — when the iron-hearted endurance is corroded by forced inactivity and maddening solitude — when the great heart is cowed by the physical lassitude and despair of a life left to rot away in the lonely darkness — who can be answerable for the level of depression to which he may sink? Savonarola, and Jerome of Prague, and Luther were men whose courage, like that of the Baptist, had enabled them to stand unquailing before angry councils and threatening kings: will any one, in forming an estimate of their goodness and their greatness, add one shade of condemnation because of the wavering of the first and of the second in the prison-cells of Florence and Constance, or the phantasies of incipient madness which agitated, in the castle of Wartburg, the ardent spirit of the third? And yet to St. John Baptist imprisonment must have been a deadlier thing than even to Luther; for in the free wild life of the hermit he had lived in constant communion with the sights and sounds of nature, had breathed with delight and liberty the free winds of the wilderness, and gazed with a sense of companionship on the large stars which beam from the clear vault of the Eastern night. To a child of freedom and of passion, to a rugged, passionate, untamed spirit like that of John, a prison was worse than death. For the palms of Jericho and the balsams of Engedi, for the springing of the beautiful gazelles amid the mountain solitudes, and the reflection of the moonlight on the mysterious waves of the Salt Lake, he had nothing now but the chilly damps and cramping fetters of a dungeon, and the brutalities of such a jailor as a tetrarch like Antipas would have kept in a fortress like Makor. In that black prison, among its lava streams and basaltic rocks, which was tenanted in reality by far worse demons of human brutality and human vice than the "goats" and "satyrs" and doleful creatures believed by Jewish legend to haunt its whole environment, we cannot wonder if the eye of the caged eagle began to film.

Not once or twice alone in the world's history has God seemed to make His very best and greatest servants drink to the very dregs the cup of apparent failure — called them suddenly away by the sharp stroke of martyrdom, or down the long declivities of a lingering disease, before even a distant view of their work has been vouchsafed to them; flung them, as it were, aside like broken instruments, useless for their destined purpose, ere He crowned with an immortality of success and blessing the lives which fools regarded as madness, and the end that has been without human honor. It is but a part of that merciful fire in which he is purging away the dross from the seven-times-refined gold of a spirit which shall be worthy of eternal bliss. But to none could this disciplinary tenderness have come in more terrible disguise than to St. John. For he seemed to be neglected not only by God above, but by the living Son of God on earth. John was pining in Herod's prison while Jesus, in the glad simplicity of His early Galilæan ministry, was preaching to rejoicing multitudes among the mountain lilies or from the waves of the pleasant lake. Oh, why did his Father in heaven and his Friend on earth suffer him to languish in this soul-clouding misery? Had not his life been innocent? had not his ministry been faithful? had not his testimony been true? Oh, why did not He, to whom he had borne witness beyond Jordan, call down fire from heaven to shatter those foul and guilty towers? Among so many miracles might not *one* be spared to the unhappy kinsman who had gone before His face to prepare His way before Him? Among so many words of mercy and tenderness might not *some* be vouchsafed to him who had uttered that Voice in the wilderness? Why should not the young Son of David rock with earthquake the foundations of these Idumæan prisons, where many a noble captive had been unjustly slain, or send but one of His twelve legions of angels to liberate His Forerunner and His friend, were it but to restore him to his desert solitude once more — content there to end his life among the wild beasts, so it were far from man's tyrannous infamy, and under God's open sky? What wonder, we say again, if the eye of the caged eagle began to film!

"Art Thou He that should come, or do we look for another?"

Jesus did not directly answer the question. He showed the messengers, he let them see with their own eyes, some of the works of which hitherto they had only heard by the hearing of the ear. And then, with a reference to the 61st chapter of Isaiah, He bade them take back to their master the message, that blind men saw, and lame walked, and lepers were cleansed, and deaf heard, and dead were raised;[1] and above all, and more than all, that to the poor the glad tidings were being preached: and then, we can imagine with how deep a tenderness, He added, "And blessed is he whosoever shall not be offended in Me" — blessed (that is) is he who shall trust Me, even in spite of sorrow and persecution — he who shall believe that I know to the utmost the will of Him that sent Me, and how and when to finish His work.

---

[1] Even if the spiritual meaning did not predominate in these expressions, as seems to be clear from the words which formed their climax, yet the recent miracle at Nain would alone suffice to justify this allusion. I may observe here that I quote from these latter chapters of "Isaiah" without thinking it necessary to call the writer of them, as Ewald does, "the Great Unnamed."

We may easily suppose, though nothing more is told us, that the disciples did not depart without receiving from Jesus other words of private affection and encouragement for the grand prisoner whose end was now so nearly approaching — words which would be to him sweeter than the honey which had sustained his hunger in the wilderness, dearer than water-springs in the dry ground. And no sooner had the disciples departed, than He who would not seem to be guilty of idle flattery, but yet wished to prevent His hearers from cherishing one depreciatory thought of the great Prophet of the Desert, uttered over His friend and Forerunner, in language of rhythmic and perfect loveliness, the memorable eulogy, that he was indeed the promised Voice in the new dawn of a nobler day, the greatest of all God's herald messengers — the Elias who, according to the last word of ancient prophecy, was to precede the Advent of the Messiah, and to prepare His way.

" What went ye out into the wilderness for to see ?

" A reed shaken by the wind ?

" But what went ye out for to see ?

" A man clothed in soft raiment ?

" Behold, they that wear soft clothing are in *kings'* houses ! [1]

" But what went ye out for to see ?

" A prophet ?

" Yea, I say unto you, and far more than a prophet. For this is he of whom it is written, Behold, I send My messenger before Thy face, who shall prepare Thy way before Thee."

And having pronounced this rhythmic and impassioned eulogy, He proceeded to speak to them more calmly respecting Himself and John, and to tell them that though John was the last and greatest of the Old Dispensation, yet the least in the kingdom of heaven was greater than he. The brevity with which the words are repeated leaves their meaning uncertain; but the superiority intended is a superiority doubtless in spiritual privileges, not in moral exaltation. " The least of that which is greatest," says a legal maxim, " is greater than the greatest of that which is least;" [2] and in revealed knowledge; in illimitable hope, in conscious closeness of relationship to His Father and His God, the humblest child of the New Covenant is more richly

---

[1] " Those in gorgeous apparel and luxury," is the slight variation in St. Luke. John, too, had been in kings' houses, but it was in hairy mantle, and not to praise, but to denounce. As Lange finely observes, John was not a reed waving in the wind, but rather a cedar half-uprooted by the storm.

[2] Maldonatus, quoted by Meyer — " *minimum maximi est majus maximo minimi.*" [189]

endowed than the greatest prophet of the Old. And into that kingdom of God whose advent was now proclaimed, henceforth with holy
and happy violence they all might press. Such eager violence —
natural to those who hunger and thirst after righteousness — would
be only acceptable in the sight of God.[1]

Many who heard these words, and especially the publicans and
those who were scorned as the " people of the earth," [2] accepted with
joy and gratitude this approbation of their confidence in John. But
there were others — the accredited teachers of the written and oral
Law — who listened to such words with contemptuous dislike.
Struck with these contrasts, Jesus drew an illustration from peevish
children who fretfully reject every effort of their fellows to delight
or to amuse them. Nothing could please such soured and rebellious
natures. The flute and dance of the little ones who played at wed-
dings charmed them as little as the long wail of the simulated
funeral. God's "richly-variegated wisdom" had been exhibited to
them in many fragments, and by many methods,[3] yet all in vain.
John had come to them in the stern asceticism of the hermit, and
they called him mad; Jesus joined in the banquet and the marriage-
feast, and they called Him "an eater and a wine-drinker." [4] Even
so! yet Wisdom has been ever justified at her children's hands.
Those children have not disgraced their divine original. Fools
might account their life as madness, and their end to be without
honor; but how is the very humblest of them numbered among the
children of God, and their lot among the saints! [5]

---

[1] Cf. Isa. lx. 8, 11 ; Luke v. 1 ; xiii. 24.

[2] The *am ha-arets*, or as we should say, " mere boors."

[3] ἡ πολυποίκιλος σοφία (Eph. iii. 10); πολυμερῶς καὶ πολυτρόπως
(Heb. i. 1).

[4] Matt. xi. 16—19; Luke vii. 31—35. The A. V., "a gluttonous man and a
wine-bibber," is perhaps a shade too strong ; the words do not necessarily mean
more than a *bon vivant*, but perhaps they correspond to expressions which connoted something more in Aramaic. φάγος does not occur in the LXX., but
οἰνοπότης is found in Prov. xxiii. 20.

[5] Wisd. v. 4, 5 ; cf. Ps. li. 4; Rom. iii. 4. I have embodied into the text, without expansion, reference, or comment, the view which seems to me the best ; and
I have followed the same method of dealing with many other passages of which
the exegesis is confessedly difficult, and to some extent uncertain. I cannot
accept Ewald's notion that the allusion is to a kind of "guessing-game," where
the children had to pay forfeit if they failed to understand the scene which their
fellows were acting.

CHAPTER XXI.

THE SINNER AND THE PHARISEE.

"Because of the savor of thy good ointments thy name is as ointment poured forth."— CANT. i. 3.

BUT not even yet apparently were the deeds and sayings of this memorable day concluded; for in the narrative of St. Luke it seems to have been on the same day that, perhaps at Nain, perhaps at Magdala, Jesus received and accepted an invitation from one of the Pharisees who bore the very common name of Simon.[1]

The cause or object of the invitation we do not know; but as yet Jesus had come to no marked or open rupture with the Pharisaic party, and they may even have imagined that He might prove of use to them as the docile instrument of their political and social purposes. Probably, in inviting him, Simon was influenced partly by curiosity, partly by the desire to receive a popular and distinguished teacher, partly by willingness to show a distant approval of something which may have struck him in Christ's looks, or words, or ways. It is quite clear that the hospitality was meant to be qualified and condescending. All the ordinary attentions which would have been paid to an honored guest were coldly and cautiously omitted. There was

---

[1] Luke vii. 36—50. Those who identify this feast at the house of Simon the Pharisee, in Galilee, with the long-subsequent feast at the house of Simon the leper, at Bethany, and the anointing of the feet by "a woman that was a sinner in the city," with the anointing of the head by Mary the sister of Martha, adopt principles of criticism so reckless and arbitrary that their general acceptance would rob the Gospels of all credibility, and make them hardly worth study as truthful narratives. As for the names Simon and Judas, which have led to so many identifications of different persons and different incidents, they were at least as common among the Jews of that day as Smith and Jones among ourselves. There are five or six Judes, and nine Simons mentioned in the New Testament, and two Judes and two Simons among the Apostles alone. Josephus speaks of some *ten* Judes and *twenty* Simons in his writings, and there must, therefore, have been thousands of others who at this period had one of these two names. The incident is one quite in accordance with the customs of the time and country, and there is not the least improbability in its repetition under different circumstances (Eccles. ix. 8; Cant. iv. 10; Amos vi. 6; *Jer. Berachôth*, f. 11, 2; Sen. *Ep.* 86; Aul. Gell. vii. 12, &c.). The custom still continues (Renan, *Vie de Jésus*, p. 385).

no water for the weary and dusty feet, no kiss of welcome upon the cheek, no perfume for the hair, nothing but a somewhat ungracious admission to a vacant place at the table, and the most distant courtesies of ordinary intercourse, so managed that the Guest might feel that he was supposed to be receiving an honor, and not to be conferring one.

In order that the mats or carpets which are hallowed by domestic prayer may not be rendered unclean by any pollution of the streets, each guest, as he enters a house in Syria or Palestine, takes off his sandals, and leaves them at the door. He then proceeds to his place at the table. In ancient times, as we find throughout the Old Testament,[1] it was the custom of the Jews to eat their meals sitting cross-legged — as is still common throughout the East — in front of a tray placed on a low stool, on which is set the dish containing the heap of food, from which all help themselves in common. But this custom, though it has been resumed for centuries, appears to have been abandoned by the Jews in the period succeeding the Captivity. Whether they had borrowed the recumbent posture at meals from the Persians or not, it is certain, from the expressions employed, that in the time of our Lord the Jews, like the Greeks and Romans, reclined at banquets,[2] upon couches placed round tables of much the same height as those now in use. We shall see hereafter that even the Passover was eaten in this attitude. The beautiful and profoundly moving incident which occurred in Simon's house can only be understood by remembering that as the guests lay on the couches which surrounded the tables, their feet would be turned towards any spectators who were standing outside the circle of bidden guests.

An Oriental's house is by no means his castle. The universal prevalence of the law of hospitality — the very first of Eastern virtues — almost forces him to live with open doors, and any one may at any time have access to his rooms.[3] But on this occasion there was one who had summoned up courage to intrude upon that respectable dwelling-place a presence which was not only unwelcome, but positively odious. A poor, stained, fallen woman, notorious in the place

---

[1] The word used is generally שָׁכַב (Gen. xxvii. 19), or יָשַׁב (1 Sam. xvi. 11, " We will not *sit round;* " cf. 1 Sam. xx. 5, 18; Ps. cxxviii. 3; Cant. i. 12, &c.); and we do not hear of reclining till the Exile (Esth. i. 6; vii. 8).

[2] The words used are ἀναπίπτειν (Luke xi. 37; John xxi. 20; Tobit ii. 1), ἀνακεῖσθαι (Luke vii. 37; cf. 3 Esdras iv. 10), ἀνακλίνεσθαι (Luke vii. 36; xii. 37; Judith xii. 15); cf. ἀρχιτρίκλινος (John ii. 8).

[3] The author had opportunities of observing this in Palestine. When we were at a Sheykh's house, the population took a great interest in inspecting us.

for her evil life, discovering that Jesus was supping in the house of the Pharisee,[1] ventured to make her way there among the throng of other visitants, carrying with her an alabaster box of spikenard. She found the object of her search, and as she stood humbly behind Him, and listened to His words, and thought of all that He was, and all to which she had fallen — thought of the stainless, sinless purity of the holy and youthful Prophet, and of her own shameful, degraded life — she began to weep, and her tears dropped fast upon His unsandalled feet, over which she bent lower and lower to hide her confusion and her shame. The Pharisee would have started back with horror from the touch, still more from the tear, of such an one; he would have wiped away the fancied pollution, and driven off the presumptuous intruder with a curse. But this woman felt instinctively that Jesus would not treat her so; she felt that the highest sinlessness is also the deepest sympathy; she saw that where the hard respectability of her fellow-sinner would repel, the perfect holiness of her Saviour would receive. Perhaps she had heard those infinitely tender and gracious words which may have been uttered on this very day [2] —" Come unto me, all ye that labor and are heavy laden, and I will give you rest." And she was emboldened by being unreproved; and thus becoming conscious that, whatever others might do, the Lord at any rate did not loathe or scorn her, she drew yet nearer to Him, and, sinking down upon her knees, began with her long dishevelled hair to wipe the feet which had been wetted with her tears, and then to cover them with kisses, and at last — breaking the alabaster vase — to bathe them with the precious and fragrant nard.[3]

The sight of that dishevelled woman, the shame of her humiliation, the agonies of her penitence, the quick dropping of her tears, the sacrifice of that perfume which had been one of the instruments of her unhallowed arts, might have touched even the stoniest feelings into an emotion of sympathy. But Simon, the Pharisee, looked on with icy dislike and disapproval. The irresistible appeal to pity of that despairing and broken-hearted mourner did not move him. It was not enough for him that Jesus had but suffered the unhappy creature to kiss and anoint His feet, without speaking to her as yet

---

[1] ἐπιγνοῦσα (Luke vii. 37).

[2] They are given by St. Matthew in close connection with the preceding events (xi. 28); it is, however, clear that St. Matthew is here recording discourses, or parts of discourses, which belong to different times.

[3] The word ἀλάβαστρον is generic, *i. e.*, it describes the use to which the little phial was put, not necessarily the material of which it was made. [Cf. χρύσει' ἀλάβαστρα (Theocr. *Id.* xv. 114) and the use of our word *box;* Herod. iii. 20; Arist. *Ach.* 1053, &c.]

one word of encouragement. Had He been a prophet, He ought to have known what kind of woman she was ; and had He known, He ought to have repulsed her with contempt and indignation, as Simon would himself have done. Her mere touch almost involved the necessity of a ceremonial quarantine. One sign from Him, and Simon would have been only too glad of an excuse for ejecting such a pollution from the shelter of his roof.

The Pharisee did not utter these thoughts aloud, but his frigid demeanor, and the contemptuous expression of countenance, which he did not take the trouble to disguise, showed all that was passing in his heart. Our Lord heard his thoughts,[1] but did not at once reprove and expose his cold uncharity and unrelenting hardness. In order to call general attention to his words, he addressed his host.

" Simon, I have something to say to thee."

" Master, say on," is the somewhat constrained reply.

" There was a certain creditor who had two debtors : the one owed five hundred pence, and the other fifty ; and when they had nothing to pay, he freely forgave them both. Tell me then, which of them will love him most ? "

Simon does not seem to have had the slightest conception that the question had any reference to himself — as little conception as David had when he pronounced so frank a judgment on Nathan's parable.

" I imagine," he said — there is a touch of supercilious patronage, of surprised indifference to the whole matter in the word he uses [2] — " I presume that he to whom he forgave most."

" Thou hast rightly judged." And then — the sterner for its very gentleness and forbearance — came the moral and application of the little tale, couched in that rhythmic utterance of antithetic parallelism which our Lord often adopted in His loftier teaching, and which appealed like the poetry of their own prophets to the ears of those who heard it. Though Simon may not have seen the point of the parable, perhaps the penitent, with the quicker intuition of a contrite heart, *had* seen it. But what must have been her emotion when He who hitherto had not noticed her, now turned full towards her, and calling the attention of all who were present to her shrinking figure, as she sat upon the ground, hiding with her two hands and with her dishevelled hair the confusion of her face, exclaimed to the astonished Pharisee —

---

[1] " Audivit Pharisaeum cogitantem " [190] (Aug., *Serm.* xcix.). " Guard well thy thoughts, for thoughts are heard in heaven."

[2] Luke vii. 43, ὑπολαμβάνω. Cf. Acts ii. 15.

"Simon! dost thou mark[1] this woman?

"I was thine own guest: thou pouredst no water over my feet; but she, with her tears, washed my feet, and with her hair she wiped them.

"No kiss gavest thou to Me; but she, since the time I came in, has been ceaselessly covering my feet with kisses.[2]

"My head with oil thou anointedst not; but she with spikenard anointed my feet.

"Wherefore I say to you, her sins — her many sins, have been forgiven; but he to whom there is but little forgiveness, loveth little."

And then like the rich close of gracious music, he added, no longer to Simon, but to the poor sinful woman, the words of mercy, "Thy sins have been forgiven."

Our Lord's words were constantly a new revelation for all who heard them, and if we may judge from many little indications in the Gospels, they seem often to have been followed, in the early days of His ministry, by a shock of surprised silence, which at a later date, among those who rejected Him, broke out into fierce reproaches and indignant murmurs. At this stage of His work, the spell of awe and majesty produced by His love and purity, and by that inward Divinity which shone in His countenance and sounded in His voice, had not yet been broken. It was only in their secret thoughts that the guests — rather, it seems, in astonishment than in wrath — ventured to question this calm and simple claim to a more than earthly attribute. It was only in their hearts that they silently mused and questioned, "Who is this, who forgiveth sins also?" Jesus knew their inward hesitations; but it had been prophesied of Him that "He should not strive nor cry, neither should His voice be heard in the streets;" and because He would not break the bruised reed of their faith, or quench the smoking flax of their reverent amazement, He gently sent away the woman who had been a sinner with the kind words, "Thy faith hath saved thee: go into peace."[3] And to peace beyond all doubt she went, even to the peace of God which passeth

---

[1] βλέπεις, not ὁρᾷς (ver. 44). Perhaps Simon had disdained even to look at her attentively, as though even *that* would stain his sanctity! The "I was thine own guest" is an attempt to bring out the force of the σοῦ εἰς τὴν οἰκίαν. The ἐπὶ τοὺς πόδας implies the pouring. Cf. Rev. viii. 3; Gen. xviii. 4; Judg. xix. 21.

[2] There is a contrast between the mere φίλημα and the καταφιλοῦσα (ver. 45).

[3] Verse 50, εἰς εἰρήνην, not only "in," but "*to* or *for* peace"; the Hebrew לְשָׁלוֹם.

all understanding, to the peace which Jesus gives, which is not as the world gives. To the general lesson which her story inculcates we shall return hereafter, for it is one which formed a central doctrine of Christ's revelation; I mean the lesson that cold and selfish hypocrisy is in the sight of God as hateful as more glaring sin; the lesson that a life of sinful and impenitent respectability may be no less deadly and dangerous than a life of open shame. But' meanwhile the touching words of an English poet may serve as the best comment on this beautiful incident: —

> " She sat and wept beside his feet; the weight
> Of sin oppressed her heart; for all the blame,
> And the poor malice of the worldly shame,
> To her were past, extinct, and out of date;
> Only the sin remained — the leprous *state*.
> She would be melted by the heat of love,
> By fires far fiercer than are blown to prove
> And purge the silver ore adulterate.
> She sat and wept, and with her untressed hair,
> Still wiped the feet she was so blessed to touch;
> And he wiped off the soiling of despair
> From her sweet soul, because she loved so much." [1]

An ancient tradition — especially prevalent in the Western Church, and followed by the translators of our English version — a tradition which, though it must ever remain uncertain, is not in itself improbable, and cannot be disproved — identifies this woman with Mary of Magdala, " out of whom Jesus cast seven devils." [2] This exorcism is not elsewhere alluded to, and it would be perfectly in accordance with the genius of Hebrew phraseology if the expression had been applied to her, in consequence of a passionate nature and an abandoned life. The Talmudists have much to say respecting her — her wealth, her extreme beauty, her braided locks, her shameless profligacy, her

---

[1] Hartley Coleridge.

[2] This tradition is alluded to by Ambrose (*in Luc.*), Jerome (in Matt. xxvi. 6), and Augustine (*De Cons. Evang.* 69), and accepted by Gregory the Great (*Hom. in Evv.* 33). Any one who has read my friend Professor Plumptre's article on " Mary Magdalene," in Smith's *Dict. of the Bible*, will perhaps be surprised that I accept even the *possibility* of this identification, which he calls " a figment utterly baseless." I have partly answered the supposed objections to the identification in the text, and mainly differ from Professor Plumptre in his view of the " seven demons." This, he says, is incompatible with the life implied by the word ἁμαρτωλός. To which I reply by referring to Luke iv. 33; Matt. x. 1, &c. Gregory the Great rightly held that the " seven demons " *may* have been applied to the " many sins," for Lightfoot has shown that the Rabbis applied drunkenness and lust to the *immediate* agency of demons (*v. supr.*, p. 193).

husband Pappus, and her paramour Pandera;[1] but all that we really know of the Magdalene from Scripture is that enthusiasm of devotion and gratitude which attached her, heart and soul, to her Saviour's service. In the chapter of St. Luke which follows this incident she is mentioned first among the women who accompanied Jesus in His wanderings, and ministered to Him of their substance;[2] and it may be that in the narrative of the incident at Simon's house her name was suppressed, out of that delicate consideration which, in other passages, makes the Evangelist suppress the condition of Matthew and the name of Peter. It may be, indeed, that the woman who was a sinner went to find the peace which Christ had promised to her troubled conscience in a life of deep seclusion and obscurity, which meditated in silence on the merciful forgiveness of her Lord; but in the popular consciousness she will till the end of time be identified with the Magdalene whose very name has passed into all civilized languages as a synonym for accepted penitence and pardoned sin. The traveller who, riding among the delicate perfumes of many flowering plants on the shores of Gennesareth, comes to the ruinous tower and solitary palm-tree that mark the Arab village of El Mejdel, will involuntarily recall this old tradition of her whose sinful beauty and deep repentance have made the name of Magdala so famous ; and though the few miserable peasant huts are squalid and ruinous, and the inhabitants are living in ignorance and degradation, he will still look with interest and emotion on a site which brings back into his memory one of the most signal proofs that no one — not even the most fallen and the most despised — is regarded as an outcast by Him whose very work it was to seek and save that which was lost. Perhaps in the balmy air of Gennesareth, in the brightness of the sky above his head, in the sound of the singing birds which fills the air, in the masses of purple blossom which at some seasons of the year festoons these huts of mud, he may see a type of the love and tenderness which is large and rich enough to encircle with the grace of fresh and heavenly beauty the ruins of a once earthly and desecrated life.[3]

---

[1] The reader will, I am sure, excuse me from the tedious task of reproducing all these venomous and absurd fictions, which are as devoid of literary as they are of historic value.

[2] Luke viii. 2.

[3] Any one who cares to see the various plays on, and derivations suggested for, the name Magdalene, can do so in Lightfoot, *Hor. Hebr.* in Matt. xxvi. 6, and Prof. Plumptre *ubi supr.* Nothing can be inferred against its meaning "of Magdala" from the ἡ καλουμένη of Luke viii. 2.

CHAPTER XXII.

JESUS AS HE LIVED IN GALILEE.

τὸ γὰρ πάθος Χριστοῦ ἡμῶν ἀπάθειά ἐστιν . . . καὶ τὸ δάκρυον
αὐτοῦ χάρα ἡμετέρα.[191] — ATHAN., *De Incarn.*

IT is to this period of our Lord's earlier ministry that those mission
journeys belong — those circuits through the towns and villages of
Galilee, teaching, and preaching, and performing works of mercy —
which are so frequently alluded to in the first three Gospels, and
which are specially mentioned at this point of the narrative by the
Evangelist St. Luke. "He walked in Galilee." [1] It was the brightest, hopefullest, most active episode in His life. Let us, in imagination, stand aside and see Him pass, and so, with all humility and
reverence, set before us as vividly as we can what manner of man
He was.

Let us then suppose ourselves to mingle with any one fragment
of those many multitudes which at this period awaited Him at every
point of His career, and let us gaze on Him as they did when He was
a man on earth.[2]

---

[1] Matt. iv. 23; ix. 35; Mark i. 39; Luke iv. 15, 44; John vii. 1: περιεπάτει
— "ambulando docebat" [192] (Bretschneider). In this part of the narrative I mainly
follow St. Luke's order, only varying from it where there seems reason for doing
so. I have, however, already stated my disbelief in the possibility of a final harmony; and in a few instances where no special order is discernible in the narrative of the Evangelists, I have followed a plan distinctly sanctioned by the practice of St. Matthew — viz., that of grouping together events which have a subjective connection. Any one who has long and carefully studied the Gospels has
probably arrived at a strong opinion as to the possible or even probable order of
events; but when he sees no two independent harmonists agreeing even in the
common chronological principles or data (*e. g.*, even as to the number of years in
Christ's ministry), he will probably feel that the order he adopts will carry no
conviction to others, however plausible it may seem to himself. I agree, however, more nearly with Lange and Stier — though by no means adopting their
entire arrangement — than with most other writers.

[2] The general idea of this chapter, and many of its details, were suggested to
me by an exceedingly beautiful and interesting little tract of Dr. F. Delitzsch,
called *Sehet welch ein Mensch.* Ein Geschichtsgemälde.[193] (Leipzig, 1869.) Some
may perhaps consider that both Dr. Delitzsch and I have given too much scope to
the imagination; but, with the exception of one or two references to early tradition, they will scarcely find an incident, or even an expression, which is not sanctioned by notices in the Evangelists.

We are on that little plain [1] that runs betwen the hills of Zebulon and Naphtali, somewhere between the villages of Kefr Kenna and the so-called Kana el-Jalîl. A sea of corn, fast yellowing to the harvest, is around us, and the bright, innumerable flowers that broider the wayside are richer and larger than those of home. The path on which we stand leads in one direction to Accho and the coast, in the other over the summit of Hattîn to the Sea of Galilee. The land is lovely with all the loveliness of a spring day in Palestine, but the hearts of the eager, excited crowd, in the midst of which we stand, are too much occupied by one absorbing thought to notice its beauty; for some of them are blind, and sick, and lame, and they know not whether to-day a finger of mercy, a word of healing — nay, even the touch of the garment of this great Unknown Prophet as He passes by — may not alter and gladden the whole complexion of their future lives. And farther back, at a little distance from the crowd, standing among the wheat, with covered lips, and warning off all who approach them with the cry *Tamê, Tamê* — "Unclean! unclean!" — clad in mean and scanty garments, are some fearful and mutilated figures whom, with a shudder, we recognize as lepers. [2]

The comments of the crowd show that many different motives have brought them together. Some are there from interest, some from curiosity, some from the vulgar contagion of enthusiasm which they cannot themselves explain. Marvellous tales of Him — of His mercy, of His power, of His gracious words, of His mighty deeds — are passing from lip to lip, mingled, doubtless, with suspicions and calumnies. One or two Scribes and Pharisees who are present, holding themselves a little apart from the crowd, whisper to each other their perplexities, their indignation, their alarm.

Suddenly over the rising ground, at no great distance, is seen the cloud of dust which marks an approaching company; and a young boy of Magdala or Bethsaida, heedless of the scornful reproaches of the Scribes, points in that direction, and runs excitedly forward with the shout of *Malka Meshichah! Malka Meshichah* — "the King Messiah! the King Messiah!" — which even on youthful lips must have quickened the heart-beats of a simple Galilæan throng. [3]

And now the throng approaches. It is a motley multitude of young

---

[1] Assochis ; now called El Buttauf.

[2] נָטָ (Lev. xiii. 45 ; Numb. vi. 9). Cf. Ezek. xxiv. 17, " cover not thy lips."

[3] I take the supposed incident in part from Dr. Delitzsch ; and after the announcement of John the Baptist (John i. 26, 32, &c.), and such incidents as those recorded in Luke iv. 41, the surmise of John iv. 29 ; vii. 41 must have been on many lips.

and old, composed mainly of peasants, but with others of higher rank interspersed in their loose array — here a frowning Pharisee, there a gaily-clad Herodian [1] whispering to some Greek merchant or Roman soldier his scoffing comments on the enthusiasm of the crowd. But these are the few, and almost every eye of that large throng is constantly directed towards One who stands in the centre of the separate group which the crowd surrounds.

In the front of this group walk some of the newly-chosen Apostles: behind are others, among whom there is one whose restless glance and saturnine countenance [2] accord but little with that look of openness and innocence which stamps his comrades as honest men. Some of those who are looking on whisper that he is a certain Judas of Kerioth, almost the only follower of Jesus who is not a Galilæan. A little further in the rear, behind the remainder of the Apostles, are four or five women, [3] some on foot, some on mules, among whom, though they are partly veiled, there are some who recognize the once wealthy and dissolute but now repentant Mary of Magdala; and

---

[1] In the Talmudic legend of the apostasy of Menahem and his 160 scholars from the school of Hillel to the service of Herod (לעבודת המלך; *Chagiga*, f. 16, 2 ; Reland, *Antt. Hebr.*, p. 251), one sign of their abandonment of the Oral Law was glittering apparel. (Jost, *Gesch. d. Judenth.* i. 259.) Professor Plumptre ingeniously illustrates this fact by a reference to Luke vii. 24 (*Dict. of Bibl.*, s. v. " Scribes ").

[2] In the Apocryphal Gospels there is a notion that Judas had once been a demoniac, whom Jesus, as a boy, had healed (Ev. Inf. Arab. c. xxxv. ; Hoffmann, *Leben Jesu nach d. Apokr.* 202). For the legendary notion of his aspect, see the story of St. Brandan, so exquisitely told by Mr. Matthew Arnold :—

> " At last (it was the Christmas night ;
> Stars shone after a day of storm)
> He sees float by an iceberg white,
> And on it — Christ ! — a living form !
>
> " That furtive mien, that scowling eye,
> Of hair that red and tufted fell ;
> It is — oh, where shall Brandan fly ? —
> The traitor Judas, out of hell."

[3] Perhaps more (Luke viii. 3, ἕτεραι πολλαὶ [194]). It is curious that no mention is made of the wife of Peter or of the other married Apostles (1 Cor. ix. 5). Of Susanna here mentioned by St. Luke, absolutely nothing further is known. Mary, the mother of James the Less, was another of these ministering women ; and it is an illustration of the extreme paucity of names among the Jews, and the confusion that results from it, that there are perhaps as many as seven Marys in the Gospel History alone. (See a fragment attributed to Papias in Routh, *Relig. Sacr.* i. 16 ; Wordsworth on Matt. xii. 47 ; Ewald, *Gesch. Christus*, p. 401, 3rd edit.) The fact that they were ministering to Him of their substance shows, among other circumstances, that there was no absolute community of goods in the little band.

Salome, the wife of the fisherman Zabdîa; and one of still higher wealth and position, Joanna, the wife of Chuza, steward of Herod Antipas.[1]

But He whom all eyes seek is in the very centre of the throng; and though at His right is Peter of Bethsaida, and at His left the more youthful figure of John, yet every glance is absorbed by Him alone.

He is not clothed in soft raiment of byssus or purple, like Herod's courtiers, or the luxurious friends of the Procurator Pilate : He does not wear the white ephod of the Levite, or the sweeping robes of the Scribe. There are not, on His arm and forehead, the *tephillin* or phylacteries,[2] which the Pharisees make so broad; and though there is at each corner of His dress the fringe and blue riband which the Law enjoins, it is not worn of the ostentatious size affected by those who wished to parade the scrupulousness of their obedience. He is in the ordinary dress of his time and country. He is not bareheaded — as painters usually represent Him — for to move about bareheaded in the Syrian sunlight is impossible,[3] but a white *keffiyeh*, such as is worn to this day, covers his hair, fastened by an *aghal* or fillet round the top of the head, and falling back over the neck and shoulders. A large blue outer robe or *tallith*, pure and clean, but of the simplest materials, covers His entire person, and only shows occasional

---

[1] The Blessed Virgin was not one of this ministering company. The reason for her absence from it is not given. It is not impossible that a certain amount of constraint was put upon her by the " brethren of the Lord," who on three distinct occasions (Matt. xii. 46; Mark iii. 21; John vii. 3 : see pp. 227, 255) interfered with Jesus, and on one of those occasions seem to have worked upon the susceptibilities even of His mother. Meanwhile her absence from Christ's journeyings is an incidental proof of the deep seclusion in which she evidently lived — a seclusion sufficiently indicated by the silence of the Gospels respecting her, and which accords most accurately with the incidental notices of her humble and meditative character.

[2] We cannot believe that Christ sanctioned by His own practice — at any rate, in manhood — the idle and superstitious custom of wearing those little text-boxes, which had in all probability originated merely in an unintelligent and slavishly literal interpretation of a metaphorical command. For further information about the *tephillin*, I may refer the reader to my article on " Frontlets " in Dr. Smith's *Dict. of the Bible*, or to the still fuller article by Dr. Ginsburg in Kitto's *Bibl. Cyclop.* s. v. " Phylacteries."

[3] This must surely have occurred to every one after a moment's reflection, yet, strange to say, I cannot recall one of the great works of mediæval art in which the Saviour is depicted with covered head. The ordinary articles of dress now are the *kumîs*, or inner shirt ; *gumbâr*, or *kaftan*, open gown of silk or cotton, overlapping in front ; *zannar*, or girdle ; *abba*, or *abaiyeh*, a strong, coarse cloak, in which the wearer usually sleeps ; and *tarbush*, or fez. (See Thomson, *Land and Book*, I., ch. ix.)

glimpses of the *ketôneth*, a seamless woolen tunic of the ordinary striped texture, so common in the East, which is confined by a girdle round the waist, and which clothes Him from the neck almost down to the sandalled feet. But the simple garments do not conceal the King; and though in His bearing there is nothing of the self-conscious haughtiness of the Rabbi, yet, in its natural nobleness and unsought grace, it is such as instantly suffices to check every rude tongue and overawe every wicked thought.

And His aspect?[1] He is a man of middle size, and of about thirty years of age, on whose face the purity and charm of youth are mingled with the thoughtfulness and dignity of manhood. His hair, which legend has compared to the color of wine, is parted in the middle of the forehead, and flows down over the neck. His features are paler and of a more Hellenic type than the weather-bronzed and olive-tinted faces of the hardy fishermen who are His Apostles; but though those features have evidently been marred by sorrow — though it is manifest that those eyes, whose pure and indescribable glance seems to read the very secrets of the heart, have often glowed through tears — yet no man, whose soul has not been eaten away by sin and selfishness, can look unmoved and unawed on the divine expression of that calm and patient face. Yes, this is He of whom Moses and the Prophets did speak — Jesus of Nazareth, the Son of Mary, and the Son of David; and the Son of Man, and the Son of God. Our eyes have seen the King in His beauty. We have beheld His glory, the glory as of the only-begotten of the Father, full of grace and truth. And having seen Him we can well understand how, while He spake, a certain woman of the company lifted up her voice and said, "Blessed is the womb that bare Thee, and the paps that Thou hast sucked!" "Yea, rather blessed," He answered, in words full of deep sweet mystery, "are they that hear the word of God and keep it."

One or two facts and features of His life on earth may here be fitly introduced.

1. First, then, it was a life of *poverty*. Some of the old Messianic prophecies, which the Jews in general so little understood, had already indicated His voluntary submission to a humble lot.[2]

---

[1] See Excursus V., "On the Traditional Descriptions of the Appearance of Jesus."

[2] It seems impossible to trace the date or origin of the later Jewish conception of a suffering Messias, the descendant of Joseph or Ephraim, which is found in *Zohar*, Bab. Targ. Cant. iv. 5, &c. It is clear that the nation had not realized the point of view which was familiar to the Apostles after Pentecost (see Acts iii. 18 ;

" Though He were rich, yet for our sakes He became poor." He was born in the cavern-stable, cradled in the manger. His mother offered for her purification the doves which were the offering of the poor. The flight into Egypt was doubtless accompanied with many a hardship, and when He returned it was to live as a carpenter, and the son of a carpenter, in the despised provincial village. It was as a poor wandering teacher, possessing nothing, that He travelled through the land. With the words, " Blessed are the poor in spirit," He began His Sermon on the Mount; and He made it the chief sign of the opening dispensation that to the poor the Gospel was being preached. It was a fit comment on this His poverty, that after but three short years of His public ministry He was sold by one of His own Apostles for the thirty shekels which were the price of the meanest slave.

2. And the *simplicity* of His life corresponded to its external poverty. Never in His life did He possess a roof which He could call His own. The humble abode at Nazareth was but shared with numerous brothers and sisters. Even the house in Capernaum which He so often visited was not His own possession ; it was lent Him by one of His disciples. There never belonged to Him one foot's-breadth of the earth which He came to save. We never hear that any of the beggars, who in every Eastern country are so numerous and so importunate, asked Him for alms. Had they done so He might have answered with Peter, " Silver and gold have I none, but such as I have that give I thee." His food was of the plainest. He was ready indeed, when invited, to join in the innocent social happiness of Simon's, or Levi's, or Martha's, or the bridegroom of Cana's feast ; but His ordinary food was as simple as that of the humblest peasant — bread of the coarsest quality,[1] fish caught in the lake and broiled in embers on the shore, and sometimes a piece of honeycomb, probably of the wild honey which was then found abundantly in Palestine. Small indeed was the gossamer thread of semblance on which His enemies could support the weight of their outrageous calumny,

xvii. 3 ; xxvi. 22, 23), and which Jesus had so often taught them (Matt. xvi. 21 ; xvii. 10—12 ; Luke xvii. 25 ; xxiv. 25—27, 46) to regard as the fulfilment of olden prophecy (Ps. xxii.; Isa. l. 6 ; liii. 2, &c.).

[1] So we infer from the " barley loaves " of John vi. 9. Barley bread was so little palatable that it was given by way of punishment to soldiers who had incurred disgrace. [" Cohortes si quae cessissent, decimatas hordeo pavit "[195] (Sueton, *Aug.* 24). " Cohortibus quae signa dimiserant hordeum dari jussit "[196] (Liv. xxvii. 13).] That the Jews had a similar feeling appears from an anecdote in *Pesachim*, fol. 3, 2. Johanan said, " There is an excellent barley harvest." They answered, " *Tell that to horses and asses.*" (See Kuinoel on John vi. 9.)

" Behold a glutton and a wine-bibber." And yet Jesus, though poor, was not a pauper. He did not for one moment countenance (as Sakya Mouni did) the life of beggary, or say one word which could be perverted into a recommendation of that degrading squalor which some religious teachers have represented as the perfection of piety. He never received an alms from the *tamchui* or *kuppa*, but He and the little company of His followers lived on their lawful possessions or the produce of their own industry, and even had a bag[1] or cash-box of their own, both for their own use and for their charities to others. From this they provided the simple necessaries of the Paschal feast, and distributed what they could to the poor; only Christ does not Himself seem to have given money to the poor, because He gave them richer and nobler gifts than could be even compared with gold or silver. Yet even the little money which they wanted was not always forthcoming, and when the collectors of the trivial sum demanded from the very poorest for the service of the Temple, came to Peter, for the didrachma which was alone required, neither he nor his Master had the sum at hand.[2] The Son of Man had no earthly possession besides the clothes He wore.

3. And it was, as we have seen, a life of *toil* — of toil from boyhood upwards, in the shop of the carpenter, to aid in maintaining Himself and His family by honest and noble labor; of toil afterwards to save the world. We have seen that "He went about doing good," and that this, which is the epitome of His public life, constitutes also its sublimest originality. The insight which we have gained already, and shall gain still further, into the manner in which His days were spent, shows us how overwhelming an amount of ever-active benevolence was crowded into the brief compass of the hours of light. At any moment He was at the service of any call, whether it came from an inquirer who longed to be taught, or from a sufferer who had faith to be healed. Teaching, preaching, travelling, doing works of mercy, bearing patiently with the fretful impatience of the stiffnecked and the ignorant, enduring without a murmur the incessant and selfish pressure of the multitude — work like this so absorbed His time and

---

[1] γλωσσόκομον (John xii. 6), properly a little box in which flute-players kept the *tongues* or reeds of their flutes, ἐν ᾧ οἱ αὐληταὶ ἀπετίθεσαν τὰς γλωττίδας [197] (Hesych.). Perhaps, as Mr. Monro suggests to me, a box may have been so called from the resemblance in *shape* to a reed mouthpiece, of which the essential point is an elastic valve which will open inwards. It seems unlikely that γλωσσόκομος should have the same meaning as γλωσσοκομεῖον. In the LXX. (2 Chron. xxiv. 8) it is used for the corban-box ; and by Aquila (Exod. xxxvii. 1) for the Ark.

[2] Matt. xvii. 24—27.

energy that we are told, more than once, that so many were coming and going as to leave no leisure even to eat. For Himself He seemed to claim no rest except the quiet hours of night and silence, when He retired so often to pray to His Heavenly Father, amid the mountain solitudes which He loved so well.

4. And it was a life of *health.* Among its many sorrows and trials, sickness alone was absent. We hear of His healing multitudes of the sick — we never hear that He was sick Himself. It is true that "the golden Passional of the Book of Isaiah" says of Him : "Surely He hath borne our griefs, and carried our sorrows ; yet we did esteem Him stricken, smitten of God, and afflicted. But He was wounded for our transgressions ; He was bruised for our iniquities ; the chastisement of our peace was upon Him, and with His stripes we are healed ; " but the best explanation of that passage has been already supplied from St. Matthew, that He suffered with those whom He saw suffer.[1] He was touched with a feeling of our infirmities ; His divine sympathy made those sufferings His own. Certain it is that the story of His life and death show exceptional powers of physical endurance. No one who was not endowed with perfect health could have stood out against the incessant and wearing demands of such daily life as the Gospels describe. Above all, He seems to have possessed that blessing of ready sleep which is the best natural antidote to fatigue, and the best influence to calm the over-wearied mind, and " knit up the ravelled sleeve of care." Even on the wave-lashed deck of the little fishing-boat as it was tossed on the stormy sea, He could sleep, with no better bed or pillow than the hard leather-covered boss that served as the steerman's cushion.[2] And often in those nights spent under the starry sky, in the wilderness, and on the mountain-top, He can have had no softer resting-place than the grassy turf, no other covering than the *tallith,* or perhaps some striped *abba,* such as often forms the sole bed of the Arab at the present day. And we shall see in the last sad scene how the same strength of constitution and endurance, even after all that He had undergone, enabled Him to hold out — after a sleepless night and a most exhausting day — under fifteen hours of trial and torture and the long-protracted agony of a bitter death.

5. And, once more, it must have been a life of *sorrow ;* for He is rightly called the "Man of Sorrows." And yet we think that there is

---

[1] Matt. viii. 17.

[2] As usual, we owe this graphic touch, so evidently derived from an eye-witness, to the narrative of St. Mark (iv. 38).

a possibility of error here. The terms "sorrow" and "joy" are very relative, and we may be sure that if there was crushing sorrow — the sorrow of sympathy with those who suffered,[1] the sorrow of rejection by those whom He loved, the sorrow of being hated by those whom He came to save, the sorrows of One on whom were laid the iniquities of the world, the sorrows of the last long agony upon the cross, when it seemed as if even His Father had forsaken Him — yet assuredly also there was an abounding joy. For the worst of all sorrows, the most maddening of all miseries — which is the consciousness of alienation from God, the sense of shame and guilt and inward degradation, the frenzy of self-loathing by which, as by a scourge of fire, the abandoned soul is driven to an incurable despair — *that* was absent, not only in its extreme forms, but even in the faintest of its most transient assoilments; and, on the other hand, the joy of an unsullied conscience, the joy of a stainless life, the joy of a soul absolutely and infinitely removed from every shadow of baseness, and every fleck of guilt, the joy of an existence wholly devoted to the service of God and the love of man — *this* was ever present to Him in its fullest influences. It is hardly what the world calls joy ; it was not the merriment of the frivolous, like the transient flickering of April sunshine upon the shallow stream ; it was not the laughter of fools, which is as the crackling of thorns under a pot — of *this* kind of joy, life has but little for a man who feels all that life truly means. But, as is said by the great Latin Father, " *Crede mihi res severa est verum gaudium,*"[198] and of that deep well-spring of life which lies in the heart of things noble, and pure, and permanent, and true, even the Man of Sorrows could drink large draughts. And though we are never told that He laughed, while we are told that once He wept, and that once He sighed, and that more than once He was troubled ; yet He who threw no shadow of discountenance on social meetings and innocent festivity, could not have been without that inward happiness which sometimes shone even upon His countenance, and which we often trace in the tender and almost playful irony of His words.[2] "In that hour," we are told

---

[1] $\delta\pi\lambda\alpha\gamma\chi\nu i\zeta o\mu\alpha\iota$ (Matt. ix. 36 ; xiv. 14 ; xv. 32 ; xx. 34 ; Mark i. 41 ; Luke vii. 13), $\delta\nu\lambda\lambda\nu\pi o\acute{\nu}\mu\epsilon\nu o\varsigma$ (Mark iii. 5), $\dot{\epsilon}\delta\tau\acute{\epsilon}\nu\alpha\xi\epsilon\nu$ (vii. 34), $\dot{\epsilon}\nu\epsilon\beta\rho\iota\mu\acute{\eta}\delta\alpha\tau o$ $\tau\tilde{\omega}$ $\pi\nu\epsilon\acute{\nu}\mu\alpha\tau\iota$ (John xi. 33), $\dot{\epsilon}\delta\acute{\alpha}\kappa\rho\nu\delta\epsilon\nu$ (ver. 35), $\ddot{\epsilon}\kappa\lambda\alpha\nu\delta\epsilon\nu$ (Luke xix. 41).

[2] *If* we could attach any importance to the strange story quoted by Irenæus (*Adv. Haer.* v. 33, 3) as having been derived by Papias from hearers of St. John, we should only see in it a marked instance of this playful and imaginative manner in speaking at unconstrained moments to the simplest and truest-hearted of His followers. The words, which have evidently been reflected and refracted by

of one occasion in His life, " Jesus rejoiced " — or, as it should rather
be, exulted — " in spirit." [1] Can we believe that this rejoicing took
place once alone ?

---

the various media through which they have reached us, may have been uttered
in a sort of divine irony, as though they were a playful description of Messianic
blessings to be fulfilled, not in the hard Judaic sense, but in a truer and more
spiritual sense. " The Lord taught, ' The days will come in which vines shall
spring up, each having ten thousand stems, and on each stem ten thousand
branches, and on each branch ten thousand shoots, and on each shoot ten thousand clusters, and on each cluster ten thousand grapes, and each grape, when
pressed, shall give twenty-five measures of wine. And when any saint shall have
seized one cluster, another shall cry, " I am a better cluster ; take me, through
me bless the Lord ' " (Westcott, *Introd.*, p. 433). Eusebius (*H. E.* iii. 39) speaks
of Papias as a weak-minded man ; and this passage is more like a Talmudic or
Mohammedan legend than a genuine reminiscence (see Hofmann, *Leben Jesu*, p.
324) ; yet it perhaps admits of the explanation I have given. The book of Papias
was called λόγων κυριακῶν ἐξηγήσεις,[199] and another fragment of it on Judas
Iscariot shows his credulity. (Neander, *Ch. Hist.*, E. Tr., ii. 430.)

[1] Luke x. 21, ἠγαλλιάσατο.

CHAPTER XXIII.

A GREAT DAY IN THE LIFE OF JESUS.

"My mystery is for me, and for the sons of my house." — *Saying attributed to Jesus in* CLEM. ALEX. *Strom.* v. 10, 64.

THE sequence of events in the narrative on which we are now about to enter is nearly the same in the first three Gospels. Without neglecting any clear indications given by the other Evangelists, we shall, in this part of the life of Jesus, mainly follow the chronological guidance of St. Luke. The order of St. Matthew and St. Mark appears to be much guided by subjective considerations.[1] Events in their Gospels are sometimes grouped together by their moral or religious bearings. St. Luke, as is evident, pays more attention to the natural sequence, although he also occasionally allows a unity of subject to supersede in his arrangement the order of time.[2]

Immediately after the missionary journey which we have described, St. Luke adds that when Jesus saw Himself surrounded by a great multitude out of every city, He spake by a parable.[3] We learn from the two other Evangelists the interesting circumstance that this was the first occasion on which He taught in parables, and that they were spoken to the multitude who lined the shore while our Lord sat in His favorite pulpit, the boat which was kept for Him on the Lake.[4]

We might infer from St. Mark that this teaching was delivered on the afternoon of the day on which He healed the paralytic, but the inference is too precarious to be relied on.[5] All that we can see is that this new form of teaching was felt to be necessary in consequence

---

[1] Papias, on the authority of John the Elder, distinctly says that St. Mark did not write chronologically (οὐ μέντοι τάξει) the deeds and words of Christ (ap. Euseb. *H. E.* iii. 39).

[2] To make the καθεξῆς of Luke i. 3 mean "in strictly accurate sequence," is to press it overduly. The word, which is peculiar to St. Luke, is used quite vaguely in chap. viii. 1; Acts iii. 24; xi. 4.

[3] Luke viii. 4. The expression of St. Matthew (xiii. 1), "the same day," or as it should be rather, "on that day," looks more definite; but the events that follow could not have taken place on the same day as those narrated in his previous chapter (much of which probably refers to a later period altogether), and the same phrase is used quite indefinitely in Acts viii. 1.

[4] Matt. xiii. 2, εἰς τὸ πλοῖον ἐμβάντα.

[5] Compare Mark ii. 13; iv. 1.

of the state of mind which had been produced in some, at least, of the hearers among the multitude. The one emphatic word "hearken!" with which He prefaced his address, prepared them for something unusual and memorable in what He was going to say.[1]

The great mass of hearers must now have been aware of the general features in the new Gospel which Jesus preached. Some self-examination, some earnest careful thought of their own was now requisite, if they were indeed sincere in their desire to profit by His words. "Take heed how ye hear" was the great lesson which He would now impress. He would warn them against the otiose attention of curiosity or mere intellectual interest, and would fix upon their minds a sense of their moral responsibility for the effects produced by what they heard. He would teach them in such a way that the extent of each hearer's profit should depend largely upon his own faithfulness.

And, therefore, to show them that the only true fruit of good teaching is holiness of life, and that there were many dangers which might prevent its growth, He told them His first parable, the Parable of the Sower. The imagery of it was derived, as usual, from the objects immediately before his eyes — the sown fields of Gennesareth; the springing corn in them; the hard-trodden paths which ran through them, on which no corn could grow; the innumerable birds which fluttered over them ready to feed upon the grain; the weak and withering struggle for life on the stony places; the tangling growth of luxuriant thistles in neglected corners; the deep loam of the general soil, on which already the golden ears stood thick and strong, giving promise of a sixty and hundredfold return as they rippled under the balmy wind.[2] To us, who from infancy have read the parable side by side with Christ's own interpretation of it, the meaning is singularly clear and plain, and we see in it the liveliest images of the danger incurred by the cold and indifferent, by the impulsive and shallow, by the worldly and ambitious, by the pre-occupied and the luxurious, as they listen to the Word of God. But it was not so easy to those who heard it.[3] Even the disciples failed to catch its full

---

[1] Mark iv. 3.

[2] See Stanley, *Sin. and Pal.*, p. 496.

[3] It is a part of the divine boldness of Christ's teaching, and the manner in which it transcends in its splendid paradox all ordinary modes of expression, that in His explanation of the parable, the seed when once sown is *identified with* him who receives it (Mark iv. 16; Matt. xiii. 20, ὁ ἐπὶ πετρώδη σπαρεὶς, "*he* that was sown on stony places" [unfortunately rendered in our version, "he that received the seed into," &c.]). See Lightfoot *On Revision*, p. 48.

significance, although they reserved their request for an explanation till they and their Master should be alone. It is clear that parables like this, so luminous to us, but so difficult to these simple listeners, suggested thoughts which to them were wholly unfamiliar.[1]

It seems clear that our Lord did not on this occasion deliver all of those seven parables — the parable of the tares of the field, of the grain of mustard-seed, of the leaven, of the hid treasure, of the pearl, and of the net — which, from a certain resemblance in their subjects and consecutiveness in their teaching, are here grouped together by St. Matthew.[2] Seven parables[3] delivered at once, and delivered without interpretation, to a promiscuous multitude which He was for the first time addressing in this form of teaching, would have only tended to bewilder and to distract. Indeed, the expression of St. Mark — " as they were able to hear it "[4] — seems distinctly to imply a gradual and non-continuous course of teaching, which would have lost its value if it had given to the listeners more than they were able to remember and to understand. We may rather conclude, from a comparison of St. Mark and St. Luke, that the teaching of this particular afternoon contained no other parables, except perhaps the simple and closely analogous ones of the grain of mustard-seed, and of the blade, the ear, and the full corn in the ear, which might serve to encourage into patience those who were expecting too rapid a revelation of the kingdom of God in their own lives and in the world; and perhaps, with these, the similitude of the candle to warn them not to stifle the light they had received, but to remember that Great Light which should one day reveal all things, and so to let their light shine as to illuminate both their own paths in life, and to shed radiance on the souls of all around.

A method of instruction so rare, so stimulating, so full of interest — a method which, in its unapproachable beauty and finish, stands unrivalled in the annals of human speech — would doubtless tend to increase beyond measure the crowds that thronged to listen. And through the sultry afternoon He continued to teach them, barely suc-

---

[1] Matt. xiii. 1—23 ; Mark iv. 1—25; Luke viii. 4—18.

[2] For the scene of their delivery at least changes in Matt. xiii. 34—36.

[3] Matt. xiii. 24—30 ; Mark iv. 26—34 ; Luke xiii. 18—21. *Eight*, if we add Mark iv. 26—29. They illustrate the various reception (the Sower); the mingled results (the tares and the net); the priceless value (the treasure and the pearl); and the slow gradual extension (the mustard-seed, the leaven, the springing corn) of the Gospel of the kingdom.

[4] Mark iv. 33.

ceeding in dismissing them when the evening was come.¹ A sense of complete weariness and deep unspeakable longing for repose, and solitude, and sleep, seems then to have come over our Lord's spirit. Possibly the desire for rest and quiet may have been accelerated by one more ill-judged endeavor of His mother and His brethren to assert a claim upon His actions.² They had not indeed been able " to come at Him for the press," but their attempt to do so may have been one more reason for a desire to get away, and be free for a time from this incessant publicity, from these irreverent interferences. At any rate, one little touch, preserved for us as usual by the graphic pen of the Evangelist St. Mark, shows that there was a certain eagerness and urgency in His departure, as though in His weariness, and in that oppression of mind which results from the wearing contact with numbers, He could not return to Capernaum, but suddenly determined on a change of plan. After dismissing the crowd, the disciples took Him, "*as He was*," ³ in the boat, no time being left, in the urgency of His spirit, for preparation of any kind. He yearned for the quiet and deserted loneliness of the eastern shore. The western shore also is lonely now, and the traveller will meet no human being there but a few careworn Fellahîn, or a Jew from Tiberias, or some Arab fishermen, or an armed and mounted Sheykh of some tribe of Bedawin. But the eastern shore is loneliness itself ; not a tree, not a village, not a human being, not a single habitation is visible ; nothing but the low range of hills, scarred with rocky fissures, and sweeping down to a narrow and barren strip which forms the margin of the Lake. In our Lord's time the contrast of this thinly-inhabited region with the busy and populous towns that lay close together on the Plain of Gennesareth must have been very striking ; and though the scattered population of Peræa was partly Gentile, we shall find Him not unfrequently seeking to recover the tone and calm of His burdened soul by putting those six miles of water between Himself and the crowds He taught.

---

¹ Mark iv. 35. If our order of events be correct, these incidents took place in the early part of March, at which time the weather in Palestine is often intensely hot. I never suffered more from heat than on one April day on the shores of the Sea of Galilee, when it was with difficulty that I could keep my seat on horseback.

² Luke viii. 19—21. This cannot be the same incident as that narrated in Matt. xii. 46—50 ; Mark iii. 31—35 (*v*. p. 223), as is shown by the context of those passages. It is, however, exactly the kind of circumstance, calling forth the same remark, which might naturally happen more than once ; and although a supposition of perpetually recurring similarities is only the uncritical resource of despairing harmonists, it may perhaps be admissible here.

³ Mark iv. 36.

But before the boat could be pushed off, another remarkable interruption occurred. Three of His listeners in succession — struck
perhaps by the depth and power of this His new method of teaching,
dazzled too by this zenith of His popularity — desired or fancied that
they desired to attach themselves to Him as permanent disciples.
The first was a Scribe, who, thinking no doubt that his official
rank would make him a most acceptable disciple, exclaimed with
confident asseveration, "Lord, I will follow Thee whithersoever Thou
goest." But in spite of the man's high position, in spite of His
glowing promises, He who cared less than nothing for lip-service,
and who preferred "the modesty of fearful duty" to the "rattling
tongue of audacious eloquence," coldly checked His would-be follower. He who had called the hated publican gave no encouragement to the reputable Scribe. He did not reject the proffered service, but neither did He accept it. Perhaps "in the man's flaring
enthusiasm, he saw the smoke of egotistical self-deceit." He pointed
out that His service was not one of wealth, or honor, or delight; not
one in which any could hope for earthly gain. "The foxes," He
said, "have holes, and the birds of the air have resting-places,[2] but
the Son of Man[3] hath not where to lay His head."

The second was already a partial disciple,[4] but wished to become
an entire follower, with the reservation that he might first be permitted to bury his father. "Follow me!" was the thrilling answer,
"and let the dead bury their dead;" that is, leave the world and the
things of the world to mind themselves. He who would follow
Christ must in comparison hate even father and mother. He must
leave the spiritually dead to attend to their physically dead.[5]

---

[1] Matt. viii. 19—22; Luke ix. 57—62. The position of the incident in the narrative of St. Matthew seems to show that it has been narrated out of its order,
and more *generally* (πορευομένων αὐτῶν ἐν τῇ ὁδῷ [100]), by St. Luke.

[2] κατασκηνώσεις, rather "shelters" than "nests;" for birds do not live in
nests.

[3] This was a title which would kindle no violent antipathy, and yet was understood to be Messianic. Cf. Dan. vii. 13; John xii. 34. (See p. 140).

[4] An ancient but otherwise groundless tradition says that it was Philip (Clem.
Alex. *Strom.* iii. 4, § 25).

[5] Some have seen a certain difficulty and harshness in this answer. Theophylact and many others interpret it to mean that the disciple asked leave to live at
home till his father's death. Such an offer of personal attendance would seem to
be too vague to be of any value; on the other hand, Sepp and others have argued
that had his father been really dead he would have been regarded as ceremonially
unclean, and could hardly have been present at all. In either case, however, the
general lesson is that drawn by St. Augustine: "*Amandus est generator, sed
praeponendus est creator.*" [201] If it was a mere question of personal attendance

The answer to the third aspirant was not dissimilar. He too pleaded for delay — wished not to join Christ immediately in His voyage, but first of all to bid farewell to his friends at home. "No man," was the reply — which has become proverbial for all time — "No man having put his hand to the plough, and looking back, is fit [1] for the kingdom of heaven." To use the fine image of St. Augustine, "the East was calling him, he must turn his thoughts from the fading West." It was in this spirit that the loving souls of St. Thomas of Aquino, St. Francis of Assisi, St. Francis Xavier, and so many more of the great saints in the Church's history consoled and fortified themselves, when forced to resign every family affection, and for Christ's sake to abandon every earthly tie.

So, then, at last these fresh delays were over, and the little vessel could spread her sails for the voyage. Yet even now Jesus was, as it were, pursued by followers, for, as St. Mark again tells us, "other little ships were with him." But they, in all probability — since we are not told of their reaching the other shore — were soon scattered or frightened back by the signs of a gathering storm. At any rate, in His own boat, and among His own trusted disciples, Jesus could rest undisturbed, and long before they were far from shore, had lain His weary head on the leather cushion of the steersman, and was sleeping the deep sleep of the worn and weary — the calm sleep of those who are at peace with God.

Even that sleep, so sorely needed, was destined to speedy and violent disturbance. One of the fierce storms peculiar to that deep hollow in the earth's surface, swept down with sudden fury on the little inland sea. With scarcely a moment's notice,[2] the air was filled with whirlwind and the sea buffeted into tempest. The danger was extreme. The boat was again and again buried amid the foam of

---

on a funeral, that was of little importance compared to the great work for which he offered himself: if it was more than this, might not the indefinite delay breed a subsequent remorse — possibly even a subsequent apostacy?

[1] εὔθετος (Luke ix. 62), literally, "well-adapted." Possibly both the aspirant and our Lord referred mentally to the story of Elisha's call (1 Kings xix. 19, 20). The parallel in Hesiod, *Opp.* ii. 60 — ἰθείην αὔλακ' ἐλαύνοι Μηκέτι παπταί-νων μεθ' ὁμήλικας [202] — is extremely striking. Yet who would be so absurd as to dream of plagiarism here?

[2] Travellers have often noticed, and been endangered by, these sudden storms. All that I had an opportunity of observing was the almost instantaneous change by which a smiling glassy surface was swept into a dark and threatening ripple. The expressions used by the Evangelists all imply the extreme fury of the hurricane (σεισμὸς μέγας, Matt. viii. 24; κατέβη λαῖλαψ ἀνέμου, Luke viii. 23). The heated tropical air of the Ghôr, which is so low that the surface of the Sea of Galilee lies 600 feet beneath the level of the Mediterranean, is suddenly filled

the breakers which burst over it; yet though they must have covered
Him with their dashing spray as He lay on the open deck at the stern,
He was calmly sleeping on[1]— undisturbed, so deep was his fatigue, by
the tempestuous darkness — and as yet no one ventured to awake Him.
But now the billows were actually breaking into the boat itself, which
was beginning to be filled and to sink. Then, with sudden and vehement cries of excitement and terror, the disciples woke Him. "Lord!
Master! Master! save! we perish!"[2] Such were the wild sounds
which, mingled with the howling of the winds and the dash of the
mastering waves, broke confusedly upon His half-awakened ear. It
is such crises as these — crises of sudden unexpected terror, met without a moment of preparation, which test a man, what spirit he is of
— which show not only his nerve, but the grandeur and purity of his
whole nature. The hurricane which shook the tried courage and
baffled the utmost skill of the hardy fishermen, did not ruffle for one
instant the deep inward serenity of the Son of Man. Without one
sign of confusion, without one tremor of alarm, Jesus simply raised
Himself on His elbow from the dripping stern of the laboring and
half-sinking vessel, and, without further movement,[3] stilled the tempest of their souls by the quiet words, "Why so cowardly, O ye of
little faith?" And then rising up, standing in all the calm of a natural majesty on the lofty stern, while the hurricane tossed, for a
moment only, His fluttering garments and streaming hair, He gazed
forth into the darkness, and His voice was heard amid the roaring of
the troubled elements, saying, "Peace! be still!"[4] And instantly
the wind dropped, and there was a great calm. And as they watched
the starlight reflected on the now unrippled water, not the disciples

---

by the cold and heavy winds sweeping down the snowy ranges of Lebanon and
Hermon, and rushing with unwonted fury through the ravines of the Peræan
hills, which converge to the head of the Lake, and act like gigantic funnels.
(Thomson, *Land and Book*, II. xxv.)

[1] There is a touch of tragic surprise in the αὐτὸς δὲ ἐκάθευδε of Matt. viii. 24.
The Evangelists evidently derive their narrative from eye-witnesses. St. Matthew
mentions the ὥστε τὸ πλοῖον καλύπτεσθαι ὑπὸ τῶν κυμάτων [203] (viii. 24);
St. Mark, τὰ δὲ κύματα ἐπέβαλλεν εἰς τὸ πλοῖον [204] (iv. 37), and the προσκε-
φάλαιον [205] (ver. 38). On this, see Smith, *Voy. of St. Paul*, p. 243.

[2] Κύριε, σῶσον, ἀπολλύμεθα (Matt. viii. 25), om. ἡμᾶς. Ἐπιστάτα,
ἐπιστάτα ἀπολλύμεθα (Luke viii. 24).

[3] This seems to be clearly involved in the τότε ἐγερθεὶς [206] of Matt. viii. 26 —
after He had spoken to those who awoke Him.

[4] There is an almost untranslatable energy in the Σιώπα, πεφίμωσο of Mark
iv. 39, and the perfect imperative implies the command that the result should be
instantaneous (φιμόω — literally, "I muzzle," 1 Cor. ix. 9).

only but even the sailors ¹ whispered to one another, " What manner of man is this ? "

This is a stupendous miracle, one of those which test whether we indeed believe in the credibility of the miraculous or nòt; one of those miracles of power which cannot, like many of the miracles of healing, be explained away by existing laws. It is not my object in this book to convince the unbeliever, or hold controversy with the doubter. Something of what I had to say on this subject I have done my little best to say elsewhere; ² and yet, perhaps, a few words may here be pardoned. Some, and they neither irreverent nor unfaithful men, have asked whether the reality may not have been somewhat different? whether we may not understand this narrative in a sense like that in which we *should* understand it if we found it in the reasonably-attested legend of some mediæval saint — a St. Nicholas or a St. Brandan? whether we may not suppose that the fact which underlies the narrative was in reality not a miraculous exercise of power over those elements which are most beyond the reach of man, but that Christ's calm communicated itself by immediate and subtle influence to His terrified companions, and that the hurricane, from natural causes, sank as rapidly as it had arisen ? I reply, that if this were the only miracle in the life of Christ; if the Gospels were indeed the loose, exaggerated, inaccurate, credulous narratives which such an interpretation would suppose; if there were something antecedently incredible in the supernatural ; if there were in the spiritual world no transcendant facts which lie far beyond the comprehension of those who would bid us see nothing in the universe but the action of material laws; if there were no providences of God during these nineteen centuries to attest the work and the divinity of Christ — then indeed there would be no difficulty in such an interpretation. But if we believe that God rules; if we believe that Christ rose; if we have reason to hold, among the deepest convictions of our being, the certainty that God has not delegated His sovereignty or His providence to the final, unintelligent, pitiless, inevitable working of material forces; if we see on every page of the

---

¹ Matt. viii. 27, οἱ ἄνθρωποι.²⁰⁷

² *The Witness of History to Christ*, Lect. I. I refer to these Hulsean Lectures only to show that the mainly non-controversial character of the present work arises neither from any doubt in my own mind, nor from any desire to shrink from legitimate controversy. At the same time let me say distinctly that I dislike and deprecate, as wrong and as needless, the violent language used by writers on both sides of this great controversy. A man may disbelieve in miracles without being either an atheist or a blasphemer ; a man may believe in them without being (as is assumed so widely) either hypocritical or weak.

Evangelists the quiet simplicity of truthful and faithful witnesses; if we see in every year of succeeding history, and in every experience of individual life, a confirmation of the testimony which they delivered — then we shall neither clutch at rationalistic interpretations, nor be much troubled if others adopt them. He who believes, he who *knows*, the efficacy of prayer, in what other men may regard as the inevitable certainties or blindly-directed accidents of life — he who has felt how the voice of a Saviour, heard across the long generations, can calm wilder storms than ever buffeted into fury the bosom of the inland lake — he who sees in the person of his Redeemer a fact more stupendous and more majestic than all those observed sequences which men endow with an imaginary omnipotence, and worship under the name of Law — to him, at least, there will be neither difficulty nor hesitation in supposing that Christ, on board that half-wrecked fishing-boat, did utter His mandate, and that the wind and the sea obeyed; that His word was indeed more potent among the cosmic forces than miles of agitated water, or leagues of rushing air.

Not even on the farther shore was Jesus to find peace or rest.[1] On the contrary, no sooner had He reached that part of Peræa which

---

[1] Matt. viii. 28—34; Mark v. 1—19; Luke viii. 26—39. The MSS. of all three Evangelists vary between Gadara, Gerasa, and Gergesa. Tischendorf, mainly relying on the Cod. Sinaiticus, reads Γεργεσηνῶν in Luke viii. 26; Γερασηνῶν in Mark v. 1; and Γαδαρηνῶν in Matt. viii. 28. After the researches of Dr. Thomson (*The Land and the Book*, II., ch. xxv.), there can be no doubt that Gergesa — though mentioned only by St. Luke — was the name of a little town nearly opposite Capernaum, the ruined site of which is still called Kerza or Gersa by the Bedawin. The existence of this little town was apparently known both to Origen, who first introduced the reading, and to Eusebius and Jerome; and in their day a steep declivity near it, where the hills approach to within a little distance from the Lake, was pointed out as the scene of the miracle. Gerasa is much too far to the east, being almost in Arabia. Gadara — if that reading be correct in Matt. viii. 28 (א, B) — can only be the name of the whole district, derived from its capital. The authority of the reading is, however, weakened (1) by the fact that it was only found in a few MSS. in Origen's time; and (2) by the probability of so well-known a place being inserted instead of the obscure little Gergesa. The ruins of Gadara are still visible at *Um Keis*, three hours to the south of the extreme end of the Lake, and on the other side of the river Jarmuk, or Hieromax the banks of which are as deep and precipitous as those of the Jordan. It is therefore far too remote to have any real connection with the scene of the miracle; and in point of fact Γεργεσηνῶν must have been something more than a conjecture of Origen's in this verse, for it is found in eight uncials, most cursives, and (among others) in the Coptic and Æthiopic versions. It must therefore be regarded as the probable reading, and St. Matthew, as one who had actually lived on the shore of the Lake, was most likely to know its minute topography, and so to have preserved the real name.

is called by St. Matthew the "country of the Gergesenes," than He was met by an exhibition of human fury, and madness, and degradation, even more terrible and startling than the rage of the troubled sea. Barely had He landed when, from among the rocky cavern-tombs of the Wady Semakh, there burst into His presence a man troubled with the most exaggerated form of that raging madness which was universally attributed to demoniacal possession. Amid all the boasted civilization of antiquity, there existed no hospitals, no penitentiaries, no asylums; and unfortunates of this class, being too dangerous and desperate for human intercourse, could only be driven forth from among their fellow-men, and restrained from mischief by measures at once inadequate and cruel. Under such circumstances they could, if irreclaimable, only take refuge in those holes along the rocky hill-sides which abound in Palestine, and which were used by the Jews as tombs. It is clear that the foul and polluted nature of such dwelling-places, with all their associations of ghastliness and terror, would tend to aggravate the nature of the malady;[1] and this man, who had long been afflicted, was beyond even the possibility of control.[2] Attempts had been made to bind him, but in the paroxysms of his mania he had exerted that apparently supernatural strength which is often noticed in such forms of mental excitement, and had always succeeded in rending off his fetters, and twisting away or shattering his chains;[3] and now he had been abandoned to the lonely hills and unclean solitudes which, night and day, rang with his yells as he wandered among them, dangerous to himself and to others, raving, and gashing himself with stones.

It was the frightful figure of this naked and homicidal maniac that burst upon our Lord almost as soon as He had landed at early dawn;[4] and perhaps another demoniac, who was not a Gadarene,

---

[1] Tombs were the express dwelling-place of demons in the Jewish belief (*Nidda*, fol. 17 *a*; *Chagigah*, fol. 3, 6). "When a man spends a night in a graveyard, an evil spirit descends upon him" (Gfrörer, *Jahrh. des Heils*, i. 408). It must not be forgotten that these δαιμόνια were expressly supposed to be spirits of the wicked dead (πονηρῶν ἐστιν ἀνθρώπων πνεύματα, [208] Jos. *B. J.* vii. 6, § 3).

[2] Compare Sir W. Scott's powerful description of the effects produced on the minds of the Covenanters by their cavern retirements.

[3] Mark v. 4, . . . διεσπάσθαι ὑπ᾽ αὐτοῦ τὰς ἁλύσεις καὶ τὰς πέδας συντετρῖφθαι.[209] St. Mark and St. Luke here give us the minute details, which show the impression made on the actual witnesses. St. Matthew's narrative is less circumstantial; it is probable that he was not with our Lord, and he may have been preparing for that winding-up of his affairs which was finished at the great feast prepared for Jesus apparently on the afternoon of this very day.

[4] Mark v. 2, εὐθέως ἀπήντησεν αὐτῷ;[210] Luke viii. 27, ἱμάτιον οὐκ ἐνεδιδύσκετο.[211] This does not necessarily mean that he was stark naked, for

and who was less grievously afflicted, may have hovered about at no great distance,[1] although, beyond this allusion to his presence, he plays no part in the narrative. The presence, the look, the voice of Christ, even before He addressed these sufferers, seems always to have calmed and overawed them, and this demoniac of Gergesa was no exception. Instead of falling upon the disciples, he ran to Jesus from a distance, and fell down before Him in an attitude of worship. Mingling his own perturbed individuality with that of the multitude of unclean spirits which he believed to be in possession of his soul, he entreated the Lord, in loud and terrified accents, not to torment him before the time.

It is well known that to recall a maniac's attention to his name, to awake his memory, to touch his sympathies by past association, often produces a lucid interval, and perhaps this may have been the reason why Jesus said to the man, "What is thy name?" But this question only receives the wild answer, "My name is Legion, for we are many." The man had, as it were, lost his own name; it was absorbed in the hideous tyranny of that multitude of demons under whose influence his own personality was destroyed.[2] The presence of Roman armies in Palestine had rendered him familiar with that title of multitude, and as though six thousand evil spirits were in him he answers by the Latin word which had now become so familiar to every Jew.[3] And still agitated by his own perturbed fancies, he

---

he may still have worn a χίτων ; but the tendency to strip themselves bare of every rag of clothing is common among lunatics. It was, for instance, one of the tendencies of Christian VII. of Denmark. Furious maniacs — absolutely naked — wander to this day in the mountains, and sleep in the caves of Palestine. (Thomson, *Land and Book*, I., ch. xi.; Warburton, *The Crescent and the Cross*, ii. 352.)

[1] As we may perhaps infer from Matt. viii. 28. There is a difference here, but no fair critic dealing with any other narrative would dream of calling it an irreconcilable discrepancy ; at any rate they would not consider that it in any way impaired the credibility of the narrative. Probably, if we knew the actual circumstances, we should see no shadow of difficulty in the fact that Matthew mentions two, and the other Evangelists one. Similar minute differences occur at every step in the perfectly honest evidence of men whom no one, on that account, dreams of doubting, or of charging with untrustworthy observation. Ἕτερόν ἐστι, says St. Chrysostom, διαφόρως εἰπεῖν καὶ μαχομένους εἰπεῖν.[212] " Per hujusmodi Evangelistarum locutiones," says St. Augustine, " VARIAS SED NON CONTRARIAS, discimus nihil in cujusque verbis nos inspicere debere, nisi voluntatem, &c." [213] (Aug. *De Cons. Evang.* ii. 28.)

[2] This duality and apparent interchange of consciousness were universal among this afflicted class. See Clem. Alex. *Strom.* i. 21, § 143, who explains Plato's notion of a language of the gods partly from the fact that demoniacs do not speak their own voice and language, ἀλλὰ τὴν τῶν ὑπεισιόντων δαιμόνων.[214]

[3] The ancient Megiddo bore at this time the name Legio, from the Roman company stationed there. It is still called Ledjûn.

entreats, as though the thousands of demons were speaking by his mouth, that they might not be driven into the abyss, but be suffered to take refuge in the swine.

The narrative which follows is to us difficult of comprehension, and one which, however literally accepted, touches upon regions so wholly mysterious and unknown that we have no clue to its real significance, and can gain nothing by speculating upon it. The narrative in St. Luke runs as follows:—

"And there was an herd of many swine[1] feeding upon the mountain; and they besought Him that He would suffer them to enter into them. And He suffered them. Then went the devils out of the man, and entered into the swine; and the herd ran violently down a steep place into the Lake, and were choked."

That the demoniac was healed — that in the terrible final paroxysm which usually accompanied the deliverance from this strange and awful malady, a herd of swine was in some way affected with such wild terror as to rush headlong in large numbers over a steep hill-side into the waters of the Lake — and that, in the minds of all who were present, including that of the sufferer himself, this precipitate rushing of the swine was connected with the man's release from his demoniac thraldom — thus much is clear.

And indeed, so far, there is no difficulty whatever. Any one who believes in the Gospels, and believes that the Son of God *did* work on earth deeds which far surpass mere human power, must believe that among the most frequent of His cures were those of the distressing forms of mental and nervous malady which we ascribe to purely natural causes, but which the ancient Jews, like all Orientals, attribute to direct supernatural agency.[2] And knowing to how singular an extent the mental impressions of man affect by some unknown electric influence the lower animals — knowing, for instance, that man's cowardice and exultation, and even his superstitious terrors, *do* communicate themselves to the dog which accompanies him, or the horse on which he rides — there can be little or no difficulty in understand-

---

[1] St. Mark, specific as usual, says "about two thousand."

[2] "All kinds of diseases which are called melancholy they call an evil spirit " (Maimon. in *Shabbath,* ii. 5). Hence it is not surprising that mechanical exorcisms were sometimes resorted to (Tob. viii. 2, 3 ; Jos. *Antt.* viii. 2,§ 5 ; Just. Mart. *Dial c. Tryph.* 85, χρώμενοι ἐξορκίζουσι . . θυμιά μασι). In *Jer. Terumoth,* fol 40, 2 (ap. Otho, *Lex. Rabb.* s. v. "Daemones"), people afflicted with hypochondria, melancholy, and brain-disease, are all treated as demoniacs, and Kardaicus is even made a demon's name. St. Peter seems to class all the diseased whom Christ cured as καταδυναστευομένους ὑπὸ τοῦ διαβόλου (Acts x. 38). For full information on the whole subject Gfrörer refers to Edzard, *Avoda Zara,* ii. 311—356.

ing that the shrieks and gesticulations of a powerful lunatic might strike uncontrollable terror into a herd of swine. We know further that the spasm of deliverance was often attended with fearful convulsions, sometimes perhaps with an effusion of blood;[1] and we know that the sight and smell of human blood produces strange effects in many animals. May there not have been something of this kind at work in this singular event?

It is true that the Evangelists (as their language clearly shows) held, in all its simplicity, the belief that actual devils passed in multitudes out of the man and into the swine. But is it not allowable here to make a distinction between actual facts and that which was the mere conjecture and inference of the spectators from whom the three Evangelists heard the tale? If we are not bound to believe the man's hallucination that six thousand devils were in possession of his soul, are we bound to believe the possibility, suggested by his perturbed intellect, that the unclean spirits should pass from him into the swine?[2] If indeed we could be sure that Jesus directly encouraged or sanctioned in the man's mind the belief that the swine were indeed driven wild by the unclean spirits which passed objectively from the body of the Gergesene into the bodies of these dumb beasts, then we could, without hesitation, believe as a literal truth, however incomprehensible, that so it was. But this by no means follows indisputably from what we know of the method of the Evangelists. Let all who will, hold fast to the conviction that men and beasts may be quite literally possessed of devils; only let them beware of confusing their own convictions, which are binding on themselves alone, with those absolute and eternal certainties which cannot be rejected without moral blindness by others. Let them remember that a hard and denunciative dogmatism approaches more nearly than anything else to that Pharisaic want of charity which the Lord whom they love and worship visited with His most scathing anger and rebuke. The literal reality of demoniac possession is a belief for which more may perhaps be said than is admitted by the purely physical science of the present day,[3] but it is not a necessary article of the Christian

---

[1] Some years ago, the dead body of a murdered lady was discovered in a lonely field solely by the strange movements of the animals which were half-maddened by the sight of the blood-stained corpse. The fact was undisputed: "the cows," as one of the witnesses described it, "went *blaring* about the field."

[2] This was a thoroughly Jewish belief. In *Bab. Joma*, 83 *b*, R. Samuel attributes the hydrophobia of dogs to demoniac possession (Gfrörer. *Jahrh. d. Heils*, i. 412).

[3] See this beautifully and moderately stated by Professor Westcott (*Charact. of the Gosp. Miracles*, pp. 72—83). He contrasts the superstitious materialism of

creed; and if any reader imagines that in this brief narrative, to a greater extent than in any other, there are certain *nuances* of expression in which subjective inferences are confused with exact realities, he is holding a view which has the sanction of many wise and thoughtful Churchmen, and has a right to do so without the slightest imputation on the orthodoxy of his belief.[1]

That the whole scene was violent and startling appears in the fact that the keepers of the swine "fled and told it in the city and in the country." The people of Gergesa, and the Gadarenes and Gerasenes of all the neighboring district, flocked out to see the Mighty Stranger who had thus visited their coasts. What livelier or more decisive proof of His power and His beneficence could they have had than the sight which met their eyes? The filthy and frantic demoniac who had been the terror of the country, so that none could pass that way — the wild-eyed dweller in the tombs who had been accustomed to gash himself with cries of rage, and whose untamed fierceness broke away all fetters — was now calm as a child. Some charitable hand

---

Josephus (*Antt.* viii. 2, § 5; *B. J.* vii. 6, § 3) with the simplicity of the Gospel narratives. A powerful series of arguments for the tenability of the view which denies actual demoniac possession may be found in Jahn, *Archaeologia Biblica* (to which I have already referred), and are maintained by the late Rev. J. F. Denham in Kitto's *Bibl. Cyclop.*, s. v. "Demons."

[1] So many good, able, and perfectly orthodox writers have, with the same data before them, arrived at differing conclusions on this question, that any certainty respecting it appears to be impossible. My own view under these circumstances is of no particular importance, but it is this: I have shown that the Jews, like all unscientific nations in all ages, attributed many nervous disorders and physical obstructions to demoniac possession which we should attribute to natural causes; but I am not prepared to deny that in the dark and desperate age which saw the Redeemer's advent there *may* have been forms of madness which owed their more immediate manifestation to evil powers. I should not personally find much hardship or difficulty in accepting such a belief, and have only been arguing against the uncharitable and pernicious attempt to treat it as a necessary article of faith for all. The subject is too obscure (even to science) to admit of dogmatism on either side. Since writing the above paragraphs, I find that (to say nothing of Dr. Lardner) two writers so entirely above suspicion as Neander and De Pressensé substantially hold the same view. "There is a gap here," says Neander, "in our connection of the facts. Did Christ really participate in the opinions of the demoniac, or was it only subsequently inferred from the fact that the swine rushed down, that Christ had allowed the evil spirits to take possession of them?" (*Life of Christ*, p. 207, E. Tr.) "That these devils," says Pressensé, "literally entered into the body of the swine is an inadmissible supposition" (*Jesus Christ*, p. 339, E. Tr.). The modern Jews, like their ancestors, attribute a vast number of interferences to the *schedim*, or evil spirits. See, on the whole subject, Excursus VII., "Jewish Angelology and Demonology."

had flung an outer robe over his naked figure, and he was sitting at the feet of Jesus, clothed, and in his right mind.

"And they were afraid" — more afraid of that Holy Presence than of the previous furies of the possessed. The man indeed was saved; but what of that, considering that some of their two thousand unclean beasts had perished! Their precious swine were evidently in danger; the greed and gluttony of every apostate Jew and low-bred Gentile in the place were clearly imperilled by receiving such a one as they saw that Jesus was. With disgraceful and urgent unanimity they entreated and implored Him to leave their coasts.[1] Both heathens and Jews had recognized already the great truth that God sometimes answers bad prayers in His deepest anger.[2] Jesus Himself had taught His disciples not to give that which was holy to the dogs, neither to cast their pearls before swine, "lest they trample them under their feet, and turn again and rend you." He had gone across the Lake for quiet and rest, desiring, though among lesser multitudes, to extend to these semi-heathens also the blessings of the kingdom of God. But they loved their sins and their swine, and with a perfect energy of deliberate preference for all that was base and mean, rejected such blessings, and entreated Him to go away. Sadly, but at once, He turned and left them. Gergesa was no place for Him; better the lonely hill-tops to the north of it; better the crowded strand on the other side.

And yet He did not leave them in anger. One deed of mercy had been done there; one sinner had been saved; from one soul the unclean spirits had been cast out. And just as the united multitude of the Gadarenes had entreated for His absence, so the poor saved demoniac entreated henceforth to be with Him. But Jesus would

---

[1] Matt. viii. 34, παρεκάλεσαν; Mark v. 17, ἤρξαντο παρακαλεῖν; Luke viii. 37, ἠρώτησαν. The heathen character of the district comes more fully home to us when we remember that Meleager and Philodemus, two of the least pure poets of the Greek anthology, were natives of this very Gadara about B. C. 50.

[2] See Exod. x. 28, 29; Numb. xxii. 20; Ps. lxxviii. 29—31.

> " We, ignorant of ourselves,
> Beg often our own harms, which the wise powers
> Deny us for our good." — SHAKSP. *Ant. & Cleop.* 1

> "God answers sharp and sudden on some prayers,
> And flings the thing we have asked for in our face;
> A gauntlet with a gift in 't." — *Aurora Leigh.*

The truth was also thoroughly recognized in Pagan literature, as in Plato, *Alcib.* ii. 138, B; Juv. *Sat.* x. 7, " Evertere domos totas *optantibus ipsis* Di faciles; '[215] and x. 111, " Magnaque numinibus vota exaudita malignis." [216] This is in fact the moral of the legend of Tithonus.

fain leave one more, one last opportunity for those who had rejected Him. On others for whose sake miracles had been performed He had enjoined silence; on this man — since He was now leaving the place — He enjoined publicity. "Go home," He said, "to thy friends, and tell them how great things the Lord hath done for thee, and hath had compassion on thee." And so the demoniac of Gergesa became the first great missionary to the region of Decapolis, bearing in his own person the confirmation of his words; and Jesus, as His little vessel left the inhospitable shore, might still hope that the day might not be far distant — might come, at any rate, before over that ill-fated district burst the storm of sword and fire [1] —when

> "E'en the witless Gadarene,
> Preferring Christ to swine, would feel
> That life is sweetest when 'tis clean." [2]

---

[1] For the fearful massacre and conflagration of Gadara, the capital of this district, see Jos. *B. J.* iii. 7, § 1.

[2] Coventry Patmore.

CHAPTER XXIV.

THE DAY OF MATTHEW'S FEAST.

"Nunquam laeti sitis, nisi quum fratrem vestrum videritis in caritate." [217] —
JEROME in Eph. v. 3 (*quoted as a saying of Christ from the Hebrew Gospel*).

THE events just described had happened apparently in the early
morning, and it might perhaps be noon when Jesus reached once
more the Plain of Gennesareth.   People had recognized the sail of
His returning vessel, and long before He reached land [1] the multitudes
had lined the shore, and were waiting for Him, and received Him
gladly.

If we may here accept as chronological the order of St. Matthew [2]
— to whom, as we shall see hereafter, this must have been a very
memorable day — Jesus went first into the town of Capernaum,
which was now regarded as "His own city."   He went at once to
the house — probably the house of St. Peter — which He ordinarily
used when staying at Capernaum.   There the crowd gathered in
ever denser numbers, filling the house, and even the court-yard which
surrounded it, so that there was no access even to the door. [3]   But
there was one poor sufferer — a man bedridden from a stroke of
paralysis — who, with his friends, had absolutely determined that
access should be made for *him;* he would be one of those violent
men who would take the kingdom of heaven by force.   And the
four who were carrying him, finding that they could not reach Jesus
through the crowd, made their way to the roof, perhaps by the usual

---

[1] Luke viii. 40.

[2] Matt. ix. 1.   Some may see an objection to this arrangement in the fact that
St. Luke (v. 17) mentions Pharisees not only from Galilee, but even from Judæa
and Jerusalem as being present at the scene.   It is, however, perfectly clear that
the Pharisees are *not* the spies from Jerusalem subsequently sent to dog His
steps (Mark iii. 2; vii. 1; Matt. xv. 1); for, on the contrary, St. Luke distinctly
says " that the power of the Lord was present to heal them."   We surmise, therefore, that they must have come from motives which were at least harmless.   If,
indeed, with $\aleph$, B, L, we read $\alpha\dot{\upsilon}\tau\dot{o}\nu$ for $\alpha\dot{\upsilon}\tau o\dot{\upsilon}s$, *this* argument falls to the
ground ; but my belief in the sequence is not changed.

[3] Matt. ix. 2—8 ; Mark ii. 1—12 ; Luke v. 17—26.

outer staircase,[1] and making an aperture in the roof by the removal of a few tiles,[2] let down the paralytic, on his humble couch,[3] exactly in front of the place where Christ was sitting. The man was silent, perhaps awestruck at his manner of intrusion into the Lord's presence ; but Jesus was pleased at the strength and unhesitating boldness of faith which the act displayed, and bestowing first upon the man a richer blessing than that which he primarily sought, He gently said to him, as He had said to the woman who was a sinner, " Be of good courage, son ;[4] thy sins are forgiven thee." Our Lord had before observed the unfavorable impression produced on the bystanders by those startling words. He again observed it now in the interchanged glances of the Scribes who were present, and the look of angry disapproval on their countenances.[5] But on this occasion He did not, as before, silently substitute another phrase. On the contrary, he distinctly challenged attention to His words, and miraculously justified them. Reading their thoughts, He reproved them for the fierce unuttered calumnies of which their hearts were full, and put to them a direct question. " Which," He asked, " is easier ? to say to the paralytic, ' Thy sins are forgiven thee ; ' or to say, ' Arise and walk ? ' "[6] May not anybody *say* the former without its being possible to tell whether the sins are forgiven or not ? but who can say the latter, and give effect to his own words, without a power from above ? If I can by a word heal this paralytic, is it not clear that I must be One who has also power on earth to forgive sins ? The unanswerable question was received with the silence of an invincible obstinacy ; but turning once more to the paralytic, Jesus said to him,

---

[1] Eastern houses are low, and nothing is easier than to get to their roofs, especially when they are built on rising ground. For the outer staircase, see Matt. xxiv. 17.

[2] Luke v. 19, διὰ τῶν κεράμων. Otherwise the ἐξορύξαντες of St. Mark might lead us to imagine that they cut through some mud partition. Possibly they enlarged an aperture in the roof. The details are not sufficiently minute to make us understand *exactly* what was done, and the variations of reading show that some difficulty was felt by later readers ; but the mere fact of opening the roof is quite an every-day matter in the East (see Thomson, *The Land and the Book*, p. 358). The objection that the lives or safety of those sitting below would be endangered (!) is one of the ignorant childishnesses of merely captious criticism.

[3] κλινίδιον (Luke v. 19), κράββατον (Mark ii. 4). Probably little more than a mere mat.

[4] Luke v. 20, ἄνθρωπε ; Mark ii. 5, τέκνον. The θάρσει, τέκνον of Matt. ix. 2, being the tenderest, is the phrase most likely to have been used by Christ.

[5] " Why does this man speak thus ? He blasphemes."— Such is probably the true reading (ℵ, B, D, L, &c.) of Mark ii. 7.

[6] This seems to me the most forcible punctuation in Mark. ii. 9.

" Arise, take up thy bed, and walk." At once power was restored
to the palsied limbs, peace to the stricken soul. The man was healed.
He rose, lifted the light couch on which he had been lying, and,
while now the crowd opened a passage for him, he went to his house
glorifying God ; and the multitude, when they broke up to disperse,
kept exchanging one with another exclamations of astonishment not
unmixed with fear, " We saw strange things to-day ! " " We never
saw anything like this before ! "

From the house — perhaps to allow of more listeners hearing His
words — Jesus seems to have adjourned to his favorite shore ;[1] and
thence, after a brief interval of teaching, He repaired to the house of
Matthew, in which the publican, who was now an Apostle, had made
a great feast of farewell to all his friends.[2]   As he had been a publican himself, it was natural that many of these also would be " publicans and sinners "— the outcasts of society, objects at once of hatred
and contempt.   Yet Jesus and His disciples, with no touch of scorn
or exclusiveness, sat down with them at the feast; " for there were
many, and they were His followers."   A charity so liberal caused
deep dissatisfaction, on two grounds, to two powerful bodies — the
Pharisees and the disciples of John.   To the former, mainly because
this contact with men of careless and evil lives violated all the traditions of their haughty scrupulosity ; to the latter, because this ready
acceptance of invitations to scenes of feasting seemed to discountenance the necessity for their half-Essenian asceticism.   The complaints could hardly have been made at the time, for unless any
Pharisees or disciples of John merely looked in from curiosity during
the progress of the meal, their own presence there would have involved
them in the very blame which they were casting on their Lord.   But
Jesus probably heard of their murmurs before the feast was over.
There was something characteristic in the way in which the criticism

[1] Mark ii. 13.
[2] Matt. ix. 11 ; Mark ii. 15 ; Luke v. 29, δοχὴ μεγάλη.[218] This shows that
Matthew had made large earthly sacrifices to follow Christ.   It seems quite clear
that the only reason why the Synoptists relate the call of Matthew in *this* place
instead of earlier, is to connect his call with this feast.   But on the other hand a
great farewell feast could hardly have been given on the very day of the call,
and other circumstances, arising especially from the fact that the Twelve were
chosen before the Sermon on the Mount, and that the call of Matthew from the
toll-booth must have preceded his selection as an Apostle, lead us to the conviction that the feast was given afterwards; and, indeed, Archbishop Newcome, in
his *Harmony of the Gospels*, p. 259, says " that Levi's call and feast were separated
in the most ancient Harmonies from Tatian, in A. D. 170, to Gerson, A. D.
1400 " (see Andrews, *Life of our Lord*, p. 211) ; and he might have added, down
to many modern commentators.

was made. The Pharisees, still a little dubious as to Christ's real character and mission, evidently overawed by His greatness, and not yet having ventured upon any open rupture with Him, only vented their ill-humor on the disciples, asking *them* "why their master ate with publicans and sinners?" The simple-minded Apostles were perhaps unable to explain; but Jesus at once faced the opposition, and told these murmuring respectabilities that He came not to the self-righteous, but to the conscious sinners. He came not to the folded flock, but to the straying sheep. To preach the gospel to the poor, to extend mercy to the lost, was the very object for which he tabernacled among men. It was His will *not* to thrust His grace on those who from the very first wilfully steeled their hearts against it, but gently to extend it to those who needed and felt their need of it. His teaching was to be "as the small rain upon the tender herb, and as the showers upon the grass." And then, referring them to one of those palmary passages of the Old Testament (Hos. vi. 6) [1] which even in those days had summed up the very essence of all that was pleasing to God in love and mercy, He borrowed the phrase of their own Rabbis, and bade *them* — these teachers of the people, who claimed to know so much — to " go and learn " [2] what *that* meaneth, " I will have mercy, and not sacrifice." Perhaps it had never before occurred to their astonished minds, overlaid as they were by a crust of mere Levitism and tradition, that the love which thinks it no condescension to mingle with sinners in the effort to win their souls, is more pleasing to God than thousands of rams and tens of thousands of rivers of oil.

The answer to the somewhat querulous question asked Him by John's disciples was less severe in tone. [3] No doubt he pitied that natural dejection of mind which arose from the position of the great teacher, to whom alone they had as yet learned to look, and who now lay in the dreary misery of a Machaerus dungeon. He might have answered that fasting was at the best a work of supererogation —

---

[1] The quotation is from the Hebrew. The LXX. has ἦ for καὶ οὐ. Comp. Matt. xii. 7 ; 1 Sam. xv. 22; Deut. x. 12 ; Prov. xxi. 3 ; Eccles. xii. 13 ; Hosea vi. 6 ; Micah vi. 8 ; passages amply sufficient to have shown the Jews, had they *really* searched the Scriptures, the hollowness and falsity of the whole Pharisaic system.

[2] Matt. ix. 13, ולמד צא. On the interesting question of the language ordinarily used by our Lord, see Chap. VII., p. 93.

[3] Matt. ix. 14—17; Mark ii. 18—22 ; Luke v. 33—39. Apparently the Pharisees, eager to seize any and every opportunity to oppose Him, and glad of a combination so powerful and so unwonted as that which enabled them to unite with John's disciples, joined in this question also (Mark ii. 19).

useful, indeed, and obligatory, if any man felt that thereby he was assisted in the mortification of anything which was evil in his nature — but worse than useless if it merely administered to his spiritual pride, and led him to despise others. He might have pointed out to them that although they had instituted a fast twice in the week,[1] this was but a traditional institution, so little sanctioned by the Mosaic law, than in it but *one single day* of fasting was appointed for the entire year.[2] He might, too, have added that the reason why fasting had *not* been made a universal duty is probably that spirit of mercy which recognized how differently it worked upon different temperaments, fortifying some against the attacks of temptation, but only hindering others in the accomplishment of duty. Or again, He might have referred them to those passages in their own Prophets, which pointed out that, in the sight of God, the true fasting is not mere abstinence from food while all the time the man is "smiting with the fist of wickedness;" but rather to love mercy, and to do justice, and to let the oppressed go free.[3] But instead of all these lessons, which, in their present state, might only have exasperated their prejudices, He answers them only by a gentle *argumentum ad hominem*. Referring to the fine image in which their own beloved and revered teacher had spoken of Him as the bridegroom, He contented Himself with asking them, "Can ye make the children of the bridechamber fast,[4] while the bridegroom is with them?" and then, looking calmly down at the deep abyss which yawned before Him, He uttered a saying which — although at that time none probably

---

[1] On Thursday, because on that day Moses was believed to have re-ascended Mount Sinai; on Monday, because on that day he returned. Cf. Luke xviii. 12 ; *Babha Kama*, f. 82 *a*.

[2] The Day of Atonement (Lev. xvi. 29 ; Numb. xxix. 7). It appears that in the period of the exile four annual fasts (in the fourth, fifth, seventh, and tenth months) had sprung up, but they certainly receive no special sanction from the Prophets (Zech. viii. 19 ; vii. 1—12). In the oldest and genuine part of the *Megillah Taanith*, which emanated from the schools of Hillel and Shammai, there is merely a list of days on which fasting and mourning are *forbidden*. It will be found with a translation in Derenbourg, *Hist. Palestine*, pp. 439—446. See too Lightfoot, *Hor. Hebr.* in Matt. ix. 14.

[3] See the many noble and splendid utterances of the Prophets to this effect (Micah vi. 6—8 ; Hosea vi. 6 ; xii. 6 ; Amos v. 21—24; Isa. i. 10—20).

[4] John iii. 29. The use of the word πενθεῖν, "mourn," instead of νηστεύειν, "fast," in Matt. ix. 15, gives still greater point to the question. Fasting was a sign of sorrow, but the kingdom of God was a kingdom of gladness, and the bridal to which their own Master had compared its proclamation was a time of joy. The disciples are the paranymphs, the children of the bridechamber, the *benî hahachunnah*, a thoroughly Hebrew metaphor for the nearest friends of the wedded pair.

understood it — was perhaps the very earliest public intimation that He gave of the violent end which awaited Him — " But the days will come when the bridegroom shall be taken away from them,¹ and then shall they fast in those days." Further He told them, in words of yet deeper significance, though expressed, as so often, in the homeliest metaphors, that His religion is, as it were, a robe entirely new, not a patch of unteazled cloth upon an old robe, serving only to make worse its original rents;² that it is not new wine, put, in all its fresh fermenting, expansive strength, into old and worn wine-skins, and so serving only to burst the wine-skins and be lost, but *new* wine in *fresh* wine-skins.³ The new spirit was to be embodied in wholly renovated forms; the new freedom was to be untrammelled by obsolete and long meaningless limitations; the spiritual doctrine was to be sundered for ever from mere elaborate and external ceremonials.

St Luke also has preserved for us the tender and remarkable addition — " No man also having drunk old wine straightway desireth new: for he saith, The old is excellent." ⁴ Perhaps the fact that these words were found to be obscure has caused the variety of readings in the original text. There is nothing less like the ordinary character of man than to make allowance for difference of opinion in matters of religion ; yet it is the duty of doing this which the words imply. He had been showing them that His kingdom was something more than a restitution (ἀποκατάστασις), it was a re-creation (παλιγγενεσία); but He knew how hard it was for men trained in the tradition of the Pharisees, and in admiration for the noble asceticism of the Baptist, to accept truths which were to them both new and strange ; and, therefore, even when He is endeavoring to lighten their darkness, He shows that He can look on them " with larger other eyes, to make allowance for them all."

---

¹ A dim hint of the same kind had been given in the private conversation with Nicodemus (John iii. 14). The word ἀπαρθῇ, clearly implying a violent termination of His career, which is here used by each of the Synoptists (Matt. ix. 15 ; Mark ii. 20), occurs nowhere else in the New Testament.

² Matt. ix. 16, ῥάκους ἀγνάφου.²¹⁹

³ οἶνον νέον εἰς ἀσκοὺς καινοὺς βλητέον (Luke v. 38). Similes not unlike this may be found in heathen literature, and we know that our Lord did not shun such existing parallels (Acts xxvi. 14). The fact, however, that His next words in St. Luke (v. 39) run into an iambic line, οὐδεὶς . . πιὼν παλαιὸν εὐθέως θέλει νέον, is probably as purely accidental as the previous iambic in verse 21, τίς ἐστιν οὗτος ὃς λαλεῖ βλασφημίας.

⁴ Leg. χρηστός. (‭א‬, B, L.)

CHAPTER XXV.

THE DAY OF MATTHEW'S FEAST (*continued*).

"Is there no physician there?" — JER. viii. 22.

THE feast was scarcely ·over at the house of Matthew,[1] and Jesus was still engaged in the kindly teaching which arose out of the question of John's disciples, when another event occurred which led in succession to three of the greatest miracles of His earthly life.[2]

A ruler of the synagogue — the *rosh hakkenêseth*, or chief elder of the congregation, to whom the Jews looked with great respect — came to Jesus in extreme agitation. It is not improbable that this ruler of the synagogue had been one of the very deputation who had pleaded with Jesus for the centurion-proselyte by whom it had been built. If so, he knew by experience the power of Him to whom he now appealed. Flinging himself at His feet with broken words[3] — which in the original still sound as though they were interrupted and rendered incoherent by bursts of grief — He tells Him that his little daughter, his only daughter, is dying, is dead; but still, if He will but come and lay His hand upon her, she shall live. With the tenderness which could not be deaf to a mourner's cry, Jesus rose[4] at once from the table, and went with him, followed not only by His disciples, but also by a dense expectant multitude, which had been witness of the scene. And as He went the people in their eagerness pressed upon Him and thronged Him.

But among this throng — containing doubtless some of the Pharisees and of John's disciples with whom He had been discoursing, as well as some of the publicans and sinners with whom He had been seated at the feast — there was one who had not been attracted by

---

[1] The note of time in Matt. ix. 18, " while He spake these things unto them," is here quite explicit ; and St. Matthew is most likely to have followed the exact order of events on a day which was to him so memorable, as his last farewell to his old life as a Galilæan publican.

[2] Matt. ix. 18—26 ; Mark v. 22—43 ; Luke viii. 41—56.

[3] Mark v. 23. Considering the position of Jairus, this little incident strikingly shows the estimation in which Jesus was held at this time even by men of leading position.

[4] Matt. ix. 19, $\dot{\epsilon}\gamma\epsilon\rho\theta\epsilon\dot{\iota}\varsigma$.

curiosity to witness what would be done for the ruler of the synagogue. It was a woman who for twelve years had suffered from
a distressing malady, which unfitted her for all the relationships
of life, and which was peculiarly afflicting, because in the popular
mind it was regarded as a direct consequence of sinful habits
In vain had she wasted her substance and done fresh injury to
her health in the effort to procure relief from many different physicians,¹ and now, as a last desperate resource, she would try what
could be gained without money and without price from the Great
Physician. Perhaps, in her ignorance, it was because she had
no longer any reward to offer; perhaps because she was ashamed in
her feminine modesty to reveal the malady from which she had been
suffering; but from whatever cause, she determined, as it were, to
steal from Him, unknown, the blessing for which she longed. And
so, with the strength and pertinacity of despair, she struggled in that
dense throng until she was near enough to touch Him; and then,
perhaps all the more violently from her extreme nervousness, she
grasped the white fringe of His robe. By the law of Moses every
Jew was to wear at each corner of his *tallîth* a fringe or tassel,
bound by a riband of symbolic blue, to remind him that he was holy
to God.² Two of these fringes usually hung down at the bottom of
the robe; one hung over the shoulder where the robe was folded
round the person. It was probably this one that she touched ³ with
secret and trembling haste, and then, feeling instantly that she had
gained her desire and was healed, she shrunk back unnoticed into the
throng. Unnoticed by others, but not by Christ. Perceiving that
healing power had gone out of Him, recognizing the one magnetic
touch of timid faith even amid the pressure of the crowd, He stopped
and asked, "Who touched my clothes?" There was something
almost impatient in the reply of Peter, as though in such a throng he

---

¹ Mark v. 26, πολλὰ παθοῦσα ὑπὸ πολλῶν ἰατρῶν. The physician Evangelist St. Luke (viii. 43) mentions that in this attempt she had wasted all her
substance (ὅλον τὸν βίον). This might well have been the case if they had
recommended to her nothing better than the strange Talmudic recipes mentioned
by Lightfoot, *Hor. Hebr. in Marc.* v. 26. (See Wunderbar, *Biblisch-talmudische
Medicin.*) The recipes are not, however, worse than those given by Luther in
his *Table Talk*, who (in the old English translation of the book) exclaims, "How
great is the mercy of God who has put such healing virtue in all manner of
muck!"

² Numb. xv. 37—40; Deut. xxii. 12. The Hebrew word is *kanephôth*, literally
"wings;" and the white tassels with their blue or purple thread were called
tsîtsîth.

³ it is not easy to stoop down in a thick moving crowd, nor could she have done
so unobserved.

thought it absurd to ask, " Who touched me ? " [1] But Jesus, His eyes still wandering over the many faces, told him that there was a difference between the crowding of curiosity and the touch of faith, and as at last His glance fell on the poor woman, she, perceiving that she had erred in trying to filch the blessing which He would have graciously bestowed, came forward fearing and trembling, and, flinging herself at His feet, told Him all the truth. All her feminine shame and fear were forgotten in her desire to atone for her fault. Doubtless she dreaded His anger, for the law expressly ordained that the touch of one afflicted as she was, caused ceremonial uncleanness till the evening.[2] But His touch had cleansed her, not her's polluted Him. So far from being indignant, He said to her, " Daughter " — and at once the sound of that gracious word sealed her pardon — " go for peace : [3] thy faith hath saved thee ; be healed from thy disease."

The incident must have caused a brief delay, and, as we have seen, to the anguish of Jairus every instant was critical. But he was not the only sufferer who had a claim on the Saviour's mercy ; and, as he uttered no complaint, it is clear that sorrow had not made him selfish. But at this moment a messenger reached him with the brief message — " Thy daughter is dead ; " and then, apparently with a touch of dislike and irony, he added, " Worry not the Rabbi." [4]

The message had not been addressed to Jesus, but He overheard it,[5] and with a compassionate desire to spare the poor father from needless agony, He said to him those memorable words, " Fear not, only believe." They soon arrived at his house, and found it occu-

---

[1] " Illi *premunt*, ista tetigit" [220] (Aug., *Serm.* ccxlv.). " Caro premit, fides tangit " [221] (*id.* lxii. 4). (Trench, *Miracles*, p. 204.)

[2] Lev. xv. 19. The Pharisees shrunk from a woman's touch, as they do now. " The *chakams* were especially careful to avoid being touched by any part of the women's dresses " (Frankl, *Jews in the East*, ii. 81).

[3] As before (Luke vii. 50), this corresponds to the Hebrew expression, לְשָׁלוֹם. Our Lord addressed no other woman by the title Θύγατερ. Legend has assigned to this woman Veronica as a name, and Paneas (Cæsarea Philippi) as a residence. An ancient statue of bronze at this place was believed to represent her in the act of touching the fringe of Christ's robe ; and Eusebius (*Hist. Eccl.* vii. 18) and Sozomen (*Hist. Eccl.* v. 21) both mention this statue, which is believed to have been so curious a testimony to the reality of Christ's miracle, that Julian the Apostate — or, according to another account, Maximus — is charged with having destroyed it.

[4] The curious word σκύλλε, something like our " worry," or " bother," is used here, and here alone (except in Luke vii. 6), by both St. Mark and St. Luke. (The ἐσκυλμένοι of Matt. ix. 36 is a dubious reading.)

[5] Mark v. 36, παρακούσας (א B, L). The word occurs nowhere else in the New Testament.

pied by the hired mourners and flute-players, who, as they beat their breasts, with mercenary clamor, insulted the dumbness of sincere sorrow, and the patient majesty of death.¹ Probably this simulated wailing would be very repulsive to the soul of Christ; and first stopping at the door to forbid any of the multitude to follow Him, He entered the house with three only of the inmost circle of His Apostles — Peter, and James, and John. On entering, His first care was to still the idle noise ; but when His kind declaration — "The little maid² is not dead, but sleepeth" — was only received with coarse ridicule,³ He indignantly ejected the paid mourners.⁴ When calm was restored, He took with Him the father and the mother and His three Apostles, and entered with quiet reverence the chamber hallowed by the silence and awfulness of death. Then, taking the little cold dead hand, He uttered these two thrilling words, "*Talitha cumi*"— "Little maid, arise!"⁵ and her spirit returned, and the child arose and walked. An awful amazement seized the parents;⁶ but Jesus calmly bade them give the child some food. And if He added his customary warning that they should not speak of what had happened, it was not evidently in the intention that the entire fact should remain unknown — for that would have been impossible, when all the circumstances had been witnessed by so many — but because those who have received from God's hand unbounded mercy are more likely to reverence that mercy with adoring gratitude if it be kept like a hidden treasure in the inmost heart.

Crowded and overwhelming as had been the incidents of this long night and day, it seems probable from St. Matthew that it was sig-

---

¹ At this time among the Jews, no less than among the Romans,

"Cantabat fanis, cantabat tibia ludis,
Cantabat moestis tibia funeribus." ²²² (Ov. *Fast.* vi.)

The Rabbinic rule provided that there should be at least two flute-players, and one mourning-woman (Selden, *Uxor. Hebr.* iii. 8). The amount of noise indicated by the θόρυβον, κλαίοντας καὶ ἀλαλάζοντας πολλὰ (Mark v. 38) recalls to us the "Quantum non superant *tria funera*" ²²³ of Hor. *Sat.* i 6, 43. The custom was doubtless ancient (Eccles xii. 5 ; Jer. ix. 17 ; Amos v. 16 ; 2 Chron. xxxv. 25). St. Luke adds the beating on the breast (viii. 52; cf. Nahum ii. 7). The custom still continues ; "they weep, howl, beat their breasts, and tear their hair according to contract" (Thomson, *Land and Book.* I., ch. viii.).

² Mark v. 39, τὸ παιδίον. She was twelve years old.

³ The Evangelists use the strong expression, κατεγέλων αὐτοῦ.

⁴ Mark v. 40, ἐκβαλὼν πάντας.

⁵ Doubtless St. Peter, who was actually present, told his friend and kinsman Mark the actual words which Christ had used. They are interesting also as bearing on the question of the language which He generally spoke.

⁶ Mark v. 42. ἐξέστησαν ἐκστάσει μεγάλῃ.

nalized by yet one more astonishing work of power. For as He departed thence two blind men followed Him with the cry — as yet unheard — " Son of David, have mercy on us." Already Christ had begun to check, as it were, the spontaneity of His miracles. He had performed more than sufficient to attest His power and mission, and it was important that men should pay more heed to His divine eternal teaching than to His temporal healings. Nor would He as yet sanction the premature, and perhaps ill-considered, use of the Messianic title " Son of David "— a title which, had he publicly accepted it, might have thwarted His sacred purposes, by leading to an instantaneous revolt in His favor against the Roman power. Without noticing the men or their cry, He went to the house in Capernaum where He abode ; nor was it until they had persistently followed Him into the house that He tested their faith by the question, " Believe ye that I am able to do this?" They said unto Him, "Yea, Lord." Then touched He their eyes, saying, "According to your faith be it unto you." And their eyes were opened. Like so many whom He healed, they neglected his stern command not to reveal it.[1] There are some who have admired their disobedience, and have attributed it to the enthusiasm of gratitude and admiration ; but was it not rather the enthusiasm of a blatant wonder, the vulgarity of a chattering boast? How many of these multitudes who had been healed by Him became His true disciples? Did not the holy fire of devotion which a hallowed silence must have kept alive upon the altar of their hearts die away in the mere blaze of empty rumor? Did not He know best? Would not obedience have been better than sacrifice, and to hearken than the fat of rams? Yes. It is possible to deceive ourselves; it is possible to offer to Christ a *seeming* service which disobeys His inmost precepts — to *grieve* Him, under the guise of honoring Him, by vain repetitions, and empty genuflexions, and bitter intolerance, and irreverent familiarity, and the hollow simulacrum of a dead devotion. Better, far better, to serve Him by doing the things He said than by a seeming zeal, often false in exact proportion to its obtrusiveness, for the glory of His name. These disobedient babblers, who talked so much of Him, did but offer him the dishonoring service of a double heart; their violation of His commandment served only to hinder His usefulness, to trouble His spirit, and to precipitate His death.

---

[1] Matt. ix. 27—31.

CHAPTER XXVI.

A VISIT TO JERUSALEM.

" Simplicity is the best viaticum for the Christian." — CLEM. ALEX. *Paed.* ii.

ANY ONE who has carefully and repeatedly studied the Gospel narratives side by side, in order to form from them as clear a conception as is possible of the life of Christ on earth, can hardly fail to have been struck with two or three general facts respecting the sequence of events in His public ministry. In spite of the difficulty introduced by the varying and non-chronological arrangements of the Synoptists, and by the silence of the fourth Gospel about the main part of the preaching in Galilee, we see distinctly the following circumstances : —

1. That the innocent enthusiasm of joyous welcome with which Jesus and His words and works were at first received in Northern Galilee gradually, but in a short space of time, gave way to suspicion, dislike, and even hostility on the part of large and powerful sections of the people.

2. That the external character, as well as the localities, of our Lord's mission were much altered after the murder of John the Baptist.

3. That the tidings of this murder, together with a marked development of opposition, and the constant presence of Scribes and Pharisees from Judæa to watch His conduct and dog His movements, seems to synchronize with a visit to Jerusalem not recorded by the Synoptists, but evidently identical with the nameless festival mentioned in John v. 1.

4. That this unnamed festival must have occurred somewhere about that period of His ministry at which we have now arrived.

What this feast was we shall consider immediately ; but it was preceded by another event — the mission of the Twelve Apostles.

At the close of the missionary journeys, during which occurred some of the events described in the last chapters, Jesus was struck with compassion at the sight of the multitude.[1] They reminded Him of sheep harassed by enemies, and lying panting and neglected in the

---

[1] Matt. ix. 35—38.

fields because they have no shepherd.¹ They also call up to the mind
the image of a harvest ripe, but unreaped for lack of laborers; and
He bade His Apostles pray to the Lord of the harvest that He would
send forth laborers into His harvest. And then, immediately afterwards, having Himself now traversed the whole of Galilee, He sent
them out two and two to confirm His teaching and perform works of
mercy in His name.²

Before sending them He naturally gave them the instructions which
were to guide their conduct. At present they were to confine their
mission to the lost sheep of the house of Israel, and not extend it to
Samaritans or Gentiles. The topic of their preaching was to be the
nearness of the kingdom of heaven, and it was to be freely supported
by works of power and beneficence. They were to take nothing
with them; no scrip for food; no purse for money; no change of
raiment;³ no travelling shoes (ὑποδήματα, *calcei*) in place of their
ordinary palm-bark sandals, they were not even to procure a staff for
the journey if they did not happen already to possess one;⁴ their
mission — like all the greatest and most effective missions which the
world has ever known — was to be simple and self-supporting. The
open hospitality of the East, so often used as the basis for a dissemination of new thoughts, would be ample for their maintenance.⁵ On

---

¹ Ver. 36, ἐσκυλμένοι . . . ἐρριμμένοι; the reading ἐκλελυμένοι is perhaps a gloss for the unfamiliar word.

² Matt. x. 1—42; Mark vi. 7—13; Luke ix. 1—6.

³ Few ordinary peasants in the East can boast of a change of garments. They
even sleep in the clothes which they wear during the day.

⁴ That this was the meaning of the injunctions appears from a comparison of
the three Evangelists. The μηδὲ ῥάβδον of Matt. x. 10 depends on μὴ κτήσησθε,
" do not *procure* for the purposes of this journey," and is therefore no contradiction to the εἰ μὴ ῥάβδον μόνον of Mark vi. 8. Keim's remarks—" Diese Wend-
ung der Dinge hat dann freilich dem Markus nicht eingeleuchtet; er ist kein
Freund der nackten Armuth. . . . aber für Mitnahme eines Stockes und
Anlegung von Sandalen spricht er sich *mit grosser fast komischer* Bestimmtheit
aus " ²²⁴ (*Gesch. Jesu*, II. i., p. 327) — are captious and shallow. As regards these
minute differences, we may observe that probably in many instances they merely
arise from the fact that our Lord used Aramaic phrases, which are capable
of trivial variation in the limits within which they were understood: *e. g.*, if here
He said, כי אם מטה, it might mean, " even if ye have a staff, it is superfluous."
(Ebrard, *Gosp. History*, p. 295, E. Tr.)

⁵ Renan notices the modern analogy. When travelling in the East no one need
ever scruple to go into the best house of any Arab village to which he comes, and
he will always be received with profuse and gratuitous hospitality. From the
moment we entered any house, it was regarded as our own. There is not an Arab
you meet who will not empty for you the last drop in his water-skin, or share
with you his last piece of black bread. The Rabbis said that Paradise was the
reward of willing hospitality. (Schöttgen, *Hor. Hebr.* 108.)

entering a town they were to go to any house in it where they had reason to hope that they would be welcome, and to salute it with the immemorial and much-valued blessing, *Shalôm lakem*,[1] " Peace be to you," and if the children of peace were there the blessing would be effective; if not, it would return on their own heads. If rejected, they were to shake off the dust of their feet in witness that they had spoken faithfully, and that they thus symbolically cleared themselves of all responsibility for that judgment which should fall more heavily on wilful and final haters of the light than on the darkest places of a heathendom in which the light had never, or but feebly, shone.

So far their Lord had pointed out to them the duties of trustful faith, of gentle courtesy, of self-denying simplicity, as the first essentials of missionary success. He proceeded to fortify them against the inevitable trials and persecutions of their missionary work.

They needed and were to exercise the wisdom of serpents no less than the harmlessness of doves; for He was sending them forth as sheep among wolves.

Doubtless these discourses were not always delivered in the continuous form in which they have naturally come down to us. Our Lord seems at all times to have graciously encouraged the questions of humble and earnest listeners; and at this point we are told by an ancient tradition,[2] that St. Peter — ever, we may be sure, a most eager and active-minded listener — interrupted his Master with the not unnatural question, " But how then if the wolves should tear the lambs ? " And Jesus answered, smiling perhaps at the naïve and literal intellect of His chief Apostle, " Let not the lambs fear the wolves when the lambs are once dead, and do you fear not those who can kill you and do nothing to you, but fear Him who after you are

---

[1] שָׁלוֹם לָכֶם (Gen. xliii. 23). It was believed to include every blessing. Have not our missionaries sometimes erred from forgetting the spirit of this injunction? It has been too caustically and bitterly said — and yet the saying may find some occasional justification — that missionaries have too often proceeded on the plan of (1) discovering all the prejudices of a people, and (2) shocking them. Doubtless this has been only due to an ill-guided zeal ; but so did not St. Paul. He was most courteous and most conciliatory in his address to the Athenians, and he lived for three and a half years at Ephesus, without once reviling or insulting the worshippers of Artemis.

[2] Clemens Romanus, xi. 5 (about A. D. 140; see Lightfoot's *Clemens Romanus*) This is one of the ἄγραφα δόγματα, unwritten traditional sayings of our Lord which there is no reason to doubt. Ἀποκριθεὶς δὲ ὁ Πέτρος αὐτῷ λέγει, Ἐὰν οὖν διασπαράξωσιν οἱ λύκοι τὰ ἀρνία; Εἶπεν ὁ Ἰησοῦς τῷ Πέτρῳ, Μὴ φοβείσθωσαν τὰ ἀρνία τοὺς λύκους μετὰ τὸ ἀποθανεῖν αὐτά.[26] The remainder of the passage is merely a reference to Matt. x. 28.

dead hath power over soul and body to cast them into hell-fire."
And then, continuing the thread of His discourse, He warned them
plainly how, both at this time and again long afterwards, they might
be brought before councils, and scourged in synagogues,[1] and stand
at the judgment-bar of kings, and yet without any anxious premedi-
tation,[2] the Spirit should teach them what to say. The doctrine of
peace should be changed by the evil passions of men into a war-cry
of fury and hate, and they might be driven to fly before the face of
enemies from city to city. Still let them endure to the end, for
before they had gone through the cities of Israel, the Son of Man
should have come.[3]

Then, lastly, He at once warned and comforted them by remind-
ing them of what He Himself had suffered, and how He had been
opposed. Let them not fear. The God who cared even for the little
birds when they fell to the ground[4] — the God by whom the very
hairs of their head were numbered — the God who (and here He
glanced back perhaps at the question of Peter) held in His hand the
issues, not of life and death only, but of *eternal* life and of *eternal*
death, and who was therefore more to be feared than the wolves of
earth — HE was with them; He would acknowledge those whom
His Son acknowledged, and deny those whom He denied. They
were being sent forth into a world of strife, which would seem even
the more deadly because of the peace which it rejected. Even their
nearest and their dearest might side with the world against them.
But they who would be His true followers must for His sake give up
all ; must even take up their cross[5] and follow Him. But then, for
their comfort, He told them that they should be as He was in the
world; that they who receive them should receive Him; that to lose
their lives for His sake would be to more than find them; that a cup

---

[1] For the συνέδρια see Deut. xvi. 18. For the power of the synagogue officers
to punish by scourging, see Acts v. 40; 2 Cor. xi 24.

[2] Matt. x. 19. The "take no thought" of the A. V. is too strong; as in Matt.
vi. 25, it means "be not *over-anxious* about."

[3] This glance into the farther future probably belongs to a much later discourse; and the coming of the Son of Man is here understood in its first and
narrower signification of the downfall of Judaism, and the establishment of a
kingdom of Christ on earth, which some at least among them lived to see.

[4] Matt. x. 29. Little birds are still strung together and sold for "two farthings"
in the towns of Palestine.

[5] If this were not a proverbial allusion (as seems probable from its use in
Plutarch, *De Ser. Num. Vind.* ix., ἕκαστος κακούργων ἐκφέρει τὸν αὑτοῦ
σταυρόν [226]), it must have been a dark saying to the Apostles at this time.
Perhaps it belongs to a much later occasion, after He had distinctly prophesied
the certainty and nature of His future sufferings.

of cold water given to the youngest and humblest of His little ones [1] should not miss of its reward.

Such is an outline of these great parting instructions as given by St. Matthew, and every missionary and every minister should write them in letters of gold. The sterility of missionary labor is a constant subject of regret and discouragement among us. Would it be so if all our missions were carried out in this wise and conciliatory, in this simple and self-abandoning, in this faithful and dauntless spirit? Was a missionary ever unsuccessful who, being enabled by the grace of God to live in the light of such precepts as these,[2] worked as St. Paul worked, or St. Francis Xavier, or Henry Martyn, or Adoniram Judson, or John Eliot, or David Schwarz?

That the whole of this discourse was not delivered on this occasion,[3] that there are references in it to later periods,[4] that parts of it are only applicable to other apostolic missions which as yet lay far in the future,[5] seems clear; but we may, nevertheless, be grateful that St. Matthew, guided as usual by unity of subject, collected into one focus the scattered rays of instruction delivered, perhaps, on several subsequent occasions — as for instance, before the sending of the Seventy, and even as the parting utterances of the risen Christ.[6]

The Jews were familiar with the institution of *Sheluchim*, the plenipotentiaries of some higher authority. This was the title by which Christ seems to have marked out the position of His Apostles. It was a wise and merciful provision that he sent them out two and two;[7] it enabled them to hold sweet converse together, and mutually to correct each other's faults. Doubtless the friends and the brothers

---

[1] Alford ingeniously conjectures that some children may have been present.

[2] Of course I do not imply that a missionary is *bound* to serve gratuitously; *that* would be against the distinct statement of our Lord (Matt. x. 10, 11); yet there *are* occasions when even this may be desirable (1 Cor. ix. 15—19; 2 Cor. xi. 9—12; 1 Thess. ii. 9, &c.). But Christ meant all His commands to be interpreted according to their spirit, and we must not overlook the fact that this method of preaching *was* (and *is*) made more common and easy in the East than for us. "Nor was there in this," says Dr. Thomson, "any departure from the simple manners of the country. At this day the farmer sets out on excursions quite as extensive without a *para* in his purse, and the modern Moslem prophet of Tarishiidehah thus sends forth his apostles over this identical region" (*The Land and the Book*, p. 346).

[3] St. Mark and St. Luke only give, at this juncture, an epitome of its first section.

[4] *Ex. gr.*, perhaps some of the expressions in verses 8, 23, 25, 38.

[5] *Ex. gr.*, verses 18—23.

[6] Cf. Mark xvi. 15—18; Luke x. 2—12; Luke xxiv. 47.

[7] The Rabbis held it a fault to journey without a friend with whom to converse about the sacred Law (*Soh. Chad.*, f. 61, 1; Schöttgen, p. 89).

went in pairs; the fiery Peter with the more contemplative Andrew; the Sons of Thunder — one influential and commanding, the other emotional and eloquent; the kindred faith and guilelessness of Philip and Bartholomew; the slow but faithful Thomas with the thoughtful and devoted Matthew; the ascetic James with his brother the impassioned Jude; the zealot Simon to fire with his theocratic zeal the dark, flagging, despairing spirit of the traitor Judas.

During their absence Jesus continued His work alone,[1] perhaps as He slowly made His way towards Jerusalem; for if we can speak of probability at all amid the deep uncertainties of the chronology of His ministry, it seems extremely probable that it is to this point that the verse belongs — "After this there was a feast of the Jews, and Jesus went up to Jerusalem."[2] In order not to break the continuity of the narrative, I shall omit the discussion here, but I shall in the Appendix[3] give ample reasons, as far as the *text* is concerned, and as far as the *time* required by the narrative is concerned, for believing that this nameless feast was in all probability the Feast of Purim.

But how came Jesus to go up to Jerusalem for such a feast as this — a feast which was the saturnalia of Judaism; a feast which was without divine authority,[4] and had its roots in the most intensely exclusive, not to say vindictive, feelings of the nation; a feast of merriment and masquerade, which was purely social and often discreditably convivial; a feast which was unconnected with religious services, and was observed, not in the Temple, not even necessarily in the synagogues, but mainly in the private houses of the Jews?[5]

The answer seems to be that, although Jesus was in Jerusalem at this feast, and went up about the time that it was held, the words of St. John do not necessarily imply that He went up for the express purpose of being present at this particular festival. The Passover took place only a month afterwards, and He may well have gone up

---

[1] Matt. xi. 1.

[2] John v. 1. Omitted by the Synoptists, who, until the close, narrate only the ministry in Galilee.

[3] See Excursus VIII., "The Unnamed Feast of John v. 1."

[4] To such an extent was this the case, that no less than eighty-five elders are said to have protested against its original institution, regarding it as an innovation against the Law (Lightfoot, *Hor. Hebr.* on John x. 22). It seems to have originated among the Jews of the dispersion.

[5] Perhaps more nearly resembling in its origin and character our Guy Fawkes' Day than anything else. Caspari calls it "ein Rache-, Fluch- und Sauffest" (*Chronol. Geogr. Einl.*, p. 113); but there is no proof that it was so at *that* time. In this particular year, the Feast of Purim seems to have coincided with a Sabbath (John v. 10), an arrangement carefully avoided in the later Jewish calendar. (See Wieseler, *Synopsis*, p. 199, E. Tr.)

mainly with the intention of being present at the Passover, although He gladly availed himself of an opportunity for being in Judæa and Jerusalem a month before it, both that He might once more preach in those neighborhoods, and that He might avoid the publicity and dangerous excitement involved in His joining the caravan of the Passover pilgrims from Galilee. Such an opportunity may naturally have arisen from the absence of the Apostles on their missionary tour. The Synoptists give clear indications that Jesus had friends and well-wishers at Jerusalem and in its vicinity. He must therefore have paid visits to those regions which they do not record. Perhaps it was among those friends that He awaited the return of His immediate followers. We know the deep affection which he entertained for the members of one household in Bethany, and it is not unnatural to suppose that He was now living in the peaceful seclusion of that pious household as a solitary and honored guest.

But even if St. John intends us to believe that the occurrence of this feast was the immediate cause of this visit to Jerusalem, we must bear in mind that there is no proof whatever of its having been in our Lord's time the fantastic and disorderly commemoration which it subsequently became. The nobler-minded Jews doubtless observed it in a calm and grateful manner ; and as one part of the festival consisted in showing acts of kindness to the poor, it may have offered an attraction to Jesus both on this ground, and because it enabled Him to show that there was nothing unnational or unpatriotic in the universal character of His message, or the all-embracing infinitude of the charity which He both practised and enjoined.

There remains then but a single question. The Passover was rapidly drawing near, and His presence at that great feast would on every ground be expected. Why then did He absent Himself from it ? Why did He return to Galilee instead of remaining at Jerusalem ? The events which we are about to narrate will furnish a sufficient answer to this question.

CHAPTER XXVII.

THE MIRACLE AT BETHESDA.

Εἰς ἀπεραντολογίαν οἱ τῶν Ἰουδαίων διδάσκαλοι ἐληλύθασι φά-
σκοντες βάσταγμα μὲν εἶναι τὸ τοιόνδε ὑπόδημα οὐ μὴν τὸ τοιόνδε,
κ. τ. λ.[227] — ORIG. *Opp.* i. 179.

THERE was in Jerusalem, near the Sheep-gate, a pool, which was
believed to possess remarkable healing properties. For this reason,
in addition to its usual name, it had been called in Hebrew " Bethesda," or the House of Mercy,[1] and under the porticos which adorned
the pentagonal masonry in which it was enclosed lay a multitude of
sufferers from blindness, lameness, and atrophy, waiting to take
advantage of the bubbling and gushing of the water, which showed
that its medicinal properties were at their highest. There is no
indication in the narrative that any one who thus used the water was
at once, or *miraculously*, healed; but the repeated use of an intermittent and gaseous spring — and more than one of the springs about
Jerusalem continue to be of this character to the present day — was
doubtless likely to produce most beneficial results.

A very early popular legend, which has crept by interpolation into
the text of St. John,[2] attributed the healing qualities of the water to

---

[1] John v. 2, ἐπιλεγομένη. There are great varieties of reading ; Tischendorf,
with ℵ, reads Βηθζαθα. Perhaps this is sufficient to account for the silence of
Josephus, who may mention it under another name. The pool now pointed out
to the traveller as Bethesda is *Birket Israel,* which seems, however, to have formed
part of the deep fosse round the Tower of Antonia. The pool *may* have been the
one now known as the Fountain of the Virgin, not far from Siloam, and connected
with it (as Dr. Robinson discovered, *Bibl. Researches,* i. 509) by a subterranean
passage. He himself had an opportunity of observing the *intermittent* character
of this fountain, which, he was told, bubbles up " at irregular intervals, sometimes two and three times a day, and sometimes in summer once in two or three
days." (*Bibl. Researches,* i. 341.)

[2] The weight of evidence both external and internal against the genuineness of
John v. 3, 4 (from the word ἐκδεχομένων [228]) seems to me overwhelming. 1. It
is omitted by not a few of the weightiest MSS. and versions (ℵ, B, D, the Cureton
Syriac). 2. In others in which it does occur it is obelised as dubious. 3. It
abounds in various readings, showing that there is something suspicious about it.
4. It contains in the short compass of a few lines no less than seven words not
found elsewhere in the New Testament, or only found with a different sense.

the descent of an angel who troubled the pool at irregular intervals, leaving the first persons who could scramble into it to profit by the immersion. This solution of the phenomenon was in fact so entirely in accordance with the Semitic habit of mind, that, in the universal ignorance of all scientific phenomena, and the utter indifference to close investigation which characterize most Orientals, the populace would not be likely to trouble themselves about the possibility of any other explanation. But whatever may have been the general belief about the *cause*, the *fact* that the water was found at certain intervals to be impregnated with gases which gave it a strengthening property, was sufficient to attract a concourse of many sufferers.

Among these was one poor man who, for no less than thirty-eight years, had been lamed by paralysis. He had haunted the porticoes of this pool, but without effect; for as he was left there unaided, and as the motion of the water occurred at irregular times, others more fortunate and less feeble than himself managed time after time to struggle in before him, until the favorable moment had been lost.[1]

Jesus looked on the man with heartfelt pity. It was obvious that the *will* of the poor destitute creature was no less stricken with paralysis than his limbs, and his whole life was one long atrophy of ineffectual despair. But Jesus was minded to make *His* Purim present to the poor, to whom He had neither silver nor gold to give. He would help a fellow-sufferer, whom no one had cared or condescended to help before.

" Willest thou to be made whole? "

At first the words hardly stirred the man's long and despondent lethargy; he scarcely seems even to have looked up. But thinking,

---

5. It relates a most startling fact, one wholly unlike anything else in Scripture, one not alluded to by a single other writer, Jewish or heathen, and one which, had there been the slightest ground for believing in its truth, would certainly not have been passed over in silence by Josephus. 6. Its insertion (to explain the word $ταραχθῇ$ [229] in verse 7) is easily accounted for ; its omission, had it been in the original text, is quite inconceivable. Accordingly, it is rejected from the text by the best editors as a spurious gloss, and indeed there is no earlier trace of its existence than an allusion to it in Tertullian (*De Bapt.* 5). (Ob. circ. A. D. 220.)

[1] Strauss and his school make all kinds of objections to this narrative. " Latterly," as Lange observes, with cutting sarcasm, " a crowd of ' critical ' remarks have been seen lying round the pool of Bethesda, like another multitude of blind, lame, and withered." They hold it impossible that the man who, as they assume, must have had some one to take him to the pool, never had any one to put him in at the right time. Such remarks are very trivial. 1. St. John says nothing of any one bringing him to the pool ; he may have lived close by, and been able to crawl there himself. 2. He does not say that the pool wrought *instantaneous* cures, or that the man had *never* been put into the troubled water.

perhaps, with a momentary gleam of hope, that this was some stranger who, out of kindness of heart, might help him into the water when it was again agitated, he merely narrated in reply the misery of his long and futile expectation. Jesus had intended a speedier and more effectual aid.

"Rise," He said, "take thy couch and walk."

It was spoken in an accent that none could disobey. The manner of the Speaker, His voice, His mandate, thrilled like an electric spark through the withered limbs and the shattered constitution, enfeebled by a lifetime of suffering and sin.[1] After thirty-eight years of prostration, the man instantly rose, lifted up his pallet, and began to walk.[2] In glad amazement he looked round to see and to thank his unknown benefactor; but the crowd was large, and Jesus, anxious to escape the unspiritual excitement which would fain have regarded Him as a thaumaturge alone, had quietly slipped away from observation.[3]

In spite of this, many scrupulous and jealous eyes were soon upon Him. In proportion as the inner power and meaning of a religion are dead, in that proportion very often is an exaggerated import attached to its outer forms. Formalism and indifference, pedantic scrupulosity and absolute disbelief, are correlative, and ever flourish side by side. It was so with Judaism in the days of Christ. Its living and burning enthusiasm was quenched; its lofty and noble faith had died away; its prophets had ceased to prophesy; its poets had ceased to sing; its priests were no longer clothed with righteousness; its saints were few. The axe was at the root of the barren tree, and its stem served only to nourish a fungous brood of ceremonials and traditions,

"Deathlike, and colored like a corpse's cheek."

And thus it was that the observance of the Sabbath, which had been intended to secure for weary men a rest full of love and peace and mercy, had become a mere national Fetish — a barren custom fenced in with the most frivolous and senseless restrictions. Well-nigh every great provision of the Mosaic law had now been degraded into a mere

---

[1] See verse 14, and below.

[2] The $κράββατον$ was probably nothing more than a mere *paillasse,* or folded *abeiyah.* To regard such a trivial effort as a violation of the Sabbath was a piece of superstitious literalism not derived from Scripture, but founded on the Oral Law.

[3] $ἐξένευσεν$ (ver. 13); literally, "swam out." Cf. Eur., *Hippol.* 471; Thuc. ii. 90.

superfluity of meaningless minutiæ, the delight of small natures, and the grievous incubus of all true and natural piety.

Now, when a religion has thus decayed into a superstition without having lost its external power, it is always more than ever tyrannous and suspicious in its hunting for heresy. The healed paralytic was soon surrounded by a group of questioners. They looked at him with surprise and indignation.

"It is the Sabbath; it is not lawful for thee to carry thy bed."

Here was a flagrant case of violation of their law! Had not the son of Shelomith, though half an Egyptian, been stoned to death for gathering sticks on the Sabbath day ?[2] Had not the prophet Jeremiah expressly said, "Take heed to yourselves, and bear *no* burden on the Sabbath day ?"[3]

Yes; but why ? Because the Sabbath was an ordinance of mercy intended to protect the underlings and the oppressed from a life of incessant toil; because it was essential to save the serfs and laborers of the nation from the over-measure of labor which would have been exacted from them in a nation afflicted with the besetting sin of greed; because the setting apart of one day in seven for sacred rest was of infinite value to the spiritual life of all. *That* was the meaning of the Fourth Commandment. In what respect was it violated by the fact that a man who had been healed by a miracle wished to carry home the mere pallet which was perhaps almost the only thing that he possessed ? What the man really violated was not the law of God, or even of Moses, but the wretched formalistic inferences of their frigid tradition, which had gravely decided that on the Sabbath a nailed shoe might not be worn because it was a burden, but that an un-nailed shoe might be worn ; and that a person might go out with two shoes on, but not with only one; and that one man might carry a loaf of bread, but that two men might not carry it between them, and so forth, to the very utmost limit of tyrannous absurdity.[4]

"He that made me whole," replied the man, " *He* said to me, Take up thy bed and walk."

---

[1] The present Jews of Palestine, degraded and contemptible as is their condition — beggars, idlers, cheats, sensualists, as the best of their own countrymen confess them to be — still cling to all their Sabbatarian superstitions : *e. g.*, " The German Jews look upon it as a sin to use a stick of any kind on the Sabbath " (Dr. Frankl, *Jews in the East*, E. Tr., ii. 6).

[2] Lev. xxiv. 10—12 ; Numb. xv. 32—36.

[3] Jer. xvii. 21.

[4] ψυχρὰς παραδόσεις φέρουσι [230] (Orig.). These instances of hard and foolish Judaic ἀπεραντολογία,[231] to which Origen expressly alludes, are preserved in the Mishna, *Shabb.* x. 5. (Gfrörer, *Jahrh. d. Heils*, i. 18).

As far as the man was concerned, they accepted the plea; a voice fraught with miraculous power ·so stupendous that it could heal the impotence of a lifetime by a word, was clearly, as far as the man was concerned, entitled to some obedience. And the fact was that they were actuated by a motive; they were flying at higher game than this insignificant and miserable sufferer. Nothing was to be gained by worrying *him.*

" *Who* is it that " — mark the malignity of these Jewish authorities [1] — not that *made thee whole,* for there was no heresy to be hunted out in the mere fact of exercising miraculous power — but "that gave thee the wicked command to take up thy bed and walk ? "

So little apparently, up to this time, was the person of Jesus generally known in the suburbs of Jerusalem, or else so dull and languid had been the man's attention while Jesus was first speaking to him, that he actually did not know who his benefactor was. But he ascertained shortly afterwards. It is a touch of grace about him that we next find him in the Temple, whither he may well have gone to return thanks to God for this sudden and marvellous renovation of his wasted life. There, too, Jesus saw him, and addressed to him one simple memorable warning, " See, thou hast been made whole : continue in sin no longer, lest something worse happen to thee." [2]

Perhaps the warning had been given because Christ read the mean and worthless nature of the man; at any rate, there is something at first sight peculiarly revolting in the 15th verse. " The man *went and told the Jewish authorities* that it was Jesus who had made him whole." It is barely possible, though most unlikely, that he may have meant to magnify the name of One who had wrought such a mighty work; but as he must have been well aware of the angry feelings of the Jews — as we hear no word of his gratitude or devotion, no word of amazement or glorifying God — as, too, it must have been abundantly clear to him that Jesus in working the miracle had been touched by compassion only, and had been anxious to shun all publicity — it must be confessed that the *primá facie* view of the man's conduct is that it was an act of needless and contemptible delation — a piece of most pitiful self-protection at the expense of his benefactor — an almost inconceivable compound of feeble sycophancy and base ingratitude. Apparently the warning of Jesus had been

---

[1] Such, as we have already observed, is all but invariably the meaning of οἱ Ἰουδαῖοι in St. John.

[2] Alford speaks here of " the sin committed thirty-eight years ago, from which this sickness had resulted;" but surely μηκέτι ἁμάρτανε means more than this: it means, " Be sinning — be a sinner — no longer."

most deeply necessary, as, if we judge the man aright, it was wholly unavailing.

For the consequences were immediate and disastrous. They changed in fact the entire tenor of His remaining life. Untouched by the evidence of a most tender compassion, unmoved by the display of miraculous power, the Jewish inquisitors were up in arms to defend their favorite piece of legalism. " They began to *persecute* Jesus *because He did such things on the Sabbath day.*"

And it was in answer to this charge that He delivered the divine and lofty discourse preserved for us in the fifth chapter of St John. Whether it was delivered in the Temple, or before some committee of the Sanhedrin, we cannot tell ; but, at any rate, the great Rabbis and Chief Priests who summoned Him before them that they might rebuke and punish Him for a breach of the Sabbath, were amazed and awed, if also they were bitterly and implacably infuriated, by the words they heard. They had brought Him before them in order to warn, and the warnings fell on *them*. They had wished to instruct and reprove, and then, perhaps, condescendingly, for this once, to pardon ; and lo ! He mingles for *them* the majesty of instruction with the severity of compassionate rebuke. They sat round Him in all the pomposities of their office, to overawe Him as an inferior, and, lo ! they tremble, and gnash their teeth, though they dare not act, while with words like a flame of fire piercing into the very joints and marrow — with words more full of wisdom and majesty than those which came among the thunders of Sinai — He assumes the awful dignity of the Son of God.

And so the attempt to impress on Him their petty rules and literal pietisms — to lecture Him on the heinousness of working miraculous cures on the Sabbath day — perhaps to punish Him for the enormity of bidding a healed man take up his bed — was a total failure. With His very first word He exposes their materialism and ignorance. They, in their feebleness, had thought of the Sabbath as though God ceased from working thereon because He was fatigued ; He tells them that that holy rest was a beneficent activity. They thought apparently, as men think now, that God had resigned to certain mute forces His creative energy ; He tells them that His Father is working still ; and He, knowing His Father, and loved of Him, was working with Him, and should do greater works than these which he had now done. Already was He quickening the spiritually dead, and the day should come when all in the tombs should hear his voice. Already He was bestowing eternal life on all that believed in Him ; hereafter should His voice be heard in that final judgment of the quick and dead which the Father had committed into His hands.[1]

Was He merely bearing witness of Himself? Nay, there were three mighty witnesses which had testified, and were testifying, of Him — John, whom, after a brief admiration, they had rejected; Moses, whom they boasted of following, and did not understand; God Himself, whom they professed to worship, but had never seen or known. They themselves had sent to John and heard his testimony; but He needed not the testimony of man, and mentioned it only for *their* sakes, because even they for a time had been willing to exult in that great prophet's God-enkindled light.[2] But he had far loftier witness than that of John — the witness of a miraculous power, exerted not as prophets had exerted it, in the name of God, but in His own name, because His Father had given such power into His hand. That Father they knew not: His light they had abandoned for the darkness; His word for their own falsehoods and ignorances; and they were rejecting Him whom He had sent. But there was a *third* testimony. If they knew nothing of the Father, they at least knew or thought they knew, the Scriptures; the Scriptures were in their hands; they had counted the very letters of them; yet they were rejecting Him of whom the Scriptures testified. Was it not clear that they — the righteous, the pious, the scrupulous, the separatists, the priests, the religious leaders of their nation — yet had not the love of God in them, if they thus rejected His prophet, His word, His works, His Son?

And what was the fibre of bitterness within them which produced all this bitter fruit? Was it not *pride?* How *could* they believe, who sought honor of one another, and not the honor that cometh of God only? Hence it was that they rejected One who came in His Father's name, while they had been, and should be, the ready dupes and the miserable victims of every false Messiah, of every Judas, and

---

[1] The distinction between οἱ τὰ ἀγαθὰ ποιήσαντες (the doers of those good deeds which cannot die) and οἱ τὰ φαῦλα πράξαντες (the slaves and victims of all that is delusive and transitory) is probably intentional.

[2] John v. 35 (cf. Matt. v. 15; Luke xii. 35). He was ὁ λύχνος ὁ καιόμενος καὶ φαίνων — the *Lamp* not the *Light* — being enkindled by Another, and so shining. " He is only as the light of the candle, for whose rays, indeed, men are grateful; but which is pale, flickering, transitory, compared with the glories of the Eternal flame from which itself is kindled" (Lightfoot, *On Revision*, p. 118). Christ is the Light from whom all lamps are kindled. " Then stood up Elias the prophet, like fire, and his word *burned as a lamp* " (Ecclus. xlviii. 1). " Lychnus orto soli non foenerat lucem " [232] (Bengel). Their " exultation " in the Baptist's teaching had been very shallow —·" they *heard*, but *did* not " (Ezek. xxxiii. 32).

Theudas, and Bar-Cochebas — and, in Jewish history, there were more than sixty such — who came in his own name.

And yet He would not accuse them to the Father; they had another accuser, even Moses, in whom they trusted. Yes, Moses, in whose lightest word they professed to trust — over the most trivial precept of whose law they had piled their mountain loads of tradition and commentary — even *him* they were disbelieving and disobeying. Had they believed Moses, they would have believed Him who spoke to them, for Moses wrote of Him; but if they thus rejected the true meaning of the written words ($\gamma\rho\acute{\alpha}\mu\mu\alpha\sigma\iota\nu$) which they professed to adore and love, how could they believe the spoken words ($\dot{\rho}\dot{\eta}\mu\alpha\sigma\iota\nu$) to which they were listening with rage and hate?[1]

We know with what deadly exasperation these high utterances were received. Never before had the Christ spoken so plainly. It seemed as though in Galilee He had wished the truth respecting Him to rise like a gradual and glorious dawn upon the souls and understandings of those who heard His teaching and watched His works; but as though at Jerusalem — where His ministry was briefer, and His followers fewer, and His opponents stronger, and His mighty works more rare — He had determined to leave the leaders and rulers of the people without excuse, by revealing at once to their astonished ears the nature of His being. More distinctly than this He could not have spoken. They had summoned Him before them to explain His breach of the Sabbath; so far from excusing the act itself, as He sometimes did in Galilee, by showing that the higher and moral law of love supersedes and annihilates the lower law of mere literal and ceremonial obedience — instead of showing that He had but acted in the spirit in which the greatest of saints had acted before Him, and the greatest of prophets taught — He sets Himself wholly above the Sabbath, as its Lord, nay, even as the Son and Interpreter of Him who had made the Sabbath, and who in all the mighty course of Nature and of Providence was continuing to work thereon.

Here, then, were two deadly charges ready at hand against this Prophet of Nazareth: He was a breaker of their Sabbath; He was a blasphemer of their God. The first crime was sufficient cause for

---

[1] "The Law," says St. Paul, "was our tutor ($\pi\alpha\iota\delta\alpha\gamma\omega\gamma\acute{o}\varsigma$) to lead us unto Christ," *i. e.* into spiritual manhood; into the maturity of the Christian life. (Dr. Lightfoot, on Gal. iii. 24, shows that the ordinary explanation of this text — however beautiful — is untenable.) Cf. John i. 46, "We have found Him of whom *Moses* in *the Law* and the Prophets did write."

opposition and persecution; the second an ample justification of persistent [1] and active endeavors to bring about His death.

But at present they could do nothing; they could only rage in impotent indignation; they could only gnash with their teeth, and melt away. Whatever may have been the cause, as yet they dared not act. A power greater than their own restrained them. The hour of their triumph was not yet come; only, from this moment, there went forth against Him from the hearts of those Priests and Rabbis and Pharisees the inexorable irrevocable sentence of violent death.

And under such circumstances it was useless, and worse than useless, for Him to remain in Judæa, where every day was a day of peril from these angry and powerful conspirators. He could no longer remain in Jerusalem for the approaching Passover, but must return to Galilee; but He returned with a clear vision of the fatal end, with full knowledge that the hours of light in which He could still work were already fading into the dusk, and that the rest of His work would be accomplished with the secret sense that death was hanging over His devoted head.

---

[1] ἐδίωκον — ἐζήτουν ἀποκτεῖναι (John v. 16, 18).

CHAPTER XXVIII.

THE MURDER OF JOHN THE BAPTIST.

" It is great sin to swear unto a sin ;
But greater sin to keep a sinful oath.
Who can be bound by any solemn vow
To do a murderous deed . . . ? "
SHAKESPEARE, 2 *Henry VI.* v. 2.

IT must have been with His human heart full of foreboding sadness that the Saviour returned to Galilee. In His own obscure Nazareth He had before been violently rejected; He had now been rejected no less decisively at Jerusalem by the leading authorities of His own nation. He was returning to an atmosphere already darkened by the storm-clouds of gathering opposition; and He had scarcely returned when upon that atmosphere, like the first note of a death-knell tolling ruin, there broke the intelligence of a dreadful martyrdom. The heaven-enkindled and shining lamp had suddenly been quenched in blood. The great Forerunner — He who was greatest of those born of women — the Prophet, and more than a prophet, had been foully murdered.

Herod Antipas, to whom, on the death of Herod the Great, had fallen the tetrarchy of Galilee, was about as weak and miserable a prince as ever disgraced the throne of an afflicted country. Cruel, crafty, and voluptuous like his father, he was also, unlike him, weak in war and vacillating in peace. In him, as in so many characters which stand conspicuous on the stage of history, infidelity and superstition went hand in hand. But the morbid terrors of a guilty conscience did not save him from the criminal extravagances of a violent will. He was a man in whom were mingled the worst features of the Roman, the Oriental, and the Greek.

It was the policy of the numerous princelings who owed their very existence to Roman intervention, to pay frequent visits of ceremony to the Emperor at Rome. During one of these visits, possibly to condole with Tiberius on the death of his son Drusus, or his mother Livia, Antipas had been, while at Rome, the guest of his brother Herod Philip — not the tetrarch of that name, but a son of Herod the Great and Mariamne, daughter of Simon the Boëthusian, who, having been disinherited by his father, was living at Rome as a private person.[1] Here he became entangled by the snares of Herodias, his brother Philip's wife; and he repaid the hospitality he had received by carrying her off. Everything combined to make the act as detestable as it was ungrateful and treacherous. The Herods carried intermarriage to an extent which only prevailed in the worst and most dissolute of the Oriental and post-Macedonian dynasties. Herodias being the daughter of Aristobulus, was not only the sister-in-law, but also the niece of Antipas;[2] she had already borne to her husband a daughter, who was now grown up. Antipas had himself long been married to the daughter of Aretas, or Hâreth, Emîr of Arabia, and neither he nor Herodias were young enough to plead even the poor excuse of youthful passion. The sole temptation on his side was an impotent sensuality; on hers an extravagant ambition. She preferred a marriage doubly adulterous and doubly incestuous to a life spent with the only Herod who could not boast even the fraction of a vice-regal throne. Antipas promised on his return from Rome to make her his wife, and she exacted from him a pledge that he would divorce his innocent consort, the daughter of the Arabian prince.

But "our pleasant vices," it has well been said, "are made the instruments to punish us;" and from this moment began for Herod Antipas a series of annoyances and misfortunes, which only culminated in his death years afterwards in discrowned royalty and unpitied exile. Herodias became from the first the evil genius of his house. The people were scandalized and outraged. Family dissensions were embittered. The Arabian princess, without waiting to be divorced, indignantly fled, first to the border castle of Machærus, and then to the rocky fastnesses of her father Hâreth at Petra. He, in his just indignation, broke off all amicable relations with his quondam son-in-law, and subsequently declared war against him, in which he avenged himself by the infliction of a severe and ruinous defeat.

Nor was this all. Sin was punished with sin, and the adulterous

---

[1] A small fragment of the Stemma Herodum will make these relationships more clear.

HEROD THE GREAT.

(=Mariamne, d. of Simon.	= Malthace (a Samaritan).	= Cleopatra.	= Mariamne,) d. of Hyrcanus.
Herod "Philip" = Herodias.	Herod Antipas. Archelaus.	Philip, Tetr. of Ituræa. = Salome.	Aristobulus.
Salome.	= d. of Aretas. = Herodias.		Herodias. Herod Agrippa I.

[2] Even the Romans regarded such unions with horror; and never got over the disgust which the Emperor Claudius caused them by marrying his niece Agrippina; but they were almost the rule in the Herodian family.

union had to be cemented with a prophet's blood. In the gay and gilded halls of any one of those sumptuous palaces which the Herods delighted to build the dissolute tyrant may have succeeded perhaps in shutting out the deep murmur of his subjects' indignation; but there was one voice which reached him, and agitated his conscience, and would not be silenced. It was the voice of the great Baptist. How Herod had been thrown first into connection with him we do not know, but it was probably after he had seized possession of his person on the political plea that his teaching, and the crowds who flocked to him, tended to endanger the public safety.[1] Among other features in the character of Herod was a certain superstitious curiosity which led him to hanker after and tamper with the truths of the religion which his daily life so flagrantly violated. He summoned John to his presence. Like a new Elijah before another Ahab — clothed in his desert raiment, the hairy cloak and the leathern girdle — the stern and noble eremite stood fearless before the incestuous king. His words — the simple words of truth and justice — the calm reasonings about righteousness, temperance, and the judgment to come — fell like flakes of fire on that hard and icy conscience. Herod, alarmed perhaps by the fulfilment of the old curse of the Mosaic law in the childlessness of his union,[2] listened with some dim and feeble hope of future amendment. He even did many things gladly because of John. But there was *one* thing which he *would* not do — perhaps persuaded himself that he *could* not do — and that was, give up the guilty love which mastered him, or dismiss the haughty imperious woman who ruled his life after ruining his peace. "It is not lawful for thee to have thy brother's wife," was the blunt declaration of the dauntless Prophet; and though time after time he might be led over those splendid floors, pale and wasted with imprisonment and disappointed hope, yet, though he well knew that it kindled against him an implacable enmity and doomed him to a fresh remand to his solitary cell, he never hesitated to face the flushed and angry Herod with that great *Non licet.*[33] Nor did he spare his stern judgment on all the other crimes and follies of Herod's life.[3] Other men — even men otherwise great and good — have had very smooth words for the sins of princes; but in the fiery soul of the Baptist, strengthened into noblest exercise by the long asceticism of the wil-

---

[1] So Josephus, *Antt.* xviii. 5, § 2. In this way it is easy to reconcile his account with those of the Evangelists.

[2] Lev. xx. 21. We know how the same fact weighed on the mind of Henry VIII.

[3] Luke iii. 19.

derness, there was no dread of human royalty and no compromise with exalted sin. And when courage and holiness and purity thus stood to rebuke the lustful meanness of a servile and corrupted soul, can we wonder if even among his glittering courtiers and reckless men-at-arms the king cowered conscience-stricken before the fettered prisoner?[1] But John knew how little trust can be placed in a soul that has been eaten away by a besetting sin; and since He to whom he had borne witness beyond Jordan wrought no miracle of power for his deliverance, it is not probable that he looked for any passage out of his dungeon in the Black Fortress,[2] save through the grave and gate of death.

Hitherto, indeed, the timidity or the scruples of Herod Antipas had afforded to John — so far as his mere life was concerned — a precarious protection from the concentrated venom of an adulteress's hate.[3] But at last what she had failed to gain by passionate influence she succeeded in gaining by subtle fraud. She knew well that even from his prison the voice of John might be more powerful than all the influences of her fading beauty, and might succeed at last in tearing from her forehead that guilty crown. But she watched her opportunity, and was not long in gaining her end.[4]

The Herodian princes, imitating the luxurious example of their great prototypes, the Roman emperors, were fond of magnificent banquets and splendid anniversaries. Among others they had adopted the heathen fashion of birthday celebrations,[5] and Antipas on his birthday — apparently either at Machærus or at a neighboring palace called Julias — prepared a banquet for his courtiers, and generals, and Galilæan nobles. The wealth of the Herods, the expen-

---

[1] History has not seldom seen similar scenes repeated. Compare the instances of Theodosius and St. Ambrose, of Attila and Leo, of Thierry and St. Columban, of Henry II. and St. Thomas à Becket, of Henry IV. of Germany and Gregory VII., &c.

[2] So the Rabbis called Machærus. (Sepp.)

[3] " But Herodias was bitterly vehement against him ($\varepsilon\nu\varepsilon\widetilde{\imath}\chi\varepsilon\nu\ \alpha\dot{\upsilon}\tau\widetilde{\omega}$; cf. Luke xi. 53), and had a settled wish to kill him; but she was not able. For Herod *was afraid* of John, knowing him to be a just and holy man, and *kept him safe*, and on hearing him used to do many things, and used to listen to him gladly " (Mark vi 19, 20).

[4] The $\gamma\varepsilon\nu o\mu\acute{\varepsilon}\nu\eta\varsigma\ \dot{\eta}\mu\acute{\varepsilon}\rho\alpha\varsigma\ \varepsilon\dot{\upsilon}\kappa\alpha\acute{\iota}\rho o\upsilon$ [234] of Mark vi. 21 refers to the pre-arranged machinations of this Herodian Jezebel.

[5] Gen. xl. 20; Herod. i. 153; Pers. *Sat.* v. 180. There can be little doubt that the unclassical $\gamma\varepsilon\nu\acute{\varepsilon}\acute{o}\iota\alpha$ means a birthday celebration (cf. Jos. *Antt.* xii. 4, § 7). Wieseler labors with great ingenuity and learning to make it mean " accession-festival " (which was also kept by the Herods, *id. ib.*, xv. 11, § 6), but fails after all to adduce any other instance of the word used in this sense.

sive architecture of their numerous palaces, their universal tendency to extravagant display, make it certain that nothing would be wanting to such a banquet which wealth or royalty could procure ; and there is enough to show that it was on the model of those

> " Sumptuous gluttonies and gorgeous feasts
> On citron table or Atlantic stone,"

which accorded with the depraved fashion of the Empire, and mingled Roman *gourmandize* with Ionic sensuality. But Herodias had craftily provided the king with an unexpected and exciting pleasure, the spectacle of which would be sure to enrapture such guests as his. Dancers and dancing-women were at that time in great request.[1] The passion for witnessing these too often indecent and degrading representations had naturally made its way into the Sadducean and semi-pagan court of these usurping Edomites, and Herod the Great had built in his palace a theatre for the Thymelici.[2] A luxurious feast of the period was not regarded as complete unless it closed with some gross pantomimic representation ; and doubtless Herod had adopted the evil fashion of his day. But he had not anticipated for his guests the rare luxury of seeing a princess — his own niece, a granddaughter of Herod the Great, and of Mariamne, a descendant, therefore, of Simon the High Priest, and the great line of Maccabæan princes — a princess who afterwards became the wife of a tetrarch, and the mother of a king[3] — honoring them by degrading herself into a scenic dancer. And yet when the banquet was over, when the guests were full of meat and flushed with wine, Salome herself, the daughter of Herodias, then in the prime of her young and lustrous beauty, executed, as it would now be expressed, a *pas seul* "in the midst of"[4] those dissolute and half-intoxicated revellers. "She came in and danced, and pleased Herod, and them that sat at meat with him."

---

[1] Mnestor, Paris, &c. Cf. Jos. *Antt.* xii. 4, § 6.

[2] See Jos. *Antt.* xv. 8, § 1 ; xix. 7, § 5.

[3] She first married her uncle Philip, tetrarch of Ituræa, then her cousin Aristobulus, King of Chalcis, by whom she became mother of three sons. The Herodian princesses were famed for their beauty.

[4] Matt. xiv. 6. In Mark vi. 22, א, B, D, L read αὐτοῦ ; but even if this were the true reading, the whole context would be sufficient to show that Keim is wrong (*Gesch. Jesu,* ii. 512) in charging St. Mark with the error of supposing that Salome was his *actual* daughter. As for the dance, Salome would but be imitating the ill-trained maidens of her own day —

> " Motus doceri gaudet Ionicos
> Matura virgo, et fingitur artibus
> Jam nunc et incestos amores
> De tenero meditatur ungui."[235] (Hor. *Od.* iii. 6, 21.)

And he, like another Xerxes,[1] in the delirium of his drunken ap
proval, swore to this degraded girl in the presence of his guests
that he would give her anything for which she asked, even to the
half of his kingdom.[2]

The girl flew to her mother, and said, "What shall I ask?" It
was exactly what Herodias expected, and she might have asked for
robes, or jewels, or palaces, or whatever such a woman loves; but to
a mind like hers revenge was sweeter than wealth or pride, and we
may imagine with what fierce malice she hissed out the unhesitating
answer, "The head of John the Baptizer." And coming in before
the king *immediately with haste* — (what a touch is that! and how
apt a pupil did the wicked mother find in her wicked daughter) —
Salome exclaimed, "My wish is that you give *me here*,[3] *immediately*,
on a dish, the head of John the Baptist." Her indecent haste, her
hideous petition, show that she shared the furies of her race. Did
she think that in that infamous period, and among those infamous
guests, her petition would be received with a burst of laughter? Did
she hope to kindle their merriment to a still higher pitch by the sense
of the delightful wickedness[4] involved in a young and beautiful girl,
asking — nay, imperiously demanding — that then and there, on one
of the golden dishes which graced the board, should be given into
her own hands the gory head of the Prophet whose words had made
a thousand bold hearts quail?

If so, she was disappointed. The tetrarch, at any rate, was plunged

---

[1] Esth. v. 3; Herod. ix. 109. Cf. Suet. *Caius*, 32.

[2] There is a remarkable parallel to this narrative in the superb banquet given
by Agrippa I. to the Emperor Caius, with the design of winning a favor. Caius
showed his sense of the compliment paid to him by offering Agrippa anything
which he liked to ask, and Agrippa used his opportunity nobly and unselfishly to
dissuade Caius from the mad attempt to set up his statue in the Temple (Jos.
Antt. xviii. 8, § 7). Caius says, τὸ δὲ πᾶν, ὅπερ ὅοι ῥοπὴν ἂν προόθείη τοῦ
εὐδαίμονος, διακονήόεται ὅοι προθυμίᾳ τε καὶ ἰόχυΐ.[236] He expected
Agrippa to ask for cities or lands, ὁ δὲ καίπερ τὰ πάντα παραόκευαόάμενος
ἐφ᾽ οἷς ᾔτηόε οὐκ ἐφανέρου τὴν διάνοιαν.[237] Finally Caius grants the
request, ἅμα τῇ θεραπείᾳ τοῦ ᾽Αγρίππα ἐνειλημμένος, καὶ ἅμα ἀπρεπὲς
ὑπολαμβάνων ἐπὶ τοόῶνδε μαρτύρων ψευδὴς γενέόθαι, κ. τ. λ.[238] The
parallels seem almost too close to be purely accidental.

[3] ὧδε (Matt. xiv. 8); ἐξαυτῆς (Mark vi. 25). We might suppose that some
scorn was intended by τοῦ βαπτίζοντος, "the man who baptizes," in verse 24,
were it not that this seems to be the general form in St. Mark (i. 4; vi. 14).

[4] "Quasi volesse crescere l' allegrezza di quel convito con un gran delitto"[239]
(Capecellatro, *La Vita di Gesù*, ii. 11). Volkmar thinks that she was a mere
child, the unconscious instrument in her mother's hands; and that the εὐθὺς
μετὰ ὅπουδῆς[240] of Mark vi. 25 implies mere ignorant girlish glee.

into grief by her request;[1] it more than did away with the pleasure of her disgraceful dance ; it was a bitter termination of his birthday feast. Fear, policy, remorse, superstition, even whatever poor spark of better feeling remained unquenched under the dense white ashes of a heart consumed by evil passions, all made him shrink in disgust from this sudden execution. He must have felt that he had been egregiously duped out of his own will by the cunning stratagem of his unrelenting paramour. If a single touch of manliness had been left in him he would have repudiated the request as one which did not fall either under the letter or the spirit of his oath, since the life of one cannot be made the gift to another; or he would have boldly declared at once, that if such was her choice, his oath was more honored by being broken than by being kept. But a despicable pride and fear of man prevailed over his better impulses. More afraid of the criticisms of his guests than of the future torment of such conscience as was left him, he immediately sent an executioner to the prison, which in all probability was not far from the banqueting hall ; and so at the bidding of a dissolute coward, and to please the loathly fancies of a shameless girl, the axe fell, and the head of the noblest of the prophets was shorn away.

In darkness and in secrecy the scene was enacted, and if any saw it their lips were sealed; but the executioner emerged into the light carrying by the hair that noble head, and then and there, in all the ghastliness of recent death, it was placed upon a dish from the royal table. The young dancing girl received it,[2] and now frightful as a Megæra, carried the hideous burden to her mother. Let us hope that the awful spectacle haunted the souls of both thenceforth till death.

What became of that ghastly relic we do not know. Tradition tells us that Herodias ordered the headless trunk[3] to be flung out over the

---

[1] St. Mark (vi. 26) uses the strong expression, $\pi\varepsilon\rho i\lambda\upsilon\pi o\varsigma\ \gamma\varepsilon\nu\acute{o}\mu\varepsilon\nu o\varsigma$.

[2] This bad age produced more than one parallel to such awful and sanguinary *nonchalance* on the part of women nobly born. Fulvia again and again ran a golden needle through the tongue of Cicero's dissevered head ; and Agrippina similarly outraged the head of her rival, Lollia Paulina (Dio Cass. xlvii. 9 ; lx. 33). It is sad to know that decapitation was regarded by the Jews with very special horror (*Sanhedr.* 7. 3). (Wetstein, *ad loc.*)

[3] $\pi\tau\tilde{\omega}\mu\alpha$ (Mark vi. 29). The tradition is mentioned by S. Jerome (*c. Ruffinum* iii. 42) and Nicephorus (i. 19). For the traditional death of "the dancing daughter of Herodias," by falling through, and having her head cut off by the ice, see Niceph. i. 20. He reports that "passing over a frozen lake, the ice broke, and she fell up to the neck in water, and her head was parted from her body by the violence of the fragments shaken by the water and her own fall, and so perished, God having fitted a judgment to the analogy and representment of her sin" (Jer. Taylor, *Life of Christ*, II. 10). But history loses sight of Salome in the court of

battlements for dogs and vultures to devour. On her, at any rate, swift vengeance fell.

The disciples of John — perhaps Manaen the Essene, the foster-brother of Herod Antipas, may have been among them — took up the corpse and buried it. Their next care was to go and tell Jesus, some of them, it may be, with sore and bitter hearts, that His friend and Forerunner — the first who had borne witness to Him, and over whom He had Himself pronounced so great an eulogy — was dead.

And about the same time His Apostles also returned from their mission, and told Him all that they had done and taught. They had preached repentance; they had cast out devils; they had anointed the sick with oil and healed them.[2] But the record of their ministry is very brief, and not very joyous. In spite of partial successes, it seemed as if their untried faith had as yet proved inadequate for the high task imposed on them.

And very shortly afterwards another piece of intelligence reached Jesus; it was that the murderous tetrarch was inquiring about Him; wished to see Him; perhaps would send and demand His presence when he returned to his new palace, the Golden House of his new capital at Tiberias. For the mission of the Twelve had tended more than ever to spread a rumor of Him among the people,[3] and specula-tion respecting Him was rife. All admitted that He had some high claim to attention. Some thought that He was Elijah, some Jere-miah, others one of the Prophets; but Herod had the most singular solution of the problem. It is said that when Theodoric had ordered the murder of Symmachus, he was haunted and finally maddened by the phantom of the old man's distorted features glaring at him from a dish on the table; nor can it have been otherwise with Herod Antipas. Into his banquet hall had been brought the head of one whom, in the depth of his inmost being, he felt to have been holy and just: and he had seen, with the solemn agony of death still rest-ing on them, the stern features on which he had often gazed with awe. Did no reproach issue from those dead lips yet louder and more terrible than they had spoken in life? were the accents which had uttered, "It is not lawful for thee to have her," frozen into

her second husband, Aristobulus (Jos. *Antt.* xviii. 5, § 4), and since God's judg-ments are not always displayed in this life, she may, for all we really know, have died, like Lucrezia Borgia, in the odor of sanctity at her little court.

[1] Perhaps this Manaen (see Acts xiii. 1 ; Jos. *Antt.* xv. 10, § 5) was a son of the Manaen who foretold to Herod the Great his future dignity.

[2] Cf. James v. 14.

[3] Mark vi 14.

silence, or did they seem to issue with supernatural energy from the mute ghastliness of death? If we mistake not, that dissevered head was rarely thenceforth absent from Herod's haunted imagination from that day forward till he lay upon his dying bed. And now, when but a brief time afterwards, he heard of the fame of another Prophet — of a Prophet transcendently mightier, and one who wrought miracles, which John had *never* done — his guilty conscience shivered with superstitious dread, and to his intimates [1] he began to whisper with horror, " *This is John the Baptist whom I beheaded: he is risen from the dead,* and therefore these mighty works are wrought by him." [2] Had John sprung to life again thus suddenly to inflict a signal vengeance? would he come to the strong towers of Machærus at the head of a multitude in wild revolt? or glide through the gilded halls of Julias or Tiberias, terrible, at midnight, with ghostly tread? " Hast thou found me, O mine enemy?"

As the imperious and violent temper of Herodias was the constant scourge of her husband's peace, so her mad ambition was subsequently the direct cause of his ruin. When the Emperor Caius (Caligula) began to heap favors on Herod Agrippa I., Herodias, sick with envy and discontent, urged Antipas to sail with her to Rome and procure a share of the distinction which had thus been given to her brother. Above all, she was anxious that her husband should obtain the title of king, [3] instead of continuing content with the humbler one of tetrarch. In vain did the timid and ease-loving Antipas point out to her the danger to which he might be exposed by such a request. She made his life so bitter to him by her importunity that, against his better judgment, he was forced to yield. The event justified his worst misgivings. No love reigned between the numerous uncles and nephews and half-brothers in the tangled family of Herod, and either out of policy or jealousy Agrippa not only discountenanced the schemes of his sister and uncle — though they had helped him in

---

[1] *Τοῖς παισὶν αὐτοῦ* (Matt. xiv. 2). The Hebrew עֲבָדִים means more than " servants," and hence is rendered by παῖς and φίλος in the LXX., and in Symmachus (1 Sam. xviii. 22 ; Esth. ii. 18) as well as by δοῦλος (Kuinoel, *ad Cor.*). This terrified surmise of the palace may have been mentioned by Chuza or by Manaen.

[2] Matt. xiv. 2 ; Mark vi. 16. That such thoughts must have been very rife is shown by the fact that when the army of Herod Antipas was disgracefully routed by Aretas, the people looked on it as a retribution for the murder of John (Jos. *Antt.* xviii. 5, §§ 1, 2).

[3] He is called βασιλεύς in Mark vi. 14 (and the courtesy title was common enough in the provinces), but τετράρχης more accurately in Matt. xiv. 1 ; Luke ix. 7.

his own misfortunes — but actually sent his freedman Fortunatus to Rome to accuse Antipas of treasonable designs. The tetrarch failed to clear himself of the charge, and in A. D. 39 was banished to Lugdunum — probably St. Bertrand de Comminges, in Gaul, not far from the Spanish frontier.[1] Herodias, either from choice or necessity or despair, accompanied his exile, and here they both died in obscurity and dishonor. Salome, the dancer — the Lucrezia Borgia of the Herodian house — disappears henceforth from history. Tradition or legend alone informs us that she met with an early, violent, and hideous death.

---

[1] "Thus," says Josephus (*Antt.* xviii. 7, § 2), "did God punish Herodias for her envy at her brother, and Herod for lending an ear to empty feminine talk." He adds that when Caius learnt that Herodias was a sister of Agrippa, he would have shown her some favor ; but the passion with which she rejected it made him banish her also.

CHAPTER XXIX.

THE FEEDING OF THE FIVE THOUSAND, AND WALKING ON THE SEA.

" Thy way is in the sea, and thy path in the great waters, and thy footsteps are
not known."— Ps. lxxvii. 19.

THE Feeding of the Five Thousand is one of the few miracles
during the ministry of Christ which are narrated to us by all four of
the Evangelists; [1] and as it is placed by St. John after the nameless
festival and just before a Passover, and by the Synoptists in immediate connection with the return of the Twelve and the execution of
the Baptist, we can hardly err in introducing it at this point of our
narrative.

The novel journeyings of the Apostles, the agitation of His own
recent conflicts, the burden of that dread intelligence which had just
reached Him, the constant pressure of a fluctuating multitude which
absorbed all their time, once more rendered it necessary that the little

---

[1] Matt xiv. 13—33; Mark vi. 30—52; Luke ix. 10—17; John vi. 1—21. The
reader will find every incident of the text either directly stated or clearly implied
in one or other of these quadruple narratives. In every important particular they
show the most absolute unanimity ; the trifling divergences, which a captious and
ungenerous criticism delights to exaggerate into glaring discrepancies, are perfectly reconcilable without any violent hypothesis, and are all more or less
accounted for in the story as here given. " The notion that genuine history is
characterized by an exact and minute attention to details," says a recent writer,
" is wholly modern. It may be doubted whether, since no narrative can give all
particulars, this method of historical composition does not, with all the affectation
of reality, present a more unreal presentation of the past, than the artless tale of
an interested but uncritical observer— whether, in short, syncretic history is not
apt to be exceedingly untrustworthy or deceptive. The more accurately two persons relate their impressions of the same great events, the wider is sure to be the
discrepancy between them. No two men see facts in exactly the same light, or
direct their attention to exactly the same circumstances " (*Paul of Tarsus*, p. 154).
He adds that, exact and patient as Thucydides is, we should have possessed two
widely differing stories of the Peloponnesian war if another observer equally
critical had devoted his attention to the same events. These slight divergencies
of the Gospel serve, however, to establish in the most satisfactory manner the
essential independence of the fourfold testimonies. They may tell against exaggerated, superstitious, and anti-scriptural theories of Inspiration ; but they are
demonstrably compatible with the most perfect truthfulness and honesty.

company should recover the tone and bloom of their spirits by a brief period of rest and solitude. " Come ye yourselves," He said, " apart into a desert place, and rest a while."

At the north-eastern corner of the Lake, a little beyond the point where the Jordan enters it, was a second Bethsaida, or " Fish-house," [1] once, like its western namesake, a small village, but recently enlarged and beautified by Philip, tetrarch of Ituræa, and called, for the sake of distinction, Bethsaida Julias. [2] The second name had been given it in honor of Julia, the beautiful but infamous daughter of the Emperor Augustus. These half-heathen Herodian cities, with their imitative Greek architecture and adulatory Roman names, seem to have repelled rather than attracted the feet of Christ; and though much of His work was accomplished in the neighborhood of consider- able cities, we know of no city except Jerusalem in which He ever taught. But to the south of Bethsaida Julias was the green and narrow plain of El Batîhah, which, like the hills that close it round, was uninhabited then as now. Hitherward the little vessel steered its course, with its freight of weary and saddened hearts which sought repose. But private as the departure had been, it had not passed unobserved, and did not remain unknown. [3] It is but six miles' by sea from Capernaum to the retired and desolate shore which was their destination. The little vessel, evidently retarded by unfavora- ble winds, made its way slowly at no great distance from the shore, and by the time it reached its destination, the object which their Master's kindness had desired for His Apostles was completely frustrated. Some of the multitude had already outrun the vessel, and were thronging about the landing-place when the prow touched the pebbly shore; while in the distance were seen the thronging groups of Passover pilgrims, who were attracted out of their course by the increasing celebrity of this Unknown Prophet. [4] Jesus was touched with compassion for them, because they were as sheep not having a shepherd. We may conjecture from St. John that on reach- ing the land He and His disciples climbed the hill-side, and there waited a short time till the whole multitude had assembled. Then

---

[1] בֵּית צַיְדָה. The same root is found in the name *Sidon.*

[2] Jos. *Antt.* xviii. 2, § 1; *B. J.* iii. 10, § 7; Plin. *Hist. Nat.* v. 15, " In lacum se fundit, quem plures Genezaram vocant, xvi. mill. pass. longitudinis, vi. mill. lat. amœnis circumseptum oppidis, ab oriente, *Juliade,*" [241] &c.

[3] Mark vi. 33, εἶδον αὐτοὺς ὑπάγοντας; Luke ix. 11, γνόντες; Matt xiv 13, ἀκούσαντες.

[4] Mark vi. 33; John vi. 2, 4.

descending among them He taught them many things, preaching to them of the kingdom of heaven, and healing their sick.[1]

The day wore on; already the sun was sinking towards the western hills,[2] yet still the multitude lingered, charmed by that healing voice and by those holy words. The evening would soon come, and after the brief Oriental twilight, the wandering crowd, who in their excitement had neglected even the necessities of life, would find themselves in the darkness, hungry and afar from every human habitation. The disciples began to be anxious lest the day should end in some unhappy catastrophe, which would give a fresh handle to the already embittered enemies of their Lord. But His compassion had already forestalled their considerate anxiety, and had suggested the difficulty to the mind of Philip.[3] A little consultation took place. To buy even a mouthful apiece for such a multitude would require at least two hundred denarii (more than £7); and even supposing that they possessed such a sum in their common purse, there was now neither time nor opportunity to make the necessary purchases. Andrew hereupon mentioned that there was a little boy there who had five barley-loaves and two small fishes, but he only said it in a despairing way, and, as it were, to show the utter helplessness of the only suggestion which occurred to him.[4]

"Make the men sit down," was the brief reply.

---

[1] "The sixth chapter of St. John's Gospel," says Mr. Bruce, "is full of marvels; it tells of a great miracle, a great enthusiasm, a great storm, a great sermon, a great apostasy, and great trial of faith and fidelity endured by the Twelve" (*Training of the Twelve*, p. 120).

[2] The ὀψία of Matt. xiv. 15 means the δείλη ὀψία or afternoon; the ὀψία of verse 23 is the second or later evening, after six o'clock.

[3] Why He should have tested the faith of Philip in particular is not mentioned; it is simply one of the unexplained touches which always occur in the narratives of witnesses familiar with their subject. Prof. Blunt, in his interesting *Undesigned Coincidences*, suggests that it was because " Philip was of Bethsaida;" this can have nothing to do with it, for Philip's native village (now Ain et-Tâbijah) was at the opposite side of the Lake. Reland's discovery (*Palaest.*, p. 564) that there were *two* Bethsaidas (one, Bethsaida Julias, at the north end of the Lake, and the other a fishing village on its western side) solves all the difficulties of Luke ix. 10 (where, however, the Cod. Sinaiticus, and the Nitrian recension of the Syriac edited by Cureton, omit the allusion to Bethsaida), Mark vi. 45, &c. (See Robinson, *Bibl. Researches*, ii. 413; Stanley, *Sin. and Pal.*, p. 382, &c.)

[4] If this παιδάριον (John vi. 9) was, as may be inferred from Mark vi. 38, *in attendance upon the Apostles*, it is very likely that he too, like Philip and Andrew, was a native of the western Bethsaida; and then perhaps our Lord's question may have been meant to see whether the simple-hearted Philip had faith enough to mention this possible resource. The ἕν is probably spurious; it is not found in א, B, D, L.

Wondering and expectant, the Apostles bade the multitude recline. as for a meal, on the rich green grass which in that pleasant spring-time clothed the hill-sides. They arranged them in companies of fifty and a hundred, and as they sat in these orderly groups upon the grass, the gay red and blue and yellow colors of the clothing which the poorest Orientals wear, called up in the imagination of St. Peter a multitude of flower-beds in some well-cultivated garden.[1] And then, standing in the midst of His guests — glad-hearted at the work of mercy which He intended to perform — Jesus raised His eyes to heaven, gave thanks,[2] blessed the loaves,[3] broke them into pieces, and began to distribute them[4] to His disciples, and they to the multitude; and the two fishes He divided among them all. It was a humble but a sufficient, and to hungry wayfarers a delicious meal. And when all were abundantly satisfied, Jesus, not only to show His disciples the extent and reality of what had been done, but also to teach them the memorable lesson that wastefulness, even of miraculous power, is wholly alien to the Divine economy, bade them gather up the fragments that remained, that nothing might be lost. The symmetrical arrangement of the multitude showed that about five thousand men, besides women and children, had been fed,[5] and yet twelve baskets[6] were filled with what was over and above to them that had eaten.

---

[1] $\dot{\alpha}\nu\acute{\epsilon}\pi\epsilon\delta\alpha\nu$ $\pi\rho\alpha\delta\iota\alpha\grave{\iota}$ $\pi\rho\alpha\delta\iota\alpha\acute{\iota}$, "they reclined *in parterres*" (*areolatim*), is the picturesque expression of St. Mark (vi. 40), who here, as throughout his Gospel, doubtless reflects the impressions of St. Peter. The word $\pi\rho\alpha\delta\iota\alpha\grave{\iota}$ occurs here only, but Theophylact's definition of it (*ad loc.*) is exactly that of a parterre $(\tau\grave{\alpha}$ $\dot{\epsilon}\nu$ $\tau o\tilde{\iota}s$ $\varkappa\acute{\eta}\pi o\iota s$ $\delta\iota\acute{\alpha}\varphi o\rho\alpha$ $\varkappa\acute{o}\mu\mu\alpha\tau\alpha$ $\dot{\epsilon}\nu$ $o\tilde{\iota}s$ $\varphi\upsilon\tau\epsilon\acute{\upsilon}o\nu\tau\alpha\iota$ $\delta\iota\acute{\alpha}\varphi o\rho\alpha$ . . . $\lambda\acute{\alpha}\chi\alpha\nu\alpha)$. The $\delta\upsilon\mu\pi\acute{o}\delta\iota\alpha$ $\delta\upsilon\mu\pi\acute{o}\delta\iota\alpha$ of the previous verse describes the orderly social grouping, *catervatim*. The words are repeated by a Hebraism, which is, however, in accordance with simple Greek idiom (cf. $\mu\acute{\upsilon}\rho\iota\alpha$ $\mu\acute{\upsilon}\rho\iota\alpha$, Æsch. *Pers.* 981; Winer, *New Test. Gram.*, p. 264, sixth edition, E. Tr.). Lightfoot compares the Hebrew שׁוּרוֹת שׁוּרוֹת used to describe the quincuncial order of vines, and of pupils in a *kerem* or "vineyard," *i. e.* school.

[2] John vi. 11, $\epsilon\dot{\upsilon}\chi\alpha\rho\iota\delta\tau\acute{\eta}\delta\alpha s$.

[3] Luke ix. 16, $\epsilon\dot{\upsilon}\lambda\acute{o}\lambda\eta\delta\epsilon\nu$ $\alpha\dot{\upsilon}\tau o\grave{\upsilon}s$.

[4] $\varkappa\alpha\tau\acute{\epsilon}\varkappa\lambda\alpha\delta\epsilon$ . . . $\varkappa\alpha\grave{\iota}$ $\dot{\epsilon}\delta\acute{\iota}\delta o\upsilon$ (Mark vi. 41). The aorist implies the instan-taneous — the imperfect, the continuous act. The fact is interesting, as giving us the only glimpse permitted us of the mode in which the miracle was wrought. The multiplication of the loaves and fishes evidently took place in the hands of Christ between the acts of breaking and of distributing the bread.

[5] Women and children would not sit down with the men, but sit or stand apart. Probably in that lonely and distant spot their numbers would not be great.

[6] It has been repeatedly noticed that all the Evangelists alike here use $\varkappa\acute{o}\varphi\iota\nu o\iota$ for the common *wicker-baskets* ($\dot{\alpha}\gamma\gamma\epsilon\tilde{\iota}o\nu$ $\pi\lambda\epsilon\varkappa\tau\acute{o}\nu$, Suid., perhaps corresponding to the Hebrew *salsillôth*, Jer. vi. 9) in which these fragments were collected: and

The miracle produced a profound impression. It was exactly in accordance with the current expectation, and the multitude began to whisper to each other that this must undoubtedly be "that Prophet which should come into the world;" the Shiloh of Jacob's blessing; the Star and the Sceptre of Balaam's vision; the Prophet like unto Moses to whom they were to hearken; perhaps the Elijah promised by the dying breath of ancient prophecy;[1] perhaps the Jeremiah of their tradition, come back to reveal the hiding-place of the Ark, and the Urim, and the sacred fire. Jesus marked their undisguised admiration, and the danger that their enthusiasm might break out by force, and precipitate His death by open rebellion against the Roman government in the attempt to make Him a king. He saw too that His disciples seemed to share this worldly and perilous excitement. The time was come, therefore, for instant action. By the exercise of direct authority, He compelled[2] His disciples to embark in their boat, and cross the Lake before Him in the direction of Capernaum or the western Bethsaida.[3] A little gentle constraint was necessary, for they were naturally unwilling to leave Him among the excited multitude on that lonely shore, and if anything great was going to happen to Him they felt a right to be present. On the other hand, it was more easy for Him to dismiss the multitude when they had

---

the word σπυρίδες, or "rope-baskets," when they speak of the feeding of the four thousand. If any one thinks it important to ask where the κόφινοι came from, the answer is that they were the very commonest possession of Jews, who constantly used them to prevent their food, &c., from being polluted. "Judaeis, quorum *cophinus* fenumque supellex"[242] (Juv., *Sat.* iii. 14; cf. vi. 542). Even in Palestine, overrun as it was at this period with heathens, such a precaution might be necessary. There was a Jewish festival named *Cophinus* (Sidonius, *Ep.* vii. 6, quoted by Mr. Mayor on Juv. *l. c.*).

[1] Gen. xlix. 10; Numb. xxiv. 17; Deut. xviii. 15, 18; Mal. iv. 5. I adopt the current Jewish explanations.

[2] ἠνάγκασε (Matthew, Mark). How unintelligible would this word be but for the fact mentioned by John vi. 15; how clear does it become when the fact there mentioned is before us; and again how imperfect would be our comprehension of what took place if we had the narrative of John alone.

[3] Compare Mark vi. 45 with John vi. 17. Tell Hûm (Capernaum) and Bethsaida (Ain et-Tâbijah) are so near together that they might make for either as was most convenient, and indeed, since the landing-place at Bethsaida was the more convenient of the two, it might be considered as the harbor of Capernaum. On the other hand, the hypothesis of Thomson and others that there was only one Bethsaida (viz., Julias) falls to the ground if we compare Mark vi. 45 ("*unto the other side*, towards Bethsaida") with Luke ix. 10, which shows that they were already at Bethsaida Julias — except, indeed, on the unlikely and far-fetched notion (adopted by Wieseler, *Chron. Syn.* p. 249; Lange, *Life of Christ*, iii. 138) that their plan was to coast along, touch at Bethsaida Julias, there take up our Lord, and then proceed to the other Bethsaida.

seen that His own immediate friends and disciples had been sent away.

So in the gathering dusk He gradually and gently succeeded in persuading the multitude to leave Him,[1] and when all but the most enthusiastic had streamed away to their homes or caravans, He suddenly left the rest, and fled from them[2] to the hill-top alone to pray. He was conscious that a solemn and awful crisis of His day on earth was come, and by communing with His Heavenly Father, He would nerve His soul for the stern work of the morrow, and the bitter conflict of many coming weeks. Once before He had spent in the mountain solitudes a night of lonely prayer, but then it was before the choice of His beloved Apostles, and the glad tidings of His earliest and happiest ministry. Far different were the feelings with which the Great High Priest now climbed the rocky stairs of that great mountain altar which in His temple of the night seemed to lift Him nearer to the stars of God. The murder of His beloved Forerunner brought home to His soul more nearly the thought of death; nor was He deceived by this brief blaze of a falsely-founded popularity, which on the next day He meant to quench. The storm which now began to sweep over the barren hills; the winds that rushed howling down the ravines; the Lake before Him buffeted into tempestuous foam; the little boat which — as the moonlight struggled through the rifted clouds — He saw tossing beneath Him on the laboring waves, were all too sure an emblem of the altered aspects of His earthly life. But there on the desolate hill-top, in that night of storm, He could gain strength and peace and happiness unspeakable; for there He was alone with God. And so over that figure, bowed in lonely prayer upon the hills, and over those toilers upon the troubled Lake, the darkness fell and the great winds blew.[3]

Hour after hour passed by. It was now the fourth watch of the night;[4] the ship had traversed but half of its destined course; it was

---

[1] Mark vi. 45, ἀπολύει, contrasted with the aorist ἀπόλυσον in verse 36.

[2] That some lingered we infer from John vi. 22. I have adopted the reading φεύγει in John vi. 15, with ℵ and the Vulgate, instead of ἀνεχώρησεν. The narrative gives the impression that the excitement of the multitude, and the necessity for exertion on the part of Jesus, were greater than is fully told. But even the received reading, ἀνεχώρησεν, involves the same conception. (Cf. Matt. ii. 12, 22.)

[3] John vi. 17, 18, κατέλαβεν αὐτοὺς ἡ σκοτία. (ℵ, D.)

[4] Between three and six; the Jews at this time had mainly given up their own division of the night into three watches (Judg. vii. 19), and adopted the four Roman watches between six p. m. and six a. m. They had only rowed twenty-five furlongs, and the Lake is about forty wide (Jos. B. J. iii. 10, § 7).

dark, and the wind was contrary, and the waves boisterous, and they were distressed with toiling at the oar,[1] and above all there was no one with them now to calm and save, for Jesus was alone upon the land. Alone upon the land, and they were tossing on the perilous sea ; but all the while He saw and pitied them, and at last, in their worst extremity, they saw a gleam in the darkness, and an awful figure, and a fluttering robe, and One drew near them, treading upon the ridges of the sea,[2] but seemed as if He meant to pass them by; and they cried out in terror at the sight, thinking that it was a phantom[3] that walked upon the waves. And through the storm and darkness to them — as so often to us, when, amid the darknesses of life, the ocean seems so great, and our little boats so small — there thrilled that Voice of peace, which said, "It is I: be not afraid."

That Voice stilled their terrors, and at once they were eager to receive Him into the ship;[4] but Peter's impetuous love — the strong yearning of him who, in his despairing self-consciousness, had cried out "Depart from me!" — now cannot even await His approach, and he passionately exclaims —

"Lord, if it be Thou, bid me come unto Thee on the water."

"Come!"

And over the vessel's side into the troubled waves he sprang, and while his eye was fixed on his Lord, the wind might toss his hair, and the spray might drench his robes, but all was well; but when, with wavering faith, he glanced from Him to the furious waves, and to the gulfy blackness underneath, then he began to sink,[5] and in an accent of despair — how unlike his former confidence! — he faintly cried, "Lord, save me!"[6] Nor did Jesus fail. Instantly, with a

---

[1] Mark vi. 48, *ἰδὼν αὐτοὺς βασανιζομένους ἐν τῷ ἐλαύνειν* — a very strong expression. Some see a difficulty in John vi. 17, " and Jesus had not come to them," and indeed it furnishes the chief ground for the suggestion that He had designed to join them at or near Bethsaida Julias; but surely it may be merely proleptic (He had not *yet* come, as He did immediately afterwards), involving perhaps in the mind of the Evangelist the silent thought that *"man's extremity* is God's opportunity." *οὔπω* is indeed the actual reading of א, B, D, L, but even *οὐκ* would be quite in accordance with St. John's manner.

[2] Job. ix. 8.

[3] Mark vi. 49, *φάντασμα*, a mere unsubstantial appearance; *τὸ μὴ ὂν ἀληθὲς ἀλλὰ σχήματι* [243] (Hesych.). Cf. Luke xxiv. 37.

[4] John vi. 21, *ἤθελον οὖν λαβεῖν* — *i. e.*, they wished to do so, and of course did. Cf. *θέλετε ποιεῖν* (John viii. 44).

[5] How unlike forgery, or falsehood, or myth, is this !

[6] "In this moment of peril," as Archbishop Trench strikingly observes, "his swimmer's art (John xxi. 7) profits him nothing ; for there is no mingling in this way of nature and grace " (*On the Miracles*, p. 299). Cf. Ps. xciv. 18.

smile of pity, He stretched out His hand, and grasped the hand of His drowning disciple, with the gentle rebuke, "O thou of little faith, why didst thou doubt?" And so, his love satisfied, but his over-confidence rebuked, they climbed — the Lord and His abashed Apostle — into the boat; and the wind lulled, and amid the ripple of waves upon a moonlit shore, they were at the haven where they would be; and all — the crew as well as His disciples — were filled with deeper and deeper amazement, and some of them, addressing Him by a title which Nathanael alone had applied to Him before, exclaimed, "Truly Thou art the Son of God."

Let us pause a moment longer over this wonderful narrative, perhaps of all others the most difficult for our feeble faith to believe or understand. Some have tried in various methods to explain away its miraculous character; they have labored to show that ἐπὶ τὴν θάλασσαν [1] may mean no more than that Jesus walked along the shore parallel to the vessel; or even that, in the darkness, the Apostles may have thought at first that He was, or had been, walking upon the sea. Such subterfuges are idle and superfluous. If any man find himself unable to believe in miracles — if he even think it wrong to try and acquire the faith which accepts them — then let him be thoroughly convinced in his own mind, and cling honestly to the truth as he conceives it. It is not for us, or for any man, to judge another: to his own Master he standeth or falleth. But let him not attempt to foist such disbelief into the plain narrative of the Evangelists. That *they intended* to describe an amazing miracle is indisputable to any one who carefully reads their words; and, as I have said before, if, believing in God, we believe in a Divine Providence over the lives of men — and, believing in that Divine Providence, believe in the miraculous, and believing in the miraculous, accept as truth the resurrection of our Lord Jesus Christ — and, believing that resurrection, believe that He was indeed the Son of God — then, however deeply we may realize the beauty and the wonder and the power of natural laws, we realize yet more deeply the power of Him who holds those laws, and all which they have evolved, in the hollow of His hand; and to us the miraculous, when thus attested, will be in no way more stupendous than the natural, nor shall we find it an impossible conception that He who sent His Son to earth to die for us should have put all authority into His hand.

---

[4] John vi. 19. Perhaps the better reading (as in the other Gospels) is ἐπὶ τῆς θαλάσσης, [244] which has the high authority of ℵ, B, C, D.

So then if, like Peter, we fix our eyes on Jesus, we too may walk triumphantly over the swelling waves of disbelief, and unterrified amid the rising winds of doubt; but if we turn away our eyes from Him in whom we have believed — if, as it is so easy to do, and as we are so much tempted to do, we look rather at the power and fury of those terrible and destructive elements than at Him who can help and save — then we too shall inevitably sink. Oh, if we feel, often and often, that the water-floods threaten to drown us, and the deep to swallow up the tossed vessel of our Church and Faith, may it again and again be granted us to hear amid the storm and the darkness, and the voices prophesying war, those two sweetest of the Saviour's utterances —

" Fear not. Only believe."

" It is I. Be not afraid."

CHAPTER XXX.

THE DISCOURSE AT CAPERNAUM.

"Gratia ejus non consumitur morsibus." [245] — AUGUSTINE.

THE dawn of that day broke on one of the saddest episodes of our Saviour's life. It was the day in the synagogue at Capernaum on which He deliberately scattered the mists and exhalations of such spurious popularity as the Miracle of the Loaves had gathered about His person and His work, and put not only His idle followers, but some even of His nearer disciples to a test under which their love for Him entirely failed. That discourse in the synagogue forms a marked crisis in His career. It was followed by manifestations of surprised dislike which were as the first mutterings of that storm of hatred and persecution which was henceforth to burst over His head.

We have seen already that some of the multitude, filled with vague wonder and insatiable curiosity, had lingered on the little plain by Bethsaida Julias that they might follow the movements of Jesus, and share in the blessings and triumphs of which they expected an immediate manifestation. They had seen Him dismiss His disciples, and had perhaps caught glimpses of Him as He climbed the hill alone; they had observed that the wind was contrary, and that no other boat but that of the Apostles had left the shore; they made sure, therefore, of finding Him somewhere on the hills above the plain. Yet when the morning dawned they saw no trace of Him either on plain or hill. Meanwhile some little boats — perhaps driven across by the same gale which had retarded the opposite course of the disciples [1] — had arrived from Tiberias. They availed themselves of these to cross over to Capernaum; and there, already in the early morning, they found Him after all the fatigues and agitations of yesterday — after the day of sad tidings and ceaseless toil, after the night of stormy solitude and ceaseless prayer — calmly seated, and calmly teaching, in the familiar synagogue. [2]

---

[1] Blunt, *Undes. Coincidences*, p. 292.

[2] And even this teaching must have been preceded by works of healing if Matt. xiv. 34—36 be in strictly chronological sequence; but a comparison of these verses with Mark vi. 53—56, would seem to show that they refer more to a period than to a particular day.

" Rabbi, when didst thou get hither?" is the expression of their natural surprise; but it is met with perfect silence. The miracle of walking on the water was one of necessity and mercy; it in no way concerned them; it was not in any way intended for them; nor was it mainly or essentially as a worker of miracles that Christ wished to claim their allegiance or convince their minds. And, therefore, reading their hearts, knowing that they were seeking Him in the very spirit which He most disliked, He quietly drew aside the veil of perhaps half-unconscious hypocrisy which hid them from themselves, and reproached them for seeking Him only for what they could get from Him — " not because ye saw signs, but because ye ate of the loaves and were satisfied." He who never rejected the cry of the sufferer, or refused to answer the question of the faithful — He who would never break the bruised reed, or quench the smoking flax — at once rejected the false eye-service of mean self-interest and vulgar curiosity. Yet He added for their sakes the eternal lesson, " Labor ye not for the meat which perisheth, but for the meat which remaineth to eternal life, which the Son of Man shall give you; for Him the Father — even God — hath sealed."

It seems as if at first they were touched and ashamed. He had read their hearts aright, and they ask Him, " What are we to do that we may work the works of God?"

"*This* is the work of God, that ye believe on Him whom He hath sent." " But what *sign* would Jesus give them that they should believe in Him? Their fathers ate the manna in the wilderness, which David had called bread from heaven."[1] The inference was obvious. Moses had given them manna from heaven; Jesus as yet — they hinted — had only given them barley-loaves of earth. But if he were the true Messiah, was He not, according to all the legends of their nation, to enrich and crown them, and to banquet them on pomegranates from Eden, and " a vineyard of red wine," and upon the flesh of Behemoth and Leviathan, and the great bird Bar Juchne?[2] Might not the very psalm which they had quoted have taught them how worse than useless it would have been if Jesus had given them manna, which, in their coarse literalism, they supposed to be in reality angels' food? Is not David in that psalm expressly showing that to grant them one such blessing was only to make them ask

---

[1] Ps. lxxviii. 24.

[2] For the Rabbinical dreams on this subject, see Buxtorf, *Syn. Jud.*, cap. 50; Bartolocci, *Bibl. Rabb.* i. 511—514; Lightfoot, *Hor. Hebr.*, p. 552. On the manna which was supposed to " serve to the appetite of the eater, and temper itself to every man's liking," see Wisd. xvi. 20, 21.

greedily for more, and that if God had given their fathers more, it was only because "they believed not in God, and put not their trust in His help;" but "while the meat was yet in their mouths, the heavy wrath of God came upon them, and slew the mightiest of them, and smote down the chosen men that were in Israel." And does not David show that in spite of, and before, and after, this wrathful granting to them to the full of their own hearts' lusts, so far from believing and being humble they only sinned yet more and more against Him, and provoked Him more and more? Had not all the past history of their nation proved decisively that faith must rest on deeper foundations than signs and miracles, and that the evil heart of unbelief must be stirred by nobler emotions than astonishment at the outstretched hand and the mighty arm?

But Jesus led them at once to loftier regions than those of historical conviction. He tells them that He who had given them the manna was not Moses, but God; and that the manna was only in poetic metaphor bread from heaven; but that His Father, the true giver, was giving them the true bread from heaven even now — even the bread of God which came down from heaven, and was giving life to the world.[1]

Their minds still fastened to mere material images — their hopes still running on mere material benefits — they ask for this bread from heaven as eagerly as the woman of Samaria had asked for the water which quenches all thirst. " Lord, now and always give *us* this bread."

Jesus said to them, "I am the bread of life. He that cometh to me shall never hunger, and he that believeth on me shall never thirst;" and He proceeds to point out to them that He came to do the Father's will, and that His will was that all who came to His Son should have eternal life.

Then the old angry murmurs burst out again — not this time from the vulgar-minded multitude, but from His old opponents the leading Jews[2] — "How could He say that He came down from Heaven? How could He call Himself the bread of life? Was He not Jesus, the son of Joseph, the carpenter of Nazareth?"

Jesus never met these murmurs about His supposed parentage and place of birth by revealing to the common crowds the high mystery of His earthly origin. He thought not equality with God a thing to be seized by Him. He was in no hurry to claim His own Divinity,

---

[1] "The bread of God is *that* which cometh down," &c., not "*he*," as in the English version.

[2] John vi. 41, 52, οἱ Ἰουδαῖοι.

or demand the homage which was its due. He would let the splendor of His Divine nature dawn on men gradually, not at first in all its noonday brightness, but gently as the light of morning through His word and works. In the fullest and deepest sense " *He emptied Himself of His glory.*" [1]

But He met the murmurers, as He always did, by a stronger, fuller, clearer declaration of the very truth which they rejected. It was thus that He had dealt with Nicodemus; it was thus that He had taught the woman of Samaria; it was thus also that He answered the Temple doctors who arraigned His infringement of their sabbatic rules. But the timid Rabbi and the erring woman had been faithful enough and earnest enough to look deeper into His words and humbly seek their meaning, and so to be guided into truth. Not so with these listeners. God had drawn them to Christ, and they had rejected His gracious drawing without which they *could* not come. When Jesus reminded them that the manna was no life-giving substance, since their fathers had eaten thereof and were dead, but that He was Himself the bread of life, of which all who eat should live forever; and when, in language yet more startling, He added that the bread was *His flesh* which He would give for the life of the world — then, instead of seeking the true significance of that deep metaphor, they made it a matter of mere verbal criticism, and only wrangled [2] together about the idle question, "How can this man give us His flesh to eat?"

Thus they were carnally-minded, and to be carnally-minded is death. They did not seek the truth, and it was more and more taken from them. They had nothing, and therefore from them was taken even what they had. In language yet more emphatic, under figures yet more startling in their paradox, Jesus said to them, "Except ye eat the flesh of the Son of Man, and drink His blood, ye have no life in you;" [3] and again, as a still further enforcement

---

[1] See some striking remarks in Lynch's *Mornington Lectures*, p. 171.

[2] ἐμάχοντο (John vi. 52). How needless their literalism was may be seen from many Rabbinic passages in Lightfoot (*Hor. Hebr.* ad loc., pp. 553, 554) (and comp. Ps. xix. 10; cxix. 3; Isa. iii. 1; Prov. ix. 5; Ezek. ii. 8, 9, &c.), *e. g.*, " Every eating and drinking in the book of Ecclesiastes is to be understood of the law of good works" (*Midr. Koheleth*, 88, 4); " Israel shall eat the years of the Messiah; " " the just eat of the Shechinah," &c.

[3] It is uncertain whether in calling Himself the Son of Man Jesus meant *Ben Adam* (Job xxv. 6; Ps. viii. 4), *i. e.*, a representative of Humanity, or *Bar Enosh* (Dan. vii. 13). The Hebrew word *enosh* represents man in his weakness (*homo*). (Grätz, *Gesch. d. Judenth.* iii. 237.) It probably conveyed to His hearers a general conception of the Messiah as the representative of Humanity alike in its feebleness and in its glory (*v. supr.*, p. 140).

and expansion of the same great truths —" He that eateth of this bread shall live for ever."

No doubt the words were difficult, and, to those who came in a hard and false spirit, offensive; no doubt also the death and passion of our Saviour Christ, and the mystery of that Holy Sacrament, in which we spiritually eat His flesh and drink His blood, has enabled us more clearly to understand His meaning; yet there was in the words which He had used, enough, and more than enough, to shadow forth to every attentive hearer the great truth, already familiar to them from their own Law, that " Man doth not live by bread alone, but by every word that proceedeth out of the mouth of God ; " and the further truth that eternal life, the life of the soul, was to be found in the deepest and most intimate of all conceivable communions with the life and teaching of Him who spake. And it must be remembered that if the Lord's Supper has, for us, thrown a clearer light upon the meaning of this discourse, on the other hand the metaphors which Jesus used had not, to an educated Jew, one-hundredth part of the strangeness which they have to us. Jewish literature was exceedingly familiar with the symbolism which represented by " eating " an entire acceptance of and incorporation with the truth, and by " bread " a spiritual doctrine. Even the mere pictorial genius of the Hebrew language gave the clue to the right interpretation. Those who heard Christ in the synagogue of Capernaum must almost involuntarily have recalled similar expressions in their own prophets; and since the discourse was avowedly parabolic — since Jesus had expressly excluded all purely sensual and Judaic fancies — it is quite clear that much of their failure to comprehend Him rose not from the understanding, but from the will. His saying was hard, as St. Augustine remarks, only to the hard ; and incredible only to the incredulous. For if bread be the type of all *earthly* sustenance, then the " bread of heaven " may well express all *spiritual* sustenance, all that involves and supports eternal life. Now the lesson which He wished to teach them was *this* — that eternal life is in the Son of God. They, therefore, that would have eternal life must partake of the bread of heaven, or — to use the other and deeper image — must eat the flesh and drink the blood of the Son of Man.[1] They must *feed on Him in their hearts by faith.*

---

[1] The following profound remark of Von Ammon will help the reader to understand this chapter. " What is true," he says, " of the *bread of heaven,* is true also of the *flesh and blood of the Son of Man ;* for these predicates are only substitutes for the original image of the *bread of life,* and are subject to the same analogical explanations as this last is " (quoted by Lange, *Life of Christ,* iii. 157). " Believe,

They might accept or reject the truth which He was revealing to their consciences, but there could be no possible excuse for their pretended incapacity to understand its meaning.

There is a teaching which is, and is intended to be, not only instructive but probationary; of which the immediate purpose is not only to *teach*, but to *test*. Such had been the object of this memorable discourse. To comprehend it rightly required an effort not only of the understanding, but also of the will. It was *meant* to put an end to the merely selfish hopes of that " rabble of obtrusive chiliasts " whose irreverent devotion was a mere cloak for worldliness; it was *meant* also to place before the Jewish authorities words which they were too full of hatred and materialism to understand. But its sifting power went deeper than this. Some even of the disciples found the saying harsh and repulsive. They did not speak out openly, but Jesus recognized their discontent, and when He had left the synagogue, spoke to them, in this third and concluding part of His discourse,[1] at once more gently and less figuratively than He had done to the others. To these He prophesied of that future ascension, which should prove to them that He had indeed come down from heaven, and that the words about His flesh — which should then be taken into heaven — *could* only have a figurative meaning. Nay, with yet further compassion for their weakness, He intimated to them the significance of those strong metaphors in which He had purposely veiled His words from the curious eyes of selfishness and the settled malice of opposition. In one sentence which is surely the key-note of all that had gone before — in a sentence which surely renders nugatory much of the pseudo-mystical and impossibly-elaborate exegesis by which the plain meaning of this chapter has been obscured, He added —

" It is the spirit that quickeneth; the flesh profiteth nothing: *the words that I speak*[2] *unto you, they are spirit, and they are life.*" Why then had they found His words so hard? He tells them: it was because some of them believed not; it was because, as He had already told the Jews, the spirit of faith is a gift and grace of God,

---

and thou hast eaten," is the formula of St. Augustine ; " believe, and thou shalt eat," that of Calvin.

[1] It will be observed that verses 26—40 are addressed mainly to the multitude , verses 43—58 to the leading Jews ; verses 61—65 to the disciples.

[2] Or perhaps " have spoken," $\lambda\varepsilon\lambda\dot{\alpha}\lambda\eta\varkappa\alpha$ (א, B, C, D, L, most versions), &c. ; but I would not, with Stier and Alford, confine $\dot{\rho}\dot{\eta}\mu\alpha\tau\alpha$ merely to " my flesh " and " my blood."

which gift these murmurers were rejecting, against which grace they were struggling even now.[1]

And from that time many of them left Him; many who had hitherto sought Him, many who were not far from the kingdom of heaven. Even in the midst of crowds His life was to be lonelier thenceforth, because there would be fewer to know and love Him. In deep sadness of heart He addressed to the Twelve the touching question, "Will ye also go away?" It was Simon Peter whose warm heart spoke out impetuously for all the rest. He at least had rightly apprehended that strange discourse at which so many had stumbled. "Lord," he exclaims, "to whom shall we go? THOU HAST THE WORDS OF ETERNAL LIFE. But we believe and are sure that Thou art the Holy One of God."[2]

It was a noble confession, but at that bitter moment the heart of Jesus was heavily oppressed, and He only answered —

"Have not I chosen you twelve, and one of you is a devil?"[3]

The expression was terribly strong, and the absence of all direct parallels render it difficult for us to understand its exact significance. But although it was afterwards known that the reproach was aimed at Judas, yet it is doubtful whether at the actual time any were aware of this except the traitor himself.

---

[1] There seems to be a special reference to Judas in these words (ver. 66), and it seems very probable that the first obvious extinction of purely temporal Messianic hopes may have been with him the turning-point of that rejection which ended in his ultimate treachery.

[2] This, and not "that Christ, the Son of the living God"— a confession which was given for the first time some months *afterwards* — is almost undoubtedly the true reading. (א, B, C, D, L, &c.)

[3] The English version is unfortunate, because it does not maintain the distinction between διάβολος, the word here used, and δαιμόνιον, which it usually renders "devil"— *e. g.*, in "He has a devil." Euthymius here explains "devil" by either "servant of the devil" or "conspirator;" and the latter meaning seems very probable. Indeed, this very word (ἐπίβουλος) is used by the LXX. to render the Hebrew *Satan* in 1 Kings v. 4; 1 Sam. xxix. 4. I have already noticed how much more lightly the Jews (and indeed all Orientals to this day) used the word "Satan" than we do. This indeed may almost be called a *modus loquendi* among them, and if Jesus spoke in Aramaic, and used the word שָׂטָן, then the reproach is not one-tenth part so fearful as it sounds to us. Thus, the sons of Zeruiah are called a Satan to David (2 Sam. xix. 22), and Hadad is called a "Satan" to King Solomon (1 Kings xi. 23, where it is merely rendered "adversary"); and in Matt. xvi. 23, the word is applied to Peter himself. "When the ungodly curseth Satan" (*i. e.*, an enemy?), says the son of Sirach (xxi. 27), "he curseth his own soul." All this is important in many ways. Further, we may observe that διάβολος occurs by no means frequently in the New Testament. (*V. supra*, pp. 193, 263, 265.)

Many false or half-sincere disciples had left Him : might not these words have been graciously meant to furnish one more opportunity to the hard and impure soul of the man of Kerioth, so that before being plunged into yet deeper and more irreparable guilt, *he* might leave Him too? If so, the warning was rejected. In deadly sin against his own conscience, Judas stayed to heap up for himself wrath "against the day of wrath, and revelation of the righteous judgment of God."

CHAPTER XXXI.

GATHERING OPPOSITION.

Ἔξωθεν παραληφθεῖδαι ἄγραφοι κενοφώνιαι.[246] — JUSTINIAN, *Nov.* 146.

ALTHOUGH the discourse which we have just narrated formed a marked period in our Lord's ministry, and although from this time forward the clouds gather more and more densely about His course, yet it must not be supposed that this was the first occasion, even in Galilee, on which enmity against His person and teaching had been openly displayed.

1. The earliest traces of doubt and disaffection arose from the expression which He used on several occasions, "Thy sins be forgiven thee." It was in these words that He had addressed the woman that was a sinner, and the sick of the palsy. On both occasions the address had excited astonishment and disapproval, and at Simon's house, where this had found no *open* expression, and where no miracle had been wrought, Jesus gently substituted another expression.[1] But it was not so at the healing of the palsied man; there an open murmur had arisen among the Scribes and Pharisees, and there, revealing more of His true majesty, Jesus, by His power of working miracles, had vindicated His right to forgive sins.[2] The argument was unanswerable, for not only did the prevalent belief connect sickness in every instance with actual sin, but also it was generally maintained, even by the Rabbis, "that no sick man is healed from his disease until all his sins have been forgiven."[3] It was, therefore, in full accordance with their own notions that He who by His own

---

[1] Luke vii. 48—50. See p. 239.

[2] Matt. ix. 6; Mark ii. 10; Luke v. 24. (See p. 269.) "But as the little bubbling and gentle murmurs of the water are presages of a storm, and are more troublesome in their prediction than in their violence; so were the arguings of the Pharisees symptoms of a secret displeasure and an ensuing war; though at first represented in the civilities of question and scholastical discourses, yet they did but forerun vigorous objections and bold calumnies, which were the fruits of the next summer" (Jer. Taylor, *Life of Christ*, II. xii.).

[3] *Nedarîm*, f. 41, 1, in Schöttg., *Hor. Hebr.*, p. 93; Keim, *Gesch. Jesu*, ii. 300.

authority could heal diseases, could also, by His own authority, pronounce that sins were forgiven. It was true that they could hardly conceive of either healing or forgiveness conveyed in such irregular channels, and without the paraphernalia of sacrifices, and without the need of sacerdotal interventions.[1] But, disagreeable as such proceedings were to their well-regulated minds, the fact remained that the cures were actually wrought, and were actually attested by hundreds of living witnesses. It was felt, therefore, that this ground of opposition was wholly untenable, and it was tacitly abandoned. To urge that there was "blasphemy" in His expressions would only serve to bring into greater prominence that there was miracle in His acts.

2. Nor, again, do they seem to have pressed the charge, preserved for us only by our Lord's own allusion, that He was "a glutton and a wine-drinker."[2] The charge was too flagrantly false and malicious to excite any prejudice against one who, although He did not adopt the stern asceticism of John, yet lived a life of the extremest simplicity, and merely did what was done by the most scrupulous Pharisees in accepting the invitations to feasts, where He had constantly fresh opportunities of teaching and doing good. The calumny was, in fact, destroyed when He had shown that the men of that generation were like wayward and peevish children whom nothing could conciliate, charging Jesus with intemperance because He did not avoid an innocent festivity, and John with demoniac possession because he set his face against social corruptions.

3. Nor, once more, did they press the charge of His not fasting.[3] In making that complaint they had hoped for the powerful aid of John's disciples; but when these had been convinced, by the words of their own prophet, how futile and unreasonable was their complaint, the Pharisees saw that it was useless to found a charge upon the neglect of a practice which was not only unrecognized in the Mosaic law,[4] but which some of their own noblest and wisest teach-

---

[1] See Ewald, *Gesch. Christus*, p. 376.

[2] Matt. xi. 19; v. *supr.*, pp. 234, 248.

[3] Matt. xi. 16, 17. See p. 273.

[4] Except on the Great Day of Atonement. The *principle* of the answer given by Jesus to the disciples of John had already been recognized as to the four yearly fasts which seem to have become usual in the time of the prophet Zechariah (Zech. viii. 19). On the bi-weekly and other fasts of the Pharisees, see Buxtorf, *Syn. Jud.*, cap. xxx. It is curious that the most ancient of the Rabbinic treatises — the *Megillath Taanith*, written before the destruction of the Temple — contains merely a list of days on which it is *forbidden* to fast; at the end of it are a certain number of days on which fasting is recommended; *but this was no part of the original work* (Derenbourg, *Hist. de Pal.* 2).

ers had not encouraged.[1] The fact that Jesus did not require His disciples to fast would certainly cause no forfeiture of the popular sympathy, and could not be urged to His discredit even before a synagogue or a Sanhedrin.

4. A deeper and more lasting offence was caused, and a far more deadly opposition stimulated, by Christ's choice of Matthew as an Apostle, and by His deliberate tolerance of — it might almost be said preference for — the society of publicans and sinners.[2] Among the Jews of that day the distinctions of religious life created a barrier almost as strong as that of caste. No less a person than Hillel had said that " no ignorant person could save himself from sin, and no ' *man of the people* ' be pious." [3] A scrupulous Jew regarded the multitude of his own nation who " knew not the Law " as accursed ; and just as every Jew, holding himself to be a member of a royal generation and a peculiar people, looked on the heathen world with the sovereign disdain of an exclusiveness founded on the habits of a thousand years, so the purist faction regarded their more careless and offending brethren as being little, if at all, better than the very heathen.[4] Yet here was one who mingled freely and familiarly — mingled without one touch of hauteur or hatred — among offensive publicans and flagrant

---

[1] *Ex. gr.*, Simeon the Just, who made the Law, Worship, and Charity the three bases of the world (*Abhôth*, i. 2), and " sa douce et vraie piété s'opposait à toute exagération, et surtout aux abstinences rigoureuses " [247] (Derenbourg, *Hist. Pal.* 51).

[2] Matt. ix. 11 ; xi. 19 ; Luke v. 30 ; vii. 34 ; xix. 7. See p. 271.

[3] לֹא עַם הָאָרֶץ חָסִיד (*Pirke Abhôth*, ii. 5). In the first clause, " no ignorant person " is literally " no empty cistern " (בּוֹר). The expression *am ha-arets*, " people of the land " (v. *ante*, p. 90), is exceedingly common in the Rabbis, and marks the arrogantly tyrannous sacerdotalism of the learned class (cf. John vii. 49). At the end of the Mishnaic tract *Horajôth* we find that a Priest takes precedence of a serving Levite, a Levite of other Israelites, an Israelite of a bastard (*Mamser*), a Mamser of the *Nethinim* (Josh. ix. 27), a Nethin of an alien (*Ger*), a Ger of a freedman ; but if the Mamser be a pupil of the Rabbis, and the High Priest an ignoramus (*am ha-arets*), then such a Mamser has the precedence of the High Priest ! " (See Lightfoot, *Hor. Hebr. in* Matt. xxiii. 14.) Their boasts as to the dignity of a *Talmîd chakam* are like those of the Stoics, which proved so amusing to Horace (*Ep.* i. 1, 106 ; Cicero, *Pro Muraena*, 29). The definition of an *am ha-arets* given in *Sota*, f. 21, 1, is one who either does not repeat the daily *Krishma*, or does not wear *tephillin*, or *tsîtsith*, or does not *wait on the learned*. See Schöttgen, *Hor. Hebr. in* John vii. 49, for yet stronger specimens of this intense spirit of Pharisaism which it was the very object of Jesus to replace by a nobler Humanitarianism (Acts x. 34). There is perhaps no kind of caste-feeling more hateful than the self-glorifying arrogance of a pseudo-erudition.

[4] Our Lord, when He said, " Let him be unto thee as a heathen man and a publican " (Matt. xviii. 17), was simply adopting a current form of expression. The amazing virulence of Jewish exclusiveness is illustrated in *Shabbath*, xiv. 4 ; *Babha Kama*, viii. 6, 4 ; 2 Esdras vi. 55, &c. (Gfrörer, *Jahrh. d. Heils* i. 214.)

sinners. Nay, more, He suffered women, out of whom had been cast seven devils, to accompany Him in His journeys, and harlots to bathe His feet with tears! How different from the Pharisees, who held that there was pollution in the mere touch of those who had themselves been merely touched by the profane populace, and who had laid down the express rule that no one ought to receive a guest into his house if he suspected him of being a sinner![1]

Early in His ministry, Jesus, with a divine and tender irony, had met the accusation by referring them to His favorite passage of Scripture—that profound utterance of the prophet Hosea, of which He bade them "go and learn" the meaning—"I will have mercy and not sacrifices." He had further rebuked at once their unkindliness and their self-satisfaction by the proverb, "They that be whole need not a physician, but they that are sick." The objection did not, however, die away. In His later days, when he was journeying to Jerusalem, these incessant enemies again raised the wrathful and scornful murmur, "This man receiveth sinners and eateth with them;"[2] and then it was that Jesus answered them and justified His ways, and revealed more clearly and more lovingly than had ever been done before the purpose of God's love towards repentant sinners, in those three exquisite and memorable parables, the lost sheep, the lost piece of money, and, above all, the prodigal son. Drawn from the simplest elements of daily experience, these parables, and the last especially, illustrated, and illustrated for ever, in a rising climax of tenderness, the deepest mysteries of the divine compassion—the joy that there is in heaven over one sinner that repenteth.[3] Where, in the entire range of human literature, sacred or profane, can anything be found so terse, so luminous, so full of infinite tenderness—so faithful in the picture

---

[1] In *Bab. Berachôth*, 43, 6, one of the six things forbidden to the pupils of the wise is "to sit at table in a company of the unlearned." Other instances of insolent self-assertion against the *am ha-arets* are given in Gfrörer, i. 191.

[2] διεγόγγυζον (Luke xv. 2), "kept angrily muttering to each other." (See *supra*, p. 270.) The contrast of this conduct with that of the Pharisees becomes more striking when we remember the extraordinary and almost ludicrous precautions which they took to secure the impossible end of avoiding every conceivable legal impurity in their *chabhoorôth*, or social meals. How ineradicable the feeling was, we may see most strikingly by observing that it still infected even some of the disciples and apostles long years after the resurrection of their Lord, who contended with Peter, saying, "Thou wentest in to men uncircumcised, and didst eat with them!" (Acts xi. 3)—the exact echo of the caste-feeling here described (cf. Gal. ii. 12.)

[3] In the lost sheep we have the stupid, bewildered sinner; in the lost drachma, the sinner stamped with God's image, but lying lost, useless, and ignorant of his own worth; in the prodigal son, the conscious and willing sinner.

which it furnishes of the consequences of sin, yet so merciful in the hope which it affords to amendment and penitence — as this little story? How does it summarize the consolations of religion and the sufferings of life! All sin and punishment, all penitence and forgiveness, find their best delineation in these few brief words. The radical differences of temperament and impulse which separate different classes of men — the spurious independence of a restless free-will — the preference of the enjoyments of the present to all hopes of the future — the wandering far away from that pure and peaceful region which is indeed our home, in order to let loose every lower passion in the riotous indulgence which wastes and squanders the noblest gifts of life — the brief continuance of those fierce spasms of forbidden pleasure — the consuming hunger, the scorching thirst, the helpless slavery, the unutterable degradation, the uncompassionated anguish that must inevitably ensue — where have these myriad-times-repeated experiences of sin and sorrow been ever painted — though here painted in a few touches only — by a hand more tender and more true than in the picture of that foolish boy demanding prematurely the share which he claims of his father's goods; journeying into a far country, wasting his substance with riotous living; suffering from want in the mighty famine; forced to submit to the foul infamy of feeding swine, and fain to fill his belly with the swine-husks which no man gave?[1] And then the coming to himself, the memory of his father's meanest servants who had enough and to spare, the return homewards, the agonized confession, the humble, contrite, heart-broken entreaty, and that never-to-be-equalled climax which, like a sweet voice from heaven, has touched so many million hearts to penitence and tears —

"And he arose and came to his father. But when he was yet a great way off his father saw him and had compassion, and ran, and fell on his neck, and kissed him. And the son said unto him, Father, I have sinned against heaven, and in thy sight, and am no more worthy to be called thy son. But the father said to the servants, Bring forth the best robe and put it on him, and put a ring on his hand and shoes

---

[1] This conception of ignominy would be far more intense to a Jew than to us. The Jews detested swine so much, that they would only speak of a pig euphemistically as *dabhar acheer,* "another thing." The husks, $\varkappa\varepsilon\rho\acute{\alpha}\tau\iota\alpha$, are the long bean-like pods of the carob-tree, or Egyptian fig (*Ceratonia siliqua,* Linn.). I have tasted them in Palestine; they are stringy, sweetish, coarse, and utterly unfit for human sustenance. They are sold by fruiterers in Paris, and are said to be used in distilling *maraschino.* The tree was called the "locust-tree," from the mistaken notion that its $\varkappa\varepsilon\rho\acute{\alpha}\tau\iota\alpha$ are the $\acute{\alpha}\varkappa\rho\acute{\iota}\delta\varepsilon\varsigma$ on which St. John fed (Matt. iii. 4; Lev. xi. 22). $\dot{\varepsilon}\delta\acute{\iota}\delta ov$, either "*ever gave*" or "*chose to give*" to him.

on his feet: and bring hither the fatted calf and kill it; and let us eat and be merry: for this my son was dead and is alive again, was lost and is found."

And since no strain could rise into sweeter and nobler tenderness — since death itself could reveal no lovelier or more consolatory lesson than it conveys to sinful man — to us it might seem that this is the true climax of the parable, and that here it *should* end as with the music of angel harps. And here it would have ended had the mystery of human malice and perversity been other than it is. But the conclusion of it bears most directly on the very circumstances that called it forth. The angry murmur of the Pharisees and Scribes had shown how utterly ignorant they were, in their cold dead hardness and pride of heart, that, in the sight of God, the tear of one truly repentant sinner is transcendently dearer than the loveless and fruitless formalism of a thousand Pharisees. Little did they suspect that penitence can bring the very harlot and publican into closer communion with their Maker than the combined excellence of a thousand vapid and respectable hypocrisies. And therefore it was that Jesus added how the elder son came in, and was indignant at the noise of merriment, and was angry at that ready forgiveness, and reproached the tender heart of his father, and dragged up again in their worst form the forgiven sins of this brother whom he would not acknowledge, and showed all the narrow unpardoning malignity of a heart which had mistaken external rectitude for holy love.[1] Such self-righteous malice, such pitiless and repulsive respectability, is an evil more inveterate — a sore more difficult to probe, and more hard to cure — than open disobedience and passionate sin. And truly, when we read this story, and meditate deeply over all that it implies, we may, from our hearts, thank God that He who can bring good out of the worst evil — honey out of the slain lion, and water out of the flinty rock — could, even from an exhibi-

---

[1] There are several touches in the original which a translation can hardly preserve, but which show the deepest insight into the angry human heart in all its mean jealousies and rancors — *e. g.*, the sharp indignant ἰδού (See!) with which the elder son begins his expostulation ; the inability to recognize his free service as anything better than a constant slavery (ἐμοὶ τοσαῦτα ἔτη δουλεύω); the position of ἐμοὶ ("you never gave *me* even a kid that *I* might enjoy myself with *my* friends!"); the use of "*this son of yours*" instead of "my brother;" the exaggerated and concentrated malignity of the ὁ καταφαγών σου τὸν βίον μετὰ πορνῶν,[248] describing his brother's wasted life in its worst and grossest form. This brutally uncharitable desire to make the worst of sin repented of, is the basest touch of all.

tion of such a spirit as this, draw His materials for the divinest utterance of all revelation — the parable of the prodigal son.[1]

The relation of Jesus to publicans and sinners was thus explained, and also the utter antagonism between His spirit and that inflated religionism which is the wretched and hollow counterfeit of all *real* religion. The Judaism of that day substituted empty forms and meaningless ceremonies for true righteousness; it mistook uncharitable exclusiveness for genuine purity; it delighted to sun itself in the injustice of an imagined favoritism from which it would fain have shut out all God's other children; it was so profoundly hypocritical as not even to recognize its own hypocrisy; it never thought so well of itself as when it was crushing the broken reed and trampling out the last spark from the smoking flax;[2] it thanked God for the very sins of others, and thought that He could be pleased with a service in which there was neither humility, nor truthfulness, nor loyalty, nor love. These poor formalists, who thought that they were so rich and increased with goods, had to learn that they were wretched, and poor, and miserable, and blind, and naked. These sheep, which fancied that they had not strayed, had to understand that the poor *lost* sheep might be carried home on the shoulders of the Good Shepherd with a yet deeper tenderness; these elder sons had to learn that their Father's spirit, however little they might be able to realize it in their frozen unsympathetic hearts, was *this:* "It was meet that we should make merry and be glad, for this *thy brother* was dead and is alive again, was lost and is found."[3]

5. But however much it might be manifest that the spirit of the Christ and the spirit of the Pharisee were inalienably opposed to each other, yet up to this point the enemies of Jesus were unable to ruin His influence or check His work. To forgive, with the same word which healed the diseases, the sins by which they believed all diseases to be caused — to join in social festivities — to associate with publicans and sinners — were not, and could not be construed into,

---

[1] I have here touched on one side of the parable only — its individual meaning. Of course it involves, on all sides, infinitely more than has here been educed from it; especially the relation of Jews to the Gentile world, and the desperately jealous fury and rancor kindled in the Jewish mind (Acts xiii. 50; xxviii. 28, &c.) by the bare mention of the truth that God could accept, and pardon, and bless the Gentiles no less than the children of Abraham.

[2] "Qui peccatori non porrigit manum — quassatum calamum confringit, qui scintillam fidei contemnit in parvulis, linum extinguit fumigans." [249] (Jer.)

[3] He will not encourage the jealous hatred which had peeped out in the elder son's half-repudiation of this relationship (" this son of thine," ὁ υἱός ϭου οὗτος, Luke xv. 30).

offences against the law. But a weightier charge, more persistently reiterated, more violently resented, remained behind — a charge of distinctly violating the express laws of Moses by non-observance of the Sabbath. This it was which caused a surprise, an exacerbation, a madness, a thirst for sanguinary vengeance, which pursued Him to the very cross. For the Sabbath was a Mosaic, nay, even a primeval institution, and it had become the most distinctive and the most passionately reverenced of all the ordinances which separated the Jew from the Gentile as a peculiar people. It was at once the sign of their exclusive privileges, and the centre of their barren formalism. Their traditions, their patriotism, even their obstinacy, were all enlisted in its scrupulous maintenance. Not only had it been observed in heaven before man was, but they declared that the people of Israel had been chosen for the sole purpose of keeping it.[1] Was it not even miraculously kept by the Sabbatical river of the Holy City? Their devotion to it was only deepened by the universal ridicule, inconvenience, and loss which it entailed upon them in the heathen world. They were even proud that, from having observed it with a stolid literalism, they had suffered themselves on that day to lose battles, to be cut to pieces by their enemies, to see Jerusalem itself imperilled and captured. Its observance had been fenced round by the minutest, the most painfully precise, the most ludicrously insignificant restrictions. The Prophet had called it " a delight," and therefore it was a duty even for the poor to eat three times on that day. They were to feast on it, though no fire was to be lighted and no food cooked. According to the stiff and narrow school of Shammai, no one on the Sabbath might even comfort the sick or enliven the sorrowful. Even the preservation of life was a breaking of the Sabbath; and, on the other hand, even to kill a flea was as bad as to kill a camel.[2] Had not the command to

---

[1] These extravagances occur in the *Book of Jubilees*, a collection of fiercely fanatical *Hagadôth* which dates from the first century. For the fable of the Sabbatic river (which probably arose from the intermittent character of some of the springs about Jerusalem) see Josephus, *B. J.* vii. 5, § 1. It might be said, however, to *violate* the Sabbath rather than *keep* it, for it only ran every seventh day.

[2] You must not walk through a stream on stilts, for you really carried the stilts. A woman must not go out with any ribbons about her, unless they were sewed to her dress. A false tooth must not be worn. A person with the tooth-ache might not rinse his mouth with vinegar, but he might hold it in his mouth and swallow it. No one might write down two letters of the alphabet. The sick might not send for a physician. A person with lumbago might not rub or foment the affected part. A tailor must not go out with his needle on Friday night, lest he should forget it, and so break the Sabbath by carrying it about. A cock must not

"do no manner of work upon the Sabbath day" been most absolute
and most emphatic? had not Moses himself and all the congregation
caused the son of Shelomith to be stoned to death for merely gathering sticks upon it? had not the Great Synagogue itself drawn up the
thirty-nine *abhôth* and quite innumerable *toldôth*, or prohibitions of
labors which violated it in the first or in the second degree? Yet
here was One, claiming to be a prophet, yea, and more than a
prophet, deliberately setting aside, as it seemed to them, the traditional
sanctity of that day of days! Even an attentive reader of the Gospels will be surprised to find how large a portion of the enmity and
opposition which our Lord excited, not only in Jerusalem, but even
in Galilee and in Peræa, turned upon this point alone.[1]

The earliest outbreak of the feeling in Galilee must have occurred
shortly after the events narrated in the last chapter. The feeding of
the five thousand, and the discourse in the synagogue of Capernaum,
took place immediately before a Passover. None of the Evangelists
narrate the events which immediately succeeded. If Jesus attended
this Passover, He must have done so in strict privacy and seclusion,
and no single incident of His visit has been recorded. It is more
probable that the peril and opposition which He had undergone in
Jerusalem were sufficient to determine His absence "until this tyranny
was overpast."[2] It is not, however, impossible that, if He did not

wear a piece of ribbon round its leg on the Sabbath, for this would be to carry
something! Shammai would not entrust a letter to *a pagan* after Wednesday,
lest he should not have arrived at his destination on the Sabbath. He was occupied, we are told, all the week with thinking as to how he should keep the
Sabbath. The Shammaites held that Sabbatism applied (1) to men, (2) to beasts,
(3) to things. The Hillelites denied the last, not holding it necessary to put out a
lamp which had been kindled before the Sabbath, or to remove fish-nets, or to
prevent the dropping of oil in a press. Rabbinical authorities for each of these
statements (though as usual the Talmud is self-contradictory about some of them)
may be found in Schöttgen; Lightfoot; Keim, *Gesch. Jesu,* ii. 297; Otho, *Lex.
Rabb.* s. v. "Sabbathum;" Buxtorf, *De Synag. Jud.,* pp. 352—356; Derenbourg,
Hist. Pal. 38. The Rabbi Kolonimos, having been accused of murdering a boy,
wrote on a piece of paper, put it on the dead boy's lips, and so made the corpse
rise and reveal the true murderer, in order to save himself from being torn to
pieces. As this had been done on the Sabbath, he spent the rest of his life in
penance, and on his death-bed ordered that for a hundred years every one who
passed should fling a stone at his tomb, because every one who profaned the Sabbath should be stoned! Synesius (*Ep.* 4) tells a story of a pilot who, in the midst
of a storm, dropped the rudder when the Sabbath began, and would only take it
again when his life was threatened. Reland (*Antt. Hebr.,* p. 518), does not quote
the story accurately.

[1] See instances in Matt. xii. 1, *et seq.;* Mark ii. 23—28; iii. 1—6; Luke vi.
1—11; xiii. 14—17; xiv. 1—6; John v. 10, *et seq.;* vii. 23; ix. 14, *et seq.*
[2] John v. 16. 18.

go in person, some at least of His disciples fulfilled this national obligation ; and it may have been an observation of their behavior, combined with the deep hatred inspired by His bidding the healed man take up his bed on the Sabbath day, and by the ground which He had taken in defending Himself against that charge, which induced the Scribes and Pharisees of Jerusalem to send some of their number to follow His steps, and to keep an espionage upon His actions, even by the shores of His own beloved lake. Certain it is that henceforth, at every turn and every period of His career — in the corn-fields, in synagogues, in feasts, during journeys, at Capernaum, at Magdala, in Peræa, at Bethany — we find Him dogged, watched, impeded, reproached, questioned, tempted, insulted, conspired against by these representatives of the leading authorities of His nation, of whom we are repeatedly told that they were not natives of the place, but "certain which came from Jerusalem." [1]

i. The first attack in Galilee arose from the circumstance that, in passing through the corn-fields on the Sabbath day,[2] His disciples, who were suffering from hunger, plucked the ears of corn, rubbed them in the palms of their hands, blew away the chaff, and ate. Undoubtedly this was a very high offence — even a capital offence — in the eyes of the Legalists. To reap and to thresh on the Sabbath were of course forbidden by one of the *abhôth*, or primary rules ; but

---

[1] Matt. xv. 1 ; Mark iii. 22 ; vii. 1. Those, however, mentioned at an earlier period (Luke v. 17) were not the same as these hostile spies. We see from Acts xiv. 19 ; xvii. 13 ; Gal. ii. 12, how common among the Jews was the base and demoralizing spirit of heresy-hunting.

[2] This Sabbath is called in St. Luke by the mysterious name of the second-first Sabbath, $\dot{\varepsilon} \nu \, \sigma \alpha \beta \beta \acute{\alpha} \tau \omega \, \delta \varepsilon \upsilon \tau \varepsilon \rho \sigma \pi \rho \acute{\omega} \tau \omega$ — *i. e.*, the first of the second, not *vice versâ* as in the English version. There is not much importance in discovering the exact significance of this isolated expression, because the time of year is amply marked by the fact that the wheat (for the context shows that it could hardly have been barley) was ripe — *i. e.*, that the time was a week or two after the Passover, when the first ripe sheaf was offered as the first-fruits of the harvest. It is probable that in the warm hollow of Gennesareth corn ripened earlier than on the plains. The reading $\delta \varepsilon \upsilon \tau \varepsilon \rho \sigma \pi \rho \acute{\omega} \tau \omega$ is itself very doubtful, and is omitted by many MSS. (especially א, B, L) and versions, including the Syriac and Coptic. Mr. Monro very ingeniously conjectures that originally the eye of a weary copyist may have been misled into it by seeing the $\delta \iota \alpha \pi \sigma \rho$. or $\delta \iota \alpha \sigma \pi \sigma \rho$., which comes near it. If this led to a misreading $\delta \varepsilon \upsilon \tau \acute{\varepsilon} \rho \omega$, the $\pi \rho \acute{\omega} \tau \omega$ may have been added as a gloss with reference to the $\dot{\varepsilon} \tau \acute{\varepsilon} \rho \omega$ in verse 6. Almost every commentator has a new theory on the meaning of the word, supposing it to be genuine. The only opinions which seem sufficiently probable and sufficiently supported to make it worth while to mention them are — 1. The first Sabbath of the second month (Wetstein). 2. The first Sabbath in the second year of the Sabbatical cycle (Wieseler). 3. The first Sabbath after the second day of unleavened bread (Scaliger, Ewald Keim, &c., following the analogy of $\sigma \acute{\alpha} \beta$. $\pi \rho \acute{\omega} \tau \sigma \nu$ in Clem. Alex. *Strom*. vi. 5, 41).

the Rabbis had decided that to pluck corn was to be construed as
reaping, and to rub it as threshing; even to walk on grass was forbidden, because that too was a species of threshing; and not so much
as a fruit must be plucked from a tree.[1] All these latter acts were
violations of the *toldóth*, or "derivative rules." Perhaps these spy-
ing Pharisees had followed Jesus on this Sabbath day to watch
whether He would go more than the prescribed *techúm ha-Shabbeth*,
or Sabbath-day's journey of two thousand cubits;[2] but here they had
been fortunate enough to light upon a far more heinous and flagrant
scandal — an act of the disciples which, strictly and technically speaking, rendered them liable to death by stoning. Jesus Himself had
not indeed shared in the offence. If we may press the somewhat
peculiar expression of St. Mark, He was walking along through the
corn-fields by the ordinary path, bearing His hunger as best He
might, while the disciples were pushing for themselves a road through
the standing corn by plucking the ears as they went along.[3] Now
there was no harm whatever in plucking the ears; *that* was not only
sanctioned by custom, but even distinctly permitted by the Mosaic
law.[4] But the heinous fact was that this should be done *on a
Sabbath!* Instantly the Pharisees are round our Lord, pointing to
the disciples with the angry question, "See! why do *they*" — with a
contemptuous gesture towards the disciples — "do that which is not
lawful on the Sabbath day?"

With that divine and instantaneous readiness, with that depth

---

[1] Maimonides, *Shabbath*, c. 7, 8; Lightfoot, *Hor. Hebr.* 206; Sepp, *Leben Jesu*,
ii. 329. Similarly, since "building" was one of the thirty-nine works forbidden
on the Sabbath, curdling milk was also forbidden, because it was a sort of build-
ing. Forbidden works were divided into "fathers" (*abhóth*, $\dot{\alpha}\rho\chi\eta\gamma\iota\varkappa\acute{\omega}\tau\alpha\tau\alpha$
$\alpha\ddot{\iota}\tau\iota\alpha$, Phil. *De Vit. Mog.* 686) and "descendants" (*toldóth*): and to build was one
of the *abhóth ;* to make cheese, one of the *toldóth.*

[2] In the Jerus. Targ., Exod. xvi. 29, the words "beyond two thousand yards"
are added, as also on Ruth i. 16. Yet the Pharisees had ingenious rules of their
own for getting over the resultant inconveniences, which may be found in the
Mishna (*Erubhín* = mixtures, or amalgamations of distances, 10 chapters). The
treatise *Shabbath* occupies 24 chapters.

[3] Mark ii. 23, $\varkappa\alpha\grave{\iota}\ \grave{\varepsilon}\gamma\acute{\varepsilon}\nu\varepsilon\tau o\ \pi\alpha\rho\alpha\pi o\rho\varepsilon\acute{\nu}\varepsilon\sigma\vartheta\alpha\iota\ \alpha\grave{\upsilon}\tau\grave{o}\nu\ \delta\iota\grave{\alpha}\ \tau\tilde{\omega}\nu\ \sigma\pi o\rho\acute{\iota}\mu\omega\nu,\ \varkappa\alpha\grave{\iota}$
$\eta\rho\xi\alpha\nu\tau o\ o\grave{\iota}\ \mu\alpha\vartheta\eta\tau\alpha\grave{\iota}\ \alpha\grave{\upsilon}\tau o\tilde{\upsilon}\ \acute{o}\delta\grave{o}\nu\ \pi o\iota\varepsilon\tilde{\iota}\nu\ \tau\acute{\iota}\lambda\lambda o\nu\tau\varepsilon\varsigma\ \tau o\grave{\upsilon}\varsigma\ \sigma\tau\acute{\alpha}\chi\nu\alpha\varsigma.$ In classical Greek, this would mean "began *to make themselves a road* by plucking."
Meyer was the first to support this rendering, and he is followed by Volkmar,
Bleek, Keim, &c., and by Bishop Wordsworth. It is doubtful, however, whether
the classical usage of $\acute{o}\delta\grave{o}\nu\ \pi o\iota\varepsilon\tilde{\iota}\nu$ can be pressed, and it must be confessed that
on this supposition the phrase would be a very curious one.

[4] Deut. xxiii. 25. I was surprised to see that the Arabs in some fields near the
summit of Gerizim looked on with perfect indifference while our weary horses
ate freely of the green springing corn.

of insight and width of knowledge which characterized His answers to the most sudden surprises, Jesus instantly protected His disciples with personal approval and decisive support. As the charge this time was aimed not at Himself but at His disciples, His line of argument and defence differs entirely from that which, as we have seen, He had adopted at Jerusalem. *There* He rested His supposed violation of the law on His personal authority; *here*, while He again declared Himself Lord of the Sabbath, He instantly quoted first from their own *Cethubhim*, then from their own Law, a precedent and a principle which absolved His followers from all blame. "Have ye not read," He asked, adopting perhaps with a certain delicate irony, as He did at other times, a favorite formula of their own Rabbis, "how David not only went with his armed followers [1] into the Temple on the Sabbath day,[2] but actually ate with them the sanctified shewbread, which it was expressly forbidden for any but the priests to eat?" If David, their hero, their favorite, their saint, had thus openly and flagrantly violated the letter of the law, and had yet been blameless on the sole plea of a necessity higher than any merely ceremonial injunction, why were the disciples to blame for the harmless act of sating their hunger? And again, if their own Rabbis had laid it down that there was "no Sabbatism in the Temple;"[3] that the priests on the Sabbath might hew the wood, and light the fires, and place hot fresh-baked shewbread on the table, and slay double victims, and circumcise children, and thus in every way violate the rules of the Sopherim about the Sabbath, and yet be blameless[4]—nay, if in acting thus they were breaking the Sabbath at the bidding of the very Law which ordains the Sabbath—then if the Temple excuses *them*, ought not something[5] greater than the Temple to excuse these?

---

[1] Some, however, have imagined that David merely *represented himself* as being accompanied by followers.

[2] This results both from the fact of the precedent being here adduced and from 1 Sam. xxi. 6 (compared with Lev. xxiv. 8, 9) It is by no means improbable that this very chapter had been read in the morning Synagogue service of the day. The service was probably over, because none of the three meals took place till then.

[3] So Maimonides, *Pesach.* 1 (following, of course, old and established authorities). Thus, too, it was lawful for the Israelites at the Feast of Tabernacles to carry their *lulabim* on the Sabbath (Reland, *Antt. Hebr.*, 486).

[4] Even Hillel had some partial insight into this truth. He settled the question (against the Beni Bathira, and the more Pharisaic Shammai), that if the Passover day fell on a Sabbath the Paschal lamb might be slain by each Israelite in his own house, because lambs were slain in the Temple on every Sabbath by the priests.

[5] μεῖζον, neuter, not masc., as in the English version (Matt. xii. 6).

And there was something greater than the Temple here. And then once more he reminds them that mercy is better than sacrifice. Now the Sabbath was expressly designed for mercy, and therefore not only might all acts of mercy be blamelessly performed thereon, but such acts would be more pleasing to God than all the insensate and self-satisfied scrupulosities which had turned a rich blessing into a burden and a snare. The Sabbath was made for man, not man for the Sabbath, and therefore the Son of Man is Lord also of the Sabbath.[1]

In the Codex Bezae, an ancient and valuable manuscript now in the University Library at Cambridge, there occurs after Luke vi. 5 this remarkable addition — " On the same day, seeing one working on the Sabbath, He said to him, *O man, if indeed thou knowest what thou doest, thou art blessed; but if thou knowest not, thou art accursed, and a transgressor of the law.*" The incident is curious; it is preserved for us in this manuscript alone, and it may perhaps be set aside as apocryphal, or at best as one of those ἄγραφα δόγματα, or " unrecorded sayings" which, like Acts xx. 35, are attributed to our Lord by tradition only. Yet the story is too striking, too intrinsically probable, to be at once rejected as unauthentic. Nothing could more clearly illustrate the spirit of our Lord's teaching, as it was understood, for instance, by St. Paul.[2] For the meaning of the story obviously is — If thy work is of faith, then thou art acting rightly : if it is not of faith, it is sin.

ii. It was apparently on the day[3] signalized by this bitter attack, that our Lord again, later in the afternoon, entered the synagogue. A man — tradition says that he was a stonemason, maimed by an accident, who had prayed Christ to heal him, that he might not be

---

[1] Mark ii. 27, 28. A similar maxim (doubtless borrowed from this, and borrowed without profit) is found in the Talmud, " The Sabbath is given to thee, not thou to the Sabbath." (See Derenbourg, *Hist. de Palest.* 144.)

[2] Compare the closely analogous expressions of St. Paul about eating εἰδωλόθυτα (1 Cor. viii. 1). Some authors have rejected this story almost with contempt; yet could it be more wrong of the man (presumably for some strong and valid reason) to work than for the Jews to feast and idle ? " It is better to plough than to dance," says St. Augustine ; " they rest from good work, they rest not from idle work " (*Enarrat. in* Ps. xcii. 2).

[3] So it would seem from Matt. xii. 9, 10 ; Mark iii. 1. It is true that the received text of Luke vi. 6 says ἐν ἑτέρῳ σαββάτῳ, but probably so vague a note of time is not intended to be pressed, and indeed the Codex Bezae omits the ἑτέρῳ. St. Luke, only aware that the incident took place on a Sabbath, may merely mean, " It was also on a Sabbath day that," &c. On the other hand, the μεταβὰς ἐκεῖθεν of Matt. xii. 9 is more often used of longer journeys. The locality of these incidents is not further indicated, but it seems certain that they took place in Galilee.

forced to beg — was sitting in the synagogue.[1] His presence, and apparently the purpose of His presence, was known to all; and in the chief seats were Scribes, Pharisees, and Herodians, whose jealous, malignant gaze was fixed on Christ to see what He would do, that they might accuse Him. He did not leave them long in doubt. First He bade the man with the withered hand get up and stand out in the midst. And then He referred to the adjudication of their own consciences the question that was in their hearts, formulating it only in such a way as to show them its real significance. " Is it lawful," He asked, " on the Sabbath days to do good or to do evil? to save life (as I am doing), or to kill (as you in your hearts are wishing to do)? " There could be but one answer to such a question, but they were not there either to search for or to tell the truth. Their sole object was to watch what He would do, and found upon it a public charge before the Sanhedrin, or if not, at least to brand Him thenceforth with the open stigma of a Sabbath-breaker. Therefore they met the question by stolid and impotent silence. But He would not allow them to escape the verdict of their own better judgment, and therefore He justified Himself by their own distinct practice, no less than by their inability to answer. " Is there one of you," He asked, " who, if but a single sheep be fallen into a water-pit, will not get hold of it, and pull it out ? How much then is a man better than a sheep?" [2] The argument was unanswerable, and their own conduct in the matter was undeniable; but still their fierce silence remained unbroken. He looked round on them with anger; a holy indignation burned in His heart, glowed on His countenance, animated His gesture, rang in His voice, as slowly He swept each hard upturned face with the glance that upbraided them for their malignity and meanness, for their ignorance and pride ; and then suppressing that bitter and strong emotion as He turned to do His deed of mercy,

---

[1] This tradition was preserved in the Gospel of the Nazarenes and Ebionites. " Caementarius eram, manibus victum quaeritans. Precor te, Jesu, ut mihi restituas sanitatem, ne turpiter mendicem cibos." [250] (Jer. *in* Matt. xii. 13.)

[2] In the Gemara it is only allowed to *pull out a* sheep if it be in danger of drowning ; planks, however, might be put in a less extreme case, and food supplied (see Reland, *Antt. Hebr.* 521). So too a man may be only healed if in peril of death (*Joma*, viii. 6). Shemaia and Abtalion had not been blamed for breaking the Sabbath to revive the snow-covered and benumbed Hillel (v. *infr.* Excursus III., "Jesus and Hillel "). Stier suggests with much probability that many exceptions may have been permitted because of Christ's words. The institution of the *erûbh* showed how ready even the Pharisees were to tamper with Sabbatical observance *when it merely suited their convenience* (v. *infr.* Excursus IX., " Hypocrisy of the Pharisees ").

He said to the man, "Stretch forth thy hand." Was not the hand withered? How could he stretch it forth? The word of Christ supplied the power to fulfil His command: he stretched it out, and it was restored whole as the other.

Thus in every way were His enemies foiled — foiled in argument, shamed into silence, thwarted even in their attempt to find some ground for a criminal accusation. For even in· healing the man, Christ had done absolutely nothing which their worst hostility could misconstrue into a breach of the Sabbath law. He had not touched the man; He had not questioned him; He had not bid him exercise his recovered power; He had but spoken a word, and not even a Pharisee could say that to speak a word was an infraction of the Sabbath, even if the word were followed by miraculous blessing! They must have felt how utterly they were defeated, but it only kindled their rage the more. They were filled with madness,[1] and communed one with another what they might do to Jesus. Hitherto they had been enemies of the Herodians. They regarded them as half-apostate Jews, who accepted the Roman domination,[2] imitated heathen practices, adopted Sadducean opinions, and had gone so far in their flattery to the reigning house that they had blasphemously tried to represent Herod the Great as the promised Messiah. But now their old enmities were reconciled in their mad rage against a common foe. Something — perhaps the fear of Antipas, perhaps political suspicion, perhaps the mere natural hatred of worldlings and renegades against the sweet and noble doctrines which shamed their lives — had recently added these Herodians to the number of the Saviour's persecutors. As Galilee was the chief centre of Christ's activity, the Jerusalem Pharisees were glad to avail themselves of any aid from the Galilean tetrarch and his followers. They took common counsel how they might destroy by violence the Prophet whom they could nether refute by reasoning, nor circumvent by law.

This enmity of the leaders had not yet estranged from Christ the minds of the multitude. It made it desirable, however, for Him to move to another place,[3] because He would "neither strive nor cry,

---

[1] Luke vi. 11, ἄνοια, a kind of senseless rage.

[2] The very form of the name, *Herodiani*, probably indicates its Roman origin; I only say "probably," because Lipsius, *Ueber den Ursprung und den Aeltesten Gebrauch des Christennamens*, argues that the termination 'is an instance of the τύπος 'Αδίανος common in barbarian, and particularly Asiatic gentile or geographical adjectives.

[3] Matt. xii. 15 (Isa. xlii. 2). It is not necessarily implied that He left *Galilee;* or if He did, the events which follow may well have occurred before He was fully aware of the extent to which the virulence of the Pharisaic party had carried them.

neither should any man hear His voice in the streets," and the hour was not yet come when he should "send forth judgment to victory." But before His departure there occurred scenes yet more violent, and outbreaks of fury against Him yet more marked and dangerous. Every day it became more and more necessary to show that the rift between Himself and the religious leaders of His nation was deep and final; every day it became more and more necessary to expose the hypocritical formalism which pervaded their doctrines, and which was but the efflorescence of a fatal and deeply-seated plague.

6. His first distinct denunciation of the principles that lay at the very basis of the Pharisaic system was caused by another combined attempt of the Jerusalem scribes to damage the position of His disciples.[1] On some occasion they had observed that the disciples had sat down to a meal without previous ablutions. Now these ablutions were insisted upon with special solemnity by the Oral Tradition. The Jews of later times related with intense admiration how the Rabbi Akiba, when imprisoned and furnished with only sufficient water to maintain life, preferred to die of starvation rather than eat without the proper washings.[2] The Pharisees, therefore, coming up to Jesus as usual in a body, ask Him, with a swelling sense of self-importance at the justice of their reproach, "Why do thy disciples transgress the tradition of the elders? for they wash not their hands when they eat bread."

Before giving our Lord's reply, St. Mark pauses to tell us that the traditional ablutions observed by the Pharisees and all the leading Jews were extremely elaborate and numerous. Before every meal, and at every return from market,[3] they washed "with the fist,"[4] and

---

[1] Matt. xv. 1—20; Mark vii. 1—23.

[2] Buxtorf, *Syn. Jud.*, p. 236. For Rabbinical rules about ablutions, and their minutiæ, see Schwab's *Berachôth*, pp. 309, 398, 436—438. They occupy a large portion of the sixth *seder* of the Talmud, which is called *Taharôth*, or "Purifications," — especially the tracts *Mikvaôth*, "lavers and baths," and *Yadaim*, or 'hand-washings," in four chapters. Yet the Talmudists admit that hand-washing (*nitilath yadaim*) is *not* necessary if the hands be clean. (Pieritz, *Gosp. from Rabbinic Point of View*, p. 111.)

[3] Some render Mark vii. 4, "And after market they do not eat (what they have purchased) until they have washed it." This is not *impossible*, but does not seem likely, although βαπτίσωνται (complete immersions *nitilôth*) implies more than νίψωνται (" wash the *hands*") in verse 3.

[4] πυγμῇ, *i. e.*, thoroughly scrubbing each hand with the closed fist; the expression seems to be borrowed from some uses of the Hebrew אֶגְרֹף, and the Syriac Version uses a similar word to render ἐπιμελῶς "carefully" in Luke xv. 8. Epiphanius (*Hœr.* xv. *ad in.*) uses the word in the sense of "frequently," and in

if no water was at hand a man was obliged to go at least four miles to search for it. Besides this there were precise rules for the washing of all cups and *sextarii*[1] and banquet-couches (*triclinia*) and brazen vessels. The treatise *Shúlchan-Arúk,* or " Table arranged," a compendium of Rabbinical usages drawn up by Josef Karo in 1567, contains no less than twenty-six prayers by which these washings were accompanied. To neglect them was as bad as homicide, and involved a forfeiture of eternal life. And yet the disciples dared to eat with "common " (that is, with unwashen) hands!

As usual, our Lord at once made common cause with His disciples, and did not leave them, in their simplicity and ignorance, to be overawed by the attack of these stately and sanctimonious critics. He answered their question by a far graver one. " Why," He said, do *you* too violate the commandment of *God* by this 'tradition' of yours? For God's command was ' Honor thy father and thy mother;' but your gloss is, instead of giving to father and mother, a man may simply give the sum intended for their support to the sacred treasury, and say, 'It is *Corban,*' and then[2]—he is exempt

---

the Vulgate it is rendered *crebro,* so that Erasmus suggested a reading πυκνῇ (?). Others follow Theophylact in making it mean " up to the elbow" (ἄχρι ἀγκῶνος). The view given above is supported by the Rabbinical passages in Lightfoot, *Hor. Hebr. ad loc.* (See Schleusner, *Lex. Nov. Test.*)

[1] ξεστῶν (Mark vii. 4), one of St. Mark's Latinisms. Earthen vessels, if in any way rendered ceremonially unclean, were not washed, but broken (Lev. xv. 12). They were so particular about the sacred vessels that one day they washed the golden candlestick, and the Sadducees remarked to them " that soon they would think it necessary to wash the sun." (*Chagiga,* iii. 8; Grätz, *Gesch. d. Jud.* iii. 458). The first and second tracts of the *Seder Taharóth,* viz., the thirty chapters of *Kelim* (vessels) and the eighteen of *Oholóth* (tents), deal with the defilements and purifications of dwellings, utensils, &c. Wotton (*Mishna,* i. 160) justly considers this the most Pharisaic " order" of the entire Mishna.

[2] Lightfoot's note on this passage is particularly valuable. He shows that our Lord is quoting a regular formula which occurs often in the tracts *Nedarîm* and *Neziróth,* both of which deal with vows. In Matt. **xv.** 6 the sentence remains thus unfinished ; it is broken off by *aposiopesis,* as though our Lord shrank from the disgraceful inferences which such a son would annex to his words, and preferred to substitute for them His own stronger declaration that their iniquitous diversion of natural charities into the channels of pious ostentation would of course undermine all parental authority. קָרְבָּן means "a gift." It is rendered δῶρον in Jos. *Antt.* iv. 4, § 4 ; *B. J.* ii. 9, § 4. To say the word " *corban,*" however rashly and inconsiderately, involved a *konam,* or vow, and some of the Rabbis had expressly taught that a vow superseded the necessity of obedience to the fifth commandment. The explanation of this and the following verse seems to be that to say, " *Be it corban,*" was a sort of imprecation by the use of which a thing was *tabooed* to any one else ; and that if it had been said to a parent even in haste or anger, the Rabbis still treated it as irrevocable.

from any further burden in their support! And many such things
ye do. Ye hypocrites!"—it was the first time that our Lord had
thus sternly rebuked them—"finely[1] do ye abolish and obliterate
the commandment of God by *your traditions;* and well did Isaiah
prophesy of you, 'This people honoreth me with their lips, but their
heart is far from me; but in vain do they worship me, teaching for
doctrines the commandment of men.'"[2]

This was not only a defence of the disciples—because it showed
that they merely neglected a body of regulations[3] which were in
themselves so opposed to the very letter of the sacred law as, in
many cases, to be more honored in the breach than the observance—
but it was the open rebuke of One who assumed a superior and
fearless authority, and a distinct reprobation of a system which
guided all the actions of the Rabbinic caste, and was more reverenced than the Pentateuch itself. The quintessence of that system
was to sacrifice the spirit to the letter, which, apart from that spirit,
was more than valueless; and to sacrifice the letter itself to mere

---

[1] καλῶς ἀθετεῖτε (Mark vii. 9), used in strong irony. The *Babha Kama*, or
"first gate," and two following treatises of the Mishna are on compensations, &c.,
and abound in such traditions which supersede the Law. Another remarkable
instance of doing away with the commandment by tradition was the unanimous
exposition of the *lex talionis* (Exod. xxi. 24; Deut. xix. 12) as meaning nothing
more than a fine. I, of course, see that the dislike to the *lex talionis* was due to
a certain moral progress through which the Greeks and Teutons also passed ; but
to profess unbounded and superstitious adoration for the mere dead letter of a law,
and then to do away with its clearest enactments by mere quibbles and fictions,
was obvious hypocrisy.

[2] The iniquity which in the Middle Ages often extorted gifts of property for
Church purposes from the ghastly terrors of dying sinners was a παράδοσις as
bad as, perhaps worse than, that which Christ denounces.

[3] As it is to this day. Dr. Frankl says of the *Ashkenazîm* and *Perúshîm* at
Jerusalem, that "they never study the Bible, and derive all their knowledge of
it from the Talmud " (p. 34). [The Karaites, however, reject this doctrine of the
Mekebalîm, and hold to the Bible only (*id.* p. 46).] "He that has learned the
Scripture, and not the Mishna, is a blockhead." "The Law is like salt, the Mishna
like pepper, the Gemara like balmy spice." (See many such passages quoted
from the *Masseketh Soferim,* and elsewhere, in Buxtorf, *Synag. Jud.,* ch. iii. ;
Carpzov. *App. Cret.,* p. 563.) — R. Menasseh Ben Israel compared the Law to the
body, the Mishna to the soul, the Cabbala to the *soul of the soul.* (Allen's *Mod.
Judaism,* p. 74.) — The *Pirke Abhôth* ordains that at five a child should study the
Bible, at ten the Mishna, at fifteen the Gemara. God Himself is represented as
studying the Talmud, and repeating the decisions of the Rabbis! (*Chagiga,* p. 15,
ap. Bartolocc. iii. 410). — In a passage of the *Babha Metsia,* f. 59, which almost
reaches sublimity in its colossal sense of conviction, the decisions of the wise are
upheld not only against miracles, but even against a voice from heaven! The
passage has been often quoted. (See Cohen, *Les Déicides,* or Schwab's *Berachôth,*
p. 72.)

inferences from it which were absolutely pernicious. The Jews distinguished between the written Law (*Torah Shebeketeb*) and the traditional Law, or "Law upon the lip" (*Torah Shebeal pih*); and the latter was asserted, by its more extravagant votaries, to have been orally delivered by God to Moses, and orally transmitted by him through a succession of elders. On it is founded the Talmud (or "doctrine"), which consists of the Mishna (or "repetition") of the Law, and the Gemara, or "supplement" to it; and so extravagant did the reverence for the Talmud become, that it was said to be, in relation to the Law, as wine to water; to read the Scriptures was a matter of indifference, but to read the Mishna was meritorious, and to read the Gemara would be to receive the richest recompense.[1] And it was this grandiose system of revered commentary and pious custom which Jesus now so completely discountenanced, as not only to defend the neglect of it, but even openly to condemn and repudiate its most established principles. He thus consigned to oblivion and indifference the entire paraphernalia of *Hagadôth* ("legends") and *Halachôth* ("rules"), which, though up to that period it had not been committed to writing, was yet devoutly cherished in the memory of the learned, and constituted the very treasury of Rabbinic wisdom.

Nor was this all; not content with shattering the very bases of their external religion, He even taught to the multitude doctrines which would undermine their entire authority — doctrines which would tend to bring their vaunted wisdom into utter discredit. The supremacy of his disapproval was in exact proportion to the boundlessness of their own arrogant self-assertion; and turning away from them as if they were hopeless, He summoned the multitude, whom they had trained to look up to them as little gods, and spoke these short and weighty words:

"Hear me, all of you, and understand! Not that which goeth

---

[1] They asserted that God had taught Moses the Law by day, and the Mishna by night (Buxtorf, *Syn. Jud.* iii.). The Mishna was supposed to consist of five main elements: — 1. Traditional interpretations. 2. Undisputed constitutions. 3. Accepted opinions derived from the thirteen ways of reasoning. 4. Decrees of Prophets and Rabbis. 5. Legal precedents. (Maimon. *Porta Mosis.* See Etheridge, *Hebr. Lit.*, p. 119.) — The object of the Gemara was to explain the Mishna, (1) lexically, (2) dogmatically, (3) inferentially, (4) mystically. According to Aben Ezra, R. Sol. Jarchi, R. Bechai, Maimonides, &c., the Law was the "Statutes" (חקים), and the Oral Law the "judgments" (טישפטים) of Deut. iv. 14. R. Josh. Ben Levi said that in Exod. xxiv. 12 "the Tables" meant the Decalogue; "the Law," the Pentateuch; "commandments," the Mishna; "which I have written," the Prophets and Hagiographa; and "that thou mightest teach them," the Gemara (*Berachôth*, f. 5 *a*). (Schwab, p. 234.)

into the mouth defileth the man; but that which cometh out of the mouth, *that* defileth a man." [1]

The Pharisees were bitterly offended by this saying, as well indeed they might be. Condemnatory as it was of the too common sacerdotal infatuation for all that is merely ceremonial, that utterance of Jesus should have been the final death-knell of that superfluity of voluntary ceremonialism for which one of the Fathers coins the inimitable word ἐθελοπερισσοθρήσκεια.[251] His disciples were not slow to inform Him of the indignation which His words had caused, for they probably retained a large share of the popular awe for the leading sect. But the reply of Jesus was an expression of calm indifference to earthly judgment, a reference of all worth to the sole judgment of God as shown in the slow ripening of events. "Every plant which my Heavenly Father hath not planted shall be rooted up. Let them alone. They be blind leaders of the blind; and if the blind lead the blind, shall they not both fall into the ditch?"

A little later, when they were in-doors and alone, Peter ventured to ask for an explanation of the words which He had uttered so emphatically to the multitude. Jesus gently blamed the want of comprehension among His Apostles, but showed them, in teaching of deep significance, that man's food does but affect his material structure, and does not enter into his heart, or touch his real being; but that "from within, out of the heart of men, proceed evil thoughts, adulteries, fornications, murders, theft, covetousness, wickedness, deceit, lasciviousness, an evil eye, blasphemy, pride, foolishness."

Evil thoughts — like one tiny rill of evil, and then the burst of all that black overwhelming torrent!

"These are the things which defile a man; but to eat with unwashen hands defileth not a man." [2]

---

[1] There is a singular and striking parallel to these words in Philo, *De Opif. Mundi,* i. 29. "There enter into the mouth," he says, expanding a saying of Plato, "meats and drinks, corruptible nourishment of a corruptible body; but there go forth from it words, immortal laws of an immortal soul, by means of which is governed the reasonable life." Compare too the fragment of Democritus, ἂν δὲ σαυτὸν ἔνδοθεν ἀνοίξῃς ποικίλον τι καὶ πολυπαθὲς κακῶν ταμεῖον εὑρήσεις . . . οὐκ ἔξωθεν ἐπιρρεόντων, ἀλλ᾽ ὥσπερ ἐγγείους καὶ αὐτόχθονας πηγὰς ἐχόντων, ἃς ἀνίησιν ἡ κακία.[252]

[2] There is a well-known difficulty about Mark vii. 19, where καθαρίζον [253] is both ungrammatical and gives a very dubious sense. If with almost all the best MSS. (א, A, B, E, F, L, &c.) we read καθαρίζων,[254] we may then connect it with the previous λέγει (ver. 18) — *i. e.* "He said this . . . purging, rendering clean, all meats" (cf. Acts xi. 5—9). It must, however, be admitted that the order of the words is a serious stumbling-block to this excellent interpretation. The only other way of explaining it is to make καθαρίζων agree with ἀφεδρῶν.[255]

CHAPTER XXXII.

DEEPENING OPPOSITION.

" Si ignobilis, si inglorius, si inhonorabilis, Christus erit meus." [256] — TERT.
Contr. Marc. iii. 17.

THERE was to be one more day of opposition — more bitter, more
dangerous, more personal, more implacable — one day of open and
final rupture between Jesus and the Pharisaic spies from Jerusalem
— before He yielded for a time to the deadly hatred of His enemies,
and retired to find in heathen countries the rest which He could find
no longer in the rich fields and on the green hills of Gennesareth.
There were but few days of His earthly life which passed through
a series of more heart-shaking agitations than the one which we shall
now describe.[1]

Jesus was engaged in solitary prayer, probably at early dawn, and
in one of the towns which formed the chief theatre of His Galilæan
ministry.   While they saw Him standing there with His eyes uplifted
to heaven — for standing, not kneeling, was and is the common Oriental attitude in prayer — the disciples remained at a reverent distance; but when His orisons were over, they came to Him with the
natural entreaty that He would teach them to pray, as John also
taught his disciples.   He at once granted their request, and taught
them that short and perfect petition which has thenceforth been the
choicest heritage of every Christian liturgy, and the model on which
all our best and most acceptable prayers are formed.   He had, indeed,
already used it in the Sermon on the Mount, but we may be deeply
thankful that for the sake of His asking disciples He here brought it
into greater and more separate prominence.   Some, indeed, of the
separate clauses may already have existed, at least in germ, among

---

[1] It seems clear from the order in which these scenes are narrated in Matt. xii.
22, seqq.; Mark iii. 11, seqq., that they took place in Galilee, and if so they cannot
well be assigned to any other period than the present.   In St. Luke they occur in
the great episode (ix. 51.—xviii. 34); but the hypothesis that this episode narrates
the incidents of one or three journeys only is not tenable, and the order suggested
by the other Evangelists seems here to be the more probable.   The only note of
time used by St. Luke is the very vaguest of all, " And it came to pass;" and the
note of place is equally so, " in a certain place."

the Jewish forms of prayer; since they resemble expressions which are found in the Talmud, and which we have no reason to suppose were borrowed from Christians.[1] But never before had all that was best and purest in a nation's prayers been thus collected into one noble and incomparable petition — a petition which combines all that the heart of man, taught by the Spirit of God, had found most needful for the satisfaction of its truest aspirations. In the mingled love and reverence with which it teaches us to approach our Father in heaven — in the spirituality with which it leads us to seek first the kingdom of God and His righteousness — in the spirit of universal charity and forgiveness which it inculcates — in that plural form throughout it, which is meant to show us that selfishness must be absolutely and for ever excluded from our petitions, and that no man can come to God as his Father without acknowledging that his worst enemies are also God's children — in the fact that of its seven petitions one, and one only, is for any earthly blessing, and even that one is only for earthly blessings in their simplest form — in the manner in which it discountenances all the vain repetitions and extravagant self-tortures with which so many fanatic worshippers have believed that God could be propitiated — even in that exquisite brevity which shows us how little God desires that prayer should be made a burden and weariness — it is, indeed, what the Fathers have called it, a *breviarium Evangelii* — the pearl of prayers.

Not less divine were the earnest and simple words which followed it, and which taught the disciples that men ought always to pray and not to faint, since, if importunity prevails over the selfishness of man, earnestness must be all-powerful with the righteousness of God. Jesus impressed upon them the lesson that if human affection can be trusted to give only useful and kindly gifts, the love of the Great Father who loves us all, will, much more certainly, give His best and highest gift — even the gift of the Holy Spirit — to all that ask Him.

And with what exquisite yet vivid graciousness are these great lessons inculcated! Had they been delivered in the dull, dry, didactic style of most moral teaching, how could they have touched the hearts, or warmed the imaginations, or fixed themselves indelibly upon the memories of those who heard them? But instead of being clothed in scholastic pedantisms, they were conveyed in a little tale

---

[1] For the proof of this, and for the Jewish prayers which most resemble (but at how wide an interval!) the Lord's prayer, see Gfrörer, *Jahrh. des Heils*, ii. 169, and the parallels adduced on Matt. vi. 9 by Lightfoot, Schöttgen, and Wetstein.

founded on the most commonplace incidents of daily life, and of a
daily life full of simplicity and poverty. Journeying at night to
avoid the burning heat, a man arrives at a friend's house. The host
is poor, and has nothing for him ; yet, because even at that late hour
he will not neglect the duties of hospitality, he gets up, and goes to
the house of another friend to borrow three loaves. But this other
is in bed ; his little children are with him ; his house is locked and
barred. To the gentle and earnest entreaty he answers crossly and
roughly [1] from within, "Trouble me not." But his friend knows
that he has come on a good errand, and he persists in knocking,
till at last, not from kind motives, but because of his pertinacity,[2] the
man gets up and gives him all that he requires. "Even so," it has
been beautifully observed, "when the heart which has been away on
a journey, suddenly at midnight (*i. e.*, the time of greatest darkness)
returns home to us — that is, comes to itself and feels hunger — and
we have nothing wherewith to satisfy it, God requires of us bold,
importunate faith." If such persistency conquers the reluctance of
ungracious man, how much more shall it prevail with One who loves
us better than we ourselves, and who is even more ready to hear than
we to pray!

It has been well observed that the narrative of the life of Christ
on earth is full of lights and shadows — one brief period, or even one
day, starting at times into strong relief, while at other times whole
periods are passed over in unbroken silence. But we forget — and
if we bear this in mind, there will be nothing to startle us in this
phenomenon of the Gospel record — we forget how large and how
necessary a portion of His work it was to teach and train His immediate Apostles for the future conversion of the world. When we
compare what the Apostles were when Jesus called them — simple
and noble indeed, but ignorant, and timid, and slow of heart to
believe — with what they became when He had departed from them,
and shed the gift of His Holy Spirit into their hearts, then we shall
see how little intermission there could have been in His beneficent
activity, even during the periods in which His discourses were delivered to those only who lived in the very light of His divine personality. Blessed indeed were they above kings and prophets, blessed
beyond all who have ever lived in the richness of their privilege,
since they could share His inmost thoughts, and watch in all its

[1] He does not return the greeting φίλε; the expression, Μή μοι κόπους
παρεχε, "don't fash me," is an impatient one: the door κέκλεισται, "has been
shut for the night:" οὐ δύναμαι, "I can't," meaning "I won't."

[2] ἀναίδειαν, "shamelessness," "unblushing persistence."

angelic sweetness and simplicity the daily.spectacle of those "sinless years." But if this blessing was specially accorded to them, it was not for their own sakes, but for the sake of that world which it was their mission to elevate from despair and wickedness into purity and sober-mindedness and truth — for the sake of those holy hearts who were henceforth to enjoy a Presence nearer, though spiritual, than if, with the Apostles, they could have climbed with Him the lonely hills, or walked beside Him as He paced at evening beside the limpid lake.

The day which had begun with that lesson of loving and confiding prayer was not destined to proceed thus calmly. *Few* days of His life during these years can have passed without His being brought into distressing contact with the evidences of human sin and human suffering ; but on this day the spectacle was brought before Him in its wildest and most terrible form. A man blind and dumb and mad, from those strange unaccountable influences which the universal belief attributed to demoniac possession, was brought before Him. Jesus would not leave him a helpless victim to the powers of evil. By His look and by His word He released the miserable sufferer from the horrible oppression — calmed, healed, restored him — " insomuch that the blind and dumb both spake and saw."

It appears from our Lord's own subsequent words, that there existed among the Jews certain forms of exorcism,[1] which to a certain extent, at any rate, were efficacious ; but there are traces that the cures so effected were only attempted in milder and simpler cases. The dissolution of so hideous a spell as that which had bound this man — the power to pour light on the filmed eyeball, and to restore speech to the cramped tongue, and intelligence to the bewildered soul — was something that the people had never witnessed. The miracle produced a thrill of astonishment, a burst of unconcealed admiration. For the first time they openly debated whether He who had such power could be any other than their expected Deliverer. " Can this man," they incredulously asked, " can *he* be the Son of David ? "[2]

His enemies could not deny that a great miracle had been performed, and since it did not convert, it only hardened and maddened them. But how could they dissipate the deep impression which it had made on the minds of the amazed spectators ? The Scribes who

---

[1] Cf. Acts xix. 13. — An energetic formula used by the Jewish exorcists is preserved in *Bab. Shabbath*, 67 *a*. (Gfrörer, i. 413.)

[2] Matt. ix. 32 ; xii. 23 (Luke xi. 15). Μήτι οὖτός ἐστι ; the words express incredulous surprise — not *nonne ?* but *num ?* Cf. John viii. 22, μήτι ἀποκτενεῖ ἑαυτόν.

came from Jerusalem, more astute and ready than their simple Galilæan brethren, at once invented a ready device for this purpose.
" This fellow hath Beelzebul " — such was their notable and insolent
solution of the difficulty, " and it is only by the prince of the devils
that He casteth out the devils." [1] Strange that the ready answer did
not spring to every lip, as it did afterwards to the lips of some who
heard the same charge brought against Him in Jerusalem, " These
are not the words of one that hath a devil."   But the people of Galilee were credulous and ignorant; these grave and reverend inquisitors from the Holy City possessed an immense and hereditary ascendancy over their simple understandings, and, offended as they had
been more than once by the words of Jesus, their whole minds were
bewildered with a doubt.   The awfulness of His personal ascendancy
— the felt presence, even amid His tenderest condescensions, of something more than human — His power of reading the thoughts — the
ceaseless and sleepless energy of His beneficence — the strange terror
which He inspired in the poor demoniacs — the speech which sometimes rose into impassioned energy of denunciation, and sometimes,
by its softness and beauty, held them hushed as infants at the mother's
breast — the revulsion of their unbelieving hearts against that new
world of fears and hopes which He preached to them as the kingdom
of God — in a word, the shuddering sense that in some way His
mere look and presence placed them in a nearer relation than they
had ever been before with the Unseen World — all this, as it had
not prepared them to accept the truth, tended from the first to leave

---

[1] Mark iii. 22 ; Matt. xii. 24.   The οὗτος is intentionally contemptuous. Beel-
zebu*l* (not Beelzebub, which is derived from the versions) is almost certainly the
right reading (א, B, &c.). But the form and true meaning of the name are enveloped in obscurity. Beelzebub is mentioned as god of Ekron in 2 Kings i. 2,
and both the LXX. and Josephus (*Antt.* ix. 2, § 1) understood this to mean "lord
of flies " (Βάαλ μυῖαν). There may have been nothing derisive in such a designation, as some even of the Greek deities were worshipped as averters of pestilent
insects (cf. Zeus Apomuios, Hercules Kornopion and Ipuktonos, Apollo Smintheus,
&c.). But Beelzebul may also mean "lord of the (celestial) *habitation*," *i. e.*,
" prince of the air " (Eph. ii. 2), and if so there is a sort of play on the word in the
οἰκοδεσπότης of Matt. x. 25. On the other hand, the name may be " lord of
dung," partly from the belief that demons haunted foul places (Matt. xii. 43 ;
Gfrörer, *Jahrh. d. Heils*, i. 139). This would be in accordance with those insulting paronomasias which the Jews, from a literal acceptation of Exod. xxiii. 13,
&c., delighted to apply to heathen idols (cf. Kir Cheres, " city of destruction,"
for Kir Heres ; Bethaven for Bethel ; Bar-coziba, "son of a lie," for Bar-chocba,
" son of a star," &c.   See my *Chapters on Language*, p. 277). The accusation is
practically the same as that of the Talmudists, that the miracles of Jesus were
wrought by magic learnt in Egypt (*Bab. Shab.*, f. 104, 2 ; 43, 1). " Latrant catuli
isti, sicut a canibus his edocti fuerunt." [257] (Lightfoot, *ad loc.*)

them the ready victims of insolent, blasphemous, and authoritative falsehood.

And therefore, in a few calm words, Jesus shattered the hideous sophism to atoms. He showed them the gross absurdity of supposing that Satan could be his own enemy. Using an irresistible *argumentum ad hominem*, He convicted them by an appeal to the exorcisms so freely, but almost ineffectually, professed by themselves and their pupils. And when He had thus showed that the power which He exercised must be at once superior to Satan and contrary to Satan, and must therefore be spiritual and divine, He warned them of the awful sinfulness and peril of this their blasphemy against the Holy Spirit of God, and how nearly it bordered on the verge of that sin which alone, of all sins, could neither here nor hereafter be forgiven. And then, after these dim and mysterious warnings, speaking to them in language of yet plainer significance, He turned the light of truth into their raging and hypocritical hearts, and showed them how this Dead Sea fruit of falsehood and calumny could only spring from roots and fibres of hidden bitterness; how only from evil treasures hid deep in darkness, where the very source of light was quenched, could be produced these dark imaginings of their serpentine malignity.[1] Lastly, and with a note of warning which has never since ceased to vibrate, He warned them that the *words* of man reveal the true nature of the heart within, and that for those, as for all other false and lightly uttered words of idle wickedness, they should give account at the last day.[2] The weight and majesty of these words — the awful solemnity of the admonition which they conveyed — seem for a time to have reduced the Pharisees to silence, and to have checked the reiteration of their absurd and audacious blasphemy. And in the hush that ensued some woman of the company, in an uncontrollable enthusiasm of admiration — accustomed indeed to reverence these long-robed Pharisees, with their fringes and phylacteries, but feeling to the depth of her heart on how lofty a height above them the Speaker stood — exclaimed to Him in a loud voice,[3] so that all could hear —

"Blessed is the womb that bare Thee, and the breasts[4] that Thou hast sucked."

"Yea"— or as we may render it —"Nay, *rather*," he answered, "blessed are they that hear the word of God, and keep it."

---

[1] Matt. xii. 34, Γεννήματα ἐχιδνῶν.

[2] Compare Matt. xii. 25—37; Mark iii. 22—30; Luke xi. 17—36.

[3] Luke xi. 27, ἐπάρασα φωνὴν.

[4] *Idem*, μασϊοί.

The woman, with all the deep and passionate affection of her sex, had cried, How blest must be the mother of such a Son! and blessed indeed that mother was, and blessed was the fruit of her womb — blessed she was among women, and blessed because she believed:[1] yet hers was no exclusive blessedness; there is a blessedness yet deeper and loftier, the blessedness of obedience to the Word of God. "How many women," says St. Chrysostom,[2] "have blessed that Holy Virgin, and desired to be such a mother as she was! What hinders them? Christ has made for us a wide way to this happiness, and not only women, but men may tread it — the way of obedience; this it is which makes such a mother, not the throes of parturition."

But the Pharisees, though baffled for a moment, did not intend to leave Jesus long in peace. He had spoken to them in language of lofty warning, nay, even of stern rebuke — to *them*, the leaders and religious teachers of His time and country. What gave such boldness to one — a mere "empty cistern," a mere *am ha-arets* — who had but just emerged from the obscure and ignorant labors of a provincial artisan? how did He dare thus to address them? Let Him at least show them some sign — some sign from heaven, no mere exorcism or act of healing, but some great, indisputable, decisive sign of His authority. "Master, we would see a sign from Thee."

It was the old question which had assailed Him at His very earliest ministry, "What sign showest Thou unto us, seeing that Thou doest these things?"[3]

To such appeals, made only to insult and tempt — made by men who, unconvinced and unsoftened, had just seen a mighty sign, and had attributed it at once without a blush to demoniac agency — made, not from hearts of faith, but out of curiosity, and hatred, and unbelief — Jesus always turned a deaf ear. The Divine does not condescend to limit the display of its powers by the conditions of finite criticism, nor is it conformable to the council of God to effect the conversion of human souls by their mere astonishment at external signs. Had Jesus given them a sign from heaven, is it likely that it would have produced any effect on the spiritual children of ancestors who, according to their own accepted history, in the very sight, nay, under the very precipices of the burning hill, had sat down to eat and to drink, and risen up to play? Would it have had any permanent significance for the moral heirs of those who were taunted by

---

[1] Luke i. 42—45.

[2] Quoted by Bishop Wordsworth on Matt. xii. 48.

[3] John ii. 18.

their own prophets with having taken up the tabernacles of Moloch, and the star of their God Remphan, though they were guided by the fiery pillar, and quenched their thirst from the smitten rock? Signs they had seen and wonders in abundance, and now they were seeing the highest sign of a Sinless Life, and yet they did but rebel and blaspheme the more. No sign should be given, then, save in prophecies which they could not understand. " That evil and adulterous generation," He exclaimed, turning to the densely crowded multitude, "should have no sign save the sign of Jonah the prophet. Saved after a day and night amid the dark and tempestuous seas, he had been a sign to the Ninevites; so should the Son of Man be saved from the heart of the earth.[1] And those men of Nineveh, who repented at the preaching of Jonah, and the Queen of Sheba, who came from the ends of the earth to hear the wisdom of Solomon, should alike rise up in the judgment and condemn a generation that despised and rejected one greater than Solomon or than Jonah. For that generation had received every blessing : by the Babylonian captivity, by the Maccabæan revival, by the wise and noble rule of the Asmonæan princes, recently by the preaching of John, the evil spirit of idolatry and rebellion which distempered their fathers had been cast out of them ; its old abode had been swept and garnished by the proprieties of Pharisees, and the scrupulosities of Scribes; but, alas! no good spirit had been invited to occupy the empty shrine, and now the old unclean possessor had returned with seven spirits more wicked than himself, and their last state was worse than the first.

His discourse was broken at this point by a sudden interruption.[2] News had again reached His family that he was surrounded by a dense throng, and was speaking words more strange and terrible than ever He had been known to utter; above all, that He had repudiated with open scorn, and denounced with uncompromising indignation, the great teachers who had been expressly sent from Jerusalem to watch His words. Alarm seized them; perhaps their informant had whispered to them the dread calumny which had thus called forth His stern rebukes. From the little which we can learn of His brethren, we infer that they were Hebrews of the Hebrews, and likely to be intensely influenced by Rabbinical and sacerdotal authority; as

---

[1] The " three days and three nights " of Matt. xii. 40, mean little more than a νυχθήμερον, or נצף — *e. g.*, from Friday evening to Sunday morning. This strange idiom has caused needless difficulties. See the passages quoted by Lightfoot (*Hor. Hebr. ad loc.*). Cf. 1 Sam. xxx. 12, 13 ; 2 Chron. x. 5, 12 ; Deut xiv. 28 ; xxvi. 12.

[2] Matt. xii. 46, Ἔτι αὐτοῦ λαλοῦντος.

yet, too, they either did not believe on Him, or regarded His claims in a very imperfect light. Is not the time again come for them to interfere? can they not save Jesus, on whom they looked as *their* Jesus, from Himself? can they not exercise over Him such influence as shall save Him from the deadly perils to which His present teaching would obviously expose Him? can they not use towards Him such gentle control as should hurry Him away for a time into some region of secrecy and safety? They could not, indeed, reach Him in the crowd, but they could get some one to call His attention to their presence. Suddenly He is informed by one of His audience — "Behold, Thy mother and Thy brethren stand without, desiring to speak with Thee." Alas! had they not yet learnt that if they would not enter, their sole right place was to stand without? that His hour was now come to pass far beyond the circle of mere human relationship, infinitely above the control of human brethren? Must their bold intrusive spirit receive one more check? It was even so; but the check should be given gently, and so as to be an infinite comfort to others. "Who is My mother?" He said to the man who had spoken, "and who are My brethren?" And then stretching forth His hand towards His disciples, He said, "Behold My mother and My brethren! For whosoever shall do the will of My Father which is in heaven, the same is My brother, and sister, and mother!"

CHAPTER XXXIII.

THE DAY OF CONFLICT.

'Εγγὺς μαχαίρας, ἐγγὺς Θεοῦ.²⁵⁸ — IGNAT. *Ad Smyrn.* 4.

UP to this point the events of this great day had been sufficiently agitating, but they were followed by circumstances yet more painful and exciting.

The time for the mid-day meal had arrived, and a Pharisee asked Him to come and lunch at his house.¹ There was extremely little hospitality or courtesy in the invitation. If not offered in downright hostility and bad faith — as we know was the case with similar Pharisaic invitations — its motive at the best was but curiosity to see more of the new Teacher, or a vanity which prompted him to patronize so prominent a guest. And Jesus, on entering, found Himself, not among publicans and sinners, where he could soothe, and teach, and bless — not among the poor to whom He could preach the kingdom of heaven — not among friends and disciples who listened with deep and loving reverence to His words — but among the cold, hard, threatening faces, the sneers and frowns, of haughty rivals and open enemies. The Apostles do not seem to have been invited. There was no sympathy of a Thomas to sustain Him, no gentleness of a Nathanael to encourage Him, no ardor of a Peter to defend, no beloved John to lean his head upon His breast. Scribe, Lawyer, and Pharisee, the guests ostentatiously performed their artistic ablutions, and then — each with extreme regard for his own precedence — swept to their places at the board. With no such elaborate and fantastic ceremonies, Jesus, as soon as He entered, reclined at the table.² It was a short and trivial meal, and outside thronged the dense multitude, hungering still and thirsting for the words of eternal life. He did not choose, therefore, to create idle

---

¹ Not "to dine with him" (which would be ὅπως δειπνήσῃ), but rather "to lunch (ἀριστήσῃ) at his house." The ἄριστον, or morning meal, was a slight repast about twelve in the day, more like the French *déjeuner* than the English "breakfast," far slighter than the δεῖπνον. Lange has understood the scenes of this chapter better than any other commentator (*Leben Jesu,* iii. v. 7).

² Luke xi. 37, εἰσελθὼν ἀνέπεσεν.

delays and countenance a needless ritualism by washings, which at that moment happened to be quite superfluous, and to which a foolish and pseudo-religious importance was attached.

Instantly the supercilious astonishment of the host expressed itself in his countenance; and, doubtless, the lifted eyebrows and depreciating gestures of those unsympathizing guests showed as much as they dared to show of their disapproval and contempt. They were forgetting utterly who He was, and what He had done. Spies and calumniators from the first, they were now debasing even their pretentious and patronizing hospitality into fresh opportunity for treacherous conspiracy. The time was come for yet plainer language, for yet more unmeasured indignation; and He did not spare them. He exposed, in words which were no parables and could not be mistaken, the extent to which their outward cleanliness was but the thin film which covered their inward wickedness and greed. He denounced their contemptible scrupulosity in the tithing of potherbs, their flagrant neglect of essential virtues; the cant, the ambition, the publicity, the ostentation of their outward orthodoxy, the deathful corruption of their inmost hearts. Hidden graves were they over which men walk, and, without knowing it, become defiled.

And at this point, one of the lawyers who were present — some learned professor, some orthodox Masoret [1] — ventures to interrupt the majestic torrent of His rebuke. He had, perhaps, imagined that the youthful Prophet of Nazareth — He who was so meek and lowly of heart — He whose words among the multitude had hitherto breathed the spirit of such infinite tenderness — was too gentle, too loving, to be in earnest. He thought, perhaps, that a word of interpolation might check the rushing storm of his awakened wrath. He had not yet learnt that no strong or great character can be devoid of the element of holy anger. And so, ignorant of all that was passing in the Saviour's mind, amazed that people of such high distinction could be thus plainly and severely dealt with, he murmured in deprecatory tones, "Master, thus saying, thou reproachest us also!"

Yes, He reproached them also: they, too, heaped on the shoulders of others the burdens which themselves refused to bear; they, too, built the sepulchres of the prophets whom their sins had slain; they, too, set their backs against the door of knowledge, and held the key, so that none could enter in; on them too, as on all that guilty generation, should come the blood of all the prophets, from the blood of

---

[1] Of course the mass of textual and other criticisms which form the Masora had existed for ages before they were collected or reduced to writing.

Abel to the blood of Zacharias, who perished between the altar and the Temple.[1]

The same discourse, but yet fuller and more terrible, was subsequently uttered by Jesus in the Temple of Jerusalem in the last great week of His life on earth; but thus did He, on this occasion, hurl down upon them from the heaven of His moral superiority the first heart-scathing lightnings of His seven-times-uttered-woe.[2] They thought, perhaps, that He would have been deceived by their specious smoothness and hypocritical hospitality; but He knew that it was not out of true heart that they offered Him even the barest courtesies of life. The fact that He was alone among them, and that He should have been, as it were, betrayed into such company, was but an additional reason why the flames of warning and judgment should thus play about their heads, which hereafter, unless they repented, should strike them to the earth. Not for an instant could they succeed in deceiving Him. There is a spurious kindness, a bitter semblance of friendship which deserves no respect. It may pass current in the realms of empty fashion and hollow civility, where often the words of men's mouths are softer than butter, having war in their heart, and where, though their throat is an open sepulchre, they flatter with their tongue; but it shrivels to nothing before the refining fire of a divine discernment, and leaves nothing but a sickening fume behind. The time had come for Him to show to these hypocrites how well He knew the deceitfulness of their hearts, how deeply He hated the wickedness of their lives.

They felt that it was an open rupture. The feast broke up in confusion.[3] The Scribes and Pharisees threw off the mask. From fawning friends and interested inquirers, they suddenly sprang up in their true guise as deadly opponents. They surrounded Jesus, they pressed upon Him vehemently, persistently, almost threateningly; they began to pour upon Him a flood of questions, to examine, to catechize Him, to try and force words out of Him, lying in ambush,

---

[1] See 2 Chron. xxiv. 20, 21; *c. infr*, Vol. II., page 246.

[2] The modern representatives and continuers of the Pharisaic sect are called *Perushím.* "They proudly separate themselves from the rest of their co-religionists. . . . *Fanatical, bigoted, intolerant, quarrelsome, and in truth irreligious, with them the outward observance of the ceremonial law is everything, the moral law little binding, morality itself of no importance.*" Such is the testimony of a Jew! (Frankl, *Jews in the East*, E. Tr., ii. 27.) "*You are a Porish,*" i. e., a Pharisee, is the bitterest reproach which one of the Chasidim can utter (*id.*, p. 35).

[3] This appears from the καὶ κεῖθεν ἐξελθόντος αὐτοῦ [259] of Luke xi. 53, which is the reading of ℵ. B, C, L, &c., instead of the much weaker reading of our version.

like eager hunters, to spring upon any confession of ignorance, on any mistake of fact — above all, on any trace of heresy on which they might found that legal accusation by which before long they hoped to put Him down.[1]

How Jesus escaped from this unseemly spectacle — how He was able to withdraw Himself from this display of hostility — we are not told. Probably it might be sufficient for Him to waive His enemies aside, and bid them leave Him free to go forth again. For meanwhile, the crowd had gained some suspicion, or received some intimation, of what was going on within. They had suddenly gathered in dense myriads, actually treading on each other in their haste and eagerness.[2] Perhaps a dull, wrathful murmur from without warned the Pharisees in time that it might be dangerous to proceed too far, and Jesus came out to the multitude with His whole spirit still aglow with the just and mighty indignation by which it had been pervaded. Instantly — addressing primarily His own disciples, but through them the listening thousands — He broke out with a solemn warning, "Beware ye of the leaven of the Pharisees, which is *hypocrisy*." He warned them that there was One before whose eye — ten thousand times brighter than the sun — secrecy was impossible. He bade them not be afraid of man — a fear to which the sad perturbances of these last few days might well have inclined them — but to fear Him who could not only destroy the body, but cast the soul also into the Gehenna[3] of fire. The God who loved them would care for them; and the Son of Man would, before the angels of God, confess them who confessed Him before men.

While He was thus addressing them, His discourse was broken in upon by a most inopportune interruption — not this time of hostility, not of ill-timed interference, not of overpowering admiration, but of simple policy and self-interest. Some covetous and half-instructed member of the crowd, seeing the listening throngs, hearing the words of authority and power, aware of the recent discomfiture of the Pharisees, expecting, perhaps, some immediate revelation of Messianic

---

[1] Luke xi. 53, ἤρξαντο δεινῶς ἐνέχειν καὶ ἀποστοματίζειν [260] (cf. Suid. *s. v.*). Theophylact explains it by ἀπὸ τοῦ στόματος κρατεῖν.[261] Vulg. "os opprimere." Classically, the word means "to dictate a repetition lesson" (Plato, *Euthyd.* 276 C).

[2] This seems to be implied by Luke xii. 1, ἐπισυναχθεισῶν τῶν μυριάδων τοῦ ὄχλου.[262] The aorist marks the sudden assemblage of the crowd.

[3] Γέεννα, Gehenna, is a corruption of the Hebrew *Gî Hinnom*, "the valley of Hinnom," outside Jerusalem, which had first been rendered infamous by Moloch worship, then defiled with corpses, lastly saved from putrefaction and pestilence by enormous fires. It thus became a type of all that was terrible and disgusting.

power, determined to utilize the occasion for his own worldly ends. He thought — if the expression may be allowed — that he could do a good stroke of business, and most incongruously and irreverently broke in with the request —

"Master, speak to my brother, that he divide the inheritance with me."

Almost stern was our Lord's rebuke to the man's egregious self-absorption. He seems to have been one of those not uncommon characters to whom the whole universe is pervaded by self; and he seems to have considered that the main object of the Messiah's coming would be to secure for him a share of his inheritance, and to overrule this unmanageable brother. Jesus at once dispelled his miserably carnal expectations, and then warned him, and all who heard, to beware of letting the narrow horizon of earthly comforts span their hopes. How brief, yet how rich in significance, is that little parable which He told them, of the rich fool who, in his greedy, God-forgetting, presumptuous selfishness, would do this and that, and who, as though there were no such thing as death, and as though the soul could live by bread, thought that "my fruits" and "my goods," and "my barns," and to "eat and drink and be merry," could for *many* years to come sustain what was left him of a soul, but to whom from heaven pealed as a terrible echo to his words the heart-thrilling sentence of awful irony, "*Thou fool, this night!*"[1]

And then our Lord expanded the thought. He told them that the life was more than meat, and the body than raiment. Again He reminded them how God clothes, in more than Solomon's glory, the untoiling lilies, and feeds the careless ravens that neither sow nor reap. Food and raiment, and the multitude of possessions, were not life: *they* had better things to seek after and to look for; let them not be tossed on this troubled sea of faithless care;[2] be theirs the life

---

[1] Luke xii. 16—21. It is not indicated, any more than in the case of Dives, that his riches were unjustly acquired : his fault lay in his forgetting the Giver ; forgetting that he was but a steward of them ; forgetting that the soul cannot live by them; forgetting how soon death might make him relax his grasp of them. It is clear that the reminiscence of Nabal's selfish folly and wretched death was in our Lord's mind. This is shown by the emphatic repetition of the μου (cf. 1 Sam. xxv. 11) and by the choice of ἄφρων = *Nabal* (id. ver. 25). The passage, too, offers sufficient resemblances to a beautiful passage in the Son of Sirach (xi. 18, 19) to establish the interesting conclusion of Stier, that our Lord was also familiar with the Apocrypha. In the original Greek of this parable there is a singular energy and liveliness, quite accordant with the mood of intense emotion under which Jesus was speaking.

[2] Luke xii. 29, μὴ μετεωρίζεσθε, "Be not like ships that toss in the stormy offing, outside the harbor's mouth."

of fearless hope, of freest charity, the life of the girded loin and the burning lamp — as servants watching and waiting for the unknown moment of their lord's return.

The remarks had mainly been addressed to the disciples, though the multitudes also heard them, and were by no means excluded from their import. But here Peter's curiosity got the better of him, and he asks " whether the parable was meant specially for them, or even for all?

To that question our Lord did not reply, and His silence was the best reply. Only let each man see that he was that faithful and wise servant; blessed indeed should he then be; but terrible in exact proportion to his knowledge and his privileges should be the fate of the gluttonous, cruel, faithless drunkard whom the Lord should surprise in the midst of his iniquities.

And then — at the thought of that awful judgment — a solemn agony passed over the spirit of Christ. He thought of the rejected peace, which should end in furious war; he thought of the divided households and the separated friends. He had a baptism to be baptized with, and His soul was straitened with anguish till it was accomplished. He had come to fling fire upon the earth, and oh, that it were already kindled! — that fire was as a spiritual baptism, the refining fire, which should at once inspire and blind, at once illuminate and destroy, at once harden the clay and melt the gold.[1] And here we are reminded of one of those remarkable though only traditional utterances attributed to Christ, which may possibly have been connected with the thought here expressed —

"*He who is near me is near the fire! he who is far from me is far from the kingdom.*"[2]

But from these sad thoughts He once more descended to the immediate needs of the multitude. From the reddening heaven, from the rising clouds, they could foretell that the showers would fall or that the burning wind would blow — why could they not discern the signs of the times? Were they not looking into the far-off fields of heaven

---

[1] Luke xii. 50, πῶς συνέχομαι. I have seen no perfectly satisfactory explanation of τί θέλω, εἰ ἤδη ἀνήφθη. It seems best to make the τί θέλω a question, and regard εἰ as equivalent to εἴθε, " would that." So those difficult words are understood by Origen (?), Meyer, Stier, Alford, &c., and, as it seems, rightly; though probably there was something far more in these utterances of deep emotion than could be rightly understood.

[2] ῾Ο ἐγγύς μου ἐγγὺς τοῦ πυρός· ὁ δὲ μακρὰν ἀπ᾽ ἐμοῦ μακρὰν ἀπὸ τῆς βασιλείας. (Didymus in Ps. lxxxviii. 8.) Traces of the same remarkable saying are found in Orig. Hom. in Jer. iii., p. 778; Ign. *ad Smyrn.* 4. (See Westcott, *Introduction*, p. 430.)

for signs which were in the air they breathed, and on the ground they trod upon; and, most of all — had they but searched rightly — in the state of their own inmost souls? If they would see the star which should at once direct their feet, and influence their destiny, they must look for it, not in the changing skies of outward circumstance, but each in the depth of his own heart.[1] Let them seize the present opportunity to make peace with God. For men and for nations the "too late" comes at last.

And there the discourse seems to have ended. It was the last time for many days that they were to hear His words. Surrounded by enemies who were not only powerful, but now deeply exasperated — obnoxious to the immediate courtiers of the very king in whose dominion he was living — dogged by the open hatred and secret conspiracies of spies whom the multitude had been taught to reverence — feeling that the people understood Him not, and that in the minds of their leaders and teachers sentence of death and condemnation had already been passed upon Him — He turned His back for a time upon His native land, and went to seek in idolatrous and alien cities the rest and peace which were denied Him in His home.

---

[1] Cf. Matt. xvi. 2, 3; Luke xii. 54—57. καύσων is the hot wind, קָרִים " ventus arens" (Jer. in Ezek. xxvii.).

CHAPTER XXXIV.

AMONG THE HEATHEN.

" They that dwell in the land of the shadow of death, upon them hath the Light shined." — Isa. ix. 2.

" THEN Jesus went thence, and departed into the regions of Tyre and Sidon." [1]

Such is the brief notice which prefaces the few and scanty records of a period of His life and work of which, had it been vouchsafed to us, we should have been deeply interested to learn something more. But only a single incident of this visit to heathendom has been recorded. It might have seemed that in that distant region there would be a certainty, not of safety only, but even of repose; but it was not so. We have already seen traces that the fame of His miracles had penetrated even to the old Phœnician cities, and no sooner had He reached their neighborhood than it became evident that He could not be hid. A woman sought for Him, and followed the little company of wayfarers with passionate entreaties — " Have mercy on me, O Lord, Thou Son of David; my daughter is grievously vexed with a devil."

We might have imagined that our Lord would answer such a prayer with immediate and tender approbation, and all the more because, in granting her petition, He would symbolically have been representing the extension of His kingdom to the three greatest branches of the Pagan world. For this woman was by birth a Canaanite, and a Syro-Phœnician; [2] by position a Roman subject; by culture and language a Greek; and her appeal for mercy to the Messiah of the Chosen People might well look like the first-fruits of that harvest in which the good seed should spring up hereafter in Tyre and Sidon, and Carthage, and Greece, and Rome. But Jesus — and is not this one of the numberless indications that we are deal-

---

[1] Matt. xv. 21—28 ; Mark vii. 24—30.

[2] The name is somewhat uncertain ; it is perhaps the opposite of Liby-phoenix —*i. e.*, the Phœnicians of Carthage (cf. *Uterque Poenus*, Hor. *Od.* ii. 2, 11), since the *province* Syro-Phœnice was not created till Hadrian's time. The readings of Mark vii. 26 differ, and Griesbach reads Σύρα Φοινίσσα. But perhaps Συροφοινίκισσα (א, A) is the safest form.

ing, not with loose and false tradition, but with solid fact ? — " Jesus answered her not a word."

In no other single instance are we told of a similar apparent cold-ness on the part of Christ; nor are we here informed of the causes which influenced His actions. Two alone suggest themselves : He may have desired to test the feelings of His disciples, who, in the narrow spirit of Judaic exclusiveness, might be unprepared to see Him grant His blessings, not only to a Gentile, but a Canaanite, and descendant of the accursed race. It was true that He had healed the servant of the centurion, but he was perhaps a Roman, certainly a benefactor to the Jews, and in all probability a proselyte of the gate. But it is more likely that, knowing what would follow, He may have desired to test yet further the woman's faith, both that He might crown it with a more complete and glorious reward, and that she might learn something deeper respecting Him than the mere Jewish title that she may have accidentally picked up.[1] And further than this, since every miracle is also rich in moral significance, He may have wished for all time to encourage us in our prayers and hopes, and teach us to persevere, even when it might seem that His face is dark to us, or that His ear is turned away.

Weary with the importunity of her cries, the disciples begged Him to send her away. But, as if even *their* intercession would be una-vailing, He said, " I am not sent but unto the lost sheep of the *house of Israel.*"

Then she came and fell at His feet, and began to worship Him, saying, " Lord, help me." Could he indeed remain untouched by that sorrow ? Could He reject that appeal ? and would He leave her to return to the life-long agony of watching the paroxysms of her demoniac child ? Calmly and coldly came from those lips, that never yet had answered with anything but mercy to a suppliant's prayer — " It is not meet to take the children's bread and to cast it to dogs."

Such an answer might well have struck a chill into her soul ; and had he not foreseen that hers was the rare trust which can see mercy and acceptance even in apparent rejection, He would not so have answered her. But not all the snows of her native Lebanon could quench the fire of love which was burning on the altar of her heart, and prompt as an echo came forth the glorious and immortal answer — " Truth, Lord ; then let me share the condition, not of the children,

[1] In Mark iii. 8; Luke vi. 17, we are distinctly told that " they about Tyre and Sidon " were among His hearers, and the witnesses of His miracles : and He had on two separate occasions at least been publicly greeted by the title, " Son of David " (Matt. ix. 27 ; xii. 23).

but of the dogs, for even the dogs eat of the crumbs which fall from their masters' table." [1]

She had triumphed, and more than triumphed. Not one moment longer did her Lord prolong the agony of her suspense. " O woman," He exclaimed, "great is thy faith: be it unto thee even as thou wilt." And with his usual beautiful and graphic simplicity St. Mark ends the narrative with the touching words, "And when she was come to her house, she found the devil gone out, and her daughter laid upon the bed."

How long our Lord remained in these regions, and at what spot He stayed, we do not know. Probably His departure was hastened by the publicity which attended His movements even there, and which — in a region where it had been His object quietly to train His own nearest and most beloved followers, and not either to preach or to work deeds of mercy — would only impede His work. He therefore left that interesting land. On Tyre, with its commercial magnificence, its ancient traditions, its gorgeous and impure idolatries, its connection with the history and prophecies of His native land — on Sarepta, with its memories of Elijah's flight and Elijah's miracles — on Sidon, with its fisheries of the purple limpet, its tombs of once-famous and long-forgotten kings, its minarets rising out of their groves of palm and citron, beside the blue historic sea — on the white wings of the countless vessels, sailing to the Isles of the Gentiles, and to all the sunny and famous regions of Greece and Italy and Spain — He would doubtless look with a feeling of mingled sorrow and interest. But his work did not lie here, and leaving behind Him those Phœnician shrines of Melkarth and Asherah, of Baalim and Ashtaroth, He turned eastward — probably through the deep gorge of the rushing and beautiful Leontes — and so reaching the sources of the Jordan, travelled southward on its further bank into the regions of Decapolis. [2]

---

[1] Ναὶ, Κύριε· καὶ γὰρ τὰ κυνάρια, κ. τ. λ. (Matt. xv. 27), " Yea, Lord ; for even the little dogs," &c. The ψίχια may possibly be the ἀπομαγδαλίαι (Ar. *Equit.* 415), or fragments of bread on which the guests wiped their hands (after thrusting them into the common dish), and then flung to the dogs.

[2] For the Leontes and the doubts as to its identification, see *Dict. of Geogr.* s. v. " Bostrenus," and Robinson, *Bibl. Res.* iii. 408—410. The reading διὰ Σιδῶνος, " He passed from the regions of Tyre *through* Sidon," in Mark vii. 31, is almost certain. The Codex Sinaiticus here concurs with the Vatican, the Codex Bezae, and the Cod. Reg. Parisiensis. Besides, the privacy which He was seeking could not well be attained by passing southwards, and so through the plain of Esdraelon, by Bethshean and over the bridge at the southern end of the Lake of Galilee. Perhaps I am wrong in assuming that the worship of Melkarth, &c., lingered on.

Decapolis was the name given to a district east of the Jordan, extending as far north (apparently)[1] as Damascus, and as far south as the river Jabbok, which formed the northern limit of Peræa. It was a confederacy of ten free cities, in a district which, on their return from exile, the Jews had never been able to recover, and which was therefore mainly occupied by Gentiles, who formed a separate section of the Roman province. The reception of Jesus in this semi-pagan district seems to have been favorable. Wherever He went He was unable to abstain from exercising His miraculous powers in favor of the sufferers for whom His aid was sought; and in one of these cities[2] He was entreated to heal a man who was deaf, and could scarcely speak.[3] He might have healed him by a word, but there were evidently circumstances in his case which rendered it desirable to make the cure gradual, and to effect it by visible signs. He took the man aside, put His fingers in his ears, and spat, and touched His tongue; and then St. Mark preserves for us the sigh, and the uplifted glance, as He spoke the one word, "Ephphatha! Be opened!"[4] Here again it is not revealed to us what were the immediate influences which saddened His spirit. He may have sighed in pity for the man; He may have sighed in pity for the race; He may have sighed for all the sins that degrade and all the sufferings which torture; but certainly he sighed in a spirit of deep tenderness and compassion, and certainly that sigh ascended like an infinite intercession into the ears of the Lord God of Hosts.[5]

Mr. Garnett calls my attention to the fact that Lucian (?), *De Deâ Syr.* ix., enumerates only three ἀρχαῖα καὶ μέγαλα ἱερὰ in Syria — those of the Syrian Hera, the Byblian Venus, and Astarte. On the other hand, Melkarth continues to be represented to a late period on coins.

[1] Pliny, *Nat. Hist.* v. 18.

[2] Gerasa, Gadara, Hippos, Pella, Gergesa, Bethshean (Scythopolis) are all said by Pliny to belong to Decapolis; the readings of one or two of the names are corrupt.

[3] Mark vii. 32—37.

[4] More exactly אֶפְּתַח, a sound hardly capable of transliteration into Greek. The conclusion which some have drawn that our Lord ordinarily spoke Greek, and that St. Mark has only preserved for us a few Aramaic words on the rare occasions on which Christ adopted the vernacular language of His people, is very precarious. Most of the Jews of that time, those at any rate who were educated and lived in the great commercial centres, spoke two languages, Greek and Aramaic, to which many of them must have added a colloquial knowledge of Latin; but we have seen reason to believe that the language most commonly used by our Lord was Aramaic (*v. supra*, p. 93.)

[5] "It was not drawn from Him," says Luther, "on account of the single tongue and ears of this poor man; but it is a common sigh over all tongues and ears, yea, over all hearts, bodies, and souls, and over all men, from Adam to his last descendant." (Stier, iii. 304.)

The multitudes of that outlying region, unfamiliar with His miracles, were beyond measure astonished. His injunction of secrecy
was as usual disregarded, and all hope of seclusion was at an end.
The cure had apparently been wrought in close vicinity to the eastern
shore of the Sea of Galilee, and great multitudes followed Jesus to
the summit of a hill overlooking the lake,[1] and there bringing their
lame, and blind, and maimed, and dumb, they laid them at the feet
of the Good Physician, and He healed them all. Filled with intense
and joyful amazement, these people of Decapolis could not tear themselves from His presence, and — semi-pagans as they were — they
" glorified the God of Israel." [2]

Three days they had now been with Him, and, as many of them
came from a distance, their food was exhausted. Jesus pitied them,
and seeing their faith, and unwilling that they should faint by the
way, once more spread for His people a table in the wilderness.
Some have wondered that, in answer to the expression of His pity,
the disciples did not at once anticipate or suggest what He
should do. But surely here there is a touch of delicacy and truth.
They knew that there was in Him no prodigality of the supernatural,
no lavish and needless exercise of miraculous power. Many and
many a time had they been with multitudes before, and yet on one
occasion only had He fed them ; and moreover, after He had done
so, He had most sternly rebuked those who came to Him in expectation of a repeated offer of such gifts, and had uttered a discourse so
searching and strange that it alienated from Him many even of His
friends.[3] For them to suggest to Him a repetition of the feeding of
the five thousand would be a presumption which their ever-deepening reverence forbade, and forbade more than ever as they recalled
how persistently He had refused to work a sign, such as this was, at
the bidding of others. But no sooner had He given them the signal
of His intention, than with perfect faith they became His ready ministers. They seated the multitude, and distributed to them the miraculous multiplication of the seven loaves and the few small fishes ;
and, this time unbidden, they gathered the fragments that remained,
and with them filled seven large baskets of rope, after the multitude
— four thousand in number, besides women and children — had eaten
and were filled.[4] And then kindly and peacefully, and with no exhi-

---

[1] Very probably near the Wady Semakh, nearly opposite Magdala.

[2] Matt. xv. 29—39 ; Mark viii. 1—9.

[3] These points have been (so far as I have observed) universally overlooked.

[4] σπυρίδες, this time not small κόφινοι, as in the previous miracle : for the
size of them compare Acts ix. 25, where St. Paul is let down the wall of Damascus

bition on the part of the populace of that spurious excitement which had marked the former miracle, the Lord and His Apostles joined in sending away the rejoicing and grateful throng.

---

in a ὅπυρίς. To suppose, as some have done, that this miracle is identical with the Feeding of the Five Thousand — both being but blurred traditions of one and the same event — is simply to deprive the Evangelists of every particle of historical value. The two miracles differ in almost every circumstance — in time, in place, in numbers, in results, in details ; and it is a striking mark of truth, which certainly would not be found in the work of inventors, that the lesser miracle is put after the greater, our Lord's object being to do a work of mercy, not to put forth a display of power.

CHAPTER XXXV.

THE GREAT CONFESSION.

" These have known that Thou has sent me." — JOHN xvii. 25.

VERY different was the reception which awaited Jesus on the farther shore. The poor heathens of Decapolis had welcomed Him with reverent enthusiasm : the haughty Pharisees of Jerusalem met Him with sneering hate. It may be that, after this period of absence, His human soul yearned for the only resting-place which He could call a home. Entering into His little vessel, He sailed across the lake to Magdala.[1] It is probable that He purposely avoided sailing to Beth saida or Capernaum, which are a little north of Magdala, and which had become the head-quarters of the hostile Pharisees. But it seems that these personages had kept a look-out for His arrival. As though they had been watching from the tower of Magdala for the sail of His returning vessel, barely had He set foot on shore than they came forth to meet Him. Nor were they alone: this time they were accompanied — ill-omened conjunction ! — with their rivals and enemies the Sadducees, that sceptical sect, half-religious, half-political, to which at this time belonged the two High Priests, as well as the members of the reigning family.[2] Every section of the ruling classes — the Pharisees, formidable from their religious weight among the people ; the Sadducees, few in number, but powerful from wealth and position ; the Herodians, representing the influence of the Romans, and of their nominees the tetrarchs ; the scribes and lawyers, bringing to bear the authority of their orthodoxy and their learning

---

[1] St. Mark says (viii. 10), " the parts of Dalmanutha." Nothing is known about Dalmanutha, though uncertain identifications of it have been attempted ; nor is anything known of Magadan, which is found in Matt. xv. 39, according to א, B, D, but does not seem a probable reading. If Magadan is a confused form of Megiddo, that must be an error, for Megiddo is in the middle of the plain of Esdraelon. Yet even in Mark the Codex Bezae reads " Magadan." Eusebius and Jerome (*Onomast.* s. v.) make Magadan a region about Gerasa, and therefore east of the Lake ; but that is impossible. The " Melegada " of D looks like a case of transposition and indeed this transposition is probably the source of the confusion, and may even account for the form Dalmanutha.

[2] Acts iv. 1, 5 ; Jos. *Antt.* xv. 8, § 1.

— were all united against Him in one firm phalanx of conspiracy and opposition, and were determined above all things to hinder His preaching, and to alienate from Him, so far as was practicable, the affections of the people among whom most of His mighty works were done.[1]

They had already found by experience that the one most effectual weapon to discredit His mission and undermine His influence was the demand of a sign — above all, a sign from heaven. If He were indeed the Messiah, why should He not give them bread from heaven as Moses, they said, had done? where were Samuel's thunder and Elijah's flame? why should not the sun be darkened, and the moon turned into blood, and the stars of heaven be shaken? why should not some fiery pillar glide before them to victory, or the burst of some stormy *Bath Kol* ratify His words?

They knew that no such sign would be granted them, and they knew that He had vouchsafed to them the strongest reasons for His thrice-repeated refusal to gratify their presumptuous and unspiritual demand.[2] Had they known or understood the fact of His temptation in the wilderness, they would have known that His earliest answers to the tempter were uttered in this very spirit of utter self-abnegation. Had he granted their request, what purpose would have been furthered? It is not the influence of external forces, but it is the germinal principle of life within, which makes the good seed to grow ; nor can the hard heart be converted, or the stubborn unbelief removed, by portents and prodigies, but by inward humility, and the grace of God stealing downward like the dew of heaven, in silence and unseen. What would have ensued had the sign been vouchsafed? By its actual eye-witnesses it would have been attributed to demoniac agency ; by those to whom it was reported it would have been explained away ; by those of the next generation it would have been denied as an invention, or evaporated into a myth.

But in spite of all this, the Pharisees and Sadducees felt that for the present this refusal to gratify their demand gave them a handle against Jesus, and was an effectual engine for weakening the admiration of the people. Yet not for one moment did He hesitate in rejecting this their temptation. He would not work any epideictic miracle at *their* bidding, any more than at the bidding of the tempter. He at once told them, as he had told them before, that "no sign

---

[1] Sepp, whose learning is strangely deformed by constant extravagances, compares the eight sects of the Jews to modern schools of thought, as follows: Pharisees = pietists ; Essenes = mystics ; Sadducees = rationalists ; Herodians = political clubs, &c.; Zealots = radicals ; Samaritans = schismatics !.

[2] John ii. 18 ; vi. 30 ; Matt. xii. 38.

should be given them but the sign of the prophet Jonah." Pointing to the western sky, now crimson with the deepening hues of sunset, He said, " When it is evening, ye say, 'Fair weather! for the sky is red;' and in the morning, 'Storm to-day, for the sky is red and frowning.' Hypocrites! ye know how to discern the face of the sky: can ye not learn the signs of the times?"[1]

As He spoke He heaved a deep inward sigh.[2] For some time He had been absent from home. He had been sought out with trustful faith in the regions of Tyre and Sidon. He had been welcomed with ready gratitude in heathen Decapolis; here, at home, He was met with the flaunt of triumphant opposition, under the guise of hypocritic zeal. He steps ashore on the lovely plain, where He had done so many noble and tender deeds, and spoken for all time such transcendent and immortal words. He came back, haply to work once more in the little district where His steps had once been followed by rejoicing thousands, hanging in deep silence on every word He spoke. As He approaches Magdala, the little village destined for all time to lend its name to a word expressive of His most divine compassion — as He wishes to enter once more the little cities and villages which offered to His homelessness the only shadow of a home — here, barely has He stepped upon the pebbly strand, barely passed through the fringe of flowering shrubs which embroider the water's edge, barely listened to the twittering of the innumerable birds which welcome Him back with their familiar sounds — when He finds all the self-satisfied hypocrisies of a decadent religion drawn up in array to stop His path!

He did not press His mercies on those who rejected them. As in after days His nation were suffered to prefer their robber and their murderer to the Lord of Life, so now the Galilæans were suffered to keep their Pharisees and lose their Christ. He left them as He had left the Gadarenes — rejected, not suffered to rest even in His home; with heavy heart, solemnly and sadly he left them — left them then and there — left them, to revisit, indeed, once more their neighborhood, but never again to return publicly — never again to work miracles, to teach or preach.[3]

It must have been late in that autumn evening when He stepped once more into the little ship, and bade His disciples steer their course

---

[1] Matt. xvi. 1—4; Mark viii. 10—13.

[2] Mark viii. 12, *ἀναστενάξας τῷ πνεύματι αὐτοῦ.*

[3] There is something emphatic both in the *καταλιπὼν αὐτοὺς*[263] of Matt. xvi. 4 and in the *ἀφεὶς αὐτοὺς*[264] of Mark viii. 13.

towards Bethsaida Julias, at the northern end of the Lake. On their way they must have sailed by the bright sands of the western Bethsaida, on which Peter and the sons of Zebedee had played in their infancy, and must have seen the white marble synagogue of Capernaum flinging its shadow across the waters, which blushed with the reflected colors of the sunset. Was it at such a moment, when He was leaving Galilee with the full knowledge that His work there was at an end, and that He was sailing away from it under the ban of partial excommunication and certain death — was it at that supreme moment of sorrow that He uttered the rhythmic woe in which He upbraided the unrepentant cities wherein most of His mighty works were done? —

" Woe unto thee, Chorazin! woe unto thee, Bethsaida! for if the mighty works which have been done in you had been done in Tyre and Sidon, they would have repented long ago in sackcloth and ashes.

" But I say unto you, That it shall be more tolerable for Tyre and Sidon at the day of judgment than for you.

"And thou, Capernaum, which art exalted unto heaven, shalt be brought down to hell: for if the mighty works which have been done in thee had been done in Sodom, it would have remained until this day.

" But I say unto you, That it shall be more tolerable for the land of Sodom in the day of judgment than for thee!' "

Whether these touching words were uttered on this occasion as a stern and sad farewell to His public ministry in the land he loved, we cannot tell;[1] but certainly His soul was still filled with sorrow for the unbelief and hardness of heart, the darkened intellects and corrupted consciences of those who were thus leaving for Him no power to set foot in His native land. It has been said by a great forensic orator that "no form of self-deceit is more hateful and

---

[1] This woe — evidently complete and isolated in character — is recorded in Matt. xi 20—24; Luke x. 12—15. St. Matthew seems to group it with the utterances at the feast of Simon the Pharisee; St. Luke with the Mission of the Seventy. It is, perhaps, hazardous to conjecture that words so solemnly beautiful and full of warning were uttered more than once ; and since the order of St. Matthew is in many places professedly unchronological, we can find no more appropriate occasion for the words than this. They have evidently the character of a farewell, and the recent visit of Jesus to the coasts of Tyre and Sidon would give them special significance here. The mention of the otherwise unknown Chorazin is an additional proof, if any were needed, of the fragmentary character of the Gospels. It is an inland town, three miles from Tell Hûm, of which the deserted ruins, discovered by Dr. Robinson, are still called Khersah.

detestable . . . than that which veils spite and falsehood under the guise of frankness, and behind the profession of religion." Repugnance to this hideous vice must have been prominent in the stricken heart of Jesus, when, as the ship sailed along the pleasant shore upon its northward way, He said to His disciples, "Take heed, and beware of the leaven of the Pharisees and Sadducees." [1]

He added nothing more; and this remark the strange simplicity of the disciples foolishly misinterpreted. They were constantly taking His figurative expressions literally, and His literal expressions metaphorically. When He called Himself the "bread from heaven," they thought the saying hard; when He said, "I have meat to eat that ye know not of," they could only remark, "Hath any man brought Him aught to eat?" when He said, "Our friend Lazarus sleepeth," they answered, "Lord, if he sleep, he shall do well." And so now, although leaven was one of the very commonest types of sin, and especially of insidious and subterranean sin, the only interpretation which, after a discussion among themselves, they could attach to His remark was, that He was warning them not to buy leaven of the Pharisees and Sadducees, or, perhaps, indirectly reproaching them because, in the sorrow and hurry of their unexpected re-embarkation, they had only brought with them one single loaf! Jesus was grieved at this utter non-comprehension, this almost stupid literalism. Did they suppose that He, at whose words the loaves and fishes had been so miraculously multiplied — that they, who after feeding the five thousand had gathered twelve handbaskets, and after feeding the four thousand had gathered seven large baskets-full of the fragments that remained — did they suppose, after *that*, that there was danger lest He or they should suffer from starvation? There was something almost of indignation in the rapid questions in which, without correcting, He indicated their error. "Why reason ye because ye have no bread? Perceive ye not yet, neither understand? Have ye your heart yet hardened? Having eyes see ye not? and having ears, hear ye not? and do ye not remember?" And then once more, after He had reminded them of those miracles, "How is it that ye do not understand?" They had not ventured to ask Him for any explanation; there was something about Him — something so awe-inspiring and exalted in His personality — that their love for Him, intense though it was, was tempered by an overwhelming reverence: but now it began to dawn upon

---

[1] Or "of Herod" (Mark viii. 15). The Herodians appear to have been mainly Sadducees.

them that something else was meant, and that He was bidding them beware, not of the leaven of bread, but of the doctrine of the Pharisees and Sadducees.

At Bethsaida Julias, probably on the following morning, a blind man was brought to Him for healing. The cure was wrought in a manner very similar to that of the deaf and dumb man in Decapolis. It has none of the ready freedom, the radiant spontaneity of the earlier and happier miracles. In one respect it differs from every other recorded miracle, for it was, as it were, tentative. Jesus took the man by the hand, led him out of the village, spat upon his eyes, and then, laying His hands upon them, asked if he saw. The man looked at the figures in the distance, and, but imperfectly cured as yet, said, "I see men as trees walking." Not until Jesus had laid His hands a second time upon his eyes did he see clearly. And then Jesus bade him go to his house, which was not at Bethsaida; for, with an emphatic repetition of the word, he is forbidden either to *enter* into the town, or to tell it to any one *in* the town. We cannot explain the causes of the method which Christ here adopted. The impossibility of understanding what guided His actions arises from the brevity of the narrative, in which the Evangelist — as is so often the case with writers conversant with their subject — passes over many particulars, which, because they were so familiar to himself, will, he supposes, be self-explaining to those who read his words. All that we can dimly see is Christ's dislike and avoidance of these heathenish Herodian towns, with their borrowed Hellenic architecture, their careless customs, and even their very names commemorating, as was the case with Bethsaida Julias, some of the most contemptible of the human race.[1] We see from the Gospels themselves that the richness and power displayed in the miracles was correlative to the faith of the recipients: in places where faith was scanty it was but too natural that miracles should be gradual and few.[2]

Leaving Bethsaida Julias, Jesus made his way towards Cæsarea Philippi. Here, again, it seems to be distinctly intimated that He did not enter into the town itself, but only visited the "coasts" of it, or wandered about the neighboring villages.[3] Why He bent His footsteps in that direction we are not told. It was a town that had seen

---

[1] Herod Philip had named his renovated capital in honor of Julia, the abandoned daughter of the Emperor Augustus.

[2] No one who has rightly considered the Gospel miracles will regard this as "a damaging concession." At any rate, if so, it is a fresh proof of the entire truthfulness of the Gospels. (Matt. xiii. 58 ; Mark vi. 5, 6 ; ix. 23, &c.)

[3] Matt. xvi. 13, μέρη, "parts," or "regions ;" Mark viii. 27, κώμας.

many vicissitudes. As "Laish," it had been the possession of the careless Sidonians. As "Dan," it had been the chief refuge of a warlike tribe of Israel, the northern limit of the Israelitish kingdom, and the seat of the idolatry of the golden calf. Colonized by Greeks, its name had been changed into Paneas, in honor of the cave under its towering hill, which had been artificially fashioned into a grotto of Pan, and adorned with niches, which once contained statues of his sylvan nymphs. As the capital of Herod Philip, it had been re-named in honor of himself and his patron Tiberius.[1] The Lord might gaze with interest on the noble ranges of Libanus and Anti-Libanus'; He might watch the splendid and snowy mass of Hermon glittering under the dawn, or flushed with its evening glow ; He might wander round Lake Phiala, and see where, according to popular belief, the Jordan, after his subterranean course, bursts rejoicing into the light : but He could only have gazed with sorrow on the city itself, with its dark memories of Israelitish apostasy, its poor mimicry of Roman imperialism, and the broken statues of its unhallowed and Hellenic cave.

But it was on His way to the northern region that there occurred an incident which may well be regarded as the culminating point of His earthly ministry.[2] He was alone. The crowd that surged so tumultuously about Him in more frequented districts, here only followed Him at a distance. Only His disciples were near Him as He stood apart in solitary prayer. And when the prayer was over, He beckoned them about Him as they continued their journey, and asked them those two momentous questions on the answers to which depended the whole outcome of His work on earth.

First He asked them —

" Whom do men say that I the Son of Man am ?

The answer was a sad one. The Apostles dared not and would not speak aught but the words of soberness and truth, and they made the disheartening admission that the Messiah had not been recognized by the world which He came to save. They could only repeat the idle guesses of the people. Some, echoing the verdict of the guilty conscience of Antipas, said that He was John the Baptist ; some, who may have heard the sterner denunciations of His impassioned grief, caught in that mighty utterance the thunder-tones of a new Elijah ; others, who had listened to His accents of tenderness and

[1] On Cæsarea Philippi see Jos. *Antt.* xv. 10, § 3 ; *B. J.* i. 21, § 3 ; and for a description of its present state, Thomson, *Land and Book*, II., ch. xvi.

[2] Matt. xvi. 13—28 ; Mark viii. 27—ix. 1 ; Luke ix. 18—27.

words of universal love, saw in Him the plaintive soul of Jeremiah, and thought that He had come, perhaps, to restore them the lost Urim and the vanished Ark: many looked on Him as a prophet and a precursor. None — in spite of an occasional Messianic cry wrung from the admiration of the multitude, amazed by some unwonted display of power — none dreamt of who He was. The light had shone in the darkness, and the darkness comprehended it not.

"But whom say ye that I am?"

Had that great question been answered otherwise — *could* it have been answered otherwise — the world's whole destinies might have been changed. Had it been answered otherwise, then, humanly speaking, so far the mission of the Saviour would have wholly failed, and Christianity and Christendom have never been. For the work of Christ on earth lay mainly with His disciples. He sowed the seed, they reaped the harvest; He converted them, and they the world. He had never openly spoken of His Messiahship. John indeed had borne witness to Him, and to those who could receive it He had indirectly intimated, both in word and deed, that He was the Son of God. But it was His will that the light of revelation should dawn gradually on the minds of His children; that it should spring more from the truths he spake, and the life He lived, than from the wonders which He wrought; that it should be conveyed not in sudden thunder-crashes of supernatural majesty or visions of unutterable glory, but through the quiet medium of a sinless and self-sacrificing course. It was in the Son of Man that they were to recognize the Son of God.

But the answer came, as from everlasting it had been written in the book of destiny that it should come; and Peter, the ever warm-hearted, the *coryphaeus* of the Apostolic choir,[1] had the immortal honor of giving it utterance for them all —

"THOU ART THE CHRIST, THE SON OF THE LIVING GOD!"

Such an answer from the chief of the Apostles atoned by its fulness of insight and certitude of conviction for the defective appreciation of the multitudes.[2] It showed that at last the great mystery was revealed

---

[1] ὁ πανταχοῦ θερμός, ὁ τοῦ χοροῦ τῶν ἀποστόλων κορυφαῖος [265] (Chrys. *Hom.* liv.).

[2] He says, not "we say," but "THOU ART" (Alford, *ad loc.*). St. Peter was "primus inter pares" — a leader, but among equals. Had he been more than this — had Christ's words been intended to bestow on him the least shadow of supremacy — how could James and John have asked to sit on the right hand and on the left of Christ in His Kingdom? and how could the Apostles on at least two subsequent occasions have disputed who among them should be the greatest?

which had been hidden from the ages and the generations. The Apostles at least had not only recognized in Jesus of Nazareth the promised Messiah of their nation, but it had been revealed to them by the special grace of God that that Messiah was not only what the Jews expected, a Prince, and a Ruler, and a son of David, but was *more* than this, even the Son of the living God.

With awful solemnity did the Saviour ratify that great confession. "Jesus answered and said unto him, Blessed art thou, Simon, son of Jonas:¹ for flesh and blood hath not revealed it unto thee, but my Father which is in heaven.² And I say unto thee, that thou art Peter (*Petros*), and on this rock (*petra*) I will build my Church, and the gates of hell shall not prevail against it.³ And I will give unto thee the keys of the kingdom of heaven; and whatsoever thou shalt bind on earth shall be bound in heaven, and whatsoever thou shalt loose on earth shall be loosed in heaven."

Never did even the lips of Jesus utter more memorable words. It was His own testimony of Himself. It was the promise that they who can acknowledge it are blessed. It was the revealed fact that they only *can* acknowledge it who are led thereto by the Spirit of God. It told mankind for ever that not by earthly criticisms, but only by heavenly grace, can the full knowledge of that truth be obtained. It was the laying of the corner-stone of the CHURCH OF CHRIST, and the earliest occasion on which was uttered that memorable word, thereafter to be so intimately blended with the history of the world.⁴ It was the promise that that Church founded on the

---

¹ So, too, Jesus addressed him on other solemn occasions (John xxi. 15—17).

² Not the common Jewish *abinu*, "our Father," but "my Father" (ὁ πατήρ μου).

³ Similar plays on words, founded on very deep principles, are common among deep thinkers in all tongues. Our Lord was probably speaking in Aramaic, in which language the phrase "gates of hell" (שַׁעֲרֵי שְׁאוֹל, *shaare sheol*) presents a pleasing assonance. If so, He probably said, "Thou art Kephas, and on this Kepha I will," &c. Many commentators, from the earliest ages downwards, have understood "this rock" to be either the confession of Peter, or Christ himself (see abundant authorities for these opinions in the elaborate note of Bishop Wordsworth); it is difficult, however, in either of these cases to see any force in the "Thou art Peter." On the other hand, to speak of a man as "the rock" is unlike the ordinary language of Scripture. "Who is a rock save our God?" (2 Sam. xxii. 32; Ps. xviii. 31; lxii. 2; Isa. xxviii. 16; and see especially 1 Cor. iii. 11; x. 4). The key was a common Jewish metaphor for authority (Isa. xxii. 22; Luke xi. 52). (Gfrörer, i. 155, 283; Schöttg., *Hor. Hebr.* ii. 894.) I shall speak further on the passage in a subsequent note, but do not profess to have fully solved its difficulties.

⁴ It is a remarkable fact that the word ἐκκλησία occurs but once again in the Gospels (Matt. xviii. 17).

rock of inspired confession should remain unconquered by all the powers of hell. It was the conferring upon that Church, in the person of its typical representative, the power to open and shut, to bind and loose, and the promise that the power faithfully exercised on earth should be finally ratified in heaven.

" Tute haec omnia dicuntur," says the great Bengel, " nam quid ad Romam ? " " all these statements are made with safety; for what have they to do with Rome ? " [1] Let him who will wade through all the controversy necessitated by the memorable perversions of this memorable text, which runs as an inscription round the interior of the great dome of St. Peter's. But little force is needed to overthrow the strange inverted pyramids of argument which have been built upon it. Were it not a matter of history, it would have been deemed incredible that on so baseless a foundation should have been rested the fantastic claim that abnormal power should be conceded to the bishops of a Church which almost certainly St. Peter did not found, and in a city in which there is no indisputable proof that he ever set his foot. The immense arrogancies of sacerdotalism; the disgraceful abuses of the confessional; the imaginary power of absolving from oaths; the ambitious assumption of a right to crush and control the civil power; the extravagant usurpation of infallibility in wielding the dangerous weapons of anathema and excommunication; the colossal tyrannies of the Popedom, and the detestable cruelties of the Inquisition — all these abominations are, we may hope, henceforth and for ever, things of the past. But the Church of Christ remains, of which Peter was a chief foundation, a living stone. The powers of hell have *not* prevailed against it; it still has a commission to fling wide open the gates of the kingdom of heaven; it still may loose us from idle traditional burdens and meaningless ceremonial observances; it still may bind upon our hearts and consciences the truths of revealed religion and the eternal obligations of the Moral Law.

To Peter himself the great promise was remarkably fulfilled. It was he who converted on the day of Pentecost the first great body of Jews who adopted the Christian faith; it was he who admitted the earliest Gentile into the full privileges of Christian fellowship.[2] His confession made him as a rock, on which the faith of many was founded, which the powers of Hades might shake, but over which

---

[1] The following texts are alone sufficient to prove finally that St. Peter in no way exercised among the Apostles any paramount or supreme authority : — Matt. xviii. 1; Eph. ii. 20; Rev. xxi. 14; 2 Cor. xi. 5; xii. 11; Gal. ii. 9, 11; Luke xxii. 24, 26; John xxi. 19—23, &c.

[2] Peter himself points to this fact as a fulfilment of Christ's promise (Acts xv. 7).

they never could prevail. But, as has been well added by one of the deepest, most venerable, and most learned Fathers of the ancient Church, " If *any one* thus confess, when flesh and blood have not revealed it unto him, but our Father in heaven, *he*, too, shall obtain the promised blessings; as the letter of the Gospel saith indeed to the great St. Peter, but as its spirit teacheth to every man who hath become like what that great Peter was." [1]

It may be said that, from that time forth, the Saviour might regard one great portion of His work on earth as having been accomplished. His Apostles were now convinced of the mystery of His being; the foundations were laid on which, with Himself as the chief corner-stone, the whole vast edifice was to be hereafter built.

But He forbade them to reveal this truth as yet. The time for such preaching had not yet come. They were yet wholly ignorant of the true method of His manifestation. They were yet too unconfirmed in faith even to remain true to Him in His hour of utmost need. As yet He would be known as the Christ to those only whose spiritual insight could see Him immediately in His life and in His works. As yet He would neither strive nor cry, nor should His voice be heard in the streets.[2] When their own faith was confirmed beyond all wavering by the mighty fact of His resurrection, when their hearts had been filled with the new Shechînah of God's Holy Spirit, and their brows, with final consecration, had been mitred with

---

[1] Origen. A · full consideration of this great utterance to St. Peter must be sought for in works professedly theological, but I may here call special attention to a calm and admirable sermon, " Confession and Absolution," by my friend Professor Plumptre (Isbister, 1874), in which he points out the distinction which must be carefully drawn between three separate things too often confounded — viz., the " Power of the Keys," the power to bind and loose, and the power to remit or retain. 1. The first (since the delivery of a key formed the ordination of a Scribe) meant the " power to open the treasury of the Divine oracles, and bring them out to Christ's disciples " (cf. Matt. xiii. 52; Luke xi. 52; Matt. xxiii. 4). To those who heard, it must have implied the *teaching* power of the Church. 2. The power to bind and loose, afterwards conferred on all the disciples (Matt. xviii. 18), gave them a power like that exercised by the Rabbis (*e. g.*, the school of Shammai, which, according to the Jewish proverb, *bound*, and the school of Hillel which *loosed*) — the power, namely, to declare what precepts are, and what are not, binding (cf. Matt. xxiii. 4; Acts x. 28). It implied, therefore, the *legislative* action of the Church. 3. The power to forgive and retain sins (John xx. 22, 23) far transcended these, and was distinctly *rejected* by the Scribes. It belongs to the *prophetic* office of the Church, and had direct reference to the gift of the Holy Spirit, and " was possible only so far as the prophetic gift, in greater or less measure, was bestowed on those who exercise it " (Plumptre, *ubi supra*, pp. 45—48). For wise views of this subject, see also Hooker, *Eccl. Pol.*, VI. iv. 1, 2.

[2] Matt. xii. 19; Isa. xlii. 1.

Pentecostal flame, then, but not till then, would the hour have come for them to go forth and teach all nations that Jesus was indeed the Christ, the Son of the Living God.

But although they now knew Him, they knew nothing as yet of the way in which it was His will to carry out His divine purposes. It was time that they should yet further be prepared ; it was time that they should learn that, King though He was, His kingdom was not of this world ; it was time that all idle earthly hopes of splendor and advancement in the Messianic kingdom should be quenched in them for ever, and that they should know that the kingdom of God is not meat and drink, but righteousness, and peace, and joy in believing.

Therefore He began, calmly and deliberately, to reveal to them His intended journey to Jerusalem, His rejection by the leaders of His nation, the anguish and insult that awaited Him, His violent death, His resurrection on the third day. He had, indeed, on previous occasions given them divers and distant intimations [1] of these approaching sufferings, but now for the first time He dwelt on them distinctly, and that with full freedom of speech.[2] Yet even now He did not reveal in its entire awfulness the *manner* of His approaching death. He made known unto them, indeed, that He should be rejected by the elders and chief priests and scribes — by all the authorities, and dignities, and sanctities of the nation — but not that He should be delivered to the Gentiles. He warned them that He should be killed, but He reserved till the time of His last journey to Jerusalem the horrible fact that He should be crucified.[3] He thus revealed to them the future only as they were best able to bear it, and even then, to console their anguish and to support their faith, He told them quite distinctly, that on the third day He should rise again.

But the human mind has a singular capacity for rejecting that which it cannot comprehend — for ignoring and forgetting all that does not fall within the range of its previous conceptions. The

---

[1] Matt. x. 38 ; John iii. 14. But now ἤρξατο δεικνύειν [266] (Matt. xvi. 21). A still further gradation, a still clearer prophecy, may be observed from time to time as the day approached (Matt. xvi. 21 ; xvii. 22 ; xx. 18 ; xxvi. 2).

[2] Mark viii. 32, καὶ παρρησίᾳ τὸν λόγον ἐλάλει.[267] Earlier and dimmer intimations were John ii. 19 (" Destroy this Temple ") ; iii. 14 (" shall the Son of Man be lifted up ") ; Matt. ix. 15 (" the Bridegroom shall be taken away from them ") ; John vi. 51 (" my flesh will I give for the life of the world ") ; Matt. xvi. 4 (" the sign of the prophet Jonas ").

[3] Matt. xvi. 21, ἀποκτανθῆναι, but in xx. 19, σταυρῶσαι. The manner of His death was, however, distinctly intimated in the metaphor of " taking up the cross," immediately afterwards (xvi. 24).

Apostles, ever faithful and ever simple in their testimony, never conceal from us their dulness of spiritual insight, nor the dominance of Judaic preconceptions over their minds. They themselves confess to us how sometimes they took the literal for the figurative,[1] and sometimes the figurative for the literal.[2] They heard the announcement, but they did not realize it. "They understood not this saying, and it was hid from them, that they perceived it not."[3] Now as on so many other occasions a supernatural awe was upon them, "and they feared to ask Him."[4] The prediction of His end was so completely alien from their whole habit of thought, that they would only put it aside as irrelevant and unintelligible — some mystery which they could not fathom; and as regards the resurrection, when it was again prophesied to the most spiritual among them all, they could only question among one another what the rising from the dead should mean.[5]

But Peter, in his impetuosity, thought that he understood, and thought that he could prevent; and so he interrupted those solemn utterances by his ignorant and presumptuous zeal. The sense that it had been given to him to perceive and utter a new and mighty truth, together with the splendid eulogium and promise which he had just received, combined to inflate his intellect and misguide his heart; and taking Jesus by the hand or by the robe,[6] he led Him a step or two aside from the disciples, and began to advise, to instruct, to rebuke his Lord. "God forbid,"[7] he said; "this shall certainly *not* happen to thee." With a flash of sudden indignation our Lord rebuked his worldliness and presumption. Turning away from him, fixing His eyes on the other disciples, and speaking in the hearing of them all — for it was fit that they who had heard the words of vast

---

[1] *Ex. gr.*, the leaven of the Pharisees (Matt. xvi. 7); the meat they know not of (John iv. 32); the sleep of death (John xi. 12).

[2] What defileth a man (Matt. xv. 17). See too John xi. 11, 16. (Lange, iii. 241.)

[3] Luke ix. 45.

[4] Mark ix. 32; Luke ii. 50; xviii. 34.

[5] Mark ix. 10.

[6] Matt. xvi. 22, $\pi\rho o\sigma\lambda\alpha\beta\acute{o}\mu\epsilon\nu o\varsigma$ $\alpha\grave{v}\tau\grave{o}\nu$.[268] There is, as Stier points out (ii. 328), a happy instinctive irony in the $\mathring{\eta}\rho\xi\alpha\tau o$ $\grave{\epsilon}\pi\iota\tau\iota\mu\tilde{\alpha}\nu$[269] of Mark viii. 32, compared to the $\mathring{\eta}\rho\xi\alpha\tau o$ $\delta\iota\delta\acute{\alpha}\sigma\kappa\epsilon\iota\nu$[270] of verse 31.

[7] Such seems to be the meaning of $\mathring{\iota}\lambda\epsilon\acute{\omega}\varsigma$ $\sigma o\iota$, $K\acute{v}\rho\iota\epsilon$ (Matt. xvi. 22). It is literally "[May God be] merciful to thee," rather than, as in the margin of the E. V., "pity thyself." The phrase is a kind of expletive, like *Di meliora! praefiscini! Di averruncent!* in Latin; and *Gott bewahre!* in German. The Hebrew expression to which it corresponds is sometimes rendered in the LXX. by $\mu\mathring{\eta}$ $\gamma\acute{\epsilon}\nu o\iota\tau o$ and $\mu\eta\delta\alpha\mu\tilde{\omega}\varsigma$ (Josh. xxii. 29; 1 Sam. xii. 23; xx. 2). (See Schleusner, *Lex. in N. T.* s. v.)

promise should hear also the crushing rebuke — He exclaimed, "Get thee behind me, Satan! thou art a stumbling-block unto me; for thy thoughts are not the thoughts of God, but of men." This thy mere carnal and human view — this attempt to dissuade me from my "baptism of death" — is a sin against the purposes of God.[1] Peter was to learn — would that the Church which professes to have inherited from him its exclusive and superhuman claims had also learnt in time! — that he was far indeed from being infallible — that he was capable of falling, aye, and with scarcely a moment's intermission, from heights of divine insight into depths of most earthly folly.

"*Get thee behind me, Satan!*" — the very words which He had used to the tempter in the wilderness. The rebuke was strong, yet to our ears it probably conveys a meaning far more violent than it would have done to the ears that heard it. The word Satan means no more than "adversary," and, as in many passages of the Old Testament, is so far from meaning the great Adversary of mankind, that it is even applied to opposing angels. The word, in fact, was among the Jews, as in the East generally, and to this day, a very common one for anything bold, powerful, dangerous — for every secret opponent or open enemy.[2] But its special applicability in this instance rose from the fact that Peter was in truth adopting the very line of argument which the Tempter himself had adopted in the wilderness. And in calling Peter an offence (σκάνδαλον), Jesus probably again alluded to his name, and compared him to a stone in the path over which the wayfarer stumbles. The comparison must have sunk deeply into the Apostle's mind, for he too in his Epistle warns his readers against some to whom, because they believe not, the Head-

---

[1] "Those whose intentions towards us are the best," says Stier, "are the most dangerous to us when their intentions are merely human" (ii. 332). How often, alas! are a man's real foes they of his own household; his friends, who love him best, become in their worldliness his worst enemies. They drag him down from heights of self-sacrifice to the vulgar, the conventional, the comfortable.

[2] For instance, in Numb. xxii. 22, 32, the same Hebrew word שָׂטָן is twice used of the angel who went to withstand Balaam; in 1 Kings xi. 14 it is used of Hadad, and in verse 23 of Rezon; in 1 Sam. xxix. 4 the Philistines use it of David. See too Ps. cix. 6, marg., &c. (*v. infr.*, p. 193). The same remark is true of the Koran. Among the Rabbis are to be found such expressions as, "When the bull rushes at a man, Satan leaps up between his horns." They always drag the notion in when they can, as in Targ. Jonath., Exod. xxxii. 19, &c. "If a woman's hair is uncovered," says R. Simeon, "evil spirits come and sit upon it" (Wetstein, *ad* 1 Cor. xi. 10). "'If that young Sheit . . ,' I exclaimed, '*about to use an epithet generally given in the East to such adventurous youths,*'" &c. (Layard's *Nineveh*, i. 287). Layard adds in a note that Sheitan is usually applied to a clever, cunning, daring fellow.

378 THE LIFE OF CHRIST.

stone of the Corner became "a stone of stumbling and a *rock of offence*" (πέτρα σκανδάλου, 1 Pet. ii. 8).

But having thus warned and rebuked the ignorant affection of unspiritual effeminacy in His presumptuous Apostle, the Lord graciously made the incident an occasion for some of His deepest teaching, which He not only addressed to His disciples, but to all.[1] We learn quite incidentally from St. Mark, that even in these remote regions His footsteps were sometimes followed by attendant crowds,[2] who usually walked at a little distance from Him and His disciples, but were sometimes called to Him to hear the gracious words which proceeded out of His mouth. And alike they and His disciples were as yet infected with the false notions which had inspired the impetuous interference of Peter. To them, therefore, He addressed the words which have taught us for ever that the essence of all highest duty, the meaning of all truest life — alike the most acceptable service to God, and the most ennobling example to men — is involved in the law of self-sacrifice.[3] It was on this occasion that He spoke those few words which have produced so infinite an effect on the conscience of mankind. "What is a man profited, if he shall gain the whole world, and lose his own soul? or what shall a man give in exchange for his soul?" And then, after warning them that He should Himself be judged, He consoled them under this shock of unexpected revelation by the assurance that there were some standing there who should not taste of death till they had seen the Son of Man coming in His kingdom. If, as all Scripture shows, "the kingdom of the Son of Man" be understood in a sense primarily spiritual, then there can be no difficulty in understanding this prophecy in the sense that, ere all of them passed away, the foundations of that kingdom should have been established for ever in the abolition of the old and the establishment of the new dispensation. Three of them were immediately to see Him transfigured;[4] all but one were to be witnesses of His resurrection; one at least — the beloved disciple — was to sur-

---

[1] Luke ix. 23.

[2] Cf. Mark viii. 34; vii. 24.

[3] The métaphorical sense cf "taking up the cross" is well illustrated by Plato, *De Rep.* ii. 362 A., ἀνασχινδυλευθήσεται. 2 Cor. iii. 18; Rom. xii. 2 could lead to no mistake.

[4] The translators of our Bible seem to have understood the Transfiguration as the first fulfilment of the prophecy, by separating it from the verses which precede it in St. Mark (ix. 1), and making it introduce the following narrative. Cf. 2 Pet. i. 16: "eye-witnesses (ἐπόπται) of His majesty" is there referred expressly to the Transfiguration, and appealed to as the confirmation of the preaching which had proclaimed "the power and coming" of Christ. See, too, 1 John i. 1; iv. 14.

vive that capture of Jerusalem and destruction of the Temple which were to render impossible any literal fulfilment of the Mosaic law. And the prophecy may have deeper meanings yet than these — meanings still more real because they are still more wholly spiritual. " If we wish not to fear death," says St. Ambrose, " let us stand where Christ is; Christ is your Life ; He is the very Life which cannot die."

CHAPTER XXXVI.

THE TRANSFIGURATION.

" And this voice which came from heaven we heard, when we were with Him
in the holy mount." — 2 PETER i. 18.

NONE of the Evangelists tell us about the week which followed
this memorable event. They tell us only that " after six days " He
took with Him the three dearest and most enlightened of His disciples,[1] and went with them — the expression implies a certain solemnity of expectation [2] — up a lofty mountain, or, as St. Luke calls it,
simply " *the* mountain."

The supposition that the mountain intended was Mount Tabor has
been engrained for centuries in the tradition of the Christian Church ;
and three churches and a monastery erected before the close of the
sixth century attest the unhesitating acceptance of this belief. Yet
it is almost certain that Tabor was not the scene of that great epiphany. The rounded summit of that picturesque and wood-crowned
hill, which forms so fine a feature in the landscape, as the traveller
approaches the northern limit of the plain of Esdraelon, had probably from time immemorial been a fortified and inhabited spot,[3] and
less than thirty years after this time, Josephus, on this very mountain,
strengthened the existing fortress of Itaburion. This, therefore,
was not a spot to which Jesus could have taken the three Apostles
" apart by themselves." Nor, again, is there the slightest intimation
that the six intervening days had been spent in travelling southwards
from Cæsarea Philippi, the place last mentioned ; on the contrary, it
is distinctly intimated by St. Mark (ix. 30), that Jesus did not " pass
through Galilee " (in which Mount Tabor is situated), till after the
events here narrated. Nor again does the comparatively insignificant
hill Paneum, which is close by Cæsarea Philippi, fulfil the require-

---

[1] Matt. xvii. 1—13 ; Mark ix. 2—13 ; Luke ix. 28—36. The " about eight days
after " of St. Luke (ix. 28) is merely an inclusive reckoning, but is one of the
touches which are valuable as showing the independence of his narrative, which
gives us several new particulars.

[2] ἀναφέρει. Comp. Luke xxiv. 51.

[3] Chisloth-tabor (Josh. xix. 12 ; Judg. iv. 6).

ments of the narrative.[1] It is, therefore, much more natural to suppose that our Lord, anxious to traverse the Holy Land of His birth to its northern limit, journeyed slowly forward till He reached the lower slopes of that splendid snow-clad mountain, whose glittering mass, visible even as far southward as the Dead Sea, magnificently closes the northern frontier of Palestine — the Mount Hermon of Jewish poetry. Its very name means "the mountain," and the scene which it witnessed would well suffice to procure for it the distinction of being the only mountain to which in Scripture is attached the epithet "holy."[2] On those dewy pasturages, cool and fresh with the breath of the snow-clad heights above them, and offering that noble solitude, among the grandest scenes of Nature, which He desired as the refreshment of His soul for the mighty struggle which was now so soon to come, Jesus would find many a spot where He could kneel with His disciples absorbed in silent prayer.

And the coolness and solitude would be still more delicious to the weariness of the Man of Sorrows after the burning heat of the Eastern day and the incessant publicity which, even in these remoter regions, thronged his steps. It was the evening hour when He ascended,[3] and as He climbed the hill-slope with those three chosen witnesses — "the Sons of Thunder and the Man of Rock" — doubtless a solemn gladness dilated His whole soul; a sense not only of the heavenly calm which that solitary communion with His Heavenly Father would breathe upon the spirit, but still more than this, a sense that He would be supported for the coming hour by ministrations not of earth, and illuminated with a light which needed no aid from sun or moon or stars. He went up to be prepared for death, and He took His three Apostles with Him that, haply, having seen His glory — the glory of the only Begotten of the Father, full of grace and truth — their hearts might be fortified, their faith strengthened, to gaze unshaken on the shameful insults and unspeakable humiliation of the cross.

There, then, He knelt and prayed, and as He prayed He was elevated far above the toil and misery of the world which had rejected Him. He was transfigured before them, and His countenance shone as the sun, and His garments became white as the dazzling snow-fields above them. He was enwrapped in such an aureole of glistering brilliance — His whole presence breathed so divine a radiance —

[1] *Πανεῖον*. The town is called on coins *Καισάρεια ὑπὸ Πανείῳ*.
[2] 2 Peter i. 18.
[3] This is evident from Luke ix. 32, 37, especially when compared with Luke vi. 12.

that the light, the snow, the lightning[1] are the only things to which the Evangelist can compare that celestial lustre. And, lo! two figures were by His side.[2] "When, in the desert, He was girding Himself for the work of life, angels of life came and ministered unto Him; now, in the fair world, when He is girding Himself for the work of death, the ministrants come to Him from the grave — but from the grave conquered — one from that tomb under Abarim, which His own hand had sealed long ago; the other from the rest into which He had entered without seeing corruption. There stood by Him Moses and Elias, and spake of His decease. And when the prayer is ended, the task accepted, then first since the star paused over Him at Bethlehem, the full glory falls upon Him from heaven, and the testimony is borne to His everlasting sonship and power — 'Hear ye Him.'"[3]

It is clear, from the fuller narrative of St. Luke, that the three Apostles did not witness the beginning of this marvellous transfiguration. An Oriental, when his prayers are over, wraps himself in his *abba*,[4] and, lying down on the grass in the open air, sinks in a moment into profound sleep. And the Apostles, as afterwards they slept at Gethsemane, so now they slept on Hermon. They were heavy, "weighed down" with sleep, when suddenly starting into full wakefulness of spirit, they saw and heard.[5]

---

[1] λευκὰ ὡς τὸ φῶς (Matt. xvii. 2); λευκὰ λίαν ὡς χιὼν (Mark ix. 3); λευκὸς . . . ἐξαστράπτων (Luke ix. 29). It is interesting to observe that St. Luke, writing for Greeks and Romans, avoids the word μετεμορφώθη [271] used by the other Evangelists, because his readers would associate that word with the conceptions with which they were familiar in Nicander, Antoninus Liberalis, and Ovid. (See Valcknaer, quoted by Bishop Wordsworth, *ad loc.*)

[2] The καὶ ἰδοὺ [272] of Matt. xvii. 3 shows how intense was the impression which the scene had made on the imagination of those who witnessed it. "The two who appeared to Him were the representatives of the Law and the Prophets: both had been removed from this world in a mysterious manner; . . . both, like the greater One with whom they spoke, had endured that supernatural fast of forty days and nights; both had been on the holy mount in the visions of God. And now they came, solemnly, to consign into His hands, once and for all, in a symbolical and glorious representation, their delegated and expiring power." (Alford.)

[3] Ruskin, *Mod. Painters*, iii. 392.

[4] Hence the merciful provision of the Mosaic law, that the outer robe was to be restored at night if taken as a pledge for debt. (See Exod. xxii. 26.)

[5] So I would render διαγρηγορήσαντες in Luke ix. 32. It is a non-classical word, and has this meaning in Byzantine writers. Or perhaps the διά may imply "waking after an interval" — "in the middle of it all." Both the context and the grammar sufficiently show that (though it occurs here only in the N. T.) it cannot mean "having kept awake," as Alford and Archbishop Trench (following Rost and Palm) render it.

In the darkness of the night, shedding an intense gleam over the mountain herbage, shone the glorified form of their Lord. Beside Him, in the same flood of golden glory,[1] were two awful shapes, which they knew or heard to be Moses and Elijah. And the Three spake together, in the stillness, of that coming decease at Jerusalem, about which they had just been forewarned by Christ.

And as the splendid vision[2] began to fade — as the majestic visitants were about to be separated from their Lord, as their Lord Himself passed with them into the overshadowing brightness — Peter, anxious to delay their presence, amazed, startled, transported, not knowing what he said[3] — not knowing that Calvary would be a spectacle infinitely more transcendant than Hermon — not knowing that the Law and the Prophets were now fulfilled — not fully knowing that his Lord was unspeakably greater than the Prophet of Sinai and the Avenger of Carmel — exclaimed, " Rabbi, it is best for us to be here ;[4] and let us make three tabernacles, one for thee, and one for Moses, and one for Elias." Jesus might have smiled at the naïve proposal of the eager Apostle, that they six should dwell for ever in little *succôth* of wattled boughs on the slopes of Hermon. But it was not for Peter to construct the universe for his personal satisfaction. He had to learn the meaning of Calvary no less than that of Hermon. Not in cloud of glory or chariot of fire was Jesus to pass away from them, but with arms outstretched in agony upon the accursed tree ; not between Moses and Elias, but between two thieves, who " were crucified with Him, on either side one."

No answer was vouchsafed to his wild and dreamy words ; but, even as he spake, a cloud — not a cloud of thick darkness as at Sinai, but a cloud of light, a Shechînah of radiance — overshadowed them, and a voice from out of it uttered, " This is my beloved Son ; hear Him." They fell prostrate, and hid their faces on the grass.[5] And as — awakening from the overwhelming shock of that awful voice, of that enfolding Light — they raised their eyes and gazed suddenly

---

[1] ὀφθέντες ἐν δόξῃ (Luke ix. 31).

[2] τὸ ὅραμα (Matt. xvii. 9). The word, which occurs eleven times in the Acts, but not elsewhere in the N. T., is applied to dreams (Acts xvi. 10 ; xviii. 9) and ecstacies (Acts xi. 5), but also to any impression on the *spirit* which is as clear as an impression on the senses (Acts vii. 31). Hence Phavorinus says, ὁράματά εἰσι προφητῶν, ὅσα ἐγρηγορότες βλέπουσι οἱ προφῆται.[213]

[3] This touch in all probability comes to us from St. Peter himself (Mark ix. 6).

[4] καλὸν in the New Testament seems sometimes to have a superlative sense. Cf. Matt. xviii. 8 ; xxvi. 24, &c., and Gen. xxxviii. 26, where בוט means " better," as " bona," in Plaut. *Rud.* iv. 4, 70. (Schleusner, s. v.)

[5] Matt. xvii. 6.

all around them,[1] they found that all was over. The bright cloud had vanished. The lightning-like gleams of shining countenances and dazzling robes had passed away;[2] they were alone with Jesus, and only the stars rained their quiet lustre on the mountain slopes.

At first they were afraid to rise or stir, but Jesus, their Master—as they had seen Him before He knelt in prayer, came to them, touched them—said, "Arise, and be not afraid."

And so the day dawned on Hermon, and they descended the hill; and as they descended, He bade them tell no man until He had risen from the dead. The vision was for them; it was to be pondered over by them in the depths of their own hearts in self-denying reticence; to announce it to their fellow-disciples might only awake *their* jealousy and their own self-satisfaction; until the resurrection it would add nothing to the faith of others, and might only confuse their conceptions of what was to be His work on earth. They kept Christ's command, but they could not attach any meaning to this allusion. They could only ask each other, or muse in silence, what this resurrection from the dead could mean. And *another* serious question weighed upon their spirits. They had seen Elias. They now knew more fully than ever that their Lord was indeed the Christ. Yet "how say the Scribes"—and had not the Scribes the prophecy of

---

[1] Mark ix. 8, ἐξάπινα περιβλεψάμενοι (cf. Matt. xvii. 8), one of the many inimitably graphic touches of truthfulness and simplicity—touches never yet found in any "myth" since the world began—with which in all three Evangelists this narrative abounds. We have proofs that on two of the three spectators this scene made an indelible impression. St. John most clearly alludes to it in John i. 14; 1 John i. 1. St. Peter (if, as I believe, the Second Epistle is genuine) is dwelling on it in 2 Peter i. in a manner all the more striking because it is partly unconscious. Thus, he not only appeals to it in confirmation of his preaching, but he uses just before the unusual word ἔξοδος for "death" [2 Peter i. 15 (cf. Luke ix. 31): it is, however, possible that δόξαν *may* here be the reading, as it seems to have been read by St. Chrysostom], and σκήνωμα (ver. 13; cf. Matt. xvii. 4) for "tabernacle;" and immediately after speaks (ver. 19) of "a light shining in a dark place," and immediately preceding the dawn—which is another, and, so far as I am aware, hitherto unnoticed trace of the fact that the Transfiguration (of which the writer's mind is here so full) took place by night. On the word ἔξοδος Bengel finely remarks, "Vocabulum valde grave, quo continetur passio, crux, mors, resurrectio, adscensio."[274] Archbishop Trench aptly compares "Post obitum, vel potius *excessum*, Romuli"[275] (Cic. *Rep.* ii. 30), and says that St. Peter by the word ἐπόπτης[276] (2 Peter i. 16) seems to imply a sort of *initiation* into holy mysteries (*Studies in the Gospels*, p. 206). Many have resolved the narrative of the Transfiguration into a myth; it is remarkable that, in this verse, St. Peter *is expressly repudiating the very kind of myths* (μῦθοι σεσοφισμένοι) under which this would be classed.

[2] "Finis legis Christus; Lex et Prophetia ex Verbo; quae autem ex Verbo coeperunt, in Verbo desinunt"[277] (St. Ambrose). (Wordsworth, in Matt. xvii. 8.)

Malachi in their favor?[1] — "that Elias must first come and restore all things?" And then our Lord gently led them to see that Elias indeed had come, and had not been recognized, and had received at the hand of his nation the same fate which was soon to happen to Him whom he announced. Then understood they that He spake to them of John the Baptist.[2]

---

[1] Mal. iv. 5. The LXX., without any authority from the Hebrew, read here 'Ηλίαν τὸν Θεσβίτην.[218]

[2] Luke i. 17, "in the spirit and power of Elias;" cf. Matt. xi. 10. The Jewish expectation of Elias is well known. A thing of unknown ownership may be kept by the finder "till the coming of Elias." He was to restore to the Jews the pot of manna, the rod of Aaron, &c., and his coming generally was to be a χρόνος ἀποκαταστάσεως[219] (cf. Acts iii. 21). See Lightfoot, *Hor. Hebr.* in Matt. xvii. 10, 11.

CHAPTER XXXVII.

THE DEMONIAC BOY.

Τινὲς δέ φασὶν ὅτι ἡ ὄψις αὐτοῦ ὡραιοτέρα γινομένη ἀπὸ τοῦ φωτός
. . . ἐφείλκετο τούς ὄχλους.[280] — THEOPHYL.

THE imagination of all readers of the Gospels has been struck by
the contrast — a contrast seized and immortalized for ever in the
great picture of Raphael — between the peace, the glory the heavenly
communion on the mountain heights, and the confusion, the rage,
the unbelief, the agony which marked the first scene that met the
eyes of Jesus and His Apostles on their descent to the low levels of
human life.[1]

For in their absence an event had occurred which filled the other
disciples with agitation and alarm. They saw a crowd assembled
and Scribes among them, who with disputes and victorious innuen-
does were pressing hard upon the diminished band of Christ's chosen
friends.[2]

Suddenly at this crisis the multitude caught sight of Jesus.
Something about His appearance, some unusual majesty, some lingering radiance, filled them with amazement, and they ran up to
Him with salutations.[3] "What is your dispute with them?" He
sternly asked of the Scribes. But the Scribes were too much abashed,
the disciples were too self-conscious of their faithlessness and failure,
to venture on any reply. Then out of the crowd struggled a man,
who, kneeling before Jesus, cried out, in a loud voice,[4] that he was
the father of an only son whose demoniac possession was shown by
epilepsy, in its most raging symptoms, accompanied by dumbness,
atrophy, and a suicidal mania. He had brought the miserable sufferer to the disciples to cast out the evil spirit, but their failure had
occasioned the taunts of the Scribes.

---

[1] Matt. xvii. 14—21 ; Mark ix. 14—29 ; Luke ix. 37—45.

[2] There were, of course, many Jews, and therefore naturally there would be
Scribes, in the kingdom of Philip.

[3] Mark ix. 14. We here follow mainly the full and vivid narrative of St. Mark.

[4] Matt. xvii. 14 ; Luke ix. 38.

The whole scene grieved Jesus to the heart. "O faithless and perverse generation," He exclaimed, "how long shall I be with you? how long shall I suffer you?" This cry of His indignation seemed meant for all—for the merely curious multitude, for the malicious Scribes, for the half-believing and faltering disciples. "Bring him hither to me."

The poor boy was brought, and no sooner had his eye fallen on Jesus, than he was seized with another paroxysm of his malady. He fell on the ground in violent convulsions, and rolled there with foaming lips. It was the most deadly and intense form of epileptic lunacy on which our Lord had ever been called to take compassion.[1]

He paused before He acted. He would impress the scene in all its horror on the thronging multitude, that they might understand that the failure was not of Him. He would at the same time invoke, educe, confirm the wavering faith of the agonized suppliant.

"How long has this happened to him?"

"From childhood: and often hath it flung him both into fire and into water to destroy him; but *if at all thou canst*, take pity on us and help us."

"*If thou canst?*"[2] answered Jesus—giving him back his own word—"all things are possible to him that believeth."

And then the poor hapless father broke out into that cry, uttered by so many millions since, and so deeply applicable to an age which, like our own, has been described as "destitute of faith, yet terrified at scepticism"—"*Lord, I believe; help thou mine unbelief.*"

Meanwhile, during this short colloquy, the crowd had been gathering more and more, and Jesus, turning to the sufferer, said, "Dumb and deaf spirit, I charge thee, come out of him, and enter no more into him." A yet wilder cry, a yet more fearful convulsion followed His words, and then the boy lay on the ground, no longer wallowing and foaming, but still as death. Some said, "He is dead." But Jesus took him by the hand, and, amid the amazed exclamations of the multitude, restored him to his father, calm and cured.

---

[1] Matt. xvii. 15, σεληνιάζεται καὶ κακῶς πάσχει.[281] This describes, at any rate, the natural side of his malady; but there is, in truth, to such maladies *no* purely *natural* side. They belong to some mystery of inquity which we can never understand. They are due, not to the στάσις [282] but to the ἀπόστασις [283] of human nature.

[2] This seems to be the force of Mark ix. 23, εἶπεν αὐτῷ τὸ εἰ δύνασαι πιστεῦσαι, πάντα δυνατὰ τῷ πιστεύοντι, which is the best reading (א, B, C, L, and some versions). For this use of τὸ see Matt. xix. 18; Luke ix. 46, &c. "As for the 'if thou canst'—all things are, &c." It is taken thus by the Æthiopic version, and "proclivi lectioni praestat ardua."[284]

Jesus had previously given to His disciples the power of casting out devils, and this power was even exercised in His name by some who were not among His professed disciples.[1] Nor had they ever failed before. It was therefore natural that they should take the first private opportunity to ask Him the cause of their discomfiture. He told them frankly that it was because of their unbelief. It may be that the sense of His absence weakened them; it may be that they felt less able to cope with difficulties while Peter and the sons of Zebedee were also away from them; it may be, too, that the sad prophecy of His rejection and death had worked with sinister effect on the minds of the weakest of them. But, at any rate, He took this opportunity to teach them two great lessons: the one, that there are forms of spiritual, physical, and moral evil so intense and so inveterate, that they can only be exorcised by prayer, united to that self-control and self-denial of which fasting is the most effectual and striking symbol;[2] the other, that to a perfect faith all things are possible. Faith, like a grain of mustard-seed, could even say to Hermon itself,[3] "Be thou removed, and cast into the waves of the Great Sea, and it should obey."

Jesus had now wandered to the utmost northern limit of the Holy Land, and He began to turn His steps homewards. We see from St. Mark that His return was designedly secret and secluded, and possibly not along the high roads, but rather through the hills and valleys of Upper Galilee to the westward of the Jordan.[4] His object was no longer to teach the multitudes who had been seduced into rejecting Him, and among whom He could hardly appear in safety, but to continue that other and even more essential part of His work, which consisted in the training of His Apostles. And now the con

---

[1] Mark ix. 38.

[2] It must, however, be noticed that the καὶ νηστεία [285] (Mark ix. 29) is a more than dubious reading. It is not found in א or B, and the corresponding verse in Matt. xvii. 21 is omitted by א, B, as well as by various versions. Tischendorf omits both. See, however, Matt. vi. 16—18; ix. 15.

[3] "Removing mountains" was among the Jews a common hyperbole for the conquest of stupendous difficulties. A great teacher was called by the Rabbis עֹקֵר הָרִים (gokêr hârîm), or "uprooter of mountains." See many instances in Lightfoot, *Hor. Hebr.* in Matt. xxi. 21.

[4] For the variety of readings on Matt. xvii. 22, ἀναστρεφομένων, συστρεφ., στρεφ., &c., see Keim, *Gesch. Jesu,* ii. 581. The παρεπορεύοντο of Mark ix. 30 is of uncertain meaning. We have already considered it in Mark ii. 23 (cf. Matt. xii. 1) [*v. supra,* p. 332]; and in Mark xi. 20; xv. 29, it means "passing by," as in Matt. xxvii. 39, the only other passage where it occurs. In Deut. ii. 14, it is simply used for הָלַךְ, "he walked."

stant subject of His teaching [1] was His approaching betrayal, murder, and resurrection. But He spoke to dull hearts ; in their deep-seated prejudice they ignored his clear warnings, in their faithless timidity they would not ask for further enlightenment. We cannot see more strikingly how vast was the change which the resurrection wrought in them than by observing with what simple truthfulness they record the extent and inveteracy of their own shortcomings, during those precious days while the Lord was yet among them.

The one thing which they *did* seem to realize was that some strange and memorable issue of Christ's life, accompanied by some great development of the Messianic kingdom, was at hand ; and this unhappily produced the only effect in them which it should *not* have produced. Instead of stimulating their self-denial, it awoke their ambition ; instead of confirming their love and humility, it stirred them up to jealousy and pride. On the road — remembering, perhaps, the preference which had been shown at Hermon to Peter and the sons of Zebedee — they disputed among themselves, " Which should be the greatest ? "

At the time our Lord took no notice of the dispute. He left their own consciences to work. But when they reached Capernaum and were in the house, then He asked them, " What they had been disputing about on the way ? " [2] Deep shame kept them silent, and that silence was the most eloquent confession of their sinful ambitions. Then He sat down, and taught them again, as He had done so often, that he who would be first must be last of all, and servant of all, and that the road to honor is humility. And wishing to enforce this lesson by a symbol of exquisite tenderness and beauty, He called to Him a little child, and set it in the midst, and then, folding it in his arms, warned them that unless they could become as humble as that little child, they could not enter into the kingdom of heaven. [3] They were to be as children in the world ; and he who should receive even one such little child in Christ's name, should be receiving Him, and the Father who sent Him.

---

[1] Mark ix. 31, ἐδίδασκεν . . . ἔλεγεν.

[2] See, for what follows, Matt. xviii. 1—35 ; Mark ix. 33—50 ; Luke ix. 46—50 ; which three passages I assume to be one and the same continuous discourse suggested by the same incidents, but told with varying completeness by the three Evangelists.

[3] The impossible tradition — mentioned by Nicephorus — that this was the martyr St. Ignatius, perhaps arose from a mistaken interpretation of his name Θεοφόρος as though it had been Θεόφορος ; but this name was derived from his celebrated interview with Trajan.

The expression "in my name" seems to have suggested to St. John a sudden question, which broke the thread of Christ's discourse. They had seen, he said, a man who was casting out devils in Christ's name; but since the man was not one of them, they had forbidden him. Had they done right?[1]

"No," Jesus answered; "let the prohibition be removed." He who could do works of mercy in Christ's name could not lightly speak evil of that name. He who was not against them was with them. Sometimes indifference is opposition; sometimes neutrality is aid."[2]

And then, gently resuming His discourse — the child yet nestling in His arms, and furnishing the text for His remarks — He warned them of the awful guilt and peril of offending, of tempting, of misleading, of seducing from the paths of innocence and righteousness, of teaching any wicked thing, or suggesting any wicked thought to one of those little ones, whose angels see the face of His Father in heaven. Such wicked men and seducers, such human performers of the devil's work — addressing them in words of more bitter, crushing import than any which He ever uttered — a worse fate, He said, awaited *them*, than to be flung with the heaviest millstone round their neck into the sea.[3]

And He goes on to warn them that no sacrifice could be too great if it enabled them to escape any possible temptations to put such stumbling-blocks in the way of their own souls, or the souls of others. Better cut off the right hand, and enter heaven maimed — better hew off the right foot, and enter heaven halt — better tear out the

---

[1] Bruce (*Training of the Twelve*, p. 234) quotes an apt illustration from the life of Baxter, whose followers condemned Sir Matthew Hale as unconverted, because he did not attend their weekly prayer meetings! " I," said Baxter, ... " that have seen his love to all good men, and the blamelessness of his life, thought better of his piety than of mine own." (*Reliquiæ Baxter*, iii. 47.)

[2] On another occasion Christ had said what seemed to be the reverse of this — viz., "He who is not with me is against me" (Matt. xii. 30). But it is easy to see that the two truths are but complementary to each other. " Qui n'a appris dans le cours d'une vie active, que, selon les circonstances et les personnes, celui qui s'abstient de concourir et se tient à l' écart tantôt donne appui et force, tantôt au contraire nuit et entrâve "[286] (Guizot, *Medit.* i. 279). Contrast the quiet insight and wisdom of this remark with Renan's " deux règles de prosélytisme tout à fait opposées et une contradiction amenée par une lutte passionnée."[287] Cf. Sueton, *Jul. Caes.* 75: " Denuntiante Pompeio, pro hostibus se habiturum qui reipublicae defuissent, ipse medios et neutrius partis suorum sibi numero futuros pronuntiavit."[288] (I owe this remarkably apposite reference to Mr. Garnett.)

[3] Μύλος ὀνικὸς (Matt. xviii. 6; Luke xvii. 2). The *rechem*, or runner-stone, *i. e.* the upper millstone, so heavy as to be turned by an ass.

right eye, and enter heaven blind — than suffer hand or foot or eye
to be the ministers of sins which should feed the undying worm or
kindle the quenchless flame. Better be drowned in this world with
a millstone round the neck, than carry that moral and spiritual millstone of unresisted temptation which can drown the guilty soul in
the fiery lake of alienation and despair. For just as salt is sprinkled
over every sacrifice for its purification, so must every soul be purged
by fire; by the fire, if need be, of the severest and most terrible
self-sacrifice. Let this refining, purging, purifying fire of searching
self-judgment and self-severity be theirs. Let not this salt lose its
savor, nor this fire its purifying power. "Have salt in yourselves,
and be at peace with one another." [1]

And thus, at once to confirm the duty of this mutual peace which
they had violated, and to show them that, however deeply rooted be
God's anger against those who lead others astray, *they* must never
cherish hatred even against those who had most deeply injured them,
He taught them how, first by private expostulation, then if necessary
by public appeal, at once most gently and most effectually to deal
with an offending brother. Peter, in the true spirit of Judaic
formalism, wanted a specific limit to the number of times when forgiveness should be granted; but Jesus taught that the times of
forgiveness should be practically unlimited. [2] He illustrated that
teaching by the beautiful parable of the servant, who, having been
forgiven by his king a debt of ten thousand talents, immediately
afterwards seized his fellow-servant by the throat, and would not
forgive him a miserable little debt of one hundred pence, a sum
1,250,000 times as small as that which he himself had been forgiven.
The child whom Jesus had held in His arms might have understood
that moral; yet how infinitely more deep must its meaning be to
us — who have been trained from childhood in the knowledge of
His atoning love — than it could have been, at the time when it was
spoken, to even a Peter or a John.

---

[1] Isa. xxxiii. 14, 15: "Who among us shall dwell with devouring fire? who
among us shall dwell with everlasting burnings? He that walketh righteously,
and speaketh uprightly, ... he shall dwell on high." We are again
reminded of that fine ἄγραφον δόγμα already quoted, "He who is near me, is
near the fire."

[2] The Rabbinic rule only admitted a triple forgiveness, referring to Amos i. 3 ;
Job xxxiii. 29 (marg., " twice " and " thrice ").

CHAPTER XXXVIII.

A BRIEF REST IN CAPERNAUM.

" Vade et scito nos esse in alio regno reges et filios regis."²⁸⁹ — LUTHER, *in* Matt. xiii.

ONE more incident, related by St. Matthew only, marked his brief stay on this occasion in Capernaum.

From time immemorial there was a precedent for collecting, at least occasionally, on the recurrence of every census, a tax of "half a shekel, after the shekel of the sanctuary," of every Jew who had reached the age of twenty years, as a "ransom for his soul," unto the Lord.[1] This money was devoted to the service of the Temple, and was expended on the purchase of the sacrifices, scapegoats, red heifers, incense, shewbread, and other expenses of the Temple service. After the return from the captivity, this *be ah*, or half-shekel, became a voluntary annual tax of a third of a shekel;[2] but at some subsequent period it had again returned to its original amount. This tax was paid by every Jew in every part of the world, whether rich or poor; and, as on the first occasion of its payment, to show that the souls of all alike are equal before God, "the rich paid no more, and the poor no less." It produced vast sums of money, which were conveyed to Jerusalem by honorable messengers.[3]

This tax was only so far compulsory that when first demanded, on the 1st of Adar, the demand was made quietly and civilly; if, however, it had not been paid by the 25th, then it seems that the collectors of the contribution (*tobhîn shekalîm*) might take a security for it from the defaulter.

Accordingly, almost immediately upon our Lord's return to Capernaum, these *tobhîn shekalîm* came to St. Peter, and asked him, quite

---

[1] Exod. xxx. 11—16. The English "tribute-money" is vague and incorrect; for the tribute was a *denarius* paid to the Roman emperor.

[2] Neh. x. 32.

[3] Philo (*De Monarch.* ii. 3) calls them ἱεροπομποί. These collections are alluded to in Cic. *Pro Flacco*, 28; Dio Cass. lxvi. 7; Jos. *B. J.* vii. 6, § 6; *Antt.* xviii. 9, § 1; and other passages collected by Wetstein, Lightfoot, &c. Taking the shekel roughly at 1s. 6d., the collection would produce £75,000 for every million contributors.

civilly, as the Rabbis had directed, "Does not your master pay the didrachmas?" [1]

The question suggests two difficulties — viz., Why had our Lord not been asked for this contribution in previous years? and why was it now demanded in autumn, at the approach of the Feast of Tabernacles, instead of in the month Adar, some six months earlier? The answers seem to be that priests and eminent rabbis were regarded as exempt from the tax; [2] that our Lord's frequent absence from Capernaum had caused some irregularity; and that it was permitted to pay arrears some time afterwards. [3]

The fact that the collectors inquired of St. Peter instead of asking Jesus Himself, is another of the very numerous indications of the awe which He inspired even into the heart of His bitterest enemies; as in all probability the fact of the demand being made at all shows a growing desire to vex His life, and to ignore His dignity. But Peter, with his usual impetuous readiness, without waiting, as he should have done, to consult His Master, replied, "Yes." [4]

If he had thought a moment longer — if he had known a little more — if he had even recalled his own great confession so recently given — his answer might not have come so glibly. This money was, at any rate, in its original significance, a redemption-money for the soul of each man; [5] and how could the Redeemer, who redeemed all souls by the ransom of His life, pay this money-ransom for his own? And it was a tax for the Temple services. How, then, could it be

---

[1] The *didrachmum* was a Greek coin exactly equivalent to half a shekel; the stater or silver *tetradrachmum* was a shekel. The stater and the Roman denarius (which was rather more than a fourth of its value) were the two common coins at this time : the actual *didrachm* had fallen into disuse. It is true that the LXX. translate *shekel* by δίδραχμον and half-shekel by ἥμισυ τοῦ διδράχμου, but it is now generally agreed that this is because they adopt the Alexandrian, not the Attic scale. The value of a *didrachm* was about eighteen-pence. (See Madden, *Hist. of Jewish Coinage*, p. 235 ; Leake, *Numism. Hellen.*, Append. 2, 3; Akerman, *Numism. Illustr. to the N. Test.*, p. 14.)

[2] So the *Pirke Abhôth*, iv. 5, quoted by Stier, ii. 362.

[3] There even seems to be some evidence (adduced by Greswell, *Dissert.* ii. 377) to show that it might be paid at either of the yearly feasts.

[4] It appears (Jost, *Gesch. des Judenth.* i. 218) that there had been a great dispute between the Pharisees and Sadducees as to whether this tax should be voluntary or compulsory, and that, after long debate, the Pharisees had carried the day. Perhaps, therefore, the demand was made of our Lord by way of testing which side he would take, and if so we may understand His words to St. Peter as sanctioning the universal principle that all gifts to God should be given "not grudgingly or of necessity." See a very interesting article by Professor Plumptre, in Smith's *Bibl. Dict.*, on "Tribute."

[5] Exod. xxx. 11, 12, *eesh kopher, naphshô*, λύτρα τῆς ψυχῆς. (Philo, *ubi supr.*)

due from Him whose own mortal body was the new spiritual Temple of the Living God? He was to enter the vail of the Holiest with the ransom of His own blood. But He paid what He did not owe, to save us from that which we owed, but could never pay.[1]

Accordingly, when Peter entered the house, conscious, perhaps, by this time, that his answer had been premature — perhaps also conscious that at that moment there were no means of meeting even this small demand upon their scanty store — Jesus, without waiting for any expression of his embarrassment, at once said to him, " What thinkest thou, Simon? the kings of the earth, from whom do they take tolls and taxes? from their own sons, or from those who are not their children."

There could be but one answer — " From those who are not their children."

" Then," said Jesus, " the sons are free." I, the Son of the Great King, and even thou, who art also His son, though in a different way, are not bound to pay this tax. If we pay it, the payment must be a matter, not of positive obligation, as the Pharisees have lately decided, but of free and cheerful giving.

There is something beautiful and even playful in this gentle way of showing to the impetuous Apostle the dilemma in which his hasty answer had placed his Lord. We see in it, as Luther says, the fine, friendly, loving intercourse which must have existed between Christ and His disciples. It seems, at the same time, to establish the eternal principle that religious services should be maintained by spontaneous generosity and an innate sense of duty rather than in consequence of external compulsion. But yet, what is lawful is not always expedient, nor is there anything more thoroughly unchristian than the violent maintenance of the strict letter of our rights. The Christian will always love rather to recede from something of his privilege — to take less than is his due. And so He, in whose steps all ought to walk, calmly added, " Nevertheless, lest we should offend them " (put a difficulty or stumbling-block in their way), " go thou to the sea and cast a hook, and take the first fish that cometh up ; and opening its mouth thou shalt find a stater:[2] that take and give

---

[1] Cf. Ps. lxix. 5 ; Aug. *Serm.* 155.

[2] A stater equals four drachmas ; it was a little more than three shillings, and was exactly the sum required for two people. The tax was not demanded of the other Apostles, perhaps because Capernaum was not their native town. The *shulchanîm*, or bankers to whom it was ordinarily paid, sat in each city to receive it on Adar 15. (Our information on the subject is mainly derived from the Mishna tract *Shekalîn*.)

unto them for Me and for thee." [1] In the very act of submission, as Bengel finely says, "His majesty gleams forth." He would pay the contribution to avoid hurting the feelings of any, and especially because His Apostle had promised it in His behalf: but He could not pay it in an ordinary way, because that would be to compromise a principle. In obeying the law of charity, and of self-surrender, He would also obey the laws of dignity and truth. "He pays the tribute, therefore," says Clarius, "but taken from a fish's mouth, that His majesty may be recognized." [2]

When Paulus, with somewhat vulgar jocosity, calls this "a miracle for half-a-crown," he only shows his own entire misconception of the fine ethical lessons which are involved in the narrative, and which in this, as in every other instance, separate our Lord's miracles from those of the Apocrypha. Yet I agree with the learned and thoughtful Olshausen in regarding this as the most difficult to comprehend of all the Gospel miracles — as being in many respects, *sui generis* — as not falling under the same category as the other miracles of Christ. "It is remarkable," says Archbishop Trench, "*and is a solitary instance of the kind,* that the issue of this bidding is not told us.*" He goes on, indeed, to say that the narrative is evidently *intended* to be miraculous, and this is the impression which it has almost universally left on the minds of those who read it. Yet the literal translation of our Lord's words may most certainly be, "on opening its mouth, thou shalt get, or obtain,[3] a stater;" and although there is no difficulty whatever in supposing that a fish may have swallowed the glittering coin as it was accidently dropped into the water,[4] nor should I feel the slightest difficulty in believing — as I hope that this book, from its first page to its last, will show — that a miracle might have been wrought, yet the peculiarities both of the miracle itself and of the manner in which it is narrated, leave in my mind a doubt as to whether, in this instance, some essential particular may not have been either omitted or left unexplained.

---

[1] ἀντὶ, "instead of" — because the money was redemption money; "for me and for thee" — not "for us," because the money was paid differently for each. Cf. John xx. 17. (Alford.) — An interesting parallel of a king paying his own tax is adduced by Wetstein.

[2] Trench, *On the Miracles,* p. 406. His entire treatment of this miracle is suggestive and beautiful.

[3] This is a thoroughly classical and largely substantiated use of εὑρίσκω. See Liddell and Scott, *s. v. ;* and for New Testament instances, see Heb. ix. 12; Luke i. 30; xi. 9; John xii. 14; Acts vii. 46.

[4] Of this there are abundant instances. There is no need to refer to the story of Polycrates (Herod. iii. 42), or to Augustine, *De Civ. Dei,* xxii. 8. Mackerel are to this day constantly caught by their swallowing a glittering piece of tin.

CHAPTER XXXIX.

JESUS AT THE FEAST OF TABERNACLES.

"Ecce Innocens inter peccatores; justus inter reprobos; pius inter impro-
bos." [290] — LUDOLPHUS, *Vita Christi*, p. 118.

IT was not likely that Jesus should have been able to live at
Capernaum without the fact of His visit being known to some of the
inhabitants. But it is clear that His stay in the town was very brief,
and that it was of a strictly private character. The discourse and the
incident mentioned in the last chapter are the only records of it which
are left.

But it was now autumn, and all Galilee was in the stir of preparation which preceded the starting of the annual caravan of pilgrims to
one of the three great yearly feasts — the Feast of Tabernacles. That
feast — the Feast of Ingathering — was intended to commemorate the
passage of the Israelites through the wilderness, and was celebrated
with such universal joy, that both Josephus and Philo call it "the
holiest and greatest feast," and it was known among the Jews as
"*the* Feast" pre-eminently.[1] It was kept for seven consecutive days,
from the 15th to the 21st of Tisri, and the eighth day was celebrated
by a holy convocation. During the seven days the Jews, to recall
their desert wanderings, lived in little *succóth*, or booths made of the
thickly-foliaged boughs of olive, and palm, and pine, and myrtle, and
each person carried in his hands a *lulab*, consisting of palm-branches,
or willows of the brook, or fruits of peach and citron.[2] During the
week of festivities all the courses of priests were employed in turn;
seventy bullocks were offered in sacrifice for the seventy nations of
the world;[3] the Law was daily read,[4] and on each day the Temple

---

[1] הֶחָג. Jos. *Antt.* viii. 4, § 1; xi. 5, § 5. See on the details of this Feast, Numb.
xxix. 12—38; Neh. viii. 15; 2 Macc. x. 6, 7; Exod. xxiii. 16; Lev. xxiii. 34, seqq.;
Deut. xvi. 13—15.

[2] Lev. xxiii. 40, marg. (*peri etz hadar* almost certainly means "citron-tree;" see
Dr. Royle's s. v. *Tappuach* in Kitto's *Bibl. Cycl.*); Jos. *Antt.* iii. 10, § 4, τοῦ
μήλου τοῦ τῆς Περσέας προσόντος; xiii. 13, § 5, κίτρια.

[3] Thirteen bullocks the first day, twelve the second, eleven the third, and so on.

[4] Neh. viii. 18. Cf. John vii. 19.

trumpets sounded twenty-one times an inspiring and triumphant blast. The joy of the occasion was doubtless deepened by the fact that the feast followed but four days after the awful and comforting ceremonies of the Great Day of Atonement, in which a solemn expiation was made for the sins of all the people.

On the eve of their departure for this feast the family and relations of our Lord—those who in the Gospels are invariably called His "brethren," and some of whose descendants were known to early tradition as the Desposyni—came to him for the last time with a well-meant but painful and presumptuous interference. They—like the Pharisees, and like the multitude, and like Peter—fancied that they knew better than Jesus Himself that line of conduct which would best accomplish His work and hasten the universal recognition of His claims. They came to Him with the language of criticism, of discontent, almost of reproaches and complaints. "Why this unreasonable and incomprehensible secrecy? it contradicts thy claims; it discourages thy followers. Thou hast disciples in Judæa: go thither, and let them too see Thy works which Thou doest? If Thou doest these things, manifest Thyself to the world." If they could use such language to their Lord and Master—if they could, as it were, thus challenge His power to the proof—it is but too plain that their knowledge of Him was so narrow and inadequate as to justify the sad parenthesis of the beloved Evangelist—"for not even His brethren believed on Him." He was a stranger unto His brethren, even an alien unto His mother's children.[1]

Such dictation on their part—the bitter fruit of impatient vanity and unspiritual ignorance—showed indeed a most blamable presumption;[2] yet our Lord only answered them with calm and gentle dignity. "No; my time to manifest myself to the world—which is *your* world also, and which therefore cannot hate you as it hates me—is not yet come. Go ye up to this feast. I choose not to go up to this feast, for not yet has my time been fulfilled."[3] So he answered them, and stayed in Galilee.

"I go not up yet unto this feast" is the rendering of the English version, adopting the reading οὔπω, "*not yet;*" but even if οὐκ,

---

[1] Ps. lxix. 8; John vii. 1—9.

[2] As Stier remarks, the μετάβηθι ἐντεῦθεν, "depart hence," of John vii. 3, is a style of bold imperative which those only could have adopted who presumed on their close earthly relationship; and they seem almost ostentatiously to exclude *themselves* from the number of His disciples.

[3] The ἀναβαίνω has the sense so frequently found in the present: "I am not for going up;" "I do not choose to go up."

"not," be the true reading, the meaning is substantially the same.[1] The οὔπω in the next clause, "my time has *not yet* been fulfilled," distinctly intimated that such a time *would* come, and that it was not His object to intimate to His brethren — whose utter want of sympathy and reverence had just been so unhappily displayed — *when* that time would be. And there was a reason for this. It was essential for the safety of His life, which was not to end for six months more — it was essential for the carrying out of His Divine purposes, which were closely enwoven with the events of the next few days — that His brethren should *not* know about His plans. And therefore He let them depart in the completest uncertainty as to whether or not He intended to follow them.[2] Certain as they were to be asked by multitudes whether He was coming to the feast, it was necessary that they should be able to answer, with perfect truthfulness, that He was at any rate not coming with *them*, and that whether He would come before the feast was over or not they could not tell. And that this must have occurred, and that this must have been their answer, is evident from the fact that the one question buzzed about from ear to ear in those gay and busy streets was, "Where is He? is He here already? is He coming?"[3] And as He did not appear, His whole character, His whole mission, were discussed. The words of approval were vague and timid, "He is a good man;" the words of condemnation were bitter and emphatic, "Nay, but He is a *mesîth* — He deceiveth the people." But no one dared to speak openly his full thought about Him; each seemed to distrust his neighbor; and all feared to commit themselves too far while the opinion of the

---

[1] Tischendorf reads οὐκ with א, D, K, the Cureton Syriac, &c.; on the other hand, οὔπω is the reading of B, E, F, G, H, &c. What seems decisive in favor of οὐκ is that it was more likely to be altered than the other; "proclivi lectioni praestat ardua." 291

[2] As early as the third century after Christ, the philosopher Porphyry, one of the bitterest and ablest of those who assaulted Christianity, charged our blessed Lord with deception in this incident; and it is therefore clear that in *his* time the reading was οὐκ (ap. Jer. *Adv. Pelag.* iv. 21). And even an eminent Christian commentator like Meyer has supposed that, in this instance, Jesus subsequently changed His purpose. The latter supposition is precarious, perhaps wholly irreverent; the former is utterly senseless. For even if Porphyry supposed that it could have happened, he must have seen how preposterous was the notion of St. John's holding such a view. It therefore seems to me a matter of no consequence whatever whether οὐκ or οὔπω be read; for it is quite clear that the Evangelist saw nothing in the language of our Lord but the desire to exclude His brethren from any certain knowledge of His plans.

[3] John vii. 11, ἐζήτουν αὐτὸν καὶ ἔλεγον, κ. τ. λ.; "they kept looking for Him, and saying," &c.

" Jews," and of the leading Priests and Pharisees, had not been finally or decisively declared.

And suddenly, in the midst of all these murmurs and discussions,
in the middle of the feast, Jesus, unaccompanied apparently by His
followers, unheralded by His friends, appeared suddenly in the Temple, and taught. By what route He had reached the Holy City —
how he had passed through the bright thronged streets unnoticed —
whether He joined in the innocent mirth of the festival — whether
He too lived in a little *succah* of palm-leaves during the remainder
of the week, and wandered among the brightly-dressed crowds of
an Oriental gala day with the *lulab* and citron in His hands —
whether His voice was heard in the Hallel, or the Great Hosanna —
we do not know. All that is told us is that, throwing himself, as it
were, in full confidence on the protection of His disciples from Galilee and those in Jerusalem, He was suddenly found seated in one of
the large halls which opened out of the Temple courts, and there He
taught.

For a time they listened to Him in awe-struck silence ; but soon
the old scruples recurred to them. " He is no authorized Rabbi ; He
belongs to no recognized school; neither the followers of Hillel nor
those of Shammai claim Him ; He is a Nazarene ; He was trained in
the shop of the Galilæan carpenter; how knoweth this man letters,
having never learned ? " As though the few who are taught of God
— whose learning is the learning of a pure heart and an enlightened
eye and a blameless life — did not unspeakably transcend in wisdom,
and therefore also in the best and truest knowledge, those whose
learning has but come from other men ! It is not the voice of erudition, but it is, as the old Greek thinker says, the voice of Inspiration
— the voice of the divine Sibyl — which, uttering things simple and
unperfumed and unadorned, reacheth through myriads of years.

Jesus understood their looks. He interpreted their murmurs. He
told them that His learning came immediately from His Heavenly
Father, and that they, too, if they did God's will, might learn, and
might understand, the same high lessons. In all ages there is a tendency to mistake erudition for learning, knowledge for wisdom; in
all ages there has been a slowness to comprehend that true learning
of the deepest and noblest character may co-exist with complete and
utter ignorance of everything which absorbs and constitutes the
learning of the schools. In *one* sense — Jesus told His hearers —
they knew the law which Moses had given them; in another they
were pitiably ignorant of it. They could not understand its princi-

ples, because they were not "faithful to its precepts."[1] And then He asked them openly, "Why go ye about to kill me?"

That determination to kill Him was known indeed to Him, and known to some of those who heard Him, but was a guilty secret which had been concealed from the majority of the multitude. *These* answered the question, while the others kept their guilty silence. "Thou hast a devil," the people answered;[2] "who goeth about to kill Thee?" Why did they speak with such superfluous and brutal bluntness? Do not we repudiate, with far less flaming indignation, a charge which we know to be not only false, but wholly preposterous and foundationless? Was there not in the minds even of this not yet wholly alienated multitude an uneasy sense of their distance from the Speaker — of that unutterable superiority to themselves which pained and shamed and irritated them? Were they not conscious, in their carnal and vulgar aspirations, that *this* Prophet came, not to condescend to such views as theirs, but to raise them to a region where they felt that they could not breathe? Was there not even then in their hearts something of the half-unconscious hatred of vice to virtue, the repulsion of darkness against light? Would they have said, "Thou hast a devil," when they heard Him say that some of them were plotting against His life, if they had not felt that they were themselves capable at almost any moment of joining in — aye, with their own hands of executing — so base a plot?

Jesus did not notice their coarse insolence. He referred them to that one work of healing on the Sabbath day,[3] at which they were all still marvelling, with an empty wonder, that He who had the power to perform such a deed should, in performing it, have risen above their empty, ceremonial, fetish-worshipping notions of Sabbath sanctity. And Jesus, who ever loved to teach the lesson that love and not literalism is the fulfilling of the Law, showed them, even on their own purely ritual and Levitical principle, that His word of healing had in no respect violated the Sabbath at all. For instance, Moses had established, or rather re-established, the ordinance of circumcision on the eighth day, and if that eighth day happened to be a Sabbath, they without scruple sacrificed the one ordinance to the other, and in spite of the labor which it involved, performed the rite of circumcision on the Sabbath day. If the law of circumcision superseded that of the Sabbath, did not the law of Mercy? If it was

---

[1] Cf. Ecclus. xxi. 11, "*He that keepeth the law of the Lord getteth the understanding thereof.*" (John xiv. 15—17, 20, 21 ; see too Job xxviii. 28.)

[2] John vii. 20, ὁ ὄχλος, not οἱ Ἰουδαῖοι.

[3] John v. 5.

right by a series of actions to inflict that wound, was it wrong by a single word to effect a total cure?[1] If that, which was at the best but a *sign* of deliverance, could not even on account of the Sabbath be postponed for a single day, why was it criminal not to have postponed for the sake of the Sabbath a deliverance actual and entire? And then He summed His self-defence in the one calm word, "Do not be ever judging by the mere appearance, but judge a righteous judgment;"[2] instead of being permanently content with a superficial mode of criticism, come once for all to some principle of righteous decision.

His hearers were perplexed and amazed, "Is this He against whose life some are plotting? Can He be the Messiah? Nay, He cannot be; for we know whence this speaker comes, whereas they say that none shall know whence the Messiah shall have come when he appears."

There was a certain irony in the answer of Jesus. They knew whence He came and all about Him, and yet, in very truth, He came not of Himself, but from one of whom they knew nothing. This word maddened still more some of His hearers. They longed but did not dare to seize Him, and all the more because there were some whom these words convinced, and who appealed to His many miracles as irresistible proof of His sacred claims.[3] The Sanhedrin, seated in frequent session in their stone hall of meeting within the immediate precincts of the Temple, were, by means of their emissaries, kept informed of all that He did and said, and, without seeming to do so, watched His every movement with malignant and jealous eyes. These whispered arguments in His favor, this deepened awe of Him and belief in Him, which, despite their authority, was growing up under their very eyes, seemed to them at once humiliating and dangerous. They determined on a bolder course of action. They sent out emissaries to seize Him suddenly and stealthily, at the first opportunity which should occur. But Jesus

---

[1] Stier quotes from the Rabbis a remark to this very effect, "Circumcision, which is one of the 248 members of the body, supersedes the Sabbath; how much more the whole body of a man?"

[2] John vii. 24, $\mu\dot{\eta}$ $\varkappa o i \nu \varepsilon \tau \varepsilon$ . . . $\dot{\alpha}\lambda\lambda\dot{\alpha}$ . . . $\varkappa \rho i \nu \alpha \tau \varepsilon$.

[3] It is a remarkable fact that the Jews have never attempted to deny the reality of the miracles which Jesus wrought. All that the *Toldôth Jeshu*, and similar books, can say is that He performed them by means of the *Shemhammephorash*, the "Tetragrammaton," or sacred name. For the preposterous legend by which they account for "that man" (as in their hatred they always call Him) having learnt the pronunciation of the name, see the translation of the *Toldôth* by Huldric (1705), or Wagenseil, *Tela Ignea Satanae*, 1681.

showed no fear. He was to be with them a little longer, and then, and not till then, should He return to Him that sent Him.¹ Then, indeed, they would seek Him — seek Him, not as now with hostile intentions, but in all the crushing agony of remorse and shame; but their search would be in vain. His enemies wholly failed to understand the allusion. In the troubled and terrible days which were to come they would understand it only too bitterly and well. Now they could only jeeringly conjecture that possibly He had some wild intention of going to teach among the Gentiles.²

So passed this memorable day; and again, on the last day of the feast,³ Jesus was standing in the Temple. On each day of the seven, and, possibly, even on the eighth, there was a significant and joyous ceremony. At early morning the people repaired to the Temple, and when the morning sacrifice had been laid on the altar, one of the priests went down with a golden ewer to the Pool of Siloam, not far from the foot of Mount Sion. There, with great solemnity, he drew three *logs* of water, which were then carried in triumphant procession through the water-gate into the Temple. As he entered the Temple courts the sacred trumpets breathed out a joyous blast, which continued till he reached the top of the altar slope, and there poured the water into a silver basin on the western side, while wine was poured into another silver basin on the eastern

---

¹ Cf. John viii. 21.

² διασπορὰ τῶν ᾽Ελλήνων (John vii. 35) means here, in all probability, " Gentile countries among which Jews are dispersed." And such a notion would seem to those bigoted Jews only too ridiculous. A modern Rabbi at Jerusalem did not know in what quarter of the globe he was living, had never heard the name Europe, and called all other parts of the world, except Palestine, *Chutselorets* (חוצה לארץ), *i. e.,* "outside the Holy Land!" (Frankl, *Jews in the East,* ii. 34, E. Tr.)

³ The feast lasted seven days, but it is uncertain whether by " the last day, that great day of the feast," the seventh day is intended, which was the proper conclusion of the feast, or the eighth, on which the booths were taken down, but on which there were special offerings and a holy convocation (Numb. xxix. 36—38). It is said that the seventh, not being distinguished from the other days, cannot be called " the great day;" but on the other hand, the *last* day of a feast is always likely to be conspicuous for the zest of its ceremonies, and there seems to be at least some indication that such was actually the case (Buxtorf, *Syn. Jud.* xxi.; see " Feast of Tabernacles " in Smith's *Dict. of the Bible*). One Rabbi (R. Juda Hakkôdesh), in the tract *Succah,* which is our chief authority on this subject, says that the water was poured out on the eighth as well as on the previous days (*Succah,* iv. 9), but the others deny this (Surenhusius, *Mischna,* ii. 276). The eighth day of the Passover, and of Tabernacles, is in Deut. xvi. 8; Lev. xxiii. 34, called *atsereth* (E. V. " solemn assembly," marg. " day of restraint ").

side. Then the great Hallel was sung,[1] and when they came to the verse " Oh give thanks unto the Lord, for He is good : for His mercy endureth for ever," each of the gaily-clad worshippers as he stood beside the altars, shook his *lulab* in triumph. In the evening they abandoned themselves to such rejoicing, that the Rabbis say that the man who has not seen this "joy of the drawing water" does not know what joy means.[2]

In evident allusion to this glad custom — perhaps in sympathy with that sense of something missing which succeeded the disuse of it on the eighth day of the feast — Jesus pointed the yearnings of the festal crowd in the Temple, as He had done those of the Samaritan woman by the lonely well, to a new truth, and to one which more than fulfilled alike the spiritual (Isa. xii. 3) and the historical meaning (1 Cor. x. 4) of the scenes which they had witnessed. He "stood and cried, If any man thirst, let him come unto me and drink. He that believeth on me, as the Scripture hath said, out of his belly shall flow rivers of living water." [3] And the best of them felt in their inmost soul — and this is the strongest of all the evidences of Christianity for those who believe heart and soul in a God of love who cares for His children in the family of man — that they had deep need of a comfort and salvation, of the outpouring of a Holy Spirit, which He who spake to them could alone bestow. But the very fact that some were beginning openly to speak of Him

---

[1] Ps. cxiii.—cxviii. Jahn, *Archaeol. Bibl.* § 355. Even Plutarch (*Sympos.* iv. 5) alludes to the κρατηροφορία.

[2] *Succah*, v. 2. The feast was called *Shimcath beth hashoabah.* The day was called the *Hosannah Rabbah,* or " Great Hosannah," because on the seventh day the Hallel was seven times sung. The origin of the ceremony is quite obscure, but it is at least possible that the extra joy of it — the processions, illuminations, dances — commemorated the joy of the Pharisees in having got the better of Alexander Jannæus, who, instead of pouring the water on the altar, disdainfully poured it on the ground. The Pharisees in their fury hurled at his head the citron-fruits which they were carrying in their hands (Lev. xxiii. 40), and on his calling his mercenaries to his aid, a massacre of nearly six thousand ensued (Derenbourg, *Hist. Pal.* 98; Jos. *Antt.* xiii. 13, § 5, κιτρίοις αὐτὸν ἔβαλλον). This unauthorized use of the fruits as convenient missiles seems not to have been rare (*Succah*, iv. 9).

[3] Cf. Isa. xliii. 20; lviii. 11; lv. 1; xii. 3; and John iv. 14; vi. 35; Rev. xxii. 17. These are the *nearest* passages to " as the Scripture hath said," which must therefore be interpreted as a *general* allusion. St. Chrysostom asks, καὶ ποῦ εἶπεν ἡ γραφὴ ὅτι ποταμοὶ, κ. τ. λ.; οὐδαμοῦ.[292] No metaphor, however, could be more intense than that offered by the longing for water in a dry and thirsty land. To see the eagerness with which men and beasts alike rush to the fountain-side after journeys in Palestine is a striking sight. The Arabs begin to sing and shout, constantly repeating the words " Snow in the sun! snow in the sun ! "

as the Prophet and the Christ, only exasperated the others. They had a small difficulty of their own creating, founded on pure ignorance of fact, but which yet to their own narrow dogmatic fancy was irresistible — "Shall Christ come out of Galilee? must He not come from Bethlehem? of David's seed?"[1]

It was during this division of opinion that the officers whom the Pharisees had dispatched to seize Jesus, returned to them without having even attempted to carry out their design. As they hovered among the Temple courts, as they stood half sheltered behind the Temple pillars, not unobserved, it may be, by Him for whom they were lying in wait, they too could not fail to hear some of the divine words which flowed out of His mouth. And, hearing them, they could not fulfil their mission. A sacred spell was upon them, which they were unable to resist; a force infinitely more powerful than their own, unnerved their strength and paralyzed their will. To listen to him was not only to be disarmed in every attempt against Him, it was even to be half-converted from bitter enemies to awe-struck disciples. "Never man spake like this man," was all that they could say. That bold disobedience to positive orders must have made them afraid of the possible consequences to themselves, but obedience would have required a courage even greater, to say nothing of that rankling wound wherewith an awakened conscience ever pierces the breast of crime.

The Pharisees could only meet them with angry taunts. "What, ye too intend to accept this Prophet of the ignorant, this favorite of the accursed and miserable mob!"[2] Then Nicodemus ventured on a timid word, "Ought you not to *try* before you condemn Him?" They had no reply to the justice of that principle: they could only fall back again on taunts — "Are you then a Galilæan?" and then the old ignorant dogmatism, "Search, and look: for out of Galilee ariseth no prophet."

Where then, as we have asked already, was Gathhepher, whence Jonah came? where Thisbe, whence Elijah came? where Elkosh, whence Nahum came? where the northern town, whence Hosea came? The more recent Jews, with better knowledge of Scripture, declare that the Messiah *is* to come from Galilee;[3] and they settle at Tiberias, because they believe that He will rise from the waters of

---

[1] Micah v. 2; Isa. xi. 1; Jer. xxiii. 5, &c.

[2] The ecclesiastical contempt of the Pharisees surpassed, in its habitual spirit of scorn, the worst insolence of Paganism against "the many."

[3] See Isa. ix. 1, 2, and this is asserted in the *Zohar.* See *supra*, pp. 75, 76.

the Lake; and at Safed, "the city set on a hill," because they believe that He will there first fix His throne.[1] But there is no ignorance so deep as the ignorance that will not know; no blindness so incurable as the blindness which will not see. And the dogmatism of a narrow and stolid prejudice which believes itself to be theological learning is, of all others, the most ignorant and the most blind. Such was the spirit in which, ignoring the mild justice of Nicodemus, and the marvellous impression made by Jesus even on their own hostile apparitors, the majority of the Sanhedrin broke up, and went each to his own home.

---

[1] So I was assured on the shores of the Sea of Galilee.

CHAPTER XL.

THE WOMAN TAKEN IN ADULTERY.

" Thus conscience doth make cowards of us all." — SHAKESPEARE.

IN the difficulties which beset the celebrated incident which follows, it is impossible for us to arrive at any certainty as to its true
position in the narrative.[1]   As there must, however, be some *à priori*
probability that its place was assigned with due reference to the order
of events, and as there appear to be some obvious though indirect
references to it in the discourses which immediately follow,[2] I shall
proceed to speak of it here, feeling no shadow of a doubt that the
incident really happened, even if the form in which it is preserved
to us is by no means indisputably genuine.[3]

---

[1] John viii. 1—11. In some MSS. it is placed at the end of St. John's Gospel; in
some, after Luke xxi., mainly, no doubt, because it fits on well to the verses 37,
38 in that chapter. Hitzig (*Ueber Joh. Marc.* 205) conjectured, very plausibly,
that the fact which it records really belongs to Mark xii., falling in naturally
between the conspiracy of the Pharisees and Herodians, and that of the Sadducees to tempt Christ — *i. e.*, between the 17th and 18th verses. In that case its
order of sequence would be on the Tuesday in Passion week. On the other hand,
if it has no connection with the Feast of Tabernacles, and no tinge of Johannean
authorship, why should so many MSS. (including even such important ones as
D, F, G) place it here ?

[2] *Ex. gr.*, John viii. 15, 17, 24, 46.

[3] The whole mass of critical evidence may be seen fully treated in Lücke's
Commentary (third edition), ii. 243—256. We may briefly summarize the grounds
of its dubious genuineness by observing that (1) it is not found in some of the
best and oldest MSS. (*e. g.*, א, A, B, C, L); (2) nor in most of the Fathers (*e. g.*,
Origen, Cyril, Chrysostom, Theophylact, Tertullian, Cyprian); (3) nor in many
ancient versions (*e. g.*, Sahidic, Coptic, and Gothic); (4) in other MSS. it is marked
with *obeli* and asterisks, or a space is left for it, or it is inserted elsewhere ; (5) it
contains an extraordinary number of various readings (" variant singula fere verba
in codicibus plerisque " [293] — Tischendorf); (6) it contains several expressions not
elsewhere found in St. John ; and (7) it differs widely in some respects — particularly in the *constant* use of the connecting δὲ — from the *style* of St. John throughout the rest of the Gospel. Several of these arguments are weakened — (i.) by
the fact that the diversities of readings may be reduced to three main recensions ·
(ii.) that the rejection of the passage may have been due to a false dogmatical
bias ; (iii.) that the silence of some of the Fathers may be accidental, and of others
prudential. The arguments in its favor are — 1. It is found in some old and

At the close of the day recorded in the last chapter, Jesus withdrew to the Mount of Olives.   Whether He went to the garden of Gethsemane, and to the house of its unknown but friendly owner, or whether — not having where to lay His head — He simply slept, Eastern fashion, on the green turf under those ancient olive-trees, we cannot tell ; but it is interesting to trace in Him once more that dislike of crowded cities, that love for the pure, sweet, fresh air, and for the quiet of the lonely hill, which we see in all parts of His career on earth.   There was, indeed, in Him nothing of that supercilious sentimentality and morbid egotism which makes men shrink from all contact with their brother-men ; nor can they who would be His true servants belong to those merely fantastic philanthropists

> " Who sigh for wretchedness, yet shun the wretched,
> Nursing in some delicious solitude
> Their dainty loves and slothful sympathies."
>
> COLERIDGE, *Religious Musings.*

On the contrary, day after day, while His day-time of work continued, we find Him sacrificing all that was dearest and most elevating to His soul, and in spite of heat, and pressure, and conflict, and weariness, calmly pursuing His labors of love amid " the madding crowd's ignoble strife."   But in the night-time, when men cannot work, no call of duty required His presence within the walls of Jerusalem ; and those who are familiar with the oppressive foulness of ancient

---

important uncials (D, F, G, H, K, U) and in more than 300 cursive MSS., in some of the Itala, and in the Vulgate. 2. The tendencies which led to its deliberate rejection would have rendered all but impossible its invention or interpolation. 3. It is quoted by Augustine, Ambrose, and Jerome, and treated as genuine in the Apostolic constitutions. St. Jerome's testimony (*Adv. Pelag.* ii. 6) is particularly important, because he says that in his time it was found " in multis et Graecis et Latinis codicibus " [294] — and it must be remembered that nearly all of these must have been considerably older than any which we now possess. The main facts to be observed are, that though the dogmatic bias against the passage might be sufficient to account for its rejection, it gives us no help in explaining its want of resemblance to the style of St. John. A very simple hypothesis will account for all difficulties. If we suppose that the story of the woman accused before our Lord of many sins — to which Eusebius alludes (*II. E.* iii. 39) as existing in the Gospel of the Hebrews — is identical with this, we may suppose, without any improbability, either (i.) that St. John (as Alford hesitatingly suggests) may here have adopted a portion of current synoptic tradition, or (ii.) that the story may have been derived originally from Papias, the pupil of St. John, and having found its way into the Gospel of the Hebrews, may have been adopted gradually into some MSS. of St. John's Gospel (see Euseb. *ubi supr.*). Many recent writers adopt the suggestion of Holtzmann, that it belongs to the " Ur-marcus," or ground document of the Synoptists. Whoever embodied into the Gospels this traditionally-remembered story deserved well of the world.

cities can best imagine the relief which His spirit must have felt when he could escape from the close streets and thronged bazaars, to cross the ravine, and climb the green slope beyond it, and be alone with His Heavenly Father under the starry night.

But when the day dawned His duties lay once more within the city walls, and in that part of the city where, almost alone, we hear of His presence — in the courts of His Father's house. And with the very dawn His enemies contrived a fresh plot against Him, the circumstances of which made their malice even more actually painful than it was intentionally perilous.

It is probable that the hilarity and abandonment of the Feast of Tabernacles, which had grown to be a kind of vintage festival, would often degenerate into acts of license and immorality, and these would find more numerous opportunities in the general disturbance of ordinary life caused by the dwelling of the whole people in their little leafy booths. One such act had been detected during the previous night, and the guilty woman had been handed over to the Scribes [1] and Pharisees.

Even had the morals of the nation at that time been as clean as in the days when Moses ordained the fearful ordeal of the " water of jealousy " [2] — even had these rulers and teachers of the nation been elevated as far above their contemporaries in the real, as in the professed, sanctity of their lives — the discovery, and the threatened punishment, of this miserable adulteress could hardly have failed to move every pure and noble mind to a compassion which would have mingled largely with the horror which her sin inspired. They might, indeed, even on those suppositions, have inflicted the established penalty with a sternness as inflexible as that of the Pilgrim Fathers in early days of Salem or Providence ; but the sternness of a severe and pure-hearted judge is not a sternness which precludes all pity ; it is a sternness which would not willingly inflict one unnecessary pang — it is a sternness *not* incompatible with a righteous tenderness, but *wholly* incompatible with a mixture of meaner and slighter motives, *wholly* incompatible with a spirit of malignant levity and hideous sport.

But the spirit which actuated these Scribes and Pharisees was not by any means the spirit of a sincere and outraged purity. In the

---

[1] It is observable that in no other passage of St. John's Gospel (though frequently in the Synoptists) are the Scribes mentioned among the enemies of Christ ; but here a few MSS. read οἱ ἀρχιερεῖς, " the chief priests."

[2] See Numb. v. 14—29.

decadence of national life, in the daily familiarity with heathen degradations, in the gradual substitution of a Levitical scrupulosity for a heartfelt religion, the morals of the nation had grown utterly corrupt. The ordeal of the "water of jealousy" had long been abolished, and the death by stoning as a punishment for adultery had long been suffered to fall into desuetude. Not even the Scribes and Pharisees — for all their external religiosity — had any genuine horror of an impurity with which their own lives were often stained.[1] They saw in the accident which had put this guilty woman into their power nothing but a chance of annoying, entrapping, possibly even endangering this Prophet of Galilee, whom they already regarded as their deadliest enemy.

It was a curious custom among the Jews to consult distinguished Rabbis in cases of doubt and difficulty;[2] but there was no doubt or difficulty here. It was long since the Mosaic law of death to the adulteress had been demanded or enforced; and even if this had not been the case, the Roman law would, in all probability, have prevented such a sentence from being put in execution. On the other hand, the civil and religious penalties of divorce were open to the injured husband; nor did the case of this woman differ from that of any other who had similarly transgressed. Nor, again, even if they had honestly and sincerely desired the opinion of Jesus, could there have been the slightest excuse for haling the woman herself into His presence, and thus subjecting her to a moral torture which would be rendered all the more insupportable from the close seclusion of women in the East.

And, therefore, to subject her to the superfluous horror of this odious publicity — to drag her, fresh from the agony of detection, into the sacred precincts of the Temple [3]— to subject this unveiled, dishevelled, terror-stricken woman to the cold and sensual curiosity of a malignant mob — to make her, with total disregard to her own sufferings, the mere passive instrument of their hatred against Jesus; and to do all this — not under the pressure of moral indignation, but in order to

---

[1] As is distinctly proved by the admissions of the Talmud, and by the express testimony of Josephus. In the tract *Sotah* it is clear that the Mosaic ordeal of the "water of jealousy" had fallen into practical desuetude from the commonness of the crime. We are there told that R. Johanan Ben Zakkai abolished the use of it (see Surenhusius, *Mischna*, ii. 290, 293).

[2] Sepp, *Leben Jesu*, iv. 2, 17.

[3] It is indeed said in the Talmud (*Sotah*, 1, 5) that adulteresses were to be judged at the gate of Nikanor, between the Court of the Gentiles and that of the women (Surenhusius, *Mischna*, iii. 189); but this does not apply to the mere loose asking of an opinion, such as this was.

gratify a calculating malice — showed on their parts a cold, hard cynicism, a graceless, pitiless, barbarous brutality of heart and conscience, which could not but prove, in every particular, revolting and hateful to One who alone was infinitely tender, because He alone was infinitely pure.

And so they dragged her to Him, and set her in the midst — flagrant guilt subjected to the gaze of stainless Innocence, degraded misery set before the bar of perfect Mercy. And then, just as though their hearts were not full of outrage, they glibly begin, with ironical deference, to set before Him their case. " Master, this woman was seized in the very act of adultery. Now, *Moses* in the Law commanded us to stone [1] *such ;* but what sayest *Thou* about her ? "

They thought that now they had caught Him in a dilemma. They knew the divine trembling pity which had loved where others hated, and praised where others scorned, and encouraged where others crushed; and they knew how that pity had won for Him the admiration of many, the passionate devotion of not a few. They knew that a publican was among His chosen, that sinners had sat with Him at the banquet, and harlots unreproved had bathed His feet, and listened to His words. Would He then acquit this woman, and so make Himself liable to an accusation of heresy, by placing Himself in open disaccord with the sacred and fiery Law? or, on the other hand, would He belie His own compassion, and be ruthless, and condemn? And, if He did, would He not at once shock the multitude, who were touched by His tenderness, and offend the civil magistrates by making Himself liable to a charge of sedition? How could He possibly get out of the difficulty? Either alternative — heresy or treason, accusation before the Sanhedrin or delation to the Procurator, opposition to the orthodox or alienation from the many — would serve equally well their unscrupulous intentions. And one of these, they thought, *must* follow. What a happy chance this weak, guilty woman had given them!

Not yet. A sense of all their baseness, their hardness, their malice, their cynical parade of every feeling which pity would temper

---

[1] The τὰς τοιαύτας is contemptuous ; but where was the partner of her crime ? The Law commanded that he too should be put to death (Lev. xx. 10). As to stoning being the proper punishment of adultery, a needless difficulty seems to have been raised (see Deut. xxii. 22—24). There is no ground whatever for concluding with Lightfoot (*Hor. Hebr.* ad loc.) that she was merely betrothed. (See Ewald, *Gesch. Christus,* 480 ; *Alterthümsk,* 254—268 ; Hitzig, *Joh. Marc.* 209.) The Rabbis say that " death," where no form of it is specified, is meant to be strangulation ; but this is not the case (compare Exod. xxxi. 14 with Numb. xv. 32—35).

and delicacy repress, rushed over the mind of Jesus. He blushed for His nation, for His race; He blushed, not for the degradation of the miserable accused, but for the deeper guilt of her unblushing accusers.[1] Glowing with uncontrollable disgust that modes of opposition so irredeemable in their meanness should be put in play against Him, and that He should be made the involuntary centre of such a shameful scene — indignant (for it cannot be irreverent to imagine in Him an intensified degree of emotions which even the humblest of His true followers would have shared) that the sacredness of His personal reserve should thus be shamelessly violated, and that those things which belong to the sphere of a noble reticence should be thus cynically obtruded on His notice — He bent His face forwards from His seat, and as though He did not, or would not, hear them, stooped and wrote with His finger on the ground.

For any others but such as these it would have been enough. Even if they failed to see in the action a symbol of forgiveness — a symbol that the memory of things thus written in the dust might be obliterated and forgotten[2] — still any but these could hardly have failed to interpret the gesture into a distinct indication that in such a matter Jesus would not mix Himself.[3] But they saw nothing and understood nothing, and stood there unabashed, still pressing their brutal question, still holding, pointing to, jeering at the woman, with no compunction in their cunning glances, and no relenting in their steeled hearts.

The scene could not last any longer; and, therefore, raising Himself from His stooping attitude, He, who could read their hearts, calmly passed upon them that sad judgment involved in the memorable words —

"Let him that is without sin[4] among you, first cast the stone at her."[5]

It was not any abrogation of the Mosaic law; it was, on the contrary, an admission of its justice, and doubtless it must have sunk heavily as a death-warrant upon the woman's heart. But it acted in a manner wholly unexpected. The terrible law stood written; it

---

[1] In the Rabbinical treatise *Berachôth*, R. Papa and others are reported to have said that it is better for a man to throw himself into a furnace than to make any one blush in public, which they deduced from Gen. xxxviii. 25. (Schwab, *Berachôth*, p. 404.)

[2] Comp. Jer. xvii. 13.

[3] It seems to have been well understood. See Wetstein *ad loc.*

[4] *i. e.*, free from the taint of this class of sins. Cf. Luke vii. 37.

[5] πρῶτος τὸν λίθον (E, G, H, K, &c.). Cf. Deut. xvii. 7. (Surenhusius *Mischna*, iv. 235.)

was not the time, it was not His will, to rescind it. But, on the other hand, they themselves, by not acting on the law, by referring the whole question to Him as though it needed a new solution, had practically confessed that the law was at present valid in theory alone, that it had fallen into desuetude, and that even with His authority they had no intention of carrying it into action. Since, therefore, the whole proceeding was on their part illegal and irregular, He transfers it by these words from the forum of law to that of conscience. The judge may sometimes be obliged to condemn the criminal brought before him for sins of which he has himself been guilty, but the position of the self-constituted accuser who eagerly demands a needless condemnation is very different. Herein to condemn her would have been in God's sight most fatally to have condemned themselves; to have been the first to cast the stone at her would have been to crush themselves.

He had but glanced at them for a moment, but that glance had read their inmost souls. He had but calmly spoken a few simple words, but those words, like the still small voice to Elijah at Horeb, had been more terrible than wind or earthquake. They had fallen like a spark of fire upon slumbering souls, and lay burning there till "the blushing, shame-faced spirit" mutinied within them. The Scribes and Pharisees stood silent and fearful; they loosed their hold upon the woman; their insolent glances, so full of guile and malice, fell guiltily to the ground. They who had unjustly inflicted, now justly felt the overwhelming anguish of an intolerable shame, while over their guilty consciences there rolled, in crash on crash of thunder, such thoughts as these:— " Therefore thou art inexcusable, O man, whosoever thou art that judgest: for wherein thou judgest another, thou condemnest thyself: for thou that judgest doest the same things. But we are sure that the judgment of God is according to truth against them which commit such things. And thinkest thou this, O man, that judgest them which do such things and doest the same, that thou shalt escape the judgment of God? or despisest thou the riches of His goodness, and forbearance, and long-suffering; not knowing that the goodness of God leadeth thee to repentance? but after thy hardness and impenitent heart treasurest up to thyself wrath against the day of wrath and revelation of the righteous judgment of God, who will render to every man according to his deeds." They were "*such*" as the woman they had condemned, and they dared not stay.

And so, with burning cheeks and cowed hearts, from the eldest to the youngest, one by one gradually, silently they slunk away. He would not add to their shame and confusion of face by watching them: He had no wish further to reveal His knowledge of the impure secrets of their hearts; He would not tempt them to brazen it out before Him, and to lie against the testimony of their own memories; He had stooped down once more, and was writing on the ground.[1]

And when He once more raised His head, all the accusers had melted away: only the woman still cowered before Him on the Temple-floor. She, too, *might* have gone: none hindered her, and it might have seemed but natural that she should fly anywhere to escape her danger, and to hide her guilt and shame. But remorse, and, it may be, an awful trembling gratitude, in which hope struggled with despair, fixed her there before her Judge. His look, the most terrible of all to meet, because it was the only look that fell on her from a soul robed in the unapproachable majesty of a stainless innocence, was at the same time the most gentle, and the most forgiving. Her stay was a sign of her penitence; her penitence, let us trust, a certain pledge of her future forgiveness. "Two things," as St. Augustine finely says, "were here left alone together — Misery and Mercy."

"Woman," He asked, "where are those thine accusers? did no one convict thee?"

"No man, Lord." It was the only answer which her lips could find power to frame; and then she received the gracious yet heart-searching permission to depart —

"Neither do I convict thee. Go; henceforth sin no more."[2]

Were the critical evidence against the genuineness of this passage far more overwhelming than it is, it would yet bear upon its surface the strongest possible proof of its own authentic truthfulness. It is hardly too much to say that the mixture which it displays of tragedy and of tenderness — the contrast which it involves between low, cruel cunning, and exalted nobility of intellect and emotion — transcends all power of human imagination to have invented it; while the pic-

---

[1] The MS. U (the Cod. Manianus in St. Mark's at Venice) has here the curious reading ἔγραψεν εἰς τὴν γῆν ἑνὸς ἑκάστου αὐτῶν τὰς ἁμαρτίας — "He wrote on the ground the sins of each one of them;" which shows how early began the impossible and irrelevant surmises as to *what* He wrote. This is the only passage where Christ is said to have written anything.

[2] "Convict" is perhaps better than "condemn" (which means "convict and sentence") here. Perhaps ἡ γυνή, the less direct address, is better than γύναι. After μηκέτι I read ἀπὸ τοῦ νῦν with D, omitting καί. But every variation of reading is uncertain in this paragraph.

ture of a divine insight reading the inmost secrets of the heart, and a yet diviner love, which sees those inmost secrets with larger eyes than ours, furnish us with a conception of Christ's power and person at once too lofty and too original to have been founded on anything but fact. No one could have invented, for few could even appreciate, the sovereign purity and ineffable charm — the serene authority of condemnation, and of pardon — by which the story is so deeply characterized. The repeated instances in which, without a moment's hesitation, He foiled the crafty designs of His enemies, and in foiling them taught for ever some eternal principle of thought and action, are among the most unique and decisive proofs of His more than human wisdom ; and yet not one of those gleams of sacred light which were struck from Him by collision with the malice or hate of man was brighter or more beautiful than this.   The very fact that the narrative found so little favor in the early centuries of Church history [1] — the fact that whole Churches regarded the narrative as dangerous in its tendency [2] — the fact that eminent Fathers of the Church either ignore it, or speak of it in a semi-apologetic tone — in these facts we see the most decisive proof that its real moral and meaning are too transcendent to admit of its having been originally invented, or interpolated without adequate authority into the sacred text.   Yet it is strange that any should have failed to see that in the ray of mercy which thus streamed from heaven upon the wretched sinner, the sin assumed an aspect tenfold more heinous, tenfold more repulsive to the conscience of mankind — to every conscience which accepts it as a law of life that it should strive to be holy as God is holy, and pure as He is pure.

However painful this scene must have been to the holy and loving heart of the Saviour, it was at least alleviated by the sense of that compassionate deliverance — deliverance, we may trust, for Eternity, no less than Time — which it had wrought for one guilty soul.   But the scenes that followed were a climax of perpetual misunderstandings, fluctuating impressions, and bitter taunts, which caused the great and joyous festival to end with a sudden burst of rage, and an

---

[1] St. Augustine (*De Conjug. Adult.* ii. 6) says that some people of weak faith removed the paragraph from their MSS., " quasi permissionem peccandi tribuerit Qui dixit Deinceps noli peccare." [225] — St. Ambrose too says that " non mediocrem scrupulum movere potuit imperitis." [296]   (*Apol. David,* ii. 1.)

[2] The Patriarch Nikon (in the tenth century) distinctly says that the passage had been expunged from the Armenian Version because it was thought pernicious for the majority ($\beta\lambda\alpha\beta\epsilon\rho\grave{\alpha}\nu$ $\tau o\tilde{\iota}s$ $\pi o\lambda\lambda o\tilde{\iota}s$).   Bishop Wordsworth thinks that the extreme severity of the Eastern Church against adultery facilitated the rejection of the passage by them.

attempt of the Jewish leaders to make an end of Him — not by public accusation, but by furious violence.

For, on the same day — the *eighth* day of the feast if the last narrative has got displaced, the day *after* the feast if it belongs to the true sequence of events — Jesus continued those interrupted discourses which were intended almost for the last time to set clearly before the Jewish nation His divine claims.

He was seated at that moment in the Treasury — either some special building [1] in the Temple so called, or that part of the court of the women which contained the thirteen chests with trumpet-shaped openings — called *shopherôth* — into which the people, and especially the Pharisees, used to cast their gifts. In this court, and therefore close beside Him, were two gigantic candelabra, fifty cubits high and sumptuously gilded,[2] on the summit of which, nightly, during the Feast of Tabernacles, lamps were lit which shed their soft light over all the city. Round these lamps the people, in their joyful enthusiasm, and even the stateliest Priests and Pharisees, joined in festal dances, while, to the sound of flutes and other music, the Levites drawn up in array on the fifteen steps which led up to the court, chanted the beautiful Psalms which early received the title of "Songs of Degrees." [3]

In allusion to these great lamps, on which some circumstance of the moment may have concentrated the attention of the hearers, Christ exclaimed to them, "I am the Light of the world." It was His constant plan to shape the illustrations of His discourses by those external incidents which would rouse the deepest attention, and fix the words most indelibly on the memories of His hearers. The Pharisees who heard His words charged Him with idle self-glorification; but He showed them that He had His Father's testimony, and that even were it not so, the Light can only be seen, only be known, by the evidence of its own existence; without it, neither itself nor anything else is visible.[4] They asked Him, "Where is Thy Father?" He told them that, not knowing *Him*, they *could* not know His Father; and then He once more sadly warned them that His departure was nigh, and that *then* they would be unable to come to Him.

---

[1] Jos. *Antt.* xix. 6, § 1. Compare Luke xxi. 1; Mark xii. 41.

[2] Pictures of these colossal lamps are given in Surenhusius's *Mischna*, ii. 260. The wicks of the four lamps which stood on each candelabrum were made of the cast-off clothes of the priests.

[3] Ps. cxx.—cxxxiv.

[4] " Testimonium sibi perhibet lux : . . . sibi ipsa testis est, ut cognoscatur lux." [297] (Aug.)

Their only reply was a taunting inquiry whether, by committing suicide, He meant to plunge Himself in the darkest regions of the grave?[1] Nay, He made them understand, it was *they*, not *He*, who were from below — *they*, not He, who were destined, if they persisted in unbelief of His eternal existence, to that dark end. "Who art thou?" they once more asked, in angry and faithless perplexity. "Altogether that which I am telling you,"[2] He calmly answered. They wanted Him to announce Himself as the Messiah, and so become their temporal deliverer; but He will only tell them the far deeper, more eternal truths, that He is the Light, and the Life, and the Living Water, and that He came from the Father — as they, too, should know when they had lifted Him up upon the cross. They were looking solely for the Messiah of the Jews: He would have them know Him as the Redeemer of the world, the Saviour of their souls.

As they heard Him speak, many, even of these fierce enemies, were won over to a belief in Him: but it was a wavering belief, a half belief, a false belief, a belief mingled with a thousand worldly and erroneous fancies, not a belief which had in it any saving power, or on which He could rely. And He put it to an immediate test, which revealed its hollowness, and changed it into mad hatred. He told them that faithfulness and obedience were the marks of true discipleship, and the requisites of true freedom. The word freedom acted as a touchstone to show the spuriousness of their incipient faith. *They* knew of no freedom but that political freedom which they falsely

---

[1] See Jos. *B. Jud.* iii. 8. § 5, τούτων μὲν ἄϊδης δέχεται τὰς ψυχὰς ὀκοτιώτερος.[298]

[2] John viii. 25, τὴν ἀρχὴν ὅτι καὶ λαλῶ ὑμῖν. A vast number of renderings have been proposed for this text. Some may be rejected at once — as Lücke's, "To begin with, why do I even speak to you?" and Meyer's, "Do ye ask what I say to you at the first?" That of De Wette, Stier, Alford, &c., is "*Essentially that which I speak*" — i. e., My *being* is My *revelation* — I am the Word. The objection to the rendering in our English version is that it makes λαλῶ, "*I am speaking*," equivalent to ἔλεξα, "I said;" but, on the other hand, we never elsewhere find Christ using such an expression as "I *am* that which I *speak*." The same objection applies to the interpretation of Augustine and others, "I am, what I am saying to you, *The Beginning*" (Rev. xxi. 6; xxii. 13; 1 John ii. 13). Lange seems to me to be right in rendering it "To start with (or, 'in the first place'), that which I represent Myself as being." Mr. Monro suggests to me the view that the question of the Jews, Σὺ τίς εῖ, evidently refers to the mysterious ἐγώ εἰμι of the previous verse (ver. 24). Treating the question as virtually an interruption, Jesus tells them (ver. 28) that they should not understand the ἐγώ εἰμι till a later experience; but returning to λόγος and λαλῶ (vv. 37, 38, 40, 43) gives a hint as to the ἐγώ εἰμι in 44, 47, and a yet fuller answer in 57, 58; yet not so full or clear as in ix. 37. On this view viii. 25 might perhaps mean, "I will tell you first of all *what I say.*"

asserted ; they resented the promise of future spiritual freedom in lieu of the achievement of present national freedom. So Jesus showed them that they were still the slaves of sin, and in name only, not in reality, the children of Abraham, or the children of God. They were absorbed with pride when they thought of the purity of their ancestral origin, and the privilege of their exclusive monotheism ;[1] but He told them that in very truth they were, by spiritual affinity, the affinity of cruelty and falsehood,[2] children of him who was a liar and a murderer from the beginning — children of the devil.[3] That home-rebuke stung them to fury. They repaid it by calling Jesus a Samaritan, and a demoniac.[4] Our Lord gently put the taunt aside, and once more held out to them the gracious promise that if they will but keep His sayings, they not only shall not die in their sins, but shall not see death. Their dull, blind hearts could not even imagine a spiritual meaning in His words. They could only charge Him with demoniac arrogance and insolence in making Himself greater than Abraham and the prophets, of whom *they* could only think as dead.[5] Jesus told them that in prophetic vision, perhaps too by spiritual intuition, in that other world, Abraham, who was not dead, but living, saw and rejoiced to see His day. Such an assertion appeared to them either senseless or blasphemous. "Abraham has been dead for seventeen centuries ; Thou art not even fifty[6] years old ; how are we to understand such words as these ?" Then very gently, but with great solemnity, and with that formula of assevera-

---

[1] Alike the Bible and the Talmud abound in proofs of the intense national arrogance with which the Jews regarded their religion and their descent.

[2] John viii. 44. Untruthfulness seems to have been in all ages a failing of the Jewish national character. "Listen to all, but *believe no one — not even me*," said the Hebrew poet Sapir to Dr. Frankl (*Jews in the East*, E. Tr., ii. 11).

[3] I am aware that some make Jesus call the Jews not " children," but " *brethren* of the devil," translating τοῦ πατρὸς τοῦ διαβόλου (ver. 44), of " the father of the devil," and rendering the end of verse 44 "*he* is a liar, and his father too ;" but I do not understand this demonology.

[4] John viii. 48, "Thou art a Samaritan " (what intense national hatred breathes in the words !), " and hast a demon." Similarly the Arabs attribute all madness to evil spirits (δαιμονᾷς = *Medjnoun enté*). (Renan, *Vie de Jésus*, 272.)

[5] Luke xvi. 22 ; Matt. xxii. 32.

[6] In some valueless MSS. this is quite needlessly corrected into "forty." It is strange that modern writers like Gfrörer should have revived the mistaken inference of Irenæus from this verse that Jesus lived fifty years on earth. The belief that He died at the age of thirty-three may be regarded as nearly certain, and it cannot even be safely conjectured from this passage either that the sorrows of His lot had marred His visage, or that the deep seriousness of His expression made Him appear older than He was. It is obvious that the Jews are speaking generally, and in round numbers : " *Thou hast not yet reached even the full years of manhood, and hast Thou seen Abraham ?* "

tion which He only used when He announced His most solemn truths, the Saviour revealed to them His eternity, His Divine pre-existence before He had entered the tabernacle of mortal flesh :

"Verily, verily I say unto you, Before Abraham came into existence, I am." [1]

Then, with a burst of impetuous fury — one of those paroxysms of sudden, uncontrollable, frantic rage to which this people has in all ages been liable upon any collision with its religious convictions — they took up stones to stone Him.[2] But the very blindness of their rage made it more easy to elude them. His hour was not yet come. With perfect calmness He departed unhurt out of the Temple.

---

[1] John viii. 58, πρὶν Ἀβραὰμ γενέσθαι, ἐγώ εἰμί. There could be no more distinct assertion of His divine nature. I have pointed out elsewhere that those who deny this must either prove that He never spoke those words, or must believe that He — the most lowly and sinless and meek-hearted of men — was guilty of a colossal and almost phrenetic intoxication of vanity and arrogance. For the Jews, more intensely than any other nation which the world has ever known, recognized the infinite transcendence of God, and therefore for a Jew, *being merely man*, to claim Divinity, would not only be inconsistent with ordinary sense and virtue, but inconsistent with anything *but sheer blasphemous insanity.* See the Author's Hulsean Lectures, *The Witness of History to Christ*, p. 85.

[2] The unfinished state of the Temple buildings would supply them with huge stones close at hand.

CHAPTER XLI.

THE MAN BORN BLIND.

" He from thick films shall purge the visual ray,
And on the sightless eyeball pour the day." — POPE.

EITHER on His way from the Temple, after this attempted assault, or on the next ensuing Sabbath,[1] Jesus, as He passed by, saw a man blind from his birth, who, perhaps, announced his miserable condition as he sat begging by the roadside, and at the Temple gate.[2]

All the Jews were trained to regard special suffering as the necessary and immediate consequence of special sin. Perhaps the disciples supposed that the words of our Lord to the paralytic whom He had healed at the Pool of Bethesda, as well as to the paralytic at Capernaum, might seem to sanction such an impression. They asked, therefore, how this man came to be born blind. Could it be in consequence of the sins of his parents? If not, was there any way of supposing that it could have been for his own? The supposition in the former case seemed hard; in the latter, impossible.[3] They were therefore perplexed.

Into the unprofitable regions of such barren speculation our Lord refused to follow them, and he declined, as always, the tendency to infer and to sit in judgment upon the sins of others. Neither the man's sins, He told them, nor those of his parents, had caused that lifelong affliction; but now, by means of it,[4] the works of God should

---

[1] It is impossible to decide between these alternatives. If it was on the *same* Sabbath, the extreme calmness of our Lord, immediately after circumstances of such intense excitement, would be very noticeable. In either case the narrative implies that the ebullition of homicidal fury against Him was transient.

[2] John v. 14.

[3] Exod. xx. 5. We can hardly imagine that those simple-minded Galilæans were familiar with the doctrine of metempsychosis (Jos. *Antt.* xviii. 1, § 3 ; *B. J.* ii. 8, § 14) ; or the Rabbinic dogma of ante-natal sin ; or the Platonic and Alexandrian fancy of pre-existence ; or the modern conception of proleptic punishment for sins anticipated by foreknowledge.

[4] The Greek idiom does not here imply, as its literal English equivalent appears to do, that the man had been born blind solely *in order* that God's glory might be manifested in his healing. The ἵνα expresses a *consequence*, not a *purpose* — it has, technically speaking, a *metabatic*, not a *telic* force. This was pointed out long

be made manifest. He, the Light of the world, must for a short time longer dispel its darkness. Then He spat on the ground, made clay with the spittle, and smearing it on the blind man's eyes, bade him "go wash in the Pool of Siloam." [1] The blind man went, washed, and was healed.

The saliva of one who had not recently broken his fast was believed among the ancients to have a healing efficacy in cases of weak eyes, and clay was occasionally used to repress tumors on the eyelids. [2] But that these instruments in no way detracted from the splendor of the miracle is obvious; and we have no means of deciding in this, any more than in the parallel instances, why our Lord, who sometimes healed by a word, preferred at other times to adopt slow and more elaborate methods of giving effect to His supernatural power. In this matter He never revealed the principles of action which doubtless arose from His inner knowledge of the circumstances, and from His insight into the hearts of those on whom His cures were wrought. Possibly He had acted with the express view of teaching more than one eternal lesson by the incidents which followed.

At any rate, in this instance, His mode of action led to serious results. For the man had been well known in Jerusalem as one who had been a blind beggar all his life, and his appearance with the use of his eyesight caused a tumult of excitement. Scarcely could those who had known him best believe even his own testimony, that he was indeed the blind beggar with whom they had been so familiar.

---

ago by Chrysostom and Theophylact, and Glassius in his valuable *Philolog. Sacr.*, pp. 529, 530, gives many similar instances — *e. g.*, Rom. iii. 4; v. 20; and comp. John xi. 4; xii. 40. It would, however, carry me too far if I attempted to enter into the subject further here.

[1] "Which," adds St. John — or *possibly* a very ancient gloss — "means Sent." It is found in all MSS., but not in the Persian and Syriac versions. The remark is rather *allusive* than *etymological*, and connects the name of the fountain with the name of the Messiah; but the possible grammatical accuracy of the reference seems now to be admitted. (See Neander, *Life of Christ*, p. 199; Ebrard, *Gosp. Hist.*, p. 317; Hitzig, *Isaiah*, 97.) Justin Martyr (*Dial. c. Tryph.* 63, p. 81) refers to the Messiah as ἀπόστολος, perhaps with a view to Isa. viii. 6. The fact that "the waters of Siloah that flow softly" were supposed, like those of other intermittent springs near Jerusalem, to have a healing power, would help the man's faith. Even Mohammedans say that "Zemzem and Siloah are the two fountains of Paradise."

[2] See Suet. *Vesp.* 7; Tac. *Hist.* iv. 8; Plin. *H. N.* xxviii. 7; and other classical passages quoted by Wetstein and subsequent commentators. Such indications as that of St. John are, under these circumstances, an invaluable mark of truth; for what mythopœic imagination, intent only on glorifying its object, would invent particulars which might be regarded as depreciatory?

They were lost in amazement, and made him repeat again and again the story of his cure. But that story infused into their astonishment a fresh element of Pharisaic indignation; for this cure also had been wrought on a Sabbath day. The Rabbis had forbidden any man to smear even one of his eyes with spittle on the Sabbath, except in cases of mortal danger. Jesus had not only smeared *both* the man's eyes, but had actually mingled the saliva with clay! This, as an act of mercy, was in the deepest and most inward accordance with the very causes for which the Sabbath had been ordained, and the very lessons of which it was meant to be a perpetual witness. But the spirit of narrow literalism and slavish minuteness and quantitative obedience — the spirit that hoped to be saved by the algebraical sum of good and bad actions — had long degraded the Sabbath from the true idea of its institution into a pernicious superstition. The Sabbath of Rabbinism, with all its petty servility, was in no respect the Sabbath of God's loving and holy law. It had degenerated into that which St. Paul calls it, a πτωχικὸν στοιχεῖον, or "beggarly element." [1]

And these Jews were so imbued with this utter littleness, that a unique miracle of mercy awoke in them less of astonishment and gratitude than the horror kindled by a neglect of their Sabbatical superstition. Accordingly, in all the zeal of letter-worshipping religionism, they led off the man to the Pharisees in council. Then followed the scene which St. John has recorded in a manner so inimitably graphic in his ninth chapter. First came the repeated inquiry, "how the thing had been done?" followed by the repeated assertion of some of them that Jesus could not be from God, because He had not observed the Sabbath; and the reply of others that to press the Sabbath-breaking was to admit the miracle, and to admit the miracle was to establish the fact that He who performed it could not be the criminal whom the others described. Then, being completely at a standstill, they asked the blind man *his* opinion of his deliverer; and he — not being involved in their vicious circle of reasoning — replied with fearless promptitude, "He is a Prophet." [2]

By this time they saw the kind of nature with which they had to deal, and anxious for any loophole by which they could deny or set aside the miracle, they sent for the man's parents. "Was this their

---

[1] Gal. iv. 9.

[2] And the Jews themselves went so far as to say that "if a prophet of undoubted credentials should command all persons to light fires on the Sabbath day, arm themselves for war, kill the inhabitants, &c., it would behoove all to rise up without delay and execute all that he should direct without scruple or hesitation." (Maimonides, *Porta Mosis*, p. 29 [Pocock]; Allen's *Mod. Judaism*, p. 26.)

son? If they asserted that he had been born blind, how was it that he now saw?" Perhaps they hoped to browbeat or to bribe these parents into a denial of their relationship, or an admission of impos· ture; but the parents also clung to the plain truth, while, with a certain Judaic servility and cunning, they refused to draw any infer- ences which would lay them open to unpleasant consequences. "This is certainly our son, and he was certainly born blind; as to the rest, we know nothing. Ask him. He is quite capable of answering for himself."

Then — one almost pities their sheer perplexity — they turned to the blind man again. He, as well as his parents, knew that the Jewish authorities had agreed to pronounce the *cherem*, or ban of exclusion from the synagogue, on any one who should venture to acknowledge Jesus as the Messiah; and the Pharisees probably hoped that he would be content to follow their advice, to give glory to God,' *i. e.*, deny or ignore the miracle, and to accept their dictum that Jesus was a sinner.

But the man was made of sturdier stuff than his parents. He was not to be overawed by their authority, or knocked down by their assertions. He breathed quite freely in the halo-atmosphere of their superior sanctity. "*We know*," the Pharisees had said, "that this man is a sinner." "Whether He is a sinner," the man replied, " *I* do *not* know; *one thing I do know*, that, being blind, now I see." Then they began again their weary and futile cross-examination. "What did He do to thee? *how* did He open thine eyes?" But the man had had enough of this. "I told you once, and ye did not attend. Why do ye wish to hear again? Is it possible that ye too wish to be His disciples?" Bold irony this — to ask these stately, ruffled, scrupulous Sanhedrists, whether he was really to regard them as anxious and sincere inquirers about the claims of the Nazarene Prophet! Clearly here was a man whose presumptuous honesty would neither be bullied into suppression nor corrupted into a lie. He was quite impracticable. So, since authority, threats, blandish- ments had all failed, they broke into abuse. " *Thou* art His disci- ple: *we* are the disciples of Moses; of *this* man we know nothing." "Strange," he replied, "that *you* should know nothing of a man

---

[1] " As if they would bind him to the strictest truthfulness " (Lange, iii. 335). " The words are an adjuration to tell the truth (comp. Josh. vii. 19)," says Dean Alford ; but he seems to confuse it with a phrase like *Al-hamdu lillâh,* " to God be the praise" (of your care), which is a different thing, and would require τὴν δόξαν. A friend refers me to 2 Cor. xi. 31 for a similar adjuration; cf. Rom. ix. 1, 5.

who yet has wrought a miracle such as not even Moses ever wrought; and we know that neither He nor any one else could have done it, unless He were from God." [1] What! shades of Hillel and of Shammai! was a mere blind beggar, a natural ignorant heretic, altogether born in sins, to be teaching *them !* Unable to control any longer their transport of indignation, they flung him out of the hall, and out of the synagogue.

But Jesus did not neglect His first confessor. He, too, in all probability had, either at this or some previous time, been placed under the ban of lesser excommunication, or exclusion from the synagogue; [2] for we scarcely ever again read of His re-entering any of those synagogues which, during the earlier years of His ministry, had been His favorite places of teaching and resort. He sought out and found the man, and asked him, " Dost *thou* believe on the Son of God?" "Why,[3] who is He, Lord," answered the man, "that I should believe on Him ? "

" Thou hast both seen Him, and it is He who talketh with thee." [4]

" Lord, I believe," he answered; and he did Him reverence.

It must have been shortly after this time that our Lord pointed the contrast between the different effects of His teaching — they who saw not, made to see; and those who saw, made blind. The Pharisees, ever restlessly and discontentedly hovering about Him, and in their morbid egotism always on the look-out for some reflection on themselves, asked "if they too were blind." The answer of Jesus was, that in natural blindness there would have been no guilt, but to

---

[1] There is no healing of the blind in the Old Testament, or in the Acts.

[2] It is true that this mildest form of excommunication (*neziphah*) was only temporary, for thirty days; and that it applied to only one synagogue. But if it were once pronounced, the time could easily be extended, so as to make it a *niddoui* (נדוי) for ninety days, and the decree be adopted by other synagogues (Gfrörer, *Jahrh. d. Heils*, i. 183). Exclusion from the synagogue did not, however, involve exclusion from the Temple, where *a separate door* was provided for the excommunicate. The last stage of excommunication was the *cherem* or *shammatta*, which was as bad as the Roman *interdictio ignis et aquae*. The Jews declare that Joshua Ben Perachiah had been the teacher of Jesus, and excommunicated Him to the blast of 400 rams'-horns. (Wagenseil, *Sota*, p. 1057). But this Joshuah Ben Perachiah lived in the reign of Alexander Jannæus, who died B. C. 79!

[3] καὶ τίς ἐστι (John ix. 36). The καὶ as often indicates a question full of surprise and emotion. See Jelf's *Greek Syntax*, § 759. Cf. Mark x. 26 (καὶ τίς δύναται σωθῆναι ; " Who *then* can be saved ? "); Luke x. 29 ; 2 Cor. ii. 2.)

[4] Professor Westcott points out the striking fact that this spontaneous revelation to the outcast from the synagogue *finds its only parallel* in the similar revelation (John iv. 26) to the outcast from the nation " (*Characteristics of the Gosp. Miracles,* p. 61).

those who only stumbled in the blindness of wilful error a claim to the possession of sight was a self-condemnation.

And when the leaders, the teachers, the guides were blind, how could the people see?

The thought naturally led Him to the nature of true and false teachers, which He expanded and illustrated in the beautiful apologue —half parable, half allegory—of the True and False Shepherds. He told them that He was the Good Shepherd,[1] who laid down His life for the sheep; while the hireling shepherds, flying from danger betrayed their flocks. He, too, was that door of the sheepfold, by which all His true predecessors alone had entered, while all the false —from the first thief who had climbed into God's fold—had broken in some other way. And then He told them that of His own free will He would lay down His life for the sheep, both of this and of His other flocks,[2] and that of His own power He would take it again. But all these divine mysteries were more than they could understand; and while some declared that they were the nonsense of one who had a devil and was mad, others could only plead that they were not like the words of one who had a devil, and that a devil could not have opened the eyes of the blind.

Thus, with but little fruit for them, save the bitter fruit of anger and hatred, ended the visit of Jesus to the Feast of Tabernacles. And since His very life was now in danger, He withdrew once more from Jerusalem to Galilee, for one brief visit before He bade to His old home His last farewell.

---

[1] Speaking of this allegory, Mr. Sanday points out the circumstance that the only other allegory in the Gospels is in John xv. "The Synoptists have no allegories as distinct from parables. The fourth Evangelist no parables as a special form of allegory" (*Fourth Gospel*, p. 167). As the phrase is ὁ ποιμὴν ὁ καλός, not ἀγαθός, perhaps it had better be rendered "*true* shepherd," rather than "good." But καλός is untranslateable.

[2] In John x. 16, there is an unfortunate obliteration of the distinction between the αὐλή, " fold," and ποίμνη, "flock," of the original.

CHAPTER XLII.

FAREWELL TO GALILEE.

" I see that all things come to an end: but thy commandment is exceeding broad." — Ps. cxix. 96.

IMMEDIATELY after the events just recorded, St. John narrates another incident which took place two months subsequently, at the winter Feast of Dedication.[1] In accordance with the main purpose of His Gospel, which was to narrate that work of the Christ in Judæa, and especially in Jerusalem, which the Synoptists had omitted, he says nothing of an intermediate and final visit to Galilee, or of those last journeys to Jerusalem respecting parts of which the other Evangelists supply us with so many details. And yet that Jesus must have returned to Galilee is clear, not only from the other Evangelists, but also from the nature of the case and from certain incidental facts in the narrative of St. John himself.[2]

It is well known that the whole of one great section in St. Luke — from ix. 51 to xviii. 15 — forms an episode in the Gospel narrative of which many incidents are narrated by this Evangelist alone, and in which the few identifications of time and place all point to one slow and solemn progress from Galilee to Jerusalem (ix. 51; xiii. 22; xvii. 11; x. 38). Now *after* the Feast of Dedication our Lord retired into Peræa, until He was summoned thence by the death of Lazarus (John x. 40—42; xi. 1—46); after the resurrection of Lazarus, He fled to Ephraim (xi. 54); and He did not leave His retirement at Ephraim until He went to Bethany, six days before His final Passover (xii. 1).

This great journey, therefore, from Galilee to Jerusalem, so rich in occasions which called forth some of His most memorable utter-

---

[1] " John x. 22—42. The Feast of Tabernacles was at the end of September or early in October. The Dedication was on December 20.

[2] See John x. 25 (which evidently refers to His last discourse to them two months before) and 40 (" again "). Besides, the expression of John x. 22, " And it was the Dedication at Jerusalem," would have little meaning if a new visit were not implied ; and those words are perhaps added for the very reason that the Dedication might be kept anywhere else.

ances, must have been either a journey to the Feast of Tabernacles or to the Feast of Dedication. That it *could* not have been the former may be regarded as settled, not only on other grounds, but decisively because that was a *rapid* and a *secret* journey, this an eminently public and leisurely one.

Almost every inquirer seems to differ to a greater or less degree as to the exact sequence and chronology of the events which follow. Without entering into minute and tedious disquisitions where absolute certainty is impossible, I will narrate this period of our Lord's life in the order which, after repeated study of the Gospels, appears to me to be the most probable, and in the separate details of which I have found myself again and again confirmed by the conclusions of other independent inquirers. And here I will only premise my conviction —

1. That the episode of St. Luke up to xviii. 30, mainly refers to a single journey, although unity of subject, or other causes, may have led the sacred writer to weave into his narrative some events or utterances which belong to an earlier or later epoch.[1]

2. That the order of the facts narrated even by St. Luke alone is not,[2] and does not in any way claim to be,[3] strictly chronological; so that the place of any event in the narrative by no means necessarily indicates its true position in the order of time.

3. That this journey is identical with that which is partially recorded in Matt. xviii. 1—xx. 16; Mark x. 1—31.

4. That (as seems obvious from internal evidence[4]) the events nar-

---

[1] *E. g.*, ix. 57—62 (cf. Matt. viii. 19—22); xi. 1—13 (cf. Matt. vi. 9—15; vii. 7—12); xi. 14—26 (cf. Matt. ix. 32—35); xi. 29—xii. 59 (compared with parts of the Sermon on the Mount, &c.). Of course the dull and recklessly adopted hypothesis of a constant repetition of *incidents* may here come in to support the preconceived notions of some harmonists ; but it is an hypothesis mainly founded on a false and unscriptural view of inspiration, and one which must not be adopted without the strongest justification. The occasional repetition of *discourses* is a much more natural supposition, and one inherently probable from the circumstances of the case.

[2] *E. g.*, x. 38—42 ; xiii. 31—35 ; xvii. 11—19.

[3] The notes of time and place throughout are of the vaguest possible character, evidently because the form of the narrative is here determined by other considerations (see x. 1, 25, 38 ; xi. 1, 14 ; xii. 1, 22 ; xiii. 6, 22 ; xiv. 1 ; xvii. 12, &c.). There seems to be *no ground whatever* for supposing that St. Luke meant to claim absolute chronological *accuracy* by the expression, παρηκολουθηκότι ἀκριβῶς, in i. 3 ; and indeed it seems clear from a study of his Gospel that, though he followed the historical sequence as far as he was able to do so, he often groups events and discourses by spiritual and subjective considerations.

[4] See, among other passages, Mark x. 17; Matt. xix. 16.

rated in Matt. xx. 17—28 ; Mark x. 32—45 ; Luke xviii. 31—34, belong not to this journey, but to the *last* which Jesus ever took — the journey from *Ephraim* to Bethany and Jerusalem.

Assuming these conclusions to be justified — and I believe that they will commend themselves as at least probable to any who really study the data of the problem — we naturally look to see if there are any incidents which can only be referred to this last residence of Jesus in Galilee after the Feast of Tabernacles. The sojourn must have been a very brief one, and seems to have had no other object than that of preparing for the Mission of the Seventy, and inaugurating the final proclamation of Christ's kingdom throughout all that part of the Holy Land which had as yet been least familiar with His word and works. His instructions to the Seventy involved His last farewell to Galilee, and the delivery of those instructions synchronized, in all probability, with His actual departure. But there are two other incidents recorded in the 13th chapter, which probably belong to the same brief sojourn — namely, the news of a Galilæan massacre, and the warning which He received of Herod's designs against His life.

The home of Jesus during these few last days would naturally be at Capernaum, His own city ; and while He was there organizing a solemn departure to which there would be no return, there were some who came and announced to Him a recent instance of those numerous disturbances which marked the Procuratorship of Pontius Pilate. Of the particular event to which they alluded nothing further is known ; and that a few turbulent zealots should have been cut down at Jerusalem by the Roman garrison was too common-place an event in these troublous times to excite more than a transient notice. There were probably hundreds of such outbreaks of which Josephus has preserved no record. The inflammable fanaticism of the Jews at this epoch — the restless hopes which were constantly kindling them to fury against the Roman Governor,[1] and which made them the ready dupes of every false Messiah — had necessitated the construction of the Tower of Antonia, which flung its threatening shadow over the Temple itself. This Tower communicated with the Temple by a flight of steps, so that the Roman legionaries could rush down at once, and suppress any of the disturbances which then, as now, endangered the security of Jerusalem at the recurrence of every

---

[1] Acts xxi. 34. Three thousand Jews had been massacred by Archelaus in one single Paschal disturbance thirty years before this time ; and on one occasion Pilate had actually disguised his soldiers as peasants, and sent them to use their daggers freely among the mob. (See Jos. *Antt.* xvii. 9, § 3 ; 10, § 2 ; xviii. 3, § 1 ; *B. J.* ii. 9, § 4.)

religious feast.[1] And of all the Jews, the Galilæans, being the most passionately turbulent and excitable, were the most likely to suffer in such collisions. Indeed, the main fact which seems in this instance to have struck the narrators, was not so much the actual massacre as the horrible incident that the blood of these murdered rioters had been actually mingled with the red streams that flowed from the victims they had been offering in sacrifice.[2] And those who brought the news to Christ did so, less with any desire to complain of the sanguinary boldness of the Roman Governor, than with a curiosity about the supposed crimes which must have brought upon these slaughtered worshippers so hideous and tragical a fate.

The Book of Job stood in Hebrew literature as an eternal witness against these sweeping deductions of a confident uncharity; but the spirit of Eliphaz, and Zophar, and Bildad still survived,[3] and our Lord on every occasion seized the opportunity of checking and reproving it. " Do ye imagine," He said, " that these Galilæans were sinners above all the Galilæans, because they suffered such things? I tell you, Nay: but, except ye repent, ye shall all likewise perish." And then He reminded them of another recent instance of sudden death, in which " the Tower in Siloam " had fallen, and crushed eighteen people who happened to be under it;[4] and He told them that so far from these poor sufferers having been specially criminal, they should all, if they did not repent, be involved in a similar destruction. No doubt, the main lesson which Christ desired to teach, was that every circumstance of life, and every violence of man, was not the result either of idle accident or direct retribution, but formed part of one great scheme of Providence in which man is permitted to recognize the one prevailing law — viz., that the so-called accidents of life happen alike to all, but that all should in due time receive according to

---

[1] The Turkish Government have, with considerable astuteness, fixed the annual pilgrimage of Mohammedans to the *Tomb* of the Prophet Moses (!) at the very time when the return of Easter inundates Jerusalem with Christian pilgrims. I met hundreds of these servants of the Prophet in the environs of the Sacred City during the Easter of 1870, and they would be a powerful assistance to the Turks in case of any Christian outbreak in the Church of the Holy Sepulchre.

[2] The same fact recurs more than once in the details of the siege of Jerusalem. It is clear, however, that some links are missing to our comprehension of this story; for one would have expected that Galilæans butchered in the Temple by a Roman Governor would have been looked upon as martyrs rather than as criminals.

[3] Job. iv. 7; viii. 20; xxii. 5.

[4] Ewald supposes that these men had been engaged in constructing the aqueduct which the Jews regarded as impious, because Pilate had sequestrated the corban money for this secular purpose (Jos. *B. J.* ii. 9, § 4).

their works.[1] But His words had also a more literal fulfilment; and, doubtless, there may have been some among His hearers who lived to call them to mind when the Jewish race was being miserably decimated by the sword of Titus, and the last defenders of Jerusalem, after deluging its streets with blood, fell crushed among the flaming ruins of the Temple, which not even their lives could save.

The words were very stern: but Christ did not speak to them in the language of warning only; He held out to them a gracious hope. Once, and again, and yet again; the fig-tree might be found a barren cumberer of the ground,[2] but there was ONE to intercede for it still; and even yet — though now the axe was uplifted, nay, though it was at its backmost poise — even yet, if at the last the tree, so carefully tended, should bring forth fruit, that axe should be stayed, and its threatened stroke should not rush through the parted air.

Short as His stay at His old home was meant to be, His enemies would gladly have shortened it still further. They were afraid of, they were weary of, the Lord of Life. Yet they did not dare openly to confess their sentiments. The Pharisees came to Him in sham solicitude for His safety, and said, "Get thee out, and depart hence; for Herod is wanting to kill thee."[3]

Had Jesus yielded to fear — had He hastened His departure in consequence of a danger, which even if it had any existence, except in their own imaginations, had at any rate no immediate urgency — doubtless, they would have enjoyed a secret triumph at His expense. But His answer was supremely calm: "Go," He said, "and tell this fox,[4] Behold, I am casting out devils, and working cures to-day and to-morrow, and on the third my work is done."[5] And then He adds,

---

[1] See Amos iii. 6 ; ix. 1.

[2] Luke xiii. 7, ἱνατί καὶ τὴν γῆν καταργεῖ; "Why does it even render the ground barren?" There seems to be a natural reference to the three years of our Lord's own ministry.

[3] The assertion was probably quite untrue. It is inconsistent with Luke xxiii. 8.

[4] Luke xiii. 32, τῇ ἀλώπεκι ταύτῃ, as though Herod were with them in person, as he was like them in cunning. "Non quod haec verba de Herode non dixerit, sed quod in personâ Herodis, quam illi sibi induebant . . . eos notaverit atque refellerit" [299] (Maldon).

[5] Vulg. "consummor;" or, perhaps, "I shall reach my goal:" such seems to be at least an admissible rendering of the difficult word τελειοῦμαι (cf. Phil. iii. 12 ; Acts xx. 24). I have given it the sense which it has in John xix. 28. The word was afterwards used of a martyr's death, as in the inscription ὁ ἅγιος Θῶμας λόγχῃ . . τελειοῦται (Routh, *Rel. Sacr.* i. 376, *ap.* Wordsworth, *ad loc.*); and even of natural death (Euseb. *Vit. Const.* 47). Cf. "Sic Tiberius *finivit*" (Tac. *Ann.* vi. 50). (Schleusner.)

with the perfect confidence of security mingled with the bitter irony of sorrow, " But I must go [1] on my course to-day, and to-morrow, and the day following; for it cannot be that a prophet perish out of Jerusalem." And, perhaps, at this sorrowful crisis His oppressed feelings may have found vent in some pathetic cry over the fallen sinful city, so red with the blood of her murdered messengers, like that which He also uttered when He wept over it on the summit of Olivet.[2]

The little plot of these Pharisees had entirely failed. Whether Herod had really entertained any vague intention of seeing Jesus and putting Him to death as he had put to death His kinsman John, or whether the whole rumor was a pure invention, Jesus regarded it with consummate indifference. Whatever Herod might be designing, His own intention was to finish His brief stay in Galilee in His own due time, and not before. A day or two yet remained to Him in which He would continue to perform His works of mercy on all who sought Him; after that brief interval the time would have come when he should be received up,[3] and He would turn His back for the last time on the home of His youth, and " set His face steadfastly to go to Jerusalem." Till then — so they must tell their crafty patron, whom they themselves resembled — He was under an invio-

---

[1] $\pi o \rho \epsilon \acute{\upsilon} \epsilon \sigma \theta a\iota$ used in a different sense from their previous $\pi o \rho \epsilon \acute{\upsilon} o \upsilon$. The $\pi \lambda \grave{\eta} \nu$ seems to mean, " Yet, though my remaining time is short, I shall not further shorten it, for," &c. Of course the " to-day," &c., means a time indefinite, yet brief.

[2] Marvellously has that woe been fulfilled. Every Jewish pilgrim who enters Jerusalem to this day has a rent made in his dress, and says, " Zion is turned into a desert, it lies in ruins ! " (Dr. Frankl, *Jews in the East*, E. Tr. ii. 2.) Sapir, the Jewish poet of Wilna, addressed Dr. Frankl thus — " Here all is dust. After the destruction of the city, the whole earth blossoms from its ruins ; but here there is no verdure, no blossom, only a bitter fruit — sorrow. Look for no joy here, either from men or from mountains " (*id.* p. 9). A wealthy and pious Jew came to settle at Jerusalem : after two years' stay he left it with the words, " Let him that wishes to have neither *aulom haze* (' the pleasures of this life ') nor *aulom habo* (' those of the life to come ') live at Jerusalem " (*id.* p. 120). — The translation is Dr. Frankl's, not mine.

[3] Luke ix. 51, $\grave{\epsilon} \nu \tau \tilde{\omega} \sigma \upsilon \mu \pi \lambda \eta \rho o \tilde{\upsilon} \sigma \theta a\iota \tau \grave{a}\varsigma \dot{\eta} \mu \acute{\epsilon} \rho a\varsigma \tau \tilde{\eta}\varsigma \dot{a} \nu a \lambda \acute{\eta} \psi \epsilon \omega\varsigma a \grave{\upsilon} \tau o \tilde{\upsilon}$ — *i. e.*, as Euthymius adds, $\dot{a} \pi \grave{o} \gamma \tilde{\eta}\varsigma \epsilon \grave{\iota}\varsigma o \grave{\upsilon} \rho a \nu \acute{o} \nu$. The word is, in the New Testament, a $\ddot{a} \pi a\xi \lambda \epsilon \gamma \grave{o} \mu \epsilon \nu o \nu$, but it is mere sophistry to make it fall in with any harmonistic scheme by giving it the meaning of " His reception by men," as Wieseler does (*Synops.*, pp. 295—297). Even Lange has now abandoned it as untenable. It can only mean what the verb $\dot{a} \nu \epsilon \lambda \acute{\eta} \phi \theta \eta$ means in Acts i. 2, 22 (cf. Mark xvi. 19), and in the LXX. (2 Kings ii. 9—11). The word occurs in the title of an Apocryphal book, the $\dot{A} \nu \acute{a} \lambda \eta \psi \iota\varsigma M \omega \acute{o} \sigma \epsilon \omega\varsigma$, or Assumption of Moses, and Irenæus speaks of $\tau \grave{\eta} \nu \ddot{\epsilon} \nu \sigma a \rho \kappa o \nu \epsilon \grave{\iota}\varsigma \tau o \grave{\upsilon}\varsigma o \grave{\upsilon} \rho a \nu o \grave{\upsilon}\varsigma \dot{a} \nu \acute{a} \lambda \eta \psi \iota \nu$. Sophocles gives several instances of its use in the *Apost. Constitutions*, and later writers.

lable protection, into which neither their malice nor his cruelty could intrude.

And He deservedly bestowed on Herod Antipas the sole word of pure unmitigated contempt which is ever recorded to have passed His lips. Words of burning anger He sometimes spoke — words of scathing indignation — words of searching irony — words of playful humor; but some are startled to find Him using words of sheer contempt. Yet why not? there can be no noble soul which is wholly destitute of scorn. The "scorn of scorn" must exist side by side with the "love of love." Like anger, like the power of moral indignation, scorn has its due place as a righteous function in the economy of human emotions, and as long as there are things of which we rightly judge as contemptible, so long must contempt remain. And if ever there was a man who richly deserved contempt, it was the paltry, perjured princeling — false to his religion, false to his nation, false to his friends, false to his brethren, false to his wife — to whom Jesus gave the name of "this fox." The inhuman vices which the Cæsars displayed on the vast theatre of their absolutism — the lust, the cruelty, the autocratic insolence, the ruinous extravagance — all these were seen in pale reflex in these little Neros and Caligulas of the provinces — these local tyrants, half Idumæan, half Samaritan, who aped the worst degradations of the Imperialism to which they owed their very existence. Judæa might well groan under the odious and petty despotism of these hybrid Herodians — jackals who fawned about the feet of the Cæsarean lions.[1] Respect for "the powers that be" can hardly, as has well been said, involve respect for all the impotences and imbecilities.

Whether "this fox" ever heard the manner in which our Lord had characterized him and his dominion we do not know; in lifetime they never met, until, on the morning of the crucifixion, Antipas vented upon Jesus his empty insults. But now Jesus calmly concluded His last task in Galilee. He summoned His followers together, and out of them chose seventy to prepare His way. Their number was probably symbolic,[2] and the mission of so large a num-

---

[1] What has been said of Agrippa is equally true of Antipas, viz., that " he had been the meanest thing the world had ever seen — a courtier of the early empire . . He had been corrupted by the influence of the Roman court, and had flattered the worst vices of the worst men in the worst age of the world's history." (*Paul of Tarsus*, p. 205).

[2] Some MSS. alter it into " seventy-two " to connect their number with the number of the Sanhedrin, and the elders appointed by Moses [about which, however, there is the same variation] (Exod. xxiv. 1). Others, with no authority but

ber to go before Him two and two, and prepare for His arrival in every place which He intended to visit, implies for this last journey of proclamation an immense publicity. The instructions which He gave them closely resemble those which He had issued to the Twelve; and, indeed, differ from them only in being more brief, because they refer to a more transitory office; in omitting the now needless restrictions about not visiting the Gentiles and Samaritans; and perhaps in bestowing upon them less ample miraculous power.[1] They also breathe a sadder tone, inspired by the experience of incessant rejection.

And now the time has come for Him to set forth, and it must be in sorrow. He left, indeed, some faithful hearts behind Him; but how few! Galilee had rejected Him, as Judea had rejected Him. On one side of the lake which He loved, a whole populace in unanimous deputation had besought Him to depart out of their coasts; on the other, they had vainly tried to vex His last days among them by a miserable conspiracy to frighten Him into flight. At Nazareth, the sweet mountain village of His childish days — at Nazareth, with all its happy memories of His boyhood and His mother's home — they had treated Him with such violence and outrage, that He could not visit it again. And even at Chorazin, and Capernaum, and Bethsaida — on those Eden-shores of the silver lake — in the green delicious plain, whose every field He had traversed with His apostles, performing deeds of mercy and uttering words of love — even there they loved the whited sepulchres of a Pharisaic sanctity, and the shallow traditions of a Levitical ceremonial better than the light and the life which had been offered them by the Son of God. They were feeding on ashes; a deceived heart had turned them aside. On many a great city of antiquity, on Nineveh and Babylon, on Tyre and Sidon, on Sodom and Gomorrah, had fallen the wrath of God; yet even Nineveh and Babylon would have humbled their gorgeous idolatries, even Tyre and Sidon have turned from their greedy vanities, yea, even Sodom and Gomorrah would have repented from their filthy lusts, had they seen the mighty works which had been done in

---

fancy, connect it with the ideal seventy nations of the world. (Lightfoot, *Hor. Hebr.*, in John vii. 37). These seventy nations are supposed to have been separated at Babel (see Targ. Ps. Jonath. in Gen. xi. 7, 8).

[1] Compare Matt. x. 5—42 with Luke x. 1—12. We must not press the fact that ἄρνας, "lambs," is in Luke x. 3 substituted for πρόβατα in Matt. x. 16. The prohibition to greet any one by the way is proverbial of any hasty mission (2 Kings iv. 29), and arose from the fact that Oriental greetings are much longer and more elaborate than ours. (Thomson, *Land and Book*, II. ch. xxiv.)

these little cities and villages of the Galilæan sea. And, therefore, "Woe unto thee, Chorazin! woe unto thee, Bethsaida!" and unto thee, Capernaum, "His own city," a yet deeper woe!

With such thoughts in His heart, and such words on His lips, he started forth from the scene of His rejected ministry; and on all this land, and most of all on that region of it, the woe has fallen. Exquisite still in its loveliness, it is now desolate and dangerous. The birds still sing in countless myriads; the water-fowl still play on the crystal mere; the brooks flow into it from the neighboring hill, "filling their bosoms with pearl, and scattering their path with emeralds;" the aromatic herbs are still fragrant when the foot crushes them, and the tall oleanders fill the air with their delicate perfume as of old; but the vineyards and fruit-gardens have disappeared; the fleets and fishing-boats cease to traverse the lake; the hum of men is silent; the stream of prosperous commerce has ceased to flow. The very names and sites of the towns and cities are forgotten; and where they once shone bright and populous, flinging their shadows across the sunlit waters, there are now grey mounds where even the ruins are too ruinous to be distinguishable. One solitary palm-tree by one squalid street of huts, degraded and frightful beyond any, even in Palestine, still marks the site, and recalls the name of the one little town where lived that sinful penitent woman who once washed Christ's feet with her tears and wiped them with the hairs of her head.[1]

And the very generation which rejected Him was doomed to recall in bitter and fruitless agony these peaceful happy days of the Son of Man. Thirty years had barely elapsed when the storm of Roman invasion burst furiously over that smiling land. He who will, may read in the Jewish War of Josephus the hideous details of the slaughter which decimated the cities of Galilee, and wrung from the historian the repeated confession that "it was certainly God who brought the Romans to punish the Galilæans," and exposed the people of city after city "to be destroyed by their bloody enemies."[2] Immediately after the celebrated passage in which he describes the lake and plain of Gennesareth as "the ambition of nature,"[3] follows a description of that terrible sea-fight on these bright waters, in which the number of the slain, including those killed in the city, was six thousand five

---

[1] The "Woe unto thee, Chorazin," and the "And thou, Capernaum," receive a very striking illustration from the photographs of the two sites by the Palestine Exploration Fund.

[2] Jos. *B. J.* iii. 7, § 31.

[3] Jos. *B. J.* iii. 10, § 8; *v. supra.*, p. 153. I here quote the translation of Whiston.

hundred. Hundreds were stabbed by the Romans or run through with poles; others tried to save their lives by diving, but if once they raised their heads were slain by darts; or if they swam to the Roman vessels had their heads or hands lopped off; while others were chased to the land and there massacred. "One might then," the historian continues, "see the lake all bloody, and full of dead bodies, for not one of them escaped. *And a terrible stink, and a very sad sight there was, on the following days over that country; for, as for the shores, they were full of shipwrecks and of dead bodies all swelled;* and as the dead bodies were inflamed by the sun, and putrified, they corrupted the air, *insomuch that the misery was not only an object of commiseration to the Jews, but even to those that hated them, and had been the authors of that misery.*" Of those that died amid this butchery; of those whom Vespasian immediately afterwards abandoned to brutal and treacherous massacre between Tarichææ and Tiberias; of those twelve hundred "old and useless" whom he afterwards caused to be slain in the stadium; of the six thousand whom he sent to aid Nero in his attempt to dig through the Isthmus of Athos; of the thirty thousand four hundred whom he sold as slaves — may there not have been many who in their agony and exile, in their hour of death and day of judgment,[1] recalled Him whom they had repudiated, and remembered that the sequel of all those gracious words which had proceeded out of His lips had been the "woe" which their obduracy called forth!

There could not but be sorrow in such a parting from such a scene. And yet the divine spirit of Jesus could not long be a prey to consuming sadness. Out of the tenebrous influences cast about it from the incessant opposition of unbelief and sin, it was ever struggling into the purity and peace of heaven, from the things seen and temporal to the things unseen and eternal, from the shadows of human degradation into the sunlight of God's peace. "In that hour Jesus rejoiced in spirit," and what a joy! what a boundless, absorbing exultation,[2] as He thought no longer of judgment but of compas-

---

[1] Since writing the above I have read the powerful descriptions of the same fact in Renan's *L'Antechrist*, p. 277. He says, "Il y a dans l'histoire peu d'exemples d'une race entière ainsi broyée."[300]

[2] ἠγαλλιάσατο. It seems clear that Luke x. 21 belongs closely to the address which closes in verse 16, though St. Luke pauses to record in the intermediate verses the return of the Seventy. This must be evident to any one who compares the passage with Matt. xi. 20—27; and unless we adopt the unlikely hypothesis that *both series* of words were uttered twice in different connections, it is clear that St. Luke's context here suits them best; and, moreover, this mark of time here given by St. Luke is slightly the more definite of the two.

sion; as He turned not with faint trust but perfect knowledge to "the larger hope;" as He remembered how *that* which was hidden from the wise and prudent had been revealed unto babes; as He dwelt upon the thought that He was sent not to the rich and learned few, but to the ignorant and suffering many; as He told His disciples, that into *His*, yea, into His own loving hands, had His Father committed all power, and that in Him they would see and know the spirit of His Father, and thereby might see and know that revelation for which many kings and prophets had sighed in vain. And then, that even in the hour of denunciation not one of them might doubt His own or His Father's love, He uttered in that same hour of rapt and exalted ecstasy, those tenderest words ever uttered in human language as God's message and invitation to His children in the suffering family of man, "Come unto me all ye that labor and are heavy laden, and I will give you rest. Take my yoke upon you, and learn of me; for I am meek and lowly in heart; and ye shall find rest unto your souls."

So, over a temporary sorrow there triumphed an infinite and eternal joy. There are some who have dwelt too exclusively on Jesus as the Man of Sorrows; have thought of His life as of one unmitigated suffering, one almost unbroken gloom. But in the Bible — though there alone — we find the perfect compatibility, nay, the close union of joy with sorrow; and myriads of Christians who have been "troubled on every side, yet not distressed; perplexed, but not in despair; persecuted, but not forsaken; cast down, but not destroyed," can understand how the Man of Sorrows, even in the days of His manhood, may have lived a life happier, in the true sense of happiness — happier, because purer, more sinless, more faithful, more absorbed in the joy of obedience to His Heavenly Father — than has been ever granted to the sons of men. The deep pure stream flows on its way rejoicing, even though the forests overshadow it, and no transient sunshine flickers on its waves.

And if, indeed, true joy — the highest joy — be "severe, and chaste, and solitary, and incompatible," then how constant, how inexpressible, what a joy of God, must have been the joy of the Man Christ Jesus, who came to give to all who love Him, henceforth and for ever, a joy which no man taketh from them — a joy which the world can neither give nor take away.

CHAPTER XLIII.

INCIDENTS OF THE JOURNEY.

"Religionis non est religionem cogere." [301] — TERT. *Ad. Scap.* 2.

WE are not told the exact route taken by Jesus as He left Gennesareth; but as He probably avoided Nazareth, with its deeply happy and deeply painful memories, He may have crossed the bridge at the southern extremity of the Lake, and so got round into the plain of Esdraelon either by the valley of Bethshean,[1] or over Mount Tabor and round Little Hermon,[2] passing Endor and Nain and Shunem on His way.

Crossing the plain, and passing Taanach and Megiddo, He would reach the range of hills which form the northern limit of Samaria; and at the foot of their first ascent lies the little town of En-gannim, or the "Fountain of Gardens."[3] This would be the first Samaritan village at which He would arrive, and hither, apparently, He had sent two messengers "to make ready for Him." Although the incident is mentioned by St. Luke before the Mission of the Seventy, yet that is probably due to his subjective choice of order, and we may suppose that there were two of the seventy who were dispatched to prepare the way for Him spiritually as well as in the more ordinary sense; unless, indeed, we adopt the conjecture that the messengers may have been James and John, who would thus be likely to feel with special vividness the insult of His rejection. At any rate the inhabitants — who to this day are not remarkable for their civility to strangers[4] — absolutely declined to receive or admit Him. Previously indeed, when He was passing through Samaria on His journey northwards, He had found Samaritans not only willing to receive, but anxious to detain His presence among them, and eager to listen to His words. But now in two respects the circumstances were different;

---

[1] Now the *Wady Mujeidah.*

[2] Along part of the *Wady Bireh.*

[3] Luke ix. 51—56. En-gannim is still a very pleasant spot, deserving its poetic name, which is now corrupted into Jenîn.

[4] So we were told on the spot, though we experienced no personal rudeness there. "They are," says Dr. Thomson, "fanatical, rude, and rebellious" (*Land and Book,* II., ch. xxx.).

for now He was professedly travelling to the city which they hated and the Temple which they despised, and now He was attended, not by a few Apostles, but by a great multitude, who were accompanying Him as their acknowledged Prophet and Messiah. Had Gerizim and not Jerusalem been the goal of His journey, all might have been different; but now His destination and His associates inflamed their national animosity too much to admit of their supplying to the weary pilgrims the ordinary civilities of life. And if the feelings of this little frontier village of En-gannim were so unmistakably hostile, it became clear that any attempt to journey through the whole breadth of Samaria, and even to pass under the shadow of their rival sanctuary, would be a dangerous if not a hopeless task.¹ Jesus therefore altered the course of His journey, and turned once more towards the Jordan valley. Rejected by Galilee, refused by Samaria, without a word He bent His steps towards Peræa.

But the deep discouragement of this refusal to receive Him was mingled in the minds of James and John with hot indignation. There is nothing so trying, so absolutely exasperating, as a failure to find food and shelter, and common civility, after the fatigue of travel, and especially for a large multitude to begin a fresh journey when they expected rest. Full, therefore, of the Messianic kingdom, which now at last they thought was on the eve of being mightily proclaimed, the two brothers wanted to usher it in with a blaze of Sinaitic vengeance, and so to astonish and restore the flagging spirits of followers who would naturally be discouraged by so immediate and decided a repulse. " Lord, wilt Thou that we command fire to come down from heaven, and *consume them*, even as Elias did?" " What wonder," says St. Ambrose, "that the Sons of Thunder wished to flash lightning?" And this their fiery impetuosity seemed to find its justification not only in the precedent of Elijah's conduct,²

---

¹ The exacerbation between Jews and Samaritans was always at its worst during the anniversaries of the national feasts ; and it often broke out into acts of open hostility. In consequence of this, the caravans of Galilæan pilgrims seem in many instances [though by no means always (Jos. *Antt.* xx. 6, § 1 ; *Vit.* 52)] to have chosen the route on the east of Jordan. The Jews accused the Samaritans of wilfully molesting their harmless travellers, even of the horrible crime of having lit false fire-signals to show the time of new moon, and of having polluted their Temple by scattering in it the bones of the dead (see Jos. *Antt.* xviii. 2, § 2 ; *B. J.* ii. 12, §§ 3, seqq.). (*Vid. supra*, p. 175.)

² 2 Kings i. 10—12. The ὡς καὶ ᾽Ηλίας ἐποίησε ³⁰² (Luke ix. 54) is omitted (perhaps on dogmatic grounds) in א, B, L. But as Bishop Andrewes says, " The times require sometimes one spirit, sometimes another. Elias' time, Elias' spirit." The notion, however, that the brothers received the name " Boanerges " (בְּנֵי רְגֵשׁ) from this circumstance is quite groundless. (See p. 207.)

but in the fact that it had been displayed in this very country of
Samaria. Was it more necessary in personal defence of a single
prophet than to vindicate the honor of the Messiah and his attendants? But Jesus turned and rebuked them. God's heaven has
other uses than for thunder. "They did not know," He told them,
"what spirit they were of." [1] They had not realized the difference
which separated Sinai and Carmel from Calvary and Hermon. He
had come to save, not to destroy; and if any heard His words and
believed not, He judged them not. [2] And so, without a word of
anger, He went to a different village; [3] and doubtless St. John, who
by that time *did* know of what spirit he was, remembered these
words of Christ when he went with Peter into Samaria to confirm
the recent converts, and to bestow upon them the gift of the Holy
Ghost.

Perhaps it may have been on this occasion — for certainly no occasion would have been more suitable than that furnished by this early
and rude repulse — that Jesus, turning to the great multitudes that
accompanied Him, [4] delivered to them that memorable discourse in
which He warned them that all who would be His disciples must

---

[1] The words are omitted in many MSS. (א, A, B, C, E, L, &c.). Alford, however, supposes that they "have been unsparingly tampered with" because they
stood in the way of ecclesiastical censures. They occur in D, and in some good
versions.

[2] John iii. 17; xii. 47.

[3] The ἑτέραν [303] (Luke ix. 56) probably implies that it was *not* a Samaritan
village.

[4] Luke xiv. 25—33. We must ask the reader to bear in mind throughout this
and the following chapter that the exact sequence of events is not here given by
the Evangelists, and therefore that the certain order in which they occurred is
not ascertainable. In a thoughtful but quite inconclusive pamphlet by the Rev.
W. Stewart (Maclehose, Glasgow, 1873) called *The Plan of St. Luke's Gospel*,
he supposes that the Evangelist arranged these unchronological incidents alpha-
betically by the leading conceptions of the paragraph — *e. g.*, ἀγαπᾶν, Luke x.
25—28, 29—37, 38—42; αἰτεῖν, xi. 1—4, 5—8, 9—13; ἀντιλέγειν, xi. 14—32, &c.
Thus under κ (κρίνειν) would fall xii. 35—38, 39—46, 47, 48, 51—53, 54—56, 57,
58, 59; xiii. 1—5, 6—9. Under χ (χαίνειν) xvi. 14, 15, 16, 17, 18, 19—31, &c. The
theory, which is worked out with as much ingenuity as it admits, will at least
serve to show how little chronological sequence is traceable in the great division
of St. Luke x.—xviii. 31. Professor Westcott (*Introd. to Gosp.*, p. 365, 3rd ed.)
arranges the contents of the section (omitting the minor divisions) as follows: —
The Universal Church; The Rejection of the Jews foreshown; Preparation (ix.
43—xi. 13); Lessons of warning (xi. 14—xiii. 9); Lessons of progress (xiii. 10—
xiv. 24); Lessons of discipleship (xiv. 25—xvii. 10); The coming end (xvii. 11—
xviii. 30). It is obviously more probable that St. Luke was guided by some such
subjective sequence, than that he should have adopted the poor expedient of an
alphabetical arrangement of unclassified fragments.

come to Him, not expecting earthly love or acceptance, but expecting alienation and opposition, and *counting the cost.* They must abandon, if need be, every earthly tie; they must sit absolutely loose to the interests of the world;[1] they must take up the cross and follow Him. Strange language, of which it was only afterwards that they learnt the full significance! For a man to begin a tower which he could not finish—for a king to enter on a war in which nothing was possible save disaster and defeat—involved disgrace and indicated folly; better not to follow Him at all, unless they followed Him prepared to forsake all that they had on earth; prepared to sacrifice the interests of time, and to live solely for those of eternity. One who believed not, would indeed suffer loss and harm, yet his lot was less pitiable than that of him who became a disciple only to be a backslider—who, facing both ways, cast like Lot's wife a longing glance on all that he ought to flee—who made the attempt, at once impotent and disastrous, to serve both God and Mammon.

As both Galilee and Samaria were now closed to Him, He could only journey on His way to Peræa, down the valley of Bethshean, between the borders of both provinces. There a very touching incident occurred.[2] On the outskirts of one of the villages a dull, harsh, plaintive cry smote His ears, and looking up He saw "ten men who were lepers," united in a community of deadly misery. They were afar off, for they dared not approach, since their approach was pollution, and they were obliged to warn away all who would have come near them by the heart-rending cry, "*Tamé! tamé!*"—"Unclean! unclean!" There was something in that living death of leprosy—recalling as it did the most frightful images of suffering and degradation, corrupting as it did the very fountains of the life-blood of man, distorting his countenance, rendering loathsome his touch, slowly encrusting and infecting him with a plague-spot of disease far more horrible than death itself—which always seems to have thrilled the Lord's heart with a keen and instantaneous compassion. And never more so than at this moment. Scarcely had He heard their piteous cry of "Jesus, Master, have mercy on us," than instantly, without sufficient

---

[1] The "hate" of Luke xiv. 26 is adopted in strict accordance with our Lord's habit of stating the great truths which He uttered in the extremest form of what, to His hearers, must even sound like paradox, in order that their inmost essential truth—their truth without any subterfuge or qualification—might be recognized, and so fixed eternally in their memory. (See *supra*, p. 215.) It was *necessary* that they should be uttered in such a way as to seize, and dominate over, the imagination of mankind for ever

[2] Luke xvii. 11—19.

pause even to approach them more nearly, He called aloud to them, "Go, show yourselves unto the priests." They knew the significance of that command: they knew that it bade them hurry off to claim from the priest the recognition of their cure, the certificate of their restitution to every rite and privilege of human life.[1] Already, at the sound of that potent voice, they felt a stream of wholesome life, of recovered energy, of purer blood, pulsing through their veins; and as they went they were cleansed.

He who has not seen the hideous, degraded spectacle of the lepers clamorously revealing their mutilations, and almost demanding alms, by the roadside of some Eastern city,[2] can hardly conceive how transcendent and immeasurable was the boon which they had thus received at the hands of Jesus. One would have thought that they would have suffered no obstacle to hinder the passionate gratitude which should have prompted them to hasten back at once — to struggle, if need be, even through fire and water, if thereby they could fling themselves with tears of heartfelt acknowledgment at their Saviour's feet, to thank Him for a gift of something more precious than life itself. What absorbing selfishness, what Jewish infatuation, what sacerdotal interference, what new and worse leprosy of shameful thanklessness and superstitious ignorance, prevented it? We do not know. We only know that of ten who were healed but *one* returned, and he was a Samaritan. On the frontiers of the two countries had been gathered, like froth at the margin of wave and sand, the misery of both;[3] but while the nine Jews were infamously thankless, the one Samaritan "turned back, and with a loud voice glorified God, and fell down on his face at His feet, giving Him thanks." The heart of Jesus, familiar as He was with all ingratitude, was yet moved by an instance of it so flagrant, so all but unanimous, and so abnormal. "Were not the ten cleansed?" He asked in sorrowful surprise; "but the nine — where are they?[4] There are not found that returned to give glory to God save this alien."[5] "It is," says Lange, "as if all these benefits were falling into a deep silent grave." The voice

---

[1] Lev. xiii. 2; xiv. 2. *V. supra*, p. 221.

[2] See the dreadful yet not exaggerated picture drawn by Dr. Thomson, *Land and Book*, IV., ch. xliii. ; Delitzsch, *Durch Krankheit zur Genesung*, § v. I had not, however, read either that little tale, or his *Ein Tag in Capernaum*, till the whole of this book was written. I mention this because there are some accidental resemblances between my language and that of Dr. Delitzsch.

[3] So it is only in the *Biut el Masakin* (" abodes of the unfortunate "), or lepers' quarter in Jerusalem, that Jews and Mohammedans will live together.

[4] Luke xvii. 17, οὐχὶ οἱ δέκα ἐκαθαρίσθησαν; οἱ δὲ ἐννέα, ποῦ;

[5] ἀλλογενής.

of their misery had awaked the instant echo of His mercy; but the miraculous utterance of His mercy, though it thrilled through their whole physical being, woke no echo of gratitude in their earthy and still leprous hearts.

But, nevertheless, this alien shall not have returned in vain, nor shall the rare virtue — alas, *how* rare a virtue! [1] — of his gratitude go unrewarded. Not his body alone, but the soul — whose value was so infinitely more precious, just as its diseases are so infinitely more profound — should be healed by His Saviour's word.

"Arise and go," said Jesus; "thy faith hath saved thee."

---

[1] Wordsworth's lines —

> "I've heard of hearts unkind, kind deeds
> With coldness still returning,
> Alas! the gratitude of men
> Hath oftener left me mourning,"

have been often quoted; but if he found gratitude a common virtue, his experience must have been exceptional.

CHAPTER XLIV.

TEACHINGS OF THE JOURNEY.

ועשו סיג לתו, " And make a fence for the Law." — *Pirke Abhôth,* i. 1.

EVEN during this last journey our Lord did not escape the taunts, the opposition, the depreciating remarks — in one word, the Pharisaism — of the Pharisees and those who resembled them. The circumstances which irritated them against Him were exactly the same as they had been throughout His whole career — exactly those in which His example was most lofty, and His teaching most beneficial — namely, the performance on the Sabbath of works of mercy, and the association with publicans and sinners.

One of these sabbatical disputes occurred in a synogogue.[1] Jesus, as we have already remarked, whether because of the lesser excommunication (the *cherem*), or for any other reason, seems, during this latter period of His ministry, to have entered the synagogues but rarely. The exclusion, however, from one synagogue or more did not include a prohibition to enter *any* synagogue; and the subsequent conduct of this *rôsh hakkenéseth* seems to show that he had a certain awe of Jesus, mingled with his jealousy and suspicion. On this day there sat among the worshippers a poor woman who, for eighteen long years, had been bent double by "a spirit of infirmity," and could not lift herself up. The compassionate heart of Jesus could not brook the mute appeal of her presence. He called her to Him, and saying to her, "Woman, thou art loosed from thine infirmity,"[2] laid His hands on her. Instantly she experienced the miraculous strengthening which enabled her to lift up the long-bowed and crooked frame, and instantly she broke into utterances of gratitude to God. But her strain of thanksgiving was interrupted by the narrow and ignorant indignation of the ruler of the synagogue. Here, under his very eyes, and without any reference to the "little brief authority" which gave him a sense of dignity on each recurring

---

[1] Luke xiii. 10—17.

[2] Luke xiii. 12, ἀπολέλυσαι.[304] The perfect implies the instantaneousness and permanence of the result.

Sabbath, a woman — a member of *his* congregation — had actually had the presumption to be healed. Armed with his favorite " texts," and in all the fussiness of official hypocrisy, he gets up and rebukes the perfectly innocent multitude, telling them it was a gross instance of Sabbath-breaking for them to be healed on that sacred day, when they might just as well be healed on any of the other six days of the week. That the offence consisted solely in the being healed is clear, for he certainly could not mean that, if they had any sickness, it was a crime for them to come to the synagogue at all on the Sabbath day. Now, as the poor woman does not seem to have spoken one word of entreaty to Jesus, or even to have called His attention to her case, the utterly senseless address of this man could only by any possibility mean either " You *sick* people must not come to the synagogue at all on the Sabbath under present circumstances, for fear you should be led into Sabbath-breaking by having a miraculous cure performed upon you ; " or " If any one wants to heal you on a Sabbath, you must decline." And these remarks he has neither the courage to address to Jesus Himself, nor the candor to address to the poor healed woman, but preaches *at* them both by rebuking the multitude, who had no concern in the action at all, beyond the fact that they had been passive spectators of it !

The whole range of the Gospels does not supply any other instance of an interference so illogical, or a stupidity so hopeless ; and the indirect, underhand way in which he gave vent to his outraged ignorance brought on him that expression of our Lord's indignation which he had not dared openly to brave. *"Hypocrite!"* was the one crushing word with which Jesus addressed him. This silly official had been censorious with *Him* because He had spoken a few words to the woman, and laid upon her a healing hand ; and with the woman because, having been bent double, she lifted herself up and glorified God ! It would be difficult to imagine such a paralysis of the moral sense, if we did not daily see the stultifying effect produced upon the intellect by the " deep slumber of a decided opinion," especially when the opinion itself rests upon nothing better than a meaningless tradition. Now Jesus constantly varied the arguments and appeals by which He endeavored to show the Pharisees of His nation that their views about the Sabbath only degraded it from a divine benefit into a revolting bondage.[1] To the Rabbis of Jerusalem He justified

---

[1] It is a curious but instructive fact that the Jews of Palestine to this day greatly resemble their Pharisaic predecessors. " I have no heart," says Dr. Thomson, " to dwell on their absurd superstitions, their intense fanaticism, or their

Himself by an appeal to His own character and authority, as supported by the triple testimony of John the Baptist, of the Scriptures, and of the Father Himself, who bore witness to Him by the authority which He had given Him.[1] To the Pharisees of Galilee He had quoted the direct precedents of Scripture,[2] or had addressed an appeal, founded on their own common sense and power of insight into the eternal principles of things.[3] But the duller and less practised intellect of these Peræans might not have understood either the essential love and liberty implied by the institution of the Sabbath, or the paramount authority of Jesus as Lord of the Sabbath. It could not rise above the cogency of the *argumentum ad hominem.* It was only capable of a conviction based on their own common practices and received limitations. There was not one of them who did not consider himself justified in unloosing and leading to the water his ox or his ass on the Sabbath,[4] although that involved far more labor than either laying the hand on a sick woman, or even being healed by a miraculous word! If their Sabbath rules gave way to the needs of ox or ass, ought they not to give way to the cruel necessities of a daughter of Abraham? If *they* might do much more labor on the Sabbath to abbreviate a few hours' thirst, might not He do much less to terminate a Satanically cruel bondage which

---

social and domestic institutions and manners, comprising an incredible and grotesque *mélange* of filth and finery, Pharisaic self-righteousness and Sadducean licentiousness. The following is a specimen of the puerilities enjoined and enforced by their learned Rabbis : — *A Jew must not carry on the Sabbath even so much as a pocket-handkerchief, except within the walls of the city.* If there are no walls it follows, according to their perverse logic, that he must not carry it at all ! To avoid this difficulty, here in Safed, they resort to what is called *erüv.* Poles are set up at the ends of the streets, and *strings* stretched from the one to the other. *This string represents a wall, and a conscientious Jew may carry his handkerchief anywhere within these strings.* I was once amused by a devout Israelite who was walking with me on his Sabbath. When we came to the end of the street the string was gone, and so by another fiction he was at liberty to go on without reference to what was in his pocket, *because he had not passed the wall.* The last time I was here they had abandoned this absurdity, probably to avoid the constant ridicule it brought upon them " (Thomson, *Land and Book,* II., ch. xix.). What a commentary on the kind of Sabbatarianism.which Christ combated ! For abundant further instances, which descend into details not only puerile but disgusting, see. Buxtorf, *Syn. Jud.,* capp. xiv.—xvi.

[1] John v. 17—47, *supra,* p. 291.
[2] Luke vi. 3—5, *supra,* p. 333.
[3] Luke vi. 9, *supra,* p. 335.
[4] It might, moreover, as they were well aware, have been avoided altogether if their Oriental laziness, and want of real earnestness, had not prevented them from rendering such tasks unnecessary by procuring a supply of water overnight. But this kind of letter-worship must of its very nature be purely artificial.

had lasted, lo! these eighteen years? At reasonings so unanswerable, no wonder that His adversaries were ashamed, and that the simpler, more unsophisticated people rejoiced at all the glorious acts of mercy which He wrought on their behalf.[1]

Again and again was our Lord thus obliged to redeem this great primeval institution of God's love from these narrow, formal, pernicious restrictions of an otiose and unintelligent tradition. But it is evident that He attached as much importance to the noble and loving freedom of the day of rest as they did to the stupefying inaction to which they had reduced the normal character of its observance. Their absorbing attachment to it, the frenzy[2] which filled them when He set at naught their Sabbatarian uncharities, rose from many circumstances. They were wedded to the religious system which had long prevailed among them, because it is easy to be a slave to the letter, and difficult to enter into the spirit; easy to obey a number of outward rules, difficult to enter intelligently and self-sacrificingly into the will of God; easy to entangle the soul in a network of petty observances, difficult to yield the obedience of an enlightened heart; easy to be haughtily exclusive, difficult to be humbly spiritual : easy to be an ascetic or a formalist, difficult to be pure, and loving, and wise, and free; easy to be a Pharisee, difficult to be a disciple; very easy to embrace a self-satisfying and sanctimonious system of rabbinical observances, very difficult to love God with all the heart, and all the might, and all the soul, and all the strength. In laying His axe at the root of their proud and ignorant Sabbatarianism, He was laying His axe at the root of all that " miserable micrology " which they had been accustomed to take for their religious life. Is the spirit of the sects so free in these days from Pharisaic taint as not to need such lessons? Will not these very words which I have written —

---

[1] They might say, If she has been bound these eighteen years, surely she might wait yet one day longer! But that very circumstance He makes an argument for the contrary, for he who loves his neighbor as himself would rather say, Not one moment longer must she suffer, if help can be afforded her! Could it be *forbidden* thus to help? The "*ought not*" of verse 16 catechetically answers, with infinite condescension, the inconsiderate, proud, and unintelligent "*ought*" of verse 14. "*Men ought*" was the theme there; so now the "*ought*" is abundantly returned; "*ought not* she, according to the law of love, which specially ordains God's works for the Sabbath, as man's labor for the remaining days, to be loosed from this misery?" (Stier, iv. 51.)

[2] Luke vi. 11, ἐπλήσθησαν ἀνοίας.[305] The attachment to the Sabbath was not all religious; it was due in part to the obstinate conservatism of an exclusive nationality, and as such it even attracted heathen notice (Ovid, *Ars Amat.* i. 415, Juv. *Sat.* xiv. 98—100).

although they are but an expansion of the lessons which Jesus incessantly taught — yet give offence to some who read them?

One more such incident is recorded — the sixth embittered controversy of the kind in which they had involved our Lord.[1] Nothing but Sabbatarianism which had degenerated into monomania could account for their so frequently courting a controversy which always ended in their total discomfiture. On a certain Sabbath, which was the principal day for Jewish entertainments,[2] Jesus was invited to the house of one who, as he is called a ruler of the Pharisees, must have been a man in high position, and perhaps even a member of the Sanhedrin. The invitation was one of those to which he was so often subjected, not respectful or generous, but due either to idle curiosity or downright malice. Throughout the meal He was carefully watched by hostile scrutiny. The Pharisees, as has been well said, "performed the duty of religious espionage with exemplary diligence."[3] Among the unbidden guests who, Oriental fashion, stood about the room and looked on, as they do to this day during the continuance of a meal, was a man afflicted with the dropsy. The prominent position in which he stood, combined with the keen watchfulness of the Pharisees, seems to show that he had been placed designedly, either to test Christ's willingness to respect their Sabbath prejudices, or to defeat His miraculous power by the failure to cure a disease more inveterate, and less amenable to curative measures, than any other. If so, this was another of those miserable cases in which these unfeeling teachers of the people were ready to make the most heart-rending shame or the deepest misery a mere tool to be used or thrown aside, as chance might serve, in their dealings with Jesus. But this time Jesus anticipated, and went to meet half way the subtle machinations of this learned and distinguished company. He asked them the very simple question —

---

[1] Luke xiv. 1—6. The others were the healing at Bethesda (John v. 10, p. 289)· the scene in the corn-field (Mark ii. 23, p. 331); the healing of the withered hand (Matt. xii. 10, p. 334), of the blind man at Siloam (John ix. 14, *supr.*, p. 420), and of the paralytic woman (Luke xiii. 14, *supr.*, p. 442).

[2] Neh. viii. 9—12. No cooking was done (Exod. xvi. 23); but, as those feasts *must* have necessitated more or less labor, the fact shows how little real earnestness there was in the Jewish Sabbatarianism; how fast and loose they could play with their own convictions; how physical self-indulgence and unintelligent routine had usurped the place of spiritual enlightenment. On the contrary, there was no inconsistency whatever in our Lord's *accepting* such invitations; there was nothing wrong in them, and nothing out of accordance with true principles; and therefore Jesus could sanction them with His presence. But had there been any true principle involved in the Jewish view, *they* ought to have *thought* them wrong.

[3] Bruce, *Training of the Twelve*, p. 27. Luke xiv. 1—6.

" Is it lawful to heal on the Sabbath day ? "

They *would* not say " Yes ; " but, on the other hand, they dared not say " No ! " Had it been unlawful, it was their positive function and duty to say so then and there, and without any subterfuge to deprive the poor sufferer, so far as in them lay, of the miraculous mercy which was prepared for him, and to brave the consequences. If they dared not say so — either for fear of the people, or for fear of instant refutation, or because the spell of Christ's awful ascendancy was upon them, or out of a mere splenetic pride, or — to imagine better motives — because in their inmost hearts, if any spot remained in them uncrusted by idle and irreligious prejudices, they felt that it *was* lawful, and more than lawful, RIGHT — then, by their own judgment, they left Jesus free to heal without the possibility of censure. Their silence, therefore, was, even on their own showing, and on their own principles, His entire justification. His mere simple question, and their inability to answer it, was an absolute decision of the controversy in His favor. He therefore took the man, healed him, and let him go.

And then He appealed, as before, to their own practice. " Which of you shall have a son,[1] or (even) an ox, fallen into a pit, and will not straightway pull him out on the Sabbath day ? " They knew that they *could* only admit the fact, and then the argument *à fortiori* was irresistible ; a man was more important than a beast ; the extrication of a beast involved more labor by far than the healing of a man. Their base little plot only ended in the constrained and awkward silence of a complete refutation which they were too ungenerous to acknowledge.

Jesus deigned no farther to dwell on a subject which to the mind of every candid listener had been set at rest for ever, and He turned their thoughts to other lessons. The dropsy of their inflated self-satisfaction was a disease far more difficult to heal than that of the sufferer whom they had used to entrap Him. Scarcely was the feast ready, when there arose among the distinguished company one of those unseemly struggles for precedence which — common, nay,

---

[1] It seems certain that υἱός, not ὄνος, is the true reading in Luke xiv. 5 ; an immense preponderance of the best MSS. (A, B, and ten uncials) and versions (the Syriac, Persian, Sahidic, &c.) is in its favor ; the apparent strangeness of the collocation is removed by certain Rabbinic parallels — *e. g.*, *Babha Kama*, 5, 6 (quoted by Sepp). There can be no question that the Jews had always *theoretically* admitted, and acted on, the very principle which our Lord asserts ; and they do so to this day — *e. g.*, the Jews of Tiberias, with all their Sabbatarianism, *bathe often* on the Sabbath.

almost universal as they are — show the tendencies of human nature
on its weakest and most contemptible side.[1] And nothing more
clearly showed the essential hollowness of Pharisaic religion than its
intense pride and self-exaltation. Let one anecdote suffice. The
King Jannæus had on one occasion invited several Persian Satraps,
and among the guests asked to meet them was the Rabbi Simeon
Ben Shetach. The latter on entering seated himself at table between
the King and Queen. Being asked his reason for such a presumptuous
intrusion, he replied that it was written in the Book of Jesus Ben
Sirach, "Exalt wisdom and she shall exalt thee, and shall make thee
sit among princes."[2]

The Jews at this period had adopted the system of *triclinia* from
the Greeks and Romans, and the "chief seat" ($\pi\rho\omega\tau\sigma\kappa\lambda\iota\sigma\iota\alpha$) was
the middle seat in the central *triclinium*. Observing the anxiety of
each guest to secure this place for himself,[3] our Lord laid down a
wiser and better principle of social courtesy, which involved the far
deeper lesson of spiritual humility. Just as in earthly society the
pushing, intrusive, self-conceited man must be prepared for many a
strong rebuff, and will find himself often compelled to give place to
modest merit, so in the eternal world, "whosoever exalteth himself
shall be abased, and he that humbleth himself shall be exalted."
Pride, exclusiveness, self-glorification, have no place in the kingdom
of God. Humility is the only passport which can obtain for us an
entrance there.

> "Humble we must be, if to heaven we go ;
> High is the roof there, but the gate is low."

And He proceeded to teach them another lesson, addressed to
some obvious foible in the character of His host.[4] Luxury, ostentation, the hope of a return, are not true principles of hospitality. A
richer recompense awaits the kindness bestowed upon the poor than
the adulatory entertainment of the friendly and the rich. In receiving
friends and relatives, do not forget the helpless and the afflicted.[5]

---

[1] Luke xiv. 7—11.

[2] Ecclus. xv. 5 ; xxxix. 4 ; cf. Prov. iv. 8. The anecdote is quoted by Sepp,
Leben Jesu, II. iii. 6.

[3] Luke xiv. 7, $\dot{\epsilon}\xi\epsilon\lambda\dot{\epsilon}\gamma\sigma\nu\tau\sigma$, "They were picking out for themselves."

[4] Luke xiv. 12—14.

[5] Our Lord knew that the conscience of each hearer, even unaided by the ordinary idioms of Oriental speech, would rightly understand the bold and sometimes
almost paradoxical form into which He purposely cast His precepts. That the
"call not thy friends" means "call not only thy friends, but also," &c., has been
admitted by all except a few fanatical commentators. Even sceptics have seen
that our Lord's sayings are not to be attacked on methods of interpretation which

Interested beneficence is nothing in the world but a deceitful selfishness. It may be that thou wouldest have won a more eternal blessing if that dropsical man had been invited to remain — if those poor lookers-on were counted among the number of the guests.

At this point one of the guests, perhaps because he thought that these lessons were disagreeable and severe, interposed a remark which, under the circumstances, rose very little above the level of a vapid and misleading platitude.[1] He poured upon the troubled waters a sort of general impersonal aphorism. Instead of profiting by these Divine lessons, he seemed inclined to rest content with "an indolent remission of the matter into distant futurity," as though he were quite sure of that blessedness, of which he seems to have a very poor and material conception. But our Lord turned his idle poor remark into a fresh occasion for most memorable teaching. He told them a parable to show that "to eat bread in the kingdom of heaven" might involve conditions which those who felt so very sure of doing it would not be willing to accept. He told them of a king who had sent out many invitations to a great banquet, but who, when the due time came,[2] was met by general refusals. One had his estate to manage, and was positively obliged to go and see a new addition to it. Another was deep in buying and selling, and all the business it entailed. A third was so lapped in contented domesticity that his coming was out of the question. Then the king, rejecting, in his anger, these disrespectful and dilatory guests, bade his slaves go at once to the broad and narrow streets, and bring in the poor and maimed, and lame and blind; and when that was done, and there still was room, he sent them to urge in even the houseless wanderers by the hedges and the roads. The application to all present was obvious. The worldly heart — whether absorbed in the management of property, or the acquisition of riches, or the mere sensualisms of con-

---

would make them repulsive to natural affection no less than to common sense. See, for other passages which require similar principles of interpretation, Matt. v. 46, 47 (Luke vi. 32—34); ix. 13; Luke xiv. 26 (comp. Matt. x. 37); John vi. 27; 1 Cor. i. 17; xv. 10. This is a well-known principle of Hebrew grammar, "Comparativus saepe ita circumscribitur, ut alterum et quidem inferius ex duobus comparatis *negetur,* alterum affirmetur, cui excellentia tribuenda est"[306] (Glass, *Phil. Sacr.,* p. 468). See Prov. viii. 10; and *supr.,* p. 439. It is of course obvious to add that the truest kindness and charity to the poor would in these days by no means consist in merely entertaining them at meals.

[1] Luke xiv. 15—24.

[2] These customs remain unchanged. The message *Tefŭddŭlû, el' asha hâder.* "Come, for the supper is ready," may be heard to this day; and to refuse is a high insult. (Thomson, *Land and Book,* I., chap. ix.)

tented comfort — was incompatible with any desire for the true banquet of the kingdom of heaven.   The Gentile and the Pariah, the harlot, and the publican, the laborer of the roadside and the beggar of the streets, these might be there in greater multitudes than the Scribe with his boasted learning, and the Pharisee with his broad phylactery. "For I say unto you," he added in His own person, to point the moral more immediately to their own hearts, "that none of those men who were called shall taste of my supper."   It was the lesson which He so often pointed.   "To be invited is one thing, to accept the invitation is another.   Many are called, but few are chosen. Many — as the heathen proverb said — 'Many bear the *narthex*, but few feel the inspiring god' (πολλοί τοι ναρθηκοφόροι παῦροι δέ τε βάκχοι)."

Teachings like these ran throughout this entire period of the Lord's ministry.   The parable just recorded was, in its far-sided and many-reaching significance, a reproof not only to the close exclusiveness of the Pharisees, but also to their worldliness and avarice.   On another occasion, when our Lord was mainly teaching His own disciples, He told them the parable of the Unjust Steward,[1] to show them the necessity of care and faithfulness, of prudence and wisdom, in so managing the affairs and interests and possessions of this life as not

---

[1] Luke xvi. 1—13. If such immense and needless difficulties had not been raised about this parable, it would have seemed almost superfluous to say that the point held up for imitation in the steward is not in his injustice and extravagance, but the foresight (φρονίμως, "prudently," not as in the E. V., "wisely") with which he anticipated, and the skill with which he provided against, his ultimate difficulties. It really seems as if commentators were so perplexed by the parable as hardly to have got beyond Julian's foolish and unworthy criticism, that it commends and sanctions cheating! What can be clearer than the very simple deductions? This steward, having been a bad steward, showed diligence, steady purpose, and clear sagacity in his dishonest plan for extricating himself from the consequences of past dishonesty : be ye faithful stewards, and show the same diligence, purpose, sagacity, in subordinating the present and the temporal to the requirements of the eternal and the future. Just as the steward made himself friends of the tenants, who, when his income failed, received him into their houses, so do *ye* use your wealth — (and time, opportunity, knowledge, is wealth, as well as money)— for the good of your fellow-men ; that when you leave earth poor and naked, these fellow-men may welcome you to treasures that *never* fail. Such seems to be the meaning of ·verse 9, which is somewhat difficult. The lesson is, in fact, the same as in the famous ἄγραφον δόγμα, "Show yourselves approved money-changers." The parables of the Unjust Judge and the Importunate Suitor (ἀναίδεια, Luke xi. 8) show quite as clearly as this parable that the lesson conveyed by a parable may be enforced by principles of *contrast*, and may involve no commendation of those whose conduct conveys the lesson. It is very probable that both these parables were drawn from circumstances which had recently occurred.

to lose hereafter their heritage of the eternal riches. It was impossible — such was the recurrent burden of so many discourses — to be at once worldly and spiritual; to be at once the slave of God and the slave of Mammon. With the supreme and daring paradox which impressed His divine teaching on the heart and memory of the world, He urged them to the foresight of a spiritual wisdom by an example drawn from the foresight of a criminal cleverness.

Although Christ had been speaking in the first instance to the Apostles, some of the Pharisees seem to have been present and to have heard Him; and it is a characteristic fact that this teaching, more than any other, seems to have kindled their most undisguised derision. They began to treat Him with the most open and insolent disdain. And why? Because they were Pharisees, and yet were fond of money.[1] Had not they, then, in their own persons, successfully solved the problem of "making the best of both worlds?" Who could doubt *their* perfect safety for the future? nay, the absolute certainty that they would be admitted to the "chief seats," the most distinguished and conspicuous places in the world to come? Were they not, then, standing witnesses of the absurdity of the supposition that the love of money was incompatible with the love of God?

Our Lord's answer to them is very much compressed by St. Luke,[2] but consisted, first, in showing them that respectability of life is one thing, and sincerity of heart quite another. Into the new kingdom, for which John had prepared the way, the world's lowest were pressing in, and were being accepted before them; the Gospel was being rejected by them, though it was not the destruction, but the highest fulfilment of the Law. Nay — such seems to be the mean-

---

[1] Luke xvi. 14, ἐξεμυκτήριζον αὐτόν.[305] The vice of avarice seems inherent in the Jewish race. To this day, says Dr. Thomson, speaking of the Jews in Palestine, "Everybody trades, speculates, cheats. The shepherd-boy on the mountain talks of *piastres* from morning till night; so does the muleteer on the road, the farmer in the field, the artisan in the shop, the merchant in his magazine, the pacha in his palace, the kadi in the hall of judgment, the mullah in the mosque, the monk, the priest, the bishop — money, money, money! the desire of every heart, the theme of every tongue, the end of every aim. Everything is bought and sold — each prayer has its price, each sin its tariff." (II. ch. xxvii.) — Quarrels about the money, complaints of the greed and embezzlement of the Rabbis, wrong distribution of the *chaluka*, or alms, and the *kadima*, or honorary pay, form the main history of the Jews in modern Jerusalem. It is a profoundly melancholy tale, and no one who knows the facts will deny it — least of all pious and worthy Jews. (*Vide* Frankl, *Jews in the East, passim.*)

[2] Luke xvi. 15—18.

ing of the apparently disconnected verse which follows [1] — even to
the Law itself, of which not one tittle [2] should fail, they were faithless, for they could connive at the violation of its most distinct provisions. In this apparently isolated remark He alluded, in all probability, to their relations to Herod Antipas, whom they were content
to acknowledge and to flatter, and to whom not one of them had
dared to use the brave language of reproach which had been used by
John the Baptist, although, by the clearest decisions of the Law
which they professed to venerate, his divorce from the daughter of
Aretas was adulterous, and his marriage with Herodias was doubly
adulterous, and worse.

But to make the immediate truth which He had been explaining
yet more clear to them, He told them the parable of the Rich Man
and Lazarus. [3] Like all of our Lord's parables, it is full of meaning,
and admits of more than one application; but at least they could not
miss the one plain and obvious application, that the decision of the
next world will often reverse the estimation wherein men are held
in this; that God is no respecter of persons; that the heart must
make its choice between the "good things" of this life and those
which the externals of this life do not affect. And what may be

---

[1] Cf. Luke vii. 29; xv. 1; Matt. xi. 12, 13. This is Luther's interpretation, and
seems to be the correct one, though Stier does not think it worthy of refutation.

[2] "Tittle," κεραία (Luke xvi. 17); *i. e.*, the smallest turn or stroke of a letter,
like the minute points which distinguish ב from כ (Orig., ad Ps. xxxiii.). (Wetstein.) — This is one of Christ's expressions which receive interesting illustration
from the Rabbis. In *Jer. Sanhedr.*, f. 20, the Book of Deuteronomy prostrates
itself before God, and complains that Solomon has robbed it of the letter *jod* (in
the letter *nashím*) by taking many wives. God answers that Solomon shall perish,
but not the letter *jod*. R. Honna said that the *jod* which God took from the name
Sarai He divided in half, giving half to Abra*h*am, half to Sara*h* (because ה (*h*) =
5, י (*yod*) = 10), &c. (Gfrörer, i. 236.)

[3] It is a curious, but perhaps accidental, coincidence that in this parable alone is
any name given; as also Lazarus is the only recipient — with the exception of
Bartimæus — of our Lord's miracles who is distinctly named. Perhaps there may
be some reference intended to names written in heaven, but forgotten on earth,
and blazoned on earth, but unrecorded in heaven (comp. the ἐτάφη of verse 22
with the silence about the burial of Lazarus). The name Lazarus, however [either
אֵזֶר לֹא, *Lo ezer* (Chald. *La*) (?), " Not help," ἀβοήθητος (Theophyl.), or better, אֵלִי עֶזֶר,
Eli ezer," God my help "], is particularly appropriate. Herberger, quoted by Stier,
says, " We have in this parable a veritable window opened into hell, through
which we can see what passes there." But inferences of this kind must be very
cautiously pressed. It is a wise and well-established rule, that " *Theologia para-
bolica non est demonstrativa.*" [308] Some see in " the five brethren " a reference to
the five sons of Annas (Jos. *Antt.* xx. 9, § 1) — an entirely questionable allusion
(Sepp, *Leben Jesu*, II. vi. 11). Some very ingenious speculations on the subject of
Lazarus may be seen in Prof. Plumtre's *Lazarus and other Poems* (note).

called the epilogue of this parable contains a lesson more solemn still — namely, that the means of grace which God's mercy accords to every living soul are ample for its enlightenment and deliverance; that if these be neglected, no miracle will be wrought to startle the absorbed soul from its worldly interests; that "if they hear not Moses and the Prophets, neither will they be persuaded though one rose from the dead." *Auditu fideli salvamur,* says Bengel, *non apparitionibus* — "We are saved by faithful hearing, not by ghosts."

This constant reference to life as a time of probation, and to the Great Judgment, when the one word "Come," or "Depart," as uttered by the Judge, should decide all controversies and all questions for ever, naturally turned the thoughts of many listeners to these solemn subjects. But there is a great and constant tendency in the minds of us all to refer such questions to the case of others rather than our own — to make them questions rather of speculative curiosity than of practical import. And such tendencies, which rob moral teaching of all its wholesomeness, and turn its warnings into mere excuses for uncharity, were always checked and discouraged by our Lord. A special opportunity was given Him for this on one occasion during those days in which He was going "through the cities and villages, teaching, and journeying toward Jerusalem." [1] He had — not, perhaps, for the first time — been speaking of the small beginnings and the vast growth of the kingdom of heaven alike in the soul and in the world; and one of His listeners, in the spirit of unwise though not unnatural curiosity, asked Him, "Lord, are there few that be saved?" Whether the question was dictated by secure self-satisfaction, or by despondent pity, we cannot tell; but in either case our Lord's answer involved a disapproval of the inquiry, and a statement of the wholly different manner in which such questions should be approached. "Few" or "many" are relative terms. Waste not the precious opportunities of life in idle wonderment, but *strive.* Through that narrow gate, none — not were they a thousand times of the seed of Abraham — can enter without earnest effort. And since the efforts, the wilful efforts, the erring efforts of many fail — since the day will come when the door shall be shut, and it shall be for ever too late to enter there — since no impassioned appeal shall then admit, no claim of olden knowledge shall then be recognized — since some of those in their spiritual pride thought that they best knew the Lord, shall hear the awful repudiation, "I know you not" — *strive ye* to be of those that enter in. For many *shall* **enter**

---

[1] Luke xiii. 22—30; Matt. xiii. 31, 32; Mark iv. 30, 31.

from every quarter of the globe, and yet thou, O son of Abraham, mayest be excluded. And behold, once more — it may well sound strange to thee,¹ yet so it is — "there are last which shall be first, and there are first which shall be last." ²

Thus each vapid interruption, each scornful criticism, each erroneous question, each sad or happy incident, was made by Jesus, throughout this journey, an opportunity for teaching to His hearers, and through them to all the world, the things that belonged unto their peace. And He did so once more, when "a certain lawyer" stood up tempting Him, and asked — not to obtain guidance, but to find subject for objection — the momentous question, " What must I do to obtain eternal life?" Jesus, seeing through the evil motive of his question, simply asked him what was the answer to that question which was given in the Law which it was the very object of the man's life to teach and to explain. The lawyer gave the best summary which the best teaching of his nation had by this time rendered prevalent. Jesus simply confirmed his answer, and said, " This do, and thou shalt live." But wanting something more than this, and anxious to justify a question which from his own point of view was superfluous, and which had, as he well knew, been asked with an ungenerous purpose, the lawyer thought to cover his retreat by the fresh question, "And who is my neighbor?" Had Jesus asked the man's own opinion on this question, He well knew how narrow and false it would have been; He therefore answered it Himself, or rather gave to the lawyer the means for answering it, by one of His most striking parables. He told him how once a man, going down the rocky gorge which led from Jerusalem to Jericho, had fallen into the hands of the robbers, whose frequent attacks had given to that descent the ill-omened name of " the bloody way," and had been left by these Bedawin marauders, after the fashion which they still practise, bleeding, naked, and half dead upon the road. A priest going back to his priestly city had passed that way, caught a glimpse of him, and crossed over to the other side of the road. A Levite, with still cooler indifference, had come and stared at him, and quietly

---

¹ Such is the general significance of καὶ ἰδού in the Gospels. It is used twenty three times in St. Matthew, sixteen in St. Luke, but not in St. Mark.

² Dante, in his *Inferno*, has finely expanded this truth : —

> "He in the world was one
> For arrogance noted ; to his memory
> No virtue lent its lustre. . . . There above
> How many hold themselves for mighty kings
> Who here, like swine, shall wallow in the mire,
> Leaving behind them horrible dispraise."

done the same. But a Samaritan journeying that way — one on whom he would have looked with shuddering national antipathy, one in whose very shadow he would have seen pollution — a good Samaritan, pattern of that Divine Speaker whom men rejected and despised, but who had come to stanch those bleeding wounds of humanity, for which there was no remedy either in the ceremonial or the moral law — came to him, pitied, tended him, mounted him on his own beast, trudged beside him on the hard, hot, dusty, dangerous road, and would not leave him till he had secured his safety, and generously provided for his future wants. Which of these three, Jesus asked the lawyer, was *neighbor* to him who fell among thieves? The man was not so dull as to refuse to see; but yet, knowing that he would have excluded alike the Samaritans and the Gentiles from his definition of "neighbors," he has not the candor to say at once, "*The Samaritan*," but uses the poor periphrasis, "He that did him the kindness." "Go," said Jesus, "and do thou likewise." I, the friend of publicans and sinners, hold up the example of this Samaritan to thee.[1]

We must not, however, suppose that these two months of mission-progress were all occupied in teaching which, however exalted, received its external shape and impulse from the errors and controversies which met the Saviour on His way. There were many circumstances during these days which must have filled His soul with joy.

Pre-eminent among these was the return of the Seventy.[2] We cannot, of course, suppose that they returned in a body, but that from time to time, two and two, as our Lord approached the various cities and villages whither He had sent them, they came to give Him an account of their success. And that success was such as to fill their simple hearts with astonishment and exultation. "Lord," they exclaimed, "even the devils are subject unto us through Thy name." Though He had given them no special commission to heal demoniacs, though in one conspicuous instance even the Apostles had failed in this attempt, yet now they could cast out devils in their Master's name. Jesus, while entering into their joy, yet checked the tone of over-exultation, and rather turned it into a nobler and holier channel. He bade them feel sure that good was eternally mightier than evil; and that the victory over Satan — his fall like lightning from heaven — had been achieved and should continue for ever. Over all evil influences He gave them authority and victory, and the word of His promise should be an amulet to protect them from every source

---

[1] Luke x. 25—37. [2] Luke x. 17—20.

of harm. They should go upon the lion and adder, the young lion and the dragon should they tread under feet;[1] because He had set His love upon them, therefore would He deliver them: He would set them up because they had known His name. And yet there was a subject of joy more deep and real and true — less dangerous because less seemingly personal and conspicuous than this — on which He rather fixed their thoughts: it was that their names had been written, and stood unobliterated,[2] in the Book of Life in heaven.

And besides the gladness inspired into the heart of Jesus by the happy faith and unbounded hope of His disciples, He also rejoiced in spirit that, though rejected and despised by Scribes and Pharisees, He was loved and worshipped by Publicans and Sinners. The poor to whom He preached His Gospel — the blind whose eyes He had come to open — the sick whom He had come to heal — the lost whom it was His mission to seek and save, — these all thronged with heartfelt and pathetic gratitude to the Good Shepherd, the Great Physician. The Scribes and Pharisees as usual murmured,[3] but what mattered that to the happy listeners? To the weary and heavy-laden He spoke in every varied form of hope, of blessing, of encouragement. By the parable of the Importunate Widow He taught them the duty of faith, and the certain answer to ceaseless and earnest prayer.[4] By the parable of the haughty, respectable, fasting, alms-giving, self-satisfied Pharisee — who, going to make his boast to God in the Temple, went home less justified than the poor Publican, who could only reiterate one single cry for God's mercy as he stood there beating his breast, and with downcast eyes — He taught them that God loves better a penitent humility than a merely external service, and that a broken heart and a contrite spirit were sacrifices which He would not despise.[5] Nor was this all. He made them feel that they were dear to God; that, though erring children, they were His children still.

---

[1] Ps. xci. 13, 14. Wetstein shows that Christ here adopted a familiar metaphor, found also in the Rabbis.

[2] ἐγγέγραπται (Luke x. 20; Rev. xx. 12, 15). See Clemens, *Ep. ad Cor.* xlv., with Dr. Lightfoot's note.

[3] Luke xv. 1, 2. This is the third instance in which this self-righteous exclusiveness is rebuked. The first was at the house of Simon the Pharisee (Luke vii. 39; see p. 238); the second at Matthew's feast (Matt. ix. 11; p. 271); and the same thing occurred again in the case of Zacchæus (Luke xix. 7). In each of these instances Jesus with a deep irony "argued with his accusers on their own premises, accepting *their* estimate of *themselves* and of the class with whom they deemed it discreditable to associate, as righteous and sinful respectively." (Bruce. *Training of the Twelve,* p. 28.)

[4] Luke xviii. 1—8.

[5] Luke xviii. 9—14.

And, therefore, to the parables of the Lost Sheep and the Lost Drachma, He added that parable in which lies the whole Gospel in its richest and tenderest grace — the Parable of the Prodigal Son.

Never certainly in human language was so much — such a world of love and wisdom and tenderness — compressed into such few immortal words.[1] Every line, every touch of the picture is full of beautiful, eternal significance. The poor boy's presumptuous claim for all that life could give him — the leaving of the old home — the journey to a far country — the brief spasm of "enjoyment" there — the mighty famine in that land — the premature exhaustion of all that could make life noble and endurable — the abysmal degradation and unutterable misery that followed — the coming to himself, and recollection of all that he had left behind — the return in heart-broken penitence and deep humility — the father's far-off sight of him, and the gush of compassion and tenderness over this poor returning prodigal — the ringing joy of the whole household over him who had been loved and lost, and had now come home — the unjust jealousy and mean complaint of the elder brother — and then that close of the parable in a strain of music — " *Son, thou art ever with me, and all that I have is thine. It was meet that we should make merry, and be glad : for this thy brother was dead, and is alive again ; was lost, and is found* " — all this is indeed a divine epitome of the wandering of man and the love of God such as no literature has ever equalled, such as no ear of man has ever heard elsewhere. Put in the one scale all that Confucius, or Sakya Mouni, or Zoroaster, or Socrates ever wrote or said — and they wrote and said many beautiful and holy words — and put in the other the Parable of the Prodigal Son alone, with all that this single parable connotes and means, and can any candid spirit doubt which scale would outweigh the other in eternal preciousness — in divine adaptation to the wants of man ?

So this great journey grew gradually to a close. The awful solemnity — the shadow, as it were, of coming doom — the half-uttered "too late" which might be dimly heard in its tones of warning — characterize the single record of it which the Evangelist St. Luke has happily preserved.[2] We seem to hear throughout it an undertone

---

[1] I have already touched on this parable (*supra*, pp 325, 326) ; but a few more words on the subject will perhaps be pardoned here.

[2] As the main events and teaching of this episode in St. Luke (ix. 51—xviii. 14) are not recorded by the other Synoptists, and as the narratives of the three meet again at Luke xviii. 15 ; Matt. xix. 13 ; Mark x. 13, it is a natural and reasonable supposition that the things narrated beyond that point belong to a time subsequent to the journey. We can, of course, only conjecture why St. Luke is almost our

of that deep yearning which Jesus had before expressed — " I have a
baptism to be baptized with; and how am I straitened until it be
accomplished!" It was a sorrow for all the broken peace and angry
opposition which His work would cause on earth — a sense that He
was prepared to plunge into the "willing agony" of the already kindled flame.[1] And this seems to have struck the minds of all who
heard Him; they had an expectation, fearful or glad according to
the condition of their consciences, of something great. Some new
manifestation — some revelation of the thoughts of men's hearts —
was near at hand. At last the Pharisees summoned up courage to
ask Him "when the kingdom of God should come?"[2] There was
a certain impatience, a certain materialism, possibly also a tinge of
sarcasm and depreciation in the question, as though they had said,
"When is all this preaching and preparation to end, and the actual
time to arrive?" His answer, as usual, indicated that their *point
of view* was wholly mistaken. The coming of the kingdom of God
could not be ascertained by the kind of narrow and curious watching[3]
to which they were addicted. False Christs and mistaken Rabbis
might cry "*Lo here!*" and "*Lo there!*" but that kingdom was
already in the midst of them;[4] nay, if they had the will and the
wisdom to recognize and to embrace it, that kingdom was *within
them.* That answer was sufficient to the Pharisees, but to His disciples He added words which implied the fuller explanation. Even
they did not fully realize that the kingdom *had already* come.
Their eyes were strained *forward* in intense and yearning eagerness
to some glorious future; but in the future, glorious as it would be,
they would still look *backward* with yet deeper yearning, not unmingled with regret, to this very past — to these days of the Son of
Man, in which they were seeing and their hands handling the Word
of Life. In those days, let them not be deceived by any "Lo there!
Lo here!" nor let them waste in feverish and fruitless restlessness
the calm and golden opportunities of life.[5] For that coming of the

---

sole authority for this period of two months; it is, however, possible that both
St. Matthew and St. Peter (who was the informant of St. Mark) were but little
with Jesus at this time, and were themselves engaged in a mission similar to that
of the Seventy.

[1] Luke xii. 49—53.
[2] Luke xvii. 20—37.
[3] Luke xvii. 20, παρατήρησις. Cf. xiv. 1.
[4] That ἐντὸς ὑμῶν may have this meaning is proved by the passage of Xeno-
phon (*Anab.* i. 10, 3) cited by Alford; but the other meaning is probably included
Cf. Rom. xiv. 17; John i. 26; xii. 35, &c.; and Deut. xxx. 14.
[5] See 2 Thess. *passim.*

Son of Man should be bright, sudden, terrible, universal, irresistible as the lightning flash; but before that day He must suffer and be rejected. Moreover, that gleam of His second advent would flame upon the midnight of a sensual, unexpectant world, as the flood rolled over the festive sensualism in the days of Noah, and the fire and brimstone streamed from heaven upon the glittering rottenness of the Cities of the Plain. Woe to those who should in that day be casting regretful glances on a world destined to pass away in flame! For though till then the business and companionships of life should continue, and all its various fellowships of toil or friendliness, that night would be one of fearful and of final separations!

The disciples were startled and terrified by words of such strange solemnity. " Where, Lord ? " they ask in alarm. But to the " where " there could be as little answer as to the " when," and the coming of God's kingdom is as little geographical as it is chronological.[1] " Wheresoever the body is," He says, " thither will the vultures be gathered together." [2] The mystic Armageddon is no place whose situation you may fix by latitude and longitude. Wherever there is individual wickedness, wherever there is social degeneracy, wherever there is deep national corruption, thither do the eagle-avengers of the Divine vengeance wing their flight from far: thither from the ends of the earth come nations of a fierce countenance, " swift as the eagle flieth," to rend and to devour. " Her young ones also suck up blood: and where the slain are, there is she." [3] Jerusalem — nay, the whole Jewish nation — was falling rapidly into the dissolution rising from internal decay; and already the flap of avenging pinions was in the air. When the world too should lie in a state of morbid infamy, then should be heard once more the rushing of those " congregated wings."

Is not all history one long vast commentary on these great prophecies ? In the destinies of nations and of races has not the Christ returned again and again to deliver or to judge ?

---

[1] See Stier, iv. 287.

[2] The Jews, and indeed the ancients generally, classed the vulture with the eagle. I cannot believe the interpretation of Chrysostom, Theophylactus, &c., that the "body" is Christ, and the gathering eagles are His saints. All that can be said for this view may be seen in Bishop Wordsworth on Matt. xxiv. 28; but a reference to Job. xxxix. 30, " Her young ones also suck up blood; *and where the slain are, there is she,*" seems alone sufficient to refute it.

[3] Deut. xxviii. 49; Job. xxxix. 30. Cf. Hab. i. 8, " They shall fly as the eagle that hasteth to eat; " Hos. viii. 1, " Set the trumpet to thy mouth. He shall fly as an eagle against the house of the Lord, because they have transgressed my covenant, and trespassed against my law." In fact, the best commentary to the metaphor will be found in Rev. xix. 17—21.

CHAPTER XLV.

THE FEAST OF DEDICATION.

Thrice blessed whose lives are faithful prayers,
　　Whose loves in higher love endure;
　　What souls possess themselves so pure,
　Or is there blessedness like theirs?—TENNYSON.

NOWHERE, in all probability, did Jesus pass more restful and happy hours than in the quiet house of that little family at Bethany, which, as we are told by St. John, "He loved." The family, so far as we know, consisted only of Martha, Mary, and their brother Lazarus. That Martha was a widow—that her husband was, or had been, Simon the Leper—that Lazarus is identical with the gentle and holy Rabbi of that name mentioned in the Talmud—are conjectures that may or may not be true;[1] but we see from the Gospels that they were a family in easy circumstances, and of sufficient dignity and position to excite considerable attention not only in their own little village of Bethany, but even in Jerusalem. The lonely little hamlet, lying among its peaceful uplands, near Jerusalem, and yet completely hidden from it by the summit of Olivet, and thus

　　　　" Not wholly in the busy world, nor quite
　　　　Beyond it,"

must always have had for the soul of Jesus an especial charm; and the more so because of the friends whose love and reverence always placed at His disposal their holy and happy home. It is there that we find Him on the eve of the Feast of the Dedication, which marked the close of that public journey designed for the full and final proclamation of His coming kingdom.[2]

It was natural that there should be some stir in the little household at the coming of such a Guest, and Martha, the busy, eager-hearted, affectionate hostess, "on hospitable thoughts intent," hurried to and

---

[1] *Peah*, f. 21, 2, quoted by Sepp, iii. 8.

[2] St. Luke, as Stier observes, may have anticipated the true order of this anecdote in order to let it throw light on the question of the lawyer, "What must I *do?*" (See Luke x. 25, 38—42.) This, if correct, is a good illustration of the subjective considerations which seem to dominate in this episode of his Gospel.

fro with excited energy to prepare for His proper entertainment. Her sister Mary, too, was anxious to receive Him fittingly,[1] but her notions of the reverence due to Him were of a different kind. Knowing that her sister was only too happy to do all that could be done for His material comfort, she, in deep humility, sat at His feet and listened to His words.

Mary was not to blame, for her sister evidently enjoyed the task which she had chosen of providing as best she could for the claims of hospitality, and was quite able, without any assistance, to do everything that was required. Nor was Martha to blame for her active service; her sole fault was that, in this outward activity, she lost the necessary equilibrium of an inward calm. As she toiled and planned to serve Him, a little touch of jealousy disturbed her peace as she saw her quiet sister sitting — " idly " she may have thought — at the feet of their great Visitor, and leaving the trouble to fall on her. If she had taken time to think, she could not but have acknowledged that there may have been as much of consideration as of selfishness in Mary's withdrawal into the background in their domestic administration ; but to be just and noble-minded is always difficult, nor is it even possible when any one meanness, such as petty jealousy, is suffered to intrude. So, in the first blush of her vexation, Martha, instead of gently asking her sister to help her, if help, indeed, were needed — an appeal which, if we judge of Mary aright, she would instantly have heard — she almost impatiently, and not quite reverently, hurries in,[2] and asks Jesus if He really did not care to see her sister sitting there with her hands before her, while *she* was left single-handed to do all the work. Would He not tell her (Martha could not have fairly added that common piece of ill-nature, " It is of no use for *me* to tell her ") to go and help?

An imperfect soul, seeing what is good and great and true, but very often failing in the attempt to attain to it, is apt to be very hard in its judgments on the shortcomings of others. But a divine and sovereign soul — a soul that has more nearly attained to the measure of the stature of the perfect man — takes a calmer and gentler, because a larger-hearted view of those little weaknesses and indirectnesses which it cannot but daily see. And so the answer of Jesus, if it were a reproof, was at any rate an infinitely gentle and tender one, and one which would purify but would not pain the poor

---

[1] Luke x. 39, ἣ καὶ παρακαθίσασα . . ἤκουεν.

[2] Such seems to be the force of ἐπιστᾶσα in St. Luke, who almost alone uses the word [xx. 1 (cf. ii. 38); Acts xxiii. 27 (cf. 1 Thess. v. 3)].

faithful heart of the busy, loving matron to whom it was addressed. "Martha, Martha," so He said — and as we hear that most natural address may we not imagine the half-sad, half-playful, but wholly kind and healing smile which lightened His face? — "thou art anxious and bustling about many things, whereas but one thing is needful;[1] but Mary chose for herself the good part, which shall not be taken away from her." There is none of that exaltation here of the contemplative over the active life which Roman Catholic writers have seen in the passage, and on which they are so fond of dwelling. Either may be necessary, both must be combined. Paul, as has well been said, in his most fervent activity, had yet the contemplativeness and inward calm of Mary; and John, with the most rapt spirit of contemplation, could yet practise the activity of Martha. Jesus did not mean to reprobate any amount of work undertaken in His service, but only the spirit of fret and fuss — the want of all repose and calm — the ostentation of superfluous hospitality — in doing it; and still more that tendency to reprobate and interfere with others, which is so often seen in Christians who are as anxious as Martha, but have none of Mary's holy trustfulness and perfect calm.

It is likely that Bethany was the home of Jesus during His visits to Jerusalem, and from it a short and delightful walk over the Mount of Olives would take Him to the Temple. It was now winter-time, and the Feast of the Dedication was being celebrated.[2] This feast was held on the 25th of Cisleu, and, according to Wieseler, fell this year on Dec. 20. It was founded by Judas Maccabæus in honor of the cleansing of the Temple in the year B. C. 164, six years and a half after its fearful profanation by Antiochus Epiphanes. Like the Passover and the Tabernacles, it lasted eight days, and was kept with great rejoicing.[3] Besides its Greek name of Encænia, it had the name of τὰ φῶτα, or the Lights, and one feature of the

---

[1] The μεριμνᾷς alludes to her inward solicitude, the τυρβάζῃ to her outward fussiness; in fact, if we may adopt such colloquial terms, "fretting" and "fussing" would exactly represent the two words. The various readings, ὀλίγων δέ ἐστι χρεία, ὀλίγων δέ ἐστι χρεία ἢ ἑνός 309 (א, B, L, the Coptic, &c.), might have risen from the notion that at any rate more than one thing would be required for the meal; but in point of fact an Eastern meal usually consists of one common dish. Altogether, it seems clear that the first and obvious meaning — as was so customary with our Lord — was meant to *involve* the high and spiritual meaning. Perhaps the ὀλίγων (supported by the consensus of א and B) may have been omitted in some MSS., from a desire to *enforce* this spiritual lesson.

[2] John x. 22. Called by the Jews *Chanûkkah.*

[3] Some account of these events may be seen in 1 Macc. iv. 52—59; 2 Macc. x. 1—8. "They decked the fore-front of the Temple with crowns of gold and with shields" (Jos. *Antt.* xii. 7, § 7)

festivity was a general illumination to celebrate the legendary miracle of a miraculous multiplication, for eight days, of the holy oil
which had been found by Judas Maccabæus in one single jar sealed
with the High Priest's seal.[1] Our Lord's presence at such a festival
sanctions the right of each Church to ordain its own rites and ceremonies, and shows that He looked with no disapproval on the joyous
enthusiasm of national patriotism.

The eastern porch of the Temple still retained the name of Solomon's Porch, because it was at least built of the materials which had
formed part of the ancient Temple.[2] Here, in this bright colonnade,
decked for the feast with glittering trophies, Jesus was walking up and
down, quietly, and apparently without companions, sometimes, perhaps,
gazing across the valley of the Kidron at the whited sepulchres of the
prophets, whom generations of Jews had slain, and enjoying the mild
winter sunlight, when, as though by a preconcerted movement, the
Pharisaic party and their leaders suddenly surrounded[3] and began to
question Him. Perhaps the very spot where He was walking, recalling as it did the memories of their ancient glory — perhaps the
memories of the glad feast which they were celebrating, as the anni-
versary of a splendid deliverance wrought by a handful of brave men
who had overthrown a colossal tyranny — inspired their ardent appeal.
" How long," they impatiently inquired, " dost thou hold our souls
in painful suspense? If thou really art the Messiah, tell us with
confidence. Tell us *here*, in Solomon's Porch, *now*, while the sight
of these shields and golden crowns, and the melody of these citherns
and cymbals, recall the glory of Judas the Asmonæan — wilt thou be
a mightier Maccabæus, a more glorious Solomon ? shall these citrons,
and fair boughs, and palms, which we carry in honor of this day's
victory, be carried some day for thee?"[4] It was a strange, impetuous, impatient appeal, and is full of significance. It forms their own
strong condemnation, for it shows distinctly that He had spoken
words and done deeds which would have justified and substantiated

---

[1] *Shabbath*, 21 *b ;* *Rosh-hashanah*, 24 *b* (Derenbourg, *Hist. Pal.* 62 ; Jos. *Antt.* xii.
7, § 7). The eight days had in reality been necessary for the work to be done.
Perhaps Pers. *Sat.* v. 180 seqq. are a description of the *Chanákkah*, though called
by mistake "*Herodis* dies " (Id. 165). See a good account of the Feast by Dr.
Ginsburg, in Kitto's *Bibl. Cycl.* i. 653.

[2] Jos. *Antt.* xx. 9, § 7. That the actual porch, in its original state, had been left
standing, is wholly improbable.

[3] John x. 24, ἐ κ ύ κ λ ω σ α ν οὖν αὐτὸν (cf. Luke xxi. 20 ; Heb. xi. 30}
καὶ ἔ λ ε γ ο ν.

[4] 2 Macc. x. 7. These *lulabim* assimilated the feast still more closely to the
Feast of Tabernacles.

such a claim had He chosen definitely to assert it. And if He had in so many words asserted it — above all, had He asserted it in the sense and with the objects which they required — it is probable that they would have instantly welcomed Him with tumultuous acclaim. The place where they were speaking recalled the most gorgeous dreams of their ancient monarchy; the occasion was rife with the heroic memories of one of their bravest and most successful warriors; the political conditions which surrounded them were exactly such as those from which the noble Asmonæan had delivered them. One spark of that ancient flame would have kindled their inflammable spirits into such a blaze of irresistible fanaticism as might for the time have swept away both the Romans and the Herods, but which — since the hour of their fall had already begun to strike, and the cup of their iniquity was already full — would only have antedated by many years the total destruction which fell upon them, first when they were slain by myriads at the destruction of Jerusalem by Titus, and afterwards when the false Messiah, Bar-Cochebas, and his followers were so frightfully exterminated at the capture of Bethyr.

But the day for political deliverances was past; the day for a higher, deeper, wider, more eternal deliverance had come. For the former they yearned, the latter they rejected. Passionate to claim in Jesus an exclusive temporal Messiah, they repelled Him with hatred as the Son of God, the Saviour of the world. That He was their Messiah in a sense far loftier and more spiritual than they had ever dreamed, His language had again and again implied; but the Messiah in the sense which they required He was not, and would not be. And therefore He does not mislead them by saying, " I *am* your Messiah," but He refers them to that repeated teaching, which showed how clearly such had been His claim, and to the works which bore witness to that claim.[1] Had they been sheep of His flock — and He here reminds them of that great discourse which He had delivered at the Feast of Tabernacles two months before — they would have heard His voice, and then He would have given them eternal life, and they would have been safe in His keeping; for no one would then have been able to pluck them out of His Father's hand, and he added solemnly, " I and my Father are one."

His meaning was quite unmistakable. In these words He was claiming not only to be Messiah, but to be Divine. Had the oneness with the Father which He claimed been nothing more than that subjective union of faith and obedience which exists between all holy

---

[1] See John v. and viii. *passim.*

souls and their Creator — His words could have given no more offence than many a saying of their own kings and prophets; but "*ecce Judaei intellexerunt quod non intelligunt Ariani!*" [310] — they saw at once that the words meant infinitely more. Instantly they stooped to seize some of the scattered heavy stones [1] which the unfinished Temple buildings supplied to their fury, and, had His hour been come, He could not have escaped the tumultuary death which afterwards befell His proto-martyr. But His undisturbed majesty disarmed them with a word : "Many good deeds did I show you from my Father : for which of these do ye mean to stone me ? " [2] Not for any good deed, they replied, "but for blasphemy, and because thou, being a mere man, [3] art making thyself God." The reply of Jesus is one of those broad gleams of illumination which He often sheds on the interpretation of the Scriptures : "Does it not stand written in your Law," He asked them, "'I said, Ye are gods?'[4] If he called them gods (*Elohim*) to whom the Word of God came — and such undeniably *is* the case in your own Scriptures — do ye say to Him whom the Father sanctified and sent into the world, 'Thou blasphemest,' because I said, 'I am the Son of God?'" And He appealed to His life and to His works, as undeniable proofs of His unity with the Father. If His sinlessness and His miracles were not a proof that He *could* not be the presumptuous blasphemer whom they wished to stone — what further proof could be given? They, nursed in the strictest monotheism, and accustomed only to think of God as infinitely far from man, might have learnt even from the Law and from the Prophets that God is near — is in the very mouth and in the very heart — of those who love Him, and even bestows upon them some indwelling brightness of His own eternal glory. Might not this be a sign to them, that He who came to fulfil the Law and put a loftier Law in its place — He to whom all the prophets had witnessed — He for whom John had prepared the way — He who spake as never man spake — He who did the works which none other man had ever done since the foundation of the world — He who had ratified all His words, and given significance to all His deeds, by the blameless beauty of an absolutely stainless life — was indeed speaking the truth when He said that He was one with the Father, and that He was the Son of God?

The appeal was irresistible. They dared not stone Him; but, as

---

[1] John x. 31, ἐβάστασαν. The word in John viii. 59 is ἦραν.
[2] John x. 32, λιθάζετε.
[3] ἄνθρωπος (ver. 33). See Lev. xxiv. 10—16.
[4] Ps. lxxxii. 6.

He was alone and defenceless in the midst of them, they tried to seize Him. But they could not. His presence overawed them. They could only make a passage for Him, and glare their hatred upon Him as He passed from among them. But once more, here was a clear sign that all teaching among them was impossible. He could as little descend to their notions of a Messiah, as they could rise to His. To stay among them was but daily to imperil His life in vain. Judæa, therefore, was closed to Him, as Galilee was closed to Him. There seemed to be one district only which was safe for Him in His native land, and that was Peræa, the district beyond the Jordan. He retired, therefore, to the other Bethany — the Bethany beyond Jordan, where John had once been baptizing — and there He stayed.

What were the incidents of this last stay, or the exact length of its continuance, we do not know. We see, however, that it was not exactly private, for St. John tells us that many resorted to Him there,[1] and believed on Him, and bore witness that John — whom they held to be a Prophet, though he had done no miracle — had borne emphatic witness to Jesus in that very place, and that all which He had witnessed was true.

---

[1] John x. 41, 42. For Bethany, *v. supra*, p. 127.

CHAPTER XLVI.

THE LAST STAY IN PERÆA.

" At evening time it shall be light."—ZECH. xiv. 7.

WHEREVER the ministry of Jesus was in the slightest degree public, there we invariably find the Pharisees watching, lying in wait for Him, tempting Him, trying to entrap Him into some mistaken judgment or ruinous decision. But perhaps even *their* malignity never framed a question to which the answer was so beset with difficulties as when they came to "tempt" Him with the problem, " Is it lawful for a man to put away his wife for every cause?" [1]

The question was beset with difficulties on every side, and for many reasons. In the first place, the institution of Moses on the subject was ambiguously expressed. Then this had given rise to a decided opposition of opinion between the two most important and flourishing of the rabbinic schools. The difference of the schools had resulted in a difference in the customs of the nation. Lastly the theological, scholastic, ethical, and national difficulties were further complicated by political ones, for the prince in whose domain the question was asked was deeply interested in the answer, and had already put to death the greatest of the prophets for his bold expression of the view which was most hostile to his own practice. Whatever the truckling Rabbis of Galilee might do, St. John the Baptist, at least, had left no shadow of a doubt as to what was his interpretation of the Law of Moses, and he had paid the penalty of his frankness with his life.

Moses had laid down the rule that when a man had married a wife, and "she find no favor in his eyes because he hath found some uncleanness (marg., ' matter of nakedness,' Heb. עֶרְוַת דָּבָר, *ervath dabhar*) in her, then let him write a bill of divorcement, and give it in her hand, and send her out of his house. And when she is departed out of his house, she may go and be another man's wife." [2] Now in the interpretation of this rule, everything depended on the

---

[1] Matt. xix. 3—12; Mark x. 2—12.

[2] Deut. xxiv. 1, 2. Literally, *ervath dabhar* is " nakedness of a matter " (blösse *im irgend etwas*). (Ewald, *Hebr. Gram.*, § 286, f.)

meaning of the expression *ervath dabhar*, or rather on the meaning of the single word *ervath*. It meant, generally, a stain or desecration, and Hillel, with his school, explained the passage in the sense that a man might "divorce his wife for any disgust which he felt towards her;"[1] even — as the celebrated R. Akiba ventured to say — if he saw any other woman who pleased him more;[2] whereas the school of Shammai interpreted it to mean that divorce could only take place in cases of scandalous unchastity. Hence the Jews had the proverb that in this matter, as in so many others, "Hillel loosed what Shammai bound."

Shammai was morally right and exegetically wrong; Hillel exegetically right and morally wrong. Shammai was only right in so far as he saw that the *spirit* of the Mosaic legislation made no divorce justifiable *in foro conscientiae*,[313] except for the most flagrant immorality; Hillel only right in so far as he saw that Moses had left an opening for divorce *in foro civili*[314] in slighter cases than these. But under such circumstances, to decide in favor of either school would not only be to give mortal offence to the other, but also, either to exasperate the lax many, or to disgust the high-minded few. For in those corrupt days the vast majority acted at any rate on the principle laid down by Hillel, as the Jews in the East continue to do to this day. Such, in fact, was the universal tendency of the times. In the heathen, and especially in the Roman world, the strictness of the marriage bond had been so shamefully relaxed, that, whereas, in the Republic, centuries had passed before there had been one single instance of a frivolous divorce, under the Empire, on the contrary, divorce was the rule, and faithfulness the exception. The days of the Virginias, and Lucretias, and Cornelias had passed; this was the age of the Julias, the Poppaeas, the Messalinas, the Agrippinas —

---

[1] The $\varkappa\alpha\tau\grave{\alpha}\ \pi\tilde{\alpha}\sigma\alpha\nu\ \alpha\grave{\iota}\tau\acute{\iota}\alpha\nu$ [311] of Matt. xix. 3 is a translation of the עַל כָּל דְּבַר (*al côl dabhar*), which was Hillel's exposition of the disputed passage. (See Buxtorf, *De Syn. Jud.* 29.) Almost the identical phrase is found in Jos. *Antt.* iv. 8,. § 23, $\varkappa\alpha\theta'\ \ddot{\alpha}s\ \delta\eta\pi\sigma\tau\sigma\tilde{\nu}\nu\ \alpha\grave{\iota}\tau\acute{\iota}\alpha s$.[312] Cf. Ecclus. xxv. 26, "If she go not as thou wouldest have her, cut her off from thy flesh."

[2] The comments of the Rabbis were even more shameful: *e. g.*, "If she spin in public, go with her head uncovered," &c.; "Even if she have oversalted his soup" (*Gittin*, 90) (Selden, *De Ux. Heb.* iii. 17). This, however, is explained away by modern commentators (Jost, *Gesch. Jud.* 264). Yet it is not surprising that it led to detestable consequences. Thus we are told in *Bab. Jômah*, f. 18, 2, that Rabbi Nachman, whenever he went to stay at a town for a short time, openly sent round the crier for a wife during his abode there (Lightfoot, *Hor. Heb. in Loc.*). See Excursus III., "Jesus and Hillel;" and Excursus IX., "Hypocrisy of the Pharisees."

the days in which, as Seneca says, women no longer reckoned their years by the consuls, but by the number of their repudiated husbands. The Jews had caught up the shameful precedent, and since polygamy had fallen into discredit, they made a near approach to it by the ease with which they were able to dismiss one wife and take another.[1] Even Josephus, a Pharisee of the Pharisees, who on every possible occasion prominently lays claim to the character and position of a devout and religious man, narrates, without the shadow of an apology, that his first wife had abandoned him, that he had divorced the second after she had borne him three children, and that he was then married to a third. But if Jesus decided in favor of Shammai — as all His previous teaching made the Pharisees feel sure that in this particular question He *would* decide — then He would be pronouncing the public opinion that Herod Antipas was a double-dyed adulterer, an adulterer adulterously wedded to an adulterous wife.

But Jesus was never guided in any of His answers by principles of expediency, and was decidedly indifferent alike to the anger of multitudes and to the tyrant's frown. His only object was to give, even to such inquirers as these, such answers as should elevate them to a nobler sphere. Their axiom, " *Is it lawful ?* " had it been sincere, would have involved the answer to their own question. Nothing is lawful to any man who *doubts* its lawfulness. Jesus, therefore, instead of answering them, directs them to the source where the true answer was to be found. Setting the primitive order side by side with the Mosaic institution — meeting their " *Is it lawful ?* " with " *Have ye not read ?* " — He reminds them that God, who at the beginning had made man male and female, had thereby signified His will that marriage should be the closest and most indissoluble of all relationships [2] — transcending and even, if necessary, superseding all the rest.

" Why, then," they ask — eager to entangle Him in an opposition to " the fiery law " — " did Moses *command* to give a writing of divorcement and put her away ? " The form of their question involved one of those false turns so common among the worshippers

---

[1] Divorce is still very common among the Eastern Jews ; in 1856 there were *sixteen cases of divorce* among the small Jewish population of Jerusalem. In fact, a Jew may divorce his wife at any time and for any cause, he being himself the sole judge ; the only hindrance is that, to prevent divorces in a mere sudden fit of spleen, the bill of divorce must have the concurrence of three Rabbis, and be written on ruled vellum, containing neither more nor less than twelve lines; and it must be given in the presence of ten witnesses. (Allen's *Mod. Judaism*, p. 428.)

[2] Gen. ii. 24. " They two " is in the LXX., but not in the Hebrew.

of the letter; and on this false turn they based their inverted pyramid of yet falser inferences. And so Jesus at once corrected them: "Moses, indeed, for your hardheartedness *permitted* you to put away your wives; but from the beginning it was not so;" and then he adds as formal and fearless a condemnation of Herod Antipas — without naming him — as could have been put in language, "Whoever putteth away his wife and marrieth another, except for fornication, committeth adultery; and he who marrieth the divorced woman committeth adultery:"[1] and Herod's case was the worst conceivable instance of both forms of adultery, for he, while married to an innocent and undivorced wife, had wedded the guilty but still undivorced wife of Herod Philip, his own brother and host; and he had done this, without the shadow of any excuse, out of mere guilty passion, when his own prime of life and that of his paramour was already past.

If the Pharisees chose to make any use of this to bring Jesus into collision with Antipas, and draw down upon Him the fate of John, they might; and if they chose to embitter still more against Him the schools of Hillel and of Shammai, *both* of which were thus shown to be mistaken — that of Hillel from deficiency of moral insight, that of Shammai from lack of exegetical acumen — they might; but meanwhile He had once more thrown a flood of light over the difficulties of the Mosaic legislation, showing that it was provisional, not final — transitory, not eternal. That which the Jews, following their famous Hillel, regarded as a Divine permission of which to be proud, was, on the contrary, a tolerated evil permitted to the outward life, though not to the enlightened conscience or the pure heart — was, in fact, a standing witness against their hard and imperfect state.[2]

The Pharisees, baffled, perplexed, ashamed as usual, found themselves again confronted by a transcendently loftier wisdom, and a transcendently diviner insight than their own, and retired to hatch fresh plots equally malicious, and destined to be equally futile. But nothing can more fully show the necessity of Christ's teaching than the fact that even the disciples were startled and depressed by it. In this bad age, when corruption was so universal — when in Rome marriage had fallen into such contempt and desuetude that a law had to be passed which rendered celibates liable to a fine — they thought

---

[1] It appears from St. Matthew that Jesus uttered this precept to the Pharisees, as well as confided it afterwards to His disciples. See Matt. xix. 9; Mark x. 11 (*vide supra*, p. 452).

[2] See Deut. x. 16; Isa. xlviii. 4; Ezek. iii. 7, &c. And yet, according to Geiger and a host of imitators, Jesus was a Rabbi of the school of Hillel, and taught nothing original! (See Excursus III.)

the pure strictness of our Lord's precept so severe that celibacy itself seemed preferable; and this opinion they expressed when they were once more with Him in the house. What a fatal blow would have been given to the world's happiness and the world's morality, had He assented to their rash conclusion! And how marvellous a proof is it of His Divinity, that whereas every other pre-eminent moral teacher — even the very best and greatest of all — has uttered or sanctioned more than one dangerous and deadly error which has been potent to poison the life or peace of nations — *all* the words of the Lord Jesus were absolutely holy, and divinely healthy words. In His reply He gives none of that entire preference to celibacy which would have been so highly valued by the ascetic and the monk, and would have troubled the consciences of many millions whose union has been blessed by heaven.[1] He refused to pronounce upon the condition of the celibate so absolute a sanction. All that He said was that this saying of theirs as to the undesirability of marriage had *no* such unqualified bearing; that it was impossible and undesirable for all but the rare and exceptional few. Some, indeed, there were who were unfitted for holy wedlock by the circumstances of their birth or constitution;[2] some, again, by the infamous, though then common, cruelties and atrocities of the dominant slavery; and some who withdrew themselves from all thoughts of marriage for religious purposes, or in consequence of higher necessities. These were not better than others, but only different. It was the duty of some to marry and serve God in the wedded state; it might be the duty of others not to marry, and so to serve God in the celibate state.[3] There is not in these words of Christ all that amount of difficulty and confusion which some have seen in them. His precepts find their best comment in the 7th and 9th chapters of the First Epistle to the

---

[1] Consider the pernicious influence exercised over millions of Buddhists to this day by Sakya Mouni's exaltation of ascetic celibacy!

[2] Matt. xix. 10—12. The Rabbis similarly distinguished between three sorts of ευνούχοι — the *seris chammah* (" of the sun," or " of nature "), the *seris adam* (per homines), and the *seris bidi shamayim* (of God). The passages of the Rabbis, quoted by Schöttgen *in loc.*, show that the metaphorical sense given to the third class is justified, and that the Jews applied it to any who practised moderate abstinence.

[3] It is well known that Origen, the most allegorizing of commentators, unhappily took this verse literally: other passages of Christ's teaching might have shown him that such an offence against the order and constitution of Providence was no protection against sensual sin; and indeed this great and holy man lived to see and to confess that in this matter he had been nobly mistaken — nobly, because the error of the intellect was combined with the most fervid impulses of a self-sacrificing heart.

Corinthians, and His clear meaning is that, besides the rare instances of natural incapacity for marriage, there are a few others — and to these few alone the saying of the disciples applied — who could accept the belief that *in peculiar times,* or *owing to special circumstances,* or *at the paramount call of exceptional duties,* wedlock must by them be rightly and wisely foregone, because they had received from God the gift and grace of continence, the power of a chaste life, resulting from an imagination purified and ennobled to a particular service.

And then, like a touching and beautiful comment on these high words, and the strongest of all proofs that there was in the mind of Christ no admiration for the "voluntary service" which St. Paul condemns, and the "works of supererogation" which an erring Church upholds — as a proof of His belief that marriage is honorable in all, and the bed undefiled — He took part in a scene that has charmed the imagination of poet and painter in every age. For as though to destroy all false and unnatural notions of the exceptional glory of religious virginity, He, among whose earliest acts it had been to bless a marriage festival, made it one of His latest acts to fondle infants in His arms. It seems to have been known in Peræa that the time of His departure was approaching; and conscious, perhaps, of the words which He had just been uttering, there were fathers and mothers and friends who brought to Him the fruits of Holy wedlock — young children and even babes [1] — that He might touch them and pray over them. Ere He left them for ever, they would bid Him a solemn farewell; they would win, as it were, the legacy of His special blessing for the generation yet to come. The disciples thought their conduct forward and officious. [2] They did not wish their Master to be needlessly crowded and troubled; they did not like to be disturbed in their high colloquies. They were indignant that a number of mere women and children should come obtruding on more important persons and interests. Women were not honored, nor children loved in antiquity as now they are; no halo of romance and tenderness encircled them; too often they were subjected to shameful cruelties and hard neglect. But He who came to be the friend of all sinners, and the helper of all the suffering and the sick, came also to elevate woman to her due honor, centuries before the Teutonic element of modern society was dreamt

---

[1] Matt. xix. 13, παιδία; Luke xviii. 15, τὰ βρέφη, "their babes."

[2] Comp. the haughty repulsion of the Shunamite woman by Gehazi (2 Kings iv. 27).

of,[1] and to be the protector and friend of helpless infancy and innocent childhood. Even the unconscious little ones were to be admitted into His Church by His sacrament of baptism, to be made members of Him, and inheritors of His kingdom. He turned the rebuke of the disciples on themselves; He was as much displeased with them, as they had been with the parents and children. "Suffer the little children," He said, in words which each of the Synoptists has preserved for us in all their immortal tenderness — "Suffer the little children to come unto me, and forbid them not, for of such is the kingdom of heaven." And when He had folded them in His arms, laid His hands upon them, and blessed them, He added once more His constantly needed, and therefore constantly repeated, warning, "Whosoever shall not receive the kingdom of heaven as a little child, shall not enter therein." [2]

When this beautiful and deeply instructive scene was over, St. Matthew tells us that He started on His way, probably for that new journey to the other Bethany of which we shall hear in the next chapter; and on this road occurred another incident, which impressed itself so deeply on the minds of the spectators that it, too, has been recorded by the Evangelists in a triple narrative.

A young man of great wealth and high position seems suddenly to have been seized with a conviction that he had hitherto neglected an invaluable opportunity, and that One who could alone explain to him the true meaning and mystery of life was already on his way to depart from among them. Determined, therefore, not to be too late, he came running, breathless, eager — in a way that surprised all who beheld it — and, prostrating himself before the feet of Jesus, exclaimed, "Good Master, what good thing shall I do that I may inherit life?" [3]

If there was something attractive in the mingled impetuosity and humility of one so young and distinguished, yet so candid and earnest, there was in his question much that was objectionable. The notion that he could gain eternal life by "doing some good thing," rested on a basis radically false. If we may combine what seems to be the true reading of St. Matthew, with the answer recorded in the other Evangelists, our Lord seems to have said to him, "Why askest

---

[1] Whereas the Essenian celibacy rose distinctly out of contempt for and distrust of woman (Jos. *B. J.* ii. 8, § 2, τὰς τῶν γυναικῶν ἀσελγείας φυλασσόμενοι [315]). The author of Ecclesiasticus speaks in the harshest tone of women.

[2] Comp. Mark. ix. 35; Luke xxii. 26; Matt. xx. 26, 27; xxiii. 11.

[3] For similar questions put to Rabbis, see Wetstein, *ad loc.* The ἀγαθὲ in Matt. xix. 16 is omitted by ℵ, B, D, L, &c., but it is found in Mark and Luke; the ἀγαθὸν in Matthew is undoubted, and perhaps the variation of readings is partly accounted for by the use of the word twice.

thou me about the good?[1] and why callest thou me good? One is the good, even God." He would as little accept the title "Good," as He would accept the title "Messiah," when given in a false sense. He would not be regarded as that mere "good Rabbi," to which, in these days, more than ever, men would reduce Him. So far, Jesus would show the youth that when he came to Him as to one who was more than man, his entire address, as well as his entire question, was a mistake. No mere man can lay any other foundation than that which is laid, and if the ruler committed the error of simply admiring Jesus as a Rabbi of pre-eminent sanctity, yet no Rabbi, however saintly, was accustomed to receive the title of "good," or prescribe any amulet for the preservation of a virtuous life. And in the same spirit, He continued: "But if thou wilt enter into life, keep the commandments."

The youth had not expected a reply so obvious and so simple. He cannot believe that He is merely referred to the Ten Commandments, and so He asks, in surprise, "What sort of commandments?" Jesus, as the youth wanted to *do* something, tells him merely of those of the Second Table, for, as has been well remarked, "Christ sends the proud to the *Law*, and invites the *humble* to the *Gospel*." "Master," replied the young man in surprise, "all these have I observed from my youth."[2] Doubtless in the mere letter he may have done so, as millions have; but he evidently knew little of all that those commandments had been interpreted by the Christ to mean. And Jesus, seeing his sincerity, looking on him loved him,[3] and gave him one short crucial test of his real condition. He was not content with the common-place; he aspired after the heroical, or

---

[1] The reading τί με ἐρωτᾷς περὶ τοῦ ἀγαθοῦ,[316] in Matt. xix. 17, seems undoubtedly the right reading (א, B, D, L, &c., the Cureton Syriac, and some of the chief Fathers). It springs naturally from the form of the young man's question; and it has certainly not been altered from doctrinal reasons, for there is no various reading in Mark x. 18; Luke xviii. 19. It is remarkable that the title "*good* Rabbi" was utterly unknown to the Jews, and does not occur once in the Talmud (Lightfoot, *Hor. Hebr. ad loc.*). There was, therefore, an obvious impropriety in the use of it by the young ruler from *his* point of view. The emphasis of our Lord's question falls on "*good*," not on "*me*;" for in the latter case it would be ἐμὲ, not με (Meyer).

[2] When the Angel of Death came to fetch the R. Chanina, he said, "Go and fetch me the Book of the Law, and *see whether there is anything in it which I have not kept*" (Gfrörer, ii. 102; Philo, i. 400).

[3] ἠγάπησεν (Mark x. 21). The word means "esteemed," and the aorist makes it mean "*was pleased with*." Origen says, "Dilexit eum, vel *osculatus est* eum;"[317] and it was the custom of the Rabbis to kiss the head of any pupil who had answered well; but this would require ἐφίλησε, not ἠγάπησε.

rather *thought* that he did; therefore Jesus gave him an heroic act to do. "One thing," He said, "thou lackest," and bade him go, sell all that he had, distribute it to the poor, and come and follow Him.

It was too much. The young ruler went away very sorrowful, grief in his heart, and a cloud upon his brow,[1] for he had great possessions. He preferred the comforts of earth to the treasures of heaven; he would not purchase the things of eternity by abandoning those of time; he made, as Dante calls it, "the great refusal." And so he vanishes from the Gospel history; nor do the Evangelists know anything of him farther. But the sad stern imagination of the poet follows him, and there, among the myriads of those who are blown about like autumn leaves on the confines of the other world, blindly following the flutter of a giddy flag, rejected by Heaven, despised even by hell, hateful alike to God and to his enemies, he sees

"l'ombra di colui
Che fece per viltate il gran rifiuto," * [318]

(The shade of him, who made through cowardice the great refusal.)

We may — I had almost said we must — hope and believe a fairer ending for one whom Jesus, as He looked on him, could love. But the failure of this youth to meet the test saddened Jesus, and looking round at His disciples, He said, "How hardly shall they that have riches enter into the kingdom of heaven." The words once more struck them as very severe. Could then no good man be rich, no rich man be good? But Jesus only answered — softening the sadness and sternness of the words by the affectionate title "children" — "Children, how hard it is to enter into the kingdom of God;"[2] hard for *any one*, but, He added, with an earnest look at His disciples, and specially addressing Peter, as the Gospel according

---

[1] λυπούμενος (Matt. xix. 22); στυγνάσας (Mark x. 22; cf. Matt. xvi. 3); περίλυπος (Luke xviii. 23).

* Dante, *Inferno*, iii. 60.

"Incontanente intesi, e certo fui
Che quest' era la setta dei cattivi
A Dio spiacenti ed a' nemici sui." [319]

This application of Dante's reference seems to me more probable than that he intended Pope Celestine.

[2] It will be seen that I follow the very striking and probably genuine reading of א, B, D, and other MSS. in Mark x. 24. The words τοὺς πεποιθότας ἐπὶ χρήμασι,[320] which our version accepts, have all the character of a gloss; and for those who "*trust* in riches" the task would not be δύσκολον, but ἀδύνατον. It is of course true that it is the *trust* in riches, not the *possession* of them, which makes it so hard to enter into the kingdom of God; but even such a mean and miserable scoffer as Lucian could see that there is always a *danger* lest those who *have* riches should trust in them.

to the Hebrews tells us, " It is easier for a camel to go through the eye of a needle, than for a rich man to enter into the kingdom of God." [1] They might well be amazed beyond measure. Was there then no hope for a Nicodemus, for a Joseph of Arimathæa? Assuredly there was. The teaching of Jesus about riches was as little Ebionite as His teaching about marriage was Essene. Things impossible to nature are possible to grace; things impossible to man are easy to God.

Then, with a touch — was it of complacency, or was it of despair? — Peter said, " Lo, we have forsaken all, and followed thee," and either added, or implied, In what respect, then, shall we be gainers? The answer of Jesus was at once a magnificent encouragement and a solemn warning. The encouragement was that there was no instance of self-sacrifice which would not even in this world, and even in the midst of persecutions, receive its hundred-fold increase in the harvest of spiritual blessings,[2] and would in the world to come be rewarded by the infinite recompense of eternal life; the warning was that familiar one which they had heard before, that many of the first should be last, and the last first.[3] And to impress upon them still more fully and deeply that the kingdom of heaven is not a matter of mercenary calculation or exact equivalent — that there could be no bargaining with the Heavenly Householder — that before the eye of God's clearer and more penetrating judgment Gentiles might be admitted before Jews, and Publicans before Pharisees, and young converts before aged Apostles — He told them the memorable Parable of the Laborers in the Vineyard. That parable, amid its other lessons, involved the truth that, while all who serve God should not be defrauded of their just and full and rich reward, there could be in heaven no murmuring, no envyings, no jealous comparison of respective merits, no base strugglings for precedency, no miserable disputings as to who had performed the maximum of service, or who had received the minimum of grace.

---

[1] The alteration to κάμιλον, " a rope," is shown to be wrong from the commonness of similar proverbs (*e. g.*, an elephant and the eye of a needle) in the Talmud, as adduced by Lightfoot, Schöttgen, and Wetstein. The explanation that the small side gate of a city, through which a laden camel could only crush with the utmost difficulty, was called a " needle's eye " is more plausible, but seems to need confirmation.

[2] The metaphor of the twelve thrones harmonized with the ideal hopes of the day. (See Lightfoot, *ad loc.*) For the Palingenesia (= " restoration of all things," ἀποκατάστασις) see Isa. xlii. 9; lxv. 17; Rom. viii. 19; Rev. xxi. 1, &c. With the whole passage compare 1 Cor. iii. 22; 2 Cor. vi. 10.

[3] See 2 Esdr. v. 42.

CHAPTER XLVII.

THE RAISING OF LAZARUS.

ἔχω τὰς κλεῖς τοῦ ᾅδου καὶ τοῦ θανάτου.[321] — APOC. i. 18.

THESE farewell interviews and teachings perhaps belong to the two days after Jesus — while still in the Peræan Bethany — had received from the other Bethany, where He had so often found a home, the solemn message that "he whom He loved was sick." [1] Lazarus was the one intimate personal friend whom Jesus possessed outside the circle of His Apostles, and the urgent message was evidently an appeal for the presence of Him in whose presence, so far as we know, there had never been a death-bed scene.

But Jesus did not come. He contented Himself — occupied as He was in important works — with sending them the message that "this sickness was not to death, but for the glory of God," and stayed two days longer where He was. And at the end of those two days He said to His disciples, "Let us go into Judæa again." The disciples reminded Him how lately the Jews had there sought to stone Him, and asked Him how He could venture to go there again; but His answer was that during the twelve hours of His day of work He could walk in safety, for the light of His duty, which was the will of His Heavenly Father, would keep Him from danger. And then He told them that Lazarus slept, and that He was going to wake him out of sleep. Three of them at least must have remembered how, on another memorable occasion, He had spoken of death as sleep; but either they were silent, and others spoke, or they were too slow of heart to remember it. As they understood Him to speak of natural sleep, He had to tell them plainly that Lazarus was dead, and that He was glad of it for their sakes, for that He would go to restore him to life. "Let us also go," said the affectionate but ever despondent Thomas, "that we may die with Him " — as though he had said, "It is all a useless and perilous scheme, but still let us go."

---

[1] John xi. 1—46, ὃν φιλεῖς (quem amas), ver. 3. The same word is only used elsewhere of the love of Jesus for the beloved disciple. Where His love for the sisters is spoken of, ἠγάπα, "diligebat" ("cared for"), is used (ver. 5). It is, however, worth noticing that three times out of four the word for even the beloved disciple is ἀγαπᾶν, and that here the φιλεῖς is not the Evangelist's own word, but put by him into the mouth of another.

Starting early in the morning, Jesus could easily have accomplished the distance — some twenty miles — before sunset. But, on His arrival, he stayed outside the little village. Its vicinity to Jerusalem, from which it is not two miles distant,[1] and the evident wealth and position of the family, had attracted a large concourse of distinguished Jews to console and mourn with the sisters; and it was obviously desirable to act with caution in venturing among such determined enemies. But while Mary, true to her retiring and contemplative disposition, was sitting in the house, unconscious of her Lord's approach,[2] the more active Martha had received intelligence that He was near at hand, and immediately went forth to meet Him. Lazarus had died on the very day that Jesus received the message of his illness; two days had elapsed while He lingered in Peræa, a fourth had been spent on the journey. Martha could not understand this sad delay. "Lord," she said, in tones gently reproachful, "if Thou hadst been here my brother had not died," yet "even now" she seems to indulge the vague hope that some alleviation may be vouchsafed to their bereavement. The few words which follow are words of most memorable import — a declaration of Jesus which has brought comfort not to Martha only, but to millions since, and which shall do to millions more unto the world's end —

"Thy brother shall rise again."

Martha evidently had not dreamt that he would now be awaked from the sleep of death, and she could only answer, "I know that he shall rise again in the resurrection at the last day."

Jesus said unto her, "I AM THE RESURRECTION AND THE LIFE: HE THAT BELIEVETH ON ME, THOUGH HE HAVE DIED, SHALL LIVE; AND HE THAT LIVETH AND BELIEVETH ON ME SHALL NEVER DIE. Believest thou this?"

It was not for a spirit like Martha's to distinguish the interchanging thoughts of physical and spiritual death which were united in that deep utterance; but, without pausing to fathom it, her faithful love supplied the answer, "Yea, Lord, I believe that thou art the Christ, the Son of God, which should come into the world."

---

[1] The "was" in John xi. 18 does not *necessarily* imply that when St. John wrote the village had been destroyed; but such was probably the case.

[2] It is an interesting incidental proof of the authenticity of the narrative — all the more valuable from being wholly undesigned — that the characters of Martha and Mary, as described in a few touches by St. John, exactly harmonize with their character as they appear in the anecdote preserved only by St. Luke (x. 38—42.) (See *supra*, p. 460.) Those who reject the genuineness of St. John's Gospel must account (as Meyer says) for this "literary miracle."

Having uttered that great confession; she at once went in quest of her sister, about whom Jesus had already inquired, and whose heart and intellect, as Martha seemed instinctively to feel, were better adapted to embrace such lofty truths. She found Mary in the house, and both the secrecy with which she delivered her message, and the haste and silence with which Mary arose to go and meet her Lord, show that precaution was needed, and that the visit of Jesus had not been unaccompanied with danger. The Jews who were comforting her, and whom she had thus suddenly left, rose to follow her to the tomb, whither they thought that she had gone to weep; but they soon saw the real object of her movement. Outside the village they found Jesus surrounded by His friends, and they saw Mary hurry up to Him, and fling herself at His feet with the same agonizing reproach which her sister also had used, " Lord, if Thou hadst been here my brother had not died." [1] The greater intensity of her emotion spoke in her fewer words and her greater self-abandonment of anguish, and she could add no more. It may be that her affection was too deep to permit her hope to be so sanguine as that of her sister; it may be that with humbler reverence she left all to her Lord. The sight of all that love and misery, the pitiable spectacle of human bereavement, the utter futility at such a moment of human consolation, the shrill commingling of a hired and simulated lamentation with all this genuine anguish, the unspoken reproach, " Oh, why didst Thou not come at once and snatch the victim from the enemy, and spare Thy friend from the sting of death, and us from the more bitter sting of such a parting ? " — all these influences touched the tender compassion of Jesus with deep emotion. A strong effort of self-repression was needed [2] — an effort which shook His whole frame with a powerful shudder [3] — before He could find words to speak, and then He could

---

[1] Martha had said, οὐκ ἂν ὁ ἀδελφός μου ἐτεθνήκει (John xi. 21, but ἀπέθανεν, א, B, C, D, &c.), " my brother would not have been dead;" Mary says, οὐκ ἂν μου ἀπέθανεν ὁ ἀδελφός (ver. 32), "*my* brother [the position of the pronoun is more emphatic] would not have died."

[2] Such seems to be the meaning of ἐνεβριμήσατο τῷ πνεύματι (ver. 33), literally, " He was indignant with himself in spirit." (Cf. Lam. ii. 6, LXX.) I fully admit, however, the difficulty of the expression, and am not prepared to deny that it may mean " He was indignant in spirit " (at the want of faith of those who were present).

[3] ἐτάραξεν ἑαυτόν. The philosophical fancies which see in this expression a sanction of the Stoic μεϛιοπάθεια, as though the meaning were that Jesus merely stirred His own emotions to the exact extent which He approved, are quite misplaced. (Comp. John xii. 27; xiii. 21.) Euthymius, an excellent ancient commentator, explains it as in the text.

merely ask, " Where have ye laid him ? " They said, " Lord, come and see." As He followed them His eyes were streaming with silent tears.[1] His tears were not unnoticed, and while some of the Jews observed with respectful sympathy this proof of His affection for the dead, others were asking dubiously, perhaps almost sneeringly,[2] whether He who had opened the eyes of the blind could not have saved His friend from death? They had not heard how, in the far-off village of Galilee, He had raised the dead ; but they knew that in Jerusalem He had opened the eyes of one born blind, and that seemed to them a miracle no less stupendous. But Jesus knew and heard their comments, and once more the whole scene — its genuine sorrows, its hired mourners, its uncalmed hatreds, all concentrated around the ghastly work of death — came so powerfully over His spirit, that, though He knew that He was going to wake the dead, once more His whole being was swept by a storm of emotion.[3] The grave, like most of the graves belonging to the wealthier Jews, was a recess carved horizontally in the rock, with a slab or mass of stone to close the entrance.[4] Jesus bade them remove this *gôlal*, as it was called. Then Martha interposed — partly from conviction that the soul had now utterly departed from the vicinity of the mouldering body, partly afraid in her natural delicacy of the shocking spectacle which the removal of that stone would reveal. For in that hot climate it is necessary that burial should follow immediately upon death,[5] and as it was the evening of the fourth day since Lazarus had died, there was too much reason to fear that by this time decomposition had set in. Solemnly Jesus reminded her of His promise, and the stone was moved from the place where the dead was laid. He stood at the entrance, and all others shrank a little backward, with their eyes still fixed on that dark and silent cave. A hush fell upon them all as

---

[1] ἐδάκρυσεν, *flevit*, " He shed tears ;" not ἔκλαυσεν, *ploravit*, " He wept aloud," as over Jerusalem (Luke xix. 41).

[2] Verse 37. Alford acutely conjectures the hostile tone of the criticism, from the use of δὲ, which St. John very frequently uses in an adversative sense, as again in verse 46.

[3] πάλιν ἐμβριμώμενος ἐν ἑαυτῷ [322] (John xi. 38).

[4] The village of Bethany is to this day called El-Azariyeh, a corruption of Lazarus, and a continuous memorial of the miracle. A deep cavity is shown in the middle of it as the grave of Lazarus. I visited the spot, but with no belief in it : that El-Azariyeh is the ancient Bethany is certain, but the tomb of Lazarus could not have been in the centre of it.

[5] Frankl mentions that, a few years ago, a Jewish Rabbi dying at Jerusalem at two o'clock was buried at 4.30. The emphatic remark of Martha may also have arisen from the belief that after three days the soul ceased to flutter in the neighborhood of the body.

Jesus raised His eyes and thanked God for the coming confirmation of His prayer. And then, raising to its clearest tones that voice of awful and sonorous authority, and uttering, as was usual with Him on such occasions, the briefest words, He cried, " LAZARUS, COME FORTH ! " [1] Those words thrilled once more through that region of impenetrable darkness which separates us from the world to come ; and scarcely were they spoken when, like a spectre, from the rocky tomb issued a figure, swathed indeed in its white and ghastly cerements — with the napkin round the head which had upheld the jaw that four days previously had dropped in death, bound hand and foot and face, but not livid, not horrible — the figure of a ,uth with the healthy blood of a restored life flowing through his ' eins ; of a life restored — so tradition tells us — for thirty more long ears [2] to life, and light, and love.

Let us pause here to answer the not unnatural question as to the silence of the Synoptists respecting this great miracle.[3] To treat the subject fully would indeed be to write a long disquisition on the structure of the Gospels ; and after all we could assign no *final* explanation of their obvious difficulties. The Gospels are, of their very nature, confessedly and designedly fragmentary, and it may be regarded as all but certain that the first three were mainly derived from a common oral tradition, or founded on one or two original, and themselves fragmentary, documents.[4] The Synoptists almost confine themselves to the Galilæan, and St. John to the Judæan ministry, though the Synoptists distinctly allude to and presuppose the ministry in Jerusalem, and St. John the ministry in Galilee.[5] Not one of the four Evangelists proposes for a moment to give an exhaustive account, or even catalogue, of the parables, discourses, and miracles of Jesus ; nor was it the object of either of them to write a

---

[1] ἐκράυγασεν (ver. 43). Comp. Matt. xii. 19 ; John v. 28.

[2] Epiphan. *Haer.* 66. See Hofmann, *Leben Jesu*, 357.

[3] On this question, see especially Meyer, p. 298.

[4] Luke i. 1.

[5] I ought, perhaps, to have explained the word *Synoptists* before. It is applied to the first three Evangelists, because their Gospels can be arranged, section by section, in a tabular form. Griesbach seems to have been the first to use the word (Holtzmann in Schenkel, *Bibel Lexicon*, s. v. " Evangelien," p. 207). But although the word, so far as I am aware, is modern, the contrasts presented by the first three and the fourth Gospels were, of course, very early observed (Clem. Alex. ap. Euseb. *Hist. Ecc.* vi. 14). Professor Westcott treats of "the origin of the Gospels" with his usual learning and candor in his *Introduction*, pp. 152—195. He there mentions that if the total contents of the Gospels be represented by 100, there are 7 peculiarities in St. Mark, 42 in St. Matthew, 59 in St. Luke. and 92 in St. John.

complete narrative of His three and a-half years of public life.   Each
of them relates the incidents which came most immediately within
his own scope, and were best known to him either by personal witness, by isolated written documents, or by oral tradition;[1] and each
of them tells enough to show that He was the Christ, the Son of the
Living God, the Saviour of the world.   Now, since the raising of
Lazarus would not seem to them a greater exercise of miraculous
power than others which they had recorded (John xi. 37) — since, as
has well been said, no *semeiometer* had been then invented to test
the relative greatness of miracles — and since this miracle fell within
the Judæan cycle — it does not seem at all *more* inexplicable that they
should have omitted this, than that they should have omitted the
miracle at Bethesda, or the opening of the eyes of him who had been
born blind.   But further than this, we seem to trace in the Synoptists a special reticence about the family at Bethany.   The house in
which they take a prominent position is called "the house of Simon
the leper;" Mary is called simply "a woman" by St. Matthew and
St. Mark (Matt. xxvi. 6, 7; Mark xiv. 3); and St. Luke contents
himself with calling Bethany "a certain village" (Luke x. 38),
although he was perfectly aware of the name (Luke xix. 29).   There
is, therefore, a distinct argument for the conjecture that when the
earliest form of the Gospel of St. Matthew appeared, and when the
memorials were collected which were used by the other two Synoptists, there may have been special reasons for not recording a miracle
which would have brought into dangerous prominence a man who
was still living, but of whom the Jews had distinctly sought to get
rid as a witness of Christ's wonder-working power (John xii. 10).
Even if this danger had ceased, it would have been obviously repulsive to the quiet family of Bethany to have been made the focus of
an intense and irreverent curiosity, and to be questioned about those
hidden things which none have ever revealed.   Something, then,
seems to have "sealed the lips" of those Evangelists — an obstacle
which had been long removed when St. John's Gospel first saw the
light.

"If they believe not Moses and the Prophets" — so ran the answer
of Abraham to Dives in the parable — "neither will they be converted though one (and this, too, a Lazarus!) rose from the dead."
It was even so.   There were many witnesses of this miracle who
believed when they saw it, but there were others who could only

---

[1] *Vid. supra,* p. 223, *n.,* where I have quoted the testimony of St. Augustine to
this effect.

carry an angry and alarmed account of it to the Sanhedrin at Jerusalem.

The Sanhedrin met in a spirit of hatred and perplexity.[1] They *could* not deny the miracle; they *would* not believe on Him who had performed it; they could only dread His growing influence, and conjecture that it would be used to make Himself a king, and so end in Roman intervention and the annihilation of their political existence. And as they vainly raged in impotent counsels, Joseph Caiaphas arose to address them. He was the civil High Priest, and held the office eleven years, from A. D. 25, when Valerius Gratus placed him in it, till A. D. 36, when Vitellius turned him out. A large share indeed of the honor which belonged to his position had been transferred to Ananus, Annas — or to give him his true Jewish name, Hanan — who had simply been deprived of the High Priesthood by Roman authority, and who (as we shall see hereafter) was perhaps the *Nasî* or *Sagan*, and was, at any rate, regarded as being the real High Priest by the stricter Jews. Caiaphas, however, was at this time nominally and ostensibly High Priest.[2] As such he was supposed to have that gift of prophecy which was still believed to linger faintly in the persons of the descendants of Aaron, after the total disappearance of dreams, Urim, omens, prophets, and *Bath Kôl*, which, in descending degrees, had been the ordinary means of ascertaining the will of God.[3] And thus when Caiaphas rose, and with shameless avowal of a policy most flagitiously selfish and unjust,[4]

---

[1] John xi. 47—54.

[2] Some have seen an open irony in the expression of St. John (xi. 49), that Caiaphas was High Priest " that same year," as though the Jews had got into this contemptuous way of speaking during the rapid succession of priests — mere phantoms set up and displaced by the Roman fiat — who had in recent years succeeded each other. There must have been at least five living High Priests, and ex-High Priests at this council — Annas, Ismael Ben Phabi, Eleazer Ben Hanan, Simon Ben Kamhith, and Caiaphas, who had gained his elevation by bribery (see Reland, *Antt. Hebr.*, p. 160, where he gives lists of the High Priests from Josephus, Nicephorus, &c.).

[3] See Jos. *B. J.* iii. 8, § 3.

[4] Some of these conspirators must have lived to learn by the result that what is morally wrong never *can* be politically expedient. The death of the Innocent, so far from saving the nation, precipitated its ruin, and that ruin fell most heavily on those who had brought it about. When the Idumeans entered Jerusalem, "Tous les membres de la caste sacerdotale qu'on put trouver furent tués. Hanan [*son* of the Gospel 'Annas'] et Jésus fils de Gamala subirent d'affreuses insultes; leurs corps furent privés de sépulture, outrage inouï chez les Juifs. Ainsi périt le fils du principal auteur de la mort de Jésus. Ce fut . . . la fin du parti sadducéen, parti souvent hautain, égoïste et cruel. Avec Hanan périt le vieux sacerdoce juif, inféodé aux grandes familles sadducéennes . . . . Grande fut

haughtily told the Sanhedrin that all their proposals were mere ignorance, and that the only thing to be done was to sacrifice one victim — innocent or guilty he did not stop to inquire or to define — one victim for the whole people,— ay, and, St. John adds, not for that nation only, but for all God's children scattered throughout the world — they accepted unhesitatingly that voice of unconscious prophecy. And by accepting it they filled to the brim the cup of their iniquity, and incurred the crime which drew upon their guilty heads the very catastrophe which it was committed to avert. It was this Moloch worship of worse than human sacrifice which, as in the days of Manasseh, doomed them to a second and a more terrible, and a more enduring, destruction. There were some, indeed, who were not to be found on that Hill of Evil Counsel,[1] or who, if present, consented not to the counsel or will of them ; but from that day forth the secret fiat had been issued that Jesus must be put to death. Henceforth He was living with a price upon His head.

And that fiat, however originally secret, became instantly known. Jesus was not ignorant of it; and for the last few weeks of His earthly existence, till the due time had brought round the Passover at which he meant to lay down His life, He retired in secret to a little obscure city, near the wilderness, called Ephraim.[2] There, safe from all the tumults and machinations of His deadly enemies, He spent calmly and happily those last few weeks of rest, surrounded only by His disciples, and training them, in that peaceful seclusion, for the mighty work of thrusting their sickles into the ripening har-

---

l'impression, quand on contempla jetés nus hors de la ville, livrés aux chiens et aux chacals, ces aristocrates si hautement respectés . . .   C'était un monde qui disparaissait. Incapable de former un État à lui seul il devait en arriver au point où nous le voyons depuis dix-huit siècles, c'est-à-dire à vivre en guise de parasite, dans la république d'autrui."[323]   (Renan, *L'Antechrist,* p. 287, who sees in all this no hand of God.)

[1] This is the name still given to the traditional site of the house of Caiaphas, where the meeting is supposed to have been held.

[2] κώμη μεγίστη, Euseb. ; " villa praegrandis," Jer. ; πολίχνιον, Jos. (Keim, III. i. 6.) — There is much uncertainty as to the position of Ephraim ; it may possibly have been on the site of the modern village of Et-Taiyibeh, which is near to the wilderness (John xi. 54), and not far from Beitîn, the ancient Bethel (2 Chron. xiii. 19 ; Jos. *B. J.* iv. 9, § 9), and about twenty miles to the north of Jerusalem (Jerome, *Onomast.*). (See Robinson, *Bibl. Res.* i. 444 seqq.) There is no necessity to suppose with Ebrard (*Gosp. Hist.* p. 360) that it was south-east of Jerusalem. (The *Kethibh*, in 2 Chron. xiii. 19, has *"Ephron ;"* the *Keri,* "Ephraim." Wieseler (*Synops.* p. 291) elaborately argues that Eusebius is right, as against Jerome, in placing it eight miles from Jerusalem, but this would hardly be far enough for safety ; and if Ephraim be Et-Taiyibeh, that is very nearly if not quite twenty miles from the Holy City.)

vests of the world. None, or few beside that faithful band, knew of His hiding place; for the Pharisees, when they found themselves unable to conceal their designs, had published an order that if any man knew where He was, he was to reveal it, that they might seize Him, if necessary even by violence, and execute the decision at which they had arrived. But, as yet, the bribe had no effect.

How long this deep and much-imperilled retirement lasted we are not told, nor can we lift the veil of silence that has fallen over its records. If the decision at which the *Beth Din* in the house of Caiaphas had arrived was regarded as a formal sentence of death, then it is not impossible that these scrupulous legists may have suffered forty days to elapse for the production of witnesses in favor of the accused.[1] But it is very doubtful whether the destruction intended for Jesus was not meant to be carried out in a manner more secret and more summary, bearing the aspect rather of a violent assassination than of a legal judgment.

---

[1] Such is the supposition of Sepp, II. iii. 31, and it derives some support from the turbid legend of the Talmud, which says that forty days before His death (the legal time for the production of witnesses) Jesus was excommunicated by Joshua Ben Perachiah, to the blast of 400 trumpets.

CHAPTER XLVIII.

JERICHO AND BETHANY.

" Those mighty voices three, —
Ἰησοῦ ἐλέησόν με,
Θάρσει, ἔγειραι, φωνεῖ σε,
ἡ πίστις σου σέσωκέ σε." [324] — LONGFELLOW.

FROM the conical hill of Ephraim Jesus could see the pilgrim bands **as**, at the approach of the Passover, they began to stream down the Jordan valley towards Jerusalem, to purify themselves from every ceremonial defilement before the commencement of the Great Feast.[1] The time had come for Him to leave his hiding-place, and He descended from Ephraim to the high road in order to join the great caravan of Galilæan pilgrims.[2]

And as He turned His back on the little town, and began the journey which was to end at Jerusalem, a prophetic solemnity and elevation of soul struggling with the natural anguish of the flesh, which shrank from that great sacrifice, pervaded His whole being, and gave a new and strange grandeur to every gesture and every look. It was the Transfiguration of Self-sacrifice; and, like that previous Transfiguration of Glory, it filled those who beheld it with an amazement and terror which they could not explain.[3] There are few pictures in the Gospel more striking than this of Jesus going forth to His death, and walking alone along the path into the deep valley, while behind Him, in awful reverence, and mingled anticipations of dread and hope — their eyes fixed on Him, as with bowed head He preceded them in all the majesty of sorrow — the disciples walked behind and dared not disturb His meditations. But at last He paused and beckoned them to Him, and then, once more — for the third time — with fuller, clearer, more startling, more terrible particulars than ever before, He told them that He should be betrayed

---

[1] Numb. ix. 10; 2 Chron. xxx. 17; Jos. *Antt.* xvii. 9, § 3.
[2] Matt. xx. 17—19 ; Mark x. 32—34; Luke xviii. 31—34.
[3] Mark x. 32. Tischendorf, Meyer, &c., accept the reading of ℵ, B, C, L, &c., οἱ δὲ ἀκολουθοῦντες,[325] as though there were *two* sets of the Apostles, of whom some in their fear had fallen behind the rest.

to the Priests and Scribes; by them condemned; then handed over to the Gentiles; by the Gentiles mocked, scourged, and — He now for the first time revealed to them, without any ambiguity, the crown-ing horror — *crucified ;* and that, on the third day, He should rise again. But their minds were full of Messianic hopes; they were so pre-occupied with the conviction that now the kingdom of God was to come in all its splendor, that the prophecy passed by them like the idle wind ; they could not, and would not, understand.

There can be no more striking comment on their inability to realize the meaning of what Jesus had said to them, than the fact that very shortly after, and during the same journey, occurred the ill-timed and strangely unspiritual request which the Evangelists proceed to record.[1] With an air of privacy and mystery, Salome, one of the constant attendants of Jesus, with her two sons, James and John, who were among the most eminent of His Apostles, came to Him with adora-tions, and begged Him to promise them a favor. He asked what they wished ; and then the mother, speaking for her fervent-hearted ambitious sons, begged that in His kingdom they might sit, the one at His right hand, and the other at His left.[2] Jesus bore gently with their selfishness and error. They had asked in their blindness for that position which, but a few days afterwards, they were to see occupied in shame and anguish by the two crucified robbers. Their imaginations were haunted by twelve thrones ; His thoughts were of three crosses. They dreamt of earthly crowns ; He told them of a cup of bitterness[3] and a baptism of blood. Could they indeed drink with Him of that cup, and be baptized with that baptism? Under-standing perhaps more of His meaning now, they yet boldly answered, " We can ; " and then He told them that they indeed *should* do so, but that to sit on His right hand and on His left was reserved for those for whom it had been prepared by His Heavenly Father.[4] The throne, says Basil, " is the price of toils, not a grace granted to ambi-tion ; a reward of righteousness, not the concession of a request."

---

[1] Matt. xx. 20—28 ; Mark x. 35—45 ; Luke xviii. 32—34.

[2] In Jos. *Antt.* vi. 11, § 9, Jonathan sits at Saul's right hand, Abner at his left. In the *Midrash Tehillin,* God is represented with the Messiah on His right and Abraham on His left (Wetstein *ad loc.*). Comp. 1 Kings ii. 19 (Bathsheba); xxii. 19.

[3] John xviii. 11 ; Rev. xiv. 10 ; Ps. lxxv. 8. "Lavacrum sanguinis" [316] (Tert. *Scorp.* 12). (Keim, iii. 43.)

[4] The English version is here not very happy in interpolating "it shall be given" (Matt. xx. 23), for the meaning is "not Mine to give *except to those for whom* it is prepared of My Father." Comp. Matt. xxv. 34 ; 2 Tim. iv. 8.

The ten, when they heard the incident, were naturally indignant at this secret attempt of the two brothers to secure for themselves a pre-eminence of honor; little knowing that, so far as earth was concerned — and of this alone they dreamt — that premium of honor should only be, for the one a precedence in martyrdom, for the other a prolongation of suffering.[1] This would be revealed to them in due time, but even now Jesus called them all together, and taught them, as He had so often taught them,[2] that the highest honor is won by the deepest humility. The shadowy principalities of earth[3] were characterized by the semblance of a little brief authority over their fellowmen; it was natural for them to lord it, and tyrannize it over their fellows: but in the kingdom of heaven the lord of all should be the servant of all, even as the highest Lord had spent His very life in the lowest ministrations, and was about to give it as a ransom for many.

As they advanced towards Jericho,[4] through the scorched and treeless Ghôr, the crowd of attendant pilgrims grew more and more dense about Him. It was either the evening of Thursday, Nisan 7, or the morning of Friday, Nisan 8, when they reached the environs

---

[1] Acts xii. 2; Rev. i. 9.

[2] Matt. xviii. 4; xxiii. 11.

[3] Mark x. 42, $o\dot{\iota}$ $\delta o\varkappa o\tilde{\upsilon}\nu\tau\varepsilon\varsigma$ $\H{a}\rho\chi\varepsilon\iota\nu$, those who profess to govern. The $\varkappa\alpha\tau\alpha$-$\varkappa\upsilon\rho\iota\varepsilon\dot{\upsilon}o\upsilon\delta\iota$ and $\varkappa\alpha\tau\varepsilon\xi o\upsilon\delta\iota\dot{\alpha}\zeta o\upsilon\delta\iota$ have a slightly unfavorable sense (1 Pet. v. 3).

[4] Matt. xx. 30—34; Mark x. 46—52; Luke xviii. 35—43. Those who have a narrow, timid, superstitious, and unscriptural view of inspiration may well be troubled by the obvious discrepancies between the Evangelists in this narrative. Not only does St. Matthew mention *two* blind men, while the others only mention one, but St. Matthew says that the miracle was performed "*as they departed from Jericho*," while St. Luke most distinctly implies that it took place *before He entered it*. But no reasonable reader will be troubled by differences which do *not* affect the truthfulness — though of course they affect the *accuracy* — of the narrative; and which, without a direct and wholly needless miraculous intervention, *must* have occurred, as they actually *do* occur, in the narratives of the Evangelists, as in those of all other truthful witnesses. Of the fourteen or fifteen proposed ways of harmonizing the discrepancies, *most* involve a remedy far worse than the supposed defect; but Macknight's suggestion that the miracle may have been performed *between the two Jerichos* — the ancient site of the Canaanite city, and the new semi-Herodian city — is at least possible. So, indeed, is the supposition that one of them was healed on entering, and the other on leaving the city. I believe that if we knew the exact circumstances the discrepancy would vanish; but even if it did not — if, for instance, Matthew had spoken of Bartimæus and his guide as "two blind men," or, in the course of time, any trivial inaccuracy had found its way into the early documents on which St. Luke based his Gospel — I should see nothing distressing or derogatory in such a supposition. For my views on Inspiration, I may perhaps be allowed to refer to my papers on the subject in Vol. I., p. 190, of the *Bible Educator.* On the fertility of Jericho, see Jos. *B. J.* iv. 8, § 3. The rose of Jericho is the *Anastatica Hierochuntia* of Linnæus.

of that famous city — the city of fragrance, the city of roses, the city of palm-trees, the "paradise of God." It is now a miserable and degraded Arab village, but was then a prosperous and populous town, standing on a green and flowery oasis,[1] rich in honey and leaf-honey, and myrobalanum, and well watered by the Fountain of Elisha and by other abundant springs. Somewhere in the vicinity of the town sat blind Bartimæus,[2] the son of Timæus, begging with a companion of his misery; and as they heard the noise of the passing multitude, and were told that it was Jesus of Nazareth who was passing by, they raised their voices in the cry, "Jesus, Thou Son of David, have mercy on us." The multitude resented this loud clamor as unworthy of the majesty of Him who was now to enter Jerusalem as the Messiah of His nation. But Jesus heard the cry, and His compassionate heart was touched. He stood still, and ordered them to be called to Him. Then the obsequious throng alter their tone, and say to Bartimæus, who is so much the more prominent in the narrative that two of the Synoptists do not even mention his companion at all — "Be of good cheer; rise, He calleth thee." With a burst of hasty joy, flinging away his *abba*, he leaped up,[3] and was led to Jesus. "What willest thou that I should do for thee?" "Rabboni," he answered (giving Jesus the most reverential title that he knew),[4] "that I may recover my sight." "Go," said Jesus, "thy faith hath saved thee." He touched the eyes both of him and of his companion, and with recovered sight they followed among the rejoicing multitudes, glorifying God.

It was necessary to rest at Jericho before entering on the dangerous, rocky, robber-haunted gorge which led from it to Jerusalem, and formed a rough, almost continuous, ascent of six hours,[5] from 600 feet below to nearly 3,000 feet above the level of the Mediterranean. The two most distinctive classes of Jericho were priests and publicans; and, as it was a priestly city, it might naturally have been expected that the king, the son of David, the successor of Moses, would be received in the house of some descendant of Aaron. But the place where Jesus chose to rest was determined by other circumstances.[6] A colony of publicans was established in the city to secure

---

[1] Ecclus. xxiv. 14.

[2] The name seems to be derived from the Aramaic *same, samia* = "blind." So Buxtorf and Hitzig, quoted by Keim, iii 52.

[3] Mark x. 50, ἀναπηδήσας (א, B, D, L, Tisch., Lachm., &c.).

[4] The steps of honor were Rab, Rabbi, Rabban, Rabboni.

[5] .About fifteen miles.

[6] Luke xix. 1—10.

the revenues accruing from the large traffic in a kind of balsam, which grew more luxuriantly there than in any other place,[1] and to regulate the exports and imports between the Roman province and the dominions of Herod Antipas. One of the chiefs of these publicans[2] was a man named Zacchæus,[3] doubly odious to the people, as being a Jew and as exercising his functions so near to the Holy City. His official rank would increase his unpopularity, because the Jews would regard it as due to exceptional activity in the service of their Roman oppressors, and they would look upon his wealth as a probable indication of numerous extortions. This man had a deep desire to see with his own eyes what kind of person Jesus was; but being short of stature, he was unable, in the dense crowd, to catch a glimpse of Him. He therefore ran forward, as Jesus was passing through the town, and climbed the low branches of an Egyptian fig, which overshadowed the road.[4] Under this tree Jesus would pass, and the publican would have ample opportunity of seeing one who, alone of His nation, not only showed no concentrated and fanatical hatred for the class to which he belonged, but had found among publicans His most eager listeners, and had elevated one of them into the rank of an Apostle. Zacchæus saw Him as He approached, and how must his heart have beat with joy and gratitude, when the Great Prophet, the avowed Messiah of His nation, passed under the tree, looked up, and, calling him by his name, bade him hasten and come down, because He intended to be a guest in his house. Zacchæus should not only see Him, but He would come in and sup with him, and make His abode with him — the glorious Messiah a guest of the execrated publican. With undisguised joy Zacchæus eagerly hastened down from the boughs of the " sycomore," and led the way to his house.[5] But

[1] Jos. *Antt.* xiv. 4, § 1; xv. 4, § 2; Justin, *Hist.* xxxvi. 3, &c.

[2] ἀρχιτελώνης. This does not necessarily imply that he had reached the rank of an actual *publicanus*, which was usually held by Roman knights, although some Jews, as we learn from Josephus, actually did attain to this rank (*B. J.* ii. 14, § 9).

[3] A Jewish name, an abbreviation of Zachariah; זַכַּי, "pure" (Ezra ii. 9); Zakkai (Jos. *Vit.* 46). Lightfoot (*Hor. Hebr. ad loc.*) thinks that he may be identified with the Zakkai whom the Rabbis mention as the father of Rabbi Johanan.

[4] The sycomore, or "Egyptian fig" (Luke xix. 4) — not to be confounded with the sycamine-tree or "mulberry" of Luke xvii. 6, or with the sycamore or *pseudo-platanus*, which is sometimes erroneously spelt sycomore — is exceedingly easy to climb.

[5] The square ruin in the wretched village of Rîha, the ancient Jericho, is (of course) called the house of Zacchæus, and is a Saracenic structure of the twelfth century.

the murmurs of the multitude were long, and loud, and unanimous.[1] They thought it impolitic, incongruous, reprehensible, that the King, in the very midst of His impassioned followers, should put up at the house of a man whose very profession was a symbol of the national degradation, and who even in that profession was, as they openly implied, disreputable. But the approving smile, the gracious word of Jesus were more to Zacchæus than all the murmurs and insults of the crowd. Jesus did not despise him: what mattered then the contempt of the multitude? Nay, Jesus had done him honor, therefore he would honor, he would respect himself. As all that was base in him would have been driven into defiance by contempt and hatred, so all that was noble was evoked by a considerate tenderness. He would strive to be worthy, at least *more* worthy, of his glorious guest; he would at least do his utmost to disgrace Him less. And, therefore, standing prominently forth among the throng, he uttered — not to *them*, for they despised him, and for them he cared not, but to his Lord — the vow which, by one high act of magnanimity, at once attested his penitence and sealed his forgiveness. " Behold the half of my goods, Lord, I hereby give to the poor; and whatever fraudulent gain I ever made from any one, I now restore fourfold." [2] This great sacrifice of that which had hitherto been dearest to him, this fullest possible restitution of every gain he had ever gotten dishonestly, this public confession and public restitution, should be a pledge to his Lord that His grace had not been in vain. Thus did love unseal by a single touch those swelling fountains of penitence which contempt would have kept closed for ever! No incident of His triumphal procession could have given to our Lord a deeper and holier joy. Was it not His very mission to seek and save the lost? Looking on the publican, thus ennobled by that instant renunciation of the fruits of sin, which is the truest test of a genuine repentance, He said, " Now is salvation come to this house, since he too is " — in the true spiritual sense, not in the idle, boastful, material sense alone — " a son of Abraham." [3]

---

[1] Luke xix. 7, ἅπαντες διεγόγγυζον.

[2] Lange and others see in the εἴ τινός τι ἐσυκοφάντησα [327] a sort of denial that he had ever cheated — a challenge to any one to come forward and accuse him; but the Greek idiom does not imply this. Συκοφαντεῖν means to gain in base, underhand, pettifogging ways (see Exod. xxii. 1—9). Fourfold restitution was more than Zacchæus need have paid (Numb. v. 7), and evidently, if he could redeem his pledge, the bulk of his property must have been honestly acquired.

[3] The legend that he afterwards became Bishop of Cæsarea is too late to be of any value (Clem. *Hom.* ii. 1, &c.).

To show them how mistaken were the expectations with which they were now excited — how erroneous, for instance, were the principles on which they had just been condemning Him for using the hospitality of Zacchæus — He proceeded (either at the meal in the publican's house, or more probably when they had again started) to tell them the Parable of the Pounds.[1]   Adopting incidents with which the history of the Herodian family had made them familiar, He told them of a nobleman who had travelled into a far country to receive a kingdom,[2] and had delivered to each of his servants a *mina* to be profitably employed till his return; the citizens hated him, and sent an embassy after him to procure his rejection.   But in spite of this his kingdom was confirmed, and he came back to punish his enemies, and to reward his servants in proportion to their fidelity. One faithless servant, instead of using the sum entrusted to him, had hidden it in a napkin, and returned it with an unjust and insolent complaint of his master's severity.   This man was deprived of his pound, which was given to the most deserving of the good and faithful servants;[3] these were magnificently rewarded, while the rebellious citizens were brought forth and slain.   The parable was one of many-sided application; it indicated His near departure from the world; the hatred which should reject Him; the duty of faithfulness in the use of all that He entrusted to them; the uncertainty of His return; the certainty that, when He did return, there would be a solemn account; the condemnation of the slothful; the splendid reward of all who should serve Him well; the utter destruction of those who endeavored to reject His power.   Probably while He delivered this parable the caravan had paused, and the pilgrims had crowded round

---

[1] Luke xix. 11—27.

[2] "A nobleman going into a far country to receive a kingdom" would be utterly unintelligible, had we not fortunately known that this was done both by Archelaus and by Antipas (Jos. *Antt.* xvii. 9, § 4).   And in the case of Archelaus the Jews had actually sent to Augustus a deputation of fifty, to recount his cruelties and oppose his claims, which, though it failed at the time, was subsequently successful (Id. xvii. 13, § 2).   Philippus defended the property of Archelaus during his absence from the encroachments of the Proconsul Sabinus.   The magnificent palace which Archelaus had built at Jericho (Jos. *Antt.* xvii. 13, § 1) would naturally recall these circumstances to the mind of Jesus, and the parable is another striking example of the manner in which He utilized the most ordinary circumstances around Him, and made them the bases of His highest teachings.   It is also another unsuspected indication of the authenticity and truthfulness of the Gospels.

[3] The surprised interpellation of the people, "Lord, he *hath* ten pounds," is an interesting proof of the intense and absorbing interest with which they listened to these parables.

Him. Leaving them to meditate on its significance, He once more moved forward alone at the head of the long and marvelling procession. They fell reverently back, and followed Him with many a look of awe as He slowly climbed the long, sultry, barren gorge which led up to Jerusalem from Jericho.[1]

He did not mean to make the city of Jerusalem His actual resting-place, but preferred as usual to stay in the loved home at Bethany. Thither He arrived on the evening of Friday, Nisan 8, A. U. C. 780 (March 31, A. D. 30), six days before the Passover, and before the sunset had commenced the Sabbath hours. Here He would part from His train of pilgrims, some of whom would go to enjoy the hospitality of their friends in the city, and others, as they do at the present day, would run up for themselves rude tents and booths in the valley of the Kedron, and about the western slopes of the Mount of Olives.

The Sabbath day was spent in quiet, and on the evening they made Him a supper.[2] St. Matthew and St. Mark say, a little mysteriously, that this feast was given in the house of Simon the leper. St. John makes no mention whatever of Simon the leper, a name which does not occur elsewhere; and it is clear from his narrative that the family of Bethany were in all respects the central figures at this entertainment. Martha seems to have had the entire supervision of the feast, and the risen Lazarus was almost as much an object of curiosity as Jesus himself. In short, so many thronged to see Lazarus — for the family was one of good position, and its members were widely known and beloved — that the notorious and indisputable miracle which had been performed on his behalf caused many to believe on Jesus. This so exasperated the ruling party at Jerusalem that, in their wicked desperation, they actually held a consultation how they might get rid of this living witness to the supernatural powers of the Messiah whom they rejected. Now since the raising of Lazarus was so intimately connected with the entire cycle of events which the earlier Evangelists so minutely record, we are again driven to the conclusion that there must have been some good reason, a reason which we can but uncertainly conjecture, for their

---

[1] Luke xix. 28.

[2] Matt. xxvi. 6—13 ; Mark xiv. 3—9 ; John xii. 1—9. This Sabbath preceding the Passover was called by the Jews *Shabbath Haggadôl*, or the " Great Sabbath." It is only in appearance that the Synoptists seem to place this feast two days before the Passover. They narrate it there to account for the treachery of Judas, which was consummated by his *final* arrangements with the Sanhedrin on the *Wednesday* of Holy week ; but we see from St. John that this latter must have been his *second* interview with them : at the first interview all details had been left indefinite.

marked reticence on this subject; and we find another trace of this reticence in their calling Mary "a certain woman," in their omission of all allusion to Martha and Lazarus, and in their telling us that this memorable banquet was served in the house of "Simon the leper." Who then was this Simon the leper? That he was no longer a leper is of course certain, for otherwise he could not have been living in his own house, or mingling in general society. Had he then been cleansed by Jesus? and, if so, was this one cause of the profound belief in Him which prevailed in that little household, and of the tender affection with which they always welcomed Him? or, again, was Simon now dead? We cannot answer these questions, nor are there sufficient data to enable us to decide whether he was the father of Martha and Mary and Lazarus,[1] or as some have conjectured, whether Martha was his widow, and the inheritress of his house.

Be this as it may, the feast was chiefly memorable, not for the number of Jews who thronged to witness it, and so to gaze at once on the Prophet of Nazareth and on the man whom He had raised from the dead, but from one memorable incident which occurred in the course of it, and which was the immediate beginning of the dark and dreadful end.

For as she sat there in the presence of her beloved and rescued brother, and her yet more deeply worshipped Lord, the feelings of Mary could no longer be restrained. She was not occupied like her sister in the active ministrations of the feast, but she sat and thought and gazed until the fire burned, and she felt impelled to some outward sign of her lòve, her gratitude, her adoration. So she arose and fetched an alabaster vase of Indian spikenard, and came softly behind Jesus where He sat, and broke the alabaster in her hands, and poured the genuine[2] precious perfume first over His head, then over His feet, and then — unconscious of every presence save His alone — she wiped those feet with the long tresses of her hair, while

---

[1] So Ewald, *Gesch. Christ.*, 401.

[2] ἀλάβαστρον μύρου νάρδου πιστικῆς πολυτελοῦς (Mark xiv. 3). Cf "*Nardi* parvus *onyx*" (Hor. *Od.* iv. 12). The possession of so expensive an unguent shows that the family was rich. It would have been under any circumstances a princely gift (Herod. iii. 120). The word πιστικῆς, if it mean "genuine," is opposed to the *pseudo-nardus* (Plin. xii. 26); but this interpretation of the word is by no means free from difficulty, and I have no better to offer. It " was so great an ecstasy of love, sorrow, and adoration, that to anoint the feet even of the greatest monarch was long unknown; and in all the pomps and greatnesses of the Roman prodigality, it was not used till Otho taught it to Nero " (Pliny, *N. H.* xiii. 35; Jer. Taylor, III. xiii.).

the atmosphere of the whole house was filled with the delicious fragrance. It was an act of devoted sacrifice, of exquisite self-abandonment; and the poor Galilæans who followed Jesus, so little accustomed to any luxury, so fully alive to the costly nature of the gift, might well have been amazed that it should have all been lavished on the rich luxury of one brief moment. None but the most spiritual-hearted there could feel that the delicate odor which breathed through the perfumed house might be to God a sweet-smelling savor; that even this was infinitely too little to satisfy the love of her who gave, or the dignity of Him to whom the gift was given.

But there was one present to whom on every ground the act was odious and repulsive. There is no vice at once so absorbing, so unreasonable, and so degrading as the vice of avarice, and avarice was the besetting sin in the dark soul of the traitor Judas. The failure to struggle with his own temptations; the disappointment of every expectation which had first drawn him to Jesus; the intolerable rebuke conveyed to his whole being by the daily communion with a sinless purity; the darker shadow which he could not but feel that his guilt flung athwart his footsteps because of the burning sunlight in which for many months he now had walked; the sense too that the eye of his Master, possibly even the eyes of some of his fellow-apostles, had read or were beginning to read the hidden secrets of his heart; — all these things had gradually deepened from an incipient alienation into an insatiable repugnancy and hate. And the sight of Mary's lavish sacrifice, the consciousness that it was now too late to save that large sum for the bag — the mere possession of which, apart from the sums which he could pilfer out of it, gratified his greed for gold — filled him with disgust and madness. He had a devil. He felt as if he had been personally cheated; as if the money were by right *his*, and he had been, in a senseless manner, defrauded of it. "To what purpose is this waste?" he indignantly said; and, alas! how often have his words been echoed, for wherever there is an act of splendid self-forgetfulness there is always a Judas to sneer and murmur at it. "This ointment might have been sold for three hundred pence and given to the poor!" *Three hundred pence* — ten pounds or more! There was perfect frenzy in the thought of such utter perdition of good money;[2]

---

[1] γλωσσόκομον (John xii. 6). *Vid. supr.*, p. 247.

[2] Matt. xxvi. 8, εἰς τί ἡ ἀπώλεια αὕτη; "Immo tu, Juda, *perditionis es*" (ὁ υἱὸς τῆς ἀπωλείας, John xvii. 12). (Bengel.) — "More than three hundred pence" would be at least £10, while the thirty pieces of silver for which Judas bargained to betray Jesus were not more than £3 16s.

why, for barely a third of such a sum, this son of perdition was ready to sell his Lord. Mary thought it not good enough to anele Christ's sacred feet: Judas thought a third part of it sufficient reward for selling His very life.

That little touch about its "being given to the poor" is a very instructive one. It was probably the veil used by Judas to half conceal even from himself the grossness of his own motives — the fact that he was a petty thief, and really wished the charge of this money because it would have enabled him to add to his own private store. People rarely sin under the full glare of self-consciousness; they usually blind themselves with false pretexts and specious motives; and though Judas could not conceal his baseness from the clearer eye of John, he probably concealed it from himself under the notion that he really was protesting against an act of romantic wastefulness, and pleading the cause of disinterested charity.

But Jesus would not permit the contagion of this worldly indignation — which had already infected some of the simple disciples — to spread any farther; nor would He allow Mary, already the centre of an unfavorable observation which pained and troubled her, to suffer any more from the consequences of her noble act. "Why trouble ye the woman?" He said. "Let her alone; she wrought a good work upon Me; for ye have the poor always with you, but Me ye have not always; for in casting this ointment on My body, she did it for My burying." And He added the prophecy — a prophecy which to this day is memorably fulfilled — that wherever the Gospel should be preached that deed of hers should be recorded and honored.

"For My burying" — clearly, therefore, His condemnation and burial were near at hand. This was another death-blow to all false Messianic hopes. No earthly wealth, no regal elevation could be looked for by the followers of One who was so soon to die. It may have been another impulse of disappointment to the thievish traitor who had thus publicly been not only thwarted, but also silenced, and implicitly rebuked. The loss of the money, which *might* by imagination have been under his own control, burnt in him with "a secret, dark, melancholic fire." He would *not* lose everything. In his hatred, and madness, and despair, he slunk away from Bethany that night, and made his way to Jerusalem, and got introduced into the council-room of the chief priests in the house of Caiaphas, and had that first fatal interview in which he bargained with them to betray his Lord. "What are you willing to give me, and I will betray Him to you?" What greedy chafferings took place we are not told, nor whether the counter-avarices of these united hatreds had a struggle before they decided on the paltry blood-money. If so, the astute Jewish priests beat down the poor ignorant Jewish Apostle. For all that they offered and all they paid was thirty pieces of silver[1] — about £3 16s. — the ransom-money of the meanest slave. For this price he was to sell his Master, and in selling his Master to sell his own life, and to gain in return the execration of the world for all generations yet to come. And, so for the last week of his own and his Master's life, Judas moved about with the purpose of murder in his dark and desperate heart. But as yet no day had been fixed, no plan decided on — only the betrayal paid for; and there seems to have been a general conviction that it would not do to make the attempt during the actual feast, lest there should be an uproar among the multitude who accepted Him, and especially among the dense throngs of pilgrims from His native Galilee. They believed that many opportunities would occur, either at Jerusalem or elsewhere, when the great Passover was finished, and the Holy City had relapsed into its ordinary calm.

And the events of the following day would be likely to give the most emphatic confirmation to the worldly wisdom of their wicked decision.

---

[1] See Exod. xxi. 32 ; Zech. xi. 12. The ἔστησαν of Matt. xxvi. 15 seems to imply that the money was paid down. No actual *shekels* were current at this time, but Judas may have been paid in Syrian or Phœnician tetradrachms, which were of the same weight (*v.* Madden). The paltriness of the sum (if it were not mere earnest-money) undoubtedly shows that the authorities did not regard the services of Judas as *indispensable.* He only saved them trouble and possible blood-shedding.

CHAPTER XLIX.

PALM SUNDAY.

" Ride on, ride on in majesty,
  In lowly pomp ride on to die ! " — HYMN.

THERE seems to have been a general impression for some time beforehand that, in spite of all which had recently happened, Jesus would still be present at the Paschal Feast. The probability of this had incessantly been debated among the people, and the expected arrival of the Prophet of Galilee was looked forward to with intense curiosity and interest.[1]

Consequently, when it became known early on Sunday morning that during the day He would certainly enter the Holy City, the excitement was very great. The news would be spread by some of the numerous Jews who had visited Bethany on the previous evening, after the sunset had closed the Sabbath, and thus enabled them to exceed the limits of the Sabbath day's journey. Thus it was that a very great multitude was prepared to receive and welcome the Deliverer who had raised the dead.

He started on foot. Three roads led from Bethany over the Mount of Olives to Jerusalem. One of these passes between its northern[2] and central summits; the other ascends the highest point of the mountain, and slopes down through the modern village of Et Tur; the third, which is, and always must have been, the main road, sweeps round the southern shoulder of the central mass, between it and the " Hill of Evil Counsel." The others are rather mountain paths than roads, and as Jesus was attended by so many disciples, it is clear that He took the third and easiest route.

---

[1] Matt. xxi. 1—11 ; Mark xi. 1—11 ; Luke xix. 28—40 ; John xii. 12—19.

[2] Traditionally called the " Hill of Offence," and by Milton, " that opprobrious hill ; " the supposed site of Solomon's idolatrous temples. It is now known as the Viri Galilæi, in reference to Acts i. 11. The " Hill of Evil Counsel " is the one on which stands the ruin of the so-called " House of Caiaphas." Williams (*Holy City*, ii. 496) notices it as a curious fact that the tomb of Annas is not far from this spot.

Passing from under the palm-trees of Bethany,[1] they approached the fig-gardens of Bethphage, the "House of Figs," a small suburb or hamlet of undiscovered site, which lay probably a little to the south of Bethany, and in sight of it. To this village, or some other hamlet which lay near it, Jesus dispatched two of His disciples. The minute description of the spot given by St. Mark makes us suppose that Peter was one of them, and if so he was probably accompanied by John. Jesus told them that when they got to the village they should find an ass tied, and a colt with her; these they were to loose and bring to Him, and if any objection arose on the part of the owner, it would at once be silenced by telling him that "the Lord had need of them." Everything happened as He had said. In the passage round the house — *i. e.*, tied up at the back of the house [2] — they found the ass and the foal, which was adapted for its sacred purpose because it had never yet been used.[3] The owners, on hearing their object, at once permitted them to take the animals, and they led them to Jesus, putting their garments over them to do Him regal honor.[4] Then they lifted Him upon the colt, and the triumphal procession set forth. It was no seditious movement to stir up political enthusiasm, no "insulting vanity" to commemorate ambitious triumph. Nay, it was a mere outburst of provincial joy, the simple exultation of poor Galilæans and despised disciples. He rides, not upon a war-horse, but on an animal which was the symbol of peace. The haughty Gentiles, had they witnessed the humble procession, would have utterly derided it, as indeed they did deride the record of it;[5] but the

---

[1] On the derivation of Bethany, *v. infra*, p. 503, *n.* There are no palms there now, but there may have been at that period. Throughout Palestine the palm and vine and fig-tree are *far* rarer than they were. Some identify Bethphage with Abu Dis. Lightfoot, apparently with Talmudical authority, makes it a *suburb* of Jerusalem. From the fact that in a journey towards Jerusalem it is always mentioned before Bethany, we might assume that it was *east* of that village.

[2] Mark xi. 4, δεδεμένον πρὸς τὴν θύραν ἔξω ἐπὶ τοῦ ἀμφόδου, not "where two ways met," as the English version translates it, following the Vulgate *bivium ;* but the Hebr. חוץ (Prov. i. 20), ἄμφοδα, αἱ ῥύμαι, ἀγυιαὶ (Hesych.).

[3] Numb. xix. 2 ; Deut. xxi. 3 ; 1 Sam. vi. 7. Comp. Ov. *Met.* iii. 12 ; Hor. *Epod.* ix. 22 (Wetstein).

[4] Comp. 2 Kings ix. 13.

[5] For instance, Julian and Sapor. In fact, the Romans had all kinds of sneers against the Jews in connection with the ass (Jos. *C. Ap.* ii. 10; Tac. *Hist.* v. 3, 4). The Christians came in for a share of this stupid jest, and were called *asinarii cultores* [328] (Minuc. Fel. *Oct.* 9 ; Tert. *Apol.* 16 ; see Keim, iii. 82). Sapor offered the Jews a horse to serve the purpose of carrying their expected Messiah, and a Jew haughtily answered him that all his horses were far below the ass which should carry the Messiah, which was to be descended from that used by Abraham when

Apostles recalled in after days that it fulfilled the prophecy of Zechariah : " Rejoice greatly, O daughter of Sion ; shout, O daughter of Jerusalem ; behold, thy King cometh unto thee; He is meek, and having salvation ; lowly, and riding upon an ass, and upon a colt the foal of an ass." [1] Yes, it was a procession of very lowly pomp, and yet beside it how do the grandest triumphs of aggressive war and unjust conquest sink into utter insignificance and disgrace !

Jesus mounted the unused foal, while probably some of His disciples led it by the bridle. And no sooner had He started than the multitude spread out [2] their upper garments to tapestry His path, and kept tearing or cutting down the boughs of olive, and fig, and walnut, to scatter them before Him. Then, in a burst of enthusiasm, the disciples broke into the shout, " Hosanna to the Son of David ! Blessed is the King of Israel that cometh in the name of the Lord ! Hosanna in the highest ! " [3] and the multitude caught up the joyous strain, and told each other how He had raised Lazarus from the dead.[4]

The road slopes by a gradual ascent up the Mount of Olives, through green fields and under shady trees, till it suddenly sweeps round to the northward. It is at this angle of the road that Jerusalem, which hitherto has been hidden by the shoulder of the hill,

---

he went to offer Isaac, and that used by Moses (Sepp, sect. vi., ch. 6). If, however, He came riding on an ass, and not on the clouds, it was to be a sign of their faithlessness (Lightfoot, *ad loc.*). The ass is not in the East by any means a despised or a despicable animal (Gen. xlix. 14 ; xxii. 3 ; 2 Sam. xiii. 29 ; Judg. v. 10) ; it is curious, however, to see that, because it was despised by Europeans and Gentiles, Josephus is fond of substituting for it $\varkappa\tau\tilde{\eta}\nu o\varsigma$ [329] and $\H{\iota}\pi\pi o\varsigma$,[330] and the LXX., with dishonest discretion, soften it down to $\H{\upsilon}\pi o\zeta\acute{\upsilon}\gamma\iota o\nu$ [331] and $\pi\tilde{\omega}\lambda o\varsigma$ [332] in Zech. ix. 9. It is clear that Jesus rode upon the foal, which by its mother's side could be led quietly along. With the $\H{\epsilon}\pi\acute{a}\nu\omega$ $a\mathring{\upsilon}\tau\tilde{\omega}\nu$ = " on one of them," comp. Acts xxiii. 24. Only inferior MSS. read $a\mathring{\upsilon}\tau o\tilde{\upsilon}$, and to understand $a\mathring{\upsilon}\tau\tilde{\omega}\nu$ of the garments is harsh. After all, however, it is doubtful whether there *were* two animals or only one ($\grave{o}\nu\acute{a}\rho\iota o\nu$, John xii. 14 ; $\pi\tilde{\omega}\lambda o\nu$ $\delta\epsilon\delta\epsilon\mu\acute{\epsilon}\nu o\nu$, Mark xi. 2 ; Luke xix. 30). It is in St. Matthew alone (xxi. 2, 7) that two animals are mentioned, and it is just conceivable that the $\varkappa a\grave{\iota}$ here may be epexegetic, and simply due to parallelism.

[1] The quotation referred to is a mixture (see Glass, *Philolog. Sacr.*, p. 969) of Isa. lxii. 11 ; Zech. ix. 9 ; and the Hebrew means literally " poor (עָנִי) and riding upon an ass, *even* upon a colt, son of she-asses." (See Turpie, *Old Test. in New*, p. 222.)

[2] Matt. xxi. 8, $\H{\epsilon}\sigma\tau\rho\omega\sigma a\nu$ . . . . $\H{\epsilon}\sigma\tau\rho\acute{\omega}\nu\nu\upsilon o\nu$.

[3] Hosanna = הוֹשִׁיעָה נָּא rendered by the LXX. $\sigma\tilde{\omega}\sigma o\nu$ $\delta\acute{\eta}$, " Oh save ! " These various cries are all from the Psalms which formed the great Hallel, (Ps. cxiii.—cxviii.) sung at the Feast of Tabernacles (Ps. cxviii. 25).

[4] In John xii. 17, the true reading (D, E, K, L, &c.) probably is $\H{o}\tau\iota$, " that " or " because," *not* $\H{o}\tau\epsilon$, " when."

bursts full upon the view. There, through the clear atmosphere, rising out of the deep umbrageous valleys which surrounded it, the city of ten thousand memories stood clear before Him, and the morning sunlight, as it blazed on the marble pinnacles and gilded roofs of the Temple buildings, was reflected in a very fiery splendor which forced the spectator to avert his glance.[1] Such a glimpse of such a city is at all times affecting, and many a Jewish and Gentile traveller has reined his horse at this spot, and gazed upon the scene in emotion too deep for speech. But the Jerusalem of that day, with "its imperial mantle of proud towers," was regarded as one of the wonders of the world,[2] and was a spectacle incomparably more magnificent than the decayed and crumbling city of to-day. And who can interpret, who can enter into the mighty rush of divine compassion which, at that spectacle, shook the Saviour's soul? As He gazed on that "mass of gold and snow," was there no pride, no exultation in the heart of its true King? Far from it! He had dropped *silent* tears at the grave of Lazarus; here He wept aloud.[3] All the shame of His mockery, all the anguish of His torture, was powerless, five days afterwards, to extort from Him a single groan, or to wet His eyelids with one trickling tear; but here, all the pity that was within Him overmastered His human spirit, and He not only wept, but broke into a passion of lamentation, in which the choked voice seemed to struggle for its utterance. A strange Messianic triumph! a strange interruption of the festal cries! The Deliverer weeps over the city which it is now too late to save; the King prophesies the utter ruin of the nation which He came to rule! "If thou hadst known," He cried — while the wondering multitudes looked on, and knew not what to think or say — "If thou hadst known, even thou, at least in thy day, the things that belong unto thy peace!"[4] — and there sorrow interrupted the sentence, and, when He found voice to continue, He

---

[1] So Josephus tells us (*B. J.* v. 5, § 6). It made those "who forced themselves to look upon it at the first rising of the sun, to turn their eyes away, just as they would have done at the sun's own rays." I came upon this spot in a walk from Bethany, not at sunrise, but under a full moon, on the night of Wednesday in Passion Week, April 14, 1870. I shall never forget the impression left by the sudden sight of the city, with its domes and minarets and twinkling lights, as it lay bathed in the Paschal moonlight.

[2] Tac. *Hist.* v. 8.

[3] John xi. 35, ἐδάκρυσεν; Luke xix. 41, εκλαυσεν.

[4] Perhaps with a play on the name Jerusalem, which might *recall* (though not derived from) יִרְאוּ שָׁלִים, "they shall see peace" (cf. Ps. cxxii. 6, 7). Such paronomasiæ are not only consistent with, but the usual concomitants of, deep emotion. See my *Chapters on Language*, pp. 269—276.

could only add, " but now they are hid from thine eyes. For the days shall come upon thee that thine enemies shall cast a trench about thee,[1] and compass thee round, and keep thee in on every side, and shall lay thee even with the ground, and thy children within thee; and they shall not leave in thee one stone upon another, because thou knewest not the time of thy visitation." It was the last invitation from "the Glory of God on the Mount of Olives," before that Shechînah vanished from their eyes for ever.[2]

Sternly, literally, terribly, within fifty years, was that prophecy fulfilled. Four years before the war began, while as yet the city was in the greatest peace and prosperity, a melancholy maniac traversed its streets with the repeated cry, " A voice from the east, a voice from the west, a voice from the four winds, a voice against Jerusalem and the holy house, a voice against the bridegrooms and the brides, and a voice against this whole people ; " nor could any scourgings or tortures wring from him any other words except " Woe! woe! to Jerusalem ; woe to the city ; woe to the people ; woe to the holy house ! " until seven years afterwards, during the siege, he was killed by a stone from a catapult. His voice was but the renewed echo of the voice of prophecy.

Titus had not originally wished to encompass the city, but he was forced, by the despair and obstinacy of the Jews, to surround it, first with a palisaded mound, and then, when this *vallum* and *agger* were destroyed, with a wall of masonry. He did not wish to sacrifice the Temple — nay, he made every possible effort to save it — but he was forced to leave it in ashes. He did not intend to be cruel to the inhabitants, but the deadly fanaticism of their opposition so extinguished all desire to spare them, that he undertook the task of wellnigh exterminating the race — of crucifying them by hundreds, of exposing them in the amphitheatre by thousands, of selling them into slavery by myriads. Josephus tells us that, even immediately after the siege of Titus, no one, in the desert waste around him, would have recognized the beauty of Judæa ; and that if any Jew had come upon the city of a sudden, however well he had known it before, he

---

[1] Luke xix. 43, χάραξ, "a palisade." (Cf. Isa. xxix. 3, 4 ; xxxvii. 33), properly only the *pali* on the *agger*, but sometimes of the entire *vallum* (cf. Isa. xxxvii. 33, LXX.).

[2] Commenting on Ezek. xi. 23, the Rabbis said that the Shechînah retired eastward to the Mount of Olives, and there for three years called in vain to the peoples with human voice that they should repent ; then withdrew for ever. (See Wetstein, p. 459 ; Keim, iii. 93.)

would have asked " what place it was ? " [1]   And he who, in modern Jerusalem, would look for relics of the ten-times-captured city of the days of Christ, must look for them twenty feet beneath the soil, and will scarcely find them.   In one spot alone remain a few massive substructions, as though to show how vast is the ruin they represent; and here, on every Friday, assemble a few poverty-stricken Jews, to stand each in the shroud in which he will be buried, and wail over the shattered glories of their fallen and desecrated home.[2]

There had been a pause in the procession while Jesus shed His bitter tears and uttered His prophetic lamentation.   But now the people in the valley of Kedròn, and about the walls of Jerusalem, and the pilgrims whose booths and tents stood so thickly on the green slopes below, had caught sight of the approaching company, and heard the echo of the glad shouts, and knew what the commotion meant.   At that time the palms were numerous in the neighborhood of Jerusalem, though now but a few remain ; and tearing down their green and graceful branches, the people streamed up the road to meet the approaching Prophet.[3]   And when the two streams of people met — those who had accompanied Him from Bethany, and those who had come to meet Him from Jerusalem — they left Him riding in the midst, and some preceding, some following Him, advanced, shouting " Hosannas " and waving branches, to the gate of Jerusalem.

Mingled among the crowd were some of the Pharisees, and the

---

[1] *B. J.* vi. 1, § 1.

[2] " Before my mind's eye," says Dr. Frankl, describing his first glimpse of Jerusalem, " passed in review the deeds and the forms of former centuries.   A voice within me said, *'Graves upon graves in graves!'*   I was deeply moved, and, bowing in my saddle before the city of Jehovah, tears fell upon my horse's mane " (*Jews in the East*, i. 351).

[3] John xii. 13, $\tau \grave{a}$ $\beta a \widehat{\imath} a$ $\tau \widehat{\omega} \nu$ $\varphi o\iota \nu \acute{\imath}\kappa \omega \nu$, " the branches of the palm-trees," which were familiar to St. John, and which, if the old derivation can stand, gave to Bethany its name.   The reading $\acute{o}\tau o\iota \beta \acute{a}\delta a\varsigma$ $\grave{\epsilon}\kappa$ $\tau \widehat{\omega} \nu$ $\grave{a}\gamma \rho \widehat{\omega} \nu$ in Mark xi. 8, though supported by אָ, B, C, L, Δ, perhaps arose from the notion that $\acute{o}\tau$. meant " grass." Dean Stanley is the first writer who seems accurately to have appreciated the facts and order of the triumphal entry (*Sin. and Palest.*, pp. 189, seqq.   See, too, Targ. Esth. x. 15 — the streets strewn with myrtle before Mordecai ; Herod. vii. 54).   The Maccabees were welcomed into Jerusalem with similar acclamations (2 Macc. x. 7). In *Kethubh.* f. 66,2, we are told of robes outspread before Nakdimon, son of Gorion (Keim, iii. 90).   A singular illustration of the faithfulness and accuracy of the Evangelists was given by the wholly accidental and unpremeditated re-enactment of the very same scene when Mr. Farran, the English consul of Damascus, visited Jerusalem at a time of great distress, in 1834.

joy of the multitude was to them gall and wormwood. What meant these Messianic cries and kingly titles? Were they not dangerous and unseemly? Why did He allow them? "Master, rebuke Thy disciples." But He would not do so. "If these should hold their peace," He said, "the stones would immediately cry out." The words may have recalled to them the threats which occur, amid denunciations against covetousness and cruelty, and the utter destruction by which they should be avenged, in the prophet Habakkuk — "For the stone shall cry out of the wall, and the beam out of the timber shall answer it." The Pharisees felt that they were powerless to stay the flood of enthusiasm.

And when they reached the walls the whole city was stirred with powerful excitement and alarm.[1] "Who is this?" they asked, as they leaned out of the lattices and from the roofs, and stood aside in the bazaars and streets to let them pass; and the multitude answered, with something of pride in their great countryman — but already, as it were, with a shadow of distrust falling over their high Messianic hopes, as they came in contact with the contempt and hostility of the capital — "This is Jesus, the Prophet of Nazareth."

The actual procession would not proceed farther than the foot of Mount Moriah (the *Har ha-beit*, Isa. ii. 2), beyond which they might not advance in travelling array, or with dusty feet.[2] Before they had reached the Shushan gate of the Temple they dispersed, and Jesus entered. The Lord whom they sought had come suddenly to His Temple — even the messenger of the covenant; but they neither recognized Him, nor delighted in Him, though His first act was to purify and purge it, that they might offer to the Lord an offering in righteousness.[3] As He looked round on all things[4] His heart was

---

[1] ἐσείσθη (Matt. xxi. 10; cf. xxviii. 4). Perhaps they recalled the attempt made upon Jerusalem by "that Egyptian" (Acts xxi. 38).

[2] *Berach.* ix. 5, quoted by Lightfoot.

[3] Mal. iii. 1—3.

[4] I follow the order of St. Matthew, in preference to that of St. Mark, in fixing the cleansing of the Temple on Palm Sunday, and immediately after the triumphal entry; and for these reasons: (1) because it is most unlikely that Jesus started late in the day; it would be very hot, even in that season of the year, and contrary to His usual habits. (2) If, then, He started early, and did not leave the Temple till late (Mark xi. 11), there is no indication of how the day was spent (for the journey to Jerusalem would not occupy more, at the very most, than two hours), unless we suppose that the incidents narrated in the text took place on the Sunday, as both St. Matthew, St. Luke, and St. John seem to imply. (3) The cleansing of the Temple would be a much more natural sequel of the triumphal entry, than of the quiet walk next day. (4) There is no adequate reason to account for the postponement of such a purification of the Temple till the following day.

again moved within Him to strong indignation. Three years before, at His first Passover, He had cleansed the Temple; but, alas! in vain. Already greed had won the battle against reverence; already, the tessellated floors and pillared colonnades of the Court of the Gentiles had been again usurped by droves of oxen and sheep, and dove-sellers, and usurers, and its whole precincts were dirty with driven cattle, and echoed to the hum of bargaining voices and the clink of gold.[1] In that desecrated place He would not teach. Once more, in mingled sorrow and anger, He drove them forth, while none dared to resist His burning zeal; nor would He even suffer the peaceful enclosure to be disturbed by people passing to and fro with vessels, and so turning it into a thoroughfare. The dense crowd of Jews — numbering, it is said, three millions — who crowded to the Holy City in the week of the feast, no doubt made the Court of the Gentiles a worse and busier scene on that day than at any other time, and the more so because on that day, according to the law, the Paschal lamb — which the visitors would be obliged to purchase — was chosen and set apart.[2] But no considerations of their business and convenience could make it tolerable that they should turn His Father's house, which was a house of prayer for all nations, into a place most like one of those foul caves which He had seen so often in the Wady Hammâm, where brigands wrangled over their ill-gotten spoils.[3]

Not till He had reduced the Temple to decency and silence could He begin His customary ministrations. Doubtless the task was

---

[1] The vast throng of foreign pilgrims, and the necessity laid on them of changing their foreign coinage, with its heathen symbols, for the *shekel hakkodesh,* "half-shekel, after the shekel of the sanctuary" (Exod. xxx. 13), would make the trade of these men at this time a very thriving one: their agio was a twelfth of each shekel. The presence of these money-makers distinctly contravened the law of Zech. xiv. 21, where Canaanite = merchant. See *supra*, p. 161, *n.*

[2] Exod. xii. 1—5. For the "booths" in the Temple Court, see Lightfoot on Matt. xxi. 12.

[3] σπηλαῖον λῃστῶν (Mördergrube, Luther) is much stronger than "den of thieves;" and if the "House of Prayer" reminded them of Jer. vii. 6, as well as Isa. lvi. 7, it would recall ideas of "innocent blood," as well as of greedy gain. The Temple was destined in a few more years to become yet more emphatically a "murderer's cave," when the *sicarii* made it the scene of their atrocities. "The sanctuary," says Josephus (*B. J.* iv. 3, § 7), "was now become a refuge, and a shop of tyranny." "Certainly," says Ananus in his speech, "it had been good for me to die before I had seen the house of God full of so many abominations, or these sacred places, that ought not to be trodden upon at random, filled with the feet of these blood-shedding villains" (*id.* § 10). "When any of the Zealots were wounded, he went up into the Temple, and defiled that sacred floor with his blood" (*id.* § 12). "To say all in a word, no passion was so entirely lost among them as mercy" (*id.* iv. 6, § 3).

easier, because it had already been once performed. But when the miserable hubbub was over, then the Temple resumed what should have been its normal aspect. Sufferers came to Him, and He healed them. Listeners in hundreds thronged round Him, were astonished at His doctrine, hung upon His lips.[1] The very children of the Temple, in their innocent delight, continued the glad Hosannas which had welcomed Him. The Chief Priests, and Scribes, and Pharisees, and leading people saw, and despised, and wondered, and perished. They could but gnash their teeth in their impotence, daring to do nothing, saying to each other that they *could* do nothing, for the whole world had gone after Him, yet hoping still that their hour would come, and the power of darkness. If they ventured to say one word to Him, they had to retire abashed and frustrated by His calm reply. They angrily called His attention to the cry of the boys in the Temple courts, and said, " Hearest Thou what these say ? " Perhaps they were boys employed in the musical services of the Temple, and if so the priestly party would be still more enraged. But Jesus calmly protected the children from their unconcealed hatred. "Yea," He answered, "have ye never read, Out of the mouths of babes and sucklings Thou hast perfected praise ? " [2]

So in high discourse, amid the vain attempts of His enemies to annoy and hinder Him, the hours of that memorable day passed by. And it was marked by one more deeply interesting incident. Struck by all they had seen and heard, some Greeks — probably Jewish proselytes attracted to Jerusalem by the feast — came to Philip, and asked him to procure for them a private interview with Jesus.[3] Chaldæans from the East had sought His cradle ; these Greeks from the West came to His cross.[4] Who they were, and why they sought Him, we know not. An interesting tradition, but one on which unfortunately we can lay no stress, says that they were emissaries from Abgarus V., King of Edessa, who, having been made aware of the miracles of Jesus, and of the dangers to which He was now exposed, sent these emissaries to offer Him an asylum in his domin-

---

[1] Luke xix. 48, ὁ λαὸς γὰρ ἅπας ἐξεκρέματο αὐτοῦ ἀκούων : [333] cf. Virg. Æn. iv. 79, " pendebat ab ore." [334]

[2] Ps. viii. 2. Did they recall the sequel of the verse, " *because of Thine enemies*, that Thou mightest still the enemy and the avenger ? " Similar emotional out-bursts of children are adduced by Schöttgen.

[3] John xii. 20—50.

[4] Stier *ad loc.* They are called Ἕλληνες, and were therefore Gentiles, not Ἑλληνισταὶ (cf. Acts xvi. 1 ; John vii. 35), or Greek-speaking Jews. In the Syriac version they are called Aramæans. That they were proselytes appears from John xii. 20 (comp. Acts viii. 27).

ions. The legend adds that, though Jesus declined the offer, He rewarded the faith of Abgarus by writing him a letter, and healing him of a sickness.[1]

St. John mentions nothing of these circumstances; he does not even tell us why these Greeks came to Philip in particular. As Bethsaida was the native town of this apostle, and as many Jews at this period had adopted Gentile appellations, especially those which were current in the family of Herod, we cannot attach much importance to the Greek form of his name.[2] It is an interesting indication of the personal awe which the Apostles felt for their Master, that Philip did not at once venture to grant their request. He went and consulted his fellow-townsman Andrew, and the two Apostles then made known the wish of the Greeks to Jesus. Whether they actually introduced the inquirers into His presence we cannot tell, but at any rate He saw in the incident a fresh sign that the hour was come when His name should be glorified. His answer was to the effect that as a grain of wheat must die before it can bring forth fruit, so the road to His glory lay through humiliation, and they who would follow Him must be prepared at all times to follow Him even to death. As He contemplated that approaching death, the human horror of it struggled with the ardor of His obedience; and conscious that to face that dread hour was to conquer it, He cried, " Father, glorify Thy name! " Then for the third time in His life came a voice from heaven, which said, " I have both glorified it, and will glorify it again." [3] St. John frankly tells us that that Voice did not

---

[1] The apocryphal letter of Abgarus to Christ is given by Eusebius (*Hist. Eccl.* i. 13), who professes to derive it from Syriac documents preserved at Edessa, and quoted by Moses Chorenensis (*Hist. Arm.* ii. 28). (Herzog, *Bibl. Encykl.* s. v. " Abgar.") The letter and reply are probably as old as the third century. Abgar says that having heard of His miracles, and thence concluded His Divine nature, " I have written to ask of Thee that Thou couldest trouble Thyself to come to me, and heal this sickness which I have. For I have also heard that the Jews murmur against Thee, and wish to injure Thee. Now I have a small and beautiful city which is sufficient for both." The reply, which is almost entirely couched in Scriptural language, begins with an allusion to John xx. 29, and after declining the king's offer, adds, " When I am taken up, I will send thee one of my disciples to heal thy sickness ; he shall also give salvation to thee and to them that are with thee." (B. H. Cowper, *Apocr. Gosp.*, p. 220 ; Hofmann, *Leben Jesu nach d. Apocr.*, p. 308.) The disease was, according to Cedrenus (*Hist.* p. 145), leprosy, and according to Procopius (*De Bell. Pers.* ii. 12) the gout.

[2] Lange (iv. 54) notices the tradition that Philip afterwards labored in Phrygia, and Andrew in Greece.

[3] John xii. 28, καὶ ἐδόξασα καὶ πάλιν δοξάσω. On the previous passage see the excellent remarks of Stier. (*Vide supr.*, pp. 110, 383.)

sound alike to all. The common multitude took it but for a passing
peal of thunder ; others said, " An angel spake to Him ; " the Voice
was articulate only to the few. But Jesus told them that the Voice
was for their sakes, not for His ; for the judgment of the world, its
conviction of sin by the Holy Spirit, was now at hand, and the Prince
of this world [1] should be cast out. He should be lifted up, like the
brazen serpent in the wilderness,[2] and when so exalted He should
draw all men unto Him. The people were perplexed at these dark
allusions. They asked Him what could be the meaning of His saying that " the Son of Man should be lifted up ? " If it meant violently taken away by a death of shame, how could this be ? Was
not the Son of Man a title of the Messiah ? and did not the prophet
imply that the reign of Messiah would be eternal ? [3] The true answer
to their query could only be received by spiritual hearts — they were
unprepared for it, and would only have been offended and shocked
by it ; therefore Jesus did not answer them. He only bade them
walk in the light during the very little while that it should still remain
with them, and so become the children of light. He was come as a
light into the world, and the words which He spake should judge
those who rejected Him ; for those words — every brief answer, every
long discourse — were from the Father ; sunbeams from the Father
of Lights ; life-giving rays from the Life Eternal.[4]

But all these glorious and healing truths were dull to blinded eyes,
and dead to hardened hearts ; and even the few of higher rank and
wider culture who partially understood and partially believed them,
yet dared not confess Him, because to confess Him was to incur the
terrible *cherem* of the Sanhedrin ; and this they would not face —
loving the praise of men more than the praise of God.

Thus a certain sadness and sense of rejection fell even on the evening of the Day of Triumph. It was not safe for Jesus to stay in the

---

[1] The Jewish *Sar ha-Olam ;* he whom St. Paul calls " the god of this world "
(2 Cor. iv. 4). The Greek κόσμος corresponds to the Hebrew *olamîm* or "aeons."
The Jews, unlike the Greeks, did not so much regard the outward beauty of Creation, as its inward significance ; for them the interest of the Universe " centered
rather in the moral than in the physical order " (Westcott, *Introd.* i. 25). (See
Eph. ii. 2.) A Mussulman title of God is " Lord of the (three) worlds " (*Rabb al
alamîn*).

[2] Comp. John iii. 14; viii. 28. Cf. "Adolescentem laudandum, ornandum, *tollen-
dum* " [335] (Letter of Dec Brutus to Cicero, *Epp. ad Div.* xi. 20).

[3] " The Law " is here a general term for the Old Testament. The reference is
to Ps. lxxxix. 36 ; comp. John x. 34.

[4] John xii. 44—50, verse 49, δέδωκε τί εἴπω (de sermone brevi, אָמַר) καὶ τί
λαλήσω (de copioso, דָּבַר). (Bengel.) The ἔκραξε (verse 44) points to the importance of the utterance. Cf. John vii. 28, 37 ; xi. 43.

city, nor was it in accordance with His wishes. He retired secretly from the Temple, hid Himself from His watchful enemies, and, protected as yet outside the city walls by the enthusiasm of His Galilæan followers, " went out unto Bethany with the Twelve." But it is very probable that while He bent His steps in the direction of Bethany, He did not actually enter the village; for, on this occasion, His object seems to have been concealment, which would hardly have been secured by returning to the well-known house where so many had seen Him at the banquet on the previous evening. It is more likely that He sought shelter with His disciples by the olive-sprinkled slope of the hill,[1] not far from the spot where the roads meet which lead to the little village. He was not unaccustomed to nights in the open air, and He and the Apostles, wrapped in their outer garments, could sleep soundly and peacefully on the green grass under the sheltering trees. The shadow of the traitor fell on Him and on that little band. Did *he* too sleep as calmly as the rest? Perhaps: for " remorse may disturb the slumbers of a man who is dabbling with his first experiences of wrong; and when the pleasure has been tasted and is gone, and nothing is left of the crime but the ruin which it has wrought, then too the Furies take their seats upon the midnight pillow. *But the meridian of evil is, for the most part, left unvexed; and when a man has chosen his road, he is left alone to follow it to the end.*"[2]

---

[1] The ἠυλίσθη ἐκεῖ of Matt. xxi. 17 does not *necessarily* imply that He bivouacked in the open air. It is, however, very probable that He did so; for (1) such is the proper meaning of the word (comp. Judg. xix. 15, 20). (2) St. Luke says, ηὐλίζετο εἰς τὸ ὄρος τὸ καλούμενον 'Ελαιῶν (xxi. 37). (3) It was His custom to resort for the night to Gethsemane, where, so far as we are aware, there was no house. (4) The retiring to Bethany would hardly answer to the ἐκρύβη ἀπ' αὐτῶν of John xii. 36.

[2] Froude, *Hist. of Engl.* viii. 30.

CHAPTER L.

" Apples of gold in PICTURES of silver." — PROV. xxv. 11.

RISING from His bivouac in the neighborhood of Bethany while it was still early, Jesus returned at once to the city and the Temple; and on His way He felt hungry.   Monday and Thursday were kept by the scrupulous religionists of the day as voluntary fasts, and to this the Pharisee alludes when he says in the Parable, " I fast twice in the week."   But this fasting was a mere " work of supererogation," neither commanded nor sanctioned by the Law or the Prophets, and it was alien alike to the habits and precepts of One who came, not by external asceticisms, but with absolute self-surrender, to ennoble by Divine sinlessness the common life of men.   It may be that in His compassionate eagerness to teach His people, He had neglected the common wants of life ; it may be that there were no means of procuring food in the fields where He had spent the night ; it may be again that the hour of prayer and morning sacrifice had not yet come, before which the Jews did not usually take a meal.   But, whatever may have been the cause, Jesus hungered, so as to be driven to look for wayside fruit to sustain and refresh Him for the day's work.   A few dates or figs, a piece of black bread, a draught of water, are sufficient at any time for an Oriental's simple meal.

There are trees in abundance even now throughout this region, but not the numerous palms, and figs, and walnut-trees which made the vicinity of Jerusalem like one umbrageous park, before they were cut down by Titus, in the operations of the siege.   Fig-trees especially were planted by the roadside, because the dust was thought to facilitate their growth,[1] and their refreshing fruit was common property.   At a distance in front of Him Jesus caught sight of a solitary fig-tree,[2] and although the ordinary season at which figs

---

[1] Plin *Hist. Nat.* xv. 21, quoted by Meyer.   On the right to pluck fruit, see Deut. xxiii. 24.

[2] συκῆν μίαν (Matt. xxi. 19), " a single fig-tree."   Compare, however, μία παιδίσκη (xxvi. 69).   The εἰ ἄρα τὶ εὑρήσει ἐν αὐτῇ (Mark xi. 13) implies a shade of surprise at the exceptional forwardness of the tree.

ripened had not yet arrived, yet, as it was clad with verdure, and as the fruit of a fig sets before the leaves unfold, this tree looked more than usually promising. Its rich large leaves seemed to show that it was fruitful, and their unusually early growth that it was not only fruitful but precociously vigorous. There was every chance, therefore, of finding upon it either the late violet-colored *kermouses*, or autumn figs, that often remained hanging on the trees all through the winter, and even until the new spring leaves had come;[1] or the delicious *bakkooroth*, the first ripe on the fig-tree, of which Orientals are particularly fond.[2] The difficulty raised about St. Mark's expression, that "the time of figs was not yet,"[3] is wholly needless. On the plains of Gennesareth Jesus must have been accustomed — if we may trust Josephus — to see the figs hanging ripe on the trees every month in the year excepting January and February;[4] and there is to this day, in Palestine, a kind of white or early fig which ripens in spring, and much before the ordinary or black fig.[5] On many grounds, therefore, Jesus might well have expected to find a few figs to satisfy the cravings of hunger on this fair-promising leafy tree, although the *ordinary* fig-season had not yet arrived.

But when He came up to it, He was disappointed. The sap was circulating; the leaves made a fair show; but of fruit there was none. Fit emblem of a hypocrite, whose external semblance is a delusion and sham — fit emblem of the nation in whom the ostentatious profession of religion brought forth no "fruit of good living" — the tree was barren. And it was *hopelessly* barren; for had it been fruitful the previous year, there would still have been some of the *kermouses* hidden under those broad leaves; and had it been fruitful *this* year, the *bakkooroth* would have set into green and delicious fragrance before the leaves appeared; but on this fruitless tree there was neither any promise for the future, nor any gleanings from the past.

---

[1] Plin. *H. N.* xvi. 27, "Seri fructus per hiemem in arbore manent, et aestate *inter novas frondes et folia* maturescunt"[336] (comp. Colum. *De Arbor,* 21). Ebrard says that it is doubtful whether this applied to Palestine (*Gosp. Hist.,* p. 376, E. Tr.); but it certainly did, as is shown by the testimony of travellers and of Jewish writers. The green or unripe fig (פֶּג, *pagh*) is only mentioned in Cant. ii. 13.

[2] בִּכּוּרוֹת (Hos. ix. 10; Isa. xxviii. 4; Nah. iii. 12; Jer. xxiv. 2, "Very good figs, even like the figs that are first ripe").

[3] There is no need whatever to render this, "it was no favorable weather for figs," "not a good fig year."

[4] *B. J.* iii. 10, § 8.

[5] Dr. Thomson, author of *The Land and the Book,* tells us that he has eaten these figs as early as April or May.

And therefore, since it was but deceptive and useless, a barren cumberer of the ground, He made it the eternal warning against a life of hypocrisy continued until it is too late, and, in the hearing of His disciples, uttered upon it the solemn fiat, "Never fruit grow upon thee more!" Even at the word, such infructuous life as it possessed was arrested, and it began to wither away.

The criticisms upon this miracle have been singularly idle and singularly irreverent, because they have been based for the most part on ignorance or on prejudice. By those who reject the divinity of Jesus, it has been called a penal miracle, a miracle of vengeance, a miracle of unworthy anger, a childish exhibition of impatience under disappointment, an uncultured indignation against innocent Nature. No one, I suppose, who believes that the story represents a real and miraculous fact, will daringly arraign the motives of Him who performed it; but many argue that this is an untrue and mistaken story, because it narrates what they regard as an unworthy display of anger at a slight disappointment, and as a miracle of destruction which violated the rights of the supposed owner of the tree, or of the multitude. But, as to the first objection, surely it is amply enough to say that every page of the New Testament shows the *impossibility* of imagining that the Apostles and Evangelists had so poor and false a conception of Jesus as to believe that He avenged His passing displeasure on an irresponsible object. Would He who, at the Tempter's bidding, refused to satisfy His wants by turning the stones of the wilderness into bread, be represented as having "flown into a rage" — no other expression is possible — with an unconscious tree? An absurdity so irreverent might have been found in the Apocryphal Gospels; but had the Evangelists been capable of perpetuating it, then, most unquestionably, they could have had neither the capacity nor the desire to paint that Divine and Eternal portrait of the Lord Jesus, which their knowledge of the truth, and the aid of God's Holy Spirit, enabled them to present to the world for ever, as its most priceless possession. And as for the withering of the tree, has the householder of the parable been ever severely censured because he said of his barren fig-tree, "Cut it down, why cumbereth it the ground?" Has St. John the Baptist been ever blamed for violence and destructiveness because he cried, "And now also the axe is laid unto the root of the tree: every tree, therefore, which bringeth not forth good fruit, is hewn down and cast into the fire?" Or has the ancient Prophet been charged with misrepresenting the character of God, when he says, "*I, the Lord, have dried up the green tree,*" [1] as

---

[1] Ezek. xvii. 24.

well as " made the dry tree to flourish ? " When the hail beats down
the tendrils of the vineyard — when the lightning scathes the olive,
or "splits the unwedgeable and gnarlëd oak " — do any but the
utterly ignorant and brutal begin at once to blaspheme against God ?
Is it a crime under *any* circumstances to destroy a *useless* tree ? if
not, is it *more* a crime to do so by miracle ? Why, then, is the Saviour of the world — to whom Lebanon would be too little for a
burnt-offering — to be blamed by petulent critics because He hastened the withering of one barren tree. and founded, on the destruction of its uselessness, three eternal lessons — a symbol of the destruction of impenitence, a warning of the peril of hypocrisy, an illustration of the power of faith ? [1]

They went on their way, and, as usual, entered the Temple ; and
scarcely had they entered it, when they were met by another indication of the intense incessant spirit of opposition which actuated the
rulers of Jerusalem.[2] A formidable deputation approached them,
imposing alike in its numbers and its stateliness.[3] The chief priests
— heads of the twenty-four courses — the learned scribes, the leading
rabbis, representatives of all the constituent classes of the Sanhedrin
were there, to overawe Him — whom they despised as the poor ignorant Prophet of despicable Nazareth — with all that was venerable in
age, eminent in wisdom, or imposing in authority in the great Coun-

---

[1] The many-sided symbolism of the act would have been much more vividly
apparent to those more familiar than ourselves with the ancient prophets (see
Hos. ix. 10 ; Joel i. 7 ; Micah vii. 1). " Even here," says Professor Westcott, " in
the moment of sorrowful disappointment, as He turned to His disciples, the word
of judgment became a word of promise. 'Have faith in God, and whatsoever
things ye desire when ye pray, believe that ye *received* them ($\dot{\epsilon}\lambda\dot{\alpha}\beta\epsilon\tau\epsilon$)' —
received them already as the inspiration of the wish — ' and ye shall have them ' "
(*Charact. of the Gosp. Miracles*, p. 25). I have dwelt at some length on this
miracle, because to some able and honest thinkers it presents a real difficulty.
Those who do not see in it the lessons which I have indicated (of which the first
two are only *implied*. not formulated, in the Gospels), regard it as a literal construction of an illustrative metaphor — a *parable* of the power of faith (cf. Luke
xxiii. 31 ; Rev. vi. 13 ; and the Koran, *Sura* 95) which has got mythically developed into a miracle. Better this, than that it should lead them to unworthy views
of " Him whom the Father hath sent ; " but if the above views be right, the difficulty does not seem to me by any means insuperable.

[2] It will be observed that I am following in the main the order of the eye-witness, St. Matthew, who, however, pauses to finish the story of the fig-tree, the
sequel of which belongs to the next day. It is, however, clear the $\pi\alpha\rho\alpha\chi\rho\tilde{\eta}\mu\alpha$
of St. Matthew is only used *relatively*.

[3] Mark xi. 27, $\pi\epsilon\rho\iota\pi\alpha\tau\upsilon\tilde{\upsilon}\nu\tau\upsilon\varsigma$ $\alpha\dot{\upsilon}\tau\upsilon\tilde{\upsilon}$; Luke xx. 1, $\dot{\epsilon}\pi\dot{\epsilon}\dot{\sigma}\tau\eta\dot{\sigma}\alpha\nu$ (cf. Acts iv.
1 ; vi. 12 ; xxiii. 27). I have already (p. 461) noticed St. Luke's use of this word
to imply something sudden or hostile.

cil of the nation. The people whom He was engaged in teaching made reverent way for them, lest they should pollute those floating robes and ample fringes with a touch ; and when they had arranged themselves around Jesus, they sternly and abruptly asked Him, " By what authority doest thou these things, and who gave thee this authority ? " They demanded of Him His warrant for thus publicly assuming the functions of Rabbi and Prophet, for riding into Jerusalem amid the hosannas of attendant crowds, for purging the Temple of the traffickers, at whose presence they connived ? [1]

The answer surprised and confounded them. With that infinite presence of mind, of which the world's history furnishes no parallel, and which remained calm under the worst assaults, Jesus told them that the answer to their question depended on the answer which they were prepared to give to *His* question. " The baptism of John, was it from heaven, or of men ? " A sudden pause followed. " Answer me," said Jesus, interrupting their whispered colloquy. And surely they, who had sent a commission to inquire publicly into the claims of John, were in a position to answer. But no answer came. They knew full well the import of the question. They could not for a moment put it aside as irrelevant. John had openly and emphatically testified to Jesus, had acknowledged Him, before their own deputies, not only as *a* Prophet, but as a Prophet far greater than himself — nay, more, as *the* Prophet, the Messiah. Would they recognize that authority, or would they not ? Clearly Jesus had a right to demand their reply to *that* question before He could reply to theirs. But they *could* not, or rather they *would* not answer that question. It reduced them in fact to a complete dilemma. They *would* not say "*from heaven,*" because they had in heart rejected it ; they dared not say "*of men,*" because the belief in John (as we see even in Josephus) was so vehement and so unanimous that openly to reject him would have been to endanger their personal safety.[2] They were reduced, therefore — they, the masters of Israel — to the ignominious necessity of saying, " We cannot tell."

There is an admirable Hebrew proverb which says, " Teach thy

---

[1] Mark xi. 27—33 ; Matt. xxi. 23—27 ; Luke xx. 1—8. The Sanhedrin had sent a similar deputation to John the Baptist, but in a less hostile spirit (*v. supra*, p. 109).

[2] Jos. *Antt.* xviii. 5, § 2 ; Luke xx. 6. The πεπεισμένος shows the permanence of the conviction ; the καταλιθάσει (which is used here only) the violent tumult which would have been caused by a denial of John's position as a prophet. Wetstein quotes from Donat. ad Ter. *Eun.* v. 5, 11, a most apposite parallel, where Parmenio, unable to deny, and unwilling to admit, protects himself by a "*nescio.*"

tongue to say, 'I do not know.' "[1]   But to say "We do not know,"
in this instance, was a thing utterly alien to their habits, disgraceful to
their discernment, a death-blow to their pretensions. It was ignorance
in a sphere wherein ignorance was for them inexcusable. They, the
appointed explainers of the Law — they, the accepted teachers of the
people — they, the acknowledged monopolizers of Scriptural learning
and oral tradition — and yet to be compelled, against their real convictions, to say, and that before the multitude, that they *could not
tell* whether a man of immense and sacred influence — a man who
acknowledged the Scriptures which they explained, and carried into
practice the customs which they reverenced — was a divinely inspired
messenger or a deluding impostor !   Were the lines of demarcation,
then, between the inspired Prophet (*nabî*) and the wicked seducer
(*mesîth*) so dubious and indistinct ?   It was indeed a fearful humiliation, and one which they never either forgot or forgave ! And yet
how just was the retribution which they had thus brought on their
own heads.   The curses which they had intended for another had
recoiled upon themselves ; the pompous question which was to be an
engine wherewith another should be crushed, had sprung back with
sudden rebound, to their own confusion and shame.

Jesus did not press upon their discomfiture, though He well
knew — as the form of His answer showed — that their " *do not
know*," was a " *do not choose to say*." Since, however, their failure
to answer clearly absolved Him from any necessity to tell them
further of an authority about which, by their own confession, they
were totally incompetent to decide, He ended the scene by simply
saying, " Neither tell I you by what authority I do these things."

So they retired a little into the background. He continued the
instruction of the people which they had interrupted, and began
once more to speak to them in parables, which both the multitude
and the members of the Sanhedrin who were present could hardly
fail to understand. And He expressly called their attention to what
He was about to say.   " *What think ye ?* " He asked, for now it is
their turn to submit to be questioned ; and then, telling them of the
two sons, of whom the one first flatly refused his father's bidding,
but afterwards repented and did it, the other blandly promised an
obedience which he never performed, He asked, " Which of these
two did his father's will ? "   They could but answer, " the first ; "
and He then pointed out to them the plain and solemn meaning of

---

[1] .לְמַד לְשׁוֹנְךָ לֵאמֹר אֵינֶנִּי יוֹדֵעַ

their own answer. It was, that the very publicans and harlots, despite the apparent open shamelessness of their disobedience, were yet showing *them* — them, the scrupulous and highly reputed legalists of the holy nation — the way into the kingdom of heaven. Yes, these sinners, whom they despised and hated, were streaming before them through the door which was not yet shut. For John had come to these Jews on their own principles and in their own practices,[1] and they had pretended to receive him, but had not ; but the publicans and the harlots had repented at his bidding. For all their broad fringes and conspicuous phylacteries, they — the priests, the separatists, the Rabbis of these people — were *worse* in the sight of God than sinners whom they would have scorned to touch with one of their fingers.

Then He bade them " hear another parable," the parable of the rebellious husbandmen in the vineyard, whose fruits they would not yield. That vineyard of the Lord of Hosts was the house of Israel, and the men of Judah were his pleasant plants ;[2] and they, the leaders and teachers, were those to whom the Lord of the vineyard would naturally look for the rendering of the produce. But in spite of all that He had done for His vineyard, there were no grapes, or only wild grapes. " He looked for judgment, but behold oppression ; for righteousness, but behold a cry." And since they *could* not render any produce, and *dared* not own the barren fruitlessness for which they, the husbandmen, were responsible, they insulted, and beat, and wounded, and slew messenger after messenger whom the Lord of the vineyard sent to them. Last of all, He sent His Son, and that Son — though they recognized Him, and could not *but* recognize Him — they beat, and flung forth, and slew. When the Lord of the vineyard came, what would He do to them ? Either the people, out of honest conviction, or the listening Pharisees, to show their apparent contempt for what they could not fail to see was the point of the parable, answered that He would wretchedly destroy those wretches, and let out the vineyard to worthier and more faithful husbandmen. A second time they had been compelled to an admission, which fatally, out of their own mouths, condemned themselves ; they had confessed with their own lips that it would be in accordance with God's justice to deprive them of their exclusive rights, and to give them to the Gentiles.

---

[1] Matt. xxi. 28—32, ἐν ὁδῷ δικαιοσύνης, minute obedience to the Law, the דֶּרֶךְ צְדָקָה of Prov. xvi. 31, &c. (Stier, iii. 113.)

[2] Matt. xxi. 33—46; Mark xii. 1—12; Luke xx. 9—19; Isa. v. 1—7 ; Ps. lxxx.

And to show them that their own Scriptures had prophesied of this their conduct, He asked them whether they had never read (in the 118th Psalm [1]) of the stone which the builders rejected, which nevertheless, by the marvellous purpose of God, became the headstone of the corner ? How could they remain *builders* any longer, when the whole design of their workmanship was thus deliberately overruled and set aside ? Did not their old Messianic prophecy clearly imply that God would call *other* builders to the work of His Temple ? Woe to them who even stumbled — as they were doing — at that rejected stone; but even yet there was time for them to avoid the more crushing annihilation of those on whom that stone should fall. To reject Him in His humanity and humiliation involved pain and loss; but to be found still rejecting Him when He should come again in His glory, would not this be " utter destruction from the presence of the Lord ? " To sit on the seat of judgment and condemn Him — *this* should be ruin to them and their nation ; but to be condemned by Him, would not this be to be " ground to powder ? " [2]

They saw now, more clearly than ever, the whole bent and drift of these parables, and longed for the hour of vengeance ! But, as yet, fear restrained them ; for, to the multitude, Christ was still a prophet.

One more warning utterance He spoke on this Day of Parables — the Parable of the Marriage of the King's Son. In its basis and framework it closely resembled the Parable of the Great Supper uttered, during His last journey, at a Pharisee's house ; but in many of its details, and in its entire conclusion, it was different. Here the ungrateful subjects who receive the invitation, not only make light of it, and pursue undisturbed their worldly avocations, but some of them actually insult and murder the messenger who had invited them, and — a point at which the history merges into prophecy — are destroyed and their city burned. And the rest of the story points to yet further scenes, pregnant with still deeper meanings. [3] Others are

---

[1] Comp. Isa. xxviii. 16 ; Dan. ii. 44 ; Acts iv. 11 ; Eph. ii. 20 ; 1 Pet. ii. 6, 7. Leaders of the people are called *pinnôth* in Judg. xx. 2, &c. Stier points out that this was the Psalm from which the Hosanna of the multitude was taken (iii. 125). The "head of the corner" (רֹאשׁ or פִּנָּה רֹאשׁ, $\varkappa\varepsilon\varphi\alpha\lambda\dot{\eta}$ $\gamma\omega\nu\acute{\iota}\alpha\varsigma$ or $\lambda\acute{\iota}\theta o\varsigma$ $\acute{\alpha}\varkappa\rho o\gamma\omega\nu\iota\alpha\widetilde{\iota}o\varsigma$) is the chief or foundation stone, sometimes placed at the angle of a building, and so binding two walls together. The $\alpha\widetilde{\upsilon}\tau\eta$ of Matt. xxi. 42 (Ps. cxviii. 23, LXX.) means "this doing," and is a Hebraism for $\tau o\widetilde{\upsilon}\tau o$ (וְאֵת) as in 1 Sam. iv. 7, LXX.

[2] Dan. ii. 34—44.

[3] The servants are ordered to go to the $\delta\iota\varepsilon\xi\acute{o}\delta o\iota$ of the roads to search for fresh guests, but we are only told that they went into the $\acute{o}\delta o\grave{\iota}$ (Matt. xxii. 9, 10) ; this delicate "reference to the imperfect work of human agents" is lost in our version. (Lightfoot, *Revision*, p. 68.)

invited; the wedding-feast is furnished with guests both bad and good; the king comes in, and notices one who had thrust himself into the company in his own rags, without providing or accepting the wedding garment, which the commonest courtesy required.[1]

This rude, intruding, presumptuous guest is cast forth by attendant angels into outer darkness, where shall be weeping and gnashing of teeth; and then follows, for the last time, the warning urged in varying similitudes, with a frequency commensurate to its importance, that " many are called, but few are chosen." [2]

Teachings so obvious in their import filled the minds of the leading Priests and Pharisees with a more and more bitter rage. He had begun the day by refusing to answer their dictatorial question, and by more than justifying that refusal. His counter-question had not only shown His calm superiority to the influence which they so haughtily exercised over the people, but had reduced them to the ignominious silence of an hypocrisy, which was forced to shield itself under the excuse of incompetence. Then followed His parables. In the first of these He had convicted them of false professions, unaccompanied by action; in the second, He had depicted the trust and responsibility of their office, and had indicated a terrible retribution for its cruel and profligate abuse; in the third, He had indicated alike the punishment which would ensue upon a violent rejection of His invitations, and the impossibility of deceiving the eye of His Heavenly Father by a mere nominal and pretended acceptance. Lying lip-service, faithless rebellion, blind presumption, such were the sins which He had striven to bring home to their consciences. And this was but a superficial outline of all the heart-searching power with which His words had been to them like a sword of the Spirit, piercing even to the dividing of the joints and marrow. But to bad men nothing is so maddening as the exhibition of their own self-deception. So great was the hardly-concealed fury of the Jewish hierarchy, that they would gladly have seized Him that very hour. Fear restrained them, and He was suffered to retire unmolested to His quiet resting-place. But, either that night or early on the following morning, His enemies held another council — at this time they seem to have held them almost daily — to see if they could not make one more combined, systematic, overwhelming effort " to entangle Him

---

[1] Zeph. i. 8.

[2] See Matt. vii. 13, 14; xix. 30; xx. 16. Those who cast forth the intruder are διάκονοι, "ministers," here representing angels; not the δοῦλοι. "Slaves" are human messengers of the earlier part of the parable, though rendered in our version by the same word.

in His talk," to convict Him of ignorance or of error, to shake His credit with the multitude, or embroil Him in dangerous relations towards the civil authority. We shall see in the following chapter the result of their machinations.

CHAPTER LI.

THE DAY OF TEMPTATIONS — THE LAST AND GREATEST DAY OF THE
PUBLIC MINISTRY OF JESUS.

"And the door was shut."— MATT. xxv. 10.

On the following morning Jesus rose with His disciples to enter
for the last time the Temple Courts. On their way they passed the
solitary fig-tree, no longer gay with its false leafy garniture, but
shrivelled, from the root upwards, in every bough. The quick eye
of Peter was the first to notice it, and he exclaimed, " Master, behold
the fig-tree which thou cursedst is withered away." The disciples
stopped to look at it, and to express their astonishment at the rapidity
with which the denunciation had been fulfilled. What struck them
most was the *power* of Jesus ; the deeper meanings of His symbolic
act they seem for the time to have missed ; and, leaving these lessons
to dawn upon them gradually, Jesus addressed the mood of their minds
at the moment, and told them that if they would but have faith in God
— faith which should enable them to offer up their prayers with perfect
and unwavering confidence — they should not only be able to perform
such a wonder as that done to the fig-tree, but even " if they bade this
mountain " — and as He spoke He may have pointed either to
Olivet or to Moriah — " to be removed, and cast into the sea, it
should obey them." But, since in this one instance the power had
been put forth to destroy, He added a very important warning.
They were not to suppose that this emblematic act gave them any
license to wield the sacred powers which faith and prayer would
bestow on them, for purposes of anger or vengeance; nay, *no*
power was possible to the heart that knew not how to forgive, and
the *unforgiving* heart could never be forgiven. The sword, and the
famine, and the pestilence were to be no instruments for *them* to
wield, nor were they even to dream of evoking against their enemies
the fire of heaven or the " icy wind of death." [1] The secret of successful prayer was faith ; the road to faith in God lay through pardon

---

[1] Some suppose that a breath of the simoom had been the agent in withering
the fig-tree.

of transgression; pardon was possible to them alone who were ready to pardon others.

He was scarcely seated in the Temple when the result of the machinations of His enemies on the previous evening showed itself in a new kind of strategy, involving one of the most perilous and deeply laid of all the schemes to entrap and ruin Him. The deadly nature of the plot appeared in the fact that, to carry it out, the Pharisees were united in ill-omened conjunction with the Herodians; so that two parties, usually ranked against each other in strong opposition, were now reconciled in a conspiracy for the ruin of their common enemy.[1] Devotees and sycophants — hierarchical scrupulosity and political indifferentism — the school of theocratic zeal and the school of crafty expediency — were thus united to dismay and perplex Him. The Herodians occur but seldom in the Gospel narrative. Their very designation — a Latinized adjective[2] applied to the Greek-speaking courtiers of an Edomite prince who, by Roman intervention, had become a Judæan king — showed at once their hybrid origin. Their existence had mainly a *political* significance, and they stood outside the current of religious life, except so far as their Hellenizing tendencies and worldly interests led them to show an ostentatious disregard for the Mosaic law.[3] They were, in fact, mere provincial courtiers; men who basked in the sunshine of a petty tyranny which, for their own personal ends, they were anxious to uphold. To strengthen the family of Herod by keeping it on

---

[1] Matt. xxii. 15—22; Mark xii. 13—17; Luke xx. 19—26. " Not the first or last instance in history, in which priests have used politicians, even otherwise opposed to them, to crush a reformer whose zeal might be inimical to both " (Neander, p. 397, Bohn). Previously we only find the Herodians in Mark iii. 6. They seem to be *political* descendants of the old *Antiochians* (2 Macc. iv. 9). (See Salvador, *Jésus Christ*, i. 162.) *Actually* they were perhaps the *Boethusîm* and their adherents, who had been allied to Herod the Great by marriage as well as by worldly interests. Herod the Great, when he fell in love with Mariamne, daughter of Simon, son of a certain Boethus of Alexandria, had made Simon High Priest by way of ennobling him. These Boethusîm had held the high-priesthood for thirty-five years, and shared its influence with the family of Annas. In point of fact, the priestly party of this epoch seem all to have been more or less Sadducees, and more or less Herodians. They had lost all hold on, and all care for, the people; and, though less openly shameless, were the lineal representatives of those bad pontiffs who, since the days of Jason and Menelaus, had tried to introduce " Greek fashions and heathenish manners " (2 Macc. iv. 13, 14).

[2] But *v. supr.*, p. 336.

[3] Their attempt to represent Herod the Great as the Messiah (!) (Tert. *Praescr.* 45, " qui Christum Herodem esse dixerunt "[337]) was a thing of the past. The *genuine* Sanhedrin, urging the command of Deut. xvii. 15, had unanimously appealed against Herod.

good terms with Roman imperialism, and to effect this good understanding by repressing every distinctively Jewish aspiration — this
was their highest aim. And in order to do this they Græcised their
Semitic names, adopted ethnic habits, frequented amphitheatres,
familiarly accepted the symbols of heathen supremacy, even went so
far as to obliterate, by such artificial means as they could, the distinctive and covenant symbol of Hebrew nationality. Thât the
Pharisees should tolerate even the most temporary partnership with
such men as these, whose very existence was a violent outrage on
their most cherished prejudices, enables us to gauge more accurately
the extreme virulence of hatred with which Jesus had inspired them.
And that hatred was destined to become deadlier still. It was already
at red-heat; the words and deeds of this day were to raise it to its
whitest intensity of wrath.

The Herodians might come before Jesus without raising a suspicion of sinister motives ; but the Pharisees, astutely anxious to put
Him off His guard, did not come to Him in person. They sent
some of their younger scholars, who (already adepts in hypocrisy)
were to approach Him as though in all the guileless simplicity of an
inquiring spirit.[1] They evidently designed to raise the impression
that a dispute had occurred between them and the Herodians, and
that they desired to settle it by referring the decision of the question
at issue to the final and higher authority of the Great Prophet.
They came to Him circumspectly, deferentially, courteously.
"Rabbi," they said to Him with flattering earnestness, "we know
that thou art true, and teachest the way of God in truth, neither
carest thou for any man ; for thou regardest not the person of men."
It was as though they would entreat Him, without fear or favor,
confidentially to give them His private opinion ; and as though they
really wanted His opinion for their own guidance in a moral question
of practical importance, and were quite sure that He alone could
resolve their distressing uncertainty. But why all this sly undulatory
approach and serpentine ensalivation ? The forked tongue and the
envenomed fang appeared in a moment. "Tell us, *therefore*" —
since you are so wise, so true, so courageous — "tell us, therefore, is
it lawful to give tribute to Cæsar, or not?" This capitation tax,[2]
which *we* all so much detest, but the legality of which these Herodians support, ought we, or ought we not, to pay it ? Which of us

---

[1] St. Luke (xx. 20) calls them ἐγκάθετοι, "*liers in ambush.*" Comp. Job xxxi. 9. ·
[2] ἐπικεφάλαιον (Mark xii. 15, Cod. Bezae); κῆνσον (Matt. xxii. 17); φόρον
(Luke xx. 22). Properly speaking, the κῆνσος was a poll-tax, the φόρος a payment for state purposes.

is in the right? — we who loathe and resent, or the Herodians who delight in it? [1]

He *must*, they thought, answer "Yes" or "No;" there is no possible escape from a plain question so cautiously, sincerely, and respectfully put. Perhaps He will answer, "*Yes, it is lawful.*" If so, all apprehension of Him on the part of the Herodians will be removed, for then He will not be likely to endanger them or their views. For although there is something which looks dangerous in this common enthusiasm for Him, yet if one, whom they take to be the Messiah, should openly adhere to a heathen tyranny, and sanction its most galling imposition, such a decision will at once explode and evaporate any regard which the people may feel for Him. If, on the other hand, as is all but certain, He should adopt the views of His countryman Judas the Gaulonite, and answer, "*No, it is not lawful,*" then, in that case too, we are equally rid of Him; for then He is in open rebellion against the Roman power, and these new Herodian friends of ours can at once hand Him over to the jurisdiction of the Procurator. Pontius Pilatus will deal very roughly with His pretensions, and will, if need be, without the slightest hesitation, mingle His blood, as he has done the blood of other Galilæans, with the blood of the sacrifices.

They must have awaited the answer with breathless interest; but even if they succeeded in concealing the hate which gleamed in their eyes, Jesus at once saw the sting and heard the hiss of the Pharisaic serpent. They had fawned on Him with their "Rabbi," and "true," and "impartial," and "fearless;" He "blights them with the flash" of one indignant word, "*Hypocrites!*" That word must have undeceived their hopes, and crumbled their craftiness into dust. "Why tempt ye me, ye hypocrites? Bring me the tribute-money." [2] They would not be likely to carry with them the hated Roman coinage with its heathen symbols, though they might have been at once able to produce from their girdles the Temple shekel. But they would only have to step outside the Court of the Gentiles, and borrow from the money-changers' tables a current Roman coin. While the people stood round in wondering silence they brought Him a denarius, and put it in His hand. On one side were stamped the haughty, beautiful features of the Emperor Tiberius, with all the wicked scorn upon the lip; on the obverse his title of *Pontifex Max-*

---

[1] Matt. xxii. 15—22; Luke xx. 19—26; Mark xii. 13—17.

[2] Mark xii. 15, 16, φέρετε . . . οἱ δὲ ἤνεγκαν.

imus! [1] It was probably due to mere accident that the face of the cruel, dissolute tyrant was on this particular coin, for the Romans, with that half-contemptuous concession to national superstitions which characterized their rule, had allowed the Jews to have struck for their particular use a coinage which recorded the name without bearing the likeness of the reigning emperor. [2] " Whose image and superscription is this ? " He asked. They say unto Him, " Cæsar's." *There*, then, was the simplest possible solution of their cunning question. " *Render, therefore, unto Cæsar the things that are Cæsar's.*" That alone might have been enough, for it implied that their national acceptance of this coinage answered their question, and revealed its emptiness. The very word which He used conveyed the lesson. They had asked, " Is it lawful to give " ($\delta o\tilde{v}\nu\alpha\iota$) ? He corrects them, and says, " Render " — " Give back " ($\dot{a}\pi\acute{o}\delta o\tau\varepsilon$). It was not a voluntary gift, but a legal due ; not a cheerful offering, but a political necessity. It was perfectly understood among the Jews, and was laid down in the distinctest language by their greatest Rabbis in later days, that to accept the coinage of any king was to acknowledge his supremacy. [3] By accepting the denarius, therefore, as a current coin they were openly declaring that Cæsar was their sovereign, and they — the very best of them — had settled the question that it *was* lawful to pay the poll-tax, by habitually doing so. It was their duty, then, to obey the power which they had deliberately chosen, and the tax, under these circumstances, only represented an equivalent for the advantages which they received. [4] But Jesus could not leave them with this lesson only. He added the far deeper and weightier words — " *and to God the things that are God's.*" To Cæsar you owe the coin which you have admitted as the symbol of his author-

---

[1] See Madden, p. 247 ; Akerman, p. 11, where plates are given. The coin would not bear the full name Tiberius, but Ti. Cæsar.

[2] See Keim, *Gesch. Jes.* iii. 136. The Essenes had a special scruple against coins which seemed to them to violate the second commandment ; and Jewish coins only bear the signs of palms, lilies, grapes, censers, &c. (See Ewald, *Gesch. Christ.*, p. 83 ; and the plates in Munk, Akerman, Madden, &c.)

[3] Maimonides, *Gezelah*, 5. " Ubicumque numisma alicujus regis obtinet, illic incolae regem istum pro domino agnoscunt." [338] In another Rabbinic tract Abigail objects to David's assertion that he is king, because the coins of Saul are current (*Jer. Sanhedr.* 20, 2). See too the curious anecdote in *Avod. Zar.* f. 6, quoted by Keim.

[4] Compare the command, given by Jeremiah (xxvii. 4—8), that the Jews should obey Nebuchadnezzar, to whom their apostacies had made them subject ; so too of Tiberius, Caligula, Nero, &c. (Rom. xiii. 1 ; 1 Pet. ii. 13, 14). The early Christians boasted of their quiet obedience to the powers that be (Justin, *Apol.* i. 17).

ity, and which bears his image and superscription; to God you owe yourselves.¹ Nothing can more fully reveal the depth of hypocrisy in these Pharisaic questioners than the fact that, in spite of the Divine answer, and in spite of their own secret and cherished convictions, they yet made it a ground of clamorous accusation against Jesus, that He had "*forbidden to give tribute unto Cæsar!*"²

Amazed and humiliated at the sudden and total frustration of a plan which seemed irresistible — compelled, in spite of themselves, to admire the guileless wisdom which had in an instant broken loose from the meshes of their sophistical malice — they sullenly retired. There was nothing which even *they* could take hold of in His words. But now, undeterred by this striking failure, the Sadducees thought that they might have better success.³ There was something more supercilious and offhand in the question which they proposed, and they came in a spirit of less burning hatred, but of more sneering scorn. Hitherto these cold Epicureans had, for the most part, despised and ignored the Prophet of Nazareth.⁴ Supported as a sect by the adhesion of some of the highest priests, as well as by some of the wealthiest citizens — on better terms than the Pharisees both with the Herodian and the Roman power — they were, up to this time, less terribly in earnest, and proposed to themselves no more important aim than to vex Jesus, by reducing Him into a confession of difficulty. So they came with an old stale piece of casuistry, conceived in the same spirit of self-complacent ignorance as are many of the objections urged by modern Sadducees against the resurrection of the body, but still sufficiently puzzling to furnish them with an argument in favor of their disbeliefs, and with a "difficulty" to throw in the way of their opponents. Addressing Jesus with mock respect, they called His attention to the Mosaic institution of levirate

---

¹ "Ut Caesari quidem pecuniam reddas, Deo temetipsum"³³⁹ (Tert. *De Idol.* xv.). (Wordsworth.)

² Luke xxiii. 2.

³ Matt. xxii. 23—33; Mark xii. 18—27; Luke xx. 27—39. Hitzig (*Ueber Joh. Marc.* 209) ingeniously conjectures that the narrative of the Woman taken in Adultery belongs to this place, so that there would have been on this day three separate temptations of Christ — the first *political*, the second *doctrinal*, the third *speculative*. But though Lange, Keim (iii. 138), Ellicott (p. 312), and others approve of this conjecture, it seems to me to have no probability. There is no shadow of external evidence in its favor; the subjective arrangement of the questions is rather specious than real; the events of life do not happen in this kind of order; and the attack of the Pharisees was in this instance *pre-arranged*, whereas the question about the adulteress rose spontaneously and accidentally.

⁴ They are scarcely mentioned except in Matt. xvi. 1.

marriages, and then stated, as though it had actually occurred,[1] a coarse imaginary case, in which, on the death without issue of an eldest brother, the widow had been espoused in succession by the six younger brethren, all of whom had died one after another, leaving the widow still surviving. " Whose wife in the resurrection, when people shall rise," they scoffingly ask, "shall this sevenfold widow be?" The Pharisees, if we may judge from Talmudical writings, had already settled the question in a very obvious way, and quite to their own satisfaction, by saying that she should in the resurrection be the wife of the first husband. And even if Jesus had given such a poor answer as this, it is difficult to see — since the answer had been sanctioned by men most highly esteemed for their wisdom — how the Sadducees could have shaken the force of the reply, or what they would have gained by having put their inane and materialistic question. But Jesus was content with no such answer, though even Hillel and Shammai might have been. Even when the idioms and figures of His language constantly resembled that of previous or contemporary teachers of His nation, His spirit and precepts differ from theirs *toto coelo*.[2] He might, had He been like any other merely human teacher, have treated the question with that contemptuous scorn which it deserved; but the spirit of scorn is alien from the spirit of the dove, and with no contempt He gave to their conceited and eristic dilemma a most profound reply. Though the question came upon Him most unexpectedly, His answer was everlastingly memorable. It opened the gates of Paradise so widely that men might see therein more than they had ever seen before, and it furnished against one of the commonest forms of disbelief an argument that neither Rabbi nor Prophet had conceived. He did not answer these Sadducees with the same concentrated sternness which marked His reply to the Pharisees and Herodians, because their purpose betrayed rather an insipid frivolity than a deeply-seated malice; but He told them that they erred from ignorance, partly of the Scriptures, and partly of the power of God. Had they not been ignorant of the power of God, they would not have imagined that the life of the children of

---

[1] Matt. xxii. 25, "There were *with us* seven brethren." On levirate marriages — so called from the Latin word *levir*, " a brother-in-law " — see Deut. xxv. 5—10.

[2] It must be steadily borne in mind that a vast majority, if not *all*, the Rabbinic parallels adduced by Wetstein, Schöttgen, Lightfoot, &c., to the words of Christ belong to a far subsequent period. These Rabbis had ample opportunities to light their dim candles at the fount of heavenly radiance, and "vaunt of the splendor as though it were their own." I do not assert that the Rabbis consciously borrowed from Christianity, but before half a century had elapsed after the resurrection, Christian thought was, so to speak, in the whole air.

the resurrection was a mere reflex and repetition of the life of the children of this world. In that heaven beyond the grave, though love remains, yet all the mere earthlinesses of human relationship are superseded and transfigured. "They that shall be accounted worthy to *obtain* that world, and the resurrection from the dead, neither marry nor are given in marriage; neither can they die any more; but are equal unto the angels; and are the children of God, being the children of the resurrection." Then as to their ignorance of Scripture,[1] He asked if they had never read in that section of the Book of Exodus which was called "the Bush," how God had described Himself to their great lawgiver as the God of Abraham, and the God of Isaac, and the God of Jacob. How unworthy would such a title have been, had Abraham and Isaac and Jacob then been but grey handfuls of crumbling dust, or dead bones, which should moulder in the Hittite's cave! "He is not the God of the dead, but the God of the living: ye therefore do greatly err." Would it have been possible that He should deign to call Himself the God of dust and ashes? How new how luminous, how profound a principle of Scriptural interpretation was this! The Sadducees had probably supposed that the words simply meant, "I am the God in whom Abraham and Isaac and Jacob trusted;" yet how shallow a designation would that have been, and how little adapted to inspire the faith and courage requisite for an heroic enterprise! "I am the God in whom Abraham and Isaac and Jacob trusted;" and to what, if there were no resurrection, had their trust come? To death, and nothingness, and an everlasting silence, and "a land of darkness, as darkness itself," after a life so full of trials that the last of these patriarchs had described it as a pilgrimage of few and evil years! But God meant more than this. He meant — and so the Son of God interpreted it — that He who helps them who trust Him here, will be their help and stay for ever and for ever, nor shall the future world become for them "a land where all things are forgotten."[2]

---

[1] Jesus proved to them the doctrine of the resurrection from the *Pentateuch*, not from the clearer declarations of the Prophets, because they attached a higher importance to the Law. It was an *à fortiori* argument, "Even Moses, &c." (Luke xx. 37). There is no evidence for the assertion that they *rejected* all the Old Testament except the Law. "The Bush" means the section so called (Exod. iii.), just as 2 Sam. i. was called "the Bow," Ezek. i. "the Chariot," &c. The Homeric poems are similarly named.

[2] R. Simeon Ben Eleazar refuted them by Numb. xv. 31 (*Sanhedrin*, 90, 6). It is, however, observable that the intellectual error, or ἀορασία, of the Sadducees was not regarded by our Lord with one-tenth part of the indignation which He felt against the moral mistakes of the Pharisees. Doubt has been thrown by

CHAPTER LII.

THE GREAT DENUNCIATION.

"Prophesy against the shepherds of Israel, prophesy." — EZEK. xxxiv. 2.

ALL who heard them — even the supercilious Sadducees — must have been solemnized by these high answers. The listening multitude were both astonished and delighted; even some of the Scribes, pleased by the spiritual refutation of a scepticism which their reasonings had been unable to remove, could not refrain from the grateful acknowledgment, "Master, thou hast well said." The more than human wisdom and insight of these replies created, even among His enemies, a momentary diversion in His favor. But once more the insatiable spirit of casuistry and dissension awoke, and this time a Scribe,[1] a student of the *Torah*, thought that *he* too would try to fathom the extent of Christ's learning and wisdom. He asked a question which instantly betrayed a false and unspiritual point of view, "Master, which is the great commandment in the Law?"

The Rabbinical schools, in their meddling, carnal, superficial spirit of word-weaving and letter-worship, had spun large accumulations of worthless subtlety all over the Mosaic law. Among other things they had wasted their idleness in fantastic attempts to count, and classify, and weigh, and measure all the separate commandments of the ceremonial and moral law. They had come to the sapient conclusion that there were 248 affirmative precepts, being as many as

---

some modern writers on the Sadducean rejection of the resurrection, and it has been asserted that the Sadducees have been confounded with the Samaritans; in the above-quoted passage of the Talmud, unless it has been altered (Geiger, *Urschrift*, 129 *n*), the reading is צדוקים, not כותיים (Derenbourg, *Hist. de Palest.* 131). Some writers have said that the Sadducees merely maintained that the resurrection *could not be proved from the Law* (מי התורה); if so, we see why our Lord drew His argument from the Pentateuch. That some Jewish sects accounted the Prophets and the *Kethubhim* of much less importance than the Law is clear from *Midr. Tanchuma* on Deut. xi. 26. (Gfrörer, i. 263.)

[1] Matt. xxii. 34—40; Mark xii. 28—34. St. Matthew says, νομικός, a word more frequently used by St. Luke than γραμματεύς, as less likely to be misunderstood by his Gentile readers; similarly Josephus calls the scribes ἐξηγηταὶ νόμου (comp. Juv. *Sat.* vi. 544).

the members in the human body, and 365 negative precepts, being as many as the arteries and veins, or the days of the year : the total being 613, which was also the number of letters in the Decalogue. They arrived at the same result from the fact that the Jews were commanded (Numb. xv. 38) to wear fringes (*tsitsith*) on the corners of their *tallith*, bound with a thread of blue ; and as each fringe had eight threads and five knots, and the letters of the word *tsitsith* make 600, the total number of commandments was, as before, 613.[1] Now surely, out of such a large number of precepts and prohibitions, *all* could not be of quite the same value ; some were "light" (*kal*), and some were "heavy" (*kobhed*). But which ? and what was the greatest commandment of all ? According to some Rabbis, the most important of all is that about the *tephillin* and the *tsitsith*, the fringes and phylacteries ; and "he who diligently observes it is regarded in the same light as if he had kept the whole Law."[2]

Some thought the omission of ablutions as bad as homicide ; some that the precepts of the Mishna were all "heavy ;" those of the Law were some heavy and some light. Others considered the *third* to be the greatest commandment. None of them had realized the great principle, that the wilful violation of one commandment is the transgression of all (James ii. 10), because the object of the entire Law is the spirit of *obedience to God*. On the question proposed by the lawyer the Shammaites and Hillelites were in disaccord, and, as usual, both schools were wrong : the Shammaites, in thinking that mere trivial external observances were valuable, apart from the spirit in which they were performed, and the principle which they exempli-

---

[1] Other Rabbis reckoned 620, the numerical value of the word כֶּתֶר (*kether*), "a crown." This style of exegesis was called Gematria (Buxtorf, *Syn. Jud.* c. ix. ; Bartolocci, *Lex. Rabb.* s. v.). The sages of the Great Synagogue had, however, reduced these to *eleven*, taken from Ps. xv., and observed that Isaiah reduced them to six (Isa. lv. 6, 7), Micah to three (vi. 8), and Habbakuk to one (ii. 4) (see *Maccoth*, f. 24). Hillel is *said* to have pointed a heathen proselyte to Lev. xix. 18, with the remark that "this is the essence of the Law, the rest is only commentary."

[2] Rashi on Numb. xv. 38—40. When R. Joseph asked R. Joseph Ben Rabba which commandment his father had told him to observe more than any other, he replied, "The law about tassels. Once when, in descending a ladder, my father trod on one of the threads, and tore it, he would not move from the place till it was repaired" (*Shabbath*, 118 *b*). These fringes must be of four threads, one being blue, which are to be passed through an eyelet-hole, doubled to make eight ; seven are to be of equal length, the eighth to have enough over to twist into five knots, which represent the five books of the Law ! &c. (Buxtorf, *ubi supra*, and Leo Modena, *Rites and Customs of the Jews*, I. ch. xi.). As for the *tephillin*, the precepts about them were amazingly minute. For the other points see *Tanch.*, f. 73, 2 ; *Jer. Berach.*, f. 3, 2.

fied; the Hillelites, in thinking that *any* positive command could in itself be unimportant, and in not seeing that great principles are essential to the due performance of even the slightest duties.

Still the best and most enlightened of the Rabbis had already rightly seen that the greatest of all commands, because it was the *source* of all the others, was that which enjoined the love of the One True God. Jesus had already had occasion to express His approval of this judgment,[1] and He now repeats it. Pointing to the Scribes' *tephillin*,[2] in which one of the four divisions contained the "*Shema*" (Deut. vi. 4) — recited twice a day by every pious Israelite — He told them that *that* was the greatest of all commandments, "Hear, O Israel, the Lord our God is one Lord;" and that the second was like to it, "Thou shalt love thy neighbor as thyself." Love to God issuing in love to man — love to man, our brother, resulting from love to our Father, God — on these two commandments hang all the Law and the Prophets.[3]

The question, in the sense in which the Scribe had put it, was one of the mere $\mu\alpha\chi\alpha\iota$ $\nu o\mu\iota\kappa\alpha\iota$, one of those "strivings about the Law,[4] which, as they were handled by the schools, were "unprofitable and vain." But he could not fail to see that Jesus had not treated it in the idle disputatious spirit or jangling logomachy to which he was accustomed, and had not in His answer sanctioned any of the common errors and heresies of exalting the ceremonial above the moral, or the Tradition over the Torah, or the decisions of Sopherim above the utterances of Prophets. Still less had He fallen into the fatal error of the Rabbis, by making obedience in one particular atone for transgression in another. The commandments which He had mentioned as the greatest were not special but general — not selected out of many, but inclusive of all. The Scribe had the sense to observe, and the candor to acknowledge, that the answer of Jesus was wise and noble. "Well, Master," he exclaimed, "thou hast said the truth;" and then he showed that he had read the Scriptures to some advantage by summarizing some of those grand free utterances of

---

[1] Luke x. 27. *V. supr.*, p. 454.

[2] The passages inscribed on the parchment slips which were put into the cells of the little leather boxes called *tephillin* were Exod. xiii. 1—10, 11—16; Deut. vi. 4—9; xi. 13—21. The sect of Perushim, or modern Pharisees, to this day $\pi\lambda\alpha\tau\acute{\nu}\nu o\nu\delta\iota$ $\tau\grave{\alpha}$ $\varphi\nu\lambda\alpha\kappa\tau\acute{\eta}\rho\iota\alpha$[340] (Matt. xxiii. 5).

[3] The expression "hangs" is probably proverbial, but some have seen in it a special allusion to the hanging *tsîtsith*, which were meant to remind them of the Law (Numb. xv. 39). (Stier, iii. 184.)

[4] Titus iii. 9.

the Prophets which prove that love to God and love to man is better than all whole burnt-offerings and sacrifices.[1] Jesus approved of his sincerity, and said to him in words which involved both gracious encouragement and serious warning, " Thou art not far from the kingdom of heaven." It was, therefore, at once easier for him to enter, and more perilous to turn aside. When he had entered he would see that the very spirit of his question was an erroneous and faulty one, and that " whosoever shall keep the whole law, and yet offend in one point, is guilty of all." [2]

No other attempt was ever made to catch or entangle Jesus by the words of His lips. The Sanhedrin had now experienced, by the defeat of their cunning stratagems, and the humiliation of their vaunted wisdom, that one ray of light from the sunlit hills on which His spirit sat, was enough to dissipate, and to pierce through and through, the fogs of wordy contention and empty repetition in which they lived and moved and had their being. But it was well for them to be convinced how easily, had He desired it, He could have employed against them with overwhelming force the very engines which, with results so futile and so disastrous, they had put in play against Him. He therefore put to them one simple question, based on their own principles of interpretation, and drawn from a Psalm (the 110th), which they regarded as distinctly Messianic.[3] In that Psalm occurs the expression, " The Lord (*Jehovah*) said unto my Lord (*Adonai*), Sit thou on my right hand." How then could the Messiah be David's son? Could Abraham have called Isaac and Jacob and Joseph, or any of his own descendants near or remote, his *lord?* If not, how came David to do so? There could be but one answer — because that Son would be divine, not human — David's son by human birth, but David's Lord by divine subsistence. But they could not find this simple explanation, nor, indeed, any other; they could not find it, because Jesus was their Messiah, and they had rejected Him. They chose to ignore the fact that He was, in the flesh, the son of David; and when, as their Messiah, He had called Himself the Son of God, they had raised their hands in pious horror,

---

[1] 1 Sam. xv. 22 ; Hosea vi. 6 ; Micah 6—8. Irenæus, *Haer.* i. 17, adds the ἄγραφον δόγμα, " I have long desired to hear such words, and have not yet found the speaker."

[2] James ii. 10.

[3] See *Midrash Tehillin ad* Ps. cx. 1 ; *Beresh. Rab.* 83, 4, quoted by Wetstein ; and the LXX. rendering of ver. 3, ἐκ γαστρὸς πρὸ Ἑωσφόρου ἐγέννησά σε [341] (Keim, iii. 158). See Ecclus. li. 10. The Chaldee Paraphrast has for Adonai, "*Meyimra*," *i. e.,* " the Word."

and had taken up stones to stone Him. So here again — since they had rejected the clue of faith which would have led them to the true explanation — their wisdom was utterly at fault, and though they claimed so haughtily to be leaders of the people, yet, even on a topic so ordinary and so important as their Messianic hopes, they were convicted, for the second time on a single day, of being "blind leaders of the blind."

And they loved their blindness; they would not acknowledge their ignorance; they did not repent them of their faults; the bitter venom of their hatred to Him was not driven forth by His forbearance; the dense midnight of their perversity was not dispelled by His wisdom. Their purpose to destroy Him was fixed, obstinate, irreversible; and if one plot failed, they were but driven with more stubborn sullenness into another. And, therefore, since Love had played her part in vain, "Justice leaped upon the stage;" since the Light of the World shone for them with no illumination, the lightning flash should at last warn them of their danger. There could now be no hope of their becoming reconciled to Him; they were but being stereotyped in unrepentant malice against Him. Turning, therefore, to His disciples, but in the audience of all the people,[1] He rolled over their guilty heads, with crash on crash of moral anger, the thunder of His utter condemnation.[2] So far as they represented a legitimate external authority He bade His hearers to respect them,[3] but He warned them *not* to imitate their falsity, their oppression, their ostentation, their love of prominence, their fondness for titles, their insinuating avarice, their self-exalting pride. He bade them beware of the broadened phylacteries and exaggerated tassels — of the long robes that covered the murderous hearts, and the long prayers that diverted attention from the covetous designs.[4] And then, solemnly

---

[1] Some of the Temple courts had room for at least 6,000 people (Jos. *B. J.* ii. 17, § 3), and it is probable that even more were assembled in them at the Passover, the torch-dance at the Feast of Tabernacles, &c.

[2] Matt. xxiii. 1—39. The attempt of Lange to bring these eight woes into allusive contrast with the eight beatitudes seems to me an instance of that misplaced ingenuity which has done much harm to sound exegesis.

[3] In the language spoken by our Lord there was a paronomasia between Moses (*Mosheh*) and *moshab*. This is another of the interesting probable indications as to the language which He ordinarily used (v. *supr.*, p. 93). There is another most marked Hebraism in Matt. xxiv. 22 (where οὐ πᾶς = οὐδείς, and σάρξ = ἄνθρωπος) and in verse 24 (δώσουσι), and xxvi. 18 (ποιῶ τὸ πάσχα).

[4] "Ye devour widows' houses." See Jos. *Antt.* xvii. 2, § 4, οἷς . . . ὑπῆρκτο ἡ γυναικωνῖτις. Most readers will recall modern parallels to this fact. As to the proselytism, see *Pirke Abhôth*, iv. 2. Ewald, *Gesch. Christ.*, p. 44, mentions that the word גיר, "to proselytize," was coined at this period. As to their immense

and terribly, He uttered His eightfold " *Woe unto you, Scribes and Pharisees, hypocrites*," scathing them in utterance after utterance with a flame which at once revealed and scorched. Woe unto them, for the ignorant erudition which closed the gates of heaven, and the injurious jealousy which would suffer no others to enter in ! Woe unto them for their oppressive hypocrisy and greedy cant! Woe for the proselytizing fanaticism which did but produce a more perilous corruption ! Woe for the blind hair-splitting folly which so confused the sanctity of oaths as to tempt their followers into gross profanity ![1] Woe for the petty paltry sham-scrupulosity which paid tithes of pot-herbs, and thought nothing of justice, mercy, and faith — which strained out animalculæ from the goblet, and swallowed camels into the heart![2] Woe for the external cleanliness of cup and platter contrasted with the gluttony and drunkenness to which they ministered! Woe to the tombs that simulated the sanctity of temples — to the glistening outward plaster of hypocrisy which did but render more ghastly by contrast the reeking pollutions of the sepulchre within ! Woe for the mock repentance which condemned their fathers for the murder of the prophets, and yet reflected the murderous spirit of

---

and pretentious self-assertion, see the numerous quotations and anecdotes from the Talmud in Gfrörer, *Jahrh. d. Heils.* pp. 144—149. One will be sufficient. They represent heaven itself as a Rabbinic school, of which God is the Head Rabbi. On one occasion God differs from all the angels on a question as to a leper being clean or unclean. They refer the decision to R. Ben Nachman, who is accordingly slain by Azrael, and brought to the heavenly Academy. He decides with God, who is much pleased. (*Babha Metzia*, f. 86 *a.*) The reader will be reminded of Pope's criticism on Milton—

> " In quibbles angel and archangel join,
> And God the Father turns a school divine."

There is a marked analogy between Rabbinism and Scholasticism. One might compare Hillel to Anselm, R. Jehuda Hakkôdesh to Thomas Aquinas, Gamaliel to Abelard, &c.

[1] The miserable quibbles by which, in consequence of such pernicious teaching, the Jews evaded their oaths, became notorious even in the heathen world. (See Martial, *Ep.* xi. 94.) The charges which our Lord uttered are amply supported by Jewish testimonies: *e. g.*, in Midrash Esth. i., f. 101,4, it is said that there are ten portions of hypocrisy in the world, of which *nine* are at Jerusalem (Schöttgen). Keim quotes some curious parallels from the Psalms of Solomon, the Assumption of Moses, and the Book of Enoch. On the Proselytism of the Jews, see Juv. *Sat.* xiv. 101. It was expressly enjoined in the *Pirke Abhôth*, iv. 2. In tithing anise they made it a question whether it was enough to pay tithes of the flower only, or also of the seed and stalk.

[2] διϋλίζοντες. Vulg. *excolantes;* cf. Amos vi. 6, πίνοντες διυλισμένον οἶνον, LXX. They filtered their water through linen to avoid swallowing any unclean insect (Lev. xi. 41—43).

those fathers — nay, filled up and exceeded the measure of their guilt by a yet deadlier and more dreadful sacrifice! Aye, on that generation would come all the righteous blood shed upon the earth, from the blood of righteous Abel to the blood of Zacharias, whom they slew between the porch and the altar.[1] The purple cloud of retribution had long been gathering its elements of fury : upon their heads should it burst in flame !

And at that point the voice which had rung with just and noble indignation broke with the tenderest pity — " O Jerusalem, Jerusalem, thou that killest the Prophets, and stonest them that are sent unto thee, how often would I have gathered thy children together, even as a hen gathereth her chickens under her wings, and ye would not![2] Behold, your house is left unto you desolate! For I say

---

[1] A Zacharias, the son of Baruch or Barachias, one of the most eminent and pious men of his day, was slain thirty-four years *after* this time by the Zealots, on a false accusation, in the midst of the Temple ($\dot{\alpha}v\dot{\alpha}$ $\mu\dot{\epsilon}\acute{o}ov$ $\tau o\tilde{v}$ $i\epsilon\rho o\tilde{v}$), and his body was flung from the Temple into the valley beneath (Jos. *B. J.* iv. 5, § 4). It is of course clear that *this* cannot be the Zacharias alluded to. Nor is there any authority for the belief of Origen, that the father of John the Baptist was martyred, or that he too was a son of Barachias. The *prophet* Zechariah was indeed a son of Berechiah (Zech. i. 1), but there is no reason to believe that he was put to death. We must therefore conclude that our Lord referred to Zechariah, *the son of Jehoiada* (which is the reading in the Gospel used by the Nazarenes), who was stoned by order of Joash " in the court of the house of the Lord." That he is referred to is clear, because (i.) this murder, in the order of the Jewish books, stood last in the Old Testament; (ii.) in dying, Zechariah had exclaimed, " *The Lord look upon it and require it ;*" (iii.) the Jews themselves had many most remarkable legends about this murder (see Lightfoot on Matt. xxiii. 35; Stanley, *Lectures on the Jewish Church*, p. 402), which made a deep impression on them, and which they specially believed to have kindled God's wrath against them (2 Chron. xxiv. 18). Consequently I believe that "son of Berechiah," which is not found (except in D) in Luke xi. 51, is a very early and erroneous gloss which has crept into the text. This is almost certainly the true explanation. In Matthew the words are omitted by א. The other suggestions — that Jehoiada had a second name, or that Zechariah was *grandson* of Jehoiada, and son of an unrecorded Berechiah — do not commend themselves by any probability. If it be asked why Jesus should have mentioned a murder which had taken place so many centuries ago, the answer seems to be that He intended to convey *this* meaning — " Your fathers, from beginning to end of your recorded history [a general expression, as we might say, ' The Jews from Genesis to Revelation '], rejected and slew God's prophets : you, as you share and consummate their guilt, so shall bear the brunt of the long-gathering Nemesis."

[2] This beautiful image also occurs in 2 Esdr. i. 30. This would be the closest parallel between the Apocrypha and any words of Christ, were it not that 2 Esdras i., ii. are interpolations found in the Latin and followed by our English version of the Apocrypha, but not found in the Arabic or Æthiopic. The germ of the image, under another form, is in Deut. xxxii. 11.

unto you, Ye shall not see me henceforth till ye shall say, Blessed is He that cometh in the name of the Lord." [1]

"Woe unto you, Scribes and Pharisees, *hypocrites.*" Some have ventured to accuse these words of injustice, of bitterness — to attribute them to a burst of undignified disappointment and unreasonable wrath. Yet is sin never to be rebuked? is hypocrisy never to be unmasked? is moral indignation no necessary part of the noble soul? And does not Jewish literature itself most amply support the charge brought against the Pharisees by Jesus? "Fear not *true* Pharisees, but greatly fear *painted* Pharisees," said Alexander Jannæus to his wife on his deathbed. "The supreme tribunal," says R. Nachaman, "will duly punish hypocrites who wrap their *talliths* around them to appear, which they are not, true Pharisees." Nay, the Talmud itself, with unwonted keenness and severity of sarcasm, has pictured to us the seven classes of Pharisees, out of which *six* are characterized by a mixture of haughtiness and imposture. There is the "Shechemite" Pharisee, who obeys the law from self-interest (cf. Gen. xxxiv. 19); the *Tumbling* Pharisee (*nikfi*), who is so humble that he is always stumbling because he will not lift his feet from the ground; the *Bleeding* Pharisee (*kinai*), who is always hurting himself against walls, because he is so modest as to be unable to walk about with his eyes open lest he should see a woman; the *Mortar* Pharisee (*medorkia*), who covers his eyes as with a mortar, for the same reason; the *Tell-me-another-duty-and-I-will-do-it* Pharisee — several of whom occur in our Lord's ministry; and the *Timid* Pharisee, who is actuated by motives of fear alone. The seventh class only is the class of "Pharisees from love," who obey God because they love Him from the heart.[2]

"Behold, your house is left unto you desolate!" And has not that denunciation been fearfully fulfilled?[3] Who does not catch an

---

[1] *i. e.* At the Second Advent (Zech. xii. 10 ; Hos. iii. 4, 5). The ποσάκις indicates that the ministry of Jesus in Jerusalem had been much fuller than the Synoptists record.

[2] *Jer. Berachôth,* ix. 7; *Bab. Sota,* f. 22 *a ; Abhôth de Rabbi Nathan,* xxxvii. (Otho, *Lex. Rab. ;* Cohen, *Déicides,* E. Tr., p. 152.) Perhaps the "Shechemite" Pharisee may be "the humpbacked" (*schikmi*) *i. e.*, "qui marchait le dos voûté comme s'il portait sur ses épaules le fardeau entier de la loi" [342] (Renan, *Vie de Jésus,* p. 204, *ed. pop.*). The passages are a little obscure, and in minor particulars the explanations differ. *Nikfi* is explained by some to mean the "flagellant" Pharisee (Derenbourg, *Hist. Pal.* p. 71). On the enormous pretensions and consummate hypocrisy of the Pharisees as a class, see *supr.,* p. 336, and Excursus IX., "Hypocrisy of the Pharisees."

[3] One poor Jew . . . stood in humble prayer, with his *tephilla* wrapped round

echo of it in the language of Tacitus — "Expassae repente delubri fores, et audita major humanâ vox *excedere Deos.*" [342] † Speaking of the murder of the younger Hanan, and other eminent nobles and hierarchs, Josephus says, "I cannot but think that *it was because God had doomed this city to destruction as a polluted city, and was resolved to purge His sanctuary by fire,* that He cut off these their great defenders and well-wishers; while those that a little before had worn the sacred garments and presided over the public worship, and had been esteemed venerable by those that dwelt in the whole habitable earth, were cast out naked, and seen to be the food of dogs and wild beasts." [1] Never was a narrative more full of horrors, frenzies, unspeakable degradations, and overwhelming miseries than is the history of the siege of Jerusalem. Never was any prophecy more closely, more terribly, more overwhelmingly fulfilled than this of Christ. The men going about in the disguise of women with swords concealed under their gay robes; the rival outrages and infamies of John and Simon; the priests struck by darts from the upper court of the Temple, and falling slain by their own sacrifices; "the blood of all sorts of dead carcases — priests, strangers, profane — standing in lakes in the holy courts;" the corpses themselves lying in piles and mounds on the very altar slopes; the fires feeding luxuriously on cedar-work overlaid with gold; friend and foe trampled to death on the gleaming mosaics in promiscuous carnage; priests, swollen with hunger, leaping madly into the devouring flames, till at last those flames had done their work, and what had been the Temple of Jerusalem, the beautiful and holy House of God, was a heap of ghastly ruin, where the burning embers were half-slaked in pools of gore.

And did not all the righteous blood shed upon the earth since the days of Abel come upon that generation? Did not many of that generation survive to witness and feel the unutterable horrors which Josephus tells? — to see their fellows crucified in jest, "some one way, and some another," till "room was wanting for the crosses, and crosses for the carcases?"— to experience the "deep silence" and the kind of deadly night which seized upon the city in the intervals of rage? — to see 600,000 dead bodies carried out of the gates? — to see friends fighting madly for grass and nettles, and the refuse of the drains? — to see the bloody zealots "gaping for want, and stumbling and stag-

---

his body and arms, *weeping as he uttered the words spoken by every Jew when he sees the Holy Land,* "WOE IS ME! THY HOLY CITIES ARE TURNED INTO DESERTS." (Frankl, ii. 344.)

[1] *B. J.* iv. 5, § 2 (Whiston). Comp. Mic. iii. 12.

gering along like mad dogs?"—to hear the horrid tale of the miserable mother who, in the pangs of famine, had devoured her own child?
—to be sold for slaves in such multitudes that at last none would buy
them?—to see the streets running with blood, and the "fire of burning houses quenched in the blood of their defenders?"—to have their
young sons sold in hundreds, or exposed in the amphitheatres to the
sword of the gladiator or the fury of the lion, until at last, "since the
people were now slain, the Holy House burnt down, and the city in
flames, there was nothing farther left for the enemy to do?" In that
awful siege it is believed that there perished 1,100,000 men, beside the
97,000 who were carried captive, and most of whom perished subsequently in the arena or the mine; and it was an awful thing to feel, as
some of the survivors and eye-witnesses — and they not Christians—*did*
feel, that "the city had deserved its overthrow by producing a generation of men who were the causes of its misfortunes;" and that
"neither did any other city ever suffer such miseries, nor *did any
age ever breed a generation more fruitful in wickedness than this
was, since the beginning of the world.*"[1]

---

[1] Every detail in these two paragraphs is taken from Jos. *B. J.* vi. 6—vi. 10,
passim. "A partir de ce moment la faim, la rage, le désespoir, la folie habitèrent
Jérusalem. Ce fut une cage de fous furieux, une ville de hurlements et de can-
nibales, un enfer."[343] (Renan, *L'Antechrist*, 506.)

CHAPTER LIII.

FAREWELL TO THE TEMPLE.

"Ecclesiâ Dei jam per totum orbem uberrime germinante Templum tamquam effoetum et vanum nullique usui bono commodum, arbitrio Dei auferendum fuit." [344] — OROS. vii. 9.

IT must have been clear to all that the Great Denunciation recorded in the last chapter involved a final and hopeless rupture. After language such as this there could be no possibility of reconciliation. It was "too late." The door was shut. When Jesus left the Temple His disciples must have been aware that He was leaving it for ever.

But apparently as He was leaving it — perhaps while He was sitting with sad heart and downcast eyes in the Court of the Women to rest His soul, troubled by the unwonted intensity of moral indignation, and His mind wearied with these incessant assaults — another and less painful incident happened, which enabled Him to leave the actual precincts of the House of His Father with words, not of anger, but of approval. In this Court of the Women were thirteen chests called *shopheroth*, each shaped like a trumpet, broadening downwards from the aperture, and each adorned with various inscriptions. Into these were cast those religious and benevolent contributions which helped to furnish the Temple with its splendid wealth. While Jesus was sitting there the multitude were dropping their gifts, and the wealthier donors were conspicuous among them as they ostentatiously offered their gold and silver. Raising His eyes, perhaps from a reverie of sorrow, Jesus at a glance took in the whole significance of the scene.[1] At that moment a poor widow timidly dropped in her little contribution. The lips of the rich contributors may have curled with scorn at a presentation which was the very lowest legal minimum. She had given two *prutahs* (פרוטות), the very smallest of current coins; for it was not lawful, even for the poorest, to offer only *one*. A *lepton*, or *prutah*, was the eighth part of an *as*, and was worth a little less than half a farthing, so that her

---

[1] Luke xxi. 1, ἀναβλέψας. Passages like "He that giveth alms in secret is greater than Moses himself;" "It is as well not to give as to give ostentatiously and openly," are quoted from the Talmud.

whole gift was of the value of less than a farthing; and with the shame of poverty she may well have shrunk from giving so trivial a gift when the rich men around her were lavishing their gold. But Jesus was pleased with the faithfulness and the self-sacrificing spirit of the gift. It was like the " cup of cold water " given for love's sake, which in His kingdom should not go unrewarded. He wished to teach for ever the great lesson that the essence of charity is self-denial; and the self-denial of this widow in her pauper condition was far greater than that of the wealthiest Pharisee who had contributed his gold. " For they all flung in of their abundance, but she of her penury cast in all she had, her whole means of subsistence." " One coin out of a little," says St. Ambrose, " is better than a treasure out of much ; for it is not considered how much is given, but how much remains behind." "If there be a willing mind," says St. Paul, "it is accepted according to that a man hath, and not according to that he hath not."

And now Jesus left the Temple for the last time ; but the feelings of the Apostles still clung with the loving pride of their nationality to that sacred and memorable spot.[1] They stopped to cast upon it one last lingering gaze, and one of them was eager to call His attention to its goodly stones and splendid offerings — those nine gates overlaid with gold and silver, and the one of solid Corinthian brass yet more precious; those graceful and towering porches; those bevelled blocks of marble forty cubits long and ten cubits high, testifying to the toil and munificence of so many generations; those double cloisters and stately pillars; that lavish adornment of sculpture and arabesque; those alternate blocks of red and white marble, recalling the crest and hollow of the sea-waves; those vast clusters of golden grapes, each cluster as large as a man, which twined their splendid luxuriance over the golden doors.[2] They would have Him gaze with them on the rising terraces of courts — the Court of the Gentiles, with its monolithic columns and rich mosaic; above this the flight of fourteen steps which led to the Court of the Women ; then the flight of fifteen steps which led up to the Court of the Priests; then, once more, the twelve steps which led to the final platform crowned by the actual Holy, and Holy of Holies, which the

---

[1] Matt. xxiv. 1; Mark xiii. 1; Luke xxi. 5, 6.

[2] *Bab. Succa*, fol. 51 *a*. (De Saulcy, *Herode*, p. 239.) The Talmudists, however, confessedly speak sometimes *literally* (לְפִי הפשט) and sometimes *hyperbolically* (לשון הנאי); and perhaps the accounts of this golden vine, and the veil which it took 300 priests to raise, are *meant* to be taken in the latter sense (see Reland, *Antt. Hebr.*, p. 139).

Rabbis fondly compared for its shape to a couchant lion, and which, with its marble whiteness and gilded roofs, looked like a glorious mountain whose snowy summit was gilded by the sun.[1] It is as though they thought that the loveliness and splendor of this scene would intercede with Him, touching His heart with mute appeal. But the heart of Jesus was sad. To Him the sole beauty of a Temple was the sincerity of its worshippers, and no gold or marble, no brilliant vermilion or curiously-carven cedar-wood, no delicate sculpturing or votive gems, could change for Him a den of robbers into a House of Prayer. The builders were still busily at work, as they had been for nearly fifty years, but their work, unblessed of God, was destined — like the earthquake-shaken forum of guilty Pompeii — to be destroyed before it was finished. Briefly and almost sternly Jesus answered, as He turned away from the glittering spectacle, "Seest thou these great buildings? there shall not be left one stone upon another which shall not be thrown down." It was the final $\dot{\varepsilon}\varkappa\chi\omega$-$\rho\tilde{\omega}\mu\varepsilon\nu$ — the "Let us depart hence" of retiring Deity. Tacitus and Josephus tell us how at the siege of Jerusalem was heard that great utterance of departing gods;[2] but now it was uttered in reality, though no earthquake accompanied it, nor any miracle to show that this was the close of another great epoch in the world's history. It took place quietly, and God "was content to show all things in the slow history of their ripening." Thirty-five years afterwards that Temple sank into the ashes of its destruction; neither Hadrian, nor Julian, nor any other, were able to build upon its site; and now that very site is a matter of uncertainty.[3]

Sadly and silently, with such thoughts in their hearts, the little band turned their backs on the sacred building, which stood there as an epitome of Jewish history from the days of Solomon onwards. They crossed the valley of Kidron, and climbed the steep footpath that leads over the Mount of Olives to Bethany. At the summit of

---

[1] This comparison is used by Josephus in that elaborate description of the Temple (B. J. v. 5) from which I have taken the above particulars. (Tac. Hist. v. 8, "immensae opulentiae templum." [345]) The splendid votive offerings of kings continued till the last: e. g., Agrippa hung up in it the golden chain presented to him by Caligula. Descriptions of the external appearance of the Temple and of Jerusalem at this time may be found in F. Delitzsch's pathetic story, Durch Krankheit zur Genesung. Eine Jerusal. Gesch. d. Herodianer-Zeit. (Leipz. 1873.)

[2] Jos. B. J. vi. 5, § 3; Tac. Hist. v. 13.

[3] Titus himself was amazed at the massive structures of Jerusalem, and saw in his conquest of it the hand of God (Jos. B. J. vi. 9, § 1). On the desolation of the Temple, compare 4 Esdr. x. 28. (Gfrörer, Jahrh. d. Heils, i. 72.)

the hill they paused, and Jesus sat down to rest—perhaps under the green boughs of those two stately cedar-trees which then adorned the summit of the hill. It was a scene well adapted to inspire most solemn thoughts. Deep on the one side beneath Him lay the Holy City, which had long become a harlot, and which now, on this day —the last great day of His public ministry—had shown finally that she knew not the time of her visitation. At His feet were the slopes of Olivet and the Garden of Gethsemane. On the opposite slope rose the city walls, and the broad plateau crowned with the marble colonnades and gilded roofs of the Temple. Turning in the eastward direction He would look across the bare, desolate hills of the wilderness of Judæa to the purpling line of the mountains of Moab, which glow like a chain of jewels in the sunset light. In the deep, scorched hollows of the Ghôr, visible in patches of sullen cobalt, lay the mysterious waters of the Sea of Lot. And thus, as He gazed from the brow of the hill, on either side of Him there were visible tokens of God's anger and man's sin. On the one side gloomed the dull lake, whose ghastly and bituminous waves are a perpetual testimony to God's vengeance upon sensual crime; at His feet was the glorious guilty city which had shed the blood of all the prophets, and was doomed to sink through yet deadlier wickedness to yet more awful retribution. And the setting sun of His earthly life flung deeper and more sombre colorings across the whole scene of His earthly pilgrimage.

It may be that the shadows of His thought gave a strange solemnity to His attitude and features as He sat there silent among the silent and saddened band of His few faithful followers. Not without a touch of awe His nearest and most favored Apostles—Peter, and James, and John, and Andrew—came near to Him, and as they saw His eye fixed upon the Temple, asked Him privately, "When shall these things be? and what shall be the sign of Thy coming, and of the end of the world?" [1] Their "*when?*" remained for the present unanswered. It was the way of Jesus, when some ignorant or irrelevant or inadmissible question was put to Him, to rebuke it not directly, but by passing it over, and by substituting for its answer some great moral lesson which was connected with it, and could alone

---

[1] Matt. xxiv., xxv.; Mark xiii. 3—37; Luke xxi. 7—38. In one of the unrecorded sayings of Christ, He answers the question thus: "When the two shall be one, and that which is without as that which is within; and the male with the female neither male nor female" (Clem. Rom. *Ep.* ii. 12; Clem. Alex. *Strom.* iii. 9, 63). (Westcott, *Introd.*, p. 431.)

make it valuable.[1] Accordingly, this question of the Apostles drew from Him the great Eschatological Discourse, or Discourse of the Last Things, of which the four moral key-notes are "Beware!" and "Watch!" and "Endure!" and "Pray."

Immense difficulties have been found in this discourse, and long treatises have been written to remove them. And, indeed, the metaphorical language in which it is clothed, and the intentional obscurity in which the will of God has involved all those details of the future which would only minister to an idle curiosity or a paralyzing dread, must ever make parts of it difficult to understand. But if we compare together the reports of the three Synoptists,[2] and see how they mutually throw light upon each other; if we remember that, in all three, the actual words of Jesus are necessarily condensed, and are only reported in their substance, and in a manner which admits of verbal divergencies; if we bear in mind that they are in all probability a rendering into Greek from the Aramaic vernacular in which they were spoken;[3] if we keep hold of the certainty that the object of Prophecy in all ages has been moral warning infinitely more than even the vaguest chronological indication, since to the voice of Prophecy as to the eye of God all Time is but one eternal Present, "one day as a thousand years, and a thousand years as one day;"[4] if, finally, we accept with quiet reverence and without any idle theological phraseology about the *communicatio idiomatum,*[346] the distinct assertion of the Lord Himself, that to Him, in His human capacity, were not known the day and the hour, which belonged to "the times and the seasons which the Father hath kept in His own power;"—if, I say, we read these chapters with such principles kept steadily in view, then to every earnest and serious reader I feel sure that most of the difficulties will vanish of themselves.

It is evident, from comparing St. Luke with the other Synoptists, that Jesus turned the thoughts of the disciples to two horizons, one near and one far off, as He suffered them to see one brief glimpse of the landscape of the future. The boundary line of either horizon

---

[1] Comp. Luke xiii. 23, 24.

[2] Matt. xxiv., xxv. ; Mark xiii. ; Luke xxi.

[3] Schott, for instance, has conjectured that the εὐθέως of Matt. xxiv. 29 is an unsuccessful representative of the Aramaic פתאם. It may be so, but the difficulty it creates is in great measure removed if, on turning to Luke xxi. 25, we see that the condensation of St. Matthew has omitted a particular which would remove the reference contained in the εὐθέως far into the future.

[4] Ps. xc. 4; 2 Peter iii. 8. St. Augustine wisely says, "Latet ultimus dies, ut observentur omnes dies." [345] †

marked the winding up of an *æon*, the συντέλεια αἰῶνος; each was a great τέλος, or ending; of each it was true that the then existing γενέα — first in its literal sense of " generation," then in its wider sense of " race " — should not pass away until all had been fulfilled. And the one was the type of the other; the judgment upon Jerusalem, followed by the establishment of the visible Church on earth, foreshadowed the judgment of the world, and the establishment of Christ's kingdom at His second coming. And if the vague prophetic language and imagery of St. Matthew, and to a less degree that of St. Mark, might lead to the impression that these two events were continuous, or at least nearly conterminous with each other, on the other hand we see clearly from St. Luke that our Lord *expressly warned* the inquiring Apostles that, though many of the signs which He predicted would be followed by the immediate close of one great epoch in the world's history, on the other hand the great consummation, the final Palingenesia, *would not follow at once*, nor were they to be alarmed by the troubles and commotions of the world into any instant or feverish expectancy.[1]   In fact, when once we have grasped the principle that Jesus was speaking partly and primarily of the fall of the Jewish polity and dispensation, partly and secondarily of the End of the World — but that, since He spoke of them with that varying interchange of thought and speech which was natural for one whose whole being moved in the sphere of Eternity and not of Time, the Evangelists have not clearly distinguished between the passages in which He is referring more prominently to the one than to the other — we shall then avoid being misled by any superficial and erroneous impressions, and shall bear in mind that before the final end Jesus placed two great events. The first of these was a long treading under foot of Jerusalem, until the times of the Gentiles (the καιροὶ ἐθνῶν, *i. e.*, their whole opportunities under the Christian dispensation) should be fulfilled;[2] the second was a preaching of the Gospel of the Kingdom to all nations in all the world.[3]   Nor can we deny all probability to the supposition that while the inspired narrators of the Gospel history reported with perfect wisdom and faithfulness everything that was essential to the life and salvation of mankind, their abbreviations of what Jesus uttered, and the sequence which they gave to the order of His utterances, were to a certain

---

[1] Luke xxi. 9, δεῖ γὰρ γενέσθαι ταῦτα πρῶτον, ἀλλ' οὐκ εὐθέως τὸ τέλος.[347] The same thing is brought out, but in obscurer sequence, by Matt. xxiv. 6; Mark xiii. 7, οὔπω τὸ τέλος.[348]   See Bossuet, *Médit. Dern.* Serm. 76.

[2] Luke xxi. 24.

[3] Matt. xxiv. 14.

extent tinged by their own subjectivity — possibly even by their own natural supposition — that the second horizon lay nearer to the first than it actually did in the designs of Heaven.

In this discourse, then, Jesus first warned them of false Messiahs and false prophets; He told them that the wild struggling of nations and those physical commotions and calamities which have so often seemed to synchronize with the great crises of History, were not to trouble them, as they would be but the throe of the Palingenesia, the first birth-pang of the coming time.[1] He prophesied of dreadful persecutions, of abounding iniquity, of decaying faith, of wide evangelization as the signs of a coming end. And as we learn from many other passages of Scripture, these signs, as they did usher in the destruction of Jerusalem, so shall reappear on a larger scale before the end of all things is at hand.[2]

The next great paragraph of this speech dwelt mainly on the *immediate* future. He had foretold distinctly the destruction of the Holy City, and He now gives them indications which should fore-warn them of its approach, and lead them to secure their safety. When they should see Jerusalem encompassed with armies — when the abomination which should cause desolation should stand in the Holy Place — then even from the fields, even from the housetops, they were to fly out of Judæa to the shelter of the Trans-Jordanic hills, from the unspeakable horrors that should follow. Nor even then were they to be carried away by any deceivableness of unright-eousness, caused by the yearning intensity of Messianic hopes. Many should cry, " Lo here! and lo there!" but let them pay no heed; for when He came, His presence, like lightning shining from the east even to the west, should be visible and unmistakable to all the world, and like eagles gathering to the carcase should the des-tined ministers of His vengeance wing their flight.[3] By such warn-

---

[1] Matt. xxiv. 8, ἀρχὴ ὠδίνων. חֶבְלֵי הַמָּשִׁיחַ, " les préludes de l'enfantement messianique "[349] (Renan, *L'Antechrist*, p. 290). As to the fulfilment of these prophecies, see Jos. *Antt.* xix. 1, § 2; Tac. *Ann.* xvi. 13; xii. 38; xv. 22; Sen. *Ep.* 91, and many other passages quoted by the commentators on this Gospel. The " Jewish War" of Josephus alone shows how accurately our Lord's words fore-shadowed the future; and Tacitus describing the same epoch (*Hist.* i. 2) calls jt " opimum casibus, atrox proeliis, discors seditionibus, ipsâ etiam pace saevum,"[350] and proceeds to speak of earthquakes (" haustae et obrutae urbes "[351]), adulteries, treacheries, violences, pollutions.

[2] See 1 Thess. v. 3 ; 2 Thess. ii. 2, &c.

[3] On the interpretation of this symbol, see p. 138 on Luke xvii. 37. That the " eagles" are primarily the Romans, finds additional illustration from the Book of Enoch xcii., where Pagan foes are compared to ravens and eagles. Legionary eagles were the very commonest symbols on Roman colonial coins, and so many

ings the Christians were preserved. Before John of Giscala had shut the gates of Jerusalem, and Simon of Gerasa had begun to murder the fugitives, so that "he who escaped the tyrant within the wall was destroyed by the other that lay before the gates" [1] — before the Roman eagle waved her wing over the doomed city, or the infamies of lust and murder had driven every worshipper in horror from the Temple Courts [2] — the Christians had taken timely warning, and in the little Peræan town of Pella, [3] were beyond the reach of all the robbery, and murder, and famine, and cannibalism, and extermination which made the siege of Jerusalem a scene of greater tribulation than any that has been since the beginning of the world. [4]

Then Jesus passed to the darkening of the sun and moon, and the falling of the stars, and the shaking of the powers of heaven — signs which may have a meaning both literal and metaphorical — which should precede the appearing of the Son of Man in heaven, and the gathering of the elect from the four winds by the trumpet-blast of the angels. That day of the Lord should have its signs no less than the other, and He bade His disciples in all ages to mark those signs and interpret them aright, even as they interpreted the signs of the coming summer in the fig-tree's budding leaves. But that day should come to the world suddenly, unexpectedly, overwhelmingly; and as it should be a day of reward to all faithful servants, so should it be a day of vengeance and destruction to the glutton and the drunkard, to the hypocrite and the oppressor. Therefore, to impress yet more indelibly upon their minds the lessons of watchfulness and faithfulness, and to warn them yet more emphatically against the peril of the drowsy life and the smouldering lamp, [5] He told them the exquisite

are still found in the East that they must have been very familiar to the Jews, who regarded them with special detestation. (Akerman, p. 15.) Cf. Jos. *Antt.* xvii. 6, § 3.

[1] Jos. *B. J.* iv. 9, § 10.

[2] On the outrages of the Zealots, see Jos. *B. J.* iv. 3, § 7. The terrifying usurpation of the Temple by these dreadful and murderous fanatics best corresponds with the βδέλυγμα τῆς ἐρημώσεως (comp. Dan. xii. 11; 1 Macc. i. 54), of which the first reference was to the profanation caused by Antiochus Epiphanes. On this "desolating wing of Abomination," see the note of Bishop Wordsworth.

[3] Euseb. (*Hist. Eccl.* iii. 5) says that they fled there in consequence of "a certain oracular utterance," and Epiphanius (*Haer.* i. 123) that they were warned by an angel.

[4] Matt. xxiv. 21. See Jos. *B. J.* v. 10, § 5, where he expressly says that there had been no generation so wicked, and no city so "plunged in misery from the beginning of the world."

[5] Matt. xxv. 8, αἱ λαμπάδες ἡμῶν σβέννυνται, not "our lamps *are gone out*," but "are smouldering," "are *being* quenched." The light of God's Holy

Parables — so beautiful, so simple, yet so rich in instruction — of the Ten Virgins and of the Talents; and drew for them a picture of that Great Day of Judgment on which the King should separate all nations from one another as the shepherd divideth his sheep from the goats. On that day those who had shown the least kindness to the least of these His brethren should be accounted to have done it unto Him. But then, lest these grand eschatological utterances should lead them to any of their old mistaken Messianic notions, He ended them with the sad and now half-familiar refrain, that His death and anguish must precede all else. The occasion, the manner, the very day are now revealed to them with the utmost plainness and simplicity: " Ye know that after two days is the Passover, and the Son of Man is betrayed to be crucified."

So ended that great discourse upon the Mount of Olives, and the sun set, and He arose and walked with His Apostles the short remaining road to Bethany. It was the last time that He would ever walk it upon earth; and after the trials, the weariness, the awful teachings, the terrible agitations of that eventful day, how delicious to Him must have been that hour of twilight loveliness and evening calm; how refreshing the peace and affection which surrounded Him in the quiet village and the holy home. As we have already noticed, Jesus did not love cities, and scarcely ever slept within their precincts. He shrank from their congregated wickednesses, from their glaring publicity, from their feverish excitement, from their featureless monotony, with all the natural and instinctive dislike of delicate minds. An Oriental city is always dirty; the refuse is flung into the streets; there is no pavement; the pariah dog is the sole scavenger; beast and man jostle each other promiscuously in the crowded thoroughfares. And though the necessities of His work compelled Him to visit Jerusalem, and to preach to the vast throngs from every climate and country who were congregated at its yearly festivals, yet He seems to have retired on every possible occasion beyond its gates, partly it may be for safety — partly from poverty — partly because He loved that sweet home at Bethany — and partly too, perhaps, because He felt the peaceful joy of treading the grass that groweth on the mountains rather than the city stones, and could hold gladder communion with His Father in heaven under the shadow of the olive-trees, where, far from all disturbing sights and sounds, He could watch the splendor of the sunset and the falling of the dew.

Spirit is dying away in the "earthen vessels" of our life. To a train of thought similar to the Parable of the Talents belongs the ἄγραφον δόγμα, "Be good money-changers" (γίνεσθε τραπεζῖται δόκιμοι).

And surely that last evening walk to Bethany on that Tuesday evening in Passion week must have breathed deep calm into His soul. The thought, indeed, of the bitter cup which He was so soon to drink was doubtless present to Him, but present only in its aspect of exalted sacrifice, and the highest purpose of love fulfilled. Not the pangs which He would suffer, but the pangs from which He would save; not the power of darkness which would seem to win a short-lived triumph, but the redeeming victory — the full, perfect, and sufficient atonement — these we may well, though reverently, believe to have been the subjects which dominated in His thoughts. The exquisite beauty of the Syrian evening, the tender colors of the spring grass and flowers, the wadys around Him paling into solemn grey, the distant hills bathed in the primrose light of sunset, the coolness and balm of the breeze after the burning glare — what must these have been to Him to whose eye the world of Nature was an open book, on every page of which He read His Father's name! And this was His native land. Bethany was almost to Him a second Nazareth; those whom He loved were around Him, and He was going to those whom He loved. Can we not imagine Him walking on in silence too deep for words — His disciples around Him or following Him — the gibbous moon beginning to rise and gild the twinkling foliage of the olive trees with richer silver, and moonlight and twilight blending at each step insensibly with the garish hues of day, like that solemn twilight-purple of coming agony into which the noon-day of His happier ministry had long since begun to fade?

CHAPTER LIV.

" So they weighed for my price thirty pieces of silver." — ZECH. xi. 12.

IT was inevitable that the burning words of indignation which Jesus had uttered on this last great day of His ministry should exasperate beyond all control the hatred and fury of the priestly party among the Jews. Not only had they been defeated and abashed in open encounter in the very scene of their highest dignity, and in the presence of their most devoted adherents ; not only had they been forced to confess their ignorance of that very Scripture exegesis which was their recognized domain, and their incapacity to pronounce an opinion on a subject respecting which it was their professed duty to decide ; but, after all this humiliation, He whom they despised as the young and ignorant Rabbi of Nazareth — He who neglected their customs and discountenanced their traditions — He on whose words, to them so pernicious, the people hung in rapt attention — had suddenly turned upon them, within hearing of the very Hall of Meeting, and had pronounced upon them — upon *them* in the odor of their sanctity — upon *them* who were accustomed to breathe all their lives the incense of unbounded adulation — a woe so searching, so scathing, so memorably intense, that none who heard it could forget it for evermore. It was time that this should end. Pharisees, Sadducees, Herodians, Priests, Scribes, Elders, Annas the astute and tyrannous, Caiaphas the abject and servile, were all now aroused; and, dreading they knew not what outburst of religious anarchy, which would shake the very foundations of their system, they met together probably on that very evening in the Palace of Caiaphas,[1] sinking all their own differences in a common inspiration of hatred against that long-promised Messiah in whom they only recognized a common enemy. It was an alliance, for His destruction, of fanaticism, unbelief, and worldliness ; the rage of the bigoted, the contempt of the atheist, and the dislike of the utilitarian ; and it seemed but too clear that from the revengeful hate of such a combination no earthly power was adequate to save.

---

[1] The name Caiaphas — a surname of the High Priest Joseph — is only another form of Kephas, " a stone " (Salvador, *Vie de Jésus*, ii. 104).

Of the particulars of the meeting we know nothing; but the Evangelists record the two conclusions at which the high conspirators arrived — the one a yet more decisive and emphatic renewal of the vote that He must, at all hazards, be put to death without delay; the other, that it must be done by subtilty, and not by violence, for fear of the multitude; and that, for the same reason — *not* because of the sacredness of the Feast — the murder must be postponed, until the conclusion of the Passover had caused the dispersion of the countless pilgrims to their own homes.

This meeting was held, in all probability, on the evening of Tuesday, while the passions which the events of that day had kindled were still raging with volcanic energy. So that, at the very moment while they were deciding that during that Easter-tide our Passover should *not* be slain — at that very moment, seated on the slopes of Olivet, Jesus was foretelling to His disciples, with the calmest certainty, that He *should* be sacrificed on the very day on which, at evening, the lamb was sacrificed, and the Paschal feast began.

Accordingly, before the meeting was over, an event occurred which at once altered the conclusions of the council, and rendered possible the immediate capture of Jesus without the tumult which they dreaded. The eight days' respite from the bitter sentence of death, which their terror, not their mercy, had accorded Him, was to be withdrawn, and the secret blow was to be struck at once.

For before they separated a message reached them which shot a gleam of fierce joy into their hearts, while we may well imagine that it also filled them with something of surprise and awe. Conscious as they must have been in their inmost hearts how deep was the crime which they intended to commit, it must have almost startled them thus to find "the tempting opportunity at once meeting the guilty disposition," and the Evil Spirit making their way straight before their face. They were informed that the man who knew Jesus, who had been with Him, who had been His disciple — nay, more, one of the Twelve — was ready to put an immediate end to their perplexities, and to re-open with them the communication which he had already made.

The house of Caiaphas was probably in or near the Temple precincts. The gates both of the city and of the Temple were usually closed at sundown, but at the time of this vast yearly gathering it was natural that the rules should have been a little relaxed for the general convenience; and when Judas slank away from his brethren on that fatal evening he would rely on being admitted without difficulty within the city precincts, and into the presence of the assembled elders. He applied accordingly to the "captains" of the Temple, the members of the Levitical guard who had the care of the sacred buildings,[1] and they at once announced his message, and brought him in person before the priests and rulers of the Jews.

Some of the priests had already seen him at their previous meeting; others would doubtless recognize him. If Judas resembled the conception of him which tradition has handed down —

> " That furtive mien, that scowling eye,
> Of hair that red and tufted fell " —

they could have hardly failed to notice the man of Kerioth as one of those who followed Jesus — perhaps to despise and to detest Him, as almost the only Jew among the Galilæan Apostles. And now they were to be leagued with him in wickedness. The fact that one who had lived with Jesus, who had heard all He had said and seen all He had done — was yet ready to betray Him — strengthened *them* in their purpose; the fact that they, the hierarchs and nobles, were ready not only to praise, but even to reward Judas for what he proposed to do, strengthened *him* in his dark and desperate design. As in water face answereth to face, so did the heart of Judas and of the Jews become assimilated by the reflection of mutual sympathy. As iron sharpeneth iron, so did the blunt weapon of his brutal anger give fresh edge to their polished hate.

Whether the hideous demand for blood-money had come from him or had been suggested by them; whether it was paid immediately or only after the arrest; whether the wretched and paltry sum given — thirty shekels, the price of the meanest slave [2] — was the total reward, or only the earnest of a further and larger sum — these are questions which would throw a strong light on the character and motives of Judas, but to which the general language of the Evangelists enables us to give no certain answer. The details of the transaction were probably but little known. Neither Judas nor his venerable abettors had any cause to dwell on them with satisfaction. The Evangelists and the early Christians generally, when they speak of Judas, seem to be filled with a spirit of shuddering abhorrence too deep for words. Only one dark fact stood out before their imagination in all its horror, and that was that Judas was a traitor; that Judas had been one of the Twelve, and yet had sold his Lord. Probably he received the money, such as it was, at once. With the gloating eyes of that avarice which was his besetting sin, he might gaze on the

---

[1] See 2 Chron. xxxv. 8; Acts iv. 1; v. 24.

[2] About £3 16s. (Exod. xxi. 32; cf. Gen. xxxvii. 28; Zech. xi. 12, 13).

silver coins, stamped (oh! strange irony of history!) on one side with
an olive branch, the symbol of peace, on the other with a censer, the
type of prayer, and bearing on them the superscription, "Jerusalem
the Holy."[1] And probably if those elders chaffered with him after
the fashion of their race, as the narrative seems to imply, they might
have represented that, after all, his agency was unessential; that he
might do them a service which would be regarded as a small convenience, but that they could carry out their purpose, if they chose,
without his aid. One thing, however, is certain: he left them a
pledged traitor, and henceforth only sought the opportunity to betray
his Master when no part of the friendly multitude was near.

What were the motives of this man? Who can attempt to fathom
the unutterable abyss, to find his way amid the weltering chaos, of a
heart agitated by unresisted and besetting sins? The Evangelists
can say nothing but that Satan entered into him. The guilt of the
man seemed to them too abnormal for any natural or human explanation. The narratives of the Synoptists point distinctly to avarice
as the cause of his ruin.[2] They place his first overtures to the Sanhedrin in close and pointed connection with the qualm of disgust he
felt at being unable to secure any pilferings from the "three hundred pence," of which, since they *might* have come into his possession, he regarded himself as having been robbed; and St. John, who
can never speak of him without a shudder of disgust, says in so
many words that he was an habitual thief.[3] How little insight can
they have into the fatal bondage and diffusiveness of a besetting sin,
into the dense spiritual blindness and awful infatuation with which
it confounds the guilty, who cannot believe in so apparently inadequate a motive! Yet the commonest observance of daily facts which

---

[1] In Matt. xxvi. 15, *ἔστησαν αὐτῷ* seems to mean "they paid," literally
"weighed" (cf. LXX., Zech. xi. 12, 13). It cannot be rendered with the Vulgate,
"constituerunt ei,"[351]† which is used to harmonize it with Mark xiv. 11 (*ἐπηγγεί-
λαντο*) and Luke xxii. 5 (*συνέθεντο*). In these matters, unimportant as regarded
their purpose, the Evangelists do not profess a rigidly minute accuracy. I should
infer, however, that Judas twice went before the priests — once to *promise* the
betrayal, and another time to *arrange its details.* Perhaps the money had been
promised on the first occasion, and paid on the second. St. Matthew only alludes
vaguely to the words of Zechariah. The supposed relation between the two
passages may be seen in Keil, *Minor Prophets*, ii. 373 (E. Tr.).

[2] We conclude that the loss of the 300 pence was the cause of the betrayal, from
the pointed manner in which the latter is narrated in immediate proximity to the
former; just as we conjecture that Nadab and Abihu were intoxicated when they
offered "strange fire," from the prohibition of strong drink to the priests immediately after the narration of their fate (Lev. x. 1—11).

[3] John xii. 6.

come before our notice in the moral world, might serve to show that the commission of crime results as frequently from a motive that seems miserably small and inadequate, as from some vast and abnormal temptation. Do we not read in the Old Testament of those that pollute God among the people "for handfuls of barley and for pieces of bread;" of those who sell "the righteous for silver and the poor for a pair of shoes?"[1] The sudden crisis of temptation might seem frightful, but its issue was decided by the entire tenor of his previous life; the sudden blaze of lurid light was but the outcome of that which had long burnt and smouldered deep within his heart.

Doubtless other motives mingled with, strengthened — perhaps to the self-deceiving and blinded soul substituted themselves for — the predominant one. "Will not this measure," he may have thought, "force Him to declare His Messianic kingdom? At the worst, can He not easily save Himself by miracle? If not, has He not told us repeatedly that He will die; and if so, why may I not reap a little advantage from that which is in any case inevitable? Or will it not, perhaps, be meritorious to do that of which all the chief priests approve?" A thousand such devilish suggestions may have formulated themselves in the traitor's heart, and mingled with them was the revulsion of feeling which he suffered from finding that his self-denial in following Jesus would, after all, be apparently in vain; that he would gain from it not rank and wealth, but only poverty and persecution. Perhaps, too, there was something of rancor at being rebuked; perhaps something of bitter jealousy at being less loved by Christ than his fellows; perhaps something of frenzied disappointment at the prospect of failure; perhaps something of despairing hatred at the consciousness that he was suspected. Alas! sins grow and multiply with fatal diffusiveness, and blend insensibly with hosts of their evil kindred. "The whole moral nature is clouded by them; the intellect darkened; the spirit stained." Probably by this time a turbid confused chaos of sins was weltering in the soul of Judas — malice, worldly ambition, theft, hatred of all that was good and pure, base ingratitude, frantic anger, all culminating in this foul and frightful act of treachery — all rushing with blind, bewildering fury through this gloomy soul.

"Satan entered into him." That, after all, whether a literal or a metaphorical expression,[2] best describes his awful state. It was a

---

[1] Ezek. xiii. 19; Amos ii. 6; viii. 6.

[2] "Satan" is sometimes, if not always, used by our Lord in senses obviously metaphorical (Matt. xvi. 23; Luke x. 18; xiii. 16, &c.).

madness of disenchantment from selfish hopes. Having persuaded himself that the New Kingdom was a mere empty fraud, he is suffered to become the victim of a delusion, which led him into a terrible conviction that he had flung away the substance for a shadow. It had not been always thus with him. He had not been always bad. The day had been when he was an innocent boy — a youth sufficiently earnest to be singled out from other disciples as one of the Twelve — a herald of the New Kingdom not without high hopes. The poverty and the wanderings of the early period of the ministry may have protected him from temptation. The special temptation — trebly dangerous, because it appealed to his besetting sin — may have begun at that period when our Lord's work assumed a slightly more settled and organized character.[1] Even then it did not master him at once. He had received warnings of fearful solemnity;[2] for some time there may have been hope for him; he may have experienced relapses into dishonesty after recoveries of nobleness. But as he did not master his sin, his sin mastered him, and led him on, as a slave, to his retribution and ruin. Did he slink back to Bethany that night with the blood-money in his bag? Did he sleep among his fellow-apostles? — All that we know is that henceforth he was ever anxiously, eagerly, suspiciously upon the watch.

And the next day — the Wednesday in Passion week — must have baffled him. Each day Jesus had left Bethany in the morning and had gone to Jerusalem. Why did He not go on that day? Did He suspect treachery? That day in the Temple Courts the multitude listened for His voice in vain. Doubtless the people waited for Him with intense expectation; doubtless the priests and Pharisees looked out for Him with sinister hope; but He did not come. The day was spent by Him in deep seclusion, so far as we know, in perfect rest and silence. He prepared Himself in peace and prayer for the awfulness of His coming struggle. It may be that He wandered alone to the hilly uplands above and around the quiet village, and there, under the vernal sunshine, held high communing with His Father in heaven. But How the day was passed by Him we do not know. A veil of holy silence falls over it. He was surrounded by the few who loved Him and believed in Him. To them He may have spoken, but His work as a teacher on earth was done.

And on that night He lay down for the last time on earth. On the Thursday morning, He woke never to sleep again.

---

[1] Luke x. 3.   [2] John vi. 70.

CHAPTER LV.

THE LAST SUPPER.

οὐκ ἔφαγε τὸν νομικὸν ἀμνὸν . . . ἀλλ' αὐτὸς ἔπαθεν ὡς ἀληθὴς ἀμνός.[352] — *Chron. Pasch.*, p. 12.

On the Tuesday evening in Passion week Jesus had spoken of the Passover as the season of His death. If the customs enjoined by the Law had been capable of rigid and exact fulfilment, the Paschal lamb for the use of Himself and His disciples would have been set apart on the previous Sunday evening; but although, since the days of the exile, the Passover had been observed, it is probable that the changed circumstances of the nation had introduced many natural and perfectly justifiable changes in the old regulations. It would have been a simple impossibility for the myriads of pilgrims to provide themselves beforehand with a Paschal lamb.

It was on the morning of Thursday — Green Thursday as it used to be called during the Middle Ages — that some conversation took place between Jesus and His disciples about the Paschal feast. They asked Him where He wished the preparation for it to be made. As He had now withdrawn from all public teaching, and was spending this Thursday, as He had spent the previous day, in complete seclusion, they probably expected that He would eat the Passover at Bethany, which for such purposes had been decided by rabbinical authority to be within the limits of Jerusalem. But His plans were otherwise. He, the true Paschal Lamb, was to be sacrificed once and for ever in the Holy City, where it is probable that in that very Passover, and on the very same day, some 260,000 of those lambs of which He was the antitype were destined to be slain.

Accordingly He sent Peter and John to Jerusalem, and appointing for them a sign both mysterious and secret, told them that on entering the gate they would meet a servant carrying a pitcher of water from one of the fountains for evening use; following him they would reach a house, to the owner of which they were to intimate the intention of the Master[1] to eat the Passover there with His disciples; and this householder — conjectured by some to have been

---

[1] Mark xiv. 14. The expression seems to imply that the owner of the house was a disciple; and still more the message, " My time is at hand."

Joseph of Arimathæa, by others John Mark — would at once place at their disposal a furnished upper room, ready provided with the requisite table and couches.[1] They found all as Jesus had said, and there "made ready the Passover." Full reasons will, however, be given in the Excursus for believing that this was not the ordinary Jewish Passover, but a meal eaten by our Lord and His Apostles on the previous evening, Thursday, Nisan 13, to which a quasi-Paschal character was given, but which was intended to supersede the Jewish festival by one of far deeper and diviner significance.[2]

It was towards the evening, probably when the gathering dusk would prevent all needless observation, that Jesus and His disciples walked from Bethany, by that old familiar road over the mount of Olives, which His sacred feet were never again destined to traverse until after death. How far they attracted attention, or how it was that He whose person was known to so many — and who, as the great central figure of such great counter-agitations, had, four days before, been accompanied with shouts of triumph, as He would be, on the following day, with yells of insult — could now enter Jerusalem unnoticed with His followers, we cannot tell. We catch no glimpse of the little company till we find them assembled in that "large upper room" — perhaps the very room where three days afterwards the sorrow-stricken Apostles first saw their risen Saviour — perhaps the very room where, amid the sound of a rushing mighty wind, each meek brow was first mitred with Pentecostal flame.

When they arrived, the meal was ready, the table spread, the *triclinia* laid with cushions for the guests. Imagination loves to reproduce all the probable details of that deeply moving and eternally sacred scene; and if we compare the notices of ancient Jewish custom, with the immemorial fashions still existing in the changeless East, we can feel but little doubt as to the general nature of the arrangements. They were totally unlike those with which the genius of Leonardo da Vinci, and other great painters, has made us so familiar. The room probably had white walls, and was bare of all except the most necessary furniture and adornment. The couches or cushions, each large enough to hold three persons, were placed around three sides of one or more low tables of gaily painted wood, each scarcely higher than stools. The seat of honor was the central one of the central *triclinium*, or mat. This was, of course, occupied by the Lord. Each guest reclined at full length, leaning on his left

---

[1] Mark xiv. 15, ἐστρωμένον; cf. στρῶσον σεαυτῷ (Acts ix. 34). The notion that the word means "paved" is an error. See Ezek. xxiii. 41, LXX.

[2] See Excursus X., " Was the Last Supper an Actual Passover ?"

elbow, that his right hand might be free.[1] At the right hand of Jesus reclined the beloved disciple, whose head therefore could, at any moment, be placed upon the breast of his friend and Lord.

It may be that the very act of taking their seats at the table had, once more, stirred up in the minds of the Apostles those disputes about precedence[2] which, on previous occasions, our Lord had so tenderly and beautifully rebuked.[3] The mere question of a place at table might seem a matter too infinitesimal and unimportant to ruffle the feelings of good and self-denying men at an hour so supreme and solemn ; but that love for " the chief seats " at feasts and elsewhere, which Jesus had denounced in the Pharisees, is not only innate in the human heart, but is even so powerful that it has at times caused the most terrific tragedies.[4] But at this moment, when the soul of Jesus was full of such sublime purpose — when He was breathing the pure unmingled air of Eternity, and the Eternal was to Him, in spite of His mortal investiture, not only the present but the seen — a strife of this kind must have been more than ever painful. It showed how little, as yet, even these His chosen followers had entered into the meaning of His life. It showed that the evil spirits of pride and selfishness were not yet exorcised from their struggling souls. It showed that, even now, they had wholly failed to understand His many and earnest warnings as to the nature of His kingdom, and the certainty of His fate. That *some* great crisis was at hand — that their Master was to suffer and be slain — they *must* have partially realized ; but they seem to have regarded this as a mere temporary obscuration, to be followed by an immediate divulgence of His splendor, and the setting up on earth of His Messianic throne.

In pained silence Jesus had heard their murmured jealousies, while they were arranging their places at the feast.[5] Not by mere verbal

---

[1] The custom of eating the Passover standing had long been abandoned. Reclining was held to be the proper attitude, because it was that of free men (Maimon. *Pesach.* 10, 1).

[2] Luke xxii. 24.

[3] Mark ix. 34; Matt. xviii. 1. See *supra*, pp. 389, 487. It is a not impossible conjecture that the dispute may have been stirred up by a claim of *Judas* as being an office-bearer in the little band.

[4] Many will recall the famous scene between Criemhilt and Brunhilt in the *Niebelungen.* In the Middle Ages blood was shed at the very altar of St. John's Lateran in a furious dispute about precedence between an abbot and a bishop.

[5] John xiii. 2. γινομένου (א, B, L. &c.) is probably the right reading, but even γενομένου cannot mean " supper being ended," as in the E. V. (see xiii. 26), but " when it was supper-time."

reproof, but by an act more profoundly significant and touching, He determined to teach to them, and to all who love Him, a nobler lesson.

Every Eastern room, if it belongs to any but the very poorest, has the central part of the floor covered with mats, and as a person enters, he lays aside his sandals at the door of the room, mainly in order not to defile the clean white mats with the dust and dirt of the road or streets, and also (at any rate among Mahometans) because the mat is hallowed by being knelt upon in prayer. Before they reclined at the table, the disciples had doubtless conformed to this cleanly and reasonable custom ; but another customary and pleasant habit, which we know that Jesus appreciated, had been neglected. Their feet must have been covered with dust from their walk along the hot and much frequented road from Bethany to Jerusalem, and under such circumstances they would have been refreshed for the festival by washing their feet after putting off their sandals. But to wash the feet was the work of slaves ; and since no one had offered to perform the kindly office, Jesus Himself, in His eternal humility and self-denial, rose from His place at the meal to do the menial service which none of His disciples had offered to do for Him.[1] Well may the amazement of the beloved disciple show itself in his narrative, as he dwells on every particular of that solemn scene. "Though He knew that the Father had given all things into His hands, and that He came from God and was going to God, He arose from the supper and laid aside His garments, and taking a towel, girded Himself." It is probable that in the utterness of self-abnegation, He entirely stripped His upper limbs, laying aside both the *simchah* and the *cetôneth*, as though He had been the meanest slave, and wrapping the towel round His waist. Then pouring water into the large copper basin with which an Oriental house is always provided, He began without a word to wash His disciples' feet, and wipe them dry with the towel which served Him as a girdle. Awe and shame kept them silent until He came to Peter, whose irrepressible emotions found vent in the surprised, half-indignant question, "Lord, dost *Thou* seek to wash *my* feet?" Thou, the Son of God, the King of Israel, who hast the words of eternal life — Thou, whose feet Oriental kings should anoint with their costliest spikenard, and penitents bathe in precious tears — dost thou wash Peter's feet? It was the old dread and self-depreciation which, more than three years before, had prompted the cry of the rude fisherman of Galilee, "Depart from

---

[1] John xiii. 1—20.

me, for I am a sinful man, O Lord ; " [1] it was the old self-will which, a year before, had expressed itself in the self-confident dissuasion of the elated Man of Rock — "That be far from Thee, Lord ; this shall not happen unto Thee." [2] Gently recognizing what was good in His impetuous follower's ejaculation, Jesus calmly tells him that as yet he is too immature to understand the meaning of His actions, though the day should come when their significance should dawn upon him. But Peter, obstinate and rash — as though he felt, even more than his Lord, the greatness of Him that ministered, and the meanness of him to whom the service would be done — persisted in his opposition : "Never, never, till the end of time," [3] he impetuously exclaims ; "shalt thou wash my feet ? " But then Jesus revealed to him the dangerous self-assertion which lurked in this false humility. "If I wash thee not, thou hast no share with me." Alike, thy self-conceit and thy self-disgust must be laid aside if thou wouldest be mine. My follower must accept my will, even when he least can comprehend it, even when it seems to violate his own conceptions of what I am. That calm word changed the whole current of thought and feeling in the warm-hearted passionate disciple. "No share with Thee ? oh, forbid it, Heaven ! Lord, not my feet only, but also my hands and my head ! " But no : once more he must accept what Christ wills, not in his own way, but in Christ's way. This total washing was not needed. The baptism of his initiation was over ; in that laver of regeneration he had been already dipped. Nothing more was needed than the daily cleansing from minor and freshly-contracted stains. The feet soiled with the clinging dust of daily sins, these must be washed in daily renovation ; but the heart and being of the man, these were already washed, were cleansed, were sanctified. "Jesus saith to him, He that is bathed ($\lambda\epsilon\lambda o\upsilon\mu\acute{\epsilon}\nu o\varsigma$) hath no need save to wash ($\nu\acute{\iota}\psi\alpha\sigma\theta\alpha\iota$) his feet, but is clean every whit. And ye are clean ; " and then He was forced to add with a deep sigh, "but not all." The last words were an allusion to His consciousness of one traitorous presence ; for *He* knew, what as yet *they* knew not, that the hands of the Lord of Life had just washed the traitor's feet. Oh, strange unfathomable depth of human infatuation and ingratitude ! that traitor, with all the black and accursed treachery in his false heart, had seen, had known, had suffered it ; had felt the touch of those kind and gentle hands, had been refreshed by the cleansing

[1] See *supra*, p. 198.
[2] See *supra*, p. 376.
[3] John xiii. 8, $o\grave{\upsilon}\ \mu\grave{\eta}$ . . . $\epsilon\acute{\iota}\varsigma\ \tau\grave{o}\nu\ a\grave{\iota}\tilde{\omega}\nu a$.

water, had seen that sacred head bent over his feet, yet stained as they yet were with the hurried secret walk which had taken him into the throng of sanctimonious murderers over the shoulder of Olivet. But for him there had been no purification in that lustral water; neither was the devil within him exorcised by that gentle voice, nor the leprosy of his heart healed by that miracle-producing touch.

The other Apostles did not at the moment notice that grievous exception — " but not all." It may be that their consciences gave to all, even to the most faithful, too sad a cause to echo the words, with something of misgiving, to his own soul. Then Jesus, after having washed their feet, resumed His garments, and once more reclined at the meal. As He leaned there on His left elbow, John lay at his right, with his head quite close to Jesus' breast. Next to John, and at the top of the next mat or cushion, would probably be his brother James; and — as we infer from the few details of the meal — at the left of Jesus lay the Man of Kerioth, who may either have thrust himself into that position, or who, as the holder of the common purse, occupied a place of some prominence among the little band. It seems probable that Peter's place was at the top of the next mat, and at the left of Judas. And as the meal began, Jesus taught them what His act had meant. Rightly, and with proper respect, they called Him " Master " and " Lord," for so He was; yet, though the Lord is greater than the slave, the Sender greater than His Apostle, He their Lord and Master had washed their feet. It was a kind and gracious task, and such ought to be the nature of all their dealings with each other. He had done it to teach them humility, to teach them self-denial, to teach them love: blessed they if they learnt the lesson! blessed if they learnt that the struggles for precedence, the assertions of claims, the standings upon dignity, the fondness for the mere exercise of authority, marked the tyrannies and immaturities of heathendom, and that the greatest Christian is ever the humblest. He should be chief among them who, for the sake of others, gladly laid on himself the lowliest burdens, and sought for himself the humblest services. Again and again He warned them that they were not to look for earthly reward or earthly prosperity; the throne, and the table, and the kingdom, and the many mansions were not of earth.[1]

---

[1] It is probable that to find the full scope of what Jesus taught on this occasion we must combine (as I have done) Luke xxii. 24—30 with John xiii. 1—17. In Luke xxii. 25 is illustrated, by the title Εὐεργέτης, "benefactor," common on the coins of the Syrian kings.

And then again the trouble of His spirit broke forth. He was speaking of those whom He had chosen; He was not speaking of them all. Among the blessed company sat one who even then was drawing on his own head a curse. It had been so with David, whose nearest friend had become his bitterest foe; it was foreordained that it should be so likewise with David's Son. Soon should they know with what full foreknowledge He had gone to all that awaited Him; soon should they be able to judge that, just as the man who receives in Christ's name His humblest servant receiveth Him, so the rejection of Him is the rejection of His Father, and that this rejection of the Living God was the crime which at this moment was being committed, and committed in their very midst.

There, next but one to Him, hearing all these words unmoved, full of spite and hatred, utterly hardening his heart, and leaning the whole weight of his demoniac possession against that door of mercy which even now and even here His Saviour would have opened to him, sat Judas, the false smile of hypocrisy on his face, but rage, and shame, and greed, and anguish, and treachery in his heart. The near presence of that black iniquity, the failure of even His pathetic lowliness to move or touch the man's hideous purpose, troubled the human heart of Jesus to its inmost depths — wrung from Him His agony of yet plainer prediction, " Verily, verily, I say unto you, that *one of you* shall betray me! " That night *all*, even the best beloved, were to forsake Him, but it was not *that;* that night even the boldest-hearted was to deny Him with oaths, but it was not *that;* nay, but one of them was to *betray* Him. Their hearts misgave them as they listened. Already a deep unspeakable sadness had fallen over the sacred meal. Like the sombre and threatening crimson that intermingles with the colors of sunset, a dark omen seemed to be overshadowing them — a shapeless presentiment of evil — an unspoken sense of dread. If all their hopes were to be thus blighted — if at this very Passover, He for whom they had given up all, and who had been to them all in all, was indeed to be betrayed by one of themselves to an unpitied and ignominious end — if *this* were possible, *anything* seemed possible. Their hearts were troubled. All their want of nobility, all their failure in love, all the depth of their selfishness, all the weakness of their faith —

> " Every evil thought they ever thought,
> And every evil word they ever said,
> And every evil thing they ever did,"

all crowded upon their memories, and made their consciences afraid.

None of them seemed safe from *anything*, and each read his own self-distrust in his brother-disciple's eye. And hence, at that moment of supreme sadness and almost despair, it was with lips that faltered and cheeks that paled, that each asked the humble question, " Lord, is it I ? " Better always that question than " Is it *he ?* " — better the penitent watchfulness of a self-condemning humility than the haughty Pharisaism of censorious pride. The very horror that breathed through their question, the very trustfulness which prompted it, involved their acquittal. Jesus only remained silent, in order that even then, if it were possible, there might be time for Judas to repent. But Peter was unable to restrain his sorrow and his impatience. Eager to know and to prevent the treachery — unseen by Jesus, whose back was turned to him as He reclined at the meal — he made a signal to John to ask " who it was." [1] The head of John was close to Jesus, and laying it with affectionate trustfulness on his Master's breast, he said in a whisper, " Lord, who is it ? " [2] The reply, given in a tone equally low, was heard by St. John alone, and confirmed the suspicions with which it is evident that the repellant nature of Judas had already inspired him. At Eastern meals all the guests eat with their fingers out of a common dish, and it is common for one at times to dip into the dish a piece of the thin flexible cake of bread which is placed by each, and taking up with it a portion of the meat or rice in the dish, to hand it to another guest. So ordinary an incident of any daily meal would attract no notice whatever. [3] Jesus handed to the traitor Apostle a " sop " of this kind, and this, as He told St. John, was the sign which should indicate to him, and possibly through him to St. Peter, which was the guilty member of the little band. And then He added aloud, in words which can have but one significance, in words the most awful and crushing that ever passed His lips, " The Son of Man goeth indeed, as it is written of Him ; but woe unto that man by whom the Son of Man is betrayed ! It were good for that

---

[1] John xiii. 24. This is the reading of many MSS. (א, A, D, E, F, &c.), and of our version ; but many good MSS. (B, C, L) read εἰπὲ τίς ἐστι ; as though St. Peter assumed that the beloved disciple, at any rate, *must* know the secret. Perhaps the true rendering should be, " Say " (to Jesus), " Who is it ? "

[2] John xiii. 23, ἀνακείμενος ἐν τῷ κόλπῳ ; ver. 25, ἐπιπεσὼν ἐπὶ τὸ στῆθος (א, A, D, &c.). The οὕτως of B, C, L makes it still more graphic. The impression made by this affectionate change of attitude may be seen from John xxi. 20 (ἀνέπεσεν), and the change from κόλπος to στῆθος marks the eye-witness.

[3] We can hardly argue frem τὸ τρυβλίον that there was only *one* dish, though this is in itself probable enough ; nor need τὸν ἄρτον (Matt. xxvi. 26) imply that there was but one loaf.

man if he had not been born!" "Words," it has been well said, "of immeasurable ruin, words of immeasurable woe" — and the more terrible because uttered by the lips of immeasurable Love; words capable, if any were capable, of revealing to the lost soul of the traitor all the black gulf of horror that was yawning before his feet. He must have known something of what had passed; he may well have overheard some fragment of the conversation, or at least have had a dim consciousness that in some way it referred to him. He may even have been aware that when his hand met the hand of Jesus over the dish there was some meaning in the action. When the others were questioning among themselves "which was the traitor?" he had remained silent in the defiant hardness of contempt or the sullen gloom of guilt; but now — stung, it may be, by some sense of the shuddering horror with which the mere possibility of his guilt was regarded — he nerved himself for the shameful and shameless question. After all the rest had sunk into silence, there grated upon the Saviour's ear that hoarse untimely whisper, in all the bitterness of its defiant mockery — not asking, as the rest had asked, in loving reverence, "*Lord*, is it I?" but with the cold formal title, "*Rabbi*, is it I?" Then that low unreproachful answer, "Thou hast said," sealed his guilt. The rest did not hear it; it was probably caught by Peter and John alone; and Judas ate the sop which Jesus had given him, and after the sop Satan entered into him. As all the winds, on some night of storm, riot and howl through the rent walls of some desecrated shrine, so through the ruined life of Judas envy and avarice, and hatred and ingratitude, were rushing all at once. In that bewildering chaos of a soul spotted with mortal guilt, the Satanic had triumphed over the human; in that dark heart earth and hell were thenceforth at one; in that lost soul sin had conceived and brought forth death. "What thou art doing, do more quickly," said Jesus to him aloud. He knew what the words implied, he knew that they meant, "Thy fell purpose is matured, carry it out with no more of these futile hypocrisies and meaningless delays." Judas rose from the feast. The innocent-hearted Apostles thought that Jesus had bidden him go out and make purchases for to-morrow's Passover, or give something out of the common store which should enable the poor to buy their Paschal lamb. And so from the lighted room, from the holy banquet, from the blessed company, from the presence of his Lord, he went immediately out, and — as the beloved disciple adds, with a shudder of dread significance letting the curtain of darkness fall for ever on that appalling figure — "*and it was night*."

We cannot tell with any certainty whether this took place before or after the institution of the Lord's Supper — whether Judas partook or not of those hallowed symbols. Nor can we tell whether at all, or, if at all, to what extent, our Lord conformed the minor details of His last supper to the half-joyous, half-mournful customs of the Paschal feast; nor, again, can we tell how far the customs of the Passover in that day resembled those detailed to us in the Rabbinic writings. Nothing could have been simpler than the ancient method of their commemorating their deliverance from Egypt and from the destroying angel. The central custom of the feast was the hasty eating of the Paschal lamb, with unleavened bread and bitter herbs, in a standing attitude, with loins girt and shoes upon the feet, as they had eaten hastily on the night of their deliverance. In this way the Passover is still yearly eaten by the Samaritans at the summit of Gerizim,[1] and there to this day they will hand to the stranger the little olive-shaped morsel of unleavened bread, enclosing a green fragment of wild endive or some other bitter herb, which may perhaps resemble, except that it is not dipped in the dish, the very ψωμίον which Judas received at the hands of Christ. But even if the Last Supper was a Passover, we are told that the Jews had long ceased to eat it standing, or to observe the rule which forbade any guest to leave the house till morning. They made, in fact, many radical distinctions between the Egyptian (פסח מצרים) and the permanent Passover (פסה דורות) which was subsequently observed. The latter meal began by filling each guest a cup of wine, over which the head of the family pronounced a benediction. After this the hands were washed in a basin of water, and a table was brought in, on which were placed the bitter herbs, the unleavened bread, the *charoseth* (a dish made of dates, raisins, and vinegar), the paschal lamb, and the flesh of the *chagigah*. The father dipped a piece of herb in the *charoseth*, ate it, with a benediction, and distributed a similar morsel to all. A second cup of wine was then poured out; the youngest present inquired the meaning of the paschal night; the father replied with a full account of the observance; the first part of the Hallel (Ps. cvii.—cxiv.) was then sung, a blessing repeated, a third cup of wine was drunk, grace was said, a fourth cup poured out, the rest of the Hallel (Ps. cxv.—cxviii.) sung, and the ceremony ended by the blessing of the song.[2] Some, no doubt, of the facts mentioned at the Last Supper may be brought into comparison with parts of

---

[1] I was present at this interesting celebration on Gerizim, on April 15, 1870.

[2] See the admirable article on the "Passover," by Dr. Ginsburg, in Kitto's *Cyclopædia.*

this ceremony. It appears, for instance, that the supper began with a benediction, and the passing of a cup of wine, which Jesus bade them divide among themselves, saying that He would not drink of the fruit of the vine until the kingdom of God should come.[1] The other cup — passed round after supper — has been identified by some with the third cup, the *Côs ha-berâchah* or "cup of blessing" of the Jewish ceremonial;[2] and the hymn which was sung before the departure of the little company to Gethsemane has, with much probability, been supposed to be the second part of the Great Hallel.

The relation of these incidents of the meal to the various Paschal observances which we have detailed is, however, doubtful. What is not doubtful, and what has the deepest interest for all Christians, is the establishment at this last supper of the Sacrament of the Eucharist. Of this we have no fewer than four accounts — the brief description of St. Paul agreeing in almost verbal exactness with those of the Synoptists. In each account we clearly recognize the main facts which St. Paul expressly tells us that "he had received of the Lord" — viz., "that the Lord Jesus, on the same night in which He was betrayed, took bread; and when He had given thanks, He brake it, and said, 'Take, eat; this is my body which is broken for you; this do in remembrance of me.' After the same manner also He took the cup when he had supped, saying, 'This cup is the New Testament in my blood; this do ye, as oft as ye drink it, in remembrance of me.'"[3] Never since that memorable evening has the Church ceased to observe the commandment of her Lord; ever since that day, from age to age, has this blessed and holy Sacrament been a memorial of the death of Christ, and a strengthening and refreshing of the soul by the body and blood, as the body is refreshed and strengthened by the bread and wine.[4]

---

[1] Luke xxii. 17.

[2] 1 Cor. x. 16.

[3] 1 Cor. xi. 23—25.

[4] The "transubstantiation" and "sacramental" controversies which have raged for centuries round the Feast of Communion and Christian love are as heart-saddening as they are strange and needless. They would never have arisen if it had been sufficiently observed that it was a characteristic of Christ's teaching to adopt the language of picture and of emotion. But to turn metaphor into fact, poetry into prose, rhetoric into logic, parable into systematic theology, is at once fatal and absurd. It was to warn us against such error that Jesus said so emphatically: *"It is the spirit that quickeneth; the flesh profiteth nothing: the words that I speak unto you, they are spirit and they are life"* (John vi. 63).

CHAPTER LVI.

THE LAST DISCOURSE.

"So the All-Great were the All-Loving too;
So, through the thunder, comes a human voice,
Saying, 'A heart I made, a heart beats here.'"
R. BROWNING, *Epistle of Karshish*

No sooner had Judas left the room, than, as though they had been relieved of some ghastly incubus, the spirits of the little company revived. The presence of that haunted soul lay with a weight of horror on the heart of his Master, and no sooner had he departed than the sadness of the feast seems to have been sensibly relieved. The solemn exultation which dilated the soul of their Lord — that joy like the sense of a boundless sunlight behind the earth-born mists — communicated itself to the spirits of His followers. The dull clouds caught the sunset coloring. In sweet and tender communion, perhaps two hours glided away at that quiet banquet. Now it was that, conscious of the impending separation, and fixed unalterably in His sublime resolve, He opened His heart to the little band of those who loved Him, and spoke among them those farewell discourses preserved for us by St. John alone, so "rarely mixed of sadness and joys, and studded with mysteries as with emeralds." "Now," He said, as though with a sigh of relief, "now is the Son of Man glorified, and God is glorified in Him." The hour of that glorification — the glorification which was to be won through the path of humility and agony — was at hand. The time which remained for Him to be with them was short; as He had said to the Jews, so now He said to them, that whither He was going they could not come. And in telling them this, for the first and last time, He calls them "little children." In that company were Peter and John, men whose words and deeds should thenceforth influence the whole world of man until the end — men who should become the patron saints of nations — in whose honor cathedrals should be built, and from whom cities should be named; but their greatness was but a dim faint reflection from His risen glory, and a gleam caught from that Spirit which He would send. Apart from Him they were nothing, and less than nothing — ignorant Galilæan fishermen, unknown and unheard of beyond their native village — having no intellect and no knowledge save that He had thus regarded them as His "little children." And though they could not follow Him whither He went, yet He did not say to them, as He had said to the Jews,[1] that they should seek Him and not find Him. Nay, more, He gave them a new commandment, by which, walking in His steps, and being known by all men as His disciples, they should find Him soon. That new commandment was that they should love one another. In one sense, indeed, it was not new.[2] Even in the law of Moses (Lev. xix. 18), not only had there been room for the precept, "Thou shalt love thy neighbor as thyself," but that precept had even been regarded by wise Jewish teachers as cardinal and inclusive — as "the royal law according to the Scripture," as "the message from the beginning."[3] And yet, as St. John points out in his Epistle, though in one sense old, it was, in another, wholly new — new in the new prominence given to it — new in the new motives by which it was enforced — new because of the new example by which it was recommended — new from the new influence which it was henceforth destined to exercise. It was Love, as the test and condition of discipleship, Love as greater than even Faith and Hope, Love as the fulfilling of the Law.[4]

At this point St. Peter interposed a question. Before Jesus entered on a new topic, he wished for an explanation of something which he had not understood. Why was there this farewell aspect about the Lord's discourse? "Lord, whither goest thou?"

"Whither I go thou canst not follow me now, but thou shalt follow me afterwards."

Peter now understood that *death* was meant, but why could he not also die? was he not as ready as Thomas to say, "Let us also go that we may die with Him?"[5] "Lord, *why* cannot I follow thee now? I will lay down my life for thy sake."

---

[1] John vii. 34; viii. 21.

[2] And it is observable that the word used is καινός, *recens*, not νεός, *novus*.

[3] James ii. 8; 1 John iii. 11.

[4] " For life, with all it yields of joy and woe,
   And hope and fear — believe the aged friend —
   Is just our chance o' the prize of learning love,
   How love might be, hath been indeed, and is ;
   And that we hold henceforth to the uttermost
   Such prize, despite the envy of the world,
   And having gained truth, keep truth ; that is all "
            R. BROWNING, "*A Death in the Desert.*"

[5] John xi. 16.

Why? Our Lord *might* have answered, Because the heart is deceitful above all things; because thy want of deep humility deceives thee; because it is hidden, even from thyself, how much there still is of cowardice and self-seeking in thy motives. But He would not deal thus with the noble-hearted but weak and impetuous Apostle, whose love was perfectly sincere, though it did not stand the test. He spares him all reproach; only very gently He repeats the question, " Wilt thou lay down thy life for my sake? Verily, verily, I say unto thee, The cock shall not crow till thou hast denied me thrice! " Already it was night; ere the dawn of that fatal morning shuddered in the eastern sky — before the cock-crow, uttered in the deep darkness, prophesied that the dawn was near — Jesus would have begun to lay down His life for Peter and for all who sin; but already by that time Peter, unmindful even of this warning, should have thrice repudiated his Lord and Saviour, thrice have rejected as a calumny and an insult the mere imputation that he even knew Him. All that Jesus could do to save him from the agony of this moral humiliation — by admonition, by tenderness, by prayer to His Heavenly Father — He had done. He had prayed for him that his faith might not finally fail.[1] Satan indeed had obtained permission to sift them all[2] as wheat, and, in spite of all his self-confidence, in spite of all his protested devotion, in spite of all his imaginary sincerity, he should be but as the chaff. It is remarkable that in the parallel passage of St. Luke occurs the only instance recorded in the Gospel of our Lord having addressed Simon by that name of Peter which He had Himself bestowed. It is as though He meant to remind the Man of Rock that his strength lay, not in himself, but in that good confession which he once had uttered. And yet Christ held out to him a gracious hope. He should repent and return to the Lord whom he should deny, and, when that day should come, Jesus bade him show that truest and most acceptable proof of penitence — the strengthening of others. And if his fall gave only too terrible a significance to his Saviour's warnings, yet his repentance nobly fulfilled those consolatory prophecies; and it is most interesting to find that the very word which Jesus had used to him recurs in his Epistle in a connection which shows how deeply it had sunk into his soul.[3]

But Jesus wished His Apostles to feel that the time was come when all was to be very different from the old spring-tide of their

---

[1] Luke xxii. 32, ἐκλείπῃ.

[2] Luke xxii. 31, ἐξητήσατο ὑμᾶς. Cf. Amos ix. 9.

[3] Luke xxii. 32, ἐπιστρέψας στήριδον τοὺς ἀδελφούς.[353] Cf. 1 Pet. v. 10.

happy mission days in Galilee. Then He had sent them forth without purse or scrip or sandals, and yet they had lacked nothing. But the purse and the scrip were needful now — even the sword might become a fatal necessity — and therefore " he that hath no sword let him sell his garment and buy one." [1] The very tone of the expression showed that it was not to be taken in strict literalness. It was our Lord's custom — because His words, which were spoken for all time, were intended to be fixed as goads and as nails in a sure place — to clothe His moral teachings in the form of vivid metaphor and searching paradox. It was His object now to warn them of a changed condition, in which they must expect hatred, neglect, opposition, and in which even self-defence might become a paramount duty ; but, as though to warn them clearly that He did *not* mean any immediate effort — as though beforehand to discourage any blow struck in defence of that life which He willingly resigned — He added that the end was near, and that in accordance with olden prophecy He should be numbered with the transgressors.[2] But as usual the Apostles carelessly and ignorantly mistook His words, seeing in them no spiritual lesson, but only the barest and baldest literal meaning. " Lord, behold here are two swords," was their almost childish comment on His words. Two swords ! — as though that were enough to defend from physical violence His sacred life ! as though that were an adequate provision for Him who, at a word, might have commanded more than twelve legions of angels ! as though such feeble might, wielded by such feeble hands, could save Him from the banded hate of a nation of His enemies ! " It is enough," He sadly said. It was not needful to pursue the subject ; the subsequent lesson in Gethsemane would unteach them their weak misapprehensions of His words. He dropped the subject, and waiving aside their proffered swords, proceeded to that tenderer task of consolation, about which He had so many things to say.

He bade them not be troubled ; they believed, and their faith should find its fruition. He was but leaving them to prepare for them a home in the many mansions of His father's house. They knew whither He was going, and they knew the way.

" Lord, we know not whither thou goest, and how can we know the way ? " is the perplexed answer of the melancholy Thomas.

---

[1] It is hardly worth observing that to render μάχαιραι " knives " in this passage is absurd.

[2] Luke xxii. 37. (Mark. xv. 28 is spurious. It is not found in ℵ, A, B, C, D.) See Excursus XI., " Old Testament Quotations."

"I am the Way, the Truth, and the Life," answered Jesus; "no man cometh unto the Father but by me. If ye had known me, ye should have known my Father also; and from henceforth ye know Him, and have seen Him."

Again came one of those naïve interruptions — so faithfully and vividly recorded by the Evangelist — which yet reveal such a depth of incapacity to understand, so profound a spiritual ignorance after so long a course of divine training.[1] And we may well be thankful that the simplicity and ignorance of these Apostles is thus frankly and humbly recorded; for nothing can more powerfully tend to prove the utter change which must have passed over their spirits, before men so timid, so carnal, so Judaic, so unenlightened, could be transformed into the Apostles whose worth we know, and who — inspired by the facts which they had seen, and by the Holy Spirit who gave them wisdom and utterance — became, before their short lives were ended by violence, the mightiest teachers of the world.

"Lord, show us the Father," said Philip of Bethsaida, "and it sufficeth us!"

Show us the Father! what then did Philip expect? Some earth-shaking epiphany? Some blinding splendor in the heavens? Had he not yet learnt that He who is invisible cannot be seen by mortal eyes; that the finite cannot attain to the vision of the Infinite; that they who would see God must see no manner of similitudes; that His awful silence can only be broken to us through the medium of human voices, His being only comprehended by means of the things that He hath made? And had he wholly failed to discover that for these three years he had been walking with God? that neither he, nor any other mortal man, could ever know more of God in this world that that which should be revealed of Him by "the only-begotten Son which is in the bosom of the Father?"

Again there was no touch of anger, only a slight accent of pained surprise in the quiet answer, "Have I been so long with you, and yet hast thou not known me, Philip? He that hath seen me hath seen the Father, and how sayest thou then, Show us the Father?"

And then appealing to His words and to His works as only possible by the indwelling of His Father, He proceeded to unfold to them

---

[1] It is almost needless to remark how utterly inconsistent are some of the modern theories about the "tendency" origin of St. John's Gospel with the extraordinary vividness and insight into character displayed by this narrative. If this discourse, and the incidents which accompanied it, were otherwise than real, the obscure Gnostic who is supposed to have invented it must have been one of the greatest and most spiritually-minded men of genius whom the world has ever seen!

the coming of the Holy Ghost, and how that Comforter dwelling in them should make them one with the Father and with Him.

But at this point Judas Lebbæus had a difficulty.[1] He had not understood that the eye can only see that which it possesses the inherent power of seeing. He could not grasp the fact that God can become visible to those alone the eyes of whose understanding are open so that they can discern spiritual things. "Lord, how is it," he asked, "that thou wilt manifest thyself unto us, and not to the world?"

The difficulty was exactly of the same kind as Philip's had been — the total inability to distinguish between a physical and a spiritual manifestation; and without formally removing it, Jesus gave them all, once more, the true clue to the comprehension of His words — that God lives with them that love Him, and that the proof of love is obedience. For all further teaching He referred them to the Comforter whom He was about to send, who should bring all things to their remembrance. And now He breathes upon them His blessing of peace, meaning to add but little more, because His conflict with the prince of this world should now begin.

At this point of the discourse there was a movement among the little company. "Arise," said Jesus, "let us go hence."

They rose from the table, and united their voices in a hymn which may well have been a portion of the great Hallel, and not improbably the 116th, 117th, and 118th Psalms. What an imperishable interest do these Psalms derive from such an association, and how full of meaning must many of the verses have been to some of them! With what intensity of feeling must they have joined in singing such words as these — "The sorrows of death compassed me, the pains of hell gat hold upon me; I found trouble and sorrow. Then called I upon the name of the Lord; O Lord, I beseech thee, deliver my soul;" or again, "What shall I render unto the Lord for all His benefits toward me? I will take the cup of salvation, and call upon the name of the Lord;" or once again, "Thou hast thrust sore at me that I might fall: but the Lord helped me. The Lord is my strength and my song, and is become my salvation. The stone which the builders refused is become the head-stone in the corner. This is the Lord's doing; it is marvellous in our eyes."

Before they started for their moonlight walk to the Garden of Gethsemane, perhaps while yet they stood around their Lord when the Hallel was over, He once more spoke to them. First He told them of the need of closest union with Him, if they would bring

---

[1] John xiv. 22. The v. l. Ἰάκωβος is curious.

forth fruit, and be saved from destruction. He clothed this lesson in the allegory of "the Vine and the Branches." There is no need to find any immediate circumstance which suggested the metaphor, beyond the "fruit of the vine" of which they had been partaking; but if any were required, we might suppose that, as He looked out into the night, He saw the moonlight silvering the leaves of a vine which clustered round the latticed window, or falling on the colossal golden vine which wreathed one of the Temple gates. But after impressing this truth in the vivid form of parable, He showed them how deep a source of joy it would be to them in the persecutions which awaited them from an angry world; and then in fuller, plainer, deeper language than He had ever used before, He told them, that, in spite of all the anguish with which they contemplated the coming separation from Him, it was actually *better* for them that His personal presence should be withdrawn in order that His spiritual presence might be yet nearer to them than it ever had been before. This would be effected by the coming of the Holy Ghost, when He who was now *with* them should be ever *in* them. The mission of that Comforter should be to convince [1] the world of sin, of righteousness, and of judgment; and He should guide *them* into all truth, and show them things to come. " He shall glorify me ; for He shall receive of mine, and show it unto you." And now He was going to His Father ; a little while, and they should not see Him ; and again a little while, and they should see Him.

The uncertainty as to what He meant carried the disciples once more to questions among themselves during one of the solemn pauses of His discourse. They would gladly have asked Him, but a deep awe was upon their spirits, and they did not dare. Already they had several times broken the current of His thoughts by questions which, though He did not reprove them, had evidently grieved Him by their emptiness, and by the misapprehension which they showed of all that He sought to impress upon them. So their whispered questioning died away into silence, but their Master kindly came to their relief. This, He told them, was to be their brief hour of anguish, but it was to be followed by a joy of which man could not rob them ; and to that joy there need be no limit, for whatever might be their need they had but to ask the Father, and it should be fulfilled.[2] To that Father who Himself loved them, for their belief

---

[1] John xvi. 8, ἐλέγξει. Cf. John viii. 9, 46; Jude 15, &c.

[2] It is one of several minute coincidences (unavoidably obliterated in the English version) which show how uniformly our Lord claimed His divine origin, that whereas He used the word αἰτῶ, " peto," of all *other* prayers to God — being the

in Him — to that Father, from whom He came, He was now about to return.

The disciples were deeply grateful for these plain and most consoling words. Once more they were unanimous in expressing their belief that He came forth from God. But Jesus sadly checked their enthusiasm. His words had been meant to give them peace in the present, and courage and hope for the future; yet He knew and told them that, in spite of all that they said, the hour was now close at hand when they should all be scattered in selfish terror, and leave Him alone — yet not alone, because the Father was with Him.

And after these words He lifted up His eyes to heaven, and uttered His great High-Priestly prayer; first, that His Father would invest His voluntary humanity with the eternal glory of which He had emptied Himself when He took the form of a servant; next, that He would keep through His own name these His loved ones who had walked with Him in the world;[1] and then that He would sanctify and make perfect not these alone, but all the myriads, all the long generations, which should hereafter believe through their word.

And when the tones of this divine prayer were hushed, they left the guest chamber and stepped into the moonlit silence of the Oriental night.

---

word used of petitions to one who is superior — the word He uses to describe His own prayers is $\dot{\epsilon}\rho\omega\tau\tilde{\omega}$, "rogo," which is (strictly speaking) the request of an equal from an equal. "'$E\rho\omega\tau\tilde{\alpha}\nu$ notat familiarem petendi modum qualis inter colloquentes solet esse. Saepius de precibus Jesu occurrit (xvi. 26; xvii. 9, 15, 20) semel tantum de precibus fidelium "[354] (Lampe). Again, when He bids His disciples believe on Him (John xiv. 1), the phrase used is $\pi\iota\sigma\tau\epsilon\acute{v}\omega$ $\epsilon\acute{\iota}\varsigma$,[355] which never occurs elsewhere except of God, whereas the ordinary belief and trust in man is expressed by $\pi\iota\sigma\tau\epsilon\acute{v}\omega$, with the dative (John i. 12; ii. 23; Matt. xviii. 6). Again, when He speaks of God as His Father the phrase always is $\dot{o}$ $\pi\alpha\tau\dot{\eta}\rho$, or $\dot{o}$ $\pi\alpha\tau\dot{\eta}\rho$ $\mu o v$; but when He speaks of God as *our* Father, the word has no article. This is most strikingly seen in John xx. 17, $\dot{\alpha}\nu\alpha\beta\alpha\acute{\iota}\nu\omega$ $\pi\rho\dot{o}\varsigma$ $\tau\dot{o}\nu$ $\pi\alpha\tau\acute{\epsilon}\rho\alpha$ $\mu o v$ $\kappa\alpha\grave{\iota}$ $\pi\alpha\tau\acute{\epsilon}\rho\alpha$ $\dot{v}\mu\tilde{\omega}\nu$;[356] where, as St. Augustine truly remarks, "Non ait Patrem *nostrum*; aliter ergo meum, aliter vestrum; naturâ meum, gratiâ vestrum "[357] (Tract. cxxi.). "Nos per illum," says Bengel, "ille singularissime et primo."[358]

[1] The E. V. misses the difference of tense and meaning in John xvii. 12, $\dot{\epsilon}\tau\dot{\eta}\rho o v \nu$, *conservabam;* $\dot{\epsilon}\varphi\acute{v}\lambda\alpha\xi\alpha$, *custodivi.*[359]

CHAPTER LVII.

GETHSEMANE — THE AGONY AND THE ARREST.

" Non mortem horruit simpliciter . . . peccata vero nostra, quorum onus illi erat impositum, suâ ingente mole eum premebant." [360] — CALVIN (*ad* Matt. xxvi. 37).

THEIR way led them through one of the city gates — probably that which then corresponded to the present gate of St. Stephen — down the steep sides of the ravine, across the wady of the Kidron,[1] which lay a hundred feet below, and up the green and quiet slope beyond it. To one who has visited the scene at that very season of the year and at that very hour of the night — who has felt the solemn hush of the silence even at this short distance from the city wall — who has seen the deep shadows flung by the great boles of the ancient olive-trees, and the checkering of light that falls on the sward through their moonlight-silvered leaves, it is more easy to realize the awe which crept over those few Galilæans, as in almost unbroken silence, with something perhaps of secresy, and with a weight of mysterious dread brooding over their spirits, they followed Him, who with bowed head and sorrowing heart walked before them to His willing doom.[2]

---

[1] The reading of St. John, πέραν τοῦ χειμάρρου τῶν κέδρων (xviii. 1 ; א, D, τοῦ κέδρου), is probably no more than a curious instance of the Grecising of a Hebrew name, just as the brook Kishon is in 1 Kings xviii. 40 called χείμαρρος κισσῶν (of the Ivies): cf. LXX., 2 Sam. xv. 23 ; Jos. *Antt.* ix. 7, § 3. We do not hear of any cedars there, but even if τῶν Κέδρων be the true reading, the word may have been *surfrappé* by the Evangelist himself ; τοῦ κεδρών is, however, the most probable reading. The Kidron is a ravine rather than a brook. No water runs in it except occasionally, after unusually heavy rains. Nor can we see any special significance — any " pathetic fallacy " — in the name Kidron, as though it meant (Stier vii. 220) " the dark brook in the deep valley," with allusion to David's humiliation (1 Kings xv. 13), and idolatrous abominations (2 Kings xxiii. 4, &c.), and the fact that it was a kind of sewer for the Temple refuse. " There," says Stier, " surrounded by such memorials and typical allusions, the Lord descends into the dust of humiliation and anguish, as His glorification had taken place upon the top of the mountain." This attempt to see more in the words of the Gospel than they can fairly be supposed to convey would soon lead to all the elaborate mysticism and trifling of Rabbinic exegesis.

[2] Luke xxii. 39.

We are told but of one incident in that last and memorable walk through the midnight to the familiar Garden of Gethsemane.[1] It was a last warning to the disciples in general, to St. Peter in particular. It may be that the dimness, the silence, the desertion of their position, the dull echo of their footsteps, the stealthy aspect which their movements wore, the agonizing sense that treachery was even now at work, was beginning already to produce an icy chill of cowardice in their hearts; sadly did Jesus turn and say to them that on that very night they should all be offended in Him — all find their connection with Him a stumbling-block in their path — and the old prophecy should be fulfilled, " I will smite the shepherd, and the sheep shall be scattered abroad." And yet, in spite of all, as a shepherd would He go before them, leading the way to Galilee?[2] They all repudiated the possibility of such an abandonment of their Lord, and Peter, touched already by this apparent distrust of His stability, haunted perhaps by some dread lest Jesus felt any doubt of *him*, was loudest and most emphatic in his denial. Even if all should be offended, yet never would he be offended. Was it a secret misgiving in his own heart which made his asseveration so prominent and so strong? Not even the repetition of the former warning, that, ere the cock should crow, he would thrice have denied his Lord, could shake him from his positive assertion that even the necessity of death itself should never drive him to such a sin. And Jesus only listened in mournful silence to vows which should so soon be scattered into air.

So they came to Gethsemane, which is about half a mile from the city walls. It was a garden or orchard[3] marked probably by some slight enclosure; and as it had been a place of frequent resort for Jesus and His followers, we may assume that it belonged to some friendly owner. The name Gethsemane means " the oil-press," and doubtless it was so called from a press to crush the olives yielded by the countless trees from which the hill derives its designation. Any one who has rested at noonday in the gardens of En-gannim or Nazareth in spring, and can recall the pleasant shade yielded by the interlaced branches of olive and pomegranate, and fig and myrtle, may easily imagine what kind of spot it was. The traditional site, venerable and beautiful as it is from the age and size of the grey gnarled olive-trees, of which one is still known as the Tree of the

---

[1] Matt. xxvi. 31—35; Mark xiv. 27—31.
[2] Zech. xiii. 7; Matt. xxvi. 32, προάξω ὑμᾶς.
[3] κῆπος (John xviii. 1); χωρίον (Matt. xxvi. 36).

Agony, is perhaps too public — being, as it always must have been, at the angle formed by the two paths which lead over the summit and shoulder of Olivet — to be regarded as the actual spot. It was more probably one of the secluded hollows at no great distance from it which witnessed that scene of awful and pathetic mystery.[1] But although the exact spot cannot be determined with certainty, the general position of Gethsemane is clear, and then as now the checkering moonlight, the grey leaves, the dark brown trunks, the soft greensward, the ravine with Olivet towering over it to the eastward and Jerusalem to the west, must have been the main external features of a place which must be regarded with undying interest while Time shall be, as the place where the Saviour of mankind entered alone into the Valley of the Shadow.

Jesus knew that the awful hour of His deepest humiliation had arrived — that from this moment till the utterance of that great cry with which He expired, nothing remained for Him on earth but the torture of physical pain and the poignancy of mental anguish. All that the human frame can tolerate of suffering was to be heaped upon His shrinking body ; every misery that cruel and crushing insult can inflict was to weigh heavy on His soul; and in this torment of body and agony of soul even the high and radiant serenity of His divine spirit was to suffer a short but terrible eclipse. Pain in its acutest sting, shame in its most overwhelming brutality, all the burden of the sin and mystery of man's existence in its apostasy and fall — this was what He must now face in all its most inexplicable accumulation. But one thing remained before the actual struggle, the veritable agony, began. He had to brace His body, to nerve His soul, to calm His spirit by prayer and solitude to meet that hour in which all that is evil in the Power of Evil should wreak its worst upon the Innocent and Holy. And He must face that hour alone : no human eye must witness, except through the twilight and shadow, the depth of His suffering. Yet He would have gladly shared their sympathy ; it helped Him in this hour of darkness to feel that they were near,

---

[1] I had the deep and memorable happiness of being able to see Gethsemane with two friends, unaccompanied by any guide, late at night and under the full glow of the Paschal moon, on the night of April 14th, 1870. It is usually argued that the eight old time-hallowed olive-trees cannot reach back to the time of Christ, because Titus cut down the trees all round the city. This argument is not decisive; but still it is more probable that these trees are only the successors and descendants of those which have always given its name to the sacred hill. It is quite certain that Gethsemane must have been *near* this spot, and the tradition which fixes the site is very old.

and that those were nearest who loved Him best. "Stay here," He said to the majority, "while I go there and pray." Leaving them to sleep on the damp grass, each wrapped in his outer garment, He took with Him Peter and James and John, and went about a stone's throw farther. It was well that Peter should face all that was involved in allegiance to Christ: it was well that James and John should know what was that cup which they had desired pre-eminently to drink. But soon even the society of these chosen and trusted ones was more than He could bear. A grief beyond utterance, a struggle beyond endurance, a horror of great darkness, a giddiness and stupefaction of soul overmastered Him, as with the sinking swoon of an anticipated death.[1] It was a tumult of emotion which none must see. "My soul," He said, "is full of anguish, even unto death. Stay here and keep watch." Reluctantly He tore Himself away from their sustaining tenderness and devotion,[2] and retired yet farther, perhaps out of the moonlight into the shadow. And there, until slumber overpowered them, they were conscious of how dreadful was that paroxysm of prayer and suffering through which He passed. They saw Him sometimes on His knees, sometimes outstretched in prostrate supplication upon the damp ground;[3] they heard snatches of the sounds of murmured anguish in which His humanity pleaded with the divine will of His Father. The actual words might vary, but the substance was the same throughout. "Abba, Father, all things are possible unto Thee! take away this cup from me; nevertheless, not what I will, but what Thou wilt."[4]

And that prayer in all its infinite reverence and awe was heard;[5] that strong crying and those tears were not rejected. We may not intrude too closely into this scene. It is shrouded in a halo and a mystery into which no footstep may penetrate. We, as we contemplate

---

[1] Matt. xxvi. 37, ἤρξατο λυπεῖσθαι καὶ ἀδημονεῖν;[361] Mark xiv. 33, ἐκθαμβεῖσθαι.[362] Cf. Job xviii. 20 (Aqu., ἀδημονήσουσιν); Ps. cxvi. 11. See Pearson, *On the Creed*, Art. iv. n. The derivation may be from ἀ δημέω, "I am carried away from myself;" or, perhaps more probably, from ἀδῆσαι, "to loathe." It is remarkable that this verse (Matt. xxvi. 38), and John xii. 27, are the only passages where Jesus used the word ψυχή[363] of Himself.

[2] Luke xxii. 41, ἀπεσπάσθη ἀπ' αὐτῶν.[364] Cf. Acts xxi. 1.

[3] Luke xxii. 41, θεὶς τὰ γόνατα.[365] Matt. xxvi. 39, ἔπεσεν ἐπὶ πρόσωπον αὐτοῦ.[366]

[4] Nothing, as Dean Alford remarks, could prove more decisively the insignificance of the letter in comparison with the spirit, than the fact that the three Evangelists vary in the actual expression of the prayer.

[5] Heb. v. 7, εἰσακουσθεὶς ἀπὸ τῆς εὐλαβείας.[367]

it, are like those disciples — our senses are confused, our perceptions are not clear. We can but enter into their amazement and sore distress. Half waking, half oppressed with an irresistible weight of troubled slumber, they only felt that they were dim witnesses of an unutterable agony, far deeper than anything which they could fathom, as it far transcended all that, even in our purest moments, we can pretend to understand. The place seems haunted by presences of good and evil, struggling in mighty but silent contest for the eternal victory. They see Him, before whom the demons had fled in howling terror, lying on His face upon the ground. They hear that voice wailing in murmurs of broken agony, which had commanded the wind and the sea, and they obeyed Him. The great drops of anguish which drop from Him in the deathful struggle, look to them like heavy gouts of blood. Under the dark shadows of the trees, amid the interrupted moonlight, it seems to them that there is an angel with Him, who supports His failing strength, who enables Him to rise victorious from those first prayers with nothing but the crimson traces of that bitter struggle upon His brow.[1]

And whence came all this agonized failing of heart, this fearful amazement, this horror of great darkness, this passion which almost brought Him down to the grave before a single pang had been inflicted upon Him — which forced from Him the rare and intense phenomenon of a blood-stained sweat — which almost prostrated body, and soul, and spirit with one final blow ? Was it the mere dread of death — the mere effort and determination to face that which He foreknew in all its dreadfulness, but from which, nevertheless, His soul recoiled ? There have been those who have dared — I can scarcely write it without shame and sorrow — to speak very slightingly about Gethsemane ; to regard that awful scene, from the summit of their ignorant presumption, with an almost contemptuous dislike — to speak as though Jesus had there shown a cowardly sensi-

---

[1] The verses (Luke xxii. 43, 44) are omitted in some of the best MSS. (*e. g.*, even A, B, and the first corrector of ℵ), and were so at a very early age. Professor Westcott thinks that the varying evidence for their authenticity points to a recension of the Gospel by the Evangelist himself (*Introd.* p. 306). Olshausen and Lange here understand the angel of "the accession of spiritual power" — "the angel of the hearing of prayer" (verse 43, ὤφθη δὲ α ὐ τ ῷ). It seems certain that an αἱματώδης ἱδρώς[368] under abnormal pathological circumstances is not unknown ; and even if it were, all that the Evangelist *says* is ἐγένετο ὁ ἱδρὼς αὐτοῦ ὡ σ ε ὶ θρόμβοι αἵματος, κ. τ. λ.[369] See Dr. Stroud, *On the Physical Cause of the Death of Christ*, p. 183 ; Bynaeus, *De Morte Christi*, ii. 33.

bility.   Thus, at the very moment when we should most wonder and admire, they

> " Not even from the Holy One of Heaven
> Refrain their tongues blasphèmous." [1]

And yet, if no other motive influence them — if they merely regard Him as a Prophet preparing for a cruel death — if no sense of decency, no power of sympathy, restrain them from thus insulting even a Martyr's agony at the moment when its pang was most intense — does not common fairness, does not the most ordinary historic criticism, show them how cold and false, if nothing worse, must be the miserable insensibility which prevents them from seeing that it could have been no mere dread of pain, no mere shrinking from death, which thus agitated to its inmost centre the pure and innocent soul of the Son of Man ? [2]   Could not even a child see how inconsistent would be such an hypothesis with that heroic fortitude which fifteen hours of subsequent sleepless agony could not disturb —with the majestic silence before priest, and procurator, and king — with the endurance from which the extreme of torture could not wring one cry — with the calm and infinite ascendancy which overawed the hardened and worldly Roman into involuntary respect — with the undisturbed supremacy of soul which opened the gates of Paradise to the repentant malefactor, and breathed compassionate forgiveness on the apostate priests ? The Son of Man humiliated into prostration by the mere abject fear of death, which trembling old men, and feeble maidens, and timid boys — a Polycarp, a Blandina, an Attalus — have yet braved without a sigh or a shudder, solely through faith in His name! Strange that *He* should be thus insulted by impious tongues, who brought to light that life and immortality from whence came the

> " Ruendi
> In ferrum mens prona viris, animaeque capaces
> Mortis, et ignavum rediturae parcere vitae ! " * [371]

The meanest of idiots, the coarsest of criminals, have advanced to the scaffold without a tremor or a sob, and many a brainless and brutal murderer has mounted the ladder with a firm step, and looked round

---

[1] Ps. xl. 13.

[2] So Celsus (ap. Orig. ii. 24), and Julian (Theod. Mops.; Munter, *Fragm. Patr.* i. 121). Vanini, when taken to the scaffold, boasted his superiority to Jesus, " Illi in extremis prae timore imbellis sudor ; *ego imperturbatus morior* " [370] (Grammond, *Hist. Gall.* iii. 211). The Jews made the same taunt (R. Isaak b. Abraham, *Chissuh Emunah,* in Wagenseil). The passages are all quoted by Hofmann, p. 439.

* Luc. *Phars.* i. 455.

upon a yelling mob with an unflinching countenance. To adopt the commonplace of orators, " There is no passion in the mind of man so weak but it mates and masters the fear of death. Revenge triumphs over death; love slights it; honor aspireth to it; grief flieth to it; fear preoccupateth it. A man would die, though he were neither valiant nor miserable, only upon a weariness to do the same thing so oft over and over. It is no less worthy to observe how little alteration in good spirits the approaches of death make: for they appear to be the same men till the last instant." It is as natural to die as to be born. The Christian hardly needs to be told that it was no such vulgar fear which forced from his Saviour that sweat of blood. No, it was something infinitely more than this: infinitely more than the highest stretch of our imagination can realize. It was something far deadlier than death. It was the burden and the mystery of the world's sin which lay heavy on His heart ; it was the tasting, in the divine humanity of a sinless life, the bitter cup which sin had poisoned ; it was the bowing of Godhead to endure a stroke to which man's apostasy had lent such frightful possibilities. It was the sense, too, of how virulent, how frightful, must have been the force of evil in the Universe of God which could render necessary so infinite a sacrifice. It was the endurance, by the perfectly guiltless, of the worst malice which human hatred could devise ; it was to experience in the bosom of perfect innocence and perfect love, all that was detestable in human ingratitude, all that was pestilent in human hypocrisy, all that was cruel in human rage. It was to brave the last triumph of Satanic spite and fury, uniting against His lonely head all the flaming arrows of Jewish falsity and heathen corruption — the concentrated wrath of the rich and respectable, the yelling fury of the blind and brutal mob. It was to feel that His own, to whom He came, loved darkness rather than light — that the race of the chosen people could be wholly absorbed in one insane repulsion against infinite goodness and purity and love.

Through all this He passed in that hour which, with a recoil of sinless horror beyond our capacity to conceive, foretasted a worse bitterness than the worst bitterness of death. And after a time — victorious indeed, but weary almost to fainting, like His ancestor Jacob, with the struggle of those supplications — He came to seek one touch of human support and human sympathy from the chosen of the chosen — His three Apostles. Alas! He found them sleeping. It was an hour of fear and peril; yet no certainty of danger, no love for Jesus, no feeling for His unspeakable dejection, had sufficed to hold their eyes waking. Their grief, their weariness, their intense excitement, had sought relief in heavy slumber. Even **Peter**, after all his impetuous promises, lay in deep sleep, for his eyes were heavy. " Simon, sleepest thou ? " was all He said. As the sad reproachful sentence fell on their ears, and startled them from their slumbers, " Were ye so unable," He asked, " to watch with me a single hour ? Watch and pray that ye enter not into temptation." And then, not to palliate their failure, but rather to point out the peril of it, " The spirit," He added, " is willing, but the flesh is weak."

Once more He left them, and again, with deeper intensity, repeated the same prayer as before, and in a pause of His emotion came back to His disciples. But they had once more fallen asleep; nor, when He awoke them, could they, in their heaviness and confusion, find anything to say to Him. Well might He have said, in the words of David, " Thy rebuke hath broken my heart; I am full of heaviness; I looked for some to have pity on me, but there was no man, neither found I any to comfort me " [1]

For the third and last time — but now with a deeper calm, and a brighter serenity of that triumphant confidence which had breathed through the High-Priestly prayer — He withdrew to find His only consolation in communing with God. And there He found all that He needed. Before that hour was over He was prepared for the worst that Satan or man could do. He knew all that would befall Him; perhaps He had already caught sight of the irregular glimmering of lights as His pursuers descended from the Temple precincts. Yet there was no trace of agitation in His quiet words when, coming a third time and finding them once more sleeping, " Sleep on now," He said, " and take your rest. It is enough. The hour is come. Lo ! the Son of Man is being betrayed into the hands of sinners." For all the aid that you can render, for all the comfort your sympathy can bestow, sleep on. But all is altered now. It is not I who wish to break these your heavy slumbers. They will be very rudely and sternly broken by others. " Rise, then ; let us be going. Lo ! he that betrayeth me is at hand." [2]

Yes, it was more than time to rise, for while saints had slumbered sinners had plotted and toiled in exaggerated preparation. While they slept in their heavy anguish, the traitor had been very wakeful

---

[1] Ps. lxix. 20.

[2] It has been asked why St. John tells us nothing of the agony ? We do not know ; but it may very likely have been because the story had already been told **as fully as it was known.** *Certainly,* his silence did not spring from any notion **that the agony was unworthy of Christ's grandeur (see xii. 27 ; xviii. 11).**

in his active malignity. More than two hours had passed since from
the lighted chamber of their happy communion he had plunged into
the night, and those hours had been very fully occupied. He had
gone to the High Priests and Pharisees, agitating them and hurrying them on with his own passionate precipitancy; and partly perhaps out of genuine terror of Him with whom he had to deal, partly
to enhance his own importance, had got the leading Jews to furnish
him with a motley band composed of their own servants, of the
Temple watch with their officers, and even with a part at least of the
Roman garrison from the Tower of Antonia, under the command of
their tribune.[1] They were going against One who was deserted and
defenceless, yet the soldiers were armed with swords, and even the
promiscuous throng had provided themselves with sticks. They were
going to seize One who would make no attempt at flight or concealment, and the full moon shed its lustre on their unhallowed expedition; yet, lest He should escape them in some limestone grotto, or in
the deep shade of the olives, they carried lanterns and torches in
their hands. It is evident that they made their movements as noiseless and stealthy as possible; but at night a deep stillness hangs over
an Oriental city, and so large a throng could not move unnoticed.
Already, as Jesus was awaking His sleepy disciples, His ears had
caught in the distance the clank of swords, the tread of hurrying
footsteps, the ill-suppressed tumult of an advancing crowd. He knew
all that awaited Him; He knew that the quiet garden which He had
loved, and where He had so often held happy intercourse with His
disciples, was familiar to the traitor. Those unwonted and hostile
sounds, that red glare of lamps and torches athwart the moonlit inter-
spaces of the olive-yards, were enough to show that Judas had betrayed the secret of His retirement, and was even now at hand.

And even as Jesus spoke the traitor himself appeared.[2] Overdo-

---

[1] ἡ οὖν σπεῖρα καὶ ὁ χιλίαρχος [372] (John xviii. 12; cf. 3); but clearly St.
John does not mean that *all the* 600 soldiers of the garrison accompanied Judas.
Of course the consent of Pilate must have been obtained with the express object
of prejudicing him against Jesus as a dangerous person. The στρατηγοὶ τοῦ
ἱεροῦ [373] of Luke xxii. 52 are Levitical officers. Critics have tried, as in so many
instances, to show that there is an error here because there was only one " captain
of the Temple " (or *ish ar ha-bait*) whose office seems to date from the Captivity
[Neh. ii. 8; vii. 2 (*sar ha-birah*); cf. 2 Macc. iii. 4]. But in 3 Esdr. i. 8, we find
οἱ ἐπιστάται τοῦ ἱεροῦ, *three* in number; and as the captain had guards
under him, to make the rounds (Jos. *B. J.* vi. 5, § 3, οἱ τοῦ ἱεροῦ φύλακες
ἤγγειλαν τῷ στρατηγῷ), [374] the name might be applied generally to the whole
body.

[2] Throughout the description of these scenes I have simply taken the four Gospel narratives as one whole, and regarded them as supplementing each other. It

ing his part — acting in the too-hurried impetuosity of a crime so hideous that he dared not pause to think — he pressed forward into the enclosure, and was in front of all the rest.[1] "Comrade," said Jesus to him as he hurried forward, "the crime for which thou art come ————— "[2] The sentence seems to have been cut short by the deep agitation of His spirit, nor did Judas return any answer, intent only on giving to his confederates his shameful preconcerted signal. "He whom I kiss," he had said to them, "the same is He. Seize Him at once, and lead Him away safely."[3] And so, advancing to Jesus with his usual cold title of address, he exclaimed, "Rabbi, Rabbi, hail!" and profaned the sacred cheek of his Master with a kiss of overacted salutation.[4] "Judas," said Jesus to him, with stern

---

will be seen how easily, and without a single violent hypothesis, they fall into one harmonious, probable, and simple narrative. Lange here adopts what seems to me to be the best order of sequence. The fact that Judas gave the signal too early for his own purpose seems to follow from John xviii. 4—9 (ἐξῆλθεν). Alford thinks it "inconceivable" that Judas had given his traitor-kiss *before* this scene; but his own arrangement will surely strike every careful reader as much more inconceivable.

[1] Luke xxii. 47.

[2] Matt. xxvi. 50, ἐφ᾽ ὅ πάρει — perhaps this is an exclamation for "What a crime!" I have taken it in the sense of an aposiopesis, "What thou art here for (do)." But perhaps ἐφ᾽ ὅ; may = ἐπὶ τί; in Hellenistic Greek (Winer, III. xxiv. 4). It is not, however, likely that Jesus would have asked a question on the purpose of Judas's coming. Observe Ἑταῖρε (Matt. xxvi. 50), "Comrade," *not* "friend" (φίλε), as most versions wrongly translate it. Never, even in the ordinary conventionalities of life, would Christ use a term which was not strictly true. There is even something stern in the use of ἑταῖρε (cf. Matt xx. 13 ; xxii. 12). Judas, in the strictest sense of the word, *had* been an ἑταῖρος ; but as Ammonius says, ὁ ἑταῖρος οὐ πάντως φίλος.[315] Hence the lines of Houdenius (*De Pass.*) —

> " Si honoras, O dulcis Domine,
> Inimicum amici nomine.
> Quales erunt amoris carmine
> Qui te canunt et modulamine ? "[316]

although exquisitely beautiful, are not strictly accurate.

[3] Mark xiv. 44, κρατήσατε . . . καὶ ἀπαγάγετε ἀσφαλῶς — one of the many slight undesigned traces of Judas's involuntary terror and misgiving. His words probably were *Schalôm alêka rabbi*, "*Peace* be to thee, Rabbi!" but there came no *alêka Shalôm* in reply : there *was* no peace for the errand on which Judas had come. Mr. Monro observes how characteristic are these snatches of dialogue like τὸ εἰ δύνασαι[317] in Mark ix. 23 (*v.* p. 387), and the τὴν ἀρχὴν ὅτι καὶ λαλῶ ὑμῖν[318] (John viii. 25; *v.* p. 416), and ἐᾶτε ἕως τούτου[319] (Luke xxii. 51; *v. infr.*, p. 583). Surely the most inventive of inventors neither could nor would invent phrases like these!

[4] The κατεφίλησεν of Matt. xxvi. 49; Mark xiv. 45, as compared with the φιλήσω before, is clearly meant to imply a fervent kiss. Something of the same kind seems to be intended by the "Rabbi! Rabbi!" of Mark xiv. 45. Κύριε [320]

and sad reproach, "dost thou betray the Son of Man with a kiss?" These words were enough, for they simply revealed the man to himself, by stating his hideous act in all its simplicity; and the method of his treachery was so unparalleled in its heinousness, so needless and spontaneously wicked, that more words would have been superfluous. With feelings that the very devils might have pitied, the wretch slunk back to the door of the enclosure, towards which the rest of the crowd were now beginning to press.

"Lord, shall we smite with the sword?" was the eager question of St. Peter, and the only other disciple provided with a weapon; for, being within the garden, the Apostles were still unaware of the number of the captors.[1] Jesus did not at once answer the question; for no sooner had He repelled the villainous falsity of Judas than He Himself stepped out of the enclosure to face His pursuers. Not flying, not attempting to hide Himself, He stood there before them in the full moonlight in His unarmed and lonely majesty, shaming by His calm presence their superfluous torches and superfluous arms.

"Whom are ye seeking?" He asked.

The question was not objectless. It was asked, as St. John points out,[2] to secure His Apostles from all molestation; and we may suppose also that it served to make all who were present the witnesses of His arrest, and so to prevent the possibility of any secret assassination or foul play.

"Jesus of Nazareth," they answered.

Their excitement and awe preferred this indirect answer, though if there could have been any doubt as to who the speaker was, Judas was there — the eye of the Evangelist noticed him, trying in vain to lurk amid the serried ranks of the crowd — to prevent any possible mistake which might have been caused by the failure of his premature and therefore disconcerted signal.

---

was the ordinary address of the Apostles to Christ; but the colder and feebler "Rabbi" seems to have been the title always used by Judas (Bengel). Cf. *supr.*, p. 562.

[1] All this is obvious from the context. The place which, since the days of St. Helena, has been pointed out as the garden of Gethsemane, may or may *not* be the authentic site; but there can be little doubt that the actual κῆπος or χωρίον had an enclosing wall.

[2] John xviii. 8. How absolutely does this narrative shatter to pieces the infamous calumny of the Jews, κρυπτόμενος μὲν καὶ διαδιδράσκων ἐπονειδέστατα ἑάλω [381] (Orig. *c. Cels.* 2, 9, quoted by Keim, III. ii. 298). Keim, without ignoring Celsus's use of Jewish calumnies, thinks that this attack is founded on John x. 39, &c.

"I am He," [1] said Jesus.

Those quiet words produced a sudden paroxysm of amazement and dread. That answer so gentle "had in it a strength greater than the eastern wind, or the voice of thunder, for God was in that 'still voice,' and it struck them down to the ground." Instances are not wanting in history in which the untroubled brow, the mere glance, the calm bearing of some defenceless man, has disarmed and paralyzed his enemies. The savage and brutal Gauls could not lift their swords to strike the majestic senators of Rome. "I cannot slay Marius," exclaimed the barbarian slave, flinging down his sword and flying headlong from the prison into which he had been sent to murder the aged hero. [2] Is there, then, any ground for the scoffing scepticism with which many have received St. John's simple but striking narrative, that, at the words "*I am He*," a movement of contagious terror took place among the crowd, and, starting back in confusion, some of them fell to the ground? Nothing surely was more natural. It must be remembered that Judas was among them; that *his* soul was undoubtedly in a state of terrible perturbation; that Orientals are specially liable to sudden panic; that fear is an emotion eminently sympathetic; that most of them must have heard of the mighty miracles of Jesus, and that all were at any rate aware that He claimed to be a Prophet; that the manner in which He met this large multitude, which the alarms of Judas had dictated as essential to His capture, suggested the likelihood of some appeal to supernatural powers; that they were engaged in one of those deeds of guilty violence and midnight darkness which paralyze the stoutest minds. When we

---

[1] John xviii. 5. One of those minute touches which so clearly mark the eye witness — which are inexplicable on any other supposition, and which abound in the narrative of the beloved disciple. To give to the "I am He" any mystic significance (Isa. xliii. 10, LXX.; John viii. 28), as is done by Lange and others, seems unreasonable.

[2] Vell. Paterc. ii. 19. Other commentators adduce the further instances of M. Antonius (Val. Max. viii. 9, 2), Probus, Pertinax, Teligny, stepson to Admiral Coligny, Bishop Stanislaus, &c. No one, so far as I have seen, quotes the instance of Avidius Cassius, who, springing to the door of his tent in night-dress, quelled a mutinous army by his mere presence. In the Talmud, seventy of the strongest Egyptians fall to the earth in attempting to bind Simeon, the brother of Joseph. Jeremy Taylor beautifully says, "But there was a divinity upon Him that they could not seize Him at first; but as a wave climbing of a rock is beaten back and scattered into members, till falling down it creeps with gentle waftings, and kisses the feet of the stony mountain, and so encircles it: so the soldiers coming at first with a rude attempt, were twice repelled by the glory of His person, till they, falling at His feet, were at last admitted to a seizure of His body." (*Life of Christ* III. xv.)

bear this in mind, and when we remember too that on many occasions in His history the mere presence and word of Christ had sufficed to quell the fury of the multitude, and to keep Him safe in the midst of them,[1] it hardly needs any recourse to miracle to account for the fact that these official marauders and their infamous guide recoiled from those simple words, " I am He," as though the lightning had suddenly been flashed into their faces.

While they stood cowering and struggling there, He again asked them, " Whom are ye seeking? " Again they replied, " Jesus of Nazareth." " I told you," He answered, " that I am He. If, then, ye are seeking me, let these go away." For He Himself had said in His prayer, " Of those whom Thou hast given me have I lost none."

The words were a signal to the Apostles that they could no longer render Him any service, and that they might now consult their own safety if they would. But when they saw that He meant to offer no resistance, that He was indeed about to surrender Himself to His enemies, some pulse of nobleness or of shame throbbed in the impetuous soul of Peter; and hopeless and useless as all resistance had now become, he yet drew his sword, and with a feeble and ill-aimed blow severed the ear of a man named Malchus, a servant of the High Priest. Instantly Jesus stopped the ill-timed and dangerous struggle. " Return that sword of thine into its place," He said to Peter, " for all they that take the sword shall perish with the sword; " and then He reproachfully asked His rash disciple whether he *really* supposed that He could not escape if He would? whether the mere breathing of a prayer would not secure for Him — had He not voluntarily intended to fulfil the Scriptures by drinking the cup which His Father had given Him — the aid, not of twelve timid Apostles, but of more than twelve legions of angels? "[2] And then, turning to the soldiers who were holding Him, He said, " Suffer ye thus far,"[3] and in one last act of miraculous mercy touched and healed the wound.

---

[1] Luke iv. 30; John vii. 30; viii. 59; x. 39; Mark xi. 18 (see p. 187, &c.).

[2] A legion during the Empire consisted of about 6,000 men. The fact that St. John alone mentions the names of St. Peter and Malchus may arise simply from his having been more accurately acquainted than the other Evangelists with the events of that heart-shaking scene; but there is nothing absurd or improbable in the current supposition, that the name of Peter may have been purposely kept in the background in the earliest cycle of Christian records.

[3] This may either mean, " Let me free for one moment only, while I heal this wounded man," as Alford not improbably understands it; or, " Excuse this single act of resistance."

In the confusion of the night this whole incident seems to have passed unnoticed except by a very few. At any rate, it made no impression upon these hardened men. Their terror had quite vanished, and had been replaced by insolent confidence. The Great Prophet had voluntarily resigned Himself; He was their helpless captive. No thunder had rolled; no angel flashed down from heaven for His deliverance; no miraculous fire devoured amongst them. They saw before them nothing but a weary unarmed man, whom one of His own most intimate followers had betrayed, and whose arrest was simply watched in helpless agony by a few terrified Galilæans. They had fast hold of Him, and already some chief priests, and elders, and leading officers of the Templeguard had ventured to come out of the dark background from which they had securely seen His capture, and to throng about Him in insulting curiosity. To these especially [1] He turned, and said to them, "Have ye come out as against a robber with swords and staves? When I was daily with you in the Temple ye did not stretch out your hands against me. But this is your hour, and the power of darkness." Those fatal words quenched the last gleam of hope in the minds of His followers. "Then His disciples, all of them" [2]—even the fiery Peter, even the loving John—"forsook Him, and fled." At that supreme moment only one unknown youth —perhaps the owner of Gethsemane, perhaps St. Mark the Evangelist,[3] perhaps Lazarus the brother of Martha and Mary—ventured, in his intense excitement, to hover on the outskirts of the hostile crowd.

---

[1] Luke xxii. 52, $\varepsilon \tilde{\iota} \pi \varepsilon \ \delta \grave{\varepsilon}$ . . . $\pi \rho \grave{o} \varsigma \ \tau o \grave{v} \varsigma \ \pi \rho o \sigma \gamma \varepsilon \nu o \mu \acute{\varepsilon} \nu o \upsilon \varsigma \ \pi \rho \grave{o} \varsigma$ $\alpha \grave{v} \tau \grave{o} \nu \ \dot{\alpha} \rho \chi \iota \varepsilon \rho \varepsilon \tilde{\iota} \varsigma, \varkappa. \tau. \lambda.$

[2] Matt. xxvi. 56, $o \acute{\iota} \ \mu \alpha \theta \eta \tau \alpha \grave{\iota} \ \pi \acute{\alpha} \nu \tau \varepsilon \varsigma$. Many readers will thank me here for quoting the fine lines from Browning's *Death in the Desert*: —

> " Forsake the Christ thou sawest transfigured, Him
> Who trod the sea and brought the dead to life!
> What should wring this from thee? Ye laugh and ask
> What wrung it? Even a torchlight and a noise,
> The sudden Roman faces, violent hands,
> And fear of what the Jews might do! Just that,
> And it is written, ' I forsook and fled.'
> There was my trial, and it ended thus."

[3] Mark xiv. 51, 52 only. As to the supposition that it was Lazarus — founded partly on the locality, partly on the probabilities of the case, partly on the fact that the $\sigma \iota \nu \delta \acute{\omega} \nu$ was a garment that only a person of some wealth would possess — see a beautiful article on " Lazarus," by Professor Plumptre, in the *Dict. of the Bible.* Ewald's supposition, that it was St. Paul (!), seems to me amazing. The word עָרוֹם, $\gamma \upsilon \mu \nu \acute{o} \varsigma$, though, like the Latin *nudus*, it constantly means " with only the *under* robe on" (1 Sam. xix. 24; John xxi. 7; Hes. $"E \rho \gamma$., 391; Virg. *G.* i. 299), is here probably *literal*.

He had apparently been roused from sleep, for he had nothing to cover him except the *sindón*, or linen sheet, in which he had been sleeping. But the Jewish emissaries, either out of the mere wantonness of a crowd at seeing a person in an unwonted guise, or because they resented his too close intrusion, seized hold of the sheet which he had wrapped about him ; whereupon he too was suddenly terrified, and fled away naked, leaving the linen garment in their hands.

Jesus was now absolutely alone in the power of His enemies. At the command of the tribune His hands were tied behind His back,[1] and forming a close array around Him, the Roman soldiers, followed and surrounded by the Jewish servants, led Him once more through the night, over the Kedron, and up the steep city slope beyond it, to the palace of the High Priest.

---

[1] John xviii. 12.

CHAPTER LVIII.

JESUS BEFORE THE PRIESTS AND THE SANHEDRIN.

הוו מתונים בדיי, "Be slow in judgment." — *Pirke Abhôth,* i. 1.

ALTHOUGH sceptics have dwelt with disproportioned persistency upon a multitude of "discrepancies" in the fourfold narrative of Christ's trial, condemnation, death, and resurrection, yet these are not of a nature to cause the slightest anxiety to a Christian scholar; nor need they awaken the most momentary distrust in any one who — even if he have no deeper feelings in the matter — approaches the Gospels with no preconceived theory, whether of infallibility or of dishonesty, to support, and merely accepts them for that which, at the lowest, they claim to be — histories honest and faithful up to the full knowledge of the writers, but each, if taken alone, confessedly fragmentary and obviously incomplete. After repeated study, I declare, quite fearlessly, that though the slight variations are numerous — though the lesser particulars cannot in every instance be rigidly and minutely accurate — though no one of the narratives taken singly would give us an adequate impression — yet, so far from there being, in this part of the Gospel story, any irreconcilable contradiction, it is perfectly possible to discover how one Evangelist supplements the details furnished by another, and perfectly possible to understand the true sequence of the incidents by combining into one whole the separate indications which they furnish. It is easy to call such combinations arbitrary and baseless; but they are only arbitrary in so far as we cannot always be absolutely *certain* that the succession of facts was exactly such as we suppose; and so far are they from being baseless, that, to the careful reader of the Gospels, they carry with them a conviction little short of certainty. If we treat the Gospels as we should treat any other authentic documents recording all that the authors knew, or all that they felt themselves commissioned to record, of the crowded incidents in one terrible and tumultuous day and night, we shall, with care and study, see how all that they tell us falls accurately into its proper position in the general narrative, and shows us a sixfold trial, a quadruple derision, a triple acquittal, a twice-repeated condemnation of Christ our Lord.

Reading the Gospels side by side, we soon perceive that of the three successive trials which our Lord underwent at the hands of the Jews, the first only — that before Annas — is related to us by St. John ; the second — that before Caiaphas — by St. Matthew and St. Mark ; the third — that before the Sanhedrin — by St. Luke alone.[1] Nor is there anything strange in this, since the first was the practical, the second the potential, the third the actual and formal decision, that sentence of death should be passed judicially upon Him. Each of the three trials might, from a different point of view, have been regarded as the most fatal and important of the three. That of Annas was the authoritative *praejudicium*, that of Caiaphas the real determination, that of the entire Sanhedrin at daybreak the final ratification.[2]

When the tribune, who commanded the detachment of Roman soldiers, had ordered Jesus to be bound, they led Him away without an attempt at opposition. Midnight was already passed as they hurried Him, from the moonlit shadows of green Gethsemane, through the hushed streets of the sleeping city, to the palace[3] of the High Priest. It seems to have been jointly occupied by the prime movers in this black iniquity, Annas and his son-in-law, Joseph Caiaphas. They led Him to Annas first. It is true that this Hanan, son of Seth, the Ananus of Josephus, and the Annas of the Evangelists, had only been the actual High Priest for seven years (A. D. 7—14), and that, more than twenty years before this period, he had been deposed by the Procurator Valerius Gratus. He had been succeeded first by Ismael Ben Phabi, then by his son Eleazar, then by his son-in-law, Joseph Caiaphas. But the priestly families would not be likely to attach more importance than they chose to a deposition which a strict observer of the Law would have regarded as invalid and sacrilegious ; nor would so astute a people as the Jews be likely to lack devices

---

[1] But nevertheless, St. John distinctly alludes to the *second* trial (xviii. 24, where ἀπέστειλεν means "sent," not "had sent," as in the E. V.; and cf. xi. 46); and St. Matthew and St. Mark imply the *third* (Matt. xxvii. 1 ; Mark xv. 1). St. Luke, though he contents himself with the narration of the third only — which was the only legal one — yet also distinctly leaves room for the first and second (xxii. 54).

[2] One might, perhaps, from a slightly different point of view, regard the questioning before Annas as mere conspiracy; that before Caiaphas as a sort of preliminary questioning, or ἀνάκρισις; and that before the Sanhedrin as the only real and legal trial.

[3] αὐλή means both the entire palace (Matt. xxvi. 58) and the open court within the πυλών or προαύλιον (*id.* 69). Probably the house was near the Temple (Neh. xiii. 4, seqq.). That Hanan and Caiaphas occupied one house seems probable from a comparison of John xviii. 13 with 15. John being known to *Caiaphas* is admitted to witness the trial before *Annas*.

which would enable them to evade the Roman fiat, and to treat
Annas, if they wished to do so, as their High Priest *de jure*, if not
de facto. Since the days of Herod the Great, the High Priesthood
had been degraded from a permanent religious office, to a temporary
secular distinction ; and, even had it been otherwise, the rude legionaries would probably care less than nothing to whom they led their
victim. If the tribune condescended to ask a question about it, it
would be easy for the Captain of the Temple — who may very
probably have been at this time, as we know was the case subsequently, one of the sons of Annas himself — to represent Annas as
the *Sagan* [1] or *Nasi* — the "Deputy," or the President of the Sanhedrin — and so as the proper person to conduct the preliminary
investigation.

i. Accordingly, it was before Hanan that Jesus stood first as a

---

[1] The title *Sagan haccohanîm*, "deputy" or "chief" of the priests, is *said* to date
from the day when the Seleucids neglected for seven years to appoint a successor
to the wicked Alcimus, and a "deputy" had to supply his place. But accident
must often have rendered a *sagan* necessary, and we find "the second priest"
prominently mentioned in 2 Kings xxv. 18 ; Jer. lii. 24 (Buxtorf, *Lex. Talm.* s. v.
סגן). Thus on one occasion, on the evening of the great Day of Atonement,
Hareth, King of Arabia, was talking to Simeon Ben Kamhith, who, being
High Priest, was rendered legally impure, and unable to officiate the next
day, because some of the king's saliva happened to fall on his vestments.
His brother then supplied his place. It is, however, doubtful whether the
title of *Sagan* did not originate later, and whether any but the real High Priest
could, under ordinary circumstances, be the *Nasi*. In fact, the name *Nasi*
seems to be enveloped in obscurity. Perhaps it corresponds to the mysterious
σάραμελ (= *Sar am El*, "Prince of the People of God"). Ewald says that Hanan
might have been *Ab Beth Dîn*, as the *second* in the Sanhedrin was called ; and
it is at any rate clear, among many obscurities, that short of being High Priest,
he might have even exceeded him in influence (cf. Acts iv. 6 ; Maimon. *Sanhedr.*
2, 4). The High Priesthood at this time was confined to some half-dozen closely-
connected families, especially the Boëthusians, and the family of Hanan, the
Kamhiths, and the Kantheras ; yet, since the days of Herod, the High Priests were
so completely the puppets of the civil power that there were no less than twenty-
eight in 107 years (Jos. *Antt.* xx. 10, § 1). Both Josephus (εἷς τῶν ἀρχιερέων,
B. J. ii. 20, § 4) and the Talmud (בני כהנים גדולים) quite bear out the language of
the Gospels in attributing the pontifical power more to a caste than to any individual. The fact seems to be that even in these bad times the office demanded
a certain amount of external dignity and self-denial which some men would only
tolerate for a time ; and their ambition was that as many members of their family
as possible should have "passed the chair." Such is the inference drawn by
Derenbourg from Jos. *Antt.* xx. 9, § 1 ; and still more from the letter of the High
Priest Jonathan, son of Hanan, to Agrippa (*id.* xix. § 4). Martha, daughter of
Boethus, bought the priesthood for her husband, Jesus, son of Gamala, and had
carpets spread from her house to the Temple when she went to see him sacrifice.
This man had silk gloves made, that he might not dirty his hands while sacrific-
ing ! (See Renan, *L'Antechrist*, 49 seqq.)

prisoner at the tribunal.[1] It is probable that he and his family had been originally summoned by Herod the Great from Alexandria, as supple supporters of a distasteful tyranny. The Jewish historian calls this Hanan the happiest man of his time, because he died at an advanced old age, and because both he and five of his sons in succession — not to mention his son-in-law — had enjoyed the shadow of the High Priesthood;[2] so that, in fact, for nearly half a century he had practically wielded the sacerdotal power. But to be admired by such a renegade as Josephus is a questionable advantage. In spite of his prosperity he seems to have left behind him but an evil name, and we know enough of his character, even from the most unsuspected sources, to recognize in him nothing better than an astute, tyrannous, worldly Sadducee, unvenerable for all his seventy years, full of a serpentine malice and meanness which utterly belied the meaning of his name,[3] and engaged at this very moment in a dark, disorderly conspiracy, for which even a worse man would have had cause to blush. It was before this alien and intriguing hierarch that there began, at midnight, the first stage of that long and terrible trial.[4]

And there was good reason why St. John should have preserved for us *this* phase of the trial, and preserved it apparently for the express reason that it had been omitted by the other Evangelists. It is not till after a lapse of years that people can always see clearly the prime mover in events with which they had been contemporary. At the time, the ostensible agent is the one usually regarded as most responsible, though he may be in reality a mere link in the official machinery. But if there were one man who was more guilty than any other of the death of Jesus, that man was Hanan. His advanced age, his preponderant dignity, his worldly position and influence, as

---

[1] John xviii. 13, 19—24.

[2] Eleazar, A. D. 16 ; Jonathan, A. D. 36 ; Theophilus, A. D. 37 ; Matthias, A. D. 42—43 ; Annas the younger, A. D. 63. The Talmudic quotations about Annas and his family are given in Lightfoot. They were remarkable for boldness and cunning (Jos. *Antt.* xx. 9, § 1), and also for avarice and meanness (*Sifr.* Deuteron. § 105). (*Jer. Pea.* 1, 6, quoted by Derenbourg, who calls them " ces pontifes détestés " [381]† [*Hist. Pal.*, p. 468].) — An energetic malediction against all these families is found in *Pesachim*, 57 *a*, in which occur the words, " Woe to the house of Hanan ! woe to their serpent hissings ! " (אוי לי מבית חנן אוי לי מלחישתן, Id. 232.) — The Boëthusians are reproached for their " bludgeons;" the Kantheras for their " libels"; the Phabis for their " fists " (Raphall, *Hist. of the Jews*, ii. 370). The passage is a little obscure, but the Talmud has many allusions to the worthlessness and worldliness of the priests of this period. (Renan, *L'Antechrist*, pp. 50, 51.)

[3] חנן, " clement," or " merciful."

[4] John xviii. 19—24.

one who stood on the best terms with the Herods and the Procurators, gave an exceptional weight to his prerogative decision. The mere fact that he should have noticed Jesus at all showed that he attached to His teaching a *political* significance — showed that he was at last afraid lest Jesus should alienate the people yet more entirely from the pontifical clique than had ever been done by Shemaia or Abtalion. It is most remarkable, and, so far as I know, has scarcely ever been noticed, that, although the Pharisees undoubtedly were actuated by a burning hatred against Jesus, and were even so eager for His death as to be willing to co-operate with the aristocratic and priestly Sadducees — from whom they were ordinarily separated by every kind of difference, political, social, and religious — yet, from the moment that the plot for His arrest and condemnation had been matured, the Pharisees took so little part in it that their name is not once directly mentioned in any event connected with the arrest, the trial, the derisions, and the crucifixion. The Pharisees, as such, disappear; the chief priests and elders take their place. It is, indeed, doubtful whether any of the more distinguished Pharisees were members of the degraded *simulacrum* of authority which in those bad days still arrogated to itself the title of a Sanhedrin. If we may believe not a few of the indications of the Talmud, that Sanhedrin was little better than a close, irreligious, unpatriotic confederacy of monopolizing and time-serving priests — the Boëthusim, the Kamhits, the Phabis, the family of Hanan, mostly of non-Palestinian origin — who were supported by the government, but detested by the people, and of whom this bad conspirator was the very life and soul.

And, perhaps, we may see a further reason for the apparent withdrawal of the Pharisees from all active co-operation in the steps which accompanied the condemnation and execution of Jesus, not only in the superior mildness which is attributed to them, and in their comparative insignificance in the civil administration, but also in their total want of sympathy with those into whose too fatal toils they had delivered the Son of God. There seems, indeed, to be a hitherto unnoticed circumstance which, while it would kindle to the highest degree the fury of the Sadducees, would rather enlist in Christ's favor the sympathy of their rivals. What had roused the disdainful *insouciance* of these powerful aristocrats? Morally insignificant — the patrons and adherents of opinions which had so little hold upon the people that Jesus had never directed against them one tithe of the stern denunciation which He had levelled at the Pharisees — they had played but a very minor part in the opposition which had sprung up round the Messiah's steps. Nay, further than this, they would be wholly at one with Him in rejecting and disconntenancing the minute and casuistical frivolities of the Oral Law; they might even have rejoiced that they had in Him a holy and irresistible ally in their opposition to all the *Hagadôth* and *Halachôth* which had germinated in a fungus growth over the whole body of the Mosaic institutions.[1] Whence, then, this sudden outburst of the very deadliest and most ruthless opposition? It is a conjecture that has not yet been made, but which the notices of the Talmud bring home to my mind with strong conviction, that the rage of these priests was mainly due to our Lord's words and acts concerning that House of God which they regarded as their exclusive domain, and, above all, to His second public cleansing of the Temple. They could not indeed *press* this point in their accusations, because the act was one of which, secretly at least, the Pharisees, in all probability, heartily approved; and had they urged it against Him they would have lost all chance of impressing upon Pilate a sense of their unanimity. The first cleansing might have been passed over as an isolated act of zeal, to which little importance need be attached, while the teaching of Jesus was mainly confined to despised and far-off Galilee; but the second had been more public, and more vehement, and had apparently kindled a more general indignation against the gross abuse which called it forth. Accordingly, in all three Evangelists we find that those who complained of the act are not distinctively Pharisees, but "*Chief Priests* and Scribes" (Matt. xxi. 15; Mark xi. 18; Luke xix. 47), who seem at once to have derived from it a fresh stimulus to seek His destruction.

But, again, it may be asked, Is there any reason beyond this bold infraction of their authority, this indignant repudiation of an arrangement which *they* had sanctioned, which would have stirred up the rage of these priestly families? Yes — for we may assume from the Talmud that it tended *to wound their avarice, to interfere with their illicit and greedy gains.* Avarice — the besetting sin of Judas — the besetting sin of the Jewish race — seems also to have been the besetting sin of the family of Hanan. It was they who had founded the *chanujôth* — the famous four shops under the twin cedars of Olivet — in which were sold things legally pure, and which they had manipulated with such commercial cunning as artificially to raise the price of doves to a gold coin apiece, until the people were delivered from this gross imposition by the indignant interference of a grandson

---

[1] Jos. *Antt.* xiii. 10, § 6.

of Hillel. There is every reason to believe that the shops which had intruded even under the Temple porticoes were not only sanctioned by their authority, but even managed for their profit. To interfere with these was to rob them of one important source of that wealth and worldly comfort to which they attached such extravagant importance. There was good reason why Hanan, the head representative of "the viper brood," as a Talmudic writer calls them, should strain to the utmost his cruel prerogative of power to crush a Prophet whose actions tended to make him and his powerful family at once wholly contemptible and comparatively poor.

Such then were the feelings of bitter contempt and hatred with which the ex-High Priest assumed the initiative in interrogating Jesus. The fact that he dared not avow them — nay, was forced to keep them wholly out of sight — would only add to the intensity of his bitterness. Even his method of procedure seems to have been as wholly illegal as was his assumption, in such a place and at such an hour, of any legal function whatever. Anxious, at all hazards, to trump up some available charge of secret sedition, or of unorthodox teaching, he questioned Jesus of His disciples and of His doctrine. The answer, for all its calmness, involved a deep reproof. "*I* have spoken openly to the world; *I* ever taught in the synagogue and in the Temple, where all the Jews come together, and in secret I said nothing. Why askest thou *me?* Ask those who have heard me what I said to them. Lo! these" — pointing, perhaps, to the bystanders [1] — "know what *I* said to them." The emphatic repetition of the "I," and its unusually significant position at the end of the sentence, show that a contrast was intended; as though He had said, "This midnight, this sedition, this secrecy, this indecent mockery of justice, are *yours*, not *mine*. There has never been anything esoteric in my doctrine; never anything to conceal in my actions; no hole-and-corner plots among my followers. But thou? and thine?" Even the minions of Annas felt the false position of their master under this calm rebuke; they felt that before the transparent innocence of this youthful Rabbi of Nazareth the hoary hypocrisy of the crafty Sadducee was abashed. "Answerest thou the High Priest so?" said one of them with a burst of illegal insolence; and then, unreproved by this priestly violator of justice, he profaned with the first infamous blow the sacred face of Christ. Then first that face which, as the poet-preacher says, "the angels stare upon with wonder as infants at a bright sunbeam," was smitten

---

[1] οὗτοι, not ἐκεῖνοι.

by a contemptible slave. The insult was borne with noble meekness. Even St. Paul, when similarly insulted, flaming into sudden anger at such a grossly illegal violence, had scathed the ruffian and his abettor with "God shall smite thee, thou whited wall;"[1] but He, the Son of God — He who was infinitely above all apostles and all angels — with no flash of anger, with no heightened tone of natural indignation, quietly reproved the impudent transgressor with the words, "If I spoke evil, bear witness concerning the evil; but if well, why smitest thou me?" It was clear that nothing more could be extorted from Him; that before such a tribunal He would brook no further question. Bound, in sign that He was to be condemned — though unheard and unsentenced — Annas sent Him across the court-yard to Joseph Caiaphas, his son-in-law, who, not by the grace of God, but by the grace of the Roman Procurator, was the titular High Priest.

ii. Caiaphas, like his father-in-law, was a Sadducee — equally astute and unscrupulous with Annas, but endowed with less force of character and will. In his house took place the second private and irregular stage of the trial.[2] There — for though the poor Apostles could not watch for one hour in sympathetic prayer, these nefarious plotters could watch all night in their deadly malice — a few of the most desperate enemies of Jesus among the Priests and Sadducees were met. To form a session of the Sanhedrin there must at least have been twenty-three members present. And we may perhaps be allowed to conjecture that this particular body before which Christ was now convened was mainly composed of Priests. There were in fact three Sanhedrins, or as we should rather call them, committees of the Sanhedrin, which ordinarily met at different places — in the *Lishcat Haggazzith*, or Paved Hall; in the *Beth Midrash* or Chamber by the Partition of the Temple; and near the Gate of the Temple Mount. Such being the case, it is no unreasonable supposition that these committees were composed of different

---

[1] Acts xxiii. 3. It is remarkable that in the Talmudic malediction of these priestly families (*Pesach.* 57; *Toseft. Menachôth,* 15) there is an express complaint that they monopolized all offices by making their sons treasurers, captains (of the Temple), &c., and that "*their servants* (עבדיהן) *strike the people with their rods.*" When Josephus talks of Hanan the son of Hanan as "a prodigious lover of liberty and admirer of democracy," the mere context is quite sufficient to show that this is a very careless, if not dishonest, judgment; as for his wonderful "virtue" and "justice," it is probable that Josephus hardly cared to reconcile his own statements with what he records of him in *Antt.* xx. 9, § 1.

[2] Matt. xxvi. 59—68; Mark xiv. 55—65. Irregular, for capital trials could only take place by daylight (*Sanhedr.* iv. 1).

elements, and that one of them may have been mainly sacerdotal in its constitution. If so, it would have been the most likely of them all, at the present crisis, to embrace the most violent measures against One whose teaching now seemed to endanger the very existence of priestly rule.[1]

But, whatever may have been the nature of the tribunal over which Caiaphas was now presiding, it is clear that the Priests were forced to change their tactics. Instead of trying, as Hanan had done, to overawe and entangle Jesus with insidious questions, and so to involve Him in a charge of secret apostasy, they now tried to brand Him with the crime of public error. In point of fact their own bitter divisions and controversies made the task of convicting Him a very difficult one. If they dwelt on any supposed opposition to civil authority, *that* would rather enlist the sympathies of the Pharisees in His favor; if they dwelt on supposed Sabbath violations or neglect of traditional observances, that would accord with the views of the Sadducees. The Sadducees dared not complain of His cleansing of the Temple: the Pharisees, or those who represented them, found it useless to advert to His denunciations of tradition. But Jesus, infinitely nobler than His own noblest Apostle, would not foment these latent animosities, or evoke for His own deliverance a contest of these slumbering prejudices. He did not disturb the temporary compromise which united them in a common hatred against Himself. Since, therefore, they had nothing else to go upon, the Chief Priests and the entire Sanhedrin *"sought false witness"* — such is the terribly simple expression of the Evangelists — " *sought* false witness against Jesus to put Him to death." Many men, with a greedy, unnatural depravity, *seek* false witness — mostly of the petty, ignoble, malignant sort ; and the powers of evil usually supply it to them. The Talmud seems to insinuate that the custom, which they pretend was the *general* one, had been followed in the case of Christ, and that two witnesses had been placed in concealment while a treacherous disciple — ostensibly Judas Iscariot — had obtained from His own lips an avowal of His claims. This, however, is no less false

---

[1] Twenty-three would be about a third of the entire number (Maimonides, *Sanhedr.* 3). Unless there be some slight confusion between the second and third trials, the πάντες of Mark xiv. 53 cannot be taken *au pied de la lettre*,[381] ‡ but must mean simply "all who were engaged in this conspiracy." Indeed, this seems to be distinctly implied in Mark xv. 1. Similarly in Matt. xxvi. 59, τὸ συνέδριον ὅλον must mean "that entire *committee* of the Sanhedrin," as may be seen by comparing it with xxvii. 1. That συνέδριον may be used simply for a small *Beth Dín* is clear from Matt. v. 22. (Jost. i. 404.)

than the utterly absurd and unchronological assertion of the tract *Sanhedrin*, that Jesus had been excommunicated by Joshua Ben Perachiah, and that though for forty days a herald had proclaimed that He had brought magic from Egypt and seduced the people, no single witness came forward in His favor.[1] Setting aside these absurd inventions, we learn from the Gospels that though the agents of these priests were eager to lie, yet their testimony was *so* false, so shadowy, so self-contradictory, that it all melted to nothing, and even those unjust and bitter judges could not with any decency accept it. But at last two came forward, whose false witness looked more promising.[2] They had heard Him say something about destroying the Temple, and rebuilding it in three days. According to one version His expression had been, "*I can destroy* this Temple ; " according to another, "*I will destroy* this Temple." The fact was that He had said neither, but "*Destroy* this Temple ; " and the imperative had but been addressed, hypothetically, to them. *They* were to be the destroyers ; He had but promised to rebuild. It was just one of those perjuries which was all the more perjured, because it bore some distant semblance to the truth ; and by just giving a different *nuance* to His actual words they had, with the ingenuity of slander, reversed their meaning, and hoped to found upon them a charge of constructive blasphemy. But even this semblable perjury utterly broke down, and Jesus listened in silence while His disunited enemies hopelessly confuted each other's testimony. Guilt often breaks into excuses where perfect innocence is dumb. He simply suffered His false accusers and their false listeners to entangle themselves in the hideous coil of their own malignant lies, and the silence of the innocent Jesus atoned for the excuses of the guilty Adam.

But that majestic silence troubled, thwarted, confounded, maddened them. It weighed them down for the moment with an incubus of intolerable self-condemnation. They felt, before that silence, as if *they* were the culprits, He the judge. And as every poisoned arrow of their carefully-provided perjuries fell harmless at His feet, as though blunted on the diamond shield of His white innocence, they began to fear lest, after all, their thirst for His blood would go unslaked, and their whole plot fail. Were they thus to be conquered by the feebleness of their own weapons, without His stirring a finger,

---

[1] *Sanhedr.*, 43 *a.* (Grätz, *Gesch. Jud.* iii. 242.) — See Excursus II., "Allusions to Christ and Christians in the Talmud."

[2] The brevity of the Evangelists prevents us from knowing whether the ordinary Jewish rules of evidence were observed. For Josephus's account of the trial of Zechariah the son of Baruch, see *Bell. Jud.* iv. 5, § 4.

or uttering a word? Was this Prophet of Nazareth to prevail against *them*, merely for lack of a few consistent lies? Was His life charmed even against calumny confirmed by oaths? It was intolerable.

Then Caiaphas was overcome with a paroxysm of fear and anger. Starting up from his judgment-seat, and striding into the midst [1] — with what a voice, with what an attitude we may well imagine! — "Answerest Thou NOTHING?" he exclaimed. "What is it that these witness against Thee?" Had not Jesus been aware that these His judges were wilfully feeding on ashes and seeking lies, He might have answered; but now His awful silence remained unbroken.

Then, reduced to utter despair and fury, this false High Priest — with marvellous inconsistency, with disgraceful illegality — still standing as it were with a threatening attitude over his prisoner, exclaimed, "I adjure Thee by the living God to tell us" — what? whether Thou art a malefactor? whether Thou *hast* secretly taught sedition? whether Thou hast openly uttered blasphemy? — no, but (and surely the question showed the dread misgiving which lay under all their deadly conspiracy against Him) — "WHETHER THOU ART THE CHRIST, THE SON OF GOD?"

Strange question to a bound, defenceless, condemned criminal; and strange question from such a questioner — a High Priest of his people! Strange question from the judge who was hounding on his false witnesses against the prisoner! Yet so adjured, and to such a question, Jesus could not be silent; on such a point He could not leave Himself open to misinterpretation. In the days of His happier ministry, when they would have taken Him by force to make Him a King — in the days when to claim the Messiahship in *their* sense would have been to meet all their passionate prejudices half way, and to place Himself upon the topmost pinnacle of their adoring homage — in *those* days He had kept His title of Messiah utterly in the background: but now, at this awful decisive moment, when death was near — when, humanly speaking, nothing could be gained, everything *must* be lost, by the avowal — there thrilled through all the ages — thrilled through that Eternity, which is the synchronism of all the future, and all the present, and all the past — the solemn answer,

---

[1] Mark xiv. 60, ἀναστάς . . . εἰς μέσον. The Sanhedrin sat on opposite divans of a circular hall; the *Nasi*, or President, who was usually the High Priest, sat in the middle at the farther end, with the *Ab Beth Din*, or Father of the House of Judgment, on his right, and the *Chakam*, or Wise Man, on his left. The accused was placed opposite to him. (See Jos. *Bell. Jud.* iv. 5, § 4; Keim III. ii. 328.)

"I am;'¹ *and ye shall see the Son of Man sitting on the right hand of power, and coming with the clouds of heaven.*" ² In that answer the thunder rolled — a thunder louder than at Sinai, though the ears of the cynic and the Sadducee heard it not then, nor hear it now. In overacted and ill-omened horror, the unjust judge who had thus supplemented the failure of the perjuries which he had vainly sought — the false High Priest rending his linen robes before the True ³ — demanded of the assembly His instant condemnation.

" BLASPHEMY ! " he exclaimed; "what further need have we of witnesses? See, *now* ye *heard* his blasphemy! What is your decision?" And with the confused tumultuous cry, " He is *ish maveth,*" " A man of death," " Guilty of death," the dark conclave was broken up, and the second stage of the trial of Jesus was over.⁴

---

¹ In Matt. xxvi. 64, Σὺ εἶπας. Alford refers to John xii. 49.

² Dan. vii. 13 : " I saw in the night visions, and, behold, one like the Son of Man came with the clouds of heaven, and came to the Ancient of Days, and they brought him near before him." Hence the hybrid term, Bar-νεφέλη, " Son of a cloud," applied to the Messiah in *Sanhedr.* 96, 6.

³ This was forbidden to the High Priest in cases of mourning (Lev. x. 6 , xxi· 10) ; but the Jewish *Halacha* considered it lawful in cases of blasphemy (גדּוּף, *gidduph*) (1 Macc. xi. 71 ; Jos. *B. J.* ii. 15, § 4). As to Joseph Caiaphas the Talmud is absolutely silent; but the general conception which it gives of the priests of this epoch agrees entirely with the Gospels. It tells how since the days of Valerius Gratus the office had constantly been bought and sold ; how the widow Martha, daughter of Boethus, gave Agrippa II. two bushels of gold *denarii* to buy it for Joshua Ben Gamala, her betrothed ; how it was disgraced by cringing meanness and supple sycophancy ; how there were more than eighty of these High Priests of the second Temple (which they quoted in illustration of Prov. x. 27), whereas there were only eighteen of the first Temple (Frankl, *Monatsschrift*, Dec. 1852, p. 588 ; Raphall, *Hist. of Jews*, ii. 368) ; and many other disgraces and enormities.

⁴ Cf. Numb. xxxv. 31.

CHAPTER LIX.

THE INTERVAL BETWEEN THE TRIALS.

"I gave my back to the smiters, and my cheeks to them that plucked off the hair; I hid not my face from shame and spitting."—Isa. l. 6.

AND this was how the Jews at last received their promised Messiah — longed for with passionate hopes during two thousand years; since then regretted in bitter agony for well-nigh two thousand more! From this moment He was regarded [1] by all the apparitors of the Jewish Court as a heretic, liable to death by stoning; and was only remanded into custody to be kept till break of day, because by daylight only, and in the *Lishcat Haggazzith*, or Hall of Judgment, and only by a full session of the entire Sanhedrin, could He be legally condemned. And since now they looked upon Him as a fit person to be insulted with impunity, He was haled through the court-yard to the guard-room with blows and curses, in which it may be that not only the attendant menials, but even the cold but now infuriated Sadducees took their share. It was now long past midnight, and the spring air was then most chilly. In the centre of the court the servants of the priests were warming themselves under the frosty starlight as they stood round a fire of coals. And as He was led past that fire He heard — what was to Him a more deadly bitterness than any which His brutal persecutors could pour into His cup of anguish — He heard His boldest Apostle denying Him with oaths.

For during these two sad hours of His commencing tragedy, as He stood in the Halls of Annas and of Caiaphas, another moral tragedy, which He had already prophesied, had been taking place in the outer court.

As far as we can infer from the various narratives, [2] the palace in

---

[1] "Millionen gebrochener Herzen und Augen haben seinen Tod noch nicht abgebüsst" [382] (Grätz, iii. 245). On the whole of this trial, see the powerful and noble remarks of Lange (iv. 309) and Keim (*ubi supra*).

[2] In this narrative again there are obvious *variations* in the quadruple accounts of the Evangelists; but the text will sufficiently show that there is no irreconcilable discrepancy if they are judged fairly and on common-sense principles. The

Jerusalem, conjointly occupied by Annas the real, and Caiaphas the titular High Priest, seems to have been built round a square court, and entered by an arched passage or vestibule; and on the farther side of it, probably up a short flight of steps,[1] was the hall in which the committee of the Sanhedrin had met. Timidly, and at a distance, two only of the Apostles had so far recovered from their first panic as to follow far in the rear[2] of the melancholy procession. One of these — the beloved disciple — known perhaps to the High Priest's household as a young fisherman of the Lake of Galilee — had found ready admittance, with no attempt to conceal his sympathies or his identity. Not so the other. Unknown, and a Galilæan, he had been stopped at the door by the youthful portress. Better, far better, had his exclusion been final. For it was a night of tumult, of terror, of suspicion; and Peter was weak, and his intense love was mixed with fear, and yet he was venturing into the very thick of his most dangerous enemies. But John, regretting that he should be debarred from entrance, and judging perhaps of his friend's firmness by his own, exerted his influence to obtain admission for him. With bold imprudence, and concealing the better motives which had brought him thither, Peter, warned though he had been, but warned in vain, walked into the court-yard, and sat down in the very middle of the servants[3] of the very men before whom at that moment his Lord was being arraigned on a charge of death. The portress, after the admission of those concerned in the capture, seems to have been relieved (as was only natural at that late hour) by another maid, and advancing to the group of her fellow-servants, she fixed a curious and earnest gaze[4] on the dubious stranger as he sat full in the red glare of the firelight, and then, with a flash of recognition, she exclaimed, "Why, *you*, as well as the other, were with Jesus of Galilee."[5] Peter was off his guard. At

---

conception of accuracy in ancient writers differed widely from our own, and a document is by no means necessarily inaccurate, because the brevity, or the special purpose, or the limited information of the writer, made it necessarily incomplete. "Qui plura dicit, pauciora complectitur; qui pauciora dicit, plura non negat." [383]

[1] Mark xiv. 66, κ ά τ ω ἐν τῇ αὐλῇ.

[2] Luke xxii. 54, μακρόθεν.

[3] Luke xxii. 55, μέσος αὐτῶν.

[4] Luke xxii. 56, ἀτενίσασα. For the other particulars in this clause compare John xviii. 17 with Matt. xxvi. 69; Mark xiv. 67. For female porters, see Mark xiii. 34; Acts xii. 13.

[5] It is most instructive to observe that no one of the Evangelists puts exactly the same words into her mouth (showing clearly the nature of their report), and yet each faithfully preserves the καὶ, which, in the maid's question, couples Peter with John.

this period of life his easy impressionable nature was ever liable to be moulded by the influence of the moment, and he passed readily into passionate extremes. Long, long afterwards, we find a wholly unexpected confirmation of the probability of this sad episode of his life, in the readiness with which he lent himself to the views of the Apostle of the Gentiles, and the equal facility with which a false shame, and a fear of " them which were of the circumcision," made him swerve into the wrong and narrow proprieties of " certain which came from James." And thus it was that the mere curious question of an inquisitive young girl startled him by its very suddenness into a quick denial of his Lord. Doubtless, at the moment, it presented itself to him as a mere prudent evasion of needless danger. But did he hope to stop there? Alas, " once denied " is always " thrice denied ; " and the sudden "manslaughter upon truth " always, and rapidly, develops into its utter and deliberate murder; and a lie is like a stone set rolling upon a mountain-side, which is instantly beyond its utterer's control.

For a moment, perhaps, his denial was accepted, for it had been very public, and very emphatic.[1] But it warned him of his danger. Guiltily he slinks away again from the glowing brazier to the arched entrance of the court, as the crowing of a cock smote, not quite unheeded, on his guilty ear.[2] His respite was very short. The portress — part of whose duty it was to draw attention to dubious strangers — had evidently gossiped about him to the servant who had relieved her in charge of the door. Some other idlers were standing about, and this second maid pointed him out to them as having certainly been with Jesus of Nazareth. A lie seemed more than ever necessary now, and to secure himself from all further molestation he even confirmed it with an oath. But now flight seemed impossible, for it

---

[1] Matt. xxvi. 70, ἔμπροσθεν πάντων; Mark xiv. 68, οὐκ οἶδα (sc. αὐτόν), οὐδὲ ἐπίσταμαι σὺ τί λέγεις.

[2] Matt. xxvi. 71, εἰς τὸν πυλῶνα; Mark xiv. 68, εἰς τὸ προαύλιον. There must be some trivial " inaccuracy," if any one cares to press the word, either here or in John xviii. 25 (εἶπον οὖν αὐτῷ), Luke xxii. 58 (ἕτερος). A wretched pseudo-criticism has fixed on the cock as " unhistorical," because the Jews are thought to have held cocks unclean, from their scratching in the dung. But not to mention that the bird may have belonged to some Roman in the Tower of Antonia, other Talmudical stories show that cocks *were* kept at Jerusalem : *e. g.*, the story of a cock that was stoned for killing an infant (*Berachôth*, 27, 1 ; see Buxtorf, *Lex. Talm.* 81, 2653). It is a condescension to notice such objections, particularly when they are supposed to rest on Talmudical authorities quoted from our imperfect knowledge of a literature which is inveterately unhistorical, and abounds in self-contradictions. See Excursus XII., " Notes on the Talmud."

would only confirm suspicion; so with desperate, gloomy resolution he once more — with feelings which can barely be imagined — joined the unfriendly and suspicious group who were standing round the fire.

A whole hour passed: for him it must have been a fearful hour, and one never to be forgotten. The temperament of Peter was far too nervous and vehement to suffer him to feel at ease under this new complication of ingratitude and falsehood. If he remain silent among these priestly servitors, he is betrayed by the restless self-consciousness of an evil secret which tries in vain to simulate indifference; if he brazen it out with careless talk, he is fatally betrayed by his Galilæan burr. It is evident that, in spite of denial and of oath, they wholly distrust and despise him; and at last one of the High Priest's servants — a kinsman of the wounded Malchus — once more strongly and confidently charged him with having been with Jesus in the garden, taunting him, in proof of it, with the misplaced gutturals of his provincial dialect. The others joined in the accusation.[1] Unless he persisted, all was lost which might seem to have been gained. Perhaps one more effort would set him quite free from these troublesome charges, and enable him to wait and see the end. Pressed closer and closer by the sneering, threatening band of idle servitors — sinking deeper and deeper into the mire of faithlessness and fear — "then began he to curse and to swear, saying, I know not the man." And at that fatal moment of guilt, which might well have been for him the moment of an apostasy as fatal and final as had been that of his brother apostle — at that fatal moment, while those shameless curses still quivered on the air — first the cock crew in the cold grey dusk, and at the same moment, catching the last accents of those perjured oaths, either through the open portal of the judgment-hall,[2] or as He was led past the group at the fireside through the open court, with rude pushing and ribald jeers, and blows and spitting — the Lord — the Lord in the agony of His humiliation, in the majesty of His silence — "*the Lord turned and looked upon Peter.*" Blessed are those on whom, when He looks in sorrow, the Lord looks also with love! It was enough. Like an arrow through his inmost soul, shot the mute eloquent anguish of that reproachful glance. As the sunbeam smites the last hold of snow upon the rock,

---

[1] John xviii. 26 (συγγενής); Luke xxii. 59 (ἄλλος τις διϊσχυρίζετο); Matt. xxvi. 73 (οἱ ἑστῶτες); Mark xiv. 70 (οἱ παρεστῶτες).

[2] The room in which Jesus was being tried may have been one of the kind called *muck'ad* in the East, *i. e.*, a room with *an open front*, two or more arches, and a low railing, the floor of which is paved *leewa'n*. (Lane, *Mod. Egyptians*, i. 22.)

ere it rushes in avalanche down the tormented hill, so the false self of the fallen Apostle slipped away. It was enough : " he saw no more enemies, he knew no more danger, he feared no more death." Flinging the fold of his mantle over his head,[1] he too, like Judas, rushed forth into the night. Into the night, but not as Judas; into the unsunned outer darkness of miserable self-condemnation, but not into the midnight of remorse and of despair ; into the night, but, as has been beautifully said, it was " to meet the morning dawn."[2] If the angel of Innocence had left him, the angel of Repentance took him gently by the hand. Sternly, yet tenderly, the spirit of grace led up this broken-hearted penitent before the tribunal of his own conscience, and there his old life, his old shame, his old weakness, his old self was doomed to that death of godly sorrow which was to issue in a new and a nobler birth.

And it was this crime, committed against Him by the man who had first proclaimed Him as the Christ — who had come to Him over the stormy water — who had drawn the sword for Him in Gethsemane — who had affirmed so indignantly that he would die with Him rather than deny Him — it was this denial, confirmed by curses, that Jesus heard immediately after He had been condemned to death, and at the very commencement of His first terrible derision. For, in the guard-room to which He was remanded to await the break of day, all the ignorant malice of religious hatred, all the narrow vulgarity of brutal spite, all the cold innate cruelty which lurks under the abjectness of Oriental servility, was let loose against Him. His very meekness, His very silence, His very majesty — the very stainlessness of His innocence, the very grandeur of His fame — every divine circumstance and quality which raised Him to a height so infinitely immeasurable above His persecutors — all these made Him an all the more welcome victim for their low and devilish ferocity. They spat in His face ; they smote Him with rods ; they struck Him with their closed fists and with their open palms.[3] In the fertility of their furious and hateful insolence, they invented against Him a sort of

---

[1] ἐπιβαλὼν (Mark xiv. 72). This seems a better meaning than (i.) " vehemently " (Matthew, Luke, πικρῶς), or (ii.) " when he thought thereon " (but cf. Marc. Aurel. *Comment.* x. 30), or (iii.) " hiding his face in his hands."

[2] Lange, vi. 319.

[3] Matt. xxvi. 67, ἐνέπτυσαν . . . ἐκολάφισαν (slapped with open palm) . . . ἐρράπισαν (struck, probably with sticks); Mark xiv. 65, ῥαπίσμασιν . . ἔλαβον al. ἔβαλλον ; Luke xxii. 63, 64, ἐνέπαιζον αὐτῷ δέροντες . . . τίς ἐστιν ὁ παίσας σε; There is a pathetic variety in these five forms of insult by blows [cf. Acts xxi. 32; xxiii. 2 ; Isa. l. 6; and the treatment of one of Annas's own sons (Jos. *B. J.* iv. 5, § 3)].

game. Blindfolding His eyes, they hit Him again and again, with the repeated question, " Prophesy to us, O Messiah, who it is that smote thee." ¹ So they wiled away the dark cold hours till the morning, revenging themselves upon His impassive innocence for their own present vileness and previous terror; and there, in the midst of that savage and wanton varletry, the Son of God, bound and blindfold, stood in His long and silent agony, defenceless and alone. It was His first derision — His derision as the Christ, the Judge attainted, the Holy One a criminal, the Deliverer in bonds.

iii. At last the miserable lingering hours were over, and the grey dawn shuddered, and the morning blushed upon that memorable day. And with the earliest dawn — for so the Oral Law ordained,² and they who could trample on all justice and all mercy were yet scrupulous about all the infinitely little — Jesus was led into the *Lishcat Haggazzith*, or Paved Hall at the southeast of the Temple, or perhaps into the *Chanujôth*, or " Shops," which owed their very existence to Hanan and his family, where the Sanhedrin had been summoned, for His third actual, but His first formal and legal trial.³ It was now probably about six o'clock in the morning, and a full session met. Well-nigh all — for there were the noble exceptions at least of Nicodemus and of Joseph of Arimathea, and we may hope also of Gamaliel, the grandson of Hillel — were inexorably bent upon His death. The Priests were there, whose greed and selfishness He had reproved; the Elders, whose hypocrisy He had branded; the Scribes,

---

¹ Wetstein quotes from *Sanhedr.* f. 93 *b*, a similar tentative applied to the false Messiah, Bar-Cochebas.

² *Zohar*, 56. See Excursus V.

³ Luke xxii. 66—71. It is only by courtesy that this body can be regarded as a Sanhedrin at all. Jost observes that there is in the Romish period no trace of any genuine legal Sanhedrin, apart from mere special incompetent gatherings. (See Jos. *Antt.* xx. 9, § 1; *B. J.* iv. 5, § 4.) But all the facts about the Sanhedrin of this period are utterly obscure. On Sabbaths and feast days they are said to have met in the *Beth Midrash*, or Temple Synagogue, which was built along the *Chêl*, or wall between the Outer Court and the Court of the Women. (Lightfoot, *Hor. Hebr.*; Keim, &c.) R. Ismael, son of R. Josè, the author of *Seder Olam*, is reported to have said that " forty years before the destruction of the Temple the Sanhedrin exiled itself (from the Paved Hall), and established itself in the *Chanujôth* " (*Aboda Zara*, 8 *b*); and this is the first of ten migrations of the Sanhedrin mentioned in *Rosh Hashana*, 31 *a*. These *Chanujôth*, four in number, are said to have been shops for the sale of doves, &c., under a cedar on the Mount of Olives, connected with the Temple by a bridge over the Kedron (*Taanith*, iv. 8). They seem to have been founded by the family of Annas, who made them very profitable, and they are called חנויות בני חני. They were destroyed by the mob when the goods of these detested priests were pillaged three years before the siege of Jerusalem. (Derenbourg, *Hist. de Pal.* 468; Buxtorf, *Lex Talm.* s. v. דין, p. 514.)

whose ignorance He had exposed;[1] and worse than all, the worldly, sceptical, would-be philosophic Sadducees, always the most cruel and dangerous of opponents,[2] whose empty sapience He had so grievously confuted. All these were bent upon His death; all filled with repulsion at that infinite goodness; all burning with hatred against a nobler nature than any which they could even conceive in their loftiest dreams. And yet their task in trying to achieve His destruction was not easy. The Jewish fables of His death in the Talmud, which are shamelessly false from beginning to end,[3] say that for forty days, though summoned daily by heraldic proclamation, not one person came forward, according to custom, to maintain His innocence, and that consequently He was first stoned as a seducer of the people (*mesith*), and then hung on the accursed tree. The fact was that the Sanhedrists had not the power of inflicting death,[4] and even if the Pharisees would have ventured to usurp it in a tumultuary sedition, as they afterwards

---

[1] These are the Sopherîm, who may perhaps have ordinarily formed a separate committee of the Sanhedrin. See Excursus XIII., "The Sanhedrin."

[2] Though Josephus was a Pharisee, we may, from its probability, accept his testimony on this point — εἰδὶ περὶ τὰς κρίσεις ὠμοὶ παρὰ πάντας τοὺς Ἰουδαίους [384] (*Antt.* xx. 9, § 1; *B. J.* ii. 8, § 14). The philosophic insouciance of a man of the world, when once thoroughly irritated, knows no scruples. Ordinarily the Sanhedrin was a mild tribunal. The members fasted a whole day when they had condemned any one to death, and many Rabbis declared themselves with strong abhorrence against capital punishments. Some of them — like R. Akiba — considered it a blot on a meeting of the Sanhedrin to condemn even one offender to death. (Salvador, *Institt. de Moïse*, ii.; *Vie de Jésus*, ii. 108.) Their savagery on this occasion was doubtless due to Sadducean influence. The *Megillath Taanith*, § 10, mentions a sort of traditional penal code of this party which seems to have been Draconian in its severity, and which the Pharisees got set aside. These Sadducean priests, like Simeon Ben Shetach before them, had "*hot hands.*" (Derenbourg, p. 106.) See Excursus XIV., "Pharisees and Sadducees."

[3] Any one who cares to look at the Talmudic falsehoods and confusion about Ben Sotada, Pandera, &c., may see them in Buxtorf, *Lex. Talm.* s. v. סמר, p. 1458, seqq.; Derenbourg, *Hist. de Pal.* 468, seqq. In unexpurgated editions of the Talmud, the name of Jesus is said to occur twenty times. See Excursus II., "Allusions to Christ and Christians in the Talmud."

[4] This is distinctly stated by the Jews in John xviii. 31, and though contemporary notices seem to show that in any common case the Romans might *overlook* a judicial murder on religious grounds (John v. 18; vii. 25; Acts xxiii. 27), yet the Jews could not always act as they liked in such cases with impunity, as was proved by the reprimand and degradation of the younger Hanan for the part which he and the Sanhedrin took in the execution of James the brother of Jesus. Döllinger (*First Age of the Church*, E. Tr., p. 420) takes a different view, and thinks that all they meant was, that they could not crucify or put to death during a feast. But whatever may be the difficulties of the subject, the Talmud seems to confirm the distinct assertion of St. John. (*Berachôth*, f. 58, 1, and six or seven other places. See Buxtorf, *Lex. Talm.* p. 514.)

did in the case of Stephen, the less fanatic and more cosmopolitan Sadducees would be less likely to do so. Not content, therefore, with the *cherem*, or ban of greater excommunication, their only way to compass His death was to hand Him over to the secular arm.[1] At present they had only against Him a charge of constructive blasphemy, founded on an admission forced from Him by the High Priest, when even their own suborned witnesses had failed to perjure themselves to their satisfaction. There were many old accusations against Him, on which they could not rely. His violations of the Sabbath, as they called them, were all connected with miracles, and brought them, therefore, upon dangerous ground. His rejection of oral tradition involved a question on which Sadducees and Pharisees were at deadly feud. His authoritative cleansing of the Temple might be regarded with favor both by the Rabbis and the people. The charge of esoteric evil doctrines had been refuted by the utter publicity of His life. The charge of open heresies had broken down, from the total absence of supporting testimony. The problem before them was to convert the ecclesiastical charge of constructive blasphemy into a civil charge of constructive treason. But how could this be done? Not half the members of the Sanhedrin had been present at the hurried, nocturnal, and therefore illegal, session in the house of Caiaphas;[2] yet if they were all to condemn Him by a formal sentence, they must all hear something on which to found their vote. In answer to the adjuration of Caiaphas, He had solemnly admitted that He was the Messiah and the Son of God. The latter declaration would have been meaningless as a charge against Him before the tribunal of the Romans; but if He would repeat the former, they might twist it into something politically seditious. But He would not repeat it, in spite of their insistance, because He knew that it was open to their wilful misinterpretation, and because they were evidently acting in flagrant violation of their own express rules and traditions, which demanded that every arraigned criminal should be regarded and treated as innocent until his guilt was actually proved.

Perhaps, as they sat there with their King, bound and helpless before them, standing silent amid their clamorous voices, one or two of their most venerable members may have recalled the very different scene when Shemaia (Sameas) alone had broken the deep silence of their own cowardly terror upon their being convened to pass judgment on Herod for his murders. On that occasion, as Sameas had

---

[1] Acts ii. 23, διὰ χειρῶν ἀνόμων προσπήξαντες.[385]

[2] Be tardy in judgment" (*Pirke Abhôth ; Sanh.* i. f. 7). בת דינא בטל דינא (*Sanh.* 95, 1 ; Buxtorf, *Lex. Talm.*, p. 515).

pointed out, Herod had stood before them, not "in a submissive manner, with his hair dishevelled, and in a black and mourning garment," but "clothed in purple, and with the hair of his head finely trimmed, and with his armed men about him." And since no one dared, for very fear, even to mention the charges against him, Shemaia had prophesied that the day of vengeance should come, and that the very Herod before whom they and their prince Hyrcanus were trembling, would one day be the minister of God's anger against both him and them.[1] What a contrast was the present scene with that former one of half a century before! Now *they* were clamorous, their King was silent; they were powerful, their King defenceless; they guilty, their King divinely innocent; they the ministers of earthly wrath, their King the arbiter of Divine retribution.

But at last, to end a scene at once miserable and disgraceful, Jesus spoke. "If I tell you," He said, "ye will not believe; and if I ask you a question, you will not answer me." Still, lest they should have any excuse for failing to understand who He was, He added in tones of solemn warning, " But henceforth shall the Son of Man sit on the right hand of the power of God." "Art thou, then," they all exclaimed, "the Son of God?"[2] "Ye say that I am,"[3] He answered, in a formula with which they were familiar, and of which they understood the full significance. And then they too cried out, as Caiaphas had done before, "What further need have we of witness? for we ourselves heard from His own mouth." And so in this third condemnation by Jewish authority — a condemnation which they thought that Pilate would simply ratify, and so appease their burning hate — ended the third stage of the trial of our Lord. And this sentence also seems to have been followed by a *second* derision[4] resembling the first, but even more full of insult, and

---

[1] Jos. *Antt.* xiv. 9, § 4; *Bab. Sanhedrin*, f. 19, *a, b*. It is on this memorable occasion that we first meet with the name of Sanhedrin. Here Hyrcanus is, with the usual Jewish carelessness, called Jannæus, and Shemaia is called Simeon Ben Shetach. There seems, however, to be inextricable confusion between the names Hillel, Pollio, Abtalion, and Sameas, Shammai, Shemaia, and Simeon.

[2] Cf. Dan. vii. 13; Ps. viii. 4; cx. 1.

[3] On this formula (*antt' amarta*, Keim), which is found in the Talmud, see Schöttgen, *Hor. Hebr.*, p. 225, and the remarks of De Quincey, *Works*, iii. 304. It is clearly more than a mere affirmation.

[4] Unless Luke xxii. 63—65 (which seems as though it refers to verse 71) describes the issue of one of the trials which he has not narrated; but, literally taken, we might infer from Matt. xxvi. 67, that those who insulted Christ after the second trial were not *only* the servants.

worse to bear than the former, inasmuch as the derision of Priests, and Elders, and Sadducees is even more repulsively odious than that of menials and knaves.

Terribly soon did the Nemesis fall on the main actor in the lower stages of this iniquity. Doubtless through all those hours Judas had been a secure spectator of all that had occurred, and when the morning dawned upon that chilly night, and he knew the decision of the Priests and of the Sanhedrin, and saw that Jesus was now given over for crucifixion to the Roman Governor, then he began fully to realize all that he had done. There is in a great crime an awfully illuminating power.[1] It lights up the theatre of the conscience with an unnatural glare, and, expelling the twilight glamour of self-interest, shows the actions and motives in their full and true aspect. In Judas, as in so many thousands before and since, this opening of the eyes which follows the consummation of an awful sin to which many other sins have led, drove him from remorse to despair, from despair to madness, from madness to suicide. Had he, even then, but gone to His Lord and Saviour, and prostrated himself at His feet to implore forgiveness, all might have been well. But, alas! he went instead to the patrons and associates and tempters of his crime. From them he met with no pity, no counsel. He was a despised and broken instrument, and now he was tossed aside. They met his maddening remorse with chilly indifference and callous contempt. " I have sinned," he shrieked to them, "in that I have betrayed innocent blood." Did he expect them to console his remorseful agony, to share the blame of his guilt, to excuse and console him with their lofty dignity? " *What is that to us? See thou to that,*"[2] was the sole and heartless reply they deigned to the poor traitor whom they had encouraged, welcomed, incited to his deed of infamy. He felt that he was of no importance any longer ; that in guilt there is no possibility for mutual respect, no basis for any feeling but mutual abhorrence. His paltry thirty pieces of silver were all that he would get. For these he had sold his soul ; and these he should no more enjoy than Achan enjoyed the gold he buried, or Ahab the garden he had seized. Flinging them wildly down upon the pavement into the holy place where the priests sat, and into which he might not enter, he hurried into the despairing solitude from which he would

---

[1] Tac. *Ann.* xiv. 10, " Perfecto demum scelere magnitudo ejus intellecta est " ³⁸⁶ (cf. Juv. *Sat.* xiii. 238). I have tried to develop this strange law of the moral world in my *Silence and Voices of God*, p. 43.

[2] Matt. xxvii. 4, Σὺ ὄψῃ. The same words were given back to *them* by Pilate (ver. 24).

never emerge alive. In that solitude, we may never know what
" unclean wings " were flapping about his head. Accounts differed
as to the wretch's death. The probability is that the details were
never accurately made public. According to one account, he hung
himself, and tradition still points in Jerusalem to a ragged, ghastly,
wind-swept tree, which is called the "tree of Judas." According to
another version — not irreconcilable with the first, if we suppose that
a rope or a branch broke under his weight — he fell headlong, burst
asunder in the midst, and all his bowels gushed out.[1] According to a
third [2] — current among the early Christians — his body swelled to a
huge size, under some hideous attack of elephantiasis, and he was
crushed by a passing wagon. The arch-conspirators, in their sanctimonious scrupulosity, would not put the blood-money which he had
returned into the " Corban," or sacred treasury, but, after taking
counsel, bought with it the potter's field to bury strangers in — a plot
of ground which perhaps Judas had intended to purchase, and in
which he met his end. That field was long known and shuddered at
as the Aceldama, or "field of blood," a place foul, haunted, and
horrible.[3]

---

[1] Acts i. 18.

[2] Said to be derived from Papias (see Hofmann, 333; Cramer, *Cat. in Acts Ap.*,
p. 12). In the Book of Jubilees the death of Cain is similarly described. (Ewald,
Gesch. Christ., p. 535.)

[3] St. Matthew, ever alive to Old Testament analogies, connects this circumstance
with passages (apparently) of Jeremiah (xviii. 1, 2; xxxii. 6—12) and Zechariah
(xi. 12, 13). It is curious that St. Matthew never *names* Zechariah, though he
three times quotes him (xxi. 5; xxvi. 31; xxvii. 9); but it was a Jewish proverb
that Zechariah had the spirit of Jeremiah, and it is possible (*vide* Wordsworth *ad
loc.*) that this passage originally belonged to Jeremiah. The right translation
seems to be, " cast it into the treasury." The notion that two fields were called
Aceldama is probably a mistake of the Harmonists. Different sites for Aceldama
have been pointed out at different times. Since Jeremiah's day pilgrims have
been shown a field with a charnel-house in it, opposite the Pool of Siloam. Papias
says that, as though the very ground were cursed, no one could pass it, ἐὰν μὴ
τὰς ῥῖνας ταῖς χερσὶν ἐπιφράξῃ.[287]

CHAPTER LX.

JESUS BEFORE PILATE.

" Per procuratorem Pontium Pilatum supplicio affectus erat." [388] — TAC. *Ann.* xv. 44.

"SUFFERED under Pontius Pilate " — so, in every creed of Christendom, is the unhappy name of the Roman Procurator handed down to eternal execration. Yet the object of introducing that name was not to point a moral, but to fix an epoch; and, in point of fact, of all the civil and ecclesiastical rulers before whom Jesus was brought to judgment, Pilate was the least guilty of malice and hatred, the most anxious, if not to spare His agony, at least to save His life.

What manner of man was this in whose hands were placed, by power from above, the final destinies of the Saviour's life? Of his origin, and of his antecedents before A. D. 26, when he became the sixth Procurator of Judæa, but little is known. In rank he belonged to the *ordo equester*, and he owed his appointment to the influence of Sejanus. His name "Pontius " seems to point to a Samnite extraction ; his cognomen "Pilatus " to a warlike ancestry. His *praenomen*, if he had one, has not been preserved. In Judæa he had acted with all the haughty violence and insolent cruelty of a typical Roman governor. Scarcely had he been well installed as Procurator, when, allowing his soldiers to bring with them by night the silver eagles and other insignia of the legions from Cæsarea to the Holy City, he excited a furious outburst of Jewish feeling against an act which they regarded as idolatrous profanation. For five days and nights — often lying prostrate on the bare ground — they surrounded and almost stormed his residence at Cæsarea with tumultuous and threatening entreaties, and could not be made to desist on the sixth, even by the peril of immediate and indiscriminate massacre at the hands of the soldiers whom he sent to surround them. He had then sullenly given way, and this foretaste of the undaunted and fanatical resolution of the people with whom he had to deal, went far to embitter his whole administration with a sense of overpowering disgust.[1]

---

[1] Jos. *Antt.* xviii. 3, § 1 ; *B. J.* ii. 9, §§ 2, 3.

The outbreak of the Jews on a second occasion was perhaps less justifiable, but it might easily have been avoided, if Pilate would have studied their character a little more considerately, and paid more respect to their dominant superstition. Jerusalem seems to have always suffered, as it does very grievously to this day, from a bad and deficient supply of water. To remedy this inconvenience, Pilate undertook to build an aqueduct, by which water could be brought from the "Pools of Solomon." Regarding this as a matter of public benefit, he applied to the purpose some of the money from the "Corban," or sacred treasury, and the people rose in furious myriads. to resent this secular appropriation of their sacred fund. Stung by their insults and reproaches, Pilate disguised a number of his soldiers in Jewish costume, and sent them among the mob, with staves and daggers concealed under their garments, to punish the ringleaders. Upon the refusal of the Jews to separate quietly, a signal was given, and the soldiers carried out their instructions with such hearty good-will, that they wounded and beat to death not a few both of the guilty and the innocent, and created so violent a tumult that many perished by being trodden to death under the feet of the terrified and surging mob.[1] Thus, in a nation which produced the *sicarii*, Pilate had given a fatal precedent of sicarian conduct; the assassins had received from their Procurator an example of the use of political assassination.

A third seditious tumult must still more have embittered the disgust of the Roman Governor for his subjects, by showing him how impossible it was to live among such a people — even in a conciliatory ' spirit — without outraging some of their sensitive prejudices. In the Herodian palace at Jerusalem, which he occupied during the festivals, he had hung some gilt shields dedicated to Tiberius. In the speech of Agrippa before the Emperor Caius, as narrated by Philo, this act is attributed to wanton malice; but since, by the king's own admission, the shields were perfectly plain, and were merely decorated with a votive inscription, it is fair to suppose that the Jews had taken offence at what Pilate simply intended for a

---

[1] These two instances are twice related by Josephus, *Antt.* xviii. 3, §§ 1, 2 *B. J.* ii. 9, §§ 2, 3, 4. Ewald has precariously conjectured that the "tower of Siloam" which fell and crushed eighteen people may have been connected with these works, and so may have furnished ground to those who desired to interpret that accident as a Divine judgment (*Gesch.* v. 40; Luke xiii. 4). It has been suggested with some probability that the *real* disgust of the Jews against the plan for building an aqueduct was due to a belief that its construction would render the city less easy of defence.

harmless private ornament ; and one which, moreover, he could hardly remove without some danger of offending the gloomy and suspicious Emperor to whose honor they were dedicated. Since he would not give way, the chief men of the nation wrote a letter of complaint to Tiberius himself. It was a part of Tiberius's policy to keep the provinces contented, and his masculine intellect despised the obstinacy which would risk an insurrection rather than sacrifice a whim. He therefore reprimanded Pilate, and ordered the obnoxious shields to be transferred from Jerusalem to the Temple of Augustus at Cæsarea.

The latter incident is related by Philo only ;[1] and besides these three outbreaks, we hear in the Gospels of some wild tumult in which Pilate had mingled the blood of the Galilæans with their sacrifices. He was finally expelled from his Procuratorship in consequence of an accusation preferred against him by the Samaritans, who complained to Lucius Vitellius, the Legate of Syria, that he had wantonly attacked, slain, and executed a number of them who had assembled on Mount Gerizim by the invitation of an impostor — possibly Simon Magus — who promised to show them the Ark and sacred vessels of the Temple, which, he said, had been concealed there by Moses.[2] The conduct of Pilate seems on this occasion to have been needlessly prompt and violent; and although, when he arrived at Rome, he found that Tiberius was dead, yet even Gaius refused to reinstate him in his government, thinking it no doubt a bad sign that he should thus have become unpleasantly involved with the people of every single district in his narrow government. Sejanus had shown the most utter dislike against the Jews, and Pilate probably reflected his patron's antipathies.[3]

Such was Pontius Pilate, whom the pomps and perils of the great yearly festival had summoned from his usual residence at Cæsarea Philippi to the capital of the nation which he detested, and the headquarters of a fanaticism which he despised. At Jerusalem he occupied one of the two gorgeous palaces which had been erected there by the lavish architectural extravagance of the first Herod. It was situated in the Upper City to the south-west of the Temple Hill, and like the similar building at Cæsarea, having passed from the use of the provincial king to that of the Roman governor, was called Herod's Prae-

---

[1] *Legat. ad Caium,* § 38. Philo calls him βαρύμηνις, and τὴν φύσιν ἀκαμπὴς καὶ μετὰ τοῦ αὐθάδους ἀμείλικτος.[389]

[2] Jos. *Antt.* xviii. 4, § 1. This was a Messianic expectation (Ewald, *Gesch. Isr.* v 171, E. Tr.).

[3] See Salvador, *Dominion Romaine,* i. 428.

torium.[1] It was one of those luxurious abodes, " surpassing all description," which were in accordance with the tendencies of the age, and on which Josephus dwells with ecstasies of admiration.[2] Between its colossal wings of white marble — called respectively Cæsareum and Agrippeum, in the usual spirit of Herodian flattery to the Imperial house — was an open space commanding a noble view of Jerusalem, adorned with sculptured porticos and columns of many-colored marble, paved with rich mosaics, varied with fountains and reservoirs, and green promenades which furnished a delightful asylum to flocks of doves.[3] Externally it was a mass of lofty walls, and towers, and gleaming roofs, mingled in exquisite varieties of splendor; within, its superb rooms, large enough to accommodate a hundred guests, were adorned with gorgeous furniture and vessels of gold and silver. A magnificent abode for a mere Roman knight! and yet the furious fanaticism of the populace at Jerusalem made it a house so little desirable, that neither Pilate nor his predecessors seem to have cared to enjoy its luxuries for more than a few weeks in the whole year. They were forced to be present in the Jewish capital during those crowded festivals which were always liable to be disturbed by some outburst of inflammable patriotism, and they soon discovered that even a gorgeous palace can furnish but a repulsive residence if it be built on the heaving lava of a volcano.

In that kingly palace — such as in His days of freedom He had never trod — began, in three distinct acts, the fourth stage of that agitating scene which preceded the final agonies of Christ. It was unlike the idle inquisition of Annas — the extorted confession of Caiaphas — the illegal decision of the Sanhedrin; for here His judge was in His favor, and with all the strength of a feeble pride, and all the daring of a guilty cowardice, and all the pity of which a blood-stained nature was capable, did strive to deliver Him. This last trial is full of passion and movement : it involves a threefold change of scene, a threefold accusation, a threefold acquittal by the Romans, a threefold rejection by the Jews, a threefold warning to Pilate, and

---

[1] Acts xxiii. 35. Verres occupied an old palace of Hiero at Syracuse (Cic. *Verr.* ii. 5, 12).

[2] Jos. *B. J.* v. 4, § 4: παντὸς λόγου κρείσσων;[390] *id.*, οὐθ' ἑρμηνεῦσαι δυνατὸν ἀξίως τὰ βασίλεια.[391]

[3] See Jos. *B. J.* ii. 14, § 8; 15, § 5, from which it appears that Florus usually occupied this palace. For the Cæsareum and the Agrippeum, see *id.* i. 21, § 1, δύο τοὺς μεγίστους καὶ περικαλλεστάτους οἴκους οἷς οὐδὲ ναὸς πῇ συνεκρίνετο;[592] *id.* v. 4, § 4, ἀδιήγητος ἡ ποικιλία τῶν λίθων ἦν.[393] Keim [Eine stolze Residenz für einen römischen Ritter] has partly reproduced the description of Josephus, III. ii. 2, 361.

a threefold effort on his part, made with ever-increasing energy and ever-deepening agitation, to baffle the accusers and to set the victim free.[1]

1. It was probably about seven in the morning that, thinking to overawe the Procurator by their numbers and their dignity, the imposing procession of the Sanhedrists and Priests, headed, no doubt, by Caiaphas himself, conducted Jesus, with a cord round His neck,[2] from their Hall of Meeting over the lofty bridge which spanned the Valley of the Tyropœon, in presence of all the city, with the bound hands of a sentenced criminal, a spectacle to angels and to men.

Disturbed at this early hour, and probably prepared for some Paschal disturbance more serious than usual, Pilate entered the Hall of Judgment, whither Jesus had been led, in company (as seems clear) with a certain number of His accusers and of those most deeply interested in His case.[3] But the great Jewish hierarchs, shrinking from ceremonial pollution, though not from moral guilt — afraid of leaven, though not afraid of innocent blood — refused to enter the Gentile's hall, lest they should be polluted, and should consequently be unable that night to eat the Passover. In no good humor, but in haughty and half-necessary condescension to what he would regard as the despicable superstitions of an inferior race, Pilate goes out to them under the burning early sunlight of an Eastern spring. One haughty glance takes in the pompous assemblage of priestly notables, and the turbulent mob of this singular people, equally distasteful to him as a Roman and as a ruler; and observing in that one glance the fierce passions of the accusers, as he had already noted the meek ineffable grandeur of their victim, his question is sternly brief: " What accusation bring ye against this man ? " The question took them by surprise, and showed them that they must be prepared for an unconcealed antagonism to all their purposes. Pilate evidently intended a judicial inquiry;

---

[1] German criticism has, without any sufficient grounds, set aside as unhistorical much of St. John's narrative of this trial; but although it is not mentioned either by Josephus or by Philo, it agrees in the very minutest particulars with everything which we could expect from the accounts which they give us, both of Pilate's own character and antecedents, and of the relations in which he stood to the Emperor and to the Jews.

[2] δήσαντες (Matt. xxvii. 2; Mark xv. 1). In sign of condemnation: such at least is the early tradition, and St. Basil derives from this circumstance the use of the *stole* (Jer. Taylor, III. xv.).

[3] Being only a procurator, Pilate had no *quaestor*, and therefore was obliged to try all causes himself. In this instance, he very properly refused to assume the responsibility of the execution without sharing in the trial. He did not choose to degrade himself into a mere tool of Jewish superstition.

they had expected only a license to kill, and to kill, not by a Jewish method of execution, but by one which they regarded as more horrible and accursed.[1] "If He were not a malefactor," is their indefinite and surly answer, "we would not have delivered Him up unto thee." But Pilate's Roman knowledge of law, his Roman instinct of justice, his Roman contempt for their murderous fanaticism, made him not choose to act upon a charge so entirely vague, nor give the sanction of his tribunal to their dark disorderly decrees. He would not deign to be an executioner where he had not been a judge. "Very well," he answered, with a superb contempt, "take ye Him and judge Him according to your law." But now they are forced to the humiliating confession that, having been deprived of the *jus gladii*, they cannot inflict the death which alone will satisfy them; for indeed it stood written in the eternal councils that Christ was to die, not by Jewish stoning or strangulation, but by that Roman form of execution which inspired the Jews with a nameless horror, even by crucifixion;[2] that He was to reign from His cross — to die by that most fearfully significant and typical of deaths — public, slow, conscious, accursed, agonizing — worse even than burning — the worst type of all possible deaths, and the worst result of that curse which He was to remove for ever. Dropping, therefore, for the present the charge of blasphemy, which did not suit their purpose,[3] they burst into a storm of invectives against Him, in which are discernible the triple accusations, that He perverted the nation, that He forbade to give tribute, that He called himself a king. All three charges were flagrantly false,

---

[1] Deut. xxi. 22, 23. Hence the name of hatred התלוי, "*the Hung*," applied to Christ in the Talmud; and Christians are called "servants of the Hung" (התלוי עובדי). Their reasons for desiring His crucifixion may have been manifold, besides the obvious motives of hatred and revenge. (1.) It would involve the name and memory of Jesus in deeper discredit. (2.) It would render the Roman authorities accomplices in the responsibility of the murder. (3.) It would greatly diminish any possible chance of a popular *émeute*.

[2] Deut. xxi. 23; Numb. xxv. 4; 2 Sam. xxi. 6; Jos. *B. J.* vii. 6, § 4. οὐκ ἀναόχετὸν εἶναι τὸ πάθος λέγοντες.[394] Some obscurity hangs over the question as to when and how the Jews had lost the power of inflicting capital punishment (John xviii. 31). The Talmud seems to imply (Lightfoot, *Hor. Hebr. in loc.*) that they had lost it by voluntarily abandoning the use of the *Lishcat haggazzith*, on account of the number of murderers whom they were forced to condemn. But this, in the usual loose Jewish way, is fixed "forty years before the destruction of the Temple" (*Aboda Zara*, f. 8, 2; Buxtorf, *Lex. Talm.*, p. 513). Others suppose that it was still permitted to them — or at any rate its use connived at — in ecclesiastical (Acts vii. 57; Jos. *Antt.* xx. 9, § 1) but not in civil cases. They had, legally, only the *cognitio causae*.[395]

[3] Cf. Acts. xviii. 14.

and the third all the more so because it included a grain of truth. But since they had not confronted Jesus with any proofs or witnesses, Pilate — in whose whole bearing and language is manifest the disgust embittered by fear with which the Jews inspired him — deigns to notice the third charge alone, and proceeds to discover whether the confession of the prisoner — always held desirable by Roman institutions — would enable him to take any cognizance of it. Leaving the impatient Sanhedrin and the raging crowd, he retired into the Judgment Hall. St. John alone preserves for us the memorable scene. Jesus, though not "in soft clothing," though not a denizen of kings' houses, had been led up the noble flight of stairs, over the floors of agate and lazuli, under the gilded roofs, ceiled with cedar and painted with vermilion, which adorned but one abandoned palace of a great king of the Jews. There, amid those voluptuous splendors, Pilate — already interested, already feeling in this prisoner before him some nobleness which touched his Roman nature — asked Him in pitying wonder, " Art *thou* the King of the Jews ? " — thou poor, worn, tear-stained outcast in this hour of thy bitter need [1] — oh, pale, lonely, friendless, wasted man, in thy poor peasant garments, with thy tied hands, and the foul traces of the insults of thine enemies on thy face, and on thy robes — thou, so unlike the fierce magnificent Herod, whom this multitude which thirsts for thy blood acknowledged as their sovereign — art *thou* the King of the Jews ? There is a royalty which Pilate, and men like Pilate, cannot understand — a royalty of holiness, a supremacy of self-sacrifice. To say " No " would have been to belie the truth ; to say " Yes " would have been to mislead the questioner. " Sayest thou this of thyself ? " He answered with gentle dignity, " or did others tell it thee of me ? " [2] " Am I a *Jew ?* " is the disdainful answer. " Thy own nation and the chief priests delivered thee unto me. What hast thou *done ?* " Done ? — works of wonder, and mercy, and power, and innocence, and these alone. But Jesus reverts to the first question, now that He has prepared Pilate to understand the answer : " Yes, He is a king ; but not of this world ; not from hence ; not one for whom His servants would fight." " Thou *art* a king, then ? " said Pilate to Him in astonishment. Yes ! but a king not in this region of falsities and shadows, but one born to bear witness unto the truth, and

---

[1] See J. Baldwin Brown, *Misread Passages of Scripture,* p. 2.

[2] This shows that Jesus, who seems to have been led immediately inside the walls of the Prætorium, had not heard the charges laid against Him before the Procurator.

one whom all who were of the truth should hear. " Truth," said Pilate impatiently, " what is *truth ?* " What had he — a busy, practical Roman governor — to do with such dim abstractions ? what bearing had they on the question of life and death ? what unpractical hallucination, what fairyland of dreaming phantasy was this ? Yet, though he contemptuously put the discussion aside, he was touched and moved. A judicial mind, a forensic training, familiarity with human nature which had given him some insight into the characters of men, showed him that Jesus was not only wholly innocent, but infinitely nobler and better than His raving sanctimonious accusers. He wholly set aside the floating idea of an unearthly royalty ; he saw in the prisoner before his tribunal an innocent and high-souled dreamer, nothing more. And so, leaving Jesus there, he went out again to the Jews, and pronounced his first emphatic and unhesitating acquittal : "I FIND IN HIM NO FAULT AT ALL."

2. But this public decided acquittal only kindled the fury of His enemies into yet fiercer flame. After all that they had hazarded, after all that they had inflicted, after the sleepless night of their plots, adjurations, insults, was their purpose to be foiled after all by the intervention of the very Gentiles on whom they had relied for its bitter consummation ? Should this victim whom they had thus clutched in their deadly grasp, be rescued from High Priests and rulers by the contempt or the pity of an insolent heathen ? It was too intolerable ! Their voices rose in wilder tumult. " He was a *mesîth ;* [1] He had upset the people with His teaching through the length and breadth of the land, beginning from Galilee, even as far as here."

Amid these confused and passionate exclamations the practiced ear of Pilate caught the name of " Galilee," and he understood that Galilee had been the chief scene of the ministry of Jesus.[2] Eager for a chance of dismissing a business of which he was best pleased to be free, he proposed, by a master-stroke of astute policy, to get rid of an embarrassing prisoner, to save himself from a disagreeable decision, and to do an unexpected complaisance to the unfriendly Galilæan tetrarch, who, as usual, had come to Jerusalem — nominally to keep the Passover, really to please his subjects, and to enjoy the sensations and festivities offered at that season by the densely-crowded capital. Accordingly, Pilate, secretly glad to wash his hands of a detestable

---

[1] In *Masseketh Sanhedrin,* vii. 10, a *mesîth* is defined as an unauthorized person (ἰδιώτης) who leads others astray. (הֵדִיוֹט אֶת הַמֵּסִית הֵדִיוֹט זֶה הַמֵּסִית.)

[2] Luke xxiii. 6.

responsibility, sent Jesus to[1] Herod Antipas, who was probably occupying the old Asmonæan palace, which had been the royal residence at Jerusalem until it had been surpassed by the more splendid one which the prodigal tyrant, his father, had built.[2] And so, through the thronged and narrow streets, amid the jeering, raging multitudes, the weary Sufferer was dragged once more.

We have caught glimpses of this Herod Antipas before, and I do not know that all History, in its gallery of portraits, contains a much more despicable figure than this wretched, dissolute Idumæan Sadducee — this petty princeling drowned in debauchery and blood. To him was addressed the sole purely contemptuous expression that Jesus is ever recorded to have used.[3] Superstition and incredulity usually go together; avowed atheists have yet believed in augury, and men who do not believe in God will believe in ghosts.[4] Antipas was rejoiced beyond all things to see Jesus. He had long been wanting to see Him because of the rumors he had heard ; and this murderer of the prophets hoped that Jesus would, in compliment to royalty, amuse by some miracle his gaping curiosity. He harangued and questioned Him in many words, but gained not so much as one syllable in reply. Our Lord confronted all his ribald questions with the majesty of silence. To such a man, who even changed scorn into a virtue, speech would clearly have been a profanation. Then all the savage vulgarity of the man came out through the thin veneer of a superficial cultivation. For the second time Jesus is derided — derided this time as Priest and Prophet. Herod and his corrupt hybrid myrmidons "set Him at nought" — treated Him with the insolence of a

---

[1] Luke xxiii. 7, *ἀνέπεμψεν*, "*remisit;*" "propriam Romani juris vocem usurpavit "[396] (Grotius): cf. Acts xxv. 21. Mutual jealousies, and tendencies to interfere with each other's authority, are quite sufficient to account for the previous ill-will of Pilate and Herod. Moreover, in all disputes it had been the obvious policy of Antipas to side with the Jews. Renan aptly compares the relations of the Herods to the Procurator with that of the Hindoo Rajahs to the Viceroy of India under the English dominion.

[2] We find the old Asmonæan palace occupied long afterwards by Agrippa II. (Jos. *B. J.* ii. 16, § 3 ; *Antt.* xx. 8, § 11). Sepp, in his fanciful way, points out that Jesus had thus been thrown into connection with a palace of David (at Bethlehem) of the Asmonæans, and of Herod.

[3] Luke xiii. 32, "This fox," *τῇ ἀλώπεκι ταύτῃ* (*v. supr.*, p. 429).

[4] Philippe d'Orleans (Egalité), a professed atheist, when in prison, tried to divine his fate by the grounds in a coffee-cup! This atheistic age *swarmed* with Chaldaei, mathematici, magicians, sorcerers, charlatans, impostors of every class. "Le monde était affolé de miracles, jamais on ne fut si occupé de présages. Le Dieu Père paraissait avoir voilé sa face ; des larves impurs, des monstres sortis d'un limon mystérieux, semblaient errer dans l'air "[397] (Renan, *L'Antechr.*, p. 325).

studied contempt. Mocking His innocence and His misery in a festal and shining robe,[1] the empty and wicked prince sent Him back to the Procurator, to whom he now became half-reconciled after a long-standing enmity. But he contented himself with these cruel insults. He resigned to the *forum apprehensionis* all further responsibility as to the issue of the trial. Though the Chief Priests and Scribes stood about his throne unanimously instigating him to a fresh and more heinous act of murder by their intense accusations,[2] he practically showed that he thought their accusations frivolous, by treating them as a jest. It was the fifth trial of Jesus; it was His second public distinct acquittal.

3. And now, as He stood once more before the perplexed and wavering Governor, began the sixth, the last, the most agitating and agonizing phase of this terrible inquisition. Now was the time for Pilate to have acted on a clear and right conviction, and saved himself for ever from the guilt of innocent blood. He came out once more, and seating himself on a stately *bema* — perhaps the golden throne of Archelaus, which was placed on the elevated pavement of many-colored marble[3] — summoned the Priests, the Sanhedrists, and the people before him, and seriously told them that they had brought Jesus to his tribunal as a leader of sedition and turbulence; that after full and fair inquiry he, their Roman Governor, had found their prisoner absolutely guiltless of these charges; that He had then sent Him to Herod, their native king, and that *he* also had come to the conclusion that Jesus had committed no crime which deserved the punishment of death. And now came the golden opportunity for him to vindicate the grandeur of his country's imperial justice, and, as he had pronounced Him absolutely innocent, to set Him absolutely free. But exactly at that point he wavered and temporized. The dread of another insurrection haunted him like a nightmare. He was willing to go half way to please these dangerous sectaries. To justify them, as it were, in their accusation, he would chastise Jesus — scourge Him publicly, as though to render His pretensions ridiculous — disgrace and ruin Him — "make Him seem vile in their eyes"[4] — and *then* set Him free. And this notion of setting Him

---

[1] Luke xxiii. 11, ἐσθῆτα λαμπράν, probably "white," as a festive color; but the notion of his being a "*candidate*" for the kingdom, is quite alien from the passage.

[2] εὐτόνως. Cf. Acts. xviii. 28.

[3] John xix. 13, "Gabbatha." The Roman governors and generals attached great importance to these tessellated pavements on which their tribunals were placed (Suet. *Jul. Caes.* 46).

[4] Deut. xxv. 3. μάστιξιν αἰκίζεσθαι [398] (Jos. *B. J.* vii. 6, § 4).

free suggested to him *another* resource of tortuous policy. Both he and the people almost simultaneously bethought themselves that it had always been a Paschal boon to liberate at the feast some condemned prisoner. He offered, therefore, to make the acquittal of Jesus an act not of imperious justice, but of artificial grace.

In making this suggestion — in thus flagrantly tampering with his innate sense of right, and resigning against his will the best prerogative of his authority — he was already acting in spite of a warning which he had received. That first warning consisted in the deep misgiving, the powerful presentiment, which overcame him as he looked on his bowed and silent prisoner. But, as though to strengthen him in his resolve to prevent an absolute failure of *all* justice, he now received a *second* solemn warning — and one which to an ordinary Roman, and a Roman who remembered Cæsar's murder and Calpurnia's dream, might well have seemed divinely sinister. His own wife — Claudia Procula [1] — ventured to send him a public message, even as he sat there on his tribunal, that, in the morning hours, when dreams are true,[2] she had had a troubled and painful dream about that Just Man; and, bolder than her husband, she bade him beware how he molested Him.

Gladly, most gladly, would Pilate have yielded to his own presentiments — have gratified his pity and his justice — have obeyed the prohibition conveyed by this mysterious omen. Gladly even would he have yielded to the worse and baser instinct of asserting his power, and thwarting these envious and hated fanatics, whom he knew to be ravening for innocent blood. That they — to many of whom sedition was as the breath of life — should be sincere in charging Jesus with sedition was, as he well knew, absurd. Their utterly transparent hypocrisy in this matter only added to his undisguised contempt. If he could have dared to show his real instincts, he would have driven them from his tribunal with all the haughty insouciance of a Gallio. But Pilate was guilty, and guilt is cowardice, and cowardice is weakness. His own past cruelties, recoiling in kind on his own head, forced him now to crush the impulse of pity, and

---

[1] Her name is given in the gospel of Nicodemus, which says she was a proselyte. On the possibility of a wife's presence in her husband's province, in spite of the old Leges Oppiae, see Tac. *Ann.* iii. 33, 34; iv. 20. For similar instances of dreams, see Otho, *Lex. Rabb.*, p. 316; Winer, *Realwört.*, s. v. "Träume."

[2] Matt. xxvii. 19, σήμερον. "Post mediam noctem visus quum somnia vera"[399] (Hor. *Sat.* i. 10, 31). "Sub auroram — tempore quo cerni somnia vera solent"[400] (Ov. *Her.* xix. 195). Perhaps she had been awakened that morning by the noise of the crowd.

to add to his many cruelties another more heinous still.[1] He knew that serious complaints hung over his head. Those Samaritans whom he had insulted and oppressed — those Jews whom he had stabbed promiscuously in the crowd by the hands of his disguised and secret emissaries — those Galilæans whose blood he had mingled with their sacrifices — was not their blood crying for vengeance? Was not an embassy of complaint against him imminent even now? Would it not be dangerously precipitated if, in so dubious a matter as a charge of claiming a kingdom, he raised a tumult among a people in whose case it was the best interest of the Romans that they should hug their chains? Dare he stand the chance of stirring up a new and apparently terrible rebellion rather than condescend to a simple concession, which was rapidly assuming the aspect of a politic, and even necessary, compromise?

His tortuous policy recoiled on his own head, and rendered impossible his own wishes. The Nemesis of his past wrong-doing was that he could no longer do right. Hounded on[2] by the Priests and Sanhedrists, the people impetuously claimed the Paschal boon of which he had reminded them; but in doing so they unmasked still more decidedly the sinister nature of their hatred against their Redeemer. For while they were professing to rage against the asserted seditiousness of One who was wholly obedient and peaceful, they shouted for the liberation of a man whose notorious sedition had been also stained by brigandage and murder. Loathing the innocent, they loved the guilty, and claimed the Procurator's grace on behalf, not of Jesus of Nazareth, but of a man who, in the fearful irony of circumstance, was also called Jesus — Jesus Bar-Abbas[3]

---

[1] We see the same notions very strikingly at work in his former dispute with the Jews about the shields — " He was afraid that, if they should send an embassy, they might discuss the many mal-administrations of his government, his extortions, his unjust decrees, his inhuman punishments. This reduced him to the utmost perplexity." (Philo, *Leg. ad Caium*, p. 38.) (τὰς ὕβρεις, τὰς ἁρπαγὰς, τὰς αἰκίας, τὰς ἐπηρείας, τοὺς ἀκρίτους καὶ ἐπαλλήλους φόνους, τὴν ἀνήνυτον καὶ ἀργαλεωτάτην ὡμότητα.) [401]

[2] Mark xv. 11, ἀνέσεισαν τὸν λαὸν.[402] History, down to this day, has given us numberless instances of the utter fickleness of crowds; but it is clear that throughout these scenes the fury and obstinacy of the people are not spontaneous.

[3] Bar-Abbas, son of a (distinguished) father; perhaps Bar-Rabban, son of a Rabbi. The reading Jesus Bar-Abbas is as old as Origen, and is far from improbable, although Matt. xxvii. 20 tells a little against it. If, however, Origen (as seems to be the case) only found this reading in verse 17, the probability of its genuineness is weakened. The ingenious combinations of Ewald, that the *Sanhedrists* desired his release, as belonging by family to their order, and the *people* because he had been imprisoned in the Corban riot (Jos. *Antt.*, *ubi supr.*), are highly uncertain.

—who not only *was* what they falsely said of Christ, a leader of sedition, but also a robber and a murderer. It was fitting that *they*, who had preferred an abject Sadducee to their true priest, and an incestuous Idumæan to their Lord and King, should deliberately prefer a murderer to their Messiah.

It may be that Bar-Abbas had been brought forth, and that thus Jesus the scowling murderer and Jesus the innocent Redeemer stood together on that high tribunal side by side.[1] The people, persuaded by their priests, clamored for the liberation of the rebel and the robber. To him every hand was pointed; for him every voice was raised. For the Holy, the Harmless, the Undefiled — for Him whom a thousand Hosannas had greeted but five days before — no word of pity or of pleading found an utterance. "He was despised and rejected of men."

Deliberately putting the question to them, Pilate heard with scornful indignation their deliberate choice; and then, venting his bitter disdain and anger in taunts, which did but irritate them more, without serving any good purpose, "What, then," he scornfully asked them, "do ye wish me to do with the King of the Jews?" Then first broke out the mad scream, "Crucify! crucify Him!" In vain, again and again, in the pauses of the tumult, Pilate insisted, obstinately indeed, but with more and more feebleness of purpose — for none but a man more innocent than Pilate, even if he were a Roman governor, could have listened without quailing to the frantic ravings of an Oriental mob[2] — "Why, what evil hath He done?" "I found *no* cause of death in Him." "I will chastise Him and let Him go." Such half-willed opposition was wholly unavailing. It only betrayed to the Jews the inward fears of their Procurator,[3] and practically made them masters of the situation. Again and again, with wilder and wilder vehemence, they rent the air with those hideous yells — "Ἆἷρε τοῦτον. Ἀπόλυσον ἡμῖν Βαραββᾶν. Σταύρωσον,

---

[1] Matt. xxvii. 21.

[2] See Isa. v. 7. These Jewish mobs could, as we see from Josephus, be very abusive. "They came about his (Pilate's) tribunal, and made a clamor at it" (*B. J.* ii. 9, § 4). "Many myriads of the people got together, and made a clamor against him, and insisted that he should leave off that design. *Some of them also used reproaches, and abused the man* (Pilate), *as crowds of such people usually do.* . . . So he bade the Jews go away, *but they, boldly casting reproaches upon him,*" &c. (*Antt.* xviii. 3, § 2).

[3] Thus, in the affair of the gilt votive shields, the Jewish leaders were confirmed in their purpose, by perceiving that Pilate's mind was wavering (Philo, *ubi supr.*). This, no doubt, is the kind of ἀνανδρία with which he is charged in *App. Constt.* v. 14.

σταύρωσον — "Away with this man." "Loose unto us Bar-Abbas." "Crucify! crucify!"

For a moment Pilate seemed utterly to yield to the storm. He let Bar-Abbas free; he delivered Jesus over to be scourged. The word used for the scourging (φραγελλώσας [1]) implies that it was done, not with rods (*virgae*), for Pilate had no lictors, but with what Horace calls the "horribile flagellum," of which the Russian knout is the only modern representative. This scourging was the ordinary preliminary to crucifixion and other forms of capital punishment.[2] It was a punishment so truly horrible, that the mind revolts at it; and it has long been abolished by that compassion of mankind which has been so greatly intensified, and in some degree even created, by the gradual comprehension of Christian truth. The unhappy sufferer was publicly stripped, was tied by the hands in a bent position to a pillar, and then, on the tense quivering nerves of the naked back, the blows were inflicted with leathern thongs, weighted with jagged edges of bone and lead; sometimes even the blows fell by accident — sometimes, with terrible barbarity, were purposely struck — on the face and eyes.[3] It was a punishment so hideous that, under its lacerating agony, the victim generally fainted, often died; still more frequently a man was sent away to perish under the mortification and nervous exhaustion which ensued. And this awful cruelty, on which we dare not dwell — this cruelty which makes the heart shudder and grow cold — was followed immediately by the third and bitterest derision — the derision of Christ as King.

In civilized nations all is done that can be done to spare every needless suffering to a man condemned to death; but among the Romans insult and derision were the customary preliminaries to the

---

[1] Matt. xxvii. 26. St Luke, with a deep touch of pathos, merely says that Pilate "gave up Jesus to their will," and then, as though he wished to drop a veil on all that followed, he does not even tell us that they led Him away, but adds, "And as they led Him away" (Luke xxiii. 25, 26).

[2] Matt. xxvii. 26. *Lora* (μάστιξ) not the ῥαβδοί (2 Cor. xi. 24, 25). It was illegal for Roman citizens, though sometimes inflicted, especially in the provinces (Acts xxii. 26.; cf. Tac. *Hist.* iv. 27; Cic. *Verr.* v. 6, 62; Jos. *B. J.* ii. 14, § 9). We are not told the number of the blows usually inflicted; they depended on the greater or less brutality of the presiding authority. The forty mentioned in the *Acts of Pilate* are clearly a reminiscence of *Jewish* customs. In John xix. 1, the word is ἐμαστίγωσεν — "ego in *flagella* paratus sum" [402]† (Vulg. Psa. xxxvii. 18); Isa. l. 6.

[3] See Cicero, *Verr.* v. 54; Hor. *Sat.* i. 3; μάστιξ ἀστραγαλωτή [403] (Athen. 153, A; Luc. *Asin.* 38); "flagrum pecuinis ossibus catenatum" [404] (Apul. *Met.* 8), "I, lictor, *colliga manus*" [405] (Liv. i. 26); "ad palum delegatus, lacerato virgis tergo" [406] (id. xxvii. 13); "verberati crucibus affixi" [407] (id. xxxiii. 36).

last agony. The "*et pereuntibus addita ludibria*" [407] † of Tacitus [1] might stand for their general practice. Such a custom furnished a specimen of that worst and lowest form of human wickedness which delights to inflict pain, which feels an inhuman pleasure in gloating over the agonies of another, even when he has done no wrong. The mere spectacle of agony is agreeable to the degraded soul. The low vile soldiery of the Prætorium — not Romans, who might have had more sense of the inborn dignity of the silent sufferer, but mostly the mere mercenary scum and dregs of the provinces — led Him into their barrack-room, and there mocked, in their savage hatred, the King whom they had tortured. It added keenness to their enjoyment to have in their power One who was of Jewish birth, of innocent life, of noblest bearing. [2] The opportunity broke so agreeably the coarse monotony of their life, that they summoned all of the cohort who were disengaged to witness their brutal sport. In sight of these hardened ruffians they went through the whole heartless ceremony of a mock coronation, a mock investiture, a mock homage. Around the brows of Jesus, in wanton mimicry of the Emperor's laurel, they twisted a green wreath of thorny leaves; [3] in His tied and trembling hands they placed a reed for sceptre; from His torn and bleeding shoulders they stripped the white robe with which Herod had mocked Him — which must now have been all soaked with blood — and flung on Him an old scarlet paludament — some cast-off war cloak, with its purple laticlave, from the Praetorian wardrobe. [4] This, with feigned solemnity, they buckled over His

---

[1] *Ann.* xv. 44.

[2] Josephus gives us several instances of the insane wantonness with which the soldiers delighted to insult the detested race among whom they were stationed (*B. J.* ii. 12, § 1; v. 11, § 1; *Antt.* xix. 9, § 1).

[3] It cannot be known of what plant this acanthine crown was formed. The *nubk* (*zizyphus lotus*) struck me, as it has struck all travellers in Palestine, as being most suitable both for mockery and pain, since its leaves are bright and its thorns singularly strong; but though the *nubk* is very common on the shores of Galilee, I saw none of it near Jerusalem. There may, however, have been some of it in the garden of Herod's palace, and the soldiers would give themselves no sort of trouble, but merely take the first plant that came to hand.

[4] Such presents were sent to allied kings (Liv. xxx. 17; Tac. *Ann.* xii. 56). (Keim.) Cf. 1 Macc. xiv. 44. — St. Matthew calls it "scarlet," St. Mark "purple." The ancients discriminated colors very loosely; or rather, very differently from what we do. Our nomenclature dwells chiefly on differences of *hue*, and their implicit analysis was of another kind. (See some excellent remarks in Mr. Gladstone's *Juventus Mundi*, p. 540; Ruskin, *Modern Painters*, iii. 225.) — For instance of similar mockery see Philo, *in Flacc.* 980, where Herod Agrippa II. is insulted in the person of an idiot, at Alexandria. Shakespeare's pathetic scene of the insults heaped upon Richard II. will recur to every English reader.

right shoulder, with its glittering fibula; and then — each with his derisive homage of bended knee — each with his infamous spitting — each with the blow over the head from the reed-sceptre, which His bound hands could not hold — they kept passing before Him with their mock salutation of " Hail, King of the Jews !" [1]

Even now, even yet, Pilate wished, hoped, even strove to save Him. He might represent this frightful scourging, not as the preliminary to crucifixion, but as an inquiry by torture, which had failed to elicit any further confession. And as Jesus came forth — as He stood beside him with that martyr-form on the beautiful mosaic of the tribunal — the spots of blood upon His green wreath of torture, the mark of blows and spitting on His countenance, the weariness of His deathful agony upon the sleepless eyes, the *sagum* of faded scarlet, darkened by the weals of His lacerated back, and dropping, it may be, its stains of crimson upon the tesselated floor — even then, even so, in that hour of His extremest humiliation — yet, as He stood in the grandeur of His holy calm on that lofty tribunal above the yelling crowd, there shone all over Him so Godlike a pre-eminence, so divine a nobleness, that Pilate broke forth with that involuntary exclamation which has thrilled with emotion so many million hearts —

" Behold the Man !"

But his appeal only woke a fierce outbreak of the scream, " Crucify ! crucify !" The mere sight of Him, even in this His unspeakable shame and sorrow, seemed to add fresh fuel to their hate. In vain the heathen soldier appeals for humanity to the Jewish priest; no heart throbbed with responsive pity; no voice of compassion broke that monotonous yell of " Crucify !" — the howling refrain of their wild " liturgy of death." The Roman who had shed blood like water, on the field of battle, in open massacre, in secret assassination, might well be supposed to have an icy and a stony heart; but yet icier and stonier was the heart of those scrupulous hypocrites and worldly priests. " Take ye Him, and crucify Him," said Pilate, in utter disgust, " for I find no fault in Him." What an admission from a Roman judge ! " So far as I can see, He is wholly innocent; yet if you *must* crucify Him, take Him and crucify. I cannot approve of, but I will readily connive at, your violation of the law." But even this wretched guilty subterfuge is not permitted him. Satan will have from his servants the full tale of their crimes, and the sign-manual of their own willing assent at last. What the Jews

---

want — what the Jews *will have* — is *not* tacit connivance, but absolute sanction. They see their power. They see that this blood-stained Governor dares not hold out against them ; they know that the Roman statecraft is tolerant of concessions to local superstition. Boldly, therefore, they fling to the winds all question of a political offence, and with all their hypocritical pretences calcined by the heat of their passion, they shout, "We have a law, and by our law He ought to die, because He made Himself a Son of God." [1]

A Son of God! The notion was far less strange and repulsive to a heathen than to a Jew ; and this word, unheard before, startled Pilate with the third omen which made him tremble at the crime into which he was being dragged by guilt and fear. Once more, leaving the yelling multitude without, he takes Jesus with him into the quiet Judgment Hall, and — "*jam pro suâ conscientiâ Christianus,*" [409] as Tertullian so finely observes [2] — asks Him in awe-struck accents, "Whence art thou?" Alas! it was too late to answer now. Pilate was too deeply committed to his gross cruelty and injustice ; for *him* Jesus had spoken enough already ; for the wild beasts who raged without, He had no more to say. He did not answer. Then, almost angrily, Pilate broke out with the exclamation, "Dost thou not speak even *to me?* [3] Dost Thou not know that I have power to set thee free, and have power to crucify Thee?" Power — how so? Was justice nothing, then? truth nothing? innocence nothing? conscience nothing? In the reality of things Pilate had *no* such power ; even in the arbitrary sense of the tyrant it was an idle boast, for at this very moment he was letting "I dare not" wait upon "I would." And Jesus pitied the hopeless bewilderment of this man, whom guilt had changed from a ruler into a slave. Not taunting, not confuting him — nay, even extenuating rather than aggravating his sin — Jesus gently answered, "Thou hast no power against Me whatever, had it not been given thee from above ; therefore he that betrayed me to thee hath the greater sin." Thou art indeed committing a great crime — but Judas, Annas, Caiaphas, these priests and Jews, are more to blame than thou. Thus, with infinite dignity, and yet with

---

[1] " It is not Tiberius's pleasure that any of our laws should be violated." (Philo, *ubi supra*, and *Leg. ad Caium*, 1014; and Tac. *Ann.* i. 9, and the boast of the Monumentum Ancyranum, "modestiam apud socios." [408]) The inscription on the *Chêl* forbidding any Gentile on pain of death to pass beyond it, has recently been discovered built into the wall of a mosque at Jerusalem, and is a relic of the deepest interest.

[2] Tert. *Apol.* 21.

[3] The position of the ἐμοὶ is emphatic (John xix. 10, 11).

infinite tenderness, did Jesus judge His judge. In the very depths
of his inmost soul Pilate felt the truth of the words — silently
acknowledged the superiority of his bound and lacerated victim. All
that remained in him of human and of noble —

> " Felt how awful Goodness is, and Virtue,
> In her shape how lovely ; felt and mourned
> His fall."

All of his soul that was not eaten away by pride and cruelty thrilled
back an unwonted echo to these few calm words of the Son of God.
Jesus had condemned his sin, and so far from being offended, the
judgment only deepened his awe of this mysterious Being, whose
utter impotence seemed grander and more awful than the loftiest
power. From that time Pilate was even yet more anxious to save
Him. With all his conscience in a tumult, for the third and last
time he mounted his tribunal, and made one more desperate effort.
He led Jesus forth, and looking at Him, as He stood silent and in
agony, but calm, on that shining Gabbatha, above the brutal agitations of the multitude, he said to those frantic rioters, as with a flash
of genuine conviction, " BEHOLD YOUR KING ! " But to the Jews it
sounded like shameful scorn to call that beaten insulted Sufferer their
King. A darker stream mingled with the passions of the raging,
swaying crowd. Among the shouts of " Crucify," ominous threat-
enings began for the first time to be mingled. It was now nine
o'clock, and for nearly three hours [1] had they been raging and wait-

---

[1] As to the hour there is a well-known discrepancy between John xix. 14, "And
it was . . . . about the *sixth* hour ; and he saith unto the Jews, Behold your
king ; " and Mark xv. 25, "And it was the *third* hour, and they crucified Him . . "
There are various suggestions for removing this difficulty, but the only ones
worth mentioning are : (α.) *That in the word " crucified" St. Mark practically
includes all the preparations for the crucifixion,* and therefore much of the trial :
this is untenable, because he uses the aorist, ἐσταύρωσαν, not the imperfect.
(β.) *That one of the Evangelists is less accurate than the other.* If no other solution
of the difficulty were simple and natural, I should feel no difficulty in admitting
this ; but as the general, and even the minute, accuracy of the Evangelists seems
to me demonstrable in innumerable cases, it is contrary to the commonest principles of fairness to insist that there *must* be an inaccuracy when another explanation is possible. (γ.) *That St. John adopts the Roman civil reckoning of hours.* But
(i.), the Romans had no such reckoning (see pp. 131, 173 ; John iv. 6, 52 ; xi. 9) ;
and (ii.), this will make Pilate's exclamation to have been uttered at six in the
morning, in which case the trial could hardly have begun at daylight, as no time
is left for the intermediate incidents. (δ.) That the Γ (third) in John xix. 14, has
by a very early error been altered into ς (sixth). This is the reading of a few
MSS. and versions, and the *Chron. Alex.* actually appeals for its genuineness not
only to τὰ ἀκριβῆ ἀντίγραφα,[410] but even to αὐτὸ τὸ ἰδιόχειρον τοῦ

ing there. The name of Cæsar began to be heard in wrathful murmurs. " Shall I crucify your King?" he had asked, venting the rage and soreness of his heart in taunts on *them.* " *We have no king but Cæsar,*" answered the Sadducees and Priests, flinging to the winds every national impulse and every Messianic hope.¹ " If thou let this man go," shouted the mob again and again, "thou art not *Cæsar's* friend. Every one who tries to make himself a king speaketh against *Cæsar.*" ² And at that dark terrible name of Cæsar, Pilate trembled. It was a name to conjure with. It mastered him. He thought of that terrible implement of tyranny, the accusation of *laesa majestas,*³ into which all other charges merged, which had made confiscation and torture so common, and had caused blood to flow like water in the streets of Rome. He thought of Tiberius, the aged gloomy Emperor, then hiding at Capreæ his ulcerous features, his poisonous suspicions, his sick infamies, his desperate revenge. At this very time he had been maddened into a yet more sanguinary and misanthropic ferocity by the detected falsity and treason of his only friend and minister, Sejanus, and it was to Sejanus himself that Pilate is said to have owed his position. There might be secret delators in that very mob. Panic-stricken, the unjust judge, in obedience to his own terrors, consciously betrayed the innocent victim to the anguish of death. He who had so often prostituted justice, was now unable to achieve the one act of justice which he desired. He who had so often murdered pity, was now forbidden to taste the sweetness of a pity for which he longed. He who had so often abused authority, was now rendered impotent to exercise it, for once, on the side of right. Truly for him, sin had become its own Erinnys, and his pleasant vices had been converted into the instrument of his punishment! Did the solemn and noble words of the

---

Εὐαγγελιότου.⁴¹¹ Unless great latitude be allowed to the word ὥς, this appears to me a possible solution; it is, however, perfectly true that the ancients, as a rule, were much looser than we are in their notes of time.

¹ " The formal equivalent of Emperor is, of course, αὐτοκράτωρ, ... but the provincials freely spoke of even the Julian Cæsars as βαόιλεύς." (Freeman, *Essays,* II. 316.)

² Agrippa I. inscribed his coins with the title φιλοκαίόαρ. (Akerman, p. 30.)

³ Tac. *Ann.* iii. 38 (and *passim*). " Majestatis crimen omnium accusationum complementum erat." ⁴¹² " He knew very well," says Agrippa (ap. Philon. *ubi supr.*), " the inflexible severity of Tiberius; " and this was some years earlier — before the gloom of the Emperor's mind had become so deep and savage as was now the case. An Apocryphal book (*Revenges of the Saviour*), with scarcely an exaggeration, says that Tiberius was " full of ulcers and fevers, and had nine sorts of leprosy." (See Tac. *Ann.* iv. 57; Suet. *Tib.* 68; Julian, *Caes.,* p. 309, &c.)

Law of the Twelve Tables [1] — " Vanae voces populi non sunt audiendae, quando aut noxium crimine absolvi, aut innocentem condemnari desiderant " [112][†] — come across his memory with accents of reproach as he delivered Bar-Abbas and condemned Jesus? It may have been so. At any rate his conscience did not leave him at ease. At this, or some early period of the trial, he went through the solemn farce of trying to absolve his conscience from the guilt. He sent for water; he washed his hands before the multitude! he said, "I am innocent of the blood of this just person ; see ye to it." Did he think thus to wash away his guilt? He could wash his hands ; could he wash his heart? Might he not far more truly have said with the murderous king in the splendid tragedy —

> " Can all old Ocean's waters wash this blood
> Clean from my hand ? Nay, rather would this hand
> The multitudinous seas incarnadine,
> Making the green — one red ! "

It may be that, as he thus murdered his conscience, such a thought flashed for one moment across his miserable mind, in the words of his native poet —

> " Ah nimium faciles qui tristia crimina caedis
> Flumineâ tolli posse putatis aquâ ! " [*][413]

But if so, the thought was instantly drowned in a yell, the most awful, the most hideous, the most memorable that History records. "*His blood be on us and on our children.*" Then Pilate finally gave way. The fatal "*Ibis ad crucem*" [413][†] was uttered with reluctant wrath. He delivered Him unto them, *that He might be crucified.*"

And now mark, for one moment, the revenges of History. Has not His blood been on them, and on their children? Has it not fallen most of all on those most nearly concerned in that deep tragedy? Before the dread sacrifice was consummated, Judas died in the horrors of a loathsome suicide. Caiaphas was deposed the year following. Herod died in infamy and exile. Stripped of his Procuratorship very shortly afterwards, on the very charges he had tried by a wicked concession to avoid, Pilate, wearied out with misfortunes, died in suicide and banishment, leaving behind him an

---

[1] Lex. xii. *De Poenis.*

[*] Ov. *Fast.* ii. 45. The custom, though Jewish (Deut. xxi. 6, 7, " all thé elders . . . shall wash their hands . . . and say, Our hands have not shed this blood, neither have our eyes seen it "), was also Greek and Roman.

execrated name.[1] The house of Annas was destroyed a generation later by an infuriated mob, and his son was dragged through the streets, and scourged and beaten to his place of murder. Some of those who had shared in and witnessed the scenes of that day — and thousands of their children — also shared in and witnessed the long horrors of that siege of Jerusalem which stands unparalleled in history for its unutterable fearfulness. " It seems," says Renan, " as though the whole race had appointed a rendezvous for extermination." They had shouted, " We have no king but Cæsar!" and they *had* no king but Cæsar ; and leaving only for a time the fantastic shadow of a local and contemptible royalty, Cæsar after Cæsar outraged, and tyrannized, and pillaged, and oppressed them, till at last they rose in wild revolt against the Cæsar whom they had claimed, and a Cæsar slaked in the blood of its best defenders the red ashes of their burnt and desecrated Temple. They had forced the Romans to crucify their Christ, and though they regarded this punishment with especial horror,[2] they and their children were themselves crucified in myriads by the Romans outside their own walls, till room was wanting and wood failed, and the soldiers had to ransack a fertile inventiveness of cruelty for fresh methods of inflicting this insulting form of death.[3]

---

[1] Euseb. *Chron.* p. 78, ποικίλαις περιπεδῶν δυμφοραῖς.[414] His banishment to Vienna Allobrogum, his tomb, his connection with Mount Pilate, &c., are all uncertain traditions. The *Paradosis Pilati, Mors Pilati,* &c., are as spurious as his " martyrdom," which is observed by the Abyssinian Church on June 25. But Evang. Nicod. i. 13, which speaks of Pilate as " circumcised in heart," shows that the early Christians were not insensible of his efforts to save Jesus. " Upon all murderers," says Bishop Jeremy Taylor, " God hath not thrown a thunderbolt, nor broken all sacrilegious persons upon the wheel of an inconstant and ebbing estate, nor spoken to every oppressor from heaven in a voice of thunder, nor cut off all rebels in the first attempts of insurrection ; but because He hath done so to some, we are to look upon those judgments as divine accents and voices of God, threatening all the same crimes with the like events, and with the ruins of eternity." (*Life of Christ,* III. xv.) — How much more true and reverent is this than the despairing cynicism which says, " Gardons-nous d'une expression si naïvement impie. Il n'y a pas plus de vengeance dans l'histoire que dans la nature ; les revolutions ne sont pas plus justes que le volcan qui éclate ou l'avalanche qui roule."[415] (Renan.)

[2] See Jos. *B. J.* vii. 6, § 4.

[3] Jos. *B. J.* v. 11, § 1, προδήλουν οἱ δτρατιῶται ἄλλον ἄλλῳ δχήματι πρὸς χλεύην καὶ διὰ τὸ πλῆθος χώρα τε ἐνελείπετο τοῖς δταυροῖς καὶ δταυροὶ τοῖς δώμαδιν.[416] " So that they who had nothing but ' crucify' in their mouths were therewith paid home in their own bodies " (Sir T. Browne, *Vulg. Err.* v. 21) The common notion, that having bought Christ for thirty pieces of silver, they were sold by thirties for one piece of silver, seems to be solely derived from a mediæval forgery called *The Revenging of the Saviour.* Still it is true that " the blood of Jesus shed for the salvation of the world became to them a curse. . . .

They had given thirty pieces of silver for their Saviour's blood, and they were themselves sold in thousands for yet smaller sums. They had chosen Bar-Abbas in preference to their Messiah, and for them there has been no Messiah more, while a murderer's dagger swayed the last counsels of their dying nationality. They had accepted the guilt of blood, and the last pages of their history were glued together with the rivers of their blood, and that blood continued to be shed in wanton cruelties from age to age. They who will, may see in incidents like these the mere unmeaning *chances* of History; but there is in History nothing unmeaning to one who regards it as the Voice of God speaking among the destinies of men; and whether a man sees any significance or not in events like these, he must be blind indeed who does not see that when the murder of Christ was consummated, the axe was laid at the root of the barren tree of Jewish nationality. Since that day Jerusalem and its environs, with their " ever-extending miles of grave-stones and ever-lengthening pavement of tombs and sepulchres," have become little more than one vast cemetery — an Aceldama, a field of blood, a potter's field to bury strangers in. Like the mark of Cain upon the forehead of their race, the guilt of that blood has seemed to cling to them — as it ever must until that same blood effaceth it. For, by God's mercy, that blood was shed for them also who made it flow; the voice which they strove to quench in death was uplifted in its last prayer for pity on His murderers. May that blood be efficacious! may that prayer be heard![1]

So manna turns to worms, and the wine of angels to vinegar and lees, when it is received into impure vessels or tasted by wanton palates, and the sun himself produces rats and serpents when it reflects upon the slime of Nilus." (Jer. Taylor, III. xv.)

[1] It is in the deepest sincerity that I add these last words. Any one who traces a spirit of vindictiveness in the last paragraph wholly misjudges the spirit in which it is written. This book may perhaps fall into the hands of Jewish readers. They, of all others, if true to the deepest lessons of the faith in which they have been trained, will acknowledge the hand of God in History. And the events spoken of here are not imaginative; they are indisputable facts. The Jew at least will believe that in external consequences God visits the sins of the fathers upon the children. Often and often in History have the crimes of the guilty *seemed* to be visited even on their *innocent* posterity. The apparent injustice of this is but on the surface. There is a fire that purifies, no less than a fire that scathes; and who shall say that the very afflictions of Israel — afflictions, alas! so largely caused by the sin of Christendom — may not have been meant for a refining of the pure gold? God's judgments — it may be the very sternest and most irremediable of them — come, many a time, in the guise, not of affliction, but of immense earthly prosperity and ease.

CHAPTER LXI.

THE CRUCIFIXION.

" Dum crucis inimicos
Vocabis, et amicos,
O Jesu, Fili Dei,
Sis, oro, memor mei." [417]
THOMAS OF CELANO, *De Cruce Domini.*

" I, MILES, EXPEDI CRUCEM " (" Go, soldier, get ready the cross "). In some such formula of terrible import Pilate must have given his final order.[1] It was now probably about nine o'clock, and the execution followed immediately upon the judgment. The time required for the necessary preparation would not be very long, and during this brief pause the soldiers, whose duty it was to see that the sentence was carried out, stripped Jesus of the scarlet war-cloak, now dyed with the yet deeper stains of blood, and clad Him again in His own garments.[2] When the cross had been prepared they laid it—or possibly only one of the beams of it—upon His shoulders, and led Him to the place of punishment. The nearness of the great feast, the myriads who were present in Jerusalem, made it desirable to seize the opportunity for striking terror into all Jewish malefactors. Two were, therefore, selected for execution at the same time with Jesus— two brigands and rebels of the lowest stamp. Their crosses were laid upon them, a maniple of soldiers in full armor were marshalled

---

[1] That Pilate sent some official account of the trial and crucifixion to Tiberius would be *à priori* probable, and seems to be all but certain (Just. Mart. *Apol.* i. 76; Tert. *Apol.* 21; Euseb. *Hist. Eccl.* ii. 2 ; Lardner, vi. 606)); but it is equally certain that the existing *Acta, Paradosis, Mors* and *Epistolae Pilati* are spurious. Tischendorf (*De Evang. Apocr., Orig.*, p. 67) thinks that, though interpolated, they may contain old materials, but I can find nothing of any interest or value in them.

[2] Some have supposed that a second scourging took place, the first being the question by torture, the second the προαικισμὸς. It seems clear, however, that Pilate had *meant* the scourging to be this preliminary to crucifixion, though, at the last moment, it suited him to let it pass as inquisitorial. Further, it is inconceivable that Jesus could have been capable of physically enduring *two* such fearful inflictions, either of which was often sufficient to cause convulsions and death It is better to regard the φραγελλώσας of Matt. xxvii. 26 as retrospective.

under the command of their centurion, and, amid thousands of spectators, coldly inquisitive or furiously hostile, the procession started on
its way.

The cross was not, and could not have been, the massive and lofty
structure with which such myriads of pictures have made us familiar.
Crucifixion was among the Romans a very common punishment, and
it is clear that they would not waste any trouble in constructing the
instrument of shame and torture.[1] It would undoubtedly be made
of the very commonest wood that came to hand, perhaps olive or
sycamore, and knocked together in the very rudest fashion. Still, to
support the body of a man, a cross would require to be of a certain
size and weight; and to one enfeebled by the horrible severity of
the previous scourging, the carrying of such a burden would be an
additional misery.[2] But Jesus was enfeebled not only by this cruelty,
but by previous days of violent struggle and agitation, by an evening
of deep and overwhelming emotion, by a night of sleepless anxiety
and suffering, by the mental agony of the garden, by three trials and
three sentences of death before the Jews, by the long and exhausting
scenes in the Prætorium, by the examination before Herod, and by
the brutal and painful derisions which He had undergone, first at the
hands of the Sanhedrin and their servants, then from Herod's body-
guard, and lastly from the Roman cohort. All these, superadded to

---

[1] Of the various kinds of cross — the *crux decussata* (X), the *crux ansata*, &c., it
is certain that the cross on which Jesus was crucified was either the *crux commissa*
(T, St. Anthony's cross), or the *crux immissa*, the ordinary Roman cross (†). The
fact that the former was in the shape of the Greek capital *tau* has given ample
room for the allegorizing propensities of the Fathers. (Cf. Lucian, *Jud. Vocal.*
12; Gesenius s. v. תו, Ezek. ix. 4.) See abundant O. T. instances of this in Just.
Mart. *Dial.* 89; Tert. *Adv. Jud.* 10, 11; Barnab. *Ep.* ix.; Clem. Alex. *Strom.* vi.
See to Theophyl. on Matt. v. 18; Sepp. *Leben Christi*, vi. 115; *Mysterium des
Kreuzes.* — I have not alluded to the so-called "invention of the cross," for the
story is intrinsically absurd, and the Jews generally burnt their crosses (Otho,
Lex. Rab. s. v. "Supplicia"). What seems decisive in favor of the shape preserved by the traditions of art for nearly 1,500 years is the expression of Matt.
xxvii. 37, that the title was put ἐπάνω τῆς κεφαλῆς αὐτοῦ.[418] I have collected all that seemed archæologically interesting on this subject in the articles
"Cross" and "Crucifixion" in Smith's *Dict. of the Bible.*

[2] Cf. Gen. xxii. 6 (Isa. ix. 6). It is not certain whether the condemned carried
their *entire* cross or only a part of it — the *patibulum*, or transom, as distinguished
from the *crux* (cf. Plaut. *fr. ap.* Non. 3, 183, "*Patibulum* ferat per urbem deinde
affigatur *cruci*"[419]). If the entire cross was carried, it is probable that the two
beams were not (as in pictures) nailed to each other, but simply fastened together
by a rope, and carried like a V (*furca*). If, as tradition says (*Acts of Pilate*, B. 10),
the hands were tied, the difficulties of supporting the burden would be further
enhanced.

the sickening lacerations of the scourging, had utterly broken down His physical strength. His tottering footsteps, if not His actual falls under that fearful load, made it evident that He lacked the physical strength to carry it from the Prætorium to Golgotha. Even if they did not pity His feebleness, the Roman soldiers would naturally object to the consequent hindrance and delay. But they found an easy method to solve the difficulty. They had not proceeded farther than the city gate,' when they met a man coming from the country, who was known to the early Christians as " Simon of Cyrene, the father of Alexander and Rufus ; " and perhaps, on some hint from the accompanying Jews that Simon sympathized with the teaching of the Sufferer, they impressed him without the least scruple into their odious service.²

The miserable procession resumed its course, and though the apocryphal traditions of the Romish Church narrate many incidents of the *Via Dolorosa*, only one such incident is recorded in the Gospel history.³ St. Luke tells us that among the vast multitude of people who followed Jesus were many women. From the *men* in that moving crowd He does not appear to have received one word of pity or of sympathy. *Some* there must surely have been who had seen His miracles, who had heard His words ; some of those who had been almost, if not utterly, convinced of His Messiahship, as they hung upon His lips while He had uttered His great discourses in the

---

¹ *Act. Pilat.* x. ἦλθε μεχρὶ τῆς πύλης.⁴²⁰

² ἠγγάρευόαν. It seems to have been a common thing for Roman soldiers to impress people to carry burdens for them (Epict. *Dissert.* iv. 1). The Cyrenians had a synagogue at Jerusalem (Acts ii. 10; vi. 9). The names Alexander and Rufus are too common to enable us to feel any certainty as to their identification with those of the same name mentioned in Acts xix. 33; 1 Tim. i. 20; Rom. xvi. 13. The belief of the Cerinthians, Basilidians, Carpocratians, and other Gnostics, that Simon was crucified for Jesus by mistake (!), is not worth notice here (Iren. *Adv. Haeres.* i. 23). One of these wild distortions was that Judas was crucified for Him ; and another that it was a certain Titian, or a phantom created by God in the semblance of Jesus. It is a curious trace of the dissemination of Gnostic and Apocryphal legends in Arabia that Mahomet treats the actual crucifixion of Jesus as an unworthy calumny. (Koran, *Surat.* 3, 4; Sale's *Koran*, i. 64, 124, " They slew Him not, neither crucified Him, but He was represented by one in His likeness.")

³ These form the subjects of the stations which are to be seen in all Romish churches, and are mainly derived from apocryphal sources. They originated among the Franciscans. The so-called Via Dolorosa does not seem to be mentioned earlier than the fourteenth century. That Jesus, before being eased of His burden, was scourged and goaded onward is but too sadly probable (Plaut. *Most.* I. i. 53, " Ita te forabunt patibulatum per viam stimulis "⁴²¹). (Cf. Jer. Taylor, *Life of Christ*, III. xv. 2.)

Temple; some of the eager crowd who had accompanied Him from Bethlehem five days before with shouted hosannas and waving palms. Yet if so, a faithless timidity or a deep misgiving — perhaps even a boundless sorrow — kept them dumb. But these women, more quick to pity, less susceptible to controlling influences, could not and would not conceal the grief and amazement with which this spectacle filled them. They beat upon their breasts and rent the air with their lamentations, till Jesus Himself hushed their shrill cries with words of solemn warning. Turning to them — which He could not have done had He still been staggering under the burden of His cross — He said to them, "Daughters of Jerusalem, weep not for me; but for yourselves weep, and for your children. For lo! days are coming in which they shall say, Blessed are the barren, and the wombs which bare not, and the breasts which gave not suck. Then shall they begin to say to the mountains, Fall on us, and to the hills, Cover us; for if they do these things in the green tree, what shall be done in the dry?" Theirs was but an emotional outburst of womanly tenderness, which they could not repress as they saw the great Prophet of mankind in His hour of shame and weakness, with the herald proclaiming before Him the crimes with which He was charged, and the Roman soldiers carrying the title of derision,[1] and Simon bending under the weight of the wood to which He was to be nailed. But He warned them that, if this were *all* which they saw in the passing spectacle, far bitterer causes of woe awaited them, and their children, and their race. Many of them, and the majority of their children, would live to see such rivers of bloodshed, such complications of agony, as the world had never known before — days which would seem to overpass the capacities of human suffering, and would make men seek to hide themselves, if it might be, under the very roots of the hill on which their city stood.[2] The fig-tree of their nation's life was still green: if such deeds of darkness were possible *now*, what should be done when that tree was withered and blasted, and ready for the burning?[3] — if in the days of hope and decency they could

---

[1] Suet. *Calig.* 32, "Praecedente titulo qui caussam poenae indicaret." 4:2 This **was** sometimes hung around the neck.

[2] Hos. ix. 12—16; x. 8; Isa. ii. 10; Rev. vi. 16. These words of Christ met with **a** painfully literal illustration when hundreds of the unhappy Jews at the siege of Jerusalem hid themselves in the darkest and vilest subterranean recesses, and when, besides those who were hunted out, no less than 2,000 were killed by being buried under the ruins of their hiding-places (Jos. *B. J.* vi. 9, § 4).

[3] The *exact* meaning of this proverbial expression is not certain. It is often explained to mean, "If, in the fulfilment of God's purposes, I the Holy and the Innocent must suffer thus — if the green tree be thus blasted — how shall the dry

execrate their blameless Deliverer, what would happen in the days of blasphemy and madness and despair? If, under the full light of day, Priests and Scribes could crucify the Innocent, what would be done in the midnight orgies and blood-stained bacchanalia of zealots and murderers? This was a day of crime; that would be a day when Crime had become her own avenging fury. — The solemn warning, the last sermon of Christ on earth, was meant primarily for those who heard it; but, like all the words of Christ, it has deeper and wider meaning for all mankind. Those words warn every child of man that the day of careless pleasure and blasphemous disbelief will be followed by the crack of doom; they warn each human being who lives in pleasure on the earth, and eats, and drinks, and is drunken, that though the patience of God waits, and His silence is unbroken, yet the days shall come when He shall speak in thunder, and His wrath shall burn like fire.

And so with this sole sad episode, they came to the fatal place, called Golgotha, or, in its Latin form, Calvary — that is, "a skull." Why it is so called is not known. It may conceivably have been a well-known place of execution; or possibly the name may imply a bare, rounded, scalp-like elevation. It is constantly called the "*hill* of Golgotha," or of Calvary; but the Gospels merely call it "a place," and not a hill.[1] Respecting its site volumes have been written, but nothing is known. The data for anything approaching to certainty are wholly wanting; and, in all probability, the actual spot lies buried and obliterated under the mountainous rubbish-heaps of the ten-times-taken city. The rugged and precipitous mountain represented in sacred pictures is as purely imaginary as the skull of Adam, which is often painted lying at the foot of the cross,[2] or as

---

tree of a wicked life, with its abominable branches, be consumed in the uttermost burning?" (Cf. Prov. xi. 31; Ezek. xx. 47; xxi. 4; and especially 1 Peter iv. 17.) (See Schenkel, *Charakterbild*, p. 30, E. Tr.) The difficulty of understanding the words was early felt, and we find an absurd allusion to them in the *Revenging of the Saviour*, where Titus exclaims, "They hung our Lord on a green tree . . . let us hang them on a dry tree."

[1] Matt. xxvii. 33; Mark xv. 22. Calvary is used by the E. V. as a rendering of κρανίον, "scull," only in Luke xxiii. 33. It is called "monticulus" in the old *Itiner. Burdig. Hieros.* vii. Renan compares the French word "Chaumont" (*Vie de Jésus*, 416). Ewald identifies it with the hill Gareb (Jer. xxxi. 39). It is hardly worth while to enter into elaborate arguments about the site, which may any day be overthrown by a discovery of the course of the second wall.

[2] "Ibi erectus est medicus ubi jacebat aegrotus" [423] (Aug.). Origen compares 1 Cor. xv. 22. There was a legend that three drops of Christ's blood fell on Adam's skull, and caused his resurrection, fulfilling the ancient prophecy quoted in Eph. v. 14, where Jerome had heard a preacher adopt the reading, "Awake, Adam that

any other of the myriads of legends, which have gathered round this most stupendous and moving scene in the world's history. All that we know of Golgotha, all that we shall ever know, all that God willed to be known, is that it was without the city gate. The religion of Christ is spiritual; it needs no relic; it is independent of Holy Places; it says to each of its children, not "Lo, here!" and "lo, there!" but "The kingdom of God is within you."

Utterly brutal and revolting as was the punishment of crucifixion, which has now for fifteen hundred years been abolished by the common pity and abhorrence of mankind,[1] there was one custom in Judæa, and one occasionally practised by the Romans, which reveal some touch of passing humanity. The latter consisted in giving to the sufferer a blow under the arm-pit, which, without causing death, yet hastened its approach.[2] Of this I need not speak, because, for whatever reason, it was not practised on this occasion. The former, which seems to have been due to the milder nature of Judaism, and which was derived from a happy piece of Rabbinic exegesis on Prov. xxxi. 6, consisted in giving to the condemned, immediately before his execution, a draught of wine medicated with some powerful opiate.[3] It had been the custom of wealthy ladies in Jerusalem to provide this stupefying potion at their own expense, and they did so

---

sleepest . . . and Christ shall touch thee" (ἐπιψαύσει). Jer. in Matt. xxvii. 33; Reland, *Palest.* 860, for the true reading ἐπιφαύσει). The words in the original are rhythmical, and as they do not occur in Scripture, they are now usually considered to be a fragment of some early Christian hymn.

[1] It was abolished by Constantine (Aur. Vict. *Const.* 41). The infamy of crucifixion is still preserved in the reproachful name *Talui* (‧ תלוי) in which the Talmud speaks of Jesus, and עובדי תלוי, "worshippers of the Hung," which they apply to Christians, though, according to *their* fable, He was first stoned, *then* hung on the tree. "Servile," "infame," "crudelissimum," "taeterrimum," "summum," "extremum," "supplicium," [424] are the names given to it by the Romans. (Cic. *Verr.* v. 66 and *passim.* See Phil. ii. 8; Cic. *Pro. Rab.* 5, "Nomen ipsum crucis absit non modo a corpore civium Romanorum, sed etiam a cogitatione, oculis, auribus." [425]) Maecenas, in one of the few interesting fragments of his verses, speaks of it as the extreme of horror, and the ultimate agony.

> "Vita dum superest bene est;
> Hanc mihi, vel acutâ
> Si sedeam cruce, sustine." [426]   (Sen. *Ep.* 101.)

[2] So Sen. *Ep.* 101; Orig. *in Matth.* 140 (Keim). Sometimes men were killed before crucifixion (Suet. *Jul. Cæs.* i. 74).

[3] St. Mark calls it ἐσμυρνισμένον οἶνον, "myrrh-mingled wine;" it is not likely that the exact ingredients would be known. St. Matthew mentally refers it to Ps. lxix. 21, ὄξος (or *possibly* οἶνον, which Tischendorf admits from א, B, D, K, L, &c.) μετὰ χολῆς. The Romans called these medicated cups "sopores" (Plin. xx. 18, Sen. *Ep.* 83, &c.).

quite irrespectively of their sympathy for any individual criminal. It was probably taken freely by the two malefactors, but when they offered it to Jesus He would not take it. The refusal was an act of sublimest heroism. The effect of the draught was to dull the nerves, to cloud the intellect, to provide an anæsthetic against some part, at least, of the lingering agonies of that dreadful death. But He, whom some modern sceptics have been base enough to accuse of feminine feebleness and cowardly despair, preferred rather " to look Death in the face " — to meet the king of terrors without striving to deaden the force of one agonizing anticipation, or to still the throbbing of one lacerated nerve.

The three crosses were laid on the ground — that of Jesus, which was doubtless taller than the other two, being placed in bitter scorn in the midst. Perhaps the cross-beam was now nailed to the upright, and certainly the title, which had either been borne by Jesus fastened round His neck, or carried by one of the soldiers in front of Him, was now nailed to the summit of His cross. Then He was stripped naked of all His clothes,[1] and then followed the most awful moment of all. He was laid down upon the implement of torture. His arms were stretched along the cross-beams; and at the centre of the open palms, the point of a huge iron nail was placed, which, by the blow of a mallet, was driven home into the wood.[2] Then through either foot separately, or possibly through both together as they were placed one over the other, another huge nail tore its way through the quivering flesh.[3] Whether the sufferer was *also* bound to the cross we do not know; but to prevent the hands and feet being torn away by the weight of the body, which could not " rest upon nothing but four great wounds," there was, about the centre of the cross, a wooden projection strong enough to support, at least in part, a human body which soon became a weight of agony.[4]

---

[1] We can but hope that the περιέζωσαν αὐτὸν λέντιον[427] of the *Acts of Pilate* (ch. 10), is true ; if so, it was exceptional, and the evidence of later martyrdoms — even of women — points the other way, as does also the Jewish custom.

[2] I write thus because the familiarity of oft-repeated words prevents us from realizing what crucifixion really was, and because it seems well that we *should* realize this. The hideous custom was probably copied by the Romans from the Phœnicians. The Egyptians simply *bound* the hands and feet, leaving the sufferer to die mainly of starvation.

[3] This was the earlier tradition, hence Greg. Naz. (*De Christ. Patient.*) calls the cross ξύλον τρίσηλον,[428] and Nonnus calls the feet ὁμοπλοκέες.[429] But Cyprian, who had witnessed crucifixions, speaks of four nails (*De Pass.*).

[4] πῆγμα. Hence the expressions ἐποχεῖσθαι ἐπὶ σταυροῦ.[430] " Sedere in cruce, sedilis excessus,"[431] &c. (Jer. Taylor, *Life of Christ*, III. xv. 2). On the other hand, there was no *suppedaneum*, or " foot-rest ; " though it is still repeated

It was probably at this moment of inconceivable horror that the voice of the Son of Man was heard uplifted, not in a scream of natural agony at that fearful torture, but calmly praying in Divine compassion for His brutal and pitiless murderers — aye, and for all who in their sinful ignorance crucify Him afresh for ever [1] — " FATHER, FORGIVE THEM, FOR THEY KNOW NOT WHAT THEY DO."

And then the accursed tree [2] — with its living human burden hanging upon it in helpless agony, and suffering fresh tortures as every movement irritated the fresh rents in hands and feet — was slowly heaved up by strong arms, and the end of it fixed firmly in a hole dug deep in the ground for that purpose.[3] The feet were but a little raised above the earth. The victim was in full reach of every hand that might choose to strike, in close proximity to every gesture of insult and hatred. He might hang for hours to be abused, outraged, even tortured by the ever-moving multitude who, with that desire to see what is horrible which always characterizes the coarsest hearts, had thronged to gaze upon a sight which should rather have made them weep tears of blood.

And there, in tortures which grew ever more insupportable, ever more maddening as time flowed on, the unhappy victims might linger in a living death so cruelly intolerable, that often they were driven to entreat and implore the spectators, or the executioners, for dear pity's sake, to put an end to anguish too awful for man to bear —

---

in modern pictures. The illustrations by G. Durrant in the popular edition of Renan's *Vie de Jésus*, though evidently meant to serve a purpose, are, in general, extremely true to Oriental life ; but those of the Crucifixion seem to me to be incorrect in many particulars. The hands were *probably* bound as well as nailed (Luc. vi. 543 — " *laqueum nodosque nocentes* ore suo rupit ; pendentia corpora carpsit Abrasitque cruces . . . Insertum manibus chalybem . . . . sustulit " [432]).

[1] The thought is more than once expressed by Mr. Browning (*A Death in the Desert*) :—

> " Is not His love, at issue still with sin,
> Closed with, and cast, and conquered, crucified
> Visibly when a wrong is done on earth ? "

[2] Infelix lignum (Liv. i. 26 ; Sen. *Ep.* 101, &c.). Now that this " tree of cursing and shame sits upon the sceptres, and is engraved and signed on the foreheads of kings " (Jer. Taylor), we can hardly imagine the disgust and horror with which it was once regarded when it had no associations but those " of pain, of guilt, and of ignominy " (Gibbon, ii. 153).

[3] Compare the old prophecy alluded to by Barnabas, *Ep.* 12, ὅταν ξύλον κλιθῇ καὶ ἀναστῇ.[433] Sometimes the sufferer was lifted and nailed after the cross had been erected (ἀνῆγον ἦγον ἦγον εἰς ἄκρον τέλος,[434] Greg. Naz., "Crucisalus ;" Plaut. *Bacch.* ii. 3, 128).

conscious to the last, and often, with tears of abject misery, beseeching from their enemies the priceless boon of death.[1]

For indeed a death by crucifixion seems to include all that pain and death *can* have of horrible and ghastly — dizziness, cramp, thirst, starvation, sleeplessness, traumatic fever, tetanus, publicity of shame, long continuance of torment, horror of anticipation, mortification of untended wounds — all intensified just up to the point at which they can be endured at all, but all stopping just short of the point which would give to the sufferer the relief of unconsciousness. The unnatural position made every movement painful; the lacerated veins and crushed tendons throbbed with incessant anguish; the wounds, inflamed by exposure, gradually gangrened; the arteries — especially of the head and stomach — became swollen and oppressed with surcharged blood; and while each variety of misery went on gradually increasing, there was added to them the intolerable pang of a burning and raging thirst; and all these physical complications caused an internal excitement and anxiety, which made the prospect of death itself — of death, the awful unknown enemy, at whose approach man usually shudders most — bear the aspect of a delicious and exquisite release.[2]

Such was the death to which Christ was doomed; and though for Him it was happily shortened by all that He had previously endured, yet He hung from soon after noon until nearly sunset, before "He gave up His soul to death."

When the cross was uplifted, the leading Jews, for the first time, prominently noticed the deadly insult in which Pilate had vented his indignation. Before, in their blind rage, they had imagined that the manner of His crucifixion was an insult aimed at *Jesus;* but now that they saw Him hanging between the two robbers, on a cross yet loftier, it suddenly flashed upon them that it was a public scorn inflicted upon *them.* For on the white wooden tablet smeared with gypsum,[3] which was to be seen so conspicuously over the head of Jesus on the cross, ran, in black letters, an inscription in the three civilized languages of the ancient world — the three languages of which *one* at least was certain to be known by every single man in that assembled multitude — in the official Latin, in the current Greek,

---

[1] And hence there are many ancient instances of men having been first strangled, or *nearly* killed, and *then* crucified; and of men who bought by large bribes this mournful but merciful privilege (Cic. *Verr.* 2, 45).

[2] See the epitome of Richter (a German physician) in Jahn's *Archaeol. Bibl.,* p. 261.

[3] Called ὄαρις, τίτλος, λεύκωμα, πίναξ.

in the vernacular Aramaic — informing all that this Man who was
thus enduring a shameful, servile death — this Man thus crucified
between two *sicarii* in the sight of the world,[1] was

"THE KING OF THE JEWS."[2]

To Him who was crucified the poor malice seemed to have in it
nothing of derision. Even on His cross He reigned ; even there
He seemed divinely elevated above the priests who had brought about
His death, and the coarse, idle, vulgar multitude who had flocked to
feed their greedy eyes upon His sufferings. The malice was quite
impotent against One whose spiritual and moral nobleness struck awe
into dying malefactors and heathen executioners, even in the lowest
abyss of His physical degradation. With the passionate ill-humor of
the Roman governor there probably blended a vein of seriousness.
While he was delighted to revenge himself on his detested subjects
by an act of public insolence, he probably meant, or half meant, to
imply that this *was*, in one sense, the King of the Jews — the greatest, the noblest, the truest of His race, whom therefore His race had
crucified. The King was not unworthy of His kingdom, but the
kingdom of the King. There was something loftier even than royalty in the glazing eyes which never ceased to look with sorrow on
the City of Righteousness, which had now become a city of murderers.
The Jews felt the intensity of the scorn with which Pilate had
treated them. It so completely poisoned their hour of triumph, that
they sent their chief priests in deputation, begging the Governor to
alter the obnoxious title. " Write not," they said, " ' The King of
the Jews,' but that ' He *said*, I am the King of the Jews.' " But
Pilate's courage, which had oozed away so rapidly at the name of
Cæsar, had now revived. He was glad in any and every way to

---

[1] Mark xv. 28 (Isa. liii. 12) is probably spurious, not being found in א, A, B, C,
D, &c. St. Mark, writing for the Romans, never once quotes from the Old
Testament.

[2] We cannot tell which of the Evangelists gives the *exact* title: it is, however,
possible that the *longest* one is accurately given by St. John (xix. 19), and that it
was the one in Aramaic, which would require least room. It is, at least, a probable conjecture that they ran as follows in the order mentioned by St. Matthew : —

ישו הנצרי מלך היהורים
'Ο βασιλεὺς τῶν 'Ιουδαίων.
Rex Judaeorum hic est. (Luke xxiii. 38.)

Professor Westcott remarks that, as given by St. Luke, it " seems like the scornful turn of the Latin title " (*Introd.*, p. 307). The true reading in St. Luke is 'Ο
βασιλεὺς τῶν 'Ιουδαίων οὗτος [435] (א). There is a monograph by S. Reyherus,
De Crucifixi Jesu Titulis, 1694. (See Hofmann, *Leb. Jes.* 375).

browbeat and thwart the men whose seditious clamor had forced him in the morning to act against his will. Few men had the power of giving expression to a sovereign contempt more effectually than the Romans. Without deigning any justification of what he had done, Pilate summarily dismissed these solemn hierarchs with the curt and contemptuous reply, " What I have written, I have written." [1]

In order to prevent the possibility of any rescue, even at the last moment — since instances had been known of men taken from the cross and restored to life [2] — a quaternion of soldiers with their centurion were left on the ground to guard the cross. The clothes of the victims always fell as perquisites to the men who had to perform so weary and disagreeable an office. Little dreaming how exactly they were fulfilling the mystic intimations of olden Jewish prophecy, they proceeded, therefore, to divide between them the garments of Jesus. The *tallith* they tore into four parts, probably ripping it down the seams ; [3] but the *cetôneth*, or under-garment, was formed of one continuous woven texture, and to tear would have been to spoil it ; they therefore contented themselves with letting it become the property of any one of the four to whom it should fall by lot. When this had been decided, they sat down and watched Him till the end, beguiling the weary lingering hours by eating and drinking, and gibing, and playing dice.

It was a scene of tumult. The great body of the people seem to have stood silently at gaze ; [4] but some few of them as they passed by the cross — perhaps some of the many false witnesses and other conspirators of the previous night — mocked at Jesus with insulting noises [5] and furious taunts, especially bidding Him come down from the cross and save Himself, since He could destroy the Temple and build it in three days. And the chief priests, and

---

[1] Such conduct on the part of Pilate would probably have been called "mythical," &c., if we did not find Philo attributing to him just the same "malicious intention to vex the people " (*Leg. ad Caium*, p. 38).

[2] At the request of Josephus, who prostrated himself at the feet of Titus, three men who had been crucified were taken down alive, and every possible effort made to save them ; but in spite of θεράπεια ἐπιμελεστάτη,[436] two of the three died (*Vit.* 75). A similar instance is narrated of Sandôkes (Herod vii. 194), and of the Convulsionnaires in the reign of Louis XV.

[3] Deut. xxii. 12. Some have imagined in this *cetôneth* a priestly garment ; but it was more probably the ordinary dress of the poor in Galilee — ἥπερ οἱ πτωχοὶ κέχρηνται τῶν Γαλιλαίων [437] (Isid.).

[4] Luke xxiii. 35, εἱστήκει ὁ λαὸς θεωρῶν [438] This seems to be clearly contrasted with οἱ ἄρχοντες and οἱ στρατιῶται.[439]

[5] Mark xv. 29, Οὐά.

scribes, and elders, less awe-struck, less compassionate than the mass of the people, were not ashamed to disgrace their grey-haired dignity and lofty reputation by adding their heartless reproaches to those of the evil few. Unrestrained by the noble patience of the Sufferer, unsated by the accomplishment of their wicked vengeance, unmoved by the sight of helpless anguish and the look of eyes that began to glaze in death, they congratulated one another [1] under His cross with scornful insolence — " He saved others, Himself He cannot save." " Let this Christ, this King of Israel, descend now from the cross, that we may see and believe." No wonder then that the ignorant soldiers took their share of mockery with these shameless and unvenerable hierarchs : no wonder that, at their midday meal, they pledged in mock hilarity the Dying Man, cruelly holding up towards His burning lips their cups of sour wine, and echoing the Jewish taunts against the weakness of the King whose throne was a cross, whose crown was thorns. Nay, even the poor wretches who were crucified with Him caught the hideous infection ; comrades, perhaps, of the respited Bar-Abbas — heirs of the rebellious fury of a Judas the Gaulonite — trained to recognize no Messiah but a Messiah of the sword, they reproachfully bade Him, if His claims were true, to save Himself and them.[2] So *all* the voices about Him rang with blasphemy and spite, and in that long slow agony His dying ear caught no accent of gratitude, of pity, or of love. Baseness, falsehood, savagery, stupidity — such were the characteristics of the world which thrust itself into hideous prominence before the Saviour's last consciousness — such the muddy and miserable stream that rolled under the cross before His dying eyes.[3]

But amid this chorus of infamy Jesus spoke not. He *could* have spoken. The pains of crucifixion did not confuse the intellect, or paralyze the powers of speech. We read of crucified men who, for hours together upon the cross, vented their sorrow, their rage, or their

---

[1] Mark xv. 31, ἐμπαίζοντες πρὸς ἀλλήλους . . . ἔλεγον.[440]

[2] In this, as in many other places, I have contented myself with silently showing that the supposed contradictions between the narratives of the Gospels do not necessarily exist. There is no contradiction in the text, yet I have only translated correctly the ὠνείδιζον (Matt. xxvii. 44), the *reproach* in which the robbers at first joined, and the ἐβλασφήμει (Luke xxiii. 39), the *furious reviling* of which only the unrepentant one was guilty. (See Lange, v. 398.)

[3] A friend supplies me with a sad and striking passage from the martyrdom of a true servant of Jesus — Savonarola. " Hic quoque non praeteribo silentio fuisse illum pendentem in ligno a puerorum multitudine saxis impetitum : a quibus antea solitus erat in templo ante praedicationis initium hymnis et laudibus excipi." [441] (Pietro Delfrini [an eye-witness], *Epist.* v. 73.)

despair in the manner that best accorded with their character; of some who raved and cursed, and spat at their enemies; of others who protested to the last against the iniquity of their sentence; of others who implored compassion with abject entreaties; of one even who, from the cross, as from a tribunal, harangued the multitude of his countrymen, and upbraided them with their wickedness and vice.[1] But, except to bless and to encourage, and to add to the happiness and hope of others, Jesus spoke not. So far as the malice of the passers-by, and of priests and Sanhedrists, and soldiers, and of these poor robbers who suffered with Him, was concerned — as before during the trial so now upon the cross — He maintained unbroken His kingly silence.

But that silence, joined to His patient majesty and the divine holiness and innocence which radiated from Him like a halo, was more eloquent than any words. It told earliest on one of the crucified robbers. At first this " bonus latro " [441] † of the Apocryphal Gospels seems to have faintly joined in the reproaches uttered by his fellow-sinner; but when those reproaches merged into deeper blasphemy, he spoke out his inmost thought. It is probable that he had met Jesus before, and heard Him, and perhaps been one of those thousands who had seen His miracles. There is indeed no authority for the legend which assigns to him the name of Dysmas, or for the beautiful story of his having saved the life of the Virgin and her Child during their flight into Egypt.[2] But on the plains of Gennesareth, perhaps from some robber's cave in the wild ravines of the Valley of the Doves, he may well have approached His presence — he may well have been one of those publicans and sinners who drew near to Him for to hear Him. And the words of Jesus had found some room in the good ground of his heart; they had not all fallen upon stony places. Even at this hour of shame and death, when he was suffering the just consequence of his past evil deeds, faith triumphed. As a flame sometimes leaps up among dying embers, so amid the white ashes of a sinful life which lay so thick upon his heart, the flame of love towards his God and his Saviour was not

---

[1] Such instances are given in Keim, III. ii. 431 — *e. g.*, Gavius, who to the last kept shouting " Civis Romanus sum " [441] ‡ (Cic. *Verr.* v. 62) ; Eleazar (Jos. *B. J.* vii. 6, § 4 ; Niger of Peræa, who showed his wounds, and entreated that he might be buried (*Id. ib.* iv. 6, § 1) ; Bomilcar, the Carthaginian, who harangued " de summâ cruce velut de tribunali in Poenorum scelera " [442] (Justin. xxii. 7). " Crederem, nisi quidam de patibulo spectatores conspuerent " [443] (Sen. *De Vit. Beat.* 19).

[2] Arab. Evang. Infant. xxiii. See the beautiful poem on this subject in Professor Plumptre's *Lazarus, and other Poems.*

quite quenched. Under the hellish outcries which had broken loose
around the cross of Jesus, there had lain a deep misgiving. Half of
them seem to have been instigated by doubt and fear. Even in the
self-congratulations of the priests we catch an undertone of dread.
Suppose that even now some imposing miracle should be wrought?
Suppose that even now that martyr-form should burst indeed into
Messianic splendor, and the King, who seemed to be in the slow
misery of death, should suddenly with a great voice summon His
legions of angels, and springing from His cross upon the rolling
clouds of heaven, come in flaming fire to take vengeance upon His
enemies? And the air seemed to be full of signs. There was a
gloom of gathering darkness in the sky, a thrill and tremor in the
solid earth, a haunting presence as of ghostly visitants who chilled
the heart and hovered in awful witness above that scene. The dying
robber had joined at first in the half-taunting, half-despairing appeal
to a defeat and weakness which contradicted all that he had hoped;
but now this defeat seemed to be greater than victory, and this weakness more irresistible than strength. As he looked, the faith in his
heart dawned more and more into the perfect day. He had long
ceased to utter any reproachful words; he now rebuked his comrade's
blasphemies. Ought not the suffering innocence of Him who hung
between them, to shame into silence their just punishment and flagrant guilt? And so, turning his head to Jesus, he uttered the
intense appeal, " O Jesus, remember me when Thou comest in Thy
kingdom." [1] Then He, who had been mute amid invectives, spake
at once in surpassing answer to that humble prayer, " VERILY, I SAY
TO THEE, TO-DAY SHALT THOU BE WITH ME IN PARADISE."

Though none spoke to comfort Jesus — though deep grief, and
terror, and amazement kept them dumb — yet there were hearts
amid the crowd that beat in sympathy with the awful Sufferer. At
a distance stood a number of women looking on, and perhaps, even
at that dread hour, expecting His immediate deliverance. Many of
these were women who had ministered to Him in Galilee, and had
come from thence in the great band of Galilæan pilgrims. Conspicuous among this heart-stricken group were His mother Mary, Mary
of Magdala, Mary the wife of Clopas, mother of James and Joses,
and Salome the wife of Zebedee. Some of them, as the hours
advanced, stole nearer and nearer to the cross, and at length the
filming eye of the Saviour fell on his own mother Mary, as, with the

---

[1] Tischendorf reads 'Ιησοῦ with ℵ, B, C, L, &c. The E. V. wrongly renders
" *into* Thy kingdom."

sword piercing through and through her heart, she stood with the disciple whom He loved.[1] His mother does not seem to have been much with Him during His ministry. It may be that the duties and cares of a humble home rendered it impossible. At any rate, the only occasions on which we hear of her are occasions when she is with His brethren, and is joined with them in endeavoring to influence, apart from His own purposes and authority, His Messianic course. But although at the very beginning of His Ministry He had gently shown her that the earthly and filial relation was now to be transcended by one far more lofty and divine, and though this end of all her high hopes must have tried her faith with an overwhelming and unspeakable sorrow, yet she was true to Him in this supreme hour of His humiliation, and would have done for Him all that a mother's sympathy and love can do. Nor had He for a moment forgotten her who had bent over His infant slumbers, and with whom He had shared those thirty years in the cottage at Nazareth. Tenderly and sadly He thought of the future that awaited her during the remaining years of her life on earth, troubled as they must be by the tumults and persecutions of a struggling and nascent faith. After His resurrection her lot was wholly cast among His Apostles, and the Apostle whom He loved the most, the Apostle who was nearest to Him in heart and life, seemed the fittest to take care of her. To him, therefore — to John whom He had loved more than His brethren — to John whose head had leaned upon His breast at the Last Supper, He consigned her as a sacred charge. " Woman," He said to her, in fewest words, but in words which breathed the uttermost spirit of tenderness, " behold thy son ; " and then to St. John, " Behold thy mother." He could make no gesture with those pierced hands, but He could bend His head. They listened in speechless emotion, but from that hour — perhaps from that very moment — leading her away from a spectacle which did but torture her soul with unavailing agony, that disciple took her to his own home.[2]

It was now noon, and at the Holy City the sunshine should have been burning over that scene of horror with a power such as it has in the full depth of an English summer-time. But instead of this,

---

[1] Although it seems to me (even apart from the authority of the Peschito) that four women are mentioned in John xix. 25 ; and although it is far from impossible that " His mother's sister " *may* mean, as Meyer conjectures, Salome herself (in which case James and John were His cousins), yet any certain decision of the point is from the nature of the case impossible.

[2] John xix. 27, εἰς τὰ ἴδια. Perhaps this furnishes us with a fresh proof that St. John was more closely connected with Jerusalem than the other Apostles, which would account for his fuller knowledge and record of the Judæan ministry.

the face of the heavens was black, and the noonday sun was "turned into darkness," on "this great and terrible day of the Lord." It could have been no darkness of any natural eclipse, for the Paschal moon was at the full ; but it was one of those "signs from heaven" for which, during the ministry of Jesus, the Pharisees had so often clamored in vain. The early Fathers appealed to Pagan authorities — the historian Phallus, the chronicler Phlegon — for such a darkness; but we have no means of testing the accuracy of these references, and it is quite possible that the darkness was a local gloom which hung densely over the guilty city and its immediate neighborhood. But whatever it was, it clearly filled the minds of all who beheld it with yet deeper misgiving. The taunts and jeers of the Jewish priests and the heathen soldiers were evidently confined to the earlier hours of the crucifixion. Its later stages seem to have thrilled alike the guilty and the innocent with emotions of dread and horror. Of the incidents of those last three hours we are told nothing,[1] and that awful obscuration of the noonday sun may well have overawed every heart into an inaction respecting which there was nothing to relate. What Jesus suffered *then* for us men and our salvation we cannot know, for during those three hours He hung upon His cross in silence and darkness; or, if He spoke, there were none there to record His words. But towards the close of that time His anguish culminated, and — emptied to the very uttermost of that glory which He had since the world began — drinking to the very deepest dregs the cup of humiliation and bitterness — enduring, not only to have taken upon Him the form of a servant, but also to suffer the last infamy which human hatred could impose on servile helplessness — He uttered that mysterious cry, of which the full significance will never be fathomed by man —

"Eli, Eli, lama sabacthani?"[2] ("My God, my God, why hast thou forsaken me?")

In those words, quoting the Psalm in which the early Fathers rightly saw a far-off prophecy of the whole passion of Christ,[3] He

---

[1] On the obvious discrepancy between the existing texts of St. John and of the Synoptists as to this reckoning of hours, see *supra*, p. 628.

[2] This utterance on the cross is the only one recorded by the two first Evangelists, and is recorded *by them alone.* שבקתני is for עֲזַבְתָּנִי. St. Mark preserves the more purely Aramaic form *Eloi.* The fact that thus in His last moments Jesus speaks in Aramaic, would seem to prove that this had been the ordinary language of His life.

[3] Tert. *Adv. Marc.* iii. 19, " Si adhuc quaeris dominicae crucis praedicationem, satis tibi potest facere vicesimus primus psalmus, *totam Christi continens passionem.*" 444 (Keim.)

borrowed from David's utter agony the expression of His own. In that hour He was alone. Sinking from depth to depth of unfathomable suffering, until, at the close approach of a death which — because He was God, and yet had been made man — was more awful to Him than it could ever be to any of the sons of men, it seemed as if even His Divine Humanity could endure no more.

Doubtless the voice of the Sufferer — though uttered loudly in that paroxysm of an emotion which, in another, would almost have touched the verge of despair — was yet rendered more uncertain and indistinct from the condition of exhaustion in which He hung; and so, amid the darkness, and confused noise, and dull footsteps of the moving multitude, there were some who did not hear what He had said. They had caught only the first syllable, and said to one another that He had called on the name of Elijah.[1] The readiness with which they seized this false impression is another proof of the wild state of excitement and terror — the involuntary dread of something great, and unforeseen, and terrible — to which they had been reduced from their former savage insolence. For Elijah, the great prophet of the Old Covenant, was inextricably mingled with all the Jewish expectations of a Messiah, and these expectations were full of wrath. The coming of Elijah would be the coming of a day of fire, in which the sun should be turned into blackness and the moon into blood, and the powers of heaven should be shaken. Already the noonday sun was shrouded in unnatural eclipse: might not some awful form at any moment rend the heavens and come down, touch the mountains and they should smoke? The vague anticipation of conscious guilt was unfulfilled. Not such as yet was to be the method of God's workings. His messages to man for many ages more were not to be in the thunder and earthquake, not in rushing wind or roaring flame, but in the " still small voice" speaking always amid the apparent silences of Time in whispers intelligible to man's heart, but in which there is neither speech nor language, though the voice is heard.

But now the end was very rapidly approaching, and Jesus, who had been hanging for nearly six hours upon the cross, was suffering from that torment of thirst which is most difficult of all for the

---

[3] It has been urged that it would be impossible to confuse *Eloi* with *Elijahu*, and that every Jew would have known what *Eloi* meant. But the first assertion is by no means self-evident under the circumstances; and as for the second, there might be many in this motley multitude — the Paschal gathering of pilgrims from all nations — to whom Aramaic was by no means familiar.

human frame to bear — perhaps the most unmitigated of the many separate sources of anguish which were combined in this worst form of death. No doubt this burning thirst was aggravated by seeing the Roman soldiers drinking so near the cross; and happily for mankind, Jesus had never sanctioned the unnatural affectation of stoic impassibility. And so He uttered the one sole word of physical suffering which had been wrung from Him by all the hours in which He had endured the extreme of all that man can inflict. He cried aloud, " I THIRST." [1] Probably a few hours before, the cry would have only provoked a roar of frantic mockery; but now the lookers-on were reduced by awe to a readier humanity. Near the cross there lay on the ground the large earthen vessel containing the *posca*, which was the ordinary drink of the Roman soldiers. The mouth of it was filled with a piece of sponge, which served as a cork. Instantly some one — we know not whether he was friend or enemy, or merely one who was there out of idle curiosity — took out the sponge and dipped it in the *posca* [2] to give it to Jesus. But low as was the elevation of the cross, the head of the Sufferer, as it rested on the horizontal beam of the accursed tree, was just beyond the man's reach; and therefore he put the sponge at the end of a stalk of hyssop — about a foot long — and held it up to the parched and dying lips.' Even this simple act of pity, which Jesus did not refuse, seemed to jar upon the condition of nervous excitement with which some of the multitude were looking on. " Let be," they said to the man, " let us see whether Elias is coming to save Him." The man did not desist from his act of mercy, but when it was done he too seems to have echoed those uneasy words.[4] But Elias came not, nor human comforter, nor angel deliverer. It was the will of God, it was the will of the Son of God, that He should be " perfected through sufferings;" [5] that — for the eternal example of all His children as long as the world should last — He should " endure unto the end."

And now the end was come. Once more, in the words of the

---

[1] Δ $\iota\psi\tilde{\omega}$. As-Sujûti, an Arabic writer, describing the crucifixion of a young Turk in 1247, says that he complained of intense thirst on the first day, and his sufferings were increased by seeing constantly before him the waters of the Baradâ, on the banks of which he was crucified. (Dr. Nicholson, in Kitto, i. 595.)

[2] Mark xv. 36, $\gamma\epsilon\mu\iota\acute{o}\alpha\varsigma$ $\acute{o}\pi\acute{o}\gamma\gamma o\nu$ $\check{o}\xi o\upsilon\varsigma$.[445] The hyssop is either a species of marjoram, or the caper-plant (*Capparis spinosa*), of which the stem is woody (Royle, *Journ. Sacr. Lit.*, Oct. 1849).

[3] The $\varkappa\alpha\lambda\acute{\alpha}\mu\omega$ [446] of Matt. xxvii. 48 = $\upsilon\acute{o}\acute{o}\grave{\omega}\pi\omega$ [447] (John xix. 29).

[4] Mark xv. 36.

[5] Heb. v. 7, 8; ii. 10; Phil. ii. 8, 9.

sweet Psalmist of Israel,[1] but adding to them that title of trustful love which, through Him, is permitted to the use of all mankind, " FATHER," He said, " INTO THY HANDS I COMMEND MY SPIRIT." Then with one more great effort He uttered the last cry — the one victorious word $T\varepsilon\tau\acute{\varepsilon}\lambda\varepsilon\sigma\tau\alpha\iota$, " IT IS FINISHED." It may be that that great cry ruptured some of the vessels of His heart; for no sooner had it been uttered than He bowed His head upon His breast, and yielded His life, " a ransom for many " — a willing sacrifice to His Heavenly Father.[2] " Finished was His holy life ; with His life His struggle, with His struggle His work, with His work the redemption, with the redemption the foundation of the new world." [3] At that moment the vail of the Temple was rent in twain from the top to the bottom.[4] An earthquake shook the earth and split the rocks, and as it rolled away from their places the great stones which closed and covered the cavern sepulchres of the Jews, so it seemed to the imaginations of many to have disimprisoned the spirits of the dead, and to have filled the air with ghostly visitants, who after Christ had risen appeared to linger in the Holy City.[5] These circumstances of amazement, joined to all they had observed in the bearing of the Crucified, cowed even the cruel and gay indifference of the Roman soldiers. On the centurion, who was in command of

---

[1] Ps. xxxi. 5. Cf. Acts vii. 59 ; 1 Pet. ii. 23.

[2] There may be something intentional in the fact that in *describing* the death of Christ the Evangelists do not use the neuter verb $\check{\varepsilon}\theta\alpha\nu\varepsilon\nu$, but the phrases, $\grave{\varepsilon}\xi\acute{\varepsilon}\pi\nu\varepsilon\upsilon\acute{\sigma}\varepsilon\nu$ (Mark xv. 37 ; Luke xxiii. 46) ; $\grave{\alpha}\varphi\tilde{\eta}\varkappa\varepsilon\nu$ $\tau\grave{o}$ $\pi\nu\varepsilon\tilde{\upsilon}\mu\alpha$ (Matt. xxvii. 50) ; $\pi\alpha\rho\acute{\varepsilon}\delta\omega\varkappa\varepsilon\nu$ $\tau\grave{o}$ $\pi\nu\varepsilon\tilde{\upsilon}\mu\alpha$ (John xix. 30) ; as though they imply with St. Augustine that He gave up His life, " *quia voluit, quando voluit, quomodo voluit.*" [448] " Oblatus est quia ipse voluit," [449] Isa. liii. 7 (Vulg.). (Bunsen, *Bibelwerk*, ix. 455.) — I have not here touched on any questions as to the suffering of Jesus in His humanity, but not in His divinity, &c. (Pearson *On the Creed*, Art. iv.) All these theological questions about the $\grave{\alpha}\nu\tau\acute{\iota}\delta o\acute{\sigma}\iota\varsigma$, $\grave{\alpha}\nu\tau\iota\mu\varepsilon\tau\acute{\alpha}\sigma\tau\alpha\acute{\sigma}\iota\varsigma$, $\pi\varepsilon\rho\iota\chi\acute{\omega}\rho\eta\acute{\sigma}\iota\varsigma$, *communicatio idiomatum,* [450] &c., seem to me far to transcend our powers of reasoning. But Christ's perfectly voluntary resignation of His own life is distinctly asserted in John x. 18.

[3] Lange, v. 420.

[4] Heb. vi. 19 ; ix. 3 ; x. 19, 20. The vail intended must be the *parocheth*, or inner vail. The Gospel to the Hebrews said that at the same moment a vast beam over the Temple lintel was shattered (Jer. *ad. Matt.* xxvii. 51). It is far from improbable that the Jewish legends of strange portents which happened " forty years " (as they say in their usual loose and vague manner) before the destruction of the Temple, are in reality the echoes and reminiscences of those which in fact took place at the death of Christ. Tertullian says to the Jews with unanswerable force, " Non potuisse cessare legem antiquam et prophetas, nisi venisset is, qui per eandem legem et per eosdem prophetas venturus aduuntiabatur " [451] (*Adv. Jud.* 6).

[5] Only in some such way as this can I account for the singular and wholly isolated allusion of Matt. xxvii. 52, 53.

them, the whole scene had exercised a yet deeper influence. As he stood opposite to the cross and saw the Saviour die, he glorified God, and exclaimed, " This Man was in truth righteous " — nay, more, " This Man was a Son of God." Even the multitude, utterly sobered from their furious excitement and frantic rage, began to be weighed down with a guilty consciousness that the scene which they had witnessed had in it something more awful than they could have conceived, and as they returned to Jerusalem they wailed, and beat upon their breasts. Well might they do so ! This was the last drop in a a full cup of wickedness : this was the beginning of the end of their city, and name, and race.

And in truth that scene was more awful than they, or even we, can know. The secular historian, be he ever so sceptical, cannot fail to see in it the central point of the world's history. Whether he be a believer in Christ or not, he cannot refuse to admit that this new religion grew from the smallest of all seeds to be a mighty tree, so that the birds of the air took refuge in its branches; that it was the little stone cut without hands which dashed into pieces the colossal image of heathen greatness, and grew till it became a great mountain and filled the earth. Alike to the infidel and to the believer the crucifixion is the boundary instant between ancient and modern days. Morally and physically, no less than spiritually, the Faith of Christ was the Palingenesia of the world. It came like the dawn of a new spring to nations " effete with the drunkenness of crime." The struggle was long and hard, but from the hour when Christ died began the death-knell to every Satanic tyranny and every tolerated abomination. From that hour Holiness became the universal ideal of all who name the name of Christ as their Lord, and the attainment of that ideal the common heritage of souls in which His Spirit dwells.

The effects, then, of the work of Christ are even to the unbeliever indisputable and historical. It expelled cruelty ; it curbed passion ; it branded suicide ; it punished and repressed an execrable infanticide ; it drove the shameless impurities of heathendom into a congenial darkness. There was hardly a class whose wrongs it did not remedy. It rescued the gladiator ; it freed the slave ; it protected the captive ; it nursed the sick ; it sheltered the orphan ; it elevated the woman ; it shrouded as with a halo of sacred innocence the tender years of the child. In every region of life its ameliorating influence was felt. It changed pity from a vice into a virtue.[1] It elevated

---

[1] " Misericordia animi vitium est "[452] (Sen. *De Clem.*). " Nec ille Aut doluit miserans inopem "[453] (Virg.).

poverty from a curse into a beatitude.[1] It ennobled labor from a vulgarity into a dignity and a duty. It sanctified marriage from little more than a burdensome convention into little less than a blessed sacrament. It revealed for the first time the angelic beauty of a Purity of which men had despaired and of a Meekness at which they had utterly scoffed. It created the very conception of charity, and broadened the limits of its obligation from the narrow circle of a neighborhood to the widest horizons of the race. And while it thus evolved the idea of Humanity as a common brotherhood, even where its tidings were *not* believed — all over the world, wherever its tidings *were* believed, it cleansed the life, and elevated the soul of each individual man. And in all lands where it has moulded the characters of its true believers, it has created hearts so pure, and lives so peaceful, and homes so sweet, that it might seem as though those angels who had heralded its advent had also whispered to every depressed and despairing sufferer among the sons of men, "Though ye have lien among the pots, yet shall ye be as the wings of a dove, that is covered with silver wings, and her feathers like gold."

Others, if they *can* and *will*, may see in such a work as this no Divine Providence; they may think it philosophical enlightenment to hold that Christianity and Christendom are adequately accounted for by the idle dreams of a noble self-deceiver, and the passionate hallucinations of a recovered demoniac. We persecute them not, we denounce them not, we judge them not; but we say that, unless all life be a hollow, there could have been no such miserable origin to the sole religion of the world, which holds the perfect balance between philosophy and popularity, between religion and morals, between meek submissiveness and the pride of freedom, between the ideal and the real, between the inward and the outward, between modest stillness and heroic energy, nay, between the tenderest conservatism and the boldest plans of world-wide reformation.[2] The witness of History to Christ is a witness which has been given with irresistible cogency; and it has been so given to none but Him.

But while even the unbeliever must see what the life and death of Jesus have effected in the world, to the believer that life and death are something deeper still; to him they are nothing less than a resurrection from the dead. He sees in the cross of Christ something which far transcends its historical significance. He sees in it the

---

[1] "Ingens vitium, magnum opprobrium pauperies"[454] (Sen.). "Blessed are the poor in spirit" (Matt. v. 3).

[2] Keim, p. 370 (abridged edition).

fulfilment of all prophecy as well as the consummation of all history; he sees in it the explanation of the mystery of birth, and the conquest over the mystery of the grave. In that life he finds a perfect example; in that death an infinite redemption. As he contemplates the Incarnation and the Crucifixion, he no longer feels that God is far away, and that this earth is but a disregarded speck in the infinite azure, and he himself but an insignificant atom chance-thrown amid the thousand million living souls of an innumerable race, but he exclaims in faith and hope and love, "Behold, the tabernacle of God is with men; yea, He will be their God, and they shall be His people." "Ye are the temple of the living God; as God hath said, I will dwell in them, and walk in them." [1]

The sun was westering as the darkness rolled away from the completed sacrifice. They who had not thought it a pollution to inaugurate their feast by the murder of their Messiah, were seriously alarmed lest the sanctity of the following day — which began at sunset — should be compromised by the hanging of the corpses on the cross. And horrible to relate, the crucified often lived for many hours — nay, even for two days — in their torture. The Jews therefore begged Pilate that their legs might be broken, and their bodies taken down. This *crurifragium*, as it was called, consisted in striking the legs of the sufferers with a heavy mallet, a violence which seemed always to have hastened, if it did not instantly cause their death. Nor would the Jews be the only persons who would be anxious to hasten the end, by giving the deadly blow. Until life was extinct, the soldiers appointed to guard the execution dared not leave the ground. The wish, therefore, was readily granted. The soldiers broke the legs of the two malefactors first,[2] and then, coming to Jesus, found that the great cry had been indeed His last, and that He was dead already. They did not, therefore, break His legs, and thus unwittingly preserved the symbolism of that Paschal lamb, of which He was the antitype, and of which it had been commanded that "a bone of it shall not be broken." [3] And yet, as He might be

[1] Ezek. xxxvii. 26; 2 Cor. vi. 16.

[2] If we must look for any reason, we may suppose that two soldiers broke the legs of a malefactor on either side first; or possibly that the cross of Jesus being a little loftier may have rendered it less easy to give the blow at once.

[3] Exod. xii. 46 (St. John also refers to Zech. xii. 10); Rev. i. 7. It is a striking circumstance that the body of the Paschal lamb was literally crucified on two transverse spits. I witnessed the Samaritan Passover on the summit of Mount Gerizim in 1870, and the bodies of the seven lambs as they were prepared for roasting looked exactly as though they were laid on seven crosses.

only in a syncope — as instances had been known in which men apparently dead had been taken down from the cross and resuscitated — and as the lives of the soldiers would have had to answer for any irregularity, one of them, in order to make death certain, drove the broad head of his *hasta* into His side. The wound, as it was meant to do, pierced the region of the heart, and "forthwith," says St. John, with an emphatic appeal to the truthfulness of his eye-witness (an appeal which would be singularly and impossibly blasphemous if the narrative were the forgery which so much elaborate modern criticism has wholly failed to prove that it is), "forthwith came there out blood and water." Whether the water was due to some abnormal pathological conditions caused by the dreadful complication of the Saviour's sufferings — or whether it rather means that the pericardium had been rent by the spear-point, and that those who took down the body observed some drops of its serum mingled with the blood — in either case that lance-thrust was sufficient to hush all the heretical assertions that Jesus had only *seemed* to die; [1] and as it assured the soldiers, so should it assure all who have doubted, that He, who on the third day rose again, had in truth been crucified, dead, and buried, and that His soul had passed into the unseen world.

---

[1] The early Fathers all appeal to this fact in refutation of the Docetae. As the effusion of lymph and blood after a *post-mortem* incision, though rare, is asserted by some physicians not to be unknown, there seems to be no need to regard the fact as miraculous. Opinions are divided as to whether the water was merely the lymph of the pericardium, or the decomposed *crassamentum* and *serum* of extravasated blood. That the circumstance is not impossible, especially if our Lord died of a ruptured heart (Ps. xxii. 14; lxix. 20) [or from a state of pleurisy?], may be regarded as proved by the letters of Sir J. Simpson and other eminent physicians to Dr. Hanna (*Last day of Our Lord's Passion*, pp. 333—343), as well as by the book of Dr. Stroud, *On the Physical Cause of the Death of Christ.*

CHAPTER LXII.

THE RESURRECTION.

"Necesse est pauca dicamus de Christo ut Deo." [455] — TERT. *Apolog.* 21.

AT the moment when Christ died, nothing could have seemed more abjectly weak, more pitifully hopeless, more absolutely doomed to scorn, and extinction, and despair, than the Church which he had founded. It numbered but a handful of weak followers, of which the boldest had denied his Lord with blasphemy, and the most devoted had forsaken Him and fled. They were poor, they were ignorant, they were hopeless. They could not claim a single synagogue or a single sword. If they spoke their own language, it bewrayed them by its mongrel dialect; if they spoke the current Greek, it was despised as a miserable *patois*. So feeble were they and insignificant, that it would have looked like foolish partiality to prophesy for them the limited existence of a Galilæan sect. How was it that these dull and ignorant men, with their cross of wood, triumphed over the deadly fascinations of sensual mythologies, conquered kings and their armies, and overcame the world?

What was it that thus caused strength to be made perfect out of abject weakness? There is one, and one only *possible* answer — the resurrection from the dead. All this vast revolution was due to the power of Christ's resurrection. "If we measure what seemed to be the hopeless ignominy of the catastrophe by which His work was ended, and the Divine prerogatives which are claimed for Him, not *in spite of,* but *in consequence of* that suffering and shame, we shall feel the utter hopelessness of reconciling the fact, and that triumphant deduction from it, without some intervening fact as certain as Christ's passion, and glorious enough to transfigure its sorrow." [1]

---

[1] Westcott, *Gospel of the Resurrection*, p. 111. He adds: "If Christ did not rise, we have not only to explain how the belief in his resurrection came to be received without any previous hopes which could lead to its reception, but also how it came to be received with that intensity of personal conviction which could invest the life and person of Christ with attributes never before assigned to any one, and that by Jews who had been reared in the strictest monotheism" (p. 112).

The sun was now on the edge of the horizon, and the Sabbath day was near. And "that Sabbath day was a high day," a Sabbath of peculiar splendor and solemnity, because it was at once a Sabbath and a Passover.[1] The Jews had taken every precaution to prevent the ceremonial pollution of a day so sacred, and were anxious that immediately after the death of the victims had been secured, their bodies should be taken from the cross. About the sepulture they did not trouble themselves, leaving it to the chance good offices of friends and relatives to huddle the malefactors into their nameless graves. The dead body of Jesus was left hanging till the last, because a person who could not easily be slighted had gone to obtain leave from Pilate to dispose of it as he wished.

This was Joseph of Arimathæa,[2] a rich man, of high character and blameless life, and a distinguished member of the Sanhedrin. Although timidity of disposition, or weakness of faith, had hitherto prevented him from openly declaring his belief in Jesus, yet he had abstained from sharing in the vote of the Sanhedrin, or countenancing their crime. And now sorrow and indignation inspired him with courage. Since it was too late to declare his sympathy for Jesus as a living Prophet, he would at least give a sign of his devotion to Him as the martyred victim of a wicked conspiracy. Flinging secrecy and caution to the winds, he no sooner saw that the cross on Golgotha now bore a lifeless burden, than he went to Pilate on the very evening of the crucifixion, and begged that the dead body might be given him. Although the Romans left their crucified slaves to be devoured by dogs and ravens, Pilate had no difficulty in sanctioning the more humane and reverent custom of the Jews, which required, even in extreme cases, the burial of the dead.[3] He was, however, amazed at the speediness with which death had supervened, and sending for the centurion, asked whether it had taken place sufficiently

---

[1] John xix. 31 ; Deut. xxi. 22, 23 ; Lev. xxiii. 7.

[2] Arimathæa, or Rama, is a place of uncertain site ; it may be Rama in Benjamin (Matt. ii. 18), or Ramathaim in Ephraim (1 Sam. i. 1), but certainly is not Ramleh in Dan.

[3] For the Greek and Roman custom, see Herod. iii. 12 ; Cic. *Tusc. Q.* i. 43 ; Plaut. *Mil. Glor.* ii. 4, 19 ; Hor. *Ep.* i. 16, 48, &c. ; Suet. *Ner.* 49 ; Juv. *Sat.* xiv. 77. For the Jewish, Deut. xxi. 23 ; Josh. viii. 29 ; Jos. *Antt.* iv. 8, § 24 ; Mark vi. 29 ; Acts viii. 2. The request of Joseph was not, however, without danger, and in later martyrdoms such a request cost men their lives, as was the case with the martyr Porphyrios. Pilate might, perhaps, have exacted a bribe (cf. Acts xxiv. 26 ; Plut. *Galb.* 28), but apparently did not do so, because the care of the Jews for burial was well known, and any violation of this usage would have been resented (Jos. *B. J.* iv 5, § 2).

long to distinguish it from a faint or swoon.[1] On ascertaining that such was the fact, he at once assigned the body, doubtless with some real satisfaction, to the care of this "honorable councillor." Without wasting a moment, Joseph purchased a long piece of fine linen,[2] and took the body from its cross. Meanwhile the force of his example had helped to waken a kindred feeling in the soul of the candid but fearful Nicodemus. If, as seems extremely probable, he be identical with the Nakdimon Ben Gorion of the Talmud, he was a man of enormous wealth;[3] and however much he had held back during the life of Jesus, now, on the evening of His death, his heart was filled with a gush of compassion and remorse, and he hurried to His cross and burial with an offering of truly royal munificence. The faith which had once required the curtain of darkness, can now venture at least into the light of sunset, and brightened finally into noonday confidence. Thanks to this glow of kindling sorrow and compassion in the hearts of these two noble and wealthy disciples, He who died as a malefactor, was buried as a king. "He made His grave with the wicked, and with the rich in His death." The fine linen (*sindón*) which Joseph had purchased was richly spread with the hundred *litras* of myrrh and perfumed aloe-wood which Nicodemus had brought,[4] and the lacerated body — whose divinely-human spirit was now in the calm of its sabbath rest in the Paradise of God — was thus carried to its loved and peaceful grave.

Close by the place of crucifixion — if not an actual part of it[5] —

---

[1] Such seems to be the significance of εἰ πάλαι ἀπέθανεν [456] in Mark xv. 44. The Martyrologies tell us that Victorinus, crucified head-downwards, lived for three days, and Paulinus and Macra for nine; but we cannot be sure of these facts. The average time of survival in the case of a healthy man seems to have been thirty-six hours; without cold, exposure, &c., the ordinary course of the mortification (which caused death) would require forty-eight hours.

[2] Another clear indication, even in the Synoptists, that this Friday was not the Passover. The *sindón* was probably of white linen, such as that in which Gamaliel II. ordered himself to be buried, in order to discourage the extravagant burial garments of the Jews. The three words used of the cerements of Jesus are σινδών (Mark xv. 46); ὀθόνια (John xix. 40); σουδάριον (xx. 7); κειρίαι is used of Lazarus (xi. 44).

[3] He and his house are said to have perished at the fall of Jerusalem; and I have already (p. 167) mentioned the dreadful story that his daughter, who had received as her dower a million denarii of gold, was seen picking the grains of corn out of the horses' dung. May not this fable point to Jewish hatred against one who in heart at least was a Christian?

[4] Even at the burial of Gamalial II. only eighty pounds of spices were burnt by Onkelos. At Herod's funeral there had been 500 spice-bearers (Jos. *Antt.* xvii. 8, § 3).

[5] ἦν δὲ ἐν τῷ τόπῳ, ὅπου ἐσταυρώθη, κῆπος [457] (John xix. 41).

was a garden belonging to Joseph of Arimathæa, and in its enclosure he had caused a new tomb to be hewn for himself out of the solid rock, that he might be buried in the near precincts of the Holy City.[1] The tomb had never been used, but, in spite of the awful sacredness which the Jews attached to their rock-hewn sepulchres, and the sensitive scrupulosity with which they shrank from all contact with a corpse, Joseph never hesitated to give up for the body of Jesus the last home which he had designed for his own use. But the preparations had to be hurried, because when the sun had set the Sabbath would have begun. All that they could do, therefore, was to wash the corpse, to lay it amid the spices, to wrap the head in a white napkin, to roll the fine linen round and round the wounded limbs, and to lay the body reverently in the rocky niche. Then, with the united toil of several men, they rolled a *gôlal*, or great stone, to the horizontal aperture; and scarcely had they accomplished this when, as the sun sank behind the hills of Jerusalem, the new Sabbath dawned.[2]

Mary of Magdala, and Mary the mother of James and Joses, had seated themselves in the garden to mark well the place of sepulture, and other Galilæan women had also noticed the spot, and had hurried home to prepare fresh spices and ointments before the Sabbath began, that they might hasten back early on the morning of Sunday, and complete that embalming of the body, which Joseph and Nicodemus had only hastily begun. They spent in quiet that miserable Sabbath, which, for the broken hearts of all who loved Jesus, was a Sabbath of anguish and despair.

But the enemies of Christ were not so inactive. The awful misgiving of guilty consciences was not removed even by His death upon the cross. They recalled, with dreadful reminiscence, the rumored prophecies of His resurrection — the sign of the prophet Jonah, which He had said would alone be given them[3] — the great utterance about the destroyed Temple, which He would in three days raise up; and these intimations, which were but dim to a crushed and wavering faith, were read, like fiery letters upon the wall, by the illuminating glare of an uneasy guilt. Pretending, therefore, to be afraid lest His body should be stolen by His disciples for purposes of imposture, they begged that, until the third day, the

---

[1] The circuit of Jerusalem is one great graveyard, and such tombs may be seen in Judæa by hundreds.

[2] Luke xxiii. 54. It was not unusual among the Jews to regard the *sunset* of Friday as the *dawn* of their Sabbath, and to give it the name of אוֹר.

[3] Matt. xii. 39.

tomb might be securely guarded. Pilate gave them a brief and haughty permission to do anything they liked;[1] for — apparently in the evening, when the great Paschal Sabbath was over — they sent their guard to seal the *gôlal*, and to watch the sepulchre.

Night passed, and before the faint streak of dawn began to silver the darkness of that first great Easterday,[2] the passionate love of those women, who had lingered latest by the cross, made them also the earliest at the tomb. Carrying with them their precious spices, but knowing nothing of the watch or seal, they anxiously inquired among themselves, as they groped their way with sad and timid steps through the glimmering darkness, "Who should roll away for them the great stone which closed the sepulchre?" The two Marys were foremost of this little devoted band, and after them came Salome and Joanna.[3] They found their difficulty solved for them. It became known then, or afterwards, that some dazzling angelic vision in white robes had terrified the keepers of the tomb, and had rolled the stone from the tomb amid the shocks of earthquake. And as they came to the tomb, there they too saw angels in white apparel, who bade them hasten back to the Apostles, and tell them — and especially Peter — that Christ, according to His own word, had risen from the dead, and would go before them, like a shepherd, into their own beloved and native Galilee. They hurried back in a tumult of rapture and alarm, telling no one except the disciples; and even to the disciples their words sounded like an idle tale. But Mary of Magdala, who seems to have received a separate and special intimation, hastened at once to Peter and John.[4] No sooner had they

---

[1] ἔχετε κουστωδίαν [458] can hardly be an imperative. It has usually been referred to some soldiers who may possibly have been lent to the Jews to act as a sort of police during the great Paschal gathering. The context seems to preclude the notion of the "guard" being composed of the Temple watchmen.

[2] Those who think it right or fair to find and to press "discrepancies" between writers who simply say the truth to the best of their power in the ordinary language of common life, may find such a discrepancy between the σκοτίας ἔτι οὔσης [459] of John xx. 1, and the ἀνατείλαντος τοῦ ἡλίου [460] of Mark xvi. 2. But such criticism scarcely deserves serious notice. I have endeavored throughout the narrative silently to show the perfect *possible* coherence and truthful simplicity of the fragmentary Gospel accounts. More than this is neither possible nor necessary. I do not hold the mechanical view of inspiration advocated in Gaussen's *Theopneustia ;* but he at least shows how simply these supposed "discrepancies" are accounted for, and how perfectly harmless are the assaults on Christian faith which take them as a basis (*Theopn.* 218—229, E. Tr.).

[3] Mark xvi. 1—7, compared (throughout the paragraph) with John xx. 1 ; Luke xxiv. 1—10 ; Matt. xxviii. 1—7.

[4] Any one who will attentively read side by side the narratives of these appearances on the first day of the resurrection, will see that they have only been pre-

received this startling news than they rose to see with their own eyes what had happened. John outstripped in speed his elder companion, and arriving first, stooped down, and gazed in silent wonder into that open grave. The grave was empty, and the linen cerements were lying neatly folded each in its proper place. Then Peter came up, and with his usual impetuosity, heedless of ceremonial pollution, and of every consideration but his love and his astonishment, plunged into the sepulchre. John followed him, and saw, and believed; and the two Apostles took back the undoubted certainty to their wondering brethren.[1] In spite of fear, and anxiety, and that dull intelligence which, by their own confession, was so slow to realize the truths they had been taught, there dawned upon them, even then, the trembling hope, which was so rapidly to become the absolute conviction,

---

served for us in general, interblended and scattered notices (see Matt. xxviii. 16; Luke xxiv. 34; Acts i. 3), which, in strict exactness, render it impossible, without many arbitrary suppositions, to produce from them a *certain* narrative of the order of events. The *lacunae*, the compressions, the variations, the actual differences, the subjectivity of the narrators as affected by spiritual revelations, render all harmonies at the best uncertain. Our belief in the Resurrection, as an historic fact, as absolutely well attested to us by subsequent and contemporary circumstances as any other event in history, rests on grounds far deeper, wider, more spiritual, more eternal, than can be shaken by divergences of which we can only say that they are not necessarily contradictions, but of which the true solution is no longer attainable. Hence the " ten discrepancies " which have been dwelt on since the days of Celsus, have never for one hour shaken the faith of Christendom. The phenomena presented by the narratives are exactly such as we should expect, derived as they are from different witnesses, preserved at first in oral tradition only, and written 1,800 years ago at a period when *minute circumstantial accuracy*, as distinguished from perfect truthfulness, was little regarded. St. Paul, surely no imbecile or credulous enthusiast, vouches, both for the reality of the appearances, and also for the fact that the vision by which he was himself converted came, at a long interval after the rest, to him as " to the abortive-born " of the Apostolic family (1 Cor. xv. 4—8). If the narratives of Christ's appearance to his disciples were *inventions*, how came they to possess the severe and simple character which shows no tinge of religious excitement? If those appearances were purely *subjective*, how can we account for their sudden, rapid, and total cessation? As Lange finely says, the great fugue of the first Easter tidings has not come to us as a " monotonous chorale," and mere boyish verbal criticism cannot understand the common feeling and harmony which inspire the individual vibrations of those enthusiastic and multitudinous voices (v. 61). Professor Westcott, with his usual profundity and insight, points out the differences of purpose in the narrative of the four Evangelists. St. Matthew dwells chiefly on the majesty and glory of the Resurrection; St. Mark, both in the original part and in the addition (Mark xvi. 9—20), insists upon it as *a fact;* St. Luke, as a *spiritual necessity;* St. John, as a *touchstone of character (Introd.* 310—315).

[1] Compare the exactly similar feature in the character of the two Apostles, in John xxi. 7.

that Christ had risen indeed. That on that morning the grave of Christ was untenanted — that His body had not been removed by His enemies — that its absence caused to His disciples the profoundest amazement, not unmingled, in the breasts of some of them, with sorrow and alarm [1] — that they subsequently became convinced, by repeated proofs, that He had indeed risen from the dead — that for the truth of this belief they were ready at all times themselves to die — that the belief effected a profound and total change in their character, making the timid courageous, and the weak irresistible — that they were incapable of a conscious falsehood, and that, even if it had not been so, a conscious falsehood could never have had power to convince the disbelief and regenerate the morality of the world — that on this belief of the resurrection were built the still-universal observance of the first day of the week, and the entire foundations of the Christian Church — these, at any rate, are facts which even scepticism itself, if it desires to be candid, can hardly fail, however reluctantly and slowly, to admit.

But as yet no eye had seen Him; and to Mary of Magdala — to her who loved most because she had been forgiven most, and out of whose soul, now ardent as flame and clear as crystal, He had cast seven devils — was this glorious honor first vouchsafed. [2] Even the vision of angels had not soothed the passion of agitation and alarm which she experienced when, returning once more to the tomb, she found that it was no longer possible for her to pay the last offices of devotion and tenderness to the crucified body of her Lord. From her impassioned soul not even the white-robed visions and angel voices could expel the anguish which she experienced in the one haunting thought, " They have taken away my Lord out of the sepulchre, and I know not where they have laid Him." With her

---

[1] And that (as the Evangelists honestly admit), in spite of such repeated forewarnings that it should be so, as we find in John ii. 18—22; vi. 61—64; x. 17, 18; xiii. 31; Matt. xii. 38—42; xvi. 13—27; xvii. 1—9; xxvi. 63, 64; Mark ix. 30—32; x. 32—34; Luke ix. 43—45. It is, of course, true that they themselves may not have heard all of these predictions, but they had heard enough to cause our Lord's exclamation ὦ ἀνόητοι καὶ βραδεῖς τῇ καρδίᾳ τοῦ πιστεύειν [461] (Luke xxiv. 25).

[2] John xx. 11—18. [Mark xvi. 9—20 is canonical, but almost certainly unauthentic. It is omitted in א, B, and in the Armenian Version. In L it is greatly altered, and in some MSS. it is marked with asterisks. Eusebius and Jerome testify to its general absence from the Greek MSS. If this external evidence be insufficient against the authority of A, C, D, Irenæus and Hippolytus, yet the internal evidence seems to be decisive — take, for instance, the fact, that in this short section πορεύομαι [462] occurs three times, θεάομαι [463] twice, and ὁ Κύριος [464] twice, though not found elsewhere in St. Mark.]

whole heart absorbed in this thought she turned away — and lo! Jesus Himself standing before her. It was Jesus, but not as she had known Him. There was something spiritual, something not of earth, in that risen and glorified body. Some accident of dress, or appearance, made her fancy that it was the keeper of the garden, and in the eager hope that he can explain to her the secret of that empty and angel-haunted grave, she exclaims to Him in an agony of appeal — turning her head aside as she addressed Him, perhaps that she might hide her streaming tears — "Oh, sir, if you took Him away, tell me where you put Him, and I will take Him."

Jesus saith to her, "Mary!"

That one word, in those awful yet tender tones of voice, at once penetrated to her heart. Turning towards Him, trying apparently to clasp His feet or the hem of His garment, she cried to Him in her native Aramaic, "Rabboni!" "Oh, my Master!" and then remained speechless with her transport. Jesus Himself gently checked the passion of her enthusiasm. "Cling not to Me,"[1] He exclaimed, "for not yet have I ascended to the Father; but go to My brethren, and say to them, I am ascending to My Father and your Father, and My God and your God." Awe-struck, she hastened to obey. She repeated to them that solemn message — and through all future ages has thrilled that first utterance, which made on the minds of those who heard it so indelible an impression — "I HAVE SEEN THE LORD!"

2. Nor was her testimony unsupported. Jesus met the other women also, and said to them, "All hail!" Terror mingled with their emotion, as they clasped His feet. "Fear not," He said to them; "go, bid My brethren that they depart into Galilee, and there shall they see Me."[2]

It was useless for the guards to stay beside an empty grave. With

---

[1] John xx. 17, Μὴ μοῦ ἅπτου. Although ἅψασθαι is used of the woman who touched the hem of Christ's garment (Matt. ix. 20), yet the "*Noli me tangere*," "Touch me not," conveys quite a false impression. It meant that the day for personal, physical presence, for merely human affection, for the grasp of human tenderness, was over now. Henceforth He was to be with His people more nearly, more intimately, because *in spirit.* "Prohibitum tangere Dominum; non eum corporali tactu Dominum, sed *fide* tangimus"[465] (Ambr.). The "for" is one of St. John's difficult causal connections, which seem to be dictated far more by the syllogism of emotion than by formal grammar. Perhaps it implies, "Be not clinging to me, for this *is but a brief interval between* my former close physical society with you, and my future spiritual union." For the τὸν πατέρα μου καὶ πατέρα ὑμῶν,[466] κ. τ. λ., see Pearson *On the Creed*, p. 42.

[2] Matt. xxviii. 9, 10. Matthew alone mentions this adoration. The προσκυνή-σαντες αὐτόν[467] of Luke xxiv. 52 are omitted in some good MSS.

fear for the consequences, and horror at all that they had seen, they fled to the members of the Sanhedrin who had given them their secret commission. To these hardened hearts belief and investigation were alike out of the question. Their only refuge seemed to be in lies. They instantly tried to hush up the whole matter. They suggested to the soldiers that they must have slept, and that while they did so the disciples had stolen the body of Jesus.[1] But such a tale was too infamous for credence, and too ridiculous for publicity. If it became known, nothing could have saved these soldiers, supposing them to have been Romans, from disgrace and execution. The Sadducees therefore bribed the men to consult their common interests by burying the whole matter in secrecy and silence. It was only gradually and later, and to the initiated, that the base calumny was spread. Within six weeks of the resurrection, that great event was the unshaken faith of every Christian; within a few years of the event the palpable historic proofs of it and the numerous testimonies of its reality — strengthened by a memorable vision vouchsafed to himself — had won assent from the acute and noble intellect of a young Pharisaic zealot and persecutor whose name was Saul.[2] But it was only in posthumous and subterranean whispers that the dark falsehood was disseminated which was intended to counteract this overwhelming evidence. St. Matthew says that when he wrote his Gospel it was still commonly bruited among the Jews. It continued to be received among them for centuries, and is one of the blaspheming follies which was repeated and amplified twelve centuries afterwards in the *Toldôth Jeshu.*[3]

3. The third appearance of Jesus was to Peter. The details of it are wholly unknown to us.[4] They may have been of a nature too personal to have been revealed. The fact rests on the express testimony of St. Luke and of St. Paul.

4. On the same day the Lord's fourth appearance was accompanied with circumstances óf the deepest interest. Two of the disciples were

---

[1] Matt. xxviii. 11—15. Those who are shocked at this suggested possibility of deceit on the part of a few hard, worldly and infatuated Sanhedrists, do not shrink from insinuating that the faith of Christendom was founded on most facile and reprehensible credulity, almost amounting to conscious deception, by men who died for the truth of what they asserted, and who have taught the spirit of truthfulness as a primary duty of the religion which they preached.

[2] Rom. vi. 4; Eph. i. 20; Gal. i. 1; 1 Cor. xv. 4—8, &c. The latter is the earliest *written* allusion to the resurrection (A. D. 54).

[3] Eisenmenger, *Entdecktes Judenthum,* i. 189.

[4] Luke xxiv. 34; 1 Cor. xv. 5.

on their way to a village named Emmaus,¹ of uncertain site, but about
eight miles from Jerusalem, and were discoursing with sad and anxious
hearts on the awful incidents of the last two days, when a Stranger
joined them, and asked them the cause of their clouded looks and
anxious words. They stopped, and looked at this unknown traveller
with a dubious and unfriendly glance ;² and when one of the two,
whose name was Cleopas,³ spoke in reply, there is a touch of surprise
and suspicion in the answer which he ventured to give. " Dost thou
live alone as a stranger in Jerusalem, and dost thou not know what
things happened there in these last days ? " " What things ? " He
asked them. Then they told Him how all their yearning hopes that
Jesus had been the great Prophet who should redeem His people had
been dashed to the earth, and how all His mighty deeds before God
and the people had ended two days back on the shameful cross. They
described the feeling of amazement with which, on this the third day,
they had heard the women's rumors of angel visions, and the certain
testimony of some of their brethren that the tomb was empty now.
" But, " added the speaker with a sigh of incredulity and sorrow —
" but Him they saw not. "

Then reproaching them with the dulness of their intelligence and
their affections, the Stranger showed them how through all the Old
Testament from Moses onwards there was one long prophecy of the
sufferings no less than of the glory of Christ. In such high converse
they drew near to Emmaus, and the Stranger seemed to be going
onwards, but they pressed Him to stay, and as they sat down to their
simple meal, and He blessed and brake the bread, suddenly their eyes
were opened, and in spite of the altered form,⁴ they recognized that

---

¹ Emmaus can hardly be Amwâs (Nicopolis), which is 160 stades (about twenty-
two miles) from Jerusalem, even if, with a few bad MSS., we read ἑκατὸν ἑξή-
κοντα ⁴⁶⁸ in Luke xxiv. 13. The name means " warm springs." *Culonieh* (see Jos.
B. J. vii. 6, § 6) seems to be a more likely site, but nothing whatever depends on
the identification of a locality so incidentally alluded to.

² Luke xxiv. 13—35, verse 17, καὶ ἐστάθησαν σκυθρωποὶ ⁴⁶⁹ (א, A, B, L, and
various versions, &c.). This, as well as the somewhat emphatic answer of Cleopas,
shows that they were not quite at their ease at the Stranger's intervention. After
the recent events such caution was very natural.

³ If, as Keim, &c., suppose, the story is mythic, &c., why was so obscure a name
as Cleopas chosen to authenticate it ? and why was the other disciple left nameless ? Would it not have been just as easy to select two of the most prominent
Apostles ? It is a mere assumption that Cleopas (or Cleopater) was the same as
Clopas, or Alphæus.

⁴ Mark xvi. 12, ἐφανερώθη ἐν ἑτέρᾳ μορφῇ.⁴⁷⁰ It must be remembered
that the Appendix to this Gospel (xvi. 9—20), though not genuine, has every
claim to our respect. Mr. Burgon's elaborate vindication of these verses (Lond.

He who was with them was the Lord. But even as they recognized Him, He was with them no longer. " Did not our heart burn within us, " they exclaimed to each other, "while He was speaking with us in the way, while He was opening to us the Scriptures? " Rising instantly, they returned to Jerusalem with the strange and joyous tidings. They found no dubious listeners now. They, too, were received with the rapturous affirmation, " The Lord is risen indeed, and hath appeared unto Simon ! "

5. Once more, for the fifth time on that eternally memorable Easter day, Jesus manifested Himself to His disciples. Ten of them were sitting together, with doors closed for fear of the Jews. As they exchanged and discussed their happy intelligence, Jesus Himself stood in the midst of them, with the words, " Peace be with you. " The unwonted aspect of that glorified body — the awful significance of the fact that He had risen from the dead — scared and frightened them.[1] The presence of their Lord was indeed corporeal, but it was changed. They thought that it was a spirit which was standing before them. " Why are ye troubled? " He asked, " and why do anxious doubts rise in your hearts ? See my hands and my feet, that it is I ; handle me, and see ; for a spirit hath not flesh and bones as ye see me have. " Even while He spoke He showed them His hands and His side. And then, while joy, amazement, incredulity, were all struggling in their hearts, He asked them if they had there anything to eat ; and yet further to assure them, ate a piece of broiled fish in their presence.[2] Then once more He said, " Peace be unto you. As my Father hath sent me, even so send I you. " Breathing on them, He said, " Receive ye the Holy Ghost. Whosesoever sins ye remit, they are remitted to them ; whosesoever sins ye retain, they are retained. "[3]

6. One only of the Apostles had been absent — Thomas the Twin.

1871) is quite unconvincing (see Mr. Hort's remarks in the *Academy*, Nov. 15, 1871).

[1] Ignatius (*ad Smyrn.*). Jesus uses the words, $οὐκ$ $εἰμι$ $δαιμόνιον$ $ἀσώματον$.[471] Some, from the mention of $σάρκα$ $καὶ$ $ὀστέα$ [472] (Luke xxiv. 39) without $αἷμα$ [473] which was the sign of the $ψυχὴ$, or " animal life "), have perhaps too rashly and literally inferred that the resurrection-body was bloodless. In a very curious translated fragment of Clemens Alexandrinus on John i. 1, a tradition is mentioned that St. John, touching the body, found no substance there ; his hand passed through it (quoted by Keim, III. ii. 568).

[2] The words $καὶ$ $ἀπὸ$ $μελισσίου$ $κηρίου$ [474] (omitted in $\aleph$, A, B, D, &c.) are of dubious authenticity.

[3] The perfects $ἀφέωνται$, $κεκράτηνται$, imply permanence of result. On this commission, see *supra*, pp. 372—374.

His character, as we have seen already, was affectionate, but melancholy. To him the news seemed too good to be true. In vain did the other disciples assure him, " We have seen the Lord. " Happily for us, though less happily for him, he declared with strong asseveration that nothing would convince him, short of actually putting his own finger into the print of the nails, and his hands into His side. A week passed, and the faithfully-recorded doubts of the anxious Apostle remained unsatisfied. On the eighth, or, as *we* should say, on the seventh day afterwards [1] — for already the resurrection had made the first day of the week sacred to the hearts of the Apostles — the eleven were again assembled within closed doors. Once more Jesus appeared to them, and after His usual gentle and solemn blessing, called Thomas, and bade him stretch forth his finger, and put it in the print of the nails, and to thrust his hand into the spear-wound of His side, and to be "not faithless, but believing. " "My Lord and my God! " exclaimed the incredulous Apostle, with a burst of conviction. " Because thou hast seen Me, " said Jesus, " thou hast believed; blessed are they who saw not and yet believed. "

7. The next appearance of the risen Saviour was to seven of the Apostles by the Sea of Galilee — Simon, Thomas, Nathanael, the sons of Zebedee, and two others — not improbably Philip and Andrew — who are not named.[2] A pause had occurred in the visits of Jesus, and before they returned to Jerusalem at Pentecost to receive the promised outpouring of the Spirit, Simon said that he should resume for the day his old trade of a fisherman. There was no longer a common purse, and as their means of subsistence were gone, this seemed to be the only obvious way of obtaining an honest maintenance. The others proposed to join him, and they set sail in the evening because night is the best time for fishing. All night they toiled in vain. At early dawn, in the misty twilight, there stood on the shore the figure of One whom they did not recognize. A voice asked them if they had caught anything. "No " was the despondent answer. " Fling your net to the right side of the vessel, and ye shall find. " They made the cast, and instantly were scarcely able to draw the net from the multitude of fishes. The incident awoke, with overwhelming force, the memory of earlier days. "It is the Lord, " whispered

---

[1] Why did they not go to Galilee immediately on receiving our Lord's message? The circumstance is unexplained, for the identification of Galilee with the peak of the Mount of Olives — now called Viri Galilæi, from Acts. i. 11 — is wholly absurd. Perhaps the *entire* message of Jesus to them is not recorded; perhaps they awaited the end of the feast.

[2] John xxi. 1—24.

John to Peter; and instantly the warm-hearted enthusiast, tightening his fisher's tunic [1] round his loins, leaped into the sea, to swim across the hundred yards which separated him from Jesus, and cast himself, all wet from the waves, before His feet.   More slowly the others followed, dragging the strained but unbroken net, with its 153 fishes. A wood fire was burning on the strand, some bread lay beside it, and some fish were being broiled on the glowing embers.   It is a sight which may often be seen to this day by the shores of Galilee.   And He who stood beside it bade them bring more fish of those which they had caught.   Instantly Simon started up, and helped with his strong arm to drag the net ashore.   And He whom they all knew to be the Lord, but whose voice and aspect made their hearts so still with awful reverence that they dared not question Him, bade them " Come and breakfast, " and distributed to them the bread and fish.

The happy meal ended in silence, and then Jesus said to His weak but fond Apostle, " Simon " — (it was no time as yet to restore to him the name of Peter) — " Simon, son of Jonas, honorest thou Me more than these ? "

" Yea, Lord, Thou knowest that I love Thee. "

" Feed My little lambs. "

Simon had felt in his inmost heart what was meant by that kind rebuke — " more than these. "   It called back to his penitent soul those boastful words, uttered so confidently among his brethren, " Although all shall be offended, yet will not I. "   Failure had taught him humility, and therefore he will neither claim a pre-eminence in affection, nor adopt the word of the Saviour's question ($\dot{\alpha}\gamma\alpha\pi\tilde{\alpha}s$), which involved deep honor and devotion and esteem; but will substitute for it that weaker word, which yet best expressed the warm human affection of his heart.   And the next time the question reminded him less painfully of his old self-confidence, for Jesus said to him only —

" Simon, son of Jonas, honorest thou Me ? "

Again the Apostle humbly answered in the same words as before —

" Yea, Lord, thou knowest that I love thee. "

" Tend my sheep. " [2]

But Simon had thrice denied, and therefore it was fitting that he should thrice confess.   Again, after a brief pause, came the ques-

---

[1] Perhaps the $\dot{\epsilon}\pi\epsilon\nu\delta\acute{\nu}\tau\eta s$ is only a subligaculum ($\lambda\iota\nu o\tilde{\nu}\nu$ $\tau\iota$ $\dot{o}\theta\acute{o}\nu\iota o\nu$ Theophyl.). It is very common in the East to work naked, or with nothing but a cloth round the waist.

[2] John xxi. 16.   The verb is $\pi o\acute{\iota}\mu\alpha\iota\nu\epsilon$, not $\beta\acute{o}\acute{o}\kappa\epsilon$.

tion — and this time with the weaker but warmer word which the Apostle himself had chosen —

"Simon, son of Jonas, *lovest* thou Me ?"

And Simon, deeply humbled and distressed, exclaimed, "Lord, Thou knowest all things ; Thou seest that I love Thee." [1]

"Feed My beloved sheep." [2] Then very solemnly He added, "Verily, verily, I say unto thee, When thou wast younger thou didst gird thyself, and walk where thou wouldest; but when thou art old thou shalt stretch out thy hands, and another shall gird thee, and shall lead thee where thou willest not."

The Apostle understood Him ; he knew that this implied the years of his future service, the pangs of his future martyrdom ; but now he was no longer "Simon," but "Peter" — the heart of rock was in him ; he was ready, even to the death, to obey the voice which said to him, "Follow Me." While the conversation had been taking place he had been walking by the side of Jesus, a few steps in front of his comrades. Looking back he saw John, his only favorite companion, and the disciple whom Jesus loved, slowly following them. Pointing to him, he asked, "Lord, and what shall he do?" The answer checked the spirit of idle curiosity — "If I will that he tarry till I come, what is that to thee? Follow *thou* Me." Peter dared ask no more, and the answer — which was intentionally vague — led to the wide misapprehension prevalent in the early Church, that John was not to die until Jesus came. The Apostle quietly corrects the error by quoting the exact words of the risen Christ. The manner of his death we do not know, but we know that he outlived all his brother disciples, and that he survived that terrible overthrow of his nation which, since it rendered impossible a strict obedience to the institutions of the Old Covenant, and opened throughout the world an unimpeded path for the establishment of the New Commandment and the Kingdom not of earth, was — in a sense more true than any other event in human history — a second coming of the Lord.

8. It may have been on this occasion that Jesus told His disciples of the mountain in Galilee, where He would meet all who knew and loved Him for the last time. Whether it was Tabor, or the Mountain of Beatitudes, we do not know, but more than five hundred of His disciples collected at the given time with the eleven, and received from Jesus His last commands, to teach and baptize throughout all

---

[1] Verse 17, οἶδας . . . γινώσκεις.

[2] John xxi. 17, προβάτια (A, B, C).

nations; and the last promise, that He would be with them always, even to the end of the world.[1]   Writing more than twenty years after this time, St. Paul gives us the remarkable testimony, that the greater number of these eye-witnesses of the resurrection were yet alive, and that some only were "fallen asleep."

9. A ninth appearance of Jesus is unrecorded in the Gospels, and is known to us from a single allusion in St. Paul alone.   "I delivered unto you," he writes to the Corinthians,[2] "that which also I received, how that Christ died for our sins, according to the Scriptures; and that He was buried, and that He rose again the third day, according to the Scriptures: and that He was seen of Cephas, then of the Twelve: after that, he was seen of above five hundred brethren at once: . . . . *after that, He was seen of James;* then of all the Apostles.   And last of all He appeared to me also, as to the abortive-born (of the Apostolic family)."   Respecting this appearance to James, we know nothing further, unless there be any basis of true tradition in the story preserved to us in the Gospel of the Hebrews. We are there told that James, the first Bishop of Jerusalem, and the Lord's brother,[3] had, after the Last Supper, taken a solemn vow that he would neither eat nor drink until he had seen Jesus risen from the dead.   Early, therefore, after His resurrection, Jesus, after He had given the *sindôn* to the servant of the priest, had a table with bread brought out, blessed the bread, and gave it to James, with the words, "Eat thy bread now, my brother, since the Son of Man has risen from the dead."[4]

10. Forty days had now elapsed since the Crucifixion.   During those forty days nine times had He been visibly present to human eyes, and had been touched by human hands.   But His body had not been merely the human body, nor liable to merely human laws, nor had He lived during those days the life of men.   The time had now come when His earthly presence should be taken away from

---

[1] The οἱ δὲ ἐδίστασαν of Matt. xxviii. 17, can only mean "but some doubted" — not, as Wetstein and others take it, whether they should worship or not, but respecting the whole scene.   All may not have stood near to Him, and even if they did, we have seen in four previous instances (Matt. xxviii. 17; Luke xxiv. 16; *id.* 37; John xxi. 4) that there was something unusual and not instantly recognizable in his resurrection body.   At any rate, here we have another inestimable proof of the candor of the Evangelists, for there is nothing to be said in favor of the conjectural emendation οὐδέ.   "Dubitatum est ab illis," says St. Leo, "ne dubitaretur a nobis"[415] (*Serm.* lxxi., ap. Wordsw. *in loc.*).

[2] 1 Cor. xv. 3—8.

[3] Or it may possibly have been James the son of Zebedee.

[4] Jer. *De Viris Illustr.* ii.   The allusion to the *sindôn* is curious.   See Excursus XV., "Traditional Sayings of Christ."

them for ever, until He returned in glory to judge the world. He met them in Jerusalem, and as He led them with Him towards Bethany,[1] He bade them wait in the Holy City until they had received the promise of the Spirit. He checked their eager inquiry about the times and the seasons, and bade them be His witnesses in all the world. These last farewells must have been uttered in some of the wild secluded upland country that surrounds the little village;[2] and when they were over, He lifted up His hands and blessed them, and, even as He blessed them, was parted from them, and as He passed from before their yearning eyes "a cloud received Him out of their sight."

Between us and His visible presence — between us and that glorified Redeemer who now sitteth at the right hand of God — that cloud still rolls. But the eye of Faith can pierce it; the incense of true prayer can rise above it; through it the dew of blessing can descend. And if He is gone away, yet He has given us in His Holy Spirit a nearer sense of His presence, a closer infolding in the arms of His tenderness, than we could have enjoyed even if we had lived with Him of old in the home of Nazareth, or sailed with Him in the little boat over the crystal waters of Gennesareth. We may be as near to Him at all times — and more than all when we kneel down to pray — as the beloved disciple was when he laid his head upon His breast. The word of God is very nigh us, even in our mouths and in our hearts. To ears that have been closed His voice may seem indeed to sound no longer. The loud noises of War may shake the world; the eager calls of Avarice and of Pleasure may drown the gentle utterance which bids us "Follow Me;" after two thousand years of Christianity the incredulous murmurs of an impatient scepticism may make it scarcely possible for Faith to repeat, without insult, the creed which has been the regeneration of the world. Ay, and sadder even than this, every now and then may be heard, even in Christian England, the insolence of some blaspheming tongue which still scoffs at the Son of God as He lies in the agony of the garden, or breathes His last sigh upon the bitter tree. But the secret of the Lord is with them that fear Him, and He will show them His

---

[1] Luke xxiv. 50. The best reading seems to be ἕως πρὸς Βηθανίαν (א, B, C, L. &c.).

[2] "It was solitude and retirement in which Jesus kept His vigils: the desert places heard him pray; in a privacy He was born; in the wilderness He fed His thousands; upon a mountain apart He was transfigured; upon a mountain He died; and from a mountain He ascended to His Father" (Petr. Cell. iv. 12, quoted by Jer. Taylor, *Life of Christ,* I. viii.).

covenant.   To all who will listen He still speaks.   He promised to be with us always, even to the end of the world, and we have not found His promise fail.   It was but for thirty-three short years of a short lifetime that He lived on earth; it was but for three broken and troubled years that He preached the Gospel of the Kingdom; but for ever, even until all the Æons have been closed, and the earth itself, with the heavens that now are, have passed away, shall every one of His true and faithful children find peace and hope and forgiveness in His name, and that name shall be called Emmanuel, which is, being interpreted,

" GOD WITH US. "

APPENDIX.

EXCURSUS I. (Pages 81, 103.)

THE DATE OF CHRIST'S BIRTH.

ALTHOUGH the date of Christ's birth cannot be established with absolute certainty, there is yet a large amount of evidence to render it at least probable that
He was born four years before our present era. It is universally admitted that
our received chronology, which is not older than Dionysius Exiguus in the sixth
century, is wrong. I ought to say here that I have not pretended to discuss the
new theories of chronology proposed by Keim; not only because I am not well
fitted for elaborate chronological inquiries, but because (i.) they would have
required inordinate space, and (ii.) they depend on views of the Gospels altogether remote from my own.

1. Our one most certain datum is obtained from the fact that Christ was born
before the death of Herod the Great. The date of that event is known with
absolute certainty, for (i.) Josephus tells us [1] that he died thirty-seven years after
he had been declared king by the Romans. Now it is known that he was
declared king A. U. C. 714; and therefore, since Josephus always reckons his
years from Nisan to Nisan, and counts the initial and terminal fractions of Nisan
as complete years, Herod must have died between Nisan A. U. C. 750, and Nisan
A. U. C. 751 — *i. e.*, between B. C. 4 and B. C. 3 of our era. (ii.) Josephus says
that on the night in which Herod ordered Judas, Matthias, and their abettors to
be burnt, there was an eclipse of the moon.[2] Now this eclipse took place on the
night of March 12, B. C. 4; and Herod was dead at least seven days before the
Passover.[3] which, if we accept the Jewish reckoning, fell in that year on April
12. But, according to the clear indication of the Gospels, Jesus must have been
born at least forty days before Herod's death. It is clear, therefore, that under
no circumstances can the Nativity have taken place *later* than February, B. C. 4.

2. The only other *certain* datum which we have is furnished by St. Luke, who
fixes the beginning of St. John the Baptist's preaching in the 15th year of
Tiberius, and says that, when Jesus began His ministry, He was about thirty
years old (Luke iii. 23).[4]

Now if the 15th year of Tiberius be dated from the death of Augustus (Aug.
19, A. U. C. 767), then Jesus was baptized A. U. C. 782; but since, as we have
seen, he *could* not have been born later than February, A. U. C. 750, this would

---

[1] *Antt.* xvii. 8, § 1.
[2] Id. xvii. 6, § 4. Ideler, *Handb. Chron.* ii. 391.
[3] Id. xvii. 8, § 4.
[4] The rendering of the English Version, "began to be about thirty years old, for ἦν
. . . ὡσεὶ ἐτῶν τριάκοντα ἀρχόμενος, is wholly untenable.

make Him at least thirty-two, an age inconsistent with the natural meaning of St. Luke's expression. There is therefore good ground to believe that St. Luke dates the year of the reign of Tiberius from his association with Augustus as joint Emperor in A. U. C. 765,[1] a method of computation which certainly existed, and would be especially likely to prevail in the Provinces. Jesus would then have begun His public teaching A. U. C. 780, a date which exactly agrees with the only secure datum about the year of His birth.

All attempts to discover the month and day of the Nativity are useless. No data whatever exist to enable us to determine them with even approximate accuracy.

The census of Quirinius, the order of the courses of priests, the cycle of lessons in the Jewish Calendar, the consulships, &c., mentioned by Tertullian, the arrival of the Magi, and the astrological conjunction which is supposed to have caused their journey, the third closing by Augustus of the Temple of Janus, and other indications which have been pressed into the service of chronology, are all too vague to be of any use, and are only likely to lead to highly uncertain or entirely erroneous results.

A *general* confirmation of the conclusion at which we have arrived may be deduced from John ii. 20, "Forty and six years was this Temple in building." Herod's reconstruction of the Temple began in the eighteenth year of his reign, probably in Cisleu, A. U. C. 734. This will bring the forty-sixth year of its continuance to A. U. C. 780, which we have already seen reason to regard as the first year of Christ's ministry, and the thirtieth of his age. There is, however, an element of doubt in this computation, owing to St. John's use of the aorist ᾠκοδομήθη, unless it be regarded as a less accurate expression for οἰκοδομεῖται (cf. Ezra v. 16).

The only difficulties in the data mentioned by Luke iii. 1, 2, are the mention of Annas as High Priest, and of Lysanias tetrarch of Abilene.

1. As regards Annas, it is true that some MSS. read ἐπὶ ἀρχιερέων, but there 'is so complete a consensus of *all* the best MSS. (א, A, B, C, D, E, &c.) in favor of ἐπὶ ἀρχιερέως, that there can be no doubt of its being the true reading. The same expression occurs in Acts iv. 6. It will then be asked, how is it that St. Luke calls *Annas* High Priest, when the office was really held by Caiaphas? The question is sufficiently answered *supra*, p. 589; but we may here observe, (i.) that Annas, having been merely superseded by the will of Valerius Gratus,[2] would, by all serious-minded Jews, be still regarded as High Priest *de jure*, according to the Mosaic Law (Numb. xxxv. 25). (ii.) That whether he held the office of *Sagan* or of *Nasî*, or not, there is sufficient evidence to show that he was at this time the most influential and powerful leader of the aristocratic, sacerdotal, and Sadducæan party at Jerusalem. (iii.) That this leading position of Annas is clearly recognized by Josephus (*Antt.* xx. 9, § 1), who, like the Evangelist, speaks vaguely about the mere puppets of civil power who at this period became titular High Priests in rapid succession.[3]

---

[1] Tac. *Ann.* 1. 3; Suet. *Aug.* 97; Vell. Paterc. 103.
[2] Annas was High Priest A. D. 7–14, and there had been three intermediate High Priests — one of whom, Eleazar, was his son—before his son-in-law, Joseph Caiaphas (Jos. *Antt.* xviii. 2, § 2) had been appointed in A. D. 24.
[3] *Vit.* 38; *B. J* iv. 3, § 9.

2. It used to be assumed that St. Luke had made some mistake about Lysanias. The facts, however, seem to be, (i.) that there was a Lysanias, King of Chalcis under Mount Lebanon, and therefore, in all probability, also tetrarch of Abilene, in the time of Antony and Cleopatra, *sixty years before* the date mentioned by St. Luke (Jos. *B. J.* i. 13, § 1); and *another* in the reigns of Caligula and Claudius, *twenty years after* St. Luke's date (Jos. *Antt.* xv. 4, § 1). We know nothing certain of any intermediate Lysanias, but there is nothing whatever to *prove* that there may not have been one; or even that this Lysanias may not be the second whom we have mentioned. Even Renan admits that, after reading the inscription of Zenodorus at Baalbek, he sees less reason to suppose that the Evangelist is in error. ("Une étude de l'inscription . . . m'a mené à croire que l'évangéliste pouvait n'avoir pas aussi gravement tort que d'habiles critiques le pensent." [476] *Vie de Jésus*, p. xiii.) The tetrarchate of Lysanias might well serve to mark a date, because, for a time, Abilene had been actually a part of Jewish territory, having been assigned in A. D. 36 by Caligula to his favorite Herod Agrippa I.

For a full commentary on these chronological data of St. Luke see Wieseler, *Chron. Synops.,* 'E. Tr., pp. 157—175. But enough has been said to show that, so far from the Evangelist having fallen into a demonstrable error, there is every reason to believe that he has independently preserved an obscure historical fact. Unless he had been perfectly well acquainted with the actual circumstances, it is inconceivable that he should have introduced so minute, and apparently superfluous an allusion, at the risk of falling into a needless blunder.

EXCURSUS II. (Page 83.)

CHRIST AND THE CHRISTIANS IN THE TALMUD.

THE name of Jesus occurs some twenty times only in unexpurgated editions of the Talmud, the last of which appeared at Amsterdam in 1645.[1]

The allusions to Him are characterized by intense hatred, disguised by intense fear. They are also marked by all the gross and reckless carelessness of these utterly uncritical and unhistorical writers.

The Christians are usually called — partly, no doubt, to conceal the allusions to them — pupils of Balaam, Minîm (heretics), Gentiles, Nazarenes.

In *Sanhedr.* 43 *a* Jesus is said to have had five disciples:— Matthaeus; Thaddaeus; נצר (which clearly means "Nazarene"); Booni — apparently meant for Nikdimon Ben Gorion (Nikodemus), or Banus; and Niki — perhaps some confusion of Nikolaitan.[2]

Our blessed Lord is called —

"That man" (cf. Acts v. 28 and פלוני, "So and so," ὁ δεῖνα).

"He whom we may not name."

"Ha-Notzrî," *i. e.,* "The Nazarene."

"The fool."

"The Hung" (תלוי). Thus Abn Ezra (on Gen. xxvii. 39) says that Constantine put on his labarum, "a figure of the hung;" and in Ps. xxx. 14, R. Bechai says

---

1 Jost, *Gesch. d. Judenth.* i. 405, 414.
2 Grätz, iii. 243. *Taanith*, f. 19, 2. See Ewald, *Gesch. Christ.*, p. 397.

that in the word קָצִיר the letter ע is suspended, to indicate that it is the "worshippers of the Hung" — *i. e.*, the Christians — who devastate the vineyard of Israel.

"Absalom."

"Ben Stada."

"Ben Pandera."

Putting into Hebrew letters the Grecised form of His name (ישוע), they made each letter the first of a Hebrew word, so as to mean "May his memory (י) be destroyed (ש), and his name (ו) blotted out (ע)."

Little is said about Jesus in the Talmud, except that He was a scholar of Joshua Ben Perachiah (who lived a century before!), accompanied him into Egypt, there learned magic, was a seducer (*mesîth*) of the people, and was first stoned, then hung as a blasphemer after forty days, during which no one had come forward to speak in his favor.[1]

The *Toldôth Jeshu* is a late and detestable compilation, put together out of fragmentary Talmudic legends, and regarded as utterly contemptible, even by the Jews themselves.[2] It is printed with a Latin translation by Wagenseil, in his *Tela Ignea Satanae;* but its blasphemies are too gross and grotesque to need further notice.

Some account of the wretched follies blasphemously indicated by the name Ben Stada, Ben Pandera, &c., may be seen in Buxtorf, *Lex. Talm.*, p. 1458, seq.

EXCURSUS III. (Page 92.)

JESUS AND HILLEL.

THE conjectural dates of Hillel's life are that he was born B. C. 75; came to Jerusalem B. C. 36; became Nasî B. C. 30; and died about B. C. 10. Geiger, a learned Rabbi of Frankfort, author of *Das Judenthum und seine Geschichte*, and *Urschrift*, says, "Jesus was a Pharisee (!) who walked in the paths of Hillel; that he uttered no new thought. Hillel, on the contrary, presents us with the picture of a genuine Reformer." This Hillel, he continues, with an undercurrent of contrast, is a really historical personage;[3] others have a halo of legend and miracle about them which merely tends to obscure and conceal their actual personality. Renan improves upon the hint, and, while he acknowledges the superiority of Jesus, says that Hillel was His real master.[4] The Messiah, it seems, was

---

[1] Lightfoot *ad Matt.* xii. 24; *Bab Sanhedr.* 67 *a*; *Shabbath*, 104 *b*; Grätz, iii. 242.

[2] "Ein elendes Machwerk." (Grätz, iii. 243.)

[3] Does M. Geiger consider it *quite historical* that Hillel knew the language of mountains, hills, valleys, trees, vegetables, wild and tame beasts, and demons (*Sofrîm*, xvi. 9); that the *Bath kôl* decided in his favor as against Shammai (*Bab. Erubhîn*, 13 *b*); that thirty of his scholars were worthy of being overclouded by the Shechina like Moses, and thirty more to make the sun stand still like Joshua (*Babha Bathra*, 134 *a*); and that such was the fiery zeal of his most eminent pupil, Jonathan Ben Uzziel, that, when he was studying the Law, birds who flew over his head were consumed (*B. Succa*, 28 *a*)? (See Otho, *Lex Rab.* 242; Buxtorf, *Lex Talm.*, p. 617; Gfrörer, *Jahrh d. Heils*, i. 37.)

[4] "Par sa pauvreté humblement supportée, par la douceur de son caractère, par l'opposition qu'il faisait aux hypocrites et aux prêtres, Hillel fut *le maître de Jésus*, s'il est permis de parler de maître quand il s'agit d'une si haute originalité " 477 (*Vie de Jésus*, p. 38).

Farther on he says, very truly, "Hillel cependent ne passera jamais pour le vrai fondateur

but the pupil and the plagiarist of a Rabbi, who, with less faults than others of his countrymen, is said to have declared "that no such Messiah would ever come."

Now I would premise at once that these questions about "originality" seem to me supremely idle and irrelevant in all cases, but most of all when they are irreverently applied to the teaching of our Lord. The originality of Jesus, even to those who regard Him as a mere human teacher, consists in this — that His words have touched the hearts of all men in all ages, and have regenerated the moral life of the world. Who but a pedant in art would impugn the originality of Michael Angelo because his Pietà is said to have resembled a statue of Signorelli; or of Raphael, because his earlier works betray the influence of Perugino? Who but an ignoramus would detract from the greatness of Milton because his *Paradise Lost* offers some points of similarity to the *Adam* of Battista Andreini? But if there are any who cannot rise above this narrow ground, it is well that they should remember that, according to the Jewish writers themselves, we can never distinguish between the maxims which Hillel originated and those which merely belonged to his school. Since they were not committed to writing till long after the death of Christ, they may easily have been due to Christian teaching, which certainly would not have been without influence on Hillel's grandson, the Rabban Gamaliel.

It needs, however, but little knowledge of the real facts to see how utterly imaginary are these Jewish conjectures. The position of Jesus towards the Rabbinism of His nation and all that occupied it — its *Hagadôth*, or legendary matter, its *Haluchôth*, or traditional customs, its puerile minutiæ, its benumbing ritual, its inflated emptiness, its irreligious arrogance, its servile second-handness, its to-and-fro balancing of conflicting opinions — is one not of submissive reverence, but of uncompromising hostility. Hillel was a "sweet and noble" Rabbi; he is the loftiest figure which Rabbinism has produced; he seems to have been really learned, humble, peaceful, and enlightened; but the distance between him and Jesus is a distance absolutely immeasurable, and the resemblance of his teaching to that of Jesus is the resemblance of a glowworm to the sun. Their whole scope and method are utterly different. Hillel rested on precedent, Jesus spoke with authority. Hillel spoke in the schools to students and separatists; Jesus in the streets and by the roadsides to publicans and sinners. Hillel confined his teaching to Jerusalem; Jesus traversed the length and breadth of Palestine. Hillel mainly occupied himself with the Levitical law, and modified its regulations to render them more easy and more palatable; Jesus taught only the moral law, and extended its application from external actions to the very thoughts of the heart. Would Christ have ever uttered a sentiment so deeply dyed in Pharisaism as this? — "No uneducated man easily avoids sin; no common person (*am ha-arets*) is pious."[1] Is not this the very echo of the haughty exclusive

du christianisme. Dans la morale, comme dans l'art, dire n'est rien, faire est tout . . . La vérité ne prend quelque valeur que si elle passe à l'état de sentiment, et elle n'atteint tout son prix que quand elle se réalise dans le monde à l'état de fait " [478] (*id.*, p. 96). Geiger's remark, baseless as it is, has, however, found great currency (Grätz, *Gesch. d. Juden*, iii.). "Jesu Sanftmuth und Demuth erinnern an Hillel, den er sich überhaupt zum Muster genommen zu haben scheint." [479] Yet it is not too much to say that there is hardly one page in any one of the Gospels which does not suffice to show its baselessness.

[1] I have already given instances (*supra*, p. 90) of the contempt poured on the poor *am ha-ratsîm*, and may add others. Their testimony was not received; they are not admitted

insolence which said, "Have any of the rulers believed on Him, or of the Pharisees? But this mob that knoweth not the Law are cursed?" Is it not the very spirit which Christ's whole life and practice combated, and which His whole teaching most utterly condemned?

1. Three main anecdotes are told of Hillel. One is that, though descended from David, he came at the age of forty-one (about B. C. 36) to Jerusalem, where he worked as a common porter, earning a *victoriatus* (about 3d.) a day, and giving half of it to the porter of the School of Shemaia and Abtalion, to admit him to their lectures. One day, at dawn in the month Tebeth — about the end of December — said Shemaia to Abtalion, "Brother, why is the school so dark? it seems to be a cloudy day." They looked up, and, darkening the window, was some semblance of a human figure lying under a mass of snow. In spite of the Sabbath they uncovered him, rubbed him with oil, and placed him near the fire. It was Hillel, who, having earned nothing the day before, and having been churlishly excluded by the porter, had climbed in the twilight into the window of the Beth Midrash, and there got buried and benumbed under a fall of snow.[1] To restore him to life by rubbing, warming, bathing him, Shemaia and Abtalion not only broke the Sabbath, but declared that he was well worthy of having the usual sabbatical rules superseded in his favor.

2. A pagan once came to Shammai, and said, "Make me a proselyte, but you must teach me the whole Law while I stand on one leg!" Shammai drove the man from his presence with blows. He went to Hillel, who replied with perfect suavity, "What is unpleasing to thee do not to thy neighbor. This is the whole Law; all the rest is commentary. Go and learn *that*."[2]

3. "Now or never," said a man to his friend; "400 zouzim[3] to the man who can make Hillel angry." "Done!" exclaimed the other It was a Friday afternoon, and Hillel was washing and combing his hair for the Sabbath. "Is Hillel there?" rudely and bluntly asked the man, as he knocked at the door. "My son," he exclaimed, hastily putting on his mantle, "what dost thou want?"

"I have a question to ask."

"Ask on, my son."

"Why have the Babylonians such round heads?"

"An important question, my son," said Hillel, laughing; "it is because they have skilful midwives."

The man turned his back on him, went off, and returned in an hour. The same rude interruption was repeated, and this time the man asked —

---

into society; no one is to take the trouble to restore to them their lost property; the terms "beasts" and "vermin" are applied to them, their wives, and their daughters; and finally, leave is given "to rend an *am ha-arets* like a fish" (עם. אריי מותר לרדעו ררג) See McCaul, *Old Paths*, pp. 6, 458, &c.

[1] *Joma*, 35 *b*.

[2] *Shabbath*, 31 *a*. — I have had repeated occasion to observe how idle is the question of "originality" in teaching of this kind; but we find the same thing long before, not only in the Pentateuch, but even in the Book of Tobit iv. 15 : "Do that to no man which thou hatest." The probable date of the Book of Tobit is two centuries before Hillel. For yet earlier and even heathen parallels to the saying, see Ewald, *Gesch. Isr.* iv. 270. It is also found to all intents and purposes in Confucius (*Doctrine of the Mean*, xx., and *Analects*, xv. 23, where he tells Tsze Kung that the one word "reciprocity" [*i. e.*, altruism] will serve him as a rule of practice for all his life) and Buddha (see Barth. St. Hilaire, *Le Buddha et sa Religion*, p. 92); see, too, Hesiod, *Opp. et Dies*, i. 284, 312, 330.

[3] A coin apparently worth a denarius, with a head of Zeus on it.

" Why have the 'Thermudians'[1] [Palmyrenes] such narrow eye-slits?"

" An important question, my son. It is because they live in the middle of a sandy desert."

A third time the man returned as before, and impudently asked —

" Why have the Africans such broad soles to their feet?"

Hillel calmly replied that it was because they live on such loose soil.

" I should have had plenty more questions to ask you were I not afraid that you would get into a passion."

Hillel only drew his mantle more closely round him, and quietly replied —

" Ask on, whatever thou hast to ask."

" So," said the man, thoroughly disarmed, "you are the Hillel whom they call the *Nasî* of Israel?"

" Yes."

" Well, then, I hope there are not many like you."

" Why, my son?"

" Because through you I have lost 400 zouzim."

" Calm thyself, my son: better that thou shouldst lose for Hillel's sake 400, ay, and 400 more, than that Hillel should lose patience."[2]

No doubt these are beautiful anecdotes, as is also the story that once for a rich man who had lost his property he hired a horse and an attendant, and, when the latter was not forthcoming, went himself three miles as his attendant.[3] Sometimes, however, we see, even in the few records of him, facts and tendencies which, however well meant, cannot be praised. Thus, in opposition to Shammai, he directed that in the bridal song the beauty of a bride should be praised, however ugly she were; and on one occasion, to avoid any question or dispute with the school of Shammai, he passed off an ox, which was going to be sacrificed for him, as a cow.[4] The Rabbis praise these proceedings, yet we feel instinctively what a shock they would have given us, how injurious they would have been to the world's morality, had they occurred in the life of Christ. He alone, of all who have ever lived in the world, could say, " Which of you convinceth me of sin?" Little as we know by comparison of a Socrates, of a Confucius, of a Sakya Mouni, of a Hillel, of a Mahomet, and *much* as we know of Jesus, yet in the scanty records of *their* lives we find much to disapprove; but there is nothing which is not divine and sinless in the fourfold record of the life of Christ.

II. Turning from Hillel's life to his teaching, we see how the notion of his being in any way a master of Christ crumbles into dust. Even his noblest answer, already recorded, is gravely defective. It may do for a summary of the *second* table of the Law, but, unlike the infinitely deeper wisdom of Jesus, it omits all reference to the first table, on which the second is alone founded, and with reference to which it is alone possible. Why did Hillel, in his famous answer, forget the Shema (Deut. vi. 4, 5), and remember only Lev. xix. 18? So did not Jesus (Matt. vii. 12; Luke vi. 31).

---

[1] This is a wrong reading for the people of *Tadmor* or Palmyra. (Buxtorf, *Lex.* s. v. Ewald, *Jahrbüch*, x. 69.)

[2] *Shabbath.* 30, 31.

[3] Other striking anecdotes are mentioned by Ewald, *Gesch. Christ.* 31—33.

[4] *Kethubôth*, 67 *b*, 16 *b.* Jost, *Gesch. d. Judenthums*, 1. 267. Delitzsch, *Jes. und Hillel*, 35 ; " Er bewegte wedelnd den Schweif des Thieres, um dessen Geschlecht zu verbergen." 48(

It is said, indeed, that Jesus sometimes applies one or other of the seven famous *middôth* (מִדּוֹת) laid down by Hillel for the interpretation of Scripture. But in point of fact these *middôth* are a mere summary of existing and perfectly obvious processes (Inference from major to minor or *vice versâ*, Matt. vii. 11, x. 29; analogy, connection, &c., Matt. xii. 5); and, in the next place, these were only contrivances to support the credit and authority of that Oral Law which Jesus utterly rejected and — it is hardly too much to say — despised. The instances in which the decisions of Christ coincide with those of Shammai are at least as numerous, and refer to subjects of greater importance (*e. g.*, Matt. v. 32; xix. 9; xviii. 17); yet who has ever thought of saying that He was a disciple of Shammai?

For instance, one of Hillel's most celebrated and elaborate decisions was on a trumpery series of questions as to whether one might or might not eat an egg which a hen had laid on a feast-day, when the feast-day came in connection with a sabbath. This precious inquiry gives its name, *Bîtsa* (egg), to an entire Talmudical treatise. Is it possible to imagine that Jesus would have treated it otherwise than with the finest yet tenderest irony? Yet in his decision on this point Hillel was more strict and more Shammaitic than Shammai himself.[1]

In some points, too, Hillel's teaching was, to say the least, very dubious. He ruled, for instance — owing to a vague expression in Deut. xxiv. 1 — that a man might put away his wife "even if she cooked his dinner badly" (*Git.* 90). It is true that Jost (*Gesch. d. Judenthums*, i. 264) and later writers interpret this to mean "bringing discredit on his home;" but the "even if" (אֲפִילוּ) evidently points to a *minimum*. His manner, too, of evading the Mosaic rules about the sabbatical year (mentioned in Excursus IX.) can only be regarded as a disingenuous shuffle. Better specimens of Hillel's teaching are —

"Separate not thyself from the congregation, and have no confidence in thyself till the day of thy death."

"If I do not care for my soul, who will do it for me? If I care only for my own soul, what am I? If not now, when then?" (*Abhôth* i. 14.)

"Judge not thy neighbor till thou art in his situation."

"Say not, I will repent when I have leisure, lest that leisure should never be thine."

"The passionate man will never be a teacher."

"In the place where there is not a man be thou a man."

"Be of the disciples of Aaron, who loved peace."

"Whoever is ambitious of aggrandizing his name will destroy it."[2]

---

[1] All ceremonializing and particularizing religions are liable to be evaporated into idle cases of casuistry. Some few years ago the Mohammedans at the Cape were agitated by such a dispute. The Sultan had sent some one to look after their spiritual condition. This person found that they were in the habit of eating cray-fish of a particular species, which in an evil hour he pronounced to be unclean. Objecting to this decision, they said that there was nothing about cray-fish in the Koran. However, he looked up a prohibition to eat spiders, and declared that for all ceremonial purposes a cray-fish *was* practically a spider. Referring the question to the curator of the Cape Museum, they were (naturally) informed that a cray-fish was *not* a species of spider. The more scrupulous, however, objected to the decision, and as far as my informant knows, the dispute may be as lively as ever to this day.

[2] Some of these (*e. g.*, the last) are obscure in the original, and admit a widely different interpretation. (Ewald, *ubi sup.*) These and others are in the *Pirke Abhôth* (Etheridge, *Hebr. Lit.*, p. 36). But it must not be forgotten that even this treatise is not older than the second century after Christ.

Hillel was undoubtedly a great and good man, and he deserved the wail uttered over his grave — "Ah, the gentle, the holy, the scholar of Ezra!"— but to compare his teaching with that of the Saviour is absurd. It was legal, casuistic, and narrow, while that of Jesus was religious, moral, and human. If Jesus uttered nothing original, as modern Jewish Rabbis are so fond of saying, how is it that, whereas the very name of Hillel is unknown except to schola˜s, the words of Jesus wrought the mightiest revolution that has ever been witnessed in the world? Had Humanity nothing better to live on than the words of Hillel, it would be dwarfed and starved indeed. The shortest and slightest of our Saviour's parables is worth all that he ever said.[1] Nay, even the least of the Old Testament prophets is transcendently greater than this "greatest and best of the Pharisees." He and his school, and Shammai and *his* school, spent a century of unprofitable and groundless jangling on the exegesis of two short words of the Law (*ervath dabhar*, Deut. xxiv. 1), without approaching a single sound principle, which would have rendered their quarrel needless: but Jesus furnished that principle, and solved the question for ever the moment that it was brought before Him (Matt. xix. 3—9). Let any candid reader consult the translation of the Talmudic treatise *Berachôth*, by M. Schwab, and see (pp. 264, 266, 314, 375, 404, &c.) the *kind* of miserably minute questions of infinitely little matters of formalism which occupied the mind and life of Hillel,[2] and calmly consider the mixture of scorn and pity with which Jesus would have treated the notion that there was in such questions any intrinsic importance. He will then be able to judge for himself of the folly and untenability of the statement that Hillel was the true master of Jesus!

EXCURSUS IV. (Page 93.)

GREEK LEARNING.

THERE is a story, several times repeated in the Talmud, that during the siege of Jerusalem in the civil war between Hyrcanus II. and Aristobulus, a box was daily let down the wall by the adherents of the latter, full of money, in return for which it was re-filled with the victims necessary for the daily sacrifice. But an "ancient" who knew "Greek wisdom" (*chôchmath Javaníth*) made the besiegers understand that the Temple would never be yielded so long as they supplied the means for continuing the daily sacrifice. Consequently, the next

---

[1] See further the admirable *brochure* of *Jesus und Hillel* by F. Delitzsch (Erlangen, 1867): Ewald, *Gesch. Christ.*, pp. 12—48; Budaeus, *Philos. Hebr.* 108, seqq.; Geiger, *De Hillel et Shammai*; Ugolini, xxi.; Grätz, *Gesch. d. Judenth.* iii. 172—179; Jost, *Gesch. d. Jud.* 254, seqq.; Herzfeld, *Gesch. d. Volkes Isr.* i. 257—261.

[2] *Ex. gr.*, Whether, when you are carrying perfumed oil and myrtles, you ought to bless first the myrtles and then the oil; whether you ought to take off your phylacteries or not in certain places of daily resort; whether you ought or ought not to be in a particular position at particular times of studying the Law; whether you ought first to wash your hands and then fill the glasses, or *vice versâ*; whether you ought to lay the napkin on the table or on the seat, &c., &c. The mere enumeration of one tithe of such points in serious dispute between the schools of Hillel and Shammai is wearisomely repulsive; yet it is of such deadening and frivolous matters — only very often unspeakably more nauseous — that the Talmud is full. One cannot blame Hillel for not being before his age; but to compare Rabbinism with Christianity, and Hillel with Christ, requires either a consummate effrontery, or a total paralysis of the critical faculty.

day, *a pig* was put in the box, which, when half-way up the wall, clung to the wall with its feet. An earthquake ensued. On this occasion the Doctors pronounced a curse on all who bred pigs, and on all who taught their children Greek wisdom. (*Sota,* 49 *b ; Menachôth* 64 *b.*)[1]

But, as Grätz (iii. 502) and Derenbourg (*Hist. Pal.* 114) point out, by " Greek wisdom " elsewhere is probably intended a sort of magic; and, in this instance, the art of secretly communicating with an enemy — as the traitorous ancient had done — by means of arrows with letters attached to them. The "ancient" is conjectured to have been Antipater.

It remains, however, true that, although the Rabbis on this, as on most other matters, contradict themselves, many of them wholly despised and discouraged Greek learning. Josephus, at the end of the *Antiquities,* distinctly tells us that they thought it slavish to be a good linguist, and, necessary as the Greek language was for commercial purposes, very few had attained it with accuracy.

Origen gives us the same testimony, saying that the Jews cared little either for the Greek language or literature.[2]

Rabbi Akiba says that no Israelite would be a partaker of eternal life who read the books of the gentiles.[3] Gamaliel was the only eminent Rabbi who permitted his pupils to read them — a circumstance to which we may possibly owe the classical quotations of St. Paul from Aratus, Menander, and Epimenides (Acts xvii. 28; 1 Cor. xv. 33; Titus i. 12).

EXCURSUS V. (Pages 214, 215.)

The Talmud and the Oral Law.

The Jews believe that the Law falls under two divisions — the Written Law (*Torah shebeketeb*), and the Oral, or that "upon the lip" (*Torah shebeal pî*), of which the latter, or "tradition," is equally authoritative with the former, or even more so.

The Talmud proper consists of the Mishna and the Gemara.

The Oral Law remained absolutely unwritten *at least* down to the time of the later Tanaîm (about A. D. 30—80), who, indeed, thought it wrong to commit it to writing. The older *Megillath Taanith* — a collection of *Hagadôth* ("legends or narrations") and *Halachôth* ("rules") on times and solemnities — is supposed to have been drawn up by Hanania Ben Hiskia in the time of our Lord. But the first who reduced the Mishna to writing was the famous Rabbi Jehuda Hakkôdesh, who died A. D. 190. His reason for doing so was the apparent danger of national extinction after the fearful massacre which ensued on the defeat of Bar-Cochebas and the capture of Bethyr; but although the reduction of the Oral Law to writing was discouraged, secret rolls (*megillôth setharîm*) of it are said to have existed before. In point of fact, laws are often, by a sort of fiction, supposed to be "unwritten" for centuries after they may be read in print.

The word Mishna means "repetition," and is usually rendered in Greek by δευτέρωσις. Maimonides divides the Oral Law into five classes — viz., (i.) *Per-*

---

[1] See Gfrörer, *Jahrh. d. Heils,* i. 114, and *Philo und die Alex. Theo.* ii. 350.

[2] *C. Cels.* ii. 34.

[3] *Bab. Sanhedr.* 90 *a.*

ushîm, explanations believed to date from Moses. (ii.) *Dinerîm,* or "constitutions," which are "modes of conduct" (*halachôth*) believed to have been delivered by Moses. (iii.) Generally received customs. (iv.) Decisions of the wise men, regarded as a "hedge about the Law" (מיג לתורה). (v.) Experimental suggestions.

Jehuda divided his immense materials into six *sedarîm,* or "orders," containing sixty-three massiktôth, or "tracts," and 525 perakîm, or "chapters" — viz.:

1. *Seder Zeraim,* or "Seeds," containing the *Berachôth,* on worship; *Peah* ("corner"), on the rights of the soil; *Terumôth,* "oblations," &c.

2. *Seder Moed,* "Festival;" containing *Shabbath, Erubhîn,* or "mixtures" (*v. infr.,* Exc. IX.); *Pesachîm,* "the Passover;" *Yoma,* "Day of Atonement;" *Sukka,* "Feast of Tabernacles;" *Bîtsa,* "an egg;" *Rosh Hashshanah,* "the new year;" *Taanîth,* "fasts;" *Chagiga,* "thank-offering," &c.

3. *Seder Nashîm,* on women; containing *Gittîn,* "divorce;" *Kethubhôth,* "wedding contracts," &c.

4. *Seder Nezikin,* on "Injuries;" containing *Babha Kama,* "the first;" *Metzia,* "the middle," and *Bathra,* "the last gate;" *Sanhedrin; Abhôda Zara,* "strange services;" *Abhôth,* "the Fathers," &c.

5. *Seder Kadashîm,* on "Consecrations."

6. *Seder Taharôth,* "Purifications," containing *Yadaîm,* or the purification of the hands, &c.[1]

The commentary on the Mishna, which is boundlessly voluminous, is called the *Gemara,* "complement," and the Mishna and Gemara together form the Talmud, or "that which should be learnt." The Jerusalem Talmud dates from about A. D. 390, and the Babylonian from about A. D. 420.

Appendices to the Mishna are called *Tosefôth;* exegetical additions to the Gemara are called *Tosafôth.* Supplements to the Mishna, consisting of commentaries (*e. g., Sifra,* a Midrash or "comment" on Leviticus, *Sifri* on Numbers and Deuteronomy, and *Mechiltha* on Exodus), are called *Baraithas.*

The language of the Talmud is uncouth, corrupt, and often unintelligible. It contains some beautiful and noble things, but far fewer than any other such enormous mass of human writings; and nothing can be conceived more tedious and unprofitable than its "desultory and confused wrangle," teeming with contradictions and mistakes. A sufficient number of Talmudic treatises have been translated to enable any reader to judge of this for himself. Lightfoot, than whom no scholar had a better right to speak, says that "the almost unconquerable difficulty of the style, the frightful roughness of the language, and the amazing emptiness and sophistry of the matters handled, do torture, vex, and tire him that reads them."

For a continuation of this subject see Excursus XII., "Notes on the Talmud."

---

[1] The principal edition and translation of the Mishna is that by Surenhusius, Amsterd. 1668—1703. It has been translated into German by Rabe (1763), and Jost (1833); and eighteen treatises have been translated into English by Rabbis De Sola and Raphall (second edition, London, 1845); Gfrörer, *Jahr. d. Heils,* i. 10. I have abridged the above account from Etheridge's *Hebr. Literat.,* pp. 117 seqq. See, too, Dr. Davidson *s. v.* "Talmud" in Kitto's *Bibl. Cycl.*

EXCURSUS VI. (Pages 134, 246.)

Traditional Description of the Appearance of our Lord.

The earliest actual descriptions of Jesus are very late, yet it is possible that they may have caught some faint accent of tradition handed down from the days of Irenæus, Papias, and St. John. Nicephorus, quoting from a description given by John of Damascus, in the eighth century, says that He resembled the Virgin Mary; that He was beautiful and strikingly tall, with fair and slightly curling locks, on which no hand but His mother's had ever passed, with dark eyebrows, an oval countenance, a pale and olive complexion, bright eyes, an attitude slightly stooping, and a look expressive of patience, nobility, and wisdom.[1] The famous letter which professes to have been addressed by "Lentulus, president of the people of Jerusalem, to the Roman Senate,"[2] though not older than the twelfth century, is yet so interesting for the history of Christian art, and so clearly derived from long-current traditions, that we may here quote it entire.

"There has appeared in our times," it says, "a man of great virtue, named Christ Jesus. . . . . He is a man of lofty stature, beautiful, having a noble countenance, so that they who look on Him may both love and fear. He has wavy hair, rather crisp, of the color of wine, and glittering as it flows down from His shoulders, with a parting in the middle of the head after the manner of the Nazarenes.[3] His forehead is pure and even, and His face without any spot or wrinkle, but glowing with a delicate flush. His nose and mouth are of faultless beauty; He has a beard abundant and of the same hazel color as His hair, not long, but forked. His eyes are blue and very bright.[4] He is terrible in rebuke, calm and loving in admonition, cheerful but preserving gravity. He has never been seen to laugh, but oftentimes to weep. His stature is erect, and his hands and limbs are beautiful to look upon. In speech He is grave, reserved, and modest; and He is fair among the children of men."[5]

---

[1] See Winer, *Realw.*, s v. "Jesus;" Nicephorus, *Hist. Eccl.* i. 40. This description, with that of the pseudo-Lentulus and John of Damascus. was edited by J. G. Carpzov, of Helmstadt, in 1777. The fullest treatment of the subject is in Dr. Lewis Glückselig, *Studien uber Jes. Christ und sein wahres Ebenbild.* Prag., 1863. (See *Quart. Rev.* 1867.) The *earliest* pictures of Christ, in the Catacombs, are purely symbolic (the Lamb, the Fish, Orpheus, &c.).

[2] No such office existed, nor did any one of that name fill any analogous position.

[3] He evidently meant Nazarites.

[4] More than one of these touches recalls the description of the youthful David (1 Sam. xvi. 12). "He was ruddy, and withal of a beautiful countenance (Heb. 'fair of eyes'), and goodly to look to." Cf. xvii. 42, and Cant. v. 10, "My beloved is white and ruddy, and chiefest (Heb. 'a standard-bearer') among ten thousand . . . His locks are bushy (Heb. 'curled'), and black as a raven. His eyes are as the eyes of doves," &c.

[5] B. H. Cowper, *The Apocr. Gospels*, p. 221; Hofmann, pp. 291–294; Hase, p. 80. — Pictures and statues of Christ are said to have originated on the gems, &c., of the Gnostics — *e. g.*, Basilidians, Carpocratians, &c.; but symbolic representations were common in the Catacombs (Iren. *c. Haer.* i. 24; Hippol., *Philosoph.* vii. 32). A statue of Christ is said to have found its way into the private *lararium* of the Emperor Alexander Severus (Lamprid., *Vit. Alex. Sever.* c. 29). The one which has acquired most fame is the supposed representation at Cæsarea Philippi (Paneas) of the healing of the woman with the issue of blood, as related in the apocryphal story of Veronica (Cowper, p. 233; Hofmann, 293, 354, 357), which Eusebius saw, but despised (*Hist. Ecc.* vii. 18), and which Julian is said to have destroyed (Sozomen, *H. E.* v. 20; Philostorg., *H. E.* vii. 3). I need merely allude to the miraculous impression on the napkin of Veronica, the shroud given by Nicodemus, &c.

EXCURSUS VII. (Page 265.)

JEWISH ANGELOLOGY AND DEMONOLOGY.

IT is the characteristic of the Oriental, and especially of the Semitic mind, to see in every event, even the mo.·· trivial, a direct supernatural interference, wrought by the innumerable unseen ministers — both good and evil — of the Divine Will. The definite form in which the belief clothed itself was, by the admission of the Jews themselves, derived from Babylon.[1]

Even the most ordinary forces and phenomena of Nature, and passions of the mind, were by them regarded as angels. Thus, in the Jer. Targum on Deut. ix. 19, it is said that, to punish the Israelites for worshipping the golden calf, God sent five angels — Indignation, Anger, Fury, Ruin, Wrath. And they would have interpreted quite literally the verse — "He maketh the winds his angels, and fiery flames his ministers" (Ps. civ. 4).

The number of the angels — the *Tsebha hashamaîm*— was immense. R. Eliezer said that at Sinai 600,000 descended, according to the number of the 600,000 Israelites;[2] and in *Bab. Berachôth* (32 *b*) we find the following story :— "According to R. Rish Lakish, Isa. xlix. 14 is to be understood as follows : The Church of Israel complains to God : 'Lord of the World, even when a man takes a second wife he thinks of the first; but thou hast utterly forgotten me.' But God answered, 'Daughter, I have 12 *mazalôth* (signs of the zodiac), and to each *massal* 30 *chêl* (commanders), and to each *chêl* 30 legions (generals), and to each legion 30 *rabatôn* (officers), and to each *rabatôn* 30 *kartôn* (captains), and to each *kartôn* 30 *kistra* (camps), and to each *kistron* I have assigned 3,650,000,000 stars. All these have I created for thy sake, and yet thou sayest I have forgotten thee.' "

This, it will be seen, makes the number of the *Tsebaoth* (or Hosts of Heaven) 12 × 30 × 30 × 30 × 30 × 30 × 3,650,000, which makes 1,064,340,000,000,000, *i. e.*, on the old English plan of notation, one trillion, sixty-four billion, three hundred and forty thousand million ; or according to the newer English plan and the French plan (recommended, says M. Littré, by Locke), one *quintillion*, &c. The factors are evidently a muddle of days, months, &c., the same factors being occasionally repeated to make sure of not being under the mark! The military terms (*castra*, &c.) have an interesting bearing on the $\Lambda\varepsilon\gamma\varepsilon\omega\nu$ of Mark v. 9; for the devils were supposed to be under similar military organization. Wier, *De Praestigiis Daemonum*, calculates that there are 7,405,926 devils.

These angels were all divided into ranks and classes,

"Thrones, dominations, virtues, princedoms, powers,"

to which there seems to be an allusion in Eph. i. 21.

The evil spirits — offspring, according to various Rabbinic legends, of Adam and Lilith, or of Sammael and Eve, or of "the sons of God and daughters of men "— were equally numerous. To them were attributed many results which

---

[1] *Rosh Hashshanah*, 56 ; Gfrörer, *Jahrh. d. Heils*, i. 124. — The facts in this Excursus are derived mainly from Gfrörer and Frankl, *Jews in the East*. Göthe's demonology in *Faust* is mainly Talmudic, and is borrowed from Eisenmenger.

[2] *Pirke Eliezer*, 41.

we should undoubtedly assign to purely natural causes, especially the phenomena of epilepsy, as is very clearly described in the Book of Enoch (xv. 8).

Their home was supposed to be the region of the middle air (John xii. 31; xiv. 30; 2 Cor. iv. 4; and especially Eph. ii. 2; vi. 12), and they were regarded as lords of the existing state of things. An exaggeration of this view led to certain Ebionite heresies, and even in the Book *Zohar* Satan is called " the second God" (*El achér ;* cf. 2 Cor. iv. 4). R. Joshua Ben Levi says that he has seven names — Lust, Impurity, the Hater, &c., and "the Man of Midnight" (Joel ii. 20, *Heb.*).

In *Bab. Berachôth* (6 *a*) we are told that if we could but see the devils no one could stand the shock. Every man has 10,000 at his right hand, and 1,000 at his left. They are remarkably powerful at night; hence no one should greet a person by night, for fear of saluting a devil (*Sanhedr.* 44 *a*). They live chiefly in ruins, and deserts and sepulchres, and under trees (especially the service-tree), and foul places.

Headache was caused by a demon named *Kardaikoos.* On the sabbath-night all hide themselves except one Asiman, who causes the birth of epileptic children.

The belief in these *Schedim,* or evil spirits, has continued unabated to this day. " There are houses in Jerusalem in which men and women cannot dwell together; the *Schedim* will not allow it; and thus they are occupied by women alone." The celebrated cabalist, Jehuda Bivas of Corfu, explained that they have no power in the West. The *chalebi*, the old traditional head-dress of the Jewish women, seems to have been invented for the express purpose of keeping off the *Schedim*, who sit on the hair of women whose heads are uncovered (see 1 Cor. xi. 10). "Its ugliness is only equalled by the difficulty of describing it : " it seems to be a sort of chignon, except that it is made entirely of linen, and conceals the hair of all who wear it.[1]

EXCURSUS VIII. (Page 284.)

The Unnamed Feast of John v. 1, and the Length of the Ministry.

"After this " (the healing of the nobleman's son), says St. John, " there was a feast of the Jews, and Jesus went up to Jerusalem."

What this feast was, is in all probability a question which, though interesting and important in settling the length of our Lord's ministry, will never receive a final answer. Whole volumes have been written on it, and to enter upon all the discussions which they open would be idle, and endless, and, after all, unconvincing. In spite of the patient thought and consummate learning which have been devoted to the consideration, the data are clearly insufficient to decide convincingly how long Christ publicly taught on earth, nor shall we ever be able to attain any *certainty* on that deeply interesting question. The few remarks which I shall make on the subject shall be as brief and clear as possible.

1. St. John groups his entire narrative round the Jewish festivals,[1] and mentions —

---

[1] See Frankl, *Jews in the East*, E. Tr., ii. 160, seqq. ; i. 227, &c.

[2] See Browne, *Ordo Saeclorum*, p. 91.

i. "The Passover of the Jews" (ii. 13), τὸ πάσχα τῶν Ἰουδαίων.

ii. "A" or "the" Feast of the Jews" (v. 1), ἑορτή or ἡ ἑορτὴ τῶν Ἰουδαίων.[1]

iii. The Passover, the Feast of the Jews (vi. 4), τὸ πάσχα ἡ ἑορτὴ τῶν Ἰουδαίων.

iv. "The Tabernacles, the Feast of the Jews" (vii. 2), ἡ ἑορτὴ τῶν Ἰουδαίων ἡ σκηνοπηγία.

v. "The Dedication" (x. 22), τὰ ἐγκαίνια.

vi. "The Passover of the Jews" (xi. 55), τὸ πάσχα τῶν Ἰουδαίων.

2. The feasts of the Jews occurred in the following order, and if we take a particular year, we can (though this cannot be regarded as *certain* or beyond dispute) fix the very day of the month and week on which they occurred. *Ex. gr.*, taking the year 28 A. D., we have —

NISAN	1.	Tues. MARCH 16.		Jewish New Year's Day.
"	14.	Mon.	" 29.	Passover; the days of unleavened bread lasting seven days.
SIVAN	6.	Wed. MAY	19.	Pentecost.
TISRI	10.	Sat. SEPT.	18.	Day of Atonement.
"	15-21.	"	23-29.	Tabernacles.
KISLEU	25.	Wed. DEC.	1.	Dedication.
VEADAR	14.	Sat. MARCH	19.	Purim.[2]

This last feast would thus be nearly a month before the Passover of the *ensuing* year, A. D. 29, in which year the Passover fell on *April 17th.*

3. Now the feast here mentioned could hardly be the Passover or the Feast of Tabernacles, because, as we have seen, St. John, when he mentions those feasts, mentions them by name; in fact, both those feasts had Greek names (πάσχα and σκηνοπηγία) familiarly known to Greek readers; and there seems to be no reason whatever why the name of either should be omitted here. It is impossible to suppose that the omission of the name is purely arbitrary or accidental. But there are still weightier reasons against the supposition that it was either of these two great feasts. For (α) if this were the Passover, St. John would omit a *whole year* of our Lord's ministry (vi. 4) without a word; and it cannot have been (β) the Feast of Tabernacles immediately succeeding the first Passover mentioned by St. John, because six months is too short a period for all the events which had intervened since the journey through Samaria (John ii. 13); nor (γ) can it have been the Feast of Tabernacles in the subsequent year, for then a year and a half would have elapsed without a single visit to Jerusalem. In short, if we assume, as we have done, that after His first Passover our Lord spent some time in Judea, and then, possibly *four months before harvest* (John iv. 35), passed through Samaria on His journey to Galilee; and if again we infer, as we seem entitled to do, that the Passover mentioned in John vi. 4 is the *second* which He attended, we must then look for this unnamed feast some time between the close of winter and the harvest — *i. e.*, between Kisleu or December and Nisan 16, on which day the first wheat-sheaf was offered, and harvest legally began.

---

[1] The reading is profoundly uncertain. The Alexandrine and Vatican Manuscripts and the Codex Bezae have not the article; on the other hand, the Codex Ephraemi and the Sinaiticus have it. Yet it is much more likely to have been *inserted* than to have been *omitted*, and if we could be sure that it did not exist in the original text, this would seem to be nearly decisive against its being the Passover or Feast of Tabernacles.

[2] Wieseler, *Chron. Syn.* E. Tr., p. 434.

If these reasons are not absolutely conclusive, they are at least very weighty, and if admitted, they at once exclude the *greater* Jewish festivals.

4. Looking, therefore, at minor feasts, there is only one for which we can see a *reason* why the name should have been omitted — viz., the Feast of Purim. The mere fact of its being a minor feast would not alone be a sufficient reason for excluding the name, since, as we have seen, St. John mentions by name the comparatively unimportant and humanly appointed Feast of the Dedication. But the name of this feast was represented by a familiar Greek word (*Encaenia*), and explained itself; whereas the Feast of Purim was intensely Jewish, and the introduction of the name without an explanation would have been unintelligible. Purim means "lots," and if St. John had merely translated the name into Greek, it might have led to very mistaken impressions. The only Greek equivalents for it were $\Phi\rho o\upsilon\rho\alpha\grave{\iota}$ or $\grave{\eta}$ $Mo\rho\delta o\chi\alpha\ddot{\iota}\kappa\eta$ $\grave{\eta}\mu\acute{\epsilon}\rho\alpha$, neither of which was generally known or understood in the Gentile world.[1] Moreover, the fact that it was the most unimportant, non-religious, and questionably-observed of the Jewish feasts, would be an additional reason for leaving the name unnoticed.

Mr. Browne, in his very learned and elaborate, but unconvincing *Ordo Saeclorum*, uses a powerful series of arguments to show that our Lord's ministry only lasted for a single year and a few weeks (pp. 342—391). He relies much on various astronomical arguments, which depend on dubious data, and on traditions which are not only conflicting, but can be easily accounted for.

Origen (*De Principiis*, iv. 5) says $\grave{\epsilon}\nu\iota\alpha\upsilon\tau\grave{o}\nu$ $\kappa\alpha\acute{\iota}$ $\pi o\upsilon$ $\kappa\alpha\grave{\iota}$ $\grave{o}\lambda\acute{\iota}\gamma o\upsilon\varsigma$ $\mu\tilde{\eta}\nu\alpha\varsigma$ $\grave{\epsilon}\delta\acute{\iota}\delta\alpha\xi\epsilon\nu$,[481] and argues for our Lord's Divinity from the fact that His brief year of teaching was found adequate — so "full of grace were His lips" — to renovate the world.[2] Such seems to have been the most ancient opinion, and yet, as Mr. Browne candidly points out, Melito, Irenæus, and others take a very different view ; and Irenæus speaks of it as a certain fact, derived by tradition from St. John, that our Lord, at the time of His death, was between forty and fifty years old (c. *Haeres*. ii. 22, 5).

The tradition as to the duration of the ministry for a single year is sufficiently accounted for by Luke iv. 19, to which expression indeed St. Clement of Alexandria directly appeals in confirmation of this view ($\kappa\alpha\grave{\iota}$ $\H{o}\tau\iota$ $\grave{\epsilon}\nu\iota\alpha\upsilon\tau\grave{o}\nu$ $\mu\acute{o}\nu o\nu$ $\H{\epsilon}\delta\epsilon\iota$ $\alpha\grave{\upsilon}\tau\grave{o}\nu$ $\kappa\eta\rho\tilde{\upsilon}\xi\alpha\iota$ $\kappa\alpha\grave{\iota}$ $\tau o\tilde{\upsilon}\tau o$ $\gamma\acute{\epsilon}\gamma\rho\alpha\pi\tau\alpha\iota$ $o\H{\upsilon}\tau\omega\varsigma$, $\grave{\epsilon}\nu\iota\alpha\upsilon\tau\grave{o}\nu$ $\delta\epsilon\kappa\tau\grave{o}\nu$ $\kappa\upsilon\rho\acute{\iota}o\upsilon$ $\kappa\eta\rho\tilde{\upsilon}\xi\alpha\iota$ $\grave{\alpha}\pi\acute{\epsilon}\sigma\tau\epsilon\iota\lambda\acute{\epsilon}\nu$ $\mu\epsilon$,[482] *Strom*. i. xxi. § 145). The tradition as to our Lord's age is derived from the surprised remark of the Jews in John viii. 57.[3] We have already seen that neither of these passages supports the inferences which have been drawn from them. This was early observed, and even Hippolytus, the scholar of Irenæus, says that our Lord died at the age of thirty-three ;[4] and Eusebius (*H. E.* i. 10), Theodoret (*in Dan.* ix. 27), Jerome (*id.*), and others agree with him.

Mr. Browne proceeds ingeniously to show that if a year's ministry be supposed,

---

[1] Purim is corrupted from the Persian word *bahre*, "lots" (cf. *pars*), which the LXX. and Josephus corrupted into $\phi\rho o\upsilon\rho\alpha\grave{\iota}$ and $\phi\rho o\upsilon\rho\alpha\tilde{\iota}o\iota$. Ewald long ago pointed out (*Morgenland. Zeitschr*. iii. 415) that it was regarded as " *a preliminary celebration of the Passover*."

[2] Even Origen does not seem to be quite consistent with himself. See *c. Cels*. ii., p. 397, and *in Matt*. xxiv. 15. (Gieseler, *Ch. Hist.* i. 55, E. Tr.)

[3] The reading $\tau\epsilon\sigma\sigma\alpha\rho\acute{\alpha}\kappa o\nu\tau\alpha$ [483] adopted by Chrysostom, Euthymius, &c., is probably a mere correction, and has no good MS. authority. The Jews only mentioned fifty as a round number, expressing complete manhood.

[4] *In Dan*. iv. Wordsw. *ad loc*.

and *if τὸ πάσχα be eliminated from* John vi. 4, St. John may then be supposed to give the feasts of a year in regular chronological order, viz: —

1. The Passover (ii. 13) . . . . March.
2. The Pentecost (v. 1) . . . . May.
3. The Feast of Tabernacles (vi. 4; vii. 2) . . . September.
4. The Dedication (x. 22) . . . . . . December.
5. The Passover of the Crucifixion . . . . March.

But it is surely and finally fatal against this view that, whatever may be the case in the quotations or allusions of some of the Fathers, there is not *the very faintest MS. authority* for the omission of τὸ πάσχα in John vi. 4.[1] Such being the case, St. John certainly and definitely mentions *three* passovers. If, as on other grounds we have seen to be probable, there was one passover in our Lord's ministry which he did *not* attend, the length of ministry was, as most inquirers have now agreed to believe, three years and some weeks, or possibly months. This would account for the remarkable specification of "three years," and a reprieve for another year, as the time during which the unfruitful tree is spared in Luke xiii. 7, 8.

EXCURSUS IX. (Page 335.)

HYPOCRISY OF THE PHARISEES.

THE very *raison d'être* [454] of the Pharisees was to create " hedges " of oral tradition around the Law. Epiphanius, inventing a very forcible word to describe their character, says that they derived their name from their ἐθελοπερισσόθρησκεία,[2] voluntary, excessive, external service; and yet, in spite of these extravagant professions, they were perfectly ready to make devices to evade the law when it interfered with their own conveniences and plans.[3] Perhaps the most flagrant instance of this is the manner in which they managed to absolve themselves from the self-imposed obligation of not exceeding the 2,000 yards at which they fixed a Sabbath day's journey.[4]

It was the custom of the Pharisees to join in *syssitia*, or common daily banquets, which they subjected to the most stringent conditions, and which they assimilated in all respects to priestly meals. But as their houses were often more than 2,000 yards from the place of meeting, and as the bearing of burdens on the Sabbath was strictly forbidden (Neh. xiii. 15; Jer. xvii. 21; Exod. xvi. 29), they would, without a little ingenuity, have been prevented from dining in

---

[1] Mr. Browne simply relies on the conjecture that it is an interpolation unknown to Irenæus, Origen, Clement, Tertullian, &c.

[2] *Hæres.* xvi. 34.

[3] " Une tendance importante des Pharisiens, *celle de transiger avec les* obligations de la Loi dans l'intérêt des nouveaux besoins " 455 (Derenbourg, *Hist. Pal.* 144). " To make a hedge round the Law " was one of the lessons of Simon the Just (*Pirk. Abhôth,* i. 1; Jost, i. 95). For some further remarks see *infr.*, Excursus XIV.

[4] This was founded on elaborate arguments drawn from Exod. xxi. 13; xvi. 29. In the latter passage, "beyond 2,000 cubits" is actually inserted by the Jer. Targum. See the excellent and thoroughly well-informed articles of Dr. Ginsburg on " Sabbath Day's Journey " and " Pharisees " in Kitto's *Bible Cyclopedia*.

common on the very day on which they most desired it. A little management quite relieved them from their difficulty.

On the evening before the Sabbath, they deposited some food at a distance of 2,000 yards from their own house, thus creating a fictitious home; from this fictitious home they could then go 2,000 yards farther to the place of meeting, thus giving themselves double the real distance! This piece of transparent hypocrisy was euphemistically described as an ideal amalgamation of distances, or "connection of places," and was called *erûbh* ("mixture," עֵרוּב), a name under which it exists to the present day.[1] In order to get over the second difficulty, a still more miserable subterfuge was adopted, by putting door-posts and lintels at the end of various streets, so that all the space between them might be regarded as one large house![2]

Could any words of burning denunciation be too strong to denounce such a playing at "fast and loose" with obligations which they professed to regard as infinitely and divinely sacred, and the violation of which they were ready to avenge by inflicting death on the transgressor? They must have thought that both their Deity and their conscience were easily cheated![3]

The Sadducees got over the difficulty, too, in a manner more daring, but infinitely less despicable, by calmly asserting that their meals were a continuation of the Temple service, and therefore claiming the benefit of the maxim, that there was "no sabbatism in the Temple."

These instances might be indefinitely multiplied: *e. g.*, if a Jew's ox is dying, he may kill it on a *holy day*, provided he eats a piece of the meat as big as an olive, to make believe that it was killed for a necessary meal. If a Jew wants to buy anything which is sold by weight or measure on a holy day, he may do so, provided that he *pays* the next day, and *does not* mention the name, weight, or measure. If a Jew wants to buy cattle, fowls, &c., on a holy day, he may do so, only he must not mention money or the *number* required. He may buy from a butcher on a holy day, only he must not say, "Give me meat for so much money," but only "*Give me a portion, or half a portion,*" and he pays for it next day.[4] Can any stretch of charity, however tender, avoid calling this the legality of evasion designed to cheat God with the letter instead of the spirit. Is the word "hypocrites" too strong for those who thus reduced shiftiness to a sacred system?

Another instance of the same kind was the way in which they treated the sabbatical year. "Before and in the time of Christ they did away with the law of remitting debts, by regarding it as a meritorious act on the part of the debtor not to avail himself of the Mosaic enactment, but to pay his debts irrespective of the sabbatical year. But not glaringly to counteract the law, these doctors enacted that the creditor should say, 'In accordance with the sabbatical year I remit thee the debt:' whereunto the debtor had to reply, 'I nevertheless wish

---

[1] Among the Jews of Palestine (especially at Safed) there are many of these contemptible trickeries.

[2] These *Erubhîn*, or "combinations" — *i. e.*, the relations of places and limits, as affecting the observation of the Sabbath — fill ten chapters of the *Seder Moed.* The invention of these is attributed to Solomon. (*Shabb.* 14, 2; Reland, *Antt. Hebr.* 524.)

[3] Similarly it is found in Hindostan that *caste* is protected with the most minute and scrupulous fidelity, *except where it clashes with ordinary interests* — as, *e. g.*, in railway travelling.

[4] See the original passages quoted in Dr. McCaul's *Old Paths*, pp. 108 ff.

to pay it,' and then the creditor accepted the payment." [1] A very ingenious farce indeed! but intolerable in men who professed an intense zeal and illimitable devotion for "every sentence, word — what say I? — every letter " — of the Mosaic legislation. Perhaps it may be said that these are simply legal fictions necessitated by a false position: but a far more shameful proof of organized hypocrisy is furnished in the advice given by Rabbi Ila to those who suffered from sensual temptations. It occurs in two separate passages of the Talmud.[2] I cannot quote the passages, but the purport of them amounts to this, that the sin of fornication is permissible if it be effectually concealed. Another Rabbinic rule about divorce is just as thin a disguise, just as cynical a concession. "A man must not marry a woman *with the intention* of divorcing her; but if he previously inform her that he is going to marry her for a season, it is lawful." [3]

Again, in spite of their boundless professions of reverence for Scripture, many of their schemes of interpretation — *gematria, notarikon,* &c. — were used to get rid of facts and meanings which they disliked. Instances of this in the **LXX.** are very numerous, and they occur frequently in the Targums. For instance: disgusted with the notion that Moses should have married an Æthiopian woman (Numb. xii. 1), Jonathan renders *Koosith* (Cushite) by "of fair face," because the letters of *Koosith* = 736, and the words *Japhath mareh* give the same sum! This was to expand the interpretation of Scripture into the number of positive integral solutions of an indeterminate equation!

Shammai, the narrow-minded rival of Hillel, was so scrupulous, that he nearly starved his little son on the Day of Atonement, and made a sort of booth of his daughter-in-law's bed that his little grandson (just born!) might keep the Feast of Tabernacles (*Succah*, ii. 9). Yet we are told that he was a luxurious and selfish man. It is easier to tithe mint than to live a holy life. Those who venture to say that Jesus was too bitter and severe against the Pharisees, must remember the saying attributed to King Alexander Jannæus, that a " real Pharisee was one who wished to play the part of Cozbi, and to receive the reward of Phinehas."

EXCURSUS X. (Page 555.)

Was the Last Supper an Actual Passover?

It is certain, and is all but universally acknowledged, being expressly stated by *all* the Evangelists, that our Lord was crucified on Friday,[4] and rose on Sunday, lying during the hours of the Jewish Sabbath in the tomb of Joseph of Arimathea. It is therefore certain that He ate His Last Supper, and instituted the Sacrament of the Eucharist, on the evening of Thursday; but was this Last

---

[1] C. D. Ginsburg, "Sabbatic Year " in Kitto, iii. 722. — For the most favorable view that can be given of these legal fictions, see R. Astruc, *Studies on the Pentateuch*; and Judah Ben Halévy, *The Khosari*, iii. §§ 46, 47, quoted by Cohen, *Les Déicides*, xi. 3

[2] *Bab. Kiddiushim*, 40 a; *Chagiga*, 16 a. See the forcible remarks of Gfrörer. "Heuchelei ist ein *Laster* zu dem die Menschen von Natur sehr geneigt sind, wird sie vollends durch geheiligte Autoritäten gebilligt, wie hier, so muss sie alle Stande ergreifen." [486] *Jahrh. des Heils*, i. 167.)

[3] McCaul, *Old Paths*, p. 376.

[4] Matt. xxvii. 62; Mark xv. 42; Luke xxiii. 54; John xix. 31. See, however, Westcott's *Introduction*, p. 323.

Supper the actual Paschal Feast, or an anticipation of it? was it eaten on Nisan 13, or Nisan 14 — *i. e.*, in the year of the Crucifixion did the first day of the Passover begin on the evening of a Thursday or on the evening of a Friday?

The question would, of course, be settled — (1) If we knew with *certainty* the date of our Lord's crucifixion, and (2) could rely on the Jewish calendars with sufficient conviction to be sure on what day of the week in that year the Passover fell. But as neither of these data can be depended on, we must turn for the solution of the question to the Evangelists alone. Let us observe, in passing, that, as all the Evangelists are agreed as to the main order of the events, the question as to whether the Last Supper was or was not the Paschal Feast, though a question of deep interest for us, is not one which directly affects the object of the Evangelists in writing the life of Christ.

Now it must be admitted that the Synoptists are unanimous in the use of expressions which admit of no natural explanation except on the supposition that the Passover *did* begin on the evening of Thursday, and therefore that Thursday was Nisan 14, and that the Last Supper was in reality the ordinary Paschal Feast.

This appears from the following passages:—Matt. xxvi. 2 — "Ye know that after two days is the *Passover;*" *id.* 17 — "Now the first day of unleavened bread the disciples came to Jesus, saying unto him, Where wilt thou that we prepare for thee *to eat the Passover?*" 18 — "I *will keep the Passover* at thy house;" 19 — "They made ready *the Passover*" [cf Mark xiv. 14—16; Luke xxii. 11—13].

St. Luke is even more explicit, for he says (xxii. 7) — "Then came *the day of unleavened bread, when the Passover must be killed;*" *id.* 15 — "With desire have I desired *to eat this Passover* [1] with you before I suffer."

And every other allusion to the day made by the Evangelists is equally plain; so that if they be correct in their statements, we must suppose that Peter and John procured from the Temple the Paschal Lamb between three and five in the afternoon, which was the *Jewish* (though not the *Samaritan*) interpretation of the expression "between the two evenings"—the time specified by the Law for the slaying of the lamb.

But now when we turn to the Gospel of St. John it seems equally indisputable on his authority that the Last Supper was *not* the Paschal Feast, and that the Passover really began on the Friday evening, and consequently that Thursday was the 13th, not the 14th, of Nisan.

For, passing over the disputed expression, "Before the Feast of the Passover," in John xiii. 1 (which is *capable*, though not naturally or probably, of another explanation),[2] we find that some of the disciples imagine that Jesus had sent

---

[1] The Greek is τοῦτο τὸ πάσχα, and therefore cannot *of itself* be meant to imply "this meal as a sort of Passover," although such a meaning may have been, and probably was, involved in the actual Aramaic words spoken by Jesus. Prof. Westcott argues that though language like this, taken alone, would clearly point to the Paschal meal, yet this natural meaning of the words could not be intended by the Evangelists, since their clear identification of the day of crucifixion, as Nisan 14, excludes such a signification (*Introduction*, p. 321). We admit at once that our difficulties may arise from imperfect knowledge of ritual and other customs which would be perfectly familiar to the Jews; but it still seems impossible to believe that the Synoptists used these expressions *knowing* that the meal eaten was not the Passover, when a word of explanation, or the slightest variation of language, would have removed all possibility of mistake.

[2] Some refer the words to ἀγαπήσας or εἰδώς; but, as Mr. Sanday remarks, we usually date *acts*, not feelings (*Fourth Gospel*, p. 202).

out Judas to "buy those things that we have need of against the feast;' [1] and that the priests and Pharisees "went not into the judgment-hall lest they should be defiled;[2] but that they might eat the Passover." St. John also says in so many words that the Friday of the crucifixion was "the preparation of the Passover;"[3] and that the following Sabbath was "a high day"[4] — evidently because it was at once a Sabbath and the first day of the Paschal Feast.

How is this apparent contradiction to be reconciled? It must, I think, be frankly confessed, that many of the solutions offered are eminently unsatisfactory, depending upon the assumption of Jewish customs and Jewish forms of speech which not only have no authority in their favor, but which even contravene such authority as we have. To go through and to sift them all would require a volume. Here I can only allude to some of the more important solutions, and then give the explanation which, after repeated and careful consideration of the question, appears to me the only satisfactory one.

1. That the day for keeping the Passover was fixed by astronomical considerations in which the possibility of error led to the observation of different days.

2. That "between the two evenings" *must* be interpreted to mean between the evening of the 13th and that of the 14th of Nisan, or between the evenings of the 14th and 15th, and therefore that the Passover might be eaten on either of those days.

3. That Jesus ate the Passover at the proper legal time, but the Jews, or some of them, in their zeal and hatred against Him, put off *their* Passover till the next evening.[5]

4. That "to eat the Passover" is an expression not confined to eating the Paschal lamb, but might be used also of eating the *chagiga*, and generally of keeping the entire feast, and that *this* explains the expressions used by St. John.[6]

5. That the supper spoken of by St. John is different from that described by the other Evangelists.

6. That when the 14th of Nisan fell on a Friday, the Paschal lamb was not killed till the 15th, in order to avoid the observance of two Sabbaths.[7]

---

[1] If the Passover had actually been eaten at that time, the expression would be quite inappropriate; and it is further probable that during the feast all ordinary business was suspended.

[2] Joseph of Arimathea did indeed "go to Pilate" on this day before the evening (Mark xv. 43); but it cannot be inferred from this that he had eaten his Passover. It may be that he did not actually enter Pilate's house, or his notions of what constituted ceremonial defilement may have been less scrupulous than those of the Pharisees: for that *some* Jews must even have gone into the judgment-hall without noticing the "defilement" is clear.

[3] παρασκευή may indeed merely mean Friday, but it is perfectly incredible that St. John should have spoken of the day of the crucifixion as παρασκευή τοῦ πάσχα in the sense of "Friday in Paschal week," if Friday had been actually "the first day of unleavened bread."

[4] In John xix. 31, μεγάλη ἡμέρα seems to represent *yom tôbh*, *i. e.*, the first or last day of an octave feast; the *intermediate* days were called *moed katôn* (Sepp).

[5] It is surprising to find this theory adopted by Bishop Wordsworth on the authority of Eusebius.

[6] The *chagiga* was eaten at other festivals also (Deut. xvi. 16), and there was nothing specifically Paschal about it.

[7] This solution is adopted by Calvin (among others); but we have no reason for supposing that this custom was adopted till some centuries later.

7. That the Last Supper was a perfectly regular Paschal meal, but was eaten, *by anticipation*, a day earlier than the usual time.[1]

Such hypotheses might be almost indefinitely multiplied, and some of them have been maintained with much learning; but none of them have commanded any general assent, either from failing to satisfy the natural probabilities of the case, or from being wholly unsupported by any adequate evidence. And even if we can *explain* how it came to happen that there could be this apparent discrepancy, it seems scarcely consistent with critical honesty to deny that the discrepancy really exists. If we construe the language of the Evangelists in its plain, straightforward, simple sense, and without reference to any preconceived theories, or supposed necessities for harmonizing the different narratives, we should be led to conclude from the Synoptists that the Last Supper *was* the ordinary Paschal meal, and from St. John that it was not.

Assuming, then, for the moment, that our decision must be formed on *conflicting* testimonies, must we suppose that strict accuracy here rests with St. John or with the Synoptists?

We answer, that it must be regarded as all but certain that St. John's language is here the most strictly correct, and that the Last Supper was *not* the actual and legal and ordinary Paschal meal, which we should suppose it to have been if the Synoptists alone had come down to us. The grounds for this conviction are the following: —

1. The extreme improbability that St. John, whose accounts of the Last Supper are incomparably more full than those of the other Evangelists, and who was more immediately and completely identified with every act in those last tragic scenes than any one of the Apostles, should yet have gone out of his way to adopt an error on a point so remarkable. There were many reasons why the Last Supper should, in the course of a few years, have come to be identified, even in the memory of the Evangelists, with the Paschal meal; there could be no reason, except the real fact of the case, why it should have been carefully and expressly *distinguished from* it.[2] Thursday, the day on which all *leavened bread* was removed from the houses, would most naturally be confused with Friday, the first day of the *Passover*, especially at a time when little or no regard was paid to chronological niceties; but, on the other hand, it is perfectly incredible that St. John could have "invented," or got into circulation, a statement conflicting with the general stream of tradition.

2. The certainty that the Friday was spent, and spent apparently without any scruples, in a scene of work, turmoil, and excitement, such as would have been

---

[1] Other theories still more baseless may be found recorded in Andrews, *Life of our Lord*, pp. 369—397 : *e. g.*, that of Rauch, that the Passover could be legally killed on the 15th as well as the 14th of Nisan ; and that of Schneckenburger, that Jesus was crucified on Wednesday and lay four days in the grave. Professor Westcott's deservedly high authority gives indeed some sanction to the tenability of this latter opinion (*Introduction*, p. 322), but Luke xxiii. 54, 56 seems alone sufficient to set it aside. Matt. xii. 40 arises from the Jewish custom of regarding "any fragment of a day, however short, as a νυχθήμερον," just as, in reckoning the years of a reign, they counted the shortest fragment of a year as a whole year. [There is something analogous to this in English law. A person born on February 20 legally comes of age at midnight on February 18.]

[2] Unless, which on other grounds seems most improbable, the Quarto-deciman controversy has anything to do with it.

wholly unsuited to the first day of a pre-eminently sacred festival.[1] Yet, if the meal of the previous evening was the Passover, Friday must have been a Feast-Sabbath, and although Feast-Sabbaths were not observed so strictly as the weekly Sabbath, yet it appears, even on the testimony of late writers like Maimonides, that a certain amount of solemnity attached to them.

3. The fact that no single circumstance is alluded to which shows that there was any observation of the day whatever as a day of solemnity or of festivity. And yet, so strict were the notions of the Jews about these Feast-Sabbaths, that even Hillel decided that if a hen laid an egg on a Feast-Sabbath it ought not to be eaten.[2] But how, Neander asks, could the first day of the principal feast be treated as an ordinary Friday? All difficulties are removed by supposing that it *was* only a common Friday, and that the next day was at once the Sabbath and the first day of the Passover feast.

4. The fact that, before any apparent discrepancy in the Gospels had been noticed, *early* Christian tradition was predominant in the assertion that the Last Supper was different from the Passover.[3]

5. The sense of inherent and symbolical fitness in the dispensation which ordained that Christ should be slain on the day and at the hour appointed for the sacrifice of the Paschal lamb.[4]

6. The fact that Jewish tradition, with no object whatever to gain by misleading us in this particular, fixes the death of Christ on the 14th Nisan,[5] the *erebh Pesach,* or evening before the Passover.

7. The fact that the language of St. Paul is most naturally interpreted on the supposition that the Last Supper was not the Passover, but another institution destined to supersede it (1 Cor. v. 7; xi. 23).

8. The fact that if Jesus had really partaken of the Passover on the very evening before His death, the Jews might fairly have argued that the observ-

---

[1] Joseph buys the "linen cloth" (Mark xv. 46). The women prepare spices and ointments (Luke xxiii. 56); Simon the Cyrenian is coming home (ἀπ' ἀγροῦ) apparently from a day's husbandry (Mark xv. 21; Luke xxiii. 26). On the Feast-Sabbaths and mode of observing them, see Lev. xxiii. 7,·8. "Ye shall do no servile work therein," is an ordinance so important that it is twice emphatically repeated. We are told that in Galilee, at any rate, the first day of the Feast was *very strictly* observed, so that even if Jewish custom had sanctioned all this buying, selling, working, &c., at Jerusalem, we should not expect to find it among the *Apostles* (John xiii. 29).

[2] In *Beza,* f. 36, and Mishna, *Jom Tobh.* 5, 2, it is expressly said that criminal proceedings were inadmissible on feast days; cf. Philo, *in Flacc.,* p. 976.

[3] So Apollinaris, Clement of Alexandria, Jul. Africanus, Hippolytus, Tertullian ("die prima azymorum quo agnum ut occiderent ad vesperam a Moyse fuerat praeceptum," 486 † *Adv. Jud.* 8), &c. See Routh, *Rell Sacr.* i. 168; Westcott, *Introduction,* p. 320. The *identification* of the Last Supper with the Passover appears to date mainly from the time of Chrysostom. Some, who refuse to see a real discrepancy, adopt one of the expedients suggested by Chrysostom, viz., either that by "Passover" St. John means the entire feast (John = Synoptists); or that Jesus ate the Passover before the proper time (Synoptists = John). (Keim, III. ii. 464; but compare 476, *n.* 4).

[4] The "ninth hour" (Matt. xxvii. 46, &c.), or three o'clock, would be the first legal moment at which the lamb could be slain according to the Jewish interpretation of "the two evenings."

[5] *Sanh.* vi. 2. (Similarly *Erebh. yôm Kippur* means the evening before the Day of Atonement.) Salvador and the author of the *Sepher Jeshuah Hannotseri* actually argued that the Romans had far more to do with the crucifixion than the Jews, because the Jews could not have crucified on *the first day of the Passover* (Sepp); but Jewish traditions themselves here contradict the erroneous common impression.

ance of the Passover, and therefore of the entire Mosaic ritual, was for ever binding on the Christian, no less than on the Jewish Church.

If, then, we conclude that the view which we derive from St. John's Gospel is literally correct, we may further consider whether it is in any way borne out by *incidental* notices preserved in the Synoptists. We find that there *is* incidental confirmation of this kind which we cannot ignore; although the force of it is undoubtedly weakened by the conflicting Jewish testimonies, as to what might and what might not be done on the days of these sacred festivals.

i. We find, for instance, that *the disciples* (John xiii. 22) suppose Judas to have left the room in order to buy what things they had need of against the feast.

ii. Not only does Judas leave the room, but he is afterwards followed by our Lord and His disciples — an action which may very possibly have become sanctioned by universal custom, but was not in accordance with the strict injunctions of the law (Exod. xii. 22).

iii. Judas hires a band composed, in part at least, of Levitical officers (Luke xxii. 52), and comes by night to arrest Jesus — an event which could hardly have been regarded as consonant with a night of peculiar solemnity.

iv. The Sanhedrin had already come to a distinct conclusion that it would be dangerous and impolitic to kill Jesus on the feast day (Mark xiv. 2); yet if the Last Supper was the Paschal meal, this was the very thing which they did. On the other hand, if the Last Supper was *not* the Passover, we see a reason for precipitating the arrest and hurrying on the execution.[1]

v. Herod Agrippa did not indeed *arrest* Peter during "the days of unleavened bread," but he expressly avoided putting him to death till the feast was over. His execution was *to be delayed till after the Passover* (Acts xii. 4).

vi. The Synoptists, while they speak of bread and wine, give not the remotest hint which could show that *a lamb* formed the most remarkable portion of the feast.[2]

vii. The general incidents of the banquet as recorded by them bear no distinctive resemblance to the very peculiar ceremonies of the Paschal feast;[3] some

---

[1] It is true that the hostile members of the Sanhedrin were quite capable of violating the sacredness of the day, or might have defended themselves by the supposed interests of religion (cf. the opinion of R. Akiba, *Sanhedr.* x. 4). But the two robbers at any rate had committed no *theological* offence.

[2] Had the lamb been there, then Peter, if not Jesus Himself, would, according to Jewish custom, have been compelled to slay the lamb with his own hands in the Temple precincts, drive through it a spit of pomegranate wood, and carry it away on his shoulders to be roasted whole. For the lambs were slain in a very solemn and formal manner. The people were admitted into the Temple only in groups, and the priests, standing in two long lines from the entrance to the altar with cups of gold and silver, passed the blood of the lambs from hand to hand, and poured it into two openings by the side of the altar. Meanwhile there were alternate blasts of trumpets and chantings of the Hallel. It is impossible to suppose that the Priests would have sanctioned for any one — and least of all for this little band of Galilæans — an isolated departure from the universal custom.

[3] *Ex. gr.* we have not a word about the lamb, the *mazzôth* or unleavened bread, the *merorîm* or bitter herbs, the sauce *charoseth*, the *hagada* or announcement, the *four* or *five* cups of wine. The "hymn," on the other hand, has been identified with the Hallel, and the " cup of blessing " in 1 Cor. x. 16 with the *côs habberâchâh*; but the first particular is inconclusive, the second expression metaphorical. The many modifications of the old memorial feast which have *now* been sanctioned for centuries by Jewish usage, have simply resulted from *necessity*. After the destruction of Jerusalem the Passover *could* not any longer be observed in accordance with the Mosaic regulations, and therefore it became a mere secondary question *to what extent* its observances could be relaxed and altered.

of them, such as the washing of the feet, and the absence of all *hurry* in the banquet, are incongruous with its meaning and character.

viii. Several incidental expressions faithfully preserved by them seem to show that this Supper was eaten because the true Passover could *not* be eaten ; such as " my time is at hand " (Matt. xxvi. 18) — as though this were a reason why He should *anticipate* the ordinary meal. Something, too, of the same kind seems to be involved in the expression of the earnest desire of Jesus to eat " this Passover with them before He suffered," particularly, if we attach any importance to the remarkable passage in Hippolytus, οὐκέτι φάγομαι τὸ πάσχα, "I shall never again eat the Passover," which, if it be a reminiscence of Luke xxii. 16, would be a prophecy that He was to be put to death before the actual Paschal feast.[1]

We conclude, then, that *the Last Supper was* NOT *the Paschal meal.* Such a meal could now have had no significance for Him, who, as the True Paschal Lamb, was now about to be offered ; nor for the Apostles, who would henceforth recognize Him in that capacity.

But, on the other hand, nothing is easier than the supposition that, before the Synoptic Gospels assumed their final form, the Last Supper (to which the metaphorical name of πάσχα was often given) should have been identified with the ordinary Jewish Passover ; and the more so if, as is most probable, Jesus had Himself spoken a few words to show that this sacrament which He thus ordained was to be *a new feast which should take the place of the ancient Passover ;* and if the near approach of the actual Passover, perhaps even the observance of one or two Paschal customs, gave a certain Paschal tinge to the actual meal. In fact, although the *memorial* (πάσχα μνημονευτικὸν) as distinguished from the *sacrificial* Passover (π. θύσιμον) was unknown until after the destruction of Jerusalem, yet the supposition of Grotius, that the meal eaten by Christ bore a *sort of general relation* to the actual Paschal meal, is by no means improbable.

To sum up, then, it seems to me, from careful and repeated study of much that has been written on this subject by many of the best and most thoughtful writers, that Jesus ate His Last Supper with the disciples on the evening of Thursday, Nisan 13, *i. e.,* at the time when, according to Jewish reckoning, the 14th of Nisan began ; that this supper was not, and was not intended to be, the actual Paschal meal, which neither was nor could be legally eaten till the *following* evening ; but by a perfectly natural identification, and one which would have been regarded as unimportant, the Last Supper, *which was a quasi-Passover, a new and Christian Passover,* and one in which, as in its antitype, memories of joy and sorrow were strangely blended, got to be identified, even in the memory of the Synoptists, with the Jewish Passover, and that St. John, silently but deliberately, corrected this erroneous impression, which, even in his time, had come to be generally prevalent. [2]

---

[1] Hippolytus expressly says ο ὐ κ ἐ φ α γ ε τὸ κατὰ νόμον πάσχα.[487] Hence the Eastern Church always used *leavened* bread at the Eucharist ; as did the Western Church also down to the ninth century.

[2] I have said nothing about the obscure and meagre history of what is called "the Paschal controversy," or dispute between the Eastern and Western Churches as to the proper time of keeping Easter, because it is now generally (though not universally) agreed that it has little or no bearing on the question before us. See Sanday, *Fourth Gospel,* p. 211; Westcott, *Introduction,* p. 320; and on the other side, Keim, III. 476—478.

EXCURSUS XI. (Page 568.)

Old Testament Quotations.

The subject of the quotations from the Old Testament by the writers of the New is far too wide to be treated in the narrow limits of an excursus. All that I purpose here to do is to furnish the reader with a few facts in support of those principles at which I have glanced more than once in the body of the work, and which appear to me to be the only ones adequate to remove the difficulties by which the subject is encompassed.

The general phenomena of these quotations have recently been examined and tabulated with great care by Mr. D. C. Turpie, in his book, *The Old Testament in the New.* He establishes the following remarkable results: — That there are in the New Testament 275 passages which may be regarded — all but a very few of them quite indisputably — as quotations from the Old; and that of these, there are *only* 53 in which the Hebrew, the Septuagint, and the New Testament agree — *i. e.*, in which the Hebrew is correctly rendered by the LXX., and quoted from the LXX. by Apostles and Evangelists. Besides these there are 10 passages where the incorrect version of the LXX. has been altered into accordance with the Hebrew; 76 where the version of the LXX. is correct, but has been varied by the New Testament writers into *less* agreement with the original; 37 where a faulty version of the LXX. has been accepted; and no fewer than 99 where the New Testament differs alike from the Hebrew and from the LXX. This result may be tabulated as follows : —

Passages in which the LXX. version is correctly accepted 53
" " " " correctly altered 10
" " " " incorrectly accepted . . . 37
" " " " incorrectly altered . . . 76
Passages in which the Hebrew, the LXX., and the New Testament all
 differ 99

Of course it will be understood that in the above tabulation, (i.) many of the differences are extremely minute, and (ii.) that the words "correct" and "incorrect" merely mean an accurate agreement or disagreement with the original Hebrew. To these must be added three passages (John vii. 38, 42, and Eph. v. 14) which can only be classed as doubtful allusions.

The important bearing of these results on the letter-worshipping theory of "inspired dictation" will be seen at once. It is hardly too much to say that while they leave untouched the doctrine of a Divine grace of inspiration and superintendence, they shatter to pieces the superstitious and anti-scriptural dogmatism which asserts that every "word and letter" of the Holy Book is *supernaturally* inspired. I dwell upon the subject — I have repeatedly referred to it — because I feel a deep conviction that to hold the theory of inspiration in this latter form is, in the first place, to deny the plain language of Scripture itself, the plain teaching of Christ, and the plain indications deducible from apostolic and prophetic usage; and in the second place, to incur the guilt of setting up a colossal and perilous stumbling-block in the path of all rational godliness.

I have, in the plainest and most candid manner, stated what seem to me the sole truly orthodox and Scriptural views on the subject of Inspiration in some

papers printed in Vol. I. of the *Bible Educator*. To those papers I must refer any theological critic who does not understand my point of view. It is impossible for me here to re-state the full arguments into which I there have entered : but it may warn insufficiently educated readers from uncharitable attacks upon my references to this subject, to know that the views which I have supported are also those of not a few of those living as well as of former theologians whose names stand highest, and whose authority is the most deservedly respected, in the Church of England. Conspicuous among the latter are the names of Luther and Calvin. Any one who will read the comment of Luther on the 20th Psalm, and that of Calvin on Psalms viii., xl., and lxviii., will perhaps be surprised to see the freedom with which they have expressed on this subject the common sense and honest view which may startle the supporters of a mechanical theory of inspiration, but would not have startled on the one hand an Origen, a Jerome, an Augustine, a Gregory of Nyssa ; or on the other, the leading intellects among the great Reformers.

EXCURSUS XII. (Page 602.)

NOTES ON THE TALMUD.

ANYTHING more utterly unhistorical than the Talmud cannot be conceived. It is probable that no human writings ever confounded names, dates, and facts with a more absolute indifference. The genius of the Jews is the reverse of what in these days we should call historical. By the change of a ר into a ד Romans find themselves transmogrified into Idumeans ; Vespasian is confounded with Titus, Titus with Trajan, Trajan with Hadrian, Herod with Jannæus. When we come to the names of the Rabbis we find an intolerable confusion of inextricable Hanans, Joshuas, and Simeons. As for events, they are, in the language of a profound and admiring student, " transformed for the edification, and even for the amusement of the audience. History is adorned and embellished by the invention of an imagination, poetic, but often extravagant ; truth is not sufficiently attractive ; everything is magnified and extended." Jerusalem, says a R. Samuel, included twenty-four cities ; each city had twenty-four quarters ; each quarter twenty-four roads, &c., &c. In Bethyr, one quarter of the city was engaged in song and dance, while, from another, torrents of blood were rolling four or forty miles to the sea.[1]

When to all these sources of doubt is added the immense uncertainty of the readings, the " lapidary brevity " of the style, the dim indirectness of the allusions, and the intentional or affected obscurity of many of the oracular utterances of the Rabbis, it may well be supposed that the Talmud must be used with caution. It is not only probable, but a well-known fact, that many of the apparently wild and absurd stories of the Talmud are only the veil adopted by timidity in the days of persecution. Jewish writers were driven to indicate

---

[1] *Gittin*, 58 *a* (Derenbourg. *Hist. de la Pal. d'après les Thalmuds*, p. 11). It is, however, **fair** to add that these and similar passages are meant to be taken not *literally* (רמי הפשט), but *hyperbolically*, in ordinary Oriental fashion (לישן הבאי). See Reland, *Antt. Hebr.*, p. 140. "If you cannot find the kernel," says Maimonides, " let the shell alone, and learn to say, ' I cannot understand this.' " The Jews themselves utterly despise many of the *Hagadôth* or legends of which the Talmud is full.

obscurely and enigmatically the teaching and the notions which they dared not publicly propound. To this class of enigmas (φωνᾶντα συνετοῖσιν) belong the story about Absalom's eye, the bone of Goliath, &c.

It has been asked by some — as, for instance, by Mr. Deutsch — whether it is fair to judge of the Talmud by brief extracts, separated from the context. I answer, first, that any one may now examine for himself whole treatises of the Talmud, both Mishna and Gemara, in translations of unquestionable fidelity ; and secondly, that my own views about the Talmud are drawn quite as much from Jewish writers, such as Maimonides, Grätz, Geiger, Jost, Munk, Derenbourg, Schwab, Cohen, Frankl, Raphall, Deutsch, Salvador, and others, as from writers like Lightfoot, Schöttgen, Otho, Surenhuys, Buxtorf, Reland, Wetstein, Gfrörer, Etheridge, Pieritz, and others. I have consulted all these writers, and the view which I derive from the professed admirers and adherents of Rabbinic literature is quite as unfavorable as that which I get even from Eisenmenger and Wagenseil.

Some excellent maxims — even some close parallels to the utterances of Christ — may be quoted, of course, from the Talmud, where they lie imbedded like pearls in " a sea " of obscurity and mud (ים התלמוד) ! It seems to me indisputable — and a matter which every one can now verify for himself — that these are amazingly few, considering the vast bulk of national literature from which they are drawn. And, after all, who shall prove to us that these sayings were always uttered by the Rabbis to whom they were attributed ? Who will supply us with the faintest approach to a proof that (when not founded on the Old Testament) they were not directly or indirectly due to Christian influence or Christian thought ? And how many of them are there which are independent of the Old Testament ? Even Mr. Deutsch, one of the most ardent admirers of the Talmud, says, " These sayings were often tender, poetical, sublime ; but they were not absolutely new ; there was not one that was not substantially contained in the canonical and uncanonical writings of the Old Testament." [1]

Sayings of this kind, which have been brought into comparison with passages in the Gospels, are among others, the following :

Matt. v. 9. — *"Love peace, and pursue it at any cost."* Hillel (*Pirk Abhôth*, i. 12) ; cf. Ps. cxxxiii. i.

Id. v. 10. — *"Remember that it is better to be persecuted than to persecute."* (*Derech Erets Rab.* ii.)

Id. v. 22. — *"Be not prone to anger."* (*P. Abhôth*, ii. 10 ; *Pesachîm*, 67.)

Id. v. 28. — A close parallel in *Massecheth Kalah*.

Id. v. 39. — *"If thy companion call thee an ass, put the saddle on thy back."* (*Babha Kama*, 8, 7.) Cf. Ecclus. xxviii. ; Prov. xx. 22 ; xxiv. 29.

Id. v. 42 ; vi. 1—4. — *"He who giveth alms in secret is greater than Moses himself."* (*Chagiga*, i., &c., &c.) Cf. Ecclus. xxix. 15, 16 ; Prov. xix. 17, &c.

Id. vi. 7. — *"It is better to utter a short prayer with devotion, than a long one without fervor."* (*Shabbath*, 10 ; *Menachôth*, 110.)

---

[1] *Remains*, p. 138. R. Joshua Ben Levi proved (to his own satisfaction doubtless) that the Oral Law had been delivered to Moses on Sinai from Exod. xxiv. 12, because there the Tables = the Ten Commandments ; the Law = Pentateuch ; commandments = Mishna ; "which I have written" = Prophets and Hagiographa ; and "that thou mayst teach them" = Gemara (*Berachôth*, 5 *a*). (Schwab, *id.* p. 234.)

Matt. vi. 31. — *"He who having but one piece of bread in his basket, says, 'What shall I eat to-morrow?' is a man of little faith."* (*Sota*, 48.) Cf. Ps. xxxiv. 10; cxlvii. 9, &c.

These instances (and they might be multiplied from many sources) are chosen from a number more in Cohen's *Les Déicides*, E. T., 150, seq. This Jewish writer urges them as diminishing the "originality" of Jesus. Such an argument, common as it is, shows a total want of culture and insight. The "originality" of the Son of God, if such a word can be used at all, consisted in this, that He saved and regenerated a corrupt and dying world, on which the whole series of Jewish doctors — Sopherîm, Tanaîm, Amoraîm, Seboraîm, and Geonîm — produced no perceptible effect, and for which, from first to last, they and their "originality" have the smallest possible significance.[1]

It is, however, fair to bear in mind (1) the heterogeneous character of the Talmud, and (2) its character as being in great measure a *corpus juris*.

(1.) As regards the first point, I cannot do better than quote some of the remarks of Mr. Deutsch, whose premature death, before he had well begun the intended work of his life — a *History of the Talmud* — cannot be too deeply regretted. He says, "All those manifold assemblies wherein a people's mental, social, and religious life are considered and developed, are here represented — Parliament, Convocation, Law Courts, Academies, Colleges, the Temple, the Synagogue, even the Lobby and the Common Room, have left realistic traces upon it. The authors of this book, who may be *counted by hundreds*, were always the most prominent men of the people in their respective generations, and thus, undesignedly and designedly, show the fulness of this people's life and progress at every turn." Elsewhere he speaks of it as "those mazes of legal enactments, gorgeous daydreams, masked history, ill-disguised rationalism, and the rest which form the Talmud and the Midrash." [2]

(2.) But it is chiefly as a *corpus juris* that the Talmud must be considered. "Speaking of it strictly as a book, the nearest approach to it is Hansard. Like Hansard, it is a law-book — a miscellaneous collection of parliamentary debates, of bills, motions, and resolutions; with this difference, that in Hansard these propositions, &c., gradually grow into an Act, while in the Talmud the Act is the starting-point. . . . The Talmud in this wise contains — besides the social, criminal, international, human and divine law, along with abundant explanations of laws not perfectly comprehended, corollaries, and inferences from the law, which were handed down with more or less religious reverence — an account also of the education, the arts, the sciences, the history and religion of this people for about a thousand years." [3]

This view of the Talmud as a sort of statute-book makes an important difference in our estimate of it. The following remarks, with which I have been favored by a friend, seem to me so original and so valuable — they seem, in fact, to place the whole controversy about the Talmud in such a completely new light — that I have asked his permission to incorporate them into this note :—

---

[1] For further remarks on this subject I may refer to my *Seekers after God*, pp. 181, 182, 320; and *Witness of History to Christ* (Hulsean Lectures), pp. 134, seqq.

[2] Deutsch. *Literary Remains*, p. 194.

[3] *Id. ib.*, p. 136.

" The Talmud seems to be *a corpus juris in which the law has not yet been differentiated from morality and religion.* There is nothing exceptional in this non-differentiation : perhaps *we* are exceptional in having outgrown the stage in which it is normal. The strange thing is the prodigious quasi-scientific productiveness of Judaism within a certain area, combined with such pre-historic, not to say embryonic backwardness in the above respect. But even in this respect the contrast is less striking if Judaism be compared with the developments and documents of Hinduism and Islam.

" 1. If we remember that the Talmud is a *corpus juris* one thing is explained immediately — namely, the rarity of moral or other truths of any value. The wonder is that there are any at all. The Statute Book is more bulky than the Talmud — at any rate the Reports are — and they contain no ' beautiful and noble things ' at all, *unless perhaps in the obsolete parts.* We don't look for such things there. If English literature had been developed analogously to Jewish, we should have the great thoughts of Hooker and Bacon, not to say of Spencer and Shakespeare, imbedded in *Coke upon Littleton.* The arrangement would be objectionable ; but not on the ground that there was so little great thought in comparison to the amount of technicality.

" 2. This first point is obvious on the most general view. But of the *fictions* of Rabbinism I cannot believe a right view is to be taken without looking at the fictions of other systems of law. Sir H. Maine has proved (*Ancient Law,* ch. ii., pp. 1—6) that legal fiction is the earliest, most imperfect, and most awkward means — but a perfectly normal means — of law reform. No example that you have adduced is more elaborate, more inconvenient, or more absurd than the devices which had by law to be employed in this country every time a man cut off an entail, from Edward IV. to 1833. Imaginary legal principles were too strong to allow us to do in a straightforward manner what the necessities of society insisted on having done in some way or other. In Judaism legal principles resisted still more stoutly, because they were more an affair of religion and morality than with us ; but the great point must have been the mischievous reaction of the fiction-system upon religion and morality themselves, which must thus have become steeped in hypocrisy. The *cause* of this would be the non-differentiation of law from morality and religion. The neglect of these considerations makes the modern books suspicious in more than one respect. They seem to treat the traditional form which conservatism obliged a piece of law to assume, as if it was the essential thing ; and they regard the social necessities which had to be provided for, as if they were rather superficially involved in the result, instead of *vice versâ.* And they seem to assume too readily that what the texts represent as *de jure* in force was operative *de facto.* These two things never go quite together, and they are peculiarly likely not to go together in a system which was more or less calculated with reference to an ideal polity, with a Jerusalem and a Temple supposed to be in existence to support it. And even the *unhistoricalness* of the Talmud (in which I suspect the writings of the Mohammedans beat it hollow for extravagance) has something answering to it at home. English law-books contain a number of historical statements, copied by one out of another, which have a very suspicious look to a reader of any sort of independence ; and in fact Rudolf Gneist says that there is a great deal of false history which, as in a manner part of the law itself, is even more directly important to the English law-student than the true.

" (3.) *Casuistry* is in a moral point of view the most disastrous, or at least the most obviously disastrous consequence of this anachronous extendedness of the province of jurisprudence; but also it is the least peculiar to Judaism. It is no great harm (besides that the thing is inevitable) if morality is a department of law, as long as things are in the early stage in which law itself is rather elastic. But when law is highly developed in precision and minuteness, morality cannot be stuffed into its pigeon holes without becoming immoral, and in fact irrational. In obedience to logic, it is made immorally as well as irrationally strict; in order to stand in any real relation to the facts of life it is made irrationally as well as immorally lax. The necessity of this laxness will be seen by taking any of the Rabbinnical examples at which you shudder most, and asking what the moralist is to do, *if he is to prescribe for the magistrate and policeman as well.* See the pleadings in ' Pascal *versus* Escobar and others,' *passim.* Pascal's position is untenable, unless it is recognized that morality is not a matter of rules at all. Here the danger of Gospel-interpreters — and it is a danger from which few of them altogether escape -— is that of representing Christ as occupying the merely negative or revolutionary position of Pascal. Now, that the action of Jesus was not merely negative or revolutionary is sufficiently proved by the result. How expressive is His saying, that there is no place reserved for those whose law-abidingness does not transcend that of the men who are before all things zealous for the Law.

" 4. The most obviously disastrous thing about Judaism, in an intellectual point of view, is not, I suppose, a *necessary* effect of its non-differentiation of law from religion and morality, though surely an easy and natural one. I mean the fact that its quasi-science is not founded even on the supposed necessities of an imaginary or obsolete state of things, but upon the interpretation of a written text. Within the 'four corners' (as our lawyers have it) of this narrow field it cuts itself off from all other intellectual culture. This distinguishes it from Hinduism and Islam in their more energetic days, and still more (thanks partly to the Greeks) from Rome. Mediæval scholasticism makes some approach to the like barrenness. One of the consequences was that folly of follies, the number-and-letter lore.

" It seems to me that the apparent eccentricities of the Talmud cannot be instructively set before the general reader without applying to them something like the above considerations, which in other applications are considered obvious enough."

This view of the Talmud is slightly touched upon by Ewald, though he makes no attempt to illustrate it by the comparative method. " When a supreme law of life," he says, " has been already given, and without troubling themselves about its ultimate foundations, men are only desirous to work it out into detail, and, if necessary, to bring it into actual life by means of a countless multitude of new regulations, . . . similar conditions everywhere produce similar re-sults. The scholastic labors of the Middle Ages and those of the Papal jurists . . are essentially the same." [1]

---

[1] Ewald, *Gesch. d. Volkes Isr.* (E. Tr., V. 196). I have already made a similar remark with-out knowing that I had been anticipated.

"Les meilleurs des hommes," says Renan,[1] "ont été des juifs ; les plus mali-
cieux des hommes ont aussi été des juifs. Race étrange, vraiment marquée du
sceau de Dieu, qui a su produire parallèlement et comme deux bourgeons d'une
même tige l'Église naissante et le fanatisme féroce des revolutionnaires de Jérusalem, Jésus, et Jean de Giscala, les apôtres et les zélotes sicaires, l'Évangile et
le Talmud! Faut-il s'étonner si cette gestation mystérieuse fut accompagnée de
déchirements, de délire, et d'une fièvre comme on n'en vit jamais?"[488] The turn
of expression is open to criticism, but the fact is striking:

EXCURSUS XIII. (Page 606.).

THE SANHEDRIN.

ORTHODOX Jews ascribe the origin of the Sanhedrin to Moses (Exod. xviii.
24—26, &c.), and identify it with the "elders of Israel" in Ezek. viii. 11, 12, and
the "elders of the Jews" in the days of Darius (Ezra vi. 8).[2] Some even saw
a germ of the Sanhedrin in the tribunal established by Jehoshaphat (2 Chron.
xix. 8—11).[3]

The Sanhedrin was the successor of the Great Synagogue, the last member of
which died in the person of Simon the Just.

In 1 Macc. xiv. 28, the assembly of the Jews, which bestowed the supreme
power on Simon, father of John Hyrcanus, is called " the great congregation of
the priests and people, and rulers of the nation, and elders of the country," corresponding to the Hebrew names *Kenéseth, Roshí Abhôth,* and *Zakain ha-Arets ;*
and it appears from coins that the Sanhedrin (the members of which are described much as in Mark xv. 1) are called the *Chebher,* or "Senate" of the
Jews. In this were included both Pharisees and Sadducees. John became a
Hellenizer (Phil-hellene : Jos. *Antt.* xiii. 11, § 3), and a Sadducee, and was the
first to adopt on his coins the Greek inscription and title of Ἰουδα Βασιλεύς.
At the end of a year he was succeeded by his brother Alexander Jannæus, who
quarrelled furiously with the Pharisees, but on his deathbed recommended his
wife Salome Alexandra to trust *true* Pharisees while she avoided the *painted* ones.
Salome accordingly gave them such privileges during her reign of nine years
that they ultimately ventured to summon her son Hyrcanus II. before their tribunal on the occasion alluded to on p. 607. It is on this occasion that we first
find the *name* Sanhedrin (סנחדרין), which, although the Talmud talks of a Sanhedrin in the days of Moses (Buxtorf, *Lex.* s. v.), is certainly not præ-Asmonæan ;
indeed, until the Hellenizing days of Jason, this Greek word would never have
been adopted by the people in place of their own term *Beth Dîn,* "House of
Judgment," or *Kenéseth haggedóla,* "the great assembly."

In the Mishna mention is made of two kinds of Sanhedrin — the provincial,
of five or seven members ; and the Grand Sanhedrin of seventy-one, with their

[1] *L'Antechrist.* p. 258. Elsewhere he says, "On peut dire de cette race le bien qu'on
voudra et le mal qu'on voudra, sans cesser d'être dans le vrai ; car . . . le bon juif est un
être excellent, et le méchant juif est un être détestable. C'est ce qui explique la possi-
bilité . . . que l'idylle évangélique et les horreurs racontées par Josephe aient été des
réalités sur la même terre, chez le même peuple, vers le même temps."[489] (p. 486.)
[2] Raphall, *Hist. of the Jews,* ii. 110.
[3] Munk, *Palestine,* 194. See Reland, *Antt. Hebr.* 243, seqq.

Nasî and *Ab Beth Dîn.* These two distinguished functionaries seem to have been regarded as representatives of the ancient *Zouggóth,* or "couples," who were in their turn representatives of the *Eshkolóth,* or "grape-clusters." The first *Nasî* under Hyrcanus II. is said to have been Joshua Ben Perachiah, and the first *Ab Beth Dîn* Nitai of Arbela.

It is said that in the Temple sat three Sanhedrins, or, as we should perhaps call two of them, "Committees of the Sanhedrin," of twenty-three members each; the Great Sanhedrin of seventy-one met in the *Lishcat Haggazîth ;* another, or a committee of the same, in a chamber which abutted on the *Chêl* (חֵיל), or division between the Court of the Gentiles and of the women; and a third at the gate of the Har ha-Beit, or Temple mountain. Derenbourg conjectures, with some probability, that the Grand Sanhedrin was but the reunion of the three inferior ones of twenty-three $(23 \times 3 + 2)$ with the two presiding officers, and that these three committees were composed, (i.) of priests, (ii.) of Levites, and (iii.) of "notables," *i. e., Sopherím, Tanaím,* &c.[1] If this conjecture be admitted, we may, perhaps, suppose that the three trials of our Lord took place before these three divisions of the Sanhedrin; or, if the trial before Hanan be regarded as purely informal and extra-judicial, then the trial before Caiaphas may conceivably be the third of these bodies which met at the foot of the Temple-mountain. It gives some support to this conjecture that in Matt. xxvi. 57, "the Scribes and elders" (= the "notables," *i. e.,* the *Sopherím,* and *Zekêním*) seem to be distinguished from "*all* the *chief priests* and elders" — *i. e.,* the Grand Sanhedrin (*id.* xxvii. 1).

But it must not be forgotten that the Sanhedrin which condemned our Lord was a dubious and hybrid kind of assembly. When the Sanhedrin had unanimously rejected the claim of Herod on the authority of Deut. xvii. 15, the Talmud (*Babha Bathra,* 3 *b*) says that he exterminated them all except Babha Ben Buta, whose eyes he put out; and that the rebuilding of the Temple was undertaken by the advice of the survivor in expiation of the atrocity.[2] Whatever the exact circumstances may have been, Herod, after the execution of Antigonus, seems to have inflicted on the Sanhedrin a frightful vengeance, from which it took them a long time to recover. It was soon after this that he thrust into the High Priesthood creatures of his own, of Egyptian and Babylonian origin, such as Simon and Joazar, the Boëthusians from Alexandria, and a certain obscure Hananel of Babylon (ἱερέα τῶν ἀδημοτέρων, Jos. *Antt.* xv. 2, § 4), who may possibly be identical with the Annas of the Gospels. For a time at least the real Sanhedrin seems to have been suspended, and its functions usurped by an assemblage of Herod's own adherents (Jos. *Antt.* xv. 7; § 4), σύναγαγὼν τοὺς οἰκειοτάτους αὐτῷ; xvii. 3, § 1, συνέδριον τῶν φίλων. The dignity of sacerdotalism might give to this spurious assemblage an appearance of dignity, but we have seen reason to believe that the Pharisees — here meaning by that title the leading doctors — took little, if any, part either in its deliberations or its

---

[1] *Hist. Pal.,* ch. vi., the facts of which I have here summarized. See too Ewald, *Gesch. d. Volkes Isr.* (E. Tr., V. 168). He says that much which is told us about the Sanhedrin in Talmudic and later writings "flows from the increasing want of the historical spirit which characterized the Jews in the Middle Ages."

[2] Josephus mentions a massacre of Pharisees (*Antt.* xvii. 2, § 4).

proceedings. They left it to the obscure Benî Bethyra,[1] the Boëthusians, the Hananites, the Kantheras, the Kamhiths, the Phabis, and their adherents. The meetings of the Sanhedrin of which Josephus speaks during this period were arbitrary, incompetent, and special gatherings. The Romans and Herod between them had abolished the old independent body.[2] It is true that Hillel, after overcoming the priestly pretensions of the Benî Bethyra, by quoting, as a last resource, the authority of Shemaia and Abtalion, is said to have been made Nasî; but Derenbourg is inclined to doubt the story altogether, and to distinguish between *Presidency of the Schools and Presidency of the Sanhedrin*.[3] At any rate, if Hillel really *was* a *Nasî* of the Sanhedrin, his political action must have been amazingly slight, considering that it is uncertain whether Josephus even recognizes his existence[4] or not.

At the time of our Lord's trial it is certain that both Hillel and Shammai were dead. They had left no successors who attained immediate prominence. We hear indeed of a Simeon, son of Hillel, but the sole recorded trait respecting him is the aphorism that "nothing is superior to silence."

EXCURSUS XIV. (Page 606.)

PHARISEES AND SADDUCEES.

THE origin of these names is buried in obscurity. All that is clear is that the Pharisees were politically descended from the *Chasidîm* (1 Macc. ii. 42 ; vii. 13), and 'were the heroic-national party; while the Sadducees were the priestly-aristocratic party, who allied themselves always with the ruling power, even when that power was anti-national in its aims.

Derenbourg, who subjects these titles to an elaborate examination, supposes that during the Graecomania which in the days of the Seleucid government began to spread more and more widely among the Jews — especially under the influence of "ungodly wretches" like Menelaus and Alcimus — the party which felt it necessary to defend the scrupulous observance of the Law by a closer "hedge," began to urge an extension of that $\dot{\alpha}\mu\iota\xi\iota\alpha$, or withdrawal from all intercourse with the heathen, which was called in Hebrew *Perishût* (פרישות), a name which thus did not imply either political detachment or worldly separation (Jos. *Antt.* xiii. 8, § 3 ; 2 Macc. xiv. 3).

The Asmonæans, however, and their party did not follow the *Tanaîm*, or Doctors, in these views which they considered exaggerated, but contented themselves with that ordinary obedience to the written law which was not inconsistent with Phil-hellenic tendencies, and for which they retained the title of *Tsedakah*, or "righteousness" (צדקה, $\delta\iota\varkappa\alpha\iota\sigma\sigma\dot{\nu}\nu\eta$: cf. Prov. xvi. 31), a name which more easily came into vogue, because the title of the last great and good Asmonæan, Simeon, had been *hatstsadîk*, "the Just."

---

[1] The well-known story of their dispute with Hillel is another indication of the hostile position held by the Doctors towards the priests.

[2] "Von Synedrien ist in der ganzen Herodäer und Römer Zeit keine Spur." 490 (Jost, i. 278.)

[3] *Nasî* was a title also given to the Chief of each tribe (Numb. iii. 24 ; xvi. 2, &c.) who in Numb. iii. 32 is called Nasî of Nasîm. (Munk, p. 195.)

[4] Josippon substitutes the names of Hillel and Shammai for the Pollio and Sameas of Josephus, *Antt.* xv. 1, § 1. (Munk, p. 545.)

But words which had originally described mere tendencies or aspirations, soon developed into the injurious party-titles of *Parouschîm* or Pharisees, and *Tsedûkîm* or Sadducees, to describe respectively the party of the Rabbis, whose tendencies were wholly patriotic [1] and popular, and that of the Priests, who were aristocratic and conservative [2] (Acts v. 17). Neither party willingly adopted names which had gradually acquired an insulting force. In our Lord's time, the names had gradually come to connote differences which were religious as well as political. The Sadducees may broadly be described as rationalists, the Pharisees as ritualists, names which, though not rigidly accurate, convey on the whole a true impression of their respective positions.

Geiger, who in his *Urschrift* and *Das Judenthum* was perhaps the first to put these parties in their true light, takes a different view of their origin. He derives the name of the Sadducees from Zadok, a descendent of Phinehas, who held the priesthood till the last unworthy representatives of Aaron's elder line were displaced by the sons of Mattathias, who belonged to the less distinguished priestly family of Joarib.[3] But the Sadducees continued to support the new power; while the Pharisees, inheriting the views of the separatists (*Nibdalîm*, who "separated themselves from the filthiness of the heathen," Ezra vi. 21), combated the pretensions, and usurped the influence of the privileged class. The difficulty in adopting this view rises from the silence of Josephus and the Books of Maccabees.

Common as is the name Pharisees in the Gospels, those who are so called seem always to have called themselves by other names in preference — such as *Sopherîm*, "scribes," *Thalmîdî chakamîn*, "pupils of the sages," and *Chabheerîm*, or "confraternities." In several passages of the Talmud they are called "plagues of Pharisees" (מכות פרושים, *J. Pea.* viii. 8 ; *J. Sota* iii. 4, &c.), and in one of these they are ranked as equally objectionable with "imbecile devotees, sly sinners, and bigoted women." But of course there were good and bad Pharisees, and while Jewish writers themselves admit that "the heavy charges which the Founder of the Christian faith brings against Pharisees are fully confirmed by the Talmud" (*Sota*, f. 22 *b*, &c.),[4] yet these were the hypocrites whom Alexander Jannæus called "dyed and varnished" Pharisees; and we may hope that Nicodemus and Gamaliel were not isolated specimens of a nobler class. The Sadducees are seldom mentioned, because with the cessation of the temporal power they practically ceased to exist as a party, although many of their distinctive views were revived by a certain Hanan, and are continued to this day by the Karaites.

The wealth, rank, connections, and offices of the Sadducees gave them much worldly influence and authority, but in all religious and ritual matters the people

---

[1] Φαρισαῖοι καλοῦνται βασιλεῦσι δυνάμενοι μάλιστα ἀντιπράσσειν [491] (Jos. *Antt.* xvii. 2, § 4).

[2] Josephus distinctly says that connection with the priesthood is the one stamp of Jewish nobility.

[3] Geiger (*Urschr.*, p. 105) shows that the story of their origin from Zadôk, a pupil of Antigonus of Socho, who carried too far his master's principle that men ought to serve God without desire for reward, is not mentioned in the Mishna or the Talmud, but is first found in the R. Nathan. If, as Epiphanius (*Haeres.* i. 4) supposes, the name is derived from צדק, "justice," the question occurs, why is it not *Tsaddîkîm* instead of *Tseaûkîm*. Köster's strange and isolated notion, that it is a Hebrew transliteration of *Stoics*, is hardly worth refuting.

[4] Raphall, *Hist. of the Jews*, ii. 117.

sided so absolutely with the Doctors or Pharisees, that the Sadducees, even against their real views, were often compelled to conform. This is the express statement of Josephus,[1] and is confirmed by the Talmud. "All your life you teach without practising," bitterly exclaimed a Boëthusian to the Priest, his father. The reply was a humiliating confession that they could not practise their real theories, but were obliged to conform to the teaching of the Doctors (חכמים). The Priest and his son in this story are believed to have been Hanan (the Annas of the Gospels), and his son Hanan the younger, who figures in Josephus in no very enviable colors, as the murderer of "James, the Lord's brother." [2]

A striking Rabbinic story (*Joma*, 71 *b*) illustrates their want of moral influence over the people. On the great Day of Atonement the High Priest, followed by the people, was leaving the Temple. Suddenly, however, the people caught sight of Shemaia and Abtalion — the "couple" of the day — walking undistinguished among the rest. Instantly they abandoned the High Priest to form an escort to the Doctors. "All hail to the men of the people," said the High Priest bitterly to them, when they took leave of him. "All hail," they replied, "to the men of the people who do the work of Aaron, and no hail to the son of Aaron who does not act like Aaron." Josephus, though his account of these two sects (*Antt.* xviii. 1, §§ 3, 4; xiii. 5, § 9; *B. J.* ii. 8, § 14) is little to be relied on, and is probably borrowed in part from Nicolas of Damascus, is yet undoubtedly right in saying that in spite of the rank of the Sadducees that had no real reverence from the people. "They influence," he says, "the well-to-do" (τοὺς εὐπόρους), "but have no popular following, while the Pharisees have the multitude as their allies."

I have several times spoken of the Sadducees as "worldly," and the epithet is justified by the ostentation which made them desire to be served in vessels of gold and silver, and to demand double dowry for every young girl married to a priest;[3] and by the greed which suffered them to grow rich at the expense of the people. Of the latter propensity two stories are told. One of them is a quarrel which they had with the Pharisees about the supply of victims for the daily sacrifice, which the Pharisees very properly said ought to be provided by the Temple treasury; whereas the Sadducees, regarding the Temple treasure as their own, wanted the victims to be paid for by separate subscriptions. Similarly the Sadducees claimed for the priests (*i. e.*, for themselves) the use of the meat-offerings, which the Pharisees said ought to be burnt on the altar. The Pharisees won the day, and appointed two festivals in honor of the double victory.[4] Thus both Pharisees and Sadducees were constantly driven into extremes by the repulsion of antagonistic errors.

Another story is that as they sold pigeons at the *chanujôth*, they multiplied to such an extent the cases in which the sacrifice of a pigeon was necessary, that the price of a single pigeon rose to a gold piece. Then R. Simeon Ben Gamaliel cried, "By the Temple I will not sleep till I have reduced their price to a denarius." Accordingly he pointed out such numerous reductions to the necessity

---

[1] *Antt.* xviii. 1, § 4.

[2] Jos. *Antt.* xx. 9, § 1; Jost, *Joma*, 1; Geiger, *Urschrift*, 112.

[3] *Abhôth de Rabbi Nathan*, v.; *Kethubhôth*, 1, 6. In the former passage we have a sort of deliberate theory of Epicureanism.

[4] *Megillath Taanîth*, §§ 1, 19. They also arranged that the Temple tribute should be received with great pomp (*Jer Snekalîm*, 45 *d*; Grätz, iii. 460).

of making this offering, that the price of a pigeon sank to the fourth of a denarius.[1] These shops are expressly called the shops of the sons of Hanan, and the
Talmud distinctly alludes to the want of uprightness in the management of them.[2]
The one maxim of the political life of a Sadducee seems to have been quietism,
even at the expense of patriotism. No wonder the priestly party were disliked
and suspected, when ever since the days of Hyrcanus and Aristobulus the people
had found cause to complain of them, that they were seeking to change the government of their nation in order to enslave them (Jos. *Antt.* xiv. 3, § 2).

Josephus, in describing the rupture between John Hyrcanus and the Pharisees
(*Antt.* xiii. 10, § 6), distinctly states that the main difference between the two
sects consisted in the acceptance by the Pharisees and rejection by the Sadducees
of the Oral Law or tradition of the elders; and although the assertion may be a
little too sweeping, it is undoubtedly founded on a real fact.

Ewald, who, in his *History of the People of Israel*,[3] enters into a full account
of the Pharisees and Sadducees, points out how the Pharisees were led to
encourage and defend hypocrisy, and conventionalize all true piety, partly
by the character of the Levitical dispensation, partly from motives of ambition,
and partly out of strong antagonism to the Sadducees. Wishing to retain the
advantages which they had received from the Asmonæan revival of national
piety, "under the influence of ambition, and devoted more or less consciously
to their own interests, *they made piety into a sort of art or trade in order permanently to secure their own power.*"

After observing that we only know the Sadducees from the reports of their
avowed enemies, he says, "It was the school of freedom of life, of thought, and
of action; but it was a freedom which sprang out of the Greek age, with its
deep moral degradation, which corresponded with it, and was acceptable to it."
But for this the Sadducees might have been of real use in counteracting the
rigidity and one-sidedness of Pharisaic development. But in their opposition to
this injurious scrupulosity they failed to note the deeper sores which at this
time were eating into the Jewish and Gentile world.

He speaks slightingly of the notices of these sects in Josephus (*Antt.* xiii. 5,
§ 9; *Vit.* 2; *B. J.* i. 5, § 2; ii. 8, § 2) as abrupt, arbitrary, and devoid of deep
knowledge, and says — too uncharitably — of Jost, Grätz, and Geiger, that their
views are baseless, "because they are themselves Pharisees, and desire to be
nothing else."

EXCURSUS XV. (Page 670.)

Traditional Sayings of Christ.

THE apocryphal sayings (ἄγραφα δόγματα) of Christ — *i. e.*, the sayings
attributed to Him by early writers, but unrecorded in the New Testament[4] —
have been collected and arranged by Prof. Westcott (*Introd. to the Gosp.*, App.
C.) with his usual care and learning. I here quote only the most remarkable, or

---

[1] *Keritôth*, i. 7.
[2] *J. Pea.* i. 6.
[3] Vol. V., p. 366, seqq., E. Tr.
[4] *Ex. gr.* Acts xx. 35.

710 APPENDIX.

those which are not mere variations of his actual words, referring all who are interested in the subject to Prof. Westcott (*l. c.*), or Hofmann (*Leben Jesu,* 317—329).

1. For the remarkable story appended in D to Luke vi. 5, *v. supra,* p. 438.

2. Cod. D also appends to Matt. xx. 28, "*But ye seek from little to increase, and that from the greater there be a less.*"

3. "*Show yourselves tried money-changers.*" (γίνεσθε τραπεζῖται δόκιμοι). (Epiphan. 44, 2.)

4. "*He that wonders shall reign, and he that reigns shall rest.*" "*Look with wonder at that which is before you.*" (Clem. Alex. *Strom.* ii. 9, 45.)

5. "*He who is near me is near the fire; he who is far from me is far from the Kingdom.*" (Orig. *Hom. in Jerem.*, iii., p. 778; Didymus in Ps. lxxxviii. 8.)

6. "*Keep the flesh pure and the seal unspotted.*" (Clem. Rom. *Ep.* ii. 8.)

7. "*For those that are sick I was sick, and for those that hunger I suffered hunger, and for those that thirst I suffered thirst.*" (Orig. *in Matt.*, I. xiii. 2.)

8. "*In whatsoever I may find you in this will I also judge you.*" (Just. Mart. *Dial.* 47.)

9. "*Never be joyful, except when ye shall look on your brother in love.*" (Jer. *in* Eph. v. 3.)

These are the most remarkable. One or two others have been quoted or alluded to in the body of the work (v. *supr.,* pp. 251, &c.), and of the remainder some are wholly unworthy of our Lord, or spring from a desire to claim His authority for false and exaggerated principles, or are mere amplifications and misquotations of His actual words.

One or two of the Mohammedan legends respecting Christ, preserved in the Koran or elsewhere, are striking — *e. g.*.

"Jesus, the Son of Mary, said, 'He who longs to be rich is like a man who drinks sea-water; the more he drinks the more thirsty he becomes, and never leaves off drinking till he perishes.'"

"Jesus once said, 'The world is like a deceitful woman, who, when asked how many husbands she had had, answered, so many that she could not count them.' And Jesus said, 'When they died, did they leave you behind?' 'On the contrary,' said she, 'I murdered and got rid of them.' 'Then,' said Jesus, 'It is strange that the rest had so little wisdom, that when they saw how you treated the others they still burned with such love for you, and did not take warning from their predecessors.'" See others in Hofmann, *ubi supr.,* p. 328. An interesting monograph might be written on the picture of Jesus as presented in the Mohammedan writings. In the Koran itself His name is frequently mentioned with those of various prophets; but the *special* references are not numerous.

INDEX.

A.

Abgarus V., King of Edessa, tradition regarding, 506, 507.
Ablutions before meals, not observed by our Lord's disciples. 337 *et seq.;* of the leading Jews, 337, 338.
Accuracy, historical, of the Evangelists, 305.
Aceldama ("Field of Blood"), 610.
Adam, skull of, at the foot of the cross, 637.
Adulteress, decision in the case of an, 406 *et seq.*, 415.
Ænon, near Salim, 170.
Age of Christ at His baptism by John, 110, *n.*
Agony in the garden, 575 *et seq.*
Allegories and Parables, 424, *n.*
Alms-giving, 538, 539.
Ambition of the disciples rebuked, 389.
Andrew, calling of, 130 *et seq.*
Andrew, the name, 135, *n.*
"Angel to the Shepherds," chapel of the, 31.
Angelology and Demonology, Jewish, 685, 686.
Anna, the prophetess, 47.
Annas (Hanan) 483, 589, 590; Christ's trial before, 591—595; his end, 631.
Antipas, son of Herod the Great, 295 *et seq.;* character and career of, 295 *et seq.;* 431, *n.;* gives a banquet, at which Salome dances, 299; wishes to see Christ, 302; spoken of as "that fox" by Christ, 431; Christ sent by Pilate to, 619; his end, 630.
Antipater, father of Herod the Great, 65, *n.*
Antonia, Tower of, 427.
Apocrypha, Christ familiar with the, 355, *n.*
Apocryphal Gospels — their character, 71, *n.*
Apostles, the calling of the first, 127—140; enumerated and characterized, 203 *et seq.;* sent out two and two, 280 *et seq.;* return from their mission, 302; questioned by Christ as to their belief in Him, 371 *et seq.;* their misunderstanding of Christ's mission, 374 *et seq.;* dispute as to which is to be the greatest, 389 *et seq.;* Christ appears after His resurrection to ten of the, 666.
Appearance of our Lord, traditional account of the, 684.

Archelaus, son of Herod the Great, 66.
Arimathæa, 657, *n.*
Ascension, the, 670, 671.
Asceticism, 104, 105.
Ass, the — how esteemed in the East, 499, 500, *n.*
Authority, Christ's, 514.

B.

Banus, a Jewish hermit, 115, *n.*
Baptism, by John, of Christ, 110 *et seq.;* by Christ's disciples, 169.
Baptism of John, from Heaven or of men? 514, 515.
Bar-Abbas, 623, 624.
Bar-jona, *see* Peter.
Barley — how esteemed in Palestine, 247, *n.*
Bartimæus, blind, and his companion healed, 489.
Baskets in use in Palestine, 308, 309, *n.*
Beelzebul, not Beelzebub, 346; *see also* Devil.
Ben-Adam, *see* Son of Man.
"Beside himself," our Lord considered, 225, 226.
"Bethania," not "Bethabara," the true reading of John i. 28, 127, *n.*
Bethany, Christ at the house of Lazarus at, 460 *et seq.;* of the present day, 480, *n*, 499, *n;* the last evening at, 546, 547.
Bethesda, Pool of (*Birket Israel*), 286, 287; Christ's miracle there, 287 *et seq.*
Bethlehem, 37, 66.
Bethphage, 499.
Bethsaida, or "Fish-house" (*Bethsaida Julias*), 306, 307, *n.*, 309, *n.*, 369.
Bethsaida (*Western*), 219, *n.*, 309, *n.*
Birth of Christ, date of the, *see* Date.
Blind man, at Bethsaida, healed, 369; blind from his birth, healed, 419 *et seq.*
Bloody flux healed, 274 *et seq.*
Blushing, 411, *n.*
Boat, Christ preaches from a, 197.
Body of Christ after the Resurrection, 666, 670, *n.*
Boyhood of Christ, 67—76.
Brahe, Tycho, star seen by, 52.
Bread of Life, Jesus the, 316 *et seq.*
Brethren of Jesus, 97—99, 144, *n.*, 206, *n.;* they try to assert a claim on Christ's actions, 255; desire to speak with Jesus, 349, 350.
Buddhist stories and the Gospel, 178, *n.*
Burial, Eastern, 480, 657; of Christ, 659.

PASSAGES OF SCRIPTURE

(NEW TESTAMENT)

QUOTED OR REFERRED TO.

ST. MATTHEW.

i. 16,	98
18,	98
19,	35, 37
20,	37
21,	45
25,	98
ii. 1,	37, 43
9,	48
11,	42, 56
12,	310
14,	66
16,	59
18,	657
22,	66, 310
23,	75
iii. 4,	326
5,	108
7,	107, 108
10,	104
11,	109
14,	111
15,	44, 112
17,	112
iv. 3,	120
4,	120
5,	122
6,	123
7,	123
10,	122
12,	127, 172, 189
13,	181, 189
15,	67, 181, 191
16,	191
18-22,	197
23,	242
24,	195
25,	157, 191
v. 1,	184, 191
1-48,	212
2,	209
3,	653
9,	700
10,	700
15,	292
18,	92
21,	209
22,	210, 596, 700
28,	700

ST. MATTHEW.

v. 32,	680
39,	700
42,	700
43,	211
46,	449
47,	449
vi. 1-34,	212
1,	112
2,	211
7,	700
9-15,	426
9,	343
16-18,	119, 388
25,	282
27,	88, 212
28,	212
31,	701
vii. 1-23,	212
7-12,	426
11,	680
12,	679
13,	518
14,	518
26,	212
27,	212
28,	213
29,	213
viii. 1-4,	219
1,	219
2,	219, 220
3,	220
5-13,	223
14,	156, 194
15,	194
17,	196, 249
19-22,	256, 426
19,	185, 201
24,	257, 258
25,	258
26,	193, 258
27,	259
28,	260, 262
28-34,	260
34,	266
ix. 1,	155, 191, 268
2,	269
2-8,	269
6,	322

ST. MATTHEW.

ix. 9,	199, 201
11,	270, 324
13,	271, 449
14-17,	271
15, 119, 272,	273, 375, 388
16,	273
18,	166
18-26,	274
19,	274
27,	278
27-31,	278
28,	278
30,	222
32-35,	426
35,	242
35-38,	279
36, 250, 276,	280
38,	222
x. 1,	240
1-42,	280
2-4,	204
3,	201, 204
4,	205, 206
5-42,	432
8,	283
9,	280
10,	283
11,	283
16,	432
18-23,	283
19,	282
23,	283
25,	283, 346
28,	281
29,	282, 680
37,	449
38,	283, 375
xi. 1,	284
2,	229
2-19,	228
3,	229, 232
5,	189
6,	232
7-9,	233
9, 10,	233
10,	385
11,	229

ST. MATTHEW.

xi. 12,	452
13,	452
16,	95
16, 17,	323
16-19,	234
18,	108, 230
19,	323, 324
20-24,	367
20-27,	367
23,	156
28,	93
29,	435
xii. 1 et seq.,	330
1,	388
3,	333
6,	333
7,	271
9,	334
10,	334, 446
11,	335
13, 15,	336
15-20,	222
16,	221
19,	374, 481
22 et seq.,	342
23,	345, 359
24,	676
25-37,	347
27,	194
30,	390
33,	165
38,	365
38-42,	662
39,	659
40,	349, 694
43,	346
46,	98, 245, 349
46-50,	255
47,	244
47-50,	350
48,	350
48-50,	144
xiii. 1,	252
1-23,	254
2,	252
20,	253
24-30,	254
31,	453

AMERICAN APPENDIX.

GIVING FIVE HUNDRED AND SIX TRANSLATIONS OF NON-
ENGLISH MATTER CONTAINED IN FARRAR'S LIFE OF CHRIST.

CORRECTIONS.

Page 135, note 2, read : ἠθέλησεν.
Page 135, note 3, line 4, read: Βηθσαίδας.
Page 272, line 7, for "than " read : that.
Page 308, note 3, read: εὐλόγησεν.
Page 322, note 1, for " *Mog.*" read: *Moy.*
Page 353, note 1, for " Vol. II., page 246," read: pp. 533, 534.
Page 453, third line from end of text, for "those " read: those who.
Page 479, note 3, line 2, read : μετριοπάθεια.
Page 546, last line, read: γίνεσθε.
Page 658, note 4, read: Gamaliel.
Page 731, Tr. No. 94, read: . . . nor would they who had come to apprehend him have
    fallen prostrate.
Page 740, Tr. No. 376, line 3, for " gives " read: givest.
Page 742, Tr. No. 417, for " shall " read: shalt.
Page 744, Tr. No. 486, read: . . . if it is thoroughly favored as here by consecrated
    authorities.

TRANSLATIONS.

730　　　　　*TRANSLATIONS.*